W9-BQW-343

HISTORY OF THE US ARMED FORCES

HISTORY OF THE US ARMED FORCES

★ ARMY ★ NAVY ★ MARINES ★ AIR FORCE ★

By James M. Morris,
Jack Murphy, Brian William Turner,
and Brooks Robards

INTRODUCTION
by Tom Carhart

Published by World Publications Group, Inc.
455 Somerset Avenue
North Dighton, MA 02764
www.wrldpub.net

Copyright ©2004
World Publications Group, Inc.

All rights reserved. No part of this publication may be reproduced, stored in a retrieval system or transmitted in any form by any means, electronic, mechanical, photocopying or otherwise, without first obtaining the written permission of the copyright owner.

ISBN 1-57215-387-3

Printed and bound in China
by SNP Leefung Printers Limited.

1 2 3 4 5 06 05 03 02

Front Cover
***Top*: A pair of F-16 Fighting Falcons fly a patrol mission while supporting Operation Enduring Freedom, November 2001 (Suzanne M. Jenkins/US Air Force).**
***2nd Row*: US Marines walk in full combat gear in Kuwaiti desert, March 2003 (Reuters/Corbis).**
***3rd Row, Left*: US Army special forces secure an important area in Najaf, Iraq, March 2003 (Reuters/Corbis).**
***Right*: US Marines arrive on a Somali beach, December 1992 (Peter Turnley/Corbis).**
***4th Row*: Aegis equipped US warships participate in a military exercise off the Florida coast, February 2001 (Reuters/Corbis).**

Back Cover
***Top Row, Left*: US Infantry soldier stands on top of his armored vehicle at Camp Virginia outside Kuwait City, March 2003 (Reuters/Corbis).**
***Right*: A crowd of workers cheer a C-47 aircraft, February 1944 (Bettmann/Corbis).**
***2nd Row*: An Air Force unit with an AH-64 Apache (George Hall/Corbis).**
***3rd Row, Left*: Troops of the 28th Infantry Division march down the Champs Elysées after Paris was liberated, August 1944 (US Army).**
***Right*: An F/A-18C Hornet launches from the flight deck aboard the USS *Abraham Lincoln*, March 2003 (Reuters/Corbis).**
***4th Row*: US Marines occupy Saddam Hussein's palace in Tikrit, April 2003 (Reuters/Corbis).**

CONTENTS

INTRODUCTION
Tom Carhart

The United States of America is a country that loves peace, yet since our Forefathers signed the Declaration of Independence, we have fought nine major wars in as many generations, not to mention numerous small wars. But the American people have a longstanding discomfort with large standing armed forces in peacetime, and have always adhered, at least in theory, to the concept of a citizen-army defending our freedoms. How is it, then, with both the American distaste for massive domestic military forces when war is not at hand and the constant need for young men to step forward at great risk and defend the American way of life, that we have been able to continually provide the needed manpower of our military? Who were and are those young men who have stepped forward and taken up arms for America?

The Revolutionary War was the first act of social violence engaged in by our new nation, and to colonial Americans, those truly were the times that try men's souls.

That war had to be fought and won, however, and the Americans who stood up for independence, who bled and died for it—for all the recognition due to the famous Minutemen and other militia members—were primarily members of the regular forces: the Continental Army, the Continental Navy, and the Continental Marines, all of whom were the predecessors of the United States Army, Navy, and Marine Corps.

For the "major" wars, such as the Civil War, World Wars I and II, Korea, and Vietnam, some form of compulsory service filled the ranks of the army while the other services mostly depended on volunteer citizen soldiers. We have also benefited from periodic activation of the heirs of the Revolutionary War militia—the National Guard and the Reserves, together termed the Reserve Components. And these volunteers have always been drawn from that same group of young men out of every generation who willingly step forward and offer their lives for our country. The concept of patriotic service, of being prepared to fight to protect and promote the welfare of a free people, is an American ideal that countless numbers of Americans have lived out in their early adulthood. Most of these young men—and in modern times increasingly women as well—have won no lasting fame, but that does not lessen the quality of their offering their lives to our country. Some of those offerings, as fate would have it, have been accepted, but all were heroes and should be so remembered.

Washington won few battles in the Revolutionary War, but he managed his Continental Army 'Regulars' well, he endured, and with the help of the French, he trapped Cornwallis at Yorktown and forced his surrender. The

War of 1812 was even more a war fought by professionals, and the Mexican-American War of 1846-48 did not involve coerced service. Although this war is not politically pretty to 21st century eyes, it was also fought mostly by the Army, although the Marine Corps played a role as well.

The inability of the American people to maintain a nation divided against itself, between slave states and non-slave states, finally resulted in secession and the Civil War. On both sides, it was the army that played the dominant role, and this was the first instance of official compulsory military service. President Lincoln sent quotas to individual states for men to fill the army, and 2 million men served for the Union, most of them volunteers. The Confederacy also had a conscription law, and over one million served in her army, but again, most of them were volunteers. However, with provisions that allowed some to avoid the military by paying for a substitute, while others could cash in on their service by collecting bounties, this first effort by the Federal government sometimes seemed, and often was, grossly unfair.

Over the following century and a half, only World War I, World War II, Korea and Vietnam have required the Selective Service to mobilize American youth for war, though a draft existed through most of the Cold War, from 1945 through 1973. But across American history, the prosecution of lesser engagements has always been left to the small professional military. Since the 1990s, however, the Reserve Components have played an increasingly important role in the potential deployment of military force into combat. This has meant our Reserves and National Guard have played major roles in the wars America has fought in Iraq and Afghanistan.

As the histories of the four branches of the nation's armed services that follow make clear, technological advances have dramatically changed the nature and the capabilities of our military until, at the dawn of the 21st century, it stands unrivalled in the world. One early major advance in military prowess sprang from flying machines, which, only some forty years after the Wright Brothers' first moments aloft, resulted in thousands of bombers flying over central Europe, covered by clouds of fighter aircraft. (Although the US Air Force was not formally established under this name until 1947, its complete history from earliest days is recounted in this volume.) Other dramatic discoveries have also had their effects: the internal combustion engine, the tank, the atomic bomb, jet propulsion, missile-firing submarines, laser rangefinders, global positioning satellites, military officers piloting rockets around and landing on the moon—the list goes on and on. But no matter the scientific breakthroughs that raise the competence of our military, there is one enduring characteristic: The human being who wears the uniform and offers his or her life for our country. These are men and women who have made a most important gift to our nation, the offering of their lives, whether they survived or made the ultimate sacrifice in uniform.

Across the more than two hundred years of American military history, this is finally their story. They will never ask to be celebrated, for selflessness is a key part of their service. But just by reading the story of the growth, development, and transformation of our forces, from ill-equipped servicemen and uncertain logistical supplies to the sleek cohorts of modern times armed with high technology wonders, they are to be honored.

Whenever we celebrate the American system of human freedoms, it is these champions who have protected and insured it, and they should be remembered for that. As you read about the dramatic history and impressive achievements of the four branches of the armed services, let us always remember the individuals who have worn their uniforms, patriotic Americans to whom we owe our deepest and most enduring gratitude.

HISTORY OF THE
US ARMY
JAMES M. MORRIS

Pages 8-9: George Washington reviews his ragged troops at the camp at Valley Forge. *This page:* An Army Airforce B-25 Mitchell bomber completes its attack run on a Japanese escort vessel.

CONTENTS

INTRODUCTION

The United States Army may be said to have been formally born on 14 June 1775 when the Second Continental Congress created George Washington's Continental Army. Its antecedents, however, extend considerably farther back in time. The North American colonists had, after all, been intermittently engaged in various forms of organized warfare for much of the preceeding century. And in a broader sense, the colonists' understanding both of what an army is and of how war should be conducted was the product of ideas that had been developed in Europe yet another hundred years earlier, when warfare was forever transformed by the introduction of the portable firearm.

Modern warfare was born during the sixteenth and seventeenth centuries when the arquebus or 'shot,' a form of man-held artillery, came into use. The early arquebus could project a one-ounce ball for a distance of up to 200 yards, although it took as long as fifteen minutes to load and fire. Its successor, the musket, represented a major step forward in weapons technology, though it, too, was unwieldy and inaccurate – besides requiring 56 separate movements to reload.

It was during the destructive Thirty Years' War between 1618 and 1648 that the first true modern army was created by Gustavus Adolphus. This Swedish leader introduced the *levée en masse* (large citizen army); the paper cartridge for use by his musketeers; and the three-rank, simultaneous-fire infantry formation for continuous volley fire. He also created well-disciplined 'divisions' of 4000-5000 men for greater maneuverability on the battlefield, cavalry units to be used as shock troops to charge enemy flanks, and three standardized classes of artillery (heavy siege guns; lighter, more mobile field guns; and regimental pieces, which could be drawn into position by a single horse). Gustavus Adolphus insisted on trained officers, regular pay for his soldiers and tighter military discipline (including banning whores from military encampments).

By the eighteenth century the technological outlines of modern warfare had clearly taken shape. Artillery (smoothbore, as opposed to later rifled artillery) now consisted almost exclusively of Gustavus' three basic types, and all were capable of firing relatively standard gauge solid iron shot for localized destruction and either grapeshot (small balls attached to one another and designed to spread on explosion) or cannister (loose pellets in a can also designed to spread) against personnel.

The flintlock musket was the standard infantry weapon. For example, the British army's 'Brown Bess' was a smoothbore musket with a 3-foot, 8-inch barrel that fired three-quarter-inch diameter balls. It had an effective range of 50 to 100 yards, and a trained musketeer could fire three rounds per minute. Attached to the barrel of the musket was a 14-inch 'ring' or 'socket' bayonet that allowed the infantryman to turn the musket into a spear without plugging the muzzle. The bayonet could be used against cavalry or against enemy personnel.

As weapons became standardized, so too did tactics. The line, which had developed out of the Greek phalanx, was the standard infantry formation in battle. Troops would march onto the battlefield in columns and then, on command, form into firing ranks. To perform this evolution in the face of bloody battle and possible death demanded rigorous training, and thus close-order drill evolved to assure proper movement and maintenance of formation while under enemy fire.

Once the two enemies' lines were drawn up, four stages of combat would normally follow. First, the artillery behind the lines of infantry would open on the enemy. Next, the infantry would advance in ranks to within 50 to 100 yards of the enemy. Third, the infantry would fire in volleys on command, usually not bothering overmuch about marksmanship at such close range. Last, the musketeers would charge the enemy with their bayonetted weapons if his line seemed ready to break. The army that did not 'cut and run' under fire and bayonet charge won the battle.

Such formalization, plus the intellectual climate of the times, forced eighteenth-century warfare into certain moral postures regarding battle. In the first place, enlightenment humanism inclined Europe toward limited warfare. It was assumed, for instance, that civilians would be immune from the violence and destruction of war. Second, the times demanded that wars only be fought for highly specific political or economic ends, never for the destruction of the enemy, his land or his people. Third, it was generally assumed that the bulk of the armies would come from the less-productive or lower social classes, rather than from the more 'solid' citizenry, thus lessening the aggregate loss to the country by battlefield woundings

America's first settlers still used the primitive matchlock arquebus.

Firearms transformed tactics, making musketeer ranks the key battle units

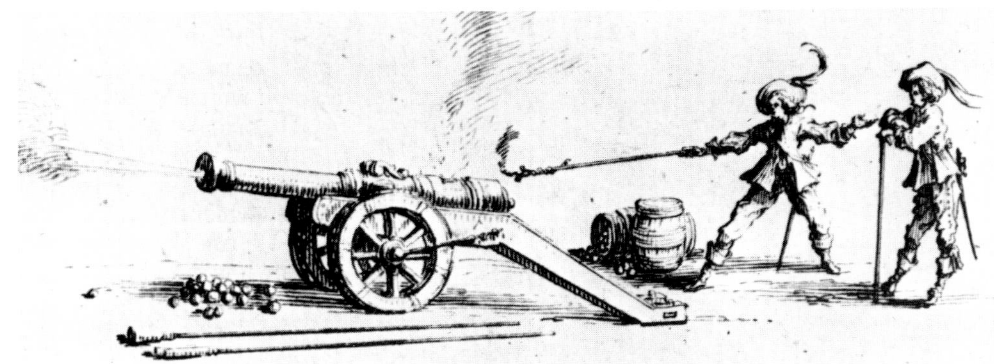

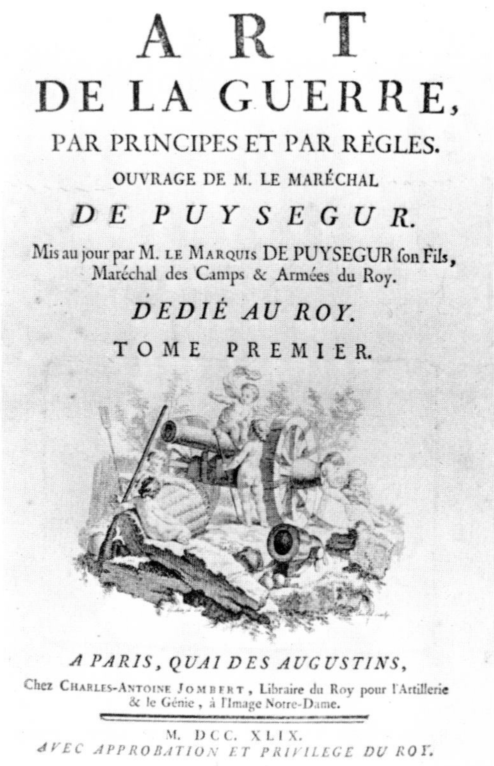
ART
DE LA GUERRE,
PAR PRINCIPES ET PAR RÈGLES.
OUVRAGE DE M. LE MARÉCHAL
DE PUYSEGUR.
Mis au jour par M. LE MARQUIS DE PUYSEGUR son Fils, Maréchal des Camps & Armées du Roy.
DEDIÉ AU ROY.
TOME PREMIER.
A PARIS, QUAI DES AUGUSTINS,
Chez CHARLES-ANTOINE JOMBERT, Libraire du Roy pour l'Artillerie & le Génie, à l'Image Notre-Dame.
M. DCC. XLIX.
AVEC APPROBATION ET PRIVILEGE DU ROY.

and deaths. Total war was a concept yet to be developed.

Technology and attitudes affected tactics, as well. Since heavy casualties of highly-trained soldiers could be expected in confrontational modes of warfare based on death-dealing artillery and musket fire, it followed that wars should be won by maneuver whenever possible. A good general was one who by movement could put his enemy in an untenable position and thus force him to surrender, his means of escape being cut off and his supply lines being cut. Thus interdiction of lines of supply and reinforcement, not the 'butcher's bill,' became the criterion of superior generalship.

The new style of warfare also produced feats of defensive engineering, especially under the influence of the fortifications designed by Sébastien Vauban, chief engineer to King Louis XIV of France. Vauban and his disciples concentrated on building low-walled forts surrounded by moats and glacis, or downward-sloping banks of earth or masonry. The only way to attack such a fort was to approach it through laboriously-dug parallel and zigzag trenches and then to place it under effective fire to breach its walls. This type of prolonged siege warfare also tended to hold down casualties and force a surrender by investment.

The eighteenth century, then, saw wars of formation, muskets, bayonets, artillery, maneuver and siege. Within these military practices and moral assumptions, the US Army was born. It would change and change again in succeeding centuries, as new technologies changed the face of war.

Above left: Mobile artillery, c. 1630.
Above: Title page of a 1749 French treatise on tactics.
Below: Linear tactics in America: a battle of the French and Indian Wars.

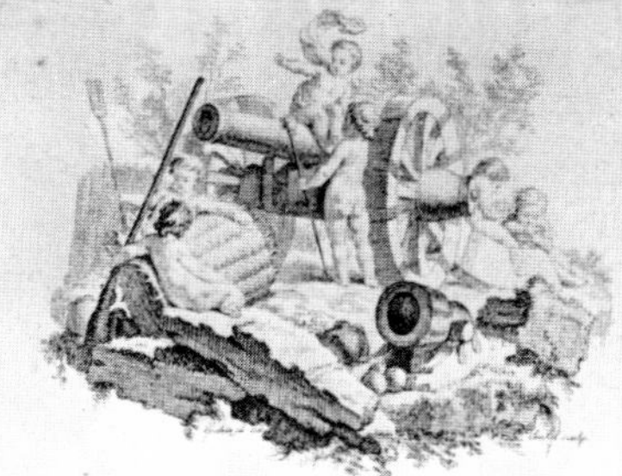

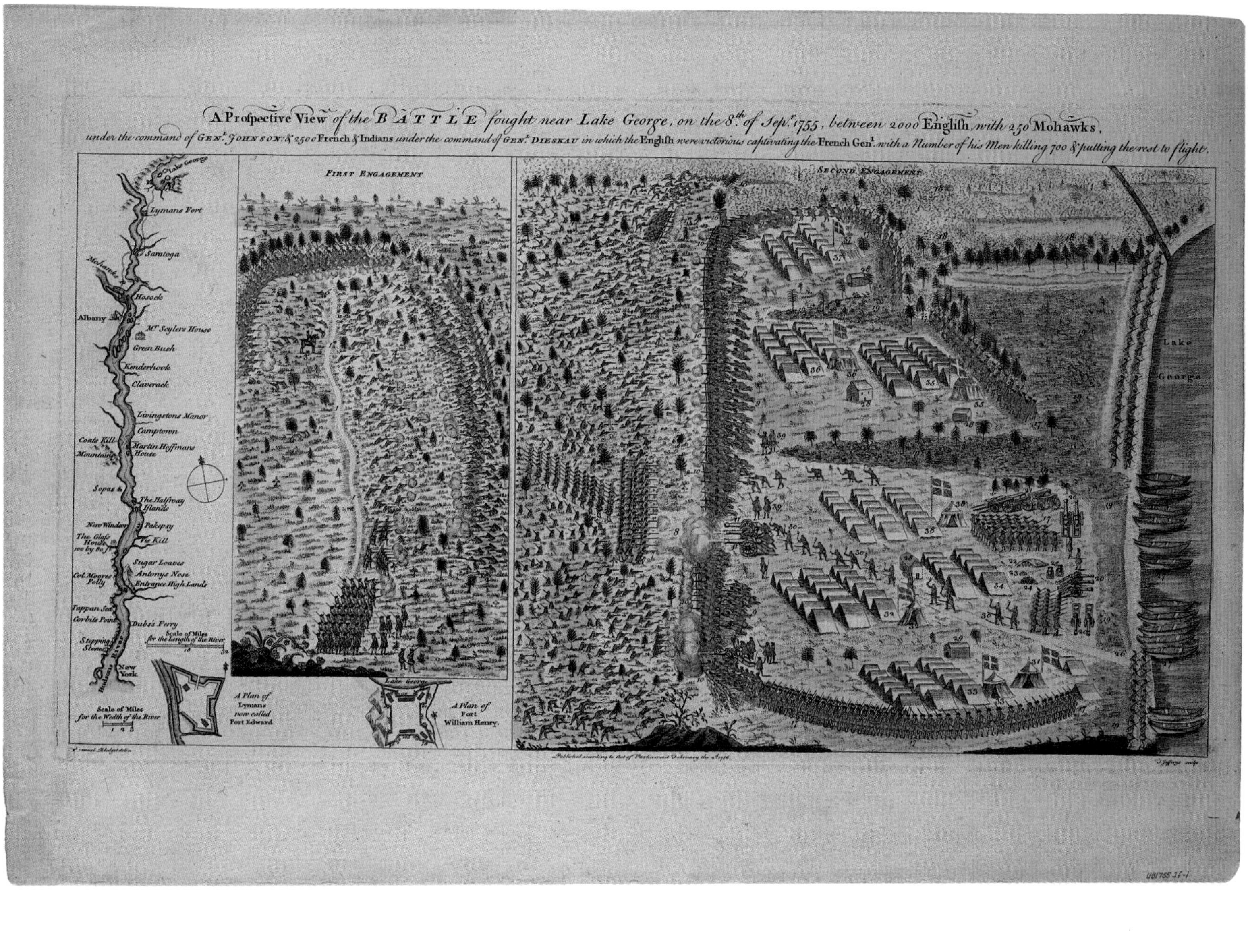
A Prospective View of the BATTLE fought near Lake George, on the 8th of Sepr. 1755, between 2000 English with 250 Mohawks, under the command of Genl. Johnson: & 2500 French & Indians under the command of Genl. Dieskau in which the English were victorious captivating the French Genl. with a Number of his Men killing 700 & putting the rest to flight.
First Engagement
Second Engagement
Lake George
Lymans Fort
Saratoga
Mohawks R.
Hosock
Albany
Mr. Seylers House
Green Bush
Kenderhook
Claverack
Livingstons Manor
Camptown
Coats Kill Mountains
Martin Hoffmans House
Sopas
The Halfway Islands
New Windsor
Pakepsy
The Glass House
Sugar Loaves
Antonys Nose
Entrance High Lands
Col. Moores Folly
Tappan Sea
Corbits Point
Dubs's Ferry
Stepping Stones
Hudsons River
New York
Scale of Miles for the Length of the River
Scale of Miles for the Width of the River
A Plan of Lymans now called Fort Edward
A Plan of Fort William Henry
Lake George

New World warfare: an Indian attack on an 18th century frontier camp.

BIRTH OF THE AMERICAN ARMY: 1607-1781

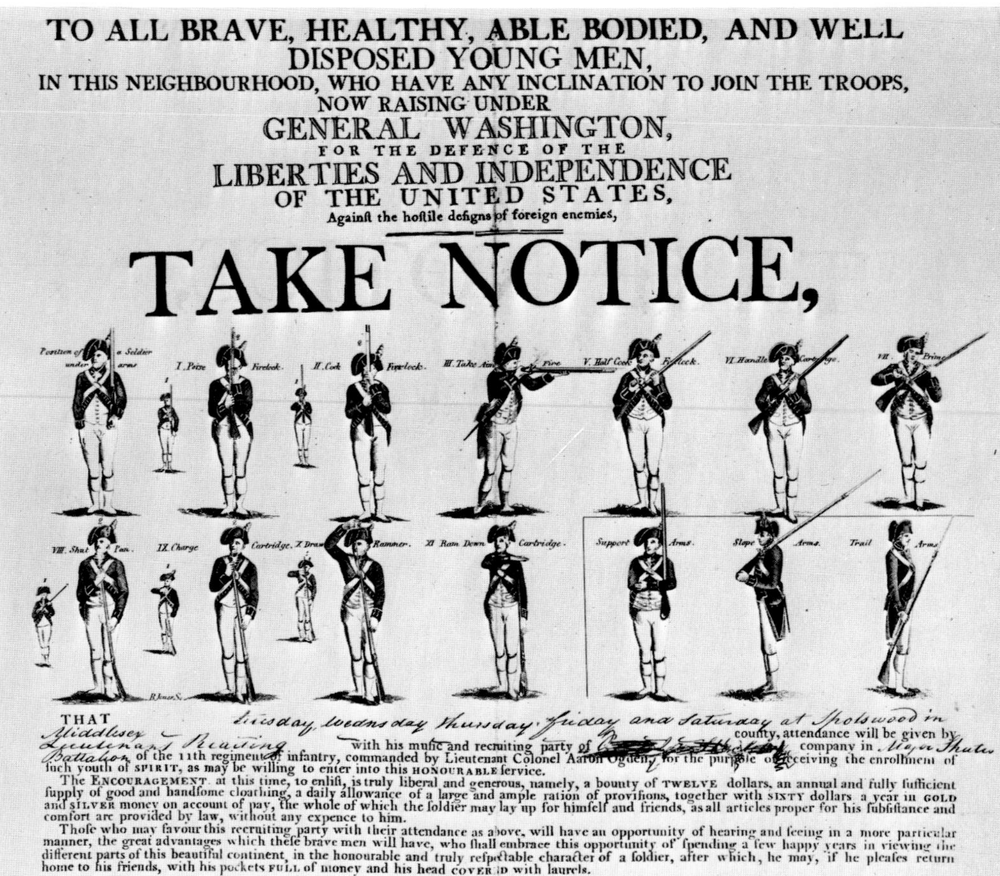

Above: **The 10 steps to arm a musket.**
Right: **An early colonial rival: Spain.**
Below: **Militia, the original army.**

From their earliest beginnings the British colonies on the North American continent had been left largely to their own devices regarding defense against their enemies, especially against the Indian tribes along the Atlantic coast who resisted the continuing encroachments of the European settlers. The early English settlements were generally small and isolated, and most military defense, perforce, had to be local defense. Aid from distant settlements or from the entire colony was available only in case of major Indian uprisings. As a result, the colonists were obliged to develop local military units, the militia, to provide for their security.

Although the tradition of the militia in English history stretched back in time to the Saxon *fyrd*, the militia in the mother country had largely fallen into disuse with the rise of professional armies in the sixteenth and seventeenth centuries. But since maintenance of a professional army would be both unnecessary and prohibitively expensive for limited campaigns against the Indians on the American frontier, colonial assemblies opted instead for local-based militias, and gradually all thirteen colonies, with the singular exception of pacifist Quaker-dominated Pennsylvania, which opted for all-volunteer units, developed a compulsory militia system under the nominal control of their central governments.

Generally speaking, in the colonial militia all able-bodied men (with the exception of sheriffs, ministers, teachers, slaves and some others) between the ages of 16 and 60 were required to report for regular training at the town or county seat. They were expected to furnish their own muskets, ammunition and other supplies. Militia musters largely consisted of marching and target practice with muskets, and they were often as much social and festive as military. The commanding officers for a colony or a military district, the colonels, were appointed by the governor with the consent of the assembly, but company-grade officers, in the best English tradition, were elected by the men.

When trouble came – usually in the form of an Indian attack on some town or settlement – the militia would be called to drive off and punish the troublemakers. Very seldom, however, would entire local militia units, or 'trainbands,' be called into active service, since the trainbands functioned more as training units for soldiering than as fighting units. Rather, volunteers chosen from the various local units would assemble to engage in the campaign. If not enough volunteers who were sufficiently young and sturdy to engage in a campaign came forth to serve, the local commander had the authority to draft enough militiamen from his unit to fill out the necessary number of men called for by the governor. Since campaigns usually lasted for only a few days, the militiamen chosen had little need for much logistical backup other than what they could carry.

Indian-fighting honed the martial skills of the early settlers.

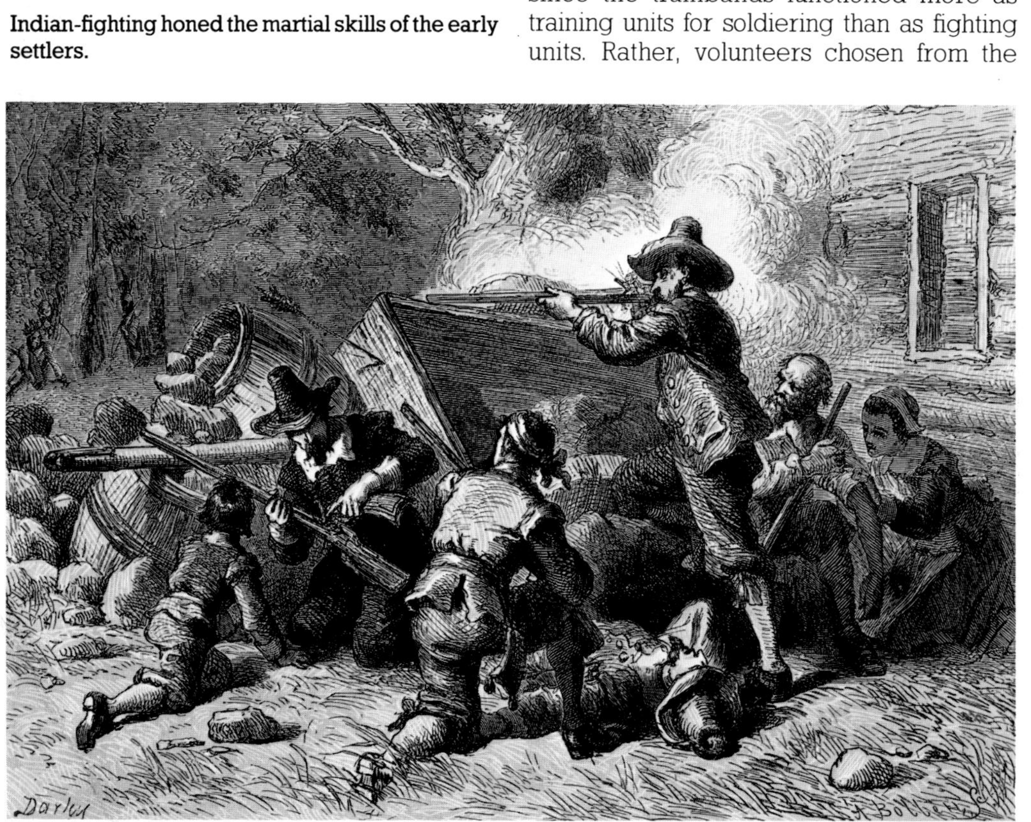

These militias were far from professional. Even the officers typically had no professional military training. But if unschooled in the niceties of conventional warfare, both the officers and their men knew their Indian adversaries and were content to forego doctrine in order to subdue opponents skilled in wilderness warfare. If the Indians fought with stealth and surprise, so too would the colonial militiamen. If the Indians used scouts to reconnoiter the path ahead to prevent a surprise of the main body, so too would the colonials employ friendly Indians or 'rangers' to do the same. If the Indians frequently slew all white men, including women and children, and burned their settlements to the ground, so would the militiamen slaughter and lay waste to Indian villages.

Despite the low level of training of the militias, whose drills became ever more casual as the Indian menace lessened, by sheer numbers and technological superiority the militiamen almost invariably defeated their Indian opponent in the colonial wilder-

ness. And thanks to this success, the militia as a defensive institution won the loyalty of the American colonists and soon became part of the social and traditional fabric of American colonial life.

Yet the colonial militia was not without its weaknesses. Since the units were uniformly seen as created for local defense, the militiamen were not inclined to respond to crises outside their own regions. This was especially noticeable in the eighteenth century as the Indian menace faded. In Virginia, for example, there was so little threat to the peace that the militia hardly existed for almost half a century, the Virginia Rangers being considered sufficient to watch the frontier. In 1713, when a threat arose from the Tuscarora Indians, Governor Alexander Spotswood was unable to raise the militia or even enlist volunteers and was forced to make peace with the tribe instead.

But even as the Indian threat receded, potential new enemies were emerging: the French and Spanish. Now the enemy would be more formidable but not near at hand, meaning that larger military forces would have to be recruited for longer times to serve at greater distances from home. Accordingly, the tendency arose to enlist recruits from outside the militia structure. Indians, free blacks and mulattoes, white servants and apprentices, plus landless whites – all were recruited as volunteers. As a result, the actual fighting that occurred was increasingly carried out by these new formations, while the old militia units became more and more social in function. If serious danger was close at hand, the militia would still respond; when it was not, the 'strollers,' 'vagabonds,' and 'drifters' were the first to be recruited for military service. How well these changes would work in practice was put to the test when the American colonies became embroiled in the English-French wars.

A frontiersman with the first native firearm, the Pennsylvania long rifle.

Colonial Wars Against the French and Indians

While the British colonists were building up their colonies along the Atlantic seaboard from Maine to Georgia in the seventeenth and early eighteenth centuries, they were not alone. To the north, along the St Lawrence River valley, the French had established colonies that eventually reached the Great Lakes country and extended down the Mississippi River to the Gulf of Mexico. To the south, the Spanish were also busy creating colonies in Florida, along the Gulf Coast, and in what is now the American southwest. Thus the English colonies were effectively ringed by potentially hostile settlements, against which they had to be on constant guard.

At the same time, the English colonists displayed a marked inclination to expand into the interior of the continent. They especially desired to cross the Appalachian mountain chain and move onto the lush, forested lands beyond. Yet this movement directly challenged the French to the north and west. The French, though fewer in number than the English, had established more favorable relations with the Indian tribes with whom they traded for furs and were thus able to recruit the Indians as allies in their border conflicts with the ever-expanding English settlers and traders.

In Europe, the English and French monarchies were now engaged in a titanic struggle for domination, and soon Europe's 'Wars for Empire' spilled over into North America, initiating a period of colonial conflict that lasted for seven decades, from 1689 to 1763. The English and their colonists warred against the French both at home and in North America, with the Spanish (trying to maintain their European and colonial greatness) often siding with the French. In four successive wars the English colonial militias were called upon to aid the mother country and her regular military forces. Given their animosity toward the French, both for their encroachments on English colonial rights and for their willingness to use savage Indians as allies, the American colonists were ready to stand beside the British land and naval forces, but often only if local grievances were involved or if the danger was perceived as affecting them seriously.

The first of the Wars for Empire was fought between 1689 and 1697. In Europe it was known as the War of the League of Augsburg; in America it was called simply King William's War. Here the northern colonies, which were most aggrieved by French attacks on their fishing rights and were most endangered by attacks by France's Indian allies on the frontier, led the way. While the British were willing to use their powerful navy to war on the French colonists in Canada in this first war, they were reluctant to supply the manpower necessary to carry out a land expedition against the French garrisons there. The New England colonies therefore accepted the task of raising a land army to attack their French neighbors. This was not strictly a militia operation, since militia units could not operate outside the colonies, but recruits were drawn largely from existing trainbands. Popular leaders were chosen to lead the operations, and the colonial assemblies put up the money for the attacks on the French. Two complementary operations were planned. One colonial expedition would attack Port Royal in Acadia (Novia Scotia) at the mouth of the St Lawrence; the second would march into Canada following the lake and river chain from the Hudson River valley to Montréal on the St Lawrence.

For the first of these operations the colony of Massachusetts raised a force of 700 men for a land and naval attack on Port Royal. Supported by the Royal Navy, the colonial troopers took the town early in 1690 but were unable to leave enough men there to retain it and it fell back into French hands. Undeterred, the Massachusetts volunteers tried again later in the same year. Now they assembled a 2000-man force, this time to take the fortress at Québec. Here they met nothing but frustrating failure. Failure also dogged the concurrent operation designed to take Montréal farther up the St Lawrence. Volunteers from New York and Connecticut were called to assemble at Albany, then move up the river chain to Montréal. Some units never arrived, and those that did march north made such slow progress through the wilderness that the whole expedition was called off. If the American phase of King William's War was inconclusive, so too was the European phase, and the French and British eventually made peace. But not for long.

Queen Anne's War, or the War of the Spanish Succession as it was called in Europe, took place between 1701 and 1713. Again it was a frustrating experience for the colonials. Again they attempted to subdue their French neighbors to the north by a two-pronged attack on the lower and upper St Lawrence citadels. The eastern prong was to sail from Boston to hit Québec by land and sea, with support from the British navy and five regiments of British regulars. The western prong was again to assemble at Albany and move overland against Montréal. Some 1500 volunteers gathered at Albany in 1709 to carry out the overland attack; an almost equal number gathered in Boston to move on Québec. Then came word that the British were not coming, as the troops were needed at home, and both expeditions had consequently to be abandoned. But the next year the colonists, with British naval support, were able to raise 1500 men and take Port Royal for a second time, and this time they held it as a permanent possession of the Crown.

The following year, 1711, the British promised naval and military aid, and the two-pronged attack scheme was revived. New England raised a force of 1500 men to join a British force of 7000 regulars. Considerable naval support was provided, but the sizeable expedition foundered on the rocks of the St Lawrence when the irresolute admiral commanding, Sir William Phips, lost his bearings in the fog in the mouth of the St Lawrence and, seeing a number of his ships go aground, gave up and brought the expedition back to Boston before sailing for home. This debacle meant that Sir Francis Nicholson, commanding the 2000 men assembled at Albany for the overland drive on Montréal, had to abandon his plans too. If the New England colonists were dismayed by these events, they were consoled by the fact that at the end of the war, in 1713, France was forced to turn over Newfoundland, Acadia, and the lands surrounding Hudson Bay to England.

Yet the French menace still remained to the north and west. Now the French began to rely more heavily on their Indian allies to harass the neighboring English colonists, especially in the Great Lakes and Ohio River regions, by supplying them with firearms. The French also maintained a string of forts designed to assure their hold on the North American interior and to protect their fur trade with their Indian friends.

After three decades of peace, the Wars for Empire broke out again in 1744, in what was called King George's War in the colonies and the War of the Austrian Succession in Europe. It ended in 1748, but in this short time the colonials demonstrated their military prowess by mounting a major expedition against Louisbourg ('the Gibraltar of the New World') on Cape Breton Island at the entrance to the St Lawrence. All of the 4000 men and most of the naval vessels in this successful operation were contributed by the New England colonies.

Predictably, colonies removed from the area of struggle were not interested in helping their compatriots: Fishing rights and French depredations were New England problems. Nevertheless, the expedition was a success, and Louisbourg fell to the colonial forces. Subsequently, when at the peace conference ending the war the British gave Louisbourg back to the French in exchange for the port of Madras in India, the colonists were outraged. Yet whatever the outcome, the colonial volunteers had proven in their typical eighteenth-century-style siege of Louisbourg that they could be a formidable fighting force, despite what the British generals thought of their rag-tag appearance and lack of professional military training.

After 1748 the French continued to strengthen their American possessions by expanding their network of forts along the Great Lakes and Ohio River valley. These included Fort Frontenac, at the eastern end of Lake Ontario, and Fort Niagara, along the crucial Niagara River. Especially important was their erection of Fort Duquesne at the confluence of the Allegheny and Monongahela Rivers (the site of present-day Pittsburgh) in 1753, thereby reinforcing their claim to the whole trans-Appalachian interior. If the mother country was still unsure whether it should push for complete French expulsion from the American interior, the colonists directly affected by the French presence had no such doubts, and conflict soon broke out anew. From 1754 to 1756 an undeclared war raged along the English-French frontier in colonial America.

Virginia, allowed by the crown to repel French encroachments upon territories claimed by her (which included western Pennsylvania), sent a militia force under Colonel George Washington to attack the French at Fort Duquesne and drive them from the area. This Virginia force was met by superior French numbers, compelled to surrender, and sent back home.

Undeterred by this loss, the British Crown dispatched a force of two regiments of regulars commanded by Major General Edward Braddock. Braddock, a veteran of four decades of honorable service on European battlefields, assembled a force of over 2000 men (which included a number of Virginia militiamen) and set out from Virginia in June 1755 through the wilderness to expel the French from Fort Duquesne.

Frustrated by being able to make only two miles per day, Braddock went ahead with an advance force of 1500 men to launch his attack. On 9 July 1755, when only seven miles from Duquesne, he and his army were suddenly attacked by an inferior force composed of less than 900 French regulars, Canadian militia and Indians firing from ambush. Braddock's forces tried vainly to form a line of fire to answer the enemy's withering fusillade. Unable to come to grips with the concealed enemy and soon facing further intense fire on their flanks, the British-militia forces suffered severe casualties, and after three hours retreated from the field in disarray, storming through their baggage train, even though no enemy was pursuing. Over 900 British and colonial troops had been killed or wounded, and 63 of 83 British officers were also casualties, including General Braddock, who was mortally wounded.

It was now obvious that highly-disciplined

Forced to surrender Fort Necessity to the French in 1754, young George Washington glumly returned to Virginia.

European troops marching in columns and firing in line on command could not be effective in the wilderness without serious modifications in tactics. Future fights would see the British regulars employing scouts, skirmishers, rangers and light troops (wearing brown and green clothing in place of the traditional British scarlet) to prevent a repetition of Braddock's costly lesson in frontier battle tactics.

The year 1755 also saw two expeditions by colonial troops against French forts in the wilderness: Crown Point on Lake Champlain and Fort Niagara between Lake Erie and Lake Ontario. Both were failures. Some 3000 colonials were assembled from New York and New England for the attack on Crown Point, but the volunteers got only as far as Lake George before they were repulsed by French forces. The expedition to Fort Niagara in the west was cancelled because of logistical problems.

In 1756 the French and British at last officially declared war. In America the conflict is remembered as the French and Indian War of 1756-1763. In Europe it is called the Seven Years' War. It was the final and decisive War for Empire. This time the British decided to concentrate their efforts on the American front. Eventually strong naval forces and 25,000 British troops were sent to the colonies for this all-out fight. These British forces were supplemented by a number of American colonial regiments placed in regular service and by colonial volunteer and militia units. The greatest number of colonial troops came from the more endangered New York and New England colonies, but most colonies fell far short of their requisitioned men, supplies and financial support.

Suffering only one important loss in the first three years of the conflict – this at Fort Ticonderoga on Lake Champlain when a combined British-colonial force of 16,000 attempted to take the fort and was repelled with heavy losses in 1758 – the British and colonial forces scored impressive victories over their French adversaries. In 1758 Louisbourg was taken in classic siege fashion by British army and naval forces, and in that same year a force of 3000 men, made up largely of colonials, captured Fort Frontenac on Lake Ontario, thus weakening the French position at Fort Duquesne. As a result, when a British and colonial force made its way to the western fort near the site of Braddock's humiliating defeat three years earlier, they found it abandoned. Occupying the fort, the British renamed the installation Fort Pitt in honor of William Pitt, their great parliamentary war leader.

By now Britain was fully committed to deciding the issue with France on the American battlefields. Again a two-pronged attack was planned against the French bastions in Canada. One army of 9000 men under Major General James Wolfe, still in his early thirties, aided by a strong naval force, advanced up the St Lawrence River to the city of Québec. Discovering a path up the sheer cliffs in front of the city, Wolfe and his men daringly scaled the escarpment on the night of 12 September 1759 and suddenly appeared before the city in traditional battle line the next morning. The French commander, Major General Louis Joseph, le marquis de Montcalm, drew up his regular and militia troops in line to face the British foe on the Plains of Abraham. Shortly after, the greatest and most decisive battle of the Wars for Empire was fought in classic European style. The less disciplined French troops could not

Britain captured Louisbourg, guardian of the St Lawrence, in 1745, only to return it to France in 1748 via the Treaty of Aix-la-Chapelle, and then to recapture it in 1758.

Britain learned harsh truths about wilderness fighting in 1755 when General Braddock and 1500 regulars were ambushed by French and Indians near Fort Duquesne (*above*). Among the nearly 900 British killed was Braddock (*left*). Three quarters of the British officers were casualties.

stand up before the withering volley fire of the British regiments. Victory went to the British regulars, although both Wolfe and Montcalm fell mortally wounded that day.

In the meantime, as the western prong of the offensive, another army of 11,000 British regulars and colonial volunteers had assembled in New York under General Jeffrey Amherst. Their mission was to capture Fort Ticonderoga and Crown Point and then advance to the St Lawrence, there to take Montréal and move downriver to assist Wolfe at Québec. Amherst first sent a detached force to capture Fort Niagara. Its success there left Fort Detroit and the other western forts isolated. He then moved on Fort Ticonderoga and Crown Point. Although the French garrisons at these outposts decided to abandon them to the stronger enemy, they retreated only as far as the Richelieu River and there set up such an effective defense that Amherst was unable to make his rendezvous with Wolfe at Québec. Only in 1760 did Amherst take Montréal, thus bringing Canada under British control and ending the colonial phase of the Seven Years' War.

When the war was finally brought to a close in 1763 by the Treaty of Paris, the extent

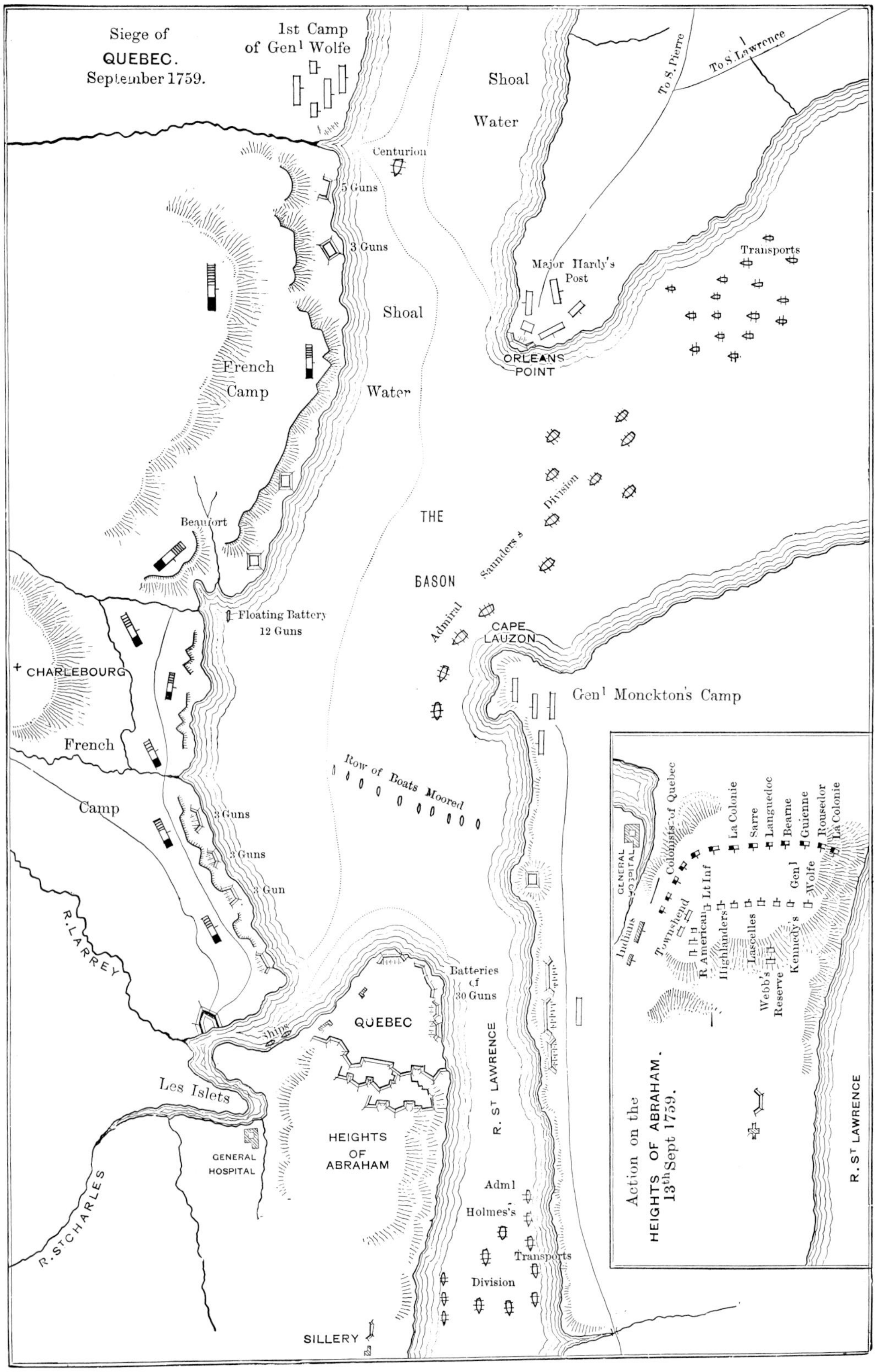

The siege of Québec, 1759. The French position in Canada was fatally affected by the loss of this fortress city.

of French defeat was reflected in the terms of peace. France was forced to relinquish her entire American empire, with the exception of small islands, Miquelon and St Pierre, south of Newfoundland. Her ally, Spain, lost Florida to Britain, but received New Orleans and the vast lands west of the Mississippi as compensation. Britain was now the dominant power on the North American continent.

These conflicts had seen the colonial volunteer-militia units carry the brunt of the land fighting in the first three wars and also make sizeable contributions in the last and decisive conflict. In the process, much had been learned. It was not that traditional eighteenth-century European-style warfare of line fire and siege had been discredited: indeed, such tactics had proved decisive in key campaigns such as those at Louisbourg and Québec. But open-field battlefield tactics had to be modified whenever fighting took place in the wilderness and against non-conventional enemies. Scouts, skirmishers, camouflage clothing, and irregular formations were shown to be absolutely necessary off the open-field battleground where the enemy utilized surprise, maneuver, and ambush as primary tactics. It had also become evident in the course of the war that supplying an army in the wilderness presented special problems. Any army moving away from its base would inevitably encounter serious difficulties unless it took its food, ammunition, and all other necessities of war with it. In short, the colonial wars had demonstrated that whereas well-equipped, well-disciplined armies still dominated the open field, control of uncultivated hinterland might well fall to him who best mastered the new tactics of guerrilla.

The American Revolution

With the Treaty of Paris of 1763 and the end of the Wars for Empire, both the American colonists and the mother country looked for-

ward to a time of peace, but differences soon arose between them over how the now-expanded American colonial territories should be governed. Britain was deeply in debt, thanks to the costs of the wars, yet at least 10,000 soldiers would now be needed to guarantee the safety of the new frontier regions and their Indian inhabitants, especially since the American colonists assumed that with the fall of New France those lands would be open to them for settlement. Since the colonists had obviously gained much by the

Right: Cap Rouge, nine miles north of Québec, was the initial base camp of British General James Wolfe.
Below: Benjamin West's famous painting of the death of Wolfe at Québec.

Two events that sparked the American Revolution: the Boston Tea Party (*top*) and the Boston Massacre (*top right*).

defeat of the French and the acquisition of their territories, it seemed only right to the Crown that some of the necessary tax burden should be borne by the colonists, especially as their taxes were significantly lower than those paid by citizens in the mother country.

Thus, as a matter of justice and fiscal responsibility, the decision was made by Crown and Parliament to raise both the internal and external taxes levied on the American colonists. The primary means employed would be both to increase taxes on trade in and out of the colonies through the Navigation Acts and to enforce these and existing tax measures far more rigorously than before. At the same time, the Crown made efforts to bring the colonies under much tighter governmental control to assure that their policies and practices would be favorable to the mother country and to the empire at large.

That was Parliament's point of view. The American colonists saw things in quite another way. They felt they had already made adequate contributions to the empire through existing taxes and through their miltiary service during the recent wars. And they did not want the British regulars on the frontier anyway. These soldiers might hold the Indians in check, but they might also keep the colonists out of coveted lands. Worse, in 1763 the government had established the Proclamation Line along the crest of the Appalachian ridge and declared the lands to the west to be a giant Indian reservation, thereby wiping out colonial land claims.

The raising of taxes and greater governmental control from London – which would lessen the amount of home rule enjoyed by the colonists – seemed to be turning the clock back and denying the colonists their legal liberties. The degree of self-government enjoyed by the colonists for a century and a half may technically have been a legal privilege, not a right, but the colonists did not see it that way. Privileges long enjoyed tend to be looked upon as rights sanctioned by time and the colonists were not about to acquiesce in the retraction of their 'rights.'

As Parliament attempted to raise taxes through such measures as the Sugar and Stamp Acts, only to be met by protests and economic boycotts which forced the mother country to back down, it became obvious that many of the colonists were willing to resist with more than polite disapproval and remonstrance. But when the Tea Act was passed in 1773, and some Bostonians responded by unceremoniously dumping shiploads of tea into the harbor, the king and Parliament decided that it was time to call a halt. Parliament then passed a number of restrictive acts, including closing the port of Boston, designed to bring Massachusetts back into subjection. These acts soon became known collectively in the colonies as the 'Intolerable Acts.' When Massachusetts was also placed under military rule, in the person of Major General Sir Thomas Gage, the stage was set for armed resistance.

The Massachusetts Provincial Congress, determined to resist coercion and military rule, ordered the colonial militia to prepare for action, if necessary, and began to collect ammunition and military supplies. These were stored at Concord, twenty miles outside of Boston. When General Gage found out through spies about the cache of forbidden supplies, he sent a force of 700 men to seize them on the night of 18 April 1775. But the minutemen, the elite among the militia, were warned of this expedition by Paul Revere and William Dawes and formed as a body on the village green at Lexington to block them. Early on the morning of 19 April the British regulars and the Massachusetts minutemen faced each other on Lexington Green. Someone – no one knows who – pulled a trigger. Immediately the regulars fired volleys and charged with their bayonets. The militiamen dispersed after suffering eight dead. The regulars marched on to Concord, destroyed what was left of the military stores, and began to march back to Boston. Along the way they came under attack by militiamen firing from houses and from behind walls and fences and were saved only by a relief force sent out from Boston by General Gage. British casualties for the day were almost 275 men; the American militiamen suffered 95, a tribute to their guerrilla tactics.

Word of what had happened spread like wildfire through the colonies. Charges of British military and governmental tyranny seemed to have been confirmed in blood. Militia from throughout Massachusetts and from the other New England colonies poured into the Boston area, and the British garrison

The beginning of the Revolutionary War: Minutemen and British regulars skirmish on Lexington Green.

found itself surrounded by a ring of determined patriots. At the same time, militia forces under Benedict Arnold of Connecticut and Ethan Allen of Vermont seized the key British forts at Ticonderoga and Crown Point. The Second Continental Congress, meeting in Philadelphia, found that it now had to decide what to do with a *de facto* army surrounding the colonies' most important port and threatening to expel the British.

But events would not wait on prolonged deliberations. As weeks passed, with the forces facing one another (the militia being supplemented by volunteer units from the neighboring colonies, and the British receiving reinforcements of 6,500 men), both sides finally decided to make moves to break the stalemate. When the British began to fortify Dorchester Heights south of Boston, the colonists moved to fortify Bunker Hill, at the neck of the Charlestown peninsula to the north. But the working party foolishly decided to fortify Breed's Hill, just across from Boston, instead, and the British resolved to drive them off. On the afternoon of 17 June 1775 General Gage sent 2200 men under Major General William Howe to carry out the operation. The Americans, roughly equal in numbers to Howe's forces, twice repelled British attacks on their fortified positions. Only on the third try was Howe successful, but he suffered a loss of over 1000 men in gaining his Pyrrhic victory. The Battle of Bunker Hill (as it mistakenly came to be called) really gained little for the British, for they were still surrounded by the 'rabble army' and unable to break out. The rebels, for their part, could not drive the British out of Boston, but they had helped create a myth (dubious, in the light of subsequent events) that an American militiaman was more than equal to any British regular.

The fighting in New England in the spring and summer of 1775 forced the Crown into a new military stance. If the colonies were determined on war, then war they would have. But it would be a conventional war fought along conventional lines, with mass British armies meeting their foes on the battlefield and the Royal Navy shutting down the colonies' commerce and supporting the British land armies up and down the coast. The British would either bring the rebellious colonial armies to decisive battle or destroy them by maneuver. Thus the rebellion would come to an end, and the pre-war political situation would be restored. In practice, the matter would not be so simple.

Bringing this British force to bear on America took some time. This left the colonies about a year to prepare themselves for the decisive conflict. Needing a regular military force to protect the colonies, the Second Continental Congress adopted the irregular New England army assembled around Boston as the Continental Army on 14

Lexington began as an American defeat: The British brushed aside the Minuteman, killing eight. But on their march back to Boston they lost 25 percent of their force to American snipers.

In storming Bunker (actually Breed's) Hill the British won a worthless objective at a cost of 1000 casualties.

June 1775. Thus the US Army, the primary defender of the nation's rights and independence, was born in a season of need as the American colonies cast their lot for freedom and prepared to defend it with their lives. At the same time, the Congress also called for volunteers from the other colonies to join the Continentals, and the next day appointed the Virginian George Washington as Commander in Chief, a move to solidify support from the southern colonies.

Whatever their political intentions, the members of the Congress had chosen a first-rate leader, brimming with dedication to the American cause and able to inspire confidence in those around him. Washington had had only a little military experience during the French and Indian War, but now he set out, with the help of four newly-appointed major generals and eight brigadiers (two-thirds of the twelve being from New England and three chosen because of their experience in the British army) to create an army on the British model.

Plans called for an army of 20,000 men, but enlistments fell far short of that goal. Many colonists were reluctant to serve even a one-year enlistment period if it meant separation from their families, farms or, businesses. By the end of the year New England militiamen were already beginning to leave the siege lines around Boston and return home, and Washington had to fill their places with other militia and volunteers. For crucial siege sup-

At Cambridge, Mass., on 15 June 1775, George Washington assumed command of the day-old Continental Army.

plies, Washington outfitted a small navy manned by army volunteers. It managed to capture a few British supply ships. He also sent Colonel Henry Knox to Ticonderoga to bring back the 50 cannon captured there.

In the meantime Washington launched a major expedition in the hope both of adding Canada to the coalition of rebellious American colonies and of gaining control of the northern axis of the potential northern invasion route from the St Lawrence down through Lake Champlain to the vital Hudson River valley. Major General Philip Schuyler from New York was given the responsibility for this expedition in June 1775, and soon 2000 men were gathered for the undertaking. The invasion, following the pattern of the earlier colonial wars against the French, was to be two-pronged. The western prong, under Brigadier General Richard Montgomery, would march from Ticonderoga north to take Montréal. The eastern prong, headed by Colonel Benedict Arnold, was to move up the Kennebec River and across the wilds of Maine to strike Québec. Montgomery managed to take Montréal by 13 November, but Arnold's forces were decimated by sickness and desertion while moving through the rugged Maine wilderness. Thus the army under Arnold numbered only 600 on that same day, 13 November, that his soldiers crossed the St Lawrence, climbed the escarpment below Québec, and encamped on the Plains of Abraham.

The British regulars and Canadian militia at Québec were unwilling to commit themselves to formal battle as Montcalm had done sixteen years before, so Arnold drew back to await reinforcement from Montgomery at Montréal. But Montgomery could bring only 300 men, and virtually no Canadians had come forward to join the American cause. With the enlistments of about half of the American force due to expire at the end of the year, Arnold and Montgomery decided to make a last desperate attempt to take the city on the night of 30 December 1775. Launched in a raging snowstorm, the attack was a dismal failure. Montgomery was killed; Arnold, wounded. When the British received reinforcements and launched a counterattack in June 1776, the American army retreated without a credible fight. The Northern Army had failed. Canada and the St Lawrence were still firmly in British hands.

The only consolation the Americans could take from the campaigns of 1775-1776 was that on 17 March 1776 the British pulled out of Boston. General Howe, Gage's successor in command, decided to take his army to Hali-

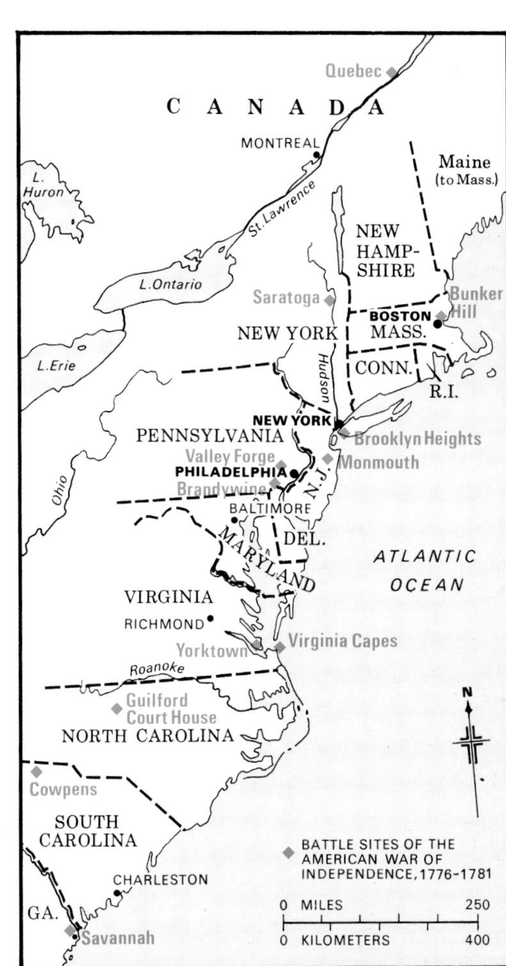

Right: Overview map of the Revolution.
Below: On 17 March 1776 the British abandoned Boston to the Americans.

Trumbull's famous scene of Congress endorsing the Declaration of Independence. The war was already a year old.

fax, Nova Scotia, to refit and await reinforcements from home. His decision to abandon Boston was aided by the fact that Washington's army had taken Dorchester Heights and Nook's Hill and had placed artillery there to harass the British below. The evacuation of Boston was not of major military significance. The British enjoyed firm control of Canada, had a major base of operations at Halifax, and were able to control the coast with the Royal Navy. Yet psychologically, the abandonment of Boston was uplifting for the rebellious colonists and made them even more confident of eventual victory.

On 4 July 1776 the Declaration of Independence was proclaimed. In one stroke it transferred a war for limited home rule into a war for independence from the Crown. Yet the weak confederation of thirteen states still faced a difficult task before independence would become reality. The new Americans were only 2.5 million in number and held more local than national loyalties, each state being jealous of its powers and prerogatives. The people were divided in their views on the war itself, with probably only one-third in favor of the revolution, one-third opposed, and one-third unwilling to commit themselves to either government. Short on war-making manufactures, the new United States of America would be hard pressed to fight a sustained war even with unanimous popular support.

Given all of this, Washington wisely realized that the one symbol of unity and center of resistance was the Continental Army, and he was determined to keep it intact at all costs. But the states were more solicitous of their own particular volunteer and militia forces (their 'lines') than toward the national military efforts. Furthermore, enlistments were short-term, desertions were frequent, opportunities for training were minimal, and the Congress insisted on playing an interfering role in running the war both through appointments of generals and determination of strategy. Military supplies were never sufficient for the army, and the Continental currency with which the soldiers were paid and supplies were purchased continually declined in value throughout the war.

Washington's Continental army was eventually authorized to consist of 110 battalions of infantry, or about 80,000 men, but it never numbered more than 30,000 men, and seldom could more than 15,000 be mustered for battle. As a result, Washington was constantly forced to use the militia units of the states to supplement his regulars. Sometimes these militia units provided sterling service; more often they did not. But though Washington bemoaned both the states' failure to support his Continentals and his need to rely on undependable militia units, this exceptional military leader somehow kept his forces together, maintained good relations with the Congress, and by patience and skill finally won the day against the British army and naval forces.

What was this Continental Army on which Washington – and the nation – depended so much? How was it organized, equipped and trained? In the beginning it was still very much a congeries of semi-local forces. Massachusetts contributed 26 battalions; Connecticut, 10; Rhode Island, three; and New Hampshire, three. The composition of each battalion, both in terms of the number of companies it included and its total strength, varied wildly. Suffice it to say that in 1775 the grand total came to about 17,000 men and officers. British regular forces in North America at the same time numbered only about 8500, but this establishment rose steadily throughout the war, reaching a total of 48,647 in 1781. Total American strength, as noted earlier, never exceeded 30,000, but this was sometimes enough to confer local superiority.

As a combat force, the Continental Army was at first almost entirely composed of infantry, the functions of cavalry and artillery being left to militia units. Indeed, it was not until 1777 that Congress finally got around to authorizing the creation of the first four regular cavalry regiments (each consisting of 360 light dragoons organized in six troops), but the need for a regular artillery branch

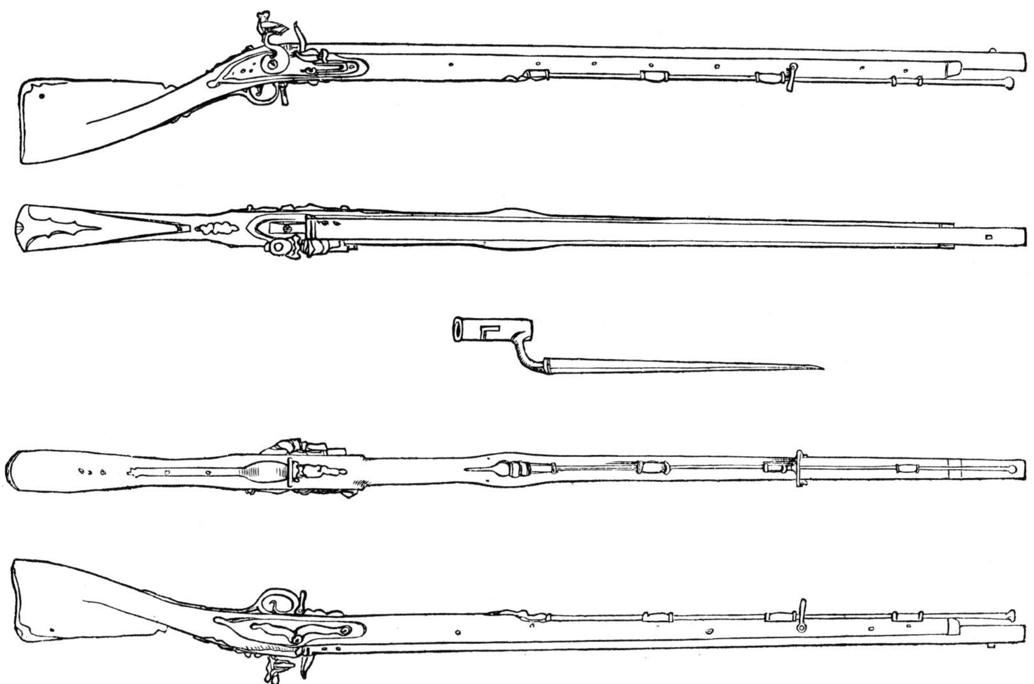

Probably the shoulder arm most widely used by both sides: Britain's Long Land ('Brown Bess') Musket.

was recognized almost from the onset of the fighting. In mid-1776, that same Colonel Henry Knox whom Washington, a year earlier, had sent scurrying to Ticonderoga to take charge of the captured British cannon, was ordered to establish a Continental Artillery. What Knox produced were four battalions, 10 companies each, armed with from six to 10 guns or howitzers per company. The contribution that this artillery branch made to American victory was of a high order and set high standards for the future.

The equipment of the Continental Army was, throughout most of the war, chaotic. Since the army had not existed before 1775 there was of course no standard infantry weapon. Captured stores of the British army's 'Brown Bess' muskets (a .753-calibre flintlock with a 44-inch-long barrel) may have formed the nucleus of the infantry's original firepower, but the majority of the Continentals' shoulder weapons was a mixed bag of odd-calibre muskets, fusils and carbines (varieties of short muskets), and the rare, deadly Pennsylvania long rifles so favored by marksmen. As the war progressed increasing numbers of French .69-calibre Charleville muskets found their way into American hands, and some American manufacturers began producing copies of both the Charleville and the Brown Bess for the Army. But at no point could Continental infantrymen be said to have had a standard shoulder arm.

The same was true of artillery. Although American manufacturers eventually began to produce standard four-, 12- and 18-pound cannon, the Continental Artillery was always primarily dependent on weapons of foreign origin, and these came in all sizes and shapes. Very loosely speaking, American artillery tended to follow the French patterns – four-, eight-, and 12-pound field guns; 16-, 24- and 36-pound siege guns; and eight-, 12- and 16-inch mortars.

As to dress, there was an insistent, but never very successful, drive towards uniformity. At first there was no standard at all. Then, in 1775, Congress recommended that all Army uniform coats be brown, with the color of the facings on the lapels and the number and arrangements of coat buttons to serve as distinguishing badges for the battalions. This recommendation was only notionally followed, some units insisting on retaining their own blue, green and even *red* coats; and in any case, the dyes used to produce the supposedly uniform brown coats were so variable that the results ranged from light sand to dark umber. Again, in 1779, Congress ordered that the standard infantry coat be blue, with distinctively-colored lapel facings for troops from each of four geographic regions (New England – white; New York and New Jersey – buff; Pennsylvania, Delaware, Maryland and Virginia – red; the southern states – blue, trimmed with white). Although this uniform often appears in later pictorial, film, and stage representations of Continental soldiery, it was never universally adopted because by 1779 the purchase of so many new uniforms was virtually beyond the government's financial means. For the remainder of the war most Continental units continued to have to cobble together what uniforms they could from existing supplies, including the nearly 30,000 uniforms provided by the French between 1776 and 1778.

Until 1778 training in the Continental Army was as haphazard as most other things about it. The low levels of training that had been

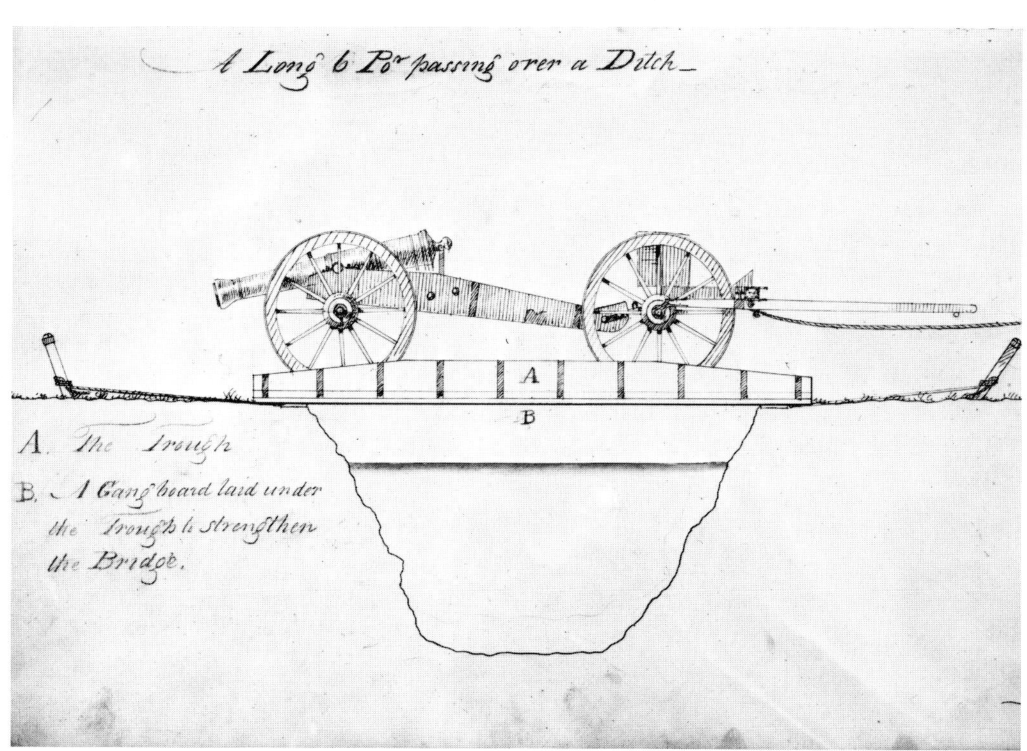

Below left: A Rhode Island artilleryman. At first only the militia served cannon.
Below: A long 6-pounder field gun.

American army uniforms, 1776-9: *right*, a brown-clad infantryman; shooting, a member of 'Morgan's Rifles.'

furnished by the pre-war militias guaranteed that Washington's new army would be largely innocent of discipline and all but the most basic military skills. The soldiers' dedication and enthusiasm may have offset some of these liabilities, but throughout the early years of the war the Continental Army was obliged to do a great deal of learning while on the job.

This state of affairs improved considerably when, at the beginning of 1778, Washington appointed Friedrich Wilhelm, Baron von Steuben, to the post of Inspector General of the Army. A former staff officer in the army of Frederick the Great of Prussia, von Steuben quickly set up at Valley Forge a training program that was at once highly professional, comprehensive, and specifically adapted to American conditions. Men trained personally by von Steuben returned to their own units and inaugurated local training programs based on what they had learned from the master, and in this way the effect of von Steuben's teachings spread through the Army with remarkable rapidity. The following year the Baron published his *Regulations for the Order and Discipline of the Troops of the United States*: it would remain the Army's official manual for the next 33 years.

So great was von Steuben's influence that it even prompted a restructuring of the Army's basic formations. After 1778 the standard battalion was to consist of eight companies of about 60 men each. The standard tactical unit would be two companies, the theoretical maximum that a single man could command by voice in the heat of battle.

Yet von Steuben was not a magician. Though he had helped to make the Continental Army far more formidable than it had previously been, it still had to confront a highly dangerous and professional adversary. And whether the Americans could ever hope to achieve victory on the battlefield continued to depend on a great many considerations that were less tactical than strategic.

That the Americans did finally prevail can in part be explained by the fact that the British were fighting a war 3000 miles from their home base, and in part by the fact that they were fighting for a cause over which public opinion at home was badly divided. The Royal Navy might assure control of the American waters and blockade the Americans' major ports, but the British army still had to destroy an army, aided by militia, that could refuse to fight and move back into the interior toward its own bases of supply almost at will. And the longer the American military forces held out, the more difficult would be the political problem of maintaining support for the war on the home front. Furthermore, as both sides realized, sitting in the wings waiting for a chance to strike if the opportunity presented itself, was France, still smarting from her losses in the Wars for Empire and hoping for an opportunity to regain her lost territories and weaken her mortal enemy across the Channel. The outcome of American war for independence, like most wars, would depend almost as much on time and will as it did on military struggle. Whether the Americans would have enough of either was the question.

In 1776 the British were finally able to bring their military and naval power to bear, but at year's end the American rebels had not been subdued and, indeed, were showing remarkable vitality. After the evacuation of Boston, General Howe remained in Halifax awaiting reinforcements for his intended attack on New York City. From there he would move north along the Hudson into Canada, thus effectively cutting off New England, the center of resistance, from the other states. From March until June Howe tarried, but in the meantime the British government ordered an expedition into the south to encourage Loyalists there to bring this section of the United States back under British rule.

The southern expedition, to be transported by a fleet under Admiral Sir Peter Parker, was delayed in starting and did not arrive in American waters until May, by which time numerous Tory forces in the south had been defeated by patriot forces. Despite this, Parker decided to attack Charleston, the largest and most influential city in the south, but his attack on the American Continental and militia army failed miserably. The Americans had established their defenses on Sullivan Island in the form of a palmetto log fort, dubbed Fort Moultrie, at the mouth of the harbor. The British landed on nearby Long Island in June but found they could not ford the waters to attack Sullivan Island and had to sit idly by while American artillery pounded the British invasion fleet. Parker was forced to give up the effort and sail north to join Howe in Halifax. For three years thereafter the south was virtually untouched by the war.

Howe, after further frustrating delays, finally set off with his invasion force for New York in late August. It was so late in the year that all he could hope to do at this point was to seize the city and its vicinity and use them as a staging area for a campaign up the Hudson-St Lawrence route the following year. Howe had an army of 32,000 men for the invasion. He was also ably supported by a powerful naval force under his brother, Admiral Richard Howe, giving him control of the critical Hudson, Harlem and East Rivers around New York. Washington, with his Continentals and militia, had only about 19,000 men to resist this British land-sea operation.

Washington made a fundamental mistake in trying to defend Manhattan Island by fortifying Brooklyn Heights on Long Island, across the East River. Brooklyn Heights, he reasoned, could dominate the lower tip of Manhattan and keep it secure. But by standing at Brooklyn Heights the American army was subject to being cut off from behind, and although the land behind Brooklyn Heights was defended by American troops, Major General John Sullivan had left the crucial Jamaica-Bedford road unguarded. Landing on 22 August 1776, Howe attacked the American position by the unguarded road and forced the defenders back upon the fortifications on Brooklyn Heights. Fortunately for the American cause, Howe delayed his main attack long enough to allow Washington to escape with his forces across the East River on the night of 29 August.

Two weeks later Howe hit the remainder of Washington's forces on Manhattan and forced them to flee north. But again his delay in pressing the attack allowed the Americans to dig in at Harlem Heights and hold off the British for another month. When, in mid-October, Howe landed behind Washington at Pell's Point, the Virginia general evacuated Manhattan and moved north to White Plains, leaving some 6000 men to guard the Hudson River at two forts situated on each side of the river: Fort Washington on the east and Fort Lee on the west bank. Howe came after Washington, forcing him to send half his

Right: Continental infantry, 1779-83.
Below: Battle of Valcour Island, 1776. The Continental Army fought a naval battle in a fruitless effort to break Britain's hold on Lake Champlain.

November, 1776: Lord Cornwallis' troops scaled New Jersey's Hudson Palisades, forcing the Americans out of Fort Lee.

army across the Hudson into New Jersey while the other half remained to delay Howe at the passes through the New York highlands upriver at Peekskill. Howe then seized Fort Washington and 3000 prisoners and forced Major General Nathaniel Greene to abandon Fort Lee. Washington's army was by now in full retreat, out of New York, across New Jersey, and down into Pennsylvania. Stragglers and deserters so sapped his forces that he had only 2000 effectives when he finally halted. The 8000 men he had left in the highlands above New York City just drifted away from the war.

The only bright spot on the American scene as 1776 campaigning came to a close was the spirited defense Benedict Arnold had made against a flotilla of boats Major General Guy Carleton had constructed to bring his sizeable force down Lake Champlain to seize Fort Ticonderoga. Carleton wanted to take 'Fort Ti' in the fall to use it as a base for a move down the Hudson the following spring. Arnold and his men built their own flotilla to challenge Carleton and, although losing in the subsequent naval action at Valcour Island in Lake Champlain, so delayed Carleton that he gave up the idea of laying siege to Fort Ti for that year and returned to winter quarters in Canada, a welcome respite for the Americans.

Despite this victory by Arnold, the American cause looked dim as the winter of 1776-1777 settled in. The British army was in control of the central reaches of the eastern seaboard, having established themselves in winter quarters in Newport, Rhode Island; in New York City; and in Perth Amboy, New Brunswick, Princeton, Trenton and Borden-

Washington crossing the Delaware on Christmas night 1776, the prelude to his brilliant surprise attack on Trenton the next morning.

town in New Jersey. Howe had every reason to be satisfied.

But Washington was not done. Hastily and desperately assembling a force of about 7000 men, both Continentals and Pennsylvania militia, he made plans to hit the British in their winter quarters. He had to do this before the end of December because many enlistments expired on the last day of the year. His plan was to make a surprise attack on the British on Christmas night at Trenton, southwest of Howe's New York base. A second force under Colonel John Cadwalader was to do the same at Bordentown, farther south. A third force was to cross opposite Trenton and prevent any escape from Washington's attack. The second and third phases of the plan misfired, but Washington's attack on Trenton was superbly effective.

Crossing the Delaware River at McConkey's Ferry, a few miles above Trenton, the American force proceeded down the east bank of the river, then split into two columns to enter the town at each end on the morning of 26 December at 0800 hours. The Hessian mercenaries were taken completely by surprise and surrendered after a fight lasting only an hour and a half. Washington took over 900 prisoners. The Hessians had lost 40 killed; the American casualty list was only four dead and four wounded.

Encouraged by this success, Washington again made an incursion with 5000 men across the Delaware on the night of 30 December. This time he found his way blocked by British garrisons under Major General Charles Cornwallis at Trenton. Delaying battle until the next day because his troops were exhausted, Cornwallis was sure that Washington had fallen into a trap and would have to fight. But Washington and his men slipped away during the night, leaving their campfires burning to deceive their enemies, and struck Princeton, to the northeast of Trenton, the next morning, inflicting heavy casualties on two British regiments.

Washington then pulled back into winter quarters at Morristown, New Jersey, and the British pulled in their outpost to positions closer to New York City for the rest of the winter. Washington had won two notable, if small, victories at Trenton and Princeton, but they had hardly changed the strategic scene in and round New York. They had, however, convinced many American British doubters of his prowess as a military commander.

The year 1777 did not produce significant victories in the field or the crushing of Washington's army that the British had expected. Instead, only Pyrrhic victories were gained, and the British grand scheme to cut off New England from the other colonies ended in defeat.

General Howe decided to capture the capital of Philadelphia, even though he was promised only 5500 reinforcements from home, instead of the 15,000 he requested. Facing him would be Washington's army of about 8000. The bitter Morristown winter had taken its toll of his troops, but replacements had been found with the coming of spring. Of equal importance, numerous foreigners had thrown in their lot with the undermanned and poorly-officered Continental forces. Some were men of limited ability on the battlefield but with pompous claims to rank and privilege; others would make valuable contributions to the war effort: Thaddeus Kosciuszko, a fine military engineer from Poland; Friedrich Wilhelm, Baron von Steuben, from Germany, who would train Washington's army at Valley Forge; and Marie Joseph du Motier, le marquis de Lafayette, from France, who became a trusted leader at Washington's side.

During June and July 1777 Washington kept his main army between Philadelphia and New York to bar Howe's path to the capital, but the British commander loaded his army on ships and sailed down to Hampton Roads and then up Chesapeake Bay to Head of Elk, southwest of Philadelphia. Washington rapidly shifted his covering army south to meet Howe and took up a blocking position at Brandywine Creek. At Brandywine on 11 September Washington's forces were flanked by Lord Cornwallis' troops, which had marched upstream and moved behind the American position, and Washington was forced to retreat to Chester, below Philadelphia. By 26 September the capital itself had fallen (the Congress having fled to York, Pennsylvania), and Howe marched into the city and disposed his troops around the surrounding area in a defensive perimeter. Washington attempted to break Howe's lines as he had done at Trenton the year before, but his attack at Germantown on 4 October misfired. Howe then tried to lure Washington

Mortally wounded in the fighting at Trenton, Hessian Col. Rall lived long enough to surrender to Washington.

Two of Washington's foreign advisors: Friedrich Wilhelm, Baron von Steuben (*left*) and Marie Joseph du Motier, le marquis de Lafayette (*below*).

and his army out into decisive combat at Whitemarsh, but the American commander would have none of it. Eventually Howe withdrew into winter quarters in Philadelphia, while Washington set up winter quarters at Valley Forge, twenty miles northwest, in a state of material and human exhaustion.

Thus by the end of Howe's 1777 campaign the British commander had successfully taken Philadelphia, but in the process he had unwittingly lain the groundwork for one of the most crucial British defeats of the war. While Howe had been carrying out his amphibious operation from the Chesapeake to take Philadelphia, he had left only a small contingent of troops in New York City, not enough to move north and join in a large operation then being carried out by Major General Sir John ('Gentleman Johnny') Burgoyne. Although apparently aware of Howe's intention of moving southwest against Philadelphia in the summer of 1777, the Crown had approved of Burgoyne's separate movement down from Canada to strike at the Americans via the Lake Champlain-Lake George route. He planned to reach Albany by the fall. His main body of almost 8000 British regulars, Hessians, Tories, and Indians would come down Lake Champlain, take Fort Ticonderoga, and then move down Lake George to the Hudson and Albany. A secondary force of about 1700 regulars and friendly Indians under Colonel Barry St Leger would sail to Oswego on the shore of Lake Ontario, move down to the Mohawk River valley to take Fort Stanwix on the upper Mohawk, just to the east of Oneida Lake, and attack Albany from the west. Facing this dual invasion force were only about 3000 Continentals led by the unpopular General Schuyler of New York.

Left: At Valley Forge von Steuben taught Continentals military drill.
Below: The Battle of Bemis Heights, 7 October 1777, the American victory that decided the Saratoga campaign.

Saratoga proved how effective the American long rifle could be in battle.

Ticonderoga fell easily to Burgoyne's forces on 27 June 1777. Pursuing the defeated American enemy to Skenesborough, Burgoyne decided, despite his heavy baggage and artillery trains, to continue overland through the wilderness. Schuyler did all he could to slow down the advancing Burgoyne, and Washington sent all possible help in the form of Continentals, but it was the New England militia, incensed at Burgoyne's use of Indians and by reports of a beautiful white woman, Jane McCrea, being scalped by one of Burgoyne's Indians, who made the difference. At Bennington, Vermont, on 16 August, the New Hampshire militia savaged a sizeable British foraging force and its relief column, Burgoyne losing about 10 percent of his command.

In the meantime the British force moving down from Oswego into the Mohawk Valley toward Fort Stanwix was running into serious difficulties. The small Fort Stanwix garrison was determined to withstand St Leger's siege, even though a courageous attempt to relieve them by New York militia under Brigadier General Nicholas Herkimer met with failure. Schuyler sent Benedict Arnold west with 900 Continentals to aid the defenders at Fort Stanwix. Arnold took advantage of a half-witted Dutchman and a friendly Oneida Indian to convince the superstitious Indians, who treated the words of madmen with special concern, that a great number of reinforcements were on their way. This caused the Indians to abandon the fight, and St Leger soon afterward gave up the siege of Fort Stanwix. Thus Burgoyne's flanking

Burgoyne's surrender at Saratoga was the war's turning point: Because of it France joined the American cause.

movement from the west had failed, and his left flank was now in serious jeopardy.

Yet Burgoyne was still determined to fight on to Albany. He crossed back to the west side of the Hudson on 13-14 September to continue south. Major General Horatio Gates, who had now replaced Schuyler by order of the Congress under pressure from New England, was waiting for him at Bemis Heights, just below Saratoga, New York. On 19 September Burgoyne attacked the positions skillfully prepared for Gates by Brigadier General Kosciuszko, in what is called the 'Battle of Freeman's Farm' and suffered serious losses.

Burgoyne had all the while been hoping for relief from New York City, but the ever-cautious Major General Henry Clinton refused to make a major move to help him. So Burgoyne was faced with an American force becoming ever stronger while his was becoming weaker, and no relief was on its way. On 7 October he tried to break out of the encircling American lines but was badly battered by the riflemen of Colonel Daniel Morgan's Continentals in what has come to be called the 'Battle of Bemis Heights.' Then, as Burgoyne withdrew back toward Saratoga, American militia worked around behind him and cut his supply lines. He was soon trapped, and surrendered on 17 October 1777, along with 6000 of his men and great quantities of supplies.

The victory at Saratoga more than made up for the loss of Philadelphia, for it was the type of clear victory the French had been awaiting before openly throwing in their lot with the American rebels. By February 1778 an alliance had been made between the two countries, and Britain's local war against her colonies had taken a giant step toward becoming a resource-draining world war.

The fortunes of war had been swinging wildly both for and against the American patriots. Now in the winter of 1777-1778, the tides of fortune seemed to be swinging against them again as George Washington and his men suffered the most agonizing months of the war in winter encampament at Valley Forge. The supply system run by the government had broken down almost completely, and without adequate food, clothing and shelter, Washington's rag-tag army endured great hardship. Yet the American army persevered and even gained strength. General Nathaniel Greene took over the post of Quartermaster General and introduced order into the chaotic supply system; and Baron von Steuben accepted the position of Inspector General and instituted his system of training to teach the men of the army the military skills they so desperately needed.

By spring 1778 General Howe had resigned his command in America and had returned to England. His successor, General Clinton, was under orders to abandon Philadelphia, to send some of his men to the West Indies and Florida to counter a new French threat there, and then to return to New York by sea. In the event, Clinton decided to return to New York by land instead, and Washington hoped a harassing action might weaken him as he came. This turned out badly when, on 27 June, an American advance force under Major General Charles Lee attacked Clinton near Monmouth Court House, New Jersey, and was badly bloodied in the day-long fight that ensued. That night Clinton's forces slipped away and within days were safely back in New York. Lee was court-martialed for incompetence.

Nor did things go better when Washington, seeking to cooperate with his new French allies, attempted to take Newport, Rhode Island, in late July and early August 1778, supported by the French fleet of Admiral Charles, le comte d'Estaing. This operation was interrupted by the arrival of a British fleet under Admiral Richard Howe. The two fleets maneuvered for battle position on 12 August but got scattered in a gale, after which Howe returned to New York, d'Estaing went to Boston and then to the West Indies, and the American land force was left to extricate itself as best it could.

After these inconclusive actions the focus of the war shifted to the south, leaving the northern armies to confront one another in a sort of stalemate. The shift reflected a change in British strategy, a return to the south where, it was still believed, Tory strength was greater. The British army, supported by the navy, was to take the key southern ports and then move inland, pacifying the outlying areas as it went, destroying any rebel armies, and bringing the population into loyalty to the Crown both by giving them protection against the rebels and by using them in keeping the peace in loyal militia units.

At first the new British strategy worked well. Charleston almost fell to British siege in May 1779, being barely saved by the return of Major General Benjamin Lincoln and his troops from Georgia. Then, in September, an attempt by d'Estaing's French fleet with 6000 troops, and 1300 Americans under Lincoln to take back the British base at Savannah resulted in an overwhelming British victory. The Americans had suffered appalling losses in an ill-conceived direct assault on the British defensive positions, and because d'Estaing thereafter sailed off to the West Indies, Clinton was free to move down the coast unmolested.

Accordingly, he drew 14,000 men from New York and Savannah in an attempt to take Charleston. His carefully-planned attack by land and sea began in February 1780. His forces first landed on John's Island, the south of the city, and then crossed over the Ashley River to put Lincoln, unwisely situated at the end of the neck of land between the Ashley River and the Cooper River to the north, under attack from behind. On 8 April 1780, the Royal Navy forced its way past lightly-defended Fort Moultrie guarding the harbor, and Lincoln was completely cut off. Under siege and with no way to get out, he was forced to surrender on 12 May. His entire force of over 5000 men was lost to the cause. This most crushing American defeat of the war was complemented by an attack on Colonel Abraham Buford's relief force of 350 Virginians by Lieutenant Colonel Banastre Tarleton's cavalry at the Waxhaws, near the North Carolina-South Carolina border. Most of the Americans were slaughtered, despite Buford's attempts to surrender.

Clinton returned to New York with about one-third of his forces, leaving Major General Cornwallis to police and pacify the south, especially South Carolina. But despite his control of the seaports and the aid of Tory units who cooperated with his forces, Lord Cornwallis found it very difficult, if not impossible, to bring the area into loyal subjugation. There were no Continentals in the area, but guerrilla bands led by Thomas Sumter, Andrew Pickens, and Francis Marion continued to operate and keep resistance alive. Realizing that the local citizenry could not be wooed back to loyalty to the Crown if the British army could not effectively protect their lives and property, Congress quickly formed a Southern Army of 4000 men under Horatio Gates. Cornwallis intercepted this Continental-militia force at Camden, South Carolina, on 16 August 1780 and badly defeated it. Gates, the hero of the northern fighting at Saratoga three year before, this time distinguished himself by fleeing 160 miles in three days after the battle. Thus by the summer of 1780 the British were beginning to have reason to think that they might win at last, despite their tenuous control over the interior of the southern states, for things were going just as badly for the Americans in the north as in the south.

The Continental currency had become worth almost nothing, and the Congress could neither pay the soldiers nor procure

This 1780 British map of Charleston shows the campaigns of 1776 and 1780. By 1780 Britain saw in the invasion of the South a likely key to victory. In fact it proved a prescription for defeat.

necessary supplies. Recruiting for the Continental army became almost impossible, even for one-year service. Army morale sank, and there were mutinies in both 1780 and 1781 that had to be put down by force. In September 1780 the hero of Québec, Lake Champlain, and Fort Stanwix, Benedict Arnold, was discovered to be a traitor. Apparently angered by lack of what he considered proper recognition of his talents, and assured of money by the British, Arnold, as commander at West Point, made arrangements to turn over that vital post on the Hudson to the enemy. His treachery was discovered before it was carried through, but Arnold got away, later to serve the British as a general officer for the last years of the war.

At this lowest point in the fortunes of the American patriots, matters suddenly began to improve in the war in the south. In October 1780 a force of Tory militia commanded by Major Patrick Ferguson was sent by Cornwallis into the interior of South Carolina to pacify the region. On 7 October this force was met by mounted militia from western North Carolinia and Virginia at King's Mountain, on the Carolinas border, and wiped out. Cornwallis had to halt his movement in the Carolina interior and retreat to Winnsboro, South Carolina, with militia dogging him every mile of the way.

Two months later General Nathaniel Greene, at last freed of his onerous duties as Quartermaster General and back on the field, arrived in Charlotte, North Carolina, to direct the continued resistance to any British moves into the interior. Cornwallis now sent a part of his army under Banastre Tarleton to find and destroy an army under Brigadier General Daniel Morgan, while Cornwallis himself led the remainder of the army cautiously into North Carolina.

Tarleton caught up with Morgan on 17 January 1781 at an open area called Cowpens, near the North Carolina border. Morgan's force was three-fourths militia, but he used them, his Continentals and his cavalry well. Placing his Continentals on a hill, with two lines of militia in front of them, he instructed the militia to fire volleys until pressed by the British advance and then to fall back through the Continentals and act as a reserve. When the British moved on the center of Morgan's line, and the militia, as instructed, fell back through the Continentals and behind the hill, it appeared to Tarleton that he had won the day. But Morgan then sent the militia around the hill to assault Tarleton's left flank, while Morgan's cavalry, under Lieutenant Colonel William Washington, came charging into Tarleton's right flank. Tarleton's forces were virtually wiped out by this classic double envelopment, though Tarleton himself managed to escape.

Morgan now joined forces with Greene in North Carolina, and together they led the over-committed Cornwallis on a futile chase through North Carolina, into Virginia, and back again, finally stopping at Guilford Court House in North Carolina to do battle on a site of Greene's choice. By this time Cornwallis had only about 2000 men, and though the ensuing battle on 15 March 1781 went to the British, their casualty count was high and their supplies were exhausted. Yet instead of moving back to Charleston to resupply and refit, Cornwallis headed for Virginia to join reinforcements sent by General Clinton. While Cornwallis moved north, Greene moved into South Carolina; soon all British posts except Charleston and Savannah had been seized by American regulars or militia.

In August 1780 the British defeated Horatio Gates, hero of Saratoga, at Camden, South Carolina, a victory that augured well for the Southern strategy.

While General Cornwallis had been busy trying to pacify the Carolinas by occupation, Clinton had been trying to do much the same in Virgina. He had had limited success until, in 1781, he sent an expedition of 1600 men into Virginia under Benedict Arnold, who raided up the James River to beyond Richmond. Clinton reinforced this contingent with another of 2600 men under Major General William Phillips. Then, in May 1781, Cornwallis unexpectedly arrived from North Carolina and took over command. All told, Cornwallis now had about 7000 men. Against such strength, General Lafayette and his 1200 Continentals, even with the aid of the Virginia militia, could do little to stop British raids throughout central Virginia.

Clinton eventually ordered Cornwallis to return to the coast to establish a base for evacuating at least part of this force back to New York. Cornwallis chose the little tobacco port of Yorktown on the York River, in from Chesapeake Bay, because of its deep anchorage. There he would await a British fleet. Lafayette, having been reinforced by 1000 men of the Pennsylviania Line under Brigadier General Anthony Wayne, followed him down from Richmond, always keeping a respectful distance. Then Washington received word that a French fleet under Admiral François, le comte de Grasse, would be coming not to New York but to the Cheasapeake from the West Indies. If de Grasse could hold off the British fleet due to sail from New York, while the American army held Cornwallis' army under siege at Yorktown, Washington might be able to compel Cornwallis to surrender before Clinton could send relief.

Washington ordered Lafayette to put Cornwallis under siege at Yorktown. He then made a feint toward New York to mislead Clinton, and, in combination with a French army of 4000 under Lieutenant General Jean Baptiste de Vimeur, le comte de Rochembeau, made a rapid march toward Yorktown. On 20 August de Grasse arrived with 24 ships in the Chesapeake and debarked 3000 French troops to aid Lafayette. When the 19 ships of the Royal Navy, under Admiral Thomas Graves, arrived at the Virginia Capes on 5 September, they found de Grasse already in the bay and waiting for them. The

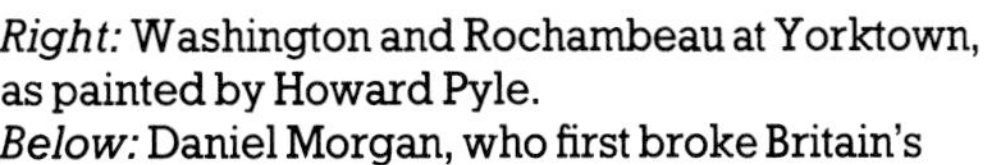

Right: Washington and Rochambeau at Yorktown, as painted by Howard Pyle.
Below: Daniel Morgan, who first broke Britain's chain of Southern successes.

Morgan's victory at Cowpens in early 1781 initiated the reversal of British fortune that culminated at Yorktown.

ensuing 'Battle of the Chesapeake' may have been indecisive from a naval point of view, but Graves was not able to force his way into the Chesapeake. Meantime, a second French fleet under Admiral Louis, le comte de Barras, arrived at the Chesapeake from Newport with reinforcements and slipped safely into the bay. There was no way that Graves could now aid the besieged Cornwallis at Yorktown; he returned to New York.

Washington now had a total of 9000 American troops (both Continentals and Virginia militia) and 6000 French at Yorktown. A formal siege began, with the digging of complex entrenchments and ever-increasing pressure on Cornwallis from the slowly advancing artillery. Cornwallis could not escape by land, and he was cut off by sea. Clinton was dilatory about sending a fleet with 4000 troops from New York to relieve him. On the very day Clinton's relief force finally left for Virginia, Cornwallis, with no other option available, began surrender talks with Washington's representatives. Two days later, on 19 October 1781, the 7000 British troops at Yorktown formally surrendered to the American commanders and their French allies, while a British band played 'The World Turned Upside Down.'

This surrender ended the formal fighting in the War for Independence. The defeat at Yorktown finally convinced the Crown and Parliament that the war against the colonists was futile. Six years of conflict had not brought the American Continental army and its militia allies to bay. The will of the colonists to resist had been bent but never broken. The French were now fully in the war, joined by the Spanish and the Dutch. British power was being challenged in two hemispheres and on half the oceans of the world. The costs were simply too high to continue the fight. The defeat at Yorktown led directly to the overthrow of the ruling British cabinet, and the new government was dedicated to bringing the war to an end on honorable terms. Avoiding possible future losses in the West Indies and in India was now considered more important than the recognition of American independence.

The peace talks that began shortly after Yorktown ended in 1783 with the Treaty of Paris, wherein Britain recognized the independence of the United States of America. A new nation had been born out of successful military conflict. It would now have to maintain its fragile independence and find its place in the family of nations. The work of the US Army was just beginning.

Right: **Plan of the siege of Yorktown.**
Below: **When Cornwallis surrendered the 7000-man Yorktown garrison Britain in effect lost the war. The American victory was mostly Washington's doing, but French help had been crucial.**

This Plan of the investment of York and Gloucester has been surveyed and laid down, and is Most humbly dedicated by his Excellency's Obedient and very humble servant,
Sebast.n Bauman. Major of the New York or 2.d Reg.t of Artillery.
4 ___ 3 18 9 & 2 6 Pr.s
5 ___ 1 18 & 2 9 Pr.s
6 ___ 1 18 & 4 9 Pr.s
7 ___ 2 18 & 2 12 Pr.s
8 ___ 2 18 & 1 9 Pr.
9 ___ 2 18 & 2 12 Pr.s
10 ___ 3 18, 2. 12, 1 6, & 1 16 In. Mor.
11 ___ 1 24 & 2 9 Pr.s
12 ___ 2 12 & 2 8 In. Howitze
13 ___ 2 18 & 1 12 Pr.
14 ___ 5 9 Pr.s
Gloucester side
15 ___ 10 18 & 1 12 Pr.
16 2 Batteries of 8 Guns diff.t calib.
17 Part of the British shipping
18 Guadaloup Frigate sunk ye night of ye 16th
19 Fowey Frigate
20 Bonetta Sloop of War
21 British Shipping as they appeared sunk
22 The Charon a 44 Gun Ship & 2 Transports set on fire by hot shot
YORK RIVER
Road from WILLIAMSBURG
Mag. St. Simons Quarters
Bar. Viominils Quarters
Bourbonnois
Soissonnois
Saintonge
Gatinois
Touraine
Agenois
Wormleys Creek
Moores House
Light Infantry
Virginia Militia
Gen. Nelsons Quarters
Gen. Lincolns Quarters
Amer. Hospital
The Field where the British laid down their Arms
Road to HAMPTON
French Hospital
French Park of Artillery
N. York Line
Gen. Steubens Quarters
Sappers & Miners
Gen. Clintons Quarters
Adj. Gen.l Q.
Count ROCHAMBEAU's Quarters
Gen.l WASHINGTON's Quarters
American Park of Artillery
Artil. Artificers
Laboratory
Magazine
Quarter M.r Gen.
Gen. Knoxs Quarters
WARWICK Road
THIS PLAN was taken between the 22nd & 28th of October, 1781.
Explanation
Blue represents the American Encampment and lines of Approach. Yellow the French. Red the British.
A. British exterior works evacuated in the night of the 29th of Sept. B. the first Parallel, thrown up by the Allied Army the
night of the 6th of Oct. C. an American Battery of three 18 & 3 24 pounders, two Howitze & two 10 inch Mortars opened the 9th. D. ano-
ther American Battery of four 18 pdrs and E. a Bomb Bat.y of four 10 in. Mortars opend the 10th. F. a French Bat.y of four 12 pdrs 6 Mortars
and Howitze opend the 9th. G. three French Batteries consisting of 16 pieces 18 & 24 pounders & 9 in. Howitz opend the 10th. H. a French
Bomb Battery of six 13 in. Mortars opend the 10th at night. I. part of the 2nd Parallel thrown up by a detachment from both
Armies on the night of the 11th. K. a Redoubt on the Enemies extream left stormed by the Americans on the night of the 14th. L. a Bas-
tion Redoubt stormed by the French the same time. M. Remainder of the second parallel was compleated the same night. N. three
French Batteries in the second parallel of 16 pieces, 18 and 24 pounders. O. a French Bomb Battery design'd for ten 13 in. Mortars. In the
Redoubt K the Americans had opend on the 15th with two 8 inch Howitze and on the 17th in the Morning with two 18 pounders, and
in the redoubt L with two 10 inch Mortars. P. an American Battery of four 18 pounders opend the 17th in the Morning. Q. another Ameri
can Battery in the second parallel, designed for seven 18 pounders, three 24 pounders, four Howitze, eight 10 inch, and ten 5½
inch Royal Mortars part of which had opend the 16th, the whole not being mounted nor the Battery compleat, when terms of Capitulation were proposed by Lord Cornwallis, and Ratified the 19th, by which 7247 British Troops, Hessians and Anspach,
became prisoners of War to the Americans, as did 840 Sailors, with a number of Shipping fall to the French. R. two French
Ships of War sent by Count de Grasse after the Capitulation to take charge of the British Marine. During the Siege
of York, Gloucester was Blockaded by American and French Troops under the command of Brigadier Gen. Choisy,
Brigadier General Weedon, and Duke de Lauzun of the French Horse.
York Town in Virginia lies in 37° 10' N. Lat.
Note. The Land within the doted lines has been laid down by survey.
100 200 400 600 800 1000
A Scale of Yards.

YEARS OF TESTING: 1783-1860

It was in the professionally-conducted Mexican War that the US Army came of age. Shown here, the storming of the city of Monterrey, 24 September 1846.

Once the war for independence had been concluded by the Treaty of Paris in 1783 the need for a standing army of any appreciable size ended, and Congress was quick to order a radical reduction in its numbers. This haste to cut the army was aided by the memory of the 'Newburgh Conspiracy' of 1782. This 'conspiracy' had begun with grumbling by some officers stationed at Newburgh, New York, about arrears in their pay. Certain of the officers had urged their peers both not to obey orders if the fighting was renewed and to refuse to disband, if so ordered by Congress, until they were paid. Washington had intervened and promised to intercede for the officers with Congress. When Congress decided to grant them their back pay and offered them full pay for five years, instead of half-pay for life, the issue evaporated. But memories of threatened military disobedience to civil authority still lingered.

A basic question facing the new nation at the end of hostilities was how large an army it needed and how that army should be constituted. Obviously a sizeable standing army, with no major enemies to fight, was both unnecessary and prohibitively expensive. What sort of force was needed to guard military supplies, control the Indians on the frontier, and generally be available to protect domestic peace? Should it be a small regular force, to be supplemented by militia in case of major trouble? This seemed to be the favored solution, but it raised the question of control of the militia, which were state forces. How much direction should the central government have over their training and use if they were to be effective militarily?

The Congress appointed a committee to come up with recommendations. Alexander Hamilton was chosen as chairman, and the committee's first major witness was George Washington. The revered general suggested that the nation would be best served by volunteer state militia units under federal control, plus a small regular army of 2630 officers and men to control the Indians and protect the nation's borders. Hamilton's committee adopted most of Washington's ideas, but Congress turned them down, primarily because of cost (at the time the regular army consisted of only 600 men guarding military supplies at West Point and other outposts). The committee then recommended the alternative of a larger force that could cost less. This would be achieved by cutting the pay of the officers. Congress again rejected its ideas.

Finally, in late June 1784, with time running out on its session, Congress agreed on an army plan. Disbanding the one existing infantry regiment and the one battalion of artillery (although leaving 80 artillerymen to

Above: Washington's mounted guard, 1784. In fact, though Congress had authorized 700, the army had but 525 men in 1784.

Below: The Battle of Fallen Timbers, 1794. 'Mad Anthony' Wayne's legion still wore uniforms much like those of 1779.

guard the military stores at West Point), the parsimonious Congress called for a new force of 700 men to constitute a regular army, the men to be drawn from volunteers from four states (Pennsylvania, New Jersey, New York, and Connecticut), under Lieutenant Colonel Josiah Harmar as commanding officer. This puny force soon proved to be inadequate to the tasks imposed upon it.

In 1786 the farmers in western Massachusetts, faced with severe economic problems, began to riot for relief from their debts. Congress responded by authorizing a 1300-man volunteer force to serve for three years, but by the time any of them reached the scene, a group of rebels led by Daniel Shays had already attacked the Springfield arsenal in January 1787. 'Shays Rebellion' was suppressed by the Massachusetts militia, but the incident clearly revealed that the tiny force of Army regulars was hardly enough to ensure domestic peace. The event, in addition to revealing the nation's military weakness, also clearly illustrated the impotence of the central government, denied taxing and enforcement powers under the Articles of Confederation. A convention, called to revise the Articles, ended by revising them out of existence and writing a new constitution.

Under the Constitution, a national army independent of the states was created, but its control was vested in both the legislative and executive branches of the federal government. Congress was given the power to declare war and to raise an army and a navy, but the Commander in Chief, in both peacetime and wartime, was the president. Congress, subsequent to the promulgation of the new Constitution and the election of executive officers and congressmen, created a single Department of War for Army and Navy. This department would persist until it became the Department of Defense after World War II.

In 1789 the new government took over the existing army of 800 men and confirmed now-Brigadier General Harmar in his rank and authority. Major General Henry Knox was appointed the first Secretary of War. While the organization of this new army was relatively simple, and procurement of supplies for the force was left in the hands of civilians for years to come, Congress did see fit to authorize creation of two federal armories for the manufacture of weapons. Armories at Springfield, Massachusetts, and at Harper's Ferry, Virginia, opened in 1794, although the nation still purchased most of its armaments abroad because of the lack of manufacturing facilities in the country.

A militia to assure domestic peace and to repel invaders having also been provided for in the Constitution, Congress passed a militia law in 1792. It provided for state militia forces to be made up of all able-bodied white men between the ages of 18 and 45, but left compliance up to the states. As a result, the state militia units were neither well-disciplined nor well-trained. Furthermore, Congress specified that members of the militia could not be compelled to serve for more than three months in any given year and forbade their use outside the United States. Although the militia was called to service by President Washington to put down a local insurrection called the 'Whiskey Rebellion' in western Pennsylvania in 1794, no real test of its effectiveness could come for a number of years.

Indian Troubles and Explorations in the West

The Indian menace in the Old Northwest had not vanished with the explusion of the French from America and the defeat of the British in 1783. If anything, it had become worse. One source of trouble was that the British, correctly arguing that the monies owed to Tories for their lost properties during the Revolution had not been paid off, as specified in the Treaty of Paris, had refused to give up the forts in the western territories. And from these forts the Indians received arms and supplies with which they stoutly resisted the incursions of the hordes of settlers now pouring into the trans-Appalachian west. For their part, the new settlers soon began issuing veiled threats that if the federal government did not protect them from the Indians they might turn to England or Spain for support. These none-too-subtle hints at secession could not be ignored by the government if it wanted to keep the nation intact.

Congress responded to President Washington's request for greater military forces to garrison the frontier by raising the number of authorized regular Army troops to 2283, but something more had to be done to curb the Indian menace. Secretary of War Knox offered an answer in the form of a major show of strength in the 'Ohio Country'. He ordered General Harmar, cooperating with Arthur St Clair, governor of the Northwest Territory, to move against the Miami Indian tribes. Their dilatory two-pronged attack, in 1790, from Fort Washington (now Cincinnati) on the Ohio River against the Miamis failed completely. The next year St Clair and Harmar assembled 600 regulars and 1400 militiamen at Fort Washington and prepared to move out once again. This punitive expedition, contrary to Knox's order for a 'rapid and decisive' stroke, traveled as sluggishly as its predecessor. In two months it had moved only 100 miles to the north, having stopped to build forts along the way and being encumbered

From Fallen Timbers to his death in 1813 Shawnee chief Tecumseh was a relentless foe of the government.

by its large baggage train, laden with the 'necessities' of civilized campaigning, including 300 women, many of them prostitutes. This force, by this time down to 1400 men, encamped on the night of 3 November near the headwaters of the Wabash River with virtually no security provided. Just before dawn the next morning, it was attacked by about 1000 Indians, who slew 600 whites and inflicted another 300 casualties. St Clair survived but soon retired from the Army, his reputation forever blemished.

Many Americans wanted to abandon the Indian wars after this painful defeat on the Wabash, but President Washington knew the issue had to be joined and resolved. So, as Commander in Chief, he ordered a third expedition against the Indians. Congress was now willing to authorize an army of 5000 men, and Washington appointed the Revolutionary War hero from Pennsylvnia, 'Mad Anthony' Wayne, as brigadier to succeed St Clair. Hardly 'mad,' although decidedly impetuous and blustery. Wayne insisted that the operation be carefully planned and that his troops be carefully trained and disciplined before his force began venturing into the wilderness.

Wayne moved his troops to Fort Washington in 1793, and the following year, with 3000 picked men, he moved north. He marched to within a few miles of Fort Miami, a recently-established post built by the British on the site of present-day Toledo, at the western tip of Lake Erie. There, on 20 August 1794, his force was attacked by Indians almost within gunshot of the fort. After repelling the first assault, Wayne and his men moved out in a bayonet charge and succeeded in driving the Indians out of their cover of fallen trees (hence the name 'Battle of Fallen Timbers') and onto the open prairie. Here his mounted militiamen decimated the Indian ranks, after which Wayne burned the Indians' villages and destroyed their crops. Cowed by this show of force, the western tribes in the Ohio Country agreed to make peace with the United States and to cede their lands to the nation. The treaty of Greenville, August 1795, ended the Indian menace for a time on the frontier, and pioneers flooded into the Northwest in unprecedented numbers.

William Henry Harrison's victory over the Indians at Tippecanoe in 1811 helped him to become president in 1840.

Inevitably, settlers soon began spilling over onto lands never ceded by the Indians. To resist them, the Indians, under the leadership of Tecumseh, chief of the Shawnees, along with The Prophet, his brother, organized a defensive Indian confederation. William Henry Harrison, governor of the Indiana territory and former army officer, decided at the urging of the settlers to strike the Indians before they could mount effective resistance, and in the summer of 1811 he organized a force of 300 regulars and 650 militia to wipe them out. Moving from Vincennes in September, and stopping to build a fort on the edge of the Indian country, Harrison and his men moved on toward Tippecanoe Creek in western Indiana, the site of Tecumseh's main village. On the morning of 7 November 1811 the Indians attacked Harrison's encampment in a wild charge that soon degenerated into furious hand-to-hand combat. Organizing a counterattack, the American forces drove the Indians from the field with the aid of their mounted militia. Harrison lost almost 70 men killed in this minor engagement. It had secured only temporary peace on the frontier, but it gained for Harrison a military reputation that would stand him in good stead when he ran for president three decades later.

The Army was also active in these years in areas beyond the Northwest territory. Spain's sale of Louisiana to France in 1800 had caused great concern in America, and especially in the West. That the immense territories west of the Mississippi should be under the domination of feeble Spain was one thing; their ownership by expansive and strong France was another. It meant, among other things, that free transit for the Western farmers down the Mississippi to New Orleans might be endangered. Worse, Spain had suspended the right of deposit of goods at New Orleans (guaranteed to America by treaty) just before transferring the land to France, meaning that American trade down the Mississippi for sale at New Orleans might be completely cut off.

When President Thomas Jefferson, therefore, approached the French government in

In fact, Tippecanoe was 'a near run thing.' A bayonet charge finally won the battle, but Harrison's losses were painfully high.

1803 about buying New Orleans for $2 million and found that Napoleon was willing to sell the whole territory for only $15 million, he overcame his constitutional scruples, partially in deference to his Western voters, and agreed to the purchase. The Army took formal possession of the territory in December 1803 and established a garrison at New Orleans. Brigadier General James Wilkinson was appointed as the first governor of the Louisiana Territory.

Now that the Louisiana Territory belonged to America, Jefferson was determined to have it explored and mapped. Accordingly, he chose Captain Meriwether Lewis and Lieutenant William Clark, both army veterans, to lead the expedition. The Lewis and Clark expedition left St Louis early in 1804, travelled up the Missouri River, crossed the Rocky Mountains, and descended to the Pacific via the Columbia River in November 1805. The explorers returned through central Montana, arriving in St Louis in September 1806. Their findings were of immense value geographically, scientifically, and politically. In the meantime, Captain Zebulon Pike was sent on a similar mission to the headwaters of the Mississippi, and then on another into present-day Colorado. As with the work of Lewis and Clark, the explorations of Pike added much to the nation's store of knowledge and established legal claim to the lands that had been traversed. But the role of the Army in the opening of the West was just beginning. It would not end until almost a century had passed, the Indians had been removed, and the trans-Mississippi territories all the way to the Pacific had been fully incorporated into the mainstream of the expanding nation.

Undeclared War with France

In 1789, the year the new Constitution was put into force in the United States, the Bourbon monarchy in France was openly challenged by the middle class, which demanded fundamental change in the government, many of the reformers taking the American Revolution as their inspiration. This was the beginning of a world-shaking French Revolution that would end only in 1799 with the coming to power of Napoleon Bonaparte. By 1793 the French had declared war against a European coalition of powers, including Britain, which were determined to restore the Bourbon monarchy to France. As France and Britain each needed to cut off supplies flowing to the other from colonies and from neutrals, both navies began to interdict trade and seize vessels on the high seas. As an emerging neutral trader, the United States soon found itself embroiled in Europe's war.

Since the British had taken the lead in seizing American merchant vessels, the Washington administration attempted to keep the United States out of war by negotiating Jay's Treaty in 1794. Although in this treaty Britain did not actually renounce the right to make seizures on the high seas, she did agree to evacuate the outposts in the American West at long last. Seeing this treaty as pro-British in intention, France now began to seize American vessels. As the nation moved into John Adams' presidency in 1797, relations between the two countries were becoming precarious. Faced with French depredations and the possibility of war, Congress was willing to re-build the neglected Navy but would only authorize the president to call out 80,000 militia for three months to augment the Army of 3300 officers and men. (This Army had only four infantry regiments of eight companies each.)

Only in 1798, with an undeclared war at sea taking place, was Congress willing to expand the infantry and the harbor defense and ordnance units and create a Provisional Army. Although the Provisional Army, headed by George Washington as lieutenant general (the aging ex-president being persuaded to come out of retirement for the

Lewis and Clark on the Columbia River. The Louisiana Purchase opened a new theater of operations for the US Army.

emergency), eventually grew to 4000 men during the next two years, it had little to do except assume a passive defense against a French enemy that never came. The Provisional Army was disbanded in June 1800, three months before the undeclared Quasi-War with France was ended by treaty.

Conflict with Britain

Thomas Jefferson, who came to the presidency in 1801, was dedicated to creating a presidency of peace and economy. The Navy was scaled back almost to nothing, and the Army was soon down to only 3000 men. Yet it was during these years that the institution most responsible for the creation of a professional army in the United States was born. In 1802 Congress authorized the organization of a Corps of Engineers, to make up for a need for trained military engineers, and assigned its ten cadets and seven officers to West Point. The resulting engineering academy evolved into the United States Military Academy, a school not only for military engineers but also for professional army officers.

Despite Jefferson's efforts to keep the United States out of Europe's wars by the use of diplomacy, his purpose was frustrated by events. The war between Britain and France resumed in 1803, and soon the harassment of American merchant ships began again, this time with the added provocation (on the part of the Royal Navy) that some American sailors were being seized from their ships and involuntarily impressed into British naval service.

Jefferson's main weapon was to deny the offenders aid by forbidding them shipments from the United States, but this embargo stratagem was a two-edged sword and hurt the American shippers and manufacturers more than it injured either the French or the British, forcing Jefferson to abandon his attempts at economic coercion. The loci of most of the rising war fever for retaliation against Britain (who most openly interfered with American neutral rights) were the American South and West. The Northeast was willing to live with occasional confiscation of American ships and cargoes by the British, but the Western and Southern farmers blamed Britain for their economic recession, allegedly because her actions prevented American agricultural products from reaching their overseas markets. The Westerners were also inflamed by rumors that the British were stirring up the Indians on the frontier. There was talk of striking back at the British by taking Canada from them.

Jefferson's successor, James Madison, actually did manage to exert sufficient pressure on Britain, through the Non-Intercourse Act, to force her to agree to respect American neutral rights on the high seas, but this was not known to the American Congress when it passed a declaration of war on Great Britain on 18 June 1812. Thus the United States entered into a war whose causes were insubstantial and ephemeral and which the nation could not and did not win.

At the outset of the War of 1812 it appeared that the United States had taken on a nation of vastly superior strength. Britain had almost 300,000 men in her regular army, plus a home militia. Her navy consisted of 700 ships (of which at least 125 were formidable ships of the line) and 150,000 men. The American army, on the other hand, had only 11,000 troops, 5000 of whom were very recent recruits. The nation was able to call up a half-million men, including 56,000 regulars and 10,000 volunteers from the militia, but the 450,000 militia called to the colors served for only very short terms and could not be used outside the country. The American navy had less than 20 ships (including only six frigates) and 4000 men, this in a war where control of the sea could be critical.

On the other hand, Britain was forced to use most of her regulars against Napoleon in Europe and in her various colonies. In Canada, a major area of wartime contention, she had only 6000 regulars, 2000 militia, and perhaps 3500 Indians to protect a frontier that stretched from the Great Lakes along the entire length of the vital St Lawrence to Québec. And because of Canada's sparse population, Major General Isaac Brock, governor of Upper Canada, was able to enlist the aid of only 10,000 Canadian militia during the war. The British navy, too, was forced to use the bulk of its strength in the war against Napoleon. In 1812 the Royal Navy had only 80 vessels in American waters, and these had to cover the Atlantic coast all the way from Halifax to Florida, escorting merchant ships, blockading American ports, and fighting off American frigates and privateers along the long coastline. Yet despite Britain's preoccupation with her greater challenge in Europe, the American challenge – whatever its strength – had to be neutralized so as not to interfere with the greater war effort. Britain committed as many forces as she could to the American war, hoping either to dispose of

Throughout the Napoleonic wars the US had troubles with Britain and France. This 1809 proclamation was premature.

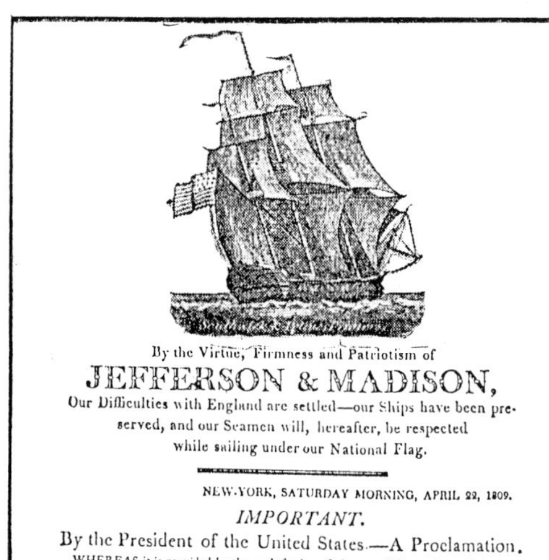

By the Virtue, Firmness and Patriotism of

JEFFERSON & MADISON,

Our Difficulties with England are settled—our Ships have been preserved, and our Seamen will, hereafter, be respected while sailing under our National Flag.

NEW-YORK, SATURDAY MORNING, APRIL 22, 1809.

IMPORTANT.

By the President of the United States.—A Proclamation.

WHEREAS it is provided by the 11th ſection of the act of Congreſs, entitled "An "act to interdict the commercial intercourſe between the United States and Great Bri-"tain and France, and their dependencies; and for other purpoſes,"—and that "in "caſe either France or Great Britain ſhall ſo revoke or modify her edicts as that they "ſhall ceaſe to violate the neutral commerce of the United States," the Preſident is authoriſed to declare the ſame by proclamation, after which the trade ſuſpended by the ſaid act and by an act laying an Embargo, on all ſhips and veſſels in the ports and harbours of the United States and the ſeveral acts ſupplementary thereto may be renewed with the nation ſo doing. And whereas the Honourable David Montague Erſkine, his Britannic Majeſty's Envoy Extraordinary and Miniſter Plenipotentiary, has by the order and in the name of his ſovereign declared to this Government, that the Britiſh Orders in Council of January and November, 1807, will have been withdrawn, as reſpects the United States on the 10th day of June next. Now therefore I James Madison, Preſident of the United States, do hereby proclaim that the orders in council aforeſaid will have been withdrawn on the tenth day of June next; after which day the trade of the United States with Great Britain, as ſuſpended by the act of Congreſs above mentioned, and an act laying an embargo on all ſhips and veſſels in the ports and harbors of the United States, and the ſeveral acts ſupplementary thereto, may be renewed.

Given under my hand and the seal of the United States, at Washington, the nineteenth day of April, in the year of our Lord, one (L. S) thousand eight hundred and nine, and of the Independence of the United States, the thirty-third.

JAMES MADISON.

By the President,
RT. SMITH, *Secretary of State.*

Sailors at mess. Britain's policy of impressing US tars enraged Americans.

the American military threat entirely, or, better, to hold the Americans at bay until the causes for their going to war were automatically removed with the defeat of Napoleon.

One way or another, the US Army would be called upon to do some heavy fighting. How well prepared it was to assume this responsibility is moot. In some respects the Army of 1812 was only a little better off than Washington's Continental Army had been in

Naval incidents multiplied in the 15 years before 1812.
Right: A US frigate *vs.* a British Sloop.
Below: An attack on a merchantman by a French corsair.

Infantry uniforms evolved steadily. By 1810 soldiers were wearing cotees and (for a few years) top hats.

1775. Years of penurious neglect had left it short of supplies, training, experienced officers, and morale. And of course it was pitifully small. Yet it enjoyed *some* advantages. Infantrymen now had a plentiful supply of standard American-made weapons, primarily the regulation .69-calibre flintlock musket and the .59-calibre flintlock cavalry pistol, furnished by the Springfield and Harpers Ferry armories, respectively. Artillery was still in a relatively chaotic state, but soon after the war began Congress created an Ordnance Department, and by 1814 the US Corps of Artillery had been born.

Also during the course of the war, some enterprising officers, such as Generals Winfield Scott and Jacob Brown – much in the manner of von Steuben before them – undertook to give their own troops intensive courses in military training. Though such professional training was never Army-wide, it produced individual units of sufficient effectiveness to cause (according to the story) one British officer at the Battle of the Chippewa River to exclaim, 'These are regulars, by God!'

In the matter of uniforms, too, the new US Army was in somewhat better case than the Continentals had been, though throughout the war uniform material was always in short supply. Now the regulation infantry uniform consisted of a short waist-length blue jacket (called a cotee) adorned with a high red collar and red cuffs, as well as a tall black leather shako and gray or white trousers. The Artillery uniforms were essentially similar, as were those of the cavalry, except that instead of the shako the cavalry's headgear was the characteristic crested and plumed dragoon's casque. If nothing else, the US Army was now beginning to *look* like an army.

And, in fact, it would behave like an army. Its performance during the war of 1812 would be spotty, at best, but at least some of those spots would be bright enough to add lustre to a burgeoning tradition in which the nation could take pride.

The War of 1812

The war began badly for the American land forces. Three offensive operations were planned against Canada for 1812. One would be launched from Plattsburg, New York, against Montréal; a second would consist of a movement from Detroit against British forces across the river in Upper Canada; a third would move from western New York across the Niagara River to attack the British forts located there. All were fiascos. Brigadier General William Hull, governor of the Michigan Territory (once a dashing Revolutionary War hero but now an aging and indecisive shell of his former self), was appointed Great Lakes commander. He arrived at Fort Detroit in July 1812 with a force of 1500 militiamen from Ohio and led them across the river into Canada soon afterwards. Facing him were only 750 British regulars, militiamen and Indians, most at Fort Malden, downriver from the Detroit crossing. Instead of moving directly against Fort Malden, Hull issued a bombastic proclamation to the people of Canada asking them to join the Americans – which was answered by musket fire – and then slowly began to make his way downriver. His opponent, General Isaac Brock, crossed over the river from Canada and cut off Hull's communications with Ohio. Then Hull received word that the 60 defenders at Fort Mackinac at the head of the Lakes had meekly surrendered to a small party of British regulars and Indians and that reinforcements had arrived at Fort Malden (Hull estimated Brock's reinforcements as ten times their actual number). Accordingly, Hull retreated to Detroit, and Brock showed up across the river and began to set up artillery units preparatory to an attack.

On the morning of 16 August 1812 the British fired but one shot into the American position and Hull ordered that the American garrison surrender. He and his regulars were taken as prisoners to Montréal; the militiamen were released on parole. To make matters worse, the day before, a small American relief force from Fort Dearborn (present-day Chicago) was massacred by Indians as they moved out for Detroit, after which the Indians returned to burn the fort. Thus, with the loss of Detroit, Mackinac, and Dearborn, the entire Northwest Territory had almost at once fallen under British control. It was hardly an auspicious beginning.

The offensive across the Niagara Frontier went no better, despite the fact that the Americans numbered 6500 troops. They were divided between Major General Stephen van Rensselaer, a New York militia officer with no fighting experience but with

By 1812 the shako had replaced the top hat and officers wore bicorns.

important political connections, and Brigadier General Alexander Smyth, an Army regular. Rensselaer's forces stood at the north end of the Frontier in and around Fort Niagara. Most of Smyth's were to the south around Buffalo. Rensselaer, as senior commander, wanted to attack across the entire 40-mile front, but Smyth refused to cooperate. Facing this insubordination, Rensselaer decided to make his attack across the river below Niagara Falls and take the heights of Queenston on his own. On 13 October 1812, 600 of Rensselaer's men were ferried across the river and climbed the heights to take Queenston. The British were quick to counterattack, but the Americans held their ground in the melee that followed. Yet Rensselaer's position was precarious. Few reinforcements were coming to aid his beleaguered troops. Because most of the New York militiamen refused to leave the territorial United States, Rensselaer could induce only 1300 men to cross the river and fight beside their comrades, and Smyth ignored Rensselaer's call for help from the regulars under his command. As a result, the besieged troops on the Canadian side of the river were forced to surrender. Some 900 of them put down their arms; 350 more had been killed or wounded.

After this debacle Rensselaer resigned and Smyth assumed command. But Smyth merely marched his men back and forth along the river, allegedly to move into position for an attack but always complaining of a lack of reinforcements. Eventually the disgusted militiamen wandered away to their homes, the volunteers were dismissed, and

The War of 1812 began badly for the US. Within months Hull (*right*) had surrendered Detroit. By October an invasion of Canada, well begun with the taking of Queenston (*below*) had collapsed, with 1250 men lost. An attack on Montréal was similarly unsuccessful.

One of the few successful American generals in the war was Jacob Brown.

the regulars were ordered into winter quarters. Smyth requested leave and received it. Within three months his name had been dropped from the Army rolls.

The attack on Montréal in 1812 was similarly unsuccessful. This force, the largest of all, was under the command of Major General Henry Dearborn. Dearborn held his force of 5000 in readiness around Albany, waiting for Rensselaer to move on Niagara. Then he slowly made his way north to Plattsburg on Lake Champlain, beginning his advance on Montréal only in mid-November. When he was within a mile and a half of the Canadian border he was challenged by 3000 British who drove back his advanced guard. At this point the New York militia announced that it would not advance into Canada, so Dearborn, evidently relieved, marched back to Plattsburg and went into winter quarters. Thus, as 1812 came to a close, the American armies had suffered three humiliating defeats against inferior forces. They would do better in the following year.

Detroit had to be retaken, so President Madison chose Brigadier General William Henry Harrison, the hero of Tippecanoe, to carry out the task. Assembling a force of 6500 men from the western territories, Harrison began to move north in October 1812. By January 1813 an advanced detachment of 1000 had moved to Frenchtown on the Raisin River, southeast of Detroit, where it came under attack by a slightly larger force of British and their Indian allies. Over 100 Americans were killed and another 500 were captured, and the campaign was marked by the ruthless slaughter of wounded American prisoners by their Indian guards. 'Remember the Raisin' became a rallying cry in the Northwest Territory, but Harrison was forced by the winter and British control of Lake Erie to defer the Americans' thirst for revenge. Harrison built Fort Meigs and Fort Stephenson at the western end of Lake Erie and waited.

A second American force, under Dearborn, was sent to capture the British naval base at Kingston at the eastern end of Lake Ontario, near its opening into the St Lawrence. But Dearborn, moving from Sackett's Harbor across the lake with a fleet assembled by Commodore Isaac Chauncey, changed his mind, and with a force of 1700 sailed to York (now Toronto) instead, turning over command temporarily to Brigadier General Zebulon Pike because of ill health. The troops landed near York on 27 April 1813 and proceeded to take the town from its 600 defenders. As the Americans moved through the town, a powder magazine exploded, killing many British and Americans, including General Pike. Apparently confused and with their leader dead, the American troops paused to burn and loot the provincial capital before leaving to attack British forts on the Canadian side of the Niagara River.

In the meantime, the stripped garrison at Sackett's Harbor, under Brigadier General Jacob Brown of the New York militia, was under attack by a force of 800 British regulars plus militia, which Sir George Prevost, the governor-general of Canada, had ferried from the Kingston base across the lake. The

Another attempt to invade Canada in 1813 petered out soon after Zebulon Pike's death at York (Montréal).

400 American regulars and 750 militiamen fought off two frontal attacks on 26 May before launching a successful counterattack that drove the British back to their ships.

While Prevost was attacking Sackett's Harbor on the eastern end of Lake Ontario, Dearborn and Chauncey, having left York, were invading Canada at the other end of the lake. At first all went well. A successful amphibious attack, led by Colonel Winfield Scott and Commander Oliver Hazard Perry of the Navy, was carried out against Fort George and Queenston on the western shore of the Niagara River. Dearborn had 4000 men

Far right: Tecumseh died in October 1813 when Harrison defeated an Anglo-Indian force on Canada's Thames River.
Right: The Navy's Oliver Hazard Perry.
Below: In September 1813 Perry defeated a British naval squadron on Lake Erie. 'We have met the enemy and they are ours,' he reported. The Army was now free to attack Upper Canada, which it did, successfully, within the month.

and could have achieved a compelling victory after taking Fort George, but he dallied, and his advance forces were routed on two separate occasions. Settling in at Fort George, Dearborn resigned his commission because of his ill health. By December both Fort George and Fort Niagara had fallen into British hands.

Farther to the west, on Lake Erie, Oliver Hazard Perry had been given the job of seizing naval control of the lake. Accordingly, he built and manned nine ships at Presque Isle and then moved his little fleet to Put-in-Bay, near Forts Meigs and Stephenson. There, on 10 September, near the southern shore of the lake, Perry met the six-ship British squadron, and in a four-hour battle disabled two of its vessels and forced the remainder to surrender. His famous message to General Harrison was: 'We have met the enemy and they are ours.'

With Lake Erie in American hands, Harrison could now attack the British in Upper Canada. Moving on the British via Detroit and Fort Malden, Harrison compelled a small 2000-man British regular and Indian force to fall back into the interior. He caught up with them on the Thames River, where, on 5 October, the British force was completely broken by a cavalry charge by mounted Kentucky militia, and over 500 British regulars and Indians were taken prisoner. Among those killed was Tecumseh, who had guided Indian resistance for the British ever since Tippecanoe, two years before.

By these operations the Americans gained control of the Northwest forts, Lake Erie and Upper Canada, but their attempt to bring Lower Canada under American domination in the fall of 1813 was an unmitigated disaster. It was supposed to be a classic two-pronged attack. One arm, 4000 men, assembled at Plattsburg on Lake Champlain under Brigadier General Wade Hampton, was to move on Montréal from the south. The second arm, 6000 men at Sackett's Harbor, under Major General James Wilkinson, was to attack down the St Lawrence as the left wing of the attack. Neither made it. Soon after leaving Plattsburg in September Hampton ran into British resistance on the Chateaugay River and retreated all the way back to Plattsburg. Wilkinson, seeing one of his detachments mauled on the St Lawrence north of Ogdensburg, gave up his part of the operation and, like Hampton, fled to Plattsburg. Both were soon dropped from the Army rolls.

In 1813 fighting also opened in a new theater, the South. Here the main American force was the Tennessee militia under its ardent Indian-hating leader, Andrew Jackson. Two thousand in number, the Tennesseans were spoiling for action, but since they

were neither permitted by Madison to move into West Florida (claimed by the United States as part of the Louisiana Purchase) nor, still less, into Spanish Florida, as Jackson wanted, they had been left in frustration in Nachez while the regulars took West Florida. Jackson and his army finally got their call to action when the Creek Indians went on the warpath in the summer of 1813, attacked Fort Mims, in the southern Mississippi Territory, and massacred more than 500 men, women, and children. Jackson caught up with the fractious Indians at Horseshoe Bend. In his attack on the 900 Indians Jackson had 600 regulars, 2000 militia, and hundreds of friendly Indians. The battle was a rout and was followed by a massacre of the Creeks. Although this campaign had no direct effect on the war, it led to Jackson's becoming a national hero and to being appointed a major general in the regular Army and commander

Above: Macdonough's victory on Lake Champlain, 11 September 1814.
Below: The battle of Lundy's Lane, 25 July 1813, one of the war's bloodiest.

Future president Andrew Jackson won his victory at New Orleans 15 days after the formal end of the War of 1812.

of the southern theater, from which position he would lead the defense of New Orleans in the following year.

Throughout 1813 the Royal Navy continued to blockade American ports and keep the miniscule American Navy off the seas. The British Navy also roamed freely up and down Chesapeake Bay, although a British attempt to take Norfolk by amphibious assault in June ended in failure, the British on that occasion consoling themselves by crossing Hampton Roads and burning the town of Hampton. Thus at sea, as well as in the North and the South, the year 1813 ended as indecisively as it had begun.

The war plan for 1814 decided upon by Madison and his cabinet was for yet another invasion of Canada, this time from the Niagara Frontier. Placed in command there was Brigadier General Jacob Brown, who had led the successful defense of Sackett's Harbor the year before. Serving under him was Winfield Scott, now a brigadier general, who had distinguished himself at Queenston. Brown was ordered to cross the Niagara River at Buffalo and capture Fort Erie before moving northward to Lake Ontario, there to join with Commodore Chauncey's naval force and seize control of the entire Niagara peninsula. Brown crossed the river with 3500 troops on 3 July 1813, took Fort Erie, and started north. Two days later his force came face to face with the troops of Sir Gordon Drummond and General Phineas Riall at the Chippewa River. The ensuing battle was fought in classic battle line style. The well-trained Americans, under the command of Scott, won the day, leaving Brown free to move on to Queenston and the junction with Chauncey.

But Chauncey declined to reinforce Brown (and nobody in Washington ordered him to do so), so Brown pulled back to the Chippewa. Then, trying to get around to the British rear, Brown's forces again collided with those of Drummond and Riall at Lundy's Lane, and a bloody slugging match ensued on the night of 25 July, each side losing over 800 men. The Americans pulled back south to Fort Erie to regroup, but the British were the first to be reinforced and soon placed the Americans at Fort Erie under heavy siege. Reinforcements, under Major General George Izard, sent to Brown from Plattsburg, did not arrive at Niagara until 5 October. By then the American position was untenable, even with the reinforcements, so early in November, Fort Erie was abandoned, and the Americans crossed back into their own territory.

When Izard had first received orders to leave Plattsburg he had protested that this would leave the Lake Champlain route wide open to the enemy. He was correct. Three days after he left, on 1 September, a major British expedition, including a naval squadron, began moving down Lake Champlain. Commanded by General Prevost, the army consisted of 12,000 veterans of the European wars. The naval units consisted of four armed brigs and twelve gunboats. Taking advantage of Napoleon's defeat and subsequent abdication, the British were now going on the offensive in America, with the goal of winning back some of the lands surrendered in the Treaty of Paris.

Facing this massive invasion force were but 3000 regulars and militia under militia brigadier Alexander Macomb. Prevost arrived at Plattsburg on 6 September. There he decided to wait until his naval force had destroyed Commander Thomas Macdonough's American flotilla before proceeding with his attacks on the American fieldworks. By skillful maneuvering and superior naval gunnery Macdonough and his men forced two large British ships to surrender and damaged enough of the others to win complete control of the lake. Realizing that even if he took Plattsburg he could not hold it without his waterborne supply line, Prevost the next day ordered his troops to return to Canada. The most dangerous British offensive on the northern frontier had been defeated by Macdonough's two-hour naval defense on Lake Champlain. The northern frontier was safe at last. Now the war shifted to the East and South.

In August 1814 a British force of 4000 men under Major General Robert Ross sailed from Bermuda, its destination Chesapeake Bay. There they were to destroy stores and attack the cities of Washington and Baltimore. The purpose of all this was to create a diversion of attention away from Prevost, who was then making his way down Lake Champlain. Ross's force sailed up Chesapeake Bay, landed on the Patuxent River, and began a march on the capital. The government tried desperately to organize defenses. It eventually collected 5000 regulars, militiamen, and sailors and marines from the navy yard to meet the attack, but the British easily brushed aside this defensive force and went on to burn the Capitol, the White House, and other government buildings.

The invaders then returned to their ships and sailed on to Baltimore. Under a major general of the Maryland militia, Samuel Smith, 10,000 militiamen had turned out to defend the city by earthworks constructed on the land approaches, while the harbor was protected by Fort McHenry, with 1000 regulars and sailors inside. On 13 September the British attacked the city after bombarding Fort McHenry for twenty-four hours but could not break the militia's defenses. Baltimore was saved, and America gained a National Anthem, thanks to Baltimore lawyer Francis Scott Key, who watched the bombardment. The British reembarked and sailed off to the West Indies, there to plan another operation, an attack on New Orleans. Taking that city would close the Mississippi to the Americans and provide the British with a valuable bargaining chip in the peace negotiations that had already begun.

The British gathered a force of 8000 regulars and 50 warships to carry out the assault on New Orleans. Andrew Jackson, as southern theater commander, assembled a force of 5000 men to oppose them. Major General Sir Edward Pakenham had been sent to America to lead the British invasion, but the expedition left Jamaica in November, before Pakenham's arrival, and began operations on 8 December. When Pakenham arrived on the scene on Christmas Day, 1814, he discovered that his troops had already been committed, thanks to decisions made by Admiral Alexander Cochrane and some subordinate army officers. Pakenham found his troops dug in on an isthmus below New Orleans with the Mississippi River on one side and a cypress swamp on the other. Opposite were the American lines, which stretched from the river to the swamp and consisted of high earthworks behind which 4500 men waited for the British attack. Jackson also had some 20 artillery pieces, nine of which were sighted on the British from across the Mississippi.

Pakenham decided on a frontal assault of 5300 men, with a secondary movement of 600 others crossing the river. When the attack came on 8 January 1815 the British were mown down by the murderous fire from behind the American parapets. Pakenham and 2000 other British regulars – over one-third of the forces making the attack – fell under the American fusilade. So great was the carnage that the officer commanding the secondary movement called it off. The British returned to the coast and attacked Fort Bowyer at the entrance to Mobile harbor, then, on hearing of the news that a peace treaty had been signed, returned to their ships and sailed for the West Indies.

Peace negotiations had in fact been going on for months at Ghent, Belgium, with neither side in a favorable enough position to agree to a peace treaty. Finally the negotiators, on Christmas Eve, 1814, had decided to accept a simple formula that had ended the war – two weeks before the Battle of New Orleans was fought.

In the War of 1812 for a second time the Army and the militia had teamed up to fight

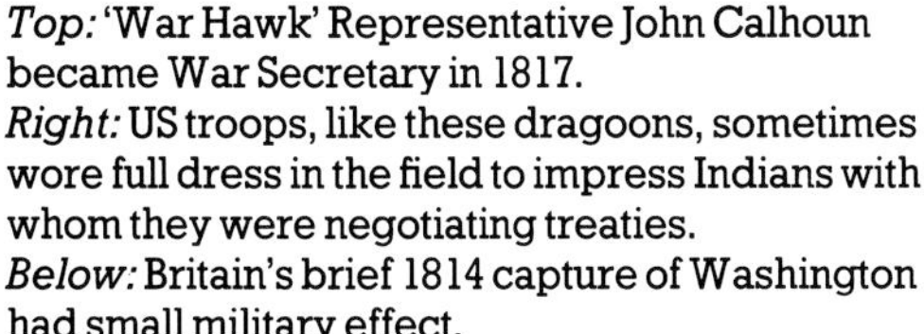
Top: 'War Hawk' Representative John Calhoun became War Secretary in 1817.
Right: US troops, like these dragoons, sometimes wore full dress in the field to impress Indians with whom they were negotiating treaties.
Below: Britain's brief 1814 capture of Washington had small military effect.

for the nation. And for a second time it became obvious that despite the militia's occasional sterling performances, as at the Battle of the Thames, the defense of Baltimore, and the Battle of New Orleans, America's future military security would depend almost entirely on how proficient its regular forces could become.

The Thirty Years' Interlude

In the immediate aftermath of the war there had been considerable popular support for the maintenance of a sizeable professional army, but as the years went on without a visible enemy on the horizon, Congress' enthusiasm paled, and by 1817 the Army had been cut to about 8200 men. By 1823 it was down to about 6000. Even as trouble began to brew with Mexico over Texas' independence and its possible annexation by the United States, there was no disposition to increase radically the size of the Army.

Nevertheless, within the Army a number of major changes were taking place. Among them was the increased attention given to the US Military Academy at West Point, where officer-engineers were being trained. In 1816 money was appropriated for new buildings, books, maps, and engineering instruments; and in that same year the cadets received regulation gray uniforms, honoring the regulars at the Chippewa and Lundy's Lane who had had to wear gray uniforms because they lacked the regulation blue. Perhaps, most important, in 1817 Brevet Major Sylvanus Thayer was appointed superintendent. Well schooled in modern military tactics and military education, Thayer introduced a number of reforms both in the organization of the corps of cadets and in its instruction. These innovations started the Academy on the road to becoming a first-rate military and educational institution, its officers competent not only in engineering but also in the three branches of combat arms: infantry, artillery and cavalry. By 1846 the Academy had graduated almost a thousand cadets, about half of whom stayed in the Army to form the backbone of a professional force.

Fortress Monroe, Virginia, at the mouth of

Chesapeake Bay, was established as an artillery school in 1824, the first of the Army's specialist schools. Also founded was the infantry school at Jefferson Barracks, near St Louis, in 1827. Unlike today's specialist schools, at both these schools whole units, not individuals, were trained for up to a year.

The man largely responsible for these major changes was John C Calhoun, Secretary of War from 1817 until 1825. Besides re-establishing the office of commanding general as part of his overall reorganization of the Army's high command, Calhoun, one of the nation's great secretaries of war, also argued forcefully for his concept of an 'expansible army.' Faced with a demand that the Army be cut to 6000 men, Calhoun insisted that this should be done by halving the number of enlisted men in each company, leaving the senior enlisted and officers as a nucleus upon which to rebuild a force of 19,000 officers and men in case of a national emergency. In the event, Congress cut the total number of companies and regiments instead, but Calhoun's idea later became the basis of plans for a ready reserve for the US military. Calhoun also pushed for the protection of America's seacoast, a weakness that had been manifest in the recent war against the British. By 1826 18 harbors and ports, from Maine to the Mississippi, had been fortified with 31 defense works.

While the nation met no foreign enemies during this period, persistent problems with the Indians remained, and three wars were fought against them before the lands east of the Mississippi were made safe. The first came in 1817, as the result of attacks made out of Spanish Florida by Seminoles, Creeks and runaway slaves on settlements in lower Georgia. The Spanish governmental officials in Florida had little control over the Indians, and British adventurers encouraged the raids, telling the Indians that southern Georgia still belonged to them. The American government reacted vigorously to these incursions, in what has come to be known as the First Seminole War. Major General Andrew Jackson, commanding the Southern Department, was instructed to remove the menace, even if he had to cross into Florida. Jackson was only too happy to comply. Assembling a force of 800 regulars, 1000 militia from Georgia and (later) 1000 militia volunteers from Tennessee, Jackson moved into Florida in February 1818, executed two British citizens whom he believed had incited the Indians, and shortly gained control of all central and western Florida, the Indians having melted away into the swamps in the face of this superior force. When Spain and Britain protested the incursion, the United States expressed its regrets but made it clear to Spain that it would either have to control the Indians or cede Florida to the United States. Spain chose the latter course, in return for a money payment.

The second of the Indian wars was known as the Black Hawk War. It took place on the Illinois and Wisconsin frontiers, on the upper Mississippi, and began when the Sac and Fox tribes, under Chief Black Hawk, moved back across the river to their former lands in Illinois, after having earlier been removed to Iowa. Black Hawk returned in 1832 with perhaps 500 warriors and 1000 women and children. Alarmed by the Indians' reappearance, the Illinois government collected 1000 militia to ride against Black Hawk, and the federal government ordered Colonel Henry Atkinson and his 500 regulars from Jefferson Barracks to march to the troubled area. (A third force of 1000 was sent from the East coast via the Great Lakes but arrived too late to take part in the conflict and was largely disabled by an outbreak of cholera among the troops.) Black Hawk moved north into the Wisconsin Territory, trying to escape back across the Mississippi, but the military caught up with him, first at Wisconsin Heights and then on the Bad Axe River, and destroyed his forces.

The third Indian war took place in the South. Labeled the Second Seminole War, it began in 1835 and dragged on until 1842. It was essentially a guerrilla war conducted by the Seminoles under their half-breed leader, Osceola, with the Indians operating out of bases in the swamps and forests of Florida. It

Left: **A US victory at Bad Axe River, 1832, ended Black Hawk's War, one of several Indian wars between 1812-60.**
Right: **Drab-looking uniforms worn by US soldiers in the frustrating Second Seminole War, 1835-42. Painting by Charles McBarron.**

George Catlin's portrait of Osceola, who successfully led the Seminoles until 1837.

began when the Seminoles repudiated a treaty by which they had agreed to move west of the Mississippi and attacked a detachment of Army regulars. Before it was over, the Army had to deploy 10,000 regulars and 30,000 militia to put down its evasive enemy. The Army persisted in marching columns of soldiers on suspected enemy strongholds, only to find the enemy gone when they arrived. Rather than face the Army in open combat, the Seminoles preferred to attack small detachments and outposts, then disappear from sight. As the war dragged on without the enemy being brought to bay, the army became increasingly desperate and ruthless in its treatment of the Indians, and Army leaders finally resorted to trickery by inviting Osceola and the other chiefs to a conference under a flag of truce and then taking them prisoner. Osceola died in captivity in 1838 at Fort Marion, Florida (later being strangely honored by having a county in western Michigan named after him), but it was the relentless campaign of extermination that finally ended the Second Seminole War.

During this same thirty-years' interlude the Army led the way into the trans-Mississippi west. There it built roads, surveyed, and built fortifications in Iowa, Nebraska, and Kansas. Fort Leavenworth, Kansas, built in 1827, served as the base for expeditions by Army engineers and explorers along the Santa Fe and Oregon Trails. The Army also made treaties with the Indians and protected settlers moving into the vast new territories opened by the Oregon Trail and to California beyond. Such officers as Lieutenant John C Fremont and Colonel Stephen W Kearny earned national reputations for their part in such endeavors.

The Mexican War

Between 1820 and 1835 some 35,000 Americans poured into the Mexican territory of Texas. At first welcomed by the Mexicans, the Americans became increasingly independent and their relations with the government became strained. When Mexico forbade any more immigration into the territory, the Texas Americans were incensed. In March 1836 they declared their independence of Mexico. Before the year was out, under the leadership of General Sam Houston, they had bested the Mexican forces that had tried to bring them back into subjection. Texas, upon winning its independence on the battlefield, then turned to the United States and asked for admission to the Union.

Much as many Americans wanted to see their fellow countrymen brought into the Union, the uncomfortable fact existed that while the United States had recognized Texas' independence, Mexico had not. If the United States accepted the Texans' request, it would be annexing Mexican territory, according to the Mexicans. Whether or not to take the risk of war with Mexico became the subject of a ten-year battle in the halls of Congress. It was a debate that, though long, could probably have only one outcome.

In November 1844, upon receiving the news that the ardent expansionist and candidate for the Democratic party, James K Polk, had won the presidential election, President John Tyler interpreted the election results as a mandate from the people for the annexation of Texas. Accordingly, he began to push for annexation, and Congress, on 1 March 1845, by joint resolution agreed to admit Texas into the Union. Mexico broke off diplomatic relations, a clear sign of an impending clash.

Anticipating that Texas would accept Congress' invitation to join the Union, President Polk ordered Brevet Brigadier General Zachary Taylor to move his forces from Louisiana into Texas to a point 'on or near' the Rio Grande. Taylor marched to the mouth of the Nueces River and set up camp. His force of regulars, volunteers, and Texas Rangers soon rose to 4000. There he waited for six months until ordered by Washington to the Rio Grande, 100 miles down the coast. The Army was now clearly on land never claimed either by Texas or by the United States, land that in the Mexicans' eyes clearly belonged to them, whatever the legality of the Texas annexation.

Setting himself up at the mouth of the Rio Grande, across the river from the Mexican town of Matamoros, Taylor built Fort Texas. Shortly afterwards, on 25 April 1846, a Mexican army crossed the river and attacked an American detachment of dragoons, killing eleven men. Taylor informed Polk that military hostilities had begun and prepared himself for major conflict.

Leaving a small detachment at Fort Texas, Taylor pulled back 18 miles to Point Isabel, where his supply ships were waiting. On his return to Fort Texas with fresh supplies and more cannon, he was met, at Palo Alto, on 7 May, by a Mexican army of some 4000 men. With his superior six-, 12- and 18-pound artillery firing cannister and solid shot, Taylor was able to outduel his opponents' artillery in a day-long battle. The Mexicans suffered almost 700 casualties, the Americans only 56. The next day the Mexicans began a full retreat, stopping briefly to put up a delaying fight at Resaca de la Palma that cost them an-

In March 1836 the 183 Texan rebels who defended the Alamo were overwhelmed by 4000 Mexican regulars. Yet Texas won its freedom soon thereafter.

other 550 casualties. The Mexican army then hastened in headlong retreat back across the Rio Grande. The Americans could not follow since they had no pontoon bridges and Taylor had neglected to acquire bridging materials or boats. When they finally crossed on 18 May the Mexican army was gone.

In the meantime, Congress, on 13 May, declared war on Mexico and authorized the expansion of the Army to 15,540 regulars and 50,000 volunteers. The American Army of 1846 was undoubtedly far better prepared to wage this conflict than it had been in either 1775 or 1812. True, it was small – only 7885 men and 734 officers distributed among eight regiments of infantry, two of dragoons and four of artillery – but it was well trained and equipped, its officers were professional, and its long years of Indian fighting had given all ranks valuable combat experience.

It had also benefited from the evolving technology of warfare. The flintlock firearm, which had dominated the field of battle since the mid-seventeenth century, was now beginning to give way to a new innovation: the percussion lock weapon. Flintlocks had always been subject to a certain amount of misfiring, either because of worn flints or because damp had gotten into the priming powder in the flashpan. And even at best, all flintlocks suffered from a small but annoying hangfire – the brief moment, after the trigger was pulled, that was required for the lock to fall forward onto the frizzen, for the spark to drop onto the priming powder and for the fire from the ignited primer to flash through the vent hole and explode the propellant charge inside the barrel. It was only a brief interruption, but often it was enough to interfere with the shooter's aim, especially if his target were moving. In the new percussion system a hammer fell directly onto a waxed paper or thin-copper cap containing fulminate of mercury, the instant explosion of which set off the propellant charge. Misfires were

Most contemporary prints wrongly show US soldiers in battle wearing dress, rather than campaign, uniforms.

radically reduced, hangfire time was shortened, and the whole reloading process was considerably speeded up. By 1841 a percussion lock musket had been ordered as the standard US infantry weapon, though during the Mexican War the older Springfield Model 1835 .67-inch calibre flintlock musket was still more prevalent, thanks mainly to General Winfield Scott's continuing prejudice against the new mechanism. The cavalry, on the other hand, took to percussion enthusiastically. Between 1833 and 1843 it adopted five different versions of the new Hall carbine (the majority being .54-inch calibre), all of them not only percussion-firing but breech-loading as well.

An infantry officer and a dragoon clad in the campaign uniforms worn in the Mexican War.

In the Corps of Artillery innovation was more tactical than technical. Since analyses of the recent Napoleonic wars seemed to suggest that the mobility of artillery could be a key factor in winning battles, by 1846 approximately half the cannons in the US Army were represented by light horse-drawn six-pounders. These weapons proved exceptionally useful in the Mexican War, though the Civil War would later demonstrate that they were not quite the be-all-and-end-all some of their proponents at first thought. Indeed, so well did the Artillery perform in the Mexican War that in 1847 Congress went so far as to authorize the formation of four more artillery regiments.

The Mexican War was the first war in which the Army was not plagued by shortages of uniforms. The standard dress uniforms looked much as they had in 1812, but for campaigning a somewhat simpler and more practical kit was adapted: the cotee and trousers (now both generally sky blue) were looser-fitting, and a soft, visored cap was worn in place of the unwieldy shako.

The Mexican War was also the first American war in which militia was not to play a major role, the augmentation of the small regular force being accomplished mainly by the recruitment of one-year volunteers. This system certainly had its disadvantages, but at least the volunteers were under direct Army control and could be professionally equipped, trained, and led. Both Generals Scott and Taylor insisted on giving all volunteers at least six hours of training each day before taking them on campaign.

At the beginning of the war the Americans planned a three-pronged attack on northern Mexico. One prong, under General Taylor – 'Old Rough and Ready' or 'Old Zack' – was to advance westward from Matamoros to Monterrey. A second, under Brigadier General John E Wool, would move from San Antonio west to the village of Chihuahua and then south. A third, under Colonel Stephen W Kearny, was to leave from Fort Leavenworth for Santa Fe and then March on to San Diego, on the California coast. Northern Mexico would then be in American hands. Only later was it decided that another expedition would be sent under Major General Winfield Scott, commanding general of the Army, to invade Vera Cruz and then proceed overland toward the capital at Mexico City. Meantime,

Future president Zachary Taylor: His campaign in Mexico was exemplary.

Several Civil War generals were Mexican veterans, among them Grant and Robert E Lee (*above*).

Polk had promoted Zachary Taylor to brevet major general and given him command of the Army in Mexico because the president feared the political ambitions of Scott, as did Taylor.

'Old Zack' made his way to Camargo, 125 miles northeast of Monterrey, to set up a base for his advance on that city. Soon he had 15,000 men assembled there, and in late August he advanced with over 6000 regulars and volunteers toward Monterrey. He reached the city on 19 September, to find it defended by 7500 Mexicans equipped with 42 artillery pieces. Taylor placed the city under siege. By 24 September the Mexican commander realized resistance was hopeless and offered to surrender the city if his troops were allowed to withdraw and if an eight-week armistice were declared. Being far from his base and having suffered the loss of 800 men to battle and sickness, Taylor agreed. But President Polk was angered by Taylor's battlefield decision and ordered that the armistice be terminated. Taylor then took Saltillo, on the main road to Mexico City. There he was joined by General Wool, who had turned south when he found that Chihuahua had been abandoned. But at this point Taylor had all of his 4000 regulars and an equal number of volunteers taken away from him: they were to join General Scott at Tampico for the invasion at Vera Cruz.

Enraged at this decision, Taylor chose to regard Scott's further order to pull back and stand on the defensive at Monterrey as 'advice.' Instead, he moved 4650 of his remaining troops south of Saltillo to Agua Nueva. Mexican General Santa Anna was then 300 miles to the south assembling a large army, but Taylor believed the Mexican leader could not march an army so far north through barren desert and would therefore move east against Scott at Vera Cruz.

Taylor realized he was wrong on the morning of 21 February 1847 when his scouts reported a great Mexican army advancing up the Saltillo road. He withdrew to the hacienda Buena Vista to await the enemy. Before the hacienda was a broad plateau; to the east was a series of mountain spurs, La Angostura being the longest and deepest; to the west was a network of gullies. Taylor had only 5000 men, many of them green volunteers; General Santa Anna had 15,000. Taylor's only apparent advantage was that his artillery was well emplaced at La Angostura.

The first day of the Battle of Buena Vista, 22 February 1847, was spent mainly in jockeying for position. The decision was reached the next day. First Santa Anna tried to break the American left wing on La Angostura, but his troops were driven off by artillery and infantry. Then he hit the plateau in the center with two divisions, and the Americans broke and ran. The battle was quickly turning into an American rout when Taylor's dragoons, the Mississippi Rifles, under Colonel Jefferson Davis, arrived on the scene and broke the Mexican cavalry charges. With reformed lines, and in the midst of a mighty thunderstorm, the Americans gradually forced the Mexicans back. Santa Anna threw fresh troops into the fray, an entire division. Again the American lines began to crack. And again the situation was saved by the Mississippi Rifles (and some troops from Indiana) galloping onto the field under the leadership of the now-wounded Davis. These mounted warriors fell upon the Mexicans and forced them to retreat, while the American artillery continued to punish them from La Angostura. That night Santa Anna began his retreat, having lost over 1500 killed and wounded, to the Americans' 800. The fighting spirit of the green volunteers, the conspicuous bravery of Zachary Taylor who stationed himself on his horse in the midst of the line, the slashing attacks by the American mounted volunteers, and punishing American artillery had won the day.

Northern Mexico was soon safely in American hands. Colonel Kearny had arrived in San Diego in December 1846 to find that the Americans in the 'Bear Flag Revolt,' the Navy's Pacific squadron, and John C Fremont's small army of 'explorers' had already wrested control of California from Mexico. And Colonel Alexander W Doniphan and his Missouri volunteers cleared the upper Rio Grande by their victory over a large Mexican force at Chihuahua shortly after Taylor's victory. Mexico City, the capital, was next.

General Scott, 'Old Fuss and Feathers,' assembled a force of over 13,000 men at Lobos island, 50 miles south of Tampico, for his attack on Vera Cruz. It was the first major joint amphibious landing in the history of the US military. Joining with a supporting naval squadron on 5 March off Vera Cruz, the unopposed landings took place on 9 March, three miles south of the city. In four hours more than 10,000 men had been rowed ashore in surf boats, along with their artillery and stores. When it was subsequently discovered that the available artillery of mortars and howitzers was insufficient to reduce Vera Cruz and its fortress of San Juan de Ulua, six naval guns were brought ashore and manhandled into position. These breached the walls of the city and fortress, and on 27 March the city fell. Scott then moved inland toward the capital.

Most brilliant of US generals in the Mexican War was Winfield Scott. He would run for the presidency in 1852.

He soon met Santa Anna's army of 12,000 men near Cerro Gordo, on the National Highway cutting through the mountains to Mexico City. Santa Anna thought his position was unassailable, but by making their way through the rough terrain around the Mexican positions, the Americans brought their heavy artillery on to the high ground above them. The result was a complete American victory, on 18 April, that forced the Mexicans to flee back toward the capital.

The road was now open to Mexico City, but at this critical point the enlistments of seven of Scott's volunteer regiments, about 4000 men, expired, and few chose to remain on the fatiguing campaign. The loss of these volunteers, plus the ravages of death and sickness among his troops, had brought Scott's force down to less than 6000. Yet he pushed on to Puebla, took the city without resistance, and there settled down to await reinforcements and the outcome of peace negotiations then underway. The reinforcements eventually came, after ten weeks, and in the meantime the peace negotiations had broken down. It was obvious that Santa Anna, now the president of Mexico, would need

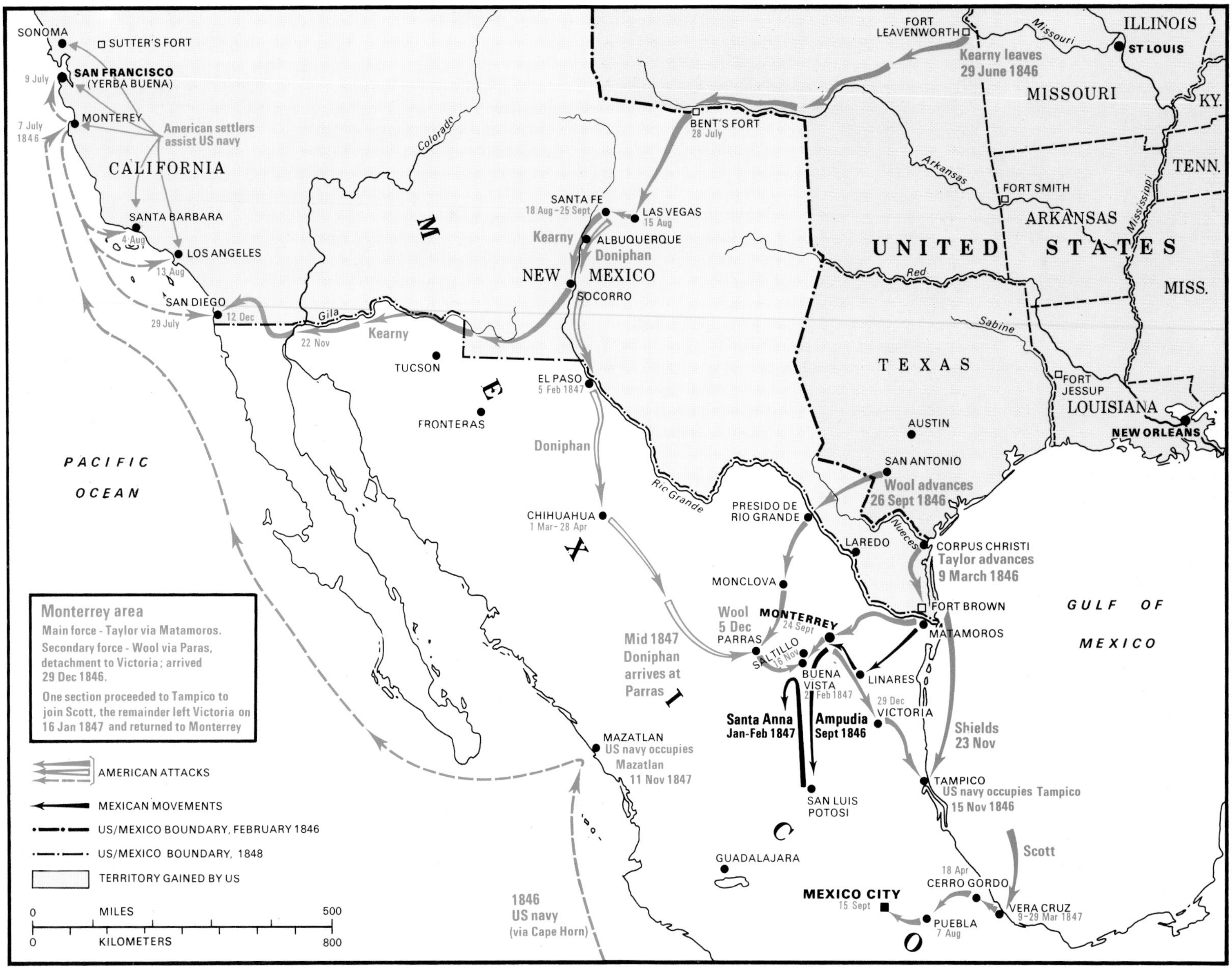

Top: General map of the Mexican War.
Left: Scott's landing at Vera Cruz: A near-perfect amphibious operation.

greater pressure before agreeing to abandon the war.

Although he had no men to guard his supply lines stretching all the way back to Vera Cruz, Scott, with his army of 10,000 men, moved on toward Mexico City on 7 August. Within three days he was only 14 miles from the city. Deciding not to attempt to take the city from the east because of its fortifications, Scott sent his forces to the south, through difficult terrain, to flank the defenses. Although sharply challenged by the Mexicans at Contreras (they lost 700 dead and had 800 taken prisoner, to only 60 American casualties), the Americans drove on. On 20 August Santa Anna's men made another gallant defensive stand at Churubusco, losing 4000 killed or wounded, but could not withstand the frontal attack of infantry and artillery launched by the Americans. Scott offered an armistice to Santa Anna, which he accepted, but when it became obvious that the Mexicans were still in no mood to acquiesce in American terms and were using the armistice to bring reinforcements, the war was resumed.

As Scott moved inland from Vera Cruz Santa Anna tried in vain to block his way to Mexico City at Cerro Gordo.

Now with only about 8000 men to challenge Santa Anna's 15,000 in the heavily fortified city, Scott persisted in his offensive. First he took an outlying defensive position called El Molino del Rey and then moved on the Castle of Chapultepec, guarding the approaches to Mexico City. On 13 September American artillery and infantry succeeded in a well-conducted three-pronged attack on the citadel, while infantry used scaling ladders to top the walls and then push on to take the Belén and San Cosmé gates to the city itself. The next day Santa Anna surrendered. Scott had proven himself a brilliant theater commander, and he had been aided in his victories by some highly promising young Army officers – Robert E Lee, George E Meade, Pierre G T Beauregard, Joseph T Johnston and Ulysses S Grant – all West Pointers who would put their battle experience in these campaigns to good use in another war yet to come.

The war with Mexico ended on 2 February 1848 with the signing of the Treaty of Guadelupe Hidalgo. By 1 August 1848 all American troops were out of the country, and the United States had gained clear title to Texas, with the Rio Grande as its recognized southern border, and to over one million square miles of new territory, including all of present-day Arizona, New Mexico, Utah, Nevada, and California, and parts of Wyoming and Colorado. The cost had been high. Almost 13,000 Americans had been lost in the war, although only 1700 had died in battle or from wounds, the rest having succumbed to disease or accident. Whatever the morality of its inception, the Mexican War resulted in impressive victories for the American Army and served as a valuable classroom for the use of new mobile artillery and fluid battle tactics.

After the Mexican War the Army resumed its duties on the frontier: defending against Indian tribes, surveying trails through the mountains and across the plains, and building forts and roads. Standing at about 13,000 men, the Army returned to its peacetime duties, while developing its service schools, new weaponry, and new doctrines. But events were soon to overtake it as the nation, wracked by controversy over the expansion of slavery into the new and expanding West, drifted toward the horror of civil war – a civil war in which the Army would fight itself.

Taylor partly owed his Buena Vista victory to the Kentucky Dragoons who twice broke Mexican infantry charges.

Sherman's March to the Sea, a brutal episode in America's bloodiest war.

THE CIVIL WAR: 1861-1865

Attempts to reconcile the many deep-seated differences between the North and South, both over the expansion of slavery and other economic and political issues, came to naught after the Mexican War, and the cleavage widened between the two sections of the country. The Compromise of 1850 over the admission of California into the Union resulted only in bad feelings. The Kansas-Nebraska Act of 1854, which attempted to allow the people in the territories to decide the issue of slavery themselves by 'popular sovereignty,' resulted only in bloody warfare in Kansas and further inflamed emotions on both sides of the Mason-Dixon Line. The rapid emergence of the Republican party and its fielding of a presidential candidate in 1856 was a sign of an impending split, for the new party was clearly a Northern party and a descendant of anti-slavery political groups going back two decades.

The Democratic party managed to win that year by straddling the issue of slavery and offering a 'neutral' and innocuous candidate, James Buchanan of Pennsylvania, for the presidency. But bad feelings continued to intensify during the next four years, especially after John Brown's vain, violent attempt to set up an asylum at Harper's Ferry for runaway slaves within slaveholding Virginia. Then, in 1860, the Republican party placed Abraham Lincoln of Illinois in nomination for the presidency and declared again against the extension of slavery. With Lincoln's victory in November, some Southern states, believing that their enemies had finally and decisively won control of the Federal government, began to draft ordinances of secession. Even before Lincoln's inauguration on 4 March 1861 seven states in the Deep South, led by South Carolina, had seceded from the Union and had formed the Confederate States of America. Two days after Lincoln's inauguration, on 6 May, the new president of the Confederacy, Jefferson Davis – an ex-West Pointer, former hero of the Mexican War, and former US Secretary of War – called for 100,000 volunteers to defend the Confederacy's existence against any attempts by the Federal government to return its citizens to loyalty to the Union.

Right: Soldiers with deadly new 1855 percussion-lock musket-rifles.

Below: As Congressional compromises failed civil war became inevitable.

The North seemed to have all the advantages as each side began to prepare itself for probable conflict. Its twenty-three loyal states had a population of 21 million people; the South had only 9 million, including over 3 million slaves whom the South would be loath to put under arms (although the slaves could be used as military laborers and kept in agricultural production, thereby freeing more white males for military duty). More important, the North had over 80 percent of the nation's factories and 67 percent of the nation's farms. And almost all of the South's factories were small and technologically primitive, making them very difficult to convert to modern war-making capacity. The North, on the other hand, had both highly skilled labor and the mechanical means to fight a technological war, plus far greater capacity for sustained and increasing production of the goods of war. The South never managed to gain industrial self-sufficiency during the course of the conflict, despite prodigious feats of improvisation.

Furthermore, the North had a developed and integrated transportation system, especially in railroads, which would play a vital role in transporting men and supplies both from the home front to the war zones and back and forth within the war zones themselves. The North also had a developed system of steamboats and barges as important ancillary means of transportation. All told, the North had over 20,000 miles of track, with adequate locomotives and rolling stock, and almost all of this railroad mileage was well integrated, with convenient intersections, good 'through' lines, and standard track gauges. The South, on the other hand, had but 9000 miles of track, little integration or standardization of track gauges, and virtually no capacity for replacing locomotives and rolling stock once they fell victim to deterioration or enemy action. Yet in the war to come transport would be all-important.

The North likewise enjoyed a preponderance of naval and maritime power. Virtually all of the American merchant marine belonged to Northerners, and the US Navy of 90 ships, while not adequate for the war, was easily capable of expansion. By 1864 the Union had a navy of 670 ships and 50,000 men, this in a war in which blockade was one of the basic strategic goals to be pursued. The Confederacy had no navy and no first-rate building and repair facilities, either at the beginning or at any time during the course of the war. Captured facilities and inland production allowed the South to scrape together a force of some 130 vessels, manned by 4000 men, but as the Federal blockade became tighter, and as the Union gained control of the inland waters in the South, there was no way the small Confederate navy could loosen this nautical stranglehold.

The election of Lincoln in 1860 was the event that triggered civil war. By inauguration day (*below*) seven rebel states had seceded. But Lincoln was to prove more dangerous to the South in war than in peace.

Given this preponderance in numbers and materiel, the Lincoln administration, with the aged Winfield Scott as General in Chief, settled on a basic three-part strategy for early victory. Part one called for capturing the Confederate capital at Richmond, Virginia. The second part called for seizure of the entire route of the Mississippi River down to the Gulf of Mexico, thus cutting the South in two and denying it support from its western territories. This was to be followed by the seizure of Chattanooga, which was to be used as a base for a second bisection of the south. The third part of the strategy, the 'Anaconda Policy,' was to impose a tight blockade on the

Above: CSA president Jefferson Davis.
Below: Recruiting for the Confederate Army in Woodstock, Virginia.

entire Confederacy, from the Chesapeake Bay to the extreme southern coast of Texas, thereby denying aid from the outside and at the same time strangling Southern commerce by denying to it its world markets, especially for cotton.

That the Union, given time to gear up for the war effort, could carry out these plans was not seriously in question. The only possible doubt was whether or not it would have the will to do so if the war became protracted. That will was supplied by Abraham Lincoln, president and Commander in Chief, who never faltered in his determination to restore the Union. The unknown Lincoln, elected to the presidency in 1860, emerged as the iron-willed Lincoln of history, who provided leadership to rally the people of the Union behind him and to pay whatever price was necessary to preserve the Union. Lincoln's hope was that the wounds of war would leave no permanent scars on the body politic, so that, after the defeat of the secessionists, the nation could again be united to pursue its destiny as the 'last best hope of mankind.' In this he never faltered, and this was undoubtedly the most important ingredient in the eventual Union victory.

Yet the South, despite its inferiority in manpower and war-making capacity, had certain advantages. For one thing, the Confederacy did not have to carry the war into the North in order to win; it had only to remain on the defensive and prevent serious Northern incursions into its territory, to hold out long enough and raise the 'butcher's bill' high enough to convince the North that the war was not worth the sacrifices demanded. In this respect the Southern secessionists stood in much the same posture as had the rebels in the American Revolution. For such an essentially defensive effort the South might, with determination, adequate production, and effective military defensive tactics, hold the North at bay for a very long time – perhaps enough time.

But to do this, the South needed both effective leadership and great self-discipline. Unfortunately for the Confederacy, Jefferson Davis, for all his manful efforts to create an effective strategy for victory, his 'offensive defensive,' lacked both the personal qualities and the organizational skills to mold a government strong enough to sustain the pressure of protracted and determined Federal force. And he was continually handicapped by the independent-mindedness of the various states of the Confederacy, which displayed an understandable but fatal tendency to see the needs of the Confederacy only in their own terms. Davis, in the midst of war, was essentially trying to mold a new

Southern Union. Whether or not it could ever have been done can never be determined, but what the outcome might have been, had the South been blessed with a Lincoln at the helm instead of a Davis, will never cease to be a subject of fascinating speculation.

The Contending Armies: 1861

When the seven Southern states seceeded from the Union, they seized all Federal properties within their borders except for Fort Pickens at Pensacola and Fort Sumter in Charleston harbor. Feeling that secession was perfectly constitutional and legal, they argued that these Federal properties were now within their jurisdictions and, as 'foreign' installations, could only exist at their sufferance. For the Federal government to abandon these posts voluntarily would be to give *de facto* recognition to the constitutionality of the South's claim. This Lincoln, as president and as a believer in the indissolubility of the Union, could not and would not do.

Lincoln informed the Confederate commissioners, sent to him a few days after his inauguration, that he would not re-supply the forts without proper notice to the Southern government, but there was no easy way out of his dilemma. If he re-supplied the forts, the South might see this as a provocative act, and the eight remaining slave states might join their confreres in leaving the Union. If he did not re-supply the forts and they were forced to surrender, he would be bowing to Southern pressure. He finally decided that the reprovisioning would have to take place and duly notified the governor of South Carolina on 8 April that a small expedition carrying supplies only, not men, would be sent.

With the moment of decision now upon the South, Confederate Brigadier General Pierre G T Beauregard, the local commander at Charleston, demanded that Major Robert Anderson, commanding at Fort Sumter, surrender the installation. Anderson refused. On 12 April 1861, in the early morning hours, the ring of batteries around Charleston harbor began a 34-hour bombardment of the fort. Anderson's guns fired back but could not equal the Confederate firepower. On 14 April Anderson surrendered the fort, after saluting the American flag with fifty guns. The following day Lincoln signed a proclamation declaring the seven Confederate states to be in rebellion and called for 75,000 militia from the states to suppress the rebellion. This call for troops caused the remaining eight states to begin the process of joining in secession, and the two sides lined up for all-out war.

President Davis' call, on 6 March, for 100,000 volunteers for twelve-month service hardly gave the South enough men to fight a war effectively. A law passed later in 1861 allowed Davis to accept up to 500,000 troops for enlistments lasting from one year to the duration of the war. Some 300,000 men stepped forward, but the great majority of these were twelve-monthers, meaning they could be going home in the spring of 1862. By 1862 the South had turned to conscription, with terms of three years' service, but still it had difficulty filling its ranks because of the provisions of its conscription laws. These provided too-generous exemptions for persons declared critical to the war effort at home (for example, that any white man owning 20 or more slaves did not have to serve). The Southern conscription laws also allowed a draftee to buy a substitute to serve for him, with no limit on the amount which could be paid the proxy. And they allowed for members of the state militia to be exempt; this was a privilege jealously guarded by some Southern governors, who placed more and more men in service as militia officers. (In some instances the numbers serving in the militia exceeded those serving in the Confederate ranks.)

Eventually some 900,000 Southerners probably served three years or more in the Confederate armies (the records are notoriously incomplete), but while 465,000 were on the rolls in 1863, with about half present for duty, by 1864 the recorded number was down to 200,000, with about half of this number having deserted or gone home. Thus by the crucial period of the war, as the Southern cause was feeling its greatest pressure, its effective army strength stood at only about 100,000 men, few enough at the beginning of the war and now grossly inadequate when compared to Northern strength.

With only about 16,000 officers and enlisted men at the beginning of the crisis, the Union Army was likewise in no condition to begin hostilities. The majority of the Army personnel were deployed in the West, six of the seven departments of the Army being located west of the Mississippi. Only 15 companies were in the Department of the East, and these were scattered along the Canadian border and the Atlantic coast. This small force was weakened by the fact that of the active officers, numbering a little over 1000, almost 300 resigned to join the Confederates (including 184 West Point gradu-

Though Lincoln had tried to avert war through conciliation, when the rebels attacked Fort Sumter in April 1861 there could be no turning back.

US regulars wore blue; Confederates, gray. But many militias, like these Zouaves, were more colorfully clad. One militia wore kilts; another, Italian plumed hats.

ates, out of a total of 824, many of whom had held high commands in the regular Army).

Knowing that the regulars, plus 75,000 militia, would be completely unequal to the task ahead, Lincoln called for an increase in the regulars to 23,000 men and for an enlistment of 42,000 volunteers for three-year stints. Congress was willing to go along with the president when it reconvened in late 1861, and proceeded to authorize him to raise a force of 500,000 men for three years. Under these provisions almost 600,000 men came forth in 1861 pledged to serve for an adequate period of time to allow them to be trained and utilized. Throughout the war the regular Army was kept intact, the Union supplementing it with volunteers at all ranks. And unlike the South, the North enacted conscription under a system whereby each state was divided into enrollment districts. If any district met its quota with volunteers (with or without cash bounties), no one would be drafted. This meant that most Union soldiers were volunteers. Less than 50,000 were drafted into Federal service, but few exemptions were allowed, although a person drafted could hire a substitute or pay the government a commutation fee of $300 to escape service. Eventually 1.5 million men served in the Union Army on a long-term basis, and as the war went on the numbers in the Union Army continued to rise, reaching 500,000 in active service by 1864. Despite their continued high place in American myth, militia units played almost no part in the Civil War: regulars, volunteers and draftees made up the ranks of the gargantuan armies needed for this fratricidal contest.

The Union Army's volunteers were drawn from partially-trained state militia units and from enthusiastic recruits from civilian life. Since the states were the basic units from which both volunteers and draftees were drawn, the military units thus formed were state units, with prominent state politicians chosen to lead them. By law, Lincoln could

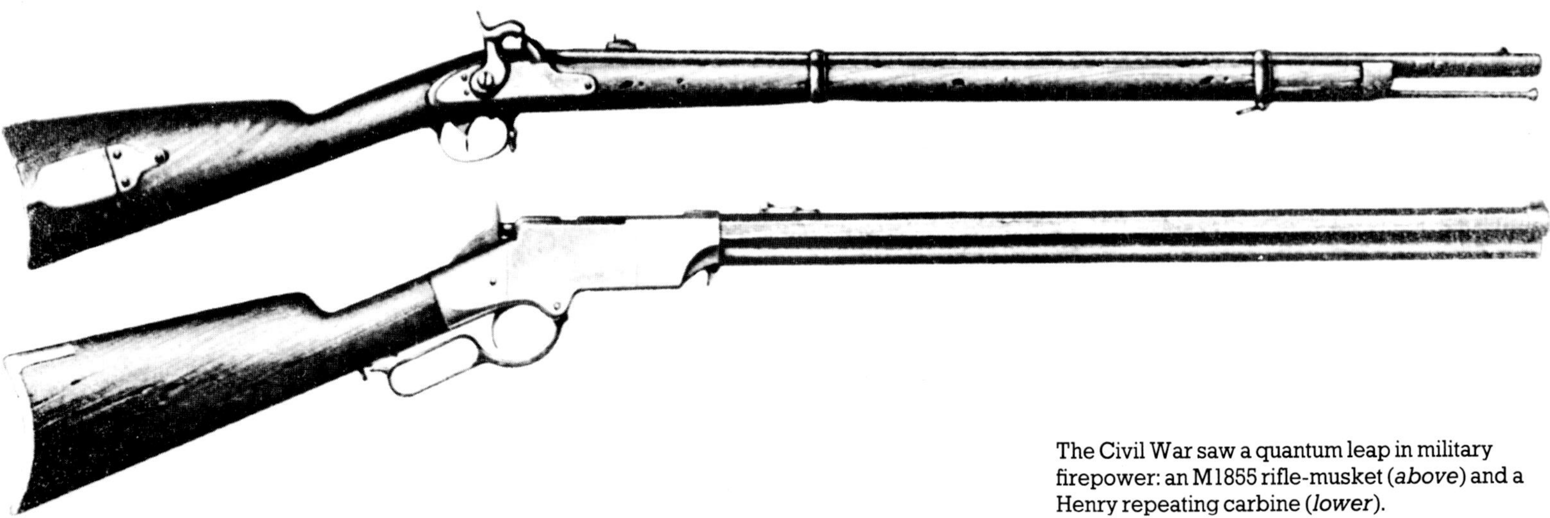

The Civil War saw a quantum leap in military firepower: an M1855 rifle-musket (*above*) and a Henry repeating carbine (*lower*).

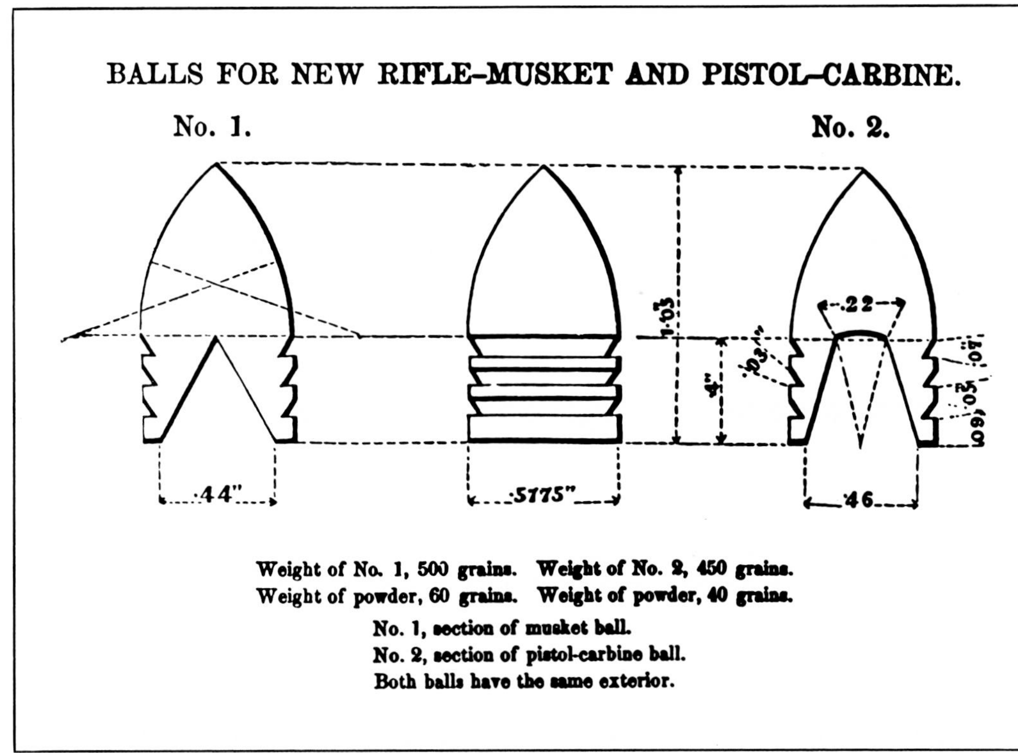

Easy to load and non-fouling, the new Minie Ball now made rifles practical as standard infantry weapons.

appoint the units' general officers, and he often chose governors or other high state officials to assure the loyalty of the states to the Union cause. Some of these politician-officers were of poor quality, while others proved to be surprisingly able. Resupply of recruits to the state-based units was carried out by the states themselves, often necessitating officers being sent back home to recruit more men for the regiments.

The state volunteer units were organized into larger theater armies based on the area in which they would be operating, e.g., the Army of the Potomac or the Army of the Tennessee. The volunteer units within the theater armies were largely made up of infantry, to which artillery and engineering units, both regular and volunteer, would be added. Special units of dragoons (mounted infantry) and Zouaves (special infantry), with distinctive and colorful uniforms and their own local-based officers, plus cavalry units, were also assigned to theater commanders.

In command over the armies thus created was the General in Chief. In fact his powers were shared with Secretary of War Edwin M Stanton and were additionally limited by the bureau chiefs (known as the General Staff), who reported to the secretary, not to him. Furthermore, Congress created its own committee to oversee the war, adding political interference into an already clumsy command system. Only in 1864 did Congress create the rank of lieutenant general and declare that this person could also be General in Chief. And only when Lincoln subsequently named Ulysses S Grant to this dual position to exercise total military control over the Army, was some measure of command unity attained. (And even then the War Department and the bureau chiefs continued to exercise considerable independence in their functions.) It was probably only Lincoln's personality and political acumen that kept the Army's high command functioning as well as it did throughout the war. In this respect the South was less fortunate.

Both the Union and Confederate Armies used essentially similar (and often identical) weapons. While at first glance it might appear that the quality of these weapons had increased only incrementally during the fifteen years since the Mexican War, in fact the improvement had been sufficient to alter the face of war. Although hardly anyone on either side realized it at the outset, the rate of fire, range and accuracy of the new weapons had now reached such levels as to make brute firepower virtually the king of battle. In the Civil War sheer attrition would come to matter as much as – and often more than – any other tactical consideration. Combat casualties would rise to unprecedented proportions – in some instances of attacks on well prepared positions, to nearly 80 percent. Indeed, the total number of battlefield deaths, about 215,000, would be higher than in any other American war save World War II, and in proportion to total population, the lethality of the Civil War would far exceed even that of World War II.

The technological advances that made these horrors possible were relatively simple: the widespread replacement of the musket by the rifle and of the flintlock by the percussion lock, the growing use of breech-loading and repeating weapons (mostly pistols and carbines), and the introduction of rifled artillery. Beginning in 1841 the Army's old smoothbore muskets began to be replaced by a succession of percussion rifles. When the Civil War began the latest of these was the .58-calibre US Model 1861, which had an effective range of nearly 300 yards and an extreme range of over 1500 yards. Rifles had, of course, been around for a long time, and it had always been known that they were very much more accurate than smoothbore muskets. But they had never been widely used by military forces because of their distressing tendency to develop clogged barrels after repeated firing. Then, in the 1830s, a French army captain, C E Minié, invented a type of non-fouling rifle bullet, and suddenly the military rifle became a practical proposition. Only a few years earlier, in the Mexican War, Ulysses S Grant had been able to say of smoothbore musketry: 'At the distance of a few hundred yards, a man might fire at you all day without your finding out.' By 1861 those days had gone forever.

Along with advances in accuracy and range came greater rapidity of fire. The percussion lock, now standard, was inherently faster and more reliable than the flintlock, and refinements in percussion lock design had advanced apace in the decades before the beginning of the war. The rate of fire of single-shot weapons was further increased by another innovation, breech loading, which was a much faster method of recharging a shoulder arm than muzzle loading had ever been. During the war breech-loading in rifles was confined mainly to cavalry carbines, the .54-calibre Burnside and the .52-calibre Sharps being the most widely used models. The apogee of rapid fire in percussion lock rifles was achieved when repeating carbines were introduced, by far the most famous of which were the six-shot .52-calibre Spencer and the classic 15-shot .44-calibre Henry. And as with rifles, so with pistols, the murderous new standards now being set by the fast-firing six-shot revolvers manufactur-

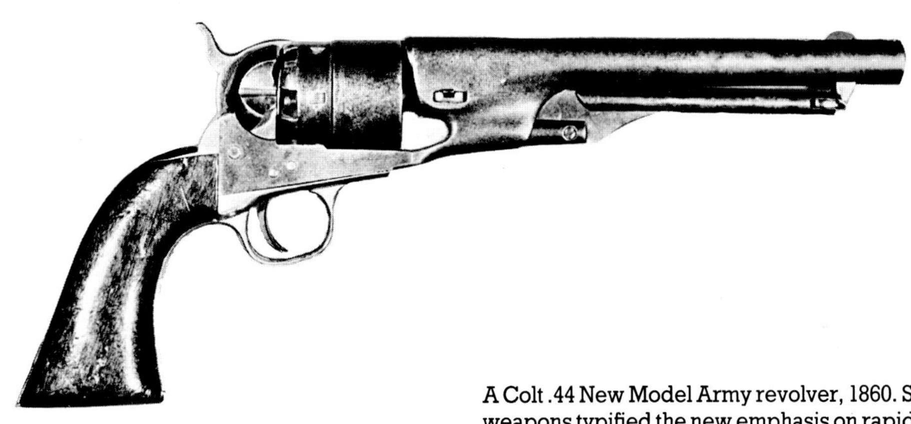

A Colt .44 New Model Army revolver, 1860. Such weapons typified the new emphasis on rapidity of fire.

The contemporary apex of rapid fire, the Gatling machine gun, was, oddly, little used in the Civil War.

ed by Remington, Starr and, above all, Samuel Colt.

Artillery was similarly transformed by technology. To be sure, probably the war's single most popular artillery piece would continue to be an old-fashioned smoothbore, the US Model 1857 'Napoleon' 12-pounder, which was both highly mobile and could still, when charged with cannister or grape, visit awesome execution on massed troops. But it is also true that by 1863 nearly half the Union Army's cannons would be new, highly accurate three-inch rifled guns with an impressive effective range of 2500 yards. A simultaneous development would be a gradual increase in the use of explosive shells, in place of old-fashioned solid shot. It was doubtless fortunate for all concerned that the technique of adding shrapnel to these explosives was still in its infancy.

Although these great advances in firepower did not much affect formations (the ideal infantry organization – seldom realized in practice – was now thought to be the three-battalion regiment, each battalion being composed of eight 100-man companies), they would significantly affect basic battlefield tactics. The special character of the new firepower favored defense. It is estimated that during the war only one out of every eight assaults on prepared positions ever succeeded, and those that did succeed often did so at frightful cost. The Civil War would never degenerate into the kind of sanguinary stalemate that characterized World War I – weapons technology had not yet evolved so far as to preclude maneuver entirely – but we can now see in retrospect how this greatest of American wars would prefigure the grisly shape of things to come.

When the Confederate capital was moved to Richmond, Virginia, only 100 miles south of Washington, it was inevitable that the initial cockpit of war would be the Northern triangle of the Old Dominion state. For the first three years of the war, fighting raged on the Potomac-Chesapeake Bay right leg of the triangle, the Blue Ridge Mountains-Shenandoah Valley left leg, and along the base formed by the James River-Richmond axis. Only in 1865 when the legs had been crushed and the Army of Northern Virginia was held under successful siege at Petersburg, south of Richmond, would the triangle collapse and the war be won.

Initially neither side was in a hurry to engage the enemy, since most of the troops in place were green recruits badly in need of training. The Federals had some 30,000 men, under the command of Brigadier General Irwin McDowell, at Alexandria, just south of Washington, and another 15,000, under the aged Major General Robert Patterson, guarding the northern end of the Shenandoah Valley. The Confederates had an army of 22,000 troops 30 miles southwest of Wash-

A 15-inch Rodman siege gun. The size and accuracy of the artillery used in the Civil War was unprecedented.

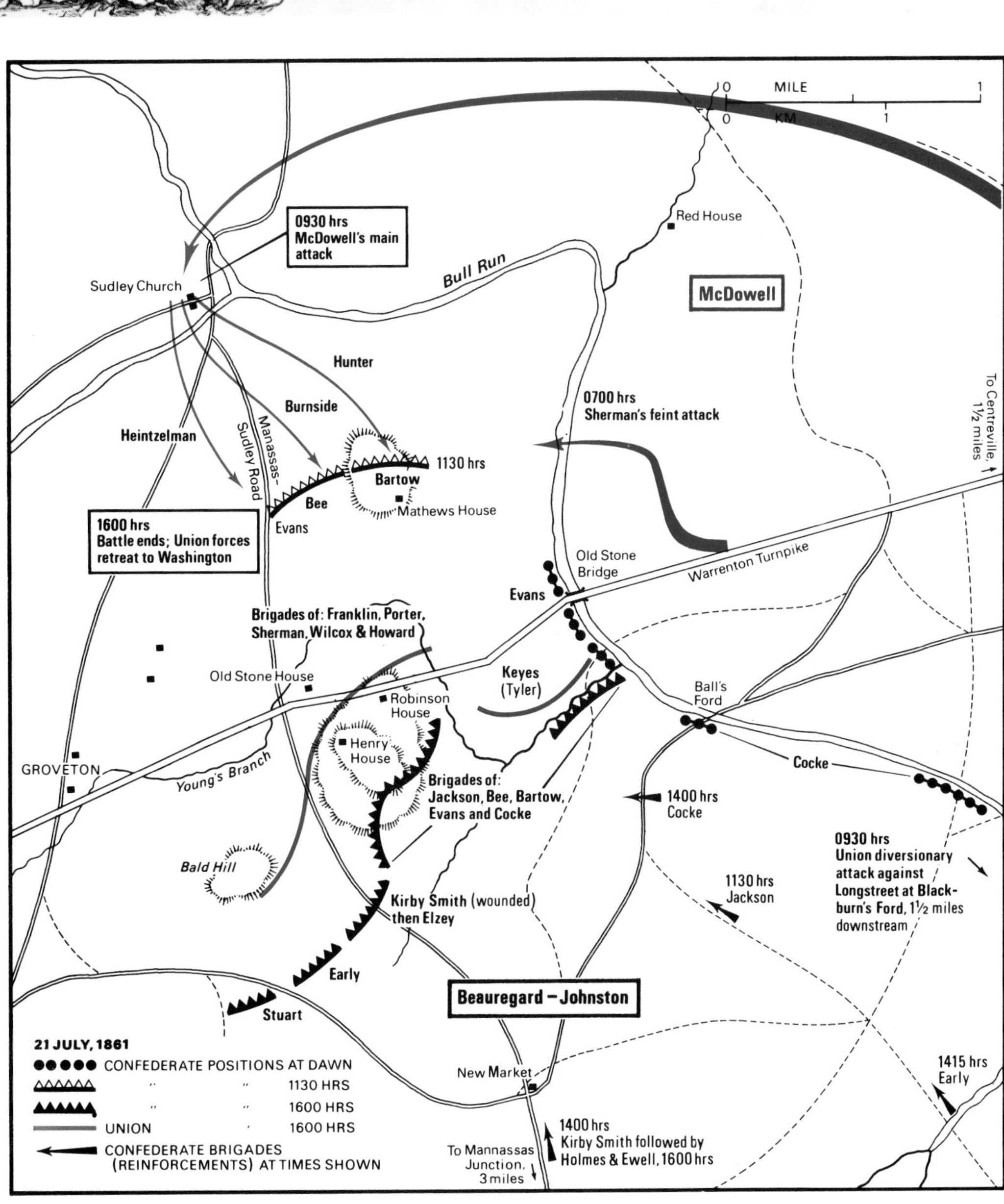

The Battle of Bull Run (*above* and *right*), the first big battle of the war, ended in a total rout of the ill-led Union forces.

ington at Manassas Junction, under Brigadier General P G T Beauregard, and another 11,000 at Winchester in the Shenandoah Valley, under Brigadier General Joseph E Johnston.

Bowing to public pressure for an offensive, and perhaps believing that one great offensive victory would break the back of Southern rebellion, in June 1861 Lincoln ordered Winfield Scott, the aging General in Chief, to order McDowell to move into the South. McDowell, hesitant to move until his troops were ready, nevertheless obeyed Lincoln's orders and prepared his plans. Assured by Scott that Patterson would not allow Johnston's forces to slip out of the Valley to join Beauregard, McDowell set out on 16 July toward Manassas, his coming well advertised to Beauregard by articles in the press. Beauregard drew up his forces behind a stream called Bull Run and waited. By 20 July he was reinforced by Johnston's forces, which had slipped away from the Valley and traveled the intervening 50 miles by rail. This meant about 30,000 men on each side would be facing one another as the two untried armies met in the initial combat of what was to be America's bloodiest war.

Both McDowell and Beauregard, as it turned out, planned to hold in the center and push their right flanks around the enemy. On the morning of 21 July Beauregard's right flank movement bogged down, but McDowell's moved well and threatened to win the field. Beauregard thereupon drew his forces to the left to reinforce his left flank (by this time running almost north to south) with 15,000 troops, sufficient to stop the 13,000 Federals and their attacks. He then ordered a sudden counterattack that forced the Federals back across Bull Run. Their retreat soon turned into a rout, and McDowell, unable to regain control of the situation, ordered his troops to retreat all the way back to Washington. As the Confederates were unable to organize an effective pursuit, the battle simply came to an end. It was forever marked by Brigadier General Thomas Jackson's having here earned the nickname 'Stonewall' for his brigade's strong defensive stand against the Union forces.

For the remainder of the summer the two armies eyed one another south of Washington, but neither would make a move until their numbers increased. Lincoln now called upon thirty-five-year-old Major General George B McClellan to command the armies around Washington. McClellan, who also assumed the office of General in Chief on 1 November when Scott retired, would soon prove himself to be an inspiring leader and trainer of men, but one sadly lacking in the judgment and aggressiveness needed in the field commander of the now-christened 'Army of the Potomac.' Lincoln was to find the first of the 'fighting generals' he needed not in the East, but in the West.

Foreshadowing of Northern Victory: 1862

The campaign of 1862 began in the west. There Brigadier General Don Carlos Buell, USA, headquartered at Louisville on the Ohio, had a force of 50,000 men undergoing training. Farther south and west, Major General Henry W Halleck, in St Louis, had another 90,000 men under his command, including 20,000 in Kentucky under Brigadier General Ulysses S Grant and another 30,000, across the Mississippi in Missouri, under Major General Samuel Curtis. The objectives of these Western armies, as part of the overall Union strategy, were to seize the Mississippi and to capture some vital rail junctions in Tennessee, preparatory to slicing through the South toward Atlanta. Facing the Union forces were 43,000 Confederates, scattered all the way from western Virginia to Kansas and under the overall command of General Albert Sidney Johnston. Near the center, and helping to protect the valuable railroad lines, were Fort Henry, on the Tennessee River, and Fort Donelson, twelve miles away to the east on the Cumberland River, just south of the Kentucky border in northern Tennessee.

By January Halleck had approved Grant's plan to move south down the Tennessee and

Top: **Ulysses S Grant, the Union's best general, was criticized for the heavy casualties he sustained.**
Right: **Details of the equipment and uniforms of Union and Confederate artillery.**
Below: **A typically lethal battle of the war was Antietam: 12,000 Union and 10,000 Confederate casualties.**

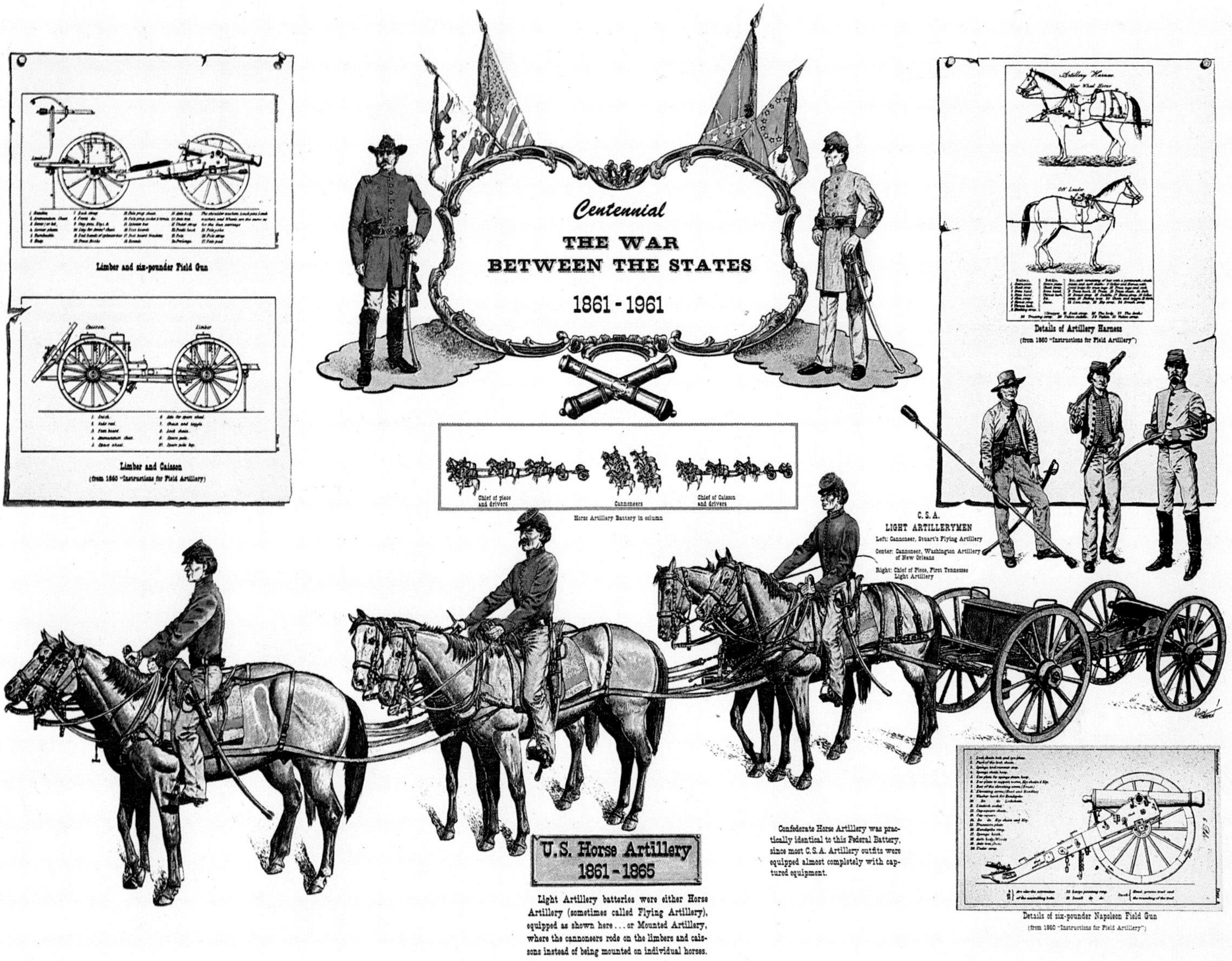

Limber and six-pounder Field Gun

Limber and Caisson
(from 1860 "Instructions for Field Artillery")

Centennial
THE WAR BETWEEN THE STATES
1861 - 1961

Chief of piece and drivers
Cannoneers
Chief of Caisson and drivers
Horse Artillery Battery in column

Details of Artillery Harness
(from 1860 "Instructions for Field Artillery")

C. S. A.
LIGHT ARTILLERYMEN
Left: Cannoneer, Stuart's Flying Artillery
Center: Cannoneer, Washington Artillery of New Orleans
Right: Chief of Piece, First Tennessee Light Artillery

U.S. Horse Artillery
1861 - 1865

Light Artillery batteries were either Horse Artillery (sometimes called Flying Artillery), equipped as shown here . . . or Mounted Artillery, where the cannoneers rode on the limbers and caissons instead of being mounted on individual horses.

Confederate Horse Artillery was practically identical to this Federal Battery, since most C.S.A. Artillery outfits were equipped almost completely with captured equipment.

Details of six-pounder Napoleon Field Gun
(from 1860 "Instructions for Field Artillery")

take Fort Henry. This would be done in cooperation with gunboats of the Navy, commanded by Flag Officer Andrew H Foote. Grant's 15,000 men jumped off in early February and, with the help of naval gunfire, took Fort Henry with no difficulty. Grant then plunged overland to take Fort Donelson, twelve miles away. Confederate reinforcements in the number of 12,000 were hurried to Fort Donelson by General Johnston, who concurrently pulled 14,000 more toward Nashville, farther up the Cumberland. Grant put the 100-acre fort and outer works under seige, and soon reinforcements from Halleck brought Grant's numbers to 27,000, about a 2-to-1 edge over his enemies. After an attempt to break out failed on 15 February, the Confederates surrendered unconditionally. Some 15,000 Confederates had fallen into Union hands, and the upper Cumberland and Tennessee rivers were now open to Union penetration.

Halleck, who had been placed in command of the whole Western theater by Lincoln, next sent Major General John Pope's Army of the Mississippi downriver to attack New Madrid and 'Island No. 10,' located on a crucial hairpin turn of the Mississippi, in co-

The capture of Fort Donelson on 15 February 1862 was Grant's first big victory in the West.

In April 1862 Confederate General Johnston surprised Grant at Shiloh and came close to defeating him.

operation with Foote's naval forces. Halleck also decided to unite Grant's Army of the Tennessee and Buell's Army of the Ohio at Shiloh (Pittsburgh Landing) north of Corinth, Mississippi, an important rail juncture, there to begin a pursuit of Johnston's Confederate forces south along a line inland and parallel to the Mississippi River. Johnston, who was aware of Halleck's plans, elected to attack Grant at Shiloh before Buell could join him. It took two days for Johnston's 40,000 untrained men to move the 22 miles north to attack Grant's army of 40,000, but, fortunately for the Southern cause, Grant was caught completely by surprise.

Early on the morning of 6 April 1862 the Union forces at Shiloh found themselves under very heavy attack by Confederates bursting out of the woods. They fell back in disarray, but then dug in to put up a fierce resistance. A Confederate victory seemed to be in the making when suddenly General Johnston fell mortally wounded. General Beauregard, assuming command, pulled back the Confederate attackers to reorganize them, but that night 17,000 of Buell's troops arrived on the scene and were ferried across the Tennessee to bring Grant's forces back up to 40,000. Grant counterattacked the next morning and drove the Confederates off the ground they had won the day before. Yet he did not pursue when the Rebel forces moved back to Corinth. Over 13,000 of the 63,000 Union troops involved in the Battle of Shiloh had become casualties, and the Confederates had suffered 11,000 casualties out of 40,000 they had committed. By far the bloodiest battle that had ever been fought in North America, Shiloh was but a harbinger of things to come.

On that same day, 7 April 1862, 'Island No. 10' fell to Pope and Foote, and, with the capture of Memphis on 6 June, the central Mississippi was firmly in Union hands. In that same month a concentration of 46 US naval vessels, under the command of Captain David G Farragut, appeared off the mouth of the Mississippi. It carried 18,000 troops under Major General Benjamin F Butler. Late in the month Farragut forced his way past two forts on the lower river and took the vital port city of New Orleans, before moving on to take Baton Rouge and Natchez. With the lower Mississippi now in Union hands only the section commanded by Vicksburg and Port Hudson remained to deny full Federal control of the entire vital waterway.

In the meantime, Halleck took over direct control of the armies in the West and ploddingly made his way to Corinth, leaving Beauregard time to evacuate the city before he arrived on 30 May. Nevertheless, the Mississippi River, and its vital shores, especially on its eastern side, were clearly coming under Union domination in this second year of the Civil War.

Yet the Confederates were far from done in the West during 1862. A giant counteroffensive was planned. It was to move out of northern Mississippi and Tennessee to penetrate the heart of the Union-held territories and bring neutral Kentucky into the Confederacy. Commanding would be General Braxton Bragg, who had replaced General Beauregard after the latter's evacuation of Corinth. Bragg moved the bulk of his forces from northern Mississippi by roundabout rail connections to Chattanooga, whence, in company with Lieutenant General Edmund Kirby Smith, he launched a drive against the forces of General Buell. Although this major offensive had resulted in furious fighting at Perryville, Kentucky, and later at Stones River, near Murfreesboro, Tennessee, no great uprising of Confederate sympathy had occurred in Kentucky. Nor was Buell's army defeated, although this army (now called the Army of the Cumberland) had been badly mauled and would require six months to recover. Nevertheless, while the Confederates still held Chattanooga, and therefore eastern Tennessee and Georgia, the great arc of land along the Ohio River and down the Mississippi was still firmly in Union hands. Thus if the Federals could capture Chattanooga, they would have a base from which to threaten a second bisection of the Confederate homeland.

In the east the year 1862 had begun with General McClellan assiduously training the 150,000-man Army of the Potomac and resisting any pressure to go on the offensive until the troops were 'ready.' Facing him at Manassas was General Joseph E Johnston's 50,000 Confederates (although McClellan kept insisting their numbers were at least twice that many). McClellan was working on a plan that would move his entire army on naval transports to the mouth of the Rappahannock River and land at Urbanna, east of Richmond. An invasion here, argued McClellan, would pull Johnston's forces south, away from the capital, to fight on ground of McClellan's choosing, and might thereby compel the surrender of Richmond. But Lincoln was insistent that a covering force of 40,000 be left near Washington to protect the capital, and then in March Johnston upset McClellan's plan by pulling his army back behind the Rappahannock, where McClellan had intended to land.

Now McClellan proposed to move his army to Fortress Monroe on Hampton Roads, at the tip of the Virginia Peninsula, and then march 75 miles up the Peninsula between the York and James Rivers to assault Richmond. Thus was born the Peninsula Campaign of 1862. Preparing to launch his expedition in March, McClellan attempted to mislead Lincoln as to how many troops he was leaving behind to protect Washington, but Lincoln peremptorily removed 30,000 men, under General McDowell, from McClellan's attack force and dispatched them to Fredericksburg on the Rappahannock to cover the capital.

McClellan still had about 100,000 men,

Right: Robert E Lee, Grant's great Southern adversary.
Below: General map of the Civil War.

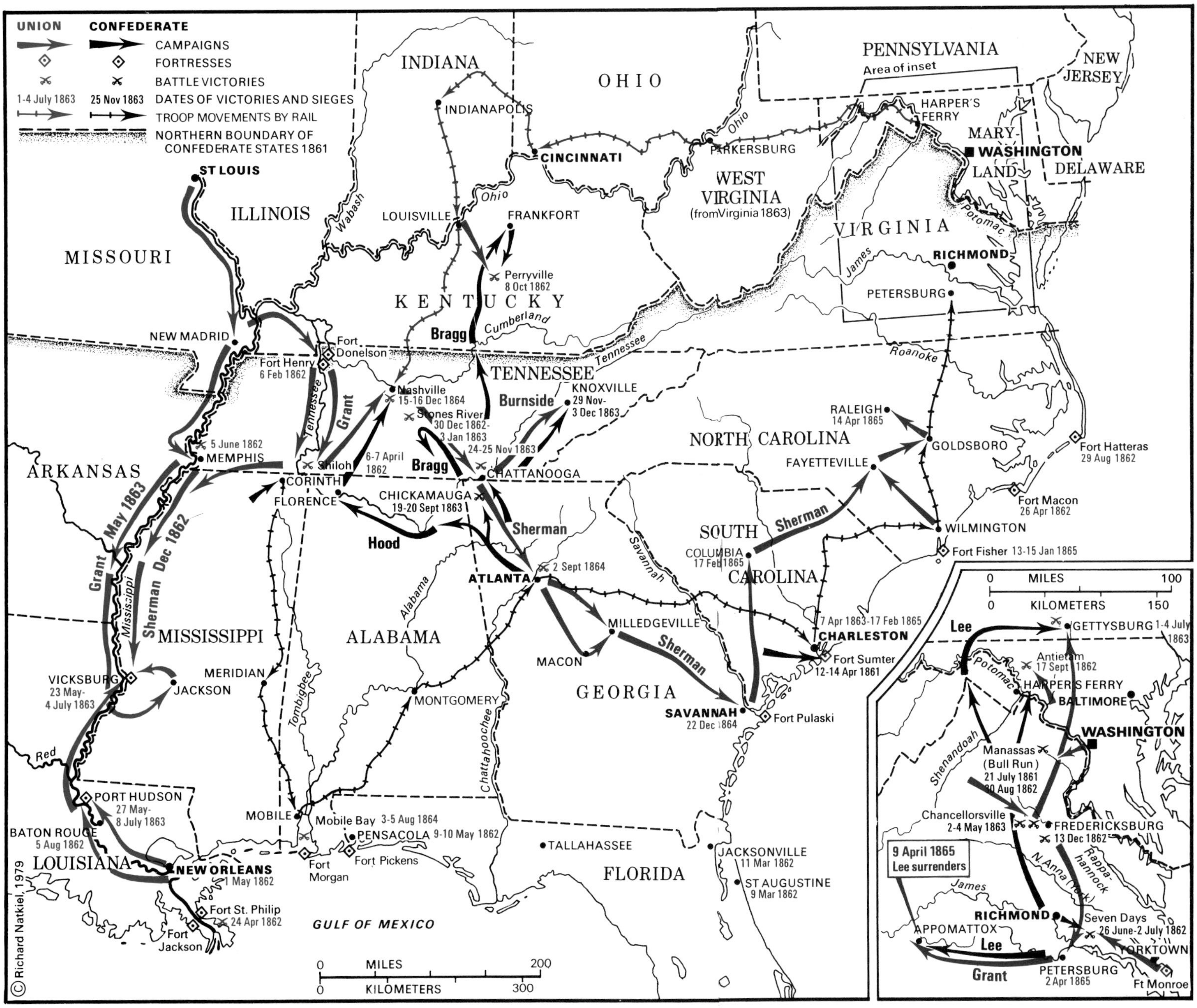

After the Battle of Fair Oaks in May 1862 Lee took over the command in Virginia from the injured Johnston.

more than enough to wage a vigorous offensive operation, but the Federal commander moved so slowly up the Peninsula that the Confederates were able to gather 70,000 troops to meet him. When he finally arrived within 20 miles of the Confederate capital in mid-May, McClellan had his forces disposed on both sides of the Chickahominy River, the northern contingent covering his communications with his base on the York River, the southern to threaten Richmond. At McClellan's pleading, Lincoln finally agreed to allow McDowell's 30,000 to move south by land and join McClellan on the Chickahominy, but the Confederate high command decided to forestall this movement by sending Stonewall Jackson and a force of 17,000 out of the Valley, on the upper left leg of the Virginia triangle, to threaten Washington as a diversion. Lincoln immediately sent three armies, under Lieutenant General John C Fremont, Major General Nathaniel P Banks, and General McDowell, to trap him west of Washington. But the Union generals were dilatory, and Jackson escaped back into the Valley, thus having successfully drawn McDowell's troops away from reinforcing McClellan.

In the meantime, on 31 May, Johnston had attacked McClellan's army at Fair Oaks and Seven Pines but could not crack their lines. As Johnston had been badly wounded in the fighting, President Davis appointed Robert E Lee to replace him. Lee and his newly-named Army of Northern Virginia at once went on a spirited offensive. Lee brought Jackson down from the Valley to reinforce himself and then struck McClellan's right wing on 25 June, setting off what has come to be known as the Seven Days' Battle (25 June-1 July 1862). Even though the attack was poorly coordinated McClellan was forced to retreat. He pulled back, not to the York River on the east, but south to the James River, where the Navy was setting up a base at Harrison's Landing. Lee followed, always shielding Richmond, but could not destroy

Lee's invasion of Maryland in 1862 was halted by the bloody battle of Antietam (Sharpsburg) in September.

McClellan's army, although taking 11,000 casualties in the attempt. The Union Army might still have moved on Richmond from this position, but Lincoln and his advisors (perhaps putting stock in McClellan's claim that Lee had 200,000 men in his army) decided to withdraw the Union army from the Peninsula and to advance on Richmond by land instead. Thus ended the Peninsula Campaign of 1862. McClellan was ordered to withdraw to join with a new united army that was being assembled just south of Washington. This force was to be commanded by General John Pope, brought from the West to rejuvenate the spirit in the Army of the Potomac.

McClellan was in no hurry to join Pope, even when it became obvious that Lee was preparing to hit Pope before McClellan's troops could arrive by water from the Peninsula. As a result, when Lee's forces attacked Pope on 29 August to begin the Second Battle of Bull Run (Second Manassas), below Washington, few of McClellan's troops had joined the hapless Pope. Despite the fact that he had 75,000 men, the Union commander engaged in fruitless piecemeal attacks on the Confederates, and when Lee, with a total of 60,000 men, suddenly assumed a determined offensive, a Union defeat soon became a Union rout. As Pope's forces struggled back into Washington, Lincoln relieved him and placed McClellan back in charge of the Eastern armies. Apparently Lincoln's theory was that if McClellan was not a fighter, he was at least a good organizer of men, and that was what was needed at the moment.

But Lee was not disposed to give Lincoln and the Federals time to recover. To shake the enemy's will, and perhaps convince Maryland to join the Confederacy, he began a move over the Potomac into Maryland, Jackson joining him after he had taken the Federal stronghold at Harper's Ferry. Now Lincoln would have to settle for McClellan to meet this new and unexpected challenge.

Yet luck seemed to be with the Unionists when a captured Confederate order revealed clearly where Lee was going and that his forces were divided, with Jackson moving toward Harper's Ferry. McClellan had only to advance rapidly across Maryland and destroy Lee's forces piecemeal before they came together, but once again he was too late and caught up with Lee at Sharpsburg, Maryland, behind Antietam Creek, only after most of Jackson's forces had joined with Lee's. Still, Lee had only 50,000 troops to McClellan's 90,000. McClellan attacked Lee, beginning early on the morning of 17 September 1862, and all day long furious fighting raged along the extended lines. Before the sun set, 12,000 Union soldiers and 10,000 Confederates had been killed or wounded; it was the bloodiest single day of the Civil War. McClellan could have used his reserves that day (which might have given him the victory), but he refused to do so. He also refused thereafter to pursue Lee, who returned in a rather leisurely fashion back across the Potomac into Virginia. Lincoln was furious: He, unlike most of his generals, realized that the destruction of the enemy's armies, not the taking of territory, was the key to Union victory. McClellan was removed, but his replacement, Major General Ambrose E Burnside, would soon display that he, too, was hardly the aggressive and determined commander Lincoln and the Union so desperately needed.

Burnside decided on a new advance on Richmond. His plan was to move to the east and south, cross the Rappahannock at Fredericksburg, and then follow the railroad line into the Southern capital. The plan was not ill-founded, but its success depended on getting the Union army across the Rappahannock at Fredericksburg before Lee intercepted him. Burnside, with his 100,000 men, won the race to Fredericksburg but dallied in crossing. This gave Lee enough time to reach the city with his 70,000 men and set up strong defensive positions on the hills around the town. Now Burnside's forces would have to cross the river under fire and climb the steep embankments in order to reach the town and confront Lee. Inexplicably, Burnside launched his main attack, on 13 December, directly against Fredericksburg itself, Lee's strongest defensive position. The Union forces were mown down in a hail of Confederate fire from the hills above. Before the day was out, Burnside had suffered an appalling 15,000 casualties. He withdrew his forces from the field, leaving the Con-

At Antietam and many other fights Thomas 'Stonewall' Jackson proved to be Lee's most valuable lieutenant.

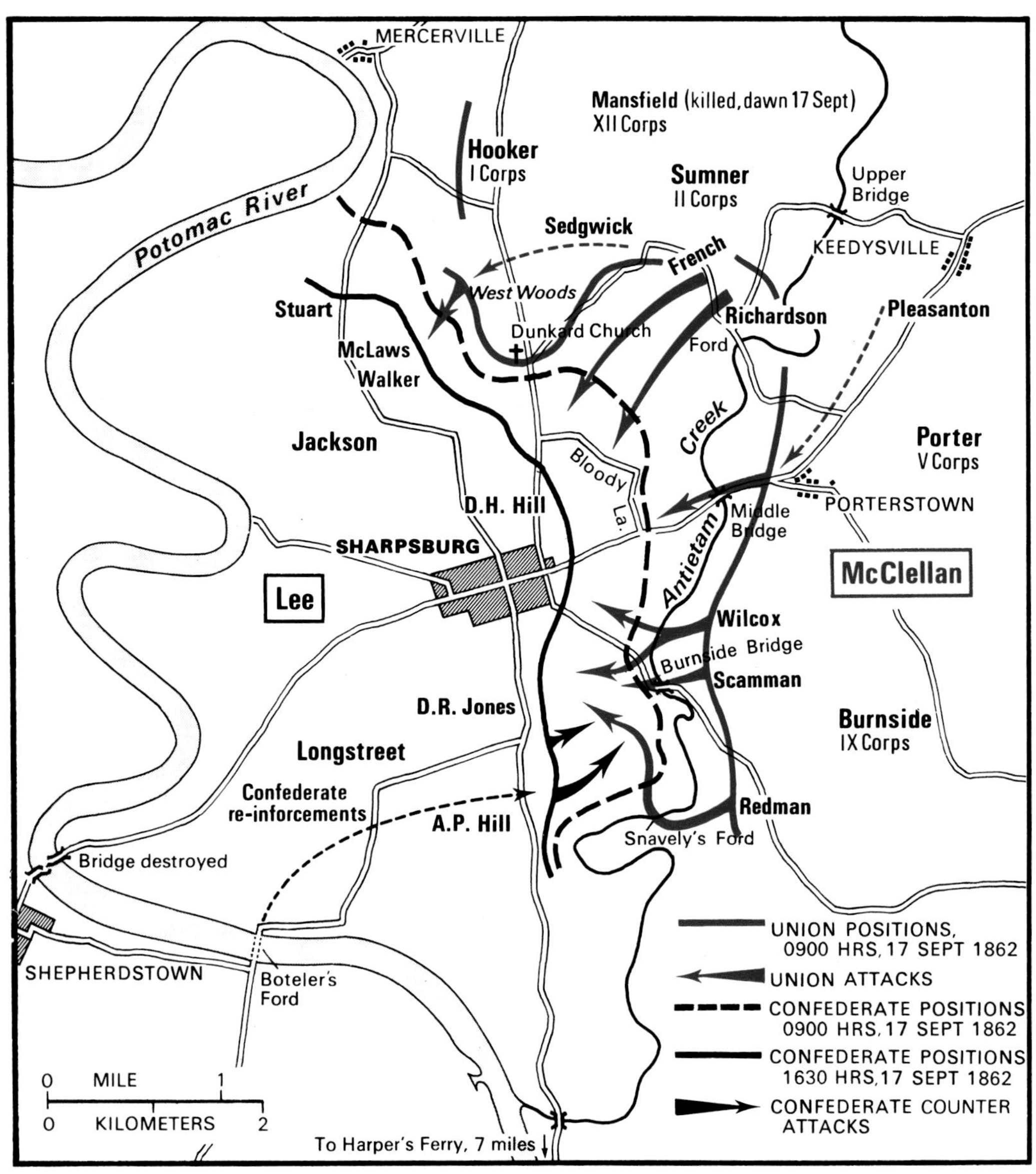

Left: Map of the Battle of Antietam.
Right: Yet another Union advance on Richmond foundered at Fredericksburg when troops were decimated crossing the Rappahannock under fire in an ill-conceived frontal attack.

federate right leg of the strategic northern Virginia triangle still intact and Richmond as safe as it had been when the year began.

Yet despite the fact that the Confederates had shown great tactical skill in reacting to Union thrusts at the heartland of the eastern theater and had scored notable victories against the enemy many times over, the Union forces were still intact and capable of replenishment. Neither had Northern will to fight been broken by dogged Southern resistance, nor had the Confederate invasion of Maryland succeeded. Furthermore, the military situation in the western theater was tilting toward eventual Union victory beyond the Appalachians. And finally, the US Navy, by neutralizing the Confederate hope for naval supremacy in Chesapeake Bay in the Battle of Hampton Roads (8-9 March 1862), and by its dogged campaign both to extend its blockade of the Confederate coast and to take key Southern port cities, was beginning to strangle the South. Thus the year 1862 had brought many victories to the Confederate cause, but foreshadowed in its events was the specter of final defeat.

The Tide Turns Against the Confederacy: 1863

As 1863 opened, General Burnside, badly shaken by his defeat at Fredericksburg the previous December, was replaced by Major General Joseph 'Fighting Joe' Hooker, a corps commander who had earned a reputation for being a fearless fighter and good organizer, as well as an inveterate braggart. Lincoln was aware of Hooker's faults but wanted a general who would at least fight. Hooker soon came up with a plan that seemed in keeping with his reputation for aggressiveness. With his army of 100,000 encamped across the Rappahannock, to the northeast of Fredericksburg, and with General Lee facing him across the river, Hooker would not repeat the suicidal frontal assault that had led to Burnside's defeat the month before. Instead, his plan called for moving three corps of his army 30 miles upriver to come in behind Lee. Two corps would remain conspicuous across the river from Fredericksburg, and two more corps would be concealed in reserve. When the enveloping right wing was in position and attacking, the troops opposite Fredericksburg would cross the Rappahannock below the city and assail Lee's front.

Hooker's campaign began in late April. The flanking army, under Hooker's personal command, made the 30-mile loop and began

Left: An 11-inch Union naval gun. The blockade came close to ruining the South.
Right: Rebel hopes of breaking the blockade with ironclads faded when USS *Monitor* defeated CSS *Virginia*.

The repulse of Pickett's charge, 3 July 1863. The Battle of Gettysburg was the turning point of the war in the East. Simultaneously Grant was winning the decisive battle in the West at Vicksburg (*inset*).

to advance on Lee from the rear, through a desolate area of scrub pine known as The Wilderness. On schedule, the corps opposite Fredericksburg crossed over and began to fight their way west toward Lee. When Lee realized what was happening, he reacted vigorously and struck hard at Hooker's force in his rear. This completely unnerved Hooker who, despite his subordinates' pleas, cancelled his offensive movement and took up a defensive position at the little town of Chancellorsville. Lee did not hesitate. Leaving a sufficient covering force at Fredericksburg, he wheeled left with 42,000 men and the cavalry of 'Stonewall' Jackson to take on Hooker and break out of the developing vise. Sensing that Hooker's extended right flank was vulnerable, Lee sent Jackson and 28,000 men to sweep around the Union right while he applied direct pressure against Hooker at Chancellorsville.

Lee was outnumbered and his forces were split, but he had surprise and audacity on his side. Hooker received reports that Confederate troops were on the move off to his right, but he assumed they were retreating from the field. That evening, 2 May, at dusk, Jackson's men came charging out of the woods on the Union right and broke through the Federal lines, yet somehow the Union forces held on. At this critical moment, the impetuous Jackson, riding out to survey the battlefield in the failing light, was mistakenly shot by his own men, who mistook him for a Federal. (He died eight days later, denying Lee his greatest cavalry commander.) The Confederate attack was blunted, and by the next day it seemed that the Union forces, being superior in numbers, might still hold their own and perhaps even break out of the trap. But Hooker had lost his nerve. Two days later, on 5 May, he began to withdraw his entire army back across the Rappahannock.

Lee, although taking 13,000 casualties at Chancellorsville, had again thwarted a Federal attempt to penetrate the right side of the triangle. Hooker had taken 17,000 casualties in a losing campaign in which he even failed to field one-third of his troops. Now the initiative seemed to have passed to the South, and Lee did not intend to give Lincoln and the Union armies time to recover.

Although some other Confederate generals wanted the Army of Northern Virginia to stand on the defensive and send aid to relieve the pressure on General Joe Johnston's forces in the West, especially around Vicksburg, Mississippi, then under siege, Lee persuaded President Davis to authorize an offensive into Pennsylvania. He argued that a major offensive into the North, coming on the heels of Chancellorsville, would break the Federal will to continue the fight. Also, it would be better for his troops to be living off the rich farmlands of Pennsylvania than off the ravaged Virginia countryside. But while Davis assented to the operation, he allowed Lee only 75,000 troops to carry it out because he did not want to leave the Virginia triangle defenseless.

Early in June 1863 Lee began his movement west into the Valley, then north across the Potomac into Pennsylvania. He sent General J E B Stuart and his cavalry out on his right flank to scout for enemy movement, but Stuart, taking advantage of latitude in his orders, attempted to ride all the way around the Federal forces paralleling Lee's line of march and thus was lost to his commander when the ensuing battle developed. Without cavalry, Lee was without his 'eyes' and could not know the location or size of the shadowing Union army. Nor could Lee know that the hesitant Hooker had just been relieved by Lincoln. To Lincoln's dismay, Hooker's response to the news that Lee was moving west and north had been to suggest that the Army of the Potomac should again move south and take Richmond. Apparently Hooker never realized that the Northern military objective had to be destruction of the Confederate

Chancellorsville: Lee's victory here in May set him on the road to Gettysburg. The death of Stonewall Jackson, accidentally shot by his own men, was, however, a blow to the South.

Top: George Meade, victor over Lee at the Battle of Gettysburg.
Right: Map of Gettysburg.

armies, not simply seizure of Confederate territories. In his place, Lincoln appointed Major General George G Meade, a corps commander and a determined fighter.

As Lee moved across the Potomac he spread his three corps, under Lieutenant Generals James Longstreet, Richard S Ewell, and Ambrose P Hill, over the Pennsylvania countryside. Learning late of the Union army's effective shadowing movement and that the Federals were close at hand, he ordered the three corps to meet at the country crossroads town of Gettysburg, Pennsylvania. On 30 June Lee's forces, approaching Gettysburg from the west, and Meade's advance forces, approaching from the southeast, first met west of Gettysburg. Meade knew that the Virginian would either have to fight or retreat and, concluding that this was as good a place as any for battle, rushed his forces forward to the little town.

On 1 July, the first day of battle, the Confederates, at this point superior in numbers, engaged the Federals to the west and north of Gettysburg. On the north, Ewell's troops succeeded in breaking the Federals' lines and pushed them south through the town and onto the heights of Culp's Hill and Cemetery Ridge, just outside the town. Lee's exhausted forces could not dislodge the equally exhausted Union soldiers from these heights, but the Confederates had scored a notable victory that first day. On the other hand, the Yankees still held the high ground and were bringing up reinforcements. Lee would either have to attack them in their superior defensive positions or give up the fight and retreat. He chose to attack.

The next day, 2 July 1863, the real fight began. General Longstreet was ordered to attack from Seminary Ridge (a mile from Cemetery Ridge, both running north and south from Gettysburg). He was to hit the Union left at or near the promontories called Little Round Top and Big Round Top. If these could be secured, the whole Union line running to the north would be subject to enfilading fire from Confederate guns. At the same time, General Ewell was to push his men up Culp's Hill on the north. But the attacks were slow in starting, and despite furious fighting at both ends of Cemetery Ridge, the Union lines held, although losing some ground.

Encouraged by these partial successes, Lee next decided to launch a grand assault by 15,000 men, under Major General George Pickett, the next day. They were to advance the full mile from their starting point on Seminary Ridge, crossing the open field between the forces, and swarming up Cemetery Ridge to the east. On the afternoon of 3 July, after a two-hour bombardment that had little effect on the Union lines, Pickett's men stepped out in line to cross the field. 'Pickett's Charge' began as a well-ordered advance, but it soon crumbled under the merciless barrage of artillery and rifle fire that poured down on the Confederate forces from the ridge above. Of the 15,000 who began the advance, only 5000 reached the crest, and these were shortly driven off. As the pitiful remnants of Pickett's troops staggered back to their lines on Seminary Ridge, General Lee could only murmur over and over, 'It's all my fault.'

The next day, 4 July, the armies eyed one another across a battlefield strewn with the human and material detritus of war. At length, Lee, rightly surmising that Meade was not about to attack his positions along Seminary Ridge, began the long withdrawal out of Pennsylvania, across the Potomac and back to the safety of Virginia. Meade followed but refused to attack, much to Lincoln's annoyance.

In this, his second offensive into the North, Lee had suffered almost 25,000 casualties. The North had lost 20,000, but whereas it could replenish its losses, the South could not. From now on Lee would have to stand on the defensive, a position which, he realized, would sooner or later lead to Confederate

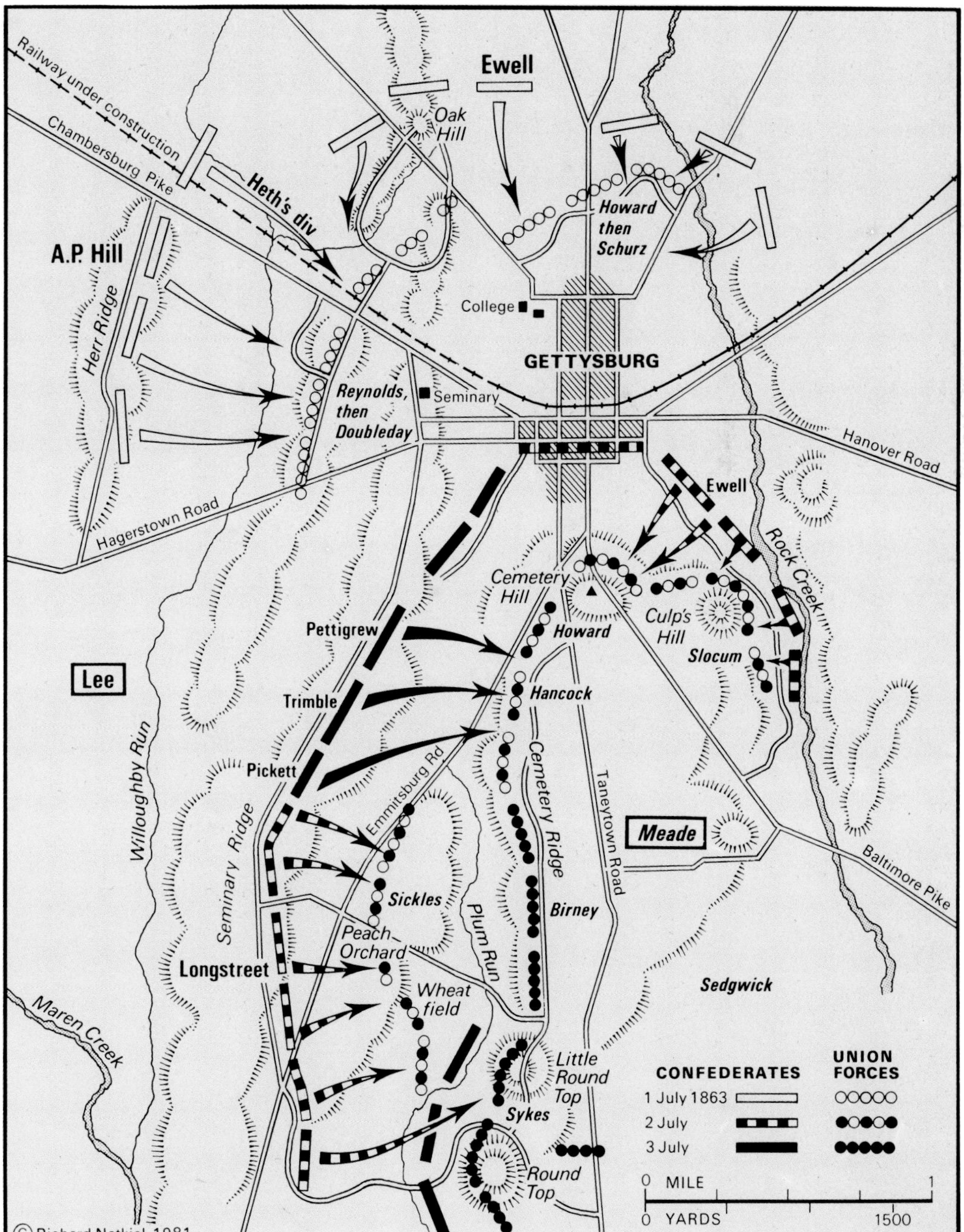

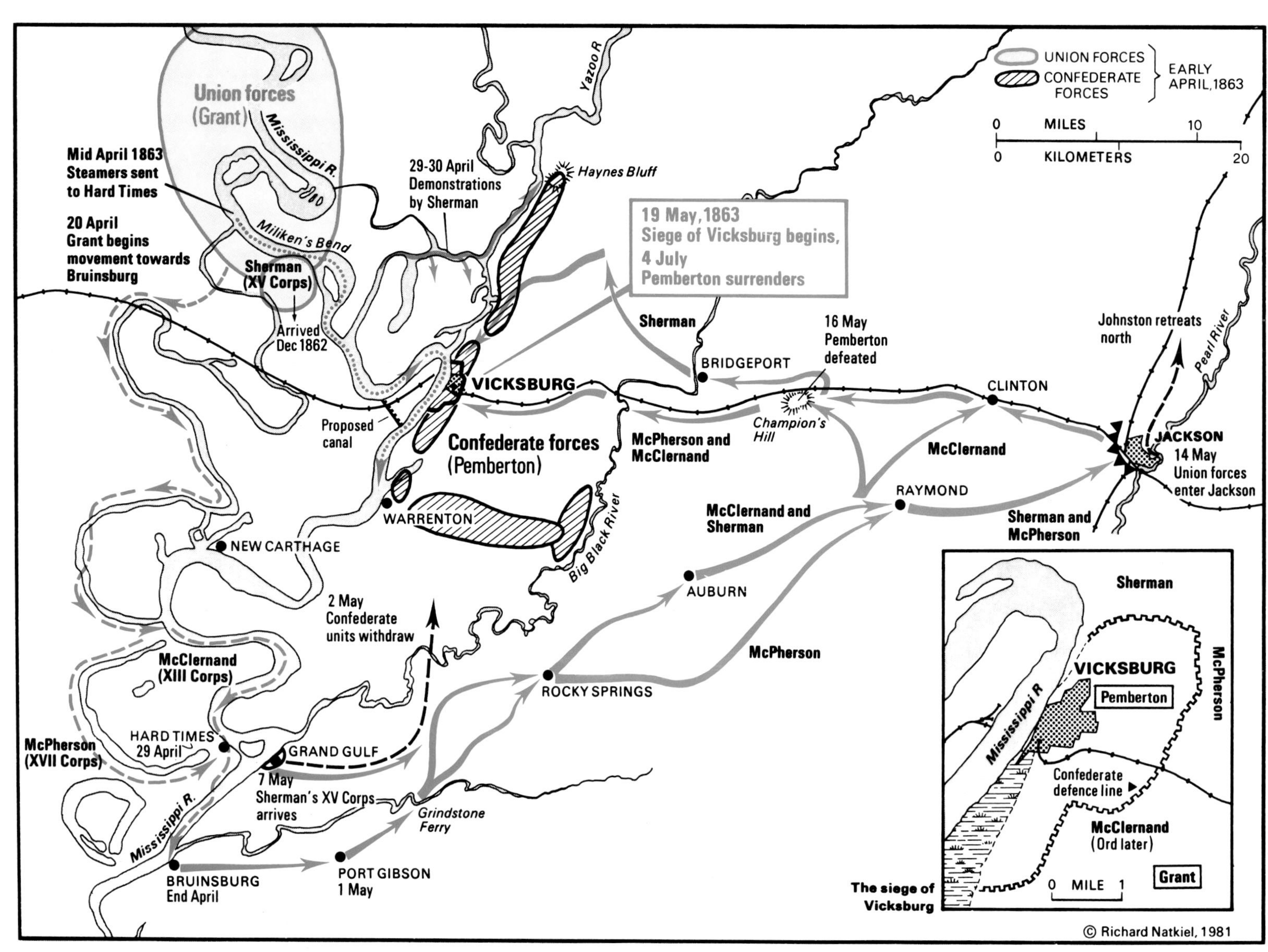

© Richard Natkiel, 1981

defeat. He had lost a crucial battle, perhaps *the* crucial battle.

While the Battles of Chancellorsville and Gettysburg were being fought, another important campaign was being conducted in the west. After the Battle of Shiloh Grant had been left with little to do by General Halleck for the latter part of 1862, but in December Halleck had finally given him permission to strike out at Vicksburg, on the Mississippi River, the last major obstacle to complete control of the Mississippi and the guardian of a corridor for supplies flowing into the Confederacy from the west. Grant first tried to take the city by marching down from Memphis toward the Alabama capital of Jackson, there to swing west against Vicksburg, while his favorite subaltern, Major General William T Sherman, advanced down the river in a simultaneous movement to hit Vicksburg as the right wing of Grant's attack. This operation failed: Sherman was repulsed, and General Joe Johnston's troops threatened Grant's supply lines so seriously that he had to retire.

Undeterred, Grant gathered his forces at Memphis and, with naval support, moved down the Mississippi in January 1863, landing on the west bank of the river in Louisiana above Vicksburg. He had with him 75,000 troops, more than all the 60,000 Confederates in Mississippi, who were divided between Vicksburg on the river and Johnston's forces inland. But Grant knew that subduing the natural fortress of Vicksburg would be no easy matter. The ground north, south, and across from Vicksburg was so low and marshy that it was very difficult, if not impossible, to traverse. The land behind Vicksburg, to the east, was high and dry but out of the reach of the Union troops. Vicksburg itself stood as a bastion high above the river, with its artillery effectively commanding the river itself and defying any force to assault it. It seemed, in short, impregnable.

During the early months of 1863 Grant tried by various strategems to get at the defenders of Vicksburg. An attempt was then made to cut a canal through the bends of the giant hairpin loop in the river below Vicksburg so as to allow the Navy to bypass the city safely and carry troops below the 'Gibraltar of the West.' But the canal, when finished, held too little water to float the naval vessels. An attempt to bring naval vessels through the narrow and winding river channels in the bayous north of the city likewise ended in failure.

Finally Grant hit on a plan. Commodore David Porter, the naval commander with him, would run his vessels past the batteries of Vicksburg at night, taking whatever punishment he must, while Grant's men would march through the swamps on the Louisiana side of the river and meet Porter's ships 50 miles below the city, there to be carried over to the eastern shore. Then Grant could strike out on firm ground to attack the Confederates. While all of this was going on, Colonel Benjamin Grierson would rapidly move his cavalry south toward Jackson and continue all the way to Baton Rouge, creating as much confusion and disruption as possible while Grant played out his hand on the river.

It was a good plan, but to make it succeed would require courage, careful timing, and not a little luck. On 16 April Porter's ships ran the gauntlet of guns pounding away from the Vicksburg shore and emerged almost unscathed below the city. Within two weeks he had joined Grant's army below Grand Gulf and ferried it across the river. While Grierson's stabbed south over 600 miles in 16 days, Grant's men made the march down through the Louisiana swamps across from Vicksburg almost without incident. Then, when Grant and his 45,000 men had been ferried to the east side of the river, he moved with lightning speed, first east to Jackson, where he drove off Johnston's forces and took the city on 14 May, then west to Vicksburg, 40 miles away, in the process fighting three major battles and winning them all. The Southern defenders were now divided, with Johnston driven northeast of Jackson and the garrison at Vicksburg, under Lieutenant General John C

Pemberton, cut off. Grant's first move was to try to take the city by assault on 23 May, but, when this failed he settled down to lay classic siege to the city.

Day and night for the next six weeks the bombardment continued, as Grant moved his siege lines ever closer to the doomed city. With no hope of aid from Johnston, with supplies running out, and with civilians resorting to eating horses and mules as their only sustenance, Pemberton finally asked for terms. He surrendered the city and garrison on 4 July 1863, one day after the great Confederate defeat at Gettysburg.

While Grant was laying siege to Vicksburg, General Nathaniel Banks and 15,000 men from New Orleans had been investing Port Hudson, farther south. With the news of the fall of Vicksburg, the defenders at Port Hudson gave up. At last the vital Mississippi River was finally and firmly in Union Hands, and the South had been cut in two. Only in the center of the great arc stretching from Virginia to New Orleans was the Confederacy holding firm.

Chattanooga, Tennessee's southern border with Georgia, was the key to the center of the Southern position. From here the Confederates could strike north to fracture the Northern lines arcing above them, and as long as this vital rail center was in the South's hands no Union offensive could be mounted into the lower South. The North was determined to take Chattanooga in this third year of the war.

Commanding the Union forces in the region was Major General William S Rosecrans. Remembering the carnage of Stones River, he dawdled, called for reinforcements at every turn, and made it clear that he was loath to make a serious effort to take Chattanooga from General Braxton Bragg and his Confederates. Finally Rosecrans had to be issued direct orders to move. He arrived at the southern Tennessee town in early September, just as Major General Ambrose Burnside occupied Knoxville to the northeast. General Bragg had pulled out of the town by the time Rosecrans got there, but he had only moved south a few miles into Georgia. There he set himself up in superb defensive positions and was soon reinforced by Longstreet's corps of 15,000 men from Virginia.

Rosecrans rushed into the mountains south of Chattanooga in pursuit of Bragg, only to find himself confronted by superior forces. He drew his men up behind Chickamauga Creek (in Indian language, 'River of Death') to await the southern attack he knew was coming. It began on 19 and 20 September as Bragg, now with 70,000 men against Rosecrans' 60,000, assaulted the Federals' lines. On the second day of the fight, Rosecrans, acting on misleading information, shifted a division from the center of his line and opened his entire position to Confederate penetration. It collapsed completely, with only the left wing, the US 19th Infantry, under Major General George H Thomas, the 'Rock of Chickamauga,' avoiding the general retreat that carried Rosecrans and his troops all the way back to Chattanooga. Thomas pulled out only when ordered to do so late the second day.

Chickamauga was a great but costly victory for the Confederates. They lost 18,000 men, an astonishing 25 percent of their forces, but the Union Army was now under siege in Chattanooga, and the South rejoiced. Yet a battle is not a campaign, and when General Grant arrived to relieve the distraught Rosecrans, 20,000 Union troops, under General Hooker, were brought in from the East, supply routes were reopened, and the situation began to change.

Grant was not a man content to sit on the defensive when offensive operations were possible; and his army had now grown to 60,000 men. The Confederate command outside Chattanooga was, on the other hand, in

Top left: **Map of the Vicksburg Campaign.**
Above: **The Union offensive into the Deep South was halted in September 1863 at Chickamauga Creek by CSA General Braxton Bragg.**

Map of Grant's Chattanooga campaign. It took Grant most of November 1863 to undo the Chickamauga disaster.

disarray, with feuding between Bragg and his generals (who thought Bragg a coward and a fool for not pursuing Rosecrans into Chattanooga after Chickamauga). President Davis had to visit the scene personally in order to try to restore harmony. The unfortunate result of his intervention was that Davis left Bragg in command but allowed the unhappy Longstreet to leave on an ill-conceived expedition to take Knoxville. This left Bragg with only 40,000 men to face the rising tide of Grant's strength.

Grant took his time. First he cleared dominating Lookout Mountain of the enemy, while simultaneously clearing his supply lines. Then, on 25 November, he moved against the main enemy line on Missionary Ridge. His plan was for General Thomas to make a demonstration in strength before the center of the Confederate line while Sherman made a wide flanking movement to encircle the enemy right. But Sherman got bogged down, so Grant ordered Thomas' troops to seize the rifle pits at the bottom of Missionary Ridge and await further orders. The Confederates in these rifle pits had been ordered to hold their places as long as possible and then to retreat up the hill to the safety of the main Confederate line of infantry and artillery at the top.

The men of Thomas' Army of the Cumberland, still smarting from criticism of their recent retreat back into Chattanooga, overran the rifle pits and then kept going right on up the hill. Even the officers got caught up in the enthusiasm of the moment and clambered up the hill with them. The Confederate infantry and artillery at the top of the hill had not been told that their skirmishers below were supposed to scamper up the hill to safety. Now they assumed that a general retreat was taking place, and they abandoned the center of Missionary Ridge to the exuberant Federals. This cracked the entire Confederate line. Bragg was obliged to retreat all the way back to Dalton, Georgia.

Bragg was soon relieved by General Joe Johnston, but the damage had been done. The Union now had firm control of Chattanooga and central Tennessee. The door to the lower South had been kicked open, and the Yankees were about to walk in.

Victory: 1864-1865

In Ulysses S Grant Lincoln had finally found a general who would fight. In March 1864 he promoted him to lieutenant general and soon thereafter appointed him to be General in Chief, replacing Halleck, who stayed on in Washington giving the armies valuable aid as a logistical coordinator. Brought east to command the Union armies, Grant remained out of Washington as much as possible by staying with General Meade's Army of the Potomac. He hoped thereby to avoid political intrigues and to take both the pulse of his own forces and those of his brilliant enemy, Robert E Lee. Grant soon thereafter came up with the plan that, with some changes demanded by Lincoln, eventually would bring the Confederates to their knees, but only after another sixteen months of hard, sanguinary battle.

Grant's plan called for three offensive movements. Meade's Army of the Potomac, stationed north of the Rapidan River near Fredericksburg, would push south toward Richmond with the objective of destroying Lee's Army of Northern Virginia. A second army under General Sherman would drive southeast from Chattanooga, first to seize Atlanta and then to strike south from that key city. A third army, under General Banks, would move up the Red River, take Shreveport and then perhaps enter Texas to warn off the French forces of Napoleon III, who had just taken control of troubled Mexico. Banks would then move back east from New Orleans to take Mobile, Alabama, and from there march north toward Mongomery and the South's heartland. This third part of the Grant strategy failed, thanks in large measure to the dilatory Banks (Mobile was eventually taken by the US Navy), but its failure had only a limited effect on the outcome of the war. The real decision of arms was reached by Grant's advance on Richmond and Sherman's march toward Atlanta and the sea.

In 1864 the Virginia triangle was finally and definitively penetrated by the Union army. Meade had 120,000 men facing Lee's 63,000 across the Rapidan and was preparing to force him out of The Wilderness and into open combat. In addition, Grant had another 33,000 men, in Major General Benjamin F Butler's Army of the James, ready to move up that river from the east to take Richmond and the vital rail center at Petersburg, south of the capital. Still another force of 23,000 Federals was in the Valley on the left leg of the triangle guarding Grant's right flank as he carried out his grand maneuver south.

As Grant, with Meade's Army of the Potomac, moved out on 4 May 1864 the General in Chief began to slide the entire Army to the left in order to gain a direct rail connection with Washington and to establish supply depots on the Chesapeake and its tributaries along the Virginia coast. Attempting to thwart Grant's lateral movement, Lee launched an attack on the Unionists on 5 May. For two days the two armies fought a series of bloody battles in The Wilderness west of Chancellorsville. The butcher's bill was staggering, but unlike previous Union commanders in the East, Grant refused to pull back, even when temporarily bested. As his southeast slide continued, the local focus of attention devolved upon the vital crossroads at Spotsylvania. Lee got there first and set up an entrenched roadblock to stop Grant. In preparation for this encounter Grant dispatched Major General Philip H Sheridan and his cavalry corps south toward Richmond to meet and destroy Lieutenant General J E B Stuart's harassing cavalry forces. In a 16-day series of running engagements that culminated in a decisive battle at Yellow Tavern, Sheridan did just that, destroying any offensive power Stuart's cavalry might have contributed to Lee's strategic defense, Stuart himself falling mortally wounded in the fray.

Grant now threw his troops against Lee's log entrenchments at Spotsylvania. For four days, beginning on 9 May, both sides took heavy casualties in a grim battle of attrition. Frustrated but hardly checked, Grant broke off the engagement on 20 May and continued his advance to the southeast. Lee raced south to meet him and dug in on the North Anna River, but Grant ignored the challenge and, continuing his slide south toward Richmond, was soon northeast of the Confederate capital. Lee followed and finally the two armies faced each other again at Cold Harbor, on an 8-mile front on Richmond's outer defenses. Grant attacked on 3 June and was again unable to break the determined Southern resistance. Since beginning his campaign a month before, Grant had suffered 55,000 casualties (to the South's 32,000), but still he persisted. Again he slipped south, now to the James River, which he crossed by a 2100-foot pontoon bridge, and established a supply base connected by rail and water to his reinforcements at City Point. By 18 June he was in position to begin siege operations against Petersburg, south of Richmond. Lee's defensive perimeter now ran from north of Richmond in a loop around the eastern part of the city and south to below Petersburg. If this line was penetrated, especially at Petersburg (the vital rail center that controlled resupply to both Richmond and Lee's army), Lee would be doomed.

To break this pressure and lift the siege, Lee, in early July, sent Major General Jubal A Early and his cavalry corps up the Shenandoah Valley to menace Washington and draw off strength from Grant's investing army. This type of distraction had worked well in 1862, but it did not work now. Both Lincoln and Grant refused to panic, and few troops were sent north to protect the capital, even though Early reached the northern outskirts of Washington before being driven off. Grant, however, was determined that such raids up the Valley should not be allowed to continue. Accordingly, he unified the capital's defenses under General Sheridan and ordered him and his army to pursue Early to the death. For the rest of 1864 Sheridan did just that, defeating Early at Winchester, Fisher's Hill, and Cedar Valley and finally putting the whole Valley to the torch to prevent Early and his men from using its resources. These 'scorched earth' tactics were effective: Never again would the Valley route be used by Confederate armies as their grand highway into the North.

While all of this was occurring in Virginia, the Union forces in Tennessee, anchored at Chattanooga and Nashville, prepared to move into Georgia. At Chattanooga General Sherman had 100,000 troops to confront General Joe Johnston's 65,000. As he moved out, on 4 May, the same day Grant was beginning his advance in the East, Sherman's

The Battle of Lookout Mountain, one of several in Grant's Chattanooga campaign that prepared the way for the decision at Missionary Ridge and the invasion of the Deep South.

targets were both Atlanta and Johnston's army. Sherman and Johnston were equally fond of maneuver and constantly tried to outflank one another as Sherman slowly pushed south, the only major battle being fought at Kennesaw Mountain, northwest of Atlanta, in late May. After 74 days of almost constant skirmishing, Johnston had held Sherman to only 100 miles of conquest. Johnston's army was still intact, and Atlanta was still in Southern hands. But this was not good enough for President Jefferson Davis, who relieved Johnston and replaced him with Lieutenant General John B Hood.

Unlike the judicious Johnston, Hood was willing to attack the tenacious Sherman head-on, but his offensives outside of Atlanta only slowed the Union juggernaut, and Federal forces soon began to encircle the city. Hood was forced to pull back, and on 1 September 1864 Union forces began to move into the city. The capture of Atlanta, along with Rear Admiral David G Farragut's dramatic seizure of Mobile Bay the previous month, gave Lincoln all the popularity he needed to assure his re-election in November.

Sherman sent 30,000 men north to General Thomas at Nashville in order to protect that valuable base in case Hood should attempt to double back and capture it. Then Sherman, with 62,000 men, began his famous 'march to the sea' at Savannah, where he was to link up with US Navy units and be transported north to join Grant outside of Richmond. Before leaving Atlanta, Sherman ordered all vital buildings burned and all railroads destroyed. This was merely a foretaste of the havoc he would create on his unopposed march to Savannah. The material destruction along his line of march was great, but the psychological destruction of Southern morale was greater. This was what Sherman wanted, for he realized that the ultimate enemy was Southern will, and he was determined to break it by bringing the war home to the middle South. Cutting himself off from resupply, he drove for the sea, leaving a shambles of Southern hopes for victory in his wake. He arrived at Savannah on the 10th of December; on 21 December the Confederates abandoned the city.

The South had only one more card to play. If General Hood could move north from Florence, Alabama, and seize Nashville, he might then be able to join Lee around Richmond and fight off the encircling Federal armies. But Hood was slow in making his move, allowing Thomas at Nashville to be reinforced and permitting the 30,000 men Sherman had sent back to get between Hood's troops and Nashville. The forces of Major General John M Schofield, head of the contingent hurrying back to Nashville, met

Left: **William T Sherman, whose march to the sea cut the South in two.**
Right: **Grant in the Wilderness, the beginning of the final Union drive to capture Richmond and end the South's will to resist.**
Below: **Joseph E Johnston, one of the greatest Confederate generals.**

Hood's army at Franklin, Tennessee, on 30 November 1864. Hood launched a frontal attack by 18,000 of his veterans on the Federals' entrenched positions. By nightfall Hood had suffered 6000 casualties, including 11 of his general officers, and Schofield was safely behind Thomas' lines in Nashville. Hood was now too weak either to attack or to try to break through to the north. His army was demoralized, and his situation was precarious.

This opportunity was not lost on Thomas. After making thorough preparations, on 15

Left, top to bottom: The battles of Richmond, Kennesaw Mountain and Spotsylvania.
Below right: Grant's victory at Petersburg doomed Richmond and the Southern cause.

December he launched a devastating three-pronged cavalry and infantry attack on Hood south of Nashville. By the second day of battle Hood's army had been reduced to a remnant and had begun a disorganized flight 200 miles south to Tupelo, Mississippi. It would never again be a fighting unit.

The new year dawned with the ports of Wilmington, North Carolina, and Charleston, South Carolina, falling to Army-Navy expeditions in January and February. Sherman, now ordered to move north by land rather than by sea, began to march toward Richmond, sweeping away the disintegrating Southern defensive forces as he made his way through the Carolinas toward juncture with Grant and Meade at Petersburg.

Around the periphery of the Richmond and Petersburg defenses the pressure on Lee and the Confederates began to mount. When the Federals broke the last rail line to the South and safety on 2 April, Lee realized he had to make a break for freedom. He struck out west along the Danville Railroad hoping somehow to join up with Johnston's forces farther south. But Grant's troops shadowed him as he moved, and Sheridan raced ahead to cut off his escape. Sheridan intercepted Lee and his forces at the little crossroads of Appomattox Court House, Virginia, on 6 April. Lee now realized that escape was impossible. It was time to speak of surrender.

Three days later, on 9 April 1865, Robert E Lee and Ulysses S Grant sat down in the drawing room of the comfortable home of Wilbur McLean in Appomattox and worked out the terms. Grant graciously accepted Lee's surrender of the Army of Northern Virginia, allowed his 28,000 prisoners to go home on parole with their horses and mules, gave them rations, and strictly forbade his soldiers from raising any cheers or firing weapons in celebration of their victory.

Five days later Abraham Lincoln, the nation's great war leader, lay dead, the victim of an assassin's bullet. Within two weeks the gallant Joseph E Johnston had surrendered his army to Sherman. By the end of May the last straggling trans-Mississippi Confederate units had given up. The Civil War was over, secession had failed, and the most frightful carnage in the nation's history had ended in an overwhelming Union victory.

West Pointers on summer encampment, 1890. The traditional gray uniform of the cadets was adopted in 1816, when the Army was short of blue cloth.

SERVING A CHANGING NATION: 1865-1898

The martial spirit and pride in military might that the Civil War had generated in the popular imagination was symbolized by the grand parade of Sherman and Meade's infantry and cavalry units up Pennsylvania Avenue in Washington. The parade lasted for two days; but America's love affair with the military was not destined to last. Although 52,000 men under General Sheridan were dispatched to the Texas-Mexican border to convince Napoleon III that his adventure in colony-making in Mexico would not be allowed by the United States (the French emperor withdrew his army from the country and left his puppet emperor, Maximilian of Austria, to face a firing squad of Mexican nationalists in 1867), and although Army units remained in the South on garrison duty, the volunteer army that had won the war was discharged, leaving only the regulars to carry on.

By late 1865 only 11,000 men (mostly United States Black troops) were still in uniform. General in Chief Grant wanted 80,000 regulars retained in the postwar Army, but the number was soon reduced by a budget-minded Congress and a peace-minded public to 54,000 in 1867, then 37,000 in 1869, and finally 27,000 in 1876.

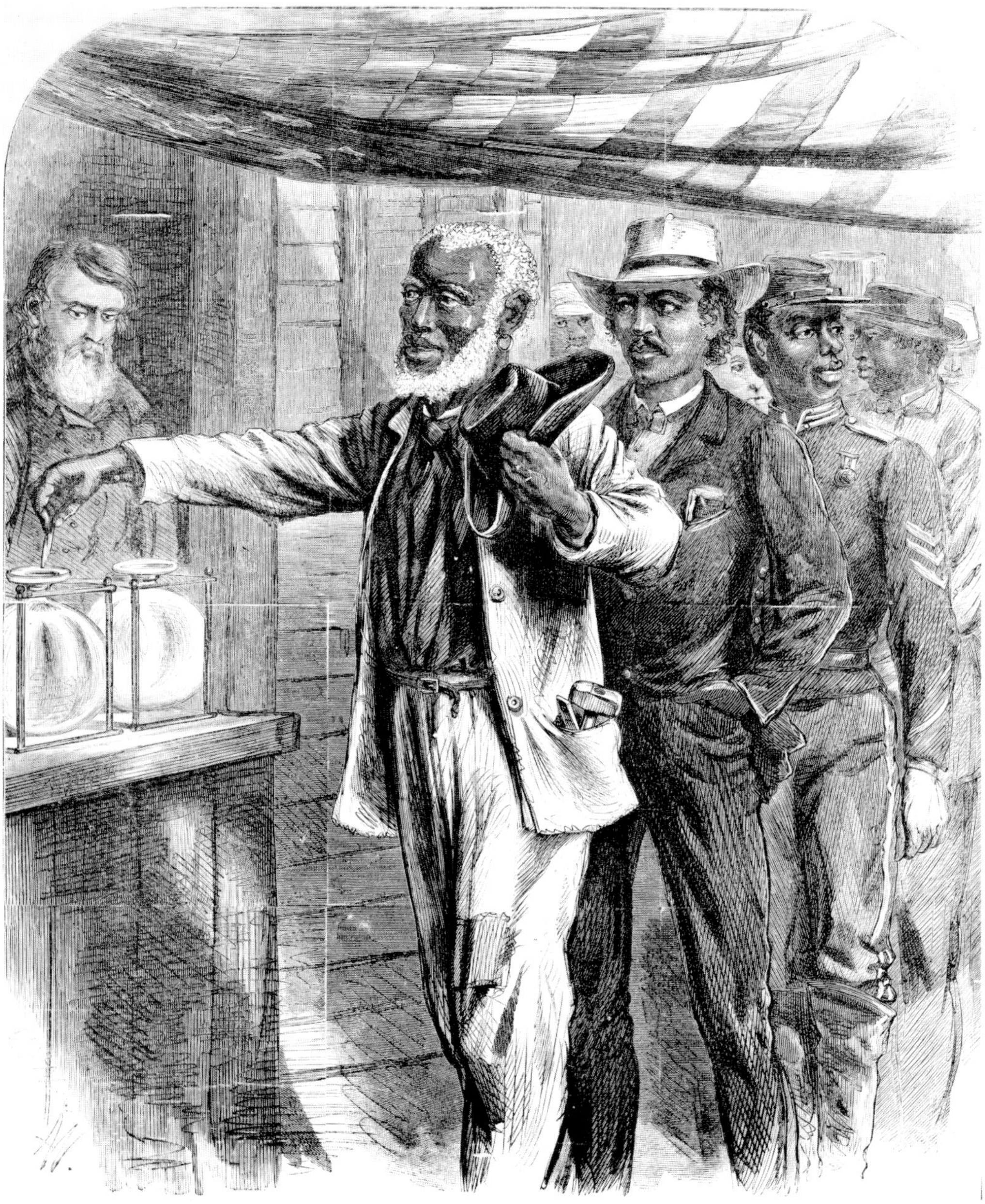

In the Reconstruction Period the Army was used to protect the voting rights of the newly-enfranchised black citizens of the Southern states.

Most Americans assumed that martial law and the Army's physical presence in the South would end with the war, but politics and Southern recalcitrance dictated otherwise. Southern resistance to accepting the outcome of the war and to the newly-mandated place of the ex-slaves in Southern society resulted in such violent opposition as to require the constant intervention of the Army to assure local peace and to guarantee civil rights to the Freedmen. The Army had assumed control of the seceded states as they had been conquered during the war and had aided the ex-slaves in many ways during the conflict. The civilian Freedmen's Bureau, created in 1865, was a legal extension of that work, an experiment in educational, vocational, and social aid to the blacks unprecedented in American history.

The work of the Freedmen's Bureau was fiercely resisted by ex-Confederates, both through the courts and through direct violence toward its personnel and those they were trying to help. This resistance was unintentionally encouraged by the lenient reconstruction policies of President Andrew Johnson who, following Lincoln's ideas on postwar reconciliation, quickly declared the Southern states reconstructed in 1865, after they had fulfilled minimal conditions, and made it known that he wanted to remove the Army as soon as possible. But to the victorious Republican party, as well as to many Army personnel and to Secretary of War Edwin M Stanton, early removal of the Army seemed almost a guarantee that there would be a quick return to the prewar Southern way of life with many of the same persons in power. The tremendous sacrifices of the war would then have been in vain.

The violence of Southern resistance to Reconstruction was expressed in the rise of the Ku Klux Klan.

This difference of opinion over treatment of the vanquished South set off a political and legal dispute, with Johnson (and many Democrats) on one side and the Radical Republican-dominated Congress and the Army high command on the other. The result was Republican-inspired federal legislation in the form of the First Reconstruction Acts of 1867. These disbanded Southern militia units (often used to resist Federal reconstruction policies) and divided the South into five military districts in which martial law superseded civil law. With the Army ruling over civil affairs (usually with great reluctance), most of the Southern states were re-admitted into the Union. But as Army rule became increasingly tainted by civilian opportunists (called 'carpetbaggers' and 'scalawags') and by alleged corruption on the part of Blacks elected to office, Southern resistance waxed.

Reacting to the Northern-based Union League's attempts to ensure the voting rights of Black voters and to the Freedmen's Bureau-backed state governments' efforts to use loyal militia units to make sure both that newly-enfranchised blacks could vote and that ineligible ex-Confederates could not, Southern die-hards soon formed activist resistance societies such as the Ku Klux Klan and the Knights of the White Camellia. These para-military units regularly beat, murdered, hanged, and raped blacks, as well as those who sympathized with them. Such terrorism led to increasing demands that the Army put down the lawless white Southern elements, even though by 1868 only 17,000 men were on duty in the former Confederate states. As directed by the Enforcement Acts of the 1870s, and especially the Ku Klux Klan Act, the Army tried manfully to stem the violence, but its numbers were simply too few to deal effectively with the problem. If the KKK gradually lost effectiveness in the South, it was more because of public revulsion from its indiscriminate violence than because of any measures taken by the Army. The Army was always hobbled in carrying out Federal policy in the South both by Northern indifference to what was happening there and by incessant demands to cut Federal expenses. Even after the influence of the KKK began to wane, the Army could do little to curb the activities of its successors, espousers of more selective violence, such as the White League and the Red Shirts.

The policy of Reconstruction finally collapsed with the disputed election of 1876, in which the Democratic candidate for president, Samuel J Tilden of New York, won the popular vote for the office over the Republican candidate, Rutherford B Hayes of Ohio, but not the electoral vote. Since the returns from four states were in dispute, the Republicans, anxious to hold on to the White House at any price, made a deal with the Southern Democrats to allow Hayes the electoral vote in return for an end to Reconstruction. This 'Compromise of 1877' led directly to the 'redemption' of the South, to the return of the Blacks to subjugation, and to the removal of the Army from its onerous duties as enforcer of political and social policies in the postwar South.

While almost one-third of the Army regulars had been stationed in the old Confederacy, the rest had been scattered all about the nation. Some were on coastal fortification duty and others were patrolling the border with Mexico, and about 9000 were stationed on the Great Plains. Although immediately after the war veterans made up the bulk of the regular forces, by the 1870s their places were largely being taken by immigrants or other persons unable to find employment. Morale and professionalism suffered accordingly. In some years desertions ran as high as one-third of the enlisted men on the rolls.

Over this mixed assemblage existed a command structure that was rife with acrimony. The line officers in the field quarreled incessantly with the staff officers who ran the various bureaus and whose duty it was to supply the more than 100 posts around the country. Both William T Sherman, General in Chief from 1869 to 1883, and Philip Sheridan, who held the office from 1884 until his death in 1888, knew of the problems created by the increasing bureaucratization and independence of the Army's staff section, but neither had the political power or the administrative ability to set matters right.

The resulting lack of coordinated and effective planning was exemplified by the Army's slowness to adopt the new and improved weaponry available in other Western countries in the late 19th century. The standard infantry weapon during the Civil War had been the muzzle-loading rifle, and after the war the Army had been content merely to convert its old muzzle-loaders into breech-loaders. Finally, recognizing the need for a more modern weapon, an Army board in 1872 recommended the single-shot 'trap-door' Springfield, so named because its breech snapped upwards like a trap door. This .45-caliber rifle still fired a black powder cartridge, despite the fact that rifles firing cartridges with smokeless powder were than available. Yet the 1873 Springfield remained the standard infantry weapon for twenty years. Not until 1893 did the Army adopt the five-shot, .30-caliber Danish Krag-Jörgensen rifle that fired smokeless powder, and not until 1897 had the 'Krag' been issued to all of the regulars. The Army was also dilatory in adopting machine guns, such as the famous Gatling Gun, and failed to see it as useful for infantry warfare. (It was viewed only as an adjunct to artillery or as useful for protecting bridges.) New breech-loading

Edwin M Stanton, Lincoln's Secretary of War, remained in office until 1868. Andrew Johnson was nearly impeached for firing Stanton, whose high-handed actions angered the president.

LOVE
TOBACCO
MANUFACTURED BY
MYERS BRO'S AND CO.
RICHMOND, VA.

Technical improvements in weaponry continued throughout the remainder of the century.
Left: **A Remington Army revolver of 1874.**
Below: **A US infantryman with a Krag bolt-action breech-loading rifle of 1896.**

rifled artillery pieces were also slow in being adopted, and, even then, black powder was still used. Indeed, the Army was even slow to change its uniforms. It was not until 1898 that khaki began to replace the blues the Army had worn on campaign ever since 1800.

But if the Army was slow in reacting to the command and equipment changes taking place in the world's other armies during these years, it nevertheless made considerable progress in its training methods. West Point, of course, still continued to turn out professional young officers (the Corps of Engineers relinquished control of the Military Academy in 1866, and thereafter its curriculum was broadened somewhat), and under Sherman and Sheridan several post-graduate professional schools for Army personnel were either revived or created. In 1868 the Artillery School at Fort Monroe was reopened (it had been closed in 1860); a Signal Corps School was opened that same year; in 1881 the School of Application for Infantry and Cavalry was opened at Fort Leavenworth (its name was changed to the General Service and Staff College in 1901); and the Army Medical School was opened in 1883. Also very important in developing a professional officer corps was the founding in 1878 of the Military Service Institution, a professional society interested in the dissemination of military knowledge through its bi-monthly *Journal*.

These same years also produced one of the most important reformers in Army history, General Emory Upton. Upton, an 1861 West Point graduate who had served under Sherman during the Civil War, was appointed commandant of cadets at the Military Academy in 1870 and served there for five years. He had earlier published *Infantry Tactics* (1867), immediately adopted by the Army as a standard text for its regulars and militia. After his West Point tour, Upton was sent on a world mission to study military systems and returned to write his greatest book, *The Military Policy of the United States*. It was not published until 1904 but was widely circulated in manuscript form before his death in 1881. *Military Policy* had a profound impact on Army thinking. It also provided

The nation's yearning for post-war reconciliation is suggested in this somewhat sentimental tobacco advertisement.

valuable ammunition against politician and ex-general John A Logman's arguments in his *Volunteer Soldier in America* (1887), which asserted that the military should be based on a strong militia and that the military academies should be closed.

Upton argued that America could no longer afford to remain unprepared in peacetime and then try quickly to gear up for war, as it had done in the past. He also asserted that the Army's command system was antiquated and that the secretary of war, the line officers, and the bureau chiefs in command should be replaced with a general staff similar to that used by the Prussians. (Though never adopted, this idea, even today, has many adherents.) He argued further that volunteers and militia, being inadequately trained and led, could no longer constitute the backbone of the Army at war and that a compact and 'expansible' professional Army was the answer, since it would provide for 100,000 properly trained and led troops for combat, the militia being only a force of last resort. Thus the regular Army, with national volunteers and draftees to supplement it, could adequately fill the bill for manpower in a 'modern' war.

Upton's ideas clearly called for a larger standing army under the control of professional soldiers, but these ideas, plus the increased cost of such a system, collided directly both with American tradition and the parsimony of Congress. As a result, few of Upton's proposals were acted upon, yet his ideas would become increasingly influential as the decades passed.

Greater professionalism was also aided by legislation. In 1882 retirement was made mandatory for officers at age 64. Promotion by examination only, for all ranks above major, came about after 1890. Regular efficiency reports on all Army officers were required by the mid-1890s. By these changes the stultifying promotion-by-seniority-only logjam was broken, and the way was opened for talented young officers to move up more quickly to command positions.

Curbing Domestic Violence

While these attempts at reform were taking place, the Army continued to be called upon to play a role in curbing America's domestic troubles. Faced with what they considered intolerable working conditions, American industrial workers began to organize into unions after the Civil War. In 1877 a great wave of railroad strikes swept across the nation, and President Hayes called upon the Army and Marines to protect Federal property endangered by the actions of the strikers. The regulars operated in small detachments and exhibited strong discipline and great restraint in putting down these strikes, winning considerable praise for their behavior.

Best known of the labor incidents in which the Army became involved was the so-called Pullman Strike of 1894. Originating in the model factory town of Pullman, Illinois, it quickly spread to many parts of the country. The most direct confrontation between the Army and the railroad strikers came in nearby Chicago. Although Illinois Governor John Peter Altgeld had protested the sending in of Army troops, President Grover Cleveland insisted on using them to assure the unimpeded passage of the US mails, and the courts sustained him. Major General Nelson A Miles, who commanded the 2000 Federal troops in Chicago and who had cautioned against using them in this situation, at first unwisely intermingled his troops with policemen and Federal marshals, but then, under orders, consolidated them for greater control. Army troops fired on a mob in only one instance, this in Hammond, Indiana, where they killed one rioter when they were about to be overwhelmed by a crowd of strikers. In retrospect, the Army's role in the Pullman strike appears commendably restrained, yet inevitably this single death occasioned some harsh criticism from labor's supporters. And it also threw into sharp relief the underlying question of whether the Army

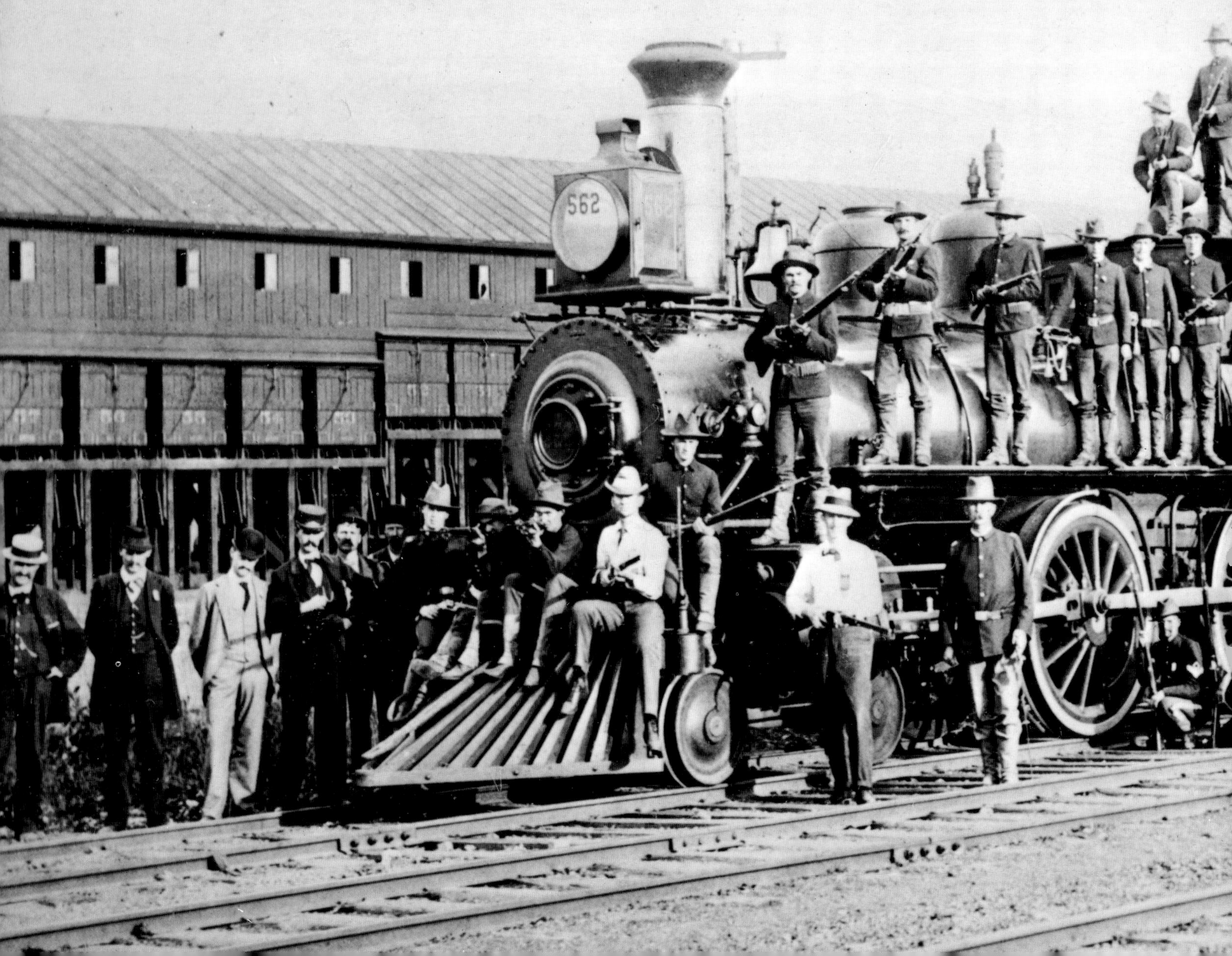

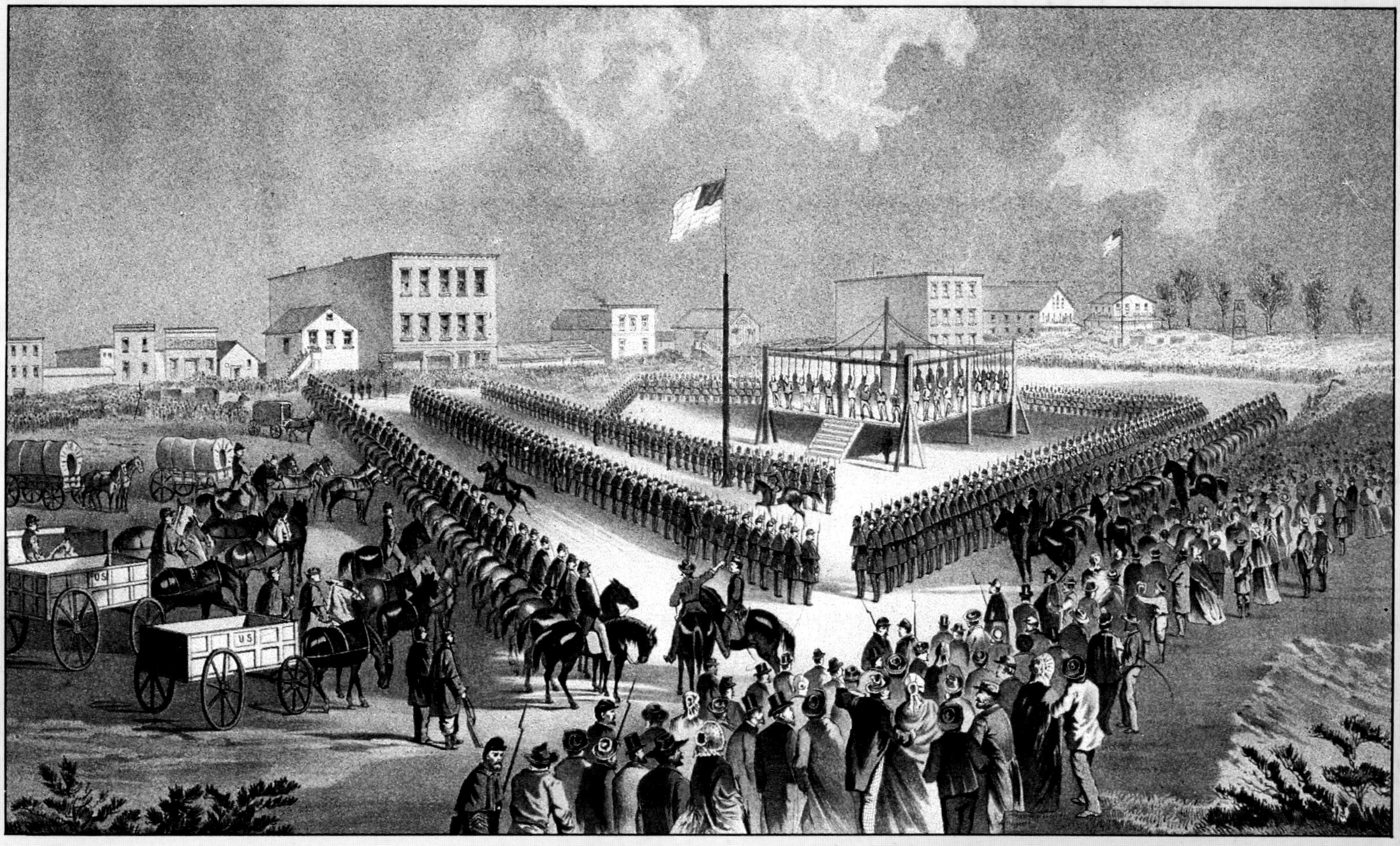

Top: This hanging of the leaders of a bloody Sioux uprising in 1862 was a foretaste of Indian troubles to come.
Below: US troops protecting a train in the Pullman strike of 1894.

The use of Army troops to intervene in labor disputes did little to enhance the Army's popularity.

really was the proper instrument for maintaining public order in such situations.

The wave of strikes also led to a revival of militia units on the state level, for by the 1870s governors and legislators began to see a volunteer militia under state control as an answer to their need for more policing power. State after state began to re-form its militia in the 1870s, almost uniformly under the name 'National Guard.' By 1879 a National Guard Association had come into being, and between 1881 and 1892 every state revised its laws to provide for a regularly organized volunteer militia free of Federal control. By the 1890s the Guard had a total enrollment of over 100,000 men, far more than the regular Army. Drawn largely from the middle class, it was a growing force that the Army, itself facing slim budgets and niggardly congressional support, had to reckon with. Although the Guard was used primarily for breaking strikes, being called out over 350 times by governors between 1877 and 1903 to handle such situations, its local prestige grew apace. The problems raised by such a military force, independent of the Army's training and control, would emerge clearly in the early 20th century as the National Guard demanded a larger and larger role in the nation's defense structure.

The Wagon Box Fight near Fort Phil Kearney in 1867 was an early post-war encounter between Army and Sioux.

The Indian Wars

West of the Mississippi lived about two million whites and roughly 270,000 Indians. Of these Indians, perhaps 100,000 were willing to fight the white man rather than accept being confined to reservations. Called upon to police the Indian lands extending from the Canadian border to Mexico were about 9000 Army troopers scattered in posts on the northern and southern Plains. Their task was made more difficult and dangerous by the fact that the Plains Indians were both mobile, usually being mounted for combat on small but sturdy ponies, and carried rifles in addition to their traditional weapons of bows and arrows and lances. In effect, they were light cavalry, and they displayed great bravery and endurance in war.

But while individualism gave the Indian warriors many advantages in combat where courage and stealth were important qualities, it also meant that alliances with other tribes were very difficult to create or sustain for long periods of time. To this disadvantage were added the facts that the white man had greater technological advantages in weapons and materiel, greater numbers, and greater political unity. Still, before the Indians had been pacified and removed from the path of frontier development, they had engaged the Army in over 950 combat actions and had inflicted 2000 casualties while suffering 6000 deaths of their own.

The Army's campaign to pacify the Indians was as thankless as it was difficult. The soldiers were always caught between the demands of the humanitarians, who condemned the Army for every Indian death, and of the frontiersmen, who only wanted the Indians removed quickly, at whatever cost in blood, and who would threaten political retribution whenever the Indians were off their reservations or engaging in warlike acts. Most individual Army officers were probably ambivalent toward their assigned duty, hating the Indian's methods of warfare and use of torture, yet admiring them as brave and resourceful warriors fighting for their homes and way of life. But government policy was clear: The Indians had to be removed from their traditional lands and confined to reservations: if they strayed, they had to be forced back; if they resisted, they had to be treated as enemies and warred upon.

In campaigning against the Indians the Army soon discovered four complementary and effective methods of dealing with their adversaries: well-planned campaigns; the use of converging columns to force the Indians to stand and fight; the destruction of the Indian's camps, food, shelter, and livestock; and the use of friendly Indians both as scouts and as regular military forces. Effective as these methods were, the Indian 'wars' nevertheless lasted from 1866 until 1890 and cost much blood and treasure.

The tribes of the southern Plains were the first to resist the flood of white settlers and the first to feel the power of the US Army. The warlike Cheyennes, Arapahoes, Kiowas, and Comanches were determined and skilled fighters, but they found it impossible to unite against the whites facing them. They were further weakened by internal dissension because many among them were willing to come to terms with the whites and accept reservation life. But by their campaigns of terror on the encroaching settlements on the southern Plains, the Indians finally convinced the government, in 1874, that the Army had to be used to return them to their reservations. The result was the year-long Red River War in which 3000 Army troops, moving in converging columns, ran down the Indians and forced them onto reservations in the Indian Territory in present-day Oklahoma.

More difficult was the Army's campaign against the Sioux confederation of 30,000 people roaming the northern Plains from the Dakotas to Wyoming. These Indians were angered by incursions into their treaty territory by miners seeking gold in the Black Hills, after its discovery there in 1875. They resented the government's apparent unwillingness to keep its own treaty promises of keeping whites out of their territory, and accordingly, under the leadership of Red Cloud, they left their reservation and migrated to Montana, joining up with the 'hunting bands' of Sitting Bull and defying governmental demands that they return to their Indian Agency homes.

To return the Sioux and their allies to their reservations, Lieutenant General Philip Sheridan, commanding the Division of the Missouri, planned an expedition of converging columns to corner the Indians and force their return to captivity. One column of 1000 men and 250 Crow and Shoshone allies, under Brigadier General George Crook, was to march north from Fort Fetterman in Wyoming. A second column, of 450 men and 25 Crow allies, under Colonel John Gibbon, was dispatched from Fort Shaw and Fort Ellis in northern and central Montana to march southeast against the Sioux encampment in southeast Montana. A third column, under Brigadier General Alfred H Terry, was to move westward from Fort Abraham Lincoln in the Dakota territory. In Terry's forces were 925 soldiers, including the 7th Cavalry Regiment, under Colonel George Armstrong Custer, and 40 Indian scouts. What the Army commanders did not realize was that they faced at least 2000 warriors (some estimate 4000) led by Red Cloud, Sitting Bull, and the Sioux's greatest war captain, Crazy Horse, all determined to fight rather than be herded back to reservation life.

On 17 June 1876 Crook's column was attacked by 1500 Sioux and Cheyenne warriors just north of the Montana border along Rosebud Creek. The ensuing six-hour fight has been named the Battle of the Rosebud. Crook's forces were saved time and again by his Crow and Shoshone allies, but were so badly mauled that Crook decided to turn back. Not knowing of Crook's defeat on the Rosebud, the other two columns moved on, intending to catch the Sioux in the Little Bighorn Valley, 50 miles to the north. Custer was ordered to move up the Rosebud River, cross over to the Little Bighorn, and descend along it. Meanwhile, Terry and Gibbon, having joined their forces, would move south up the Bighorn to its mouth, thus trapping the Indians as Custer drove them north. Custer came upon the Sioux encampment on Sunday, 25 June, a day before Gibbon and Terry could get into position, but apparently did not realize either the number of Indians gathered there or their determination to fight. He split his command of 600 riders into three columns. The largest column, about 230 men, was kept under his personal command.

Beginning the attack, one column under Captain Frederick W Benteen was sent off to the left to prevent the Indians' flight in that direction. A second column under Major Marcus A Reno was sent forward to attack the Indian encampment directly. Reno met fierce resistance and had to be reinforced by Benteen and the pack train from the rear. (Custer had refused to bring a Gatling Gun and its supporting platoon along because it would have limited his mobility.) The survivors of these two columns held out until two days later when the forces under Terry and Gibbon arrived on the scene. In the meantime, Custer's own column, moving to the

Perhaps the two most famous foes of the Indian Wars: Sitting Bull, *left*, and George A Custer, *below*. Their 10-year antagonism would culminate on the slopes of the Little Big Horn, in the most famous battle of the Indian Wars.

Above: Burying the dead at Wounded Knee, 1890. This was the last major battle (massacre?) of the Plains wars.
Right: Otto Becker's famous American icon, *Custer's Last Stand*.
Below: Geronimo, right, and three of his Chiricahua Apache band, 1886. The Apache wars lasted from 1861-1900 and were of unparalleled savagery.

right and blocked by the terrain from seeing the number of Indians he was facing, was suddenly encircled by thousands of Sioux under Crazy Horse, and in a two-hour fight was wiped out to the last man. The Battle of the Little Bighorn, in which over 50 percent of the 7th Cavalry was killed, became celebrated as the greatest Indian victory in American history.

After the battle, as the news of the 'massacre' on the Little Bighorn stunned the nation in the midst of its Centennial celebration, public indignation was whipped to a frenzy by the survivors' stories of Sioux 'atrocities' in distant Montana Territory. The Army poured troops into the territory, and a winter campaign was mounted under the leadership of General Crook and Colonel Nelson A Miles. It broke the back of Indian resistance, aided by the fact that the Indians had dispersed after the Little Bighorn battle to celebrate, hunt, and resume their way of life. By the spring of 1877 almost all the Sioux, including the great warriors Sitting Bull and Crazy Horse, had surrendered and had been herded onto reservations.

Other campaigns against non-Plains Indians continued during these years: the Modoc War of 1872-1873; the Nez Percé War of 1877 in the Northwest; and the Bannock, Sheepeater and Ute Wars in Idaho and Colorado in 1878-1879. The last major campaign was carried out by the Army against the Apaches in the Southwest. Widely and rightly regarded as exceptionally fierce warriors, and led by their great chief Cochise, the Apaches had finally agreed to cease resistance and accept reservation life in 1872, but some elements of the tribe, led by Geronimo, refused to surrender and continued to kill and loot. Assigned to bring Geronimo and his renegade Apaches to bay, General Crook enlisted friendly Apaches to aid him, dispensed with wagons in favor of mule trains to follow the Indians wherever they went in the mountains and deserts, and determined to pursue Geronimo and his warriors and give them no rest until he subdued them (once even crossing the border into Mexico in hot pursuit of his quarry). His strategy worked, and, although Crook was not in the territory when the event occurred, Geronimo and his men finally surrendered in 1886.

The surrender of Geronimo marked the end of regular warfare against the Indians, although isolated actions occurred for a few years thereafter. The final flareup between the Indians and the Army occurred in 1890 when a group of Sioux on a reservation in South Dakota, intoxicated by the preachings of the new Ghost Dance religion that promised a resurgence of Indian glory (and that the Indians would be immune to the white man's bullets), left their reservation. They were intercepted by a body of soldiers at Wounded Knee Creek and told to relinquish their weapons. Fighting broke out when an Indian's rifle discharged as it was being wrested from him by two soldiers. Before the subsequent melee was over, 200 Indians had been killed or wounded (including many women and children), and 62 soldiers had become casualties. Thereafter the Sioux returned to their reservations. The Battle of Wounded Knee was perhaps a grimly fitting end to a bitter and tragic chapter of American history.

The Army's campaigns against the Indians, like its other occupations during the thirty years that followed the Civil War, were essentially domestic and aimed at maintaining internal order. It had not been called upon to perform its most essential function: waging war with foreign enemies. Yet events in the Caribbean, in Mexico, in Europe, and on the American political scene were shortly to catapult the Army onto foreign shores and to give it a major role in America's emergence to world power.

WARRIORS ON A WORLD STAGE: 1898-1919

Moving to the front, France, 1918.

While America's internal frontier was expanding to the Pacific Ocean, her economic expansion beyond the nation's borders was also inexorably drawing her into an orbit of much wider responsibilities in hemispheric and world affairs. Commerce was rapidly increasing both with Central and South America and with the Orient, as well as with most European nations. In the wake of this economic expansion came political, social and humanitarian concerns in areas of the world previously regarded as peripheral to the nation's interests. Such concerns were not totally disinterested, considering American economic investments throughout the world, and were at times predicated on a belief in American superiority to others, but whatever their genesis, they inevitably impelled the United States toward a policy of increasing foreign intervention, and one of the chief instruments of intervention became the US Army.

War with Spain

Since the 1820s the nations of Latin America had been engaged one by one in throwing off the yoke of Spanish domination. By 1896 only Cuba and Puerto Rico remained Spanish colonies in the New World, and the peoples on both islands felt the passion for political freedom already won by their hemispheric brothers. The Cuban people had attempted rebellion unsuccessfully in the 1860s and 1870s, and in 1895 they rose again to try to throw off Spanish rule.

From the beginning, the Cuban revolutionaries worked to get the USA involved in their new rebellion. Without American aid the revolution could not succeed against superior Spanish military power. Accordingly, the Cuban revolutionary *junta* (council) established an office in New York City to promote the Cuban cause, to raise money and volunteers in America, and to issue propaganda designed to implicate the United States in the island's struggle.

Spain's behavior aided the rebel's cause. Spanish attempts to put down the rebellion in 1896 were extremely harsh, and Spanish cruelties in Cuba were prominently reported in America's major 'yellow press' newspapers, currently engaged in a circulation war and trying to out-sensationalize one another. Feeling the pressure of popular enthusiasm for the Cuban cause, Congress adopted a resolution in 1896 saying that the United States should recognize the belligerency of Cuba (thereby granting her *de facto* recognition as a separate power and denying that the conflict was a civil war and, as such, solely a Spanish affair). But President Grover Cleveland disregarded this congressional initiative, as did his successor, William McKinley. Neither wanted war with Spain over the issue of Cuban independence.

Yet events moved beyond McKinley's

power to control them. He had refused to make too much of the insulting contents of a letter from the Spanish minister in Washington, Enrique Dupey de Lôme, to a friend in Havana. (The letter had been stolen from the post offfice in Havana and printed in William Randolph Hearst's *New York Journal*, despite the illegality of its receipt and printing.) But the American people reacted with great anger to this defamation, and their anger turned to fury when the battleship *Maine* blew up in the harbor at Havana on 15 February 1898, with the loss of the lives of 260 American sailors.

The American press was immediately filled with insinuations that the Spanish had deliberately blown up the *Maine*. An American investigating commission reported that the ship had been rocked by an external explosion from a 'submarine mine' placed against the hull outside the ship's powder magazines, but it could not say who had done

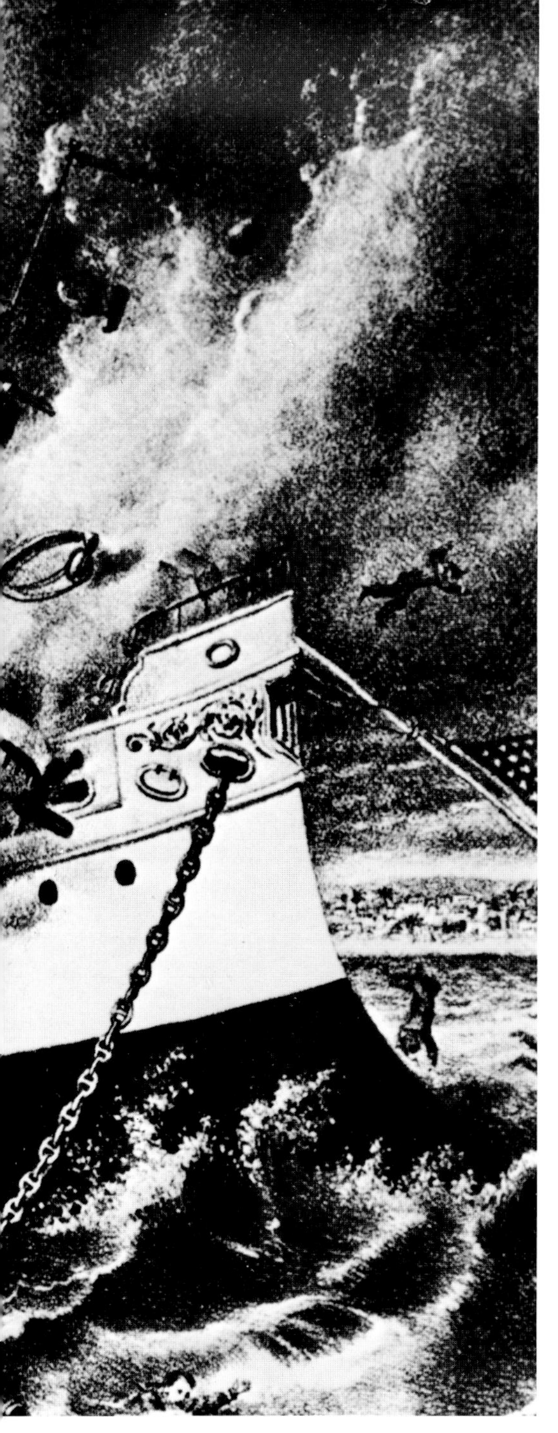

Top: **Regulation uniforms for infantry and artillery, 1899. In fact, troops wore casual non-standard kits while on active campaign.**
Left: **The explosion of USS *Maine* in Havana harbor, 15 February 1898, was widely blamed in the US on Spanish sabotage.**

the deed. A Spanish investigating team reported that the explosion was internal. The *Maine* had not been blown up, they argued, but had blown itself up, perhaps from a coal gas explosion (a very real possibility, as naval records now make clear).

Whatever had happened to the *Maine*, McKinley was now obliged to put more pressure on Spain to resolve her troubles in Cuba and offered to mediate between Spain and her rebellious colony. He wanted to avoid war if at all possible, but he could not convince Congress to cease beating the war drums. On 11 April 1898 the president finally sent an ambiguous war message to Congress, and on 20 April the bellicose Congress passed a resolution declaring Cuba free and authorizing the president to use the Army and Navy to enforce its declaration. Armed with this legislative authority, McKinley ordered a naval blockade of Cuba. Spain reacted with a declaration of war on the United States. The United States reciprocated, and the Spanish-American War, the 'splendid little war,' as Secretary of State John Hay would later call it, was on.

While the Navy, having been in the process of rebuilding and expanding since the 1880s, was basically prepared for war, the Army was not. It did not even have a mobilization plan. Spread out over the West in small garrison units and inexperienced in tropical warfare, amphibious operations, or combined operations with the Navy, the 26,000 officers and men of the regular Army were hardly in a position even to train new recruits adequately for war, much less to carry out major operations in the Caribbean themselves. The Army's feverish attempt to prepare for conflict were further confused by the question of the readiness and participation of the various state Guard units, since it was not at all clear whether these units were forbidden by law from operating outside the continental United States.

The wartime Army, as authorized by Congress, consisted of both regular and volun-

The sunken *Maine* became a symbol for anti-Spanish 'war hawks' in the US.

teer soldiers. Guard units as such were not called up, but if enough men of a Guard unit enlisted as volunteers the Army kept them together as a special unit. During the course of the short war the regulars were expanded to 59,000 (of 65,000 authorized) and volunteers totalled 216,000, including 10,000 special volunteers dubbed 'Immunes' (men allegedly possessing immunity from tropical diseases). Lacking coordination by a general staff and with no mobilization plans, the regular Army's attempts to train the volunteers pouring into newly-built camps in the South ran into grave difficulties. Shortages of basic training equipment, poor sanitary facilities, inadequate food supplies, and shortages in weaponry led inevitably to inadequate preparation for combat.

Major General Nelson A Miles, Commanding General of the Army, wanted to assemble and train a special force of 80,000 at Chickamauga Park, Georgia. This force was to land in Cuba in October, after the unhealthy rainy season had passed, there to work with the Navy and the Cuban rebels to defeat the Spanish. But Secretary of War Russell M Alger, backed by a groundswell of public opinion that demanded immediate action, overruled him and ordered that expeditionary forces be sent to Southern ports to prepare for an immediate attack on Cuba, even though no strategic plan of operations against the Spanish had yet been developed.

While the Army was still wallowing in confusion, the Navy won the first decisive victory of the war half a world away in the Philippines. Responding to orders from Acting Secretary of the Navy Theodore Roosevelt to prepare for operations in the Far East in case of war with Spain, Commodore George Dewey of the Asiatic Squadron had his vessels and men ready to go when war was declared. Sailing out of Hong Kong upon receipt of orders on 24 April 1898, Dewey's fleet steamed into Manila Bay, in the Philippines, on the night of 30 April and the next morning destroyed the entire Spanish fleet anchored there. In a matter of five hours Spanish naval power in the Pacific had ceased to exist, and the harbor of Manila was safely in American hands. Since Dewey's 1700 men were too few to take the capital city of Manila, they settled down to wait for the Army to arrive from the West Coast, meantime trying to discourage the British, French, and German naval units now arriving in Manila Bay from making any claims to sovereignty in the Philippines.

By late July 15,000 Army regulars and volunteers under the command of Major General Wesley Merritt had arrived in the Manila area. Constituted as the VIII Corps, Merritt's forces soon found that they would probably have less trouble with the Spanish

For the war with Spain the Army was expanded by 216,000 volunteers.

Right: Inadequately prepared Tampa, Florida, was designated the staging area for the Cuban invasion.

Below right: While the Army was still assembling, the Navy, on 1 May 1898, won a great victory at Manila Bay.

army garrison in the Philippines, whose commander was perfectly willing to surrender to overwhelming force as long as Spanish honor could be upheld, than with the guerrilla forces of Emilio Aquinaldo, who had been fighting the Spanish and who assumed that American help had been sent to drive out the Spanish in order to give the Filipinos their independence. That was not, in fact, the intention of the McKinley administration, which feared that if the Filipinos were granted their independence they would be too weak to sustain it against pressure from various European powers.

The peaceful surrender of the Spanish garrison at Manila was worked out in a carefully-planned scenario designed to salvage Spanish honor. The US Navy would place Manila under fire but would hit nothing in the city; the Spanish Army would 'defend' Manila against the American troops but promised not to hit any of them. The plan almost failed because of lack of cooperation by Aquinaldo's forces, but Manila finally fell to Merritt's VIII Corps on 13 August 1898, with almost no casualties on either side, and the next day the formal surrender of the city was accepted. This was two days after an armistice ending hostilities had been signed between Spain and the United States, giving Spain the argument at the peace conference in Paris that the United States had no claim to the Philippines, since its capital had not been taken when the armistice was agreed upon. But this claim was brushed aside, and the ensuing Treaty of Paris transferred sovereignty of the Philippine archipelago from Spain to the United States.The United States had thus become a Far Eastern power almost by accident. It was, however, an accident that would have important historic consequences.

While these momentous events were taking place in the western Pacific, the Army was engaged in making the United States a major Caribbean power, as well. Under orders from the secretary of war who, as we have seen, wanted immediate action, the Army began planning for an expedition from Tampa to land somewhere in the vicinity of Havana, on the north side of the island. With considerable difficulty, the Army began to move men, equipment, horses, weapons, and food to that totally inadequate port city on the Gulf of Mexico. But then it was decided that no expedition could be launched until the Spanish fleet, which had sailed from Europe under the command of Admiral Pascual Cervera, could be located and destroyed by the US Navy.

Not until May was word received that the admiral had evaded the Navy's blockading vessels and had slipped into Santiago harbor, on the southern shore of the island. Since the ship channel there was narrow and the harbor was both mined and guarded by forts, the Navy now had to call upon the Army to destroy the forts from the land side and then

The most famous volunteer of the war was Teddy Roosevelt, seen here with some of his 'Rough Riders.'

to come around behind the city of Santiago de Cuba, at the head of Santiago Bay, and Force Cervera out of the harbor.

The War Department reacted to the Navy's request for aid at Santiago by embarking V Corps, under Major General William R Shafter, from Tampa with all possible dispatch, which in this case meant two weeks. Although V Corps was probably the best-prepared of all units, the port of embarkation at Tampa was a shambles, thanks to bad planning, inadequate rail and loading facilities, and lack of priorities for loading the available vessels according to combat needs at the point of debarkation. Nevertheless, Shafter's force of 17,000 men finally sailed out on 14 June 1898 and arrived off Santiago six days later. Amphibious landings were made at Siboney and Daiquiri, east of Santiago, beginning on 22 June. Fortunately for the Americans, their landings were unopposed, even though the Spanish had 36,000 troops in the Santiago area.

From their landing sites the American forces marched west to San Juan Heights, guarding Santiago from the east. Pausing to bring up supplies, Shafter laid out his plans. Brigadier General Jacob F Kent's infantry division was to attack the Heights on the left, while Brigadier General Joseph Wheeler's dismounted cavalry made a grand frontal assault. In the meantime Brigadier General Henry Lawton's infantry was to seize the town of El Caney, two miles to the north, then turn south-westward to support Wheeler's right flank. When the attack was made on 1 July it was marked by Wheeler's and Kent's infantry receiving minimal field artillery support, and none was requested from the Navy. Lawton was delayed at El Caney and joined the main units only after the battle was over. Nevertheless, while black troopers from the 10th and 19th Cavalry Regiments joined Colonel Theodore Roosevelt's volunteer Rough Riders in storming nearby Kettle Hill, Kent's infantry eventually charged up San Juan Hill and broke the Spanish defenses.

Despite the American victories of 1 July, Shafter wanted to withdraw to higher ground both to save his troops from enemy fire emanating from the Santiago defenses and from the effects of the tropical diseases that were decimating his troops. Alger denied his request. With the Army reluctant to move forward and the Navy unwilling to enter Santiago Bay to destroy Cervera's fleet, strategic decision-making seemed at an impasse. Then Cervera, under orders to escape if Santiago appeared to be in danger of falling, on 3 July began an ill-fated dash for freedom out of Santiago Bay. Within two hours his entire fleet, four cruisers and two destroyers, had been either put out of commission or sunk by US naval gunfire.

With the American Army approaching from the land and the American Navy now able to sail into Santiago Bay, the Spanish military leaders agreed to quit, and on 16 July surrendered the 23,000 troops in the Santiago area without further fighting. This was a welcome relief for the American troops, who were being rapidly debilitated by malaria, typhoid, and yellow fever. During the course of the Cuban fighting 5462 Americans died. Of these, only 379 were battle casualties the remainder being victims of disease. The magnitude of this health problem led directly both to the Medical Corps' successful project to find the causes of yellow fever and to the Army's long-term concern with tropical medicine.

A Gatling gun in action at El Caney, 1 July 1898. In this opening battle of the Cuban campaign Spanish troops resisted more fiercely than expected.

While Shafter and V Corps were gaining victory around Santiago, General Miles was preparing to seize Puerto Rico. Sailing from Guantanamo Bay, Cuba (seized earlier from the Spaniards by US Marines), Miles landed on 25 July at Guanica with 3000 troops. He met so little opposition that by 13 August he had captured the entire island, much to the delight of the Puerto Ricans, who welcomed the American troops with open arms.

Since 24 April Spain had lost two battle fleets, 23,000 troops, Santiago, Manila, and Puerto Rico. Now Spain felt that it was time to stop fighting and attempt to regain at the bargaining table what was being lost on the battlefields. In this she was disappointed. In the Far East the United States took from Spain both the Philippines and Guam in the Marianas. In the Caribbean the United States

took Puerto Rico and insisted that Cuba be given her independence (although the United States would control Cuban foreign affairs until 1934). The ensuing Treaty of Paris ratified these American gains and calamitous Spanish losses. For America it had indeed been a 'splendid little war.'

But if Spain was forced to acquiesce, Emilio Aquinaldo and his Filipino insurgents were by no means ready to accept the decisions of Paris regarding their country. They had fought for Philippine independence, not for American domination. Clashing first with Army units outside Manila in February 1899, the 40,000 rebels on the main island of Luzon forced the army to carry out extensive campaigns against them. The Filipinos made good use of their knowledge of the jungle, and even though they were handicapped by primitive weapons, their hit-and-run raids were very successful. By the summer of 1899 over 35,000 Army troops were engaged in battles against the Filipinos, and not until fall was the insurgents' power broken on Luzon. Fighting on the other islands did not finally come to an end until 1902.

Left: Contrary to what many people believe, the taking of San Juan Hill was *not* the war's decisive battle.
Left below: The US naval victory at Santiago led to Spain's surrender.
Below: After defeating Spain in the Philippines, the US was obliged to go on fighting Filipino insurgents.

Even while this unfortunate conflict between the Filipinos and the Army was taking place, the American government was taking steps to introduce governmental, medical, educational and economic reforms that would revolutionize life in the islands. Self-government was gradually introduced, and within two decades the archipelago was well along the road to the full independence that was finally granted at the end of World War II. Thus the Philippines and the United States began their formal association in mutual warfare and ended it in friendship and respect.

The Boxer Rebellion

A clear sign of America's new interest in the Far East was Secretary of State John Hay's announcement, in September 1899, of an 'Open Door' policy, whereby the United States sought to guarantee equal trading rights in China for the occidental powers and Japan. Hay subsequently insisted publicly that all the major powers interested in securing privileges in China had agreed that China's territorial integrity would be respected, that is, that China would not be dismembered by the great powers. Yet though the United States perceived that her own interests would be best served by upholding China's national integrity, events would soon force the Americans to behave in a contrary way and resort to armed intervention.

Resentful of Western incursions upon their sovereignty (Britain, Russia, France, Portugal, Japan, and Germany had all made claims to parts of China), nationalistic Chinese calling themselves the Fists of Righteous Harmony, with the tacit approval of the Manchu Dowager Empress, Tzu Hsi, began attacks on all foreigners. Leaving a trail of the blood of foreign missionaries and their Christian converts, the 'Boxers,' as the Westerners called them, soon swept the countryside of 'foreign devils' and placed the foreign legations in the capital of Peking under siege. Defending the 500 foreigners and 3000 Chinese Christians in the Legation Quarter were only about 450 troops assigned to the foreign legations. The call for outside help went out as 140,000 angry Boxers and Chinese imperial troops began to attack the legations' defenses.

Although the United States reiterated its determination not to assist in the dismemberment of China under the pretext of protecting the foreign nationals, it nevertheless dispatched naval units and Marines to assist in

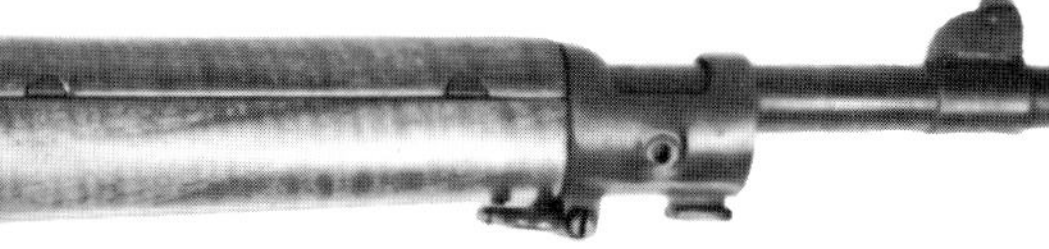

The 1903 Springfield rifle replaced the Krag. As late as World War II it was still the preferred sniper's gun.
Right: Poor sanitation caused more US Army deaths in Cuba, the Philippines and China than did enemy action.
Below: Boxers and Marines battle in Peking during the 1900 Rebellion.

taking the port city of Tientsin and attempting to break through to Peking. When this small expedition of 2000 men failed (the Chinese stopped the relief force before Peking and cut them off from the rear) the western powers realized that a more sizeable expedition was necessary. Accordingly, President McKinley dispatched the 9th Infantry, the 14th Infantry, and some artillery units from the Philippines to China, while other units were transported directly from the United States. Eventually some 2500 soldiers and Marines, under Major General Adna R Chaffee, were assembled and took part in the re-seizure of Tientsin on 14 July 1900.

These American soldiers represented about 10 percent of a 25,000-man army of British, French, Russian, German, Austrian, Italian, and Japanese troops. This 'International Relief Force' began the 80-mile march on Peking in early August to lift the Boxers' siege and rescue the nationals in the legation compound. American soldiers, especially the 14th Infantry and the 5th Artillery, played key roles in the fighting in and around Peking, and by 15 August the expeditionary forces had seized the heart of the capital and relieved the beleaguered foreign nationals and Chinese Christians from their 55-day siege. The Boxers had been decisively defeated, though mopping-up operations in the provinces continued for months.

American troops played little part in these latter operations, since McKinley was anxious to get the soldiers back to the Philippines. Nor were many Americans involved in the international army of occupation that stayed in north China until the Boxer Protocol had been signed and outside forces were withdrawn in September 1901. Nevertheless, under the Protocol signed by the Dowager Empress, all the powers were allowed to maintain a fortified legation area in Peking, and a small American contingent remained in China until 1938 carrying out these duties. The victorious powers also imposed a reparations agreement on China that cost the weakened country $333 million. Of this total the United States received only $25 million and used the money solely to educate Chinese youths both in China and in the United States.

The Boxer Expedition was hardly a major chapter in the history of the nation or of the Army, but it clearly revealed the new role the United States was undertaking in the world, since for the first time the nation had taken part in an international military operation beyond its borders. If America's armed forces were to be committed internationally, they would have to be changed and modernized in order to fulfill their new responsibilities.

Modernization and Reorganization

If the Spanish-American War had reassured the Navy about its combat-readiness, the war had certainly not done the same for the Army. Among the many deficiencies the war had revealed were several that related to weaponry. Accordingly, in 1903 the Army began to replace its old Krag rifles with the improved bolt-action Springfield M1903 rifle, a .30-calibre five-round weapon capable of high-velocity sustained fire. In 1911 it also replaced the .38-calibre revolver as the standard sidearm with the efficient and brutally powerful .45-calibre seven-round Colt automatic pistol. The Army also adopted the M1902 3-inch gun as its standard field artillery piece, and it upgraded its coastal defense forces not only with improved installations but also by equipping its fortifications with new 16-inch rifled guns for greater range and accuracy. By this time, and none

too soon, the Army was well along in replacing black powder with smokeless for all its weapons.

The Army also moved toward use of the airplane, first by establishing an Aeronautical Division within the Signal Corps in 1908 and then, in 1914, by establishing a separate Aviation Section in the Signal Corps. Even so, thanks to Congressional parsimony, by the time the Army entered World War I in 1917 it still lagged far behind the other belligerents in planes, pilots, organization, and combat doctrine.

The Army was also slow in adopting a modern machine gun to replace the Gatling. John Moses Browning had patented a recoil-operated machine gun as early as 1901 and formally offered it to the Army in 1910. But the Army, not realizing the supreme importance

Left: The Army was still being called into labor disputes, as at this IWW-led 1912 strike in Lawrence, Mass.
Below: Five years after this Wright Brothers' biplane first flew the US Army's Signal Corps established its new Aeronautical Division. In 1909 it acquired 'Aeroplane No 1'.

of this new class of weapon, took no action. In fact, the Army was not to get a modern machine gun until 1917, well after its crucial role in battle had been made manifest to all.

Perhaps more important to the modernization of the Army during this period was the work of fundamental reorganization of the service's high command structure. This was begun by Secretary of War Elihu Root after a special commission under Grenville M Dodge had revealed glaring deficiencies in administration and supply in the late war with Spain. Immediately upon being appointed to his post in 1899, Root began to move with determination toward basic reform in the Army's command structure. The heart of the 'Root reforms' was attained in 1903, when Congress approved creation of the office of a Chief of Staff who was to be responsible to the president, through the Secretary of War, for all Army functions. The position of Commanding General, with its built-in and necessary separation from the Secretary of War, was discarded. Previously the Commanding General had been responsible for the troops, while the Secretary of War had been responsible for administration of the Army. Now the administrative bureau chiefs would no longer be independent of the chief field officer in the Army. An important adjunct to the Chief of Staff's powers was the creation of a General Staff for overall planning, although just how influential this body might be would become clear only after the energetic Major General Leonard Wood was appointed Chief of Staff in 1912.

HARPER'S WEEKLY

EDITED BY GEORGE HARVEY

Guernsey Moore

The Army dress uniform, as shown on a *Harper's Weekly* cover of 1909. Képis had by now given way to visored caps.

Reform also came to the Army with the establishment of more special schools for further and more effective training of officers. Included were the Army War College (1900) and a General Staff and Service College at Leavenworth, Kansas (1901), as well as schools in coast artillery, cavalry and field artillery, medicine, engineering, and signals.

Secretary Root also tried to dispel some of the confusion about the roles of the Army, the National Guard and the volunteers. Spurred by military reformers, Congress in 1903 passed the Dick Act which authorized two separate militia groups. The organized militia (National Guard), under both state and federal controls, would receive federal funds by accepting Army standards for officers and enlisted men, organizing along Army lines, meeting for drill at least twice a month, and prescribing summer camp for its enrollees. In emergencies the Guard could be called up for nine months' service, although the geographic limitation – that Guard units could not serve outside the United States – remained. The reserve, or unorganized mili-

Left: Francisco 'Pancho' Villa, the Mexican rebel leader who goaded the US into sending the Army into Mexico.
Above: Villa's pursuer, Gen. John J Pershing. To the right, General Leonard Wood, the first great Army Chief of Staff.
Far right: Pershing's personal aide in 1916 was George S Patton.

tia, consisted of all males ages 18 to 45 who were not enrolled but could be called for federal or state service when needed.

Subsequent legislation in 1908 and 1914 allowed the president to assign units of the Guard to foreign service and to appoint all Guard officers while the Guard was in federal service. Army reformers then turned to the idea of organized reserves as a workable alternative to the Guard, and the Reserve Act of 1912 allowed regulars to move into federal reserve units to shorten their terms of active service. To be sure, this alternative held little attraction at the time, although it would later become an important component of the Army, and in 1914 only 16 enlisted men were in the federal reserve. Thus, although significant steps had been taken, the essential problem of how to create an adequate reserve force to supplement the 75,000 regular Army officers and enlisted men in case of war emergencies still remained.

Latin American Interventions

Ever since the end of the Spanish-American War the Army's involvement in hemispheric affairs had been growing. It had taken the lead in Cuba in re-establishing government and in eradicating disease before its occupation duties ended in 1902. It subsequently returned to Cuba between 1906 and 1909, in the form of the 5000-man 'Army of Cuban Pacification,' to re-establish law and order when rebellion again swept the island. For the same reason it returned to the island in both 1912 and 1917.

The Army also took over the construction of the Panama Canal in 1907, under the inspired leadership of Colonel W Goethals. This came about as the result of a successful Panamanian revolution against Colombia in 1903 and a subsequent treaty with the United States which allowed the nation a ten-mile wide strip of land and the right to build the long-sought-after canal from the Atlantic to the Pacific Oceans. The new interoceanic canal was opened in 1914, a standing tribute to the Army Corps of Engineers.

Less glorious, but important for field experience, was the Army's role in the United States' difficulties with Mexico between 1911 and 1916. As revolutionary movements rocked northern Mexico in 1911, President William Howard Taft ordered the Army to assemble three brigades at San Antonio, Texas, in case trouble spilled across the border. The Army discovered to its horror that it took six months to assemble 13,000 officers and men at that location. This assemblage was not called into action, but the difficulties in mobilization compelled the Army to make a number of changes in its plans for bringing its troops together.

Then, in 1914, President Woodrow Wilson attempted to aid the enemies of the government in Mexico City by allowing them to buy arms in the United States. When this led to a minor incident at the Gulf port of Tampico, Wilson imposed a naval blockade on part of the Mexican coast. When a German freighter subsequently approached the port of Veracruz with ammunition destined for the

government of President Victoriano Huerta, Wilson ordered that the port be seized. In April 1914 8000 US soldiers and Marines carried out his orders and captured Veracruz. The major Latin American powers of Argentina, Brazil, and Chile stepped in to mediate the dispute, and the troops were withdrawn.

Two years later, in order to goad the United States into invading Mexico again so that he could 'save' the country and seize power, Francisco ('Pancho') Villa, a rebel opposing the government of President Venustiano Carranza, conducted a series of raids across the border into New Mexico and Texas. President Wilson duly ordered the Army, under Brigadier General John J ('Black Jack') Pershing, into Mexico in March 1916 to 'assist' the Mexican government in running down Villa. This Army of 10,000 men never caught up with Villa, but it became embroiled in a number of clashes with Carranza's Mexican army instead. With the Army unable to catch Villa and the clashes with the Mexican army becoming a sizeable embarrassment to the United States, Wilson finally ordered the Army out of Mexico early 1917. If the 'punitive expedition' in Mexico had added no laurels to the reputation either of the nation or the Army, at least it revealed some serious weaknesses in the Army's capacity to wage war. And it was important for the Army to understand these weaknesses, for it would shortly be called upon to wage a very large war indeed.

World War I

World War I was at first only Europe's war. It was begun in 1914 almost exclusively for the narrow national interests of the major powers involved: Britain, France, Germany, Austria-Hungary, and Russia. None was solely guilty of starting the war; none was innocent of provocative acts or of accepting the war as a means of striking out at its national competitors for territory, trade, and economic dominance. But all the well-developed war plans of the major combatants promising quick victory proved to be faulty in execution. The war settled down into a bloody stalemate on France's eastern border (the 'Western Front') and on Germany's and Austria-Hungary's borders with Russia (the 'Eastern Front'). Neither the Central Powers (Germany, Austria-Hungary and Turkey) nor the

America's reluctance to be drawn into the war in Europe is well expressed in this 1915 political cartoon. Yet well before 1917 the nation had begun to shift over to a war footing.

Allies (Great Britain, France, Russia, and – later – Italy) were strong enough to win. But neither side was weak enough to lose. All sides had underestimated the effectiveness of the machine gun as a defensive weapon capable of neutralizing infantry power as no weapon had ever done before, and hundreds of thousands of young men were uselessly fed into the maw of death.

Unable to force a decision on the Western Front, Britain sought to bring Germany to her knees by imposing a stringent naval blockade. Germany was determined to break the blockade and, in turn, to cut Britain off from outside aid by using the only weapon available to her, the U-boat. When use of the U-boat led the German navy into a number of sinkings of neutral vessels, and of the British liner *Lusitania* in May 1915, the outcry from America was so great that Germany promised to curb her submarine warfare. But in early 1917, with every indication present that Russia would soon be forced out of the war by internal revolution against Czar Nicholas II (thus collapsing the Eastern Front), and with low morale and even mutinies in the French and British armies working in its favor, the German government decided that the time was ripe for breaking the stalemate on the Western Front both by massive attacks there and by cutting off Britain completely from outside aid. This meant a resumption of unrestricted submarine warfare by Germany and probably open intervention by the United States. But Kaiser Wilhelm II and his advisors were willing to take the risk, believing that the issue would be settled in their favor before the United States could send enough troops to Europe to save their French

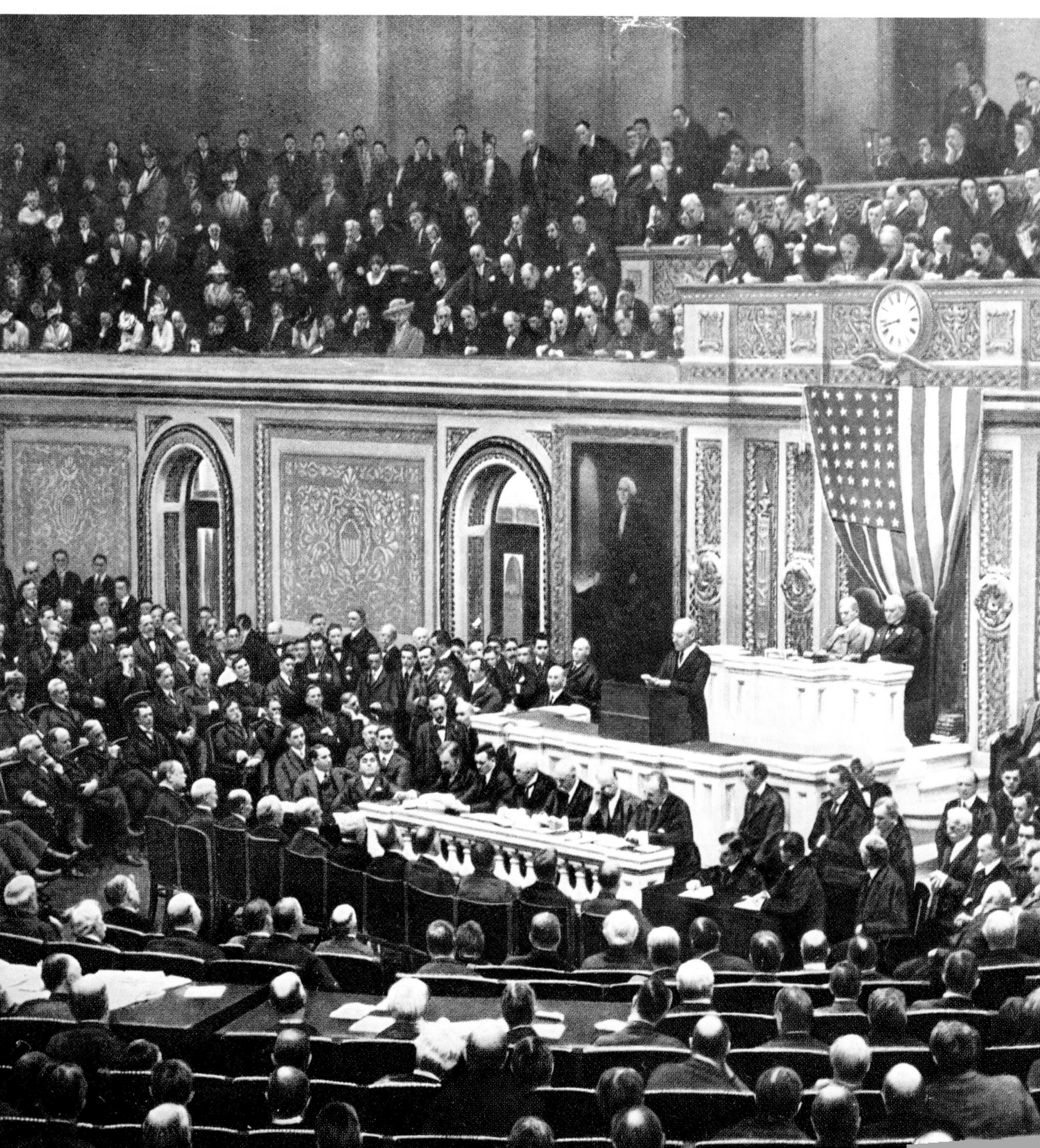

and British allies. In February 1917 Germany made its declaration of unrestricted submarine warfare, and on 6 April the United States went to war against Germany.

But even while avoiding involvement in the European war for three years, the United States had taken important steps toward in-

Right: Once America entered the war, bellicose patriotism ran high.
Below: A wave of German torpedoings of US ships in 1917 caused Congress finally to declare war on 2 April.

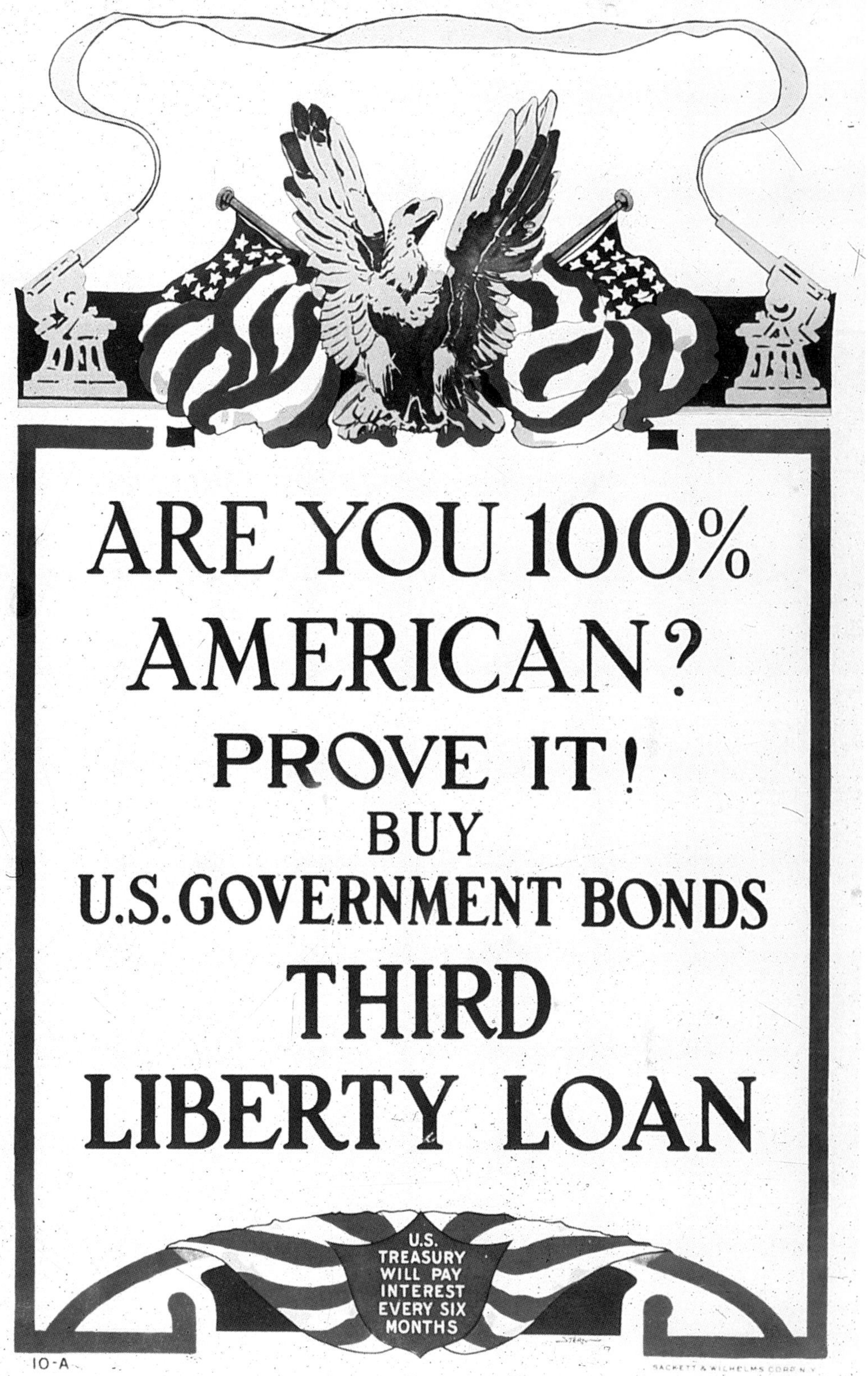

ARE YOU 100%
AMERICAN?
PROVE IT!
BUY
U.S. GOVERNMENT BONDS
THIRD
LIBERTY LOAN

U.S.
TREASURY
WILL PAY
INTEREST
EVERY SIX
MONTHS

10-A

volvement in future conflicts. Of special significance was the National Defense Act of 1916, an ambiguous legislative and political compromise that nonetheless was a crucial step in the US Army's preparation for World War I. Rejecting the 'expansible' army concept of a regular nucleus expandable with volunteers, the legislation of 1916 called for strengthening the regular Army within five years to 175,000 men, with 300,000 the goal in wartime. It also provided for a federally-funded and federally-organized National Guard of 400,000 men under both state and federal controls and subject to call by the commander in chief. Additionally, it provided for an officer reserve corps and another for enlisted men, and for a volunteer army in case of war. Finally, the Reserve Officers' Training Corps (ROTC) program, an extension of the Gettysburg and Plattsburg training programs, in which businessmen and college students had participated in officer training programs on a voluntary basis, was also established by the act. In sum, this act not only provided the basic framework for military recruitment and organization during World War I, but also formed the framework for Army forces during the remainder of the century. Regulars, Guardsmen, reservists, and volunteers (including draftees) would henceforth be part of the Army in wartime, whatever the encumbrances of the system.

When the USA entered the war in April 1917 the Army was hardly ready for instant action. Including those Guardsmen in federal service on the Mexican border, it numbered slightly more than 200,000, with another 100,000 Guardsmen still in state service. A small and under-trained contingent, the 1st Infantry Division, under the commander of the American Expeditionary Force, General Pershing, was sent to France in June as a token of American support for her allies, while at home the Army was frantically attempting to expand to necessary strength and to train recruits to battlefield standards. Manpower came from the Guard and the reserves, from volunteers, and from draftees called up under the Selective Service Act of May 1917. Unlike its Civil War predecessors, this draft law made no provisions for substitutes and bounties and mandated that those drafted would serve the duration of the war. Administration of the draft, and the onerous job of calling up individuals for service or granting them occupational exemptions, was vested in local citizen boards. Men

Above: Map of Belleau Wood.
Left and below: Two examples of the foreign equipment used by America in the war: a Renault FT-17 tank and the SPAD 13 fighter plane flown by Eddie Rickenbacker.

Authors of the 1918 German offensive: Field Marshal von Hindenburg (*left*) and General Ludendorff.

between the ages of 21 and 30 (later 18 and 45) were subject to this 'selective service.' The act also increased the regular Army strength to 286,000, National Guard strength to 450,000, and volunteer strength to a million. These numbers were steadily raised as the necessities of war dictated, and before the war ended the Army's peak strength rose to 3.6 million men in 62 divisions.

Training for this rapidly-expanding force through the year and a half of war was a major problem, with inadequate facilities and too few training personnel. Shortages of weapons forced the Army to supplement its Springfields with British Lee-Enfield rifles; to accept the Allies' machine guns because the Browning machine gun only reached full production in mid-1918; to use upwards of 2200 British and French artillery pieces, since only 100 of American manufacture were available for the battlefields; and to employ French tanks and Allied planes almost exclusively. Indeed, some of this foreign equipment would continue in service in the US Army for several years after the end of the fighting in Europe.

The wartime emergency also forced a change in the army's organization, resulting in the further subjugation of the bureau chiefs to the Chief of Staff. Largely responsible for these changes were Secretary of War Newton D Baker and General Peyton C March, Chief of Staff after March 1918. Armed with the legislative authority and with the backing of Baker, March insisted that all bureau chiefs were subordinate to the General Staff and could report to the Secretary of War only through him. March also reorganized and strengthened the personnel and organization of the General Staff so that at long last it became what Elihu Root had envisioned, a true general staff with real authority over the Army. Unfortunately for the war effort, General Pershing had been sent to Europe with what he understood to be almost total authority over his troops, and he steadfastly resisted March's authority. Only when Pershing returned to take over March's position after the war would 'Black Jack' acquiesce in final authority being given to the Chief of Staff.

As General Pershing led his troops to France he was ever mindful of fact that he had been ordered to maintain his troops as a 'separate and distinct component' of Allied forces, and he insisted on this to his British and French counterparts, General Sir Douglas Haig and General Henri Philippe Pétain. He also insisted that his troops undergo further training before being committed to battle. Accordingly, he chose as the American sector of the Western Front the area of Lorraine between the Argonne Forest and the Vosges Mountains southeast of Paris. This was to the right of the French sector in the middle, the British occupying the northernmost sector of the long line. In this 'quiet' area, Pershing could complete the training of his men without too much danger of a German attack from across the line, even though the enemy commanded the St. Mihiel salient protruding into the American positions.

Pershing demanded a training period of at least six months, much to the consternation of the British and French, who wanted the American troops in the line as soon as possible. As Pershing saw it, his men had to be proficient not only in trench warfare, with such weapons as the machine gun, the hand grenade, and the mortar, but also had to master the use of the rifle and bayonet in preparation for the day when the American 'doughboys' would go on the offensive.

Recognizing that the British and French armies, as well as their own, were approaching exhaustion in early 1918 and that the US Army might well swing the balance against

Pershing decorating Colonel Douglas MacArthur for bravery on the Chateau Thierry front. MacArthur was then the commander of the famous 42nd, or 'Rainbow,' Division.

them when it got to full strength on the Western Front, the German army commanders, Generals Paul von Hindenburg and Erich von Ludendorff, decided that they had to strike a fatal blow at their enemies before it was too late. Accordingly, they prepared a massive 3.5 million-man offensive against the British and French on the Western Front. The attack was launched on 21 March 1918 along a 50-mile front against the British on the north, and in the ensuing battle the Germans severely strained, but could not break, the Allied line, despite giving and receiving horrible casualty totals. Ludendorff struck again in April, establishing a salient against the British in Flanders, on the Lys River. Before his final blow at the British in Belgium, Ludendorff planned a diversionary attack on the French northeast of Paris in an area known as the Chemin des Dames. To his own surprise, his 27 May attack knifed through the French lines, and within three days he was at the Marne River at Chateau-Thierry, less than 50 miles from Paris, the deepest penetration since August 1914.

Rushed to the aid of the French were two divisions of American soldiers and Marines, sent by Pershing at the request of Marshal Ferdinand Foch and placed in the line to stop the German offensive. Here at Chateau-Thierry, the green American troops showed great coolness under fire and played a major part in stopping the Germans. (One officer who particularly distinguished himself was Colonel Douglas MacArthur of the 42nd, or Rainbow, Division.) The Americans then went on the offensive in Belleau Wood and acquitted themselves equally well. When Ludendorff made his last offensive efforts to break the Allied lines in June and July, American troops again played a stellar role in stopping him. By that time, ten American divisions were on the line, with 250,000 arriving each month, and the British and French positions were still intact. Ludendorff had lost his race to defeat the enemy before American numbers began to play their role on the Western Front.

Having stopped the German drive, the Allies quickly went over to the offensive. Indeed, planning was underway even before the German offensives had been halted. The result was one of the most dramatic turnarounds in military history. Within days the defender became the attacker. Foch, as overall Allied commander, had two grand objectives: to eliminate the three salients (against the British on the north, the French in the middle, and the Americans in the south) and then drive on the Germans so rapidly that they would have to flee back into Germany, abandoning their supplies and thus finding themselves in no position to continue the war into 1919.

His first attack – to clear the Marne salient – was made by the French, aided by eight American divisions. Begun on 18 July, this so-called Aisne-Marne Offensive had completely obliterated the Marne salient by 6 August. The second offensive, in the north, the Somme offensive against the Amiens salient, was a French-British affair aided by one American division. It, too, was also a smashing success, with the British using 400 tanks in the first massed tank offensive in military history. The third offensive was carried out by the Americans against the St. Mihiel salient in the south, beginning on 12 September. Some 550,000 troops, aided by 260 tanks under Lieutenant Colonel George S Patton, Jr and 1500 planes controlled by Colonel William ('Billy') Mitchell, pushed east to destroy this salient in four days. The Americans were then directed to move north, keeping the Meuse River on their right and the rugged Argonne Forest on their left. Their new objective was to capture the rail junction of Aulnoye and Mézières so as to cut off the German retreat, while the British moved south toward the Americans in a giant

The Chateau Thierry battles included episodes of fierce street fighting.

Far larger than any previous battle in US history was the great 47-day fight for the Argonne Forest.

pincer movement to trap the Germans and the French put pressure on the center of the line. A total of 220 Allied divisions took part in this triple offensive.

The plan called for the Americans to make a giant shift, from facing east for the St. Mihiel offensive to turning north for the 'Meuse-Argonne offensive,' in a space of only ten days. They had to be in position at Verdun, 50 miles away, when the offensive began on 26 September. This shifting of 600,000 men, with all their supplies and equipment, was carried out successfully, thanks in large measure to Colonel George C Marshall of Pershing's staff, and the offensive jumped off on time. In the drive across the 24-mile front (which was gradually expanded to 90 miles as the troops penetrated the German defenses) the Americans eventually used 1.25 million troops (larger than any single American Army in any previous war) on a front far wider than had ever been attempted in any previous American conflict. The rugged hand-to-hand battle through the dense woods and choked streams of the Argonne went on for 47 days before the three German defensive lines were penetrated.

Although the American offensive was slowed by rain, mud, and logistical jams and foul-ups, once the Argonne Forest was cleared on 10 October the Americans continued to drive towards the Meuse River crossings and the key villages with their valuable railheads. The fighting here produced a national hero, in the person of Pfc Alvin C York, who killed 25 Germans and captured 132 more in a single engagement. By 5 November the Americans had crossed the Meuse, the villages of Aulnoye and Mézières having fallen to the British and the French in the meantime, and were speeding toward Sedan on the French-German border.

By now the entire German defensive position along the Western Front was collapsing. Faced with revolution both at home and in the military, the German government of Kaiser Wilhelm fell, and the new republican government asked for surrender terms. On 11 November 1918, at 1100 (in the eleventh month, on the eleventh day, at the eleventh hour), the war ended. The US Army, along with the Navy and Marines, had played a significant part in the Allied victory. After much fumbling during the early months of the war, the Americans had fought with determination, skill, and great courage and made of their Army a world-class war machine.

Compared to British losses of 947,000 men, French losses of 1.4 million, Russian losses of 1.7 million, German losses of 1.8 million and Austria-Hungarian losses of 1.2 million, the American casualty list of 50,280 killed and 200,000 wounded had not been great. But

The surrender of the German fleet in 1918, as seen from a US ship. World War I forever ended Germany's hopes of becoming a great naval power.

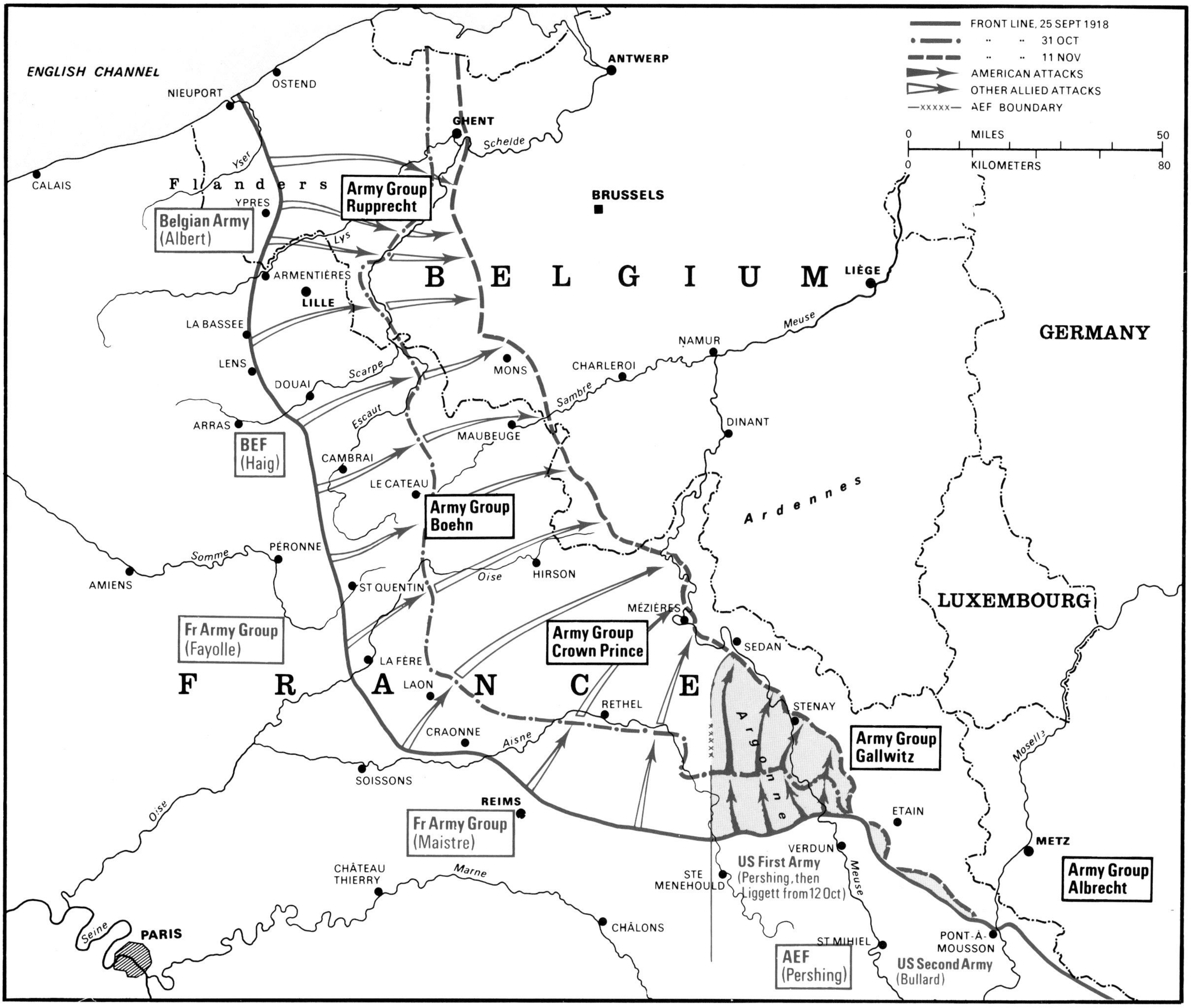

Above: Map of the last allied offensive in 1918. The US Army had captured St Mihiel on 12 September. By 10 October they were through the Argonne and a month later were over the Meuse.
Right: A US machine gun emplacement. The weapon is a French Hotchkiss 8mm, typical of the foreign equipment in US service.

American intervention had nevertheless been crucial to victory.

For the first time the American military had been called upon to play a major role in a great war fought far beyond its borders. If its military success was subsequently squandered by diplomatic failure, the laurels the Army won on the battlefields of France were honestly gained, and the lessons it learned about modern technological warfare – including the use of automatic weapons, armor, artillery, and the airplane – would shape its development in the decades to come. The US Army had come a long way since 1898 and its clumsy attempts to fight a war against weakened Spain. Within two more decades it would face a vastly greater challenge, this time on a planetary scale.

A famous image of World War II: St Paul's during the Blitz.

WORLD WAR II IN EUROPE: 1939-1945

With the Armistice of November 1918 the demand to 'bring the boys home' was felt in all parts of the nation. Demobilization began almost immediately, despite the Army's fervent but futile plea for a regular force of 600,000 men and a three-month universal military training (UMT) program to assure an adequate strength in the event of future war. But with the defeat of Germany, and no perceived threat from any other front, such requests were futile. America, in the words of President Warren Harding, who succeeded Woodrow Wilson, wanted 'normalcy,' not involvements. Within a year after the end of the war over three million men had been demobilized, and the Army stood at only 19,000 officers and 205,000 enlisted men. It was a regular volunteer force again.

Some of the US troops in Europe at the end of the war were kept on for occupation duty in Germany and Austria, but the last of these had been withdrawn by January 1923. Meanwhile, American troops had joined with those of other nations in trying to aid pro-Allied and anti-Bolshevik 'White' forces in Russia during the civil war that broke out after the fall of the Romanov dynasty and the subsequent seizure of power by Nikolai Lenin's Bolsheviks in November 1917. At Murmansk-Archangel, in northern Russia, 5000 American soldiers under British command joined other Allied troops in aiding the White Armies against the Red armies between August 1918 and June 1919. A second American-Allied force moved into Russia's Far Eastern regions via Vladivostock in August 1918 and remained until April 1920. Here the 10,000 American servicemen and their Allied counterparts, like their comrades in northern Russia, were unsuccessful in helping to defeat the Red Armies, brilliantly led by Leon Trotsky. More substantial Allied intervention on behalf of the anti-Bolsheviks might have led to the Communists' defeat, but the exhausted Western forces, reflecting the war-weary spirit of the time, had little stomach for further fighting anywhere after the bloodletting of the Western Front. Peace seemed more important than principle, and the boys came home, leaving Russia to her fate.

The Peacetime Army

A fundamental reorganization of the Army in the aftermath of the war was embodied in the National Defense Act of 1920, adopted by

Congress after months of careful study and necessary compromise. The act established the Army of the United States as the basic land component of the nation's military forces, this Army to consist of three elements: the regular Army, the National Guard, and the officer and enlisted reserve forces. This scheme would assure a small professional force of regulars for emergencies and for on-line training of the other components, plus a massive force ready for call-up in the event of greater conflicts. The regular Army was authorized an enlisted strength of 280,000 men and an officer strength of 17,000, although the actual numbers in any year would be regulated by the appropriations of Congress. The Guard units were allowed a strength of 436,000, although they averaged only about 180,000 active Guardsmen during the interwar years. Few men enlisted in the reserves at the non-commissioned ranks, but some 100,000 officers were enrolled as reserve officers, most coming from ROTC or CMTC (Citizens' Military Training Camp) programs (the latter consisting of four years of summer camp training for prospective officers).

Practice was less impressive than theory. Thanks to limited funds, the regular Army numbered only 12,000 officers and 125,000 enlisted men by 1922; it remained at about that level until the possibility of conflict in the late 1930s forced an expansion in the size of the Army. But the Army did undertake some useful reorganization during this period. In addition to its existing major branches of infantry and artillery, it added three new branches: the Air Service, the Chemical Warfare Service, and the Finance Department, though the embryonic tank corps that had evolved during World War I was absorbed by the infantry. The position of Chief of Staff was strengthened when Pershing came to that office in 1921, and the General Staff was reorganized by him into five divisions: personnel, intelligence, training and operations, supply, and war plans (the last-named for long-range strategic planning). Training continued in the service's 31 special branch schools, while the command and General Staff School at Leavenworth (the old General Staff and Service College, renamed in 1928), the new Army War College, and the Army Industrial College provided capstone training for the Army's highest officers.

The creation of the Air Corps was particularly significant. Its foremost champion was Brigadier General William ('Billy') Mitchell. Mitchell, along with General Sir Hugh Trenchard of the Royal Air Force and Italy's General Guilio Douhet, was an untiring exponent of air power, believing that it alone would win or lose future wars. Mitchell attempted to prove this thesis by challenging the Navy to test the resistance of ships to aerial bombardment. The Navy had already been quietly examining this question, but now it was forced by Mitchell's open garnering of publicity to allow the Army Air Service to join in the testing. In celebrated bombing experiments in 1921 off the Virginia Capes,

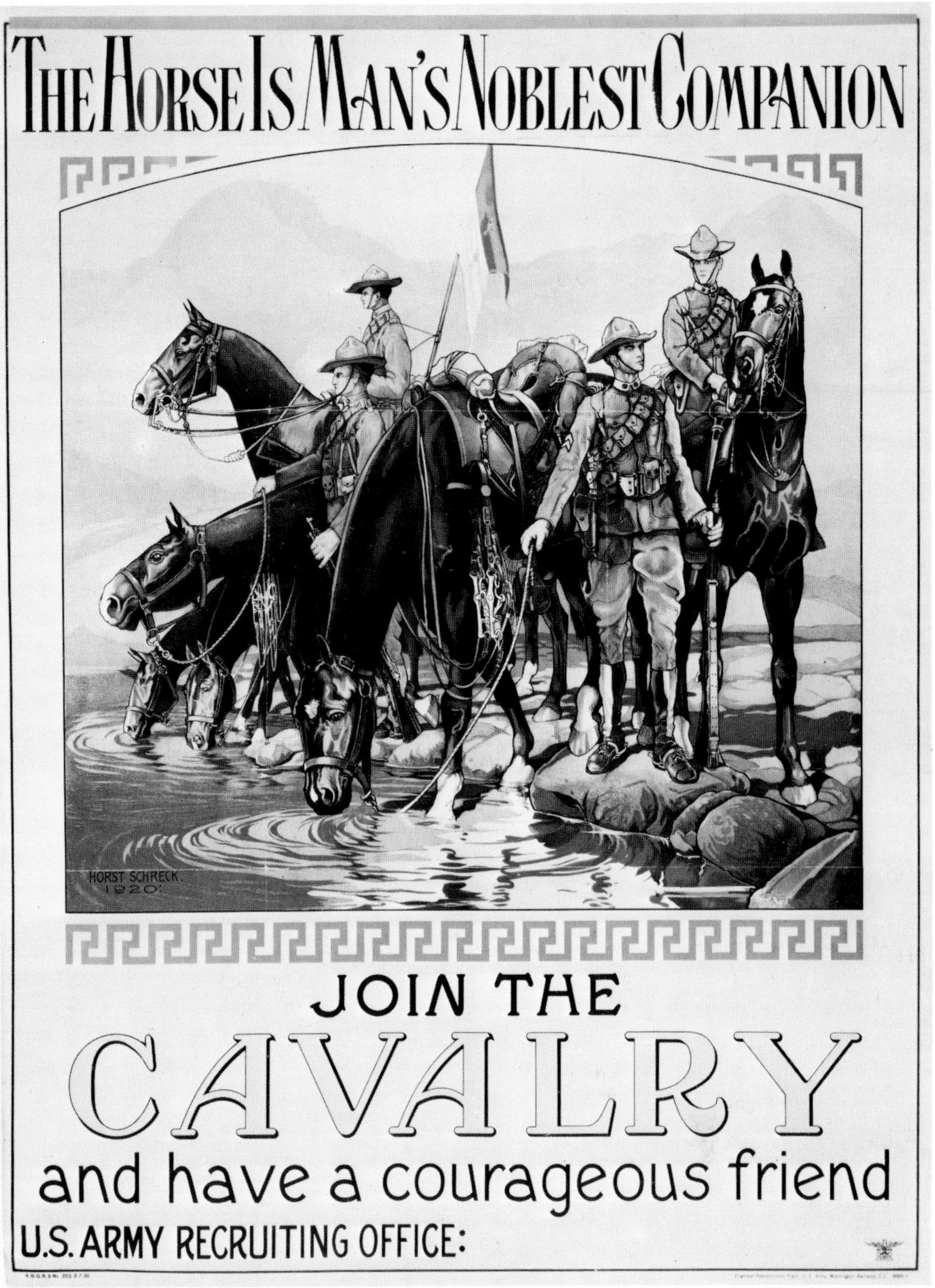

US military posture in the immediate post-war years was confused. Despite continuing foreign commitments, as in Russia (*below*), the Army was cut drastically and had a hard time in attracting recruits (*right*). At the same time, prophets such as General Billy Mitchell (*top left*), advocate of airpower, were vainly warning of basic changes in military technology. Mitchell's famous court martial did not, however, result solely from an opposition to his ideas. His conduct probably was, as charged, insubordinate.

THE HORSE IS MAN'S NOBLEST COMPANION
HORST SCHRECK. 1920.
JOIN THE
CAVALRY
and have a courageous friend
U.S. ARMY RECRUITING OFFICE:

Rapid progress in tank design between the wars fostered development of anti-tank guns: here, a wartime 57mm gun.

Mitchell's Air Service pilots dropped bombs on an old German battleship, the *Ostfriesland*, and sank it. While this success was by no means a valid indication of a naval vessel's ability to withstand aerial bombardment (the *Ostfriesland* was at anchor and unmanned), Mitchell made the most of the Air Service's 'victory' over the surface navy in his comments to the press.

Mitchell's penchant for notoriety hardened the opposition within the military to his extreme position. Chief of Staff Pershing named Major General Mason M Patrick as head of the Air Service in order to curb Mitchell's runaway enthusiasm. Patrick and many others in the Army were air power devotees, but they hardly agreed with Mitchell that an independent air service was necessary or that air power had made all other military power obsolete. Patrick was perfectly willing to accept the Air Service's subordination to ground commanders, but Mitchell was not, and he said so publicly. The result was Mitchell's court martial for insubordination; when convicted, he resigned from the Army in 1926.

In the meantime, however, a special board, appointed by President Calvin Coolidge and chaired by Dwight D Morrow, upheld continued development of air power. In 1926 the Air Corps Act gave the Army Air Corps full and equal status with the other branches of the Army and equal access to the Chief of Staff. It also provided for 17,000 officers and men and 1800 airplanes. Army air power was off and winging by 1927 and continued to develop and expand in the crucial 1930s.

The Army's development of armored fight-

The Army's first 'modern' bomber, the 213 mph all-metal Martin B-10, joined the Air Corps in 1934.

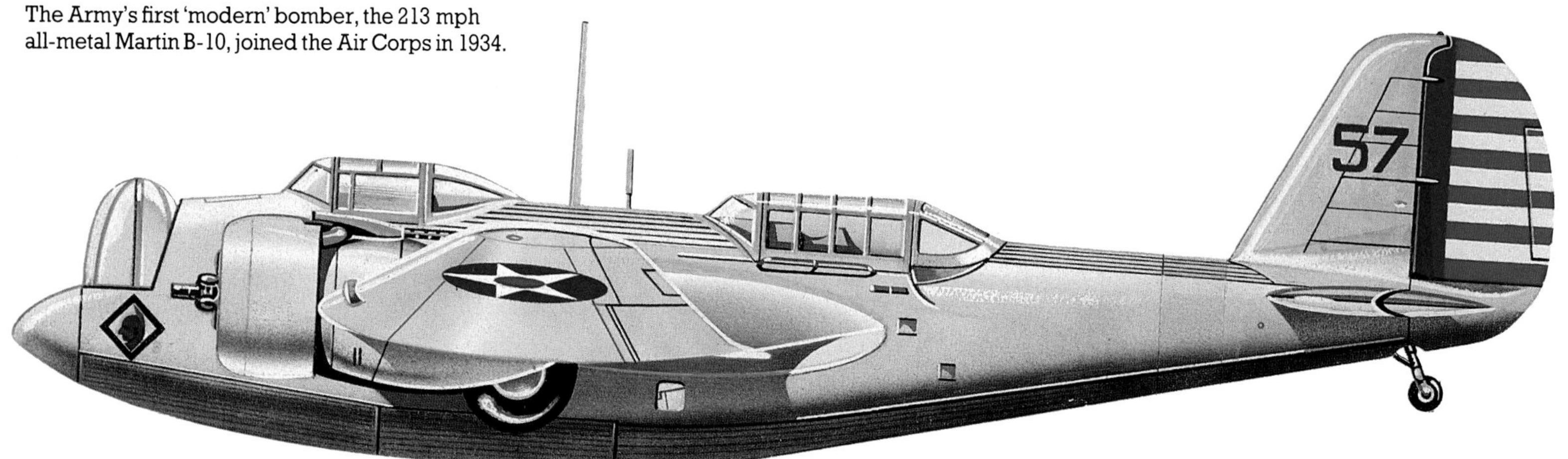

George Patton called the 1935 Garand semi-automatic rifle 'the greatest battle implement ever devised.'

ing vehicles during these same years was considerably less successful. By 1920 the Tank Corps of 5000 vehicles and 20,000 men of World War I had almost disappeared, with only 2600 men and some 700 tanks in the Army's arsenal. In the ensuing years the Tank Corps was, as we have seen, disbanded, and armored units were used only for support of infantry. Steps were taken to mechanize the Army's various ground forces in the 1930s, but little money was made available for the creation of special armored units. As a result, on the eve of World War II the US Army lagged behind its major European counterparts not only in the quantity of armor available, but also in the quality of its design. In 1940, for example, the principle US battle tank, the M3 Grant, still carried its main offensive armament in its hull, rather than in an independently traversable turret. Throughout the war the US armor strove mightily to make up for the developmental deficiencies of the 1930s, but the main wartime American tank, the M4 Sherman, never was the equal of the German Panthers and Tigers.

In other categories of weapons, the army fared better during the decade before the war. In 1936 the old Springfield rifle began to be replaced by the excellent .30-calibre gas-operated semi-automatic Garand M1. Since the end of World War I the standard automatic squad weapon had been the .30-calibre Browning Automatic Rifle, but by the early 1930s this somewhat unwieldy gun was being supplemented by the famous .45-calibre Thompson sub-machine gun, the 'Chicago piano' of gangster legend, with its impressive cycling rate of 800 rounds per minute. At about the same time the Army began receiving what were to be its standard mortars, the 81 mm M1 and the 60 mm M2. And at the end of the decade the Army added to its inventory several artillery pieces that would play significant roles in the coming war: the 37 mm M3 anti-tank gun (later to be supplanted by the more powerful 57 mm M1 AT gun, as well as by Bazookas and recoilless rifles); that all-purpose workhorse, the 105 mm M3 howitzer; and, for heavy support, the 155 mm Long Tom and the massive 8-inch howitzer.

The Air Corps made equally good technical progress. As early as 1934 it was receiving deliveries of a bomber as advanced as any in the world, the Martin B-10, an all-metal twin-engine monoplane with retractable landing gear. Two years later it got its first versions of the Boeing B-17, the 'Flying Fortress,' destined to become the most famous American heavy bomber of World War II. By 1937 it had begun to equip its fighter squadrons with aircraft of 'modern' design (*ie.* fast all-metal cantilever monoplanes with enclosed cockpits and retractable landing gear), and by the end of the decade it had acquired several types whose names would shortly become known throughout the world – among them, the Curtiss P-40 Tomahawk, the Bell P-39 Airacobra, and the Lockheed P-38 Lightning.

Indeed, the major problems of the inter-war Army always had less to do with quality than with quantity. For most of the period it remained a small force, incapable of playing any major role in the nation's foreign affairs. To be sure, Congress in 1935 authorized the Army to increase its regular enlisted strength

An M3 Grant medium tank. Pre-war US tank designs lagged behind those of Germany, Russia, England and France.

to 165,000 and in subsequent years progressively loosened its purse strings for the purchase of new equipment. Yet it was not until after war had actually broken out in Europe, in September 1939, that the government took steps to increase the Army's strength significantly above the 1935 levels, and it was not until 1940 that conscription was begun. As events were to prove, these actions were taken only just in time.

The Road to War

Neither during the self-indulgent 'Roaring Twenties' nor in the grim depression-ridden years of the early 1930s had the American people given much serious attention to the possibility of the nation's becoming involved in another war. Yet there was no want of ominous portents. Mussolini's militant Fascisti had seized power in Italy in 1922. Japan's government was falling increasingly under the influence of a military clique that made no secret of its expansionist ambitions. And, most menacing of all, in 1933 the sinister Adolf Hitler became the absolute leader of Germany.

In 1935 Hitler proceeded to remilitarize the Rhineland, despite the provisions of the Versailles treaty. The French and British were hesitant and unwilling to challenge him. That same year Mussolini's Italian Army invaded the east African nation of Ethiopia, easily routing its primitive defenders and meeting with no firm or meaningful resistance from the League of Nations or from the nations which had signed the Kellogg-Briand Pact of 1927 outlawing warfare forever. In 1937 Japan invaded China, serving notice that it would use military force to establish a Japanese Far Eastern empire. In 1938 Hitler carried out his annexation of Austria (a move outlawed by Versailles) in the face of only muted protest from the European democracies. In that same year he demanded and got the Sudetenland from Czechoslovakia, Britain and France acceding, despite the vehement objection of the Czechs over losing their only natural defense against expansionistic Germany. Then, despite, his promises not to do so, in March 1939 he seized the remainder of Czechoslovakia. It finally became clear to Europe's statesmen that Hitler could never be trusted, nor could he be restrained either by reason or diplomacy.

The most serious check to Hitler's ambitions, and hence the best hope of peace, lay in the fact that he still had the Soviet Union to challenge him in the east, for reigning over Russia was Joseph Stalin, the self-proclaimed implacable enemy of Nazism. Yet in August 1939 Germany and Russia signed a friendship pact providing for the division of Poland and for the Soviet right to expand into Finland and the Baltic countries. On 1 September 1939 the German armies invaded Poland. At long last the European democracies, allied to Poland, decided to go to war to stop Hitler and his Axis partners.

However strong the desires of the American people to isolate themselves from Europe's war, advances in military technology alone meant that isolation was now increasingly difficult to maintain. If any nation in the Western Hemisphere allowed an aggressor airbases or submarine bases from which to operate, or if he seized them by force, not only America's vital Panama Canal but also the continental United States itself would be within enemy striking range. When President Roosevelt, in late 1939, approved the military's strategic hemispheric defense plan called RAINBOW (each nation was give a color and each possible combination of enemies and allies was studied for possible American military reaction), America had already abandoned in fact the idea of 'fortress America,' whether it realized it or not.

When the European war began, on 1 September 1939, Roosevelt issued a declaration of American neutrality, as well as a declaration of limited national emergency. The latter allowed him to raise the numbers in the regular Army to 227,000 and in the Guard units to 235,000 to help ensure America's neutrality. But as the nation watched Hitler's war against his neighbors succeed beyond anyone's expectations, official neutrality became increasingly compromised. The government

sought to aid embattled England and France, and neutrality legislation was amended to permit them to buy munitions in America. These purchases were initially on a 'cash and carry' basis, but American loans were soon forthcoming, in the form of the Lend-Lease program of March 1941, that kept the nation's European friends afloat. Roosevelt went one step further in September 1940 by trading fifty old American four-stack destroyers to the British in return for long-term leases on eight British bases, one in Newfoundland and seven in the Caribbean. This gave England anti-submarine weapons she desperately needed and furnished Roosevelt with the argument that he was putting the US in a stronger defensive posture in the Americas. Less openly (as a matter of fact, very secretly), Roosevelt not only extended American naval patrols ever farther out into the Atlantic, but also ordered the Navy to surreptitiously aid the British in their war against German U-boats. America was in an undeclared naval war in the North Atlantic months before the official outbreak of hostilities in 1941.

As America inched closer and closer to all-out war, the US Army found itself mobilizing and reorganizing in order to meet the challenges facing it. Thanks to larger Congressional appropriations for manpower; to the calling up of the National Guard and reserves to federal service in 1941; and to the passage of the Selective Service and Training Act of 1940, the nation's first peacetime draft legislation, by mid-1941 the Army had 1.5 million officers and men in its ranks. The Army Air Forces was expanding rapidly, an Armored Force was belatedly created, and the other combat arms command (infantry, field artillery, coast artillery, cavalry, and antiaircraft and tank destroyers) were likewise expanding and being trained under the leadership of Chief of Staff General George C Marshall. By late 1941 the Army had 27 infantry, five armored, and two cavalry divisions, plus 35 air groups.

Above: By the late 1930s the Air Corps' best fighter was the Curtiss P-40.
Right: General Hideki Tojo, leader of the aggressive military faction that came to power in Japan in the 1930s.

Meantime, the scope and fury of the war in Europe grew apace. Hitler moved through Norway, Denmark, and the Low Countries in the spring of 1940, after a six-month winter lull, and drove the French out of the war within six weeks. The small British force in France was salvaged to fight again by the 'miracle' evacuation from the beaches of Dunkirk. Now Britain was Hitler's target, but his attempt to defeat the island nation through air power (the Battle of Britain, August-September 1940) ended in failure, forcing the German dictator to abandon his plans for invasion. Unable to win in the West, in June 1941 Hitler turned east and attacked his 'ally,' the Soviet Union. The magnitude of his early successes in this vast campaign suggested that he might yet be able to realize his dream of becoming the master of Europe, and perhaps of the world.

America Goes to War

On 7 December 1941 a great Japanese naval armada launched a surprise air attack on the American naval base at Pearl Harbor, while other Japanese forces struck at the Philippines, Guam in the Marianas, and Wake Island in the central Pacific. An American public, aroused as never before in its history, vowed in the aftermatch of Pearl Harbor to bring the Japanese down and to avenge the American soldiers, sailors and Marines in the far-off Pacific who had been the initial victims of Japanese treachery. Hitler sensed this was a good time to declar war on the United States. Preoccupied with Japan, it might now be unable to continue sending war materials to the British and Russians. He was convinced, as was Kaiser Wilhelm in 1914, that he could conquer Europe before the United States could react with sufficient strength. He accordingly declared war on the United States and was followed by Mussolini.

World War II had now entered a new and fatal phase for the Axis powers. Admiral Isoroku Yamamoto, Japan's naval chief, had warned his countrymen against bringing America into the war because of her moral, industrial and military potential. He had told his fellow military chieftains that they might well run wild for six months to a year, but when America awoke and recovered from the initial attacks on her, the Axis could not win. Yamamoto was an accurate prophet. The USA rose up in wrath to strike down the enemies of freedom with a power unprecedented in world history and joined with her allies to reverse the tide of war and bring the Axis enemies to their knees.

During World War II, 16.3 million Americans served in the nation's armed forces. Of these, 11.2 million served in the Army, 4.1 million in the Navy, 669,000 in the Marine Corps, and 330,000 in women's auxiliary corps. When the war ended in August 1945, 12 million men and women were in uniform. Most of these were brought into the military through the draft, since formal volunteering ended by law in 1942. Under the selective service legislation of World War II all males aged 18 to 64 were required to register; the operative upper age limit was initially 44, then it was dropped to 38. Locally-administered draft boards registered 36 million males. Of these, 10 million were drafted for service. Approximately one-sixth of America's males were in uniform during the course of the war. Deferments for occupational skills were given generously because the war effort required the efforts of efficient workers in the factories and on the farms in unprecedented numbers. During the course of the war the nation's civilian and military workforce jumped from 60 million to 75 million (the total population was 130 million), with the industrial work force rising by 10 million men and women.

During the war, American industry produced for American and Allied fighting men 1200 combatant naval vessels, 82,000 landing craft, 96,000 bombers 88,000 fighters, 23,000 transport planes, 2600 cargo ships, 700 tanker ships, 86,000 tanks, 120,000 artillery pieces, 2.4 million trucks and jeeps, and 14 million shoulder weapons. Of these, 37,000 tanks, 792,000 trucks, 43,000 aircraft, and 1.8 million rifles were sent to America's allies. As the United States scored feats of productivity to arm itself and its war companions, it truly became the 'Arsenal of Democracy.'

When World War II broke out in 1939 many Americans hoped the US would be able to stay at peace. But Franklin Roosevelt (*top*) understood the aims of Adolf Hitler (*right*) better and tried to prepare the country for an almost certain US involvement. Any hopes that Hitler might be stopped by Anglo-French armies were dashed by the fall of France in 1940 (*below*).

Left: The US was in an undeclared war with German U-Boats by 1941.
Below: Adm. Isoroku Yamamoto, author of the Pearl Harbor raid that at last brought America into the war.

Phase I: North Africa

American war efforts in North Africa and the Mediterranean, which began in November 1942 with American landings in North Africa as part of Operation TORCH, represented the result of long American-British debate and compromise over the most effective joint strategy to be followed in defeating Hitler and his Axis allies. Prior to 1938 American military planners had been primarily concerned with fighting Japan and had assumed that the nation would go on the offensive in the Pacific and on the defensive in the Atlantic in any future war. In 1938 this scenario began to change, as the danger of Hitler to America's European friends became more visible. By 1940 a plan called RAINBOW 5, which envisioned a war of the United States, Britain and France against Germany, Italy and Japan, had emerged as accepted grand strategy. It called for defense of the Western Hemisphere, a strategic defensive in the Pacific until the European Axis powers were defeated, and a projection of American armed force on to Africa or the European continent. Roosevelt, as Commander in Chief, had approved of RAINBOW 5 by early 1941, and staff talks between American and British commanders were underway.

In planning its grand strategy against Germany, Britain had first thought in terms of using its seapower to blockade the Continent, as it had done so effectively in World War I, and of using strategic airpower to cause Germany's political and economic collapse. By the end of 1940 it was clear that such ideas were mere wishful thinking, and British planners were looking in other directions. While they were convinced by 1941 that an invasion of the Continent would eventually be needed to defeat the Germans, the Mediterranean theater of operations was given more immediate priority. Egypt had to be retained as a staging area for the Empire's resources; there was a possibility that French leaders in Syria, Lebanon, and Algeria could be brought over to the Allied side; and Greece had to be retained to deny Hitler the oil of the oil fields in Rumania and the Persian Gulf countries. If the Axis powers conquered Egypt and the Persian Gulf, Britain would be staring at defeat. The Mediterranean had to be kept out of Hitler's and Mussolini's hands, but the question of how to do so was still moot.

When Prime Minister Winston Churchill and the British war chieftains met in Washington with President Roosevelt and the American military leaders in December 1941, the whole strategic situation was examined in detail. The leaders agreed that the European theater of war had primacy for the time being; that the U-boats had to be defeated to assure that valuable supplies could get through to Britain; and that somehow, somewhere, an Anglo-American offensive against German land forces had to be mounted. But the Allies could not agree on where or when the offensive should take place. The more impetuous Americans wanted to strike directly at Hitler by invading the Continent as soon as possible. The British wanted first to put pressure on the periphery, build up for an invasion, and then hit the Germans only when Allied preponderence of men and materiel gave them a fair chance of success.

Undeterred by British arguments, American military planners continued to push for a direct blow at Nazi Germany, and by March 1942 they had developed several bold plans, one for a massive cross-channel invasion in the spring of 1943 and another for an earlier and smaller invasion to be launched in September 1942 if Russia were about to be defeated on the Eastern Front or if Germany were crumbling internally. But the British still were reluctant to endorse the American plans fully because, they insisted, the Mediterranean had to be protected. Any of these plans would draw too many men away from the Mediterranean theater. By mid-1942 the British had rejected any landings on the Continent during that year, at least. The war in North Africa was now going very badly for the British Eighth Army, so any invasion of the Continent was out of the question.

But President Roosevelt was determined that the Americans had to get into European action in 1942. He had promised this to Soviet Foreign Minister Vyacheslav Molotov. The German offensive in Russia was enjoying great success and pressure had to be taken off the Russian defenders. Also, the American public was demanding action. Accordingly, he sent his personal delegate, Harry Hopkins, along with General Marshall and Admiral Ernest J King, Chief of Naval Operations, to London with orders to come up with some agreement for a joint offensive in the European theater in 1942. He was willing to accept a peripheral Mediterranean invasion if necessary. Churchill, in response, resurrected a British plan for an invasion in North Africa called GYMNAST, and Roosevelt bought the idea, much to the consternation of American military planners. One of them, Major General Dwight D Eisenhower, said the day of this decision 'could well go down as the blackest day in history.'

Throughout World War II the Army's Chief of Staff would be the brilliant and respected George C Marshall.

Thus was born Operation TORCH (ex-GYMNAST), an invasion of North Africa to be carried out in November 1942. It was intended to open the Mediterranean for the Allies; give them bases for bombing German-controlled areas in southern Europe; distract the Germans away from the hard-pressed Russians; and perhaps lead to the invasion of Sicily and Italy and the collapse of Hitler's southern front. Eisenhower, named to command the operation, set D-Day for 8 November. The US Army, which had been rapidly building its strength for eleven months since Pearl Harbor, was going into action at last.

The American-British invasion of North Africa came at a crucial time in the Mediterranean war. The British had long been fighting in the North African desert, that flat, almost trackless 150-mile-wide wasteland stretching 400 miles from Alamein in Egypt to Derna in Libya. In 1940, after some initial setbacks, they had succeeded in routing the Italian forces in North Africa, but this victory had only prompted a German riposte, and early in 1941 General Erwin Rommel and his crack armored troops, the Afrika Korps, began to arrive in North Africa. By late April 1941 they had driven the British army all the way back across the coast, encircling and bypassing the British garrison at the port of Tobruk in Libya, as they pushed to the Egyptian border. In June and again in November 1941 furious battles took place as the British tried to relieve Tobruk. The battles exhausted Rommel's forces, and in December he was forced to retreat to El Agheila. But the British were too exhausted to chase and destroy him, and, after resting and being reinforced, in the first six months of 1942 Rommel fought his way back across the desert, chased the British to El Alamein, 60 miles west of Alexandria in Egypt, and this time took the port of Tobruk by siege. Rommel then attacked the British lines in July 1942 and was beaten back in the First Battle of El Alamein. The Eighth Army stopped Rommel's second offensive on 13-17 July. It was the farthest Rommel would go: Now was the time for the British to counterattack.

When General Sir Claude Auchinleck refused to press hard against Rommel until his troops had been rested, Churchill relieved him, and Lieutenant-General Bernard Law Montgomery was brought in to lead the Eighth Army (Churchill's first choice being killed in a airplane crash). At El Alamein Rommel was at the end of a tenuous 1400-mile supply line and wanted to pull back, but Hitler insisted that he 'defend every inch of ground.' So as Montgomery built up his men and supplies, Rommel could neither match him nor retreat, the result being the Afrika Korps' defeat at Alam Halfa and (Second) El Alamein in late 1942. Rommel was then forced to retreat all the way back across Libya to the Mareth Line in southern Tunisia, and, as he fled, the Americans and British launched Operation TORCH in his rear. Rommel was at the Mareth Line and dug in, but now an army was advancing from the west, and the Germans were in a trap.

As we have seen, TORCH was a strategic compromise between the British and American high commands. Once decided upon, however, plans had moved forward quickly. The objectives of the invasion forces were to gain a foothold on the North African coastal plain over a 900-mile front; to seize Casablanca, Oran, and Algiers, the three largest ports in Morocco and Algeria; and then to speed to the east to take northern Tunisia. This would trap the German and Italian forces in North Africa and take them out of the war.

The invasion of North Africa aimed to cut off the eastward escape route of German General Erwin Rommel (*left*). The invaders were ferried to North Africa by a huge naval armada (*below*) divided into three separate task forces, each destined for a different landing spot.

The invasion force, called Western Naval Task Force, was scheduled to land in the vicinity of Casablanca, in Morocco, and was under the command of Major General George S Patton, Jr. It assembled in Hampton Roads, Virginia, and sailed on 23 October 1942 with 35,000 men. The Center Task Force, containing 39,000 American and British soldiers, sailed from Scotland. In command of these landing forces was Major General Lloyd R Fredendall, US Army. They were to land east and west of Oran in Algiers and take the city. Eastern Task Force also sailed from the British Isles. It had 33,000 men and was under the command of Major General Charles W Ryder of the US Army. Its destination was Algiers. Once the landings had taken place, all Allied troops in Algiers would become the British First Army, under Lieutenant General Kenneth Anderson, and would race for northern Tunisia.

One of the great unanswered questions before the landings was whether or not the French troops, now under collaborationist Vichy command, would fight the Allied invaders. Attempts were made to dissuade them from doing so through contacts with General Henri Giraud and Admiral Jean Francois Darlan, commanding French forces in North Africa. The meetings were only partially successful, resulting in spirited French defense in Algiers and Morocco before Admiral Darlan agreed to switch sides and bring his 200,000 French troops over to the Allies. It also resulted in Darlan's being assassinated by a compatriot for dealing with the invading Allies.

The landings in North Africa went well for the Americans and British. In Algeria the French around Algiers laid down their arms on 8 November, the day of the invasion, and Oran fell two days later after stern resistance. The city of Casablanca and its surrounding area was in American hands by 11 November, although the landing of men and supplies from ship to shore was so clumsily managed that the Americans were fortunate

Top: Oran/Mers-el-Kebir was one of the three main Allied landing points.
Below: The North African landings.

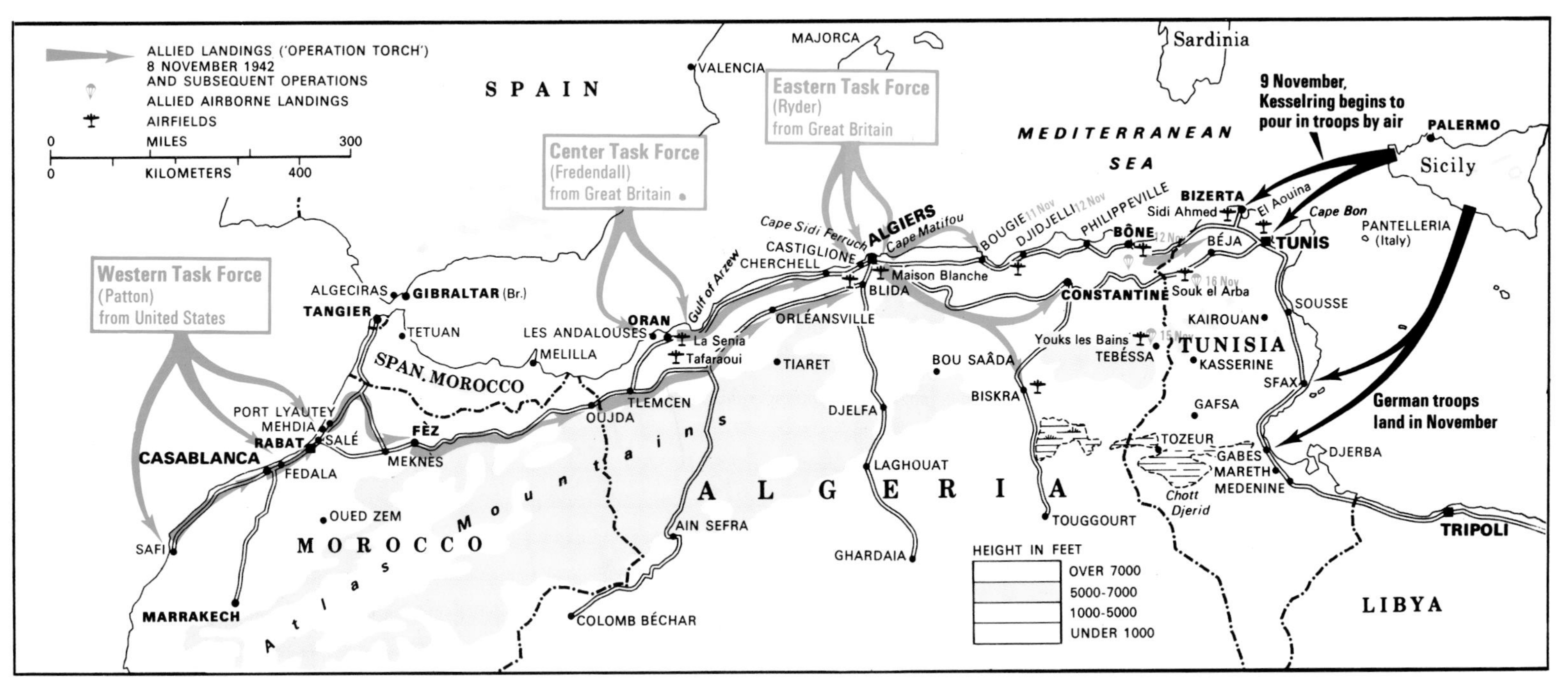

Both General Patton (*left*) and General Eisenhower saw their first major actions of World War II in the 1943 Tunisian Campaign.

the French were not able to put up a fight.

Unfortunately, the chase to the east by First Army to capture the Germans in Tunisia soon bogged down, and Field-Marshal Albert Kesselring, commanding the southern Wehrmacht from Italy, was able to reinforce his troops in northern Tunisia. The Allies had only two weeks to cover the 450 miles to the key coastal cities of Tunis and Bizerta before winter rains and mud set in. Thanks to massive logistical problems and the superiority of German tanks, especially the Panzer IV, over Allied armor, Anderson was forced to call a halt in early December far short of his goal. As the Allies made efforts to reinforce First Army in Tunisia, the Germans dug in to stop them. They also still held the Mareth Line in the south, and here Montgomery refused to force his Eighth Army against the Germans until he had overwhelming superiority in numbers.

In February 1943, taking advantage of poor disposal of troops along the American lines outside Tunis and Bizerta, Rommel and General Juergen von Armin of V Army launched an attack through the center of the Allied north-south line. Their intention was to break through to the sea and isolate and destroy the leading elements of First Army, thus breaking the encirclement of Tunis and Bizerta. Their Valentine's Day attack almost succeeded, the American and British soldiers being bloodied in the Battle of Kasserine Pass. Fortunately for the Allied troops, von Armin refused to support the operation fully and Rommel lost his nerve. Otherwise the German counterattack might well have led to a disastrous Allied defeat. Even so, the green US 2nd Army Corps lost 6500 men killed, wounded or captured in the battle; another 4000 British soldiers who came to their aid were also lost. It was a baptism of fire the survivors would never forget, but one that led the Army to engage in more extensive training for its troops before further engagements with their determined enemy.

In the aftermath of Kasserine Pass Rommel was removed by Hitler, and George Patton took over 2nd Corps. Under the leadership of General Sir Harold Alexander, the Allies subsequently went on the offensive again. As First Army began a determined push from the west, Eighth Army flanked the Germans at the Mareth Line. Together they began to push the Germans and their Italian allies ever north and west toward the shores of the Mediterranean. Despite dogged defenses by the German forces (Hitler ordered that there would be no retreat), the Allies continued to press on and also began to cut the Axis lines of air and sea supply from Sicily and Italy. On 7 May 1943 the British moved into Tunis and the Americans entered Bizerta. One week later the last German and

The tough veterans of Rommel's Afrika Korps nearly defeated US and British troops at the Kasserine Pass.

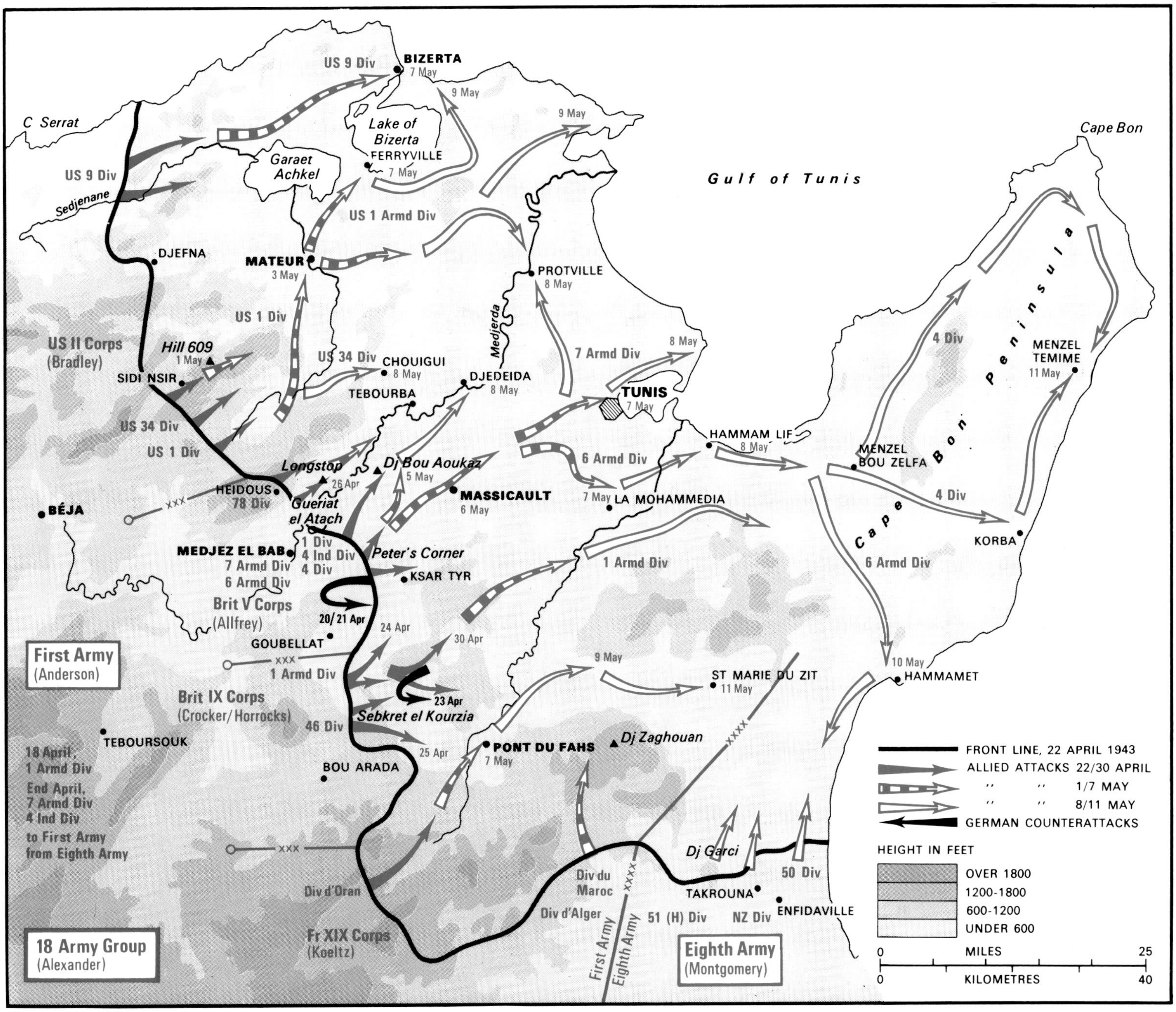

Top: The final stages of the Tunisian campaign. *Below:* US paratroopers preparing for the invasion of Sicily. The surround on the USAAF insignia seen on the truck would soon be changed from yellow to red and then, finally, to blue.

Italian forces had surrendered. The battle for North Africa was over, but not before the Axis saw 40,000 killed, wounded or missing and 275,000 captured in the Tunisian campaign alone. Allied casualties stood at 66,000. Operation TORCH and the taking of North Africa had been a very expensive undertaking, but many military lessons had been learned, and, most important, the British and Americans now threatened Hitler's southern flank.

Phase II: Sicily and Italy

While the fighting was still raging in North Africa, in January 1943 Roosevelt, Churchill and the American and British Combined Chiefs of Staff met in Casablanca to discuss grand strategy. As before, the American mili-

A big Landing Ship Tank (LST) is in the foreground of this photograph of invasion craft heading for Salerno.

tary leaders wanted an invasion of France, and, as before, the British wanted to operate on the periphery until Allied forces were ready for such a large undertaking. The result was a compromise: Sicily would be invaded. The seizure of Sicily would make the Allies' Mediterranean supply lines more secure, divert Germans from the Russian front, and put pressure on Italy, already reeling from its North African losses, to drop out of the war. Accordingly, plans were drawn up for the invasion.

The British Eighth Army, under Lieutenant General Montgomery, would attack on the southeast corner of Sicily, south of Syracuse, and drive to the north. The American Seventh Army, under General Patton, would land on Sicily's southern coast to protect the Eighth Army's flank and rear, a secondary role the fiery Patton hardly appreciated. Facing the Allies would be nine Italian divisions of dubious quality and two crack German divisions of 30,000 men, the Hermann Goering armored divisions and the 15th Panzer Grenadiers of mechanized infantry. D-Day was set for 10 July 1943.

Operation HUSKY, the invasion of Sicily, was to be the largest amphibious operation in history to date. Some 80,000 troops with 7000 vehicles, 600 tanks and 900 artillery pieces would be landed in 48 hours. Seven Allied divisions would make up the assault waves. HUSKY would also include the first large-scale Allied airborne operation of the war, with 4600 men making their air assaults via planes and gliders.

The airborne troops were to land in the dark three hours before the dawn invasion. The paratroop phase of the operation was a near fiasco. The 3400 American paratroopers under Colonel James M Gavin, were scattered all over southeast Sicily, thanks to inadequate aircrew training and to American naval crews shooting at their own planes. And almost half the British gliders scheduled to land near a key bridge south of Syracuse were released early and fell into the sea, although the bridge was taken and held by 87 brave men until relief arrived. Tragedy occurred again the following night when, the two major amphibious landings having been made with little opposition, 144 American planes carrying in 2000 American paratroopers were fired upon by nervous gunners, despite being in a 'safe' corridor and displaying proper recognition lights. In this blunder off Gela, 23 planes were shot down and 27 were damaged, and a total of 229 paratroopers lost their lives.

It was hardly an auspicious start for the invasion, but Allied power was preponderant, and the Germans and Italians were forced to withdraw gradually to the northern coast of the island, despite being reinforced by 50,000 additional German soldiers. Even so, the Axis forces had slowed Montgomery's drive up the Sicilian east coast to a crawl, and Patton could only sit on his left and protect his flank. Finally, Patton convinced Alexander that the Seventh Army should be unleashed, to drive for Palermo, on Sicily's northwest corner. Patton moved with lightning speed across Sicily, only to find that the Germans had pulled out of Palermo for Messina, at the other (northeast) corner of the island. Patton and the Seventh set out in pursuit, and, although slowed by terrain and determined German resistance, arrived in Messina to

Mark W Clark, who commanded the 5th Army in Sicily and Italy, was one of the more controversial US generals.

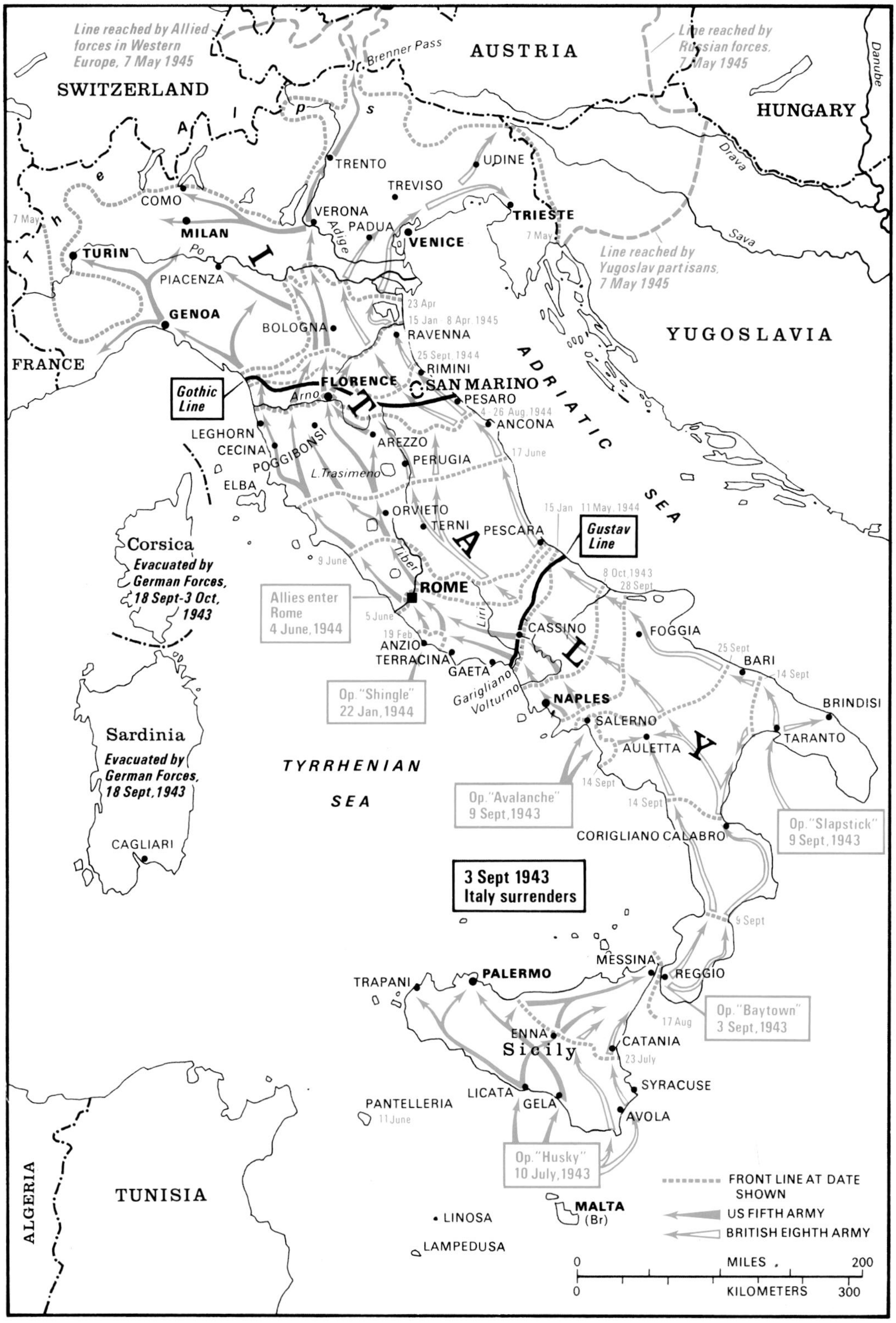

complete the conquest of Sicily on 17 August, two hours ahead of the British. Montgomery was furious at having been thus upstaged, but of somewhat greater importance was the fact that 45,000 Germans and over 70,000 Italians had gotten away across the narrow Strait of Messina to fight again. Even so, 157,000 of their comrades had been killed or captured in the campaign in Sicily, and American casualties had been only 19,000. In many ways Sicily had proved to be a cakewalk. Italy would be another story.

While the campaign for Sicily was underway, Mussolini was deposed (in July 1943) to placate the war-weary Italian people. King Victor Emmanuel II appointed Field Marshal Pietro Badoglio in his place. Badoglio pledged to continue the war, but it was widely and correctly assumed he would try to end Italy's involvement as soon as possible. Hitler, dismayed by this turn of events, ordered the rescue of the imprisoned Mussolini and set him up as a puppet ruler in northern Italy, while at the same time directing the German armies to stand by to take over in Italy. When, therefore, Badoglio announced the signing of surrender terms on the eve of the Allied invasion of the country, the Germans immediately moved eight divisions into central and southern Italy, disarmed the Italians, and prepared to fight off the invaders.

The British Eighth Army crossed the Straits of Messina from Sicily on 3 September 1943 in a diversionary and largely useless invasion, there to move up to the instep of Italy to join with the main assault force further to the north. Meanwhile the British 19th Corps and the US 6th Corps, together constituting the Fifth Army, under Lieutenant General Mark W Clark, USA, prepared for the main invasion at Salerno, 25 miles south of Naples. As the 70,000-man force of Operation AVALANCHE hit the beaches of Salerno on 9 September 1943, backed by 82 British and American naval vessels, it ran into fierce resistance from the four German divisions that were waiting for the invasion. Only after four days of bitter fighting on the Salerno beachhead did Field-Marshal Kesselring withdraw his forces north of Naples to a line running across the entire Italian peninsula. On this 'Gustav Line' Kesselring gave the Allies the first of many lessons in brilliant flexible defensive maneuvers. Throughout the remainder of the year Kesselring's X Army held firm, only giving up territory at horrible cost to the Allies, who were also battered by one of the worst Italian winters in decades.

The linchpin of the Gustav Line (or 'Winter Line') was the area of Cassino, crowned by the Benedictine abbey called Monte Cassino, whose history went back to the 6th century and time of St. Benedict himself. Frustrated by the bloody stalemate and convinced that the Germans were using Monte Cassino as an artillery spotting post, General Sir Harold Alexander finally gave the order to bomb it out of existence. In one of the most controversial actions of the war (the Germans, in fact, were not using it as an observation post) the bombing took place on 15 February 1944. Some 660 tons of bombs and artillery ordinance leveled the famed religious house. But even as it lay in ruins, the

Left: Map of the Italian campaign.
Below: German paratroopers such as these defended Monte Cassino.

Germans fought on along the Gustav Line, and it was not until three months later that Monte Cassino fell into Allied hands and the Gustav Line was decisively conquered.

In the meantime, the Allies tried to end-run the Gustav Line, in Operation SHINGLE, by invading along the coast north of the line at Anzio. Some 40,000 soldiers of the US 6th Corps, including the British 1st Division and the American 3rd Division, invaded on 22 January 1944 in a hastily-mounted operation. The initial landings went well, but on 16 February Kesselring's improvised XIV Army counterattacked with 125,000 men and almost drove the 100,000 Allied soldiers into the sea. For three months the Germans held the British and American forces on a narrow beachhead, subjecting them to day and night shelling and nightly air raids. The Allies suffered 59,000 casualties at Anzio, one-third of them from disease, exhaustion and neurosis, before they finally broke out on 23 May. Even then, an opportunity for ending the stalemated war in Italy was lost when General Clark, instead of moving east to trap the German X Army behind Cassino, decided instead to take the capital of Rome for its propaganda value. Kesselring got his troops out, and the long Italian war continued to drag on.

The Allies finally broke Kesselring's Gothic Line north of Florence in September 1944, but the onset of winter weather meant that German resistance in Italy would continue into the next year. Only in the spring of 1945 was the Allied movement into northern Italy continued, and only after weeks of heavy fighting did the Germans finally surrender. The end came on 2 May 1945.

The Italian campaign was one of the longest and costliest of the European war. It lasted for twenty months and caused tens of thousands of casualties. It was beyond doubt the most frustrating campaign of World War II and did not end until the fall of Germany itself. Whatever the strategic wisdom of Salerno, Anzio, the bombing of Monte Cassino, and the long, slogging fight up the Italian peninsula, it had at least tied down part of Hitler's Wehrmacht while the long-awaited cross-channel invasion was launched in June 1944. But few veterans of the Italian campaign

Twelfth Air Force B-25s pass a fiery Mt Vesuvius as they head for their target, Monte Cassino. The bombing of Monte Cassino's old abbey proved militarily useless.

would remember things that way. Their memories were of death, disease, cold, and German resistance that, until the last, seemed as though it would never end.

Phase III: The Normandy Invasion and Breakout

During the weeks preceding the invasion of Sicily, at the Trident Conference in Washington, the American military planners finally got their go-ahead for an invasion of the Continent when Roosevelt and Churchill agreed on a landing to be carried out in 1944 Operation BOLERO, the build-up phase for the cross-channel invasion, had been underway since April 1942. Now with OVERLORD agreed upon, preparations began in earnest, and by the summer of 1944 1.5 million American soldiers and airmen, plus 500 million tons of supplies and equipment, had been landed in Britain to supplement the 1.75 million British and 175,000 Commonwealth troops already assembled there. Planning for the invasion was vested first in COSSAC (Chief of Staff to Supreme Allied Commander), then in SHAEF (Supreme Head of the Allied Expeditionary Force), when General Eisenhower was appointed Supreme Commander in January 1944. Montgomery had coveted the job, but the political leaders agreed that the top position had to go to an American. Thus Montgomery was to command Allied ground forces under Eisenhower during the invasion.

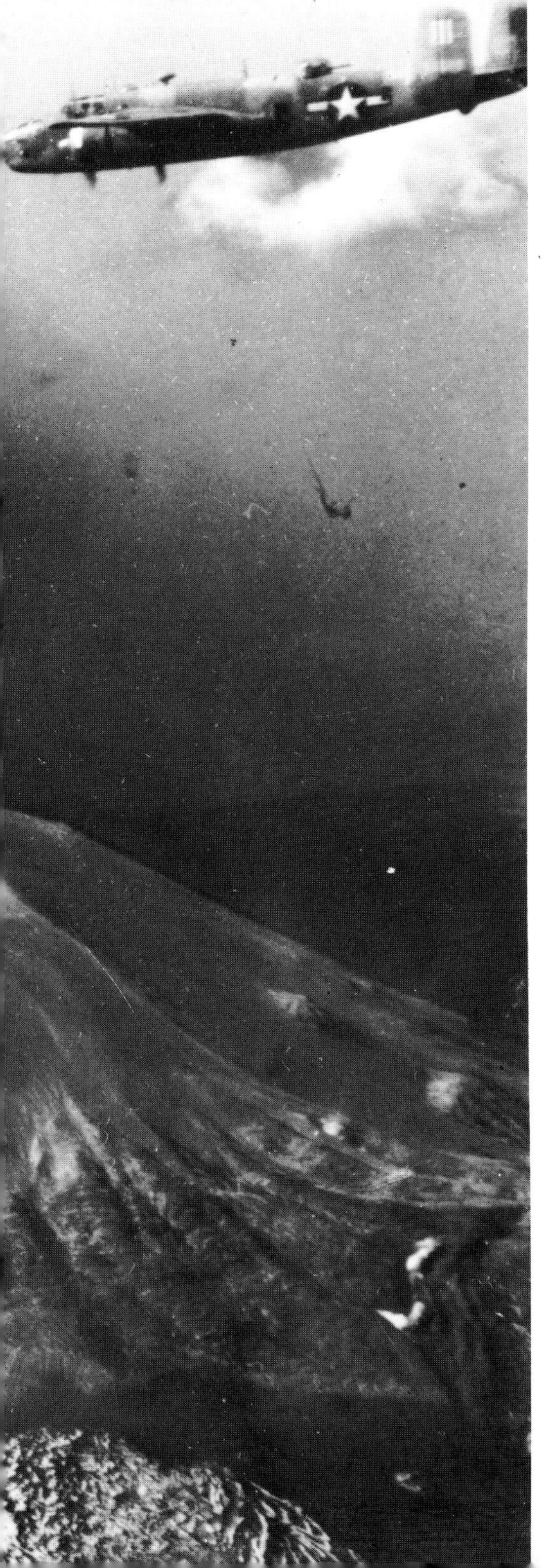

From Italy the 12th Air Force could raid many European targets. This B-26 lost an engine to flak over Toulon.

Many months of preparation went into the massive operation. After extensive study and debate it was decided to land on the coast of Normandy, directly south of England, instead of in the Pas-de-Calais area on the Belgian border. Normandy was close to fighter bases in southern England, would be easier to supply and reinforce, had suitable beaches for landings, contained the potentially useful port of Cherbourg, and was manned by fewer German defenders than the Pas-de-Calais. But even as the decision for Normandy was made and preparations began, some American and British bomber chiefs were voicing opposition to OVERLORD itself. They argued that the whole invasion was a gigantic mistake because strategic bombing could take out German cities and war potential in time, making invasion unnecessary. As of early 1944, however, there was insufficient evidence to support their contention, so Operation OVERLORD was on. The troops were being assembled. Special armored equipment, such as sea-going

Sherman tanks with canvas flotation collars to enable them to 'swim' to the beaches, Shermans with chain flails on front-mounted drums to clear mine fields, and Churchill tanks with 290 mm mortars to be used against pillboxes had been developed. And in order to provide safe anchorages for supply vessels after the initial landings, floating piers, caissons, and blockships had been readied.

To convince the Germans that the main invasion would take place in the Pas-de-Calais area, Operation FORTITUDE was brought into play. It called for the creation of a fictitious army of 50 divisions and a million men, complete with camps and equipment, under Lieutenant General George Patton, in Kent. It also included extensive bombing of the Pas-de-Calais area, at a 2-to-1 ratio over bombings of Normandy, in the weeks preceding D-Day. On the night before D-Day motor launches would set out for France towing balloons with reflectors that gave off images of ships on radar. Royal Air Force bombers would drop aluminum foil strips to simulate airplanes on radar scopes, and dummy paratroopers would be dropped all over the area. In the event, FORTITUDE fooled the Germans completely, holding them in place for the 'real' invasion in the Pas-de-Calais while the American and British troops gained a foothold on the Normandy beaches.

Although the German defenses along Hitler's 'Atlantic Wall' were the most formidable man-made barrier in the West, and although Field-Marshal Gerd von Rundstedt had 15,000 strong points manned by 300,000 troops along the Wall, the German chain of command was weak. German air power was controlled solely by Air Marshal Hermann Goering, who was back in Germany, and four of the seven armored divisions in the Atlantic defenses were assigned directly to Wehrmacht headquarters, i.e., to Hitler himself, rather than to General Erwin Rommel, commander of Army Group B in the invasion area. Thus when crucial decisions had to be made

Right: A 5th Army tank destroyer, a form of self-propelled artillery used to fight German panzers. _Below:_ By September 1944 US troops in Italy had only reached the Arno. Still ahead lay the final German defenses, the formidable Gothic Line.

18

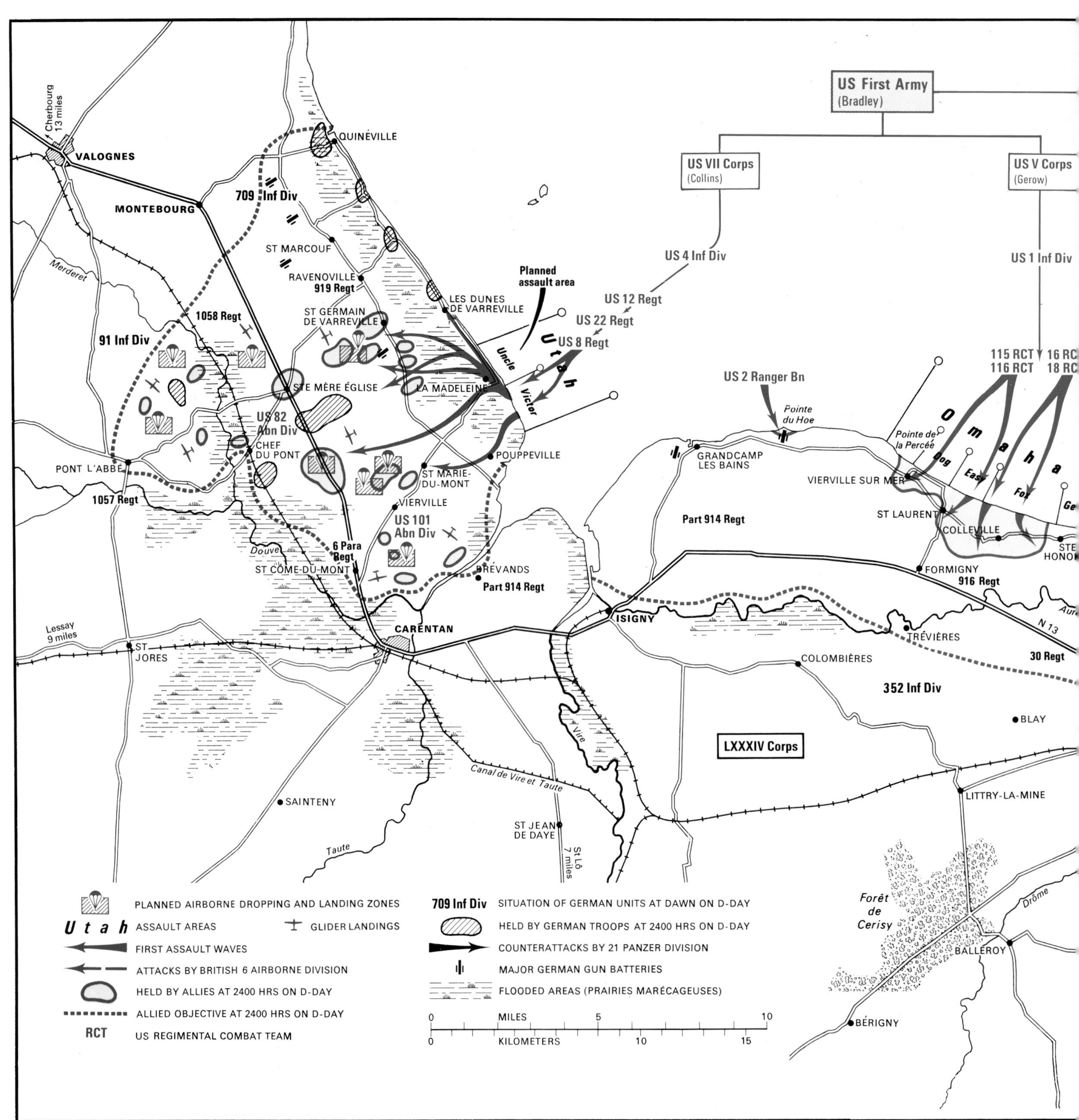

on the battlefield, they could not always be carried out. Had German reaction been more rapid and effective, and had Hitler not been convinced until it was too late that the real invasion site was the Pas-de-Calais area, OVERLORD might not have succeeded.

Although several times delayed because of bad weather, D-Day was finally set for 6 June 1944 by Eisenhower, and early that morning airborne troops led off Operation NEPTUNE, the code name for the assaults themselves. The British 6th Airborne Division landed on the left, or east, flank of the invasion area and took the Caen Canal and the Orne River bridges with ease, while the American 82nd Airborne Division, under Major General Matthew Ridgway, landed near Sainte-Mere-Eglise at the base of the Cotentin Peninsula, and the 101st Airborne, under Major General Maxwell Taylor, landed nearby to anchor the right flank of the Normandy landing areas. After naval and air bombardment of the beaches and the areas behind them, 176,000 soldiers began landing from 4,000 landing craft at 0630 in the morning. Fortunately for the Allies, the Germans were unable to react quickly because Hitler's chief of operations, General Alfred Jodl, had countermanded Rundstedt's orders to move two armored divisions to Normandy at the very moment the landings were beginning. On Utah Beach, on the far right flank, the 23,000 men of the US 7th Army Corps, under General J Lawton ('Lightning Joe') Collins, had a fairly easy time of it, thanks to effective pre-dawn bombardment and confusion spread in the German ranks by the airborne landings behind the beachheads. Only 197 casualties were suffered the first day, and a substantial beachhead on the Cotentin Peninsula was achieved when the infantry succeeded in joining up with their airborne comrades.

Omaha beach, to the east, was another story. There the 5th Army Corps, under

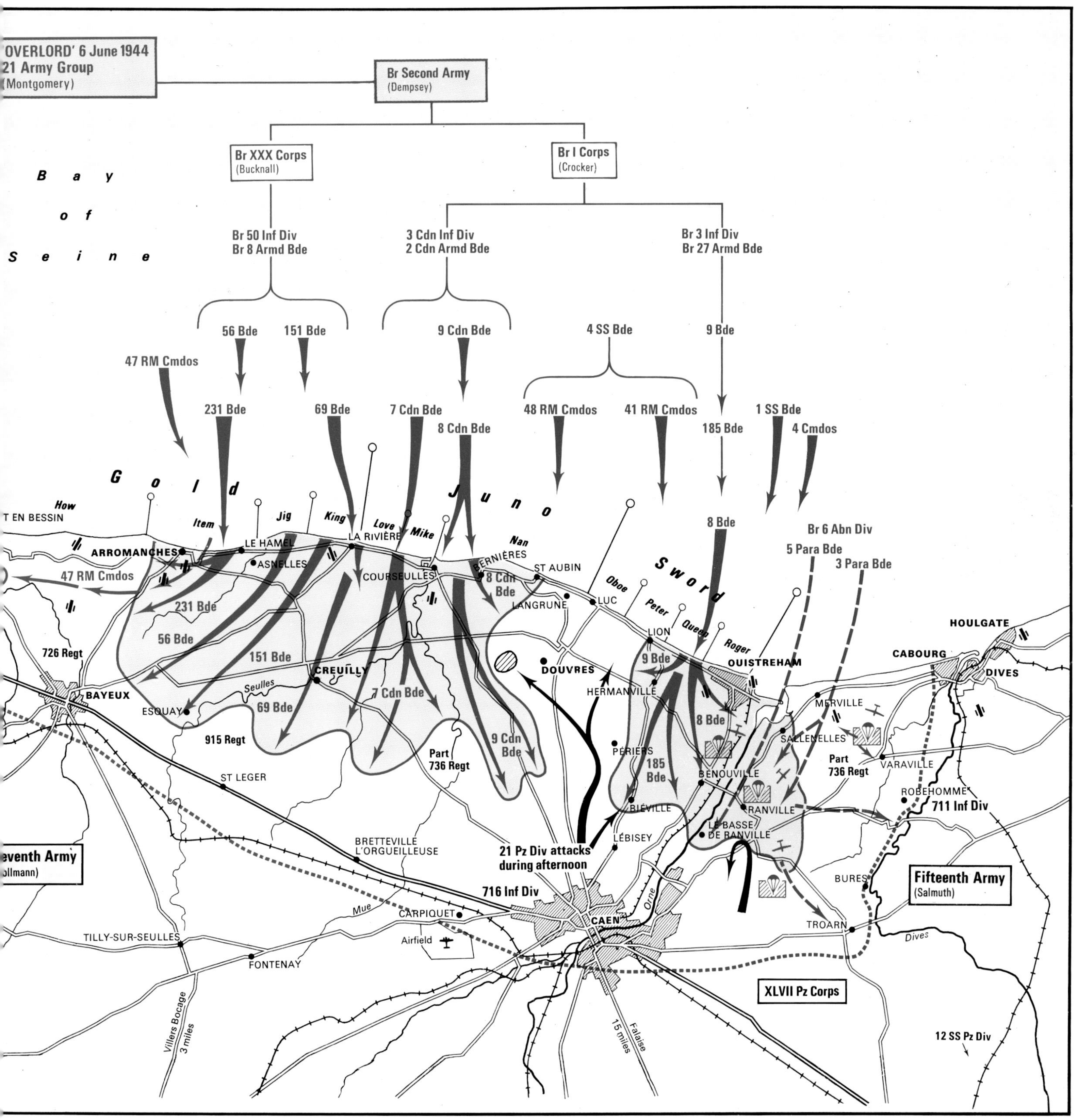

Major General Leonard T Gerow, ran into a firestorm of artillery and machine gun fire. With the initial waves pinned down on the 300-yard pebbled beach and unable to move out because of enemy fire, succeeding waves of men and equipment began to pile up. By 0900 Bradley was ready to call off the invasion on Omaha beach, but SHAEF never received his message, and the battle went on. Gradually the soldiers fought their way through the obstacles with their light weapons and established a defensible beachhead, but the cost was 3000 casualties that first day. Had the American commanders not refused to use the specialized armored equipment available to them, the casualty count would undoubtedly have been lower. But by the same token, had the Navy's destroyers not come in to bottom-scraping depths to cover the soldiers on the beach, the count would have been far higher, and perhaps the beachhead would have been lost.

To the left and east of the American Utah and Omaha Beaches the British Second Army, under General Miles Dempsey, landed on Gold, Juno, and Sword Beaches. Their landings were not difficult, but they subsequently had to beat off countless German armored counterattacks in order to maintain their positions and seize the city of Caen, the intended pivot-point for the great Allied swing west into the heart of France. Although delayed by fierce German resistance, the British, like the Americans, were greatly aided in the first days of fighting by the fact that Hitler steadfastly refused to believe that this was the 'real' landing and would not unleash his reserves against the Normandy beachheads.

In the days and weeks that followed the landings in Normandy, the Allies slowly but surely improved their positions until it was clear they could not be pushed back into the sea. While the Russians continued to drive ever closer to Germany from the east, Hitler

Top: German propaganda claimed West Wall defenses were impregnable, but few were as formidable as this.

now found his Western enemies firmly in France and equally determined to invade the Fatherland. Yet despite the Allies' successes in OVERLORD, and despite personal testimony from von Rundstedt and Rommel that the situation in Normandy was hopeless and that the Germans should fall back to better defensive positions, Der Führer ordered that there be no retreat.

By 29 June the US 7th Army Corps had taken the port of Cherbourg, at the top of the Cotentin Peninsula, and the British were encircling Caen, the key to holding the Normandy beaches. By 18 July the American 7th and 8th Corps had fought their way through the almost impenetrable hedgerow country, the *bocage*, and had reached St-Lô. In August the American First Army had moved into Brittany, while the new Third Army, organized under General Patton, swung around to the left and headed east.

Hitler now attempted a counterattack toward Avranches, but this succeeded only in destroying 10,000 German soldiers and causing another 50,000 to be wounded in the 'Falaise Gap,' where the British First and Second Armies, on the north, and Patton's Third Army, on the south, converged to trap the German forces. By 20 August Patton was

Top: D-Day troops in a landing craft.
Below: Special intakes helped this M4 Sherman tank to get through the tidal waters, but it finally foundered in the soft sand of a Normandy beach.

on the Seine at Fontainebleau, and on 25 August Paris was liberated, the honor of first entering the city being given to the Free French forces who had fought alongside the Allies. By the end of July, over a million Allied soldiers were on French soil, backed up by 150,000 vehicles and some million tons of supplies. The cry was now 'On to Berlin.'

In the meantime, Operation ANVIL, an amphibious landing on the southern French coast between Cannes and Toulon, had taken place. This 15 August 1944 invasion was carried out by the US Seventh Army, under Major General Alexander M Patch. Once the landings had been made successfully, the accompanying French 2nd Corps was allowed to pass through the Seventh Army and lead the advance through Marseilles and up the Rhône to Lyons and Dijon. They linked up with the Third Army in September and then continued to march north and east on the Third Army's flank toward Germany. All of France was being liberated, and it looked as though the war might be over in 1944, but in fact many months would have to pass and many thousands of people would have to die before Europe would see peace again.

Phase IV: The Final Drive on Germany

No sooner had the Allies broken out of the Normandy beachheads and begun to sweep east across France, with the British on the left and the Americans on the right, than a dispute broke out among the commanders as to how next to proceed against the German enemy. Montgomery and Bradley preferred operating on a narrow front on the left, while the right merely maintained pressure on the German defenders. Circling left around through Belgium and Holland toward the vital Ruhr Basin north of Cologne, they would aim to beat the Russians into Berlin. Patton and other American generals preferred to advance on a broader front, Montgomery's 21st Army Group seizing the Channel ports on the left flank, while the American armies advanced in a series of moves against the Saar, the Ruhr, and the Rhineland.

Eisenhower opted for the second strategy. On the left the British moved into Belgium, seizing Brussels and Antwerp, with its giant port facilities. At the same time, the US First and Third Armies pushed vigorously ahead on the center and right, the Third Army crossing the Meuse at Verdun and entering the area of the great American victories of 1918. But now Montgomery's advance against the Germans in the channel ports and along the 60-mile Scheldt Estuary was beginning to slow down. Without control of the Scheldt the great port of Antwerp was useless because the estuary controlled all shipping into the city. As a result, the American First and Third Armies were soon running short of fuel, and their advances too slowed to a walk, despite the unlimited opportunities for victory which lay before them.

In order to speed up the bloody, slow-moving offensive in Belgium and Holland,

Paratroops, eight miles from Utah Beach at Carentan, pass the bodies of comrades killed by German snipers.

Montgomery devised and had approved by SHAEF Operation MARKET-GARDEN, a combined ground-airborne operation to open a narrow 60-mile front through which the British 30th Corps would rush to turn the north end of the Siegfried Line, or West Wall. The key to the success of the operation was the swift capture of the bridges at Veghel, Zon, Grave, Nijmegen, and Arnhem in the Netherlands by British and American airborne troops, so as to allow the 30th to pass through swiftly. This was to be one of the most ill-fated operations of the entire war.

On 17 September 1944 the American 101st Airborne Division jumped behind the German lines and captured the Veghel and Zon bridges, and the next day the 30th Corps, coming up from the south, linked up with them. On 17 September, too, the American 82nd Airborne dropped to take the Grave bridge, and two days later the 30th Corps had made its way to this location, as well. By 20 September the now-combined British-American forces had also taken the Nijmegen bridge. So far, the operation seemed to be going well, but farther to the north, at Arnhem, disaster was building.

The British 1st Airborne Division had landed to take it on 17 September, but the Germans had quickly rushed reinforcements into the area. In short order the British airborne forces had been cut off, with the 30th Corps unable to cut through to rescue them. On 25 September a remnant of the besieged 1st Airborne, about 2200 men, managed to withdraw across the Neder Rhine to British lines, but they left many comrades behind within the swiftly-closing German encirclement. The next day the British pocket was wiped out: the 1st Airborne had lost 7000 men killed, wounded or captured in the vicinity of Arnhem. And in the meantime General von Rundstedt had brought 86,000 men of the XV Army into the vicinity of the Scheldt Estuary, where they contributed to the prolonged and

Right: The campaign in France would show the colorful Patton to be one of the war's greatest commanders.
Below: The Normandy breakout.

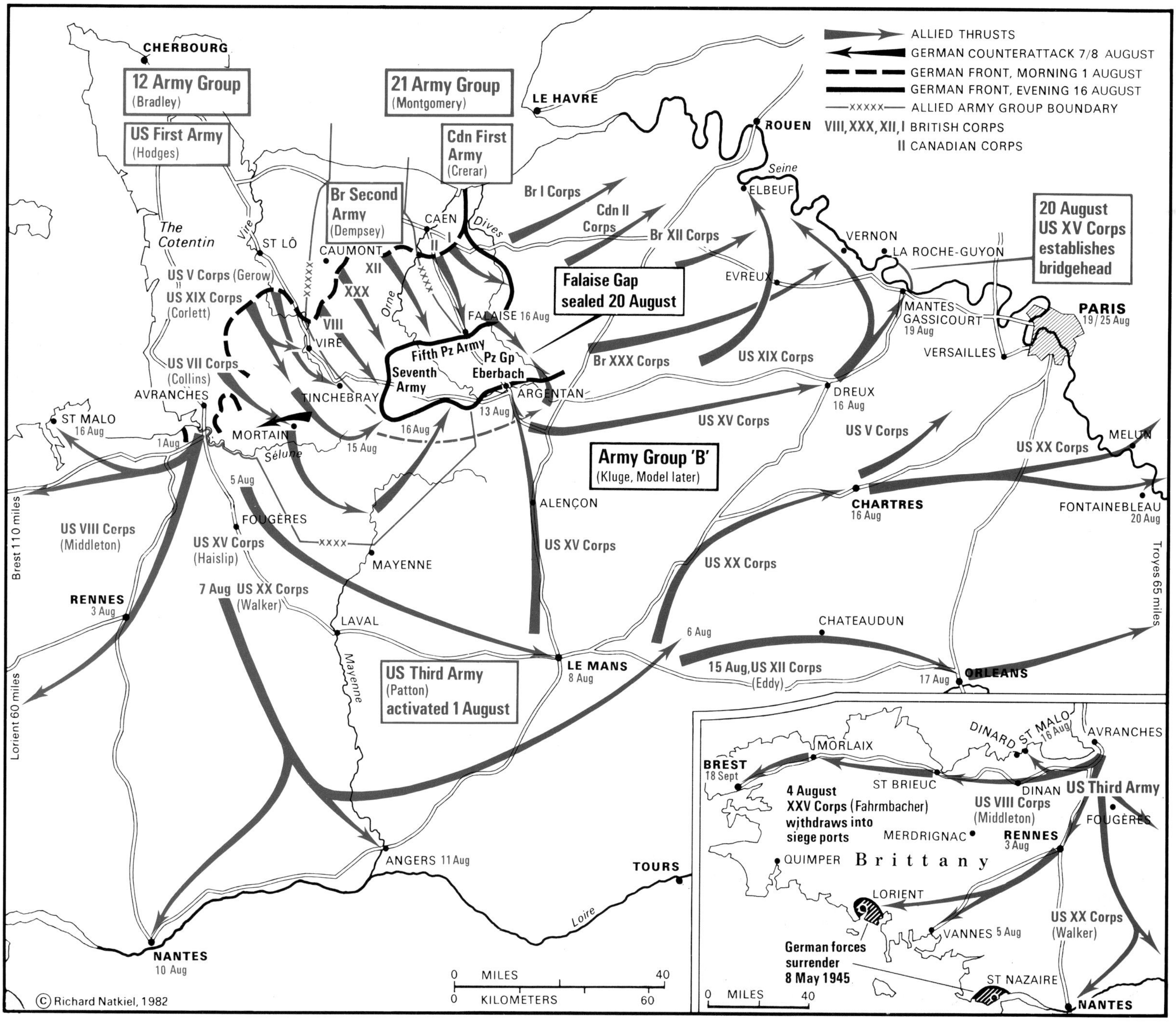

Paris was liberated on 25 August 1944. The honor of first entering the city was given the Free French. Four days later there was a great victory march down the Champs Elysées. Shown here, troops of the 28th Infantry Division.

stubborn defense of that vital area and continued to deny the Allies the use of Antwerp. In the aftermath of the fighting, MARKET-GARDEN was stoutly defended by the British and Montgomery as a proper move, but controversy over the operation continued for decades thereafter.

Although Antwerp was still useless to the Allies, while the Arnhem operation was underway the Canadian First Army continued clearing the Channel ports. During September they drove the Germans out of Dieppe, Le Havre, Boulogne, and Calais, the latter city of great importance as the launching site for the V-1 rockets now being fired on Britain. But not until 8 November was the Scheldt Estuary taken, primarily by Canadian troops, and not until 26 November was it cleared of mines and made usable. These delays held up the American armies to the south and east, forcing them to rely on the 'Red Ball Express' of trucks to bring them gasoline and other supplies all the way from Cherbourg, 350 miles away. And now the Allies found that winter was moving in. The end of the war would not come in 1944: They would have to wait out the winter and resume the offensive in the spring.

But Hitler had other plans. He was contriving a giant counteroffensive intended to break through the densely forested and semi-mountainous Ardennes region in Belgium and Luxembourg and drive all the way to Antwerp 100 miles to the west, thus splitting the advancing Allied armies. He would then destroy the British and American armies piecemeal before turning to face the Russians advancing from the east. Hitler's generals were opposed to this daring operation because they were convinced they did not have the numbers and supplies to mount such a massive counteroffensive. But Hitler insisted, and the Germans began to scrape together men and equipment from all over the Reich to carry out the unexpected and daring Ardennes offensive.

By the time the German offensive jumped off, on 16 December 1944, to begin what has come to be called the 'Battle of the Bulge,' 25 divisions, including 10 armored divisions, had been secretly assembled behind their lines. The VI SS Panzer Army, under General Josef Dietrich, and the V Panzer Army, under Lieutenant-General Hasso von Manteuffel, were to spearhead the attack directly through the American lines, while VII Army and XV Army protected their flanks. A Panzer brigade of 20,000 men, led by Lieutenant-Colonel Otto Skorzeny and dressed as Americans, was to commit sabotage and spread confusion behind the American lines. Over 250,000 men, 1900 artillery pieces, and 970 tanks and armored assault guns were to take part in the offensive, and some 1500 planes were promised in order to assure local air superiority. Hitler intended to run

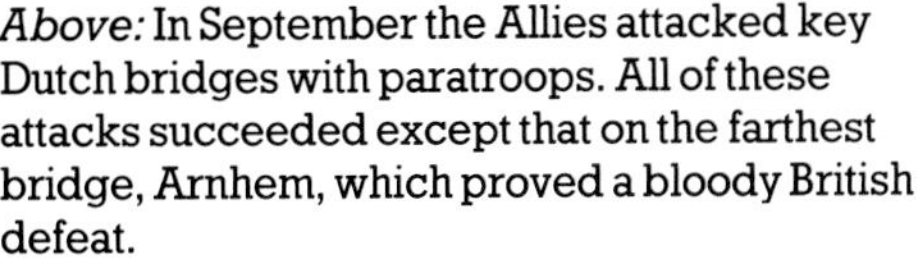

Above: In September the Allies attacked key Dutch bridges with paratroops. All of these attacks succeeded except that on the farthest bridge, Arnhem, which proved a bloody British defeat.
Right: A German Panther tank.

the show himself, the nominal commander, Field-Marshal von Rundstedt, having been placed in that position only for his prestige and morale-building power among the German troops.

While the Germans were building up for their Ardennes offensive, the Americans had been suffering badly in their attempt to take the Hurtgen Forest. They had sustained 24,000 casualties in this offensive (that lasted from 2 November to 13 December), and they lost 9000 more men to disease or battle fatigue. The 8th Corps of the First Army, against whom the German attack was to be directed, was thinly stretched and plagued with faulty intelligence as to what the Germans were up to. (An intelligence officer who told the First Army commander, Lieutenant General Courtney H Hodges, 'It's the Ardennes,' was sent off to Paris for a rest.) In miserable winter weather, marked by low clouds, fog, and heavy snowfalls that grounded Allied airpower over the Ardennes, on 16 December the Germans launched the most famous counterattack of the war.

Only 83,000 Americans stood as defenders when the 250,000 Germans attacked on a 60-mile front, with the communications centers and road junctions of Saint-Vith and Bastogne as their first objectives. The initial attacks carried all before them, despite desperate efforts by the American troops to halt the onslaught. In some areas of the front the Germans had a 6-to-1 advantage. Wave after wave of Germans drove out of the Ardennes, some of them following Hitler's orders for a 'wave of terror and fright' in which 'no human inhibitions should be shown.' This resulted in the slaughter of 140 American prisoners by SS Panzer troops in what came to be known as the 'Malmedy Massacre.' Behind the Allied lines all was confusion as the Germans poured through, with Eisenhower desperately trying to transfer troops into the Ardennes as soon as he and his advisors finally realized that a major German offensive was underway.

Men of an SS unit ready to open fire with their machine gun.

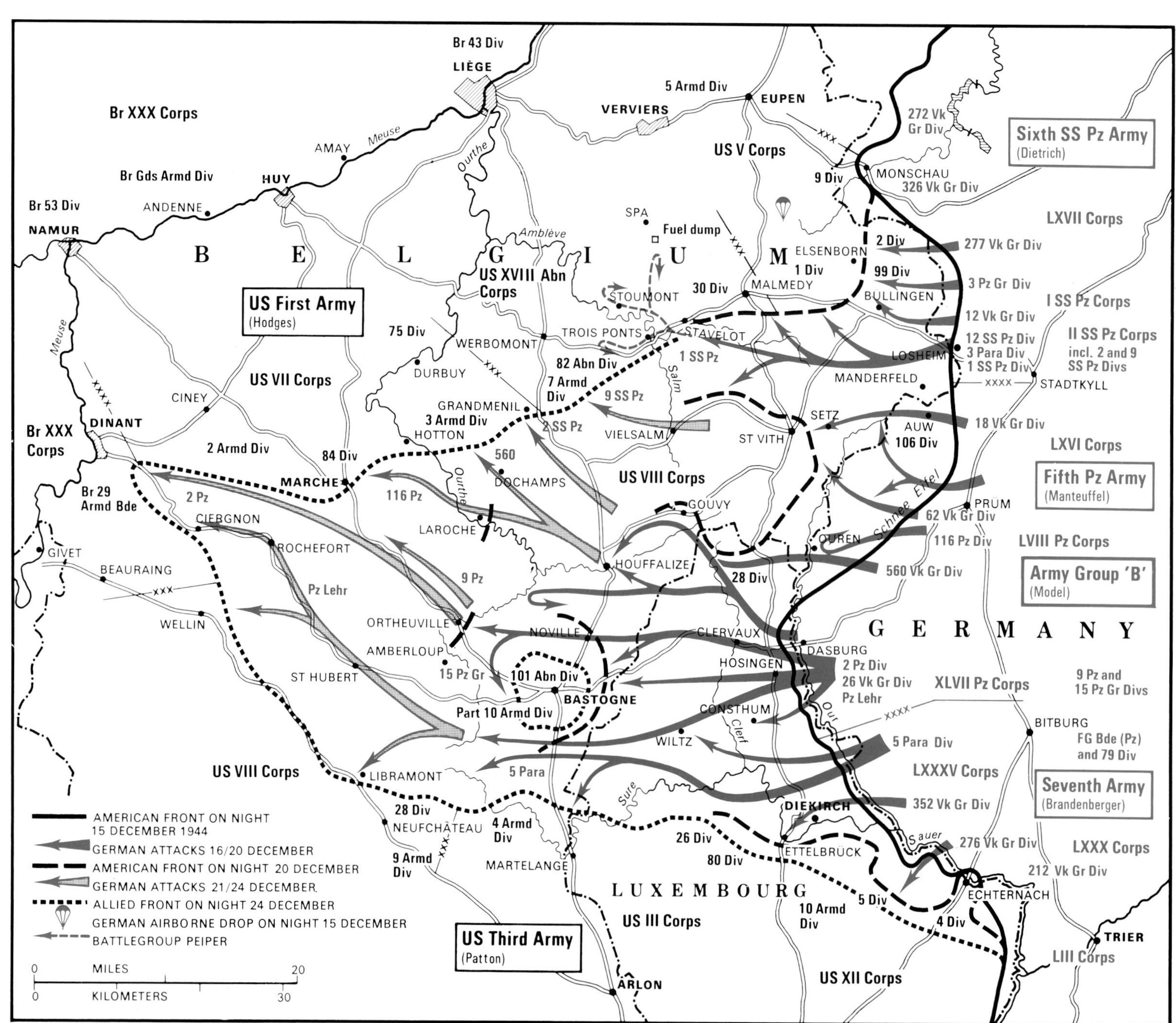

Saint-Vith was the key to the northern Ardennes. Every available unit was sent to its defense, including the 7th Armored Division. Within three days of the opening of the offensive, Eisenhower also ordered the 82nd Airborne, now in reserve and recovering from MARKET-GARDEN, into the Saint-Vith area. Once they arrived, they and the 7th Armored Division held out near the tiny town against continued German attacks until 23 December, thereby throwing the entire German attack off schedule.

Thirty miles southwest of Saint-Vith, at Bastogne, another drama was being played out. On 18 December 3000 men of the 101st Airborne Division, the 'Screaming Eagles,' began moving toward the area to relieve its defenders. In command was Brigadier General Anthony C McAuliffe. By 20 December the entire 11,000-man 101st, along with some men of the 10th Armored Division, was in place and ready to take on the German attacks. For two days they held out against all odds, cheered by the knowledge that 'Georgie' Patton was sending the 4th Armored Division to their rescue from the south. When the Germans sent a surrender ultimatum to McAuliffe, his written reply simply said 'Nuts!' To be sure Germans understood, the American officer delivering the reply said, 'If you don't understand what "Nuts" means, in plain English it is the same as "Go to hell,"' adding, 'And I will tell you something else – if you continue to attack we will kill every goddam German that tries to break into this city!'

The siege of Bastogne was not lifted until 26 December, when Patton's armored units fought their way into the city. The 4th Armored Division lost 1000 men in carrying out the rescue, and they found 2000 more Americans dead in and around Bastogne. But at Bastogne and Saint-Vith the Americans had fatally disrupted the German timetable. By Christmas Day the Panzer armies had been stopped, with dry fuel tanks, 30 miles short of Antwerp, and, as the skies cleared, the Allies soon had complete control of the air. On 30 December the First Army began to counterattack from the North, while the Third Army moved in from the south. By 16 January the giant pincers had met at Houffalize, north of Bastogne. On 28 January 1944 the Battle of the Bulge was declared officially over. The Germans had suffered over 100,000 casualties, to the Americans' 81,000. Hitler's grand counteroffensive had failed, and the last great reserve of German men and equipment was gone.

In February and March 1945 the Allies began to cross the Rhine into Germany. The 21st Army Group, under Montgomery, moved from the north into the vital Ruhr. To the south the US 12th and 6th Army Groups continued to press toward Cologne. When units of the US First Army discovered the bridge at Remagen over the Rhine intact on 7 March and crossed over and held it, Eisenhower shifted the attack south to support this opening. Patton's Third Army crossed at Nierstein on 22 March, and by early April the

Above: **Map of the Battle of the Bulge.**
Right: **A US 105mm howitzer in action during the German advance.**

General Anthony McAuliffe, famous at Bastogne for one word: 'Nuts!'

east bank of the Rhine had been cleared of German troops.

In line with American promises to Stalin, Roosevelt and Eisenhower had decided they would not conduct a race for Berlin with the Russians and that the Allies would stop at the Elbe (a decision that dismayed and angered the less naive British). Nevertheless the drive into Germany continued during April and early May, and all along the western terrain the Allied armies were soon breaking through the weakened German resistance. On 25 April American and Russian troops met at Torgau, on the Elbe east of Leipzig. On 30 April Hitler committed suicide as the Russians fought their way into Berlin, and on 4 May Montgomery accepted unconditional surrender from the representatives of Admiral Karl Dönitz, Hitler's successor, at Luneberg Heath. The Allied war against Germany ended on 8 May 1945, and by 11 May all Germans had lain down their arms.

Between D-Day and 8 May 1945, 5.4 million Allied troops had been poured into Western Europe, supported by 970,000 vehicles and 18.2 million tons of supplies. In this last year of the European war, in which the US Army had over 3 million men in the theater, the Americans had suffered 568,000 casualties, including 135,000 dead. America's allies suffered 179,000 casualties, including 60,000 dead. German losses were probably equal to or greater than the total Allied losses. No one on the Allied side doubted that the sacrifices had been well worth while.

The Army Air Force over Europe

Whatever doubts remained from the military debates of the 1930s about the importance of air power were largely erased during the first year of the war. The German Luftwaffe had played a stellar role in the Blitzkriegs against Poland, the Low Countries and France; and in the Battle of Britain the fate of England, and possibly the outcome of the war, had been decided by the RAF. As a consequence, there was little sentiment in the US to stint the air services, and General Henry ('Hap') Arnold, chief of the Army Air Forces (as the Air Corps was re-christened in June 1941), now received unqualified support for airpower both from the Army and the Congress. By the time of America's entry into the war in December 1941 the nation had an Air Force of 354,000 men and 2800 planes. At peak strength, in early 1945, it would have 2.4 million men and nearly 800,000 planes.

Shortly after Pearl Harbor the Eighth Air Force was formed, and Brigadier General Ira Eaker was sent to England to set up its headquarters. Eaker was a strategic bombing enthusiast who had stood beside Billy Mitchell during his court martial. Since then his belief had not flagged, which placed him in close agreement with Air Chief Marshal Arthur Harris of the Royal Air Force Bomber Command.

Not until August 1942 did Eighth Air Force and Eaker (who had now replaced General Carl ('Tooey') Spaatz as Eighth Air Force commander) have enough men and four-engined Boeing B-17 Flying Fortresses in

Right: The drive into Germany.
Below: Snow-clad Shermans lined up for counterattack near St Vith, one of the key US positions in the battle.

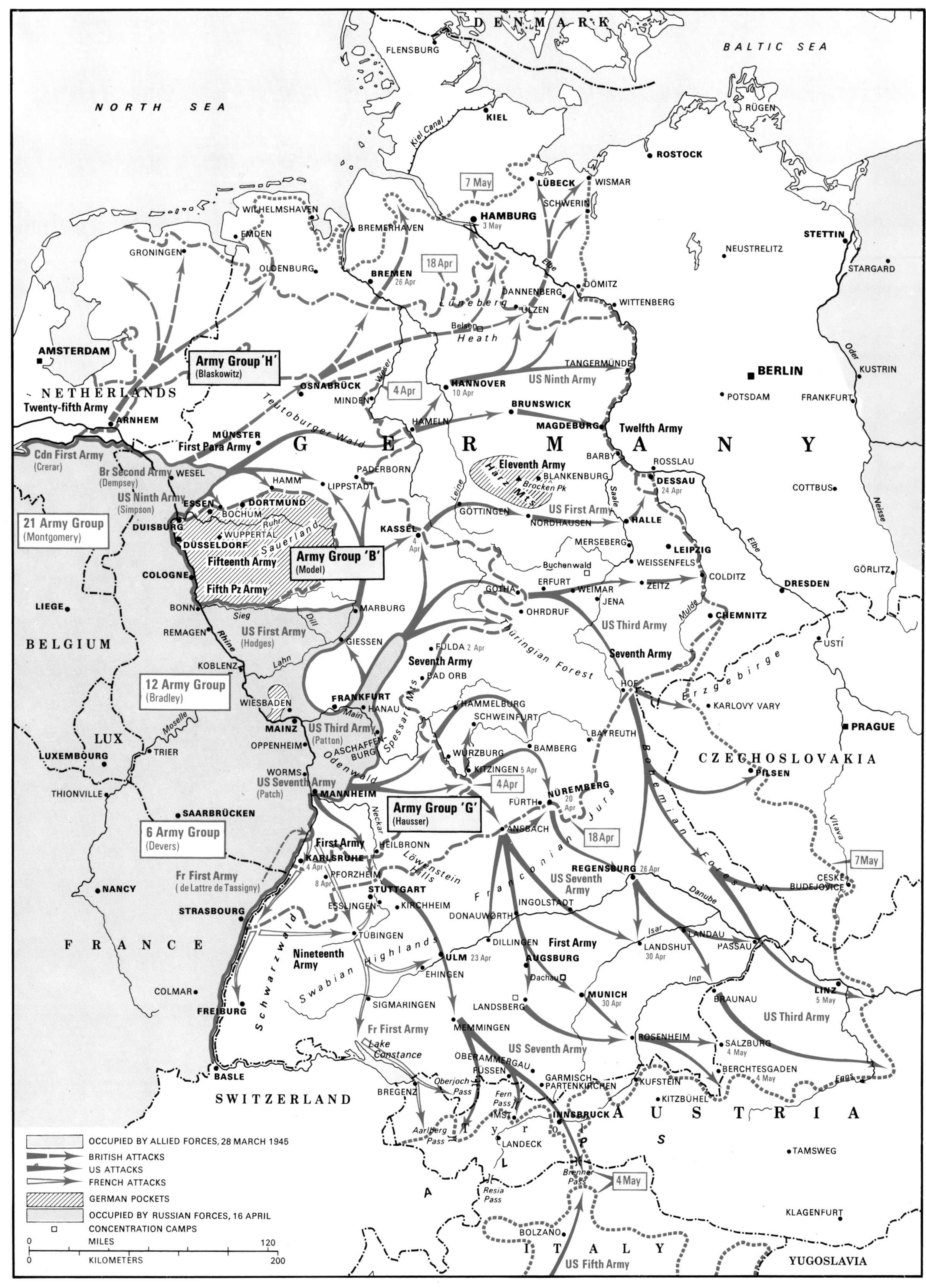

DENMARK
BALTIC SEA
NORTH SEA
NETHERLANDS
BELGIUM
LUX
FRANCE
SWITZERLAND
GERMANY
CZECHOSLOVAKIA
AUSTRIA
ITALY
YUGOSLAVIA
ALPS
Army Group 'H' (Blaskowitz)
Army Group 'B' (Model)
Army Group 'G' (Hausser)
21 Army Group (Montgomery)
12 Army Group (Bradley)
6 Army Group (Devers)
Cdn First Army (Crerar)
Br Second Army (Dempsey)
US Ninth Army (Simpson)
US First Army (Hodges)
US Third Army (Patton)
US Seventh Army (Patch)
Fr First Army (de Lattre de Tassigny)
Twenty-fifth Army
First Para Army
Fifteenth Army
Fifth Pz Army
Eleventh Army
Twelfth Army
Seventh Army
First Army
Nineteenth Army
US Fifth Army
7 May
18 Apr
4 Apr
4 May
7May
OCCUPIED BY ALLIED FORCES, 28 MARCH 1945
BRITISH ATTACKS
US ATTACKS
FRENCH ATTACKS
GERMAN POCKETS
OCCUPIED BY RUSSIAN FORCES, 16 APRIL
CONCENTRATION CAMPS
MILES 0 120
KILOMETERS 0 200

L
337675
N
VE
L
297059
S
S

Right: The victors: (L to R) Omar Bradley, Dwight Eisenhower, George Patton.
Below: Almost as vital as the ground war was the battle raging in the sky. Here, B-17s of the 381st Bomb Group.

England to make their first bombing raid, on Rouen in France. A dozen more followed, as the Americans learned the art of high-level daylight bombing. In the meantime, four-engined Consolidated B-24 Liberators had joined the B-17s. Liberators were slightly faster than the 'Forts' and had a greater bomb capacity, but the B-17 could operate at greater altitudes and could defend themselves better. Together these two bomber types would form the backbone of the American air offensive against Germany in the years that followed.

By late 1942 the Eighth had nearly 300 bombers in England, and its air crews were gaining in proficiency daily as they raided more and more targets in France. But Eaker had yet to realize his dream of launching his daylight precision bomber fleets against Germany itself. Indeed, he was beginning to encounter a growing sentiment in both England and America against this ever being done. The problem had to do with the lack of long-range fighters. Neither the Americans nor the British yet had fighters able to escort bombers beyond the borders of Germany, and it was widely held that the losses Ger-

B-24s had better range than B-17s, but their weaker defenses made them less favored for raids deep into Germany.

man day fighters could inflict on unescorted bomber formations would prove not merely unacceptable but probably appalling. It was for this reason that the British had long ago abandoned daylight strategic bombing entirely, confining their long-range heavy bomber operations to the hours of darkness. They strongly urged the Americans to do the same, but Eaker and other precision bombing enthusiasts scorned the inaccuracy of night bombing and insisted that their Forts could take care of themselves in air combat. In the end, Roosevelt and Churchill, at the Casablanca Conference (January 1943), agreed to give the Eaker faction a chance to prove their contentions about the viability of unescorted daylight bombing. To what extent they succeeded in doing so is still moot, but in the process of trying they undeniably visited fearsome destruction on Germany.

The Eighth Air Force's daylight bombing campaign against Germany began in earnest in June 1943. Kiel, Warnemünde, Hannover, Oschersleben, Kassel, and various points in the strategic Ruhr Valley were among the targets struck during the next 60 days. Perhaps the most famous raid of this period was the attack on Hamburg, conducted in conjunction with the RAF in late July. In that battered city superheated air from burning buildings was drawn into a gigantic convection current that produced tornadic winds of 150 mph and temperatures of 1800° Fahrenheit. Approximately half the city and 50,000 people were destroyed in this attack.

So far, bomber losses had been significant but far from intolerable. This was to change in August, as the Luftwaffe fighter defenses began to organize to meet the new challenge. The climactic day was 17 August 1943 (the same day the invasion of Italy began). The Eighth Air Force had been assigned two targets deep in Germany. The first was Regensberg, site of a major Messerschmitt aircraft manufacturing complex. Although the introduction of drop tanks had begun to extend the ranges of Allied fighters significantly, Regensburg was still well beyond their radius, and the 146 B-17s had to fly unescorted over Germany most of the way to the target. Luftwaffe Messerschmitt Bf 109s and 110s, Focke-Wulf Fw 190s, and Junkers Ju 88 nightfighters kept the Forts under continuous attacks. Seventeen Forts were lost, and casualties to aircrews on surviving planes were heavy. But this was only the warm-up.

The second raid that day, on the Schweinfurt ball-bearing factories, also deep in Germany, was to have been launched 10 minutes after the Regensburg bombers flew off, but weather delayed the bombers' takeoffs for more than three hours, thus negating any advantage to be had from simultaneous attack. Some 300 German fighters were waiting for the 230 Flying Fortresses as they crossed the German border. They hectored the Forts unmercifully all the way to Schweinfurt and back, shooting down 36. Although the Americans did considerable damage to both Regensburg and Schweinfurt, 53 of the 376 B-17s sent out on these two missions were shot down, and 47 others never flew again. So great was the damage to the bombers on this single day that the Americans did not return to German skies for another two months. When they did, on 14 October, in the form of another giant raid on Schweinfurt by 291 Flying Fortresses, the results were much the same. Some 60 American bombers were lost, to only 38 German fighters. Further raiding deep into Germany in 1943 was suspended until the range of fighters could be sufficiently extended to escort bombers all the way to their targets.

The Eighth Air Force was by no means the only US Army air force operating in the European Theater. In the summer of 1942, while the Eighth was assembling in England, the nucleus of a US Army Middle East Air Force was being established in North Africa. Composed at first of a handful of B-17, B-24, B-25 (a twin-engine medium bomber built by

North American) and P-40 units, it grew rapidly. After the battle of El Alamein it was redesignated the Ninth Air Force, and by August of 1943 it had become so large that it had to be subdivided, some of its units being given to the newly created Twelfth Air Force, while the remainder of the Ninth was transferred to England to supplement the Eighth Air Force's growing daylight bombing offensive across the Channel. Since, unlike the Eighth, the Ninth had, in addition to its heavy bombers, a large medium bomber component, it was able to mount nearly continuous low-level short-range attacks against targets in France and the Low Countries, even at times when, either for reasons of policy or bad weather, the heavies were grounded. And after D-Day, when the mediums could operate from bases on the continent, they, too, were able to join in the aerial assault on Germany. By the end of the war the Ninth was a very large and powerful organization, indeed, containing no fewer than 11 Bomb Groups and 18 Fighter Groups (three more than the Eighth).

While the Eighth and Ninth assailed Hitler's Reich from the west, the Twelfth kept up the attack from the south, now, increasingly from bases in Italy. By the beginning of 1944 it, also, had grown so large that it had to be subdivided, the heavy bomber units and their fighter escort groups being transferred to a new command, the Fifteenth Air Force, while the Twelfth continued to operate an impressive collection of medium, attack and fighter units.

With respect to daylight raids by unescorted heavy bombers flying deep into enemy territory, the experience of the Mediterranean air forces was much the same as that of the air forces flying out of England. Perhaps the most memorable example was the great raid mounted against Rumania's Ploesti oil refineries in August 1943 (the same grim month as the Regensburg and Schweinfurt raids). Of the 165 unescorted B-24s that finally made it to the target 43 were downed by

A bomber's-eye-view of the Eighth Air Force's most notoriously dangerous and expensive target, Schweinfurt.

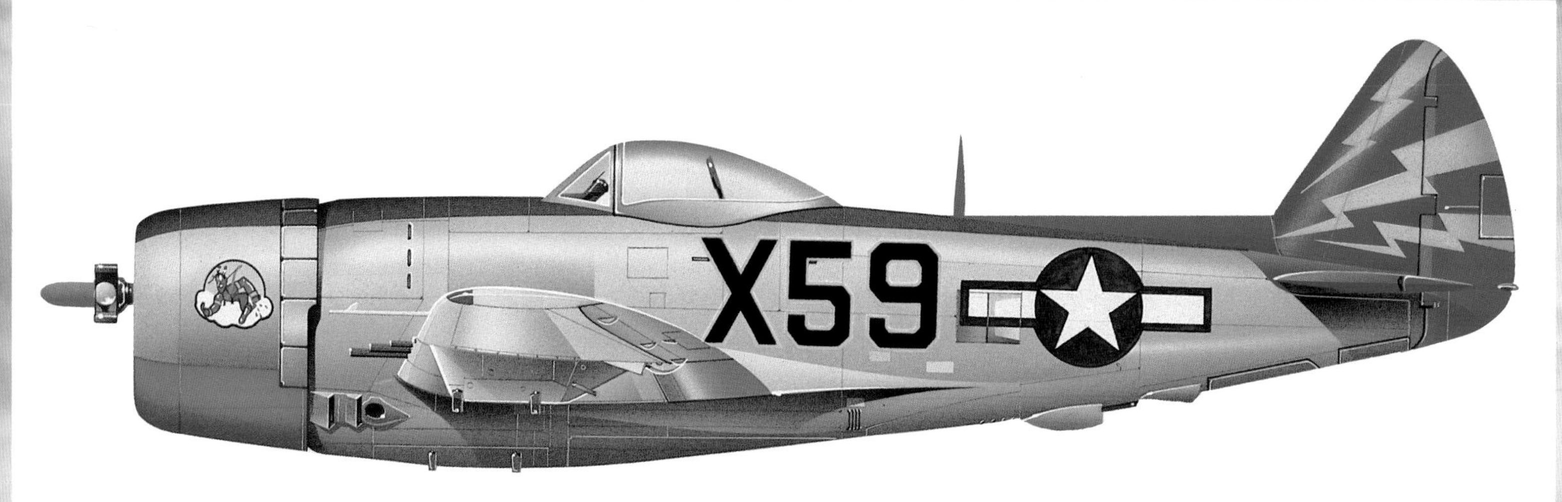

The P-47 Thunderbolt fighter (*above*) lacked the range to escort bombers deep into Germany. But any Luftwaffe hope of halting the raids ended when the long-range P-51 Mustang appeared.

enemy flak and fighters and eight more were so badly shot up they had to crash land in Turkey; and of the 114 that managed to straggle back to their bases more than half had sustained serious damage.

By the end of August it was plain that, despite the contentions of enthusiasts, the future of daylight strategic bombing would, after all, depend on the provision of suitable fighter escort. Of the American fighters available in 1943, the big Lockheed P-38 Lightning had the necessary range but could not maneuver with Lufwaffe fighters on equal terms, while the more formidable Republic P-47 Thunder bolt decidedly did *not* have the range. Yet there was hope in the offing, in the form of North American's spectacular new P-51 Mustang, an American-designed airframe powered by Britain's famed Rolls-Royce Merlin engine, that promised not only unparalleled speed and maneuverability but a range that put virtually the whole of Germany

YM

Above: **Messerschmitt Bf 110 fighters, one of many air-defense types used.**
Left: **By 1945 Mustang-escorted B-24s could raid Berlin almost at will.**

within its combat radius. Mustangs began to appear in the ETO in early 1944, and within six months they had radically changed the character of the European air war. Allied bomber losses dropped sharply, while Luftwaffe fighter losses soared to such levels that German industry was hard put to make them good. What could not be made good, of course, was the relentless loss of trained German fighter pilots. The Luftwaffe was, in effect, hemorrhaging to death, while the whole of Germany lay increasingly exposed to the fury of the Allied air offensive.

Although British and American air strategists protested, Allied air power in 1944 was largely turned to supporting OVERLORD. The Eighth and Ninth Air Forces, along with their British air colleagues, flew over 200,000 sorties to cripple the main transportation lines in France and northwest Europe. They virtually shut down rail traffic in France, although always bombing at a 2-to-1 ratio on the Pas-de-Calais area over the Normandy area to preserve the landing site deception. They also flew against the German rocket-launching sites in northwest Europe, and on D-Day 8000 bombers and fighters flew over 14,000 sorties in support of the amphibious landings, having already played their deceptive role in Operation FORTITUDE farther north. In the days that followed, the Allies had complete air superiority over the Normandy beaches, a major factor in the success of the invasion.

Major daylight strategic bombing of Germany resumed with a vengeance in 1945. The declining Luftwaffe tried desperately to limit the destruction. One hope for turning the tide of air battle was the development of the Messerschmitt Me 262, the world's first jet fighter, but Hitler delayed development of this remarkable plane until late 1944, insisting it should be used as an offensive bomber, since it had the ability to carry a bomb. Once in the skies, the Me 262s proved to be very effective against their propeller-driven adversaries, but there were never enough of them even to begin to threaten Allied air supremacy.

Aircraft of the RAF and all four of America's European air forces now ranged virtually at will over Germany. In February Allied strategic bombers dropped nearly 125,000 tons of bombs on German cities, while medium and attack bombers added approximately another 30,000 tons. By March the Eighth Air Force alone was capable of sending 1500 heavy bombers over Germany in a single day, and the RAF of dropping nearly 5000 tons of bombs on a single target. The gruesome Anglo-American attack on Dresden, made in mid-February, is perhaps the best remembered of these late-war raids. In it, 1600 acres of the old city were leveled and about 70,000 persons lost their lives.

On 16 April 1945 the air offensive against Germany ended. There was by then hardly anything left to destroy. Exactly how great a contribution aerial bombardment made to Germany's eventual collapse is still a matter of debate, but none denies that that contribution was significant. The 73,000 American airmen – as well as the like number of RAF fliers – who were killed during the European bombing offensive certainly did not give their lives in vain. Yet it was to be in the Pacific, rather than in Europe, that the truly decisive role of air power would at last be demonstrated.

The fight for Bougainville.

WORLD WAR IN THE PACIFIC: 1941-1945

In September 1941 the military rulers of Japan made a fateful decision. Unless the United States reversed its policy of resisting Japanese expansion in the Far East, American outposts in the Pacific would have to be attacked and destroyed, for they stood as barriers to the fulfillment of the Japanese dream of dominating the western Pacific. Not satisfied with her conquests of Manchuria, Korea, Formosa, and the Ryukyu Islands prior to 1921, in the next ten years Japan had seized large portions of northern China and important Chinese southern seaports and had then moved into French Indochina, with the acquiescence of the Vichy government in France.

Now it was time to complete the Japanese empire in the Pacific by seizing the American-owned Philippine Islands and Guam, the Dutch East Indies, Borneo, New Guinea, Burma, Thailand and Malaya, plus Wake Island in the central Pacific and the Gilbert and Solomon Islands in the southwest Pacific. With these conquests completed, Japan would rule the Pacific for decades to come. As her leaders and people saw it, this was her destiny.

Seizing Far Eastern territories from the British and Dutch did not seem too dangerous an undertaking, since these nations were tied up with their war against Hitler. The problem was the United States. American ownership of the Philippines, Guam, and Wake meant that the Americans had territories and military installations within the area coveted by Japan. As long as the Americans stood astride and on the flank of the Japanese routes of conquest, Japanese holdings, both real and anticipated, would be endangered. If, therefore, the United States would not acquiesce in Japan's Far Eastern plans (and it would not: American hostility to Japanese expansionism became clearer and clearer after 1939), Japan would have both to seize American territories in the western Pacific and neutralize her military bases in the central Pacific.

The first six months of the Pacific War saw Japan everywhere triumphant over her Western foes.

Such brave defenses as that of Wake Is. (*right*) salved American pride but were no substitute for victory.

Of course this would mean war, but, it was hoped, within six months the Japanese army and navy would have realized all of Japan's objectives in the Pacific. The Americans and their severely weakened European allies would be left on the periphery of Japan's empire, with no alternative but to accept her conquests. America could launch a counter-offensive only from the Hawaiian Islands or from her own West Coast, and it would have to extend all the way across the vast reaches of the Pacific. This would be a nearly impossible task, especially in the absence of significant help from the British, French, or Dutch. America would thus have to accept the inevitable and learn to live with Japan's conquests.

These strategic calculations gave birth to a Japanese plan to attack Pearl Harbor, the Philippines, and Guam early in December 1941, and simultaneously to mount offensives against the British, Dutch and Australian territories west and south. The western and central Pacific would be firmly in Japanese hands by mid-summer 1942. The plan was audacious to the point of being breathtaking, and it almost succeeded.

At 0755 on the clear Sunday morning of 7 December 1941 the Japanese launched a superbly executed surprise attack on the giant American naval base at Pearl Harbor. Within two hours most of the US Pacific Fleet's battleships were either sunk or severely damaged, 18 warships overall. In addition, 177 Army and Navy planes were destroyed, 159 damaged, and over 2,000 sailors and Marines were dead or dying. Intelligence information that a Japanese attack was imminent, information that in retrospect would appear to be crystal clear, had produced no advance warning. Radar blips picked up by the Army Aircraft Warning Service's five mobile radar units on the northern tip of Oahu (blips that indicated great numbers of planes coming from the north) were first misunderstood and then ignored. The Americans were totally unprepared.

At the Army's Schofield Barracks, Hickam Field and Wheeler Field, as elsewhere on Oahu, the enemy struck without warning. Army Air Force bombers and fighters at the airfields had been lined up wingtip to wingtip as protection against sabotage. They made perfect targets for the Japanese airmen, who wiped them out in the first waves. Almost no American aircraft were able to rise to meet the enemy. A flight of B-17s arriving from the mainland, stripped of armor and ammunition for the long over-water haul, became a prime target as the Flying Fortresses flew into the area to land at Hickam Field. One was destroyed as it crash landed, another landed on a golf course, and the others set down anywhere they could on any

The Japanese attack on Pearl Harbor (*right and top right*) so crippled the US Pacific Fleet that no retaliatory action was possible.

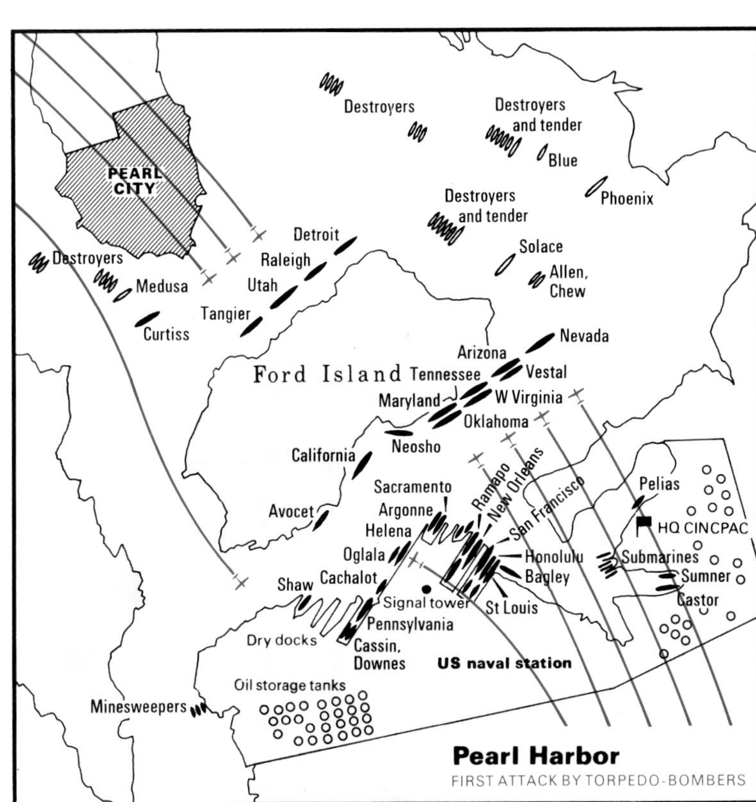
PEARL CITY
Destroyers
Destroyers and tender
Blue
Phoenix
Destroyers and tender
Detroit
Raleigh
Utah
Tangier
Destroyers
Medusa
Curtiss
Solace
Allen, Chew
Nevada
Arizona
Ford Island
Tennessee
Vestal
Maryland
W Virginia
Oklahoma
Neosho
California
Sacramento
Argonne
Helena
Avocet
Ramapo
New Orleans
San Francisco
Pelias
HQ CINCPAC
Oglala
Cachalot
Shaw
Honolulu
Bagley
Submarines
Sumner
Castor
Signal tower
St Louis
Pennsylvania
Dry docks
Cassin, Downes
US naval station
Oil storage tanks
Minesweepers
Pearl Harbor
FIRST ATTACK BY TORPEDO-BOMBERS

small airstrips available in the Hawaiian Islands.

Like his naval counterpart, Admiral Husband E Kimmel, Lieutenant General Walter C Short, the Army commander in Hawaii, was soon relieved of command and held accountable for the devastation. He had not consulted with Kimmel and had failed to put his men on full war alert prior to the raid. Whatever Short's real guilt in the controversial matter as to why the military was not ready for the attack, the grim fact remained that the Army, like the Navy, was in no position either to protect the Hawaiian Islands against further attack or invasion or to begin the process of fighting back against the forces of Nippon.

Defeat: Guam, Wake, the Philippines

On that same December day, at 1220 in the afternoon, 108 Japanese bombers and 84 fighters swept in over Clark Field northwest of Manila, the capital of the Philippines, on the island of Luzon. Below they found 18 B-17s, over 50 P-40 fighter planes and 30 other aircraft all neatly lined up in rows. Not one defensive aircraft was in the air to oppose them, despite the fact that the news of Pearl Harbor had by now been flashed throughout the Pacific command. In short order, and with their only challenge coming from feeble antiaircraft fire, the Japanese planes swooped down to destroy General Douglas MacArthur's air force parked on the ground. Only 17 B-17s sent south to a base on Mindanao, the southernmost main island in the Philippines, were saved from destruction. As at Pearl Harbor, the Americans in the Philippines had been caught unprepared. Plans had been underway for a B-17 attack on the Japanese air forces on Formosa, but they had been delayed by a lack of reconnaissance photographs. Now, the thousands of Army personnel in the Philippines, along with their naval and Filipino comrades, were left without air cover as the Japanese prepared to launch their invasion of the archipelago.

Almost at the same time, the 400-plus naval and Marine garrison on Guam in the Marianas, some 1,500 miles east of Manila, was attacked by over 5,000 Japanese troops. Within two days the island fell.

Wake Island, a small atoll 2,300 miles west of Hawaii, then being converted to a naval aircraft station, was scheduled for attack on 8 December. On the island were 450 Marines, 1200 civilians from the construction crews working on the islands, and a handful of Army Signal Corps and naval personnel. They were hit first in the forenoon by Japanese aircraft from Kwajalein, in the Marshall Islands, 600 miles away. Three days later a Japanese invasion squadron of 13 vessels arrived off Wake. Although the Marine defenders, with valuable aid from the Navy and Army personnel, held off two invasion attempts with their accurate gunnery, sinking one ship and damaging five others, they could not stop the inevitable. Air raids continued on the besieged garrison, and finally, on 23 December, a major Japanese invasion was launched. The island fell that day, and 1555 Americans were taken prisoner.

The main Japanese target, though, was the Philippines. Here General Douglas MacArthur, former Army Chief of Staff, Field Marshal of the Philippine army, and now commander of the American-Philippine army forces, had only about 25,000 regulars on hand. These consisted of the Philippine Division of the US Army, 12,000 Filipino Scouts (members of the US Army), a division of Philippine Army regulars, and a few Marines. With these few men he would have to hold off a major Japanese invasion force.

Lieutenant General Masaharu Homma led the 43,000 men of his Japanese 14th Army ashore on Lingayen Gulf, north of Manila, on 22 December. Homma's forces soon had the Northern Luzon Force, under Major General Jonathan ('Skinny') Wainwright, in retreat. Meanwhile, a second force landed at Lamon Bay, 70 miles southeast of the capital. The American and Filipino forces could not stop the Japanese moves toward Manila, despite their bravest efforts, so MacArthur ordered all his forces back, some taking up positions on the Bataan Peninsula at the northern end of Manila Bay, while others moved onto the fortress island of Corregidor – 'The Rock' – in

the middle of the entrance to the bay. This meant abandoning the city of Manila, but MacArthur felt he had no choice if the garrison was to hold out long enough for aid to arrive. By 2 January Manila had fallen.

Although faced with shortages of food, ammunition and medicine, 15,000 American troops and their 65,000 Filipino allies dug in on Bataan to await the Japanese juggernaut. Army headquarters was deep inside the 1400-foot reinforced Malinta Tunnel on Corregidor, and from there the defense of Bataan and Corregidor would be directed. Beginning on 11 January, the Japanese again and again mounted artillery and infantry attacks against the American and Filipino positions on Bataan, first at the northern end of the peninsula and then, when this line had to be abandoned, across the center. Slowly the American-Filipino forces were pushed back, but they took a grim toll of Japanese as they went. By mid-February Homma had lost over 7000 dead and wounded, and he had still not taken Luzon. He called a two-month halt and asked Tokyo for reinforcements.

During the lull the American and Filipino soldiers tried to strengthen themselves for the offensive that was sure to come, but MacArthur's army was slowly falling victim to

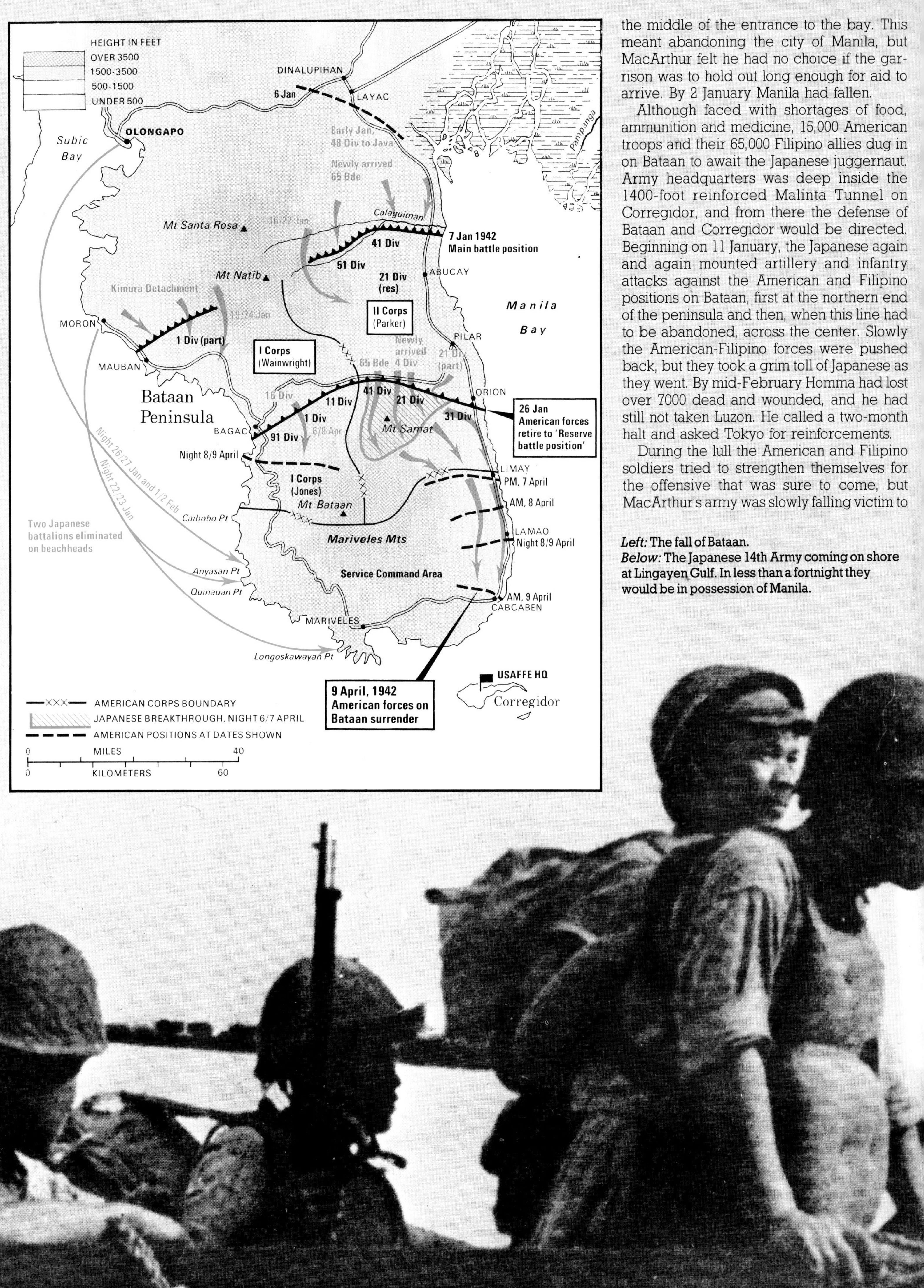

Left: The fall of Bataan.
Below: The Japanese 14th Army coming on shore at Lingayen Gulf. In less than a fortnight they would be in possession of Manila.

disease, as supplies of medicine, especially precious quinine, ran out. And morale, too, was sinking, particularly after a radio broadcast from President Roosevelt in late February revealed that reinforcements were not coming. Then MacArthur himself was ordered out of the Philippines by Roosevelt: He was to go to Australia to assume command of forces that would launch a grand counteroffensive against Japan. MacArthur reluctantly followed orders. On 11 March he turned over command on Luzon to General Wainwright and, with his family, left by PT boat for Mindanao, to the south, and thence by Flying Fortress to Darwin, Australia. Before leaving his beloved Philippines, MacArthur promised Wainwright he would return, a vow the flamboyant general reiterated upon arriving in Australia: 'I came through, and I shall return.' This public promise would cast a long shadow over subsequent Pacific strategy.

Back in the Philippines the suffering and dying went on. The revitalized forces of General Homma renewed their offensive on Bataan on 3 April, and six days later Major General Edward King, who had replaced Wainwright as Bataan commander when Wainwright replaced MacArthur on Corregidor, surrendered what was left of the American-Filipino forces in his command, 76,000 men. For another month the 13,000 defenders on Corregidor and its three surrounding fortified islands were subjected to constant artillery barrages. Then, on 5 May, Japanese troops and tanks rolled ashore. Two days later Wainwright was forced to surrender not only Corregidor and its defenders but the entire Philippine archipelago to General Homma. The Philippines had fallen after five months, but not before the Army troops there, along with their Navy, Marine and Filipino comrades, had written a glorious chapter in defensive warfare, and not before several thousand troops slipped away to fight the Japanese as guerrillas until MacArthur fulfilled his promise to return.

For those soldiers forced to surrender in the Philippines, the suffering was only beginning. The 13,000 men on Corregidor were left without food for a week and were then driven through Manila like animals before being shipped by train to a harshly-run POW camp at Cabanatuan, north of Manila. Here, within two months, 2000 American prisoners died of hunger and disease. The 76,000 American and Filipino prisoners from Bataan underwent a worse fate, the infamous Bataan Death March to Camp O'Donnell, 65 miles away. Most were forced to walk and to endure the cruelty of the Japanese guards who, in their contempt for any soldier who would surrender, frequently stabbed and shot those who straggled. At least 7000 Americans and Filipinos died on the Death March.

By the end of the war, of the 25,600 Americans captured in the Philippines, on Wake Island, and elsewhere in the Pacific (22,000 of these in the Philippines), 10,650 died in captivity, a grim figure of over 41 percent. The saga of the Corregidor and Bataan prisoners was but a foretaste of the cruelty and fanaticism of the Pacific war that was about to unfold.

Left: The surrender of Corregidor.
Below: One of Col. James Doolittle's 16 B-25s taking off from USS *Hornet* for the famous first raid on Tokyo. The raid did little damage, but its effect on enemy morale was considerable.

The Solomons Campaign

The Americans were able to strike back at Japan on 18 April 1942, in an astonishing raid by 16 land-based Army B-25 bombers led by Lieutenant Colonel James H Doolittle. They flew 700 miles from the carrier *Hornet* to bomb Tokyo and four other major Japanese cities. The raid served to buttress American morale early in the war, but it caused little damage. The Navy also scored some minor victories in the Pacific, but none great enough to offset the grim fact that most of the miniscule American Asiatic Fleet, including the cruiser USS *Houston*, had either been destroyed in the Battle of the Java Sea on 27-28 February or in other isolated actions that occurred as Japanese forces swept inexorably down through the southwestern Pacific. The meager British and Dutch forces working with the Asiatic Fleet were also decimated.

The Japanese armies moved on. Malaya, Singapore, the Dutch East Indies, Rangoon, Hong Kong, more of China, the remainder of the Philippines, and New Britain all fell to the Japanese forces. Only at sea could the Americans score any victories: first in the Battle of the Coral Sea on 4-8 May 1942, when an American task force was able to turn back a Japanese invasion force steaming for Port Moresby on New Guinea, and then, a month later, in the mid-Pacific, when two American carrier task forces (with only three carriers between them) sank four Japanese carriers in the Battle of Midway. Although no one realized it at the time, the Battle of Midway represented the turning point of the Pacific war. Japanese expansion had been stopped,

and the Japanese navy had been seriously weakened. From this point on, the Americans and their Allies would be gradually shifting to the offensive in the Pacific, and American superiority in numbers and in warmaking capabilities would begin to make itself felt.

Yamamoto had had his six months. Now it was the Allies' turn. As the Japanese were, at first slowly, and then with increasing speed, pushed back from their farthest perimeter of conquest to their home island base, the US Army would be called upon to play a major role in this bloody war of reconquest.

The first step back came in the Solomon Island chain, deep in the south Pacific northeast of Australia. The Japanese had begun to menace both Australia and New Zealand by seizing New Britain Island and the port of Rabaul from the Australians, capturing the towns of Lae and Salamaua, on the northeast shore of New Guinea, and bombing Port Moresby, on the southeast coast of New Guinea. In March 1942 the Japanese had seized the Solomon islands of Guadalcanal and Tulagi, intending to use them as airbases to interdict Allied traffic to Australia and to endanger the other island chains along the shipping routes from America. The Japanese had to be ousted from Guadalcanal and Tulagi, and thus was born the first American offensive operation of the Pacific War, hastily mounted and, initially, small in scale.

The assignment was given to the 1st Marine Division, and on 7 August 1942 the Leathernecks began their assaults on Guadalcanal and on Tulagi, 20 miles to the north, across Sealark Channel. The Japanese reacted violently, rushing reinforcements to the area and trying by every means to dislodge the marines from the islands, especially Guadalcanal, with its vital airstrip, Henderson Field. No fewer than six major naval battles were fought as the Japanese tried to cut off the Marines from reinforcement by sea, while at the same time bringing in more troops and supplies of their own.

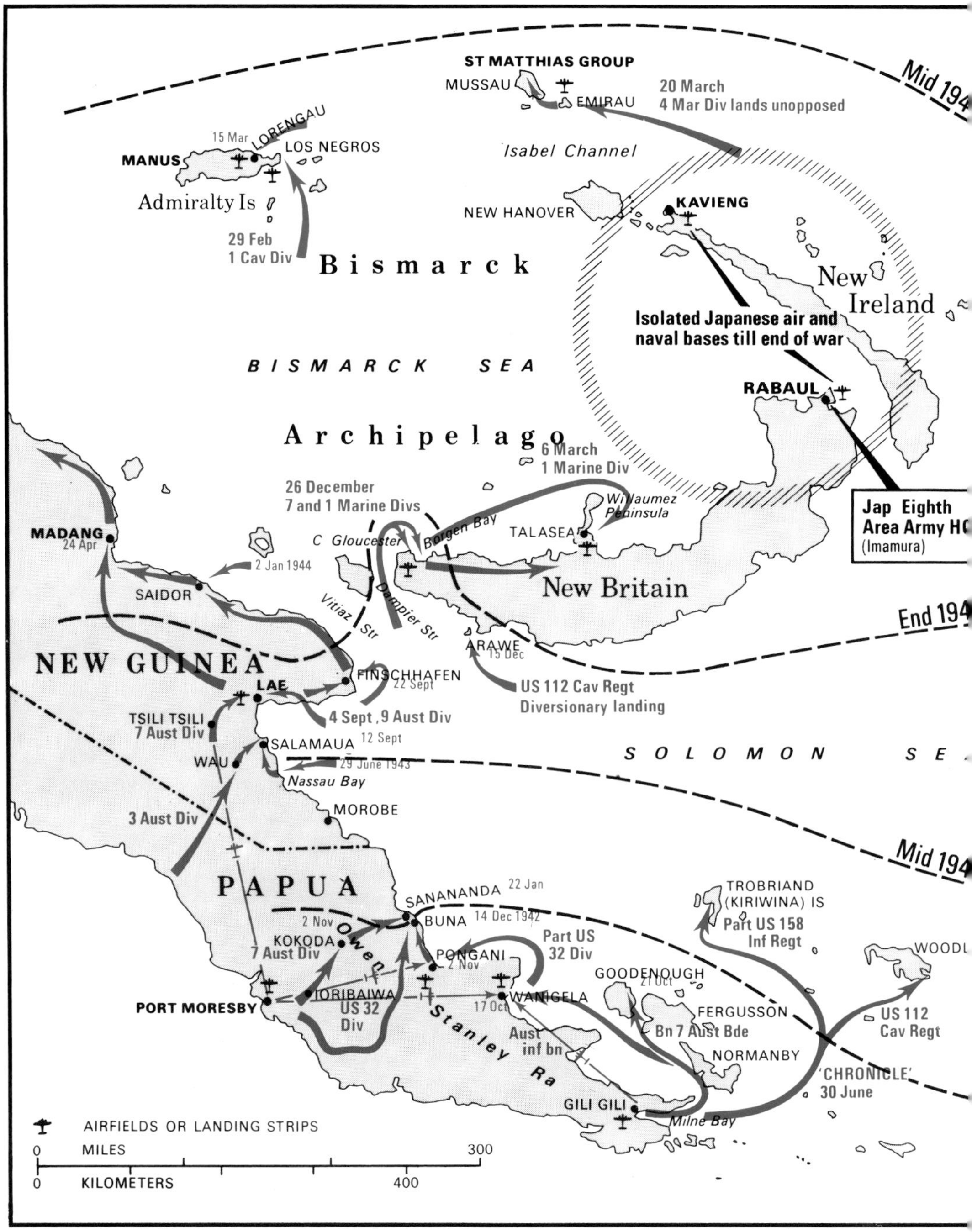

Right: The South Pacific offensives
Below: Wounded US soldiers returning from the front in New Guinea, 1942.

In early December the 1st Marine Division was withdrawn from the island, its place being taken by the 2nd Marine Division and the Army's Americal and 25th Divisions, Major General Alexander M Patch commanding. Patch immediately sent his troops against rugged Mount Austen, a 1500-foot peak, still in Japanese hands, that overlooked Henderson Field, six miles away. There the soldiers ran into savage opposition, a bitter indoctrination into the fighting quality of the Japanese soldier. Patch finally decided to bypass the mountain and go after the main Japanese force that was escaping to the west, but the 13,000 Japanese (all that were left of 36,000 crack troops) managed to get away when their navy moved in to evacuate them. Guadalcanal and nearby Tulagi were now freed of Japanese, and the Americans had a solid hold on the southern Solomons. The

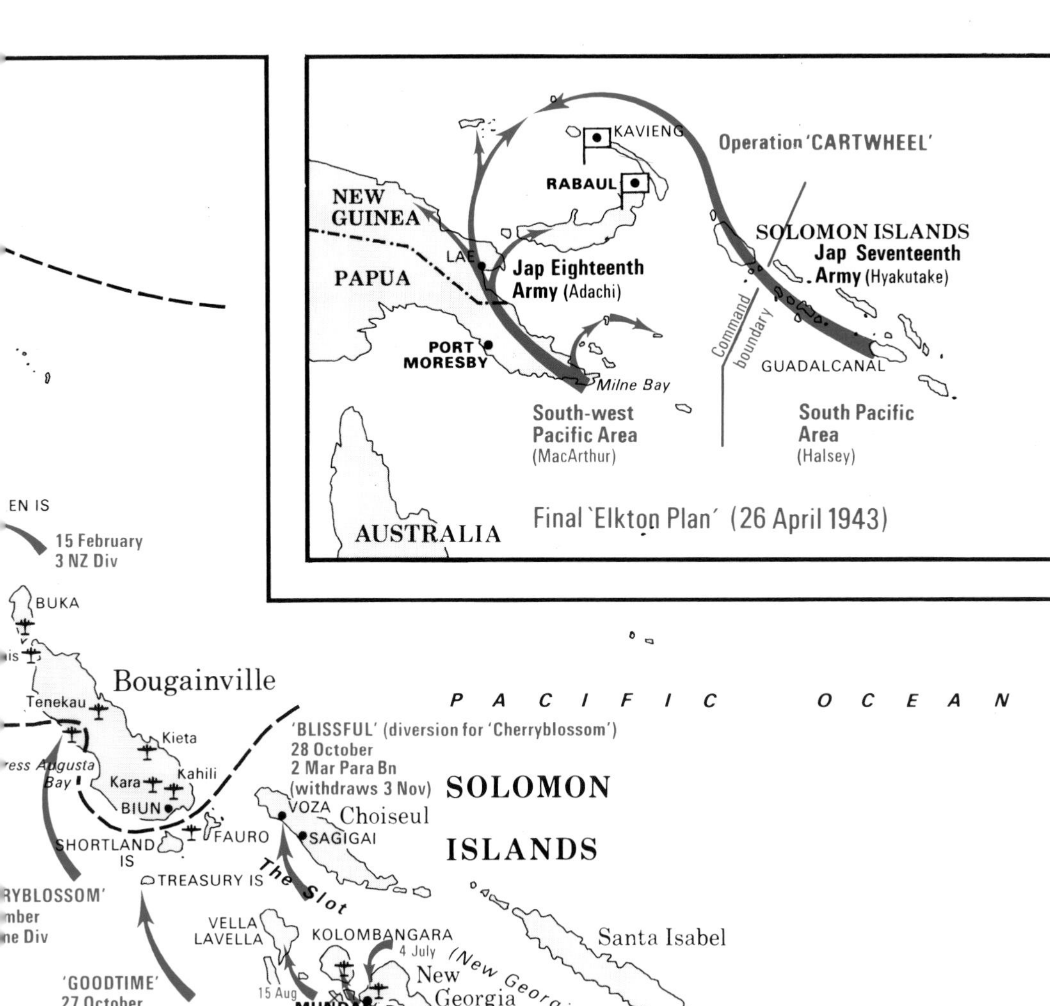

routes to Australia were safe, and the US Army had entered the Pacific war in force, the beginning of a commitment that would last for three more years and would involve the Army in dozens of major operations throughout the Pacific fighting area.

New Guinea and the Solomons Ladder

While the Japanese were being expelled from the lower Solomons, Australia, aided by ground and air units of the US Army, was fighting desperately to halt the spread of Japanese power in New Guinea. In July 1942 Japanese troops had begun landing on the northern coast of Papua, the easternmost part of New Guinea, near the small mission station at Gona. Their objective was to cross the Owen Stanley mountain range, rising in places to 13,000 feet, and to take the town of Port Moresby on the southern shore. With Port Moresby in hand, they could attack Australia, only 300 miles away across the Torres Strait. The Japanese had tried to take Port Moresby once before by water, but the invasion fleet had been turned back in the Battle of the Coral Sea in early May. Now, two months later, they had begun a second operation to seize the vital Allied base by land instead.

The only route for the 100-mile trek from Gona to Port Moresby was a perilous trail, the Kokoda Track, over the mountains. In places it was so narrow one could traverse it only by holding onto branches to avoid falling hundreds of feet down into the jungle gorges below. Yet the Japanese were as determined to make this daunting trek and take Port Moresby as the Australians were to prevent them from doing so.

Through late July, all of August, and into September 1942 the Japanese resolutely pushed against the Australian defenders. By 17 September they had reached Ioribaiwa, only 30 miles from Port Moresby. But here the Japanese overland drive was stopped. The Japanese troops were utterly exhausted, and their supply lines were providing only a trickle of the food and material they needed, thanks in large measure to incessant attacks conducted by MacArthur's Fifth Air Force, under Major General George C Kenney.

The Japanese, meanwhile, had also suffered defeat in their attempt to seize Milne Bay, on the southeast tip of Papua, in early September. Here 1300 American troops had stood side by side with their 7700 Allied comrades to stop a Japanese amphibious attack and force the survivors back to their ships. The failure at Milne Bay, combined with the constant necessity of moving more troops to Guadalcanal, meant that the Japanese outside Port Moresby could not be reinforced. With no aid possible, and with his troops suffering from disease and starvation, Major General Tomitaro Horii accepted the

By mid-1943 the Solomons advance had gone from Guadalcanal to New Georgia. Here, the 43rd Infantry hits Rendova.

Long before the island had been fully secured, Seabees were building vital landing strips on Bougainville.

high command's decision to retreat. He began to lead his weary and despondent men back across Papua to the northern shore, pursued all the way by the 7th Australian Division.

Once back on the northern shore, the Japanese turned to meet their pursuers in the Buna-Gona area. The US Army dispatched units of the 32nd Infantry Division, transported by the Fifth Air Force, to small fields in the Buna area. While the 7th Australians advanced on nearby Gona, the Americans began their attacks on the well-emplaced Japanese at Buna on 19 November 1942. When they failed to break through, General MacArthur, on 30 November, named newly-promoted Lieutenant General Robert L Eichelberger to command the American troops at Buna. His final words to Eichelberger reflected his determination: 'I want you to take Buna, or do not come back alive.'

General Eichelberger whipped the disheartened American troops into shape and launched a devastating attack on 5 December. This, coupled with spectacular Australian victories at Gona, had the Japanese in retreat by Christmas, and by 22 January the Japanese had been driven out of Papua. The cost had been high: 3000 men had been killed and 5400 wounded.

The Buna-Gona victories coincided with the defeat of another Japanese drive, this time from Lae and Salamaua, in Northeast New Guinea, toward Port Moresby (a defeat in which the Fifth Air Force played a major role by bringing in reinforcements to the Australians at the mountaintop airstrip at Wau to stop the Japanese drive). Together, the Allied forces had managed one of the most significant triumphs of the Pacific war. But at the end of the bloody fighting, MacArthur pledged 'No more Bunas.' He kept his word.

After the successes of Guadalcanal and Papua, jubilant American strategists began to think in terms of mounting major offensive campaigns. MacArthur wanted to drive up New Guinea, through the Philippines, and on to the Japanese home islands. The Navy wanted to storm across the central Pacific, conquering islands and building airbases and anchorages as they went, until Japan was within bomber and carrier-based aircraft range. The outcome of this high-level strategic argument was that the Joint Chiefs of Staff decided on a compromise, a giant two-pronged movement toward Japan. MacArthur would advance toward the Philippines along the island chains in the southwest Pacific, while the Navy, assisted by the Army and Marines, would fight its way across the Pacific from the east.

The two giant pincers would converge on the Philippines, although a decision was deferred on whether to liberate the Philippines or bypass them. In any event, both the Army and the Navy now had clear mandates for action, and by the spring of 1943 they were on the move. For the Army the first part of the job meant clearing New Guinea and moving 'up the Solomons ladder' toward the great Japanese base at Rabaul on New Britain, a task that would require the cooperation of both the Navy and the Marines. It would take longer than anyone then realized.

The plan was that MacArthur's forces would clear the Huon Peninsula, including the Japanese base at Lae, in Northeast New Guinea, and then move across the Vitiaz and Dampier Straits to land on the western end of New Britain Island. Rabaul was on the eastern end of the island. Meanwhile, Halsey's forces would move up through the Solomons, with Rabaul also as their target. On 30 June 1943 elements of the 41st Infantry Division landed 60 miles below Lae at Nassau Bay. They soon joined with Australian troops (which had crossed the mountains) and moved toward Lae. On that same day 5000 troops of Lieutenant General Walter Krueger's Sixth Army took the undefended islands of Kiriwina and Woodlark in the Trobriand Islands east of New Guinea, and both were soon equipped with airstrips.

On New Guinea the American and Australian troops advanced toward Lae during July and August. Then, in September, an amphibious landing was made by the Australians 20 miles east of Lae, while the Army's 503rd Airborne Regiment parachuted in 20 miles west of the city (the Fifth Air Force dropping 1,700 paratroopers in one minute). Although the Japanese were ordered to evacuate the base at Lae, 9000 withdrew into the mountains, and it took the American-Australian force until the end of the year to complete the capture of the Huon Peninsula.

On 15 December 1943 soldiers of the 112th Cavalry Regiment finally crossed the Vitiaz and Dampier Straits and landed at Arawe on New Britain. MacArthur and the Army were now less than 300 miles from Rabaul. On 25 December MacArthur sent the 1st Marine Division, the Guadalcanal veterans, to take Cape Gloucester, on the western tip of New Britain, which they did after three weeks of fighting. MacArthur, with the Straits securely in American hands, now had gained clear naval passage west and north.

In the meantime Halsey's forces were moving up the Solomons toward Rabaul, in the process undergoing some of the roughest fighting of the Pacific campaign. The islands of New Georgia, Kolombangara, and Bougainville were considered the primary steps up the Solomons ladder, but no one realized how costly seizing these steps would be. In Halsey's assault on New Georgia, Marines were landed on the night of 20 June 1943 at Segi Point. Their object was to make their way behind crucial Viru Harbor by D-Day, 30 June, but the jungle delayed them, and they arrived too late. Similarly, the assault troops that landed on the island of Rendova, across from Munda Point on New Georgia, to set up artillery cover also found the jungle and mud too much to handle. It took four days for them to set up their 155mm guns and commence firing on their objective, the Japanese airfield on Munda. By that time, the troops of the 43rd Infantry Division had already landed on New Georgia itself, but they too soon became bogged down by the jungle morass and met fierce Japanese resistance. An American all-out attack on Munda, launched on 9 July, failed completely. Thoroughly frustrated, Halsey removed the commander of the Munda operation and sent in the 37th and 25th Divisions to help out, but not until 5 August were the determined Japanese defenders blasted from their well-prepared jungle entrenchments and the airfield taken. Some 10,000 Japanese had held off 40,000 Americans for five weeks.

Fearful that an attack on Kolombangara, with its 10,000 defenders, would result in another such blood bath, Halsey decided to bypass the island and take nearby Vella Lavella instead. The American landing on Vella Lavella on 15 August 1943 met with almost no opposition, Kolombangara was neutralized and the Americans had learned, almost by accident, the tactic of leapfrogging.

Bougainville, only 250 miles from Rabaul by air, still remained, and it could not be bypassed. It had six airfields and was defended by 40,000 well-seasoned veterans of the China wars. Yet Halsey was able to throw the Japanese somewhat off balance at first. He sent the 2nd Marine Parachute Battalion to take the island of Choiseul, southeast of Bougainville, on the night of 27 October, for a while convincing the Japanese that it was the site of the major landing. He also fooled the enemy completely by making his main landings at Cape Torokina, on the western coast of the 125-mile-long island, rather than at Buin, on the southern part of the island, where the Japanese had major installations. But on Bougainville, as on the other islands, Japanese resistance was furious. The 3rd Marine Division and the Army's 37th Division were quickly subjected to the kind of bloody combat their fellow soldiers had experienced before them on New Georgia. Although the Americans were able to establish a perimeter at Cape Torokina, the Japanese counterattacked to drive them back into the water, and the battle raged for 17 days be-

An artist's impression of the landing on Bougainville, the start of one of the bitterest of the Solomons' battles.

fore the Japanese were driven off. Protracted fighting followed. In fact, Bougainville was not fully secured until April 1944, by which time the Japanese had lost 7000 dead, the Americans 1000.

But long before the fighting ended, the Americans had built three airfields on Bougainville, and from them the airmen could both strike at Rabaul and support MacArthur's move across the Vitiaz and Dampier Straits to New Britain on 15 December 1943. Then, with Rabaul at last within easy striking distance of land-based and carrier-based planes, the decision was made simply to bypass it. It had been effectively neutralized as a naval, air, and land staging area, and MacArthur was free to resume his advance on the Philippines.

Across the Pacific

The first objectives in the Navy's central Pacific offensive were the Gilbert Islands, over 1500 miles southwest of Hawaii and 500 miles southeast of the Marshall Islands. The two main targets in the Gilberts were Makin Atoll, to the north, and Tarawa Atoll, 100 miles to the south. The taking of Makin was assigned to the Army; the Marines were to seize Tarawa.

There were only 300 soldiers and 400 laborers on Makin. Assaulting them would be the 165th Regimental Combat Team of the 27th Infantry Division, a contingent of 6500 men. But the expected one-day fight beginning on 20 November 1943 (as the battle for Bougainville was raging in the Solomons), took four days, as radio equipment failed and men and artillery were misused by the undertrained troops. The overall landing commander, Marine Major General Holland M ('Howlin' Mad') Smith, was contemptuous of the slow action of the 27th Division (which had a 20-to-1 advantage in numbers over the enemy) and said so. But Smith soon found that he had greater problems on his hands when the Marines attacked tiny Betio, in the Tarawa Atoll to the South.

The attack on Betio, the first Marine amphibious assault in the central Pacific, turned into a bloodbath. It took three days of furious fighting to dig out the Japanese from an island of less than half a square mile in area. The defenders had been virtually untouched by pre-invasion naval and air bombardment, and now they held to their defensive blockhouses, pillboxes, and caves to their deaths, taking a grisly toll of Marines in the process. By the time the fighting was over 4700 Japanese troops and laborers had died in their places. Over 1000 Marines were dead, and some 2200 had been wounded. But at least some valuable lessons were learned at Tarawa, such as the need for more reliable radio equipment and secure communications command vessels, for high-trajectory

The Gilberts were the first target of the Central Pacific offensive. Army troops had some trouble taking Makin (*above*), but nothing like the bloodbath that faced the Marines on Tarawa (*right*).

artillery rounds that gave greater penetration of emplacements, and for amtracs (armored amphibian tractors with propellers and caterpillar tracks) to replace the flimsy Higgins assault boats that often could not cross coral reefs. Such lessons would serve both the Marines and the Army well as they drove across the central Pacific. Amphibious warfare would, in their hands, reach unimagined levels of tactical sophistication.

On 1 February 1944 Kwajalein Atoll came under US attack. At the northern end of the atoll the 4th Marine Division assaulted and secured the islands of Roi and Namur, giving them control of the Japanese airbase there. Meanwhile, the Army's 7th Division took Kwajalein Island. Neither assault met much resistance, and few Americans died.

With barely a pause, Admiral Nimitz ordered Rear Admiral Marc A Mitscher's fast carrier task force's planes to attack the major naval base at Truk, 1100 miles west. They responded with a pounding of Truk that netted over 40 ships sunk and 200 planes destroyed on the ground. This left Nimitz's forces free to take Eniwetok Island, in the western Marshalls, 380 miles beyond Kwajalein, without harassment. The job of taking Eniwetok and nearby Engebi and Parry Islands was given to the 106th Infantry

Left: Landing craft evolved steadily throughout the war. Here, LVTA-1s, small amphibian tanks with 37mm guns.
Below: The invasion of Saipan.

of the 27th Division and to the Marines of the 22nd Regiment. It took just one day of combat to seize these islands. Soon all of the Marshall Islands were either taken or bypassed, and the central Pacific drive rolled on toward the Marianas Islands, the final steppingstones to the Philippines.

The Marianas Islands lie 1500 miles east of Manila Bay. Once their main islands of Saipan, Tinian, and Guam were taken, the Americans could cut Japanese supply lines to the south, isolate Truk to the southeast, and build airfields from which to bomb the Japanese home islands with the new long-range Boeing B-29 Superfortresses. The Navy's Fifth Fleet, that had assembled for the attack on the Marianas, included over 600 ships. The Marines of the 2nd, 3rd, and 4th Divisions and the Army's 27th Division totaled over 127,000 men.

Nimitz scheduled the first attack for Saipan, in the middle of the island group. Invading to engage the 32,000 Japanese soldiers and naval troops on the island would be the 2nd and 4th Marine Division. On 15 June 1944 the Marines launched their attacks on Saipan and were able to establish a beachhead, despite furious Japanese opposition and counterattacks. To try to save the defenders, the Japanese First Mobile Fleet and Southern Fleet sailed out of bases in the southwest Pacific to take on the American Fifth Fleet in a decisive battle to save the Marianas. The Japanese fleets contained much of what was left of the once-great Imperial Fleet. The result of this major Japanese naval sortie was the two-day Battle of the Philippine Sea, 19-20 June, in which Mitscher's Task Force 58 decimated the First Mobile Fleet and destroyed its air power in what the Americans called 'The Great Marianas Turkey Shoot.'

In the meantime the advance up the island of Saipan from the southern landing points was bogging down. 'Howlin' Mad' Smith put the blame on the Army's 27th Division, in the center of the northward-thrusting American line, the same unit he had previously castigated for its slowness on Makin. This time 'Howlin' Mad' demanded and got the relief of the 27th Division's commander, Major General Ralph Smith. The 27th thereafter began to advance, but on the morning of 7 July had to face the most furious *banzai* attack of the war. Some 3000 Japanese, drunk with *sake* and faithful to their commander's wish that they follow him in death, charged the American lines at Tanapag Harbor. The death-seeking Japanese were stopped only by furious hand-to-hand fighting and 105mm howitzers fired into their ranks at point-blank range. When Saipan was finally declared secure on 9 July 1944, over 16,000 Americans had been killed or wounded. The Japanese dead numbered 29,000.

On 24 July nearby Tinian was invaded by 15,000 Marines. It fell within a week. In the meantime Guam, to the south, had been invaded by elements of the 3rd Marine Division, the 1st Provisional Marine Brigade and the Army's 77th Division. It took two weeks of hard fighting and the death of 3500 Japanese troops before the island fell.

With the Marianas now in American hands, the Philippines seemed the next logical target. But Nimitz insisted, over Halsey's protests, that the Palau Islands in the western Carolines be taken to protect his southern flank. The result was disastrous for the 1st Marine Division, given the task of invading the island of Peleliu, the largest island in the chain, on 15 September 1944.

The Japanese were absolutely determined to hold Peleliu, and the 6500 seasoned soldiers on the island were instructed that they were to fight from prepared positions to the last man, taking as many Marines with them as they could. They carried out their orders to the letter, and after six days of bitter fighting still controlled much of the island, despite the heroic efforts of the Marines to drive them from their positions. At this point the Army's 321st Regimental Combat Team of the 81st Infantry Division was sent in. More savage fighting followed, but the Japanese could not be dislodged, even though by the end of October only 700 Japanese remained alive. By then the Marines had suffered so many casualties they could fight no more. The 81st Division took over, and the gallant 1st Marine Division was pulled out.

Slowly and carefully the 81st reduced the remaining Japanese positions, and within a month the battle had been won. But the battle for Peleliu cost the Americans over 1200 Marines and about 275 soldiers dead and over 6000 of both services wounded. Whatever the justification for the decision to invade Peleliu, unlike the similar blood bath of Tarawa ten months before, this time few Americans at home took note of the carnage. All eyes were now riveted on the action in the Philippines. True to his promise, MacArthur had returned. The road that he had traveled had been strewn with difficulties. He had negotiated it with genius.

Victory in New Guinea

While the great right arm of the American Pacific strategy was moving across the central Pacific, MacArthur, in the southwest Pacific, had taken Papua New Guinea, including much of the Huon Peninsula west of Buna-Gona, and was in the process of neutralizing Rabaul by his landings on the western end of New Britain Island. But the remainder of New Guinea remained a Japanese stronghold, and it had to be taken. MacArthur had to get at least to Hollandia, halfway up the coast, before he would have a jump-off point for the island of Mindanao in the southern Philippines. Accordingly, as the Australian troops moved west on an inland route through New Guinea, MacArthur and the US Army moved along the north coast in a simultaneous paralleling movement.

He first sent the 126th Regimental Combat Team of the 32nd Division to assault the town of Saidor in order to trap a major Japanese troop concentration between his troops and the Australians. This failed, and many of the enemy got away to Madang, up the coast, but MacArthur, in a surprise move in February 1944, sent his army to take the Admiralty

A wounded Marine on Peleliu, site of a bloody battle in which nearly 1200 Marines and 275 Army soldiers died.

Islands, to the north. This gave him air bases from which to launch the Fifth Air Force against the Japanese stronghold at Madang. After Madang had been duly bombed, MacArthur launched his land attack. Led by the 1st Cavalry Division (Armored), the attack succeeded, despite fierce Japanese resistance. The Japanese commander moved his forces west to prepare himself for MacArthur's next move up the coast. He assumed the new targets would be Hansa Bay and Wewak.

But MacArthur had other plans: he would bypass these intermediate points and strike directly at Hollandia, 500 miles up the coast. With invaluable aid from General Kenney's Fifth Air Force, which neutralized Japanese air power in the target area, and with the Navy's Task Force 58 standing by, Hollandia was invaded on 22 April 1944 and taken with little trouble. The 1st Division, the 24th Division, and the 163rd Regimental Combat Team made up the force that landed in three locations in the Hollandia area.

Although 55,000 Japanese of the Eighteenth Army were still between himself, at Hollandia, and the pursuing Australians, MacArthur did not hesitate to move west from Hollandia towards the Vogelkop Peninsula, at the far west end of New Guinea. Along the way he was obliged to fight many battles, and resistance was often savage, as on the island of Biak in Geelvink Bay, just east of the Vogelkop Peninsula, where 11,000 Japanese troops fought ferociously until late July. Meanwhile, MacArthur had convinced President Roosevelt that the left flank of the American advance in the Pacific – his flank – should now move on to Mindanao, then to Leyte, in the central Philippines, and finally to Luzon, in the north of the archipelago. MacArthur thus prevailed over the Navy's preference for bypassing the Philippines and striking for Formosa instead.

But first something still had to be done about the Japanese Eighteenth Army and other scattered units which remained in New Guinea. The Eighteenth Army had launched an attack on the 32nd Division, the 124th Regimental Combat Team, the 31st Division, and the 112th Cavalry Regimental Combat Team at Aitape. The intention was to dilute American strength and halt the Army's outward thrust toward the Philippines. The assault started on 10 July and ended only on 9 August. In that one month, 10,000 Japanese were lost, against an American toll of 400 dead and 25,000 wounded. Completely decimated and exhausted by their futile efforts, the remainder of the Japanese force fled back toward Wewak and then into the New Guinea mountains. At the end of the war what remained of this Japanese army finally surrendered to the Australians.

With New Guinea under effective control as of late July 1944, MacArthur turned north toward Mindanao. In early September, as MacArthur's forces were preparing to attack Morotai, in the Moluccas, so as to protect the left flank of his route north to Mindanao, the general received a message from Admiral Halsey, whose Third Fleet was already carrying out air attacks on the Philippines. The central part of the archipelago was wide open, said Halsey, and he had urged the Joint Chiefs to change the Pacific strategy to bypass Mindanao and strike directly at Leyte. Nimitz and the Joint Chiefs, then meeting with Roosevelt and Churchill, agreed. MacArthur was given the green light to invade Leyte.

The decision to liberate the Philippines also entailed an important shift in the central Pacific strategy. Nimitz' forces, having advanced over 4500 miles from Hawaii to the Palaus in ten months of fighting, were now to veer north to strike the Bonin Islands and seize Iwo Jima as a fighter base to protect the bombers flying out of the Marianas against Japan. They were also to take Okinawa and other islands in the Ryukyu Island chain, less than 400 miles from the Japanese homeland. The altered two-prong strategy, if successful, would ring Japan with air and sea power preparatory to an invasion of the home islands in 1945.

The Philippines

Four American Army divisions, under Lieutenant General Walter Krueger, commander of the Sixth Army, hit the beaches on Leyte, in the central Philippines, on 20 October 1944. Air cover was provided by General Kenney's Fifth Air Force and by naval task forces under Admiral Halsey. The Japanese reacted quickly to the invasion, fearing that the entire archipelago would be lost if Leyte fell to the Americans. Ground and air units were hurried to Leyte, while the Japanese mustered their last naval units to destroy the invasion fleet off the invasion beaches. In the ensuing Battle of Leyte Gulf

(23-25 October) the Japanese decoyed Halsey's main force far off to the north of the Philippines, while sending two sizeable squadrons through straits in the central and southern parts of the islands to converge at Leyte Gulf and destroy the invading Americans. But for the gallantry of the sailors on the relatively few fighting ships left behind at Leyte Gulf, the beachhead on Leyte might well have been lost and the Army units isolated. In fact, the Japanese Navy accomplished nothing at Leyte Gulf but its own destruction.

On Leyte itself the reinforced Japanese continued to hold out and slowed the American drive to a crawl until December, when the 77th Division made a surprise landing on Leyte's west coast. This effectively broke the

MacArthur's strategy was almost as dependent on amphibious operations as was Halsey's.
Right: MacArthur inspects the beach after his landing in Dutch Borneo.
Below: US troops pouring out of an LST to invade Middleburg Is.

stalemated war, although some Japanese units held out for several more months. In the meantime MacArthur and the Army were moving onto the main island of Luzon. After seizing a supporting airfield in December, four divisions landed on Lingayen Gulf, north of Manila, on 9 January 1945. MacArthur's forces on Luzon quickly built to more than five divisions in a matter of days. He then began his move down the Central Plains toward Manila. Many of the intervening Japanese forces fled to the mountains, but 20,000 Japanese naval and army service troops decided to fight it out in Manila. This resulted in a month-long campaign that left the city virtually destroyed and 100,000 civilians dead, many executed by the Japanese.

Meanwhile, the 503rd Parachute Infantry struck to retake Corregidor, the 38th Division landed near Subic Bay to secure the Bataan Peninsula, and the 11th Airborne hit southern Luzon. As the Japanese moved into the

Left: Generals MacArthur and Horace Fuller viewing damage done by naval gunfire to a Japanese supply dump at Hollandia, New Guinea. MacArthur used naval support brilliantly
Below: The invasion of Leyte.

An LST with landing pontoons lashed to her side heading for Okinawa, the costliest island battle of the war.

mountains, MacArthur continued to pour in reinforcements. Eventually 11 divisions, three regimental combat teams, and thousands of Filipino guerrillas were used against the Japanese in this, the largest land war in the Pacific theater. Japanese resistance in most areas of Luzon had ended by June 1945, after General Eichelberger's new Eighth Army had taken over from General Krueger's exhausted Sixth Army. At war's end, some 50,000 Japanese were still holding out in Luzon's mountains.

With the American Army in full control of the Philippines, and the Navy in full control of the surrounding seas, the fate of Japan was effectively sealed. Yet a good deal of blood remained to be spilled before the war in the Pacific finally came to an end.

Iwo Jima and Okinawa

Iwo Jima, in the Bonin Islands, 660 miles southeast of Tokyo, was the key to supplying fighter protection to the B-29s attacking the Japanese home islands. The task of taking the island was assigned to the 70,000 Marines of the 4th and 5th Divisions. They launched their attacks on 19 February 1945, reinforced by the 3rd Marine Division, and ran into fanatical Japanese resistance. A month of hard fighting was required before the tiny eight-square-mile island was secured. About 6800 Americans were killed on Iwo Jima. Almost all of the 22,000 Japanese defenders died in the savage fighting.

A landing by the 77th Division was made on the Kerama Islands, off Okinawa, on 26 March. The main amphibious assaults on crucial Okinawa were made on Easter Sunday, 1 April 1945. The Army's 7th and 96th Divisions and the Marines' 2nd and 6th Divisions made the initial landings. Overall command was in the hands of the Tenth Army commander, Lieutenant General Simon B Buckner. To the surprise of the American forces, the defending 130,000-man Japanese Thirty-second Army made no effort to impede their landings. Instead, the Japanese pulled back into entrenched positions in the hills, where they fought the Army and Marine units almost to a standstill, especially on the southern part of the island. Meanwhile, Japanese aircraft subjected the Navy to *kamikaze* attacks that resulted in the sinking of 25 ships and the damaging of more than 150. Ashore, the Japanese held out along the Shuri Line and on the Oroku Peninsula, until finally withdrawing for a last stand on the Kiyamu Peninsula, on the southern tip of the island. The soldiers and Marines pursued them over the craggy surfaces of southern Okinawa, blasting and burning the Japanese out of their caves and entrenched positions, until the enemy finally surrendered on 22 June. In 83 days the Japanese had lost at least 110,000 men killed; the Army and Marines, over 7600 killed and 31,807 wounded. *Kamikaze* and other air attacks had accounted for an additional 4300 naval personnel dead and another 7000 wounded.

The combatants on both sides now knew what the next steps would be: stepped up aerial bombing, followed by an invasion of the home islands. For this, bloodily-won Okinawa would be the staging area.

The Pacific Air War

American air power in the Pacific was roughly handled by the Japanese in the opening days of the war. Of the 231 USAAF aircraft

Nearly 6800 Marines died on Iwo Jima to give B-29s a forward base.

based on Oahu on 7 December 1941, 97 were destroyed and 88 were heavily damaged. On the same day the Navy lost 80 aircraft, 50 percent of its total in Hawaii. The situation was even worse in the Philippines: Major General Lewis H Brereton's 249-plane Far Eastern Air Force lost 67 percent of its aircraft in the first hours of the Japanese attack on 8 December, and by Christmas FEAF had virtually ceased to exist.

Almost as dismaying as the devastation itself was what America was learning about the calibre of the Japanese Army and Navy air arms. Far from being composed of the second-rate pilots and third-rate planes attributed to them by most western 'experts' before the war, they proved to be equipped with large numbers of formidably modern aircraft flown by battle-tested veterans. The single Japanese warplane that best symbolized this unpleasant reality was the Imperial Navy's Mitsubishi A6M Zero, which was not only revealed to be the most advanced carrier-based fighter in the world, but seemed likely to prove technically superior to most of the USAAF's land-based fighters, as well. And there were several other Japanese types which were, in their own combat categories, almost as impressive as the Zero. Thus America and her allies entered the Pacific air war in a state of such quantitative and qualitative inferiority that none could predict when the tables might be turned.

By the beginning of 1942 the Army had only two significant concentrations of air power left in the Pacific: the Hawaiian Air Force, still trying to recover from the damage it had sustained during the Pearl Harbor attack, and a motley collection of bomber and fighter squadrons that was being hastily assembled in Australia to help meet the looming threat of Japanese invasion. On 2 February the Hawaiian group was redesignated the Seventh Air Force: In time it would become the principal Army air component of the right half (*ie.* the Central Pacific wing) of America's vast two-pronged offensive against Japan. Similarly, the Australian group, which would be christened the Fifth Air Force in September, would become MacArthur's principal air weapon in the left-hand wing of the great offensive.

It was General Kenney's Fifth that was to see the most combat. When it was activated in the autumn of 1942 it had only 75 operational fighters and 80 bombers, and these were already engaged in a precarious struggle for supremacy in the New Guinea skies with what was then perhaps Japanese military aviation's most elite formation, the daunting Lae Air Wing. Despite heavy casualties the Fifth survived this trial by fire and was able subsequently to give valuable support to US and Australian troops in their successful Buna-Gona campaign. By the end of the year the Fifth had established a major airbase on New Guinea (at Dobodura) and its

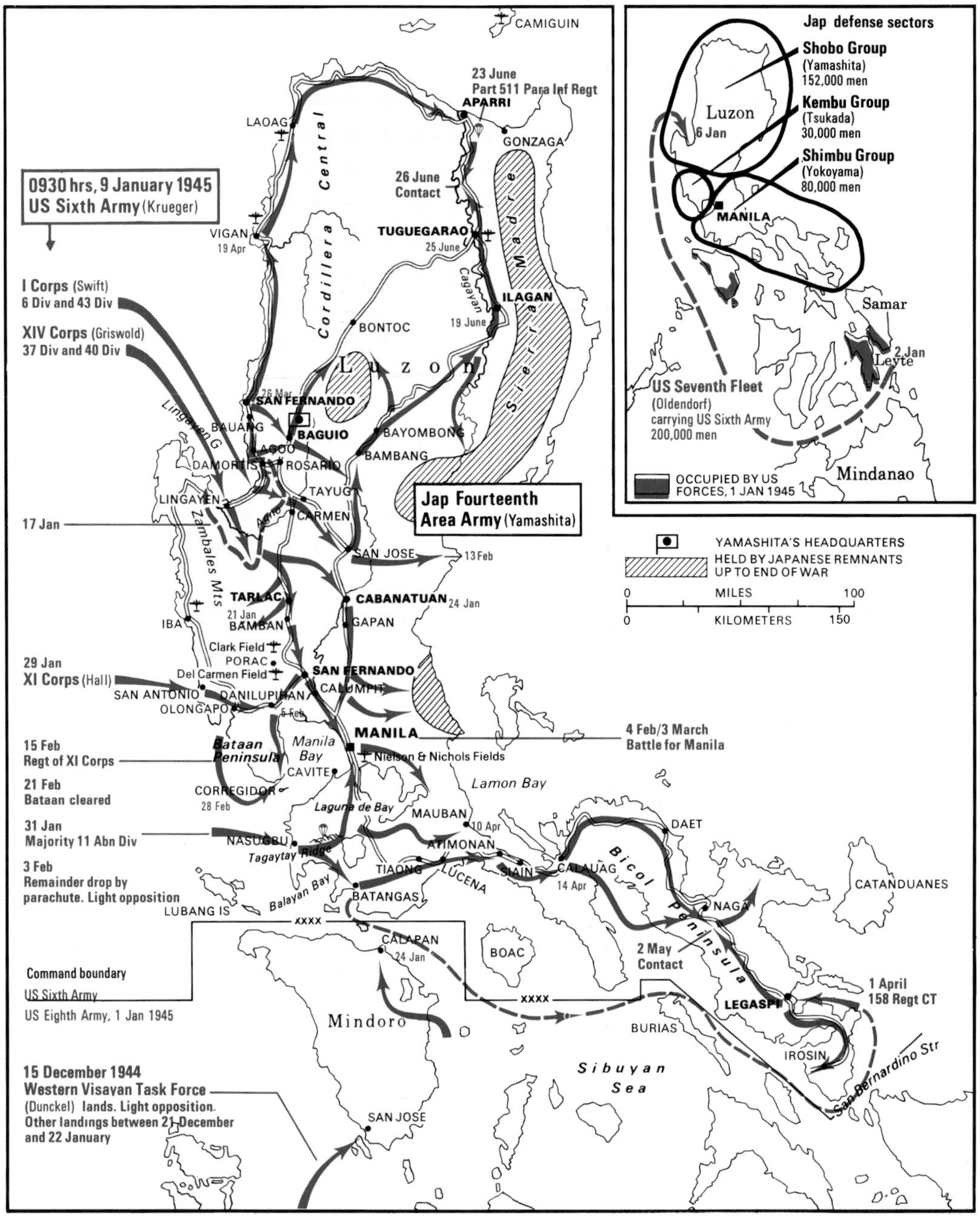

Right: The Luzon campaign.
Below: US cruisers shell Bataan and Corregidor.

The Bell P-400 was no match for the brilliant Mitsubishi A6M Zero (*below*).

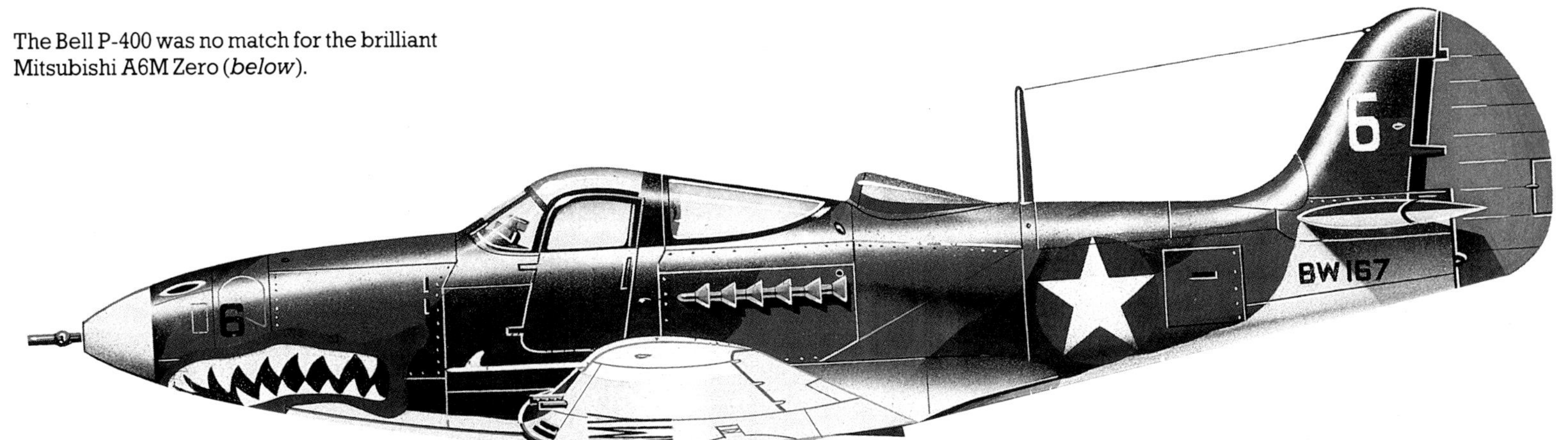

B-17s and B-24s were making regular raids on the big Japanese base at Rabaul, a bombing campaign that would continue with mounting intensity for the next 12 months until Rabaul ceased to be a significant factor in the prosecution of the war. Simultaneously, throughout 1943 and 1944 the Fifth gave often crucial close support to MacArthur's ground forces as they leap-frogged their way to victory along New Guinea's north coast.

In aerial combat the Fifth also made steady progress in overcoming the qualitative deficiencies that had plagued it at the outset. Pilots and aircrews, now highly proficient veterans, devised new tactics to offset the technical limitations of their equipment. To be sure, some hopelessly outclassed machines, such as the Bell P-39s and the Douglas A-24s, had to be withdrawn, but the marginal inferiorities of other types were gradually dissipated through incremental technical improvements and ever more refined tactical employment. The case of the Lockheed P-38 is perhaps the most striking example of what improved tactics could accomplish. This ponderous twin-engine fighter was plainly no match for the agile Japanese fighters in dogfights, but it could at least operate at significantly higher altitudes. This single advantage permitted the P-38 pilots to perfect a spectacularly successful 'bounce' tactic, in which the American fighters would come down on their enemies in thunderous power dives, make single firing passes, and then, using the great speed accumulated in the dives, zoom back up to the safety of altitudes where the Japanese could not follow. In time the Fifth would receive fighters much superior both to the P-38 and the Zero, but the fact remains that the Fifth's two highest-scoring aces – indeed, the highest-scoring aces in American history – Major Richard Bong and Major Thomas McGuire, made most of their kills in P-38s.

Quantity eventually came to favor the Fifth (as it did all US air forces) as much as quality. By early 1944 it comprised 803 fighters, 780 medium and heavy bombers, and 328 transports, a ten-fold increase over its inventory eighteen months earlier. By the end of 1944 this massive force was ashore on Leyte, and six months later it was joining the Seventh and other Pacific air forces on Okinawa and Ie Shima in the Bonin Islands in preparation for the final assault on Japan.

The route by which the Seventh Air Force had come to the Bonins was somewhat more circuitous. Obliged to follow the island-hopping course of the central Pacific arm of America's two-pronged grand strategy in the Pacific, the Seventh was constantly on the move and sometimes widely dispersed. The roster of its various bases – among others, Midway, Espiritu Santo, Guadalcanal, Makin, Kwajalein, Iwo Jima, and Okinawa – reads like a capsule history of the Central Pacific campaign itself. Since the Seventh was smaller than the Fifth, and less continuously engaged with the enemy, its contribution to victory is not so easily expressed in raw statistics. Yet in strategic terms, that contribution was considerable.

There were other US Army air forces active in the Pacific, as well. The Tenth and Fourteenth Air Forces, operating in the China-Burma-India theater, may not have played major parts in America's grand offensive strategy but made important contributions to the crucial campaigns being fought by her British and Chinese allies on the Pacific's Asian perimeter. The Thirteenth Air Force wrote some glorious chapters in the history of the bitter air war over the Solomons before joining forces with the Fifth in the battle for the Philippines. Finally, there was the new XXI Bomber Command, already in place in the Marianas even before the Fifth and Seventh finally converged in the Bonins in the late spring of 1945. To the XXIst would go both the honor of ending World War II and the onus of ushering in the awesome new age of the atom.

The End of the Pacific War

During the summer of 1945 the 1000 Boeing B-29 Superfortresses of XXI Bomber Command (which was made part of the Twentieth Air Force in July) conducted almost daily raids on the cities of Japan from the Marianas, Okinawa, and Iwo Jima, aided by carrier-based planes from the American and British Pacific Fleets. Simultaneously American planes, surface ships, and submarines shut down any outside help for the beleaguered Japanese in the home islands. Already plans were being made for the invasion of Japan itself. Now that the war had ended in Europe, all of the Allied might could and would be applied for this most massive invasion in world history. Casualties on the Allied side were estimated to reach 1.5 million, and on the Japanese side, up to 10 million military and civilian, ten percent of the population. All expectations were that the Japanese would display even more fanaticism in protecting their home islands than they had shown in defending their Pacific possessions, for their '*Ketsu-Go*' ('Decisive Battle') home defense plan was designed to cause such high Allied casualties as to induce the Americans to give up the fight and go home.

Left: The greatest US Pacific aces flew Lockheed P-38s, yet the plane's European record was only mediocre.
Below: US air power alone neutralized Japan's giant naval base at Rabaul.

Over 193,000 men of the Sixth Army, including seven Army and three Marine divisions, were set to strike the southernmost Japanese home island of Kyushu on 1 November 1945 in Operation OLYMPIC. Some 457,000 men would follow. They would be backed by the Fifth Fleet, with 3033 vessels (even more than at Normandy) and 2000 carrier-based planes. Some 6000 land-based planes would also participate in the operation. On 1 March 1946 the US Eighth and First Armies, with 14 divisions, would land on the main island of Honshu in the Yokohama-Tokyo area as part of Operation CORONET. It was estimated that Japanese resisistance would end only after many months of shocking bloodshed.

All plans for invasion were cut short when, on 6 August 1945, a Twentieth Air Force B-29 dropped an atomic bomb on the city of Hiroshima. Despite the weapon's unprecedented destructive power, the Japanese government refused to surrender. Two days later the Russians declared war on Japan and invaded Manchuria. On 9 August a second B-29 dropped an atomic bomb on the city of Nagasaki. Although the Japanese still had over two million men (including seven regular divisions and seven reserve divisions) under arms and willing to defend their homeland, plus 10,500 operational aircraft (5000 to be used in *kamikaze* attacks), the devastation wrought by the atomic bombs was so great that the Japanese government, not knowing how many more weapons of this type America had at its disposal, asked for peace. Japan formally accepted the Allied terms on 14 August 1945.

With the signing of the surrender terms on board the US battleship *Missouri* in Tokyo Bay on 2 September the Pacific war came to an end. As in the European phase of the war, the US Army, cooperating with its American sister services and those of the Allied nations, had brought a stubborn foe to its knees at a terrible cost in blood. Some 235,000 Army personnel had lost their lives in the war effort in the European and Pacific theaters. But victory had been won, and now it was time to look to a world without war.

Top: From first to last the workhorse USAAF fighter in the Pacific was the Curtiss P-40. Here, a P-40 M Warhawk.
Right: Nagasaki, 9 August 1945.

Top: Kobe, 1946. Even before Hiroshima, conventional bombing had lain waste many Japanese cities.
Below: History's most famous bomber.

Korea, 1950: Four M26 tanks firing on a Communist observation post.

COLD WAR AND GLOBAL COMMITMENT: 1945-1985

Peace had returned in 1945 with the defeat of Germany and Japan, but the world had changed significantly. Most of Europe's major powers had been brought close to prostration by the bloodletting of the war. Elsewhere in the world, people who had been living under European political and economic domination for decades or centuries were eager to take advantage of their masters' exhausted condition to demand more freedom, if not outright independence. Moreover, the destruction of the short-lived German and Japanese empires had left power vacuums in western Europe and in the Far East that must, in the nature of things, somehow be filled.

In America, a vague fear, waiting only to be confirmed, began to arise that the Russian Communists, now victoriously standing astride eastern and central Europe, would surely seize the moment to ensnare millions of people in their expanding power network. True, the United Nations, with its emphasis on peaceful solutions to future quarrels between nations, had been created in San Francisco, but few Americans were willing to put their complete trust in an organization that looked so suspiciously like the old League of Nations. Furthermore, the United Nations included as a signatory peacekeeper the Soviet Union, a nation that had given ample evidence in word and deed that its commitment to peace might be less than total.

Perhaps it would all work out, but the United States would have to keep its guard up and learn to live with the fact that America had inherited the mantle of protector of freedom in the postwar world. Few realized how high the price would be for playing that role.

Harry S Truman, whose presidency saw the end of World War II and the dawn of the Cold War and the Atomic Age.

Demobilization and Readjustment

Whatever the state of the world, it was widely expected that the GIs of World War II would quickly be returned to their homes and families, now that the fighting had stopped. The Army devised a method of releasing individual troops on the basis of their length of service, time in combat, overseas deployments, and number of dependents. But the scheme was hardly in place before increasing public pressure forced the high command to release men even faster, so that by the end of 1945 half of its eight million men under arms had been separated. When the Army tried to slow down the return of troops from overseas early in 1946 in order to meet its worldwide commitments, the attempt was met by protests and demonstrations in all the former theaters of war. Quick release procedures were resumed, and another 25 percent were discharged by mid-1946.

Because President Harry Truman's budgets mandated a postwar Army strength of only one million men (instead of the four million the Army had planned on during the war), the Army cut the remainder of its draftees. By mid-1947 the Army counted only 680,000 ground troops and 300,000 airmen. It was all-volunteer and pared down for peacetime duty. The Navy and Marine Corps suffered corresponding reductions in manpower, and little money was available for acquisition and maintenance of equipment in any of the services.

While the strength of the military was being curtailed, action was taken to bring unity to the nation's armed forces in both planning and operating. Under the provisions of the National Security Act of 1947, the Air Force was created as a co-equal service with the Army and the Navy. (The Navy retained control over the Marine Corps, despite the objections of the Army, which wanted responsibility for all ground troops.) The Act also created the National Security Council to co-ordinate and integrate national security policies. NSC members were the Secretary of State, the Secretary of Defense (a new position with cabinet rank), the secretaries of the three military branches, and other agency heads appointed by the President.

A second body created by the Act was the National Military Establishment. It was headed by the Secretary of Defense and included the secretaries of the services. Under the Secretary of Defense were the Joint Chiefs of Staff, represented by the military chiefs of the Army, Navy, and Air Force. The Joint Chiefs were charged with giving advice to the Secretary of Defense, the National Security Council and the President, not with running the services. Under the first Secretary of Defense, James V Forrestal, each branch was accorded its area of responsibility: the Army for land warfare; the Navy for sea and sea-based operations, plus the Marine Corps; and the Air Force for strategic air warfare, tactical air support for the Army, and air transportation. Area commands were

established throughout the world, wherein a single commander appointed by the Joint Chiefs of Staff would exercise coordinating control within that geographical region.

The National Security Act was amended in 1949 because it had left the Secretary of Defense with too little power to enforce co-operation in the federated military service system now established. The office was also weak because the three civilian secretaries of the services had direct access to the President, thus bypassing the Secretary of Defense. The amendments of 1949 strengthened the office of Secretary of Defense by converting the National Military Establish-

Even as Americans enjoyed such post-war pleasures as dancing to Rock 'n Roll (*below*) they were haunted by the looming spectre of the atom bomb (*left*).

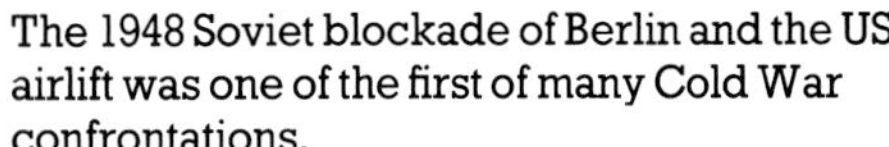
The 1948 Soviet blockade of Berlin and the US airlift was one of the first of many Cold War confrontations.

ment into the Department of Defense, with the Secretary of Defense holding full cabinet rank and the service secretaries clearly placed below him. The Army, Navy, and Air Force retained their autonomy, but were also plainly and directly under the Secretary of Defense. The Joint Chiefs of Staff (now with another member, in the person of a chairman without a vote) still held a somewhat amorphous position. The JCS was charged with co-ordinating military strategy and planning but had no responsibility for their being carried out. That responsibility lay with the Secretary of Defense, the three service secretaries, and the various chiefs of staff.

As part of this unification process, three interservice schools for senior officers were created to assure joint service planning and execution: the Armed Forces Staff College for planning, the Industrial College of the Armed Forces for mobilization of resources, and the National War College for execution of military plans. In these same years other important changes were also made. A new Uniform Code of Military Justice was enacted in 1950, and President Truman ordered all services to become racially integrated. All-black units ceased to exist in the Navy and in the Air Force in June 1950, and in the Army by 1954.

While unification and reorganization were proceeding apace in the five years after World War II, the size of the services (with the exception of the new Air Force, which seemed to promise more defense for less money with its atomic bombers ready to fly anywhere in the world) continued to decline, particularly after the advent of cost-conscious Secretary of Defense Louis A Johnson, who succeeded James Forrestal in 1949.

President Truman had, in 1945, called for UMT (universal military training) for one year for all young men in order to assure an adequate and trained military force, but the idea had died after years of acrimonious debate in Congress. The Army was, accordingly, forced to depend on the National Guard and the reserves to supplement its regulars, but restricted budgets held down the Guard to only 325,000 members in undertrained and underequipped units, and the reserves to only 186,000 men. And, under the budget-cutting axe, the Army found that by 1950 its regulars only amounted to 591,000 men and women, despite the continuing need for it to provide occupation forces in Germany, Japan, and Korea. The Navy and Marine Corps were similarly undermanned and underequipped, and even the Air Force, despite its favored status, faced serious deficiencies in planes and materiel. All of this erosion was still taking place, when the escalating Cold War finally spilled over into actual combat in Korea. Again peacetime neglect produced near-disastrous results.

Cold War, Containment, and Korea

Disputes over occupation forces and policies did not arise in Japan because of President Truman's insistence that Japan come under American occupation alone after the war, but situations in Germany and Korea foreshadowed inter-Allied tensions that eventually led to open hostility. The American, French, and British zones of occupation in western Germany and in the capital of Berlin, far inside the Soviet occupation zone in eastern Germany, experienced swift disarmament and restoration of German rule under Allied tutelage. In eastern Germany, however, the Soviet Union steadfastly erected barriers to reunification of the entire country by its insistence upon Soviet domination of the eastern section of the nation, which it ruled as a client state. After Russia's failure to oust the Western powers from Berlin by a blockade of the city in 1948-49 – a blockade broken by an Allied airlift of food and supplies for the people of Berlin – there emerged two separate and distinct German states, the German Federal Republic, made up of the Western zones of occupation, and the German Democratic Republic, a Soviet-dominated Communist regime in the east.

Briton Klaus Fuchs was among several Soviet spies who helped to break the American monopoly of atomic secrets.

Lack of Soviet co-operation also prevented reunification of the peninsula of Korea after its Japanese conquerors had been removed in 1945. The Russians moved onto the peninsula north of the 38th parallel as a temporary zone of occupation, while American soldiers from Okinawa moved in south of that line. Despite wartime agreements that Korea would be reunited and free, meetings in late 1945 revealed that the Soviets saw the 38th parallel as more than just a temporary boundary between occupation zones. In fact they would not agree to a reunited Korea unless the initial interim government was Communist-dominated. As a result, the 38th parallel developed into a *de facto* boundary between a Communist-dominated North Korean government, and a pro-Western South Korean government.

These disputes in Germany and Korea over occupation policies gave clear warning that the Soviets viewed occupation as a means of aggrandizement and control. They helped to initiate a broadening postwar confrontation between Soviet and Western blocs that hardened into a semi-permanent Cold War.

Western fears of Soviet aggressive intentions in the aftermath of the war seemed con-

Above: The US suffered what was then seen as a Cold War defeat when Mao Tse-tung's Communist Party came to power in mainland China.

firmed by Soviet policy in eastern Europe. Here, one state after another was drawn behind what Winston Churchill called the 'Iron curtain' in a celebrated speech at Fulton, Missouri, in 1946. And it soon became clear that Russia and her 'satellites,' as the dominated central and eastern European countries came to be called, were playing a leading part in attempting to bring Greece into the Soviet orbit via a civil war. Russia was also supporting Mao Tse-tung in his attempts to overthrow the pro-Western government of Chiang Kai-shek in China. The American response to Communist aggrandizement was a policy of 'containment,' i.e., helping friendly governments resist encroachments on their sovereignty by the Soviet Union or other Communist states.

Containment assumed an economic stance in 1947 when Congress, at the urging of President Truman, put up $400 million in aid to Greece and Turkey to assist these two countries in their fight against Communist incursions. This trail-blazing step soon became known as the 'Truman Doctrine' and, since it was couched in terms of helping free people throughout the world resist outside forces, placed the United States squarely in opposition to Soviet and Communist expansionism. The next year the principle was specifically extended to Europe, when the United States adopted the Marshall Plan, whereby $16 billion was funneled to Europe to help the Western democracies get back on their feet economically to resist Com-

Sensational spy trials such as that of the Rosenbergs (*left*) fostered the anti-Communist demagoguery of men like Joseph McCarthy (*top left*).

The formidable T-34/85 tank was one of the modern weapons the Soviets had supplied to their North Korean ally.

munist encroachments. Congress finally became convinced of the necessity of such aid when the Soviet Union staged a coup and overthrew the government of Czechoslovakia, putting a Communist government in its place in April 1948.

The year 1948 also saw a permanent division of Korea when the Soviet Union refused to allow free elections in the country to establish a unitary government, even though the elections would be supervised by the United Nations. Accordingly, the UN held an election in South Korea later that year and established the Republic of Korea in the south. The Soviet Union, in turn, established a Communist government in the north, the Democratic People's Republic, and the temporary occupation boundary of 1945 became a permanent political boundary. Both Russia and the United States withdrew their occupation troops in 1949.

Containment also took on a military form in these years when, in 1947, the United States and 21 American republics signed the Inter-American Treaty of Reciprocal Assistance (the Rio Pact) to resist collectively any armed attack on any of the signatory powers. And the next year saw the US enter into a military alliance with five Western European democracies in the Brussels Treaty, the forerunner to the North Atlantic Treaty Alliance, signed in 1949. Under the provisions of NATO (the North Atlantic Treaty Organization), the United States, Canada, and ten European democracies pledged their mutual help in case of attack, the expected aggressor being the Soviet Union or one of its satellites. By 1949, too, the United States was sending Army advisory groups to friendly nations under the Mutual Defense Assistance Program. And containment took on a new urgency in this pivotal year when the Soviet Union exploded its own atomic bomb and when Chiang Kai-shek was driven off the mainland of China onto the island of Taiwan (Formosa) by the forces of Mao Tse-tung, who quickly signed a treaty of mutual assistance with the Soviets.

While the Western powers had continued to disarm, the Soviet Union, along with the Communist Chinese and the leaders of Russia's puppet states in the East and West, had maintained and extended their military strength. By 1950 Russia had an army of over two and a half million men, to America's 640,000, and 9000 warplanes, to America's 3300. The Cold War atmosphere was now very tense. The question was whether confrontation would somehow spill over into actual warfare. That question was answered on 25 June 1950 when thousands of soldiers of the North Korean army swept across the length of the 38th parallel in a well-planned invasion of South Korea.

The North Korean government had been waging clandestine warfare against the Republic of Korea government of Syngman Rhee with little success for two years before the invasion. Perhaps misreading American willingness to defend South Korea, the invasion in force of 25 June, aided by Soviet-built T-34 tanks and perhaps encouraged by Soviet advisors, swept all before it in the days that followed. The ROK (Republic of Korea) army, basically a constabulary force and not well trained or equipped, numbered only 95,000 men; the North Korean army had at least 135,000 regulars plus as many as 100,000 trained reserves. Within three days the South Korean capital of Seoul, 35 miles below the 38th parallel on the western shore of the peninsula, had been entered by the main North Korean force, while parallel attacks were taking place down the center and eastern shore of the country.

The United Nations Security Council had condemned the invasion and had authorized force to meet it. (The Soviet Union was absent and unable to cast a veto on UN reaction to the invasion because it had walked out of the Security Council six months earlier over the UN's unwillingness to replace Nationalist China's delegation with one from Communist China.) By this time President Truman had already ordered General Douglas MacArthur in Tokyo to use all available American forces to stop the North Korean drive, including the use of ground, air, and naval forces. Concurrently Truman had ordered the Seventh Fleet to stand off Taiwan to prevent both the Chinese Communists from attacking the Nationalists on Taiwan and the Nationalists from attacking the Communists on the mainland, since either move would have widened the conflict. Truman was also putting the wheels in motion to back up MacArthur's stand with more soldiers and supplies. As the feisty Truman saw it, if South Korea fell, the policy of containment would be rendered worthless. It was a time of testing for America and the Western democracies.

In Japan MacArthur had available to him one armored division and three infantry divisions in his Eighth Army command, but all were undermanned and underequipped. He also had little tactical air support, since the Air Force units in Japan were primarily defensive and only equipped with short-range interceptors. But with North Korean units marching down the Korean peninsula, and

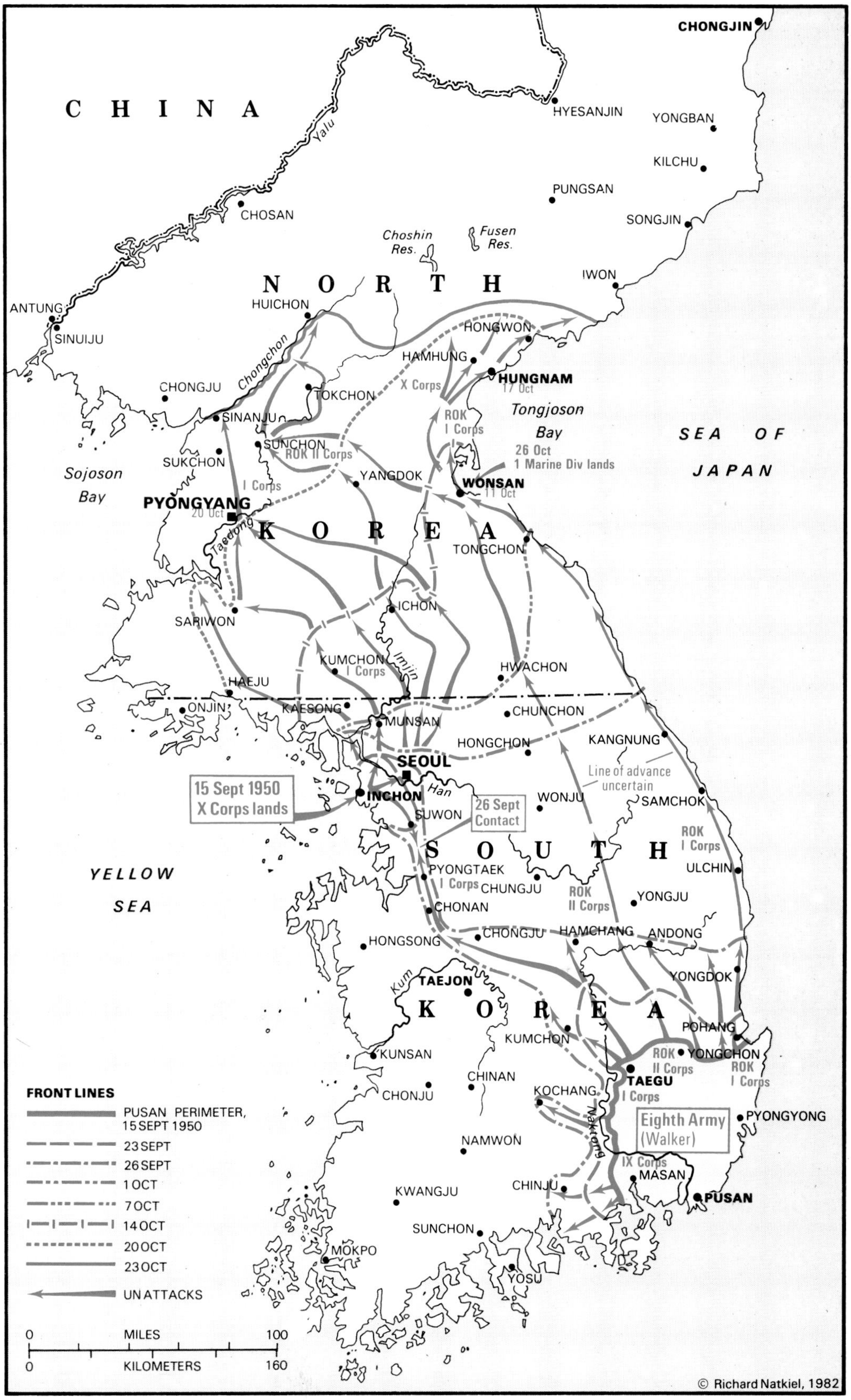

Right: The Korean War.
Left: A 57mm recoilless rifle in action against a Communist position in Korea.
Below: Some US 'Cold Warriors' of the Korean War period. L to R: Philip Jessup, Dean Acheson, John F Dulles and Charles Bohlen.

© Richard Natkiel, 1982

with the ROK forces only able to delay them slightly, something had to be done. MacArthur began to feed in elements of the Eighth Army piecemeal. Lieutenant General Walton H Walker was named Eighth Army commander in charge of both American and South Korean forces, but he could only slow, not stop, the North Korean drives. American armored and infantry units facing the enemy were constantly forced to withdraw to avoid capture in double envelopments by the numerically superior enemy forces.

By early August the Americans had suf-

Left and below left: **MacArthur's brilliant landing at Inchon in September 1950 turned the war around in a day.**

fered 6000 casualties (and the South Koreans 70,000), and General Walker's forces had been almost pushed out of South Korea. They held only a small area in the south behind the 'Pusan perimeter,' a line around the vital resupply port of Pusan. This 140-mile-long curved perimeter of American and ROK troops, however, proved strong enough to hold off the enemy and allow MacArthur time to feed in more troops and supplies. As additional Army troops, plus Marines, British infantry, and armor, assembled behind the line, Navy and Air Force planes mastered the techniques of close air support for the defenders below. Although it was not clear at the time, the tide was beginning to turn against the North Koreans. Now MacArthur was about to make the finest strategic coup of his long and distinguished career.

Even while ROK and American units were being forced back toward Pusan, MacArthur was planning his offensive. The farther the North Korean forces advanced to the south, the more vulnerable they were to envelopment, and in this MacArthur saw his opportunity. He quickly assembled X Corps, commanded by his chief of staff, Major General Edward M Almond, out of the 7th Infantry Division, the 1st Marine Division, and almost 9,000 ROK soldiers. Its purpose: to stage an amphibious landing at Inchon, the Yellow Sea port on the west coast of Korea only 25 miles from the capital of Seoul, far behind the enemy lines. Since most major highways and rail lines converged at Seoul, seizing the city would cut off the North Korean invaders to the south and force them to retreat through the mountains of eastern Korea. Ideally, most of them would be trapped and destroyed.

MacArthur's plan for the invasion at Inchon was as dangerous as it was audacious. Inchon had to be captured quickly, but the port could be approached only through mile-wide mud flats on which ships could easily be stranded, especially since the tides at the port rose and fell an incredible 30 feet. Furthermore, the harbor was guarded by defenses on the island of Wolmi-Do at its mouth, and, once ashore, the assaulting forces would have to clamber over a high seawall into the built-up urban area. Resupply could come in only at high tide every 12 hours: At falling, low, or early rising tidal periods the port was useless for reinforcement. And X Corps would be the last of MacArthur's reserves.

Most of MacArthur's Army and Navy colleagues were adamantly opposed to the operation, some estimating its chances of success at 500-to-1, but MacArthur was given the go-ahead, and the landings took place as planned on 15 September 1950. They were

Right: **After Inchon the Allies were able to make use of new offensive possibilities. Here, paratroops of the 187th Airborne make a drop in Korea in April 1951.**

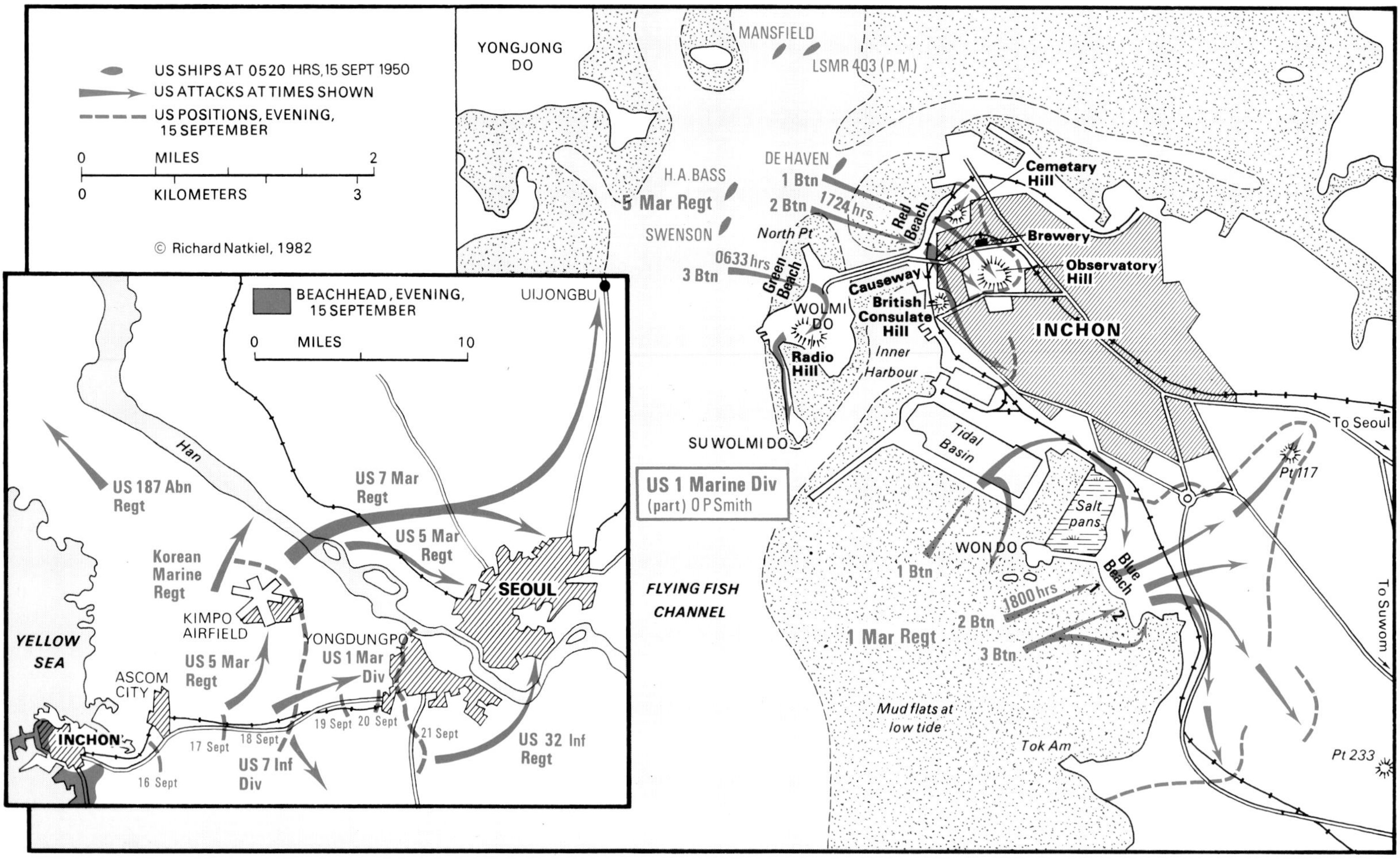

US SHIPS AT 0520 HRS, 15 SEPT 1950
US ATTACKS AT TIMES SHOWN
US POSITIONS, EVENING, 15 SEPTEMBER
BEACHHEAD, EVENING, 15 SEPTEMBER
© Richard Natkiel, 1982

successful beyond anyone's imagining. The 1st Marine Division and the 7th Infantry Division troops met only light resistance, quickly established a beachhead for re-supply, and began to sweep inland toward strategic Kimpo Airfield and Seoul, despite heavy fighting. Within two weeks, by 29 September, MacArthur was able to turn over the capital once again to President Rhee. In the meantime, General Walker's Eighth Army broke out of the Pusan perimeter and swept north. Some 30,000 North Koreans managed to escape back across the 38th parallel, but another 135,000 were killed or captured in MacArthur's superbly executed trap.

South Korea had been effectively cleared of the invading North Korean forces, but what now should be the next step? President Truman wanted to limit the war to the defense of South Korea, fearing that a move into the north might bring North Korea's supporters, China and Russia, into the war. On the other hand, the enemy troops who had escaped, combined with their reserves in the north, could still mount a considerable threat to the existence of the South Korean government. Furthermore, reunification of all of Korea *was* a long-standing American and United Nations goal. Faced with a difficult choice, the President told MacArthur, on 27 September, that he could enter North Korea but was to use only ROK forces as he neared the Chinese or Soviet borders on the north. Within two weeks the United Nations had given its *de facto* approval to the move to the north by calling for a restoration of peace and security throughout the entire country.

By late October American and ROK forces had moved deep into North Korea and in places were only 50 miles from the Chinese border. At a conference between Truman and MacArthur held on Wake Island on 15 October the general assured the president that Communist Chinese warnings that they might intervene only constituted sabre-rattling bluffs. Yet ground commanders of US and ROK units were already finding Chinese soldiers among the increasingly-stubborn defenders they faced as they approached the Yalu River, the northern border of the country.

By early November it was clear that thousands of Chinese 'volunteers' were fighting alongside the North Koreans, although still not in sufficient strength to check seriously the United Nations Command's armies push-

Top: The Inchon landing.
Below: House-to-house fighting near Seoul after the Chinese offensive.

ing north. But by late November the scale of the Chinese intervention had increased dramatically. Now some 300,000 Chinese troops had crossed into North Korea. It was, MacArthur said, an 'entirely new war.' He ordered his troops back from the Yalu to prevent their being overwhelmed or captured by the swarming Chinese. Once again the Allies were in retreat.

The American and ROK withdrawal from North Korea was carried out in good order, despite the severe Korean winter, but Chinese pressure was intense. The X Corps was withdrawn from Hungnam by sea to Pusan in a dramatic evacuation, and the United Nations force soon found itself back in the vicinity of the 38th parallel, having lost all of its territorial gains in the north. On 24 December General Walker was killed in a traffic accident, and Lieutenant General Matthew B Ridgway, the paratrooper commander of World War II fame, was hurriedly flown in to take his place as the head of Eighth Army. Although Ridgway found his UN lines to be thin and weak, he took all possible steps to protect the 38th parallel and Seoul. But Chinese attacks on New Year's Eve 1950 forced him to pull back even farther, and on 4 January 1951 the Chinese swept into the capital.

Despite this setback Ridgway managed to take advantage of weak Chinese logistical support and to end their incursions, stopping them roughly along the old 38th parallel line. With Ridgway holding that line the President and the Joint Chiefs decided to accept a stalemated war rather than become engaged in a major conflict with China or Russia. But MacArthur demurred. He was fully prepared to escalate the war in order to win, and his suggested options included blockading China, launching air attacks on China's war industries, using Chinese Nationalist troops in Korea, and allowing Chinese Nationalist troops to attack the Chinese mainland.

The President and the military chiefs rejected MacArthur's proposals. Since Ridgway had stabilized the front and there was diminishing danger of the UN forces being driven off the peninsula, the decision was made to stay and defend South Korea, but widening the war was out of the question. Even under these strategic limitations Ridgway was able to make some gains by cautious offensive moves north of the 38th parallel after recapturing Seoul in March 1951.

President Truman considered sending out feelers for a negotiated settlement at this point, but MacArthur maintained his bellicose public stance. He even sent an offer for peace talks to the enemy commanders, its tone being that of a victor addressing the vanquished. MacArthur's arrogant assumption of a nearly independent diplomatic-political role highly displeased the peppery president, but Truman held his fire. But then, despite presidential orders that all comments on national policy be cleared beforehand by his office, MacArthur informed the Republican party leader in the House of Representatives that he favored the use of Nationalist Chinese forces and that he was at odds with official policy for a limited war in Korea. (There could be, he said, 'no substitute for victory.') President Truman, on 11 April 1951, relieved the general from command and appointed General Ridgway in his place.

The 'firing' of General MacArthur seemed to crystallize national sentiment over the Korean War. The nation was already bitterly divided over a limited war in which there seemed no chance of gaining a clear-cut victory. To millions of Americans MacArthur was the symbolic martyr to a misguided policy of no-win warfare. The old general returned to the United States as a hero, to be feted with the largest parade ever staged down Fifth Avenue in New York City and to be invited to address Congress. It was great show, a heaven-sent issue for the opposition Republicans, and a catharsis for a nation involved in a military situation fraught with controversy and frustration. Eventually, after memories of MacArthur's return and dramatic speech before Congress had dimmed (at the conclusion of the speech he had announced that, like an old soldier, he would 'just fade away'), and after the Korean hostilities had ended, most Americans concluded that, in the long run, Truman had done the right thing in releasing the hero-general from his duties.

But while the Truman-MacArthur controversy flared at home, the Army, the Marines, and the ROK forces were still fighting on in Korea. Chinese and North Korean troops continued to attack the UN positions, and Lieutenant General James A Van Fleet, the new Eighth Army commander, and his soldiers beat off these attacks and then advanced north of the 38th parallel to the 'Kansas-Wyoming line,' terrain suitable for tenacious defense. There the fighting stopped in June 1951, and the peace talks began.

Delays by the Communists precluded setting an armistice date throughout the summer, and hostilities flared now and again into the fall. The North Korean and Chinese forces finally agreed on an armistice on 27 November (to begin in 30 days along whatever battle line existed at that time), but further negotiations for fixing the armistice date broke down. Through the winter of 1951-52 the negotiations dragged on, the major issue of contention being the United Nations proposal that prisoners of war who did not wish to be sent home would be set

By the end of 1951 the Korean front had stabilized a little north of the 38th parallel. The static war that followed consisted largely of small raids and artillery duels (*below*).

Eisenhower 'goes to Korea,' January 1953. In his presidential campaign he had promised to end the increasingly unpopular no-win war.

free, as provided for in the Geneva Convention of 1949. The Communists vigorously objected to this proposal. Negotiations continued through the summer of 1952; finally, in October 1952, the talks went into recess.

The negotiations were only resumed after the election of Dwight D Eisenhower as president in November 1952. In his run for the presidency Eisenhower had promised to 'go to Korea' and do something about the stalemated war, and in January 1953, before his inauguration, he flew to Korea to confer with General Mark Clark, now the Far East commander. Clark was ready to resume the war, but Eisenhower was not. He wanted an armistice and was willing to use threats to get it. After taking his oath of office, he informed the Communists in China, the Soviet Union, and North Korea via diplomatic channels that if an armistice were not forthcoming the United States would 'move decisively without inhibition in our use of weapons' and without necessarily confining its actions to Korea. In March 1953 continued American persistence finally led to an agreement for renewal of the talks, although battles flared through July. An armistice agreement was finally signed on 27 July 1953, and fighting ended that day.

In the 37 months since the original North Korean invasion, 142,000 American men had been killed, wounded, or captured, about 75 percent being Army personnel. The North Koreans and Chinese had lost about one and a half million men, the vast majority Chinese. In all, about two million American fighting men were committed to the war. When the line of demarcation was drawn in 1953 (slightly south of the 38th parallel on the western side of Korea and slightly north of the parallel across the center and eastern end of the peninsula) it signaled that the United States had, at the least, contained an aggressor and defended a friend.

Yet precisely what the legacy of the controversial Korean War would be was unclear when the fighting finally ended in 1953. What was very evident, however, was that the world was becoming an increasingly dangerous place, that America had fallen heir to active leadership among the Western democracies, and that the American military would play a major role in world affairs in the decades to come. It now seemed probable that limited wars fought under a nuclear umbrella might become permanent features of the post-war world.

New Technologies, New Postures, New Problems

The years 1953 to 1963 represented a decade of fundamental realignment both within the Army and within the American military establishment. Korea was fought largely on a World War II basis, although within the new American political-military strategy of containment. But rapid changes in the 1950s and 1960s in armaments, technologies, and mission concepts forced the American military to adapt to new modes of warfare occasioned by the presence of atomic weapons of overwhelming destructive power. These called for a basic alteration of the traditional American concept of victory in war. The gradually escalating conflict in Vietnam would demonstrate to what extent freedom of military action had become hostage to political calculation, though, to be fair, it should be added that politics may not have been solely responsible for the lack of a clearcut US victory in Vietnam.

There was no question, even after the Korean War, that the United States would continue to resist Communist and Soviet expansionism as a matter of duty. The only question was how. Surely nuclear weapons would play the largest part in America's

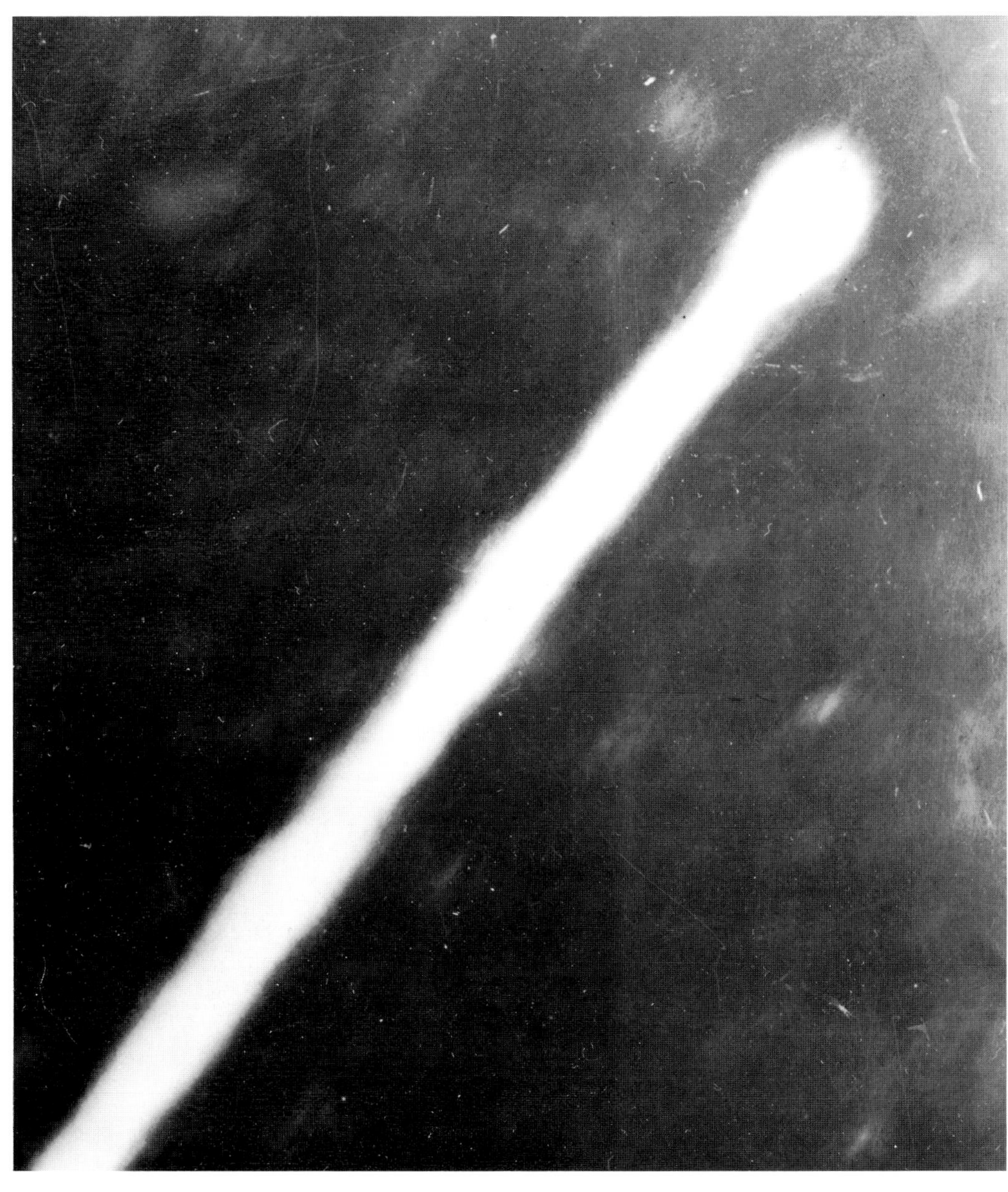

plans for deterrence. Such weapons could be delivered by the Air Force's newer long-range bombers operating from Strategic Air Command (SAC) bases at home, in Europe, and on the periphery of the Soviet empire. Intercontinental ballistic missiles (ICBMs) and the Navy's submarines armed with ballistic missiles could also be used as delivery systems. The Air Force had functional ICBM systems by 1960 with the solid-fuel, concrete-silo-survivable 'Minuteman' on the ways, and the Navy carried 1500-mile-range 'Polaris' missiles in its nuclear-powered submarines.

As a secondary echelon of nuclear deterrence it was also necessary to deploy in Western Europe and in the Far East shorter-range IRBMs (intermediate range ballistic missiles), Air Force planes with tactical nuclear bombs, and carrier-based aircraft. These steps, of course, required the co-operation of America's allies in Europe through NATO, and in the Far East in the form of the Southeast Asia Treaty Organization (SEATO), formed in 1954. Other regional alliances were also formed during these years, so that the United States was bound by commitments to aid its allies against Communist aggression throughout the world.

Emphasis on nuclear deterrence meant de-emphasis on the build-up of conventional forces, which were cut back to meet the administration's goal of reducing military spending from its Korean War levels. The Army, for example, was forced to cut six divisions during the 1950s. Crucial to the Eisenhower defense policy of nuclear superiority, as enunciated by Secretary of State John Foster Dulles, was greater emphasis on intelligence gathering to assess Soviet capabilities and intentions. This was gained partially through high-flying reconnaissance planes, such as the U-2, which could fly at 70,000 feet and take crystal-clear photographs of Russian military installations. Radio intelligence, spies and, by 1960, a functioning satellite reconnaissance program were also used.

For land power in case of war, the Eisenhower administration, ever mindful of trying to get 'more bang for the buck,' looked to reduced regular forces and the greater utilization of reserves and the National Guard. These forces were enlarged through laws of 1952 and 1956 that allowed men to spend part of their active duty time with reserve units or the Guard. This raised the number of reservists and Guardsmen in active training to one million, but did nothing to answer the Army's need for greater firepower and mobility on the battlefield.

The Army, therefore, used its limited funds to modernize its armored divisions and to procure armored personnel carriers for its infantry. Perhaps most important, the Army quickly moved to adopt the helicopter for carrying troops and for vertical envelopment techniques in battle. 'Helos' had been used in Korea for reconnaissance and medical evacuation missions, but newer, larger, and more dependable helicopters opened vistas of troop movement and tactics never seen before. The Army also formed 'sky cavalry' units for close fire support, using helicopter gunships. The Army believed, with the Marines, that the helicopter represented the wave of the future in infantry tactics. Thus the

New challenges to US security arose at the end of the 50s. *Top:* the trail of a Soviet space rocket. *Below:* Fidel Castro, Cuba's new ruler, soon became a Soviet client.

Eisenhower years, despite the administration's tilt toward nuclear weaponry and a strategy of massive retaliation, produced significant steps toward modernization and crystallization of the Army's role in the nation's defense posture.

When John F Kennedy came into the White House in 1961 he brought with him a concept of military strategy at variance with that of Eisenhower. Kennedy and his advisors believed that the strategy of massive retaliation not only brought with it the deadly danger of overreaction, but also left the nation unready for lower level, localized conflicts that could best be contained by conventional, non-atomic means. He called his new strategy 'flexible response.' The concept included not only matching or superseding the Russians in atomic capabilities through increased warheads, better missiles and more accurate targeting, but also having multi-use conventional forces at the ready at all times. This combination, of course, would cost more, but the young president believed that increased defense spending, combined with domestic tax cuts, would bring the economy out of the doldrums, making 'flexible response' good domestic policy too.

Three months after his inauguration in 1961 John Kennedy had to face the humiliating Bay of Pigs failure.

Conscious, however, of the potential waste inherent in defense spending, Kennedy (no doubt influenced by the movement toward more efficiency promised for the business world by systems analysis and budgeting) brought with him to Washington a new breed of managers for the Department of Defense, each fully convinced that greater national defense at restricted costs could be gained by cost analysis and its application. This approach to defense would bring more centralization and systemization to the American military, as well as an unprecedented amount of civilian decision-making.

Kennedy's point man for the 'new look' in military matters was his Secretary of Defense, Robert S McNamara, former head of Ford Motor Company. McNamara brought with him to Defense an entire upper-tier team of management-systems-engineering experts, soon dubbed 'defense intellectuals' by their admirers and 'whiz kids' by their critics. As Kennedy's first-line advisor on military matters, McNamara instituted a number of reforms, such as budget requests based on strategic functions. Having budget requests that were 'function based' gave McNamara's analysts a quantifiable end by which to measure cost effectiveness and, presumably, military worth. But the result was that weapons systems were often chosen for their lower cost relative to a given end, rather than for their optimum combat effectiveness. For example, the Air Force and the Navy found themselves ordered to produce a model for a fighter plane (the TFX) that would serve both services, even though both argued that, given their different missions, each needed an airplane specifically suited to their respective combat roles. Though the military chiefs resisted McNamara's planning-programming-budgeting system (PPBS) and argued against its efficiency in combat situations, and even though McNamara's 'revolution' caused vast disarray in the military services, it remained in place during the Kennedy years and was carried over into the presidency of Lyndon B Johnson, who succeeded Kennedy after the popular leader's assassination in 1963.

What would eventually prove to be of greatest consequence for the military and the nation was that under both Kennedy and Johnson the principles of systems analysis tended also to be applied to many aspects of foreign policy and to military decisions in Vietnam. This approach had far-reaching implications for the effective conduct of war, where non-quantifiables play an equal or greater role than quantifiables. McNamara's quantifiable analyses also led the nation into a labyrinth of 'assured destruction' requirements for atomic warheads and delivery systems, all based on a number of hypotheses regarding Russian capabilities and intentions. In the end, 'assured destruction' wound up looking much like the old 'massive retaliation' quantified.

'Flexible response' also sent unclear signals to America's allies. France, for example, became fearful that the United States might not use its full arsenal to defend Western Europe, and under Charles de Gaulle France not only pulled its troops out of their integrated status in NATO and forced NATO to move its headquarters out of the country, but also set France on the road to developing its own nuclear arsenal.

Yet whatever its shortcomings, 'flexible response' led to some measurable improvements in America's conventional non-nuclear forces. For the Army this meant development of infantry and armored divisions with greater mobility and firepower. The Army

also joined the Air Force in 'Strike Command,' whereby two Army airborne divisions were wedded operationally to the Tactical Air Command (TAC) and the Military Airlift Command (MAC) for greater tactical striking power. The 'air cavalry' tactic of using armed helicopters in conjunction with ground forces was also developed and refined. And since the administration had been shocked by the unreadiness of Army Reserve and National Guard units called up at the time of the crisis over the building of the Berlin Wall in 1961 (the Air Force and Navy reserves made a much better showing), Kennedy and McNamara concentrated on trying to improve the reserves and the Guard, paring their numbers somewhat but emphasizing increased training and readiness for those who remained.

Fortunately for the nation there was no conventional Soviet challenge to the nation's new defense posture. The abortive Bay of Pigs invasion of Cuba by Cuban refugees to topple Fidel Castro in April 1961 proved

Left: Kennedy's Secretary of Defense, Robert McNamara, advocated flexible response and function-based budgets.
Below: The worst crisis of the Cold War erupted when the USSR attempted to send MRBMs to Cuba. Here, missile crates on the Soviet ship _Kasimov_.

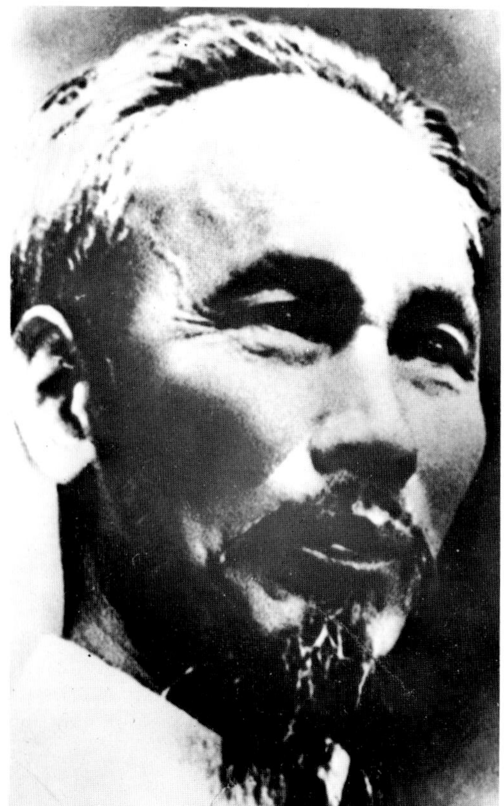

Top: A US reconnaissance photograph of a Cuban missile site, October 1962.
Left: North Vietnamese leader Ho Chi Minh. The Kennedy years saw a sharp rise in US involvement in Vietnam.

nothing about the military because it was almost entirely a CIA-conducted operation. The nation's military leaders were not privy to the planning and execution of the invasion except in the most peripheral sense.

Despite the painful failure of the Bay of Pigs operation, Kennedy remained convinced that counterinsurgency was a valid and valuable military-diplomatic tool. This led to his personal interest in the development of the Army's Special Forces, an elite and highly-trained force to be used for sabotage, counterintelligence, and counter-guerrilla action. Thus the 'Green Berets' found a champion in Kennedy, and by late 1961 they were at work in South Vietnam.

If America was spared any very serious conventional military challenges during the Kennedy years, the nation nevertheless had to face what was probably its most alarming nuclear confrontation. This was the Cuban missile crisis of October-November 1962. It began when military intelligence revealed that allegedly defensive missile sites being installed in Castro's Cuba by the Soviets were in fact being readied for offensive medium-range nuclear missiles. Calling to full alert the Strategic Air Command's bombers with nuclear payloads, putting the Army's NATO forces with tactical nuclear weapons on guard to protect Western Europe, and imposing a naval blockade on Cuba with the Navy's carrier battlegroups and submarines, Kennedy was able to force the Russians to withdraw the missiles from Cuba in return for a promise not to invade the island and to remove American missiles from Turkey. This successful use of America's entire spectrum of responses in complementary fashion, combined with effective threats of escalation, was taken by many as proof that 'flexible response' was meeting America's national defense needs. Yet in retrospect it is difficult to say just how serious the Soviet threat ever actually was. If it were a dangerous but essentially frivolous probe, the success of the American response would fall short of proving the absolute validity of the nation's overall defensive strategy.

Crucial to the Army and to the nation were

steps taken during the Kennedy years that would drag the United States deeper and deeper into a quagmire in Southeast Asia. From this the nation would extricate itself only in 1975, after the fighting there had removed one president from office, fractured the national consensus on both foreign policy and national defense goals, left the US with an unacceptable casualty list from a conflict in which America was clearly defeated and humbled, and caused a shuddering among the nation's allies as they came to doubt America's willpower and ability to defend itself and them.

The Vietnam War

American involvement in Vietnam began in 1950 with modest aid being offered to the French, who were trying to regain control over their former colony of French Indochina in the face of Vietnamese determination that this would not be allowed to happen. Only a few Americans were involved at first. These included Army officers and enlisted men in the Military Assistance Advisory Group sent to dispense military and financial aid. Opposed to the French and their puppet emperor, Bao Dai, were Communist forces called the Viet Minh. Their leader was the venerable Communist and Vietnamese leader Ho Chi Minh. Under Ho, the Viet Minh claimed jurisdiction over the entire country in the name 'the Democratic Republic of Vietnam.' The French, with weak support at home, were finally driven to the conference table in 1954, after they suffered a humiliating defeat at the fortress of Dien Bien Phu.

The conference held at Geneva to settle the conflict was attended by all the major nations, plus delegates from the Democratic Republic of Vietnam and the State of Vietnam (the Bao Dai government). The resulting Geneva Accords ended the fighting, set up a temporary demilitarized zone at the 17th parallel, with the Viet Minh administering Vietnam to the north and the French to the south, and provided civilians with the right to choose whether to live in the south or the north. Free elections were to be held in two years to determine the permanent government of the reunited country. Both Vietnamese governments objected to any permanent division of the country, and the South Vietnamese government, in particular, objected to the elections, since it believed that truly free elections would never be allowed in Ho Chi Minh's north. The United States declined to push them on this matter.

'Non-combatant' US advisors teaching grenade drill to South Vietnamese soldiers in the late 50s. By 1965 US forces would be openly at war and fighting the enemy face-to-face.

Thus Vietnam was divided into two countries. Some 100,000 South Vietnamese moved north (Ho Chi Minh calling on Viet Minh agents to stay in the south in their guerrilla base areas), and 800,000 North Vietnamese moved south. To strengthen the South Vietnamese government, about 400 Americans remained in the south to train the South Vietnamese army of 200,000 men and to provide economic aid to the government, now led by Ngo Dinh Diem. Initially, the American intention was simply to help South Vietnam to maintain its independence in the face of Communist aggression from the north. No one imagined that this was a commitment that would last until 1975 and eventually draw the United States into armed conflict on a massive scale.

The government of Ngo Dinh Diem proclaimed itself a republic and initiated steps to

Above: The 'Ho Chi Minh Trail' in Laos, the enemy's main supply route.
Right: General William C Westmoreland commanded US forces in Vietnam 1964-8.
Far right: The Vietnam War.

gain control over the countryside by suppressing dissidents, resettling refugees, and making modest land reforms. When the time for the scheduled national elections came up in 1956, President Diem insisted that free elections could not be held in the north and refused to participate. The United States backed him, and it appeared that the Communists would have to acquiesce in the inevitability of a divided Vietnam.

But Ho Chi Minh, having consolidated his power in the north by stern repression, now gave the green light to the Viet Minh in the south to rise once again and to attack the Diem government. Soon the South Vietnamese government was being seriously harassed by Ho's Viet Cong (Vietnamese Communist) insurgency campaigns within, and by his movement of regular North Vietnamese troops into the South. Local authority over South Vietnam was challenged by VC assassinations, sabotage, terror, and small-scale military attacks, all carried out under a thinly-disguised Communist organization labeled the 'National Front for the Liberation of South Vietnam' (NLF). Under this pressure the United States sent more advisors to Vietnam to aid the South Vietnamese military in its counterinsurgency efforts. Until 1960 the US advisors operated only in rear-echelon organizational training units; thereafter they began gradually to be drawn into the field to help stiffen the South Vietnamese army against its enemies in the countryside.

By 1960 the Viet Cong was enjoying marked success by terrorizing Vietnamese civilians into aiding and protecting them, and the government of President Diem was hard pressed to resist the growing danger from the north. Ho Chi Minh, on the other hand, allowed no dissent at home and enjoyed the support of both China and the Soviet Union in carrying out his campaign to bring down the Diem government and reunite Indochina under his banner.

Reacting to these unfavorable developments, President Kennedy decided to increase American support to Diem. By 1962, 11,000 men, the great majority of them from the Army, were serving as part of the Military Assistance Command, Vietnam (MACV), then under General Paul D Harkins. These troops, many of them Green Berets, now began to work directly with South Vietnamese regular and irregular forces in the field. But the military situation still failed to improve. Since the Communists had control of large sections of Laos, they were able to dominate the frontier along the long common border between that country and Vietnam and thus establish and maintain a supply route in 'neutral' territory. Their 'Ho Chi Minh Trail' ran all along the western border of South Vietnam. With it they could re-supply their regular or insurgent forces at will without outside interference. On the other side, the 60,000 South Vietnamese troops trying to control infiltration into South Vietnam in the highlands and along the frontier were hard pressed to do so effectively.

Seeking to aid the South Vietnamese in destroying VC enclaves in the south, the US in 1962 began to ferry their troops to the enemy by means of helicopters such as the CH-21 Shawnee and the UH-1 Huey. Armed helos were also added to the vertical envelopment forces. By early 1963 the United States was clearly in the war, and some progress was being made against the North Vietnamese, but the government of President Diem was at the same time becoming more and more unpopular. In view of this, and hoping to restore political stability in South Vietnam, President Kennedy gave his tacit blessing to a plot to overthrow Diem.

In the resulting coup both Diem and his brother Nhu were murdered by the conspirators (a development Kennedy insisted he never intended), but the result was not the political stability anticipated. Instead, there followed a year and a half during which numerous South Vietnamese generals jockeyed for control and influence, creating a splendid opportunity for the Viet Cong to reassert itself and extend its influence.

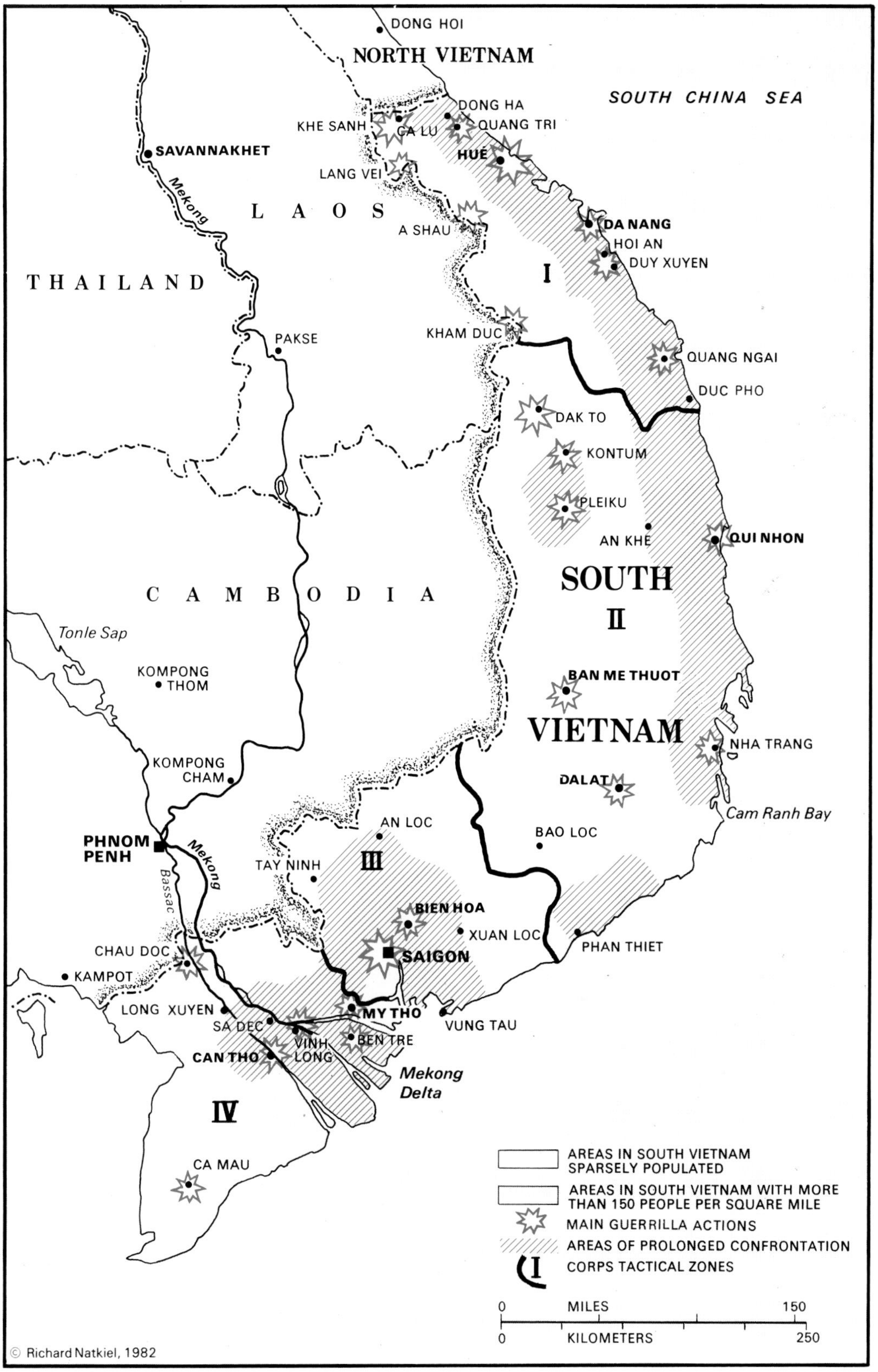

As the North Vietnamese continued to pour regular army units and insurgents into the south, the South Vietnamese government, even with 23,000 American advisors, seemed unable to stop their gradual extension of control over the countryside. President Lyndon B Johnson, Kennedy's successor, was unsure how to react. He did not want to escalate the war, since it would endanger his domestic programs, but he did not want to be saddled with losing it. In the event, he took advantage of an August 1964 attack by North Vietnamese patrol boats on American destroyers carrying out electronic surveillance missions in the Gulf of Tonkin to gain from Congress almost *carte blanche* authorization to repel attacks on US forces and to curb aggression in Southeast Asia. But even with the Tonkin Gulf Resolution he still seemed unsure of what to do and was not inclined – as was his Secretary of Defense, Robert McNamara – to listen to the military's suggestions. By the spring of 1965 he was forced by events to make his decision.

Under pressure of major North Vietnamese and Viet Cong victories in the central highlands of Vietnam, Johnson, in February 1965, ordered both that American Army and Marine combat troops should go into direct action against the enemy and that military targets in North Vietnam should be

The helicopter was a crucial weapon in Vietnam. Here, troops on a 'search and destroy' mission land from UH-IDs.

bombed. Within three months Air France B-52s were also hitting enemy enclaves in South Vietnam. Yet pressure by the North Vietnamese continued to threaten the existence of the South Vietnamese government, and still more US ground troops had to be committed to the fight. By the end of 1965, 180,000 American troops were in Vietnam, and more were on the way.

For a time it appeared that perhaps the situation might be saved. A government had emerged, under Army General Nguyen Van Thieu and Air Force Marshal Nguyen Cao Ky, that promised some stability and a willingness to allow a return to civilian rule once the war was over. And new tactics were being developed. In order to thwart the Viet Cong and North Vietnamese Army in the south, General William C Westmoreland, commander of US forces since the year before, ordered 'search and destroy' operations to hold off any further incursions and destroy enemy enclaves.

But despite notable victories over the enemy, such as the Army's successful seizure and holding of the Ia Drang Valley in the central highlands in the late summer of 1965 (which proved the feasibility of massed helicopter transport of infantry troops), the combined US and South Vietnamese forces could not destroy the invading and infiltrating enemy forces. They could not break the enemy's will and compel him to call a halt to the war, especially when his supply ports in North Vietnam and Cambodia and his Ho Chi Minh Trail were still politically off limits for destruction by superior American air power.

Thus the war dragged on, and by February 1968 American military personnel in Vietnam totaled over 490,000 men. South Vietnamese regulars and militia totaled another 640,000. By this time as many as 180,000 North Vietnamese had been killed and another 70,000 had been captured, but the 240,000 Communist combatants still in the field could not be subdued. Now both time and American impatience with a long, indecisive war were Ho Chi Minh's greatest allies. As he had said in 1945, 'If we have to fight, we will fight. You will kill ten of our men and we will kill one of yours, and in the end it will be you who will tire of it.'

The American soldier, although backed by excellent medical care (less than 1 per cent of battle casualties died in the war) and equipped with new armored personnel carriers, the new automatic M16 rifle, new anti-tank rockets, superbly effective Claymore anti-personnel mines, helicopter gunships, and other technological improvements, was caught in a war in which the enemy was always elusive, ready to take casualties, and willing to fight on. Worse, the American soldier was hamstrung by the government's inability to clarify the strategic goal of the fighting and dying; the inability of the American public, influenced by media coverage that by and large was not sympathetic to the cause, to comprehend the nature of the war; and the willingness of the military high command to accept policy decisions that brought the fighting men no closer to final victory.

Left: Both weather and terrain made Vietnam a difficult theater. Here, a mortar fires in monsoon-sodden jungle.

Some clear American successes had been scored in 1966 and 1967 when sizable units moved out of their base camps against enemy strongholds, and the pacification programs carried out by the civilian-military units under CORDS (Civil Operations and Revolutionary Development Support) seemed to be effective in rooting out Viet Cong influence in the villages of South Vietnam, but still the war went on. Indeed, although taking casualties as high as 10-to-1 over American forces in the field, North Vietnmaese troops, reflecting Ho Chi Minh's prophetic warning, showed every sign of continuing, and by 1967 they were preparing for a major offensive to begin with the lunar new year (*Tet*) in early 1968.

The Tet Offensive that began on 30 January 1968 was built around a series of massive attacks on South Vietnamese cities. Its object was both to bring about a general uprising against the government and to encourage anti-war sentiment in the United States. It failed in the former but succeeded in the latter. In their pre-dawn attacks in the provinces and in the Saigon and Mekong Delta areas, the 84,000 North Vietnamese and Viet Cong attackers struck the capital, 36 provincial capitals, and dozens of other cities and hamlets. Particularly hard hit were the cities of Saigon and Hue. Fighting was heavy in all locations, but, to the dismay of the North Vietnamese, the US and South Vietnamese soldiers, Marines, and Rangers, aided by massive close air support, inflicted heavy losses on the enemy. Especially noteworthy were the vigorous defenses put up around the Green Beret camp at Dak To, around the Marine base camp at Khe Sanh, and in Hue and Saigon. By the time the month-long offensive had died out, the Communists had suffered 32,000 troops killed and 6000 captured, against only 4000 killed on the American and South Vietnamese side.

The Tet Offensive had been an overwhelming Communist defeat, and soon the American and South Vietnamese pacification program in the countryside was reinstated with greater vigor than before, but the picture of initial military losses presented to the American public by the media, coming on top of general American disenchantment with the war, spurred vigorous demands at home for a complete pull-out from Vietnam. Thus an American and South Vietnamese military victory was interpreted as a great defeat at a crucial time in the continuing public debate over Vietnam. It became, in fact, a strategic psychological victory scored by the Communists. Understandably, many US servicemen saw this as a form of betrayal.

An M113 APC pulls an M48 tank out of the mud. Although Vietnamese terrain was unsuitable for armor, tanks often proved indispensable in battle.

Top: Bombing of Haiphong, April 1972, as seen from an American B-52.
Above left: Vietnam exposed some weaknesses in US equipment. The postwar Bradley M2 is a more battle-worthy personnel carrier than the old M113.
Below left: Vietnamese aftermath: Boat People.

The Tet Offensive also meant the end of the presidency of Lyndon B Johnson, who announced in March 1968 that he would not be a candidate for re-election, that he was curbing the air offensives against North Vietnam, and that he would welcome talks with the Communists. He was succeeded by Richard M Nixon who promised throughout his campaign against Hubert H Humphrey, the 'peace' candidate for the Democrats, that he had 'secret plans' and would end the war 'with honor.'

President Nixon had no secret plans, but he was determined to remove the American fighting men from the war and pursue peace through diplomacy. Aided by an impending Russo-Chinese split and by popular support for his announcement that he was determined to end the draft in favor of an all-volunteer Army, Nixon moved toward diplomatic solutions and toward a policy of 'Vietnamization,' wherein the South Vietnamese army, with American financial and advisory aid, would henceforth shoulder the burden of the fighting.

Withdrawal of American troops began in the summer of 1969 as the Army, now under General Creighton Abrams, held off the enemy by isolated actions against North Vietnamese base camps. Nixon also allowed the Air Force to begin pounding the Ho Chi Minh Trail and to destroy the 'neutral' Cambodian port of Sihanoukville, in both cases severely damaging the North Vietnamese ability to carry on its war against the south. Finally, Nixon authorized American and South Vietnamese troops to wipe out major North Vietnamese enclaves, across the border in Cambodia called the 'Parrot's Beak' and the 'Fish Hook.'

Even as the Americans were pulling out of Vietnam, anti-war sentiment continued to grow at home. News of the My Lai massacre of 400 villagers in 1968 (wherein the officer in charge had not been court martialed and punished by his superiors) leaked out to damage the Army's reputation, and the 'Pentagon papers,' revealing Defense Department uneasiness over the conduct of the war, were purloined and published. Now the North Vietnamese decided on another Major offensive to achieve final victory. This 'Easter Offensive' of 1972 by the North Vietnamese was bloodily rebuffed by surprisingly effective South Vietnamese troops. It was also foiled by President Nixon's decision to allow the military to mine the major North Vietnamese harbor of Haiphong, a move the generals had been urging for years. The resulting Air Force raids on North Vietnamese targets and Haiphong were spectacularly effective and, of great significance, neither the Soviet Union nor China made more than mild protests.

In the meantime presidential advisor Henry Kissinger continued to explore the diplomatic route to peace. By October 1972 it looked as though his efforts had been successful, but when the North Vietnamese balked and continued their military activity, Nixon loosened the Air Force once again, and Operation LINEBACKER II, in which Air Force and Navy planes flew 1800 sorties and dropped 20,000 tons of bombs on North Vietnam, mostly in the Hanoi and Haiphong areas, was carried out. This led the North Vietnamese to agree to end the fighting. America would withdraw, and all other issues would be settled by the Vietnamese themselves. By December 1972 American forces in Vietnam had declined from a wartime high of 565,000 to only 24,000.

America was finally out of the war. A sum of $1 billion was delivered to President Thieu in military aid, and the fighting, now again waged by the original combatants, went on. Nixon won re-election in 1972 but resigned in the wake of the Watergate scandals in 1974, with Gerald R Ford inheriting the weakened presidency. Congress, responding to anti-war and anti-military sentiment in the aftermath of Vietnam, was keeping a tight clamp on military spending, actually reducing the Pentagon's budget in terms of real purchasing power by 37 percent between 1968 and 1974. Congress also passed the War Powers Act in 1973, requiring Congressional approval of overseas troop deployments for longer than 60 days, a severe curb on the president's power as commander-in-chief and as chief diplomatic official in the government.

The year 1973 also saw the end of the draft and the implementation of the 'all volunteer' armed forces, an experiment that at least doubled the cost for each soldier in uniform. The new enlistees tended, if anything, to be somewhat less educated than the former inductees, yet they would have to handle weapons and equipment of unprecedented sophistication. Added to this were problems of integrating more black and female recruits into the service units, of dealing with the widespread availability and use of drugs by military personnel, and of trying to teach military discipline to young men and women coming out of a permissive society. The result was widespread dissatisfaction and disorientation in the services.

A resounding blow to American prestige came in April 1975 when the US-backed South Vietnamese government fell to a concerted North Vietnamese attack, Congress having refused President Ford's request for $700 million in emergency military monies to aid its South Vietnamese ally. (The use of American forces in combat in Southeast Asia had been flatly prohibited by Congress in 1973.) Americans watched on their television sets as Marine helos dropped into Saigon to evacuate the last Americans from the war-stricken country. Vietnamese refugees fought desperately to escape the city in the face of the terror of a holocaust that would surely follow their 'liberation' by the North Vietnamese. The tribulations of their compatriots, the 'boat people,' would intensify the impression of American failure in the months to come.

Since the conflict began in 1950, some 2.6 million American military personnel had served in South Vietnam. Over 47,000 had died there in battle, another 10,000 had died from accidents and disease, and 154,000 had been wounded. The war had cost the

Men of the 82nd Airborne Division on Grenada, October 1983. US casualties in this invasion: 18 dead, 67 wounded.

American government $410 billion. The South Vietnamese had lost 200,000 killed as soldiers, but over one million South Vietnamese of all sorts had died as war casualties. The North Vietnamese had expended 800,000 lives in gaining their victory. As American Marines lowered the flag and departed from Saigon on the last day of the Vietnam War, an American colonel on diplomatic assignment in Hanoi remarked to a North Vietnamese officer, 'You know you nevered defeated us on the battlefield.' The North Vietnamese officer replied, 'That may be so, but it is irrelevant.'

What was relevant was that by the Vietnam War the anti-Communist alliance system, including NATO, had been seriously weakened. SEATO was dead, with Far Eastern nations looking elsewhere than to America for their security needs. The domestic consensus in favor of 'containment' and the necessity of aiding America's allies was shattered, as the American politicians and the people they represented vowed 'no more Vietnams.' And the American military forces sank into public disfavor, being unfairly burdened with the 'loss' of Vietnam. Only in the next decade would the Army and its sister services regain a modicum of their former prestige. Whether the damage done to the American consensus about containment or to the Western alliance system can be wholly repaired remains to be seen. But there is reason to be optimistic.

The Army's new main battle tank, the 45mph M1 Abrams, began to enter service in 1980. It was armed with a 105mm gun.

Soldiers at the Ready

When he assumed the presidency in January 1977 President Jimmy Carter brought to the White House and to American diplomacy a desire to move international relations and American policy in more humane directions. Accordingly, he tried manfully to curb the spread of nuclear weapons and, at the same time, to reduce American outlays for defense purposes. Although dollar growth of the defense budget went up slightly under the first two Carter budgets, because of inflation real outlays actually declined. In addition, Carter cancelled the B-1 bomber program, curtailed the Navy's shipbuilding and replacement plans, stretched out procurement of MX missiles and tactical aircraft, and reduced spending in the military for operations and weapons maintenance. Indeed, during the first two years of the Carter administration, the military, including the Army, was virtually placed on hold while the new president tried to translate the international power struggle into some less menacing form of competition.

But the president's hopes were frustrated by events. First came the jolt of withdrawing support for the Shah of Iran only to have him replaced by the radical and violently anti-American Ayatollah Khomeini in 1979. This was followed by the seizure of American embassy personnel in Tehran and their being held hostage for 444 days by the Muslim fundamentalist leader and his followers. Further frustration was later added to the situation in the form of a bungled inter-service attempt to rescue the 53 hostages from the Iranian capital of Tehran in April 1980. As a result, Carter backed off from withdrawing the one American Army divison from South Korea and placed American troops in the Sinai after the Camp David agreements to assure peace there betwen Israel and Egypt. The final shock came with the Soviet invasion of Afghanistan in December 1979, which led Carter to reassessment of his policies and to recommending an increase in real spending on defense.

Now convinced of the need to augment American military power, Carter also increased military aid to Israel, Egypt, and Saudi Arabia to forestall spread of Soviet influence in the Middle East; authorized a Rapid Deployment Joint Task Force of up to 200,000 troops for world emergencies; and began to stockpile military supplies at the newly-leased American base at Diego Garcia in the Indian Ocean. But severe damage had been done to the military by the inadequate budget appropriations of Carter's first two years in office. Disturbed by Carter's perceived inability to handle America's problems, for all his good intentions, the voters turned to Ronald Reagan, the Republican candidate in 1980, and placed him, with his promises to 'rearm America,' in the White House.

During his years in office Reagan kept that promise. Military budgets placed heavy emphasis on weapons procurement and on substantial pay and benefit increases for personnel penalized by years of heavy inflation. Real growth in defense spending under the first three Reagan budgets stood at eight to 12 per cent, and defense spending moved to over seven per cent of the nation's GNP. The Militrary also moved to implement cruise missile and B-1 bomber programs, with Reagan's support, and both MX ICBMs and Pershing II intermediate-range missiles have been deployed, the former in fixed silos at home and the latter on European soil under NATO auspices. In addition, the president called for an anti-ICBM space-based laser or energy beam defense system called the Strategic Defense initiative, dubbed 'Star Wars' by the media. Nor did the Reagan administration hesitate to project American power abroad. It supported both friendly governments and anti-Communist counter-insurgency operations in Central America. It sent US Marines into Lebanon in 1982 (a move that ended in disaster with the bombing of their headquarters in October 1983); and it sent a multi-service force onto the Caribbean island of Grenada, also in October 1983, to deflect a Cuban Communist takeover of the island, already being converted into a military base of operations, an altogether more successful operation.

Operation URGENT FURY, the invasion of

Above: Men of the 82nd Airborne fire rounds from their preferred artillery weapon – the compact M102 105mm light howitzer – into the Grenadian hills during the 1983 invasion.
Right: Small forces from other Caribbean nations joined the US in the Grenadian operation.

Grenada, may have been more successful than the attempt to free the hostages from Teheran in 1980 or the landing of Marines in Lebanon in 1982, but the multi-service operation revealed serious shortcomings in American military operations. These led to probing criticism from outside the military and much soul searching within. The result was some very positive changes in US military doctrine during Reagan's remaining years in the White House.

The 1983 invasion of the tiny Caribbean island came about after Maurice Bishop and his socialist movement were otherthrown by left-wing extremists in October 1983. American policy makers had already been concerned about Soviet and Cuban presence on the island, and since a large airport complex had recently been constructed there, it was feared that Soviet aircraft might now be permitted to operate from the airfield and endanger shipping in the Caribbean and Central America and perhaps even along the southern coast of the United States. Furthermore, there were on the island about 600 American students and tourists whose safety would have to be assured.

Above: **Happy American students surround a US soldier on Grenada. Ensuring that the students would not be taken hostage by the enemy was one of the US Military's primary concerns during the invasion, an objective that the US Army was able to accomplish successfully.**
Opposite: **American troops in Greenville, Grenada, after taking the town on 25 October.**

When the Organization of Eastern Caribbean States asked the United States to join in military action to restore democracy and political stability on Grenada, Reagan gave the order for American forces to invade to protect the Americans, neutralize the island, and reestablish political harmony and democracy. In the ensuing operation that began on October 25, Marines (assisted by token forces of six area nations) attacked the northern end of the island while Army Rangers and members of the 82nd Airborne Division attacked on the south–even though the American students at St George's University Medical School and the other American nationals were in the capital at the center of the island. It took three days before the island was secured, despite relatively light opposition from Grenadan and Cuban defenders.

Secretary of Defense Caspar Weinberger claimed that the job had been 'well done,' but there was criticism from the Senate Armed Services Committee, which pointed to poor coordination between the Army and Navy, noting that there was no single service commander with the authority to make tactical decisions. Poor radio communication between the services had also been a major problem, resulting in ground forces not being able to call in supporting naval gunfire. And incredible logistical foul-ups marred the whole operation.

The long-term importance of Operation URGENT FURY lay not in its restoring stability to Grenada or in its thwarting foreign designs in the Caribbean but in the impetus it gave to changes in America's military forces, especially in the areas of command and coordination. The Packard Commission (officially the President's Blue Ribbon Commission on Defense Management, created in 1985 to assess the organization of the Department of Defense and chaired by former Deputy Secretary of Defense David Packard), and the Senate Armed Services Committee, subsequently recommended that DOD be reorganized and that unified commands be created for vitally needed cooperation between the armed forces.

The same year Senators Barry Goldwater (R) of Arizona and Sam Nunn (D) of Georgia, each the respected party leader on the Senate Armed Services Committee, endorsed a comprehensive staff study drawn up by the Department of Defense regarding it s organization and decision-making processes. Thus early in Ronald Reagan's second term in office a fundamental rethinking of the roles of all the armed services was underway. And it would not be long before the fruits of this rethinking would be put to the a fiery test.

Two US M2 Bradley Fighting Vehicles churn through the Saudi Arabian desert during the tense months prior to the start of the war with Iraq in early 1991.

VICTORIOUS PROFESSIONALS 1985-PRESENT

The year 1985 may well prove to be a watershed in the history of the world, for in that year, though no one yet realized it, the very assumptions on which East-West relations had been based ever since the end of World War II began to change. In essence, US policy toward the Soviet Union had not significantly varied since 1947, when American diplomat George Kennan called for 'containment' of Soviet expansionism by military, diplomatic, and economic means. Kennan predicted that if the West could contain the USSR long enough, the internal weaknesses of the Communist system would eventually force the system to change. Events in 1985 and thereafter seemed to bear out Kennan's theory.

In 1985 Mikhail Gorbachev came to power in the USSR and called for change not only in terms of *glasnost* (openness to public debate) but also of *perestroika* (restructuring of the Soviet system). It soon became clear that Gorbachev also included on his agenda the idea of downgrading hostility toward the West at least in part because the arms race, with its consequent high expenditures, was causing an unacceptable strain on the Soviet economy.

In the months and years that followed, Gorbachev and his reformers, while holding off challenges from old guard Communist leaders, were confronted both with growing demands for political and economic liberalization within the Soviet Union and with secessionist movements in various parts of of the polyglot empire. By the end of 1989 the Soviet puppet governments of all the USSR's European satellites had either been overthrown or fatally compromised, and the hated Berlin Wall had been torn down. The Warsaw Pact was formally dissolved in 1991, and by the end of 1992 the USSR itself had disintegrated into a commonwealth of independent non-communist states.

Yet the fall of the Soviet Union and the end of the Cold War did not automatically end America's security concerns. The mighty ex-Soviet war machine, including its atomic weaponry, was now divided among the unstable nations that made up the new Trans-Ural Confederation of Independent States. But since neither the future character of the CIS nor that of any of its member governments was predictable, how all this military power might be used was unknown.

The Army's Manpower

Unlike previous eras in its history, by the 1980s the US Army was moving to take full advantage of the military skills not only of its active duty personnel but also of its reserve and National Guard units. The all-volunteer Army, in which civilian pay and benefits would have to match or exceed those of the civilian economy, resulted in higher cost-per-soldier expenditures. At the same time, the cost of its equipment and weaponry – from the single bullet to high-technology helicopters and missiles – was soaring to new heights. Army planners, therefore, opted for a smaller but highly trained regular force, supplemented as necessary by fully trained and integratable reserve and Guard forces.

The backbone of the modern Army would be its active duty personnel, standing at 781,000 in 1985 (but due for cuts in the budget deficit years that followed). These men and women in armor, cavalry, air cavalry, mechanized infantry, light infantry, airborne, Ranger, special forces, aviation, and artillery battalions would form the core of the Army's fighting forces. There was evidence of improvement in the caliber of the regular forces in that over 91 percent of the Army's recruits were now high school graduates, and officers in the field reported that these regulars were among the best they had ever commanded. The Army had come a long way since the recruiting doldrums of the 1960s and 1970s.

Backing up the on-line regulars were 261,000 reservists in combat, combat-support, and general-support units which supplemented the regulars in all battalions except air cavalry, airborne infantry, motorized infantry, and Ranger units. By 1987 there were more reserve than active battalions in cavalry, light infantry, and field artillery and an equal number of special forces reserve units. Another 285,000 men and women served in the Individual Ready Reserve (IRR), being subject to call according to their military occupational specialities. Over 80 percent of the Army's reservists were high school graduates, and the Army was moving to provide them with 'the latest' equipment, so that they could be fully integrated into regular fighting units when called to duty.

As with the reserves, the National Guard soldiers were better trained and better equipped than ever before. Numbering over 452,000 paid members in 1986, the guardsmen were expected to be deployable in 30 to 60 days from call-up. They represented 43 percent of the Army's combat units (including 50 percent of its armored cavalry regiments) and 20 percent of its support units. Like the reservists, they were now furnished with some of the latest weaponry in the Army's arsenal and were better trained than ever before. Guard units, like their reserve counterparts, regularly took part in major exercises both in the United States and abroad, and the Army National Guard was also moving to build its own aviation (helicopter) force of 6600 soldiers by 1991.

A soldier at the Air Assault School at Fort Campbell, KY, is instructed in rappelling.

Opposite top: **Army trainees man a forward area radar during an air defense exercise. Such radars give early warning to batteries of anti-aircraft guns or missiles.**
Opposite: **US Air Assault troops practice rappelling down from a UH-60 Black Hawk.**

New Weapons

The weapons that had been developed to give this new-model Army the firepower and mobility it wanted were formidable indeed. Heading the list of new armored vehicles was the M1A1 Abrams main battle tank. By 1985 the Army had 35 battalions of Abrams tanks and was shooting for 7400 of the behemoths by the early 1990s. First produced in 1982, the M1 Abrams weighed in at 60 tons, but its 1500-horsepower engine could drive it at up to 45 miles per hour. Armed with either a 105mm rifled gun or a 120mm smoothbore gun and two machine guns, the Abrams could move and fight equally well in daylight or dark because it was equipped with a laser range finder, a ballistic computer, and thermal-imaging night sights. Furthermore, the Abrams had a 27 percent lower silhouette than its lighter and less powerful predecessor, the M60 Patton. As the Gulf War would illustrate, the Abrams could outduel any tank in existence, including the Soviet-built T-72.

Supplementing the Abrams main battle tank were M2 and M3 Bradley fighting vehicles designed to carry infantrymen and their weapons into war with speed and safety. The Bradleys, replacements for the earlier M113 APCs (armored personnel carriers), were armed with a machine gun, a 25mm cannon, and twin launchers for TOW (Tube-launched, Optically tracked, Wire-guided) missiles and had a cross-country speed of 41 miles per hour. They also had double armor plating of aluminium and steel and were fully

Above: **The mighty US M1A1 Abrams main battle tank would silence its many critics with its splendid performance in the 1991 Gulf War.**
Opposite: **A US soldier stands guard with his TOW (Tube-launched, Optically-tracked, Wire-guided) anti-tank missile launcher.**

amphibious. Also in the armored category and delivering firepower against the enemy on the battlefield were the 155mm M109 and 203mm M110 self-propelled howitzers, these supplementing the non-armored, towed 155mm M114 howitzers, the 155mm M198 howitzers, and the 105mm M101 and M192 howitzers.

In the air, the new Army of the 1980s featured two 'stars,' the AH-64A Apache attack helicopter and the UH-60 Black Hawk combat assault transport helicopter. The Apache, which entered the Army's air inventory in the early 1980s, had a maximum speed of 192 miles per hour and a range of 380 miles, despite its loaded weight of nine tons. Its two-man crew, equipped with a laser target designator, forward-looking infrared sensors, and pilot night-vision capabilities, carried combat ordnance of 8 Hellfire radar-guided anti-tank missiles, 38 2.75-inch Hydra rockets, and 1200 rounds of ammunition for its 30mm cannon. The Apache would prove itself to be a first-class anti-tank weapon in the Gulf War.

The UH-60 Black Hawk, with a crew of three, could cruise at 150 knots and lift an 11-man infantry squad or a 105mm howitzer and its crew into combat. In the 1980s it became the workhorse of the Army's vertical assault combat operations.

These machines were rapidly displacing the Vietnam-era AH-1 Cobra attack helicopter, the UH-1 Iroquois utility and transport helicopter, and the OH-58 Kiowa multi-role helicopter as technology proceeded apace. And by the late 1980s the Army had begun development of the even newer LHX (light helicopter experimental) in two versions, a scout-attack version and a light assault version, intending to procure 4200 of these fast machines for the combat of the future.

The Army's missile inventory of the 1980s was headed by the Patriot tactical air defense missile. First deployed in early 1985, the Patriot was a medium- and high-altitude ground-to-air missile. Mobile and having all-weather capability, it functioned by command guidance from the ground to mid-course; then, as it neared its target, it would inform ground radar of its location relative to the target, and a ground computer system would direct it to the kill. Though not really meant to be an anti-missile weapon, the Patriot missile would attain a better than 80 percent success rate when deployed against Iraqi Scud missiles in the 1990-91 Gulf War.

Also in the Army's missile inventory were the Hawk, a medium-range, surface-to-air missile, the Chaparral, a self-contained, heat-seeking anti-aircraft missile, and the Stinger, a man-portable guided missile weighing only 35 pounds, as well as many types of TOW missiles.

Coming on line in the 1980s to aid ordnance targeting for the Army in combat were JSTARS (joint surveillance and target attack radar system) for deep target intelligence and JTACMS (joint tactical missile system), used in cooperation with the Air Force in attacking deep targets.

The Army's chief shoulder weapon continued to be the M16A2 rifle. With a 5.56mm caliber (the NATO standard for rifles), the M16 in its improved version had a maximum range of 500 meters, and it was also fitted with a new 3-round burst device. In 1982 the Army adopted the light M249 5.56mm automatic squad rifle as a second weapon for its infantry; it could fire an astounding 700 rounds per minute. The standard hand weapon was the 9mm Beretta, a replacement for the venerable Colt .45.

The Army in the Unified Command Structure

Two catalysts for change in the Army's place in the military structure for the late 1980s were the Packard Commission's report, calling for strengthening of the authority both of unified and specified commanders and of the Joint Chiefs, and the Senate Armed Services Committee's report entitled *Defense Organization: The Need for Change*, issued in 1985. President Reagan endorsed the substance of both reports and

Below: **AH-64 Apaches, probably the world's most sophisticated attack helicopters.**
Bottom: **The UH-60 Black Hawk began replacing the UH-1 Iroquois (the "Huey" of Vietnam fame) as the Army's standard all-purpose helicopter in the early 1980s.**

urged Congress to act on them. As a result, Senator Barry Goldwater and Representative William Nichols of the House Armed Services Committee co-sponsored a bill endorsing most of the recommendations contained in the reports. The Goldwater-Nichols Department of Defense Reorganization Act of 1986 was quickly passed by both houses of Congress and was signed into law by President Reagan in October 1986.

By this landmark legislation not only were the office of the chairman of the Joint Chiefs strengthened and duty in unified staff billets required for general-officer rank in the services, but also unified and specified commands were either strengthened or created to direct all American forces worldwide with greater efficiency. The Goldwater-Nichols Act strengthened the four unified commands and one specified command already in place, and in the years thereafter four more unified commands and another specified command were added.

The US Army was slated to play a major role in seven of these ten commands, and its current field manual, *FM 100-5: Operations,* now assumes joint operations throughout. In fact, a multi-service combat operations doctrine for synchronized deep attack had been a keystone of Army-Navy cooperation since the origination of AirLand Battle doctrine in the early 1980s, a fact reflected in *FM 100-5: Operations.*

So great has been the effect of the multiservice commands system on all US military operations that it is now almost impossible to understand fully how any given service functions without first understanding how it fits into these integrated structures. The unified commands in which the Army plays a significant part are the Pacific Command, the European Command, the Southern (ie Latin American) Command, the Central (ie southwest Asian and northern Indian Ocean) Command, the Space Command, the Special Operations Command, and the Transportation Command. In addition, the Army is the primary component of one of the specified commands, the Forces Command. It is certainly worth taking a closer look at these particular organizations.

The US Pacific Command (USPACOM) was created in 1947 as an outgrowth of the unified command practices which developed in that theater during World War II. Its area of responsibility includes not only the Pacific Ocean but also the Indian Ocean area and the Asian land-mass, approximately 52 percent of the surface of the earth. Its commander in chief and his staff are located on Oahu, Hawaii, and about 380,000 defense personnel are assigned to this theater of operations. Directly under the Commander in Chief Pacific Command are subordinate Army, Navy, Marine, and Air Force commanders, all also located on Oahu, with the Army's subordinate unit, US Army Western Command, headquartered at Fort Shafter. Two subordinate unified Army commands report directly to the Commander in Chief Pacific Command: these are US Forces Korea and US Forces Japan.

Above: **Throughout the 1980s all US armed services trained with South Korean forces in annual Team Spirit exercises. Here, US and ROK Marines practice landings.**
Opposite: **An Army air assault team begins its perilous descent from a hovering UH-60 Black Hawk helicopter.**

Traditionally, Pacific Command's primary strategic mission was to cope with whatever regional military challenges the USSR or North Korea might present. The collapse of the Soviet Union greatly reduced one part of the threat but did not completely dispel it, since a formidable array of ex-Soviet land, sea, air and nuclear power still remained in place in the Far East. Although this potent force was nominally under the control of the new CIS, neither the future character of the CIS nor even its survival was certain, and how its military forces might be used was therefore unguessable.

On the Korean peninsula the North Korean government has over 800,000 troops in its Korean People's Army. It is, by some estimates, the fifth largest army in the world, with 70 infantry divisions or separate brigades and 80,000 special operations forces. Some 65 percent of its ground forces are south of Pyongyang and thus constitute a potential threat to the South Korean capital of Seoul. South Korea has only about 650,000 troops, and its armed forces are outnumbered by the North Koreans in tanks by about a 3:1 margin, in field artillery by a 2:1 margin, and in aircraft by about 400 planes.

Standing at the side of the South Koreans are the 31,500 men and women of the US Eighth Army, along with 2200 Marines and 11,000 Air Force personnel, cooperating since 1978 with their allies under the ROK/US Combined Forces Command. For over a decade the American and South Korean forces have been carrying out their annual Team Spirit exercises with combined forces numbering as many as 200,000 soldiers, including more than 6000 members of the US Army.

US Pacific Command also shares responsibility for the security of Japan, with over 46,000 American combatants (mostly from the Marine Corps and Air Force) stationed on the home islands and Okinawa, plus almost 15,000 military personnel stationed in the Philippines.

Multi-service and multi-national cooperation under unified command is also the hallmark of US European Command (USEUCOM) headquartered at Stuttgart-Vaihingen, Germany. European Command is essentially America's commitment to NATO, but its area of responsibility extends far beyond the borders of western Europe, for this unified command has responsibility for 13 million square miles, from the tip of Norway through the Mediterranean Sea and parts of the Middle East all the way to the southern tip of Africa.

In 1990 there were over 344,000 troops from the Army, Navy, Marine Corps, and Air Force in western and southern Europe. Almost 216,000 of these men and women (63 percent) were Army troops at 82 different sites, with some 207,000 stationed in Germany alone. The primary mission of European Command was originally deterence of aggression from the Soviet Union and its satellites on western Europe. Accordingly, the soldiers in this command have been especially well equipped with sophisticated weapons such as M1 Abrams tanks, multiple launch rocket systems (MLRSs) and Patriot air defense missiles. Their US Navy counterparts have also been equipped with powerful armadas, including the carrier task forces of the Sixth Fleet in the Mediterranean which deploy versatile F/A-18 Hornets, A-6 Intruders, A-7 Corsairs, and F-14 Tomcats and

which include ships armed with such impressive weapons as the 700-mile-range Tomahawk cruise missile. The Air Force too, has been stationing such state-of-the-art aircraft as F-15 Eagles and F-16 Fighting Falcons in the theater to play its part in gaining air superiority in case of conflict.

Equally important to the success of NATO defense has been the skill of the troops of the many nations involved in the alliance. USEUCOM has conducted a large number of training exercises each year, usually with NATO allied troops taking part. The Autumn Forge exercises have at times involved more than 200,000 troops and 400 NATO ships, as well as many thousands of air sorties. Because rapid reinforcement from the United States would be crucial if the US became involved in a general war in Europe, Reforger (REturn of FORces to GERmany) exercises have also been held annually, with as many as 20,000 troops sent to Germany from the United States to test the nation's rapid deployment capabilities. And to assure adequate equipment and supplies once the troops arrive, more and more heavy artillery equipment has been pre-positioned in the theater, with the Army striving to have enough supplies in Europe for six full divisions (60,000 to 100,000 soldiers).

How the forces of European Command will be structured in the future depends on two basic factors. One is strong political pressure in the United States to draw down the number of American military stationed in Europe and thereby save monies spent on national defense (especially in view of the relative economic health of many of the nation's NATO allies, now able to do more in their own defense). The other is the depth and duration of the changes occurring in the still-unstable republics that have replaced the Soviet Union. But until events prove conclusively that a high level of American defensive aid to western Europe is no longer necessary, the areas under the jurisdiction of European Command will continue to be of strategic importance to the US.

Becoming ever more important to American interests beyond its borders are events taking place in Latin America, the area of responsibility of US Southern Command (SOUTHCOM), established in 1963. This unified command has three components: US Army South, the US Southern Air Force, and US Naval Forces Southern Command. US Army South includes approximately 7000 troops and is headquartered at Fort Clayton, Panama City. Its primary mission is to protect the Panama Canal until it is turned over to the Republic of Panama on 31 December 1999. It also supports other missions in 12 Latin American nations, operates the Jungle Operations Training Center at Fort Sherman, Panama, and regularly carries

Top: An MP of the 82nd Airborne crouches behind his M60 during the annual Reforger exercises conducted by NATO armed forces in the Federal Republic of Germany.
Left: Men of the 1st Infantry de-train in Germany to take part in a Reforger exercise.

out multi-national training exercises with names such as Blazing Trails, Kindle Liberty, and Blue Horizon.

Southern Command receives only a small fraction of the Department of Defense budget (0.1 percent), but its missions proved to be of considerable importance in the 1980s, particularly in the two Central American hotspots of Panama and Nicaragua. While difficulties with the Panamanian government of Manuel Noreiga eventually led to successful American military intervention with Operation JUST CAUSE in 1989, the Nicaraguan situation fostered a good deal of insecurity in Central America and led to devisive policy debates in Congress. It is still not clear whether the problem has been completely lain to rest.

After the Sandinistas took power in Nicaragua in 1979 by overthrowing the regime of General Anastasio Somoza, their Marxist-Leninist government, with the aid of Soviet, Cuban, North Korean, Libyan, and PLO advisors, built an army of 80,000 men (120,000 if reservists and militia are counted) equipped with modern Soviet weapons and

Right: US and German troops, standing in the shadow of an M60 tank, discuss tractics during a Reforger exercise.
Below: An Ml Abrams main battle tank in the 1982 Reforger exercise. Such field testing helped to provide information that resulted in the much-improved MlAl Abrams.

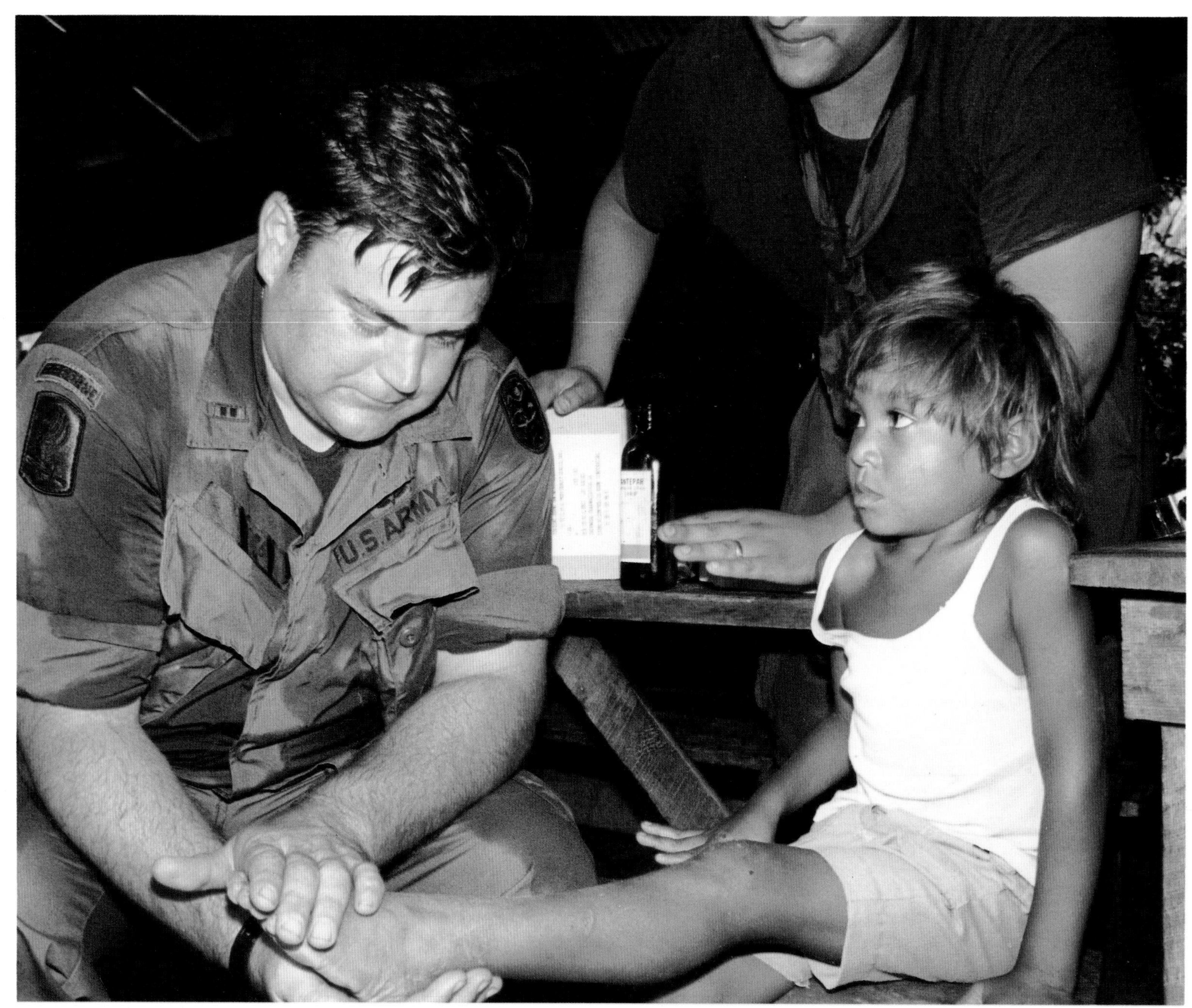

deploying more armored vehicles than in all the rest of Central America combined. Alarmed by the rise of what it considered a new base for potential Soviet subversion – or even direct aggression – in the Americas, the Reagan administration was overtly hostile to the new Nicaraguan government and gave direct military and humanitarian aid to Nicaragua's anti-Sandinista contra rebels. At one point, in March 1988, two battalions of the 82nd Airborne Division out of Fort Bragg, North Carolina, and two battalions of the 7th Infantry Division (Light) from Fort Ord, California, 3200 soldiers in all, were airlifted into Honduras in Operation GOLDEN PHEASANT to stop Sandinista soldiers from making incursions into Honduras in pursuit of contras. By early 1990, however, the Sandinistas had lost power in a Nicaraguan national election, and whatever threat they represented was, if not permanently ended, at least temporarily much reduced.

Fidel Castro's Cuba had also become a secondary problem for the United States and Central America by the early 1990s, despite as many as 14,000 Soviet military personnel stationed there and Soviet aid of $4 billion each year. Neither Cuba's authoritarian political system nor its collapsing economy provided very attractive models for other Latin Americans, and there was even some doubt about how much longer the USSR would be willing or able to underwrite the inflexible Castro regime.

Whatever the outcome of the Latin American people's struggles for democracy and economic growth as the area emerges to stand on its own in the affairs of the world, Southern Command continues to support American and friendly interests – political, economic, maritime, and military – against those who would turn Latin America's problems into an excuse for violence and further exploitation of its citizens.

US Atlantic Command, established in 1947, is almost entirely a sea command. Its responsibility is to guard US interests in the Atlantic Ocean from the North to the South Pole, an area of 45 million square miles. Headquartered in Norfolk, Virginia, USLANTCOM regularly has but a handful of Army personnel, but it is authorized, as needed, to call up

A member of one of Southern Command's MEDCAP team gives medical treatment to a village lad during the course of an Army exercise conducted in Honduras in 1983.

as many as three combat-ready Army divisions under Army Forces Atlantic.

US Central Command (CENTCOM) was created in 1983 as the successor to the Rapid Deployment Force of the Carter years. It is the unified command for American interests in Southwest Asia, the Persian Gulf, and the area around the Horn of Africa. It is charged with ensuring the uninterrupted flow of oil through the Strait of Hormuz, the Gulf of Oman, and the Persian Gulf: with promoting security for friendly states in the area: and with responding to military challenges such as that posed by Iraq in 1990.

CENTCOM, headquartered at MacDill Air Force Base in Tampa, Florida, has no troops but its own but has the authority to call on and direct more than 400,000 personnel from all the armed services, including ground forces, fighter and bomber wings, Marine amphibious forces, Army Rangers, special forces from the Army, Air Force and Navy, carrier battle groups, and other US Navy forces.

Shipboard pre-positioning and planning for logistical support for Middle East operations has also always been within the purview of Central Command in its preparation of any military eventuality in the 19 countries that constitute its area of authority.

As with other unified commands, CENTCOM has carried out extensive exercises not only in the United States (eg. Gallant Eagle) but also in the Middle East, with its biennial Bright Star exercises utilizing up to 20,000 soldiers, sailors, and airmen, as well as nationals from allied countries in the region. That unified commands in general and Central Command in particular were well prepared for coordinated air, land, and sea warfare was dramatically illustrated by the Gulf War of 1990-91.

The US Space Command, a unified command charged with US military space operations, ballistic missile defense planning, and directing space support operations for the Joint Chiefs and other unified and specified commands, was created in 1985. Headquartered at Peterson Air Force Base, Colorado, with its nerve center in Colorado Springs, SPACECOM has three components: the Air Force Space Command and the Army Space Agency, both at Colorado Springs, and the Naval Space Command located at Dahlgren, Virginia. The existing North American Aerospace Defense Command (a US-Canadian cooperative radar early warning system designed to thwart trans-polar ICBMs) has been retained to work closely with the Space Command, the commander of each being dual-hatted to assure close coordination of information. The Army plays a slightly smaller role than the Air Force and Navy in Space Command.

The key to the success of this unified command is its ability to gather, assess, and coordinate all space-based intelligence. This information is then disseminated to the Joint Chiefs and the commanders in the field for maximum use in carrying out the technologically sophisticated warfare that marks the present stage of military development. Its role in the Gulf War was vital to the success of that operation.

The US Special Operations Command (SOCOM), mandated in the Goldwater-Nichols Act, came into being in 1987 to provide coordinated covert operations within the American military. Special forces carrying out covert operations had been enthusiastically supported by President Kennedy in the early 1960s, but they were largely subsumed by conventional operations and fell increasingly into disuse and fragmentation in Vietnam and in the years that followed. The

Right: Egyptian troops salute US colors during Bright Star 80, one of a series of exercises that were conducted in the Middle East to hone US desert-fighting skills.

Right: Men of the 101st Airborne unload a UH-60 Black Hawk from a transport aircraft after Bright Star 81. Such desert exercises proved their worth in the 1991 Gulf War.

debacle of the Desert One hostage rescue attempt in Iran in April 1980 revealed their weaknesses and led to the Holloway Commission recommending that special forces coordination, training, and mission specificity were absolutely imperative. With the Reagan administration pushing for these goals, emphasis was again placed on special operations forces working in a unified manner, and Special Operations Command thus came into being.

The SOCOM has four major components: the Army's 1st Special Operations Command at Fort Bragg, North Carolina: the Naval Special Warfare Command at Coronado, California: the 23rd Air Force at Hurlburt Field, Florida: and the Joint Special Operations Command at Pope Air Force Base, North Carolina.

The Army's 1st Special Operations Command is the largest of all and is composed of active duty, reserve, and National Guard forces. Included are eight special forces groups, a Ranger regiment, a psychological operations group, and aviation and support groups. Cross-training and joint exercises with other special operations forces and with conventional forces are regular parts of the rigorous training given its personnel.

Also created in 1987 was the US Transportation Command (TRANSCOM), designed to provide airlift, sealift, and terminal services, plus commercial air and land transportation, for deploying and sustaining American forces anywhere in the world. The Transportation Command, headquartered at Scott Air Force Base, Illinois, has three major components. These are the Air Force's Military Airlift Command, the Navy's Military Sealift Command, and the Army's Military Traffic Management Command, headquartered at Falls Church, Virginia. With a heavy emphasis on coordination, pre-planning, and full use of data processing, and relying heavily on reserve forces to supplement the regulars in keeping the logistical pipeline flowing, the relatively new Transportation Command proved in the Gulf War that it would do the job even when faced with exceptional difficulties.

In addition to the unified commands, there are also two specified commands in America's military system. These are the Strategic Air Command (SAC) and the Forces Command (FORSCOM). The Strategic Air Command, headquartered at Offutt Air Force Base, Nebraska, is 'all Air Force,' with 54 units at 39 bases in the continental United States and 16 overseas. With military personnel numbering 124,000, it is America's long-range bomber and intercontinental ballistic missile strike force. As such, it flies more than 2000 aircraft (including B-1, B-2, and B-52 bombers, as well as numerous tankers and reconnaissance aircraft), and it controls over 1000 ICBMs (including Peacekeeper, Minuteman II, and Minuteman III missiles).

The second specified command is Forces

Command. Created in 1987 and headquartered at Fort McPherson, Georgia, FORSCOM's primary mission is to train, equip, and prepare the Army's forces for deployment overseas in support of forward-based contingents. In this capacity, it is in charge of 19 major installations and 1 million soldiers, that is, all the active, reserve, and Guard forces in the continental United States, Alaska, Puerto Rico, and the Virgin Islands.

Its active component is made up of over 250,000 men and women in six armies, three corps, 12 divisions, and four separate brigades. Its reserve component is made up of over 300,000 soldiers in 25 commands, 12 training divisions, and 3 separate infantry brigades. Its Guard component consists of 450,000 guardsmen in 10 divisions, 17 brigades, and four armored cavalry regiments. All must be trained, equipped, and mobilized to augment forward-deployed troops at any time.

A second mission of FORSCOM is defense

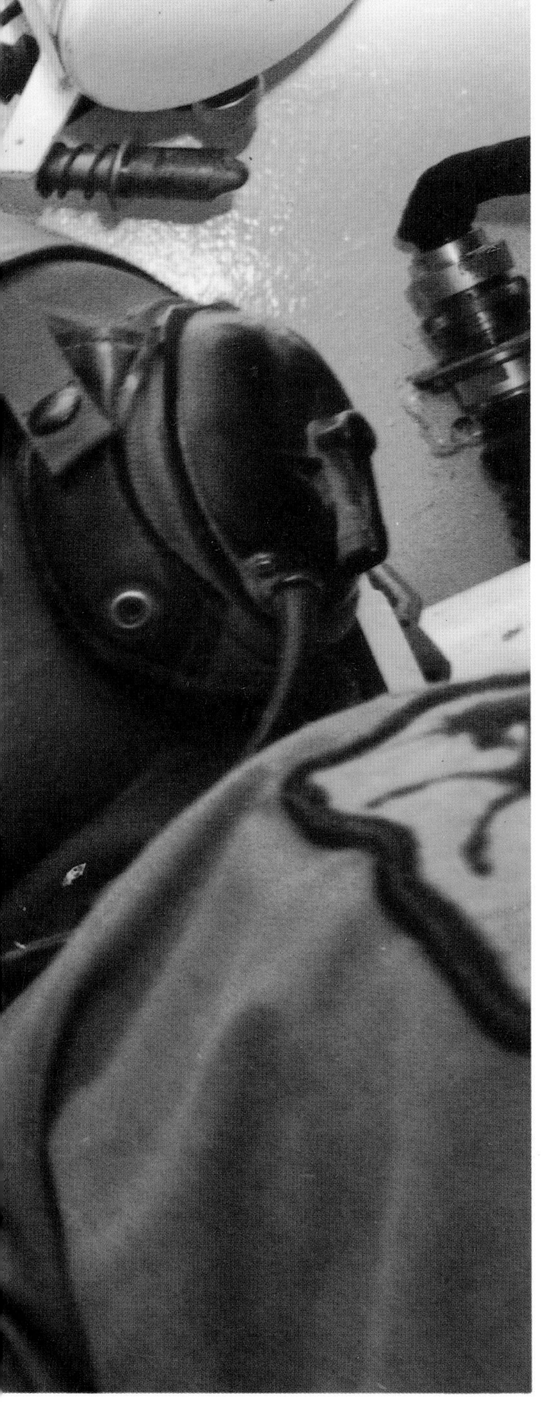

Above: President George Bush observes a mock tank battle in the Mojave desert.
Left: The complex gunner's station in the turret of an Abrams tank. Operating modern hi-tech weaponry requires very high levels of skill which must be maintained by both constant training and practice.

of the continental United States and Alaska. To this end it coordinates its efforts with the five continental armies and state units and with the Canadian Forces Mobile Command.

Training for combat-readiness and deployment being its primary goal. Forces Command supervizes training for all its constituent units. Its National Training Center at Fort Irwin, California, is the Army's premier training facility and also operates as a joint training center for all the military services under direction of the Department of Defense. FORSCOM also carries out joint training exercises through the Joint Readiness Training Center at Fort Chaffee, Arkansas, and through amphibious training exercises with the Navy's US Pacific and US Atlantic Commands at Coronado, California, and Little Creek, Virginia. In addition, it conducts joint exercises with the Air Force, as well as deploying its US-based forces overseas to participate in joint training exercises such as Team Spirit in Korea, Reforger in Europe, and Bright Star in the Middle East.

Forces Command is perhaps the best illustration of how the traditional separation in the Army between regulars, reservists, and guardsmen is becoming a thing of the past and how service mission exclusivity, interservice rivalries, and lack of cooperation are coming to an end under the impact of the unified and specified command structures. The positive results of these structural changes became manifest in Panama in 1989 and in the Middle East the following year.

Panama: Operation JUST CAUSE

In February 1988 the Republic of Panama came under the right-wing dictatorial rule of General Manuel Antonio Noriega, whose main sources of power were his 'Dignity Battalions' of about 8000 pro-Noreiga irregulars and his army, the Panama Defense Forces. Once he was in authority, there seemed no easy way to get rid of Noriega. When Pana-

manian voters went to the polls and overwhelmingly voted him out of office, Noreiga simply voided the election and refused to allow the winning candidates to be sworn into office. Meantime, Noreiga had been indicted by two US federal grand juries on charges of dealing in illicit drugs and laundering drug profits through Panamanian banks. The United States government wanted him brought to justice.

US-Panamanian relations deteriorated steadily and reached a crisis when Noreiga's men killed an American serviceman and when, in response to US protests, Noreiga made the foolish gesture of declaring war on the United States, American military units stationed within the country, supplemented by additional forces from the outside, were ordered by President George Bush on 17 December 1989 to invade Panama in what came to be called Operation JUST CAUSE. Bush's purposes were fourfold: to protect American citizens, to support the thwarted democratic institutions in Panama, to ensure the continued operation of the Panama Canal, and to apprehend General Noreiga.

Long before the H-hour of 1:00 am on 20 December 1989 the 13,000 American troops in Panama were preparing to move against Noreiga, and steps were being taken to airlift in another 9000 troops from bases around the United States. Indeed, some 4500 troops, plus tanks and attack helicopters, had been shipped into Panama in the months before the operation got underway. So well planned and executed was Operation JUST CAUSE that within seven hours after the combined-service operation was launched the 9000 additional American troops had parachuted or been flown into Panama, the initial assault had been completed, Panama City was under the effective control of American troops, the PDF had been neutralized, and Noreiga was on the run and hiding from the American soldiers. JUST CAUSE clearly showed that the changes in force development, unified command, and training regimens instituted in the 1980s were capable of paying rich dividends.

Left: **Panamanian strongman General Manuel Antonio Noriega in March 1988, a month after he had assumed dictatorial power in the strategically important republic.**
Below: **A UH-60 Black Hawk clatters over the streets of Panama City in the aftermath of operation JUST CAUSE, the US invasion of Panama on 20 December 1989.**

Directing the invasion of Panama was the commander in chief of the Southern Command, General Maxwell Thurman. Days before H-hour special operations forces were shadowing Noreiga's moves, carrying out reconnaissance missions in and around Panama City and the canal, and watching the movements of PDF units. On Tuesday, 19 December, huge Air Force transports were landing at Howard Air Force Base at 10-minute intervals bringing soldiers and supplies into the area.

The on-site and augmenting troops were divided into five task forces, each with its own mission. Task Force Red was ordered to seize the airfield at Rio Hato 90 kilometers southwest of the capital and Torrijos International Airport in the city. To capture the Rio Hato airfield, Army Rangers parachuted in and attacked the two companies of PDF forces there, in the process being aided by Air Force F-117A Stealth fighters which dropped concussion bombs on the defenders, the first combat mission for the new radar-invisible fighters. Some 250 PDF prisoners were taken at Rio Hato as the airfield was secured, and within two hours giant C-130s were landing with additional equipment and supplies. The secondary task of TF Red, the seizure of Torrijos International Airport, was carried out by the men of the 82nd Airborne Division from Fort Bragg, North Carolina, who jumped in two waves and secured the facility.

The men of Task Force Bayonet had three assignments when they started out a little after midnight. First, they attacked the Comandancia, Noreiga's military command building in the heart of Panama City, with tanks and howitzers supported by gunships and attack helicopters. Second, elements of the Navy's special operations Seals (SEA, Air and Land capability) units attached to TF Bayonet rushed Patilla Airport, a private facility in the capital, securing the airstrip and destroying Noreiga's Learjet to preclude his escape by air. Four Seals were killed in this operation because an intelligence failure left them without warning that they would be up against armored troops. In the meantime, other Seals disabled boats that might have been used by Noreiga for an escape by sea. Third, TF Bayonet troops carried out an airborne assault via Black Hawk helicopters to cut off PDF troops at Fort Amador south of the Comandancia, while also securing the United States Embassy, Southern Command headquarters, and the headquarters of US Army South at Fort Clayton.

Task Force Pacific was given the task of reinforcing the on-site troops at Torrijos Airport. They carried this out by jumping in two waves of paratroopers of the 82nd Airborne Division from Air Force C-141 transports. Critics later pointed out that the 82nd could just as well have been landed at the airport

Right: **On the third day of the invasion of Panama a US soldier in Panama City pauses in front of a poster of General Noriega. Two days later, Noriega would seek asylum in the Vatican nunciature in Panama City.**

Above: An American NCO positions his men outside the Marriott Hotel in Panama City. Some 100 civilians, many Americans, had been held in the hotel by Noriega forces.
Left: Chairman of the Joint Chiefs of Staff General Colin Powell (l) holds a briefing on the Panama invasion in Washington, DC.

rather than carrying out a dangerous night-time jump. Whatever the validity of that criticism, the soldiers of the 82nd joined up with Rangers and other special forces to block the PDF forces from Fort Cimarron from reaching the city. In this blocking operation the soldiers received valuable assistance from AC-130 gunships, which helped drive the PDF forces back to the fort.

While all this was going on Task Force Semper Fidelis, consisting of Marine Corps rifle and light infantry companies stationed in the area, assisted by a TF Bayonet contingent and the Marine's First Fleet Antiterrorism Security Team, blocked the Bridge of the Americas in the southern part of the city to prevent a PDF counterattack on Howard Air Force Base.

Across Panama, at the northern end of the canal, Task Force Atlantic was carrying out its part of the combined operation. Composed of elements of the 82nd Airborne Division and of the 7th Infantry Division, plus other special units, TF Atlantic seized the canal facilities near Colon from PDF infantry and naval infantry units. They also seized the valuable Madden Dam, which feeds the canal locks, and Gamboa Prison, where they released 45-50 political prisoners arrested in the earlier attempt to overthrow Noreiga.

In the days that followed these successful assaults PDF forces and Dignity Battalion soldiers continued to hide from the Americans and carry out sniping attacks in Panama City. Much media attention was focused on the successful American operation to secure the Marriott Hotel where some 100 people, many of them Americans, were rescued from Panamanian forces.

Yet the assault on Panama was really over on the first day, as General Colin L Powell, the chairman of the Joint Chiefs of Staff, announced to the American people on television that evening. The one great task remaining was the capture of the elusive Manuel Noreiga. But with his forces killed, captured, or in hiding, he had already been effectively deposed and neutralized, much to the delight of the Panamanian people. A democratically elected government was, in fact, already in power in Panama City, the president-elect, Guillermo Endara, having taken the oath of office at the headquarters of US Army South at Fort Clayton on the evening of the first day of the battle.

With his forces smashed and nowhere to go, Noreiga finally sought refuge in the nunciature of the Vatican on 25 December. Although being thus protected from arrest by the laws of sanctuary, he could not escape, especially as the nunciature was immediately surrounded by American troops. He finally surrendered to US Drug Enforcement Administration authorities on the evening of 3 January 1990 and was flown by an Air Force plane to federal custody in Florida to face the drug charges placed against him.

Operation JUST CAUSE was over. In the successful combined operation only 23 Americans had been killed in action, and 330 had been wounded. Since this was largely an Army operation, it is not surprising that 18 of the soldiers killed and 288 of those wounded were Army personnel. JUST CAUSE had not been without its failures, especially in intelligence, but it had justified the combined forces concept adopted and trained for in the 1980s. As General Edward Meyer, former chief of staff of the Army, said, 'The Panama operation outlined the rationale for the type of forces we will require in the future.'

The Gulf War: the Background

Iraq, a nation of 18 million persons, of whom about one-half are Shiite Muslims, one-fourth Sunni Muslims, and about one-fourth Kurds with their own language, culture, and separatist tendencies, had been governed since 1979 by the Sunni Saddam Hussein in a thoroughly dictatorial fashion. He professed strongly anti-Western and anti-Israeli sentiments and allowed such renowned terrorists as Abu Nidal refuge in Iraq. But when his 1980 invasion of neighboring Iran bogged down, he was forced to turn to the West and other countries for help. The United States was inclined to be sympathetic to his pleas for aid because the Iran of Ayatollah Khomeini seemed the greater threat to American interests in the Middle East. Besides, there was hope expressed that Hussein might now be more inclined to moderation in his dealings with the West.

In 1982 the United States removed Iraq from its list of countries that supported terrorism, and two years later it restored full diplomatic relations with Hussein's government. By the late 1980s the United States had even agreed to share intelligence information with the Iraqis. When the Iran-Iraq war finally petered out in August 1988, with Iran more-or-less the winner, it appeared that Hussein had indeed moderated his views toward the West and Israel.

But such was not the case. Hussein quickly made it clear that he saw himself as the leader destined to bring the Arab nations back to their deserved glory, by force if necessary, to assume control over the region's oil reserves, and to drive the Israelis out of the Middle East. He did not demobilize his million-man army at the close of the war but, rather, began to spend billions on new weapons (including Soviet Scud missiles, T-72 tanks, and MiG-29 fighters) and pushed ahead Iraqi research and development of chemical and nuclear weapons.

On 17 July 1990 Hussein issued a violent verbal attack on the United Arab Emirates and Kuwait, bitterly accusing the latter of building military installations on Iraqi territory, of stealing billions of dollars worth of oil from the Iraqi portion of the Rumaila oil field that spans their joint border, and of overproducing oil, this driving the world price of crude down. More ominously, he began to amass 30,000 troops along the Kuwaiti border.

Although it had earlier declined to impose sanctions on Hussein, despite his bellicosity, the Bush administration was clearly disturbed by Hussein's threats to Kuwait and to peace in the Middle East. On 25 July the administration sent US Ambassador to Iraq, April Glaspie, to talk with the Iraqi president. Hussein refused to back down but did promise that he would not invade Kuwait

Top: Captured members of Noriega's army, the Panama Defense Forces, mill about in a temporary prison compound.
Above: Iraqi President Saddam Hussein (l) confers with his foreign minister, Tariq Aziz, at a 1987 Arab summit meeting held to discuss the Iran-Iraq War.

Above: On 9 August 1990 the UN Security Council declares Iraq's annexation of Kuwait to be null and void.
Opposite top: Among the first US troops to arrive in Saudi Arabia after the invasion of Kuwait were members of the 82nd Airborne.
Opposite: A massive tent city in Saudi Arabia housing elements of the 1st Cavalry.

while his current discussions with President Hosni Mubarak of Egypt were continuing. This promise was cynically broken when hundreds of Iraqi tanks and other vehicles rolled across the border into Kuwait on 2 August 1990. The Gulf crisis had come to a head.

The Gulf War: DESERT SHIELD, 2 August 1990-14 January 1991

As Saddam Hussein's force of tanks, armored vehicles, and infantry rolled into Kuwait City, the capital, they quickly seized government buildings, the central bank (where the Iraqis confiscated millions in foreign currency and gold bars), the international airport, and the Dasman palace of Sheik Jaber al-Ahmed al-Sabah. Al-Sabah, the Emir of Kuwait, fled to Saudi Arabia by helicopter: his younger brother, Sheik Fahd, was killed defending the palace. Hussein then announced the annexation of Kuwait as the 19th providence of Iraq.

The United Nations Security Council demanded the immediate withdrawal of all Iraqi forces from Kuwait, but Hussein had no intention of doing so. By annexing Kuwait he had doubled his oil reserves, which now constituted 20 percent of the world's oil supply. If he were next to invade Saudi Arabia, which seemed alarmingly likely, he would control 40 percent.

Hussein had counted on the supposition that the United States would be unwilling to take a strong military stand against him. As he said, 'Yours is a society that cannot lose 10,000 dead in one battle.' He may or may not have been right, but the Bush administration and the American military, having learned some lessons from the Vietnam experience of two decades before, had no intention of fighting a high-casualty, protracted war of attrition this time around. War with Iraq, if it came, would be fought on an entirely different basis.

Nor were Hussein's suppositions about the weak response that other countries would make to his aggression borne out. The United Nations, with almost universal support from its member states, including the Soviet Union (more in need of Western economic aid than of the continued friendship of Iraq), not only placed a complete trade and financial embargo on Iraq but continued to strengthen its stand thereafter.

Indeed, Hussein failed to get any significant support even from fellow Arabs. Saudi Arabia, under King Fahd, heretofore conciliatory and unwilling to take any action that would endanger its regional friendships and oil revenues, quickly decided to join the US and UN in opposing the Iraqi invasion of Kuwait. Soon thereafter 12 Arab League nations, led by Egypt's President Hosni Mubarak, demanded that Iraq withdraw from Kuwait and pledged their military forces to defend Saudi Arabia and any other Arab state threatened by Iraq. Five nations abstained from these resolutions, but only Saddam Hussein's Iraq, Muammar Qaddaffi's Libya, and Yasir Arafat's Palestine Liberation Organization voted against them. Jordan's King Hussein tried desperately, if none too skilfully, to stay neutral on that occasion and in the months to come, but non-Arab Turkey, a well-armed member of NATO with little to fear from Saddam Hussein, also joined the coalition being fashioned by President Bush, agreeing to stop Iraq's pipeline across Turkish territory to the Mediterranean.

Thus within weeks a diplomatic and military ring had been formed around Saddam Hussein and Iraq. Yet he still would not back down. If, he reasoned, he could hold what he had and withstand the embargo by causing defections within ranks of the states that had agreed to impose it, he could still emerge victorious and in control of Kuwait. And in the end, it was his army that would be his final trump card.

On the eve of Iraq's invasion of Kuwait, Saddam Hussein had 5000 tanks, including over 1000 modern T-72s with 125mm guns; 6000 armored personnel carriers; 5000 artillery pieces, including Soviet-made multiple rocket launchers and G5 howitzers with a range of 24 miles purchased from South Africa; and some 600 aircraft (these included a limited number of Mig-25 and Mig-29 high-performance fighters and Su-24 and Su-25 attack planes).

Hussein also had Soviet- and French-made surface-to-air missiles in his inventory, plus Soviet Scud surface-to-surface missiles, capable of carrying warheads of 1000 pounds of conventional explosives and modified to fly beyond their designed range of 300 miles.

MILITARY AIRLIFT COMMAN

He also had supplies of poison gas (mustard, tabun, and sarin) and binary chemical weapons, and he was prepared to use them, as evidenced by his earlier use of poison gas against the Iranians and then even against his own people (as in the case of the 5000 Kurds gassed to death in the town of Halabja). There was also some evidence collected by Western intelligence sources which indicated that he might soon have nuclear weaponry.

President Bush had forged and then held together the coalition formed against Iraq, hoping military action would not be necessary, but he nevertheless began working through his military leaders, and especially through Colin L Powell, the chairman of the Joint Chiefs of Staff, to build up American forces in the Middle East should it become necessary to confront Hussein. Responsibility for this operation fell to CENTCOM and its commander in chief, General H Norman Schwarzkopf, 'the Bear', soon to become one of the best known officers in the US military.

Although CENTCOM's war plans had been originally designed to counter an attack by the Soviet Union through Iran toward the Persian Gulf, they proved to be applicable, with modifications, to the new problem. They called for combat aircraft to be flown to Oman, Saudi Arabia, or Kuwait and for two airborne units to be sent to the Southwest Asia on short notice (the 82nd Division of paratroopers and the 101st Airborne Division, the latter being heavily equipped with troop-transport and anti-tank helicopters, plus specially designed dune buggies and light Sheridan tanks). Three 15,000-man Marine brigades would also be flown into the area, there to be supplied with equipment from three flotillas of ships prepositioned at Diego Garcia in the Indian Ocean. Follow-on equipment in the form of tanks, trucks, and other heavy vehicles would be transported via eight roll-on/roll-off ships docked in the United States and immediately available.

As the UN embargo went into effect in the fall of 1990, and while the United States and its allies persisted in their efforts to solve the problem without war, the overall strategy of the Bush administration in Operation DESERT SHIELD took shape. First, the US would act through the United Nations to build a multi-national military force in Saudi Arabia to protect that country and to free Kuwait by military force if necessary. Second, other nations in whose co-interest the actions were being taken would be asked to help pay for the operation: Germany and Japan, plus Saudi Arabia and Kuwait, promised to pay $51 billion to help defray America's cost. Third, to maintain the coalition aligned against Iraq, Saddam Hussein's demands at 'linkage' between the Kuwait question and the Israel-Palestine question would be rejected. The United States would promise to work toward a settlement of the Palestinian issue diplomatically after, and only after, Kuwait had been liberated.

By December 1990 American troops in the Gulf totalled 540,000 men and women. Added to these US combatants were the 1st Armored Division, as well as planes and ships, from Britain; the light armored 6th Division, as well as planes, tanks, APCs, and warships, from France; ships from Argentina, Australia, Belgium, Denmark, Greece, Italy, the Netherlands, Norway, Poland, Portugal, and Spain; and warships and planes from Canada. From the Middle East were added two armored divisions and a commando regiment from Egypt; an armored division from Syria; and men, planes, tanks, and ships from various other countries in the region. This represented the greatest multi-national force assembled for warfare since the end of World War II.

Still Hussein would not back down. The United Nations on 29 November gave him until 15 January to get out of Kuwait, and on 12 January, Congress gave President Bush the authority to use the American military to carry out UN Resolution 678 for the freedom of Kuwait. A last-minute flying mission by UN Secretary General Javier Perez de Cuellar on 13 January to plead directly to Hussein to

CENTCOM chief General H. Norman Schwarzkopf led the allied coalition against Iraq in both the buildup phase (DESERT SHIELD) and the combat phase (DESERT STORM).

A Patriot missile roars from its launcher. Though mainly an anti-aircraft weapon, the Patriot did well against Iraq's Scud surface-to-surface missiles.

withdraw from Kuwait also failed. All possibilities for a peaceful solution had been exhausted. Now DESERT SHIELD was about to become DESERT STORM.

The Gulf War: DESERT STORM, 15 January-27 February 1991

DESERT STORM began with an air assault that lasted from 15 January through 23 February. The American-coalition offensive started in the early morning darkness of 16 January when dozens of Tomahawk cruise missiles from the battleships *Wisconsin* and *Missouri* were launched against Baghdad. Simultaneously, hundreds of landbased and seabased planes and AH-64 Apache helicopters, all equipped with special radar units and infrared sensors for night vision, swept in on the Iraqi capital. This was the beginning of an aerial attack that for the next five weeks would average 3000 sorties per day.

After one week the coalition air forces had inflicted such heavy losses on the Iraqi air force that it faced complete annihilation. Over 130 Iraqi pilots flew their planes to sanctuary in Iran – where the Iranian government promptly confiscated them. The coalition air offensive was technologically aided by American and Saudi AWACs planes able both to see all friendly and enemy movement in the air and on the ground and to direct coalition attack planes against Iraqi targets.

The air offensive made good use of such amazingly sophisticated ordnance as Paveway laser-guided bombs capable of following anti-aircraft laser beams to their sources and destroying them, HARM antiradiation missiles that followed enemy air defense radar beams to destroy them; GBU-15 'smart' bombs using a TV guidance system to strike their targets with precision; BLU-82 'daisy-cutter' bombs that released their explosives above ground, destroying everything and everyone below; Maverick missiles with infrared sensors; and laser-guided Hellfire missiles capable of taking out a tank from five miles away.

By the fifth week of the air war about 200 tanks were being eradicated each night; untold numbers of artillery pieces had been destroyed along the Iraqi lines; reinforcement trucks with food, water, and medicine could not move up to supply the Iraqis night or day; enemy communications had largely been wiped out; and the Iraqi troops in their trenches were being pounded unmercifully, knowing full well that a ground attack was sure to follow.

Hussein's reaction to the air assault was to fire his Scud missiles at Israel and Saudi Arabia. His hope in launching the missiles into Israel was to draw that country into the war and thus split the Arabs away from coalition arrayed against him. But, not without heated debate between Israeli political and military hardliners and moderates, the Israeli government decided not to retaliate (unless chemical warheads were used) and to let the coalition forces knock out the Scud launchers and defeat Iraq without Israel's help. To help convince Israel of the wisdom of its stand, the coalition forces made a concerted effort to find and destroy the Scud launch sites (the Americans thought there were only a few dozen Scuds; actually there were over 200 in Iraq's arsenal) and also rushed in Patriot surface-to-air missile units and their crews from Germany to help protect the Israeli population. Except for a solitary hit on a US Army

barracks in Dhahran, wherein 28 American servicemen were killed, the Scuds did very little damage to Israel, Saudi Arabia, or the coalition forces.

Hussein's only other response was a 29 January four-unit armor attack on Khafji, a city of 35,000 people six miles below the Kuwait-Saudi Arabia border, in the hope both of forcing the Americans and their allies into a land war before they were ready and of stopping the increasingly effective air campaign against his nation. One armored unit made it into now-deserted Khafji and held it for two days before being driven out by coalition air and ground forces; the other three armored units were stopped in their tracks and destroyed before they could even arrive at their objective.

On 22 February, President Bush announced that the Iraqi leader would have until noon (EST) the next day to begin withdrawing from Kuwait. If not, the offensive against him would continue, a clear signal that the land war was about to begin. Still Hussein would not give in and ordered his forces to begin dynamiting the oil wells of Kuwait in an act of wanton destruction. Thus the die was cast.

While the coalition air units had been pummeling Iraqi airfields, command and control centers, missile sites, storage facilities, and chemical plants, General Schwarzkopf and his CENTCOM staff had been busy refining the details of their projected land offensive. Basically Schwarzkopf's forces, consisting of some 500,000 Americans, 20,000 Syrians, 35,000 Egyptians, 40,000 Saudis, 35,000 British, 10,000 Frenchmen, 7000 Kuwaitis, and 17,000 soldiers from other nations, would carry out three operations.

The first element of the plan was that a 17,000-man Marine amphibious force carried in 33 Navy ships off Kuwait in the Persian Gulf would *not* make an amphibious landing as the Iraqis supposed (the Leathernecks had carried out highly-publicized practice landings on key islands off the Kuwaiti coasts). They would, instead, remain in place to draw Iraqi forces out of the center of the line along the southern border of Kuwait to guard against landings on the eastern shore of the country. In effect, thanks to this feint, many of the Iraqi troops and their defensive ordnance would be facing the wrong direction.

Second, an offensive would be launched into southern Kuwait by Kuwaiti, Syrian, Saudi and other Arab units with the US Marines.

Third, and perhaps the most audacious move of the campaign, General Schwarzkopf lined up the remainder of his assault forces in a 200-mile line well to the east, between the Tapline Road and the Kuwaiti-Saudi Arabian

Left top: **Wreckage in Riyadh, Saudi Arabia, caused by an Iraqi Scud missile that got past the defending Patriot batteries.**
Left center: **An Iraqi personnel carrier wrecked in the battle for Khafji.**
Left: **An armada of fuel and supply trucks follows the US 1st Armored Division as it moves into position to strike into Iraq in the final days of DESERT STORM.**

Officers of the 1st Armored Division work out some of the battle tactics that helped make the Gulf War so amazingly brief.

border, so that they could be used to sweep forward north and then east in a grand envelopment of the enemy forces in southern Iraq and Kuwait. This move was possible because the air campaign had severely interfered with the Iraqi command's ability to know where the coalition forces were at any given moment, and, therefore, to make informed guesses about their intentions. Schwarzkopf later, somewhat loosely, referred to this as a 'Hail Mary' maneuver.

A 'Hail Mary' play in football is a desperation play wherein the quarterback can only pray that a receiver far away in the end zone will be able to catch his pass, but there was no hint of desperation in this brilliantly planned flanking tactic.

By 0400 on 24 February, jump-off time, the coalition ground forces were lined up along the Kuwaiti-Saudi Arabian border from east to west as follows: a Joint Forces unit (Saudis, Kuwaitis, Omanis, and soldiers of the United Arab Emirates); the 2nd marine Division; the Tiger Brigade of 2nd Armored Division; the 1st Marine Division; and a second Joint Forces unit (Saudis, Syrians, Eqyptians, Kuwaitis, Pakistanis). Farther west along the Iraq-Saudi Arabian border, the forces lined up from east to west were: the British 1st Armored Division; VII Corps, consisting of the 1st Infantry Division (Mech), known throughout the Army as 'The Big Red One,' and the 1st Cavalry Regiment; the 1st Armored Division; and XVIII Corps, consisting of the 24th Infantry Division (Mech), the 3rd Armored Cavalry Regiment, the 101st Airborne Division (Air Assault), the 82nd Airborne Division, and the French 6th Light Armored Division.

At 4:00 in the morning of 24 February the attack began, with the 1st and 2nd Marine Divisions breaching the Iraqi deep barrier system along the south central border of Kuwait. They were supported by the Tiger Brigade of the 2nd Armored division, which advanced between them. At the same time, at the far end of the line out to the west, the French 6th Armored and the 2nd Brigade of the 82nd Airborne Division, closely followed by the rest of the 82nd, launched an overland attack toward the As Salman airfield 50 miles inside Iraq. Simultaneously, the Joint Arab Forces along the southern Kuwaiti border near the Gulf broke through Iraqi fortified lines and headed straight up the coast toward Kuwait City.

Four hours later, at 8:00 on the morning of 24 February, the 101st Airborne 'Screaming Eagles' launched the largest helicopter assault in military history as 4000 men were airlifted 60 miles into Iraqi territory to establish a forward supply base. They would then move toward a point on the Euphrates River only 150 miles from Baghdad.

In the afternoon of 24 February the Joint Forces in the center of the line (Saudis, Syrians, Eqyptians, Kuwaitis, and Pakistanis) crossed the border into southwestern Kuwait. To their left, VII Corps also began to penetrate and then rush through the Iraqi defenses, cutting through the Iraqi minefields with no difficulty as it raced north. Meanwhile, the 24th Infantry Division (Mech) tore through on the left and pushed deep into the interior of Iraq.

Much of the success of these attacks could be credited to special forces teams which for weeks had been reconnoitering far behind the enemy lines in helicopters and muffled dune buggies (FAVs, or fast attack vehicles) and now carried out direct-action sabotage and range-spotting missions as the coalition forces pushed into Kuwait and Iraq. Another important factor was that the total allied air cover made it almost impossible for Iraqi forces to move without endangering themselves, even at night.

By the end of the first day the entire network of Iraqi fortified lines had been penetrated and coalition forces were racing north deep into Kuwait and Iraq. Military leaders in the field and from CENTCOM all the way up to the Joint Chiefs and the Department of Defense were frankly astonished at the success of the first day's fighting, as, indeed, was the whole world.

Days two and three, 25 and 26 February, brought more successes to the coalition forces. The Arab Joint Forces on the east drove north toward Kuwait City while the 2nd Marines, the Tiger Brigade, and the second Arab Joint Forces group on their left, paralleled their moves deep into Kuwait. To their left VII Corps, in the center of the line, continued to drive rapidly northward, then swept to the east to confront Hussein's elite Republican Guards in northern Kuwait. Still farther left on 25 and 26 February, the American armored and cavalry divisions continued to drive deep into Iraq before also wheeling right to take on other Republican Guard units in the southeastern corner of that country and in northern Kuwait. Meantime, the 82nd Division was blocking any counterattacks or reinforcements from the north, and the 24th Infantry (Mech) was sealing off the Tigris-Euphrates valley and preventing the escape of Iraqi forces fleeing north.

Everywhere that the coalition forces moved during these first three days they found their Iraqi adversaries usually willing to surrender with little or no resistance. Deprived of food, water, and medical care and dazed and frightened by five weeks of constant terror from the skies, they seldom put up stiff resistance when faced with the overwhelming firepower and maneuverability of the coalition forces. It is estimated that as many as 100,000 Iraq soldiers

Above: **Some of the 100,000 Iraqi troops who surrendered to the allied coalition forces during the 100-hour land war.**
Below: **Use of such sophisticated weapons in the Gulf War as the Tomahawk cruise missle was a foretaste of what combat might be like in the next century.**

surrendered during the ground war, this number matching the 100,000 Iraqi dead and the 100,000 who deserted during the four-day land war.

By the fourth day of the land war, 27 February, it was clear that the fighting was coming to an end. As XVIII Corps was moving into southern Iraq and the city of Basra, VII Corps, in the center, met and soundly defeated the Republican Guards in an all-out tank battle. The 1st Marine Division seized Kuwait International Airport while the 2nd Marine Division blocked all exits from the city in order to allow the Arab Joint Forces from the south and west the honor of moving up to recapture the capital city. President Bush that evening declared that at midnight the fighting would end. The 100-hour land war was over.

Reflections on the Gulf War

An outpouring of analyses and commentaries followed the end of the Gulf War, and from these certain salient conclusions have emerged that both clarify what occurred and have important implications for the decisions the United States must make when considering the nation's armed forces in the years to come:

1. The Gulf War was an overwhelming military victory for the US and coalition forces and surely resurrected both the military services' pride in themselves, much damaged in the aftermath of Vietnam, and the nation's pride in its armed forces. But the United States must still face the fact that the nation has a plentitude of military obligations to itself and to millions of people around the world. These obligations must be upheld whether or not future wars are ultimately termed 'good' or 'bad'. The United States' military services are not an expensive luxury; they are an expensive necessity.

2. Despite all the criticism of spending for the military in the 1980s, and particularly for its emphasis on high technology and expensive weaponry, the Gulf War proved that such spending is absolutely critical if a modern military establishment is to be maintained. The high-technology weaponry used by the nation's armed forces in the Gulf War may not in itself have spelled the difference between victory and defeat, but it certainly spelled the difference between less than a hundred US military deaths in the war and the thousands that would inevitably have

been suffered had not such weapons and the trained personnel able to man and maintain them been available.

3. Success in the Gulf War was largely a result of applying the doctrines of coordinated combined-service warfare that had been patiently fashioned for a decade and a half. AirLand Battle worked. Centralized command worked. The ability to deploy highly trained and highly motivated soldiers, sailors, airmen, and Marines worked.

4. The victory in the Gulf War must be credited to all members of the armed services, from the lowest rifleman or technician to the members of CENTCOM and the Joint Chiefs. But it must also be credited to George Bush, not only for forging and holding together a coalition of disparate nations for months on end until a victory had been achieved, but also because, unlike Lyndon Johnson in Vietnam, he established the parameters of the war and then let the military fight it. Sound military theory and practice demand such a controlled stance on the part of the supreme commander in all military conflicts, great or small.

5. Saddam Hussein's military incompetence undoubtedly contributed much to the ease with which he was defeated, but we must be wary of drawing the wrong conclusions from that fact. General Schwarzkopf was certainly right when he said at a news conference regarding Hussein as a military leader: 'He is neither a strategist, nor is he schooled in the operational art, nor is he a tactician, nor is he a general, nor is he a soldier. Other than that he's a great military man. . . .' But in its next war the United States might not be so lucky.

6. The war fought in the deserts of the Middle East was almost tailor-made for the application of overwhelming ground and air power, plus rapid, almost unimpeded, maneuverability. Any future wars, large or small, will probably not be fought under the same conditions. The US must therefore be prepared for all military contingencies through the now-proven doctrine of flexible response. If not, it could face a defeat somewhere else every bit as great as its victory in the Gulf War.

Continued Challenges of the 1990s

The Gulf War had, indeed, been won in decisive and dramatic fashion. The Army, along with the other US armed forces, won accolades from the public, who had viewed the successes of the war on television. For the first time since the Vietnam War the nation's fighting forces had faced a major challenge, and no one could doubt that they had won a resounding victory over a dangerous foe. Perhaps of greater importance, the Gulf War illustrated that the military had learned from its mistakes of the recent past, had made substantial changes in its war-making capabilities, and had shown that it was capable of preparing for future conflicts realistically, rather than 'fighting the last war.' This change of outlook has been crucial to the Army and its sister services, their bywords for the 1990s and beyond being change and adaptability when faced with new challenges-some in historically familiar areas, some not - in a rapidly changing world.

A member of the 10th Mountain Division guards a street in Mogadishu, Somalia, in 1993.

One of the most unsettled areas of the world in the 1990s is sub-Saharan Africa. Nation after nation has seen political instability, turmoil, civil war, and famine in the decades since the rapid decolonization movement took hold in the aftermath of World War II with its resulting weakening of the former colonialist European powers. Chaos and heartbreak have been the watchwords of these countries, caught between their former subservient stage of development from their colonial days and the political and economic demands of the late 20th century. One of the most unfortunate of these nations is Somalia.

Gaining its independence from Great Britain in 1960, Somalia, on the eastern horn of Africa, witnessed nothing but chaos thereafter. Born out of the former British Somaliland and a former Italian possession, the new Somali Republic in 1969 fell under a one-man rule that lasted until January 1991 when Gen Muhammed Siyad Barrah fled from the capital of Mogadishu. Thereafter it fell into civil war between rival factions, the most dangerous being the Somali National Alliance led by Mohammed Farah Aidid. An estimated 40,000 casualties bore grisly witness to military bloodshed, banditry, and drought.

Faced with the likelihood of mass starvation of 1.5 million people in Somalia, the United Nations secretary general declared the country to be 'without a government' in July 1992 and accepted the United States' offer

Above: **Army troops land in Port-au-Prince, Haiti, in September 1994.**
Below: **Members of the 10th Mountain Division patrol the streets of Port-au-Prince, Haiti.**

to send in troops to ensure delivery of food to the starving populace. Thus, at the direction of President Bush, Operation RESTORE HOPE was launched by the US in December 1992. The Army eventually sent in 25,000 troops, the first consisting of 10,000 soldiers from the 10th Mountain Division (Light Infantry) from Fort Drum, New York. Troops from Canada, France, Italy, and Belgium joined them. The next year the UN took control of the humanitarian mission and attempted to convince all sides in the civil war to engage in negotiations to end the bitter fighting.

In March 1993 the United States began to withdraw its peacekeeping forces, leaving that duty to the Untied Nations, although 3,000 American logistical and 5,000 other troops remained behind. But violence between the tribal factions seeking to control the country continued, encouraged by weak UN decision-making and a failure to capture Gen Aidid in May. Firefights between US soldiers and Somali guerrillas in the streets of Mogadishu intensified, culminating in a series of tragic incidents in which 18 US soldiers were killed and 78 wounded in an ambush in Mogadishu on 3-4 October, causing Congress to call for a withdrawal of all US forces.

President Bill Clinton thereupon made the decision to withdraw all US forces from Somalia by mid-March 1994. By that time all United Nations-sponsored troops had pulled out of the country, leaving its people still mired in the horror of civil war and famine. The American forces had done their best to carry out their humanitarian mission and had enjoyed some success, but it was a mission launched without the military being given the authority to bring the country out of chaos and ruin by disarming the various political factions that kept the nation in chaos. The lives of US soldiers, it seemed, had been lost in vain, and Somalia's survivors were left with a future without hope of peace and stability.

The problem faced by the United States in the Caribbean nation of Haiti dated back to 1986 when the 26-year dictatorship over that country ended when President Jean-Claude Duvalier fled into exile and a military junta seized control. After further rapid turnovers of government, in 1990 a priest, Jean-Bertrand Aristide, was elected president but within a few months had been expelled as another military junta seized control. Thereafter conditions in Haiti deteriorated rapidly, economically and politically, forcing 35,000 Haitians to flee their native land for the United States. At first welcomed, their increasing numbers persuaded first President Bush and then President Clinton to have them returned to their homeland or to temporary shelter at the Navy's Guantanamo Naval Base in Cuba.

As conditions in Haiti continued to deteriorate, the United Nations imposed a near-total embargo of the country, and in 1994 the UN Security Council authorized a multinational force under US control and command to restore democracy in Haiti and secure the return of Aristide to office. President Clinton alerted the Army and the other services to prepare for an invasion, a move not approved of by most Latin American governments, the US Congress, and American public, according to the polls. Nevertheless, plans for carrying out Operation SUPPORT DEMOCRACY went forward, and on 14 September 1994 Clinton announced that an invasion of Haiti was most certainly forthcoming. Two days later, however, a special US delegation headed by ex-President Jimmy Carter, ex-chairman of the JCS General Colin Powell, and the influential Senator Sam Nunn of Georgia arrived in the Haitian capital of Port-au-Prince. Faced with a clear warning from the delegation that US land, sea, and air forces would be loosed on Haiti if the military junta did not come to terms with the UN resolution, four days later the military leaders agreed to leave office, paving the way for the restoration of Aristide.

The first US troops to land in Haiti to ensure that the agreement would be carried out and that order would be maintained were 3,000 soldiers of the Army's 10th Mountain Division from Ft. Drum, New York. They landed on 19 September 1994 and they were followed by 15,000 more troops from 25 countries. Only minimum bloodshed followed, and on 15 October Aristide was returned from exile in the United States to be restored to power. Thereafter the UN sanctions were lifted, and by 31 March 1995, all foreign troops had left Haiti (except for some assigned to police duties).

The most troubling and controversial use of the Army in the 1990s came when 18,500 of its men and women were sent as peacekeepers into Bosnia-Herzegovina in late December 1995 and early 1996 as part of a United Nations protection force 21,000 strong. With the breakup of Yugoslavia and the declaration of independence by Croatia and Slovenia in 1991, fighting between ethnic Croats and ethnic Serbs began with Serbia sending arms and supplies to Serbian rebels in Croatia.

troops already being stationed there. Fearing more instability in the volatile Middle East, on 7 October President Clinton announced that US air, land, and sea forces would be sent to Kuwait to protect its territory against any move by Saddam Hussein. Accordingly, in Operation VIGILANT WARRIOR of October-December 1994 some 40,000 ground troops, including the 24th Infantry Division (Mechanized); 28 Navy ships; and 650 aircraft were sent into the area to join the 12,000 US men and women already on duty there. Many of these latter were members of Operation SOUTHERN WATCH, inaugurated in August 1992, in which Air Force and Navy air crews patrol a 'no-fly' zone over southern Iraq to ensure Saddam Hussein's compliance with the United Nations Security Resolution 688. Faced with this show of strength, the Iraqi dictator backed down and began to withdraw the Republican Guards from the border area, and, in turn, the Defense Department

Left: **The 1st Armored Division crosses the Sava River into Bosnia, 30 December 1995.** *Below:* **A US soldier on Operation JOINT ENDEAVOR speaks with a Bosnian child in early 1996.**

The next year Serbia and Montenegro proclaimed themselves to be the Federal Republic of Yugoslavia and sent supplies to Serbian rebels in Bosnia and Herzegovina. Within three years some 200,000 people had been killed or wounded in the ensuing fighting. The continued bloodletting between Serbs, Muslims, and Croats, and campaigns 'of ethnic cleansing' in which Serbian forces killed all Muslims and non-Serbs in areas under their control, led to the United Nations imposing sanctions and finally calling for the creation of a multinational military force to impose peace on the troubled countries.

As a result, the 18,500 Army troops were dispatched to Bosnia in Operation JOINT ENDEAVOR, part of a larger United Nations force already in the country and the first time Army troops served in Eastern Europe in appreciable numbers. Aiding in the peacekeeping were Navy jets off carriers in the Adriatic and Air Force planes stationed in Italy that overflew the UN-occupied areas to ensure the safety of the troops on the ground. The massive air strikes in Operation DELIBERATE FORCE by these planes and those of other NATO nations in August 1995 on Serb positions had resulted in the lifting of the siege of Sarajevo and drove the Serbs to the negotiating table, resulting in the Dayton Accord in November of that year. According to this accord, a ceasefire was to be put in place and 60,000 NATO troops, about 20,000 of them from the US, were on duty in the troubled remains of Yugoslavia.

As 1996 came to a close, US troops remained on station in Bosnia, the promise made by President Clinton when the troops were dispatched that the deployment of US forces would be for no more than a year now long forgotten. It appeared that US and UN military intervention in the former Yugoslav state had led to few longterm positive results, and the combatants only waited to resume their ethnic warfare at the first opportunity.

But if the Army's mission to Bosnia led to no positive results, its role in Kuwait in 1994 showed it and the other US military forces to be extremely effective when given a role commensurate with their designated missions, training, and capabilities. In October 1994 Saddam Hussein began to deploy 20,000 of his Republican Guards to just north of the Kuwaiti border, 50,000 regular Iraqi

limited the deployment of US troops to 13,000 ground forces, 275 combat aircraft, and one aircraft carrier battle group. These UN sanctions imposed on Iraq remained in effect, to be lifted only when that nation disposed of its weapons of mass destruction, recognized as inviolable the border between itself and Kuwait, and acknowledged Kuwait's rights of sovereignty over its territory.

Hussein continued to challenge the terms laid down by the United Nations. He occasionally sent Iraq's planes into the no-fly zones, he occasionally had his radar "lock onto" Coalition planes flying over their inspection zone, and in a few instances even fired on these planes. In the case of all serious incidents, the US military responded with either airplane or missile attacks on Iraqi military installations. Although none of these incidents involved the US Army, thousands of US Army personnel remained stationed in Saudi Arabia and Kuwait in the event they would be needed to deter a more serious challenge by Hussein.

As in the case of Haiti, US Army troops are sometimes assigned to intervene in what are effectively civil wars in other nations. This can be a controversial move, both domestically and internationally, but the United States has long maintained its right and responsibility to do so, especially with countries with which its has a "special relationship." One such country is Liberia in Africa, which was founded by former slaves from the United States. In the spring of 1996, civil war broke out in Liberia. In April US Army paratroopers were flown in to bolster the small US Marines guard unit assigned to the US embassy in Monrovia. Shortly thereafter a large force of Marines arrived to relieve the Army troops of this duty.

A more persistent trouble spot involved the new nations that had once formed Yugoslavia. Serbia continued to be plagued by so much internecine violence that the original plan to withdraw all US troops had to be set aside. In December 1997, President Clinton announced that the US Army troops would remain in Bosnia-Herzegovina for an indefinite term. Meanwhile, in the Former Yugoslav Republic of Macedonia (FYROM), which split off from Serbia in 1991, the United States continued to maintain a force of some 500 US Army troops because of ethnic divisions and violence there.

Things remained relatively calm in these two states until in February 1998 a virtual civil war broke out in the Serbian province of Kosovo between the Serbians and the ethnic Albanians there. Although the ethnic Albanians were the majority in terms of population, the Serbians had the overwhelming advantage of the military units and police assigned there by Slobodan Milosevic, president of Serbia. As the violence spiraled out of control and Serbia refused to accede to the demands of a treaty negotiated in Rambouillet, France, in February-March 1999, NATO on 24 March 1999 launched air strikes against Serbia and the Serbian forces in Kosovo. In fact, the vast majority of the air strikes were made by US forces—Air Force, Navy, and Marines—but as Milosevic continued to resist, on 27 April President Clinton called up 25,000 Army reservists. Meanwhile, the Army had assigned 24 Apache helicopters and their supporting units (including tanks, armored vehicles, and howitzers) to the Albania-Kosovo border region. In the end, these Apache helicopters were never sent into action over Kosovo because NATO was never able to gain total control of the airspace there; in other words, the US forces could not be certain that they might not take casualties. (In fact, one of the Apache helicopters crashed on a training mission in Albania.) By the time the bombing and the fighting stopped on 10 June, the only US Army "casualties" of the Kosovo action turned out to be three soldiers captured by Serbians while on patrol along the Kosovo-Macedonia border; after being held by the Serbians for a month, they were released unharmed. Some 7,000 US Army troops were then quickly assigned to southern Kosovo as part of the NATO-sponsored

Above: **US Army soldiers in Skopje, Macedonia in April 1999 continued peacekeeping efforts in this troubled region.**
Below: **Shown through a night vision lens, Special Forces troops embarked on a night raid near Kandahar, Afghanistan, 20 October 2001.**
Opposite, top: **US Special Forces troops took to horseback to cross the Afghan terrain as they assisted members of the Northern Alliance in November, 2001, as part of Operation Enduring Freedom.**
Opposite, bottom: **Troops of the 1st Battalion 87 10th Mountain Division arrived at Bagram Airfield in Afghanistan on 16 December 2001, where they were to take over from the departing Marines.**

Soon thereafter, members of the Army's Special Operations Force began to be inserted into Afghanistan—their exact numbers and missions kept secret for security reasons.

Meanwhile, US Army troops throughout the world were not only on high alert but in some cases were receiving special training for possible assignments in Afghanistan. Among these were members of the 82nd and 101st Airborne Divisions, which were likely to be among the first to be sent in if large units were called for. And as it happened, during October 2001, units of the US Army were among the 65,000 military personnel from 10 different countries in Exercise Bright Star, a multi-national exercise held biennially in northern Egypt. Scheduled long before the events of September 11, this was the largest and most significant such exercise conducted by the US forces in the Middle East, and the US personnel clearly participated with a special focus, given the situation in Afghanistan. Although the first major US ground forces put into Afghanistan were Marines, on 28 November the first units of the Army's 10th Mountain Division began to enter northern Afghanistan, and more units of the US Army soon followed.

Kosovo Force (KFOR), under which Kosovo was divided into five regions to be controlled temporarily by troops from five NATO members (USA, Britain, France, Italy, Germany).

After the activities in the Balkans calmed down, the Army, along with the rest of the US military branches, seemed to go into a state of hiatus. Matters such as cutbacks in the defense budget, closing of bases, and declining active duty personnel seemed to dominate the news, along with public policy issues such as gays ("Don't ask, don't tell") and sexual harassment in the military. When the new administration of President George W. Bush took over in January 2001, still other issues came to the fore. The new secretary of defense, Donald Rumsfeld, for example, was a proponent of developing multiservice military units that would be prepared for rapid deployment in the early stages of an overseas crisis. At the same time he indicated that among his priorities were "quality-of-life" issues—improving pay and other conditions to maintain re-enlistment and morale in what appeared to be a largely peaceful world.

On 11 September 2001, three of four terrorist-hijacked airplanes crashed into the World Trade Center and the Pentagon and brought the United States, and indeed, the world, to a state of highest alert. The crash into the western part of the Pentagon, killed some 80 Army personnel and civilians associated with the Army. In addition to responding to the disaster at the Pentagon, personnel of the Army Corps of Engineers were at "Ground Zero" in New York within two hours after the hijacked airliners struck the World Trade Center. They continued for weeks afterward to provide support for many aspects of the recovery operations.

Meanwhile, the Army was prepared to move into action from the moment President George W. Bush declared a war on terrorism and launched Operation ENDURING FREEDOM against Osama bin Laden and his Taliban protectors in Afghanistan. The operation began on 7 October with air and missile strikes from US Air Force and Navy personnel, while the Army participated in the preparation and dropping of emergency food supplies into Afghanistan. On 19 October, a small unit of US Army Rangers parachuted into southern Afghanistan on a daring night raid on two Taliban sites. The US soldiers met with some resistance but suffered only mild casualties, including two paratroopers who were injured in the jump. Two Rangers were killed in a helicopter crash in Pakistan that same night in an unrelated accident.

Operation Iraqi Freedom

Despite the overwhelming success of the US-UN forces in driving the Iraqis out of Kuwait in the Persian Gulf War in 1991, subsequent efforts to disarm Saddam Hussein met with nothing but frustration for the next decade. Saddam had accepted the United Nations Resolution 687 in April 1991 that required Iraq to destroy or dismantle all biological, chemical, and nuclear weapons or nuclear-weapons-usable material and also forbade the development of any such weapons in the future (Iraq had previously used chemical weapons against the Kurds in 1988 and against Iran in 1986), but the Iraqi government persistently failed to comply with this resolution. Additionally, in 1992 the United States, Great Britain, and France established "no-fly" zones in northern and southern Iraq to protect Shiite and Kurdish

Muslims from attack by Iraqi planes and helicopters. Furthermore, UN economic sanctions on Iraq were also in place by that time, and UN weapons inspectors were on the ground.

In 1998 Iraq announced that it would no longer cooperate with the UN inspectors and demanded that the UN end its economic sanctions. The Iraqi government eventually allowed the inspectors back in under threat of US military intervention, but, as it turned out, they were subject to less than full cooperation. Then at the end of 1999 the UN established a new weapons inspection organization called the UN Monitoring, Verification and Inspection Commission (UNMOVIC), and Hans Blix of Sweden was named as its head in January 2000. Still, full cooperation by Iraq was not forthcoming.

After the terrorist attacks on New York City and the Pentagon on 11 September 2001, pressure against terrorists and their facilitators began to build in the United States. This led to further confrontation between the United States and Iraq. In September 2002 President Bush asked Congress for the authority to use force against Iraq. This was forthcoming the following month with overwhelming majorities in both houses of Congress. Meanwhile, at the United Nations a new measure, Resolution 1441, was passed by the Security Council, which found Iraq in "material breach" of earlier resolutions and called for new inspections. As all of this diplomatic action was occurring, plans were well underway to deploy 62,000 US troops to the Gulf region to join 60,000 already there, and by December American military assets were steadily being moved into the area.

In January 2003 Blix reported to the UN that no "smoking gun" evidence of weapons of mass destruction had been found, but also that there was no proof that earlier weapons had been dismantled. On 5 February 2003,

Above: A convoy of US Army 3rd Infantry M1A1 Abrams tanks crosses the Euphrates river as hundreds of armored vehicles move towards the outskirts of Baghdad on 6 April 2003. *Right:* US Army soldiers sort through their MREs for breakfast at Forward Ammo and Refueling Point (FARP) Shell in southwest Iraq. *Below:* Army medics carry a wounded US Army soldier to a helicopter.

Secretary of State Colin Powell told the Security Council that intelligence data made it clear that Iraq did not intend to disarm and was hiding its weapons from the UN inspectors. Standing firmly with President Bush was British Prime Minister Tony Blair. On 24 February the US, Britain, and Spain proposed a new resolution to the Security Council ordering Iraq to disarm peacefully, and on 7 March Blair, backed by the US and Spain, added an amendment setting 17 March as the deadline for Iraqi disarmament. France threatened to veto any resolution authorizing the use of force against Iraq and was backed by Russia, China, and Germany.

On 16 March President Bush met with Prime Minister Blair and Spanish Premier Jose Maria Aznar in the Azores. They decided to give diplomacy one more day to work and expressed a willingness to go to war against Iraq with or without UN approval. The next day all US efforts to secure UN approval were abandoned, and Bush gave Hussein and his sons the final ultimatum to leave the county within 48 hours or face war, explaining, "We are acting because the risks of inaction would be far greater." On 18 March the British House of Commons backed Blair on a 412-149 vote to use "all means necessary" to disarm Hussein. Clearly, Gulf War II was about to begin.

The US-led war against Iraq began on 19 March 2003, with a surprise air assault on targets in Baghdad in an attempt to eliminate Iraqi President Saddam Hussein. In addition to the military support of Britain and Australia, the Bush administration claimed to have the support of a coalition of at least 35 other nations in its preventative attack on Iraq. The president also outlined goals beyond disarming Iraq, saying that the actions were taken to help the Iraqis achieve a "united, stable and free country."

The first days of the ground campaign that began on 20 March were marked by massive air strikes on Baghdad and by the advance of coalition ground troops over Iraq's southern border with Kuwait. As the massed coalition forces consisting of heavily-armed units from the US Army's 3rd Infantry Division, the 101st and 82nd Airborne Divisions, and the Marine 1st Expeditionary Force thereafter moved northwest toward Baghdad, ground- and helicopter-borne British and US Marines covered their right flank with attacks on Basra in the southeastern corner of the country. All of these forces initially ran into stout resistance and took numerous casualties. Still, they moved steadily forward against Iraqi opposition, the ground forces utilizing heavy armored vehicles such as the M1A1 Abrams Main Battle Tank (MBT), the M113 Armored Personnel Carrier (APC), and the M2 Bradley Mechanized Infantry Vehicle (MICV). Also employed were Apache and Cobra attack helicopters, Kiowa light observation helicopters, A-10 "Warthog" jets, and heavy artillery pieces, plus the latest in technology in their superior sighting and killing weaponry. These air and ground assets were more than sufficiently supplemented by support units and the fierce determination of the Army's and Marines' "grunts" to overcome all resistance while sparing, as far as possible, civilian casualties.

On 21 March the US-led forces launched a massive air assault against Baghdad that lasted for three hours. More than 1,300 cruise missiles and bombs from B-2 Spirit bombers and F-117 Nighthawk stealth fighter-bombers, Tomahawk sea-launched cruise missiles, and air-launched missiles from B-52 bombers were unleashed in a major air assault on the Republican Guard headquarters, facilities of the Special Republican

Below: **A convoy of the US Army's 3rd Infantry Division's Engineer Brigade drives under highway signs that show the direction into Baghdad's city center and Baghdad's airport as troops advance towards Iraq's capital on 6 April 2003.**

Left: A soldier guides heavy US Army engineering equipment during a desert sandstorm in the north of the city of Najaf in central Iraq, 24 March 2003.
Below: A US soldier watches as Kurdish Peshmerga volunteer fighters fire on an Iraqi army post close to the village of Khazer, 3 April 2003.

Guard, and other bulwarks of Saddam's government. By 24 March soldiers from the 3rd Infantry Division had reached the outskirts of Karbala, about 50 miles south of Baghdad. Troops movements were slowed by fierce sandstorms and high winds on 25-26 March, but missiles continued to pour into Baghdad throughout these days as the coalition troops approached the capital city.

On 26 March the US opened a northern front, parachuting more than 1,000 members of the Italian-based US 173rd Airborne Brigade into Kurdish-held territory in northern Iraq to secure an airfield in the region so that cargo planes could deliver military equipment to the area. And between 28 March and 2 April US and British aircraft bombarded Iraqi Republican Guard targets outside of Baghdad in preparation for the coming ground assault on the city. By 7 April US ground forces had entered Baghdad and taken over one of Hussein's palaces. In the days that followed, more of the capital had fallen into coalition hands—dramatically symbolized on television worldwide on 9 April when Iraqi citizens, aided by an American armored recovery vehicle, pulled down a statue of Saddam Hussein in the heart of Baghdad—and the air and ground forces had moved on northward to seize Saddam's ancestral home town of Tikrit.

When Tikrit and other Iraqi cities fell into coalition hands it was clear that all organized resistance by the Iraqi soldiers and members of the Republican Guard was rapidly coming to an end, some 270,000 coalition forces now deployed in the region. By

Above: **Rescued POWs (left to right) Patrick Miller, Shoshana Johnson and James Riley at US Army hospital in Landstuhl, Germany, 18 April 2003. The soldiers were freed after 22 days of imprisonment.**

16 April, units of the Army's 4th Infantry Division had also entered the fray; originally deployed in ships off the coast of Turkey, when Turkey denied access to US ground forces, the ships carrying the 4th Infantry Division had to make their way down through the Suez Canal and then on to Kuwait, from where they made their way quickly across southern Iraq to engage in action north of Baghdad. For the war was far from over as pockets of resistance remained and terror bombers and snipers continued to harass the American and British soldiers in Baghdad and other towns and villages of Iraq. Still, it was clear that after three weeks of fierce fighting that Operation Iraqi Freedom had been brought to a successful conclusion. Only mopping up residual pockets of resistance, getting humanitarian aid to the people of Iraq, and establishing a new government remained to be accomplished.

The "butcher's bill" for Operation Iraqi Freedom had been comparatively light. The Pentagon announced on 22 April that 131 American troops had been killed in Iraq (116 in action with Iraqi forces), and some 500 had been wounded. Still, much more was left to be done in the weeks and months ahead: ending all resistance by the remainder of Saddam's forces; identifying, isolating and eliminating Iraq's weapons of mass destruction (General Tommy Franks, the commander of CENTCOM based in Qatar, placed the number of possible hiding places at 2,000-3,000); capturing and eliminating terrorists both in Iraq and beyond, including those with ties to the al Qaeda terror network; getting humanitarian aid to the Iraqi people; and aiding the Iraqi people in attaining a representative self-government that would not be a threat to themselves or to their neighbors.

The Army Looks to the Future

Throughout the world, whenever they are called upon, Army personnel are conscious that end of the Cold War has not meant the end of conflict or personal danger to themselves. New and better conventional vehicles and weapons and theater ballistic missiles possessed by increasing numbers of nations have now been joined by the threats of chemical and biological weapons, not to mention the methods of terrorists. All these continue to endanger not only US lives and security but also those of the nation's friends and allies throughout the world. Given the realities of the 21st century, the US Army, as a basic component of the international defense system, is committed to remaining the best-trained and best-equipped army in the world. It is clear that the Army intends to maintain its proud tradition as the bulwark of America's land fighting forces while preparing itself for the future.

HISTORY OF THE US NAVY

JAMES M. MORRIS

Page 264-265: The USS *Constitution* rakes the crippled *Guerriere* off Nova Scotia, 19, August 1812.
This page: The USS *Raleigh*, with pontoons lashed to her sides, lists to port after Japan's devastating raid on Pearl Harbor.

CONTENTS

INTRODUCTION

To understand the role of the US Navy in the nation's history, it is essential to review briefly the crucial role that sea power has played in the destiny of other leading nations throughout history. Sea power—the ability to control the nation's sea lanes with sufficient strength to ensure its vital interests—has been and remains a key ingredient in the fate of nations whether in ancient, medieval or modern times. The historical record amply demonstrates that nations seldom rise to major status and are never able to maintain a position of pre-eminence if they disregard their naval and maritime potential. Mastery of the sea has always been a dynamic power factor, and nations that neglect their navies do so at the peril of their present and future well-being.

Sea Power in Early Times

Man's destiny has always been tied to the sea. Iron-Age men fashioned boats of planks and added oars for paddling and rudders for steering. Egyptian *kepen* 207 feet in length, with keels and double masts, carried goods up and down the Nile by about 1400 BC. Indeed, all ancient peoples located on rivers and seas recognized the need to trade and colonize on near and distant waters. Trade and colonies, moreover, demanded protection, so navies were born. Ramses III, for example, had a well-organized naval force and turned back the Libyans, Syrians and Philistines from Asia Minor in the Battle of Pelusian in the late twelfth century BC. The Cretans (or Minoans), however, were probably the leading sea power in those times. Their powerful fleet patrolled the sea lanes from the Dardanelles in the east to the Strait of Bonifacio, between Corsica and Sardinia, in the west. The Cretans were succeeded as sea lords by the Phoenicians, who controlled the North African coast and circumnavigated the African subcontinent from the Red Sea all the way to the Gates of Hercules (Gibraltar). They were effectively challenged by the Greek states, with their mighty war vessels of two, three, and more banks of oars and triple-pronged rams at their bows. The Romans, too, built a powerful navy that they used to good effect in their Punic Wars against the Carthaginians, wars finally lost by the North African power when Hannibal's ineffective navy lost control of the coast of Spain and thereby endangered his lines of supply.

As the Middle Ages dawned in the Mediterranean and Western world, and economic and political stagnation settled over the land, some commerce still continued to flow to and from the Baltic and North Seas and the Levant to the east. Wheat, wines, timber, tin and wool moved by sea from northern to southern European ports, there to be exchanged for

Below: **British forces, joined by men from the New England colonies, land to capture Louisburg, Cape Breton Island, from the French in 1745.**

sugar, cheeses, oil, oranges, spices and fine cloth from India, Egypt and the Barbary Coast. The oar-powered galley gradually lost its position of dominance in commerce and defense to the wind-powered 'round ship' with up to four masts, a forecastle at the bow and an after-castle at the stern. Trade was further facilitated by the development of such navigational instruments as the 'log' to measure a ship's speed by the time required to pass knots spaced 49 feet apart on a thrown line, and the astrolabe, which gave a relatively accurate measure of latitude. The sextant was also developed—the compass was known from China—and seamen could now venture farther and farther from protective shorelines in search of trade and conquest. Although full-time navies disappeared in this period of political and economic confusion, tradesmen-warriors like the fierce Vikings still plied the seas. Often naval forces were decisive, as in William of Normandy's conquest of England with over 1000 vessels in 1066, or in the case of the Third and Fourth Crusades in the late twelfth and early thirteenth centuries, as ships carried warriors and supplies to the Middle Eastern battlefields.

The effects of naval power were also graphically demonstrated during France's long and eventually successful Hundred Years' War against England (1337–1453). The fortunes of the two antagonists rocked back and forth from French victories at LaRochelle and Cherbourg in the late fourteenth century to English victories with a rebuilt navy in the early fifteenth. Final French victory came with command of the seas under the naval rebuilding program of Jacques Coeur. Sea power and national power strode hand in hand through the Middle Ages, as they had through ancient times, although some emerging land-based monarchs were loath to see the connection—until the discovery, claim and colonization of North America made the relationship too obvious to deny.

European Nations Discover the New World

If we discount as highly improbable the story that North America was first discovered in the sixth century by the Irish monk St Brendan and his compatriots in a *curragh* (a ribbed, oak-tanned oxhide vessel with a mast and sail), the first Europeans to touch North American shores were undoubtedly Norsemen from Greenland under the leadership of Leif Ericsson about the year 1000. Having established a tiny settlement at L'Anse aux Meadows on the northern tip of the Newfoundland coast, the Norse made three more voyages to the area, but the tiny colony eventually languished. Only centuries later did other powers rediscover the Western Hemisphere. This time the Europeans came to stay and to build new lands.

Although the search for new sea lanes for Far Eastern trade was the major dynamic in propelling European powers far west of their Atlantic shores—the old trade routes through the Mediterranean Sea and the Levant having been cut by the victorious Ottoman Turks, to whom Constantinople itself fell in 1453—science and technology also played a major role in the opening of the New World. Most of the credit must go to the Portuguese Prince Henry 'the Navigator,' who established what might well be called an oceanographic institute at Sagres early in the fifteenth century. Here this Portuguese monarch quizzed ship captains about the seas and navigation; assembled mathematicians, cartographers and ship designers; collected all the geographic books available, including those of Herodotus, Marco Polo and Ptolemy; amassed *portolani* (sea charts) from seamen; encouraged the development of the triple-masted, lateen-sail caravel; and aided in the development of the cross-staff for better reckoning of latitude than was possible with the primitive astrolabe. As a result of the work at Sagres, Portuguese and other European sailors could now sail farther still, often hundreds of miles into the Atlantic. The door to reaching the fabled East by an all-water route was cracking open. Yet westward from Europe across the uncharted Atlantic, they would find not the fabulous lands described by Marco Polo, but an even more bounteous continent soon to be opened to European development.

The man responsible for opening the Western Hemisphere to colonization and trade was Christopher Columbus, an experienced Italian mariner sailing for Their Most Catholic Majesties of Spain, Ferdinand and Isabella. His first epoch-making voyage of 1492–93, in which he was aided in many ways by Martin and Vincente Pinzon of Palos, his home port, brought him fame and promise of more royal support, even though it was unclear whether 'Hispaniola' was really off the coast of Japan as Columbus believed. Three subsequent follow-up voyages brought only disease and death, hostility from the native peoples, mismanagement and finally disgrace and an obscure death for Columbus.

But the New World had been opened, and those European nations with available maritime and naval power hastened to claim and develop it as they could. In 1497 John Cabot, an Italian sailing under the colors of Henry VII of England, made a voyage of exploration along the North American coast but disappeared on a second voyage the following year. In the decades that followed, other voyages set forth under the flags of Portugal, Spain, England and France; by the middle of the sixteenth century it was clear that, rather than being an archipelago off the eastern coast of China or Japan, a New World, an entire continent, had been discovered, a continent that had no fabled but illusory 'Northwest Passage' to the Orient. The belief in this passage had led many early discoverers up the river and bay systems of the eastern coast on voyages of futility. The names of Giovanni da Verrazzano, Jacques Cartier, Martin Frobisher and others stand as testimony to European determination to explore this new land for gold, glory and national honor.

As it became obvious that the New World was a treasure house of wealth and possibilities for nations to extend themselves outward by colonization, the European monarchs gave their backing to enterprising individuals and groups who would undertake the task. Although the Spanish, Portuguese and French were early in the field, and thus seized the lion's share of territories stretching almost from pole to pole, it was English enterprise that claimed the eastern coast of North America from latter-day Maine to Georgia. This solid and expanding foothold developed into a series of settlements in the most favorable locations along the coast and also in the Caribbean. These colonies eventually developed into the most permanent and wealthy extensions of European control in all of North America.

England's New-World Colonies

Although Sir Walter Raleigh's colony at Roanoke in the Carolinas saw three groups of settlers arrive in the years 1585–87, a relief expedition in 1590 found no survivors; thus England's first sizable attempt at colonization failed. Despite this failure, the growing power of England could not be denied, and, after defeating her long-time rival Spain's Armada in 1588 she moved steadily to create colonies in North America. England had an expanding population, capital available for new ventures and a monarchy interested in colonial development. Above all, she had seized the maritime and naval initiative from her competitors and thereafter would not be denied.

Yet England's position as a maritime power and colonizer was still subject to dispute by other nations, especially France and Spain. France was in a splendid position to challenge England for 'God, gold, and glory,' and Spain still represented a considerable threat. As England began to plant colonies along the Eastern Seaboard, beginning in 1607 at Jamestown and continuing through the seventeenth century, France was doing the same to the north along the St Lawrence River Valley and into the Great Lakes and Mississippi River regions—thus effectively hemming in the English to the north and west. Spain continued its rule in the south and southwest, down through Mexico and Central America and on to the great South American continent. This eventually led to major conflicts as the English, French and Spanish North American colonies became part of the great struggles for empire.

Above: **Christopher Columbus (1451–1506) made his first landfall in the New World on 12 October 1492 at Watling's Island in the Bahamas.**

In the meantime, the English colonists, from the rocky New England coastal colonies, through the broadening and fertile expanse of the middle colonies, into the region as far south as Georgia, found their lives inexorably tied to the seas. The Atlantic Ocean had served them originally only as the pathway to Europe and the source of resupply and reinforcement, but soon these land-oriented agrarian peoples discovered that the rivers and seas represented an indispensable element in their growth and prosperity. The virgin lands could not be exploited without river craft to take the colonists and their goods to and from the interior. Boats of all types skimmed up and down rivers carrying goods and people to farms and plantations. At the mouths of rivers great and small, coursing sometimes hundreds of miles into the rich interior, bays of all sizes served as anchorages for ships to take the colonists' goods to market and bring back from Europe or other colonies the manufactures and supplies they needed.

Furthermore, especially in New England but also down the coast, the colonists found an abundance of fish. They used them first for their own sustenance and later for trade along the coast and even with Caribbean and European ports. Fishing became an important occupation and fish surpluses soon became an important trade commodity.

The rise of colonial trade internally, with the Caribbean colonies and with England and other European countries, led, in turn, to the birth and growth of a shipbuilding industry. In England timber was becoming scarce. In the American colonies, especially New England, timber of all the necessary kinds was plentiful and near the coast where shipbuilders could ply their lucrative trade. So successful was this colonial industry that by the late seventeenth century many English vessels were being built in colonial shipyards, and English shipwrights began an exodus from the mother country to the building yards of the American colonies in search of the higher wages available there.

By the end of the seventeenth century, then, the English colonies hugging the Atlantic shores and stretching inland to the Appalachian Mountains found themselves bound to the sea. This despite the fact that only 10 percent of the colonial population earned its living directly in trade, fishing, shipbuilding and allied industries. Agricultural goods from the Middle Colonies, the 'breadbasket colonies,' and from farms and plantations north and south found their markets via coastal and ocean vessels sailing the Atlantic expanse. Tobacco, rice and indigo from Southern farms and plantations reached their domestic or European markets by a myriad of vessels. In turn, farmers and plantation gentry obtained supplies for farm or table—supplies of incredible variety, for tastes simple or extravagant—via the coastal and ocean sea lanes. Fishermen sold their surplus in the markets of the colonies and the world. Shipbuilders, shipowners and seamen plied their skills to the benefit of all. Without trade upon coastal, Caribbean and Atlantic waters, the emerging English colonial economy would have ground to a halt. Whoever would disturb that trade network or challenge it in any way would endanger the expanding colonies.

To protect these precious trade routes, the North American colonists looked to the mother country. After all, they were English colonies under English law and protection. The Crown and Parliament agreed. The American colonies, an integral part of the Empire, were precious sources of supplies to England and a major market for its manufactured goods. Both the mother country and the colonies recognized their vital interdependence, and considered their political and economic ties sacred and worthy of spirited defense. Challenges came from outside, not from inside, the system at this point.

England, the Colonies and the Wars for Empire

The challenge for North America came primarily from France. Catholic France was the natural enemy of Protestant England. In addition, either the French would dominate Europe and the colonies in trade and power, or England would. The two nations stood as hearty young gladiators in the arena that was Europe, each determined that the other would not dominate, each determined that he would not be overcome. On the sidelines stood Spain and Holland, willing to intervene to regain lost glory and right old wrongs should either major contestant falter. In this posture the great Wars for Empire between France and England, the titanic clashes of major powers in a life-and-death struggle for domination of Europe and the colonies, began in 1689 and continued intermittently until 1763. In these wars the colonists stood by their mother country. Her protection was their protection; her destiny was their destiny.

Both nations were ready for the great conflict that began in 1689. When Louis XIV of France had come to the throne in 1661, the French Navy was in a sad condition. Louis's navy had but a handful of ships, officers and seamen. Thirty years later the Sun King's Navy could challenge both England and Holland, separately or together. This miracle had been achieved by subsidizing shipbuilding, improving naval bases, enhancing the quality of both officers and men and establishing all the auxiliary industries needed for maritime and naval strength. At the same time, Louis had built up the French colonies by various forms of government assistance. By the 1680s France had a true navy and was a power to be reckoned with.

England, on the other hand, had allowed her navy to languish after having rebuilt it in the wake of the three disastrous Anglo-Dutch Wars from the 1650s to 1674. She had embarked on a major naval program in 1677, only to see it falter in the face of domestic difficulties between 1678 and 1684. But from 1678 on, the British Navy began to revive under the capable direction of Charles II, James II and their brilliant aide Sir Samuel Pepys. By the onset of the first of the great wars for empire, the British were rearmed and 'at the ready' for any challenge Louis XIV and France might make.

As Louis made his move into the Netherlands in an attempt to expand his kingdom in 1689, he faced not only neighboring

Holland but also England in the person of William of Orange (now ruling there as the husband of Mary II after the Glorious Revolution had overthrown the Stuart king James II). This offensive set off the War of the League of Augsburg—referred to in the colonies as 'King William's War'—which lasted until 1697 and was fought in both Europe and America.

The British Navy was well occupied at home in the early months of the war with James II's attempt to regain the throne by an invasion of Ireland with French naval help. Although the colonies as a whole were hardly disturbed by the war, the seagoing colonists smarted over raids by privateering vessels out of French Canada, which ranged American waters from the St Lawrence to the West Indies preying on commercial and fishing vessels. As the principal victims, colonists from Massachusetts, Connecticut and New York took matters into their own hands in April 1690 and provided eight small ships and 800 men for an attack on Port Royal, Nova Scotia, the privateers' base of operations. The attack, led by Sir William Phips, was unopposed, and the following month the colonists demonstrated the religious antagonism inherent in the conflict by plundering the local Catholic church and smashing its altar. Their subsequent attack, with 34 ships and 2000 men, upon the great citadel of Quebec turned into a fiasco, and the volunteers returned home to sit out the rest of the war without any major French threat to their lives or fortunes. The European phase of the war dragged on for another seven years.

Even the formal end of the war, however, brought no end to French privateering and attacks on colonial fishermen, so

Below: **The Spanish Armada sails from Ferrol, July 1588.**

the colonists were happy to join with the mother country when the War of the Spanish Succession—'Queen Anne's War' in the colonies—broke out in 1702. This war, which lasted until 1713, originated when King Charles II of Spain willed his throne to the grandson of Louis XIV to protect his country from being partitioned by the various European Powers. This arrangement, vehemently opposed by England and Holland as a move by Louis to expand to the south, set off the war. France and Spain were on one side, England and Holland on the other. The English colonists in America took up the cause again by engaging in three operations involving naval power, the latter two utilizing British naval units directly. In the first, Colonel William Rhett of Charleston, South Carolina, was commissioned a vice-admiral in 1706 to command a home-grown flotilla against five Spanish ships raiding the town. The defense was successful, and the South Carolinians mounted a successful retaliatory expedition the following year against Pensacola in Spanish Florida.

In the second action, the American colonists and British naval and military units joined forces in 1710 to stage an amphibious operation against Port Royal, Nova Scotia (returned to France after the previous war). The expedition consisted of four frigates, 30 transports and 1400 men under the leadership of Colonel Francis Nicholson, a British soldier. The operation was quick and successful, aided by the fact that the French had only 300 men in the town and no naval support. Privateering was effectively thwarted again.

The third operation also involved the Royal Navy. Nine warships plus 12,000 army troops (including five regiments of crack British soldiers) and colonial volunteers, launched a major attack on Quebec to gain control of the St Lawrence. They left Boston in July 1711 and arrived on 22 August, only to find themselves completely lost in the fog and gales of the Gulf of St Lawrence. After losing eight of his 60 transports and 900 men in the fog and confusion, the commanding admiral, Hovenden Walker, gave up and returned with his ships and men to England. Given this misuse of seapower, the British and their colonists could only count as good fortune the fact that French naval power had declined drastically during the course of the war and thus played no part in the defense of Quebec. What had been a fiasco could have been a disaster.

The war ended in 1713, and Louis XIV died two years later. The fundamental conflict was suspended for a quarter of a century as each nation recovered from the strains of war and regirded itself for the inevitable renewal of the fight. Domination of Europe and of the colonies had not been settled.

In 1744 the wars for empire broke out again. Austria and Prussia had joined the old combatants of England (now Great Britain after the Act of Union of 1707), France and Spain. Prussia's desire for Austrian territory had been added to the list of issues involved. The war was known in Europe as the War of the Austrian Succession and in America as 'King George's War.' It lasted for four years, until 1748.

The battles that raged in Europe were large land engagements, but in the American colonies they took the familiar form of Indian attacks on the frontiers and privateering on the coastal waters. The only major engagement in which the colonies were involved was an attack on Louisbourg on Cape Breton Island, a keystone

of French power and a base for privateering, near the mouth of the St Lawrence. In this attack of April 1745, the colonial land and naval forces from New England were aided by the Royal Navy, which blockaded Louisbourg while the fortress was besieged by the colonials. Only one French warship arrived, and it was easily captured. The successful siege ended in June, and the chaplain of the colonial forces personally chopped to pieces the altars and images in the town's Catholic church. When Louisbourg was returned to France by the Treaty of Aix-la-Chapelle which ended the war, the American colonists were outraged—1000 of their compatriots had died in the prolonged siege of the city. Yet no one could deny the important part the Colonial and Royal Navies had played in the successful siege of 1745, nor could they deny the importance of the Royal Navy thereafter in protecting the colonists from depredations and even invasions by French and Spanish forces.

Right: **General James Wolfe whose victory at Quebec set the seal on the British success in the French and Indian War.**
Below: **British warships on the St Lawrence during the siege of Quebec in 1759. The city fell on 13 September.**

When war broke out again in 1756 after an uneasy peace of only eight years, naval power again played a major role in the outcome of this fourth and decisive phase. Disgusted with British naval lethargy early in the conflict in the face of a revived French naval effort, the Crown named William Pitt as Minister of War. The new minister surrounded himself with young, tough military men who were anxious to carry the fight to the enemy. A fleet of 40 ships under the command of Vice-Admiral Edward 'Old Dreadnought' Boscawen, accompanied by 14,000 soldiers under Jeffrey Amherst and James Wolfe, easily overran Louisbourg in July 1758 and moved on to take the citadel of Quebec. This was accomplished by September 1759, after a giant British fleet that included 49 men-of-war closed off any chance of French reinforcements reaching their besieged comrades. Quebec fell, then Montreal the next year, then all of French Canada. When a huge French invasion fleet was later scattered by the Royal Navy before reaching England's home shores, the writing was on the wall for the French in this Seven Years' War (the 'French and Indian War' in colonial parlance). Having allowed its navy to be weakened while the British Navy grew ever stronger, the French could not sustain their campaigns for empire. They were forced to sue for peace, and the resulting Peace of Paris of February 1763 stripped from them virtually all their North American possessions, including all of Canada. They were left with only a few islands off Newfoundland and in the Caribbean. The French had suffered a devastating defeat by sacrificing their fleet to the demands of their land armies. Given another chance a decade later, they did not repeat their mistake.

Britain, on the other hand, now lord of all India and North America east of the Mississippi thanks to her naval prowess and control of the sea, allowed her fleet to deteriorate thereafter. She paid the price, as her American continental colonies slipped from her authority and demanded their political freedom.

Above: The most famous of the US Navy's early battles; the action between the *Bonhomme Richard* and the *Serapis*.

A RELUCTANT NAVAL POWER

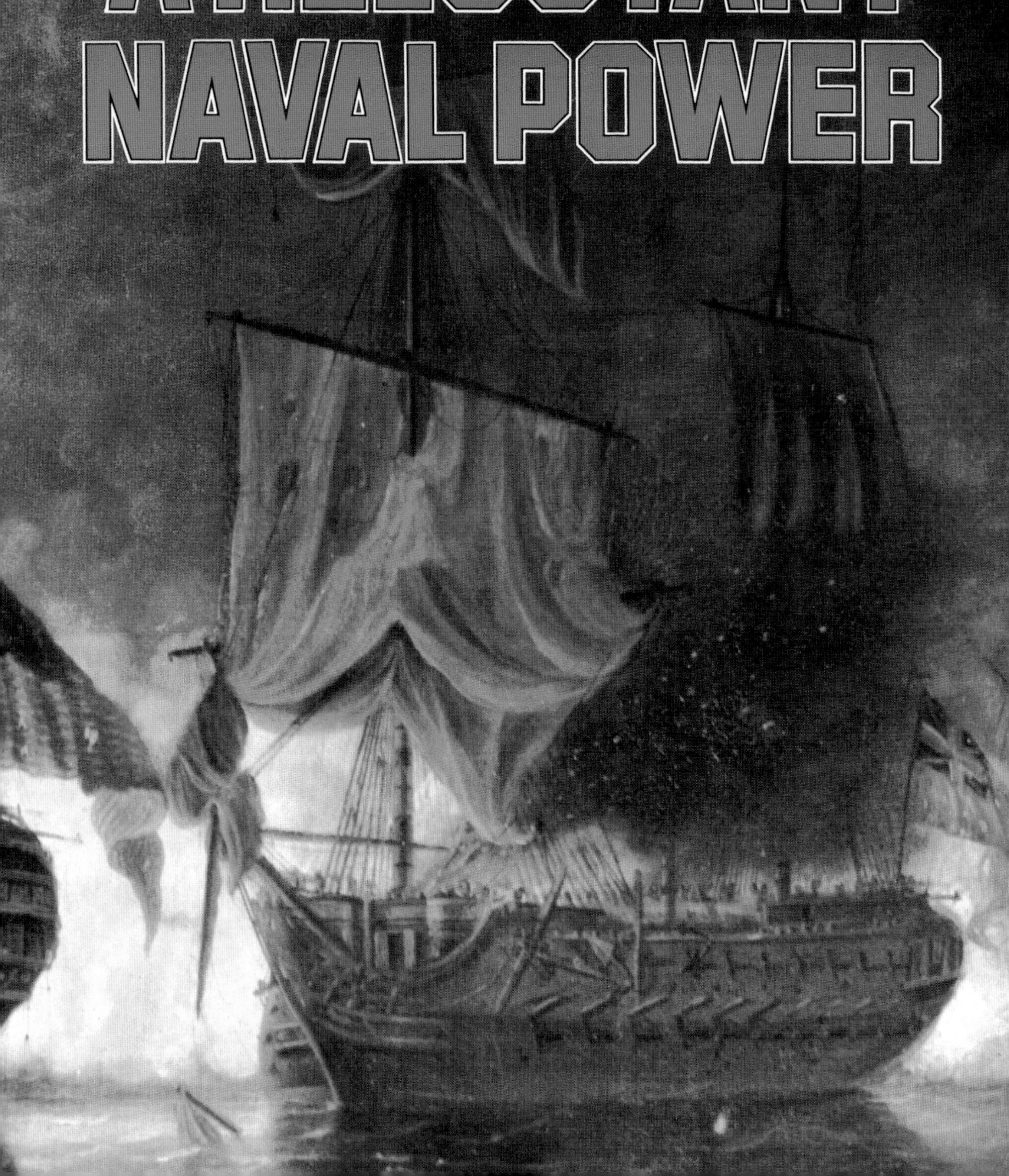

COLONISTS AND REVOLUTIONARIES

Troubles broke out in the colonies in 1775, troubles caused largely by the Crown's decision to pay off its heavy war debts and its new costs of garrisoning expanded American territories by having the colonies pay a greater share in taxes, with higher rates and strict enforcement. This was a fundamental change in policy within the mercantile system of colonial trade and manufacturing—from one of demanding minimal taxes to one of imposing heavier taxes and stricter control. As trouble loomed large because of colonists' resistance to this change, the British Navy was in poor shape to help impose the Crown's will upon them. After the Peace of Paris of 1763, the navy had been cut back to the bone in an effort to save money, and naval administration itself became a victim of graft and corruption. John Montagu, the Earl of Sandwich, First Lord of the Admiralty from 1771 to 1778, allowed the navy to languish still further.

When, therefore, the colonists rose in rebellion in 1775 to resist British efforts to control them by force of arms, Vice-Admiral Samuel Graves in Boston had only 29 ships available to blockade and control the 1800-mile coastline of North America. And in subsequent months and years the naval situation continued to be tight, especially when the French joined the fray in 1778; what began as a limited colonial police action became a world war, with the British fighting the Americans, the French, the Spanish and the Dutch.

Below: **General Benedict Arnold commanded the American forces in the Battle of Valcour Island in October 1776.**

On the other hand, the rebellious colonies had no saltwater navy at all at the beginning of the conflict and were hard pressed to create one thereafter. Their efforts were feeble at best, whether in the form of the Continental Navy or the various independent small navies created after the conflict began by eleven of the colonies. The key to eventual victory for the Americans lay in a freshwater victory on Lake Champlain, and in the French Navy that would match British naval power and finally outduel it in the critical Battle of the Chesapeake (1781) that broke the back of British determination to put down the American rebellion.

American naval efforts were always small and basically ineffective on the Atlantic coastal waters and high seas. It is safe to say that the colonies' saltwater navies had no appreciable effect on the outcome of the Revolution. Although Massachusetts colonists may have thrilled at Jeremiah O'Brien's capture of the schooner *Margaretta* at Machias, Maine, in June 1775, the victory was of limited practical consequence. So were the exploits of the small vessels sent out by General George Washington to seize British supplies early in the war. Congress did not move effectively to remedy the situation until shocked by the bold bombardment of the town of Falmouth, Maine, in October of that year. Following this incident, ships were purchased and others were ordered built on 13 October 1775—marking this date as the birthday of the US Navy. The Naval Committee (which ran the Continental Navy throughout the rebellion independent of Washington's control) finally got around to appointing officers for the American vessels, although many assignments were patently political. The officers were typically relatives of the men in charge of naval affairs.

Esek Hopkins, for example, was a man of limited naval background but a brother of the politician Stephen Hopkins of Rhode Island, a member of the seven-man Naval Committee. Yet Esek Hopkins was given command of the 24-gun frigate *Alfred*. In February 1776 he left the Delaware with seven support vessels under orders to drive Lord Dunmore's fleet out of Chesapeake Bay and then clear the Carolina coast. Bypassing the Virginia Capes to avoid the British forces, Hopkins went to the Bahamas instead and captured the city of Nassau, most of the valued gunpowder there having been removed by the local governor before his attack. Making his way north again, Hopkins and his squadron were attacked off New London in the middle of the night of 6 April 1776 by a lone British ship, the 20-gun frigate *Glasgow*. After a four-hour exchange of fire and chase, the *Glasgow* sailed away to the protection of the British fleet at Newport, and Congress faced the unpleasant duty of court-martialing Hopkins for allowing the vessel to escape. Hopkins and his fleet made for Providence to rebuild and never sailed again as a squadron. Hopkins ultimately resigned his command.

If the American Navy could not stand up to its British counterpart in head-to-head engagements—as indeed it could not, and most vessels soon bobbed quietly in protected harbors under effective British blockade—the same could not be said for American privateers. Privateers were vessels given legal permission (letters of marque) to raid British commerce and supply vessels. They were virtually the only consistent naval offensive the Americans could muster on coastal waters and the high seas, the British Navy having bottled up the regular seaborne fighting forces. Soon sloops, schooners and converted fishing vessels under state congressional authority were busily raiding British commerce along the coast, off the Gulf of St Lawrence, in the warm Caribbean and even in European waters. It was a lucrative business and an effective weapon of war. Soon the British were forced to convoy their supply vessels and arm their merchantmen to beat off the American raiders, who even then found that by clever decoying they could seize an occasional merchant prize. During the war about 2000 American privateers took over 2200 British ships. But these measures could not win the war, and by summer of 1776 the situation on land and sea looked desperate for the infant American nation.

Even David Bushnell's amazing inven-

Above: **The British line bears down during the Battle of Valcour Island.**

tion, the *Turtle*, an innovative one-man submarine of double-shell oak-stave construction, with a ballast tank for descending and ascending, a depth gauge, a snorkel breathing tube, and a screw to bore into an enemy ship's hull to attach a time-fuse bomb, failed in its purpose. Commanded by an army sergeant, Ezra Lee, the *Turtle* was towed down the Hudson River, then cut free to assault Admiral Richard ('Black Dick') Howe's squadron in New York Harbor on the night of 6 September 1776. Although the outgoing tide swept Lee far beyond his target, by turning the manual propeller he was able to make his way back to the British squadron and to a point directly under the hull of Howe's flagship, HMS *Eagle*, of 64 guns. Lee must have been exhausted by his ordeal with the tide, but he went to work operating the screw mechanism on top of the *Turtle* to attach the explosive charge. The screw hit metal strapping on the hull and would not penetrate, and, since dawn was approaching, Lee abandoned the effort and made for shore. The *Turtle* was the first submarine to survive a war mission, but she failed to effect the outcome of the naval war. Neither numbers nor technology could come to the aid of the beleaguered American armies, as the British seized control of American ports almost at will and blockaded the coastal cities.

American and French Naval Victories

At this point, however, one of the most crucial American victories of the Revolution occurred. In June 1776, while the Americans were in full retreat from Canada after a failed invasion attempt, the Continental Congress decided the American forces should make a stand at Lake Champlain. The pursuing British Army under General Guy Carleton wanted to gain control of Lake Champlain and Lake George, plus Fort Ticonderoga and Albany. With these as a base, the British

Below: **The British revenue schooner *Gaspée* is captured and burned by a party of American protesters in June 1772.**

Left: **John Paul Jones indignantly refuses to surrender to the** ***Serapis*****: 'I have not yet begun to fight.'**

could then move at will down the Hudson from Albany and up the river from New York City to cut the colonies in two. Sensing the urgency of the situation, the Continental Congress authorized the building of an American defensive fleet on Lake Champlain. It was to be commanded by one of the most renowned American military leaders, General Benedict Arnold. Carpenters were sent from Philadelphia, and naval stores and arms were shipped from New York and Connecticut. Within six weeks a naval squadron of ten new vessels and five existing vessels was ready.

Arnold maneuvered his fleet into position between Valcour Island and the New York shore of Lake Champlain and waited for the British, descending with their inland fleet. On 11 October 1776, the 30-ship British fleet came on. Arnold allowed them to pass Valcour before attacking, so that the British would have to beat back against the wind. The fight raged from 11:00 o'clock in the morning until dusk. The outnumbered Americans were beaten, and that night Arnold and his remaining vessels slipped away. The British caught them two days later and completed the destruction of the tiny fleet, but in losing, Arnold had won. He and his men had delayed the British by forcing them to build a fleet to match the American flotilla. This postponed the attack on Fort Ticonderoga and Albany until too late in the season to continue campaigning. The British were forced to withdraw. Had Albany been taken in 1776, it could have served as a base from which to continue the northern offensive the following year, and undoubtedly the colonies would have been cut asunder. Arnold and his 'navy' had bought a precious year for the colonial cause.

When the British moved down the Lake Champlain route the next year, they were forced to start far north and eventually met defeat at the Battle of Saratoga in October 1777. Saratoga, in turn, brought the dawdling French into full alliance with the Americans now that it appeared the British could be defeated and the French could exact vengeance for the losses of the Seven Years' War. With the French Navy in the war to counterbalance the overwhelming British naval predominance against the Americans, victory seemed possible. France entered the alliance with the United States in 1778 with a rebuilt navy. By then the French Navy had 80 ships of the line and 67,000 men and was a force to be reckoned with. Early French naval engagements, however, were not promising. Admiral Charles le Comte d'Estaing arrived off New York in April 1778 with the Toulon fleet but refused to enter harbor to take on Admiral Richard Howe's fleet. Moving instead to Newport, Rhode Island, he bottled up the British fleet there and bombarded the city. But when Admiral Howe brought up his fleet to challenge d'Estaing, neither antagonist would attack and both were scattered in a storm. Howe returned to New York and d'Estaing moved to the Caribbean, with no damage done on either side.

Nor did the fortunes of war appear to favor the Americans and their French allies during the remainder of the year. Nicholas Biddle's 32-gun frigate *Randolph* was destroyed by the 64-gun ship of the line HMS *Yarmouth*. An American expedition under Dudley Saltonstall to the mouth of the Penobscot River in Maine to destroy a British base being built there turned into a complete fiasco when a small British squadron's arrival forced the Americans to run upriver and surrender or burn their craft. Then in August 1778 d'Estaing's fleet was finally goaded into attacking the British at Savannah, Georgia, with 20 ships of the line and 5500 troops. Attempting a bombardment from the land and a storming of the British lines, the French were driven into a swamp and lost over 1000 men. Disgusted at the fortunes of war, d'Estaing sailed home.

American fortunes improved but little in 1779, although 23 September of that year

Right: **A feature of the battles on the Great Lakes was the use of small gunboats, as shown in this view of the Battle of Valcour Island.**

Above: **The 10-gun sloop *Sachem* of the Continental Navy *circa* 1776–77. Note the design of the flag.**
Left: **Lieutenant John Paul Jones presides as the Stars and Stripes is hoisted for the first time aboard the *Lexington*, 4 July 1776.**

saw the greatest sea victory of the American cause. The man responsible was John Paul Jones (born John Paul, Jr). Having gone to sea in 1761 at the age of 13 from his native Scotland, Jones sailed in the Atlantic and Caribbean trades for many years and attained a captaincy by the age of 21. When the war with Britain broke out, Jones secured a commission in the Continental Navy. Having served well as a lieutenant on the *Alfred*, he was given command of the sloop *Ranger* in 1777 and sailed for Europe to harass British trade on His Majesty's home waters. Since the French and the Americans had signed their alliance before Jones arrived in 1778, he was able to use French ports as his bases of operation and to raise havoc in the waters around the British Isles. Giving up command of the *Ranger* on the promise of a more formidable vessel, Jones was disappointed that his new ship was the old 900-ton East India merchant vessel *Duc de Duras*. He promptly rechristened her *Bonhomme Richard* to honor his patron Benjamin Franklin, Ambassador to Paris and author of *Les Maximes du Bonhomme*

Richard (The Sayings of the Gentleman Richard).

Undaunted by this disappointing command assignment, Jones set sail on 14 August 1779 with his squadron: the *Bonhomme Richard*; a new American frigate, the *Alliance*, under an erratic Frenchman named Pierre Landais (an honorary citizen of Massachusetts); three French naval vessels and two French privateers. The squadron attained some success in capturing British vessels. Then, on the evening of 23 September, it fell in with a Baltic convoy off Flamborough Head on the Yorkshire coast. The convoy was guarded by the new 44-gun frigate *Serapis* and a small sloop. Ordering an attack, Jones soon found his companion vessels fleeing the scene, leaving the 42-gun *Bonhomme Richard* to fight the enemy alone.

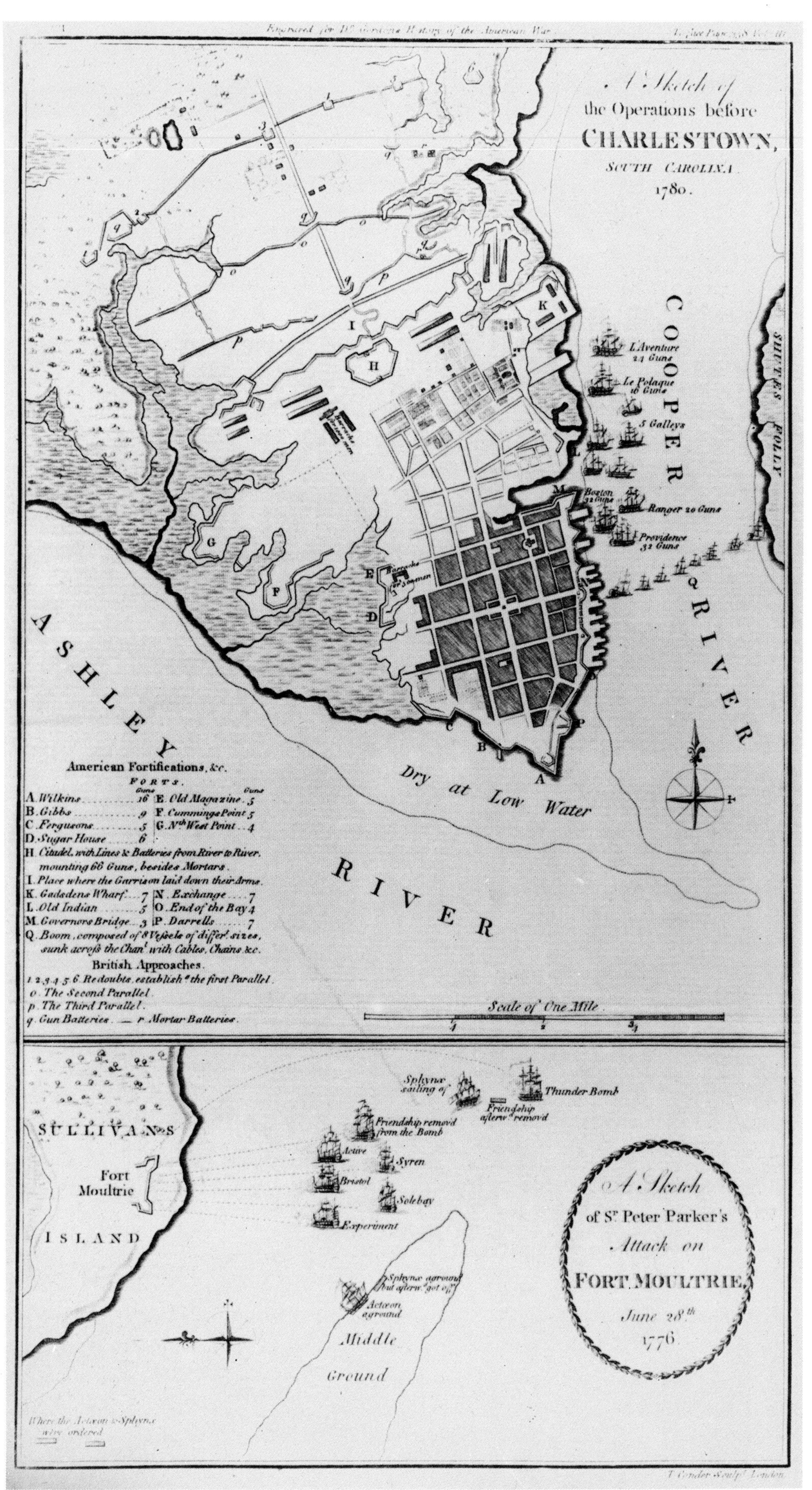

In the furious duel that followed for three and a half hours, the *Serapis* and *Richard* broadsided one another with their withering fire, reducing both ships to floating wreckage. The *Richard* also suffered broadsides from Landais's *Alliance*, which returned to the scene of battle and began firing on the wrong ship. Finally one of Jones's sailors from the *Richard* crawled out to the end of a yardarm that hung over the deck of the *Serapis*—the two ships by then hopelessly entwined—and dropped a grenade onto the gun deck of the British frigate. The horrible explosion that resulted forced the brave and capable Captain Richard Pearson of the *Serapis* to haul down his colors and present his sword to Jones in surrender of his vessel. The *Bonhomme Richard* was so battered by the battle that she sank two days later.

John Paul Jones's splendid victory created the first and only genuine naval hero of the Revolutionary War. His stirring rejection of Captain Pearson's offer to accept his surrender midway through the battle, 'I have not yet begun to fight,' embodied the embattled spirit of the new nation in an hour of failing fortunes.

After his glorious victory over the *Serapis*, Jones went on to command two other American vessels during the war, then served as a rear admiral in the Russian Black Sea fleet before dying in poverty and obscurity in Paris in 1792 at the age of 45. As a symbol of the spirit of the Revolution, Jones's body was brought back to America early in the twentieth century at the behest of President Theodore Roosevelt (who was promoting a powerful navy in any way he could) and entombed in a marble sarcophagus on the grounds of the United States NavalAcademy at Annapolis, Maryland. After a century of neglect, the brave and resourceful sea captain returned to his adopted country for the honors he deserved as an almost solitary light of fighting hope during the dismal middle years of America's fight for independence.

Through all these years of revolutionary conflict, the effective privateers continued their work, and by 1780 the war was beginning to turn. The French with the assistance of the Spanish, gained command of the Caribbean, as d'Estaing's returned fleet battled Admiral George B Rodney to a draw in those waters in April. In July d'Estaing moved in and took final control of Newport. Rodney would not even challenge his control. The basic strategic reality was that by 1780 the British were involved in a world war against the Americans, the French, the Spanish and the Dutch. This meant that the Royal Navy was attempting to cover the Baltic and North Seas, the north and south

GREAT
ENCOURAGEMENT
FOR
SEAMEN.

ALL GENTLEMEN SEAMEN and able-bodied LANDSMEN who have a Mind to diſtinguiſh themſelves in the GLORIOUS CAUSE of their Country, and make their Fortunes, an Opportunity now offers on board the Ship RANGER, of Twenty Guns, (for France) now laying in Portsmouth, in the State of New-Hampshire, commanded by JOHN PAUL JONES Eſq; let them repair to the Ship's Rendezvous in Portsmouth, or at the Sign of Commodore Manley, in Salem, where they will be kindly entertained, and receive the greateſt Encouragement.--The Ship Ranger, in the Opinion of every Perſon who has ſeen her is looked upon to be one of the beſt Cruizers in America.---She will be always able to Fight her Guns under a moſt excellent Cover; and no Veſſel yet built was ever calculated for ſailing faſter, and making good Weather.

Any Gentlemen Volunteers who have a Mind to take an agreable Voyage in this pleaſant Seaſon of the Year, may, by entering on board the above Ship Ranger, meet with every Civility they can poſſibly expect, and for a further Encouragement depend on the firſt Opportunity being embraced to reward each one agreable to his Merit.

All reaſonable Travelling Expences will be allowed, and the Advance-Money be paid on their Appearance on Board.

In CONGRESS, March 29, 1777.

Resolved,

THAT the Marine Committee be authoriſed to advance to every able Seaman, that enters into the Continental Service, any Sum not exceeding FORTY DOLLARS, and to every ordinary Seaman or Landſman, any Sum not exceeding TWENTY DOLLARS, to be deducted from their future Prize-Money.

By Order of Congress,
JOHN-HANCOCK, President.

Above: **Recruiting poster for the USS *Ranger*.**
Right: **Map of the siege of Yorktown.**
Below right: **Esek Hopkins, first commander of the US Navy.**

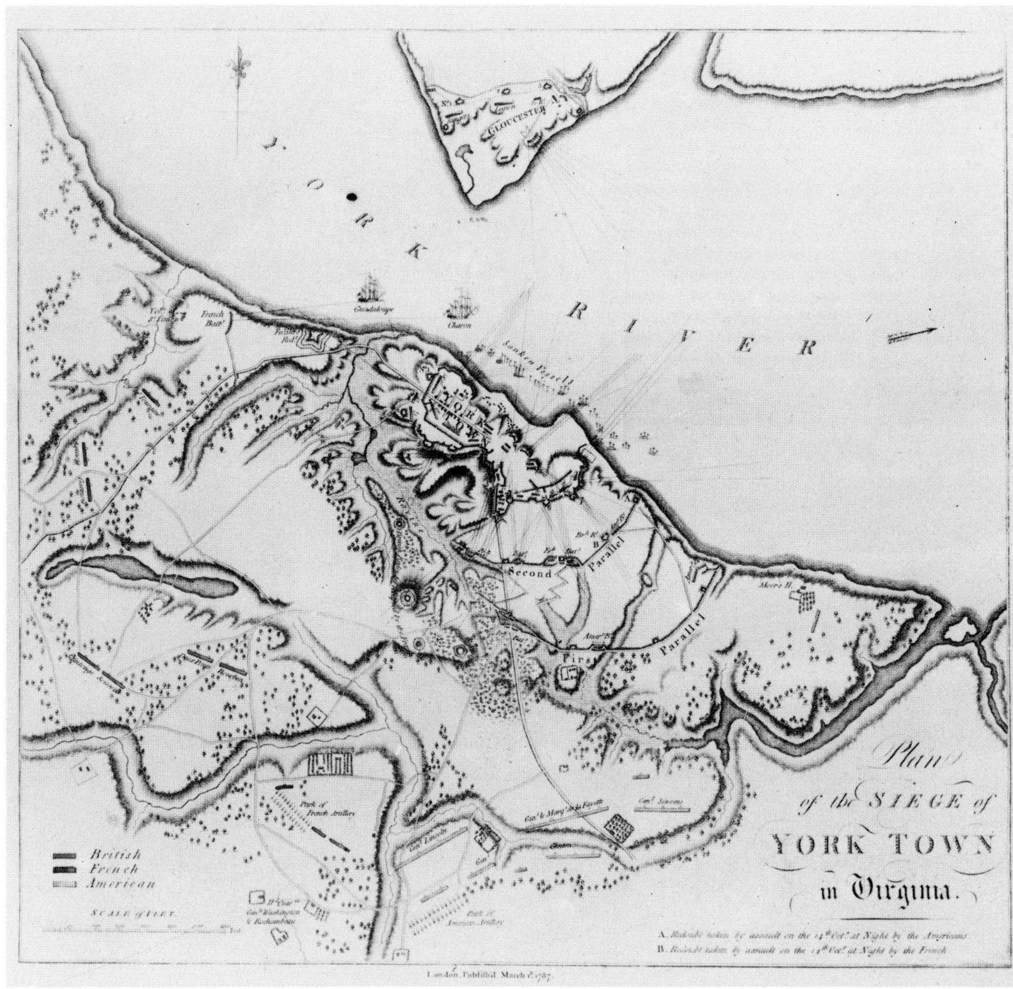

Atlantic, the Caribbean, the Mediterranean Sea and the Indian Ocean. Increasing war weariness at home and rising opposition in Parliament to a prolonged conflict with the nation's best customers, plus Britain's naval weakness, finally spelled crucial defeat for the king and his war party. The occasion was Lord Charles Cornwallis's ostensible 'triumphal march' through the Tory Southern states, which ran into unexpected resistance and moved to Yorktown, Virginia.

Cornwallis had chosen well in moving his army to Yorktown as a base for evacuation by the Royal Navy. He could defend himself against the troops pursuing him, and the harbor could accommodate the fleet that would take him out. But two events occurred which Cornwallis did not count on. First, Washington, correctly estimating the situation, rapidly moved his troops from the New York area—along with those of Lieutenant General de Rochambeau from Newport—and placed Cornwallis's Army under heavy and relentless siege. Second, Admiral Francois Joseph Paul de Grasse, leaving the Spanish fleet to guard the Caribbean in his absence, moved to the Chesapeake to prevent the British fleet from entering to save Cornwallis. When the weakened British fleet arrived off Capes Henry and Charles—Admiral Rodney, then ill, having sailed home with four ships of the line, and six other vessels having been diverted to escort a Jamaican convoy home to England—its commander,

Left: **Maps of the British attacks on Charleston, SC, in 1776 (lower) and 1780. American weakness in major vessels prevented intervention in either case.**

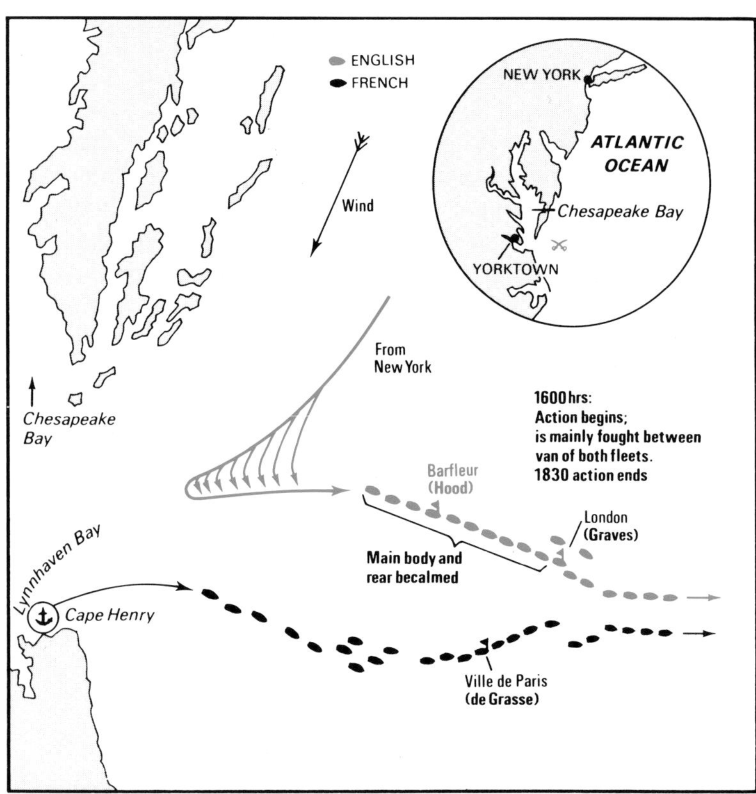

Above: Captain John Barry.
Above left: Map of the Battle of Chesapeake Bay which made possible the victory at Yorktown.
Right: Another broadside from the *Bonhomme Richard* strikes the largely dismasted *Serapis.*

Admiral Thomas Graves, found de Grasse's fleet inside and waiting.

On 5 September 1781 the critical 'Battle of the Capes' was fought. Thanks to British tactical errors—Graves engaged only part of his line of battle—the French Navy's hold on the entrance to Chesapeake Bay could not be broken. Cornwallis's lifeline had been snapped. Furthermore, de Grasse was able to draw off Graves's fleet for five days, allowing a French fleet under Admiral de Barras to slip into the Chesapeake and reinforce the French naval squadron there. Defeated and now outnumbered, Graves sailed back to New York to refit, and as the American and French forces numbering 15,000 men drew the noose tighter and tighter around Cornwallis's 7000 troops, the British commander bowed to the inevitable and asked for terms of surrender. On 19 October 1781 the ceremonies were held. The American war for independence, for all practical purposes, had been won.

Additional fighting at sea took place after that date, most importantly the great British-French sea battle in the Caribbean known as the Battle of the Saints in 1782, but the issue had been decided. The Parliamentary majority that had persisted in the war since 1775 had been discredited, the British nation was deeply in debt, privateers were still wreaking havoc with merchant vessels on the high seas and the vaunted Royal Navy was stretched thin across the face of the earth. The war against the former colonists could be won only by military exertions beyond the willpower and capacity of the nation. It was time to quit.

Dividing the Americans from their French allies, who wanted to pursue the war until lands and rights lost in previous conflicts were restored to the Bourbon Kingdom, the British signed the Treaty of Paris with the American envoys on 3 September 1783. American independence was recognized. The jubilant Americans, now free of the mother country, turned to peacetime pursuits once again. During the war approximately 60 ships had seen service with the Continental Navy. They had captured over 200 enemy vessels. But with the return of peace, it was widely believed that a naval force was both prohibitively expensive and superfluous. Therefore, all the remaining vessels under commission were sold off except the *Alliance*, which would be used to show the flag and protect American trade. But the cost of maintaining even this frigate was soon seen as being too high for the infant nation, so she was sold off on 1 August 1785. With her sale, the Continental Navy came to an end, the state navies having already been disbanded.

Although the leaders of the successful rebellion were extolled for generations as national heroes—as one would expect—quickly forgotten were the military lessons of the war. Chief among these was that the nation had almost lost the war in the first two years for lack of a navy—indeed, would have lost the war if the British Government had shown greater resolution in suppressing the revolt—and that final victory was attained only through control of the sea. Naval power, in this case French naval power, was the crucial ingredient. The new American nation would pay dearly in the years ahead for forgetting these lessons.

Right: The *Alliance* fires on the closely engaged *Serapis* and *Bonhomme Richard.*
Below: Jones' first command for the Continental Navy, the brig *Lexington.*

FOR NATIONAL RIGHTS AND EXPANSION

Six short years after the Treaty of Paris was signed came an event that was destined to have cataclysmic effects on the European heartland and to pull the infant American nation into another armed conflict. In 1789 the French nation, loaded down with war debts and saddled with a monarchy unwilling or unable to respond effectively to the forces swirling around it, fell into domestic revolution. The French Revolution lasted for ten years, ending only with the rise to power of Napoleon Bonaparte. In the process, the rebellion led to war on all fronts and catapulted the United States into the turmoil of war with first the French, then the British. Between these two conflicts, the new United States was also forced to humble the Barbary pirates from the northern coast of Africa in order to uphold American rights.

The Federalists, the Quasi-War and the Rebirth of the Navy

As the Revolutionary War came to an end and Americans returned to their peaceful pursuits, most of them gave little thought to the nation's lack of naval power. There were problems in that Britain was not living up to all the terms of the Treaty of Paris, Spain was closing the Lower Mississippi to American commerce and the Barbary pirates were plundering American ships on the Mediterranean and holding their crews for ransom. But the fact that a respectable American naval force could help to solve these problems was perceived only dimly, if at all. Besides, the government established under the Articles of Confederation had no real taxing power to support national defense—or any other national interest—and required the consent of nine of the thirteen states to take substantial action on anything. Thus the Navy was nonexistent under the Articles. Fortunately, the fundamental weaknesses of the Articles became apparent to enough states so that a convention was called in Philadelphia in 1787 to alter the Articles in favor of a centralized government more responsive to compelling national needs. The convention altered the Articles right out of existence and created a new central government under a new Constitution: it received the support of the states and came into effect in 1789.

The new national government embodied many fundamental changes in powers, including those of national defense. Under the Constitution, the Commander in Chief of the armed forces was the President, and the Congress was empowered to levy and collect taxes for national defense, although it could appropriate money to the military for only up to two years. Congress was specifically empowered to raise and support an army and a navy. Defense had become primarily a national obligation under the new document.

Although the United States now had the legal power to create an army and a navy, this did not mean that either was forthcoming or adequately financed. The Federalists, under the leadership of Alexander Hamilton and backed by the merchant classes, were clearly in favor of a navy to support and defend the nation's commercial interests. America's shipping, they argued, had to be protected against seizure of its vessels and depredations by the Mediterranean potentates. Coastal shipping and fishing rights in the Atlantic could be upheld only by naval force. A navy, in fine, could enforce the respect America was due as a sovereign power.

The Republicans, however, were opposed to any substantive military power. Drawing their strength from the inland reaches of the country, and fearful of aristocratic power as embodied in an officer corps, besides being ardent friends of France, or Francophiles, the Jeffersonians were in no mood to build a powerful navy. They argued that it would be expensive and unnecessary, since no European power would send a sizable fleet to America's shores. Perhaps a small naval force to punish the Barbary pirates and guard American ports might be acceptable, but any expenditure beyond that would be foolish and superfluous.

Even as Europe slipped into war in 1793 and British and French naval units began to seize neutral American shipping, the Republicans refused to rethink their stance on an American navy; their aversion to land-based forces was also largely un-

Below: Building the USS _Philadelphia_, _circa_ 1800. American frigates were usually larger than other nations' – an obvious advantage.

Above: **The American ship *Planter* beats off an attack from a French privateer in July 1799 during the Quasi-War.**

changed. The continuing capture of American vessels by the Barbary pirates, and the cavalier attitude of France and Britain toward American neutral rights on the high seas, finally forced the dominant Federalists to re-create a small navy, but only over the opposition of the non-commercial frontier Republicans.

Six new 204-foot frigates, eventually to sail under the names *Constitution*, *Constellation*, *United States*, *Congress*, *President* and *Chesapeake*, were authorized in 1794. Designed by Joshua Humphreys, an experienced Philadelphia shipbuilder, these vessels were to be strong in construction to stand up to enemy equals and swift of sail to escape when outgunned or outclassed. Despite a lessening of tensions with Morocco and Algiers the next year, shipbuilding continued in a dilatory fashion (the *United States*, *Constellation* and *Constitution* were launched in 1797) so that America had some naval muscle to bare when warfare between the British and French spilled over and American rights had to be defended on the high seas.

When John Jay's attempt to settle outstanding problems with Britain met with only partial success—and, indeed, the United States received no assurances from the British that they would stop taking American vessels bound for France on the high seas—France was incensed. The Jay Treaty of 1795 had significantly decreased the danger of war with Britain, but had increased the danger of war with France, which saw it as a pro-British move on the part of the United States. France continued to take American merchant vessels trading with Britain, and President John Adams's attempt to solve the bones of contention with France ended in an aborted attempt at negotiations. Thus America fell into the Quasi-War, or Undeclared War, with France in 1798 when Congress authorized the seizure of armed French vessels.

Although the Quasi-War was of little military significance (the United States eventually seized 80-plus French ships, mostly in the West Indies), it did result in the real rebirth of the US Navy. Congress completed the building of the Humphreys-designed frigates and built, bought or rented more than four dozen other vessels, all of which acquitted themselves well in protecting American convoys and tangling with French vessels. Captain Thomas Truxtun won notable victories in the *Constellation* over the 40-gun *L'Insurgente* in the West Indies (1799) and over *La Vengeance* off Guadeloupe in 1800. Of greater importance in the long run, Congress also created a separate Navy Department in 1798. Benjamin Stoddert, a wealthy Maryland merchant, was appointed by President Adams as its first secretary. Stoddert not only brought the Navy into being as a regular force and directed its operations, but also made plans for new and larger vessels that could stand up to the largest French or British ships of the line. He also planned to build a complete shore establishment of shipyards and warehouses for the fledgling Navy, spreading them along the eastern shore for both defensive and political purposes. When the Undeclared War ended with the Convention of 1800, the United States had a navy, one that had proved its mettle in protecting American seagoing interests. But dark clouds appeared on the new navy's horizon: the fragmentation of the Federalist Party, and popular opposition to the Alien and Sedition Acts, clearly pointed to victory for the anti-navy Republicans under Jefferson.

The Jeffersonians, the Barbary Wars and Trouble with England

Benjamin Stoddert had envisioned a respectable naval force with at least three dozen major vessels, including numerous ships of the line. His Republican successor (after Jefferson's 'Revolution of 1800') had other ideas more in line with his party's values and ideas. Secretary of the Navy Robert Smith, who held the office from 1801 to 1809, presided over the scuttling of Stoddert's plans as unnecessary luxury. Not long after Jefferson's inauguration and Smith's assumption of office, the US Navy had been reduced to six ships and a handful of officers and men.

But Jefferson's dream of a miniscule navy guarding America's coast as proper for a frugal and peaceful people evaporated in the face of renewed Barbary raids on American vessels in the Mediterranean. Soon the attacks by Tripoli, Tunis, Morocco and Algiers forced the land-oriented president to reverse himself and call for a naval force to deter the Barbary Powers. Navy monies were doubled, and an American squadron under the command of Captain Richard Dale was dispatched to punish the Mediterranean pirates. The ineffectual Dale was soon replaced by the equally inept Captain Richard V Morris and finally by Captain Edward Preble. Only then did pacification of the region begin in earnest. The most noteworthy event of this naval police action created a hero for the American public. When Commodore William Bainbridge's frigate *Philadelphia* ran aground off Tripoli on 31 October 1803 and its 307-man crew was captured by the local pasha, Lieutenant Stephen Decatur and a small party worked themselves alongside the hapless *Philadelphia* on a dark night in February 1804 and burned her, thus restoring American honor. While few other actions were of this magnitude, the US naval presence finally convinced the potentates (in 1805) to refrain from attacking American vessels and to return the captured officers and crew of the *Philadelphia*—as long as an agreed-upon $60,000 bribe was paid and America would resume offering annual 'presents' to the African leaders. (Trouble with the Barbary pirates did not end until

Left: **The** ***United States*** **at her commissioning ceremony in 1797.**
Right: **Sailors from the USS** ***Constitution*** **storm aboard the French privateer** ***Sandwich*** **in the West Indies in May 1800.**

1815–16, when squadrons under Commodores Stephen Decatur and William Bainbridge used a show of force to compel Algeria, Tunis and Tripoli to desist.)

The Barbary Wars of 1801–05 demonstrated graphically that naval power, especially when projected into an enemy's home waters, was a very effective protection for national interests. Yet even in the face of British and French violations of America's maritime rights, the Republicans persisted in their anti-naval stand until America stumbled into war all over again —a war that might well have been avoided had the nation been negotiating from strength rather than from weakness.

As of 1805 the American merchant fleet was in a flourishing state. While British and French forces battered away at each other on land and sea (October 1805 saw Horatio Nelson's great victory over the French fleet and that of her Spanish ally off Cape Trafalgar), the Americans were shipping goods from Spanish, Dutch and French colonies in the Caribbean and Far

Right: **Stephen Decatur, hero of actions against the Barbary pirates and the British.**
Below: **The battle between the** ***Constellation*** **and** ***L'Insurgente*****, 9 February 1799, from a painting by Charles Patterson.**

Above: **Commodore Richard Dale, one of the first US commanders in the wars with the Barbary pirates.**

East into Napoleon's France and the ports of his allies. These goods were usually landed in American ports first and then reshipped to Europe (a practice known as the 'broken voyage') in exchange for manufactured goods. American products were also being carried by American ships to the ports of the belligerents, so trade had never been better.

But Britain, fighting for her life against France and her allies, saw no good in such practices. Since she could never raise land armies large enough to conquer Napoleon on the Continent, he would have to be defeated on the seas. That meant stopping American neutral vessels from carrying their cargoes into European ports.

The first incident triggered by American shipping practices came in May 1805 when the *Essex* out of Salem, on a broken voyage from Barcelona to Havana, was seized in the Caribbean by the British. A British admiralty court condemned the cargo, saying it was never intended for the American market, although most of the port duties paid were returned. The Americans were incensed by this action, and a few mariners gave up broken voyages, but most continued on their way.

When France and England subsequently blockaded one another's coasts and ports, American trading vessels were subject to seizure by both sides, but most continued to sail anyway, since great profits could be made by successful vessels. American neutral rights were not being honored by the belligerents, but open war was avoided.

All this began to change after the *Chesapeake* affair of 1807. Given the harsh living and disciplinary conditions on British warships, the Royal Navy was forced to man its ships largely by impressment. An impressed sailor was one who was simply seized on land or sea and forced into the King's service. Both impressment and seizure of deserters were allowable under British law, but the *Chesapeake* affair illustrated the peril of enforcing these statutes.

The *Chesapeake* was a new 38-gun American frigate being outfitted at Norfolk on Hampton Roads. A British squadron patrolling in Chesapeake Bay had orders to search for deserters outside American territorial waters and suspected that some British deserters had signed on the *Chesapeake*. Accordingly, HMS *Leopard* passed out of the bay and waited for the American vessel to emerge. As she did so on 22 June 1807, the captain of the *Leopard* informed Commodore James Barron, the *Chesapeake*'s commander, that he would send a crew aboard to search for the deserters. When Barron refused this request, saying that his crew had been recruited in Boston and he knew of no British deserters aboard, the British fired three broadsides into the *Chesapeake*, which was completely unprepared for battle, and forced Barron to haul down his flag to save his ship. The British then boarded the American vessel and took four men as deserters (one of whom was indeed just that). Whatever the legality of the British actions—they had fired a preliminary warning shot across the bow of the *Chesapeake* and Barron had not hove to—the American nation reacted violently to the event. Jefferson ordered all British warships out of American waters and forbade any further entry. Through James Monroe, American Ambassador to England, he demanded reparations and an end to impressment. The British disavowed the actions of the *Leopard*, but steadfastly refused to give up impress-

Right: **The engagement between the *Chesapeake* and the *Leopard*.**
Below: **The USS *Experiment* and the British *Louisa Bridger* in a night battle, 16 November 1800. The *Experiment* believed the *Louisa Bridger* to be French.**

Above: The *Philadelphia* burns in Tripoli as Decatur and his men escape.

ment. Within months they had specifically ordered the impressment of all British sailors on any neutral vessel. Insulting as this seemed to the Americans, the British were fighting a war for survival, and the Treaty of Tilsit of that year (1807), whereby Russia became an ally of France, made their situation even more perilous. British survival took precedence over American neutral rights in their eyes, and America, without a navy to challenge these practices, would simply have to live with the consequences.

Below: A party from the *Enterprise* set out to board a Tripolitan pirate in 1801.

Even at this, Jefferson could not be convinced of the need for a strong navy, but proposed instead that the nation should only guard her shores against foreign naval encroachments. Accordingly, Congress appropriated money for 188 small gunboats ('Jeffs,' as they came to be called) for inshore patrol. Only 50 feet long, with two 32-pound cannons and crews of 20, the tiny crafts' gunwales were only two feet above water when fully loaded. But the gunboats were cheap—a major consideration. They could also be stored under sheds when not deployed. They were useless against any regular enemy naval force, but might at least be used to keep American vessels in port during an embargo, even if they could not keep enemy vessels out. Thomas Jefferson continued to put his faith in moral persuasion and withholding of American ships and goods, rather than in armed force.

Jefferson's attempts at economic embargo were exercises in futility. His Embargo Law of December 1807, designed to cut off the British from American foodstuffs and raw materials, stopped all exports from the United States by land and sea. Unfortunately for this short-sighted policy, his embargo leaked like a sieve and brought great hardship, not to the British, but to those Americans who depended upon foreign trade and the merchant marine for their livelihood. And Jefferson's gunboats and miniscule navy could not begin to make the embargo effective, no matter how they tried. Faced with an embarrassing and frustrating defeat, Jefferson decided to change to a selective embargo instead. It worked no better than his previous attempt at economic coercion.

The War of 1812

President James Madison, Jefferson's successor, could do no better. The Non-Intercourse Act of 1809 and Macon's Bill Number Two of 1810 only made matters more confusing without guaranteeing American rights. American ships and cargoes were still being seized. Nor did a new short-term full embargo in the spring of 1812 seem to work. But, ironically, it was working better than the Americans realized. On 16 June 1812 the British revoked their Orders in Council authorizing the seizure of American ships, because crop failures at home made American foodstuffs imperative. But two days later, not knowing of this British action, the American Congress declared war on Great Britain. Seizures of American ships, continued British impressment of American seamen, an agricultural depression that the Western farmers blamed on British interference with trade, the desire of the 'War Hawks' in Congress to restore 'national honor' and a belief that the British were stirring up the Indians on the American frontier all combined to lead America into the ill-conceived War of 1812.

Faced with fighting a major power with only sixteen ships in commission, plus the useless 'Jeff boats'—the British had over 600 men-of-war—the navy turned to squadron patrols to harass British vessels on the North Atlantic sea lanes. Captain John Rodgers proved the value of such operations early in the war by drawing the British Halifax, Nova Scotia, naval squadron hundreds of miles to the east to allow American merchantmen to speed safely home to American ports. And American

Right: Scenes from the battle of HMS *Java* with the *Constitution*. Above, the *Java* loses her foremast in an attempt to board the more heavily armed *Constitution*, becomes unmanageable and is totally dismasted by the *Constitution*'s broadsides, below.

hopes for naval superiority were raised by the victory of the large 44-gun frigate *Constitution*, under Captain Isaac Hull, over HMS *Guerriere*, 38 guns, off Nova Scotia on 19 August 1812. American privateers were also busy. By the end of 1812, almost 600 vessels were preying on British commerce (including the famous *Rossie* out of Baltimore under Captain Joshua Barney); during the course of the war over 1300 British vessels were claimed.

But despite these efforts by the ship-poor United States, Britain reacted with vigor and had soon clamped a tight blockade on the Atlantic coastal ports and bays. There were occasional American naval victories like that of the USS *United States* under Commodore Stephen Decatur over

Left: **A privateer captures a British brig, a typical action during the War of 1812.**
Below: **Close action during Perry's victory on Lake Erie.**

Right: **Thomas Macdonough, victor in the battle at Plattsburgh Harbor, Lake Champlain on 11 September 1814.**

HMS *Macedonian* (25 October 1812) and the USS *Constitution* under Commodore William Bainbridge over HMS *Java* two months later, but the dominance of British seapower was soon obvious. The reinforced British squadrons in American waters had blockaded America's ports. Neither naval nor commercial vessels were able to break out from New York to New Orleans. Not even Captain James Lawrence's spirited duel between his *Chesapeake* and HMS *Shannon* off Boston harbor could crack the blockade strangling the American nation. (This was the engagement in which Lawrence, in the midst of defeat, bravely encouraged his crew by shouting 'Never strike the flag of my ship!' 'Don't give up the ship!') The British Navy controlled the seas and even received supplies from American citizens opposed to the war, especially in New England where numerous American vessels continued to sail under British license. The British also demonstrated graphically the importance of their strategic advantage by sailing up Chesapeake Bay to attack and burn Washington and then bombard Baltimore in August 1814.

Only on inland waters did American forces have notable success. On 10 September 1813 Master Commandant Oliver Hazard Perry, with a home-built fleet, defeated a British lakes squadron off Put-in-Bay. He immortalized the Battle of Lake Erie by transferring his motto flag, 'Don't Give Up the Ship,' from his battle-wrecked *Lawrence* to the *Niagara* to continue the fight until victory was won. Perry's victory, marked by his stirring message 'We have met the enemy and they are ours,' was also a great strategic victory for the United States, ensuring control of the Northwest Territory. Perry then proceeded to transport American forces under General William Henry Harrison across Lake Erie to Ontario, where they won an impressive land victory over the British in the crucial Battle of the Thames the following month.

A home-built American naval force also won well-deserved laurels in the Battle of Lake Champlain in September 1814. A 10,000-man British force had marched down from Montreal via the Richelieu River to Plattsburg, New York, the key to control of Lake Champlain. The commander of the British forces, General Sir George Prevost, sent a naval force of 14 gunboats under Captain George Downie against an equal contingent under Captain Thomas Macdonough to seize control of the lake. Gaining the tactical advantage by superior maneuvering of his vessels, and aided by the fact that his crews were

Right: **American and British privateersmen in a bloody boarding action.**

trained seamen, Macdonough captured most of the British force, retained control of the lake for the Americans and forced Prevost back into Canada. Thus the British were denied the valuable bargaining chip of control extending from eastern Maine to Lake Champlain at the peace negotiations then being held at Ghent, Belgium. American naval forces also played an important role in Andrew Jackson's defeat of General Edward Pakenham at the Battle of New Orleans (fought two weeks after the Treaty of Ghent had been signed on Christmas Eve, 1814) by anchoring Jackson's right flank on the Mississippi River.

As the War of 1812 ground to a halt—a war that tactically and strategically might be termed a draw at best—it was evident that the US Navy had played an unimpressive role in the conflict. The strategies of static defense by small gunboats and the extensive use of privateers against commerce had not brought the British to bay. It was realized that only a powerful trained naval force would command the respect of other nations and defend American interests in time of war. The big heavily gunned frigates had, in fact, done the job, although sheer lack of numbers of these and other first-rate vessels had allowed the British effectively to dominate American coastal waters. Congress, realizing at last the imperatives of command of the sea, authorized the building of seven 74-gun ships of the line in 1816. The year before it had reorganized the navy under a Board of Navy Commissioners (all officers) to advise the secretary of the navy on personnel, shipbuilding and administrative affairs. (The board functioned until 1842, when the bureau system was adopted.) Having won widespread public favor, the US Navy was ready to play a major role in the affairs of the nation.

Standing Down but Keeping Station

Although the Navy stood in this advantageous position at the end of the nation's second great conflict with Great Britain, there was an inevitable decrease in naval defense enthusiasm with no major foes to challenge American interests at home or abroad for the next three decades. In addition, a nationwide fervor for economic development emerged as the United States began to shift to industry in the North, and agricultural expansion in the South and West became boundless. The nation also suffered the severe Panic of 1837. These factors largely account for the Navy's failure to reach its potential in the years prior to the Civil War. The nation did not abandon its Navy—it realized its important role in protecting American commerce on the sea lanes of the world—

Above: **Typical uniforms of the War of 1812. In the foreground a lieutenant carrying a speaking trumpet used for passing orders to men working in the rigging.**

but allowed only a moderate growth of the force. As a result, the Navy made certain notable gains in the period 1815 to 1861 and played a number of key roles in American expansion, but it never enjoyed sufficient public and political favor to develop its full potential as a peace-keeping force.

Ships continued to be built, although the pace was usually dilatory. The seven vaunted 74-gun vessels so enthusiastically authorized by Congress in 1816 were slow in coming: three were still not completed

Above: Captain Isaac Hull of the *Constitution*.
Left and above left: Final scenes in the battle of the *Java* and *Constitution*. The *Java* tries to get under way with a jury sail but, after being forced to surrender and the surviving crew having been taken off, she is blown up.

Left: **'Macdonough Pointing the Gun' (during the fighting on Lake Champlain), from an engraving by F F Walker.**

by 1861. The US Navy could properly boast of the largest warship in the world when the 120-gun *Pennsylvania* was launched in 1837, but the overall pace of building never appreciably quickened. Steam warships also came to the navy during this period: the USS *Fulton*, a 700-ton sidewheeler (1837); the wood paddle-wheel sister ships *Missouri* and *Mississippi*, authorized in 1839; the sloop *Princeton*, which first utilized John Ericsson's screw propeller (1843); and the *Michigan* for use on the Great Lakes, a sidewheeler launched on Lake Erie in 1843 as the first iron-hulled steam warship in the US Navy (she continued to sail the Lakes until 1923). But while the navy occasionally made modest leaps forward, especially during the abbreviated tenures of such naval secretaries as Abel P. Upshur (1841–43) and George Bancroft (1845–46), the overall pace of development was sluggish. The navy was on 'Slow Ahead.'

During these years various squadrons were established for patrol duty: the Mediterranean (1815), the East India (1817), the Pacific (1821), the West Indies (1822), the Brazil (1826), the Home (1843, which absorbed the West Indies Squadron) and the African (1853). Engaged in protecting American commerce, suppressing pirates in the Caribbean, attempting to halt the illegal slave trade from Africa and 'showing the flag' in foreign ports, the naval squadrons quietly conducted the nation's business during thirty years of peace. It was also during this time that Lieutenant Charles Wilkes carried out a very successful voyage of exploration (1838–42) to Antarctica, the South Pacific and the Northwest coast on behalf of the navy and the nation. Also along the scientific line, Naval Lieutenant Matthew Fontaine Maury continued to develop the sciences of navigation and oceanography, which led to his recognition as 'Pathfinder of the Seas.'

Although the number of naval vessels in commission hovered at only about fifty during this period—spread thinly over the face of the world—naval personnel played key roles in expanding American influence, especially in the Pacific. In 1826 the USS *Peacock*, under the command of Captain Thomas ap Catesby Jones, was ordered to Hawaii to protect commerce there. Jones, on his own, negotiated a treaty with the regents of the child monarch giving Americans certain key rights in the islands. Although the treaty was never even submitted to the Senate, the Americans in the islands and the Hawaiians lived by it anyway. Then in 1842 President John Tyler asserted the 'Tyler Doctrine' of American priority over all other powers in the islands. As a result, Hawaii fell into the American sphere of influence after 1842, a step aided and upheld by the US Navy.

The navy was also present at the opening of China to the Western Powers. The British broke the back of Chinese resistance to the inroads of English trade, especially in opium, in the Opium War of 1839–42 and forced the Chinese Government to open treaty ports to them and to let them trade freely. Commodore Lawrence Kearney arrived in China in 1842 to open negotiations for like privileges for the Americans. He was followed soon after by Caleb Cushing, with four American warships. to resume the negotiations. Cushing, as Commissioner to China, negotiated the Treaty of Wanghia in 1844, gaining trading rights that were very profitable to the Yankee merchants. Although the Chinese were really only bowing to the inevitable in opening their land to outsiders, the navy had played an important role in expanding America's commercial and diplomatic rights in the Far East.

Right: Perry leaves the badly damaged _Lawrence_, taking his flag to the _Niagara_. _Below:_ The _Niagara_ (center) bursts through the British line in the Battle of Lake Erie.

It was also in the crucial decade of the 1840s that the navy took a giant step toward full maturity with the opening of the United States Naval Academy at Annapolis, Maryland. Until then, naval officers had learned their trade at sea, but this time-honored method had many drawbacks, not the least of which was inadequately prepared officers. When an experiment by which young men of promise were sent to sea in small ships ended with the son of the secretary of war and two others being hanged for mutiny in 1842, resistance to a formal academy such as the Army had maintained at West Point since 1802 began to break down. Objections to a naval academy as too expensive and too likely to turn out an antidemocratic military caste (a charge long borne by West Point) withered. Under the inspired leadership of Secretary of the Navy George Bancroft, opposition was overcome and an academy with regular courses and a 2–3–1 curriculum (two years at Annapolis, three years at sea and one year on a practice ship) was authorized. Fort Severn at Annapolis was transferred to the navy, all midshipmen not attached to ships were ordered there by Secretary Bancroft, and in October 1845 the Academy formally began its work of educating naval officers. A proud naval tradition had begun.

Men of the USS *Constitution* (right) cheer as their ship goes into action with HMS *Guerriere* (below). Many of the American successes in the War of 1812 were owed to the American emphasis on accurate gunnery, whereas British standards had declined since the victory at Trafalgar in 1805.

War with Mexico

Above: **The landing force at Tabasco comes under fire.**

In the meantime, trouble was brewing to the south. Ever since Texas had proclaimed her independence from Mexico in 1836, relations between the United States and her southern neighbor had been strained. Even though the US Navy had observed strict neutrality toward both belligerents during the Texas war of independence, even allowing the Mexican Government to obtain logistical supplies from New Orleans, Mexico was highly suspicious of American intentions toward the Texas republic peopled largely by ex-Americans, many of whom wanted the new nation in the Union. When, therefore, the United States annexed Texas in 1845 and the two nations began to dispute the location of the new state's southern boundary, the situation went from bad to worse. In January 1846 President James K Polk sent General Zachary Taylor and his men into the disputed territory and, with the help of the navy, Taylor proclaimed a blockade at the mouth of the vital Rio Grande River. When blood was spilled in Mexican attempts to assert its boundary claims, the United States declared war in May 1846. Whatever the rightness or wrongness of American actions in beginning the conflict—fiercely debated then and still debated today—the navy played a key role in winning this war of American expansion.

Once war was declared, the navy discovered that its deep-draft frigates and ships of the line were of limited value, since they could not cross the eight-foot sandbars found at the mouths of the Mexican rivers on the Gulf. Small steamers, schooners and brigs that could be used effectively on close blockade had to be purchased. This was crucial, since Commodore David Connor was under orders to seal off the Mexican Gulf Coast and capture its major ports. However, no challenge to Connor's orders or the navy could come from Mexico, whose navy was too small to engage the American forces. During the course of the war, not one Mexican naval vessel ever put to sea on Gulf waters. The major challenge to the blockaders came from the weather:they kept station outside the Mexican ports in the dry season (October to April) when violent northers caused acute discomfort and in the rainy season (April to October) when the 'vomito', or yellow fever, threatened to immobilize whole crews. But by buying steamers and swift, shallow-draft schooners for tight blockading, the navy was able to seal off the coast to Mexican exports and to supplies from outside.

It took the US Navy two tries to capture the fort at Alvarado, south of the major Mexican port of Vera Cruz—Commodore Matthew C Perry relieving Commodore Connor in the interim—and the taking of

Below: **Steamers tow landing barges across the sand bar before the landing at Tabasco.**

Vera Cruz itself via a joint army-navy effort called for ingenuity and new naval tactics to carry out this giant amphibious landing successfully. Special double-ended, flat-bottomed landing craft forty feet in length and stackable in threes for transporting had to be hurriedly built for the purpose. When an over-the-beach assault by sailors, marines, and soldiers finally took place on 9 March 1847, a line of fire was directed at the shoreline as the surfboats carried the men ashore. The surfboats were then pulled back off the beach by their crews, hauling on ropes attached to kedge anchors dropped offshore for this purpose. All 8600 men were carried ashore in eleven hours without incident—aided by the fact that the Mexicans had decided not to defend the beach. (This was the largest amphibious operation carried out by the navy until World War II.)

As the troops worked their way around Vera Cruz and the forts guarding the northern and southern ends of the city and laid it under siege, the navy was called upon to undertake two vital operations. Naval guns were unloaded from the ships and dragged three miles over the sand into assigned position, from which their crews delivered steady and accurate fire against the city walls. In a two-day stretch before Vera Cruz surrendered, the naval batteries delivered 1000 shells and 800 round shot (45 percent of all ordnance expended) at the city's walls and forts. Meanwhile, naval units in harbor also delivered withering fire on the city, moving directly beneath the guns of the Castle of San Juan de Ulloa to do so. When the city surrendered on 29 March 1847, opening the way for the armies to move inland against the capital of Mexico City, the navy could rightly boast of having played a significant role in the fall of Vera Cruz. During the remainder of the war on the Gulf Coast, the navy continued its tight blockade and sealed off the remaining port cities by taking Alvarado, Tuxpan and Tabasco, the latter two operations requiring movement up rivers and the use of landing parties. By June 1847 the Gulf Coast was secure. The Navy had done its duty in exemplary fashion.

On the Pacific Coast, the war and the navy's part in it was a quagmire of confusion. The first misfire came in 1842, when the commander of the Pacific Squadron, Commodore Thomas ap Catesby Jones, took the port of Monterey under the mistaken belief that war had broken out (the city was returned to Mexican officials with apologies). The squadron comman-

Below: **Another view of the landing at Tabasco. Sidewheelers were very suitable for the Gulf Coast because of their shallow draft.**

der in 1845, Commodore John D Sloat, was reluctant to make any unauthorized moves unless a war was definitely in progress. By June 1846, however, Sloat had become convinced that the war was on and rendered aid to the Americans in California as they proclaimed the 'Bear Flag Republic.' His men occupied Monterey before he found out that Captain John Charles Fremont of the Topographical Engineers, the surveyor-turned-revolutionary, was under no orders whatever to help the rebels. Turning over his command to Commodore Robert F Stockton, who had arrived shortly before, Sloat sailed home.

Cooperating with Fremont, the pompous Stockton made everyone's job more difficult by his inflammatory proclamations to the citizens of California. But he was able to use the crew of his *Congress* to take Santa Barbara, San Pedro and Los Angeles for the American cause. Los Angeles was subsequently lost and had to be painfully retaken, but when San Diego also fell to Stockton's men, California was secure and sewn up in a tight blockade. Subsequently, naval forces under Commodore W Branford Shubrick, who replaced Stockton in January 1847, took key ports in Baja California and on the Mexican West Coast and held them until word was received in March 1848 of the armistice signed at Guadalupe Hidalgo the month before.

The navy had done well in the war. Its ships and men had transported the armies to their destinations and had played a major role at Vera Cruz. They had gained control of the seas and prevented reinforcement on both coasts by a tight blockade. Amphibious operations had been learned by trial and error in the Vera Cruz operation. All this had been accomplished despite a lack of supplies and directed coordination. And as a result of the 'Bear Flag' revolt and the taking of California (in addition to the new Oregon Territory to the north), the nation now had a Pacific water frontier and the navy had a bigger job than ever in protecting America's enlarged Pacific interests.

Above: The Stars and Stripes flies over the beach at Vera Cruz as the landing parties continue to stream ashore.

The Opening of Japan

By this time many groups in America were interested in further Pacific expansion, particularly in opening the fabled land of Japan, closed to the outside world for two

Below: The warships *Levant*, *Savannah* and *Cyane* (R to L) lie offshore as men from the ships land at Monterey, 7 July 1846.

Above: **Perry and his interpreter in discussion with Japanese commissioner Hayashi.**

centuries. Protestant missionary societies wanted the kingdom opened to spread the Christian gospel among its people; whaler crew members from vessels that had sunk in Japanese waters were being held there; coaling stations were needed for steam vessels plying the sea lanes to China; and Yankee merchants saw great profits in opening the land to American goods. Although America's first attempt to make contact with the aloof kingdom failed miserably when Commodore James Biddle was openly rebuffed in 1846, the Government was determined to try again and turned to the Navy to do the job.

The naval officer chosen to lead the expedition was Commodore Matthew Calbraith Perry, one of the heroes of the Mexican War. Selected because he had diplomatic experience and because President Millard Fillmore liked him, Perry accepted the assignment with enthusiasm and began his preparations in 1852. He would command the sail-steamer *Mississippi* as his flagship, and eventually left from Norfolk on 24 November 1852 with two steam sidewheelers, four sailing sloops-of-war and three supply ships scheduled to join him in the Far East. Perry not only prepared himself thoroughly for his duties by wide reading and talking to whaling captains about the Japanese, but also supplied himself with scientists and artists to observe and record everything they saw. In addition, he carried a letter from the President and gifts for the Emperor of Japan, plus a Frenchman as his chef and an Italian musician as his bandmaster. Armed with credentials as envoy extraordinary and minister plenipotentiary to Japan, Perry sailed in the hope of opening Japanese ports to American trade, obtaining protection for American seamen and gaining coaling stations in the Japanese islands. Making his way across the South Atlantic, then around Africa and across the Indian Ocean to Hong Kong, Canton and Shanghai, Perry provisioned his fleet and left on 17 May 1853 for the Japanese-controlled island of Okinawa in the Ryukyu chain. Using this visit as a dress rehearsal for later negotiations (and to set up talks on a coaling station on Okinawa in case his mission to Japan fell through), Perry approached the Okinawan officials in great pomp and splendor to convince his imperial hosts of his importance. (This Perry believed, was absolutely necessary for impressing the ruling Japanese shoguns.)

On 2 July Perry's fleet of four vessels sailed for Japan. It arrived six days later and anchored just outside Yedo (Tokyo) Bay. This first visit to Japan, which lasted from 8 through 17 July 1853, was designed solely to impress the Japanese officials and their emperor. Negotiations could come

later. Perry would deliver President Fillmore's letter, state his demands, sail away and return the following spring with a greater force of ships when they arrived on station. To impress the Japanese, Perry kept himself invisible from the nation's officials; he was being imperious, not arrogant, by design. He would deal only with high officials in delivering his letter from the President; upon landing to do so, he was accompanied in great ceremony and dignity by 250 sailors and marines, plus the fleet band, to a specially constructed building (under the floor of which ten samurai warriors were concealed in case of trouble). Having delivered the letter, Perry announced that he would return in the spring with more ships to conduct negotiations. Returning to his four-ship fleet, Perry moved it up the bay to test the channel and to show the Japanese he would not be ordered out. He then returned to China.

As promised, Perry returned the following year. He appeared at Yokosuka on 13 February 1854 with ten ships. Again assuming an imperious manner, Perry was now ready to negotiate. Although he originally insisted on the talks being held in the capital city of Edo, Perry compromised and settled on Yokohama, south of Edo, when the Japanese protested that the Emperor would be overthrown if the parley were held in the capital. The commodore made his ceremonious landing on Japanese soil with 500 sailors and marines forming a long corridor of march and the 'Star Spangled Banner' booming from the band. Perry did not forget to order a 21-gun salute to the Emperor, and gifts (including a miniature railway on a 350-foot circular track and a working telegraph setup) were presented by the Americans. Although the Japanese at first refused to open their ports to American trade, Perry persisted in his demands. The resulting Treaty of Kanagawa (31 March 1854) included the opening of two treaty ports for trade, care of American victims of shipwreck and most-favored-nation status (any privilege extended to any other nation was automatically given to the United States). As Perry's fleet sailed away on 10 April 1854, he could well be pleased with his accomplishments. The opening wedge for Japanese trade had been driven by this officer-diplomat who had learned the art of Oriental negotiating. (A full commercial treaty followed in July 1857, with negotiations carried out by Townsend Harris.) As Perry resigned his command and sailed home in September 1854 by commercial steamer, he had earned the accolades heaped upon him. Like the nineteenth-century navy he represented so well, Perry's accomplishments had not been spectacular, but they had been solid. He had served the nation in peace and in war and had helped her become a major expansive power. His achievements, like the navy's had helped engender a deep national confidence in America's future. That national confidence would soon be sorely shaken, as the country found itself in the throes of Civil War.

Below: The USS _Hartford_ photographed _circa_ 1861, three years after she came into service. The _Hartford_ was a typical example of the hybrid steam/sail warships of her day.

CIVIL WAR, AT SEA AND ON INLAND WATERS

The Civil War between the government of the United States and the Confederate States of America was long in coming. The Northern and Southern states had been wrestling with the issues dividing them for over four decades. The question of the expansion of slavery had been argued since 1819, when Southern slaveholders had attempted to expand their 'peculiar institution' into the Louisiana Purchase territories, specifically into Missouri. This move had been strongly opposed by Northern interests who objected to slavery in lands they hoped to develop as free-labor territories and states. This early controversy had been worked out in the famous Compromise that allowed slavery in Missouri but forbade it in all other areas north of the line 36°30′ (the southern border of Missouri), but the issue continued to smolder in the decades that followed.

The Compromise of 1850 and the Kansas-Nebraska Act led to outright border conflict instead of peace; the Supreme Court's Dred Scott decision and the exploits of the abolitionist fanatic John Brown only inflamed the issue further. Northern abolitionists and Southern 'fire-eaters' fueled the controversy, and when Abraham Lincoln was elected President in 1860 as the candidate of the Northern-based Republican party, the Southern states, led by South Carolina, began to secede from the Union. Additional dissension centered on sectional differences over the tariff (the North wanted it higher; the South wanted it lower), aid to the railroads (the North generally pro; the South generally con) and the nature of the Constitution (the North arguing that federal power was supreme, the South that final power resided in the states). Believing they had the Constitutional right to leave the Union, various Southern states passed ordinances of secession after Lincoln's election and proceeded to form a new central government. The issue had finally been joined—despite the unsuccessful efforts of representatives from the border states to bring about a compromise of some kind—and everyone tensely awaited further developments.

The Nation Divides

In the harbor off Charleston, South Carolina, stood Fort Sumter, a federal military installation under the command of Major John Anderson, United States Army. South Carolina, having seceded and joined the Confederacy, claimed that Fort Sumter was now foreign military installation on its sovereign territory and demanded that it be evacuated. President Lincoln, believing that the very act of secession was

invalid because not provided for in the Constitution, argued that South Carolina and the Confederate States were wrong and steadfastly refused to order evacuation of the fort by the federal troops garrisoned there. Undeterred by the fact that a chartered merchant steamer, the *Star of the West*, had attempted to provision and reinforce the troops at Fort Sumter in January 1861 and had been fired upon and turned back, Lincoln ordered reinforcements to Fort Sumter by sea on 8 April 1861. President Jefferson Davis of the Confederacy instructed General P T Beauregard to try to persuade the Federals to leave peacefully before the reinforcements arrived, but Major Anderson refused the request. Accordingly, on 12 April the Confederate batteries along Charleston Harbor opened fire and compelled the Union troops to surrender the next day. Shooting had begun. Both sides, believing they were right, had refused to give in and now called for troops to defend their rights on the battlefield. The Civil War was fated to last for four years and ended only when over half a million men had died and as many had been wounded. It was fought from Texas to Virginia and from Pennsylvania to the waters of the Gulf Coast before the issues had been settled. The US Navy played a major role in the conflict before the hard-fought Union victory was achieved in 1865.

Given the relative economic strength of each section of the country, the South would be hard pressed to emerge victorious. The North had a population of 23,000,000, the South only 9,000,000, of whom about 3,500,000 were slaves whom Southerners dared not put under arms.

MEN WANTED

FOR THE

NAVY!

All able-bodied men not in the employment of the Army, will be enlisted into the Navy upon application at the Naval Rendezvous, on Craven Street, next door to the Printing Office.

H. K. DAVENPORT,
Com'r. & Senior Naval Officer.

New Berne, N. C.,
Nov. 2d, 1863.

Left: **Union ships bombard Fort Royal, SC, 7 Nov 1861. After its capture Fort Royal became an important base for the blockade.**
Right: **Naval recruiting poster.**
Below: **9-inch Dahlgren smooth-bore guns, aboard the USS *Hartford*.**

In critical railroad mileage the North had 22,000 miles of track, the South only 8000. The North had 90 percent of the nation's manufacturing facilities, crucial to modern warfare, the South only 10 percent. The North owned virtually all the merchant vessels, the South but few. Faced with these discrepancies, the South realized it could win only by fighting a basically defensive war. It would have to force the North into a grand strategy that carried the war into the South to compel submission, a strategy that was expensive in money and manpower. The South also looked for help from abroad, since they believed that the British in particular would be forced to break any Federal blockade to attain their supply of cotton, the South's most important export. If the Southerners could go on the defensive, get outside help and hold out long enough so that the North would tire of the conflict and let them go their way in peace, they could win despite the economic and population differences. It would be a test of will, and the South would win.

Mindful of all this, Lincoln and his planners developed their own grand strategy. First, Union armies would march on the South and cut it into separate pieces while taking a considerable toll of Southern troops, troops very hard to replace in a white population of only 5,500,000. Second, the US Navy would clamp a tight blockade on the Southern coasts, allowing no cotton out and no foreign supplies in, at the same time using river forces to help the army cut the South into pieces by controlling its river systems, especially the vital Mississippi. Thus strangled by the aptly named 'Anaconda Plan,' and hatcheted apart by Northern land offenses, the South would be forced to surrender and the Union would be saved. Thus strategies were set, and each power geared up for a war to the finish which, both sides were sure, would last but a few months at most.

Although the Union Navy was in a weakened state at the beginning of the war due to declining naval appropriations, it was stronger than the virtually nonexistent Confederate Navy. The North had only 42 warships in commission at the start of hostilities (23 of which had steam power), and the number of naval personnel stood at only 7500. These vessels, sporting 455 guns, were spread out on station, however—only 12 in the Home Squadron and the rest in the East Indies and the Pacific. But the Union had at least the nucleus of a powerful navy capable of rapid expansion thanks to the Northern industrial base. The Union Navy also had over 1200 trained officers, even after losing 321 of the 671 officers of Southern background who resigned their commissions when the war broke out. Working on this base, Lincoln's Secretary of the Navy, Gideon Welles from Connecticut, ordered all seaworthy vessels to duty, purchased many others for conversion into war vessels and began construction on others. By December 1861 the Union fleet had over 250 vessels and 22,000 men and continued to expand during the course of the war, adding over 200 new vessels with over 1500 guns to the navy's inventory. These included 74 mighty ironclads.

The South, on the other hand, was hard pressed for naval power as the war began and was unable to add to its sea forces in any appreciable way. Although 321 naval officers in federal service 'went South' after Fort Sumter, they had virtually no vessels or crews to command. Although Southern forces had seized a few small vessels, the entire Southern naval contingent consisted of less than a dozen at hand. But Stephen R Mallory of Florida, the Confederate naval secretary, was undaunted. The former US Senator and chairman of the Senate Naval Affairs Committee, after failing in his attempts to buy ironclad steamers from England and France, ordered the construction of ironclads, floating batteries and gunboats for Southern defense and contracted for the building of swift, heavily gunned commerce raiders in England. It would take miracles to build an effective naval force in the industry-poor South, but Mallory was determined to try. He was heartened by the fact that the Confederates had seized the Pensacola naval yard (even though it was only a small repair yard) and that the important Norfolk (Gosport) naval yard had fallen to the Confederates with little difficulty with its large drydock intact, thanks to the dawdling of old Commodore Charles S McCauley. In the process the South had seized the partially burned screw frigate *Merrimac* and almost 1200 cannon, including 300 powerful Dahlgren guns. It was not enough, but it was at least a start.

Southern Commerce Raiding and Blockade Running

Faced with no chance of building a navy powerful enough openly to challenge the Union Navy in direct combat, the South turned instead to privateering, the traditional response of the weaker naval power. Privateering, or commerce raiding, could accomplish two things. It would gain some supplies for the Southern cause, but, more importantly, it would serve as a very

Below: Union ships withdraw before the Confederate ironclad _Manassas_ and fire ships in an action near the mouth of the Mississippi on 12 October 1861.

effective irritant to Northern commerce, making shipping unsafe and driving marine insurance rates up, thus undermining Northern support for the war. It might well also draw off Union naval vessels from their blockades of Southern ports. Commerce raiding, combined with blockade running and Union defeats at the hands of the Southern armies, would eventually bring victory, it was hoped, to the Southern cause.

Although Southern commerce raiders were always few in number—never more than 30 operating at any one time—some achieved great success and notoriety. The *Florida*, for example, set sail from her building ways at Liverpool in 1862 (thanks to the negligence and even connivance of the British authorities, who allowed Confederate agents to contract for ships and equipment with British builders and suppliers) and in the next two years captured 37 Northern vessels, inflicting a loss of over $3 million on the ships' owners. The *Florida* came to an inglorious end, though. Captured by Union vessels in a Brazilian port in 1864, she was taken to Norfolk, by then in Union hands. When the Brazilian Government rightly protested the taking of the ship in a neutral port, the United States agreed to return her to the South. However, she was 'accidentally' hit by an army transport in Hampton Roads and sank at her moorings when her watercocks were 'accidentally' opened by a Union naval officer. The *Florida* still rests today in the mud off Hampton, Virginia.

The most famous of all Southern privateers was the *Alabama*, also built in England in 1862. She escaped just before the arrival of British Foreign Office orders for her detention (the British finally bowing to American pressure to prevent such non-neutral acts). Sailing the seas of the world, this swift eight-gun barkentine-rigged ship with a retractable propeller enjoyed remarkable success for two years under Captain Raphael Semmes of Maryland. She met her match, however, when she issued a challenge to the USS *Kearsarge*, a steam corvette, in June 1864 off the coast of Cherbourg, France. The *Kearsarge* was heavily gunned and manned by well-trained seamen. In addition, she had an armor belt of chain and heavy planking to protect her vital engines. As the vessels steamed out to do battle on the morning of 19 June 1864, excited crowds watched the epic battle in the making from the Cherbourg waterside and the cliffs. The two powerful vessels steamed in circles, matching broadside for broadside, until the heavy and accurate gunnery of the *Kearsarge* proved too much for the famed *Alabama*. After the wounded were removed, she sank in the early afternoon and Southern commerce raiding and morale suffered a devastating blow.

The testimony at the hearings of the 'Alabama claims' at Geneva after the war

Above: **The *Merrimac* (nearest) makes a clumsy attempt to ram the *Monitor* (right).**

Right: **Farragut stands nonchalantly in the rigging of the heavily engaged *Hartford* at the Battle of Mobile Bay.**

Above: **The CSS *Florida* sinks a Union clipper. The contemporary caption describes the *Florida* as a 'British pirate.'**

showed that 11 Southern commerce raiders built in Britain during the war had captured over 250 Northern vessels and caused a loss of over $17 million to American maritime commerce, although by 1863 the British had reversed their policy and had seized Confederacy-bound vessels including two powerful 'Laird Rams' designed to break the blockade. Impressive as these statistics appear, however, the fact remains that while the American merchant marine was sorely wounded by these Southern vessels, with many shipowners 'fleeing the flag' to foreign registry, and marine insurance rates skyrocketed, the commerce raiders never drew the blockading vessels off station or affected the war in any major way. They were an irritant and a source of Southern pride to be sure, but they did not play a significant role in the outcome of the war.

The same was true of the blockade runners. Although the Federal blockade of the Southern coast was proclaimed by May 1861, from the Virginia Capes to the Rio Grande, for the first year of the war there were few ships on station and blockade running involved little risk. But from 1862 to 1864 more ships arrived to fill out the four blockading squadrons (North Atlantic, South Atlantic, East Gulf and West Gulf), and the practice became hazardous indeed. In the final year of the war the remaining Southern ports of Mobile, Savannah, Charleston, and Wilmington, North Carolina, were added to the US Navy's list of captured ports—New Orleans having been taken in 1862—and blockade running came to a complete halt.

Yet even during the early years when successful blockade running was possible,

Left: **The Confederate attack on Union forces at Memphis is driven back, 6 June 1862, opening up the Mississippi to the Union advance.**

it failed to help the Confederate cause in any appreciable way. Using the Southern ports of New Orleans, Mobile, St Augustine, Savannah, Charleston and Wilmington as bases of operation, blockade-running captains sailed to such neutral ports as Nassau, Havana and Bermuda to exchange Southern cotton for goods needed in the South. Even though the US Navy kept these neutral ports under surveillance, blockade runners were able to sneak in and out at night using local pilots for navigation and steam power for speed. The fast, shallow-draft paddle-wheelers, sometimes with telescoping funnels and painted gray, were usually able to best the Navy's blockades at both ends of their runs and carry into the Southern ports not only 'hardware' (munitions) but, significantly, silks, laces, linens, corset stays and other goods in high demand. Of the 84 steamers in the trade between 1861 and 1864, 37 were captured, 25 met with debilitating accidents and 22 continued to operate. While they operated, the blockade runners made fabulous profits for their owners and crews. Shipowners could repay the cost of their vessels by only one or two successful voyages, captains could make as much as $5000 per month, and crew members could receive $100 per month plus a $50 bonus per trip (a Confederate soldier was paid only one-tenth of this amount).

The reasons for these high profits and wages reveal the weakness of blockade running as a Southern stratagem. While

the Southern cause desperately needed iron, steel, copper, guns, ammunition, engines and medicines, more money could be made in carrying luxury items to the Southern populace than in bringing in war items for the Confederate Government—to be paid off in depreciated Confederate dollars. Salt that could be purchased by enterprising blockade runners in Nassau for $7.50 per ton could be sold at Richmond for $1700 per ton. Coffee that sold in Nassau at $240 per ton brought $5500 per ton in the Confederate capital. Wilmington, North Carolina, held weekly auctions that drew speculators from all over the South to its wharves to bid on goods brought in through the blockade. There the speculators paid premium prices for coffee, tea, fresh meats, fine cloth and corset stays. Try as it might, the Confederate Government could not stop this trade in luxury goods. While only a fraction of Southern cotton was able to reach its market, the return trips by the blockaderunners were markedby venality of the worst kind. Thus the Southern war effort gained little by this increasingly dangerous but profitable trade and was forced to depend on its own marginal resources to sustain its armies in the field.

Union Strategy of Blockade

While the commerce raiders and blockade runners produced some hope for the Confederate cause in the early stages of the war, the Federal strategy of seizing Southern ports and imposing a strict blockade gradually became effective and inexorably drew a noose around Southern imports and exports, thereby dooming the rebellion. Initially utilizing Fort Monroe in Virginia at the entrance to the Chesapeake Bay as its base of operations, the North gradually began to attack, seize and shut up the 89 harbors, ports and bays along the 3500-mile Atlantic and Gulf coastlines that marked the South's water boundaries and its sea link to the outside world. In August 1861 a joint army-navy expedition left Fort Monroe to seize Fort Clark on Hatteras Inlet and its companion installation Fort Hatteras, thereby to deny exit by Confederate vessels from Albermarle and Pamlico Sounds. After a four-day bombardment and an amphibious assault, Fort Clark fell to the Union forces. Fort Hatteras fell to the attackers three days later, and the North Carolina waters were cut off from use as an outlet to the Atlantic sea lanes. Two months later an expedition was mounted from Fort Monroe against Port Royal, South Carolina, headed by General William T Sherman and Captain Samuel F Du Pont. When the city fell to the Union forces on 7 November 1861, the blockading squadron had a secure base to use against Savannah and Charleston. Other ports were taken along the Atlantic in subsequent months so that

Above: The action at Memphis. The *Van Dorn* was the only ship to escape the Union victory.

Below: The CSS *Atlanta*, which surrendered to the USS *Weehawken* at Warsaw Sound in the Wilmington River, Georgia, in June 1863.

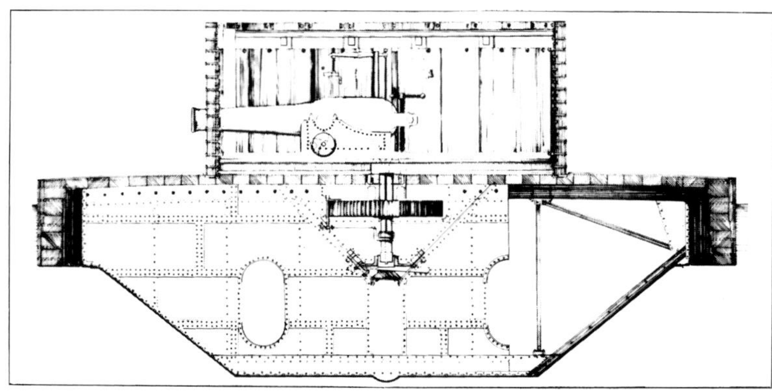

Above: **Secretary of the Confederate States Navy, Stephen R Mallory.**

by March 1862 only Savannah, Charleston and Wilmington were left on the Atlantic coast, although the major ports of Mobile and New Orleans were still open on the Gulf. An attempt to put Charleston out of action without military confrontation had failed. In December 1861 and January 1862, the Union Navy had brought 35 old hulks to Charleston (mostly old whalers) to be sunk in the harbor channel to seal it off to shipping. Towed into position in the outer harbor, the stone-ballasted vessels were sunk in place. Unfortunately for the Union cause, the old hulks disintegrated and the harbor currents cut new channels around them—thus the 'Stone Fleet' experiment proved a failure and the vital port of Charleston remained open.

But if the Union attempts at blockade showed signs of eventually strangling the South, the Confederate leaders held out high hopes for a new naval weapon that could break the Union blockade. It might also assure Southern control of Chesapeake Bay, thereby opening Richmond via the James River to the sea, hampering Union military operations in northern Virginia, and menacing the Federal capital at Washington. That new weapon was the ironclad *Virginia*.

Monitor vs *Virginia (Merrimac)*

When the Union forces abandoned the Gosport navy yard in April 1861, they left behind the scuttled 40-gun steam frigate *Merrimac*, which had been burned to the waterline. The Southern forces raised her hull and placed her in dry-dock where marine engineers worked to salvage her engines. By July 1861 orders had been issued to naval constructor John L Porter and Lieutenant John M Brooke to convert her into an ironclad. Accordingly, a 170-foot shed with angled sides of 45 degrees was constructed on her cut-down hull. The angled walls were of pine two feet in thickness covered by four inches of plate iron. As she neared completion in February 1862, the ship measured 257 feet in length and 57 feet in beam, drew 23 feet of water, had six smoothbore Dahlgrens and two rifled guns broadside and two rifled guns fore and aft. She could make six knots. Captain Franklin Buchanan, founder of the Naval Academy and an experienced officer, was given command of the rechristened CSS *Virginia* and drew a crew from army and navy ranks. The new ironclad had only to be tried in combat.

Early on the morning of 8 March 1862, the *Virginia* made her way down the Elizabeth River from Gosport and entered Hampton Roads. On blockade duty there were numerous Union vessels: the 50-gun frigate *Congress*, the 50-gun *St Lawrence* and the 24-gun sloop *Cumberland*, backed up by the steam frigates *Roanoke* and *Minnesota*, each of 46 guns. As the *Virginia* moved into range by early afternoon, the Union vessels found that their broadsides only bounced off the Confederate ironclad, and the land batteries along the shore from Newport News Point to Hampton, plus the guns of Fort Monroe and Fort Wool nearby, could do no better. The *Virginia* moved in, broadsided the wooden *Congress* and *Cumberland*, rammed the hapless *Cumberland* and slowly destroyed the resisting Union vessels under merciless fire. The *Roanoke* and *St Lawrence* never got into position, and the *Minnesota* was never in range. Finally the lowering tide forced the victorious ironclad back to base to continue the one-sided fight the next day. But as the sun rose the next day over Hampton Roads, a new combatant had entered the field of battle on the Union side. The second phase of the Battle of Hampton Roads was about to begin.

Top: **The *Monitor* in July 1862 showing the dented turret from the battle with *Merrimac*.**
Above: **Midships section through the *Monitor*'s twin turret showing the raft construction.**

Sitting under the protective guns of Fort Monroe on that clear Sunday morning of 9 March 1862 was the tiny *Monitor*. Knowing of the Confederate plans for the *Merrimac* from espionage reports and even from Southern newspaper accounts, the Federal Government had belatedly begun work on its own iron vessel. John Ericsson drew the plans as building went along in the Greenspoint shipyard on Long Island, and the diminutive vessel was completed in only 100 days. It was 172 feet in length and 41 feet in beam, drawing only 10 feet of water. On its flat deck almost at water's edge was a revolving turret nine feet high and twenty feet in diameter, with openings for two retractable 11-inch Dahlgrens. Steam powered, the small iron vessel left New York City on 6 March under the command of Captain John L Worden with a crew of 58 men. Although it nearly foundered in heavy seas on its trip south, the *Monitor* arrived at dusk on 8 March as the day's battle was ending, and Captain Worden was ordered to engage the *Virginia* the next day if she appeared.

As the two ironclad vessels approached one another that mild Sunday morning to begin the battle, they soon found that neither could gain the advantage. The *Monitor* was difficult to hit, and when a shot did strike her turret it just bounced off. Likewise, the *Virginia* suffered no damage as shots merely glanced off her sloping sides. After a prolonged exchange of fire, each tried to ram the other, but Worden's *Monitor* missed the *Virginia*'s vulnerable propellers, and the *Virginia* (now under Lieutenant Catesby ap Roger Jones, replacing Captain Buchanan who had been wounded the day before) rammed the *Monitor* only to see her slip out from underneath her thrusts. Finally both vessels withdrew, each claiming victory. The *Virginia* had clearly won the battle on 8 March, but the battle of 9 March was at best a draw. Nevertheless, the *Monitor* had prevented the destruction of the remainder of the blockading fleet and her presence precluded any chance of the Confederates moving up Chesapeake Bay. She must be credited with a strategic victory despite the tactical draw.

In the weeks that followed, the *Monitor* refused to be drawn into a second round with the *Virginia* and kept her station under the guns of Fort Monroe as guardian of the Chesapeake. The *Virginia*, on the other hand, defended the James River and the water approaches to Richmond until Union forces descended on Norfolk as part of the Peninsula Campaign. To prevent her capture, she was scuttled in the lower James on 11 May 1862, never to be recovered. At the end of the year the

Above: **The unsuccessful Union attack on Fort Sumter, 7 April 1863. Five ships were put out of action including the flagship *Keokuk*.**
Below: **S F du Pont, the previously highly successful commander of the South Atlantic blockading squadron, was relieved after the failure at Fort Sumter.**

Above: Officers of the USS *Kearsarge* photographed at Cherbourg in June 1864. Captain Winslow is third from left.
Left: One of the *Kearsarge*'s 11-inch Dahlgren smooth-bore guns seen on the same occasion as the picture above.
Below: Ship's crew of the USS *Choctaw*.

Monitor foundered in a storm off Cape Hatteras as she was being towed to Charleston by the steamer *Rhode Island* to take part in operations there. (She has recently been discovered and efforts are being made to preserve her as an underwater historical site if she cannot be rescued from her watery grave.)

Although both the vessels that had broken new ground at the Battle of Hampton Roads were lost soon thereafter, they played a major role in the evolution of modern navies. They introduced into naval architecture the revolving turret, protective armor plate and the protective deck, rifled guns and all-heavy-gun vessels. They proved that while iron might not be able to beat iron, iron could clearly beat wood in naval warship construction. Ironclads went on to play a significant role in naval construction for the duration of the war and, in the long run, iron (and then steel) vessels would replace the 'wooden walls' of the world's traditional navies. Iron plus steam would spell the eventual end of the old sailing navy. Technology was the ultimate winner of the Battle of Hampton Roads.

Fall of the Southern Ports

Meanwhile Northern attempts to close Southern ports by capture and blockade continued apace. Even as the ironclads were dueling in Virginia waters, a Union fleet was assembling off New Orleans, preparing to capture that vital Southern port at the mouth of the Mississippi. It was built around Flag Officer David G Farragut's flagship, the screw sloop USS *Hartford*. Located at the mouth of the river were Forts St Philip and Jackson, 90 miles south of New Orleans. These would have to be taken first. When mortar bombard-

ments of the forts failed to reduce them, Farragut determined to run by them at night, leaving them isolated and vulnerable. Accordingly, after two gunboats had broken a boom of logs and chains stretched across the river, Farragut made his move past the forts on the night of 24 April 1862. His large ships having been dragged over the mud bars at the mouth of the river, the squadron proceeded in line-ahead fashion to run the gauntlet of Confederate guns. The 17 Union naval vessels had their precious steam engines protected against shot with hay and planking, and the ships suffered no appreciable damage. Since army troops had meanwhile been transported via the bayous to a point five miles above the forts, Forts St Philip and Jackson were besieged and neutralized. New Orleans itself was then easily taken by 1 May, when the troops of General Benjamin F Butler garrisoned the town. Believing that defense of New Orleans was unnecessary, since Union forces could not pass the forts, Richmond had made no further provisions for defending the most important port of the Confederacy.

The second great Gulf port city, Mobile, Alabama, fell to the Union Navy in August 1864. Again the naval commander was David Farragut. In his flotilla were four ironclads of the *Monitor* type and 14 wooden vessels. Mobile Bay was guarded by the Confederate ironclad *Tennessee*, three wooden paddlesteamers and 180 'torpedoes,' or floating kegs filled with gunpowder. Forts Morgan and Gaines also guarded the bay.

On 5 August 1864 Farragut, standing high in the rigging of the *Hartford* to direct the battle, ordered his ships into action to force their way into the bay. When the steam sloop *Brooklyn* came to a halt on seeing the floating mines, Farragut called out, 'Damn the torpedoes. Go ahead!' and the invading force pressed on. Although the ironclad *Tecumseh* was destroyed by one of the mines, the other vessels proceeded and within three hours had passed the forts and were anchored in Mobile Bay. The Confederate ironclad *Tennessee*, captained by Franklin Buchanan, who had commanded the *Virginia* on the first day of the Battle of Hampton Roads, approached to do battle. It was disabled after an hour of fierce fighting, and Union control of the bay was complete. By 23 August the forts had been bombed into submission by Union warships and land batteries, and Mobile was taken out of the war.

Savannah fell to a combined Union naval-army force three months later. The joint expedition was headed by General William T Sherman and Admiral John A Dahlgren. When Sherman's forces captured Fort McAllister guarding the sea approaches to the city on 13 December 1864, it was obvious that Savannah would fall to the Union forces. Complete surrender of the Georgia port city was attained by Christmas. Even while the siege of Savannah was taking place to the south, joint army-navy operations had begun against Wilmington, North Carolina. Wilmington was very important to both sides because of its direct railroad connection

Above: **Rear Admiral David Glasgow Farragut photographed in 1863.**

with Richmond. Leading the naval squadron was the fiery Admiral David Dixon Porter. In December an initial land attack on Fort Fisher guarding the harbor failed, because the army could not make good its attacks on the doughty fortress; the next month Porter carried out an intense three-day bombardment of the fort followed by a two-pronged land attack. While the 2000 Federal sailors and marines on the east side of the island failed to breach the walls and fled in panic, the action there drew most of the defenders to that side of the fortress, allowing the soldiers to breach the west wall and compel surrender. Wilmington was finished as a Southern port, leaving only Charleston open for the Confederate cause.

By February 1865 it was Charleston's turn to fall under the intense pressure of Union Army-Navy power (an aborted attempt had been made to take the city by the navy alone in 1863). After a sustained naval-battery bombardment against Fort Moultrie on Sullivan's Island on 17 February 1865, landing parties found it deserted. Land operations by the army were gradually successful, and the Union troops first broached the defensive lines around the city and then took Fort Johnson and

Above: **The Union fleet forges on relentlessly during the Battle of Mobile Bay.**

finally Fort Sumter. The fall of this fortress where hostilities had begun four bloody years before was more than symbolic. When Charleston fell, the South had lost its last useful port. It was sealed off completely from the sea and from outside help. Successful Union Army offenses in Virginia during these months, and General Sherman's slashing march to the sea, ensured that the south could not resist much longer. The Anaconda Plan and the piecemealing of the South by Union armies had worked.

Ironclads on the Western Waters, 1861–62

In the meantime the Union armies' successes on the battlefield, which ultimately brought the Confederates to their knees in 1865, had been aided in many ways by naval power. The Mississippi River and its major tributaries were crucial waterways both to Southern resistance and to Northern offensive operations. Lincoln called the Mississippi 'the backbone of the Rebellion' and was determined to seize it. Accordingly, Union strategy on the inland waters called for working down the river from Cincinnati and Cairo, Illinois, and up the river from the Gulf of Mexico to snap the backbone of the South.

A squadron under Flag Officer Andrew Foote was assembled in November 1861 at Cairo—but under the authority of the War Department, not the navy, since this was to be a land operation and the ships of the squadron were to assist the army. It consisted originally of eight new ironclad gunboats 175 feet in length and drawing only six feet of water for riverine use. Mounting 13 guns, and with bows, machinery and paddlewheels protected by two-and-a-half-inch iron plating, the gunboats, named for cities along the Ohio and Mississippi Rivers, were expected to play a vital role in assisting the Union armies as they penetrated the South.

The first use of gunboats to support the Northern armies came at Forts Henry and Donelson, only twelve miles apart on the Tennessee and Cumberland Rivers. Each had been designed to halt penetration upstream into Tennessee and the middle South. In January 1862 General Henry W Halleck, in command in the West, ordered Flag Officer Foote to attack Fort Henry on the Tennessee with his gunboats while General Ulysses S Grant and his troops cut it off from the rear. The joint attack took place on 6 February and was successful, but the Confederate commander had meanwhile removed his troops to Fort Donelson. Nevertheless, the Union gunboats chased the protecting Confederate gunboats all the way up the Tennessee to Florence, Alabama, capturing three steamers in the process and forcing the Confederates to burn six more. The combined army-navy attack on Fort Donelson on the Cumberland eight days later was also successful, the Confederates being forced to surrender over 12,000 troops, but Halleck would not permit Foote's gunboats to proceed upriver against Nashville. Consequently, the Union lost a splendid opportunity to seize that unprotected vital rail center. When Halleck changed his mind two days later, Foote was back in Cairo and the chance to take Nashville was gone. Nevertheless, the geographic heart of the South had been penetrated, and the land war switched to its rivers for the next year.

Meanwhile, joint army-navy operations continued on the Mississippi. In March 1862 naval gunboats played a key role in taking Island Number 10 near the Kentucky-Tennessee border. The South had made this tenth island on the Mississippi below the mouth of the Ohio a virtually impregnable bastion of defense. Located on the upper part of a double hairpin turn, the island had a low fortress with five artillery batteries. This fortress was supported by five batteries on the Tennessee side of the river plus a floating battery. Well dug in, the Confederates resisted for two weeks and thereby kept General John Pope's Union Army on the west side of the river. Finally, in early April 1862, two of Foote's gunboats, the *Carondelet* and the *Pittsburg*, ran the gauntlet through the Confederate batteries, got behind the fortress and silenced the Southern guns, allowing Pope to cross with his troops. The capture of Island Number 10, one of the strongest Confederate fortifications, took place at the same time the Federals beat off a spirited counterattack at Shiloh, Tennessee, with the help of two wooden steamers

Above: **The twin-turret monitor USS** ***Monadnock.***
Right: **Rear Admiral David Porter, highly successful commander of the Union Mississippi Squadron in the Vicksburg campaign.**

and began a move toward the vital rail center at Corinth, Mississippi. The water-land road to gaining the Mississippi and adjoining lands to the east was opening, but many months of hard warfare remained before the river and her eastern shore-lands fell to Union forces.

Two months later the Union Army-Navy forces took Fort Pillow, halfway between Island Number 10 and Memphis, but only after a fierce gunboat ram attack by the Confederates on the Union gunboat squadron had been beaten off and after the Confederates had abandoned the site—Union forces had taken Corinth, making the fort untenable. The Union forces then moved downriver to Memphis.

On 4 June 1862 one of the most spectacular battles of the river war took place before the city. The Union ironclads were now under the command of Flag Officer Charles Davis (Foote had been wounded at Fort Donelson and was relieved of command, never to return to action). They were aided by an Army Ram Fleet under Colonel Charles Ellet. The Ram Fleet consisted of steamboats converted to ramming vessels, with the ram running from bow to stern for greater strength. In the colorful battle before the enthralled citizens of Memphis, the Confederate gunboat fleet lost three vessels by fire or ramming. The remaining gunboats fled downriver. The defenseless city was forced to surrender, and Union gunboats controlled the Mississippi except for the great citadel at Vicksburg, Mississippi. Union naval vessels controlled the upper and middle river and convoyed steamers with troops and supplies along its waters. They also held New Orleans and the lower Mississippi, but as long as Vicksburg was in Confederate hands the South was not cut in two and could continue to resist Northern encroachments on its territories.

Vicksburg and Victory

Vicksburg was located on a high bluff on the eastern side of the Mississippi, just below a hairpin turn. With the winding, entangling Yazoo to the north and a mass of impenetrable bayou rivers to the west, it was a source of unending frustration for Grant, his generals and his troops. Beginning in November 1862, the Union

Below: **The wooden hull of an ironclad is burned on the stocks as the Confederates abandon Savannah, 21 December 1864.**

Above: **The USS *Malvern*, flagship of the North Atlantic blockading squadron, in 1865.**

forces tried three times to cut channels through the watery bayous across the river to get south of the city. Each time they failed. One attempt by Union gunboats to sail down the swollen Yazoo to the solid ground north of Vicksburg was also beaten back. Finally, Grant decided to march his men along the western shore of the river to well below Vicksburg, but this meant that the Federal gunboats would have to run the fierce barrage of Confederate batteries high above them to get below the city and protect the troops as they crossed back to the eastern shores.

The daring maneuver, led by Rear Admiral David Dixon Porter, was carried out on the night of 16 April 1863. A flotilla of nine gunboats, one ram and three steam transports, with coal barges lashed to their sides and wet hay stacked around their boilers, made the dangerous run past the guns of Vicksburg. Despite the hail of artillery raining down upon them, the squadron steamed through, losing only one steamer in the process. On 22 April the maneuver was repeated, this time with six steamers loaded with supplies, and again only one vessel was lost. These courageous moves allowed Grant to land south of Vicksburg and then to put it under siege, after taking the capital city of Jackson to the east and beating off the Confederates at Champion's Hill as the Union forces moved back west. The merciless siege placed both the Confederate troops of General John Pemberton and the civilian population under prolonged and relentless artillery fire from army units on land and naval units below the city. Vicksburg finally fell on 4 July 1863—one day after the great Union victory at Gettysburg, Pennsylvania—with 31,000 men, 172 cannons and 60,000 rifles surrendered to the Union forces. Four days later Port Hudson, south of Vicksburg, also fell, and Abraham Lincoln proclaimed that 'The Father of Waters goes again unvexed to the sea.'

General Grant gave full credit to the naval forces for his incredible victory. The Mississippi River was now in Union hands. The South had been cut in two. Its western states would gradually die in isolation,

Below: **The Confederate blockade runner *Lord Clyde* was captured and renamed first USS *Advance* and later USS *Frolic*.**

Above: **USS *Camanche* ready for launch at San Francisco in November 1864.**

their precious men and supplies being denied to the Confederate cause. Union land forces could now move to sunder the remaining Southern states, while bringing their crushing weight down upon General Robert E Lee's Army of the Potomac. This would take almost two years, but the Confederate foundation had been broken. The dual Union strategy of blockading the Confederate coastline and isolating the embattled Southern states was working ever more effectively. It was now only a matter of time. The end came in April 1865 when General Lee, after leading the Southern forces in splendid resistance to the advancing armies of U S Grant in the east, surrendered at Appomattox Court House in Virginia. The Civil War was over.

The US Navy had amassed a sterling record during the four-year conflict. Expanding its number of vessels to 671, its officer corps to 9000 men and its enlisted ranks to 51,000, it had captured or destroyed over 1500 Southern vessels of all types. It had co-operated with the massive Northern land armies on both the seacoasts and the inland waters, and it had clamped an effective blockade on the South that had cut her off from outside help and left her to her own inadequate resources. In the process, the Navy had learned valuable lessons: that unprotected wooden vessels were now obsolete against ironclads, that passive defense of harbors was completely inadequate in modern warfare, that a successful blockade could be imposed only by clear command of the seas, that steam was beginning its conquest over sail power and that modern navies could no longer be created in a short time given the demands of modern technology. The Civil War triumphs of the US Navy had catapulted her into becoming a major national defense force. The question was whether or not she could maintain that eminence in the changed conditions in the aftermath of the war.

Below: The battlecruiser *Guam* at sea toward the end of World War II.

A NAVAL POWER BORN TO GLORY

THE NATION BUILDS A NAVY

In 1865, at the end of the Civil War, the US Navy had over 700 ships in its inventory, including 65 ironclads; by 1880 it had only 48 capable of firing a gun and stood twelfth in the world in naval power—behind Chile and China. The US Navy had been effectively scuttled in fifteen years.

The American people decided after Appomattox that a sizable navy was simply too expensive. The nation was deeply in debt due to the war and was embroiled in the massive problems of reconstructing the South. These matters—plus labor strife, farmer agitation and political corruption—were perceived as more important than foreign affairs, and, besides, any potential enemies were 3000 miles across the ocean. Peace seemed inevitable, or at least there were no war clouds on the horizon. If peace was assured and money was tight, the solution was obvious: get rid of 'useless' warships. A navy could always be re-created quickly if the need arose, they argued, overlooking the fact that modern naval and weapon technology had made such ideas obsolete.

The Navy's 'Dark Ages'

Gideon Welles continued as navy secretary and presided over the dismantling of the fleet. A total of 400 ships of the blockading fleet had been broken up or sold off within nine months of the end of the fighting. The mighty ironclads were moored and left to rot, while other river craft were disposed of. By the time Welles left office in 1869, only 52 warships were still in commission. And Adolph E Borie and George M Robeson, President Grant's appointees as navy secretaries, left the job of running the service largely to Vice-Admiral David Dixon Porter, who turned his considerable power against existing research and development programs. Monitors (the low-freeboard turreted gunships developed during the war on the design of Ericsson's *Monitor*) and sailing cruisers would serve the navy well. Modern steam-powered vessels would not, as symbolized by the dismissal of chief engineer Benjamin F Isherwood, the father of the Civil War steam navy, in 1869.

This resistance to steam power on the part of the flag admirals in the navy's 'dark ages' (1865 to 1882) is often criticized as an example of pure reactionism, yet it is understandable in view of the times and their current state of technology. For example, the steam-powered sloop of war USS *Wampanoag* was an Isherwood-created vessel that set a world steam speed record of 17.7 knots in 1868. But it was rejected for naval use nonetheless by a special naval board on steam machinery under Rear Admiral Louis Goldsborough in 1869, because it was a coal burner. Soon thereafter it was removed from the active list and sold.

But this action and other examples of the rejection of steam power did not represent mere stupidity or crass defense of a sailing navy on the part of the admirals. Whatever their attachments to a sailing navy, the admirals were also aware that in the case of the *Wampanoag* her steam plant constituted one-third of her total weight, took up almost half her total length below decks and burned over six tons of coal per

hour at top speed. The admirals knew that while commercial vessels could afford to devote a great amount of weight and space to machinery and coal, a fighting ship needed that valuable space for armament and ammunition, to say nothing of crew's quarters, ship's stores and other requirements. Steam power and greater speed could be a boon to a commercial vessel, but might well leave a ship of war sadly deficient in its primary function. Furthermore, the naval decision-makers during this period worried about the fact that spare parts for steam machinery could not be found in most areas of the world in which the ship might sail and could not be fabricated upon the ships themselves. And what of coal supply? Coal stations were not available on the ocean lanes of the world at this time, nor would they be for a number of years. And coal was expensive, an important consideration in times of declining budgets approved by Congress. Furthermore, naval and steam engineering was far from an exact science in these years, and many 'experts' testified that steam had many shortcomings.

Added to these technical and professional factors was the overriding fact that the American people saw little need for any sizable navy, much less a more expensive steam navy, and this attitude was reflected by their representatives in Washington. Domestic problems, expansion to the West and economic hard times took priority over naval concerns in the minds of the people. Only when American economic expansion led to worldwide investments and interests would the nation awaken to its global destiny and support a strong navy again as a necessary means of achieving that destiny. Thus, while Europe's navies turned toward iron, steel, steam and high-technology ordnance, the American Navy stuck mainly to wood, sail and existing gunnery to carry out its limited functions and awaited new leadership backed by new attitudes that would pull it out of the doldrums.

Showing the Flag and Other Duties

During this period of quiescence, however, the now-reduced navy was busy 'showing the flag' and carrying out other important national duties in all parts of the world. In 1866 the monitors built for Civil War service were sent on extended cruises to show the flag. The *Miantonomah* successfully crossed the Atlantic to visit various European ports, ending up in Russia where an attempt was made to sell her to Czar Alexander II for his imperial fleet. The *Monadnock*, after rounding Cape Horn and visiting a number of South American ports, joined the Asiatic fleet. In 1871 Rear Admiral John Rodgers took the Asiatic fleet into 'forbidden' Korean waters to investigate the disappearance of American merchant crews and to attempt to make a treaty of friendship. His efforts came to nothing, however, as the Koreans fired on his squadron while he was achored in the Salee River near Seoul. Rodgers answered with a 600-man landing party of marines and sailors who attacked the offending forts. In this warlike atmosphere, negotiations were impossible (and a typhoon was approaching), so Rodgers sailed away. Only in 1881, a decade later, was a trade treaty agreed upon and the safety of American crews assured when Commodore Robert W Shufelt returned to the 'Hermit Kingdom.'

The only important warlike action taken by the Navy occurred in 1873–74 in what has come to be known as the '*Virginius*

Above: Old salts yarning aboard the *Enterprise circa* 1887.

Left: The USS *Jeannette* sinking after being crushed in the Arctic Ice in June 1881.
Right: Officers of the USS *Constellation* pose with welcoming officials during a visit to Cork, Ireland, in 1880.

Right: **Negotiations during the Korean Expedition in 1871. F Low, minister to China (right).**
Bottom: **Boats from the USS *Tennessee* take a landing party ashore at Panama in April 1885 to protect American property following disturbances.**

affair.' The *Virginius* was an American vessel flying the American flag that was engaged in carrying 'filibustering' mercenaries into Cuba to fight the Spanish authorities there. Spotted by a Spanish cruiser, the *Tornado*, in Cuban waters, the *Virginius* fled with the Spanish vessel in hot pursuit, only to be captured off Jamaica. The Spanish authorities in Santiago, rightly suspecting that the mercenaries had been on their way to Cuba to aid the revolutionaries and that the ship was actually Cuban-owned with false papers, proceeded to have the captain, two members of the crew and 50 passengers (30 of whom were probably Americans) tried and then executed by a firing squad. As the nation reacted in rage to this 'dishonor to the flag,' the navy was ordered to assemble off Key West to fight if necessary—although the mission was virtually impossible, since its ships were armed with smoothbore cannon good only in a close fight and their top speed was only 4.5 knots. The situation was calmed only when the commander of the USS *Wyoming* left Colon in Panama and sailed into Santiago to protest the Spanish Government's actions. Although he took this action strictly on his own initiative, the *Wyoming* was soon backed up by the *Juniata* and the *Kansas*. This ended the threat of more executions and quieted events sufficiently so that diplomacy could take over. The Spanish Government paid an indemnity, even though it proved the origin and intent of the ship and passengers. The affair was ended—to the navy's credit—and war talk faded.

Providing a lighter touch during these years was the saga of the gunboat *Wateree*. While anchored in the harbor at Arica, Peru, in 1868, the vessel found herself sitting on the harbor floor as a giant tidal wave was preceded by a rush of all the water out of the harbor. Looking up from their embarrassing position, the crew of the *Wateree* was terrified to see a giant wall of green water rushing toward them. The tidal wave picked up the small vessel and deposited it high and dry on land 47

Above: **Band from the North Atlantic Squadron, Camp Osceola, near Pensacola, April 1888.**

feet above the harbor. Although the crew successfully defended the gunboat against attack by local Indians, they were unsuccessful in their attempts to launch her. The enterprising captain, therefore, gave up and sold the *Wateree* to a local businessman who converted the vessel into a hotel while the crew found a way home.

On a weightier note, the navy attempted serious negotiations during this period to 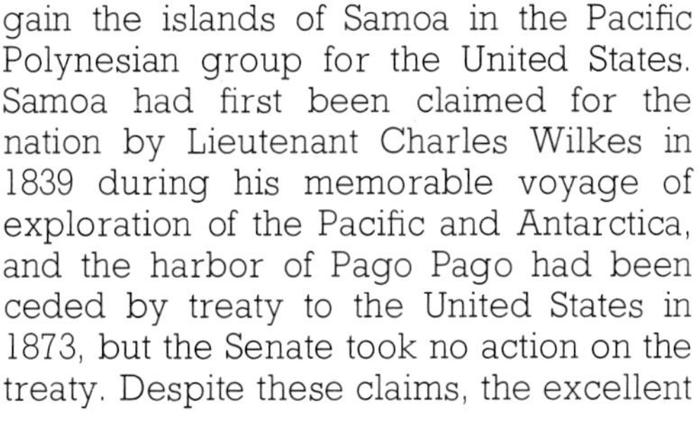 gain the islands of Samoa in the Pacific Polynesian group for the United States. Samoa had first been claimed for the nation by Lieutenant Charles Wilkes in 1839 during his memorable voyage of exploration of the Pacific and Antarctica, and the harbor of Pago Pago had been ceded by treaty to the United States in 1873, but the Senate took no action on the treaty. Despite these claims, the excellent harbor was also coveted by the British and the Germans, and all three powers claimed sovereignty and had commercial treaties with the local rulers, the United States gaining hers in 1878. By the late 1880s the disputed ownership had resulted in American, British and German warships being sent to Samoa to bolster their nations' claims. In March 1889 a hurricane struck the islands and the anchorage at Apia, wrecking three German ships and three American cruisers. Great as the loss was, naval presence in Samoa assured American rights; when an agreement was forthcoming later in the year and a joint protectorate was set up over the islands, the nation received valuable Pago Pago and surrounding territories as a coaling station on the sea lane to Australia and later developed it into an important naval base. Thus a naval-diplomatic move in the 1870s bore rich fruit in the decades that followed.

Naval Renaissance

By the early 1880s, certain fundamental economic and perceptual changes mandated a more favorable political climate that created a 'New Navy.' By this time the American economy was growing to full industrial and commercial maturity. American businessmen, solidly backed by the public, were looking beyond the seas for new markets and new sources of foodstuffs and raw materials. They saw no reason why the dynamic American economic expansion should stop at the water's edge. New markets in new lands would lead to greater prosperity and prestige. And, they were coming to realize, new and improved foreign trade meant that the nation needed a navy.

The first naval secretary to respond to

the new economic imperatives was William H Hunt, who served from 1881 to 1882. In his brief tenure, Hunt got things moving by creating a naval board under Admiral John Rodgers to consider the navy's needs and make recommendations on ship types and numbers. Although Congress cut the recommendation severely, it did authorize the construction of three steel cruisers (the *Atlanta*, *Boston* and *Chicago*) and a dispatch boat (the *Dolphin*) in 1883, the famous 'ABCDs' which constituted the first ships of the New Navy. Hunt's work was continued by William E Chandler, his successor, often called the 'Father of the New Navy' for his continued support of the ABCD construction and for fostering the establishment of the Naval War College on Coaster's Harbor Island in Newport, Rhode Island. The War College,

Left: **Officers' uniforms *circa* 1899. From left: Lt JG, Lt and Capt Marines, Chief Engineer, Rear Adm, Commander and Surgeon.**
Below: **USS *Chicago* seen during the New York Naval Review 1889.**

Right: **Enlisted men's uniforms including steward (left) and master at arms, with rifle.**

under Rear Admiral Stephen B Luce, was the beginning of an intellectual renaissance in naval circles, not only because it attracted aspiring officers to learn naval strategy, tactics and logistics in a systematic and demanding environment, but also because Luce brought Captain Alfred Thayer Mahan to the staff.

Mahan, whose father, Major Dennis Hart Mahan, was long a dominant figure in the classrooms of the United States Military Academy at West Point, displayed brilliant insights into naval affairs. He tied them to theories of national power and greatness in his lectures on sea power and history developed over the years at Newport. These ideas were eventually brought to public attention in 1890 with the publication of Mahan's epic *The Influence of Sea Power upon History, 1660–1782*, a book which demonstrated historically his belief that a nation could become great and maintain her strength only if she had sea power to expand and protect her vital economic interests. Mahan's words were tantamount to Holy Writ to the students who sat before him. He influenced not only generations of naval and civilian leaders in the United States, but also military and political leaders of all the major nations. In creating the Naval War College and placing it under Admiral Luce, Secretary Chandler had built more than he ever dreamed.

Chandler's successor, William C Whitney, who served from 1885 to 1889, extended Chandler's work by authorizing 30 ships superior in design, armament, ordnance and speed to any that had preceded them. Included were the two heavy-armored cruisers (or second-class battleships) *Maine* and *Texas* authorized in 1886. Each displaced 6000 tons. Another ship,

Right: **(L to R)** ***Amphitrite*, *Puritan*, *Montgomery*** **and** ***Ericsson*** **in 1893.**
Below: **The USS** ***Palos*** **tows landing barges during the Korean Expedition, 10 June 1871.**

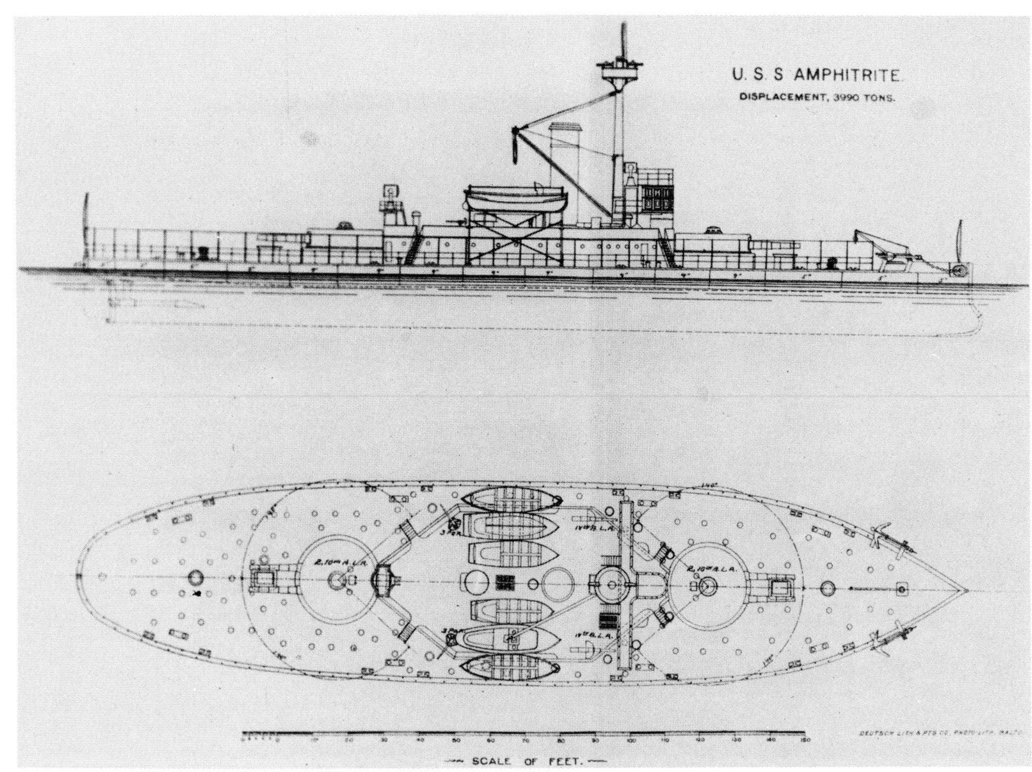

Above: **Plans of the *Amphitrite*, already obsolete when she came into service in the early 1890s.**

the cruiser *Charleston*, authorized in 1885, was the first American naval vessel to sport no sails. Whitney's work, in turn, was extended by Benjamin F Tracy, 1889–93, who was a devotee of Mahan and believed with him that the nation's shores could best be defended by creating a force of capital ships to meet any enemy far at sea. These mighty vessels could also protect American commerce on the sea lanes of the world. To Tracy, this meant armored battleships to destroy enemy fleets and carry the fight to their shores. Even with the help of influential friends in both political parties, Tracy was unable to build two great fleets, as he had hoped (for the Atlantic and the Pacific). But he did gain Congressional authorization for three 10,000-ton armored 'coastal battleships,' the *Oregon*, *Indiana* and *Massachusetts*, followed by the larger and more heavily gunned 11,400-ton *Iowa*. Tracy also obtained authorization for three armored cruisers of 7000 to 9000 tons.

Although the Panic of 1893 temporarily wreaked havoc on naval expansion, Hilary A Herbert, naval secretary from 1893 to 1897, continued the push for an even larger navy. In 1895 Congress authorized the construction of two *Kearsarge*-class battleships of 11,500 tons (the *Kearsarge* and the *Kentucky*) and the following year authorized the building of three more battleships of the *Illinois* class (the *Illinois*, the *Alabama* and the *Wisconsin*). Thus through good times and bad, under Democratic and Republican Administrations, the new navy continued to grow. By the mid-1890s the nation had awakened to its economic interests and saw the Navy as a vital instrument in extending itself upward and outward into the affairs of the world. No longer did European nations have a monopoly on steel-hulled, heavily armored, speedy steam vessels with breech-loading rifled guns and more efficient powders. The United States had a ranking navy superior to most, and looked for the day it would stand equal to Britain's great Royal Navy. Farm boys and city lads left their farms, small towns and great cities to 'join up' and be part of America's expanding naval presence. Shipyards buzzed with the work of creating the behemoths of the seas and their smaller companion vessels that carried American colors to the four corners of the globe. America had 'navy fever' and a pride in her new-found status.

War with Spain

The new navy would get the chance to prove its mettle in the Spanish-American war of 1898. Trouble had long been brewing on the island of Cuba in the Caribbean. For decades the Cubans had been actively resisting their Spanish overlords. Cuba and Puerto Rico were the last New World possessions of the once-great Spanish Empire, an empire that had been steadily slipping from the control of the mother country as one colony after another rose in revolution, beginning in the 1820s. Spain was as determined to retain Cuba as the Cuban people were to gain their independence. But to gain their freedom against a stronger mother country, Cuba needed help, a 'big brother' to equal or surpass Spanish strength. That friend could be the nearby United States, which had declared its right to oversee Latin American affairs as early as 1823 in the Monroe Doctrine. The trick for the Cuban revolutionaries was to get the Americans interested, then involved, in their cause.

This they attempted to do by operating a propaganda headquarters out of New York City where they sold 'Cuban bonds' and generally labored hard to keep the American public aware of the troubles in their homeland. They were aided by the stringent measures that Spanish authorities inflicted on the Cuban people. These were loudly trumpeted by the American newspapers, as they tried to surpass one another in sensationalistic stories of Spanish atrocities. The Spanish military commander in Cuba, General Valeriano Weyler, became well known in American homes under such unfortunate names as 'Butcher Weyler,' 'the human hyena' and 'the mad dog of Spain.'

President Grover Cleveland resisted public pressure and Congressional attempts to get the nation involved in the Cuban revolution, although he warned

Right: **Admiral George Dewey, whose victory at Manila Bay was achieved at the cost of only eight American wounded.**
Below: **The wreck of the *Maine*.**

the Spanish Government that the United States could not tolerate such disturbing events so close to its shores. His successor, William McKinley, a Republican, followed the same policy of avoiding war, but was soon overcome by events. On 9 February 1898 a letter was released to the American press by the Cuban revolutionary 'junta' operating in the United States. Written by Dupey de Lome, the Spanish Minister in Washington, to an editor friend in Cuba, it had been stolen from the post office in Havana and turned over to the junta. The letter contained many slurs against President McKinley and immediately caused a great public outcry, which did not subside even when de Lome was immediately recalled.

One week later, on 15 February 1898, with public opinion still wrathful over the de Lome letter, the USS *Maine*, reclassified as a second-class battleship after launching, was rocked by a terrific explosion while anchored in the harbor at Havana. Some 260 of the 350 men aboard were killed. Captain Charles Sigsbee of the *Maine* stated that the explosion could have been internal or external and urged caution until a complete investigation could be launched. A Spanish board of inquiry determined that from the bent hull plating it was clear that the explosion had been internal. An American naval board of inquiry concluded that the cause of the explosion was probably external, specifically a 'submarine mine' clandestinely fastened to the hull of the vessel, but they could not determine who might have done the deed. This made little difference to the American public, since they soon became convinced from American newspaper accounts that the Spanish were the culprits. The cry 'Remember the *Maine*!' rumbled across the country and into the halls of Congress.

Still William McKinley refused to panic or to urge war, because Spain was willing to make some reforms in Cuba. But finally he collapsed under the frenzied call for war and on 9 April 1898, 'in the name of humanity,' recommended American intervention in the troubled situation. Congress was only too happy to comply and passed a resolution declaring Cuba to be free (but with an amendment by Senator Henry Teller that the United States had no intention of taking Cuba as its own) and authorizing the Commander in Chief to use the armed forces to make Cuba's freedom a reality. When the navy immediately set up a blockade around the island, Spain declared war on the United States; the United States reciprocated the next day, 25 April 1898. The Spanish-American War, the 'splendid little war,' was on.

Having been allocated $30 million by Congress in the crisis, the navy began construction on three battleships plus numerous torpedo boats and torpedo boat destroyers. In short order it also purchased or chartered 50 steamers to be used as transports (about one-half were of foreign registry, a sad commentary on the state of the US merchant marine) and purchased or chartered a number of fast liners to be armed and converted into scouts and auxiliary cruisers. Crewing for the expanding navy was no problem, as naval militia from various states soon stepped forward.

Above: **Examining the wreck of the** ***Maine.***
Below: **The battleship** ***Oregon*** **rounding the Horn en route to join the fleet at Santiago.**

Above: **The action off Cardenas on 11 May 1898. L to R, the *Winslow*, *Hudson* and *Wilmington*.**

The initial steps taken by the navy were for defensive purposes. A 'flying squadron' was assembled in Hampton Roads under Commodore Winfield S Schley. Its job was to protect the East Coast from Spanish attack, since it was known that Spanish Admiral Pascual Cervera had left the Cape Verde Islands on 29 April although his destination was unknown. Fearing a bombardment of seaboard cities, many wealthy Americans sent their valuables inland for safety, and all along the coast cities demanded naval protection.

In the meantime, the North Atlantic Squadron under Rear Admiral William T Sampson assembled at Key West to intercept Cervera and begin action in the Caribbean waters as necessary. The Asiatic Squadron under Commodore George Dewey was stationed in Hong Kong and ready for action in the Far East, having been instructed as early as December by the assistant naval secretary—the bellicose and dynamic New York politician Theodore Roosevelt—to stand at combat readiness.

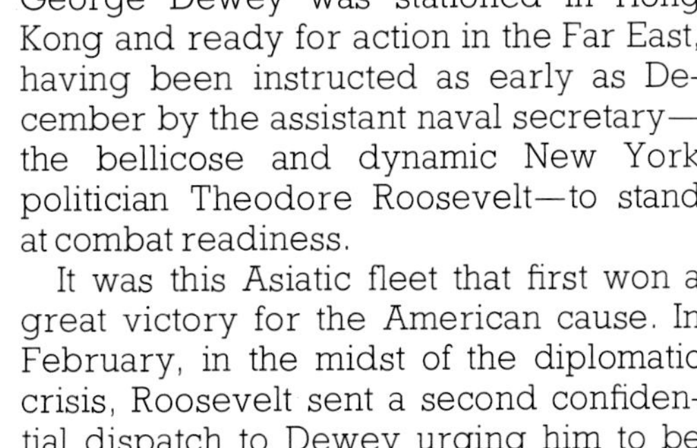

It was this Asiatic fleet that first won a great victory for the American cause. In February, in the midst of the diplomatic crisis, Roosevelt sent a second confidential dispatch to Dewey urging him to be prepared for immediate action. Thus when war was declared, and naval secretary John D Long ordered the fleet to the Philippines to destroy the Spanish fleet stationed in that faraway archipelago, Dewey was ready to go. On 27 April 1898 Dewey left his anchorage at Mirs Bay near Hong Kong and headed for the Philippine capital of Manila. His squadron consisted of four protected cruisers and three auxiliary vessels. Waiting to meet him was a weak Spanish contingent of only two protected cruisers and five obsolete smaller vessels. On the night of 30 April, Dewey's fleet passed the protecting Spanish batteries on Corregidor and El Fraile without incident and anchored in Manila Bay.

The next morning, 1 May, Admiral Dewey said to the captain of his flagship, the *Olympia*, 'You may fire when ready, Gridley,' and the Battle of Manila Bay began. The American fleet made five maneuvers past the anchored Spanish fleet, which did not have turreted guns and so could utilize only half its ordnance.

Below: **The bombardment of Matanzas on 27 April 1898 by the *New York*, *Cincinnati* and *Puritan*.**

Below: **The landing fleet lies offshore as men of the 71st Regiment reach the beach at Sibboney on 22 June 1898.**

Even at that, the greater range and accuracy of the American naval guns made the outcome a foregone conclusion. The order was given to cease fire to count ammunition and survey the Spanish fleet, and, as the smoke from the guns slowly lifted, the Americans were astonished to see that almost the whole Spanish fleet had been destroyed. Renewing the fray, Dewey's ships finished off the remainder of the Spanish fleet by 12:30 in the afternoon. The navy had scored a tremendous victory—admittedly against a weak enemy—and America had a new hero named George Dewey, quickly promoted to Acting Rear Admiral by President McKinley.

The Spanish were forced to surrender control of Manila Bay with the destruction of their fleet, but Dewey had sovereignty over the Spanish Philippines only within the range of his guns. Surrender of the capital and of the archipelago would have to wait for an occupying force, so Dewey gathered his squadron before Manila to impose a tight blockade on the Bay—and to keep other foreign powers like Germany out, so they could not make claim to the Philippines. Not until three months later did the US Army arrive and Manila surrender (only to lead to greater troubles, when the Filipino insurgents fighting the Spanish discovered that the Philippines would not be turned over to them). But it had been a memorable and dashing victory, and the navy enjoyed great esteem.

Within two weeks of this engagement in the Far East, reports reached the navy that Cervera's squadron was heading for the Caribbean. Despite the best efforts of Sampson's and Schley's squadrons, Cervera made it safely into the port of Santiago on the southern coast of Cuba. As he was soon discovered by Sampson and Schley and blockaded in the harbor at Santiago, a basic problem surfaced. Cervera could not come out of harbor, as the superior American naval force would destroy him, but the Americans could not get into the harbor to drive him out because of the long, narrow configuration of the harbor and shipping channel and the

Right: Destruction of the Spanish fleet at Manila Bay. At left the USS _Olympia_, _Baltimore_ and _Boston_.
Below: Wreck of the _Merrimac_ in the channel at Santiago.

Above: The American battleships prepare to engage in the Battle of Santiago.
Left: Dewey on his flagship at the outset of the Manila Bay engagement.

guns positioned on the hillsides to fire against any incoming force. So the navy blockaded Santiago Harbor and waited for the army to arrive and launch a ground attack against the city of Santiago, making Cervera's position untenable.

By mid-June the naval transports had brought General William R Shafter's 17,000 men to the southern coast of Cuba and disembarked them over the surf, the horses being slung over the side by cranes to swim ashore (many swam out to sea). If all went well with the land maneuvers, Cervera's fleet of four cruisers and two

Below: Battle of Santiago. The *Cristobal Colon* comes under fire from the *Oregon* and *Iowa* (left). *Texas* (right) is also engaged.

torpedo boat destroyers would soon be forced to flee—into the guns of the five American battleships, three armored cruisers and two protected cruisers steaming in a giant circle outside the harbor. In order to make their escape impossible, however, a daring plan was concocted. The collier *Merrimac* was to be deliberately sunk in the channel by naval constructor Lieutenant Richmond Pearson Hobson and a skeleton crew. Unfortunately, the *Merrimac* sank off the channel and Hobson and his men were captured, although the Spanish defenders treated them as heroes for their brave attempt.

With the American expeditionary force finally making its way around the city of Santiago, the Spanish military commander ordered Admiral Cervera to make a run for it—although how he would get out and where he would go was far from clear. On 3 July at 9:30 in the morning the Spanish fleet came steaming out and turned west. Although the American fleet had grave difficulty in getting into parallel position—a battleship and a cruiser almost collided in the thick smoke disgorged by the coal-fired warships—the Spanish fleet was soon under intense gunfire. By 1:30 in the afternoon the entire fleet had been either destroyed or beached, the hapless Spanish sailors being shot in the water by Cuban revolutionaries as they swam for shore. This pitched naval battle saw over 600 Spanish killed and another 1700 taken prisoner. American casualties amounted to one man killed and one wounded. It was a most one-sided victory.

Having little to do thereafter, the navy continued to blockade Santiago Harbor until the city surrendered on 17 July. Thereafter, they transported the army troops to Puerto Rico where they were joyfully received. Meanwhile, a fleet had been assembled in Spain and had sallied forth to retake Manila Bay, but when word arrived of Cervera's defeat and of American intentions to send a squadron to the coast of Spain, the fleet was recalled—having already passed through the Suez Canal—by the government. The war was effectively over in both the Philippines and the Caribbean. A peace protocol was signed between the governments of Spain and the United States on 12 August 1898. As later characterized by the American diplomat John Hay, it had been a 'splendid little war.'

Responsibilities Near and Far

What most Americans did not realize as the war came to an end with the Treaty of Paris (signed in November 1898 and approved by the Senate in February 1899) was that the United States had now become a Far Eastern power as well as the major Caribbean power. Despite some misgivings, the United States took the Philippines from Spain—fearing either internal convulsions or outside domination by some other power; it also took Guam. And during the course of the war, American reluctance to take Hawaii (seen as late as 1893 when a 'spontaneous' revolution aided by the marines of the USS *Boston* overthrew the native government and the revolutionists asked for recognition and annexation) had been overridden by the need for a secure coaling station: the islands had been annexed. Uninhabited Wake Island had been taken at the same time and Midway back in 1867; the United States now had a clear line—Hawaii, Midway, Wake, Guam—to the Philippines and the Far East. America was now a Pacific and Far Eastern power, with all this would entail in the decades to come down to the present day. At the same time, she had become dominant in the Caribbean by taking Puerto Rico and placing Cuba under US protection and guidance. None of this had been foreseen as the nation drifted toward war over atrocities against the Cuban people, but it was the new reality. America was no longer isolationist; its responsibilities were rapidly becoming worldwide.

Among other things, this meant that the US Navy had major commitments that followed the flag. The navy was now bigger than ever before, and its impressive victories at Manila Bay and Santiago had forged a special place for it in American affections. It was ready to come of age.

A mark of the navy's new status was that public opinion seemed to support 'a navy second to none but Britain's.' This 'Big Navy' sentiment was strengthened by the presence of Theodore Roosevelt in the White House after the assassination of William McKinley in 1901. Roosevelt was an avid disciple of Alfred Thayer Mahan, and pushed naval primacy as no president had ever done in peacetime through his speeches and appointments. Roosevelt also used the navy to promote his ideas of American dominance in the Caribbean, leading to frequent American intervention in that area.

American naval thinking had clearly abandoned the doctrine of a passive defensive posture plus commerce raiding. Manila and Santiago showed what could be done by taking the fight to the enemy.

American naval strategists and tacticians of the early twentieth century envisioned epic and decisive sea battles in which the stronger, faster and more heavily gunned fleet would emerge victorious. This view was shared by naval strategists worldwide and led to the building of vessels suitable for such climactic duels.

With the construction of the British *Dreadnought* (launched in 1906) all other battleships were rendered obsolescent. The *Dreadnought* was the first giant 'all-big-gun' ship. She was larger (17,900 tons), longer (490 feet), faster (21.5 knots) and more heavily armored (11-inch steel hull and turret coverage) than anything afloat

Below: Painting of the USS ***Iowa*** as she would have appeared in 1898 in a typical contemporary paint scheme of tan and light gray.

Scenes from the cruise of the Great White Fleet. *Above*, the *Georgia* (BB.15); *Below*, the fleet leaves Hampton Roads. *Right*, Roosevelt addresses the crew of the *Connecticut* on their return.

or building. All the navies of the world were forced to shift to dreadnought construction to match or supersede her. The United States was no exception. In addition to building battleships, the Navy retained its armored cruisers for scouting, commerce raiding and anti-torpedo duty with the fleets, and added destroyers, submarines and airplanes. The United States not only had a bigger navy by 1914—including 17 modern battleships built or building—it also had a better navy.

The US Navy was very active in the years 1898–1914, carrying out America's new commitments in the Far East and acting as one of Theodore Roosevelt's 'big sticks' in the Caribbean. Between 1899 and 1902 the navy, operating out of San Francisco, abetted military efforts to put down the Filipino insurgency against American control by support and blockading activities in that wartorn archipelago. In 1900 over 2500 naval personnel joined the international force which put down the nationalistic Boxer Rebellion in China against outside nations' interference in the affairs of that hapless country. In 1903 the Navy played a major role in obtaining the Panama Canal for the United States.

Many attempts had been made to build a canal somewhere across the Central American isthmus, but all had failed for one reason or another. The latest attempt had been made by the bankrupt French De Lesseps Company, which retained the right to build the canal. American interest in a canal intensified during the Spanish-American War when the *Oregon*'s 'dash' from Bremerton, Washington, to Key West, Florida, around Cape Horn took 25 days. From a naval point of view this was clearly unacceptable, because it meant that the United States would have to maintain two fleets, one in the Atlantic and one in the Pacific, unless a cut-through was obtained. Political leaders agreed, and accord was reached with Great Britain in the Hay-Pauncefote Treaty of 1901 that the United States could build an isthmian canal on its own. The problem was Colombia, of which Panama was a part, which held out for the highest possible amount of money. Reacting to Colombian obstinacy, Roosevelt—with the assistance of the French, who wanted their bankrupt company compensated, and with an eye on the 1904 election campaign—inspired a local revolt by the Panamanians, who wanted the canal, against their Colombian overlords. The Navy actively aided the revolution by preventing Colombian ships from reinforcing the tiny garrison in Panama, and the revolutionary regime and its Republic of Panama were recognized three days later, on 6 November 1903, by the United States. Shortly thereafter the Hay-Bunau-Varilla Treaty was

signed, by which the US obtained a 10-mile strip of land for a canal for $10 million and a $250,000 annual annuity. Roosevelt now had a green light to 'make the dirt fly,' and the great task of building the canal began. It was completed in 1914, to the delight of the American people, merchant shippers (who cut 9000 miles off the trip from New York to San Francisco and 6000 miles off the trip from New York to Manila) and the navy, which could now expeditiously move its forces from ocean to ocean by a fast and secure passage.

The navy was also active in 'America's lake,' the Caribbean, during these years in bringing the US Marines to Cuba, Santo Domingo, Haiti and Nicaragua to restore order and forestall European intervention. The navy also bombarded and seized the port of Vera Cruz during the Mexican crisis of 1914, when President Woodrow Wilson moved against the government of General Victoriano Huerta after it attempted to buy a large quantity of arms to use against its domestic enemies.

Wherever and whenever called upon, the navy served well during the years before World War I in carrying out its duty of protecting American interests as determined by US political leaders. And the American people were proud of and confident in the Navy as never before in the nation's history. Indicative of this pride was the Roosevelt-inspired cruise of the Great White Fleet from December 1907 to February 1909, designed to display America's new national and naval power. The fleet of 16 battleships and 10 auxiliary vessels, all painted gleaming white as a sign of peace, assembled at Hampton Roads for a great send-off by the President himself. The tour took the vessels around the coast of South America and up the west coast of the United States, then across the Pacific to Hawaii, New Zealand, Australia, the Philippines and Japan. Wherever it went, the fleet made ceremonious port calls to entertain and be received by political leaders. It created a grand impression, although the American sailors displayed a propensity to sample the 'low' culture rather than the 'high' culture of the port cities. After a fervent welcome everywhere, especially in Japan, the Great White Fleet made its way home via the Suez Canal and the Mediterranean, to drop anchor with synchronized precision in Hampton Roads before a beaming Theodore Roosevelt. It had been a 'good show,' and Roosevelt could leave office that March 1909 with a navy dominant in the Western Hemisphere and coming to power in the Pacific. Roosevelt was proud of his navy. It had come of age. The American people shared his pride and enthusiasm. It was with this self-assurance that the nation soon found itself embroiled in the carnage of World War I.

Above: **Japanese and American officers pose on the quarterdeck of the USS *Missouri* during the Great White Fleet's visit to Yokohama in October 1908.**
Below: **The battleship *Connecticut* (right) and Russian ships in Messina Harbor in January 1909**

Top: The USS *Kentucky* showing the highly unconventional arrangement of the armament with the secondary turrets superimposed above the main weapons.
Above: The *Kearsarge* pictured around the turn of the century.

A PARTNER IN THE GREAT CRUSADE

Building upon the foundation created by Theodore Roosevelt, the navy's most enthusiastic presidential patron and publicist, his successor William Howard Taft continued to support a powerful sea force. Their patronage took the form mainly of support for big battleships, a reflection of the prevailing assumption that control of the seas would be seized and maintained by these titans, locked in mortal gun duels on the high seas.

Battleships and Other Weapons

During Roosevelt's time, the American battleship navy matured and in 1909 the *Michigan* and *South Carolina*, of 16,000 tons and armed with eight 12-inch guns in twin-stacked turrets fore and aft, came off the building ways to join the fleet. These imposing battleships were followed by the 20,000-ton *Delaware* and *North Dakota* with ten 12-inchers. And this was not the end, for the *Arkansas* and *Wyoming* of 26,000 tons and twelve 12-inch guns followed soon after.

Not only were the new battleships more heavily armed than ever before, but their gunnery power and accuracy were greatly improved, due largely to the determined efforts of naval officers William S Sims and Bradley K Fiske. As a lieutenant Sims found American gunnery so deficient at the turn of the century that he began a one-man campaign to improve it. He persisted to the point where his career was almost ruined by conflict with senior admirals on the issue. He was saved by the favorable notice of President Roosevelt, who made him inspector of target practice and then his personal naval aide. Under Sims's leadership, training methods were improved and the navy adopted continuous-aim firing and 'dotters' for training purposes, which measured gun-crew accuracy without expending ammunition. Bradley Fiske invented a valuable telescopic gun sight and the optical range finder. By World War I a gun-control officer perched high on the ship's foremast could aim and fire the vessel's big guns simultaneously to an effective range of almost 20,000 yards (over 11 miles). Thanks to these and other developments, the US Navy's battleships were equal to those of any other nation and received a major share of the limited shipbuilding funds doled out by Congress in the pre-war years.

Yet while battleships received most of the attention, the navy did not entirely neglect other weapons then coming into use in the forces of the great powers. Submarines began to join the fleets in the pre-World War I era. The father of the American submarine was a civilian, John P Holland. Although his first boat, the 85-foot *Plunger*, was launched in 1897, it was unworkable because of mandated naval speeds that necessitated a triple-screw

Top: The battleships *Iowa*, *Indiana* and *Massachusetts* on a visit to Kiel in 1911.
Above left: Eugene Ely ready to fly off the USS *Pennsylvania*, 18 January 1911.
Above: The battleship *Illinois* enters a floating dock for repairs in 1902.
Main picture: An early Lake submarine passes the battleship *Kearsarge* during the 1905 review of the Atlantic Fleet.

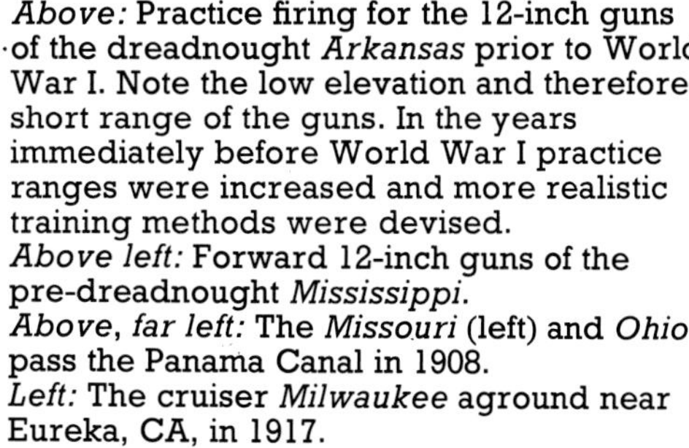

Above: **Practice firing for the 12-inch guns of the dreadnought *Arkansas* prior to World War I. Note the low elevation and therefore short range of the guns. In the years immediately before World War I practice ranges were increased and more realistic training methods were devised.**
Above left: **Forward 12-inch guns of the pre-dreadnought *Mississippi*.**
Above, far left: **The *Missouri* (left) and *Ohio* pass the Panama Canal in 1908.**
Left: **The cruiser *Milwaukee* aground near Eureka, CA, in 1917.**

steam plant to allow the submarine to run on the surface at 15 knots. But Holland, on his own, had been developing a simpler model, the *Holland*, which had a single torpedo tube, a surface speed of seven knots and a range of 1500 miles. Although the boat had no periscope, and thus had to surface every few minutes to take bearings, the *Holland* was purchased by the Navy in 1900, and improvements to submarine technology and operations followed swiftly thereafter. The invention of the gyrocompass made underwater cruising possible, and the adaptation of the diesel engine for surface power greatly improved the boats' safety. Life aboard the primitive undersea boats was cramped, unhealthy and always dangerous, and naval doctrine saw no use for submarines except against enemy warships or in protecting harbors, but the submarine had certainly come to stay in the US Navy by the time World War I broke out in 1914.

Air power had also joined the fleet although, like the submarines, only in a minor capacity. As in so many other naval projects, Theodore Roosevelt played a role. As assistant secretary of the navy in 1898, he interested both the army and the navy in the work of Professor Samuel P Langley of the Smithsonian Institution toward an 'aerodrome' (airplane). But the navy would not pursue it further at that time because the apparatus was 'only fit for land service.' Only in 1910, seven years after the Wright brothers' successful flight at Kitty Hawk, was the Navy bestirred to look into the possibilities of air flight from ships. On 14 November 1910, as the cruiser *Birmingham* sat in Hampton Roads, Eugene Ely, a civilian flier, took off in his Curtiss pusher biplane from an inclined platform over her bow and landed safely on the beach. Two months later, on 18 January 1911, Ely took off from shore and landed safely on a platform erected on the stern of the cruiser *Pennsylvania* as she lay at anchor in San Francisco Bay. Ely's plane was brought to a halt on the 120-foot platform by catching his 'arresting gear,' trailing below the plane, on cables stretched over the 'deck,' each cable attached to 50-pound sandbags. One hour later Ely flew off the ship. The basic idea behind the modern aircraft carrier had been proved.

But although it was quickly recognized that the new airplane could perform valuable service to the fleet by acting as its 'eyes' for reconnaissance purposes—miles beyond what lookouts in the fleet could possibly see even with binoculars—and by freeing cruisers from scouting duty, landing an airplane on a deck was still a very dangerous proposition. Accordingly, development turned toward floatplanes, or seaplanes, which could be launched from a shipboard ramp or catapult at sea to do their work, then be recovered by landing near the mother ship on their floats or pontoons. The seaplane

Above: A Goodyear B-type airship in 1917.
Left: Admiral Sims, the notable gunnery specialist, and members of his staff in London in 1918.

would then be hoisted aboard ship by a crane. By 1913 fleet operations at Guantanamo Bay, Cuba and other locales had proved that airplanes could take photographs, sight enemy submarines and surface vessels, perform wide scouting missions aloft for extended periods and be recovered in moderate seas. The next year five seaplanes attached to the naval squadron at Vera Cruz, by President Wilson's investment of the port in his quarrel with the Mexican Government under General Huerta, proved that air reconnaissance over hostile territory was invaluable. Although air power would subsequently play only a minor role in naval operations during World War I, it had won a place for itself—albeit a limited place—in the emerging navy even before the conflict began. It was not until the 1920s and 1930s that naval air power really came into its own.

The naval weapon that did come to play the major role in World War I was the lowly and unglamorous destroyer. The destroyer was a smaller vessel that had evolved as a counterweapon to the torpedo boat. Initially it was referred to as a 'torpedo boat destroyer.' Torpedo boats had come into use since the 1870s, when the invention of self-propelled torpedoes had been wedded to small, fast boats designed to deliver them against fleet vessels. The torpedo boat destroyer was the answer to stopping the small maneuverable torpedo boat, because it had greater size, speed and firepower than its prey. It could also perform valuable duty by screening the larger vessels while underway. The first American destroyer

Left: Practice with 6-pounder anti-torpedo boat guns on the *Illinois* before WWI.

joined the fleet in 1902—the 420-ton *Bainbridge*. It had two 3-inch guns and two 18-inch torpedo tubes and could make an amazing 29 knots. By 1914 the destroyer had been significantly improved in size and seaworthiness, and the navy had three dozen of these trim vessels on duty. Thus by the outbreak of war in 1914, the navy, while heavy in battleships and comparatively lacking in cruisers, had taken significant steps in developing submarine and air power. It had also begun to balance out its fleet with destroyers. Like the great European navies, it saw great surface-ship warfare as the probable scenario in the event of hostilities. But, as events were to prove, it could give a good account of itself when the fortunes of war forced it to make significant changes.

Europe Goes to War

'The Great War' to Americans living through it—'The War to End All Wars' and to 'Make the World Safe for Democracy' in the mind of President Woodrow Wilson—began in the summer of 1914 with the assassination by Serbian terrorists of the Austrian Archduke Franz Ferdinand in the little Bosnian town of Sarajevo. Austria, to gain satisfaction for the death of the heir apparent and end Serbian agitation against her, made impossible demands on the Serbian Government, which looked to her ally Russia for aid. Germany, backing Austria, sought assurances from Russia and France that they would not enter the dispute. When neither would comply, Germany—fearing a two-front war, and relying on its Schlieffen Plan of hitting France first and then turning toward Russia in case of conflict—declared war on both powers. In attacking France, Germany moved across Belgium, and this brought Britain into the conflict. Soon the secondary nations joined in, and a world war was on. Imperialism, an inflated sense of national pride, an entangling alliance system, and, critically, a desire finally to 'have it out' led to bloody warfare that would leave millions dead on the battlefields of Europe before ending in 1918.

The great land strategies of the European powers soon broke down. The rapid German sweep across northern France, designed to encircle and destroy the vaunted French Army, slowed, then stalled and finally ground to a halt on the Western Front. On the Eastern Front plans also went awry, resulting in Germany's fighting on two fronts. Even joined by Austria and Turkey, Germany was too weak to win and too strong to lose, and the war quickly settled into a bloody stalemate with the combatants, especially in France and Belgium, engaged in merciless, unending trench warfare.

On the seas, too, grand strategies did not work out as planned. Britain, as an island power with a great navy, was faced with the necessity of keeping her sea lanes open against commerce raiders, containing the German High Seas Fleet and blockading Germany's ports. Germany, on the other hand, technically superior to the British fleet although numerically inferior, had to shut off British commerce with her Dominions and all neutrals, especially the United States. Both saw the North Sea as the critical water mass to command while waiting for the great sea battles that would give them naval domination and eventual victory.

Above: **Secretary of the Navy Josephus Daniels addresses a meeting in 1917.**

After some preliminary confrontations in the North Sea, in the Falklands in the far South Atlantic and in the Dogger Bank, the great test of sea strength came on 31 May and 1 June 1916: in the Battle of Jutland,

Below: **The SS *Albert Watts* on fire near Genoa in November 1917. Note the guns fore and aft denoting the presence of a USN armed guard.**

Above: **A U-boat's torpedo strikes home on a freighter. Merchant ships sailing independently were easy victims.**

the Germans tried to break the British blockade and humble her fleet in one grand engagement. The German High Seas Fleet of 22 battleships and 77 other vessels was commanded by Vice-Admiral Reinhard Scheer, the British Grand Fleet of 28 battleships and 120 other ships by Admiral Sir John Jellicoe. In this first real test of the great battleship fleets, the Germans attempted to draw the British into a trap off the coast of Denmark and managed to win a narrow victory in a shifting series of surface combats. Cutting through the British fleet, Scheer's forces returned safely to port, but the importance of the battle lies chiefly in what occurred thereafter. The British, having failed to defeat the German High Seas Fleet, were forced to keep their Grand Fleet concentrated in home waters and the North Sea (with 100 valuable destroyers in support that could have been used against submarines) in case the High Seas Fleet re-emerged to do battle. The Germans, unwilling to risk their valuable surface fleet again in head-to-head combat, turned to the submarine as a means of destroying supplies coming into Britain and breaking the British blockade of their homeland. Thus the stage was set for the United States, as the leading neutral trader and supplier to Britain and her allies, to be drawn slowly but inexorably into the war.

When hostilities broke out in Europe in the summer of 1914, President Wilson declared American neutrality, giving the United States the legal right to trade with any and all belligerents. But Wilson himself, an ardent Anglophile, was hardly neutral and was inclined to downplay British violations of neutral rights (such as redefining contraband lists to suit their purposes, mining the North Sea, opening private mail and 'blacklisting' firms that traded with Germany). He focused his attention—and the nation's—on German use of submarine warfare. Wilson's attitudes, plus American trade with England and France, American investments in the Allied cause and well-publicized stories of German 'atrocities' against civilians, turned America more and more against the Central Powers.

In February 1915 the German Government announced that the waters around the British Isles would be considered a war zone and enemy ships traveling through them were subject to sinking without warning. Although Germany backed up its words with repeated sinkings, Americans continued to travel into these waters on Allied vessels, disregarding the warnings. On the afternoon of 7 May 1915, the British Cunard liner *Lusitania* was sunk within sight of the coast of Ireland by the German submarine U-20. She sank in 20 minutes, taking with her to her watery grave 1198 victims, including 128 Americans. Whether or not the *Lusitania* was indeed carrying munitions and thus liable to attack, the Americans and President Wilson were incensed at the callous deed. The German Government agreed to pay an indemnity and to stop unrestricted submarine warfare, but the damage had been done. The memory of the *Lusitania* and its victims was burned into the American consciousness. There it smouldered until early 1917 when Germany, sensing the time was right with the Eastern Front about to collapse because of the impending revolution in Russia, broke the military deadlock. Believing that any American military aid would be too little too late—the ratio of British merchant ships sunk to

Above: Admiral Mayo, C-in-C US Atlantic Fleet (left) and Rear Admiral Strauss seen during a visit to a hospital in Scotland.
Above right: The minesweeper *Tanager* at work in heavy seas.

German submarines lost was then 15:1 and Germany estimated that Britain could be overcome in five months if the subs were unleashed—Germany resumed unrestricted submarine warfare in January. This finally brought America into the war on 6 April 1917 at President Wilson's request, and the United States stepped to the side of the Allied powers.

Above: A US Navy airship patrols over a convoy en route to Europe.
Below: US 'four stacker' destroyers on convoy duty.

America Joins the Crusade

But as it did so, it found that the US Navy was hardly ready for all-out war. Part of the reason was Wilson's naval secretary, Josephus Daniels, a land-lubbing small-town newspaperman from North Carolina. Wilson had little respect for military men and their opinions, and his choice of Daniels was unfortunate in many ways. Known for his reformism, pacifism, populist agrarianism and support of Prohibition, Daniels brought some controversial ideas to the navy. He introduced compulsory basic education courses on every ship and at every duty station and, to make the service more 'democratic,' cut out the officers' wine mess in July 1914, since the enlisted men's grog had been curtailed during the Civil War. Daniels also fought in Congress against the establishment of an office of Chief of Naval Operations with any real power, believing that civilian control would be endangered. On the other hand, Secretary Daniels made some positive contributions prior to 1917. First, he fought for the naval preparedness program as embodied in the Naval Act of 1916, which called for the construction of 156 ships (including 10 battleships, 16 cruisers, 50 destroyers and 67 submarines) in three years—although he resisted all efforts to construct ships for ASW (anti-submarine warfare) duty and dallied on preparing existing vessels and crews for combat. Second, he chose as assistant naval secretary Franklin D Roosevelt, a New York politician and naval enthusiast looking for a way to further his blossoming career; Roosevelt was a disciple of decisive naval power. He did a fine job as a buffer between the officers and Daniels and the politicos both before and during the war and studied the navy well in the process. This experience would benefit both him and the navy after 1933, when Roosevelt would be Commander in Chief.

Thus when the war began in 1914, the US Navy under Daniels was building but ill prepared for major conflict. There were no war plans (Wilson had forbidden the military to make contingency plans), few ASW vessels, and no apparatus set up to co-operate with the British; only one-third of the navy's vessels were fit for duty and 90 percent of its ships were inadequately manned. Despite this, the Navy went to its task and played a substantial role in winning World War I.

By the time the United States entered the war, Germany's unrestricted warfare with her 120 subs was taking a tremendous toll of British merchant vessels. In the first three months of 1917, almost 1,300,000 tons of shipping had been sunk, and the toll was rising fast. Britain faced starvation if the German submarines could not be contained or destroyed. That was the message received by Admiral William S Sims, sent to London by President Wilson to survey the naval situation, when he met with Admiral Sir John Jellicoe, the First Sea Lord, on 10 April 1917 at the Admiralty. If sub-seeking destroyers were not sent to contain the menace, Britain might lose the war. Although the British had 200 destroyers, 100 were attached to the Grand Fleet at Scapa Flow in the Orkney Islands on the northern tip of Scotland, and the remainder were spread thinly in patrolling the waters around the British Isles, in the Mediterranean and in the North Atlantic. This was simply not enough.

Above: **A Curtiss H-16 flying boat at Queenstown Naval Air Station, Ireland in 1918.**

Below: **A typical World War I convoy with an escorting USN destroyer farthest from the camera.**

Above: The USS *Covington* sinking off Brest on 2 July 1918 after being torpedoed by the German submarine U-86.
Left: King George V and Admiral Rodman inspect the crew of the *New York*.

Destroyers, Convoys and Mines

Sims moved quickly in two directions. First, he cabled home to the navy to send every available destroyer to Britain. Despite the reluctance of Secretary Daniels and Admiral William S Benson, Chief of Naval Operations, to make such a commitment, the government finally decided to honor Sims's request. On 4 May 1917 six American destroyers constituting Destroyer Division 8 arrived at the Queenstown naval base in Ireland. They were commanded by Joseph K Tausigg, Commander, USN, and were the first of dozens that would follow in the months ahead. With destroyers available, the German submarines could be sunk or neutralized. Second, Sims convinced the British and the French that they must convoy ships carrying men and supplies. Although the Admiralty had first rejected this on the grounds that convoys were limited in speed to that of the slowest vessel and merchant captains could not maintain their positions, the Allies finally became con-

vinced in May 1917—after a trial run by a convoy from Gibraltar—that the stratagem would work with more destroyers available for escort duty. They further found that merchant captains could keep station very well. Convoying thus became standard practice, with the Americans playing an important role in protecting the vessels under escort.

Soon American destroyers, operating from bases from the Mediterranean to Scotland, were co-operating well with their British counterparts under the overall command of Vice-Admiral Lewis Bayly of the Royal Navy. Under Captain Joel Pringle, as Bayly's US Chief of Staff, the destroyers operated smoothly as part of the British naval defense force, with Bayly proclaiming his affection for the Yank destroyermen by referring to them as 'my Americans.' This co-operation, plus the use of the newly developed contact mine (equipped with copper wire tendrils that exploded the device on contact with metal) and depth charges (steel cylinders containing 300 pounds of explosives and detonated by the increased water pressure as they sank), gradually contained the submarine menace, and Britain could hold out and fight back. Sinkings of Allied ships declined from 875,000 tons in April 1917, to 458,723 tons in October 1917, to 277,934 tons in April 1918. The submarines were clearly on the run, and American destroyers and companion submarine chasers were proving their worth. The work was not glamorous for the officers and crews of the workhorse vessels, but it was helping to win the war on the sea.

The US Navy also made a major contribution to the sea-war effort by helping to lay a great minefield across the North Sea from Norway to Scotland, a distance of 240 miles: this kept the German U-Boats from getting out to sea, 'shutting the hornets up in their nests,' in the words of President Wilson. Mining the North Sea was originally rejected by the British because it would call for an impossible total of 400,000 mines, but when the copper-wire tendril mine (invented by Ralph C Browne of the United States) became available, the picture changed. Now 100,000 mines would do the job. Accordingly, the operation was carried out between June and October 1918, the Americans laying over 56,000 mines and the British over 13,000. Although it is impossible to determine how many German vessels fell victim to the mines, the barrier effectively closed the North Sea and had a great negative psychological effect on the German people and on the German Navy. The US Navy also contributed a division of five battleships to the Grand Fleet at Scapa Flow, and a few US submarines served in European waters as well. These vessels, along with the naval cruisers on convoy duty in the western Atlantic protecting the American merchant marine's 'bridge of ships' to the war zone, played a crucial supporting role in the naval war against the Central Powers.

As the Germans and their allies began losing the war at sea, they were also being slowly pushed back on the Western Front as French, British and American army units threatened to break their defensive lines and move into the fatherland itself. There revolutions threatened to break loose in reaction to starvation and the prolonged war effort. The Imperial Government had to call a halt. Kaiser Wilhelm II left the country, and a new interim government asked for an armistice: when it was agreed to, the fighting ended.

The Great War was over. The US Navy had proved its mettle again from the highest admiral to the lowest seaman. The crews of the bobbing, sub-chasing destroyers stalking their prey; the men on the great dreadnoughts at anchor in Scapa Flow awaiting an enemy that never came; the more than 6000 American naval aviators who flew planes and blimps on reconnaissance and convoy-protecting missions; the 12,000 'yeomanettes' who supported the men at sea by donning US Navy uniforms; and the 14-inch-gun crews in France wearing the 'Woozlefinch' insignia, whose railroad-mounted guns lobbed 1400-pound shells onto the German front lines—all had served meritoriously as part of America's naval contribution to the 'war to end all wars.' Peace arrived to general rejoicing at 11:00 on the morning of 11 November 1918.

Above: The submarine *L-3* leads a flotilla into an Irish base in 1918.
Right: Admiral Strauss, Commander Mine Force, and members of his staff.
Below right: Tugs help the USS *Mount Vernon*, damaged by torpedo, to dock at Brest.
Bottom right: Naval railway battery in France.
Below: The destroyer *Shaw* after a collision.

RETRENCHMENT AND REBIRTH

One of the most dramatic events of modern naval history took place in June 1919 at Scapa Flow, Scotland, home port of the British Grand Fleet. Pursuant to the provisions of the Treaty of Versailles, the defeated German High Seas Fleet had sailed into the Forth in perfect order on 21 November 1918 to be turned over to the victors. Ten battleships, 17 cruisers, 50 destroyers and 102 submarines made up the incredible armada which eventually anchored at Scapa Flow. Then, on 21 June 1919, obeying the command of Vice-Admiral Ludwig von Reuter, the captain of every ship ordered its seacocks opened: all 179 vessels began to sink to the bottom of the Flow in protest against the victors' Treaty. Only four ships were salvaged. The German Navy was no more.

This gesture of defiance meant that only the United States was now in a position to challenge Britain's control of the seas. But perhaps the scuttling at Scapa Flow had a greater and unintended symbolic value, for in the early 1920s a movement arose, especially in England and the United States, advocating that all the world's navies should be scuttled, or at least scaled back drastically in the name of peace. The 1920s, a time of self-imposed American isolation from world affairs, became the decade of naval disarmament; the 1930s would become the decade of naval rearmament, as the nation began to realize its worldwide obligations once again in the face of the growing tensions inspired by Hitler's regime and the clear territorial ambitions harbored by Japan.

Disarmament Cripples the Navy

In early 1919 the US Navy had 16 dreadnoughts and 13 more building. It was awaiting 12 new battle cruisers authorized in 1916. Britain, with 33 dreadnoughts and nine battle cruisers, was preparing to build four great 48,000-ton battle cruisers and four more battleships. Japan was looking toward two great naval squadrons of battleships and battlecruisers—one squadron of each—to be completed by 1928. A capital-ship naval race was underway even though the war was over. In all three countries movements designed to halt such building and to scale down the naval budgets sprang up. Peace could not be gained by more weapons of war, argued

Below: The battleship USS *Washington* under construction in 1922. She was cancelled before completion under the terms of the Washington Naval Treaty.

Above: The battleship *Nevada*, first battleship to be built on the 'all or nothing' principle of armor protection, carries President Wilson to France in December 1918.
Top left: The *Ostfriesland* finally sinks during the Mitchell tests.
Above left: The mast of the USS *Michigan* collapsed during a storm in 1918. Between the wars modernization replaced the cage masts on most US battleships with stronger, more rigid tripods.

the pro-disarmament forces, and prosperity demanded a relief from the crushing tax burdens they imposed. By 1921 the pressure for disarmament had become irresistible.

An invitation to a worldwide disarmament conference to cut back the world's navies and to clear the air over Japanese intentions in the Far East was issued by the Harding Administration in August 1921, after a resolution by Senator William Borah of Idaho had crystallized popular support for such a meeting. As the delegates from nine nations assembled in the nation's capital the following month, the American secretary of state, Charles Evans Hughes, electrified the conferees in his opening speech by saying that the United States would be willing to scrap 30 battleships (15 built and 15 building, for 845,740 tons) if the other powers would move in the same direction. Hughes went on to propose that the British and the Japanese follow suit and outlined exactly how they should do it. Britain was to scrap 19 capital ships (583,375 tons) and Japan 17 ships (447,928 tons). Since no agenda had been agreed upon previously, Hughes's breathtaking suggestions became the basis for negotiations, and eventually three separate agreements were made before the Washington Naval Conference adjourned in February 1922.

Two of the agreements dealt with Far Eastern problems. The 'Four Power Treaty' bound the United States, Great Britain, France and Japan to recognize and

Left: A phosphorus bomb explodes above the old battleship _Alabama_ during tests in 1923. _Right:_ Nieuport 28 flying off a battleship (probably _Arizona circa_ 1921).

respect one another's possessions in the Far East and to settle any disputes that arose by joint conference. The 'Nine Power Treaty,' accepted by the same four nations plus Italy, China, Belgium, the Netherlands and Portugal, pledged to maintain the 'Open Door' in China, a doctrine first promulgated by American secretary of state John Hay in 1899 to protect China's integrity. The third treaty dealt with naval disarmament.

This 'Five Power Treaty' agreed to on 6 February 1922 called for a ratio of 5:5:3:1.75:1.75 in capital ships (the nations involved according to their ratios being the United States, Britain, Japan, France and Italy). In standard displacement tonnage the agreement specified 525,000 tons, 525,000 tons, and 315,000 tons for the greater powers and 175,000 tons each for France and Italy. In addition, no capital ships (battleships and battle cruisers) could be constructed for ten years and no capital ships retained could be over 35,000 tons or carry ordnance greater than 16 inches. The aircraft carrier ratio was set at 135,000 tons, 135,000 tons, 81,000 tons, 60,000 tons and 60,000 tons, with no carriers except for any two per country to be over 27,000 tons. The two excepted carriers could go to 33,000 tons apiece, but under no circumstances could any nation's maximum tonnage be topped. No cruiser could be over 10,000 tons or be armed with more than 8-inch guns. And no battleships or carriers could be replaced before twenty years of age. This treaty was to remain in effect for ten years, any nation seeking to disavow its provisions being bound to give two years' notice. Thus the Five Power Treaty brought a virtual end to capital-ship construction and postponed any naval building rivalry for fifteen years, even though Japanese movements into China in the early 1930s made a mockery of the other two treaties.

Cutting Back

The desired naval-limitation agreement having been gained, the Harding Administration went to work cutting back the US Navy to treaty strength through naval secretary Edwin C Denby, although Congress deserves the major blame for putting the axe to the navy in these years. Congress made it almost impossible even to modernize personnel and refused to fund 16 cruisers needed by the navy. Denby did manage to get the collier *Jupiter* converted to the navy's first carrier (the inadequate *Langley*) and instituted plans for converting the hulls of two battle cruisers into the new 33,000-ton carriers *Lexington* and *Saratoga*. But given Congress's control of the purse strings, there was little else he could do.

The navy did not fare better under President Calvin Coolidge, who knew little about it and showed no signs of wanting to cure that deficiency. In newer vessels it received only the two carriers, 10 light cruisers and three submarines, plus the five battleships authorized at the end of the war, but little else. Coolidge also called for a second disarmament conference to limit cruisers, submarines and destroyers. It met in Geneva in 1927 but came to nothing, due partly to skillful lobbying by William B Shearer representing American shipbuilding interests. Coolidge, angered by the failure at Geneva, called for building more cruisers of the treaty tonnage

***Main picture:* A battleship lets loose a full broadside during firing practice in the mid-1920s.**

TEXAS
IDAHO
ARKANSAS
MISSISSIPPI
MELVILLE
STODDERT
WYOMING
BIRMINGHAM
PARTRIDGE

Left: The battleship _California_ fitting out at Mare Island Navy Yard, CA, in 1920. The _California_ was armed with twelve 14-inch guns and saw service throughout the Pacific War after being badly damaged at Pearl Harbor.

limit of 10,000 tons each and backed a Navy General Board call to bring the navy up to treaty strength. But neither he nor his naval secretary, Curtis D Wilbur, made a spirited fight for the newer vessels, and a '15-cruiser' bill was signed only in February 1929, as Coolidge was about to leave office.

Herbert Hoover, his peace-loving Quaker successor, was a disaster for the US Navy. Believing that the failure of the Geneva conference would result in another arms race, he met with British Prime Minister Ramsay MacDonald to discuss the problem; this resulted in the London Naval Conference of 1930. Meeting in the shadow of the Kellogg-Briand Peace Pact, wherein warfare had been denounced as an instrument of national policy, this conference set to work to limit all naval vessels not covered by the Washington Naval Conference, especially cruisers.

From the London Naval Conference came limitations on light (6-inch-gun) and heavy (8-inch-gun) cruisers, an agreement on parity among the three powers present regarding submarines, and a ratio of 10 (United States):10 (Britain):7 (Japan) on destroyers. Battleships were further reduced to 15:15:9, and the capital-ship building holiday was extended to 1936. Thus naval building programs had finally been contained—or so it seemed. But the London Naval Treaty also contained Article 21, which allowed any signatory to scuttle its limitations if threatened by any non-signatory power, and if one signatory went beyond its limits, all others could do so. This 'escalator clause' was an open door to self-willed expansion, especially as Japan, in 1933, announced her intention to withdraw from the treaty when it expired. Japan had begun her conquest of Manchuria in 1931, and none of the signatories to the three Washington Naval Conference agreements had moved to stop her. Since the subsequent League of Nations Disarmament Conference of 1932–34 and the London Naval Conference of 1935–36 were both failures, it was clear to all by the mid-1930s that naval arms limitation was falling apart in the face of national aggressions. Only then did the United States turn again to rebuild its truncated navy to deal with the realities of world power politics.

The US Navy in general was sadly lacking in 1933, with only 101 newer vessels, 9000 officers and 81,000 men. It had not even been built up to treaty limits in the decade since the Washington Naval Conference, standing at only 65 percent of authorized strength. President Hoover had told his naval secretary, Charles Francis Adams, to cut spending and return appropriated funds in an attempt to cut expenses during the deepening Depression. The year 1932 was the nadir of the modern US Navy. Only one branch of the navy had been growing in strength throughout the period of decline. This was naval aviation.

Left: Ships of the Atlantic and Pacific Fleets at anchor in Panama Bay in January 1921.

Naval Air Power

The Navy's experience with air power during World War I was limited, as we have seen, but the public and air enthusiasts were enthralled by the relatively high rate of damage (for the low expenditure of money) promised by air power (an approach that would later come to be called 'more bang for the buck'). With tactical and strategic theorists worldwide making fabulous claims that airplanes would soon render both armies and navies obsolete, the navy could hardly turn away from a weapon which, at the least, could aid them appreciably in fleet operations. But well-publicized tests off the Atlantic coast in 1921 against ships—including bombing attacks by Army Brigadier General Billy Mitchell's crews on the old German battleship *Ostfriesland*, and later on the modern battleship *Washington*—were largely inconclusive. Ships were hard to hit from the air and when properly compartmentalized could take tremendous damage and remain afloat—a lesson that had to be taught to such myopic devotees of air power as Mitchell, who drew his ideas from the theories of General Giulio Douhet of Italy. The navy was not about to reject air power; it was too busy adding it to its fleets.

Common sense won out over those

Below: The airship _Los Angeles_ landing on the aircraft carrier _Saratoga_. The long endurance of airships was useful for patrolling.

admirals who still envisioned great sea battles with big-gun vessels slugging it out to a decisive conclusion, as well as over those admirals who saw the airplane as making the armed vessel obsolete. The navy took the middle course. In the 1920s such carriers as the *Langley*, then *Lexington* and *Saratoga*, came on line, and carrier pilots were being trained at Pensacola. From the naval aircraft factory at Philadelphia came better catapults, arresting gear and metal alloys for the 'skins' of the planes. Fighter planes and torpedo and dive bombers were built, tested and added to the carrier squadrons, and long-range scouting and patrol planes joined the air inventory to replace the great dirigibles as scouts. (Three of the navy's four great lighter-than-air ships unfortunately crashed in storms, one of which claimed as a victim Rear Admiral William A Moffett, chief of the Navy's Bureau of Aeronautics.) Between 1926 and 1930 the navy purchased over 100 airplanes, and Pensacola could not possibly train all the young ensigns who wanted to add gold wings to their uniforms. Pensacola was also overrun with senior officers who sought their pilot or aerial-observer wings as a means of promotion. The 'Pensacola admirals' were 'having their tickets punched,' a practice not unknown since the beginning of command and seniority structures. The Navy somehow survived the 1920s, even adding an air arm; the 1930s saw its renaissance.

Far left: **The aviator Charles Lindbergh pictured in 1929 aboard the carrier *Saratoga*. In the background, one of the ship's 8-inch gun turrets.**
Left: **US fleet at Colon in 1933. At right the carriers *Saratoga* and *Lexington*.**
Below: **Battle line during maneuvers in the 1920s. The 32,000-ton battleship *Pennsylvania* is the leading ship.**

Resurgence in the Face of Danger

The impetus for rebuilding the US Navy after 1933 came from three factors: President Franklin D Roosevelt's commitment to naval power; the grim necessity of putting men back to work after the Great Depression, with shipbuilding playing a significant role in New Deal recovery efforts; and the deteriorating world situation, as aggression became the rule of the day in Europe, the Mediterranean area and the Far East. The first two require little explanation, since Roosevelt had demonstrated his naval enthusiasm and know-how as assistant secretary during World War I. The renaissance in ship-

Above: Battleships maneuvering off Hawaii in 1925, a photograph taken from the *Oklahoma*. Next ahead is the *Nevada*. *Top:* The *Tennessee* fires a full 14-inch broadside.

building got under way in June 1933 under a $238 million National Recovery Administration program to build 32 warships and continued from that point. The third factor requires amplification.

As of 1933 Germany had fallen under the leadership of Adolf Hitler and his Nazi cohorts on a platform of repudiating the Versailles Treaty and seeking to regain German superiority in European affairs. A decade before, Italy had fallen under the rule of the Fascist dictator Benito Mussolini who wanted to re-create the Roman Empire in the Mediterranean whatever the cost. In Russia, Josef Stalin was firmly entrenched in power and dedicated to spreading Marxist Communism throughout the world. And in Japan a military clique had already taken Manchuria as part of its public goal of establishing a great Far Eastern Empire at the expense of its neighbors. All these developments contained overt challenges to world peace and to the ideals and traditions of the American people. If power was not checked by power, the face of the world would be sadly altered by the grim hand of totalitarian aggression.

As the 1930s continued, aggression escalated. In 1933 Japan took the northern provinces of China. In 1935 Mussolini's mechanized troops overran the hapless natives of Ethiopia. In that same year Hitler announced he was repudiating the arms restriction on Germany imposed by the Treaty of Versailles and announced a submarine-building program. The next year he marched boldly into the demilitarized Rhineland. In 1936 Spain fell into civil war and the Russians, Germans and Italians hastened to help the combatants. In November of that year Japan and Germany joined forces in the Anti-Comintern Pact, with Italy standing close by as an ally. In 1937 Japan continued its attacks on China, and an American gunboat, the USS *Panay*, was attacked and sunk on the Yangtse River by Japanese planes. In 1938 Hitler took control of Austria by his famous *Anschluss* and forced the Czechs to give up the Sudetenland (with the approval at Munich of England and France). The following year, despite his promises, he took the Czech provinces of Bohemia and Moravia. In April 1939 Italy invaded tiny Albania, and the Germans and Italians joined hands as the Axis Powers. Russia gave Germany the green light to move east on 23 August 1939 when she signed a non-aggression pact with Hitler—she was also promised half of Poland—and Hitler responded on 1 September by invading Poland. Britain and France finally decided to curb Germany by honoring their guarantees of Polish independence. World War II began.

Through all of this President Roosevelt was walking a tightrope between military preparedness and the overwhelming desire of the American public to stay out of the troubles of the world. As the situation deteriorated in Europe and the Far East, the isolationism of the 1920s came to full flower, as the American people balked at being pulled into Europe's troubles again. This sentiment received new life in 1934, when the report of the Senate committee chaired by Gerald P Nye stated—on very slanted evidence—that American munitions makers and bankers had conspired to drag the United States into World War I. The next year Congress passed a neutrality act that forbade American exports of arms and ammunition to any belligerents—be they aggressors or victims—and allowed no American vessels to carry armaments to any belligerents. It also restricted travel by Americans on the vessels of belligerents. While this amounted to a *de facto* surrender of America's rights on the high seas, the neutrality law would ostensibly keep America out of any situation that might embroil her in war. That was the whole idea. And as the events of the middle 1930s made the world situation ever more dangerous, with Germany, Japan and Italy on the move, American opinion showed continued determination to stay out of war, and neutrality legislation was only marginally liberalized. Roosevelt, as a result, had to 'sell' naval rearmament until 1939 as a make-work boost to the economy, and thereafter as a means of protecting American interests in an increasingly lawless world. In this he was eminently successful. The US Navy grew at an ever-accelerating pace from 1933 to 1941.

During the 1920s, as mentioned, the navy was allowed to add to the fleet to some extent, especially in cruisers. While

Main picture: **Battleship Division 5 at firing practice off San Diego in 1925–26. The leading ships are *Maryland*, *Colorado* and *West Virginia*.**

Above: Fleet at anchor in Guantanamo Bay, Cuba, for maneuvers in 1927.
Left: Curtiss R-type floatplane being hoisted aboard the carrier *Langley*.
Right: UO-1 observation aircraft, in service in the 1930s.

completing work on 10 *Omaha*-type cruisers of only 7500 tons, the Navy laid down eight heavy cruisers of 10,000 tons, and in 1929 began work on Coolidge's 15 heavy cruisers, six of the *Phoenix*-class 'treaty cruisers' of 10,000 tons and nine of the 10,000-ton *Portland* class. Work also began that year on the *Ranger*, a smaller carrier of 14,500 tons. Thus by early 1933 the Navy had 342 ships (1,000,270 total tons) with another 16 vessels being built (78,060 tons). These 342 ships included 15 battleships, three carriers, 20 cruisers, 222 destroyers and 82 submarines.

Rebuilding the Fleet

Impressive as this might seem, the navy was hardly at adequate strength to defend the nation's worldwide interests, and so benefited greatly by the building programs of the 1930s. Under the National Recovery Administration funding of 1933, the navy was authorized one heavy and three light cruisers, and, most importantly, two new aircraft carriers of 19,900 tons, to be named the *Enterprise* and the *Yorktown*. The Vinson-Trammel Act of 1934 called for a US Navy of full treaty strength in all types of vessels and authorized construction of new battleships and carriers. The carrier *Wasp* was authorized in 1936 and the *Hornet* followed; the new battleship *North Carolina* was laid down in 1937.

In 1935 Congress funded 24 destroyers and 12 submarines, and in 1936, in addition to funding the *Wasp*, provided monies for two light cruisers, 15 destroyers and six submarines. As the world situation continued to deteriorate, Congress passed the Vinson Act, or 'Twenty Percent Naval Expansion Act,' in 1938 calling for an increase in naval tonnage of 20 percent (46 warships and 26 auxiliaries) and funded eight more destroyers and four subs. Money for more vessels followed in 1939: by July of that year the resurgent US Navy had 373 ships in its inventory (15 battleships, 5 carriers, 37 cruisers, 221 destroyers and 94 submarines) in an aggregate tonnage of 1,277,290. Building were 77 vessels of another 458,880 tons, including 8 battleships, 2 carriers, 4 cruisers, 43 destroyers and 20 subs. In a little over six years, the US Navy had increased its tonnage by over 25 percent, modernized existing vessels and now had a more balanced fleet of faster and more heavily gunned ships. Furthermore, a dozen bases were being constructed or improved throughout the navy's areas of concern.

But Europe's war and Japanese aggressions prodded Roosevelt to do even more to prepare the US Navy for trouble if it came. In June 1940 Congress authorized a 21-vessel battleship fleet and the next month, in the Vinson-Walsh Act, or the 'Two-Ocean Navy Act,' authorized another increase in warship tonnage, this time by another 70 percent, up to 3,049,480 tons. Included were the giant *Essex*-type carriers of 27,000 tons, plus *Iowa*-class battleships, heavy cruisers, destroyers and 1500-ton fleet submarines. Under the prompting of Roosevelt and the perilous state of world affairs, the Navy was being pushed to combat readiness if war could not be avoided.

Aiding the Nation's Friends

World events were not waiting on the navy, while President Roosevelt maneuvered to render all possible aid to the Allies without getting America directly involved in the war. In October 1939 the United States and 21 Latin American nations signed the Declaration of Panama, declaring Western Hemisphere waters to be inherently free from hostile acts by warring nations and establishing a 300-mile neutrality zone off their shores. These waters would be patrolled by warships and planes to enforce the Declaration. That

Right: The carrier *Langley* in Pearl Harbor in 1928. The *Langley*'s navigating bridge was at the bow under the overhang of the flight deck.
Below: Flotilla vessels and cruisers of the Pacific Fleet in March 1925.

Left: Martin T4M-1 torpedo-bombers landing on the carrier *Lexington* in January 1929.
Right: Curtiss F6C fighters and Martin T3M torpedo planes aboard the *Lexington* during the carrier's maiden cruise in April 1928.
Below: The minesweeper *Owl* under way during the Fleet Review, 4 June 1927.

Above: **The airship *Los Angeles* and two blimps in flight over the light cruiser *Raleigh* during maneuvers in October 1930.**

same year saw American neutrality legislation altered to permit the sale of American arms, but only for cash and only on the buyer's vessels. However, the changes also forbade American merchant vessels from carrying arms and barred US citizens from combat zones. America would protect its own turf, but was still strenuously avoiding war.

This ambivalence became more difficult to maintain in late 1939 and early 1940, as Poland, then Finland, were overrun, followed by Germany's invasion in quick order of Denmark, Norway, the Netherlands, Belgium and France—the latter coupled with an Italian invasion from the south. Things looked bleak for the Allied Powers when the evacuation of 300,000 British troops at Dunkirk left the home islands in dire straits, France capitulated to Germany on 22 June 1940, leaving Hitler astride the Continent from the English Channel to the plains of Poland, and Japanese aggression continued virtually unchecked in China. The United States Government responded by joining the Latin American nations in the Declaration of Havana of June 1940, in which the signatory powers stated that an act of aggression by any non-American nation upon any American nation would be considered an act of aggression on all. In September 1940 the US passed the Burke-Wadsworth Bill instituting the peacetime draft for all men between the ages of 21 and 35 (although the law specified that draftees could not be used outside the Western Hemisphere except on American possessions).

While these measures brought America much closer to preparedness and drew a line around the territory which the Axis Powers were forbidden to cross, they offered no help to the hard-pressed British facing the onslaught of German power, especially on the seas, where British resistance met mammoth pressure in the form of German submarine attacks on vital commerce.

With this in mind, Franklin Roosevelt and British Prime Minister Winston Churchill worked out an agreement known as the 'destroyer deal.' As announced by the President on 3 September 1940, 50 older American destroyers would be transferred to Britain by executive agreement in return for 99-year leases on eight Western Hemisphere bases belonging to Britain, one in Newfoundland and seven in the Caribbean. Roosevelt, furthermore, extended American neutrality patrols farther out to sea in search of submarines, the pilots reporting any sightings on open radio frequencies so that British ships could pick up the information. After his successful re-election to an unprecedented third term in office that fall, Roosevelt, in his 'Four Freedoms' speech of 6 January 1941, called for America to supply ships, planes, tanks and guns to nations fighting for those freedoms against 'aggressors' (there was no room for doubt about the identity of these protagonists).

America took other crucial steps toward full involvement in the war in the Lend-

Right: **The crowded flight deck of the *Saratoga*. The *Lexington* and *Saratoga* were designed to carry 78 aircraft and could comfortably fit in more.**

Lease Act of March 1941, wherein the 1939 provision of 'cash and carry' was dropped for nations fighting the aggressors; in forming an agreement with Denmark for America to construct air bases in Greenland for patrol duty; and in Roosevelt's extending the area of the ships and planes of the neutrality patrol up to 2000 miles from the American coast. This was well within the area defined by Germany as the war zone earlier that year. Furthermore, American scout planes within the zone were informing the nearest British base when a German ship or sub was spotted, so that convoys could avoid the area and British planes and ships could seek to destroy it.

It was a decidedly pro-Allied neutrality game that Roosevelt was playing in the North Atlantic, marked by the shifting of many US Navy vessels from the Pacific to the Atlantic. By the fall of 1941—the 'Atlantic Charter' decrying Nazi tyranny having been drawn up by Roosevelt and Churchill in Newfoundland—the United States was in an undeclared war on Germany through Roosevelt's extended neutrality patrol.

The US Navy was virtually the only American force carrying on the undeclared war. When the USS *Greer* was attacked in the North Atlantic by a German submarine on 4 September 1941, Roosevelt told the Navy to 'shoot on sight' any hostile craft attacking American ships or any ships under American escort. Whatever the legality of the last part of the order, the naval war in the North Atlantic was becoming very dangerous. The attack on

Below: **The *Yorktown* (CV.5) pictured in Hampton Roads in October 1937.**

the *Greer* was followed by attacks by German subs on the destroyer *Kearney* (after the *Kearney* had dropped depth charges) and on the destroyer *Reuben James* in October 1941. The attack on the *Kearney* prompted Roosevelt (who did not reveal to the public the circumstances of the incident) to say, 'We Americans have cleared our decks and taken our battle stations.' The sinking of the *Reuben James* prompted Congress to allow American merchant vessels to be armed and to sail to any and all belligerent ports. America, already in an undeclared naval shooting war, stood at the threshold of all-out involvement in warfare against Nazi Germany. Then devastation fell from the skies onto the US Navy base at Pearl Harbor in the Pacific, and the undeclared naval war against Hitler's Germany in the North Atlantic turned into a conflict against all the Axis Powers worldwide. The US Navy faced its greatest challenge as the smoke from the devastated Pacific Fleet marked the incredible destruction of the 'day that will live in infamy.'

REGAINING THE PACIFIC SEAS

Japan had long been determined to extend its holding and influence in the Far East, and the year 1940 saw a resurgence of this aggressive expansionism. As a spokesman for the Japanese militarists, Prince Fumimaro Konoye announced the area of Japanese interests as the expansive Greater East Asia Co-Prosperity Sphere, stretching from the home islands and Manchuria south through the Dutch East Indies and into central Pacific waters. In the very heart of this projected Japanese empire were the Philippines and the American island of Guam in the Marianas. Then in September 1940 an agreement was made with the Nazi-dominated Vichy regime in France for the Japanese to take over Indochina, and the Imperial Japanese Government became a partner in the Axis military alliance.

No letup occurred in 1941. Despite President Roosevelt's freezing of all Japanese assets in the United States as a warning to Japan to cease its march of conquest, the Japanese moved into Indochina, and the war-minded General Hideki Tojo became Prime Minister. The American Government, with its attention focused on the deteriorating military situation in Europe—Hitler turned his fury on Britain to gain final control of the Continent for his 'Thousand-Year Reich'—shored up US military forces in the Philippines as best it could. This included placing all US Army forces in the Far East under the authority of the imperious Lieutenant General Douglas MacArthur—top man in his West Point class, World War I decorated hero, former Army Chief of Staff, experienced Far Eastern military leader, and hitherto Field Marshal of the Philippine Army. A few submarines were also sent to the Philippines to reinforce the Navy's Asiatic fleet under the command of Admiral Thomas C Hart. But, all in all, it would be a pitifully weak army-navy defensive team that would face the Japanese if, as expected, their primary target was the Philippine archipelago. In the meantime, Washington carefully watched events in the Pacific and tried to perceive Japanese intentions.

Below: **Japanese Zero fighters ready for take off from a carrier at the start of the Pearl Harbor attack.**

Pearl Harbor

The Japanese leaders were looking at another objective. Their original Pacific plans had, indeed, called for a sweep through the Philippines en route to the conquest of the rich Dutch East Indies, fending off American naval attacks on their left flank as they moved south. But these plans were scuttled in favor of a more daring strategy that came from the mind of Admiral Isoruko Yamamoto, Commander in Chief of the Combined Fleet. Pearl Harbor, America's great naval base in the Hawaiian Islands, was chosen as the new primary target. With the American fleet at Pearl Harbor destroyed, the Japanese would have virtually no opposition as they moved south; before the Americans could challenge them, their position in the Pacific would be impregnable.

Accordingly, plans were drawn up for a lightning air strike on the American naval and air bases on Oahu. An advanced cover force would lead to the target area a strike force of six carriers, two battleships and three cruisers plus escorts. This impressive armada began to gather in November 1941 in Hitokappu Bay in the Kuriles; on 26 November, under strict radio silence, the vessels steamed out of the bay to sail east, southeast, then south. The target: Pearl Harbor and the unsuspecting American fleet. Target date: 7 December 1941.

Moving steadily on their charted course, the phantom fleet was refueled en route. Late Japanese intelligence reports indicated that eight US battleships, nine cruisers, 20 destroyers and 41 other vessels were anchored at Pearl Harbor. Diplomatic negotiations between Washington and Tokyo being deadlocked, the coded message 'Climb Mount Niitaka' ('Proceed with attack') was sent out. On 7 December 1941 (Hawaiian date) between 6:00 and 7:15 in the morning, 360 planes (81 fighters, 104 horizontal bombers, 40 torpedo bombers, and 135 dive bombers) took flight from the decks of the six Japanese carriers 200 miles due north of the islands, formed up, and headed for Pearl Harbor. At 7:55 they attacked the quiet naval base with full fury. The greatest surprise attack in history had begun.

Between 7:55 and 9:45 the American fleet and air bases—not sufficiently warned despite ominous signs of trouble with Japan—underwent a devastating air raid without being able to put up a creditable defense. With little difficulty, the Japanese dive bombers first neutralized the airfields on Oahu; the American planes had

Right: **The destroyers *Cassin* and *Downes* and (behind) the battleship *Pennsylvania* in the flooded dry dock at Pearl Harbor after the attack.**

Above: A large column of smoke fills the sky above Battleship Row as the Japanese attack reaches its height.

Above: Rifle-armed soldiers and sailors keep watch for a renewed Japanese attack as the ships of Battleship Row burn in the background.
Below: Damage-control parties strive to control fires aboard the battleship *Nevada* at Pearl Harbor.

been neatly lined up in rows as a precaution against sabotage. At the same time the first waves of torpedo planes zoomed in at low altitude to ram their deadly ordnance into the hulls of battleships and cruisers moored side by side along the docks, the outside vessels taking the worst punishment. Pearl Harbor became an inferno of blazing ships as surviving crew members tried desperately to save the vessels and to man their antiaircraft weapons. After the initial half-hour attack, a 15-minute lull ensued; then the chaos of death began again at 8:40 as the Japanese horizontal bombers went to work, followed by a second wave of torpedo bombers. At 9:15 the dive bomber attacks resumed, lasting for an agonizing half hour. By 9:45 it was all over. The Japanese planes—only 29 of which had been lost—returned to their carriers, leaving behind them the burning wreckage of the Pacific Fleet.

In less than two hours the Japanese attackers had sunk or severely damaged eight battleships, three cruisers, three destroyers, four other vessels and 188 American aircraft. The Navy and Marine Corps suffered over 2000 men killed and over 700 wounded that day; the Army had almost 200 killed and over 400 wounded. The only consolation the American military leaders could draw from the dreadful day of death was that the Japanese had not destroyed the fuel storage tanks and naval repair shops on Oahu and that the three American carriers all happened to be deployed away from Pearl Harbor. The Pacific Fleet could be rebuilt to fight back.

Opposite: Map of the Battle of the Coral Sea.
Below: The Japanese carrier *Shokaku* under attack during the Coral Sea battle.
Bottom: The crew of the *Lexington* abandon ship, Coral Sea, 8 May 1942.

Early Actions

Within three days of Pearl Harbor America had declared war on Japan, Germany and Italy had declared war on the United States, and the United States had declared war on Germany and Italy. America had now joined the Allies in the worldwide fight against the Axis powers. By 1 January 1942 the Allies had confirmed their wartime intentions in the Declaration of Washington, which included the decision to concentrate first on Hitler and the Atlantic front. This priority was set because the German war machine, extended on four fronts, was a greater immediate danger. In the Pacific the Americans would wait until Europe had been taken care of, holding all the territory they could while slowing down the Japanese movements. American Forces went on the offensive in the Atlantic and on the defensive in the Pacific.

To lead this demanding military mission for the Navy, the stern taskmaster Admiral Ernest J King was brought in as Commander in Chief, US Fleet, on 30 December and the next month was also given the job of Chief of Naval Operations. King's man in the Pacific after 31 December was Admiral Chester W Nimitz, Commander in Chief, Pacific Fleet (Cincpac), moved up from Chief of the Bureau of Navigation to replace Admiral Husband E Kimmel, in disgrace and under investigation in the aftermath of the Pearl Harbor debacle. Time would show that this was a brilliant appointment. Admiral Hart was retained as commander of the Asiatic fleet for the time being as he was fighting a fine delaying action against the strong initial Japanese movements south. This team would be in charge of stalling the Japanese juggernaut in the Pacific. If they could not do the job, the way back to victory would be virtually impossible. Nimitz's task as Cincpac was to see that the Navy's job in the Pacific was done and done right.

Despite the rebuilding programs of the 1930s, the Navy had a mammoth job to gear up both men and ships for the fight ahead. Within a year of Pearl Harbor, 900,000 volunteers had been added to the prewar naval ranks of 325,000 officers and men. This called for rapidly expanding the four existing training sites and building three more. The additional officers needed would come partly from the V-5 (aviation cadet), V-7 (reserve midshipmen) and V-12 (general officer) programs on the nation's college campuses. Maintaining adequate trained manpower for the fleet was not a major problem for the Navy throughout the war once the multitudinous training programs had been set up.

Naval shipbuilding received top priority from the wartime administration, as industry turned to building the American war machine. Faced with the loss of virtually its entire Pacific battleship fleet at Pearl Harbor, the Navy was left with its carriers as the nucleus of Pacific power (the Atlantic Fleet had eight battleships and four carriers). Accordingly, it had only seven big carriers available for both oceans, although several large *Essex*-class flat-tops were building. The Navy turned to converting merchant vessels into 'baby flat-tops' or 'jeep carriers' for convoy escort, airplane transport and fleet support roles. Light also in cruisers, destroyers, submarines, landing craft, fighters, dive bombers and torpedo bom-

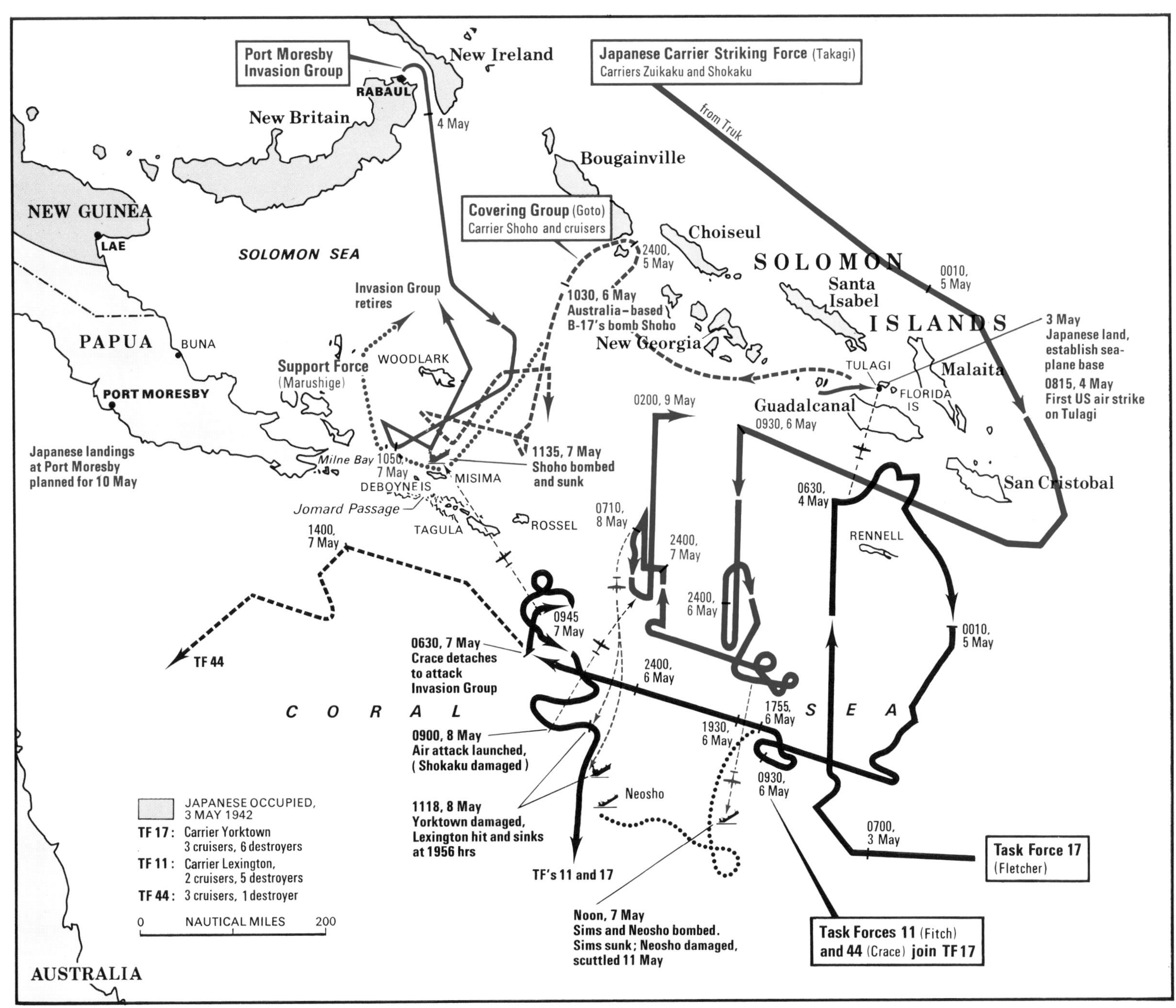

bers, the Navy began or accelerated building programs on all types of vessels and airplanes, so that by late 1942 it was gaining the muscle it needed. By 1943 giant fleets built around fast carriers would begin to dominate Pacific waters, but in the meantime the Navy was buying time until the balance of naval power could swing its way.

During the first six months of the war America's Pacific forces were fighting with their backs to the wall. Guam, Wake and Hong Kong were taken shortly after Pearl Harbor, and the Japanese marched down the Malayan Peninsula toward Singapore; the American Philippines were another prime target. Seeking to slow down the enemy a British naval force consisting of the new 35,000-ton battleship *Prince of Wales* and the battlecruiser *Repulse* threw themselves in the way of the Japanese fleet moving down through Malayan waters on 10 December, only to be sunk by Japanese bombers and torpedo planes. In January 1942 four old American destroyers launched an attack on the Japanese in the Makassar Strait west of Borneo and sank five ships in an amazing display of gallantry. The following month a weak Allied naval force under Rear Admiral Karel Doorman of the Royal Netherlands Navy tried valiantly to stop the Japanese in the Battle of the Java Sea. All the Allied cruisers, including the USS *Houston*, were lost. With the Allied defensive fleet gone, the Dutch East Indies were soon in Japanese hands.

In the critical Philippines the American forces grimly awaited their turn. Soon Army and Filipino ground forces were encircled on the Bataan Peninsula, and the 4th Marine Regiment was holding out on Corregidor at the entrance to Manila Bay. With the Philippines about to fall to the Japanese juggernaut, General MacArthur was ordered out to make his way to Australia, from which point he could direct a counteroffensive. What remained of the American forces surrendered in May 1942, and General Jonathan Wainwright and his 70,000 men were forced to undergo the infamous Bataan Death March.

While this was taking place, the Japanese in the early months of 1942 had moved far south into the Solomon Islands and northern New Guinea and threatened both Port Moresby on Papua New Guinea and Australia itself. If these fell, defeat of the Japanese would be virtually impossible. No one knew this better than the Pacific fleet commanders.

To gain some idea of Japanese strength along the sea lanes to Australia and to lift civilian morale by showing that somebody was 'doing something,' an American carrier force built around the *Enterprise* under the command of Vice-Admiral William F Halsey staged a raid on the Marshall and Gilbert Islands halfway between Hawaii and Australia in February 1942.

They followed this up the same month with a raid on Wake and Marcus Islands in the central Pacific. In March a task force that included the *Lexington* and *Yorktown* raided northern New Guinea. None of

Top: A destroyer comes alongside the damaged *Lexington* to help take the crew off. *Above:* The *Lexington* finally blows up. Better damage-control procedures might have saved the ship.

these raids caused significant damage, but they did lift morale at home. The same is true of Lieutenant Colonel James Doolittle's raid on Tokyo of 18 April 1942. The 16 B-25 Army bombers that lifted off the deck of the *Hornet*, 650 miles out at sea, to bomb Tokyo and then fly another 1100 miles to China did little damage, but they did give Americans a great deal of much-needed hope in the dismal early months of 1942.

When the Americans discovered, by breaking the Japanese naval code, that the enemy was launching invasion forces against Port Moresby in southern New Guinea and the island of Tulagi in the Solomons to the east, they decided to thwart those plans as best they could. The result was the Battle of the Coral Sea of 7–8 May 1942. Rear Admiral Frank Jack Fletcher and the *Yorktown* task force, and Rear Admiral Aubrey W Fitch in command of the *Lexington* task force, were ordered to strike at the two enemy task forces. Halsey, with the *Enterprise* and *Hornet* (back from the Tokyo raid) was ordered to follow. He arrived too late. The opposing American and Japanese forces found one another on 7 May and launched their attacks. This was the first naval engagement in history in which surface ships never fired a shot at one another and, indeed, never saw one another. When it was over after two days of air attacks on the fleets, the Japanese had lost the new small carrier *Shoho* and another had been badly damaged. The Americans saw the *Yorktown* badly damaged and lost a tanker, a destroyer and the *Lexington* on the second day—the *Lexington* the victim of two torpedoes plus an enormous explosion caused by ruptured aviation fuel lines. (Most of the crew were saved.) The Battle of the Coral Sea was a strategic victory for the Americans despite their heavy losses because it stopped the invasion of Port Moresby. But now the Americans had only four carriers left in Pacific waters (*Yorktown*, *Hornet*, *Saratoga*, *Enterprise*); the Japanese had nine. Within one month this imbalance had been largely nullified in the Battle of Midway, the Navy's greatest victory in World War II.

The Battle of Midway

The Japanese wanted the island of Midway as a forward base for an attack on Hawaii; they also wanted to lure the American fleet out to its own destruction. The First Carrier Striking Force of four carriers (*Akagi*, *Kaga*, *Hiryu*, *Soryu*) plus two battleships, three cruisers and 11 destroyers was under the command of Vice-Admiral Chuichi Nagumo, who had led the attack on Pearl Harbor. Its mission was to attack Midway by air and devastate the American fleet if it showed up. The Midway Invasion Force (Second Fleet) under Vice-Admiral Nobutake Kondo would move in from the west with 5000 men in 12 transports with two battleships, a light carrier and numerous cruisers and destroyers as escorts. A third armada, the Second Carrier Striking Force, would move on American positions at Attu, Adak and Kiska far north in the Aleutians as a diversion. It would consist of two light carriers, three cruisers and six destroyers. In the rear would come the Main Force (First Fleet) of nine battleships plus numerous cruisers and destroyers under the command of Admiral Yamamoto himself, who had personally approved the invasion-entrapment plans. In addition, 16 submarines would station themselves between Pearl Harbor and Midway to the northwest. If the Americans came out to do battle, Yamamoto had more than enough firepower to put them down (although he believed that the *Yorktown* as well as the *Lexington* might have been sunk in the Battle of the Coral Sea and that the *Hornet* and the *Enterprise* were still in the Solomons area). If not, the submarine screen could stop them or at least give warning if any carriers sallied forth.

Unknown to Yamamoto, Admiral Nimitz had learned both his plans and his target date: 4 June 1942. This was due to the

Above: The small Japanese carrier *Shoho* takes a torpedo hit from an American aircraft, 7 May 1942.
Below, main picture: A Japanese Val dive-bomber attacks the USS *Hornet* during the Battle of Santa Cruz, 26 October 1942.

Above: **The *Yorktown* on fire after the first Japanese attack during the Battle of Midway. These fires were brought under control.**

superior sleuthing of cryptologist Commander Joseph Rochefort and his assistants at Pearl Harbor. Nimitz knew that he had only two carriers (*Hornet* and *Enterprise*), plus the damaged *Yorktown* if she could be patched up in time, with which to stop the attack. The recently repaired *Saratoga* was at San Diego to form a new task force and undoubtedly could not get back in time. Against these the Japanese could throw perhaps 10 carriers, plus 23 cruisers and 11 fast battleships. Rather than scatter his fleet to protect Oahu, Nimitz decided not to take the bait of the Aleutians invading force and concentrate his forces on the Japanese left flank. If the four carriers of the First Carrier Striking Force were to be taken out of action, the Midway invasion force and the combined fleets would be without air cover. Put the carriers down and the whole Japanese operation would fail. It was a long shot, but Nimitz had no choice. If he scattered his thin fleet, the Americans could do nothing to stop the Japanese.

Accordingly, when Task Force 16 including the *Hornet* and *Enterprise* returned to Pearl Harbor on 16 May, Nimitz gave command of the force to Rear Admiral Raymond Spruance (Halsey being hospitalized with a skin ailment) and told him to put himself on Nagumo's flank and hit him while his planes were off raiding Midway. Task Force 16 left Oahu on 28 May. When Task Force 17 returned to Pearl Harbor under Admiral Fletcher, Nimitz gave the repair crews three days to get the *Yorktown* ready again (the estimates had all concluded it would take 90 days). Three days later, on 30 May, the *Yorktown* and Task Force 17 left the Pacific base to meet Spruance and Task Force 16 at the rendezvous point 200 miles north of Midway. The stage was set for a titanic clash.

As the American task forces arrived on station, it became a matter of waiting. In the meantime Rear Admiral Robert A Theobald's North Pacific Force was steaming north to intercept the attack on the Aleutians, but Theobald, believing the Aleutians landing was a ruse and that the enemy would hit Dutch Harbor far to the east or else Alaska, placed his force 400 miles south of Kodiak: as a result, he was out of the fight altogether. As the *Saratoga* task force left San Diego on 1 June, it would arrive too late to help.

Although all this was not known by Nimitz, Spruance and Fletcher at the time, it was clearly up to the two carrier task forces, plus some Army B-17s on Midway, to stop the invasion. Yet Nimitz had a glimpse of victory. His Operation Plan No. 29–42, while stipulating an attack of attrition on the Japanese striking force, included the enticing idea that, with luck, maybe the Japanese fleet could be caught while recovering its attacking planes, thus grounding the remaining Japanese carrier planes until recovery of the fuel-shy first wave was completed. Furthermore, the Japanese might still believe the carriers were far south in the Solomons (a US cruiser in the Coral Sea was broadcasting on carrier air-group frequencies to give that impression). Then complete surprise would be possible. As the battle turnd out, this is exactly what happened. A shot of luck, unbelievable gallantry and correct command decisions won the day for the undersized American naval forces.

On 3 June the Japanese invasion fleet was spotted 700 miles west of Midway: Army B-17s attacked the enemy ships, although no damage was done. But at least Admiral Nimitz knew the Japanese were coming right on schedule and could be expected the next day.

At six o'clock on the morning of 4 June Navy Catalina scout planes found the Japanese strike force 180 miles northwest of Midway and coming down hard at 135 degrees. Nimitz correctly surmised that they had launched their first wave and did not know of the American carriers on their flank, since they were not turning to meet them. By 6:25 Midway was under heavy air attack. A half hour later Spruance launched his planes from the *Hornet*, *Enterprise* and *Yorktown*. By 8:20 Nimitz knew that Nagumo would either have to launch his reserves (if his search planes had discovered the American carriers), leaving the returning first-strike planes in the air on low fuel, or he would have to

Above: **Japanese torpedo bombers pass near the already damaged *Yorktown*.**
Below: **The Japanese *Hiryu* shortly before she was sunk.**

recover, refuel and rearm the first strike planes for a second strike, leaving the second-wave planes waiting. If he chose the first, he would lose planes to the sea; if he chose the second, he would lose at least an hour. He chose the latter. If only the American planes arrived on time, Nimitz knew, the Japanese would be in an extremely vulnerable position.

Although 35 dive bombers from the *Hornet* could not find the Japanese fleet and flew on to Midway, the 15 old TBD Devastator torpedo bombers from the *Hornet* sighted the enemy at 10:25 am and attacked with no fighter cover. They skimmed in over the water to launch their torpedoes, with Japanese fighters and antiaircraft guns contesting them every inch of the way. Ten of 14 torpedo bombers from the *Enterprise* joining in the attack were shot down; 35 of 41 from the *Yorktown* met the same fate; all the torpedo bombers from the *Hornet* were lost. And they had done no damage whatever. But their gallant sacrifice won rich dividends, because they had pulled the Japanese fighter cover down just as dive bombers from the *Yorktown* and *Enterprise* happened to discover the Japanese fleet. No fighters were up to oppose them. Down they plummeted through clear skies. The *Akagi* was hit by three bombs and soon turned into a raging inferno of fuel oil and torpedoes left on deck in rearming the first wave for a strike on the American carriers. Admiral Nagumo was forced to transfer his flag to a nearby cruiser, and the survivors of the fiery holocaust abandoned ship. She sank the next morning.

At almost the same time the *Akagi* was hit, the *Kaga* and *Soryu* were struck by the American dive bombers. Again the ships quickly became infernos from the bombs, torpedoes and aviation fuel. Nagumo had refused to launch an attack on the American carriers with his reserves as soon as he discovered they were in the area; he had waited until the first wave was recovered, re-fueled and armed with armor-piercing bombs and torpedoes. This took two hours. Just as his carriers were turning into the wind to launch, the *Yorktown* and *Enterprise* bombers hit them. It was like throwing a match into a powder keg.

Shortly thereafter, at 10:50 am, Japanese dive bombers from the fourth and trailing carrier, the *Hiryu*, were launched against the American carriers. They found their prey—the *Yorktown*. Eighteen dive bombers hit her with two bombs that stopped her dead in the water. Within

***Above:* An escorting cruiser moves in to assist the burning *Yorktown*.**

minutes Admiral Fletcher had shifted his flag from the doomed vessel to the cruiser *Astoria*. But the *Yorktown* refused to go down. Two hours later her men had repaired her boilers and she was making 20 knots and preparing to launch her fighters. At this point she was attacked again by torpedo planes; a third wave hit her once more an hour later and she was abandoned. But for a second time she refused to go down, and was not sunk until three days later while being towed to Pearl Harbor. A Japanese sub evaded her destroyer screen to put her down.

The *Hiryu* may have been carrying on gallantly as the last carrier in the group, but at 5:00 in the afternoon of 4 June her turn came. She was hit by 24 American planes in four waves, took four bomb hits and had to be abandoned. She was deliberately sunk the next morning by a Japanese submarine.

Four Japanese carriers were sunk or sinking: the American flank attack had worked perfectly. But the battle was not over. What if Yamamoto detached his fast battleships and cruisers from the Midway Invasion Force to attack the American carrier task forces in their state of exhaustion? Correctly guessing that this would happen, Spruance and Fletcher moved to the east. The Japanese battleships and cruisers came on in hot pursuit the night of 4 June, but had to abandon their search early the next morning for fear of being caught in daylight without air cover. As they turned back west, American air-search crews reported that all Japanese ships were moving northwest; Yamamoto had called off the invasion.

But Spruance was not done. He came barreling through to catch the fleeing Japanese fleets and put them under air attack. The next day, 6 June, American air strikes sank the cruiser *Mikuma* and battered the *Mogami* unmercifully. Still Yamamoto could salvage at least a partial victory if Spruance kept coming. Task Force 16 could run into a trap of bombers stationed on Wake Island plus the firepower of his First Fleet (at this point, indeed throughout the entire battle, the Pacific command had no idea that the First Fleet was in the rear area). Yamamoto even had English-language distress signals sent out to lure the Americans into the trap. But Spruance refused to take the bait. Fearing attacks on his task force from the land-based bombers, he turned back east 400 miles from Midway. The battle was over, even though the Japanese from the Second Carrier Striking Force landed and took Attu and Kiska the next day, 7 June—while Theobald's Force was 1000 miles away.

Above: A Hellcat fighter comes in to land on a new _Essex_ class carrier.
Above right: R to L, Admiral Halsey, Secretary Knox and Admiral King.
Right: A landing officer brings a plane in to land on the carrier _Wasp_.
Below: The Japanese heavy cruiser _Mikuma_ sinking after the Battle of Midway.

Above: **Dauntless dive bombers head for the Japanese aircraft carrier fleet at Midway. What seems to be a burning Japanese ship can be seen below.**

When the score was tallied up, the American Navy had won an overwhelming victory, perhaps the greatest in its history. While losing the *Yorktown*, one destroyer, 147 aircraft and 307 men, American naval forces had pounded the Japanese with heavy losses: four carriers and one heavy cruiser sunk, one heavy cruiser wrecked, one battleship and three destroyers damaged, 322 aircraft lost and 2500 men killed. This last factor was especially crucial, since among the casualties were the elite of Japanese naval pilots. Time would prove that they could never be adequately replaced—a critical factor in a naval war dominated by the antagonists' air power. Admiral Yamamoto, in trying to obtain two objectives, Midway and the American fleet, had gained neither. The Battle of Midway reversed the entire course of the Pacific war: the US took the offensive. It was the Navy's finest hour in World War II.

Battles for Guadalcanal

The Japanese military forces had reached their farthest point of expansion by the summer of 1942, although no one realized it at the time. But both sides understood clearly that if the Japanese secured complete control of the Solomon Islands east of New Guinea, they would be able to cut the supply lines to Australia and wreck Allied plans for a counteroffensive from that base of operations. Furthermore, the Americans wanted to wrest Guadalcanal in the south Solomons from the Japanese to establish a base for the right arm of a two-pronged movement north through the Solomons. (The left arm under General MacArthur would move from Australia along the coast of New Guinea, then turn right to take the large Japanese base at Rabaul on New Britain Island). Accordingly, the first giant amphibious operation of the war was planned with the islands of Guadalcanal and Tulagi, Ganutu and Tanambogo, twenty miles to the north, as the targets. It was set for early August 1942. Two Navy task forces were to aid 19,000 Marines in the landing: an air support force built around the carriers *Hornet*, *Wasp* and *Enterprise* and an amphibious support force built around seven cruisers. The Marine landing on 7 August went well, and by the next day Tulagi, the other tiny islands and the airfield on the north edge of Guadalcanal had been taken (renamed Henderson Field, it was the focus of fighting for the next four months). The Navy's SeaBees (Construction Battalions) went to work to finish the field for American use. But early next morning, a Japanese strike force of seven cruisers and a destroyer came racing down 'The Slot' through the

Below: **The carrier *Wasp* sinks after a torpedo attack from the Japanese submarine *I.19* in the Solomons in September 1942.**

Right: The flight deck of the carrier *Saratoga* at dawn before an attack on Rabaul in November 1943.

Above: **President Roosevelt examines a captured Japanese flag, taken after an amphibious operation.**

waters of the central Solomons and attacked the unsuspecting amphibious force as it lay south of Guadalcanal—the carrier fleet having been pulled back by Admiral Fletcher for refueling.

In the resulting Battle of Savo Island, the Allied amphibious fleet was severely mauled, losing four cruisers in a matter of hours. Unaware that the American carriers were not in the area, Vice-Admiral Gunichi Mikawa withdrew before attacking the unprotected transports. A severe defeat could easily have been a disaster. But Rear Admiral Kelly Turner, expecting more trouble for his battered men and ships, withdrew the naval amphibious support force before the supply ships were completely unloaded, leaving the Marines and SeaBees to their own devices on Guadalcanal. After a ten-day stage of rebuilding by both combatants, marked by light attacks by each side, the Japanese returned in force. Six sea battles were eventually fought before the control of the south Solomons was finally decided.

The first of these, the Battle of the Eastern Solomons of 24 August 1942, was fought 150 miles east of Guadalcanal. As a Japanese occupation force and two screening forces moved toward the island, Admiral Fletcher's planes from the *Enterprise* and *Saratoga* attacked the enemy forces and sank the small carrier *Ryujo* and a destroyer. This blunted the planned attack, although the *Enterprise* was badly damaged by Japanese aircraft. The Japanese were forced to abandon their attempt to recapture Guadalcanal at this time. The second engagement, the Battle of Cape Esperance, took place on 11–12 October. An American naval force—less the carriers *Saratoga* (damaged by a torpedo on 31 August and forced out of action for three months) and *Wasp* (torpedoed and sunk by a Japanese sub on 15 September)—took on a Japanese force that was part of the 'Tokyo Express'—cruisers and destroyers that moved in nightly to reinforce Japanese positions and shell American troops on Guadalcanal. The American cruiser-destroyer task force sank a Japanese cruiser and destroyer, losing one destroyer in the battle. Undeterred, the Japanese continued to resupply and reinforce their Guadalcanal forces. The situation was growing critical as they fiercely contested the American presence on Guadalcanal. The Navy had to gain control of the air and water around the island, or America's toehold in the Solomons would be lost.

Two weeks later, sensing the time was right for a massive move to expel the hard-pressed Americans, Admiral Yamamoto sent a giant force of four carriers, four battleships, 14 cruisers and 44 destroyers to deliver a knockout blow to the Navy and push the Marines off Guadalcanal. Admiral Halsey, now in command in the area, sent Admiral Thomas C Kinkaid to meet them with two carriers, two battleships, nine cruisers and 24 destroyers. The resulting air melee, known as the Battle of the Santa Cruz Islands, took place on 26 October 1942 and ended with American loss of the *Hornet* and new damage to the *Enterprise*. In this carrier-plane battle the Americans suffered a tactical defeat when Kincaid was forced to withdraw, but they won a strategic victory in that over 100 Japanese planes and crews went down—a crucial loss to the Japanese Navy. While this third battle was taking place, the Marines were beating off Japanese reinforcements. The Guadalcanal campaign was beginning to turn around, despite the losses in the Battle of the Santa Cruz Islands.

The fourth and fifth battles, known as the Naval Battles of Guadalcanal, took place on

Above: The assault transport *McCawley* on exercises in 1943.
Right: Arming a Dauntless dive bomber aboard the *Enterprise* in August 1942.

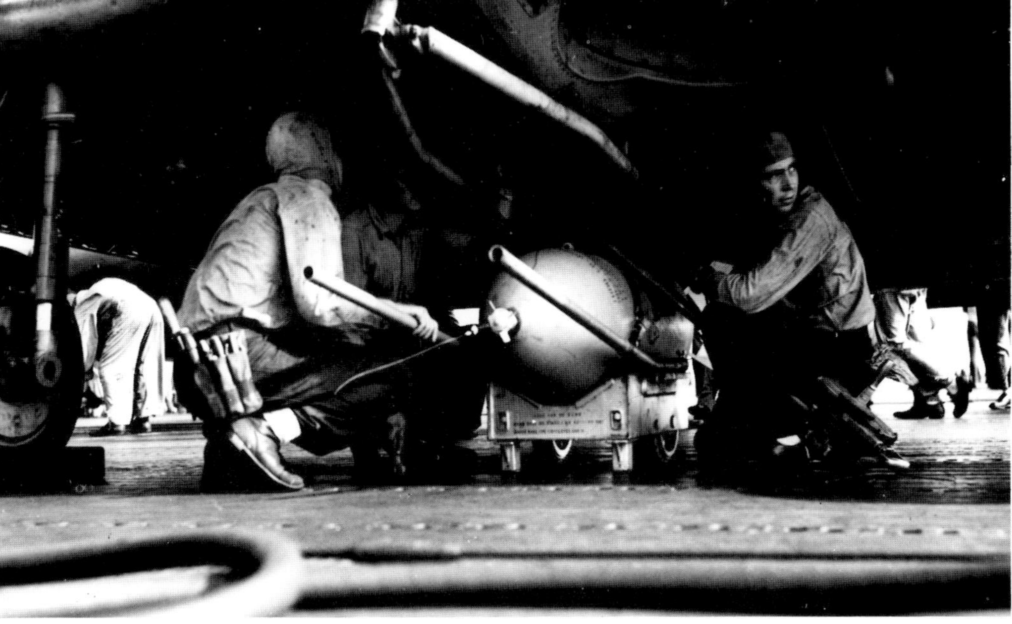

12–15 November. The first was a wild brawl of only 14 minutes, in which an American force of five cruisers and eight destroyers under Rear Admiral Daniel J Callahan attempted to derail the Tokyo Express and its 13,500-troop replacement force bound for Guadalcanal. The Japanese lost one battleship and two destroyers in the furious and desperate fighting; the Americans lost the cruisers *Atlanta* and *Juneau* and four destroyers. But the Jap-

Below right: The heavy cruiser *Quincy* seen a few days before she was sunk in the Battle of Savo Island, 9 August 1942.
Below: Training with Goodyear blimps at Moffet Field, CA, in 1944.

anese were forced to retreat without reinforcing Guadalcanal. The second battle took place on 14 November. Again the Japanese were attempting to reinforce Guadalcanal, and again the American naval forces were assigned the task of stopping them. In this surface ship-to-ship battle American and Japanese units pounded at one another again, both sides suffering heavy losses, but as the Japanese invasion force scattered, Guadalcanal was secure at last.

The sixth engagement, the Battle of Tassafaronga of 30 November 1942, was a clear Japanese victory of eight destroyers over an American cruiser-destroyer force in the dark of night, but it made no appreciable difference in the campaign. American naval forces had gradually but definitely gained control of the sea and air in the southern Solomons to the point where the Japanese could no longer contest them. So many ships had been sunk in the waters just north of Guadalcanal that the area was given the nickname 'Iron-bottom Sound.' When the Army took over Guadalcanal from the Marines with 50,000 troops in January, and the Tokyo Express was finally derailed at the same time by patrol torpedo (PT) boats and aircraft, the dogged battle for Guadalcanal was over (9 February 1943). American military forces now had their staging area in the southern Solomons and could begin to move north.

Island Hopping

For the next year and a half, combined American forces in the Pacific carried out a giant ocean-wide, two-pronged movement against the Japanese possessions. The left prong of the movement consisted of General Douglas MacArthur's Southwest Pacific Forces clearing the enemy from the north shore of New Guinea and moving into the Bismarck Sea. As he moved, his right flank was covered by the South Pacific Forces under Admiral Halsey fighting their way through the Solomon Island chain to meet MacArthur's forces in the Admiralty Islands. The two would then roll northwest toward the Philippines. In the meantime, the right prong, the Central Pacific Forces under Admiral Spruance, moved from Pearl Harbor in a westerly and southwesterly direction to take the Marshall, Gilbert and Marianas island chains from the Japanese, then advanced west to meet the left pincer at the Philippines, while also driving to the northwest toward the Japanese home islands. During this gigantic offensive campaign the Japanese would be pushed inexorably back by a series of amphibious landings on certain key islands and bases while the Allies deliberately neutralized or bypassed others to let them 'die on the vine' with severing of their supply lines to the rear.

To carry out its Pacific-wide strategy successfully, the US Navy had to expand constantly, procuring more ships, men

Above: The battleship *Iowa* and a sister ship at sea in 1944.
Left: Crewmen of the carrier *Yorktown* in May 1943. Several of the US ships sunk early in the war were remembered in the names of more modern replacements.
Below: The *Massachusetts* during a shore bombardment.

and equipment from the shipyards, factories and homes of America. These were forthcoming in abundance. By mid-1943 the fast carrier task force had been formed and was proving a powerful weapon. Usually consisting of up to a dozen heavy and light carriers with hundreds of planes on board, as many as six great battleships for firepower and dozens of escorting cruisers and destroyers with necessary support vessels, these mighty armadas cruised at 25 knots, taking the war to the Japanese with devastating force. By that same year the Navy had 18,000 aircraft of improved quality; during 1944 the number reached 30,000. Grumman Avenger torpedo bombers, Grumman F6F Hellcats and Vought Corsairs and their crews could match and excel anything the Japanese could launch. Navy personnel approached three million in 1943, including 100,000 WAVES (Women Accepted for Voluntary Emergency Service). Utilization of scientific inventions made the armadas' ships and weapons even more effective. The use and improvement of radar, sonar, variable-timed fuses, rockets and hundreds of other developments made the deadly work of the Navy more effective than ever before. Behind all this the ever-improving logistical stream of unglamorous oilers, transports and freighters carrying the millions of tons of supplies and hundreds of thousands of soldiers and Marines facilitated the mission of pushing back the Japanese. As the Pacific conflict turned into a war of strategy, firepower, manpower and logistics—in short, into a war of attrition—the Americans began advancing as a gigantic force across the broad waters of the Pacific.

By the summer of 1943, the Americans and their Australian and New Zealand allies were prepared to begin 'island

Below: A Navy Liberator patrol aircraft takes off from Guadalcanal on a photo-reconnaissance mission in 1943.

Above: **Final briefing for pilots aboard the *Lexington* before a mission during the Gilberts operations in December 1943.**

hopping toward the Philippines and the Japanese home islands. They were indirectly aided by the death of Admiral Isoruko Yamamoto (18 April 1943) shot down by an Army P-38 pursuit plane over Bougainville in the Solomons. The great strategist of the Japanese Pacific war was out of the fight, the victim of an intercepted code message and an ambush. His replacement was more defensive-minded than the great Yamamoto—a fact much to the Allies' advantage.

The summer/fall 1943 objective for the left prong of the Pacific strategy was the central Solomons. Munda, Kolombangara and Vella Lavella were taken or neutralized, and the great Japanese base at Rabaul on New Britain was pounded by American planes, neutralized and finally bypassed. To the west, Bougainville with its 60,000 defenders was invaded by amphibious forces on 1 November after its airfields had been knocked out: it was secured in two months. In all these operations the US Navy carried out very successful preliminary air attacks to soften up the enemy positions, covered the landings with bombardments and air cover, and supplied and protected the land forces as they struggled toward their objectives. The Army, Navy, and Marines were learning that precisely co-ordinated preparation and execution were critical in amphibious warfare. The summer of 1943 also saw the Aleutians wrested from the Japanese by American naval and army units with co-operation from Canadian forces. US Navy bombardment and landing-support operations were as critical to Allied amphibious victory here in the north as they were in the South Pacific.

The central Pacific right prong of the grand strategy began to move in the fall of 1943. After intermittent air attacks through October and early November from the new giant *Essex*-class carrier fleets, American forces moved to take Makin and Tarawa in the Gilbert Islands in mid-November. After heavy air and sea bombardments of the islands, the Army landed on Makin and the Marines hit Tarawa on 20 November. Makin, lightly defended, was relatively easy, but Tarawa was a nightmare. The attacking waves of Marines came up against reinforced pillboxes, bunkers and dugouts virtually untouched by preliminary bombardment. They suffered very heavy casualties. Only when the naval air and sea bombardments were resumed were the Japanese dug out of their fortified emplacements. But the Americans learned their lessons from the Tarawa experience. Armor-piercing shells and rockets were needed against reinforced fortifications, better across-the-beach landing craft were required, and improved preinvasion reconnaissance of the enemy's defenses was absolutely essential. Tarawa was a grim teacher of the realities of amphibious warfare.

By early 1944 MacArthur's forces had worked their way across the coast of northern New Guinea and had turned west to take the Admiralty Islands. With Rabaul bypassed and the Admiralties taken, the Solomon Island chain was in American and Allied hands. Success was achieved by seizure of key bases, leaving others to wither without support; this was possible because the Japanese Navy could no longer contend with the ever-increasing power of the US Navy, which concentrated increasingly on supplying air cover, sea bombardment and transport and landing support to invading soldiers and marines. The Pacific war was gradually turning around as naval offensive and support power developed into an unbeatable weapon of modern amphibious warfare.

As MacArthur advanced in the South Pacific, Spruance and the Central Pacific Forces continued westward. The major islands of the Gilberts secured, the target shifted to the Marshall Islands to the northwest. Little was known of the Marshalls, which consist of over 1000 atolls and five major islands, because they had been

Above: Flight-deck scene aboard the light carrier _Monterey_ in late 1943. _Monterey_ and her sisters were converted from hulls laid down for light cruisers.
Right: The light cruiser _St Louis_ leaves Tulagi Harbor.

taken by Japan from Germany after World War I and been closed to all outsiders since 1935. It was rightly believed they had been converted into a complex of naval and air bases. The decision was to concentrate on Kwajelein Atoll in the southwest Marshalls, since it could be converted into a giant staging area, and on Eniwetok at the far northwestern edge of the group. Learning from previous experience, on 20–21 January 1944 Kwajalein was bombed and shelled as no Japanese stronghold had ever been hit before. It paid off: over three-fourths of the Japanese defenders died before any Americans began to hit the beach on 31 January. Although the soldiers and Marines assaulting Kwajalein Atoll took heavy casualties, the Japanese lost over 8000 men in one week. Kwajalein was taken. Eniwetok fell two weeks later. Overwhelming naval bombardment and air power, plus flinty determination by the land forces, had brought the Marshalls into American hands.

Next stop in the central Pacific was the Mariana Islands 1000 miles due west and only 1500 miles from the Japanese home islands. First Saipan, then Guam and Tinian, would be assaulted. On 11–12 June 1944 the airfields and defenses of all three islands came under murderous bombing from the planes of the American fast-carrier task forces moving into the area. Two days of concentrated shelling of Saipan and Tinian from the vessels of the surface fleet followed. On 15 June the Marines landed on Saipan, on the 16th, soldiers of the 27th Army Division. They were faced by 30,000 determined Japanese defenders. It took three weeks of hard fighting to secure an island of only 72 square miles, the last days being marked by the horror of over 3000 Japanese suicides, mostly civilians who chose to die by leaping from the bluffs of the northern coast to the rocky shore 830 feet below rather than submit to capture. (They had been told the Americans would torture and execute them if they surrendered.)

Tinian and Guam were the next targets, and the Mariana Islands would soon be in American hands and prepared as staging areas for the next offensives. Giant airfields in the Marianas would put Japan itself within reach of long-range American bombers.

Above: Aircrew aboard the *Ticonderoga* relax in the carrier's ready room in November 1944.

For the Japanese, the successful American onslaughts in the Gilberts and Marshalls had been serious reverses, but now the Americans simply had to be stopped. From the Marianas they could link up with MacArthur's forces moving north from New Guinea to assault the Philippines. And they could swing north, using their bomber and naval power to attack the islands off the Japanese coast, like Okinawa.

Below: A Japanese patrol boat sinking after being torpedoed by the submarine *Seawolf* in April 1943.

From there, the Allies could launch frequent, death-dealing air attacks on Japan's home islands. With the whole war effort endangered, the Japanese Navy was called upon to stop the Americans in the Marianas before the whole Japanese outer defense perimeter collapsed. The result was the Battle of the Philippine Sea of 19–20 June 1944.

Warned by his scouting submarines that a Japanese carrier group was approaching the Marianas, Admiral Spruance detached Rear Admiral Marc A Mitscher's Task Force 58, consisting of 15 carriers and seven battleships, to meet them. On the morning of 19 June the Japanese launched an initial 69 planes against the American force, and 'The Great Marianas Turkey Shoot' began. Navy Hellcats shot down 25 of this first wave of planes before they even saw the American fleet. Most of the remaining planes fell victim to American anti-aircraft guns fitted with the new VT (proximity) fuses that detonated anywhere within 70 feet of the target. Yet wave after wave of Japanese planes—piloted by very inexperienced crews due to a critical shortage in the fleet—tried to penetrate the American defenses. About 320 Japanese planes went down or were wrecked on landing, to only 27 American planes lost; American submarines sank two carriers during the battle. The Japanese withdrew, but Mitscher's air crews found them late the next day. Two hundred and sixteen American planes took to the air and caught up with the retreating Japanese fleet. One carrier was sunk and another damaged. Critically low on gasoline, the carrier pilots returned to Task Force 58 after sunset. Many could not find the fleet and landed in the dark. Seventy-three planes were lost in the murky Pacific waters, but all except 16 pilots and 33 crew members were rescued. Despite the danger of being sunk by submarines if the lights were turned on, Mitscher saved his remaining pilots by ordering full illumination, and the Battle of the Philippine Sea came to a successful conclusion. The Japanese sea menace in the Marianas removed, Tinian fell on 1 August and Guam nine days later. From the newly constructed airstrips on Saipan, Army B-29s would begin bombing the Japanese home islands by November.

Submarine Warfare

While American surface ships were waging their giant two-pronged offensive against Japanese naval and military units across the Pacific waters, American fleet

Right: Planes of the carrier *Enterprise* during the raid on Marcus Island in 1942.
Below: Enlisted men exercise on the deck of the *Yorktown* during operations in 1943.

LCM 53

Far left: US personnel inspect the battered shoreline of Kwajalein after its capture from the Japanese in February 1944.
Left: One of the battlecruiser *Alaska*'s Curtiss SC-1 float planes taxis in to be recovered during the Iwo Jima operation in March 1945.
Main picture: The oiler *Cahaba* refuels the battleship *Iowa* and an aircraft carrier in the Pacific in 1945.

Above: **A pilot of VF.17 describes a successful air battle near Rabaul to one of his buddies in February 1944.**

submarines of the 311-foot *Gato*, *Balao* and *Tench* classes were achieving their own remarkable victories. American submarines early in the war were few in number, and captains and crews were frequently frustrated by too few torpedoes and by failures of the magnetic exploder, depth-control mechanism or contact exploder in the standard Mark 14 torpedoes.

Below: **The USS** ***Barb*** **leaves Mare Island on her last war patrol in July 1945.**

These flaws made the torpedoes run below their target or fail to detonate, but improvements in both boats and weaponry soon turned the submarines into one of the most effective classes of weapons in the American naval arsenal.

American subs had no hesitancy in attacking Japanese warships. They also served invaluable rescue and intelligence-gathering functions across the Pacific and even in Japanese home waters. Fleet-movement and weather information gathered by submarines played a valuable role in the Navy's Pacific strategy. But the primary mission of the submarines was to destroy the Japanese merchant marine.

Japan, an island nation, was as vulnerable to economic strangulation as Britain. Without its merchant fleet to bring in raw materials from its far-flung subject states and to supply its garrisons defending the empire, it could not even function, much less win the war. Japan had to import 24 percent of its coal, 88 percent of its iron ore and almost 90 per cent of its oil. Strangely, given this vulnerability, the Japanese had never developed effective antisubmarine warfare (ASW) resources and did little to remedy the deficiency during the war. As a result, American submarines could range far and wide against the Japanese economic lifelines.

Operating on single patrol missions or, after 1943, in small 'wolf packs,' the 1500-ton diesel fleet submarines—each with 24 torpedoes, a 20-knot surface and 8.75-knot submerged speed, and a cruising range of 10,000 miles—stalked their prey. The newer boats had radar that permitted them to attack at night on the surface, or they could fire their deadly ordnance from periscope depth. By late 1943 the toll of Japanese merchant shipping began to rise and the Japanese were ill-equipped to contain the destruction. Vice Admiral Charles A Lockwood, commander of the Pacific Fleet's submarines, turned them loose on the ships carrying oil from the Dutch East Indies and Borneo in 1944; soon tankers were being sunk faster than they could be replaced, their valuable crude oil lost to the Japanese war cause. In one month alone, October 1944, one-third of all Japanese tankers afloat were sunk.

Right: **Ships of Task Force 58, the main carrier force, at anchor in the South Pacific early in 1944.**
Below right: **The devastating effects of heavy naval bombardment seen on Kwajalein immediately after its capture.**

During the Pacific war, 288 American submarines—with crews of 80 officers and men each—sank 276 warships and over four million tons of Japanese merchant shipping, some vessels approaching or topping 100,000 tons to their credit. In addition, mines planted by submarines, surface vessels or aircraft sank another two million tons. The price paid was only 59 American submarines.

By 1945 the Japanese war machine was wobbling under the blows of American submarine warfare against its lines of supply. Whether or not this unrestricted submarine warfare was the most important factor in Japan's defeat, as some experts claim, there is no doubt that the crews of the 'silent service,' co-operating with their naval surface and air comrades, were disabling the Japanese effort in the later months of the war.

Final Assaults

By the summer of 1944 the US Navy was approaching full strength. It had over 1100 combatant ships including 23 battleships, 22 carriers, 63 'jeep carriers,' 52 cruisers, over 700 destroyers and destroyer-escorts, over 34,000 planes and 59,000 pilots, over 200 subs and almost 40,000 landing craft. Personnel stood at approximately 3,500,000 men and women. In the Pacific the pincers of the Allied grand strategy were moving ever more rapidly toward the Philippines, as MacArthur moved up from New Guinea to take Morotai in the East Indies and the Central Pacific Forces prepared to move in from the Marianas in support of this drive; the Atlantic Fleet, having helped put down the German submarine menace, was assisting the final drive on Nazi Germany.

On 20 October 1944 MacArthur's army landed on the southwest coast of the island of Leyte to surprisingly little resistance. As promised two and a half years earlier, he had returned to the Philippines. At this, the Japanese activated their complicated Sho-Go (Victory) Plan to isolate the landing force on Leyte Gulf and destroy the defending American Seventh Fleet under Vice-Admiral Thomas C Kinkaid. One Japanese fleet of five battleships under Vice-Admiral Takeo Kurita was to cut through the Sibuyan Sea in the center of the archipelago from the west, pass through San Bernardino Strait and assault Kincaid from the north. A second fleet of battleships under Vice-Admiral Shoji Nishimura was to join Vice-Admiral Kiyohide Shima's three carriers and two destroyers to traverse the Mindanao Sea further south, enter Leyte Gulf through Surigao Strait and thus catch Kincaid in a trap between the two fleets. Meanwhile, a fleet of four carriers under Admiral Jisaburo Ozawa would approach from the home islands to the north to lure Halsey's Third Fleet away from Leyte Gulf. The resulting battle—actually four separate actions—is know as the Battle for Leyte Gulf of 23–26 October 1944: in many respects it was the greatest naval battle ever fought.

The Japanese Southern Force under Nishimura made its way through the Mindanao Sea, with Shima trailing behind, heading for Surigao Strait and Kinkaid's southern flank. Kinkaid ordered Rear Admiral Jesse B Oldendorf, with six old battleships salvaged from the Pearl Harbor attack, to stop him. As the Japanese units approached shortly after midnight on 24 October, the battlewagons and their escorts were waiting in Surigao Strait. American destroyers and PT boats launched torpedo boats against Nishimura's force while the battleships' 14- and 16-inch radar-directed guns blasted away. The Japanese lost two battleships and two destroyers and failed to force the Straits. Admiral Shima's fleet arrived hours later and joined Nishimura's retreating ships without firing a shot.

In the meantime Kurita's Center Force was moving through the Sibuyan Sea south of Luzon as the northern wing of the entrapment plan, but Halsey, taking the Japanese bait, moved north to meet Ozawa's Northern Force of carriers (not knowing the Japanese were almost without aircraft due to losses in the Battle of the Philippine Sea). Halsey believed that Kinkaid was covering San Bernardino Strait, the eastern exit from the Sibuyan Sea. Kinkaid, believing Halsey had left a task force at the Strait, was not covering it either: it was wide open.

On through the Sibuyan Sea came Kurita.

Right: The fast minelayer USS _Shannon_ moves through a Pacific fleet anchorage on the eve of the landings on Okinawa.
Main picture: Bombarding targets on the Japanese mainland in July 1945.
Bottom left: The carrier _Bunker Hill_ after being hit by kamikazes off Okinawa on 11 May 1945. Aircraft carriers were particularly vulnerable because of their aviation fuel stores.
Bottom right: _LST.829_ heads for the shore during the Okinawa landings.

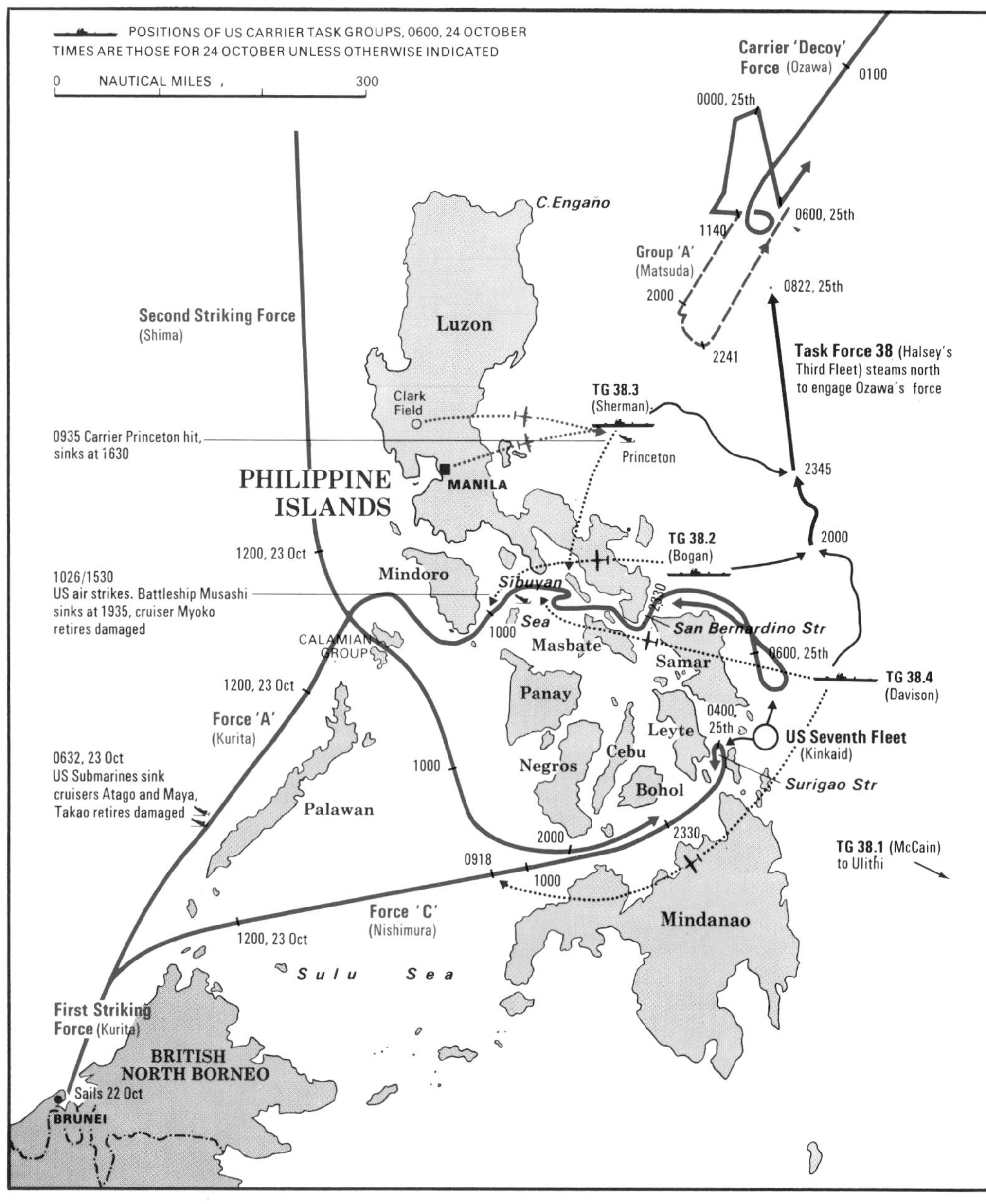

He was attacked by American planes on 24 October and lost the battleship *Musashi* in this second action. But he kept coming despite his losses, sailing through the open San Bernardino Strait under cover of darkness and turning south toward Leyte Gulf. As he rounded the island of Samar with his four battleships, seven cruisers and 11 destroyers and prepared to attack Kinkaid's unsuspecting fleet, he was finally spotted at sunrise on 25 October by a small 'jeep carrier' group and its escorts. They sounded the alarm and tore into Kurita's force with their puny weapons. Fortunately, Kurita thought he was fighting Halsey's main force and stopped to do battle rather than rushing through to hit Kinkaid. Kinkaid threw everything available into the desperate fight to stop Kurita off Samar, while beseeching Halsey to return to help him. In furious fighting in which two jeep carriers were lost, Kurita was stopped and retreated back through San Bernardino Strait.

Halsey, meanwhile, was far to the north chasing Ozawa's decoy force off Cape Engaño. Although Halsey's planes put down the four carriers in handy fashion, he continued chasing the surviving vessels north. Kinkaid was still calling frantically for help in his desperate situation off Samar. Halsey finally broke off the chase and turned south, but too late to catch Kurita as he made his escape back through San Bernardino Strait.

When the Battle for Leyte Gulf was over, the Japanese had lost three battleships, four carriers, nine cruisers and ten destroyers. The Imperial Japanese Navy was virtually finished as a fighting force. The road to Tokyo was open. But the cost of victory for the Americans would still be high because, ominously, the Japanese in the Battle for Leyte Gulf had used kamikaze attacks for the first time. Kamikaze—'Divine Wind'—pilots mostly had little training in flight. Their only mission was to dive their planes onto enemy ships in heroic suicidal attacks. Many American sailors would die in the last year of the Pacific war before the dreaded kamikaze raids ended with Japan's surrender.

Now that the Philippines were accessible and the Japanese fleet was staggering, there was a need for forward bases for landings on Japan itself and air bases to give fighter protection to the B-29s flying from the Marianas. The first to fall to American assault was tiny Iwo Jima in the Bonin Islands, almost midway between Saipan and Tokyo. The island had been bombed methodically from carrier- and land-based planes from the Marianas since June 1944; the invasion took place on 19 February 1945 after fierce naval shelling and bombing by B-29s. The little island of only eight square miles, defended by 20,000 Japanese, was assaulted by an

Top left: **Map of the Battle of Leyte Gulf.**
Left: **Unloading equipment from an LST at Middleburg Is, New Guinea, in Aug 1944.**

880-ship armada and 220,000 men. Because the Japanese were so well dug-in and fought tenaciously, it took five weeks and Marine casualties of 5500 killed and almost 14,000 wounded before the island fell; the Navy lost 90 men before the bloody fighting ended. Long-range bombers could now fly to Japan with continuous fighter-plane cover.

Okinawa was next. This island, only 350 miles from Japan, would be the staging area for the great assault on the Japanese home islands. It had to be taken. The Americans—aided by the Royal Navy—assembled a mammoth force of 1200 ships and 181,000 assault troops to do the job. After the usual fierce bombardments, 50,000 soldiers and Marines landed on Easter Sunday, 1 April 1945, to face 110,000 well-entrenched Japanese troops. Here the full fury of the kamikaze suicide planes fell on the American fleet. Hundreds dove through the skies at the lumbering transport and supply ships and at the combat vessels. Before Okinawa was secured on 21 June, 34 ships had been sunk, 368 more had been damaged. Over 12,000 Americans had died and 35,000 had been wounded (including almost 10,000 sailors killed, missing or injured) in securing the island. It had been a horrendously costly victory, and the Navy dreaded what would come when they turned to the next task—attacking the Japanese home islands. American commanders estimated that the invasion scheduled for late 1945

Right: Firefighters on the USS _Intrepid_ after a kamikaze hit, 25 November 1944.
Below: The Japanese _Ise_ or _Hyuga_ under attack off Cape Engaño, 25 October 1944. Both had been converted to carrier/battleship with a small flight deck aft.

Above: LSM.311 **and other landing ships approach the beach at Leyte on 20 Oct 1944.**

or early 1946 would require the largest amphibious force ever assembled, even larger than the one that had landed at Normandy the year before. Approximately five million men would be needed, of whom about one million would be lost. It would be the largest invasion in history across the largest expanse of water, resulting in record casualties. By July 1945 the Navy had set about its most challenging task with grim determination by carrying out carrier task-force raids on Japanese airfields and industries in conjunction with British carriers and US Army Air Force B-29 raids from Saipan. Meanwhile, Okinawa was being prepared as a great airbase and staging area for the invasion.

Then on 6 August the *Enola Gay* dropped an atomic bomb with the explosive force of 20,000 tons of TNT on Hiroshima. Three days later the Army Air Force dropped a second atomic bomb of similar destructive power on Nagasaki. On 14 August 1945 the Navy's war—the nation's war—in the Pacific came to an end. Significantly, the formal Japanese surrender document was signed on the deck of a US Navy battleship; the *Missouri*, in Tokyo Bay on 2 September 1945. The curtain was rung down on the Navy's greatest challenge and most memorable years of sacrifice and glory.

Above: A destroyer lays a smoke screen during the Leyte landings.
Below: Pilots of the USS *Hornet* rushing to their planes for a mission in the China Sea in February 1945.

CARRYING THE WAR TO HITLER

While the US Navy was fighting its way across the Pacific in the months after Pearl Harbor, it also had responsibilities in another whole theater of action—the Atlantic Ocean. Now, if never before, the United States had to accept its role as a continental island-nation in the midst of the world's two great oceans. And now, if never before, a potential world power was going to have its naval forces tested by two highly dedicated and heavily armed enemies on opposite shores. How the US Navy met the challenge of the Japanese across the Pacific has been recounted; how it met the challenge of the Germans in the Atlantic must now be considered. In the first months of World War II, as we have seen, the USA was not involved—at least formally—and the action was largely in the Atlantic Ocean and between the British and the Germans. But the results of those engagements must be explained if the role of the US Navy in the war in Europe and on the Atlantic is to be understood. For, to anticipate, that role is so unexpected that what we shall see is a US Navy that hardly exchanges a shot with a major German ship, but that nevertheless ends up playing a crucial role in defeating the Germans.

When World War II broke out on 1 September 1939, the German Navy was not prepared for the battles it would be called upon to fight. In 1938 Grand Admiral Erich Raeder, head of the navy, had presented Hitler with two overall plans for naval development. One called for the production of naval weapons of war to be used against commerce—weapons like

Above: Type VII U-boats like *U-101* formed the backbone of the German submarine force. *Above left:* Admiral Raeder led the German Navy in the early years of the war until Dönitz took over at the start of 1943. *Below: U-203* sets out on patrol from Brest at the start of April 1943, at the height of the Battle of the Atlantic.

Above: **The destroyer *Gleaves* on her way to the Canadian escort base at Argentia.**

submarines, surface raiders and minelayers. If war with Britain was envisioned in the near future, this type of vessel would be needed to destroy her ocean-going commerce, as had been attempted in World War I. The second plan, Plan Z, called for a great surface fleet to match or exceed that of any other nation, especially Great Britain, in open combat. But this would call for a major shipbuilding program and would take up to ten years to complete.

Hitler chose Plan Z. Why he did so remains a mystery. Perhaps he felt that war with Britain could be delayed or even avoided. Whatever his reasoning, Hitler was subsequently stunned by England's declaration of war upon Germany after the invasion of Poland; thus the German Navy was called upon to change its strategic and tactical missions as soon as World War II began.

At the outbreak of the fighting, Germany had a sizable Plan Z surface fleet building —and scheduled for completion by 1945— but not large enough to gain control of the seas and drive off blockaders from the nation's coast. The navy had only five battleships commissioned and two building, eight cruisers, 26 merchant ships usable as armed cruisers and a number of auxiliary vessels. Furthermore, the Germans had only 56 submarines, these under the command of Admiral Karl Dönitz. These were hardly sufficient to close down the waters around Britain and in the North Atlantic. Although caught without adequate numbers of ships and trained men, the German Navy sailed out to do its best in the early months of the war. Its job: destroy British commerce by all possible means.

The British, on the other hand, had two counterobjectives: keep the sea lanes open at all cost and blockade the North Sea exits to keep the German fleet bottled up in the Baltic.

Surface Raiding

Merchant vessels approaching the British coast from the British Dominions or from neutral ports became the targets of the German surface fleet. After a brief and ruinous flirtation with single sailings, the British quickly returned to convoying, the stratagem so successful in World War I. But German surface raiders were still a constant danger, even to convoys; this was made obvious by the cruises of the 'pocket battleships' *Deutschland* and *Graf Spee* as they began to attack merchant shipping on the high seas.

During the fall of 1939 the *Graf Spee* was sinking thousands of tons of shipping in the South Atlantic; a sizable British and French contingent was assigned to hunt her down. This force included two carriers and eight cruisers at various times. On 13 December 1939 three British cruisers found the *Graf Spee* outside the River Plate that flows between Uruguay and Argentina on the east coast of South America, they took her on. A spirited duel of big guns punctuated a series of battle maneuvers by each side. As a result, two of the cruisers were badly damaged by the *Graf Spee*'s 11-inch guns; the German battleship also sustained numerous hits. The *Graf Spee* limped away to the safety of the neutral port of Montevideo with two of the British cruisers in pursuit. Despite intense diplomatic pressure from Germany, the government of Uruguay ordered the *Graf Spee* out of its waters within three days. Being short of ammunition, the captain of the *Graf Spee* decided to scuttle his vessel rather than try to fight his way out. The scuttling took place outside the harbor on 17 December 1939, and—with the *Deutschland* returning to German waters —German surface raiding was abandoned for several months.

In the fall of 1940 serious German surface raiding was renewed when the pocket battleship *Scheer* slipped into the North Atlantic to prey on British convoys, followed a month later by the heavy cruiser *Hipper*. Although neither ship was able to effect great damage in the North or South Atlantic, they did remind the British that surface raiding could raise havoc with convoys if not quickly contained.

In the spring of 1941 Admiral Raeder implemented his plan for a great surface-raiding mission that would completely disrupt or even shut down the North Atlantic sea lanes. He would send the giant new battleship *Bismarck*, along with the heavy cruiser *Prinz Eugen*, into the Atlantic. Here they would be joined by the battleships *Scharnhorst* and *Gneisenau* to lay waste the British supply lines. Although the *Scharnhorst* could not be repaired in time for sailing, and the *Gneisenau* was taken out of action by a torpedo from a British plane, Raeder ordered the two remaining ships out to Bergen in occupied Norway. From there they were to break through the Royal Navy's blockade, move north of Iceland and pounce upon convoys in the North Atlantic. The *Scharnhorst* was to join them as soon as possible.

Warned as to what was afoot, and fearful of the destruction that would await their convoys if this German naval squadron were not stopped, the British alerted every ship available in the Home Fleet and North Atlantic to hunt down the *Bismarck* and *Prinz Eugen*. On 23 May the two German raiders were spotted moving down through the Denmark Strait between Greenland and Iceland by two British cruisers, which shadowed them south. The German raiders were met next morning by the battle cruiser *Hood* and the battleship *Prince of Wales*. The *Hood* was sunk in a fiery explosion of her magazines from the long guns of the *Bismarck*, and the *Prince of Wales* suffered crippling damages. Out of the fight, the *Prince of Wales* made her way toward Iceland, while the two British cruisers continued shadowing the *Bismarck* to report her location. Stunned by the loss of the *Hood*, the Admiralty ordered various ships from Gibraltar and two battleships from convoying duty to run down the *Bismarck* and her companion. But the *Prinz Eugen* slipped away to the south, and the *Bismarck* temporarily gave her dogged shadows the slip. By sheer luck, British persistence and radio-direction-finder signals, the trail of the *Bismarck* was picked up again as she headed toward the French coast, and all British forces available were directed toward her probable course.

Right: **Crew of the USS *Kearney* inspect damage caused by a U-boat torpedo on the night of 16–17 October 1941.**

At 10:30 on the morning of 26 May 1941 the great German battleship was spotted 750 miles west of France. Shadowed now by the cruiser *Sheffield*, the *Bismarck* was hit by air attacks from the carrier *Ark Royal* in an effort to slow her down. They jammed her rudders. The British ships caught up with the *Bismarck* that night and launched ineffective torpedo attacks against the crippled giant. But by the next morning the battleships *Rodney* and *King George V* had arrived on the scene; they began to pound away at the damaged battleship. The hapless vessel was finally put down by a torpedo from the cruiser *Dorsetshire*.

However, in a humiliating display of ineptitude, the British allowed the *Scharnhorst*, *Gneisenau* and *Prinz Eugen* to slip out of the port of Brest on the French coast and run for home right through the English Channel without being properly attacked. Although two of the vessels hit mines off the Dutch coast and sustained damage, they made it to port safely, much to the consternation of the British. But even this heroic dash could not convince Hitler or the German Navy that surface-raider warfare was worth the price, though the battlecruiser *Scharnhorst* eventually sallied out in December 1943 to attack an Arctic convoy off the North Cape and was soon sunk by the British battleship *Duke of York* along with her escorting cruisers and destroyers.

The last major German surface combatant, the new battleship *Tirpitz*, was bombed by British carrier planes while under repair in Alten Fjord in the north of Norway on 3 April 1944. Moved to Tromso Fjord further south for more repairs, she was bombed and capsized at her moorings on 12 November 1944.

German surface raiding by major combatant ships had come to an effective end on 27 May 1941 with the death of the *Bismarck*, despite these later forays. For the remainder of the war, and throughout the time America was fighting side by side with her British allies, the German menace took the form of deadly unrestricted submarine warfare. Germany had reverted to her most effective weapon of World War I, but now she proved herself capable of a more widespread and deadly use of the U-boat—the *Unterseeboot*, as the Germans call the submarine. If the United States and Britain could not contain the submarine campaign as they had in World War I, Britain could not survive. If Britain were to capitulate, the European war would undoubtedly be lost. That was the challenge to the United States and to her navy in the Atlantic as the nation joined the Allies in December 1941 and fought desperately until the U-boats were finally matched, then overwhelmed, in the agonizing years that followed.

Battle of the Atlantic, 1939–41

Although Admiral Dönitz as submarine commander had 56 operational U-boats at the beginning of the war—rather than the 300 he considered the minimum necessary—only 22 of them were both ready and suitable for North Atlantic patrols. Accordingly, he was able to keep less than ten submarines on duty during the early months of the war. They attained some successes against ships sailing without convoys, but lost nine of their number in the process before turning to aid in the invasion of Norway in the early months of 1940. The capitulation of Norway, Holland, Belgium and France gave Dönitz the opportunity to rebase his U-boats nearer their patrol areas in the Atlantic. Great heavily fortified submarine pens were created at five locations on the Bay of Biscay on the west coast of France, and secondary bases were constructed in Norway. Dönitz now had bases closer at hand to their targets, resulting in less time in transit and more at destruction.

With more subs available thanks to the French bases in particular, by the summer of 1940 Dönitz was able to send out his boats to hunt the convoys in 'wolf packs.' They successfully bore down on and sank ship after ship in the North Atlantic convoys by having one submarine shadow a convoy until all subs in the area could close in for a co-ordinated kill. The night surface attack was the favored tactic. In reaction to this increasing menace, the British extended their escort patrols farther out to sea; any vessels marginally suitable for convoy duty were added to the fleet and Churchill made his desperate request to Roosevelt for 50 American destroyers. Still the sinkings continued, especially among independent ships. Furthermore, the 600-mile-wide 'Black Pit' in the mid-Atlantic, where long-range air patrols could not reach, remained a favorite haunt of U-boats against both independents and convoys. In rapid succession 17 of 34 merchantmen in convoy SC-7 were sunk in the summer of 1940, followed by 14 of 49 in another convoy (HX-79), by packs of German subs.

For Dönitz's subs on the Northwestern Approaches, this was the 'Happy Time.' A total of 217 merchant vessels of over a million tons was sent to the bottom with the loss of only six U-boats in the summer and fall of 1940. Still, 2000 merchantmen a day were at sea for Britain, and convoys were getting through despite the wolfpacking technique. Dönitz waited during the winter months of 1940–41 until better weather and more boats should signal a new and stronger effort in the North Atlantic. Here, he believed, the war would be won or lost. As spring 1941 approached, however, Dönitz found that his enemies had improved their antisubmarine warfare (ASW) activities and had thereby made raiding on the Northwestern Approaches increasingly costly. Accordingly, he shifted the U-boats' area of operations farther to the west beyond the range of coastal-based patrol planes. Dönitz would now concentrate his submarines in those areas where he could do the most damage while sustaining the fewest casualties. He was determined to carry out a war of attrition on the North Atlantic sea lanes, constantly moving his subs to where they could do maximum damage to the British commercial lifeline.

In the meantime the United States was moving closer to involvement in the North Atlantic war. The 'destroyers for bases' deal of July 1940 had given way to Lend-Lease legislation in March 1941.

This allowed the British to buy war goods on credit. While this was taking place, Roosevelt had also sent military representatives to England for 'exploratory talks' that resulted in co-ordinated plans for American participation in the Atlantic if America entered the war. These talks, in turn, led to others including the 'ABC-1 Staff Agreement' of January 1941, which spelled out what the United States would do short of war and in the event of war. This included both the idea of Germany as the prime enemy if she and Japan were to make war on the United States and on Britain and the pledge that the United States would soon escort convoys in the North Atlantic.

By February 1941 the agreed-upon neutrality patrols were being carried out by the US Atlantic Fleet under Admiral Ernest J King; by July American naval units were escorting convoys from Newfoundland to Iceland. The eastern end of the patrol area was anchored by American airplanes flying from Reykjavik, Iceland. Combined with the fact that the Americans were broadcasting every U-boat sighting on open channels, this convoying, as we have seen, put America into an undeclared naval war. The attack on the US destroyer *Greer* (4 September 1941) 200 miles southwest of Iceland—after the destroyer had shadowed U-652 for three hours—was only the signal that the undeclared war was on. The torpedoing of the destroyer *Kearney* and the sinking of the USS *Reuben James* in October, both on convoy duty, made no appreciable change in the basic situation, but it enabled Roosevelt to place the Germans in a worse light before the American public while refusing to reveal what was really going on in the North Atlantic. But since the Admiralty was now experimenting with escort carriers to cover convoys in the 'Greenland gap,' (an experiment that was costing the Germans many precious U-boats) Dönitz decided in December 1941 to shift his submarine campaigns to North American waters now that America was in the war. The hunting would be good: the Americans would see the battle of the Atlantic at close range for the first time. Operation *Paukenschlag* ('drumroll'), as Admiral Dönitz named it, was about to begin.

Battle of the Atlantic, 1942–45

Having utilized its slender ASW resources in convoy escort missions across the North Atlantic sea lanes, the US Navy was in no position to protect American coastal waters in the early months of the war. Furthermore, in building up the Navy in the late 1930s and early 1940s, efforts had been concentrated largely on building large combat vessels. Escort vessels, particularly the smaller but effective destroyer-escorts, had been neglected on the assumption they could always be hurriedly built if needed. As a result, the east coast shipping lanes were essentially both undefended and indefensible when the German submarines began to lurk in American waters early in 1942.

Although there were never more than a dozen German submarines operating in the Eastern Sea Frontier (the Navy's designation for the Atlantic coast command area) at any time, the damage they did to the unprotected tankers and freighters moving along the coast with raw materials and oil for east-coast industrial centers was astounding. Having no reason to wolfpack, the individual U-boats lay offshore and submerged during the day, then moved in on the merchant vessels on the surface at night, dispatching them with torpedoes or gunfire. The offshore waters from Cape Hatteras to Cape Breton Island in Nova Scotia were their hunting grounds. The Carolina Capes were a favorite haunt. German submarines often found the unarmed merchant vessels running with lights on; frequently they were clearly silhouetted by the lights of eastern seaboard cities. Only in April 1942 were shore lights dimmed, much to the chagrin of port-city merchants and caterers to vacation pleasure-seekers. The toll of sinkings off the East Coast in what the German submarine crews called the 'Second Happy Time' rose rapidly, reaching 87 vessels of 514,366 tons in the first four months of 1942.

The Navy was trying its best to stop the slaughter, but it was woefully lacking in ASW vessels and aircraft. Only about 100 vessels of all descriptions from naval destroyers and Coast Guard cutters all the way down to converted yachts were available to fight the submarine onslaught. Less than 200 army and naval aircraft were also available. Furthermore, the naval commander of the Eastern Sea Frontier originally refused to adopt convoying and attempted to seek out the prowling subs by 'hunter groups.' But the April 1942 total of 23 ships sunk off the East Coast without the destruction of a single U-boat finally led to a change in tactics.

Right: U-boat ace Gunther Prien is congratulated on his return from sinking the British battleship *Royal Oak* in the fleet anchorage at Scapa Flow in 1939.
Below: The heavy cruiser *Prinz Eugen* arrives at Brest in June 1941 after separating from the *Bismarck* soon after the engagement with *Hood* and *Prince of Wales*.

Utilizing 34 small corvettes and trawlers provided by the British and equipped with asdic (the equivalent of sonar) regular convoying and extended air cover during defensible daylight hours, total sinkings were cut drastically along the east coast. The German submarines had little choice other than to 'keep their heads down' in these waters and so were shifted to the Caribbean and Gulf of Mexico by Admiral Dönitz. Here they were enormously successful. In May 1942 alone, 41 ships of 220,000 tons were sunk in the Gulf of Mexico, over half being tankers sunk off the Passes of the Mississippi. When defensive convoys were instituted for these areas as well, the U-boats—still well supplied with fuel and food by 1700-ton supply submarines called 'milk cows,' which allowed them a longer and wider latitude of operations—moved into the southern Caribbean to continue their deadly work against much-needed merchant cargoes in that area. Driven from this hunting ground by naval convoying and air patrols, the German subs moved farther south along the Brazilian coast to pick off ships sailing independently along the coastal or transatlantic routes. By late 1942 this area too was becoming dangerous for submarines, thanks to convoying and effective air patrols, so Dönitz recalled his boats from American waters. The battle of the submarines against their pursuers returned to the mid-Atlantic, where Dönitz hoped to find easier pickings again, for the Black Pit was still beyond the land-based air cover from North American, Icelandic and British air bases. Here the U-boats would concentrate their efforts in early 1943. Since German submarine production had reached 30 boats per month, Dönitz felt he was now ready to take appreciable losses and put down the mid-Atlantic convoys. But Allied naval

Main picture: **An Atlantic convoy pictured from a US battleship early in 1944.**

forces had also increased productivity and technology. Most surface ASW vessels now had radar, and the increased numbers of ships meant that British Antisubmarine Support Groups of six to eight fast destroyers, corvettes and frigates could be formed to seek out submarines and aid convoys under attack. Soon escort carriers would be added to their numbers.

Employing picket lines on both sides of the sea lanes to attack convoys moving through the Black Pit without air support, Dönitz's crews enjoyed considerable early success, sinking 807,000 tons of shipping in November 1942 alone. But as the Atlantic war moved into 1943, the Allies discovered that fewer but larger convoys, aided by Antisubmarine Support Groups utilizing radar and radio detection systems (HF-DF—'huff duff'—high-frequency direction finders) to home in on the broadcasting submarines, plus air cover from escort carriers and long-range aircraft like B-24 Liberators equipped with radar and depth charges, meant safer passages. The turning point in the Battle of the Atlantic came in April 1943 when the 'kill ratio'—between merchants sunk to casualties sustained—simply became too high for the German submarine packs. Losing 41 submarines to the new Allied tactics in 'Black May' 1943, Dönitz ordered his submarines south to attack Central Atlantic convoys. Improved submarine technology, he felt, would soon permit him to return to the North Atlantic to resume his attacks on the Allies' lifelines across those waters.

But in the Central Atlantic hunting grounds southwest of the Azores, German submarines found only frustration in the summer and fall of 1943. for the US Navy—which from 1 April 1943 had responsibility for this area—had developed 'hunter-killer groups' to combat the submarine menace. These groups, made up

Below: **Crewmen loading provisions on *PC.556* before a patrol in the Atlantic in October 1942.**
Bottom: **A meeting of the US-British Combined Chiefs of Staff in Washington. Admiral King, second from camera on right, represents the US Navy.**

of destroyers, destroyer-escorts and escort carriers, were very effective against both attacks and 'milk cow' submarines. The air power packed by the groups was overwhelming, and U-boat losses mounted rapidly. In three months the Germans lost 15 submarines while sinking only one convoyed merchant vessel.

Meanwhile, U-boats operating in the Bay of Biscay were also coming under sustained and killing pressure thanks to the work of the Royal Air Force Coastal Command and its use of newly perfected ultra-high-frequency radar units and an 80-million-candlepower searchlight used against the subs in night attacks. American aircraft co-operated closely with the British in carrying out this antisubmarine warfare off the coast of France. Altogether 18 German submarines were lost at this time in the Bay of Biscay. The sub pens of western France were now of much less value to the U-boat forces.

During the critical year 1943 the German Navy lost 237 U-boats, and the Battle of the Atlantic was won through Allied co-operation. Although U-boat operations continued through 1944, the combination of antisubmarine support groups, hunter-killer groups, larger convoys under better escort, improved radar and sonar detection systems and above all, virtually round-the-clock air cover from co-ordinated carrier- and land-based planes was simply too much for the beleaguered crews of the German undersea forces. Wherever Dönitz moved his attack submarines, the Allies were there to beat him and cast his vital U-boats into the depths of the Atlantic. By 1945 the German submarines were a no more than occasional menace to the vital Allied convoys.

During the course of the war 1175 U-boats sailed for the Reich. Of these, 781 were lost, 191 to American forces, the remainder to other Allied air and naval forces. German U-boats sank 14,573,000 tons of shipping, only about one-fourth from ships sailing in convoy. On the other hand, over 300,000 voyages were made across the Atlantic by Allied merchant vessels in support of the war. The safe passage of these ships in convoy—increasingly unmolested as the Battle of the Atlantic was won by Allied naval and air power and virtually untouched in the final 18 months of the war—spelled victory for Allied forces in Europe. Dönitz was correct when he said the battle for Europe would be decided in the North Atlantic. With the defeat of his U-boat forces after their easy victories of 1941–42 on these waters, Allied offensives could continue until the final defeat of the Third Reich.

Above: **View of the quarterdeck of the battleship *Massachusetts* during a lull in the battle of Casablanca.**

North African Offensives

Perhaps less dramatic but equally important to the Allied victory in Europe were US Navy efforts in support of mammoth amphibious landings as opening steps to giant land offensives in Africa and Europe. These operations eventually carried the war into Germany itself.

From the very beginning of World War II, American military planners wanted to strike directly at the heart of German mili-

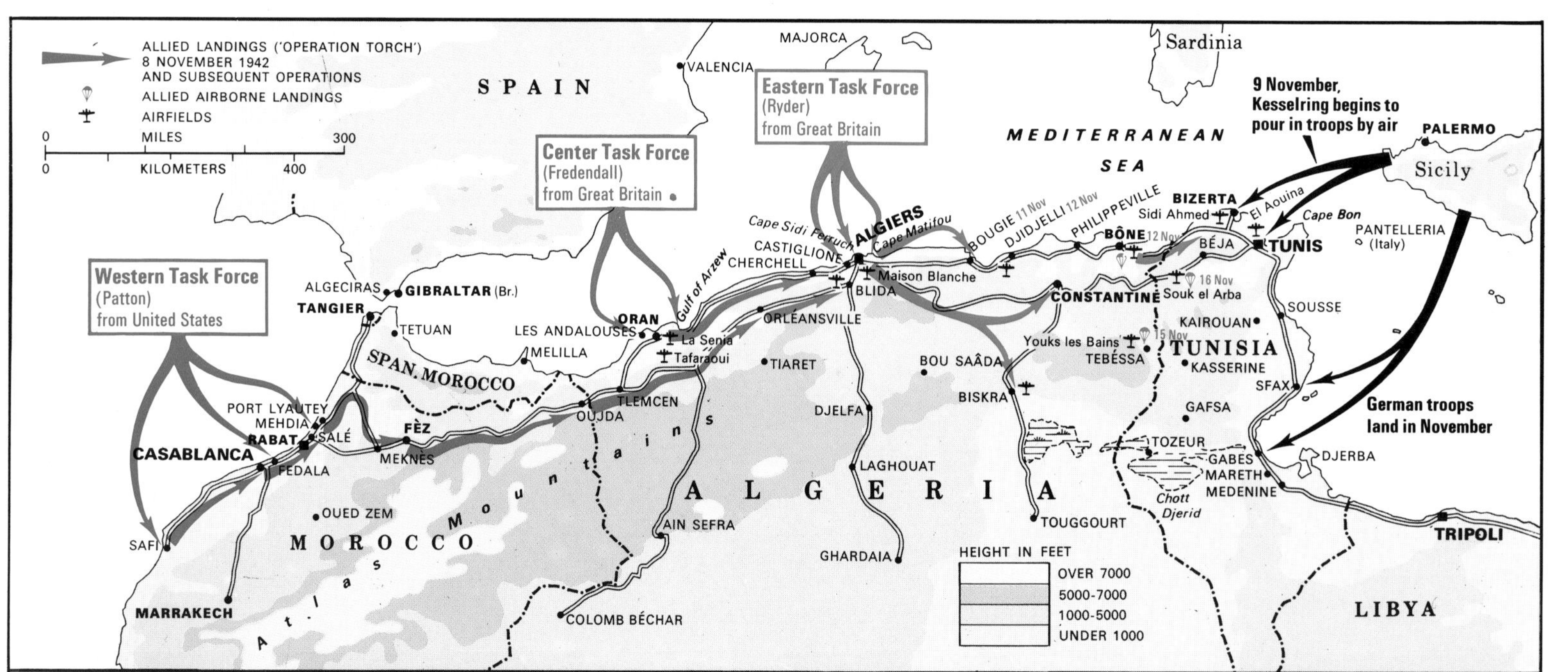

tary power by launching an invasion of Nazi-occupied France. The British, on the other hand, preferred to follow a grand strategy of hitting the Nazi behemoth on the periphery in the Mediterranean and reducing its strength by attrition before launching a mighty invasion in force—either in the 'soft underbelly' of Italy or in France—to drive into Germany itself. The Americans suspected that the British were more interested in saving their Near East empire by waging a peripheral Mediterranean war first, but they could not avoid the hard reality that until Axis military strength was seriously weakened and Allied military strength overwhelming, no invasion of the Continent stood a chance of succeeding. Thus, with the blessing of President Roosevelt and to the relief of Prime Minister Churchill, a decision was made to put off Operation SLEDGEHAMMER (seizing a beachhead in France in 1942) and Operation ROUNDUP (a drive into Germany in 1943) in favor of Operation TORCH (an invasion of North Africa in 1942). This strategy would pressure German forces in the Mediterranean and get the Americans actively into the European war in 1942. The American public was demanding action; as Roosevelt saw it, Operation TORCH was the answer.

Allied planning called for a three-pronged invasion striking simultaneously at Casablanca in French Morocco (outside Gibraltar on the west coast of Africa) and at Oran and Algiers, Algeria, on the Mediterranean. All were major ports and, very importantly, beyond range of the *Luftwaffe* in Sicily. From these points a drive to the east would move into Tunisia. The object was to catch General Erwin Rommel with his Afrika Korps and the Italian Army between the combined British-American forces from Algeria and the British Eighth Army advancing west across North Africa from Egypt. For this invasion, Western Naval Task Force (American Task Force 34), led by Rear Admiral Kent Hewitt, was to sail directly from the United States with 35,000 men to the beachheads in Morocco; the Navy was also assigned the task of covering the landings. Center Naval Task Force

Above: **A damaged and irrepairable F4 Wildcat pushed overside from the *Santee*.**

Below: **The crowded flight deck of the USS *Chenango* on the eve of the Torch landings.**
Bottom left: **Map of the Torch landings.**

***Above:* Transports and warships at anchor in the harbor at Mers-el-Kebir near Oran. *Bottom right:* The crowded deck of an escort carrier, probably the *Santee*, during Operation Torch in November 1942.**

(British) was to sail from Britain with 39,000 American troops to hit Oran. Eastern Naval Task Force (British) was also to sail from Britain with 23,000 British and 10,000 Americans to invade Algiers.

Western Task Force would be under control of the US Navy in the person of Admiral Royal E Ingersoll, Commander in Chief, Atlantic Fleet, until the mid-Atlantic, at which time the entire operation would come under the direction of Lieutenant General Dwight D Eisenhower, Commander in Chief, Allied Forces. Eisenhower would then delegate control to his deputies in each area. This would ensure that in these amphibious operations control of an entire sector in the landings—military and naval, American and British—would be under one man for better co-ordination and mutual support. The inter-service command squabbles that so often characterized Pacific amphibious operations were not to be found in the European theater.

Planning and training for the three amphibious operations went on through 1942, but time was short for learning complicated landing patterns, and the landings might be stoutly resisted. The hope that the Vichy French troops would not fight the invading Allies could not be taken for granted. All three major ports had to be taken to secure solid bases of operations before moving on to the east. Invasion was set for 8 November 1942, the latest date possible before winter weather made beach landings impossible. More time was needed for training the soldiers and sailors in amphibious techniques, but time was not available; the invasion forces were assembled despite the unsatisfactory level of preparation.

The three attack groups of Western Naval Task Force (destined for Mehdia and the airfield at Port Lyautey nearby, 90 miles north of Casablanca; Fedala, 15 miles north of Casablanca; and Safi, 150 miles to the southwest) left Hampton Roads on 23–24 October 1942 and joined a naval covering group of one battleship and two cruisers three days later at sea. The next day, 28 October, a carrier group built around the *Ranger* and four jeep carriers joined the armada. Reaching the African coast on 7 November, the group split up to approach the three target cities the next day.

The landings early in the morning of 8 November were marked by predictable confusion as the undertrained naval crews piloting small plywood 'Higgins boats' and 50-foot steel LCMs (Landing Craft, Mechanized) tried to put men and equipment on the beaches in the dark. Subsequent invasions would use LSTs (Landing Ships, Tank) and other specialized vessels to get the Army's men and equipment off expeditiously, but the forces in Morocco had no such luxury and paid for it in confusion and casualties. Beach landings had to be made in order to swing around behind the cities to take them from the rear.

Despite the fact that the Vichy French did, indeed, resist strenuously, and despite the confusion in landing both men and equipment, the Fedala, Mehdia and Safi landings were successful. Much of the credit must go to the offshore naval covering units for effective support of the soldiers on the beaches. US Navy gunfire silenced batteries along the Fedala shore; put the great French battleship *Jean Bart*, firing her 15-inch guns from Casablanca harbor, out of commission; reduced the batteries at El Hank west of Casablanca and at Fedala; and stopped one French counterattack at Safi and another at Mehdia. The naval attack and covering groups also had to beat off attacks by one French cruiser, seven destroyers and eight submarines against the invasion fleet. All French vessels except one were severely damaged in the confused melee; the Americans lost no ships. On 10 November the damaged *Jean Bart* was sunk by dive bombers from the *Ranger*; next day the French forces in Morocco surrendered. The Casablanca landings had proved a useful baptism of fire for the American forces. Certainly a great many of the mistakes made here were not repeated in later assaults.

The landings at Oran and Algiers also revealed the paramount importance of amphibious co-ordination and close naval support throughout the entire landing and securing phases of the operations, although the fighting here was less hectic than in Morocco. The French Admiral Francois Darlan, Commander in Chief of the Armed Forces of Vichy France, ordered a cease-fire for all French troops in Africa on 10 November, convinced of the wisdom of such a move by an American diplomat, Consul-General Robert Murphy. Operation TORCH was over, and American and British troops now moved on toward Tunisia to drive the Germans and Italians out of North Africa. It took six months of hard fighting to overcome the last Axis resistance on 13 May 1943, but the first giant—if indirect—step had been taken toward the German heartland.

The Invasion of Sicily

While the North African campaign was still in full swing, Roosevelt, Churchill and their chiefs of staff met at the Casablanca Conference (14–25 January 1943) to work out future strategy for the European war. The Americans still wanted a cross-Channel invasion of France in mid-1943, but the British argued that the Allies would have only 25 divisions available by then to face a 44-division German resistance. Therefore, the British said, the peripheral strategy should continue with an assault on either Sicily or Sardinia to erode German resistance and simultaneously aid Russia by pinning down more German troops in Western Europe. A successful seizure of Sicily in particular might well knock Italy out of the war and bring in Turkey on the Allied side. Although not fully convinced of the wisdom of such a strategy, the Americans agreed—but only if more men and supplies were diverted to the Pacific campaigns. Thus a bargain was struck, and Operation HUSKY, the invasion of Sicily 90 miles across the Sicilian Channel from Tunisia, was agreed upon as the next major operation for 1943.

Although Allied commanders were hampered in meeting to discuss strategy for HUSKY by the North African campaign in full swing, plans were finally worked out. The narrow Strait of Messina between Sicily and Italy was the ideal location for a landing—seizing the city of Messina on the west coast of the Straits would seal off all Italian and German troops on the island before they could be evacuated. But this was rejected because of doubt that Allied planes could cover a landing in that area. Accordingly, it was decided that British forces would land on the southeast coast of Sicily on the Gulf of Noto below the important port of Syracuse to seize that crucial city. They would then move north along the coast to capture Messina.

American troops, meanwhile, were to attack along a 37-mile beachhead on the southern coast of Sicily, taking the towns of Licata, Gela and Scoglitti along the Gulf of Gela. For these massive operations over 470,000 troops were assigned, more than the number used at Normandy a year later. After seizing their beachheads, American forces were to move west and north to take the western end of the island and its capital, the north-coast port of Palermo. They would then move east to Messina as the left wing of a giant pincer to meet with the British at Messina and seal off the island. Invasion was set for 10 July 1943.

Although US Navy planners were unhappy about supporting an invasion force over such a wide area, they were cheered by the arrival of many new craft: LSTs (Landing Ships, Tank), LCTs (Landing Craft, Tank), LCIs (Landing Craft, Infantry), LCVPs (Landing Craft, Vehicles and Personnel), LCMs (Landing Craft, Mechanized) and hundreds of newly developed DUKWS (called 'ducks'—not an acronym, but the first four letters of the serial numbers on these amphibious cargo trucks from General Motors). The new vessels, able to unload men and equipment on the beaches, or run up on to the beaches with supplies in the case of the DUKWS, might allow them to seize and hold their beaches. On the other hand, naval planners were very annoyed by the night-time invasion plan that would preclude supporting bombardment. They were also disturbed about the Army Air Force's decision not to give close tactical air support to the troops in favor of 'sealing off the beachhead' by bombing behind the landing areas to prevent reinforcement. The Army shared the Navy's skepticism of such a use of air power—close air support having proved so critical in the Morocco landings—but both services were overridden. Air Force pilots were specifically forbidden to answer naval or land-force requests for support unless approved by Air Force headquarters in North Africa. Even air support from Allied carriers was denied.

On 8 July 1943 the two great amphibious armadas left from various North African ports for their assigned invasion points on Sicily. A total of almost 1400 ships and over 1800 landing aircraft were involved. Facing the 470,000-man invading force were 240,000 Italian and German troops, far from a comfortable margin for the Allied invaders. The Allies would be aided by the fact that the 180,000 Italian defenders had little stomach for a serious defense.

H-Hour, 2:45 am on 10 July, found the American vessels rolling in a heavy swell; misery and confusion were rampant in the assault boats, but the landings proceeded on schedule. Resistance on the Gulf of Gela beachhead was fierce but short-lived, as American troops overran pill-

boxes and gun emplacements with the help of naval units offshore, who were finally allowed to fire when it was obvious that surprise was over. When 'false beaches,' or sandbars, offshore and the target beaches themselves hampered unloading, the DUKWs proved a godsend for the invasion forces. Nothing stopped their crews from delivering their three-ton loads of vital equipment and ordnance.

The Navy scored its most successful contribution to the Sicilian campaign—and taught the Army a valuable lesson in close naval support——when German tanks counterattacked the beachhead at Gela on the morning of 11 July. Lieutenant General George Patton, in charge of the Army's forces, agreed to let the Navy try to handle the problem. Aided by seaplane spotting, the cruiser USS *Boise* and two destroyers opened up with a hailstorm of six-inch shells and obliterated the enemy tanks in short order. Even Patton was impressed.

The British also had a hard time landing because of rough seas in the Gulf of Noto, but faced little resistance onshore: by nightfall of D-Day they had taken the valuable port city of Syracuse. The race to Messina and the capture of the Axis forces was now on. Patton's Seventh Army moved up the southwest coast and took Port Empidocle on 16 July, then raced 100 miles north to capture Palermo on 22 July. By 23 July Patton was moving east along the northern shore of Sicily accompanied by several US Navy light cruisers and destroyers to provide fire support. The Navy also tried to entrap enemy forces by making three amphibious landings ahead of the Seventh Army's advance; these failed in their objective for various reasons, but did expedite the rapid withdrawal of enemy forces.

Meanwhile, General Bernard Montgomery's British Eighth Army got bogged down on its northern thrust. Held off by crack Axis troops, they could make little progress. By 3 August German and Italian forces were withdrawing, and when Patton beat Montgomery into Messina on 17 August—to the delight of the former and the consternation of the latter—45,000 German and over 60,000 Italian troops had already been evacuated across the three-mile Strait of Messina to fight again on the Italian peninsula. Despite this failure, the swift subjugation of Sicily, combined with a massive Allied air raid on Rome, convinced King Victor Emmanuel III to depose Benito Mussolini as *Duce* and take him into 'protective custody.' Hitler, knowing that the new government under Marshal Pietro Badoglio would not seriously pursue the war on the mainland, ordered additional troops into Italy and soon replaced Italian troops in France, Yugoslavia and Greece with his own. Operation HUSKY had been a phenomenal success. Allied communications in the Mediterranean were now secure, Italy was about to fall out of the war and Hitler's forces were spread ever thinner over his shrinking empire. In Churchill's memorable phrase, the Allies were 'closing the ring.'

The Invasion of Italy

The decision to invade Italy (Operation AVALANCHE) after securing Sicily had been made even before Allied forces launched HUSKY. American planners had preferred a cross-Channel invasion of France, but British arguments—that an invasion of the Italian mainland would definitely drive that country out of the war and force Hitler into spreading his forces even thinner—had won the day. Churchill and Roosevelt had agreed—that was all-important in these cases—and Italy was placed next on the agenda, but the Americans insisted on using no additional troops and naval units besides those already in the Mediterranean to carry out the operation. They also insisted on beginning to build up troops and supplies in Britain for the invasion of France. This was granted, and D-Day for the long-awaited invasion of France was set for 1 May 1944. But first came the invasion and conquest of Italy, which proved to be a formidable and supremely frustrating task.

As final plans were worked out, Italy

Below: Landing operations at Salerno. A landing craft from the USS *James O'Hare* unloads despite incoming German artillery fire.

would be invaded at two points. General Montgomery's Eighth Army would cross the Strait of Messina on 3 September 1943 and invade at Reggio on the toe of the 'boot.' The main attack, by American and British forces, would come on 9 September at the Gulf of Salerno, a quarter of the way up the boot, from which a drive would be made for Naples, Italy's best port, just 35 miles north. American forces, now called the Fifth Army, were under Lieutenant General Mark W Clark. Negotiations were also under way with Marshal Badoglio to pull Italy out of the war at the same time as the Salerno landings, with the Italian troops switching sides; quick action by Hitler prevented this, as most Italian units were soon disarmed. Only a few Italian naval and airforce units joined the Allied forces.

But the Germans, expecting Italy to be the next target, had reinforced the *Wehrmacht* there. Field Marshal Albert Kesselring, in command of German forces in the south of Italy, did not get all the troops he requested from Hitler, but still had enough strength to more than contest the Allied landings at Salerno. The beaches were mined and wired, the Gulf of Salerno was mined and gun positions bristled in the hills above the beaches.

The Allied amphibious forces, under overall command of Admiral Hewitt, were divided into a British force of two divisions to land on the north beach and drive left toward Naples, with an American force of like size to land to the south and move right to meet Montgomery's forces coming up from Reggio, plus two divisions in reserve. A naval landing force of 26 transports, 120 LSTs and 90 LCTs would carry them ashore, backed by a support force including three American cruisers, a British carrier group and a British covering group. H-Hour was again before sunrise, at 3:30 am; much to Admiral Hewitt's amazement, the amphibious landings were again to be without previous naval bombardment. Army arguments for surprise prevailed, and the German divisions waiting behind the Salerno beaches were not shelled; in the American sector there was not even naval gunfire as the troops crossed the beaches. According to plan, the assault forces deployed from North African and Sicilian ports on 3–6 September. Even the news of Italy's capitulation on 8 September, the day before the invasion, did little to soften the trials of those soldiers and sailors assigned to the assault on the Italian mainland.

Fighting on the two designated beaches was fierce and waged at point-blank range, although the British forces to the north received the help of naval gunfire as the US Navy's amphibious group commander ordered destroyers and rocket-launching craft to open fire after German artillery opened up. The beachheads in Allied hands at the end of the day had been preserved by American and British naval gunfire that knocked out German batteries, machine gun nests, infantry and tanks. Fighting off both conventional and new, devastating glide bombs delivered by the *Luftwaffe*, the naval forces held their ground for three crucial days while the beachhead was reinforced and widened. Unlike Sicily, this time there were carrier-based planes for tactical support of ground troops. The climax of the battle came on 13–14 September when a major German counterattack with tanks failed. Credit must go to effective naval gunnery support, dogged resistance by the foot soldiers and effective air support. Kesselring's tanks and infantry were pounded by naval artillery until 16 September, when he ordered his troops back to a defensive position behind the Volturno River. At the cost of 13,000 dead, missing and wounded. the Salerno beachheads were taken. Naples, Italy's most valuable port, fell to the allies on 1 October 1943.

Yet despite the conquest of Naples and Italy's capitulation (much of the Italian fleet was now interned at Malta), the battle for Italy was far from over. Topography favored the German defenders, and as they backed off from the Volturno River line to a more permanent barrier 40 miles north of Naples, the Winter Line, the whole Allied land offensive slowed to a crawl. Seeking to break the developing stalemate, an amphibious operation against Anzio—to end-run the German line—was planned. But only one division could be assigned to the assault on this port city 37

Above: The Italian submarine *Nichelio* surrenders to the Allied forces during the Salerno operation.
Right: Sunrise over Salerno Bay. Two USN tugs are among the nearest ships.

miles south of Rome: beaching and landing craft were being transferred to Britain, so the Fifth and Eighth Armies had to move effectively to support it from their positions south of the Winter Line or the whole mission would surely fail. Postponed in November when these two armies could not move because of resistance and rain, the project was revived with a 22 January 1944 invasion day. By this time a two-division force had been scraped together for the landings and sufficient LSTs, LCIs and LCTs had been assembled. From H-Hour at 2:00 am throughout the day, the landings went remarkably well despite the lack of naval bombardment. By evening 36,000 troops were ashore, and in the next few days tons of tanks, guns and supplies followed.

But Kesselring was determined to throw the Allied invaders into the sea. He counter-attacked with fury. Army units and naval gunfire held him off, and the beachhead was saved, thanks largely also to the Navy's new scheme of loading trucks and DUKWs in Naples and ferrying them on LSTs directly to Anzio and the beachhead. For weeks the Navy's ferry service ran the gauntlet into Anzio to keep the offensive alive. Yet not until the rains had stopped in mid-May 1944 and the Allies had 27 divisions built up in Italy were they able to force the Germans back from their defensive lines. Only on 4 June 1944, two days before the Normandy invasion, did Allied troops enter Rome. The whole Italian campaign had proved to be a long, bloody virtual stalemate. Yet it drew off German strength by tying down 25 divisions of the *Wehrmacht* and ultimately helped lead to Germany's defeat. Frustrating as they had been, however, the Salerno and Anzio landings had further educated Allied naval, ground and air forces in the intricacies of effective amphibious landings against a determined enemy with maneuverability and effective firepower. The landings in France in 1944 represented the finished product of two years of costly interservice schooling in modern warfare: armies, navies and air forces had to work as one.

The Landings in France

Planning for the long awaited cross-Channel invasion of France had been going on since early 1943. When General Eisenhower was given command of Operation OVERLORD in December 1943, it was to be the definitive operation to take Germany out of the war. After the first assaults by five divisions, 50 divisions were to pour into Europe to destroy the Nazi war machine once and for all. It followed, therefore, that the initial landings on French soil had to be carried out with overwhelming force and intricate precision to attain both immediate and ultimate objectives. It was in view of these considerations that Operation ANVIL (the projected assault on southern France in

Above right: DUKWs landing supplies at Anzio come under German artillery fire.
Right: The cruiser USS *Biloxi* during her shakedown cruise in October 1943.
Below: The escort carrier *Kasaan Bay* seen framed by the signal flags of her sister-ship the *Tulagi* off southern France, during Operation Anvil, 15 August 1944.

the Toulon-Marseille area)—later renamed Operation DRAGOON—was postponed. Eisenhower originally envisioned this invasion as a major diversion, but landing craft for OVERLORD were in such short supply that the two operations could not be carried out simultaneously. DRAGOON was finally launched two months after OVERLORD, on 15 August 1944.

After much study, the landing site chosen for OVERLORD was a stretch of the Normandy coast east of the Cherbourg Peninsula. It was directly south across the English Channel from Portsmouth and the Isle of Wight in southern England. Although the area beyond the beaches, the *bocage* country of earthen walls and thick hedgerows of trees, would present some problems, Normandy gave ready access for cutting off the Cherbourg Peninsula to the west and the port of Cherbourg itself; troops could also move east from the Normandy beaches toward Le Havre and up the coast to take other key ports.

Plans for NEPTUNE-OVERLORD D-Day (NEPTUNE designating the naval part of the operation) called for three paratroop divisions to be dropped during the night before the invasion: one British division to seize the Orne River crossings and the Caen canal, the American 82nd and 101st Airborne Divisions to seize the causeways leading from the beaches to lands beyond and to capture various bridges on the Cherbourg Peninsula. The American First Army on the morning of the first day would seize Utah and Omaha Beaches to the west, and the British Second Army would take Gold, Juno and Sword Beaches on their left.

Naval support, predominantly British, would include pounding the German defenses before and during the invasion—naval gunfire was now finally accepted by the Army as crucial—and carrying the landing forces to the beach, then reinforcing them steadily thereafter with trips across the Channel. NEPTUNE would be an immense undertaking. Anglo-American naval units were also to keep German naval forces away and sweep the mines from the invasion channels to the beaches. For this great combined naval operation, over 2700 vessels from battlewagons to landing craft were available, the vessels to be armed, loaded and assembled all along the southern coast of England and at points as far away as the Thames Estuary on the east and Belfast, Northern Ireland, on the west. All had to converge via precise timetables if the invasion were to succeed.

D-Day was originally scheduled for 1 May 1944, but was delayed a month until 5 June for more training of the landing crews. H-Hour was from 6:30 to 7:55 in the morning depending on tidal conditions on the beaches. At the last minute, weather conditions dictated a 24-hour delay, but on 6 June 1944 the long-awaited invasion began precisely on schedule.

On 31 May, 54 old ships had left Scotland to be sunk off the invasion beaches to form a breakwater. They had been followed by 150 minesweepers that would advance to clear the Channel for the invasion forces. By 3 June the fire-support ships were underway, and the troop convoys with almost 200,000 men aboard began to form in the Channel south of the Isle of Wight.

Above: **Coast Guard landing craft head for Normandy, June 1944.**
Right: **The pre-landing bombardment, D-Day.**
Below: **A small part of the Allied invasion fleet lying off the English coast before setting out for France.**

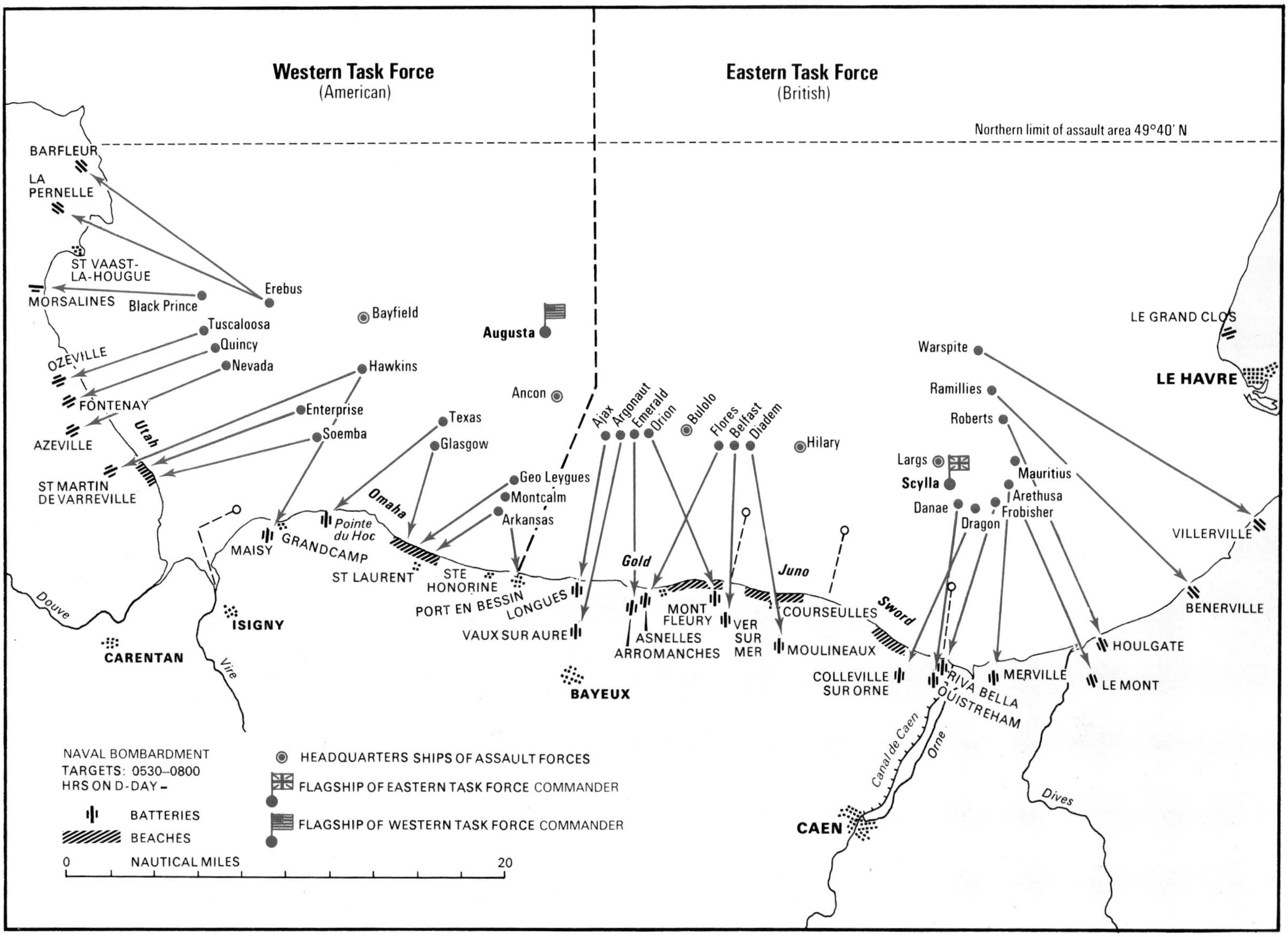

Western Task Force
(American)

Eastern Task Force
(British)

Northern limit of assault area 49°40′ N

BARFLEUR
LA PERNELLE
ST VAAST-LA-HOUGUE
MORSALINES
Black Prince
Erebus
Bayfield
Augusta
Tuscaloosa
Quincy
Nevada
Hawkins
OZEVILLE
FONTENAY
AZEVILLE
Utah
Enterprise
Soemba
ST MARTIN DE VARREVILLE
Texas
Glasgow
Ancon
Geo Leygues
Montcalm
Arkansas
Omaha
Pointe du Hoc
MAISY
GRANDCAMP
ST LAURENT
STE HONORINE
PORT EN BESSIN
LONGUES
VAUX SUR AURE
Douve
ISIGNY
CARENTAN
Vire
Ajax
Argonaut
Emerald
Orion
Bulolo
Flores
Belfast
Diadem
Hilary
Gold
MONT FLEURY
ASNELLES
ARROMANCHES
VER SUR MER
Juno
COURSEULLES
MOULINEAUX
BAYEUX
Largs
Scylla
Warspite
Ramillies
Roberts
Mauritius
Arethusa
Danae
Dragon
Frobisher
Sword
COLLEVILLE SUR ORNE
RIVA BELLA
OUISTREHAM
MERVILLE
HOULGATE
LE MONT
BENERVILLE
VILLERVILLE
LE GRAND CLOS
LE HAVRE
Canal de Caen
Orne
Dives
CAEN

NAVAL BOMBARDMENT TARGETS: 0530–0800 HRS ON D-DAY –
BATTERIES
BEACHES
HEADQUARTERS SHIPS OF ASSAULT FORCES
FLAGSHIP OF EASTERN TASK FORCE COMMANDER
FLAGSHIP OF WESTERN TASK FORCE COMMANDER
0 NAUTICAL MILES 20

LSTs landing cargo over the Normandy beaches in the first days of the invasion.

US 96
US 262
US 310

Above: **Landing operations at Omaha beach showing the technique of unloading from grounded LSTs.**

Despite the 24-hour weather delay, the mighty combined armadas formed up on schedule and moved across the Channel the night of 5–6 June . By 3:00 am on D-Day the fire-support ships were in place. The invasion of France was about to begin, not in the Pas-de-Calais area to the north as the Germans expected but in Normandy. Here the final fate of Germany would be decided.

The British and American paratroopers were dropped on schedule at 1:30 and 4:00 am, while out in the Channel troops began to pour into the landing craft. Between them and the beaches were the naval support vessels, the US battleships *Texas*, *Arkansas* and *Nevada*, plus three US heavy cruisers, two British battleships, five cruisers and 22 destroyers, all lined up to rake the German emplacements behind the American beaches with their murderous fire. British vessels were covering their target beaches to the east. Gunboats and LCTs were to accompany the landing craft and cover the beaches with fire support as the troops made their way ashore through the surf. By 6:00 the naval bombardment was underway.

Covered by this withering fire and many tons of bombs from hundreds of heavy bombers, the troops waded ashore right on schedule at 6:30 in the morning. Utah Beach proved to be relatively easy for the invading forces, but Omaha Beach was heavily fortified and strenuously defended. Tanks dropped by LCTs ahead of the infantry either sank despite their flotation belts, or were knocked out by heavy shelling. The troops on the LCVPs that followed were also shelled unmercifully and the DUKWs accompanying the waves of infantry with artillery were almost all wiped out. But naval gun power saved the day for the thousands of infantrymen hugging the sands of Omaha Beach as their bombardments, directed by spotters in Spitfires flying from England, decimated German emplacements and prevented reinforcements from moving up to push the Allied forces off the beachheads. Sometimes moving as close as 1000 yards from shore to blast away at targets called in by ground spotters, or targets of opportunity, 12 American and British destroyers tore holes in the defensive lines and allowed the ground troops to advance.

By nightfall 34,000 troops were in the beachhead at Omaha; 21,300 were on Utah. The American beachheads were secure, and for days thereafter thousands of tons of equipment and supplies passed over the beaches from the naval armadas running back and forth to England. The British beaches were easier to assault, but here too naval bombardment before and during the landings ensured eventual success. But if vast quantities of men and equipment did not continue to flow into the invasion area, the whole operation would be stymied, for Hitler now belatedly decided that the Normandy landings were not a mere diversion and began to pour crack troops into the area to push the Allies out.

However, the Americans and their British allies were prepared to reinforce the cross-Channel landings in a new and effective way. Even before the first day's action had ended, the old merchant ships ('Gooseberries'), having been towed across the Channel, were being sunk to form artificial breakwaters parallel to the beaches. 'Phoenixes,' enormous concrete box-like caissons, and 'Bombardons,' huge steel floats used to form floating breakwaters, had accompanied them in their slow towed procession from the English coast. Collectively these devices formed 'Mulberries,' artificial harbors off Omaha and Gold beaches, within which Allied ships could safely unload the tons of supplies needed by the invading forces. By 17 June these supplies were flowing ashore to support the expanding offensive; although the worst storm in 50 years destroyed the Mulberry off Omaha Beach two days later, the precious supplies continued to move ashore across Gold Beach.

Furthermore, the navies had discovered while awaiting the construction of the Mulberries that LSTs could be beached at high tide and then unloaded as the tide receded, so off-loading proceeded apace both before and after the storm of 19 June, and the operation was saved. In the first 30 days, the navies carried 929,000 men, 177,000 vehicles and almost 590,000 tons of supplies to the beachheads at Normandy. The breakout from the beachheads and the Cherbourg Peninsula was now possible. During these same crucial early days the US Navy with three battleships, two heavy cruisers (plus two British cruisers) and 11 destroyers had destroyed the heavy coastal batteries at Cherbourg on 25 June and, with the advancing Army units, had compelled the surrender of the city the next day.

The American armies moved west to cut off the Cherbourg Peninsula and south across the French countryside, turning east after 7 August at Avranches to begin forcing the Germans back toward the Rhine and their own borders. Meanwhile, British forces to the east along the Channel beat off a German counterattack, and as one army moved south to link up with the Americans, another advanced northeast toward Le Havre. By late August 1,500,000 Allied troops had broken out and were moving toward Paris and the Rhine. They were knocking on Hitler's door.

Once OVERLORD had been safely launched and secured, landing craft and naval units headed for the Mediterranean to assist in Operation DRAGOON. D-Day was set for 15 August 1944. American and French forces would make the landings between Toulon and Cannes, 50 miles to the northeast. From there the soldiers would move inland to capture the great harbor at Marseilles to the west, then drive up the Rhone Valley to Dijon to meet General Patton's Third Army for the drive into Germany.

Above: **General Eisenhower and Secretary of the Navy Forrestal following a conference in France in August 1944.**

The invasion went more easily than expected. Preceded by extensive aerial bombing and landings behind the beaches by 5000 British and American paratroopers, the main assault groups went ashore at 8:00 in the morning. Before the troops touched shore to meet limited resistance, a full two hours of naval and aerial bombardment had preceded them. The bombardment was deadly and effective: destroyers and LCIs drenched the beaches with fire to knock out any remaining emplacements just before the troops moved ashore. The naval bombarding forces were aided by the planes of seven British and two US escort carriers that spotted for them and also attacked German reinforcements behind the lines. Air supremacy was almost complete, as it had been at Normandy.

The capture of the ports of Toulon and Marseilles required naval bombardment in support of land and air forces assaulting the cities, but by 28 August both had capitulated and the French-American forces were moving northward up the Rhone. By 11 September contact had been made with Patton's Third Army, and German troops in southwest France were sealed off. The two Allied army units joined up to march in tandem toward the German homeland.

Operations OVERLORD and DRAGOON had been phenomenal successes. The Germans were now being hounded from the west and southwest by the American, British and French Armies. To the east and southeast the Russian offensives were also picking up speed. It was now just a matter of time before the Third Reich fell to the Allies. The German's last-ditch attempt to split the Allied forces in mid-December in the Battle of the Bulge temporarily threw the Allied offensive into retreat and confusion in the Ardennes region at the French-Belgium border, but the great German war machine had been fatally crippled by this time. It finally collapsed on 7 May 1945, when a surrender document was signed in Eisenhower's headquarters at Reims by Field Marshal Jodl. The next day, 8 May 1945 at 11:01 pm, the war ended in Europe.

As in the Pacific campaigns, entering their final stages as American forces moved inexorably toward the Japanese home islands, the US Navy had played a major role in securing the peace of the world. From the U-boat wars to the landings at Morocco, Algiers, Sicily, Italy and France, the Navy had served with distinction and pride. As the world began to breathe the clear air of peacetime once again, the Navy looked to its new duties on a now radically changed world scene.

Below: **The USS *Tide* sinking off Omaha after hitting a mine, 7 June 1944.**

U.S.S. MIDWAY
Queen of the Seven Seas
COMMEMORATIVE WAR BONDS
SOLD HERE

Launching of the large carrier *Midway* in March 1945, too late for service in World War II.

NEW NAVAL MISSIONS

THE COLD WAR AND THE CHANGING NAVY

In the summer of 1945, when victory in Europe was newly won and American military forces were fully geared up for the final assault on Japan, the Navy had almost 3,400,000 officers and men on duty. There were approximately 1200 major ships and 40,000 aircraft of all types in its inventory. Five years later active duty personnel had shrunk to 375,000: 90 percent of the Navy's World War II personnel had been discharged to civilian life. Major combatant vessels numbered fewer than 250, aircraft only 4300. The greatest naval force in history has been slashed to prewar levels, while responsibilities had continued, even increased, in many areas of the world. Additionally, during these five crucial postwar years the Navy had been forced to battle for its very existence as an American fighting force. All signs pointed toward rough seas in maintaining its position as the nation's first line of defense.

Demobilization and Air Attacks

At the end of World War II the American people, in an atmosphere of victory and euphoria, seemed to conclude that a strong military was no longer necessary. Forgetting the lessons of their own history, that peace can be maintained and national interests ensured only through adequate military—and especially naval—strength, they demanded that the government 'bring the boys home' as fast as possible so the nation could return to peaceful pursuits now that overseas threats had been eliminated.

Accordingly, the Navy's first job after hostilities ended in August 1945 was 'Operation Magic Carpet,' utilizing all vessels available—including even carriers and battleships—to ferry the fighting men home. In one year alone, the Navy carried over 2,000,000 men and women back to the United States; in the Far East it transported 400,000 Chinese, Japanese and Korean soldiers back to their homelands. The boys were coming home, peace was in the air and demobilization proceeded apace. In addition to cuts in ships and personnel, the Navy also saw its operating budget drop from $45 billion in 1946 to $14.5 billion in 1947, then to $11.5 billion in 1948. Construction contracts were cancelled on almost 10,000 ships and small craft. Some 2000 other vessels were retired from active service and 'mothballed' in various anchorages along the coasts. Even more were simply declared surplus and sold off for scrap. The Navy had not undergone such a drastic cut in ships, personnel and budget since the end of the Civil War.

An even greater threat to a viable naval defense force was posed by the new atomic bomb and the devotees of air power, who felt their day had finally come. There was widespread public acceptance of the idea that the atomic bomb had made all other weapons obsolete, and that sufficient air power to deliver the deadly bomb against any aggressor was all that was necessary to ensure peace. Air enthusiasts promulgated the theory that strategic bombing had really won the war: if this were true, it followed that the Navy and its fast carrier task forces—as well as the Army and the Marine Corps—were now superfluous. Since the Air Force alone could deliver 'the bomb' (then weighing five tons), air power must grow while the other services were phased down or out, victims of their own vulnerability in the face of new technology. Air Force generals publicly asked why any navy at all was needed.

The Navy's admirals fought back with cold hard facts and technological counterattack. Demobilization, attacks from air enthusiasts and the advent of atomic power would not spell the demise of the Navy if its leaders could prevent it. And world events moved toward confirming the Navy's view that a strong sea force was critical to the nation's security.

The Cold War Begins

Despite fervent hopes in the West that Russia's co-operation with the Allies during World War II would effect a change in her government's attitudes and goals espoused since the revolution of 1917, Kremlin leaders still dreamed of a Communist-dominated world. War-devastated Europe and the Far East offered splendid opportunities to take significant steps in that direction. So did anticolonial nationalistic ambitions of peoples in the Near East, Southeast Asia and Africa. These aspirations could be utilized to further Soviet ambitions, particularly when Western Europe lay prostrated by its wartime efforts.

Any lingering Western complacency in the face of Russian expansion was shaken when a 1948 coup in Czechoslovakia drew that country into the Soviet orbit. Furthermore, in June 1948 the Soviets clamped a blockade on the city of Berlin—contrary to all agreements among the Allies—to display their intention of complete control over the future of Germany. If the Allied occupying powers—Great Britain, France and the United States—could be forced from the divided capital city, it would be a clear sign that Russia was the dominant power in all of the former Reich.

Faced with a decision to withdraw or

Below: A feature of the design of the _Midway_ was the siting of the guns below the flight deck to avoid blast damage to the aircraft.

remain in Berlin, the Allies carried out an 11-month airlift of supplies into the city. This kept the population alive and Allied claims to joint governing powers intact. By the time the Soviets backed down and lifted the blockade in May 1949—the Western powers meanwhile having created the Federal Government of Germany at Bonn as a sign that Western Germany was a viable and permanent entity outside the Russian-dominated East Germany orbit and control—ten million tons of supplies had been airlifted into the beleaguered city. US Navy and Air Force planes carried 70 percent of these vital supplies; British planes accounted for the rest. It had been a grueling test of will that the Allies had won, and a valuable lesson in Soviet intentions.

While these challenges to US and Western goals and determination were primarily within the purview of the Army and Air Force, checking Communist expansion in the Mediterranean Basin fell largely to the Navy. As early as April 1946 the Navy had shown the flag at Istanbul, the capital of Turkey, in the form of the battleship *Missouri*, which visited the strategic city ostensibly to return the body of the Turkish ambassador (who had died in Washington), but in reality to demonstrate America's interest in Communist activities in the area. Russia had demanded from the Turkish Government a share of control over the historic and strategic

Above: **The submarine *Cusk*, *circa* 1948, fitted with a hangar and launch ramp for the Loon cruise missile.**

Straits and Dardanelles. The *Missouri* was there to show that the United States backed the Turkish Government in its refusal to acquiesce in such an arrangement. The message was received in the Kremlin.

Following a visit by the carrier *Franklin D Roosevelt* to Greece that fall to demonstrate American support of the Greeks in their fight against a Communist-led insurgency, the Navy announced that deployments could henceforth be expected in the Mediterranean. The Navy was returning to the *Mare Nostrum* as an instrument of diplomacy after a century of absence. This US naval presence became more pronounced in 1947, when the insurgents threatened to overthrow the Greek government and thereby other pro-Western governments in the area, including Turkey with its hold on the historic waterway from the Black Sea. Refusing to allow this, or to allow the eastern Mediterranean to fall into Soviet hands, President Harry S Truman announced the 'Truman Doctrine': the United States would help free peoples everywhere resist threats by totalitarian governments, whether openly or through armed minorities within a government. Since Greece was then in a civil war against Communist rebels supplied by the Communist Government in Yugoslavia (at that time a Soviet puppet state), there was no doubt that America was serving notice that Greece and Turkey would not be allowed to fall under Soviet domination. Subsequently supplies and military advisers were sent to Greece, and the US Navy continued to patrol the eastern Mediterranean.

With the assignment of an American carrier to the Mediterranean on a permanent basis late in 1947, bolstered the next year by additional vessels, the Sixth Fleet was born and the American presence in the Mediterranean became a military and diplomatic fact of life thereafter. In effect, the American Navy took over the task of guarding the southern flank of the gradually emerging Western defense line designed to resist Soviet attempts to expand either toward Western Europe or into the Mediterranean Basin. When NATO was created two years later, the US Navy continued this function for the Western alliance, a duty it maintains to this day.

All these actions in Europe and the Mediterranean resulted in a gradual awakening of the American people to the consequences of Russian 'expansionism of opportunity.' Clearly, different options of effective reaction had to be fashioned to meet the challenge. Both economic aid and formal military alliances emerged in what came to be called the Cold War.

Economic aid took the form of the Marshall Plan of June 1947. The plan flowed from a suggestion by Secretary of State George C Marshall that economic assistance be offered to European countries to get them back on their feet after the wartime destruction, thereby lessening the threat of radical reactions against their governments. While this US aid was offered to all countries in Europe in need of economic reconstruction, the Soviet Union refused the offer of help and prevented its puppet states from accepting it too, binding them, instead, to the Molotov Plan administered by Russia. By 1954 the European Recovery Program (the embodiment of the Marshall Plan) had spent over $34 billion on nonmilitary aid (and over $14 billion in military aid) and was a phenomenal success, helping to rebuild the shattered economies of the Western European nations and keeping many of them, particularly Italy, from falling under Communist control.

Military aid took the form of the North Atlantic Treaty Organization (NATO), created in 1949 with 11 Western European nations joining the United States in a mutual defense pact, obviously against Soviet aggression. The North Atlantic Treaty Pact, the first peacetime military alliance the United States had ever entered into, allowed any or all nations to come to the aid of any member state if that state became the victim of aggression. To this day NATO defense forces, heavily supported by the United States, have continued to play a stellar role in providing a shield against outside aggression for the people of Western Europe. Without US naval power to project American determination to Europe's shores, NATO would be a shell without substance.

With world events, and particularly Soviet aggressive moves in Europe and in the Mediterranean, propelling the United States into a role as defender of the peace and security of the West, the US Navy, with its potential for controlled and flexible response, had demonstrated its value in a convulsive post-World War II situation. Yet the Navy constantly had to beat off flank attacks by its sister services in order to exist as a separate and effective arm of America's national defense structure.

Unification Attacks and the 'Revolt of the Admirals'

Unification of the armed services for better co-ordination and economy had been discussed for decades. Over four dozen bills supporting unification had been proposed from the 1920s to the end of World War II. But as the war came to an end with the Army Air Force claiming major credit for defeating enemy forces by strategic bombing—and smarting under its control by the Army—the issue became more pronounced. The Air Force wanted unification as a means of gaining independence from the Army; it also wanted unification to strip the Navy of its air arm. The Army, on the other hand, supported unification not only to let the air forces go, but also to take over the Navy's amphibious Marine Corps. The Navy, stripped of its air function (representing 30 percent of its men and materiel) and of the Marines, would be left with only surface combatant, submarine, convoy-escort and surface-support services. The Navy did not oppose unification as such, but it did resist losing its air arm and its Marines. It argued that it could not

Opposite: The _Forrestal_ at sea in 1959.
Below: An F2H Banshee comes in for a hard landing on the _Midway_ in 1953.

carry out its traditional and necessary functions of control of the seas and projection of power without its air and amphibious arms. Nor could the other two services carry out these functions either, leaving the military forces severely limited in anything less than an all-out atomic war.

Unification came about in the National Security Act of 1947, which provided for a National Military Establishment of three departments, Army, Navy and Air Force; a civilian secretary of defense to oversee all three services and sit in the cabinet as principal adviser to the President in all defense and national security matters; three civilian secretaries of the Army, Navy and Air Force; and a Joint Chiefs of Staff to co-ordinate military strategy and logistics. The Navy's continued existence as a multifaceted fighting force was assured under this legislation, which specifically provided for continuation of the Navy's air arm and the Marine Corps. The Navy could live with this arrangement, especially as the first secretary of defense was James V Forrestal, a financier who had come to Washington as naval undersecretary and had become secretary of the navy in 1944 upon the death of Frank Knox. Things proceeded rather well among the unified services for two years under Forrestal's leadership, although the generals and admirals fought one another continually for a fair share of the declining defense allocations of a parsimonious Congress. The act was amended in 1949 to change the NME to the Department of Defense and to provide a chairman for the Joint Chiefs of Staff.

The Navy had thus parried one serious threat against it in the early stages of unification, but threats to its existence were to continue, as it found out only two years later. In 1949 Forrestal suffered a nervous breakdown from overwork and was forced to resign. President Truman appointed as his replacement a West Virginia lawyer-politician active in veterans' affairs, Louis A Johnson. Johnson's appointment came primarily as a reward for his activities as a fund-raiser during Truman's 1948 presidential campaign. The secretary of the navy at the time was John L Sullivan, who had taken the post in 1947. Sullivan shared the admirals' profound distrust of the Air Force's reliance upon massive retaliation in the form of the B-36 bomber with an atomic payload as the primary answer to America's defense needs. And Sullivan was fully committed to naval air power for both strategic and tactical purposes. He approved the building of a 60,000-ton supercarrier to implement the Navy's plans for multiple missions built around newly developed jet fighters. On 18 April 1949 the keel for the supercarrier, to be named the *United States*, was laid with due ceremony at Newport News Shipbuilding in Virginia. The modern naval air age was about to begin. But the Navy never figured on the pro-Air Force Louis Johnson, who had every intention of merging naval aviation with the Air Force and putting the Marines into the Army to save money, even if he had to 'crack heads' to do so. Johnson was determined to have 'real unification' and save over a billion dollars in the process, a fine claim for one who aspired to higher office.

Five days after the laying of the keel for the *United States*, the tactless Johnson, backed with a two-to-one vote in the JCS, summarily cancelled the contract on the carrier. John L Sullivan was out of town and had not been consulted. With this act, the issue of unification was rejoined. Sullivan was furious and resigned forthwith, blasting Johnson for his pro-Air Force and pro-Army prejudices. Johnson followed up the carrier cancellation by revealing that plans were underway to transfer Marine air units to the Air Force. Soon thereafter, the secretary of the army told a Senate committee that the Marines should be part of the Army.

The Navy was resolved to fight to the death over these issues; it got its chance to voice its concerns when the House

Left: Crewmen of the carriers _Saratoga_ (top) and _Independence_ commemorate the establishment of US Navy aviation.
Below: A typical task group of the late 1950s based around the USS _Valley Forge_.

Armed Services Committee launched an investigation of Johnson's connection with the procurement of the B-36; Johnson had been a director of the company that received the B-36 contracts. The committee, headed by Georgia Congressman Carl Vinson, cleared Johnson of any wrongdoing, but opened the hearings to extended comment on the whole question of the role of each of the armed services with their respective missions in the nation's defense posture. Navy leaders took advantage of this opportunity to make their case—and vent their frustrations.

Although Francis P Matthews, a banker and businessman from Nebraska and Truman's new secretary of the navy (although he had absolutely no background in naval affairs), backed secretary of defense Johnson during the Vinson hearings, the admirals came out swinging. Vice-Admiral Arthur Radford, Commander in Chief, Pacific Fleet, called the B-36 a 'billion-dollar blunder.' Naval witnesses argued time and again against a single weapon and delivery system and pointed out that unification would not work without allowing each service to proceed with weapons development and testing according to its needs. In this 'revolt of the admirals,' both active duty officers and retired line admirals like King, Nimitz, Spruance and Halsey argued for balanced forces and centered their criticisms on reliance on the B-36 as the heart of America's strategic defense posture. With a maximum speed of only 375 miles per hour and a ceiling of 40,000 feet, they argued, the B-36 was extremely vulnerable to the new Russian MiG-15 jet fighter. The Air Force argued strenuously for the efficiency of the B-36 strategy, and General Omar N Bradley, chairman of the joint chiefs of staff, even asserted that the Marines should be absorbed by the Army since large-scale amphibious operations would never again occur in warfare. For siding with his naval colleagues in the fight, Admiral Louis E Denfield was fired by Matthews as Chief of Naval Operations.

But the Navy was helped by the essential logic of its arguments, and by the fact that during the course of the hearings the Soviet Union exploded an atomic device. The American atomic monopoly was gone, and use of the A-bomb against Russia or its satellites could bring atomic retaliation. The name of the game had been changed dramatically, and the Vinson Committee's report of March 1950 reflected both the Navy's well-argued case for its multi-reaction capabilities and the new atomic realities that opened the door to conflicts of less-than-atomic proportions. The report noted the Navy's needs for means of flexible response and recommended that

Above: **Terrier surface-to-air missiles ready to launch on the *Josephus Daniels*.**

a supercarrier be built when funds became available. It also charged the Air Force with being unbalanced in favor of strategic, as opposed to tactical, power. Finally, it declared that Louis Johnson had violated the law by canceling the *United States* contract.

The Navy stood vindicated: its right to exist as part of a balanced defense force was never again challenged. More importantly, by its fight it had awakened the Congress and the nation to the realities of modern military power and the need for a flexible response at sub-atomic levels. The proper functions of the Army, the Navy and the Air Force were now in a better perspective. Even the generals and admirals understood one another better. The 'revolt of the admirals' had worked out for the best, but Congressional support for more adequate funds for the military services whereby they could respond to all types of threats to the peace were slow in coming. Only when North Korea invaded South Korea on 25 June 1950 and propelled the United States into limited warfare did it become obvious that American forces were simply not prepared for conventional warfare challenges, and that the Navy's demands for flexible response had been right on target.

War in Korea, 1950–53

The conflict in Korea rose out of World War II, after which the Russians accepted the surrender of Japanese troops in Korea north of the 38th parallel; the United States accepted their surrender south of that line. Free elections to determine the fate of the peninsula fell through when the Soviets refused to go along with the United Nations supervision of the process in the north. Thus evolved a *de facto* situation wherein two governments came into being—one in the north supported by the Russians and one in the south supported by the United States—with both claiming sovereignty over the entire country.

This stalemate was broken on 25 June 1950, when 110,000 North Koreans with over 1000 artillery pieces, more than 100 Soviet-built tanks and 100 tactical aircraft swept across the 38th parallel into South Korea. It is clear that both the Soviet Union and China had given the green light to the North Korean Government, perhaps to test American determination to back up her words with action, or perhaps because on three occasions since 1947 high American officials had declared Korea to be outside the American defense perimeter. As the well-trained troops swept south against an increasingly demoralized and hapless South Korean Army, American determination to resist Communist expansion was put to the test. The capital city of Seoul, on the western coast just below the 38th parallel, was quickly overrun, and it appeared that the country would be conquered with breakneck speed.

Reacting swiftly to the invasion, the United States took the matter to the United Nations Security Council: on 26 June (in the absence of the Soviets, who were boycotting the organization) that body condemned the invasion and the next day directed member states to furnish assistance to the Republic of Korea in repelling the attack. By this time President Truman had already acted, ordering General Douglas MacArthur in Japan to take over all American forces to direct the defense of South Korea. As he said, 'We've got to stop the sons of bitches no matter what.' The President also ordered the US Seventh Fleet into the Formosa Strait to prevent the Chinese Communists from attacking the Nationalists, or vice versa, during the Korean confusion; either act would have expanded the conflict into World War III. But Truman's determination to halt the aggression by military means rested with US military forces that had been hard hit by budget-pruning for five years.

With the United States taking the lead in the defense of South Korea (to be joined by forces from Britain, Greece, Turkey and 16 other nations) and furnishing the bulk of land, naval and air forces, supplies

Right: The battleship *Iowa* off the Korean coast in May 1952.
Bottom: Map of the Inchon landings.

and money, the fate of South Korea obviously depended on American military strength and how soon it could be assembled. MacArthur's Army units stationed in Japan were at only 50 percent of combat readiness, the Fleet Marine Force was down to only 24,000 men, the Air Force F-80 jets were based in Japan and could remain over any Korean target for 15 minutes at the most and the Seventh Fleet had only one large *Essex*-class carrier, two cruisers, 12 destroyers and a few minesweepers and auxiliary craft in the area. The British had one carrier available to aid the American naval efforts.

Despite the small arsenal available for the job, the Navy went to work. While the Army and Marines poured men and supplies into the defense perimeter established around Pusan on the southern tip of the Korean Peninsula, the Navy began gunfire missions in support of the land forces—there was little to fear from North Korean naval efforts, which involved only four dozen small and insignificant craft—and air strikes were launched from the carriers. On 5 July American naval forces received orders to establish a blockade of the entire Korean coastline to prevent reinforcement by sea of the North Korean forces. Thus the pattern for the Navy was set in the first days of the war. It was to furnish surface gunfire support for land units; transport Army, Marine and Air Force personnel and equipment to the fighting areas; and furnish tactical air support to the land forces by cutting North Korean supply lines from the north.

The Air Force found itself hamstrung to a large extent because there was little occasion for strategic bombing in this type of war and because its fighters, based in Japan, did not have the range to attack targets in Korea effectively. Carrier-based Navy planes, either jets or piston-driven, had no such problem and played a stellar role—along with the bombarding cruisers and destroyers hitting shore batteries, enemy convoys and bridges, and the land forces fighting a desperate defensive battle around Pusan—in bringing the North Korean offensive to a halt. The

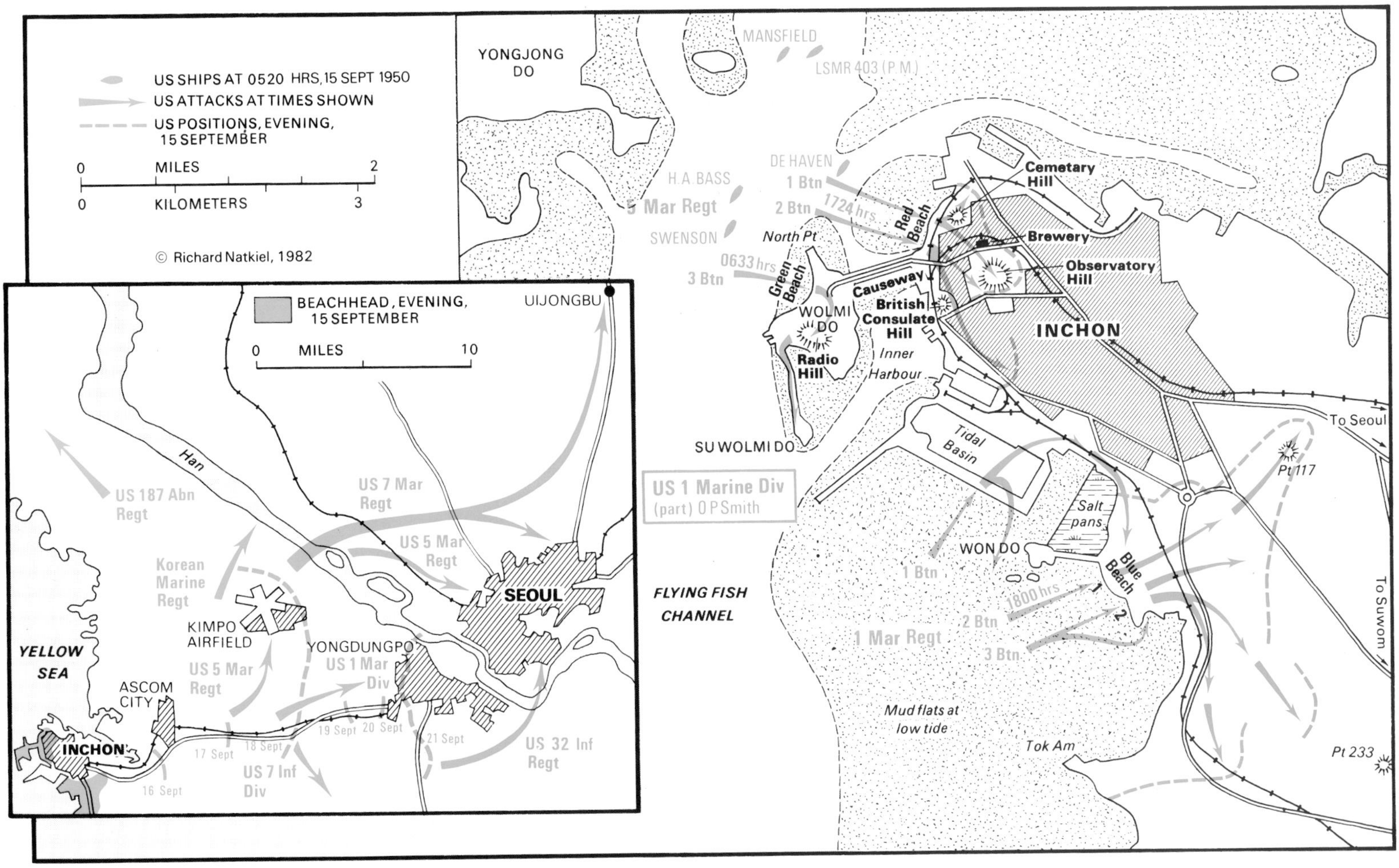

US SHIPS AT 0520 HRS, 15 SEPT 1950
US ATTACKS AT TIMES SHOWN
US POSITIONS, EVENING, 15 SEPTEMBER
0 MILES 2
0 KILOMETERS 3
© Richard Natkiel, 1982
BEACHHEAD, EVENING, 15 SEPTEMBER
0 MILES 10
UIJONGBU
Han
US 187 Abn Regt
US 7 Mar Regt
US 5 Mar Regt
Korean Marine Regt
KIMPO AIRFIELD
SEOUL
YONGDUNGPO
US 1 Mar Div
US 5 Mar Regt
YELLOW SEA
ASCOM CITY
INCHON
16 Sept
17 Sept
18 Sept
19 Sept
20 Sept
21 Sept
US 7 Inf Div
US 32 Inf Regt
YONGJONG DO
MANSFIELD
LSMR 403 (P.M.)
H.A. BASS
DE HAVEN
5 Mar Regt
1 Btn
2 Btn
1724 hrs
Red Beach
SWENSON
North Pt
0633 hrs
3 Btn
Green Beach
Cemetary Hill
Brewery
Observatory Hill
Causeway
WOLMI DO
British Consulate Hill
INCHON
Radio Hill
Inner Harbour
SU WOLMI DO
Tidal Basin
US 1 Marine Div (part) O P Smith
To Seoul
Pt 117
Salt pans
WON DO
Blue Beach
1800 hrs
FLYING FISH CHANNEL
1 Btn
2 Btn
3 Btn
1 Mar Regt
To Suwon
Mud flats at low tide
Tok Am
Pt 233

Above: **The *New Jersey* off Korea in May 1951. All four *Iowa* class ships served during the Korean War.**

carrier-based planes also scored a coup by knocking out most of the North Korean Air Force on the ground in an effective bomb-and-rocket attack on the main North Korean air base near Pyongyang. Any lingering doubts about the Navy's capability of providing effective support in a limited war below the atomic threshold, and of taking the war to the enemy, vanished in the opening weeks of the Korean conflict.

Even at this, the Navy's greatest role in Korea was still to come. Since the situation had stabilized around Pusan by the end of the summer of 1950, General MacArthur decided that the time had come to strike a decisive blow against the enemy. He planned to do so in classic style, with a giant attack on the enemy flank to isolate the North Korean forces by cutting them off from reinforcements. The site chosen for the vast amphibious landing on the enemy's flank was Inchon, a port city on the western shore of Korea near the capital of Seoul. Strategic Kimpo Airbase was nearby. The Marines would land at Inchon and push inland, while the Eighth Army would break out at Pusan, catching the North Koreans in MacArthur's vise. The landing was scheduled for 15 September 1950.

But carrying out an amphibious landing at Inchon would be a terrific gamble—some military officers estimated its chances of success at 5000 to 1—because of the 29-to-36-foot tides found there and because the assaulting Marines would be forced to land not on a beach but against a giant sea wall, well defended by enemy forces. The tremendous tides also meant that dangerous currents in the harbor would be a problem and, given the tidal depths, landings could be made only a few days each month and only for a few hours on those days, assuming the naval amphibious landings units could successfully navigate the tortuous channels within the harbor with their ever-threatening mud flats that could ground a vessel without warning. The odds-makers were not far off in their estimates of success, given the complexity of the operation, but the decision to proceed had been made by MacArthur, the commander, and the Navy prepared for the landing.

Softening up of enemy positions in the Inchon area began on 10 September, as planes from the fleet began hitting the island fortress of Wolmi-do within Inchon Harbor. American and British cruisers and destroyers added their guns to the bombardment by hitting gun emplacements in the harbor area. In the grey dawn of 15 September, the 230-vessel invasion fleet appeared off Inchon, a fleet scraped together from the entire Pacific command. Wolmi-do and its garrison of 400 men was the first target. After more pounding by naval guns and aircraft, the Marines moved ashore at 6:30 in the morning and by 8:00 had taken the fortress. The city of Inchon was next; after preliminary softening up, the Marines hit the target with its perilous sea wall that evening. Despite heavy enemy fire, they climbed up and over the walls and moved on the city and Kimpo Airfield. Aided by close naval support, including air strikes, they had taken the city by midnight. Kimpo fell shortly thereafter, and the rail line to Seoul was cut. Sea and air control had aided the Marines in bringing about one of the most successful amphibious landings in American history. Only 22 men were killed, fewer than 200 wounded.

With American units closing in on the capital of Seoul, and the Eighth Army under Lieutenant General Walton H Walker moving north (supported by naval gunfire directed at the east coast road), the

Below: **The *Iowa* during the Korean War. Note the helicopter on the quarterdeck.**

North Korean Army beat a hasty retreat. In an attempt to catch them, MacArthur decided on another amphibious landing—this time at Wonsan, a port city on the eastern coast of Korea north of the 38th parallel. This operation was delayed for eight crucial days because the harbor was strewn with 3000 mines, and the Navy had only a handful of minesweepers available. By the time the task was completed, the ROK (Republic of Korea) armies had encircled the city, forcing the defenders to flee to the north.

During these military actions, three important decisions had been made by President Truman. First, he announced on 27 July that the use of atomic bombs would not be permitted in the war. This was a clear sign to all—especially China—that he would not escalate the war to new heights: it would be fought only along conventional lines. Second, on 12 September he relieved Secretary of Defense Johnson of office for supporting a preventive war against the Soviets. Johnson was replaced by General George C Marshall, who brought higher morale and greater efficiency and co-operation to the department of defense. Third, having decided to attempt political unification of the Korean Peninsula, on 27 September he authorized MacArthur to operate north of the 38th parallel (an order approved by the UN), but specifically forbade the general to cross into Manchuria or to allow any air or naval action north of the Yalu River.

Truman backed up his orders not to provoke Chinese or Russian intervention by attacks on Manchuria via a meeting with MacArthur on Wake Island in October. MacArthur assured the President that neither the Chinese nor the Russians would cross the border, despite the fact that Chou En-lai, the foreign minister of China, had already warned that the Chinese would enter if Americans crossed the 38th parallel. MacArthur was wrong. On 27 October 1950 thousands of Chinese 'volunteers' began crossing the border into North Korea. Within a month the American Army and Marine forces were forced into controlled retreat. The Eighth Army fell back across the 38th parallel, leaving men of the First Marine Division with the task of fighting their way out of the Chosin Reservoir on the east coast and making their way through eight Chinese armies to the port of Hungnam 35 miles away. Thanks to close air support from naval fliers who harassed the Chinese at every turn, the Marines made their way into Hungnam, where every vessel available had been dispatched to ferry them out. Setting up a curtain of fire around the town with naval guns and firepower, the relief force under Rear Admiral James H Doyle was able to evacuate over 100,000 American and ROK troops and 91,000 civilians from Hungnam by Christmas Eve. They were carried to safety at Pusan.

From this point on, the conflict settled into a war of attrition with the battle line just north of the 38th parallel. Before long it was a stalemate, and peace talks began in July 1951, but not before General MacArthur had been ingloriously fired by President Truman for advocating—publicly—the use of atomic weapons in Manchuria and the utilization of Chiang Kai-shek's 500,000 troops in Korea or

Below: **A Navy Corsair about to make a rocket attack on a North Korean bridge in September 1951.**

Main picture: The *Essex* class carrier *Leyte* seen in the mid-1950s.
Below: An A-4 Skyhawk being prepared for launch from the USS *America*.
Below left: The *Missouri* blasts enemy positions at Chonjin, 21 October 1951. The *Missouri* was the only US battleship in commission at the start of the Korean War.

against China itself. The nation was as split over the Truman-MacArthur controversy as it was over the war itself, which ultimately cost the United States 142,091 casualties—killed, wounded, captured or missing.

Once peace talks began, the fighting gradually died away except for a few months when negotiations broke down and the battles were resumed. General Matthew B Ridgway, MacArthur's successor, had no intention of expanding the scope of the war, and Vice-Admiral C Turner Joy, heading the UN delegation, assumed the unenviable job of carrying out negotiations with the communist delegation, the enemy knowing full well that any significant enlargement of the war by the United States was politically impossible. The stalemate was finally ended with the signing of a formal truce on 27 July 1953, placing the truce line almost where the border had been before the fighting began 37 months before.

It had been a frustrating war for a rather bewildered American public, but the communists had been stopped cold in their first attempt to enlarge by force. Truman, however, by refusing to use America's greatest strategic striking power, had sent a message to would-be aggressors that they could escape responsibility for their warmongering by using proxies without fear of American retaliation. This unintended message of America's willingness to use only limited means in limited wars was not lost on either China or Russia, as the next two decades would show.

As the Navy surveyed its part in the conflict, it could not but be proud. It had done its job on limited resources, and done it well. The war had also revealed that the Navy did, indeed, need greater financial support to provide the ships, weapons and personnel to carry out its multiresponse mission. In Korea it had proved that it could do the jobs assigned—shore bombardments, close air support, transportation and supply of ground troops, amphibious landings—as no other service could. To talk of the Navy as being obsolete was now patently ridiculous. The Army knew it; the Air Force knew it; and the American public knew it. The Navy's new wartime mission was its old mission updated.

Upholding American Commitments in the 1950s

During the remaining years of the 1950s, the Navy was called upon to uphold American and noncommunist world rights in the Far East, in the Mediterranean and in the North Atlantic. It did this without firing a shot. The imposing Seventh Fleet in the Far East, the Sixth Fleet in the Mediterranean and the vessels assigned to NATO for European duty stood at the ready to deter Communist aggression and localize conflicts wherever they occurred. Not only were American commitments maintained within the NATO alliance, the nation also made an agreement with the Philippines (which gained its independence on 4 July 1946) whereby 23 military and naval bases, including Subic Bay, would be maintained on a 99-year-lease basis by the United States in the archipelago, thus ensuring an ongoing American presence in the Far East. The United States signed a mutual defense pact with Australia and New Zealand called ANZUS in 1951. Furthermore, in 1954 the United States joined Britain, France, Australia, New Zealand, the Philippines, Thailand, and Pakistan in the South East Asia Treaty Organization (SEATO) which, while not a defense alliance—since it provided only for consultation in the face of aggression—served to keep the United States in naval alliance with the other member countries. In each case it was expected that the Navy would be called upon to bear a heavy burden in supporting America's friends in the face of communist aggression.

Left: The carrier *Kitty Hawk* refuels her escorting destroyers *McKean* (right) and *Harry Hubbard* during exercises in October 1962.

The nation and the Navy also became actively involved to the point of intervention in many areas of the world. In 1954 the Navy prepared to intervene by carrier strike force to aid the French army of 12,000 surrounded at the fortress of Dien Bien Phu in Vietnam by 50,000 communist forces, but the decision was made at higher levels to forego unilateral intervention.

Later in the year and into 1955, after the abortive Geneva Conference resulted only in a division of Vietnam along the 17th parallel, the Navy carried out Operation 'Passage to Freedom' by using its vessels to relocate 800,000 people from North Vietnam in the south and to remove tons of military equipment to South Vietnam from the north. Then in 1958 the Chinese Communists began a military buildup across from the Nationalist-controlled islands of Quemoy and Matsu, only four miles off the Chinese coast. The communists saw the islands as stepping stones to the conquest of Taiwan; the Nationalists saw them as springboards to their return to the mainland. When bombing of the islands by the communists began on 23 August 1958, the Seventh Fleet was called upon to aid the 100,000 Nationalist defenders on the islands without getting into a shooting war with the communists. The Navy helped convoy supplies to the islands from Taiwan by carrying amphibious tractors close to shore, from which point they could make their way in. The Navy also flew sorties from its five carriers in the air space over Taiwan, thus freeing the Nationalist air forces to deal with the communists' Russian-built MiGs. The crisis soon died as China turned to attack Tibet and the frontiers of India.

The Navy was also called upon to act in the Mediterranean in 1958. The Middle East was quickly becoming a hotspot, with the Americans in full support of Israel against her Arab neighbors and the Soviets trying to break out into the eastern Mediterranean by supporting nationalist and anti-Western colonial movements throughout the area. At stake, too, was the

Below: Terrier missile fired from the carrier *Constellation* during her shakedown cruise in 1962.

rich supply of oil which the Western nations had developed in the area and which the Soviets were seeking to deny to the oil-starved Free World countries. On 14 July 1958 an armed revolt ended the pro-Western government in Iraq. The President of Lebanon, Camille Chamoun, believed the coup had been staged with the help of Egyptian president Gamal Abdel Nasser (closely tied to Russia) and, fearing the same might happen in his country, asked the United States for military aid. In line with the 'Eisenhower Doctrine' of 1956—which said that the United States would aid any Middle Eastern Government threatened by communism if aid was asked for—the Sixth Fleet was ordered into the area. It was an imposing sight, with its three carriers plus escorting cruisers and destroyers and amphibious ships loaded with Marines as it approached the Lebanese shore on 15 July. By afternoon the Marines were landing on the beaches near Beirut under cover of Navy jets overhead. Eventually 14,000 Marines moved into Lebanon and remained there until the situation stabilized and the threat of a coup passed. Although there was no resistance to the landings—indeed, the Marines were greeted only by scantily clad sunbathers and ice-cream vendors—the Navy demonstrated clearly that it could move quickly and effectively to trouble spots on incredibly short notice. Thanks to this swift response, the Russian pledges of assistance to the Egyptians were revealed as hollow promises. The lesson was not lost on a disappointed Nasser. Nor was it lost on the Soviets, who decided that a multiple-response fleet in the Mediterranean was indispensable to success in that area.

Thus during the Eisenhower years the Navy was able to play an effective role in countering the Soviet military threat in line with the President's basic desire to protect the Free World within the framework of necessary national economic stability and balanced budgets. Money was tight, but all three services were allowed to move forward in research and development of the weapons systems they needed in the event of either nuclear or sub-nuclear confrontations. The US Navy stayed on station as in the past, although now it was increasingly armed with weapons of the atomic age.

Birth of the Nuclear Navy

Atomic research had not stopped with the development of the atomic bomb, but had proceeded apace from that point. If the development of atomic power for warfare by the United States had needed any impetus, it was supplied when the Soviets exploded an atomic device of their own in 1949. In 1952 the USA demonstrated the first hydrogen bomb. Then in 1954 the Russians exploded a hydrogen bomb, prompting President Eisenhower to demand military armaments that would deter attack by the Soviets. The race for nuclear superiority in weaponry was on.

The Navy had been working on atomic power for vessels since the late 1940s, particularly on an atomic-powered submarine. Such a submarine could remain submerged as long as necessary, because it drew its steam power from a nuclear reactor that required no oxygen and gave off no exhaust. The need to surface periodically had always been the greatest tactical weakness of submarines. Remaining submerged for days or weeks on end, an atomic submarine would be virtually impervious to attack. The trick was to produce an atomic reactor suitable for the limited space available in a sub. The man who spearheaded the Navy's project for atomic-powered submarines was Hyman G Rickover.

Rickover was the Navy's leading expert on nuclear propulsion and chief of the Nuclear Propulsion Division of the Bureau of Ships. At the same time he was head of the Naval Reactors Branch of the Atomic Energy Commission. In this dual military-civilian capacity, he could both demand that each agency fulfill his goals and coordinate the research of both organizations. Always crusty and demanding (to the point of frequent insufferability, according to many who had to deal with him) he constantly prodded his researchers on and saw his dream come true with the launching of the atomic submarine *Nautilus* at Groton, Connecticut, in 1954. The black-hulled boat, with a sleek 'sail' replacing the old conning tower, was taken out for trials in January 1955 and passed with flying colors. It was a proud day for this son of a Polish immigrant, who had graduated from Annapolis in 1922 and begun his brilliant career in marine engineering shortly thereafter. Now he had placed the United States in the lead in the atomic sub

race. Rickover must have drawn satisfaction, too, from the fact that he had been passed over for promotion to rear admiral and had faced mandatory retirement in 1953, only to be saved by a spirited outcry from the public and Congress. Whatever the merits of Rickover's personality and his way of doing business, there was no doubting his accomplishments. He was leading the Navy into the atomic age.

Work on nuclear-powered submarines and their technology continued at a brisk pace in the years that followed. In 1958 the *Nautilus* proved her ability to stay submerged for long periods of time while navigating with pinpoint accuracy, when she sailed from the Pacific to the Atlantic under the polar ice cap. Later that year the *Skate* rose from the sea to surface at the North Pole. Perhaps the most dramatic demonstration of the atomic submarine's ability to remain submerged and navigate accurately came two years later, when the *Triton* made a complete circumnavigation of the globe underwater, cover-

Left: The USS *Grayback* enters San Diego harbor carrying a 400-mile range Regulus I cruise missile.
Below: The USS *Ethan Allen*, name ship of the second US Navy class of nuclear-powered, ballistic-missile submarines.

25

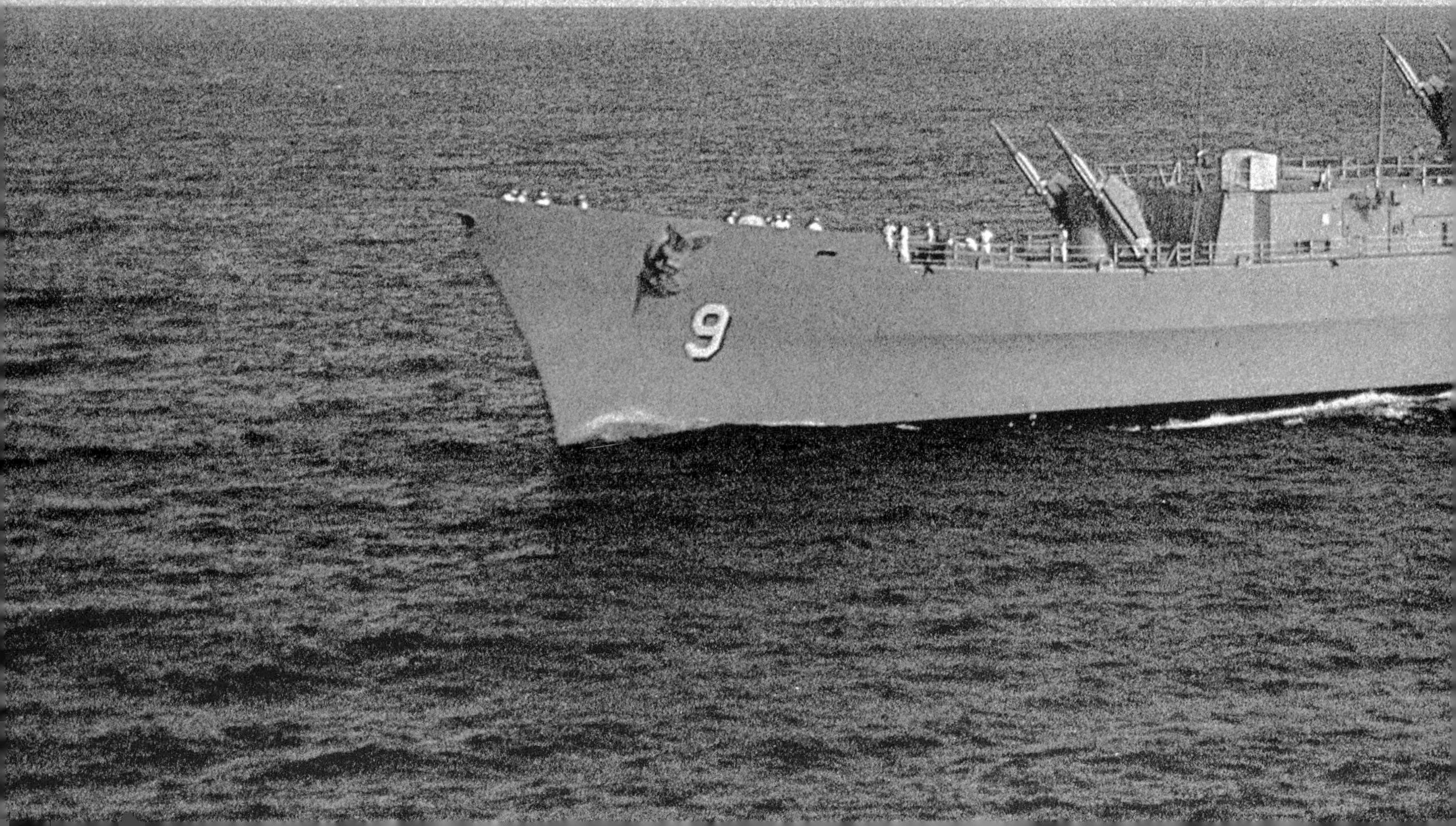

Left: The nuclear-powered *Bainbridge* at sea in 1979.
Below: The *Long Beach* showing the square-sided superstructure that was for many years a recognition feature of this nuclear-powered cruiser. The installation of new radars in the early 1980s has changed this profile however.

GJ
GL
AB
AF
NAVY
AF
8413
AF
8395
NAVY
101
AF
8402
NAVY
106
NAVY
105
AF
8398
NAVY
109
NAVY
112
NAVY
111

Above: The *Lafayette* class ballistic-missile submarine USS *Nathan Hale* (SSBN.623).
Left: F-4 Phantom II aircraft at the forward end of the *Enterprise*'s massive flight deck in April 1962.

ing the 36,000 miles in 83 days, her inertial navigation system making the feat possible.

Nor did the Navy pass up the chance to develop atomic-powered surface vessels in these years. In 1957 the keel was laid for the *Long Beach*, a cruiser with a nuclear propulsion plant buried in her sleek hull. The 17,000-ton vessel was not only the first nuclear surface ship in the Navy's inventory when she joined the fleet in 1961, but also the first cruiser built for the service since World War II. Her main batteries consisted of guided missiles rather than guns. She was followed into the surface fleet by the giant atomic-powered carrier *Enterprise*, whose keel was laid in 1958 and who joined the fleet in 1962. This 1123-foot giant of almost 90,000 tons was powered by eight reactors and could steam at 30 knots and go two years without refueling. Her angled flight deck (an innovation copied from the British) had four powerful steam catapults that allowed her to launch a plane ever 30 seconds. The *Enterprise* added a new and powerful dimension to the Navy's arsenal and dictated that other ships in carrier task forces of the future would have to match her in speed and mobility. Together they would be armadas of the 1960s and beyond. Having also launched the guided-missile frigate *Bainbridge* with nuclear power generation, the Navy had demonstrated by the early 1960s that nuclear power had come to stay on the oceans, and that the US Navy would command the lead in new firepower and technology.

But the secret of the tremendous potential of these new naval craft lay in the simultaneous development of the guided missile. Not satisfied with having nuclear submarines equipped with short range Regulus missiles (which required them to surface in order to fire their ordnance), Admiral Arleigh A Burke, Chief of Naval Operations from 1955 until 1961—and the chief figure in the 'revolt of the admirals' less than a decade before—pushed for guided missile research and development that would allow missile firing from beneath the sea. Success was attained in 1960 when the submarine *George Washington*, in a test off the Florida coast, fired the first Polaris missile from a submerged position. From this point on, the matching of atomic submarine propulsion with accurate long-range ballistic missiles gave the Navy one of the most advanced and secure weapons systems in the world. Other and more powerful submarines, surface vessels and ballistic missiles would follow, but the pattern had been set in these years of trial and rearmament for the Navy.

In 1956 President Eisenhower had set the tone and direction of defensive weaponry when he outlined the weapons of the future, weapons to deter aggression in either nuclear or sub-nuclear confrontations. He had argued for balanced forces consisting basically of strategic air power, guided missiles, supercarriers, atomic submarines capable of launching missiles with atomic warheads, plus a sizeable army, a capable Marine force for land operations and a strengthened Air Force tactical capability. With these coming into place in the Navy and its sister services by the end of the 1950s, it was clear that the questions of national defense reorganization and of the types of weapons that were necessary to maintain an adequate military readiness in all situations had been answered by conflict, compromise and the grim realities of world events. The greatest teacher had been the Korean War. The greatest gainer had been the American people and their friends around the world who, feeling a sense of direction and purpose, had shouldered the burden of the defense of the non-communist world as part of their historical legacy. But the calm assurance of the 1950s gave way to the turbulent 1960s and 1970s, and with them came new problems for the nation—and for the armed services that protected American interests.

Aircraft maintenance in the cavernous hangar of the USS *Enterprise* in 1964.

CONFLAG
STA. No 4
AE
AE
7745
9543
3307

DECADES OF TURMOIL

'Let every nation know, whether it wishes us well or ill, that we shall pay any price, bear any burden, meet any hardship, support any friend, oppose any foe to assure the survival and the success of liberty.' With these soul-stirring words of his inaugural address, John F Kennedy made his debut as President of the United States in 1961. The former World War II naval officer and Congressman and Senator from Massachusetts had beaten out Vice-President Richard M Nixon by a whisker in the 1960 presidential elections and now came to the nation's helm. To the Navy and the entire defense establishment, the implications of the new President's words were clear: America, having rediscovered its world mission and its resolve, was about to take the offensive for liberty. Yet time would show that this was a false start. Not until almost twenty years of trial and confusion, both internal and external, had passed would the nation appear to rediscover its sense of direction. The 1960s and 1970s would prove to be decades of internal confusion and of commitments without conviction: and the Navy and its sister services would undergo further purgatories before America began to awaken to the realities of worldwide responsibilities in the late twentieth century.

The McNamara 'Revolution' and Caribbean Crisis

Robert S McNamara, Kennedy's choice for secretary of defense, had compiled an outstanding record as a brilliant systems analyst and organizer from his early student days at Berkeley and Harvard to his stint as president of Ford Motor Company after World War II. The aggressive McNamara was the embodiment of the new style of industrial manager who based his decisions on systems and cost analysis. As a leader in scientific management, he attracted a legion of young, dynamic men of the same mold who followed him to Washington to flesh out his personal staff, which soon expanded to 1600 persons. With the young president's support, McNamara's drive to introduce modern principles of management to the Pentagon met little resistance from above, but plenty of resistance from below.

To the Navy, McNamara's 'whiz kids' (plus the burgeoning professional staffs

Right: **Soviet-made *Komar* class missile patrol boats photographed in Cuba on 3 November 1962.**
Below right: **Missile equipment being removed from Cuba, 6 November 1962.**
Below: **Suspicious crates opened by the crew of a Soviet freighter to expose comparatively innocuous bomber aircraft, not missiles.**

KRONSTADT PC

4 KOMAR PGMG

6 MISSILE TRANSPORTERS

TRUCK

TRUCK CRANE

TRUCK

of permanent Congressional committees) represented a clear danger to the services —and thereby to the nation—by operating on two false premises: first, that management by civilians in areas of professional military expertise and judgment would result in essentially sound military decisions. Military critics argued that theoretically sound managerial decisions could well be poor military decisions, especially with over-direction taking away the proper sphere of judgment from experienced leaders and competent field commanders on the spot. The second false premise was that military decisions are essentially quantifiable. Military leaders preferred to rely on previous performance and prudential judgment of the situation in view of overall strategies. To quantify the unquantifiable (whether in weapons procurement, strategic or tactical options, or personnel decisions) was both foolhardy and usually counterproductive. Many, if not most, of the crucial problems faced by the armed services, they argued, did not yield to systems analysis.

But these objections did not deter the defense secretary and his assistants. If the admirals (or generals) could not produce quantifiable proof that a proposed weapons system or tactical analysis would or would not work (at least on paper), or that a particular type of ship or plane was or was not cost-effective because of its particular role in wartime deployments or diplomatic situations, the assumption was made at Defense that the military leaders could not know what they were talking about. Admirals and generals would function only to offer suggestions to their civilian superiors. Time would prove that the admirals and generals stood on solid ground in their resistance to excessive civilian control and systems analysis processes, but many tragedies would occur before the service leaders would regain attention as professionals in their own right.

During President Eisenhower's time a plan had been hatched for the United States to support anti-Fidel Castro Cubans in attempting an invasion of the island to overthrow the Caribbean dictator, who had come to power in 1959. By late 1960, 'Operation Pluto' had been formulated by the Central Intelligence Agency. Free Cuban airplanes would carry out pre-invasion air strikes against Castro's 30-plane air force, and a 1500-man invasion force, trained covertly in Guatemala, would land at Bahia de Cochinos (The Bay of Pigs) on the southern coast of Cuba. This invasion, according to CIA operatives, would set off an anti-Castro uprising, and the capital of Havana would soon fall to the invaders. At this point all planning was tentative and subject to cancellation by the White House.

By 1961 final planning for the invasion was well under way, without the Navy having been informed that this combat operation had been approved in the highest government circles and that they were to support it to assure its success. The Navy received virtually no critical information on the invasion plans, the military being told simply to 'Stay the hell out of it.'

The invasion attempt on 17 April 1961 was a notorious fiasco. United States naval units were sent to the area to assist the civilian-directed operation, but Kennedy then refused to authorize US naval aircraft standing by on the deck of the carrier *Essex* to give critical air cover as the invasion proceeded on 17 April. Survivors of the invasion forces were soon trapped on the swampy terrain at the Bay of Pigs landing site and within three days had been rounded up and thrown into prison camps by the Castro forces. (They were ransomed by the United States in December 1962 for $53 million in food and medicine.) American prestige was damaged both in Latin America and throughout the world. More importantly, the aborted invasion attempt pushed Castro even closer to viewing the Soviet Union as his protector. Soon thereafter the Soviets were permitted to begin installing nuclear ballistic missiles on Cuban soil.

Although Operation Pluto proved conclusively that military operations should be planned by military professionals, not civilian amateurs, and that no commitment should be made unless the country was willing to follow through with sufficient force to accomplish the objective, the embarrassing lesson was apparently lost

Right: **The Soviet freighter** ***Metallurg Anasov*** **with missiles and related equipment on deck after leaving Cuba on November 1962.**
Below: **The similarly laden** ***Komsomol*** **pictured in the Mediterranean.**

on civilian White House advisors, although perhaps not on President Kennedy who, when the next Cuban problem intruded itself, worked closely with the Navy and other services to effect a solution.

During the summer of 1962 it became obvious to US intelligence forces that something ominous was happening in Cuba. Dozens of Russian ships had arrived bringing men, fighter planes and surface-to-air missiles to the island. Inquiries to the Soviet Union brought assurances that the weapons were only defensive in nature, but refugees from Cuba insisted that something very menacing was taking place. Finally, on 14 October, a high-flying U-2 American reconnaissance plane took photographs that revealed clearly the rapid preparation of long-range missile sites—one type of missile being readied was capable of a 1000-mile range, and another had a 2000-mile range. America at this time enjoyed a clear superiority in ballistic missiles, with 130 ICBMs (intercontinental ballistic missiles), 144 Polaris missiles in Navy subs and about 1500 strategic bombers. But in one bold stroke Soviet Premier Nikita Khrushchev could neutralize that lead by placing the entire United States within two-to-three minute warning range of Soviet missiles. Eighty million Americans could be killed in a single pre-emptive strike.

After examining the options—a 'surgical' air strike on the missile sites, a blockade of Cuba, or an invasion of the island—Kennedy decided that a blockade, or 'quarantine' as he called it, was the proper response. He asked Admiral George W Anderson, Jr, CNO, if the Navy could do the job: Anderson responded, 'The Navy will not let you down.' While the government informed the United Nations, the Organization of American States and the nation's major allies what was in the offing, the Air Force put four tactical aircraft squadrons and its ICBM crews on alert. The Army began moving thousands of troops to embarkation points in Georgia and Florida; the Navy alerted its Polaris crews and formed 180 ships, including eight carriers, into Task Force 136 to carry out the blockade. In all, some 480 ships eventually took part in the operation, and almost 400,000 military personnel went on alert.

With the military at the ready, and with Air Force B-52s in the air, Kennedy went before the nation via television on the evening of 22 October 1962 to inform the American people and all nations that the Soviet Union had placed offensive missiles in Cuba and that the island would be quarantined until they were removed. To give the Russians time to think it over and back down, Kennedy announced that the naval blockade would begin $1\frac{1}{2}$ days hence, on 24 October at 9:00 in the morning, EST.

Tension mounted steadily as two dozen ships from Russia neared the announced quarantine line northeast of Cuba (first established at 800 miles from the island, then reduced to 500 miles when it was realized that some Russians ships underway would reach the deeper line before 24 October). As work continued on the missile sites, Kennedy informed Khrushchev on 23 October that he had OAS support and that Soviet ships would not be fired upon for the purpose of sinking them, but would be disabled. Furthermore, he said, the US Navy would force Soviet submarines to the surface or depth charge them. The Navy put the quarantine into effect as scheduled on 24 October, stopping and boarding all Soviet-chartered ships approaching the island; those without offensive weaponry were allowed through. Most turned back. No Soviet ship with offensive weapons crossed the line, and six subs were forced to the surface after they had been picked up and warned by signal to surface and identify themselves or be depth charged. Finally, on 28 October Krushchev announced that he would remove the missiles under UN supervision if Kennedy would pledge not to invade Cuba (at that moment 30,000 Marines were poised offshore for invasion). Although Castro remained in power after the Cuban confrontation, the Russians had clearly backed down. The missile crisis was over, although American forces would stay on alert for another three weeks, and the US Navy would monitor removal of the missiles from Cuba.

The crisis had been the supreme example of flexible response by a balanced naval force. The Navy, co-operating with the Air Force and Army, had again proved its versatility. Nuclear war had been avoided because other options had been available. The Navy had not let the President—or the nation—down, as Admiral Anderson had promised; it had performed its duty in exemplary fashion.

Into the Quagmire of Vietnam

American involvement in South Vietnam began as far back as the closing months of World War II, when American military-intelligence agents moved into the country to encourage uprisings against the occupying Japanese and worked briefly with the communist guerrilla leader Ho Chi Minh. As the French tried to re-establish control over their colony at the end of the war by putting down Ho's guerrilla forces who threatened to take it over, the US made the fateful decision in 1950, under President Truman, to extend economic and military aid to the French—probably in reaction to the 'loss' of China to the communists the year before. By 1954 communist forces under Ho had won a resounding victory over the French fortress at Dien Bien Phu (the United States refusing to carry out last-minute bombings, or to commit American ground forces to aid in the defense in the absence of clear support from other allies of the French): the French were forced to close their war at the bargaining table. The Geneva Conference of that year divided the beleaguered country into North Vietnam and South Vietnam, and the French began to leave.

In response to the perceived danger of spreading communism, the United States formed the South East Asia Treaty Organization (SEATO) early the next year, allying itself, Australia, France, New Zealand, Pakistan, the Philippines, Thailand and Great Britain. Also in 1954 the United States enthusiastically endorsed Ngo Dinh Diem as Prime Minister of South Vietnam. Diem, a highly regarded anticommunist patriotic leader for many years, was overwhelmingly elected President the following year but soon proved to be authoritarian in his governing style. Still, he seemed the best man for US support in

Below: **A US Navy *Swift* boat engages a shore target in South Vietnam. The *Swift*-type patrol boats were armed with 0.5-inch machine guns and an 81mm mortar.**

Above: A US Navy assault support patrol boat operating in the Mekong Delta in November 1967. In the background a Chinook transport helicopter.
Below: The carrier *Franklin Roosevelt* pictured in the Gulf of Tonkin in 1966.

the difficult situation wherein Ho and North Vietnam refused to accept the concept of a divided Vietnam and waged incessant guerrilla warfare against the government of South Vietnam.

American advisers continued to visit South Vietnam in search of a means of winning counterinsurgency victories, but their job was made more difficult by Diem's refusal to make the reforms that would win him wider popular support in his clash with the North Vietnamese forces, and by Ho's claims to be the real leader of all of the Vietnamese people. In 1961 Vice-President Lyndon B Johnson visited the South Vietnamese leader and returned to tell President Kennedy that more economic aid should be extended, but that military intervention on a large scale should not be tried. He added, however, that the United States had to stand by its friends and assist South Vietnam in its struggle against communism. Kennedy, fearing a communist victory, decided to increase the number of American advisers in South Vietnam from a total of 1000 to 16,000 over a two-year period.

By the end of 1962, almost 10,000 advisers were in Vietnam, but the war against the North Vietnamese insurgents was still going badly. Convinced that the basic problem was the uncooperative government of Ngo Dinh Diem (who surrounded himself with family members in power positions, including especially Ngo Dinh Nhu, his brother, and his brother's wife, the diminutive but fiery Madame Nhu), the White House, the State Department and the Central Intelligence Agency endorsed a coup by South Vietnam's military against Diem. Kennedy, perhaps naively, assumed that the worst fate awaiting Diem would be exile. Instead, the military leaders arrested Diem and Nhu early in the morning of 2 November 1963, as they were praying in a church, and assassinated both in cold blood in the rear of an armored personnel carrier. The US had now taken a major and bloody step into responsibility for the war halfway around the world. Ironically, Kennedy himself would

fall to an assassin's bullet before the month was out.

Before the end of this fateful month, 23,000 Americans had been assigned to Vietnam; two-thirds of them were military, but fewer than 800 were naval personnel. American presence and responsibility were growing; soon it would escalate rapidly as a decision was evolving to accept a face-off between communism and democracy in this far-off divided land. The key step was the Tonkin Gulf Resolution, passed by Congress on 7 August 1964 by virtually unanimous votes.

The occasion was an attack three days earlier by North Vietnamese torpedo boats on American destroyers patroling international waters in the Gulf of Tonkin. Ordering retaliatory air strikes against the torpedo boat bases (64 sorties were launched from American aircraft carriers), Johnson asked Congress for authority to 'take all necessary steps, including the use of armed forces' to prevent further North Vietnamese aggression. The resulting resolution opened the door to further escalation of American support to the government of South Vietnam. By July 1965 the President had committed 100,000 combat troops; by the end of 1965 the number had climbed to 250,000; by 1968 the total commitment stood at 550,000 men, including 38,000 naval personnel. America was in a full land war in Asia against guerrilla forces from the north. The Army and the Marines took the brunt of the fighting, but the Navy played a major role in the conflict for a full decade.

Naval support for the war effort centered on the planes of Task Force 77, lying 100 miles offshore on 'Yankee Station' in the Gulf of Tonkin. From this point the Navy flyers flew combat support missions for the Army and Marine Corps. The planes also bombed Hanoi industrial plants, as well as tactical military targets along the guerrillas' supply lines including railroads, bridges and truck convoys. To the consternation of the pilots and their commanding officers, the planes were forbidden to hit certain areas designated 'sanctuaries,' including the important port of Haiphong where large supplies of arms and equipment were unloaded from Soviet and satellite vessels. Nor was this crucial harbor ever mined until May 1972, just before the close of the war, even though the operation could have been accom-

Above: **USN inshore patrol boat *PCF.38* during Operation Slingshot, Vietnam, February 1969.**
Left: **The *New Jersey* bombards a target near Tuyhoa in March 1969 during her last spell on the gun line in Vietnam in March 1969.**

Below: ***PCF.43*** **at high speed on an inland river in Vietnam in February 1969.**

plished with ease from the air. Haiphong was 'off limits' to bombing because of White House fears that a Russian vessel might be hit, setting off an incident with the Soviets.

In addition to using air power, the Navy also brought the battleship *New Jersey* into the war zone, utilizing her nine 16-inch guns against shore targets. Minesweepers, patrol boats and Coast Guard cutters were deployed along the extensive coastline to interdict junks and other vessels carrying supplies to the Viet Cong forces. Meanwhile, shallow-draft converted landing craft outfitted with machine-guns, 20- and 40-mm cannon, and 81mm mortars—in a throwback to Civil War tactics—patroled the Mekong Delta and the waters near Saigon to interdict supplies and, working with the US Army, to carry out raids on the enemy forces. Other shallow-draft vessels patroled the rivers of the Mekong Delta on similar missions. America's 'brown-water navy' served with as much distinction as their 'blue-water' comrades in the troublesome war that was Vietnam.

Yet the basic frustrations suffered by the naval—and other service—forces in this 'no win' war were the result not of military decisions, but of civilian decisions imposed upon the military who had to do the fighting. In the 1950s, in addition to the concept of 'flexible response' by which military reaction was matched to the challenge at hand, another doctrine had emerged—that of 'strategic gradualism,' which argued that response should be escalated in stages with pauses between each escalation. Eventually, according to the theory developed by the academicians responsible for the idea, the enemy would realize he could not win without the danger of ever-greater escalation and would come to the conference table. This theory, which in effect denied the principle of the vigorous offensive to compel the enemy to do your will, was not accepted by the military leaders. They saw it as giving the enemy the opportunity to prepare his defenses for the next escalation. And, as Paul B Ryan has argued effectively in his *First Line of Defense*, 'If it potentially lowered the level at which diplomacy would give way to shooting, it also opened the door to a progressive stepping up of the use of force.'

Unfortunately, President Johnson, savoring historical recognition as the founder of the Great Society and therefore desiring to limit the war and its consequent costs, embraced the theory despite the advice of his military leaders. With Robert McNamara at his side to quantify the escalations and tactics used, Johnson moved into civilian control of the war in a manner unprecedented in American history. So closely did Johnson and McNamara control the fighting that the President is reported to have said that the American military 'could not even bomb an outhouse without my approval.' Civilian interference also saw such phenomena as Air Force B-52s used for tactical air support while the Navy's carrier planes carried out strategic bombing of enemy targets. Added to these problems was the fact that Johnson, believing the war must be fought and won in South Vietnam only—despite the fact that Laos and Cambodia were being used as staging areas, and that the obvious source of aggression was inside North Vietnam—prohibiting bombing the two neighboring, supposedly 'neutral,' countries and in 1968 forbade any bombing inside North Vietnam.

Above: **The ammunition ship *Mount Katmai* transfers supplies to the *New Jersey*.**
Right: **Spectacular full broadside from the *New Jersey* against a target in Vietnam.**

***Above:* The last act of the Vietnam War. Refugees come aboard the USS *Hancock* during the humiliating evacuation before the fall of Saigon to the Communists in 1975.**

As American casualty lists climbed and the cost of the war reached $30 billion per year by 1968, forceful opposition began to break out at home, and Johnson announced he would not run for re-election. Hubert H Humphrey got the Democratic nomination, but he lost to Richard M Nixon for the Republicans. From this point on, the American commitment in Vietnam was de-escalated as Nixon sought to 'Vietnamize' the war. In 1970 Nixon sent troops into Cambodia and Laos to neutralize the communist sanctuaries there—despite unfavorable reaction at home—and by 1971 he had cut troop and naval strength in Vietnam by half. In 1972 he kept to the troop withdrawal schedule, despite a heavy Communist offensive, by increasing the number of naval planes on 'Yankee Station' and by authorizing the bombing of North Vietnam. This was soon followed by orders to mine the harbor of Haiphong and six other ports and to hit power plants in the Haiphong area. Meanwhile, he also arranged a detente with Russia and China, and in January 1973 announced the end of the war. In 1975 the whole of South Vietnam fell to the Communists, for good or ill, a controversial chapter in American history came to an end.

During the course of this long and frustrating war, the Navy and her sister services distinguished themselves in the most trying circumstances ever encountered by American military forces at war. Without public support or understanding, and hobbled by well-meaning but ineffective civilian controls, the services were nevertheless blamed for the whole debacle. Yet as Clausewitz had pointed out long before, once a nation decides on war it must set its goals in the conflict and then let the military carry out the war in the most effective way. If a nation is unwilling or unable either to define its goals in warfare or to allow the military to carry out these goals, it should never engage in war. The problem in Vietnam lay not in the military, but in the nation and the government that it was attempting to serve.

Duties Elsewhere—Plus Z-grams

While the Navy was carrying out its assigned duties in Vietnam waters—losing 83 pilots and crewmen killed and at least 200 others missing in action, and suffering the loss of 300 planes and over 1000 damaged—it also continued to carry out its responsibilities elsewhere in the world, although stretched increasingly thin by the Far Eastern conflict. In 1965 President Johnson ordered a Navy amphibious task force to the Dominican Republic to prevent a Castro-type takeover of the provisional government installed there after the murder of the dictator Raphael Trujillo (the ostensible reason was to assure the safety of American lives and property in that troubled land).

In June 1967 the problems of civilian versus military control of vessels were highlighted when an American intelligence-gathering ship, the USS *Liberty*, was bombed and strafed in broad daylight by Israeli planes during the Six-Day War fifteen miles off the coast of Egypt. Israel claimed it was all a case of mistaken identity as her pilots assumed the ship was Egyptian—despite her markings and the fact she was clearly flying the American flag. Thirty-four men died and about 170 were wounded in the incident. American naval vessels had been ordered to stay

100 miles from the coast the day before, but the *Liberty* was under the direct control of the Joint Reconnaissance Center in Washington, not the Navy. The *Liberty* had been sent at least five messages from nonnaval sources to pull back from the coast, but apparently never received any of them and remained hovering in the danger zone. Had the ship been under the command of the Sixth Fleet, it would have been pulled back and the incident and loss of lives would never had occurred. The Navy pointed this out to McNamara, who apparently missed the point completely. Divided command structure had claimed 34 victims.

The same type of incident occurred only seven months later, on 23 January 1968, when another intelligence-gathering ship, the lightly armed USS *Pueblo*, was captured by North Korean vessels off the coast of that nation after a less than all-out defense by its crew. The 83-man crew and all its secret equipment fell to the captors, and the officers and crew spent a year in a North Korean prison before being released. Investigation of the incident revealed that the ship was under a score of federal civilian agencies plus the Navy, and that with no one taking charge of her destination or mission she had sailed into waters too distant for US naval forces to come to her rescue. Divided command structure had claimed its second ship and crew, this amid the turmoil of the Vietnam war already becoming untenable for much the same reasons. When the *Mayaguez* was seized off Cambodia in 1975, the American reaction would be swift and decisive: perhaps something was learned from the *Liberty* and *Pueblo* incidents.

The elevation of Richard M Nixon to the presidency in 1969 brought some lessening of American commitments around the world, but little aid to the Navy greatly

Main picture: **The first Trident submarine, the USS *Ohio*, at speed on the surface.**
Bottom: **Scene inside the missile compartment of the *Ohio*. Each missile carries up to eight independently targetable warheads.**

HODE ISLAND
SSBN
AL DYNAMICS
NH
BOAT DIVISION

Launch of the *Los Angeles* class nuclear-powered attack submarine USS *Portsmouth*. The *Los Angeles* class is the latest type of attack submarine to be built for the US Navy and production is continuing. In the background the partially-complete Trident submarine *Rhode Island*.

Above: **The nuclear-powered *Truxtun* was initially described as a frigate but was redesignated as a cruiser (CGN) in 1975.**

weakened by the protracted Vietnam conflict. The Navy was critically short on replacement vessels and necessary hardware. On the one hand, the new administration announced the Nixon Doctrine in July 1969: henceforth the US would keep its treaty commitments by providing a nuclear shield from all-out aggression and supplying aid to its allies, but it would not bear the burden of fighting for any nation in a limited war. On the other hand, the Navy (now relying on a basic strategy of nuclear submarines and an all-purpose defense fleet as part of the Nixon Doctrine) would have to carry out its missions with a smaller force. The impact of this new austerity became clear in August 1969, when the Navy was forced to decommission 100 vessels and discharge over 70,000 men.

While undergoing these cutbacks, the Navy was also forced to adjust to the policy moves inaugurated by its newly appointed chief of operations, Admiral Elmo R Zumwalt, Jr. 'Bud' Zumwalt was chosen over the heads of a number of more senior officers; at 49 he was the youngest officer ever to hold that position. The new secretary of defense, Melvin Laird, had met the admiral while Zumwalt was serving as commander of naval forces in Vietnam and had been greatly impressed by the dynamic young officer. Standing with Laird and Zumwalt was Rhode Island politician John H Chaffee, the new Secretary of the Navy, who apparently agreed with the projected policy changes of his new Chief of Naval Operations and gave him free rein to put them into practice, despite objections from senior admirals.

Believing that the Navy should adopt more forward-looking social attitudes in tune with the times, and make naval life more attractive to its men and women by eliminating 'Mickey Mouse' regulations, Zumwalt soon inaugurated a stream of new directives to the service (non-affectionately dubbed 'Z-grams'). Beards were allowed, as were 'non-regulation' haircuts; civilian clothes were permitted on liberty; committees were established aboard ships to discuss human relations problems; and a more relaxed attitude toward traditional discipline became manifest. In line with affirmative action and equal opportunity standards in the civilian community, efforts were made to bring more minority and underprivileged youths into the service (the Navy, like the other services, had become racially integrated after World War II). When this goal was not met quickly, enlistment standards were lowered, thus bringing into uniform many young men who had less than adequate backgrounds for an increasingly technological Navy. When these minorities could not qualify for technical training specialities and were shunted into low-skill jobs, they interpreted it as demeaning, racially inspired and a breach of promises made to them.

Matters came to an unfortunate head in 1972, when four racially inspired riots took place aboard naval vessels, and there was widespread evidence of additional disobedience, riot and even mutiny in the fleet. Once the glare of publicity surrounding the incidents had subsided, and the consequent Congressional investigation had concluded, the new secretary of the navy, John Warner (who had replaced Chafee earlier in the year), along with Zumwalt, reimposed higher enlistment standards and purged the Navy of its marginal performers, who were at the heart of the problem, through early discharge. But many senior admirals felt that substantial damage had been done by utilizing the Navy as a laboratory-cum-showplace for 'enlightened social policies' and that the service would suffer the effects of Zumwalt's policies for years. Few doubted the wisdom of Zumwalt's instituting longer homeporting and similar measures, but many questioned whether the flood of Z-grams pushing for too much too fast had ultimately served the Navy well at a crucial time in its existence.

Despite these internal adjustments, the Navy continued to do its duty, sometimes under rather strained conditions with Washington ever coaching from the sidelines. In the fall of 1973 the Arab forces of Syria and Egypt, attempting to regain lands lost to Israel in the Six-Day War of 1967, attacked the Israelis with Soviet-supplied armor and artillery. Fearing that Israel would be conquered, President Nixon ordered an airlift of American equipment to the tiny nation, but found to his consternation that many allies, fearing retaliation by the various Arab oil-producing states if they interfered, refused to help the US aid Israel and denied rights to land and refuel airlift cargo planes on their soil.

At the same time the airlift was assembled, the Sixth Fleet was sent into the eastern Mediterranean, but White House directives (probably issued by Secretary of State Henry Kissinger, as the Nixon Administration was reeling from the effects of Vice-President Spiro Agnew's resignation under fire) severely limited the fleet commander's maneuvers. When the chairman of the Joints Chiefs requested permission to move the fleet closer to the war zone so as to evacuate Americans in the embattled area if necessary, he was

Right: **The ammunition ship *Kaleakala* under way off the coast of Oahu.**
Below: **The nuclear cruisers *Arkansas* (nearest), *Mississippi* and *Texas* during exercises in the Caribbean in 1981.**

65

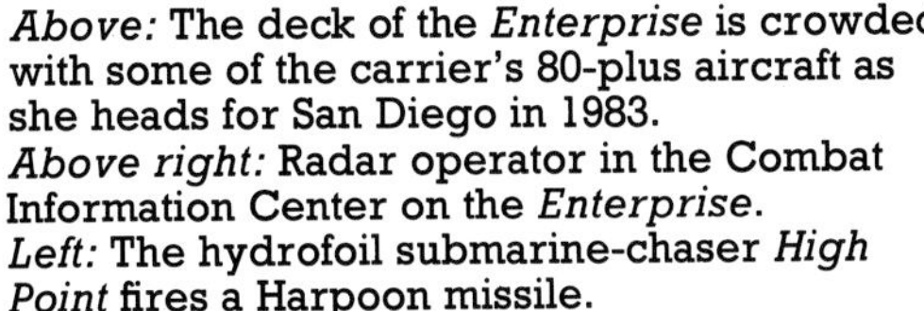

Above: **The deck of the** ***Enterprise*** **is crowded with some of the carrier's 80-plus aircraft as she heads for San Diego in 1983.**
Above right: **Radar operator in the Combat Information Center on the** ***Enterprise.***
Left: **The hydrofoil submarine-chaser** ***High Point*** **fires a Harpoon missile.**

persistently refused by the White House. Only when it appeared that the Soviet Union might send troops to Suez to extricate Egyptian army units from encirclement was the Sixth Fleet hurriedly augmented by a carrier task-force group and a destroyer task-force group—a belated attempt to increase American naval strength in the troubled area to equal the recently reinforced Russian fleet. When the conflict ended a month later in a shaky truce and the fleets dispersed, it was obvious that while the Sixth Fleet had demonstrated the Navy's ability to carry out a flexible response by a force in place without firing a shot, it was also clear that the Russians had successfully challenged American dominance in the Mediterrnean. Stability had been reintroduced into the volatile area thanks to American naval presence, but whether this presence would remain viable in these waters in the face of a continuing Soviet naval buildup was another question. For their part, the Arab nations repaid the United States for its help to Israel by a five-month oil embargo that graphically illustrated the dependence of the Western nations and Japan on the oil resources of this crucial area of the globe.

The Onset of Détente

In the midst of these controversies of the early 1970s a decided change in American foreign policy was taking place. This new policy, while ostensibly pointing to a less confrontational posture between the United States and Russia, also resulted in far less clarity in American foreign-policy goals. This confusion in goals, in turn, made the tasks of the Navy and also of its sister services even more difficult in the years which lay ahead.

In an effort to ease budget-breaking nuclear rivalry for both countries, the US turned away from its two-decade policy of containment of communist expansion in favor of a policy of détente, or relaxation of tensions between the two powers. This, it was hoped, would lead to more understanding between the two nations and a relaxation of the mutual distrust that stood in the way of world peace and security. In 1972 President Nixon journeyed to Moscow, where he signed the first Strategic Arms Limitation Treaty (SALT I) as an initial step toward curbing nuclear rivalry.

Yet the concept of détente in no way hindered the Soviets from aiding and sponsoring revolutionary regimes in Africa and the Middle East. Actually, the Soviet Navy continued to display an ever-widening presence in those areas and on the sea lanes of the world. Meanwhile, the US Navy was expected to continue its worldwide vigilance with more sophisticated weaponry on budgets deliberately restrained, not only for domestic priorities but to illustrate America's good intentions. It was an anomalous situation in which the Navy and the nation found itself: the era of détente was to introduce relaxed tensions and increased good will at the same time the Soviets were taking measures to increase tension in key areas of the world and thus destroy good will.

In August 1974 Richard Nixon resigned the presidency, turning over the office to

Below: **The guided-missile frigates** ***Jack Williams*** **(nearest),** ***Antrim*** **and** ***Oliver Hazard Perry*** **with the Atlantic Fleet in 1982.**

Gerald R Ford, the popular House Minority Leader selected as Vice-President the year before on Spiro Agnew's resignation.

President Ford—and the entire nation—underwent the anguish of seeing thousands of refugees from South Vietnam flee their homeland (along with the US embassy staff) as Saigon and the entire country of South Vietnam fell to the North Vietnamese Communist forces in March 1975. Americans noted with pride that the Seventh Fleet rescued hundreds of these refugees from death or imprisonment in the wake of the communist takeover, but the riveting scenes of the terror-stricken flight of America's erstwhile allies was a memory that would not go away.

President Ford did, however, win abundant if temporary praise six weeks after the inglorious fall of Vietnam in the *Mayaguez* incident of May 1975. The *Mayaguez* was a US container vessel seized sixty miles off the coast of Cambodia in the Gulf of Siam by Cambodian Communists. Its crew of 39 was interred. The US Government tried to gain the ship's release through China and the United Nations; when this failed, Ford ordered a Marine-Navy combat unit with Air Force helicopter aid to regain the ship and free her crew. When the lost ship was sighted at Tang Island, 34 miles off the mainland, a Marine assault team was carried to the site by a destroyer escort. They boarded the ship, only to find it abandoned. Meanwhile, planes from the *Coral Sea* blasted Cambodian positions ashore and sank three gunboats. A Marine assault team was landed at Tang Island at the same time. Finding none of the crew, but soon engaged in a brisk exchange of fire with the Cambodians, the Marines were helicoptered out under naval protective fire. The crew, meanwhile, had been picked up from a fishing boat off Tang Island, so the *Mayaguez* incident ended as an American victory of sorts, although 41 American servicemen died in the episode.

Above: **The USS *Leahy*, name ship of a class of nine cruisers, built in the early 1960s and still in service.**

Left: The carrier *Constellation* and the support ship *Niagara Falls*.
Below: The experimental amphibious assault landing craft JEFF-B. Hovercraft have, as yet, seen little service with the military.

The Carter Years

Despite this show of determination and force, and despite his obvious attempts to give the nation a sense of direction and healing, Ford lost the presidency to Governor James E Carter of Georgia in 1976. For the Navy, having an Annapolis graduate at the helm of the ship of state gave reason for optimism that the needs of the service might at last be met, or at least understood. But it was not to be, and the Navy found the years from 1976 to 1979 as confused and confusing as any it had lived through since 1960.

As a candidate, Carter had pledged to cut the defense budget by $5 billion. When he became president, he slashed Ford's shipbuilding program from 157 to 67 ships. Considering that the defense budget had been steadily declining—from $115.7 billion in 1970 to $104.4 billion in 1972, to $100.8 billion in 1974—and raised only to $104.7 billion in 1976, it was obvious that the recent modest gains made by the services were about to be reversed. At the same time the nondefense budget had grown from about $80 billion in 1950 to over $150 billion in 1960, then to about $250 billion in 1970, and finally to almost $350 billion in 1975. By 1980 the defense budget would stand at about $145 billion, while the nondefense budget had skyrocketed to over $400 billion. In 1960 defense represented 49 percent of the federal budget; by 1980 it had fallen to only 23 percent. Yet it was the defense budget that received almost all the blame for the tremendous budget deficits and accompanying inflationary pressures. During these same years, it is interesting to note, the Navy's share of the Department of Defense budget remained at almost the same figure and in constant dollars actually declined slightly.

What made the situation more perilous for the Navy—and the nation—was the fact that the Soviet Union had awakened to its need for sea power and was building its navy with mounting vigor. By 1973 Soviet expenses for defense purposes actually exceeded those of the United States; by 1980 its defense budget stood at the equivalent of 175 billion American dollars. While President Carter and his party colleagues in Congress were canceling nuclear carrier construction in 1978, delaying cruise missile construction, closing down the B-1 bomber program and agreeing to restrict the range of cruise missiles in the SALT II talks, the Soviet Union continued to build its military forces to and beyond American levels in almost all areas.

At the end of World War II the Soviet Navy was a weak coastal-defense force, which it remained until the 1960s. However, during this period of naval quiescence, Nikita Krushchev in 1953 appointed as commander-in-chief of the Soviet Navy Admiral Sergei G Gorshkov, who would hold this position into the 1980s. For the next ten years this 'Mahan of the Russian Navy' argued that a naval buildup was indispensable if the Soviet Union was to defend itself and project its power around the globe. Concrete results had been attained by 1961, when the Soviets had commissioned their first nuclear submarine and installed air-to-surface missiles on their long-range patrol bombers to guard their shores.

While this essentially defensive power was satisfactory, the importance of a credible offensive and sub-surface fleet, and the consequences of their lack, were dramatically illustrated in the Suez crisis of 1956 and the Cuban missile crisis of 1961. The Russian embarrassment in the Middle East and her backdown in Cuba were due to American preponderance in surface vessels. Not only could the US Navy surface fleet interdict vessels, it was covered by mighty air power supplied by the carriers. As Gorshkov explained in *The Sea Power of the State* some years later, Russia had effective nuclear-missile submarines but needed attack submarines, powerful missile-carrying surface ships, carriers and long-range missile-bearing planes to protect the missile subs against ASW agents of any type. The targets of the better-protected Soviet nuclear-missile submarines would be land targets or bases, destruction of which would deny enemy ships and planes their logistical bases and thereby render them helpless. (By 1978 the Soviet Navy would have 58 nuclear-missile submarines, up from 0 in 1960; the United States, in contrast, would have only 41 in 1978, up from two. By 1979 the Soviets had 142 nuclear-powered subs; the United States had 109, 23 percent fewer).

At the same time he was obtaining his new vessels, Gorshkov also obtained long-range ballistic missiles for his submarines. With a 4200-mile range by the mid '70s his boats could lurk in home waters like the Barents Sea without ever having to expose themselves to detection or destruction on the sea lanes of the world. With such weapons as ballistic-missile submarines protected by surface fleet vessels and attack submarines (which could fire long-range missiles at enemy fleets or battle groups), and Backfire long-range reconnaissance bombers equipped with air-to-surface missiles, Gorshkov by the late 1970s had a major striking force capable of victory in an all-out nuclear confrontation, a force also capable of lesser responses according to the circumstances. The Soviet Navy had come a long way since the humiliations of the late 1950s and early 1960s.

While the Soviet fleet was growing in

Above: Loading a Phalanx multibarrel antiaircraft gun.
***Right:* The ammunition ship *Mount Baker* and the *Nimitz*. US carriers cannot accommodate all their aircraft in the hangar, some must be kept parked on deck.**

***Below:* A torpedo-armed SH-60B SeaHawk antisubmarine helicopter, the latest US Navy shipboard ASW helicopter.**

size and capability, the US Navy was shrinking from over 900 ships in 1970 to approximately 460 ships in 1978. American tonnage in carriers slipped from 2 million in 1964 to 1.4 million in 1978; surface vessels took the greatest drop, from 2.3 million tons to 1 million tons, in those same years. Submarines slipped slightly in tonnage, as did amphibious vessels. From a total tonnage of 6 million in 1964, the Navy could claim only 3.9 million tons in 1978. The Soviet Union had climbed from 1.7 million to 2.3 million tons, leaving the American fleet only 41 percent larger than the Soviet fleet (down from 72 percent larger in 1964). But when America's tonnage preponderance in aircraft car-

Right: **A Sea King antisubmarine helicopter lowers its dipping sonar during an anti-submarine-warfare exercise in 1982.**

Above: **The attack submarine *Phoenix* is launched from General Dynamics yard at Groton, CT, in 1980. Three Trident submarines can also be seen under construction.**

riers (1.4 million tons) was subtracted, the Soviet fleet was almost the same size as the American. And it must be noted that the Soviet fleet far outstripped the American in all types of submarines. By 1978, it seemed clear, the United States no longer had a two-ocean navy; with luck, it had a one-and-a-half-ocean navy, and no one could predict the outcome in case of a Soviet-American clash.

Part of the Navy's difficulty in the 1970s lay, however, within itself. During this trying decade it was constantly accused of waste in ship and weaponry procurement, of 'going first class' at the taxpayers' expense. Cost overruns and expensive delays in delivery were charges frequently leveled against the Navy, whose blame of civilian contractors as the culprits impressed few. The shipbuilders and contractors, in turn, blamed the higher costs on the Navy for changing specifications over and over again during construction. Wherever the truth lay in these charges and countercharges, the Navy suffered severely through bad publicity.

Nor was the Navy helped by criticism that it was a divided service, with the aviation admirals dominating their surface and submarine counterparts and clinging to the carrier task force strategy, come what may. Disunity also seemed the order of the day, as the public witnessed disagreements between certain admirals and Admiral Hyman Rickover, who even at the age of eighty could not be retired because of Congressional support. Rickover's charges in the media spotlight inclined the public to believe that high-ranking admirals were not being honest; he excoriated waste and inefficiency in every area of naval procurement and implied that the admirals were covering up. Such suspicions were made more plausible by the charge that senior military officers retired to well-paying jobs with defense contractors and thereby created a secret network of collusion, widely believed to exist since President Eisenhower's 1950s charges of a military-industrial complex. Eisenhower was actually referring to problems generated by increasing investment of the national economy in defense production, thereby endangering the national economy, but the existence of a 'conspiracy' had been an article of faith for antimilitary opinion-makers for two decades.

Part of the problem lay, too, in the fact that most Americans simply did not understand the role of the Navy—and its sister services—in the post-World War II situation. The nation had been on a warlike standing—with its attendant budgets—almost continuously since 1941. The Navy

could make a case for more ships, men and weaponry to protect the sea lanes, project American force where necessary and aid allies throughout the world, but who was listening? The Navy might well work out plausible scenarios as to what could happen in any of a dozen hotspots at any time when it would be called upon to respond quickly and powerfully, but such reasoning was beyond the concerns of most Americans (and not a few Congressmen and media representatives). The deterrent potential of a Trident submarine that could carry 24 ballistic missiles and operate anywhere in the oceans seemed less compelling than the fact that the 560-foot boat carried a price tag of $1 billion. Continued faith in the spirit and wisdom of détente, and negative fallout from the debacle of Vietnam, combined to propel the Navy into the last years of the 1970s on a wave of criticism, with nothing but flak bursts on the horizon. Then, almost overnight, the nation awakened to a fundamental reassessment.

Above: **The *Kitty Hawk* class carrier *John F Kennedy* with F-14, A-6 and A-7 aircraft among those on deck.**

By 1979 world events had begun to show the American people that neglect of their Navy had made them very vulnerable. The United States, they began to realize, was forced to import over three million barrels of oil from the Middle East each day, one-third of which had to pass through the Hormuz Strait from the Persian Gulf to the Arabian Sea. Furthermore, the Soviets seemed to be moving into the area, while American naval defense forces in the Indian Ocean were minimal at best. In response, the Navy offered to form a Fifth Fleet in the Indian Ocean, since this vital body of water could not be protected by the Seventh Fleet stationed in the Far East. This vulnerability in the Middle East

Below: **The *Pegasus* class hydrofoil *Taurus* on trial at Elliot Bay, Washington. She is armed with Harpoon missiles.**

and Persian Gulf became a major concern in 1978–79, when Iran fell into revolution and under the control of the fanatical religious leader the Ayatollah Khomeini. In November 1979 Americans watched newsreel coverage of the storming of the US embassy and the capture of 66 fellow citizens. That same month a mob burned the US embassy at Islamabad, Pakistan. This was followed the next month by a Soviet invasion of Afghanistan. In every case the US was in no position to retaliate effectively.

The invasion of Afghanistan was an attempt to stem a nationalist revolt against a docile communist regime in the capital of Kabul: the Russians were taking no chances on losing this subject state, but the invasion, with the other events breaking upon American complacency, had effects felt throughout the nation. President Carter, sincere in his humanitarian idealism, now recognized that human rights can never be protected without means of punishing or discouraging the aggressor. By 1980 the dovelike Congress, which had for years turned a deaf ear to the Navy's warnings about the consequence of weakness, was becoming more hawkish in mood. Requests for nuclear aircraft carriers, long-range attack planes, antisubmarine warfare systems for planes, submarines and surface ships, and better pay and benefits for naval officers and crews for greater retention rates in technical specialities, now received a favorable hearing. The military budget began to rise to meet the Services' needs. All this was carried out against the background of Carter's State of the Union message of January 1980, in which he announced the 'Carter Doctrine'. henceforth the Persian Gulf region was considered germane to the vital interests of the United States, and

Above: **The guided missile destroyer USS *Cochrane* (*Charles Adams* class).**
Left: **Stern view of the *Leahy* showing her after missile launcher and two radar trackers.**

any attempt by any power to gain control of it by force would be repelled. Although the President asked America's allies to share the burden of defending the Persian Gulf region, it was clear that the US Navy would be the chosen instrument for implementing that doctrine in the volatile Middle East: it would have to be strengthened to do the job.

The altered mood in Congress and in the White House reflected a new commitment and the realization that, despite the spirit of détente and American efforts to influence Soviet action by restraint of its warmaking capabilities, Soviet ambitions had not changed. Whether this new attitude of firmness on the part of the American public with its concomitant support of the military—including especially the Navy with its mammoth job of protecting American interests around the globe through capacity for instant readiness and reaction—would continue through the 1980s and beyond could not be gauged, but clearly a change of heart and mind appeared to be taking place. The 'new cold war' was on. The election to the presidency of Ronald Reagan over Jimmy Carter in November 1980 seemed to confirm a reversal of opinion.

The Present and Future of the Navy

In 1978 the Navy had released an assessment of its needs for the foreseeable future. Entitled 'Sea Plan 2000,' the plan spelled out the Navy's tasks in the years ahead: to maintain stability by forward deployment

Above: **The battleship *New Jersey* and the frigate *Meyer Kord* shortly after the *New Jersey* recommissioned in 1983.**

of carrier battle groups in the Atlantic and Pacific, Northeast and Southeast Asia, the Mediterranean and the Indian Ocean; to contain crises by US superiority at sea by either the use of force or a show of force; and to deter major war by supporting allies on the flanks of the Soviet Union and by maintaining the ability to threaten Soviet forces. These would be accomplished by more and better ships coupled with technological improvements in antimissile and antisubmarine-warfare defense systems. The Navy proposed three options to the nation. Option 1 called for a 1 percent per year real naval growth rate to 439 ships by the year 2000 (a minimal level); Option 2 called for a 3 percent per year growth rate to 535 ships (a moderate level); and Option 3 proposed a 4 percent per year growth rate to 585 ships (the optimum defense level). Sea Plan 2000, calling for a balanced fleet of conventional and atomic weaponry, argued essentially that national defense capabilities had to square with national goals, and that choosing the first option would mean a pullback in US commitments; the second option meant that the US could probably match the Soviets in naval strength; the third option was the best guarantee of the protection of American interests.

While Sea Plan 2000 represented alternatives in a measured, nonalarmist manner and undoubtedly impressed many members of Congress, talk of a SALT II agreement and public apathy precluded any widespread appreciation of the Navy's argument—until the events of 1979 brought about a new consciousness of the effects of allowing America's military and naval strength to erode.

Thus the early years of Ronald Reagan's presidency saw the beginning of an American naval renaissance. The President himself set the tone when he said, 'Freedom to use the seas is our nation's lifeblood. For that reason, our Navy is designed to keep the sea lanes open worldwide . . . [and] we must be able in time of emergency to venture into harm's way and to win.' Reagan's support of a reborn and powerful navy of 600 warships —'a 600-ship Navy' became a popular rallying cry for enthusiasts—was not without an ironic twist, since the President had no naval background. His predecessors from 1961 to 1981—five presidents—were all ex-naval officers—including an Annapolis graduate—and none of them gave comparable support to their former service branch and its unique and critical missions.

Reagan's arguments for a larger and more effective navy as crucial to the national interest were bolstered by the effectiveness of Great Britain's 1982 defense of her claims to the Falkland Islands against counterclaims and occupation by Argentine military forces. Although Britain lost six ships to Argentine jets and missiles (which revealed her reliance on short-range aircraft and lack of long-range surveillance forces to protect her main

Below: **The nuclear-powered guided-missile cruiser *Arkansas*.**

NAVY
727
501

Two of the US Navy's most important current aircraft.
Main picture: An F/A-18 Hornet in flight over Lake Tahoe. The F/A-18 is scheduled to replace both the A-7 and the F-4 in US Navy carrier air groups.
Top left: An E-2C Hawkeye of Carrier Airborne Early Warning Squadron 122 in flight. Each carrier normally embarks some four of these aircraft.

fleet components), the islands were reclaimed in a spectacular demonstration of the mobile, multipurpose forces that only a navy could supply and especially of how submarine power could neutralize a surface fleet. The lesson was not lost on knowledgeable observers.

In September 1982 1200 US Marines were sent into Lebanon as part of a multinational peacekeeping force, as that harried Middle Eastern nation saw renewed conflict between internal and external forces trying to claim it for their own ends. When the Marine contingent came under fire from the militia factions commanding the hills beyond Beirut International Airport in 1983, it was the big guns from the recommissioned battleship *New Jersey* that gave them relief, even as a sizable US fleet stood offshore to reinforce and protect them. The naval forces remained on station after the Marines were withdrawn from Beirut early in 1984.

With greater public and political backing evident, the Navy moved into the mid-1980s with a revitalized building program including two additional 91,000-ton *Nimitz*-class nuclear carriers capable of simultaneous air action against air, land, surface and subsurface enemies; the potential of 15 battle groups built around 15 deployable carriers; almost 100 fast attack submarines in service or building of the *Los Angeles*-class nuclear-powered variety (to be used against either enemy submarines or surface vessels); a fleet of over 39 operational ballistic-missile submarines, including the new *Trident* boats

Above: **The *Forrestal* class carrier *Ranger* at high speed on maneuvers.**
Above right: **The cruiser *Horne* (CG.30), a unit of the *Belknap* class.**
Right: **The USS *Ticonderoga* at sea. The *Ticonderoga* is the first ship to be fitted with the AEGIS air-defense system which can control as many as 18 Standard antiaircraft missiles simultaneously.**

with Trident I and II missiles, armed also with deadly Mark 48 torpedoes for self-defense; and one reactivated and re-armed battleship in commission (the *New Jersey*), another on its way (the *Iowa*), and two more scheduled for recommissioning in 1984 and 1985. In addition, *Spruance*- and *Kidd*-class destroyers, *Perry*-class frigates, and Aegis cruisers were joining the fleet, which by 1983 had 490 ships and 76 under construction.

These new and modernized vessels were armed with highly effective A-6E Intruder and A-7E Corsair attack bombers; F-14 Tomcat fighters armed with Phoenix missiles effective at ranges of up to 100 miles; and new F/A-18 Hornet fighter and attack aircraft, Harpoon air- or surface-to-surface missiles, Tomahawk tactical antiship and land attack missiles, acoustic-homing ASW torpedoes, attack and ASW shipborne helicopters like the SH-3 Sea King, and the latest and most effective computerized radar guidance systems available for these weapons. Furthermore, the Aegis cruiser/SM2 weapons system which joined the fleet with the commissioning of the *Ticonderoga* in 1983 offered superb defensive capabilities

47

Right: An S-3A Viking makes the 200,000th carrier landing for the type, aboard the USS *Kitty Hawk*.
Second right: An A-7E Corsair light attack aircraft in flight over the carrier *America*. The A-7 can carry up to eight tons of ordnance.
Main picture: An A-6E Intruder medium attack aircraft. From 1963 to 1996, this was the workhorse of the US Navy's carrier force; with night-attack and all-weather capability, it served from Vietnam to the Persian Gulf.

10
VA-82 MARAUDERS
NAVY
AMERICA

02
AG
158533
NAVY
VA 65

Right: The *Spruance* class destroyer *Elliot* at sea in 1978. By early 1984 there were 31 *Spruance* class ships in service with the Navy. *Main picture:* An F-14A Tomcat of VF.2 in flight. Each carrier normally operates 24 Tomcats in the fighter role with an additional small detachment assigned to reconnaissance. *Bottom:* Two Tomcats ready for launch on the forward catapults of the nuclear carrier *Nimitz.*

to fleets against co-ordinated high-density air attacks and Soviet antiship cruise missiles, thus protecting the heart of any carrier battle group. By 1988 almost 1900 new and effective aircraft would be added to the fleet, looking to 14 fully equipped and modernized carrier wings by that time. And all these ships and weapons were being acquired under a new direct-contract approach that forced contractors to assume more of the burden for cost overruns, thus eliminating many of the publicity problems so burdensome in the troubled two decades before.

Backed by a rediscovered national sense of direction and commitment, and by a political system responding to that force, the Navy was in full renaissance by the mid-1980s. In the words of Admiral Thomas B Haywood, Chief of Naval Operations: 'We are a Navy on the move, with a full head of steam. We are a Navy with confidence. We are a Navy determined to be the finest professional force at sea, today and in the future.' The US Navy would, as always, do its duty.

NEW CHALLENGES, NEW RESPONSES

The first four years of the Reagan administration were years of resurgence for the Navy, not only in its budget, ships and hardware but also in its sense of self-confidence. The popular president was clearly aware of the importance of a strong naval force in a still-dangerous world, and in his secretary of the navy, John Lehman, he had an articulate and persuasive advocate for naval power to the Congress. Building a '600-ship navy' seemed a realizable and popular goal. But Ronald Reagan's second term in office saw the Navy's fond dreams disappointed. Thanks both to domestic and foreign events, the buildup of the Navy that had marked Reagan's first term in office was replaced by a contraction in his second, even though the Navy's obligations had in no way diminished and may even have grown.

The World-War-II battleship USS *Missouri* was recommissioned in May 1986. She was armed with Tomahawk and Harpoon missiles.

1985: Year of Change

The year 1985 was pivotal for the Navy and America's other three armed forces. In that year Mikhail Gorbachev came to power in the Soviet Union and began his historic drive for fundamental change in his nation through both *perestroika* (restructuring of the Soviet system) and *glasnost* (openness to public debate). Doubtless the new Soviet president was in part moved by necessity, for his nation's economy was in shambles after 70 years of inefficient centralized control. But whatever Gorbachev's motives may have been, and however he imagined the course that domestic reform might take, he soon found that the desire for wholesale reform was so strong among the people of the various republics making up the USSR, to say nothing of the satellite states, that control of events both within and without became increasingly difficult. Within six years secessionist movements had broken out in the Baltic states; the Russian Republic and other constituent Soviet states were demanding more autonomy; the eastern European satellite nations were declaring their independence of Soviet overlordship; the hated Berlin Wall had been torn down and Germany had been reunited; and the Warsaw Pact, the core of the Soviet land defense system, had been formally dissolved.

Now the nations that had worked so diligently to contain Soviet expansionism for 45 years had to decide how to react to these events. How were they to adapt their national

Top left: **Soviet leader Mikhail Gorbachev. who came into power in 1985.**
Above and left: **Among the most powerfully symbolic gestures made by Gorbachev in his effort to end the Cold War was the tearing down of the Berlin Wall in November 1989.**

defense postures to the new Soviet reality – whatever it might prove to be? America's strategists, including the Navy's, were forced to rethink their assumptions after 1985. Events worldwide, however, suggest that the need for a global strategy remained.

That same year also saw the beginning of a fundamental restructuring of all the US military services in an effort to eliminate once and for all the lack of inter-service coordination that had so often plagued American military operations in the past. Criticism of America's command structure had been considerable during the Vietnam war, and it became a focus of renewed attention after the debacle of the Iranian hostage rescue attempt in 1980. The clamor intensified two years later when the abortive and tragic intervention in Lebanon ended in the bombing deaths of 241 Marines, and it rose to a crescendo with the American invasion of Grenada in 1983, a small-scale operation that revealed, despite all the talk about cooperation and coordination between the services in combined operations, that the reality was far different.

Operation URGENT FURY, the invasion of Grenada to free the tiny Caribbean island from left-wing radicals, to put an end to Soviet and Cuban influence and presence there and to assure the safety of some 600 American students and tourists, began on 25 October 1983 and ended three days later. The invasion was planned as primarily an Army and Marine Corps operation, backed by tactical air cover from the *Independence* carrier group and by naval gunnery and logistical support. But in the event, inter-service coordination proved lamentable. No service commander present had overall tactical authority, and lack of integrated radio communications precluded the ground forces from being able to call in naval gunfire. The publicity given the obvious foul-ups on Grenada gave the final push to reorganizing the American military.

In 1985 the Packard Commission (chaired by David Packard, former deputy secretary of defense) was created to assess the organization of the Department of Defense. Its conclusions matched those of the Senate Armed Services Committee: DOD had to be reorganized, and unified multi-service commands had to be created. When, that same year, Senators Barry Goldwater (R-AZ) and Sam Nunn (D-GA), the leaders of the Senate Armed Services Committee, threw their support behind a DOD staff report authorizing DOD reorganization, the die was cast. Eight unified commands (the European, Pacific, Atlantic, Southern, Central, Space, Special Operations and Transportation Commands) and two specified commands (the Strategic Air Command and Forces Command) were subsequently created or completed. Henceforth, unified commanders would control all service activities in their areas of operation, a reform that bore fruit dramatically in the Gulf War when General H Norman Schwarzkopf of Central Command directed the warmaking activities of all the services in the five-month conflict with Iraq.

A follow-on reorganizational change that affected all the services and their strategic and tactical roles was made the next year when Congress passed the Goldwater-Nichols Defense Reorganization Act of 1986. This legislation gave the chairman of the Joint Chiefs of Staff the final decision-making power over all the US military and made him the president's principal military advisor. Henceforth, decisions at the JCS level would be made by one man, not by committee consensus. Furthermore, the Joint Staff was now to work for the chairman alone, not for the JCS as a body. (Service on the Joint Staff was also made a prerequisite for flag rank in all the services.) At the same time, the commanders of the unified and specified commands were given complete authority over all operations, training and logistics within their commands, the individual service commanders thus losing their operational authority. These reforms signaled that henceforth interservice and intraservice cooperation and coordination would be the rule, not the exception.

Nineteen eighty-five may have introduced changes that would ultimately benefit the Navy, but at the time, the year seemed to offer the service scant good news. Certainly the Walker spy case was not good news.

The leader in the Walker espionage ring was John A Walker, Jr, a naval warrant officer and cryptologist with top secret clearance, who began spying for the Soviet Union in the mid-1960s. He was aided by Jerry A Whitworth, a radioman and satellite communications expert who had retired from the Navy in 1983. Also implicated were Arthur J Walker, John's brother and a retired lieutenant com-

Above: A big US Air Force C-141 Starlifter removes evacuees from Grenada in 1983 (in the foreground, an Army CH-47 helicopter). The Grenada operation underscored the need for better interservice coordination.
Below: Navyman John A Walker, Jr (left) is taken to his trial for espionage in 1985.

mander, and Michael L Walker, John's son, who stole secret documents from the Oceana Naval Air Station in Virginia and from the carrier *Nimitz.*

Tried for espionage in Norfolk, the four received long prison sentences in November 1985, but naval and intelligence officials are still trying to assess the damage inflicted on the Navy's code systems and underwater warfare capabilities by the Walker spy ring. Critics pointed out that the Navy's internal anti-espionage safeguards had obviously broken down in this case and wondered how national security might be further compromised when some 900,000 naval personnel had access to classified materials, 139,000 of them to top secret documents. The shadow of the Walker case hung over the Navy long after prison doors had swung shut on the foursome involved.

The other bad news in 1985 involved naval appropriations. The Balanced Budget and Emergency Control Act of 1985, the Gramm-Rudman-Hollings Act (or 'Gramm-Rudman'), arose from wildly escalating federal budget deficits during President Reagan's first term in office. Urged by David A Stockman, his budget director, to spur economic growth and take the nation out of increasing deficits by cutting taxes that stifled incentive while also cutting federal spending, Reagan embraced the first economic principle without attending sufficiently to the second. Reagan, to be sure, received enthusiastic assistance in keeping federal expenses high from the Democratically-controlled Congress, which not only increased defense spending at an average rate of 8.9 percent per year for four years but increased non-defense spending at a much higher rate. Thus, even though tax revenues went up as the result of economic expansion, the federal debt continued to grow alarmingly. Clearly, something had to give.

The result was Gramm-Rudman, which aimed to reduce the annual federal deficits from $171.9 billion to 0 in four years. According to the law, if the federal budgets did not hit their descending target amounts each year, automatic cuts in spending would have to take place.

Two things, however, doomed Gramm-Rudman's laudable goals. First, the legislation exempted monies for Social Security, veterans' compensation and benefits, interest on the national debt and Medicare from the automatic cut provisions. Since this amounted to about half the budget, the other half would have to take double cuts to meet the legislation's goals. Thus a 10 percent automatic cut would mean in actuality a 20 percent cut for defense or any other non-protected expenditure, surely a draconian and unworkable measure. Second, the Supreme Court the next year 'de-fanged' Gramm-Rudman by invalidating the automatic triggering provision of the law that mandated across-the-board cuts, thereby leaving the Congress free to spend as before.

The Gramm-Rudman-Hollings Act thus turned out to be a law without effect, and the budget deficit continued to climb higher and higher, reaching almost $3 trillion in 1990. The debates engendered by Gramm-Rudman did, however, provide a forum for those Congressmen and special interest groups opposed to spending for defense. They launched a concerted campaign for balancing the budget by reducing spending for the military – even though the savings thus realized would in fact be small and would in any case be spent on domestic projects, *ie,* not used to balance the budget or be applied to the federal debt. In fact, the defense budget, in growing from $161 billion to $300 billion in the decade, rose from only 23 percent of the federal budget to 26.1 percent. Put another way, it represented an increase from 5.2 percent of the nation's GNP to only 5.7 percent, and it meant no increase whatever in constant dollars. But the campaign to decrease military spending continued, with the Navy, like its sister services, forced constantly to retrench, regardless of the cost to national security.

The Libyan Challenge Met

Whatever its problems with reorganization, spies, and budget-cutting, the Navy in the meantime had to continue to carry out its duties on the waterways of the world. These included the Mediterranean Sea and the persistent problem of terrorism encouraged and supported by Muammar Qaddafi, the unstable and dangerous fundamentalist military dictator of Libya.

Ever since he had come to power in a coup in 1969, Qaddafi had displayed an obsession for lessening Western influence in North Africa and the Middle East, for expanding Libya's role in these regions and for destroying Israel. As a result, US relations with Libya began to deteriorate, especially as evidence mounted that Qaddafi was playing a direct role in organized terrorism not only in North Africa and the Middle East but indeed throughout the world. Definite ties were established between Qaddafi and terrorist

Far left: Michael Walker, part of the John Walker spy ring, goes to jail.
Below: Libya's Muammar Qaddafi.

organizations in no less than 36 countries, including Japan, Ireland, Germany, Italy and Nicaragua.

It was he who provided the money, arms and air transportation for the terrorists who carried out a massacre at the 1972 Olympic Games in Munich, and his support for other terrorist activities continued in the years that followed. In 1981 it was discovered that Qaddafi had even sent an assassination team to the United States to kill President Reagan, Secretary of Defense Caspar Weinberger and other top government leaders.

Then, on 7 October 1985, members of the Palestinian Liberation Organization highjacked the Italian cruise ship *Achille Lauro* and murdered an American passenger in cold blood. When the highjackers were caught (the Boeing 737 carrying them from Egypt to Tunisia being forced to land at an Italian naval air station in Sicily by four Navy F-14 Tomcat fighters from the carrier *Saratoga*), apparent ties to Libya were discovered. This was followed two months later by terrorist attacks on airport lobbies in Rome and Vienna in which 18 persons were killed (including five Americans) and more than 100 were wounded. Qaddafi praised the attacks and gave refuge to Abu Nidal, the mastermind behind them.

Ever since 1973 and the Yom Kippur War, Qaddafi had been arguing that the Gulf of Sidra, south of a line between Tripoli on the west and Benghazi on the east, belonged to Libya alone, with no right of international passage through its waters. This claim was in direct contradiction to all international conventions regarding the use of the world's seas, and the United States, having no intention of honoring such a specious assertion, had deliberately ignored Qaddafi's proclaimed 'line of death' by conducting Sixth Fleet exercises in the Gulf of Sidra in order to prove its right of navigation there. This had led to minor incidents over the years, including an unprovoked air-to-air missile attack by two Libyan Su-22 fighters on US Navy F-14's in August 1981, an engagement that saw the Libyan planes expeditiously destroyed by American Sidewinder air-to-air missiles from the Tomcats. Libyan terrorism and harassment of the Sixth Fleet continued even after this incident – until 1986, when President Reagan decided finally to do something about it.

Early that year Reagan ordered all US citizens to leave Libya and told five US oil companies to begin moving out. He also directed the JCS to prepare military contingency plans to be used against that country and sent a second, then a third, carrier task force into the Mediterranean. Unable to force the US to accede to his demands and unable to confront it successfully with his military hardware, Qaddafi moved in other directions.

In late March 1986 he directed his operatives around the world to begin attacks on American citizens and installations. On 3

April, Syrian terrorists exploded a bomb on a TWA flight from Rome to Athens, killing four Americans. Qaddafi congratulated them and promised further escalation of violence against American citizens. He made good on his promise two days later when a discotheque in West Berlin was bombed, leaving two US soldiers and one Turkish civilian dead and another 229 persons wounded, including 78 Americans. Citing 'incontrovertible evidence' of Libyan complicity in the bombing, Reagan ordered the US military to carry out attacks on terrorist targets in Libya. The resulting raids took place on the night of 14 April 1986.

The US Navy was already in the area in force for Operation ELDORADO CANYON, the previous month having conducted a four-day exercise in the Gulf of Sidra with 30 vessels, including the carriers *Coral Sea*, *Saratoga* and *America*. Missile boat attacks had been leveled at the US warships, and at least two of the Libyan craft had been sunk. Land-based missiles had also been fired at the American fleet, and Libyan jets had tried unsuccessfully to penetrate the American air screen. The US naval forces were therefore primed for immediate action when the word came down to take out a number of terrorist sites in Libya.

Above: Senior officers on board USS _America_ tensely await reports of bombing results during the joint USN-USAF airstrike on selected targets in Libya on 14 April 1986.
Opposite: USS _Saratoga_ refuels at sea off the Libyan coast in March 1986.

Only those Libyan installations which were clearly terrorist in their activities were targeted: strictly military installations were excluded, and tactical orders made it clear that civilians, as far as possible, were not to be injured in any way. The United States wanted to make it clear to the populace of Libya that Qaddafi's terrorist mechanisms, not the Libyan nation, its army or its people, were the objects of the raids to be made on Tripoli and Benghazi.

Chosen as the instruments for the attacks were Navy and Air Force tactical jets. Tactical aircraft would be able to inflict the most damage on the designated targets with the least amount of collateral damage. Nighttime was chosen for the attacks because the Libyan Air Force pilots had little proficiency at nighttime operations, because civilians would be off the streets of the cities and because Libyan anti-aircraft defenses would be limited to hand-held SAMs that could not be effectively aimed in the dark.

Assigned to carry out the Navy's part in the simultaneous attacks on the five designated targets were versatile A-6E Intruders. The Air Force's variable-sweep 'swing-wing'

The wreckage of Muammar Qaddafi's personal headquarters in Tripoli's Azizyah Barracks after the April 1986 US airstrike.

Libyans inspect the damage wrought on a Benghazi airfield by Navy A-6E Intruders during the April 1986 airstrike.

F-111F attack aircraft, flying out of Great Britain, was the tactical weapon of choice for that service because of its long-range, high-payload, low-level and high on-target precision capabilities. The Air Force was brought in to cooperate with the Navy in carrying out the raids not because the Air Force demanded 'a piece of the action,' as reported by the media, but because the Navy did not have enough tactical aircraft to hit all the necessary targets simultaneously while carrying out its other duties. Its A-7 Corsairs and F/A-18 Hornets would be flying air defense-suppression missions, while its F-14 Tomcats and other F/A-18s would be providing combat air patrol to protect the three-carrier fleet.

In the ensuing five-target, 12-minute, one-pass-over-target raid, six Navy A-6Es from the *America* attacked the Benghazi Military Barracks, an alternaite site for terrorist command and control headquarters, while six more Intruders from the *Coral Sea* hit Benina Airfield outside Benghazi to assure that its MiG fighters would not rise to attack the American forces. On the western side of the Gulf of Sidra at Tripoli three Air Force F-111Fs attacked the Sidi Bilal Terrorist Training Camp, an aquatic commando school outside the city, while three more F-111Fs bombed the Aziziyah Barracks, the command and control center for Qaddafi's worldwide terrorist activities and his headquarters at the time of the attack. Tripoli Military Airfield, home of Qaddafi's terrorist transportation system, was the target of five more F-111Fs. Only one American aircraft was lost in the operation, this an F-111F which disappeared during the flight from England to Libya.

The raids of 14 April 1986 must be scored a success. While Qaddafi escaped with his life from the Aziziyah Barracks, the American air attacks both destroyed important terrorist installations in Libya and, perhaps more important, demonstrated to Qaddafi that he could continue to sponsor overt terrorism only at considerable personal risk. Incidents of terrorism dropped sharply in the aftermath of the combined Navy-Air Force raids on Libya of April 1986.

The lightning air offensive against the Libyan strongman-terrorist also demonstrated that American military forces could work together smoothly and effectively. Cooperation and coordination had been the watchwords of Operation ELDORADO CANYON from initial planning to successful execution. Interservice cooperation may have been imposed officially only in 1985, but the Libyan operation of April 1986 showed that the Navy and the Air Force were already well along the road now mandated for them.

Convoys and Conflict in the Middle East

The Mediterranean was not the only hotspot for the US Navy in the mid-1980s. Simultaneously, it was called to dangerous duty in the Persian Gulf to protect the giant tankers carrying a large portion of the world's oil supply out of the Gulf during the long eight-year war between Iran and Iraq.

The Iran-Iraq War began in September 1980 when Iraqi forces under President Saddam Hussein attacked the neighboring Islamic Republic of Iran, then under the sway of a fanatical Muslim fundamentalist leader, the Ayatollah Khomeini. The Iraqi offensive began with a series of victories, but Iran launched successful counteroffensives, and the conflict settled into a war of attrition. Since 90 percent of Iran's oil exports transited the Persian Gulf (whereas Iraq exported most of its oil through overland pipelines), its Kharg Island loading facility and other ports on the Persian Gulf – plus the ships of nations buying oil from Iran – became prime targets for Iraq's air force. On the other hand, since Iran borders all of the eastern coast of the Gulf, it was in a position to attack vessels trading with Iraq's allies, Saudi Arabia and Kuwait, either by air or by land-based weaponry. Thus all ships trading with either of the belligerents or with Iraq's allies were in danger of being attacked and sunk.

President Reagan, determined that American-flagged vessels should not be successfully attacked while in the international waters of the Persian Gulf and that the critical narrow Strait of Hormuz at the lower end of the Gulf should not be closed, ordered addi-

Below: Khorramshahr, Iran, scene of bitter fighting early in the bloody eight-year war between Iraq and Iran that began in 1980.
Right: A US patrol boat and the frigate USS *Taylor* escort re-flagged Kuwaiti tankers through the dangerous waters of the Persian Gulf during the Iran–Iraq War.

A view of the damage done to the frigate USS *Stark* after she was hit by an Exocet missile launched by an Iraqi Mirage in the Persian Gulf on 17 May 1987. Over 30 naval personnel were killed.

tional American naval vessels into the Persian Gulf. (A small US naval force had regularly sailed the Gulf since 1949 to demonstrate America's interest in the continued flow of oil to the markets of the Free World.) He also moved a carrier battle group near to the Strait in the waters of the North Arabian Sea. By 1985 the Navy's Middle East Force was stationing four frigates and destroyers in the Gulf on a regular basis, rotating these surface vessels in and out on a four-month basis.

By 1987 attacks on ships in the Gulf by both Iran and Iraq had escalated sharply – from five in 1981 to 179 in 1987 – the Iraqis mainly using aircraft and the Iranians mainly using mines, fast attack boats and land-based, Chinese-built, sea-skimming Silkworm missiles with 1100-pound warheads. Kuwait in particular was being hard hit by the tanker war, and President Reagan in May 1987 offered to have Kuwaiti vessels reflagged under the American ensign and stated that the United States Navy would protect these vessels in the Gulf.

By this time the Navy had more than 30 vessels in the Persian Gulf and North Arabian sea: a carrier, a battleship, their escorts, destroyers and frigates for escorting within the Gulf and minesweepers. In addition, a Marine amphibious force and the Navy's special forces Seals were also in the area and ready to move. Nor was the United States alone in sending naval vessels to protect the valuable exports of the Gulf nations: nine British destroyers and minesweepers and six French, six Italian, five Belgian and five Dutch naval vessels were also carrying out convoying and minesweeping duties in the strife-torn area.

That convoy duty during the tanker war could be dangerous was dramatically prove on the night of 17 May 1987 when the guided missile frigate *Stark* (FFG-31), on picket duty in international waters and outside the belligerents' declared war zones, was attacked by an Iraqi F-1 Mirage jet, which fired two Exocet missiles into the vessel, killing 37 men.

Subsequent investigation revealed that the missiles had apparently been fired in error by the Iraqi pilot. But though the *Stark* had been warned of the approach of the Iraqi jet by an AWACS plane, its chaff launchers were never fired, its Phalanx Gatling gun was only in standby mode, its fire control radar was not turned on, its 50 caliber machine guns were not loaded, its incoming missile audible signal had been turned off by its operator and the attacking plane had not been warned off until too late.

The ship was saved by the heroic damage control efforts of the crew, but the '*Stark* incident' demonstrated that the Persian Gulf was too dangerous a place for relaxed procedures. Thenceforth US Navy ships escorting convoys or on picket duty in the Gulf stood on high alert at all times.

Attacks on ships in the Gulf tapered off somewhat after the *Stark* incident, and in February 1988 the battleship *Iowa* and her escorts rotated out of the North Arabian Sea and were not replaced. Leaving the area, too, was the USS *Okinawa*, used as a platform for the Navy's Sea Stallion minesweeping helicopters. With the American presence being cut to 16 command and combat vessels in the Gulf, it appeared that the danger of further incidents might also be lessened.

But on 14 April 1988 the frigate *Samuel B. Roberts* (FFG-58) sailed into a minefield in the central Persian Gulf about 65 miles east of Bahrain. It hit an Iranian-built 385-pound mine which exploded on the port side of the keel. The detonation opened a hole 23 by 30 feet in the hull, destroyed 15 feet of the ship's keel and almost cut the frigate in two. The commanding officer reported that the force of the blast lifted the stern of the 445-foot vessel 10 to 12 feet. Ten sailors were injured in the explosion and resulting fire, but the ship was saved by the damage control efforts of the crew. The heavily damaged frigate was sent home in July aboard the chartered heavy lift ship *Mighty Servant II*.

Meanwhile, convinced that Iran was responsible for the damage to the *Roberts*, the

Captain Glen Brindel of the USS *Stark* was criticized by some after the Iraqi attack for not having readier air defenses.

military command authorities ordered a retaliatory attack on Iran. Operation PRAYING MANTIS was carried out four days later, on 18 April 1988. Nine Navy ships, plus contingents of Marines and Navy Seals, were assembled for the operation by the Joint Task Force Middle East commander. The sailors and Marines were ordered to sink the Iranian frigate *Sabalan* or any suitable substitute and to neutralize three Iranian gas-oil separation platforms being used as surveillance posts.

Two of the oil platforms were taken in textbook fashion, with naval gunfire forcing the Iranians on them to flee or surrender. Marine and Seal teams moved onto the platforms from helicopters to gather intelligence information and then demolish the structures. But on the third platform a stray shot hit a compressed gas tank, causing it to burn and incinerating its gun crew. After the assaults on the platforms, one of the naval groups (three vessels) sank an Iranian patrol boat after it had attacked the group with anti-ship missiles. Another group, with the aid of two A-6 Intruders, attacked and sank an Iranian frigate. One Intruder had left the frigate dead in the water from missile strikes, and then the other hit the frigate with Harpoon anti-ship missiles at the same moment one of the surface destroyers did the same.

Operation PRAYING MANTIS took place at the same time that Iraq was retaking the strategically valuable Fao Peninsula from Iran. It may be assumed that these virtually simultaneous defeats helped to convince the Iranians that they could not win the war and should negotiate a peace agreement with Iraq. This, in any case, is what they did, but before 1988 was over and the war had ended, the greatest tragedy of the Persian Gulf tanker war occurred, the downing of an Iranian airliner by missiles fired by the USS *Vincennes* on 3 July.

Certain facts about the incident are beyond dispute. There is no question that the *Vincennes* (CG-49), a guided missile cruiser of the *Ticonderoga* class fitted with the ultra-sophisticated Aegis antiaircraft weapons system, brought down the Iran Air Airbus, Flight 655, killing all 290 passengers and crew aboard. It is also clear that the airbus was in a commercial flying corridor when it was struck and that it was actually gaining altitude when it was identified and fired upon and was not descending, as interpreted by the inexperienced tactical information coordinator in the *Vincennes*'s combat information center.

In defense of the Navy and the ship's crew, however, other facts must be recalled in order to place the tragedy in its context of taking place in the 'fog of war.' First, the radar units on Aegis-equipped vessels track an airplane's course and speed, not its altitude; this has to be determined by continual monitoring in the vessel's combat information center. Second, the airliner was tagged as a 'target unknown' and was closing on the ship on a

Above: The frigate USS *Samuel B Roberts*, as she appeared in her 1986 sea trials.
Below: Severely damaged by an Iranian mine, the *Samuel B Roberts* is taken home for repairs on the deck of the chartered heavylift ship *Mighty Servant II* in July 1988.

CG-49
HOME OF
AIR AEGIS

constant bearing and on a classic attack path; furthermore, it was flying on the very edge of the commercial corridor (not in the center of the corridor as airliners usually did), and its altitude was lower than normal commercial flights. Third, the *Vincennes* was under attack by two Iranian gunboats at the time of the sighting, giving the impression that a coordinated attack might be underway (the Middle East Force had been alerted to a possible Iranian suicide attack over the 4 July weekend). Fourth, Iranian F-14 fighters had been flying out of Bandar Abbas airfield, from which the airliner had just taken off, in the days preceding 3 July. Fifth, an Iranian P-3 radar plane was on patrol in the area, a type of plane used to guide Iranian attack planes to their targets. Sixth, the *Vincennes* challenged the approaching plane to identify itself seven times, warning it that it was in danger. In addition, a nearby US frigate, the *Sides*, challenged it five times. Neither received a reply, nor did the plane change its course or take evasive maneuvers. Seventh, the two missiles fired by the *Vincennes* were launched after a full seven minutes had passed from first sighting, and then only when the plane was a mere seven nautical miles away from the cruiser. Finally, the ship's IFF (Identify Friend or Foe) radar incorrectly identified the Airbus as an F-14, and visual confirmation was impossible because of hazy weather and a ceiling of 200 feet. All in all, the *Vincennes* incident of 3 July 1988 must be marked down as a tragic mistake occurring in the heat of combat in a long-troubled war zone.

On 20 August the conflict between Iran and Iraq was halted under a United Nations cease-fire agreement, and by December US Navy convoying in the Persian Gulf had come to an end. It had been a long and troubling deployment for the Navy, but no one could then foresee that it was but a prelude to the much larger and potentially more dangerous deployment that would have to be made in the same waters in under two years time.

Background to the Gulf War

Matching Libya's Muammar Qaddafi in his hatred of the West and of Israel, and equally determined to be the leader who would bring the Arab world to new heights of power and glory, was Saddam Hussein of Iraq. Ruler of a nation of 18 million persons and composed one-half of Shiite Muslims, one-quarter of Sunni Muslims, and one-quarter of dissident Kurds with their own language and culture, Hussein had come to power in 1979 as head of the Sunni-dominated Baath Socialist party, and in the years that followed he had rapidly made himself into a full-fledged dictator, ruling through a combination of terror and propaganda and bloodily suppressing all potential opposition. He had also become one of the Arab world's most zealous advocates of playing 'oil politics' as a means of humbling the hated West.

Although more temperate Arab statesmen attempted to distance themselves from Hussein, realizing that the Western nations and Japan were their best customers for their oil, he became a popular figure among many Muslims in the Middle East, especially when he launched his invasion of Iran in 1980. The leaders of the Western nations, too, treated Hussein warily, but when his war with Iran bogged down and he toned down his anti-Western and anti-Israeli rhetoric, there seemed to be reason for optimism that he would moderate. Accordingly, his pleas for Western aid in his war with Iran were received favorably, and many nations began to sell him military equipment. Even the United States, still seeing the Ayatollah Khomeini as a greater danger to American interests, also moved closer to Hussein, removing Iraq from its list of 'terrorist-supporting' countries. By the late 1980s American agencies were actually sharing intelligence information with the Iraqi leader.

But when the Iran-Iraq War ended in 1988 Hussein soon made it clear that he had in no way moderated and was still dedicated to aggressive pan-Arabism, to gaining control of the area's oil supplies and to driving the Israelis out of the Middle East. He did not demobilize his million-man army, began to spend billions of dollars on new weapons (most bought from the Soviets) and placed renewed emphasis on developing chemical and nuclear weapons. (He had already displayed his willingness to use poison gas against dissident Kurdish villagers in 1987 and 1988, the number of victims running into the hundreds, and perhaps thousands.)

Further proof of Hussein's belligerent intentions came from his frequent speeches in which he displayed bitter anti-American and anti-Israeli animosity. These public pronouncements, while making the Iraqi leader increasingly popular to some Arabs, annoyed and alarmed such moderate Arab leaders as President Hosni Mubarak of Egypt and King Fahd of Saudi Arabia. Their concerns deepened when, in July 1990, Hussein turned his verbal fire on the heads of state of the United Arab Emirates and Kuwait, whom he accused of overproducing oil and thus driving the world price of crude down. He followed this by massing 30,000 of his troops on the border of neighboring Kuwait. Approached by the American ambassador to Iraq, April Glaspie, to ascertain his intentions, Hussein assured her that he would not invade Kuwait while his current talks with President Mubarak were still ongoing.

This promise was cynically broken when,

Iraqi dictator Saddam Hussein. During the Iran–Iraq War the US tended to support Iraq, a policy it would eventually regret.

Wreckage left by Iraqi bombers in Hamadan, Iran, in 1982. Soviet- and French-equipped, Iraq's air force was locally formidable.

***Left:* The cruiser *Vincennes*. On 3 July 1988, in a tragic case of war's confusion, the *Vincennes* downed an Iranian airliner that was mistaken for an attacking warplane.**

on 2 August 1990, Hussein's tanks and infantry rolled into Kuwait, his soldiers looting, burning and raping as they went. The Emir of Kuwait, Sheik Jaber al-Ahmed al-Sabah, fled the country, and Hussein, after giving a number of excuses for the invasion, announced that Kuwait had been annexed as the 19th providence of Iraq.

The Gulf War: DESERT SHIELD, 2 August 1990 – 14 January 1991

The United Nations Security Council demanded the immediate withdrawal of Iraqi troops from Kuwait, and US President George Bush froze all Iraqi and Kuwaiti assets in the United States. Bush also banned the importation of any Kuwaiti oil into the country, as did the Western European nations and Japan, but Hussein refused to back down. With the seizure of Kuwait he controlled 20 percent of the world's oil supply; if he also seized neighboring Saudi Arabia he would control 40 percent. Hussein undoubtedly believed that despite strong protests from the United Nations, the United States and other countries, no one would seriously oppose his *fait accompli*, but even if they did, he was convinced that his million-man army could defend Iraq and his new possession against any outside force.

The United Nations, with almost universal support (including the Soviet Union), placed a trade and financial embargo on Iraq. And the leaders of most other Arab states also refused to accept his seizure of Kuwait: this was, after all, not an ideological confrontation between East and West but simply an unprovoked attack made by one Arab nation on another. Using the overwhelming condemnation of Iraq by virtually all the nations of the world, and, most important, by the Arab nations, President Bush was thus able to organize a powerful coalition to demand the freedom of Kuwait.

US President George Bush responded to the August 1990 Iraqi invasion of Kuwait with speed and determination, swiftly building an international anti-Iraq coalition.

Above: **King Fahd of Saudi Arabia was one of the first to join the anti-Iraq coalition.**
Top right: **Chairman of the JCS US General Colin Powell greets crewmen on board the battleship USS *Wisconsin* in the Persian Gulf during the DESERT SHIELD buildup.**
Right: **CENTCOM commander General H Norman Schwarzkopf greets USAF reinforcements newly arrived in Saudi Arabia.**

One of the first of the Arab leaders to step to the side of the United States and the United Nations was King Fahd of Saudi Arabia, who needed no further convincing after the American secretary of defense, Richard B Cheney, showed him satellite photographs proving that Hussein was massing troops on the Saudi border. Faud not only closed the Iraqi pipeline running across his country to the Red Sea but also agreed to allow American and coalition forces to use his territory as a military staging area to force Hussein out of Kuwait. Other Arab nations fell into line, as did Iraq's non-Arab neighbor to the north, Turkey, which agreed to cut off Iraq's other pipeline leading to the Mediterranean. Hussein was left with only Jordan's King Hussein, Libya's Muammar Qaddafi and the Palestine Liberation Organization's Yasir Arafat to support his actions.

Still he would not back down. He would, he was convinced, win as he had won his war with Iran. He had 5000 tanks (including over 1000 modern, Soviet-built T-72s), 6000 armored personnel carriers, 5000 artillery pieces, 600 aircraft (some of them late model Soviet Mig-25 and MiG-29 fighters and Su-24 and Su-25 bombers), French- and Soviet-made surface-to-air missiles, improved Scud surface-to-surface missiles capable of carrying a 1000-pound warhead far beyond their 300-mile designated range, chemical artillery shells and perhaps nuclear weapons (the Israelis had wiped out Iraq's French-built nuclear reactor at Osirak in a lightning air raid on 7 June 1981, but no one knew if another secret facility had been built).

As President Bush was working diplomatically to build up the coalition of nations arrayed against Iraq, the American military commanders, led by General Colin L Powell, chairman of the JCS, were working to build up their forces in the Middle East. Central Command, led by the Army's General H Norman Schwarzkopf, had been designed to forestall a Soviet push into the Middle East, but its plans were quickly modified to fit the new situation. Air Force combat units and Army airborne units (the 82nd Division and the 101st Division) were dispatched to Saudi Arabia, and three 15,000-man Marine brigades were flown in, soon to be followed by their equipment, which was brought to them by three flotillas of pre-positioned ships from Diego Garcia in the Indian Ocean. At the same time, Navy ships steamed into the area, both to enforce the UN embargo and to help move thousands of tanks, trucks and other heavy vehicles and tons of supplies into the area under the direction of the integrated Military Transportation Command.

Operation DESERT SHIELD (as it was officially designated on 7 August 1990) quickly expanded as thousands of troops and millions of tons of supplies and equipment began to move into Saudi Arabia. By December the greatest multinational military force assembled for warfare since World War II

Left: Sixteen-inch shells in the barbette of the No 1 turret of the recommissioned battleship *Wisconsin* in the Persian Gulf.
Above: Tomcats, Intruders, Prowlers and two Hawkeyes crowd the flight deck of the USS *Independence* as she cruises in the Gulf of Oman in 1990 during the tense months of Operation DESERT SHIELD.
Below: A freighter rushes Navy small craft to the Persian Gulf in August 1990.

had been drawn together in the Middle East. The coalition forces included not only the half-million American men and women from the four services, along with their equipment, ordnance, and logistical backup, but also planes, ships, and the 1st Armoured Division (including the 'Desert Rats' of the 7th Armoured Brigade) from Great Britain; planes, ships and the armored Daguet Division from France; ships from Argentina, Australia, Poland and eight NATO countries; two armored divisions and a commando regiment from Egypt; an armored division from Syria; and men, planes, tanks, and ships from a number of other Middle Eastern countries which had joined the operation.

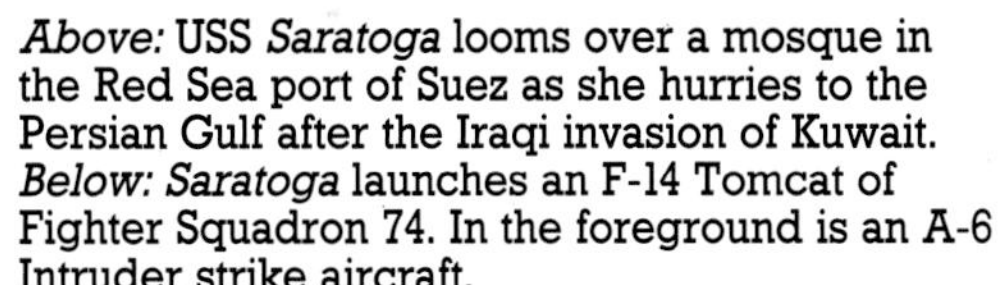

Above: **USS *Saratoga* looms over a mosque in the Red Sea port of Suez as she hurries to the Persian Gulf after the Iraqi invasion of Kuwait.**
Below: ***Saratoga*** **launches an F-14 Tomcat of Fighter Squadron 74. In the foreground is an A-6 Intruder strike aircraft.**

On 29 November the United Nations gave Iraq until 15 January to get out of Kuwait. Hussein was unimpressed. On 9 January a meeting between the American secretary of state, James A Baker, and Tariq Aziz, the foreign minister of Iraq, came to nothing. Even when, on 12 January, the US Congress gave President Bush explicit authority to use the American military to carry out UN Resolution 678 calling for Iraq to leave Kuwait, Hussein would not back down. Finally, a last-minute attempt at personal diplomacy by UN Secretary General Javier Perez de Cuellar just two days before the United Nations deadline also came to nothing.

Diplomacy, embargo and the threat of war had all failed to persuade Hussein to loosen his grip on the tiny, oil-rich nation. Now the 'Mother of All Battles,' as Baghdad Radio called it, was about to begin.

The Gulf War: DESERT STORM, 15 January – 27 February 1991

By the early morning of 15 January 1991, when operation DESERT STORM began, the Navy had six carrier battle groups in place or moving into position. In the Red Sea were the task forces built around the *John F Kennedy* (CV-67), the *Saratoga* (CV-60) and the *America* (CV-66). In the Persian Gulf were the *Midway* (CV-41) and the *Ranger* (CV-61), soon to be joined by the *Theodore Roosevelt* (CVN-71) and the *America*, which would be shifted to the Gulf from the Red Sea. Generally, aircraft flying from the Red Sea battle groups would concentrate on targets in western Iraq and the Baghdad area, while those in the Persian Gulf would hit targets in southeastern Iraq. Unlike Vietnam, in this war all air strikes would be theater-wide and under the joint coordinated command of the Joint Forces Air Component Commander, no aircraft flying on nationally-directed or service-specific missions or routes.

Also active in the battle area were a vast array of Navy and coalition ships. All ships (except those in the southern end of the Persian Gulf) were under the tactical control of Commander US Naval Forces Central Command, Vice Admiral Henry H Mauz, Jr, who was succeeded by Vice Admiral Stanley R Arthur. In all, some 120 American and 50 allied ships were on station when DESERT STORM began. The US vessels active in the war during the course of the operation, besides the six carrier battle groups, included two battleships, the *Wisconsin* (BB-64) and the *Missouri* (BB-63); numerous frigates, cruisers and destroyers; submarines; two hospital ships (*Comfort* and *Mercy*); 31 amphibious task force vessels; commercial vessels with assault logistical equipment; and two embarked MEBs (Marine Expeditionary Brigades).

From the earliest days of the air campaign, Navy aircraft flew often and with great effectiveness as part of the US-coalition air offensive. Navy Tomahawk land-attack cruise missiles (TLAMs) streaked into Iraq to land precisely 'on target' over 80 percent of the time; carrier-based Navy E-2C Hawkeye airborne early-warning surveillance planes helped direct the sorties carried out by Air Force, Marine, Navy and coalition attack planes; P-3 Orions flew long-range land and sea target-identification missions; and EA-6B Prowlers jammed enemy radar sets. A-6E Intruders and F/A-18 Hornets worked in tandem in attacking hardened aircraft shelters and bridges, the Intruders laser-targeting the shelters and bridges while the Hornets dropped laser-guided bombs on them. Swing-wing F-14 Tomcats, meanwhile, flew combat air patrols over surface combatants, made reconnaissance flights and attacked mobile Scud missile sites in western Iraq. A-6E Intruders and A-7E Corsairs fired SLAMs (stand-off land attack missiles) with great success.

Within two weeks, by 30 January, some 33,000 coalition sorties had been flown, Navy aircraft accounting for 4700 of them. Of the 31 designated strategic targets in Iraq, including chemical, biological and possibly nuclear sites, all had been hit and/or destroyed. Over half of Hussein's command and control centers had been put out of action. Some 29 air-defense installations had been hit, 38 of 44 airfields had been bombed, 70 hardened aircraft shelters had been destroyed and 33 of 36 key bridges had been bombed. Only 10 percent of Iraq's supplies were reaching its beleaguered troops in Kuwait (themselves under daily air attack), and 29 Iraqi aircraft had been shot out of the sky without the loss of a single coalition aircraft in aerial combat.

In addition, Navy A-6E Intruders had disabled an Iraqi mine-layer and an intelligence-gathering tanker, had destroyed Silkworm missile sites on the Kuwaiti coast, had attacked three Iraqi landing craft running for safety in Iran and had hit the Iraqi Al Kalia naval station. By the time the air campaign was over, coalition forces had rendered Iraqi naval forces 'combat ineffective' by sinking or destroying 14 Iraqi combatant ships, seven auxiliaries and four amphibious vessels.

In the meantime, the battleship *Missouri* had moved in and lobbed 16-inch shells with great accuracy into concrete bunkers on the Kuwaiti coast. The *Missouri* was relieved after three days by the *Wisconsin*, which continued the bombardment and then supported a Marine Corps probe of Iraqi defenses in southern Kuwait. The battleships' accurate gunnery was largely due to the use of RPVs (remotely piloted vehicles) which

An aerial view of USS *Wisconsin*. At the start of DESERT STORM *Wisconsin* hit Iraq with scores of Tomahawk cruise missiles.

Navy A-7 Corsair strike aircraft prepare for a night launch from USS *John F Kennedy* during the first 24 hours of DESERT STORM, the combat phase of the war with Iraq.

Above: General Schwarzkopf briefs the press on DESERT STORM naval engagements as of 30 January 1991.
Right: A pilot of a Marine AV-8B Harrier vertical/short take-off jet prepares to launch from the amphibious assault ship USS *Nassau* during the final days of Operation DESERT STORM.
Below: An A-6E Intruder strike aircraft is poised on USS *Saratoga*'s catapult before taking off for an operation over the Kuwaiti theater.

Above: Crewmen of the assault helicopter carrier USS *Guadalcanal* man 3-in/50-cal guns for air defense.
Left: A helicopter of helicopter carrier USS *Tripoli* tows a minesweeping sled.

spotted their fall of shot. (At one point in the war, frightened Iraqi troops surrendered to a RPV, probably the first time in the history of warfare when humans capitulated to a robot.)

In the ground war of 24-27 February coalition land forces moved north directly into Kuwait from the Kuwaiti-Saudi Arabian border toward Kuwait City, while other coalition forces of the VII and XVIII Corps swept deep into Iraq in a grand left envelopment that forced Hussein to accept a cease fire in only three days. US naval forces also played vital roles in support of this ground offensive. These included moving toward the northern Persian Gulf to carry out a grand feint to convince the Iraqis that an amphibious landing on Kuwait's eastern shore was about to take place. As part of this feint, the *Missouri* moved up to its bombardment station while Amphibious Task Forces 2 and 3, with the 4th and 5th Marine Expeditionary Brigades on board, moved into position to effect a landing. Thanks to wide media coverage of earlier amphibious exercises on 24 January (the extensive media coverage deliberately assisted by Central Command), when the real offensive began a month later Hussein and his commanders were convinced that an amphibious landing on the Kuwaiti coast was imminent. As a result, on 24 February 50,000 Iraqi defenders badly needed elsewhere were left looking out to sea for a Marine landing that never came (although, as General Schwarzkopf later made clear, the Marines were combat ready and would have been landed on the Kuwait coast if they had been needed).

The Navy also supplied valuable aid to the coalition land forces in their movements into Kuwait and Iraq. A-6Es and F-18s provided close air support for the advancing troops, while other Intruders joined coalition aircraft in striking Iraqis fleeing north from Kuwait City toward Basra. And all the while the battleships continued to blast away at their designated targets in Kuwait and Iraq.

In sum, the Navy had held off any further advance by Hussein during the early weeks of DESERT SHIELD, had accounted for one-fourth of all sorties (26,000 of 103,000) flown during DESERT STORM, had expended 1100 16-inch shells, had fired nearly 300 Tomahawks from the Persian Gulf and Red Sea and had delivered and/or escorted some 95 percent of all matériel (18 billion pounds) arriving by sea for the support of DESERT STORM. Its losses amounted to one F-14 Tomcat, one F/A-18 Hornet and four A-6E Intruders downed by antiaircraft fire and one Intruder, two Hornets and four helicopters lost to non-combat causes. Two vessels, an amphibious assault ship, the *Tripoli* (LPH-10) and the Aegis missile cruiser *Princeton* (CG-59), hit mines while guiding the battleships into position in the northern Gulf, but both were saved through the damage control efforts of their crews. To the US Navy, as well as to the Army, the Air Force and the Marine Corps, the American people extended a heartfelt 'well done' for both DESERT SHIELD and DESERT STORM.

Rescue in Liberia: Operation SHARP EDGE

During August 1990, while the Navy and Marines were reacting to Iraq's invasion of Kuwait and building up for DESERT SHIELD, they were also called upon to effect a rescue mission in the West African nation of Liberia. Liberia has enjoyed a special relationship with the United States dating back to 1822, when it was established as a resettlement haven for freed American slaves. Liberia in the 20th century also assumed importance as the site of major American rubber plantations and of US telecommunications stations.

Headed by ex-army sergeant Samuel K Doe since his successful coup in 1980 (and subsequently as elected president since 1986), the Liberian government in 1989 faced a growing insurgency led by Charles Taylor and his National Patriotic Front of Liberia (NPFL). By 1990 the dissidents had begun to advance toward the capital city of Monrovia, and by early August the rebel NPFL and a splinter group, led by Prince Johnson and calling itself the INPFL were close to seizing the capital. Johnson was also threatening to

Firefighters of the assault helicopter carrier *Tripoli* prepare for damage control after the ship hit a mine in the Persian Gulf on 18 February 1991.

Navy divers plunge into the waters of the Persian Gulf to inspect damage done to the hull of USS *Tripoli* by an Iraqi mine.

take American hostages, a fearsome prospect, since the rebels had recently killed about 200 civilians at the Lutheran Church of Monrovia. Accordingly, on 4 August the US ambassador requested that the US government send troops to protect the embassy and to evacuate both US citizens and some other foreign nationals.

By the time the requisite orders went out, the 22nd Marine Expeditionary Unit (Special Operations Capable) and Amphibious Squadron Four (consisting of the amphibious vessels *Saipan* (LHA-2), *Ponce* (LPD-15) and *Sumter* (LST-1181) and the destroyer *Peterson* (DD-969) were already off the Liberian coast, well-briefed on their mission, and ready to effect their tasks. They had been dispatched from Toulon, France, on 27 May to be in position to react to events in Liberia if necessary.

Operation SHARP EDGE began on the evening of 4 August. Seven Ch-46 helicopters and one Ch-53D helicopter with Marine rifle platoons aboard landed at the US telecommunications office and swiftly evacuated 21 US citizens to the Navy vessels waiting six miles off shore. Simultaneously, more Ch-46s and Ch-53Ds landed 234 Marines at the US embassy. Here they set up heavy weapons and mortars to cover the building and grounds and evacuated 40 US and foreign nationals from the embassy compound. These operations were carried out under the watchful eyes of AH-1T attack helicopters and a command helicopter.

From 6 August through 21 August the helicopter crews, working with the ground Marines, continued to evacuate American citizens and foreign nationals from Monrovia. On 11 August Charles Taylor of the NPFL offered to turn over European diplomats and their families still in Monrovia to the Americans at the town of Buchanan just down the coast from the capital. The *Saipan* and *Peterson* were deployed to five miles off the coast of Buchanan, and a Seal force was sent in to carry out negotiations with the NPFL and agree on a landing zone for the helicopters. After four Ch-46s brought out 96 persons, Operation SHARP EDGE was for all major purposes an end.

During the operation more than 1600 American and foreign citizens had been evacuated without incident, and all US facilities in Liberia had been protected. In a situation that had all the earmarks of potential violence and international misunderstanding, the Navy and Marines had come through. SHARP EDGE may not have attracted much attention in the United States in the summer of 1990, considering the momentous events taking place in the Persian Gulf at that time, but it proved to the Navy and to its Marines that training, rehearsal and coordination were the keys to successful security and evacuation missions in foreign countries.

The Fall of the Soviet Union

While in the early months of 1991 the world's attention was riveted on the dramatic events unfolding in the Middle East, events of even greater historical magnitude were taking shape in the Soviet Union. *Perestroika*, Mikhail Gorbachev's attempt to restructure the collapsing Soviet economy along more market-oriented lines, was proving to be a therapy applied in doses that were both too little and too late. Again and again, when confronted with painful key decisions Gorbachev temporized. Price controls were *not* removed, the ruble was *not* made genuinely convertible, rules governing the right to acquire private property were hopelessly muddled and national production priorities remained fixed on heavy industry rather than being switched to badly-needed consumer goods. Meanwhile, the pace of economic collapse was accelerating: by 1990 the Soviet budget deficit had reached catastrophic proportions, nearly 20 percent of the reeling nation's total GNP.

But if *perestroika* was foundering, *glasnost* must, from Gorbachev's point of view, have seemed to be succeeding all too well. Not only had it opened the way for an alarming upsurge in the expression of strong national-

Evacuated by a Navy helicopter from civil-war-torn Liberia in August 1990, US and other foreign civilians are set safely down in neighboring Sierra Leone.

USSR President Mikhail Gorbachev shakes hands with Russian President Boris Yeltsin in the aftermath of the abortive 1991 coup that almost undid them both.

ist sentiments in most of the USSR's constituent republics, it had also made possible the emergence of a nationwide liberal reform movement that was becoming increasingly critical of Gorbachev's many hesitations and inconsistencies.

As tensions between Gorbachev and the liberals mounted during the second half of 1990, the Soviet president made the critical error of turning to Communist Party conservatives for political support. The ideological gulf that separated Gorbachev from the conservatives was in reality much too wide to be bridged by any but the flimsiest and most emphemeral alliance of expediency, but the fact that Gorbachev had shown himself willing to make concessions to the right vastly increased both the size and the intensity of the liberal opposition to his regime and his own style of leadership.

The early months of 1991 witnessed a mounting series of confrontations between the liberals and the government, with the climax coming in March, when, along with a clumsy (and somehow rather halfhearted) threat of resort to armed force, the government attempted to bully the Russian parliament into ousting the republic's president, Boris Yeltsin, who had become the liberals' de facto leader. But the time when such tactics could easily succeed in the USSR had passed. The parliament resisted, 100,000 Muscovites took to the streets in protest and then all the nation's coal miners went on strike. Appalled, Gorbachev hastened to try to compose his differences with Yeltsin and to placate the liberals by proposing a new 'Union Treaty' that would considerably expand the powers of the republics at the expense of those of the central government. The liberals and the country in general reacted favorably. Now it was the turn of the conservatives to be appalled.

The conservatives' response took the form of an armed coup d'état. Launched in mid-August, just days before the Union Treaty was due to be signed and while Gorbachev was vacationing on the Crimea, it met with overwhelming popular resistance, and after 72 hours it collapsed. Far from restoring the authority of the Soviet government, the failed rightist coup had succeeded in destroying it completely.

In the months that followed, republic after republic declared its independence, and the question of what role the Gorbachev government had left to play in national life became ever more difficult to answer. By mid-December, Yeltsin had persuaded all the newly-sovereign republics save the three Baltic states and Georgia to join Russia in a loose-knit confederation to be called the Commonwealth of Independent States. This fragile entity came into being on 25 December 1991. Mikhail Gorbachev resigned as head of state, the red flag flying over the Kremlin was hauled down and the once-mighty Soviet Union, shaper of so much twentieth-century history, was no more, dead at the age of 74.

Successes and Failures in the Post-Cold War Years

The dramatic victories of the military forces of the United States and their coalition partners in the Gulf War overshadowed all other events during the post-Cold War years as the nation gloried in the overwhelming defeat of the forces of Saddam Hussein, thereby liberating Kuwait and maintaining the balance of power in the Middle East. The Gulf War also testified to the fact that the American forces that forged a swift and decisive victory over the Iraqi dictator had, indeed, learned valuable tactical lessons from their past failures in the Middle East and elsewhere. This Gulf War success, however,

During the attempted right-wing coup in August 1991 an armed bodyguard protects Russia's President Boris Yeltsin.

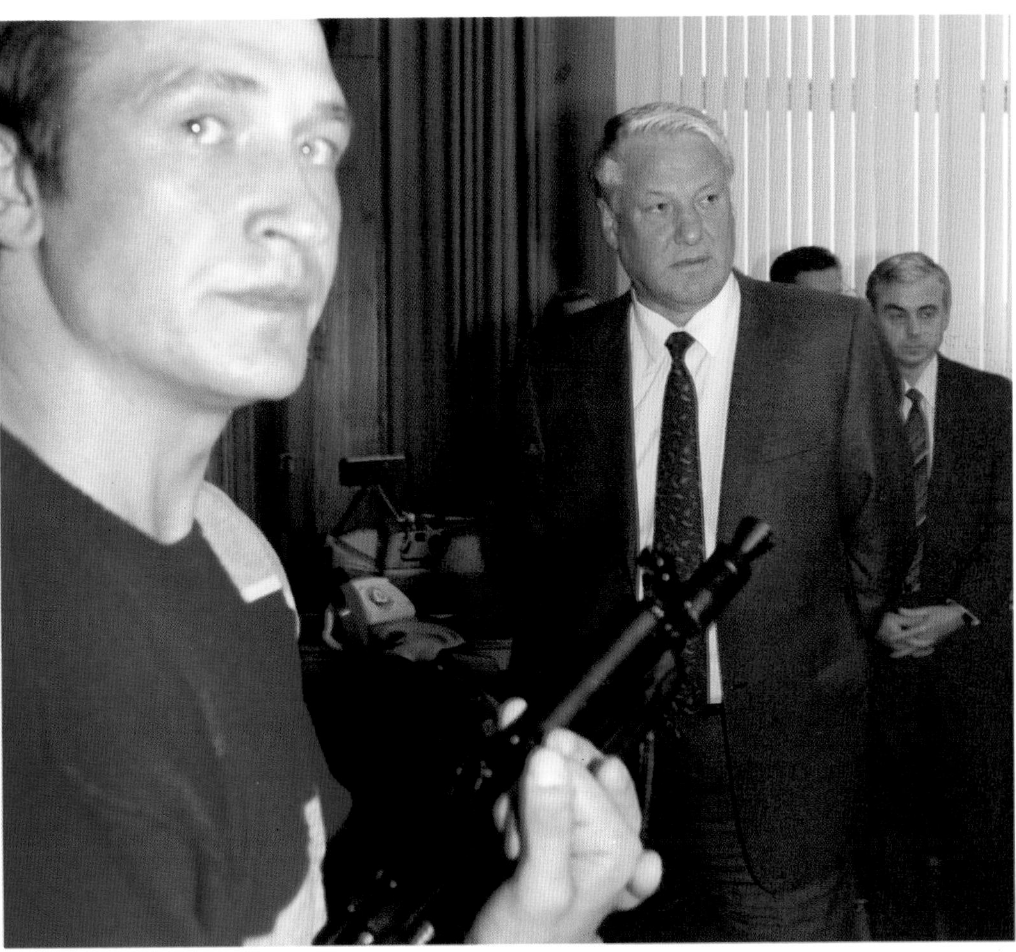

was not unique. It was matched by others. In these, too, the Navy played a prominent role in carrying out the new American military creed that joint operations would be the norm in present and future operations.

One of these instances of success came in the troubled Caribbean nation of Haiti. Here a military coup in 1991 had deposed the president, Jean-Bertrand Aristide. A subsequent United Nations economic embargo resulted in deteriorating living conditions for the people of that already-distracted nation. As a result, thousands of Haitians began to flee their native land by boat. Their destination: the United States. President George Bush initially talked in terms of welcoming them, but their increasing numbers led him and then President Bill Clinton to have them stopped and returned to Haiti or to temporary shelter on the US Navy's Guantanamo Naval Base on Cuba. By August 1994 the numbers of Haitian refugees there had reached 16,500, and the Navy's facilities there were being strained to the breaking point.

Supported by a United Nations Security Council resolution, a multinational force (including the US Navy) prepared to invade the island to restore democratic rule and President Aristide. Fortunately, the ruling military junta in Port-au-Prince backed down in the face of a warning by a US delegation led by former president Jimmy Carter, General Colin Powell, and Senator Sam Nunn of Georgia, that the island would be invaded to restore democratic government there. US Army troops were landed, Aristide was returned to power from exile in the United States, and the sanctions against the island were lifted. Order had been restored in Haiti and a freely elected government had been returned to power. Both in aiding the Haitian refugees from tyranny and in utilizing the threat of force to re-democratize a suffering Caribbean nation, the Navy had played a leading role.

Success could also be claimed by the Navy in 1994 when it played a key role in restoring Middle East stability as Saddam Hussein again threatened Kuwait and the Middle East status quo. In October of that year, probably to apply pressure on the United Nations to lift the sanctions it had imposed on Iraq after the Gulf War, Saddam Hussein began to place 20,000 of his Republican Guards just north of the Kuwaiti border, joining some 50,000 additional Iraqi troops already stationed there. On 7 October 1994, President Bill Clinton announced that American troops would be sent to Kuwait to prevent a second Iraqi attempt to seize that state, and by 12 October 40,000 troops, 650 aircraft, and 28 Navy ships had been dispatched to the area to join the 12,000 American military already there. Faced with this show of strength and determination, Hussein backed down and withdrew his Republican Guards from the border. Once more in the troubled Middle East, total American military strength had achieved a notable, if limited, victory. Combined with signs that Arab-Israeli hostility might be lessening, such as the Gulf Cooperation Council's decision to begin to ease its four-decade-old Arab boycott of Israel, these peacekeeping tasks in the Middle East

US Navy Hawkeyes and Vikings make one of their final flights over the Cubi Point Air Station at soon-to-be-abandoned Subic Bay in the Philippines in March 1992.

were, at the least, hopeful indications that stability in that perennial hotbed of conflict might eventually be reached.

A third area of the word in which the Navy and the other military services scored some successes was Central Europe, specifically in Bosnia, Croatia, and Serbia, three countries that had emerged from the breakup of Yugoslavia at the end of the Cold War and had engaged in continuing warfare for dominance and/or cultural homogeneity since then. Then American military first became involved in the situation in July 1992 when, pursuant to a UN resolution, attempts were made to aid the civilian victims of the fighting in Bosnia-Herzegovina in Operation PROVIDE PROMISE. This humanitarian operation involved Navy, Marine Corps, and Air Force flights into Bosnia-Herzegovina with supplies and foodstuffs and the assignment of a Navy fleet hospital there in an attempt to alleviate the suffering of non-combatants in this centuries-old Balkan cultural conflict.

This was followed shortly after by Operation DENY FLIGHT, in which US Navy carrier-based aircraft supported the multinational mission of enforcing a no-fly zone over Bosnia. This operation saw the USS *Theodore Roosevelt* (CVN-71) battle group, including two destroyers, the USS *Arleigh Burke* (DDG-51) and the USS *John Rodgers* (DD-983), and the guided missile cruiser USS *Mississippi* (CGN-40), steam into the Adriatic to provide effective support to the ground troops involved in the area. This operation was set to continue as long as American ground forces remain in the former Yugoslav state.

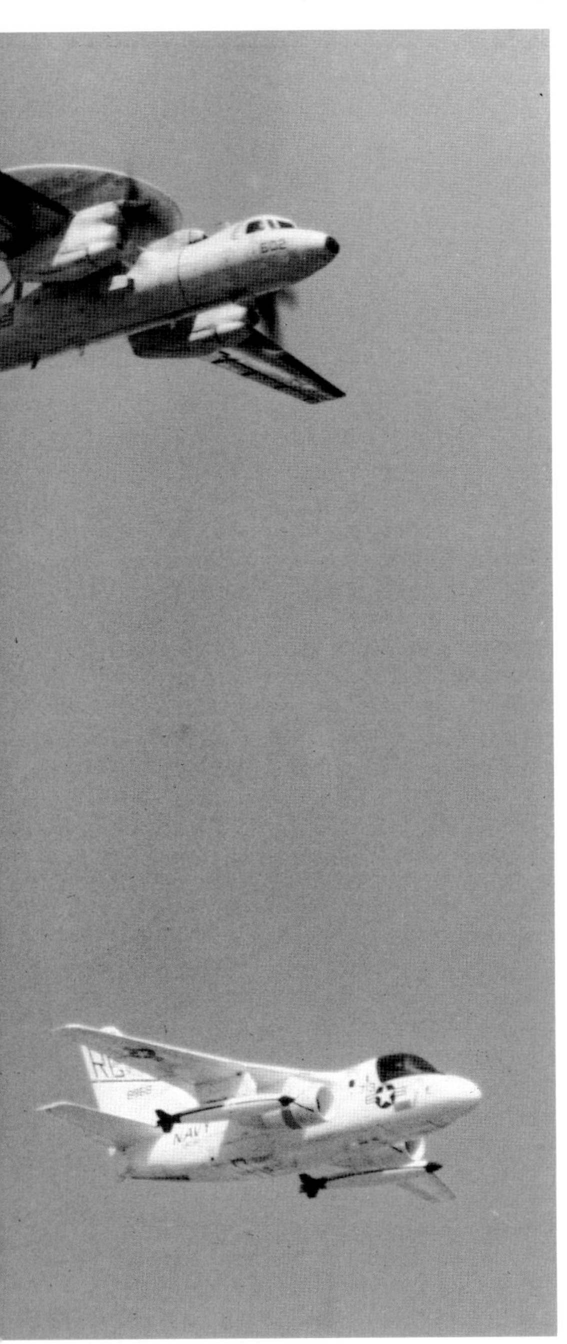

Filipino protesters demand that Americans give up their Philippine bases. When the US finally bowed to such pressure in 1992, it lost some major military assets in Asia.

Operation SHARP GUARD, inaugurated in 1993 in the wake of a UN resolution of embargo against the factions fighting in former Yugoslavia, witnessed US and NATO naval forces in the Adriatic enjoy success in cutting off the fighting factions from clandestine arms shipments by sea, although successful overland and air transport of arms seriously weakened the combined effort to diminish the fighting prowess of the combatants there. In addition to the *Theodore Roosevelt* battle group, Navy nuclear-powered attack submarines and patrol aircraft provided surveillance and reconnaissance aid to the surface craft involved in this low-profile operation.

Probably the most dramatic success in these Balkan operations was the rescue of Air Force Captain Scott O'Grady, shot down in his F-16 Fighting Falcon by a Serb surface-to-air missile in June 1995. After a harrowing six days of eluding Serb forces, O'Grady made voice contact with American military units. In response, a joint Navy/Marine force in helicopters flying off the USS *Kearsarge* (LHD-3) effected a daring rescue of the downed pilot, skimming back to the *Kearsarge* at 130 knots, often only 20 to 30 feet off the surface, to avoid small arms and antiaircraft artillery fire and surface-to-air missiles. O'Grady's gratitude for his rescue was matched by the nation's awe over his being snatched from his pursuers in only five minutes on the ground and with no casualties.

The year 1995 also saw aggressive retaliatory action against Serbian forces in August and September after a mortar attack on Sarajevo. Operating off the carriers *Theodore Roosevelt* and USS *America* (CV-66), Navy aircraft joined with others from the Marine Corps, Air Force, and NATO allied forces to pound the enemy positions for three weeks. This joint force air attack, named Operation DELIBERATE FORCE, enjoyed remarkable success, the manned aircraft in 3,515 sorties being supplemented by 13 Tomahawk land-attack cruise missiles fired from the Aegis cruiser USS *Normandy* (CG-60). Operation DELIBERATE FORCE played a significant part in convincing the Bosnian Serbs to begin peace talks, which finally resulted in the Dayton Accord that molded a framework for a possible settlement in the former Yugoslav state. US Navy forces continued on watch in the Adriatric, along with their British and French counterparts, as US and allied ground forces attempt to ensure a measure of safety to the non-combatants caught up in a seemingly endless cultural war.

While thus enjoying considerable success in carrying out its designated duties in the

Army soldiers on the deck of the USS *Dwight D Eisenhower* (CVN-69) enroute to Haiti in Sept. 1994.

mid-1990s, including aiding in the evacuation of the last UN personnel from Somalia in early 1995, maintaining Operation SOUTHERN WATCH in the Arabian Gulf, and aiding the Coast Guard in its drug interdiction efforts, the Navy was also buffeted by internal failures in the form of social and personnel problems that too often obscured its accomplishments and damaged its reputation with Congress and the American people.

On 19 April 1989 a turret explosion on the battleship USS *Iowa* (BB-61) resulted in the death of 47 men. In the aftermath of the tragedy the Navy rushed to judgment and blamed a dead sailor (supposedly intent on suicide) for the explosion, when in fact the explosion was caused by a problem with the powder bags. Two years later the Navy leadership's competence and honesty were again called into question in the Tailhook scandal.

At the Tailhook Association's convention in Las Vegas in 1991 ('tailhookers' are Navy carrier aviators) a number of unprofessional and unlawful sexual activities occurred with senior officers at least in the vicinity. When a young female officer complained of being unwillingly groped and fondled by male members of the Association, her complaints were initially ignored, then an internal investigation was completely botched. Eventually, as a result of further investigation into the matter, the Chief of Naval Operations was forced to resign two months before his normal retirement date, a number of junior and middle-grade officers were brought up on charges and court-martialed, and, unfortunately, 'tailhookers' who were not in attendance at Las Vegas (some were not even in the United States when the events occurred) had their promotions delayed or denied.

But 'Tailhook,' as it came to be known in the media, was not the only embarrassing incident for the Navy in personnel matters during these years. At the Naval Academy a female midshipman had been manacled to a urinal in 1989, only one of a number of instances of sexual harassment of female midshipmen reported to authorities. Further, a major cheating scandal was uncovered at Annapolis in December 1992, and then a drug scandal in 1995. Additionally, numerous charges have been leveled at senior Navy officers and enlisted for sexual harassment and improper sexual actions in recent years, the problem exacerbated by the assignment of women to combatant ships; this problem may only get worse if a study presently underway determines that women should be placed aboard submarines with their necessarily close living conditions.

These problems, along with those imposed by the Clinton dictum that homosexuals must have equal opportunities within the armed forces, apparently claimed another victim with the suicide of Chief of Naval Operations Jeremy M Boorda on 16 May 1996. The first CNO to rise from the enlisted ranks, Boorda was faced with the task of solving the complex social and personnel problems imposed on the Navy (to a large degree by idealists with little or no experience with or knowledge of unique naval operating environments) when he took command in 1994. He also had to shoulder other burdens placed upon him as the Navy sought to refine its mission and maintain it against the other services in the post-Cold War world and in the face of budgetary cuts dating back to the Bush administration years. Boorda did an outstanding job for two years in wrestling with these problems and reestablishing the Navy's pride in itself. But these tasks took their toll, and when questions arose over the 'V' insignia (signifying combat action in the Vietnam War) he wore on two of his commendation awards (Boorda already having removed them), the popular CNO took his own life in May 1996, depriving the Navy of an able commander striving to restore the service to its proper place of honor in the nation's eyes and to its proper and necessary role in America's military establisment.

On Duty Station

During the last half of the 1990s, the Navy would find itself called upon to perform in a number of situations that could not have been anticipated when in 1775 the Naval Committee took charge of the forerunner of the U.S. Navy, the Continental Navy. U.S. Navy ships continued to maintain a constant presence in the Arabian (Persian) Gulf in support of Operation SOUTHERN WATCH, the operation initiated in the aftermath of the Gulf War in order to enforce UN-mandated sanctions against Iraq and enforce the 'No-Fly Zone.' In fact, it was frequently violated by Saddam Hussein's air force, and planes from the U.S. Navy carriers and missiles from surface ships would just as promptly respond by attacking Iraq. Other Navy ships continued to interdict ships in the Gulf region suspected of violating the embargo against Iraq. And in response to the bombing of two American embassies in Africa, in August 1998 the Navy sent planes and missiles against terrorist training centers in Afghanistan and a suspected chemical weapons facility in Sudan.

Constant training exercises were carried out to test and tune up the Navy's capabilities to meet all kinds of emergencies and hostilities—from deploying strategic reserve forces to testing for future ship designs and technologies. Relatively new were the increasing numbers of joint training exercises with foreign navies. Indicative of the great depth, reach, and commitment of the U.S Navy were exercises in which various elements participated in wide-flung regions in the month of June 2001: some ships participated with 14 other European nations in a training exercise in the Baltic Sea; other ships participated in Exercise Alexander the Great with Greek forces in the Mediterranean; still others participated with ships of 13 nations in the Mine Countermeasure Exercise in the waters off Singapore.

There were also the new 'humanitarian' missions of the Navy. In August 1999, the Navy carried troops and supplies to aid the victims of Turkey's horrendous earthquake. In February 1999, U.S. Navy ships carried supplies to aid the victims of a terrible earthquake in India. More historical than humanitarian, Navy divers helped to recover the steam engine of the USS *Monitor* off Cape Hatteras, where the Federal ironclad had sunk 10 months after its famous Civil War battle with the CSS *Merrimack*.

Right: **Haitians hold a rally at a camp at the Guantanamo Bay Naval Station in Cuba in 1994.** ***Below:*** **An F/A-18C Hornet flies past oil fields over Kuwait. The aircraft is from Strike Fighter Squadron 147 (VFA-147), embarked aboard the aircraft carrier USS *Nimitz* (CVN-68).**

In the spring of 1999, however, the U.S. Navy did find itself engaged in more conventional duty. Ships of the Navy's 6th Fleet had been a presence in the Adriatic Sea off Yugoslavia since 1996, as part of Operation JOINT ENDEAVOR to enforce the Dayton Peace Accord for Bosnia. But when Serbian forces

Sailors escort Air Force Captain Scott O'Grady aboard the USS *Kearsarge* (LHD-3) after Marines rescued the downed pilot during Operation DENY FLIGHT in June 1995.

supported by Yugoslavia's President Slobodan Milosevic began to attack and kill the Albanian-Moslem people of the province of Kosovo, NATO launched Operation ALLIED FORCE, designed to force the Serbians to cease their aggressive activities. Thus, the guided missile cruiser USS *Philippine Sea* commenced firing Tomahawk missiles on 24 March. This fleet was soon joined by more U.S. ships, including the aircraft carrier USS *Theodore Roosevelt,* from which U.S. Navy aircraft were launched to conduct night strikes. Other Navy ships carried the Marines who were brought ashore in Albania and Macedonia as part of the NATO ground forces that were ready to move into Kosovo if necessary.

On 9 June the Yugoslav military commanders signed an agreement to withdraw their forces from Kosovo, so no American ground forces were required to engage in combat, but the Navy could take pride in having brought things to this point. The Navy then continued to stand by as the combat phase of NATO's operations was converted to the peacekeeping Operation JOINT GUARDIAN, in which the Navy's Amphibious Readiness Group 2 deployed U.S. Marines to Kosovo to help enforce the peace and provide stability.

On 9 February 2000 occurred one of those accidents that every Navy-related person—among others—would regret. The USS *Greeneville,* a *Los Angeles*-class attack submarine, was on a Distinguished Visitor Cruise off the coast of Diamond Head, Oahu, Hawaii. Such cruises are designed to demonstrate the Navy's capacities to various influential individuals, and in this instance the commanding officer (CO) of the submarine decided to demonstrate an 'emergency surfacing maneuver'—a very quick raising of the submarine to the surface. After performing the routine checks to make sure that no surface vessels were nearby, the CO gave the command for a quick ascent. Just as the submarine neared the surface, there was a loud bump. The submarine had come up directly under a Japanese vessel, the *Ehime Maru,* which was in these waters on an educational voyage. The Japanese vessel sank almost immediately, and although most of the 35 Japanese crew and students aboard were eventually picked up by the submarine, nine persons went down with the ship, which sank in almost 2,000 feet of water. (The U.S. Navy would later aid in recovering the bodies of the Japanese.)

It was a devastating experience for all concerned. The CO of the submarine was one of the most experienced and respected of all submariners, so questions immediately arose. How could such an error have been committed? And did the presence of those 16 civilians contribute to the accident? A court of inquiry concluded that the accident was caused by two factors: inadequate acoustic and visual search of the area before surfacing, and inadequate contact management by the ship's responsible personnel. In both instances, the CO was basically at fault. Although he was not given any formal punishment, he resigned from the Navy, an unfortunate ending to an otherwise commendable career.

Then, on 12 October 2000, yet another accident unsettled not just those who sail the world's seas but all Americans. The USS *Cole* was an *Arleigh Burke*-class destroyer assigned to the waters of the Persian Gulf —part of Operation SOUTHERN WATCH that was keeping an eye on Iraq. The *Cole* was anchored for a refueling in the port of Aden, the capital of the nation of Yemen, when a smaller vessel approached it. Before the crew of the *Cole* challenged this unknown boat, it came along midship portside and exploded with tremendous force that ripped a gaping hole in the hull of the *Cole*. Needless to say, the occupants of the small boat were killed instantly, but so too were 17 crew members (including two female sailors); 39 others were injured. Quick action by the crew prevented the *Cole* from sinking, and eventually it was brought back to a shipyard in Mississippi for repairs (carried on a special Norwegian heavy transport ship, the M/V *Blue Marlin*) where it would be repaired and sent back to sea in the fall of 2001.

It was apparent virtually from the moment of impact that this was the handiwork of terrorists: The U.S. Navy knew very well that they presented a constant threat in that part of the world—had, in fact, chosen Aden for refueling because it seemed safer than other ports in the region. So again, the question immediately arose: How had this happened? In January 2001, a special U.S. Navy Judge Advocate General Manual (JAGMAN) investigation announced its findings that the *Cole*'s commanding officer's decisions had been both reasonable and appropriate and therefore no punitive actions were warranted against him or the crew. At the same time, the JAGMAN indicated that a number of lessons had been learned, specifically that the Navy should do a better job in both training and equipping its personnel for dealing with the new risks.

On 1 April 2001, the Navy was involved in yet another unfortunate incident, when a Chinese fighter jet collided with one of its reconnaissance aircraft some 80 miles off the Chinese island of Hainan. The jet crashed into the sea and the Chinese pilot, although he parachuted free, was never found. The American plane made an emergency landing on Hainan, where its 24 crew members were detained for 11 days. After the crew members were released, China finally consented to having the plane taken apart and removed. From the beginning, China insisted that American actions had caused the collision, but most objective observers accepted the American version—that the Chinese pilot had flown too close and caused the accident.

As it happened, the next time Navy personnel found themselves assaulted they were not on either ships or planes in a 'high-threat environment.' Rather, they were the Navy personnel and civilian employees who had reported to work in the Pentagon the morning of 11 September 2001. Shortly after the two planes crashed into the

World Trade Center in New York City, an airliner piloted by suicidal hijackers came crashing into the side of the Pentagon, killing 189 people, of whom 33 were Navy personnel and 9 were civilian employees or contractors with the Navy Department. It was a dual disaster unprecedented in American history, although for the Navy it inevitably recalled the Japanese surprise attack on Pearl Harbor in 1941. Another unsettling link to the Navy's history was the discovery that at least a couple of the hijackers almost certainly had been involved in the attack on the USS *Cole* the previous October.

The Navy would get some satisfaction when it was called to participate in what President George W. Bush would designate as Operation ENDURING FREEDOM, the campaign against terrorists in general and, most immediately, the individuals responsible for those suicidal hijackings. On 7 October 2001, U.S. Navy ships in the Arabian Sea off Pakistan commenced firing Tomahawk missiles and launching airplanes on the Taliban outposts and forces in Afghanistan. The first planes were from the carriers *Enterprise* and *Carl Vinson*; the first missiles were from the guided-missile carrier *Philippine Sea* and the destroyer *John Paul Jones*. Other ships would soon join them in an operation that continued on into 2003.

Operation Iraqi Freedom

Operation Iraqi Freedom of 2003 was essentially a ground war fought on virtually land-locked Iraqi soil with the targets being the capital city of Baghdad and the government of Saddam Hussein. Still, the US Navy—along with the US Air Force, the US Coast Guard, and Great Britain's Royal Navy—played important roles in this three-week war fought by the coalition ground forces and in their eventual victory. To appreciate this mode of warfare, it is important to realize that the American military's emphasis on joint force operations for the last 30 years faced its greatest test in Iraq and proved their effectiveness in dramatic style. And to understand this brief war marked by controversy at both home and abroad—although polls consistently showed that the vast majority of American citizens were solidly behind the conflict—it is important to survey its background to understand why and how America became militarily involved in this Middle Eastern country in 2003.

Going back 12 years, despite the success of the US-UN forces in driving the Iraqis under Saddam Hussein out of Kuwait in 1991, subsequent efforts to disarm Hussein met with frustration after frustration in the years that followed. The United Nations Resolution 687 of April 1991 required Iraq to destroy or dismantle all biological, chemical, and nuclear weapons or nuclear-weapons-usable material. It also forbade the development of such weapons in the future. But the Iraqis continually failed to comply with this resolution despite UN economic sanctions in place and UN weapons inspectors being on the ground.

By 1998 the Iraqis were demanding an end to the economic sanctions imposed upon their country and forced the UN weapons inspectors to leave the country, allowing them to return only under the threat of US military intervention. Despite the fact that in 1999 a new UN weapons inspection organization was formed, the UN Monitoring, Verification and Inspection Commission (UNMOVIC), and Hans Blix of Sweden was named to head it the following year, full cooperation by Iraq was not forthcoming from the Baghdad regime.

The terrorist attacks on New York City and the Pentagon on 11 September 2001, led to increased confrontations between Iraq and the United States. Unwilling to countenance

Below: U.S. Navy and Marine Corps security personnel patrol past the damage done by the terrorist bombing attack on the USS *Cole* in Aden, 12 October 2000.

Above: **A U.S. Navy CH-46 Sea Knight search and rescue helicopter flies ahead of the aircraft carrier USS *Carl Vinson* in the Arabian Sea in October 2001.**
Below: **An F/A-18C Hornet launching from the aircraft carrier USS *Carl Vinson* (CVN 70) in a strike against al Qaeda terrorist training camps and military installations of the Taliban regime in Afghanistan as part of Operation ENDURING FREEDOM.**

more possible terrorist attacks on the American people, in September 2002 Bush asked Congress for the authority to use force against Iraq. This authorization was forthcoming the following month with overwhelming majorities in both houses of Congress. Meanwhile, at the United Nations a new measure, Resolution 1441, was passed by the Security Council. It stated that Iraq was in "material breach" of the earlier UN resolutions and called for new inspections. As all of this diplomatic interplay was taking place, plans were well underway by the American government to deploy an additional 62,000 troops to the Persian Gulf region to join the 60,000 already there, and weapon-laden Navy ships and their crews were being deployed to the area.

On 5 February 2003, Secretary of State Colin Powell told the UN Security Council that intelligence data made it clear that Iraq was not going to disarm and, in fact, was hiding its weapons of mass destruction from the inspectors. Standing firmly beside President Bush in his determination to challenge Iraq was Tony Blair, the prime minister of Great Britain. On 23 February the United States, Great Britain, and Spain proposed to the Security Council that a resolution be passed ordering Iraq to disarm. Blair backed this up on 7 March by proposing an amendment setting 17 March as the deadline for Iraq's compliance. France, however, served notice that it would veto any resolution authorizing the use of force against Iraq, and Germany, China, and Russia stood with France on this issue.

On 16 March President Bush met with Prime Minister Blair and Spanish Premier Jose Maria Aznar in the Azores. They announced they would give diplomacy one more day to work, and then, they made it clear, they would go to war to disarm Iraq with or without UN approval. The next day Bush gave Saddam Hussein and his sons a final ultimatum to leave the country within 48

hours or face war. The president explained, "We are acting because the risks of inaction would be far greater." On 18 March the British House of Commons backed Blair on a 412-149 vote to use "all means necessary" to disarm Hussein. The buildup of US military forces, including US Navy ships in the eastern Mediterranean and the Persian Gulf was by this time well underway.

What the United States chose to call Operation Iraqi Freedom began on 19 March 2003, with an air assault on targets in Baghdad designed to eradicate Saddam Hussein. Tomahawk Cruise missiles were fired from US Navy ships in the Persian Gulf and the Red Sea. This opening air assault was approved by Great Britain, Australia, and at least tacitly by the 35 other nations the Bush administration claimed were in support of the use of armed force against Iraq. And by this time President Bush had widened the goals of the war, now asserting that the military action being taken was being carried out to help the Iraqi people achieve a "united, stable and free operation Iraqi Freedom country."

When the ground war commenced on 20 March, standing by—in the Eastern Mediterranean, the Red Sea, the Persian Gulf, and the Indian Ocean—was a 70-odd ship coalition armada, including 60,000 US maritime men and women manning these ships in support of the ground forces under the direction of Vice Admiral Timothy Keating, Commander, US Naval Forces Central Command and Commander, US Fifth Fleet. The first days of the ground war were marked not only by the advance of coalition forces north from Kuwait into Iraqi territory—the Navy's SEALS and British Royal Marine commandoes at the same time seizing oil shipping facilities on the al-Faw peninsula—but also by massive air strikes on Baghdad. The Navy played a major role in this airborne offensive, firing satellite-guided, long-range Tomahawk cruise missiles from its carrier task forces, each consisting of an aircraft carrier and its accompanying surface and sub-surface

Above: A briefing in the Mission Planning room aboard the USS _Harry S. Truman_ in support of Operation Iraqi Freedom in the Mediterranean Sea, 19 March 2003.
Below: An F/A-18C Hornet launches from the flight deck aboard the aircraft carrier USS _Abraham Lincoln_, 20 March 2003.

vessels, in the area. Two were located in the eastern Mediterranean: the USS *Theodore Roosevelt* (CVN-71) and the USS *Harry Truman* (CVN-75). Three were positioned in the Persian Gulf: the USS *Kitty Hawk* (CV-63), the USS *Constellation* (CV-64), and the USS *Abraham Lincoln* (CVN-72). Each carrier had aboard about 75 warplanes, consisting of F/A-18 Hornets, F-14 Tomcats, S-3 Vikings, and other fixed wing and rotary blade aircraft. These were used to attack targets in Baghdad and, later, elsewhere in Iraq; to provide air support for advancing coalition troops; and to fly surveillance and reconnaissance missions. These initial air strikes of 20 March were devastating but merely a preview of what was to come. The next day a massive, three-hour air assault on Baghdad in which more than 1,300 cruise missiles and bombs from B-2 Spirit bombers, F-117 Nighthawk stealth fighter-bombers, the Navy's Tomahawk cruiser- and destroyer-launched cruise missiles, and air-launched missiles from B-52 Bombers were targeted on the Republican Guard headquarters, the facilities of the Special Republican Guard, and other symbols of Saddam's government.

In the days to come, hundreds of sorties would be flown from US Navy carriers based in the Persian Gulf, both on missions to support ground troops and to take out

Above: The aircraft carriers USS *Kitty Hawk* (front) and USS *Constellation* in the Gulf region, 13 April 2003.

Below: An F/A-18C Hornet attempts an arrested landing aboard the aircraft carrier USS *Kitty Hawk* on 23 March 2003.

Opposite, Top: American flags fly as a Tomahawk cruise missile is fired at Iraq from MK-41 vertical launching system aboard the Aegis guided-missile cruiser USS *Mobile Bay,* 21 March 2003.

Opposite, Bottom: An aviation ordinance man checks his list near rows of laser guided bombs in the hangar bay before they are loaded onto jets on the USS *Kitty Hawk* in the northern Gulf, 21 March 2003.

selected Iraqi targets. US naval forces would also be conducting a comprehensive mine-clearing effort to ensure safe passage into the Iraqi port city of Umm Qasr for ships bringing in humanitarian aid to the Iraqi people, and the Coast Guard would be providing coastal security patrols, conducting navigational surveys of the Iraqi waterways, and escorting the ships carrying in critical humanitarian supplies into Iraq. Another invaluable contribution of the US Navy was its hospital ship, the USNS *Comfort*, stationed throughout the hostilities in the Persian Gulf and providing life-saving medical services both to coalition military forces and Iraqi military and civilians.

After the first week of ground operations in which coalition forces moved up from the south toward Baghdad, a northern front was opened when more than 1,000 members of the US 173rd Airborne Brigade dropped into Kurdish-held territory in northern Iraq, and by 7 April US ground forces had entered Baghdad in force. By this time there were some 250,000 US and British troops in the Gulf Region with thousands more arriving daily. After securing the city to the delight of many if not most of its citizens—as shown worldwide on 9 April with the dramatic toppling of Saddam Hussein's statue in the heart of Baghdad by the citizens of the city with the aid of an American armored recovery vehicle—the ground forces moved on to complete Operation Iraqi Freedom by seizing the city of Tikrit, the ancestral home of Saddam Hussein.

The war was far from over, although US naval vessels had launched more than 7,000 air sorties and, along with British ships, having fired more than 800 Tomahawk cruise missiles (only 10 of which failed to reach their

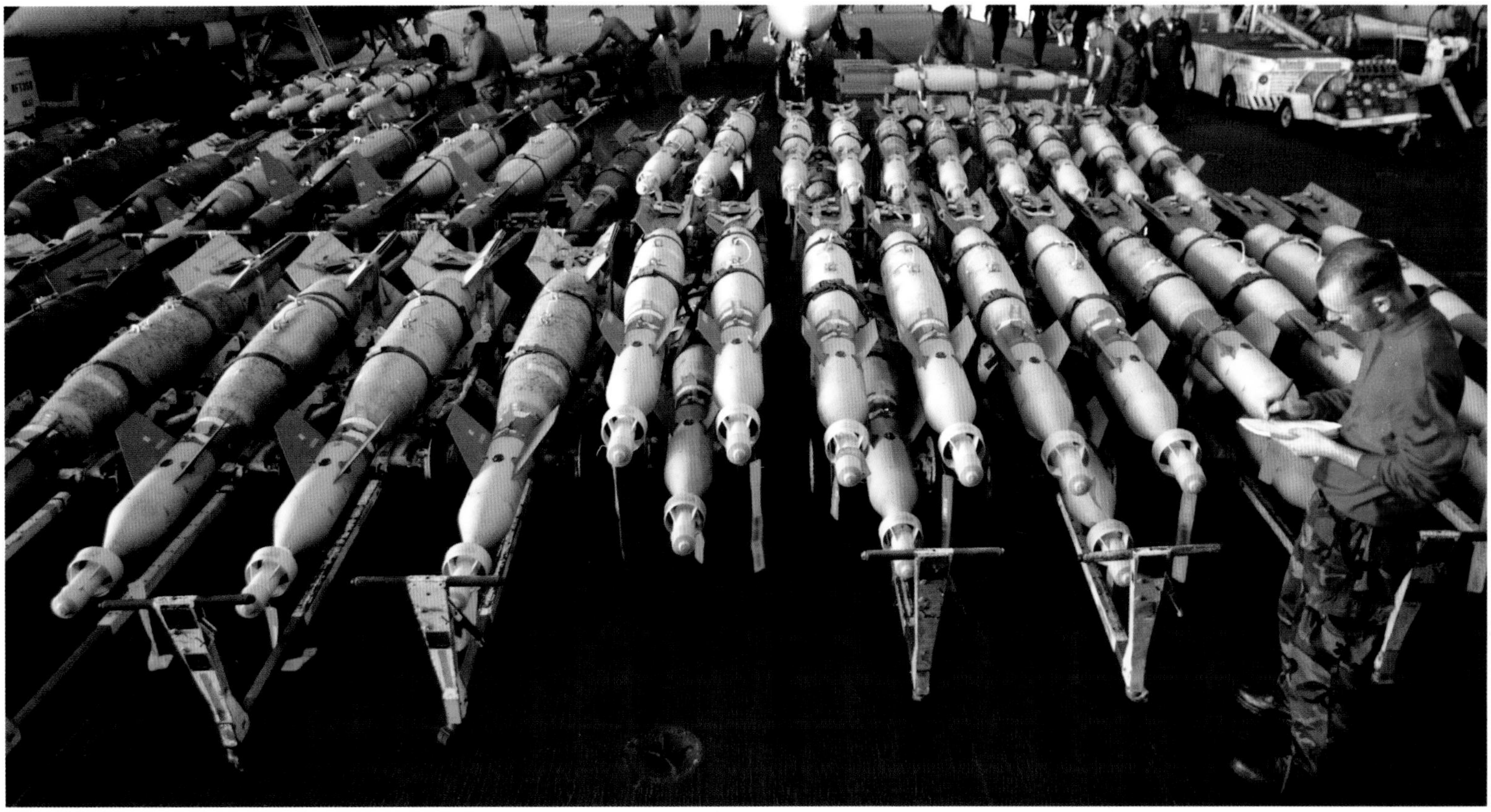

Above: Military Sealift Command vehicle transport ship USNS *Gilliand.*

target). By mid-April some US vessels were being ordered back to their home ports, having little or nothing to do in the campaign. It was clear that Saddam Hussein's tyrannical rule was over as his country lay in ruins.

The price in blood for the United States was 131 American troops losing their lives (116 in action with Iraqi forces) according to the Pentagon on 22 April, along with some 500 wounded. Much still had to be done to finish the war and put Iraq back together. The coalition forces now faced the tasks of ending the futile resistance of Saddam's remaining loyalists; finding and eliminating Iraq's weapons of mass destruction; capturing and eliminating terrorists both in the Middle East and worldwide, including those with ties to the al Qaeda terror network; and funneling in humanitarian aid to the Iraqi people and assisting them in establishing a representative government in their homeland.

The Navy in the 21st Century

The war against terrorists was called 'the first war of the 21st century,' a recognition that there were to be new technologies, new procedures, new rules in the wars of the future. How well prepared is the U.S. Navy for this future? To address the challenges, the Navy periodically sets forth its priorities, which now more than ever stress its commitment to systematic innovation, the solution of difficult interoperability and integration problems, and the steady pursuit of promising scientific and technological initiatives.

High on the list of objectives is increasing and improving Navy-Marine Corps integration in areas from warfighting doctrine to procurement strategies. Through greater integration, the Naval Services seek increased flexibility of their striking power, for example, by restructuring Navy-Marine Corps carrier air wings. These new wings and their supporting units will be tailored to provide a range of crisis-response options. In the Information Technology world, the Department will replace its numerous independent local networks with a Navy/Marine Corps Intranet (NMCI) capable of more efficiently and less expensively supporting more than 400,000 Navy and Marine Corps users. NMCI will provide better 'speed of action' and significantly improve security through implementation and enforcement of standardized information-assurance practices.

The Navy and the Marine Corps have ongoing initiatives to translate such capstone concepts as Network-Centric Warfare (NCW) and Operational Maneuver into reality. The Naval War College's Navy Warfare Development Command (NWDC) and the Marine Corps Combat Development Command (MCCDC) are tasked to refine these concepts and also develop future warfare ideas. NWDC's Maritime Battle Center (MBC) and the Marine Corps Warfighting Laboratory (MCWL) also explore candidate concepts, tactics, techniques, and procedures for the application of advanced technologies. Navy Fleet Battle Experiments (FBEs) and Marine Corps Advanced Warfighting Experiments (AWEs) test these new doctrines and ideas in the field, assess the utility of new technologies, explore new operational capabilities and organizational arrangements, and feed the empirical results back to the Development Commands.

Both the Navy and the Marine Corps strongly support joint experimentation initiatives. Extending the Littoral Battlespace (ELB) Advanced Concept Technology Demonstration (ACTD) involves a wireless network connecting ships at sea, aircraft, and ground forces (both small units and individual Marines). This system holds exceptional potential for increased information exchange among all forces in a Joint Task Force organization. For example, the IT21 initiative will provide a reliable and ubiquitous network to all afloat commanders for rapid data flow among sensors, weapons, and command and control nodes and is key to the reprioritization of Command, Control, Communications, Computers, Intelligence, Surveillance and Reconnaissance (C4ISR) programs to execute the NCW concept.

Carriers and large-deck amphibious ships are also being fitted with identical or very similar command, control, and communications (C3) subsystems. Improving configuration management and software standardization will improve the speed of information flow and provide a common view of the battlespace. C4ISR systems for joint, allied, and coalition forces must be analyzed and agreed upon to make interoperability a reality.

Advances in science and technology underpin transformation of the Navy. Such advances may significantly affect disparate areas, from warfighting tactics and techniques to propulsion plants to overall platform cost and design. Some of these include:

Unmanned Aerial Vehicles (UAVs) and Unmanned Underwater Vehicles (UUVs). Technology, especially in the areas of sensors and processing, has moved forward at an amazing pace.

Integrated Power Systems (IPS). Electric propulsion, envisioned for future surface and submarine platforms, will enable integrated powering of all propulsion, combat systems, and ship services, thus enhancing warship capability.

Electro-Magnetic Aircraft Launching System (EMALS). Beginning with the first of the next-generation aircraft carrier, CVNX-1, EMALS will replace steam catapults that are currently used to launch carrier aircraft. EMALS will significantly reduce weight, catapult manning requirements, and life-cycle costs.

DD-21 will be the first major U.S. surface combatant designed as a single, integrated system. This holistic approach, encompassing the ship, all shipboard systems, crew, associated shore infrastructure, and all joint and allied interfaces, has the potential to reduce manning as well as operating and support costs by up to 70 percent.

Doctrinal interoperability issues may be even more complex than technological ones. One of the challenges facing the Naval Services in the next few years is thinking through the operational and organizational implications of employing netted Centric Warfare. Certainly, naval forces have been operationally netting via tactical data links for decades. However, the extraordinary advances in information technology, particularly the networking of multiple systems, leveraged through efforts like IT21 and the NMCI, promise to increase the combat effectiveness of naval and joint forces far beyond what earlier data links enabled.

Some of these advanced systems and technologies were put to the test in Operation ENDURING FREEDOM. The planes from the carriers, F-14s and FA-18s, for instance, were armed with the newest in Guided Bomb Units: some of their precision-guided bombs were directed by lasers aimed by the pilots, but the more sophisticated were guided remotely by satellite. But in the end, all fighting services are only as good as the personnel within them. As of April 2002, the Navy had some 381,500 active-duty personnel and 154,300 in the ready reserve. Like all branches of the U.S. government, the 21st-century Navy was confronted with new strains on its budget, but it did not intend to skimp on its payscale or re-enlistment incentives. It is also now recognized that the effective integration of reserve elements with active components is indispensable, as demand for military forces increases and the active force stabilizes at a reduced level.

From the years of its birth in the late 1700s the U.S. Navy has seen times of splendid victory and times of humiliating defeat, times of widespread support and times of public neglect, times of internal strength and professional pride and times of troubles, times of strong leadership and times of weak leadership. Yet throughout its existence it has served the nation well and honorably in war and in peace, working through all problems to carry out its mandate of defending the nation on waters near or far. As the 21st century commences, the United States Navy will again take up whatever challenges it faces in the future and play a stellar role with the other armed forces in serving the nation whose name it so proudly bears.

Below: **Military Sealift Command vehicle transport ship USNS *Gordon*.**

HISTORY OF THE US MARINES

JACK MURPHY

Page 518-519: Marines debark from a UH-1 helicopter in Vietnam.
This page: A Marine detachment from the USS Chicago pictured in 1892.

CONTENTS

Above: Marines land ashore at Birbera, Somalia, during Operation Bright Star, the US-Egyptian exercises.

INTRODUCTION

America is in essence an island state, separated by the world's oceans from most of its allies and trading partners. Right from the start, it has had to be ready to protect its economic and political relationships in places all around the globe. The facts of geography make America a maritime nation; the necessities of geopolitics require that it not only maintain unrestricted access to the seven seas, but also remain capable of defending that access when necessary.

That is how the Corps serves the nation—as a force in readiness, always prepared to fight, anywhere, anytime.

Throughout the nearly 200 years-long history of the Marine Corps it has formed what is, compared with the other services, a tiny organization, made up—in the words of a Marine recruiting poster—of 'a few good men.' The Corps's concern for quality over quantity was foreshadowed in the document of the Continental Congress that created the Continental Marines, predecessors of the present Corps; it specified '*that particular care be taken* [to enlist] such as are good seamen, or so acquainted with maritime affairs as to be able to serve to advantage by sea, when required.'

It is no coincidence that many of the Marine Corps's more famous actions and expeditionary services have taken place in periods when the United States has not been involved in a formal state of war; the Corps works hard at maintaining a 'cutting edge' that keeps it ready to be first to fight. The key factors in achieving the Corps's constant state of readiness are those 'few good men' to which the recruiting poster refers. Though the technology of warfare changes, the need for the trained, disciplined fighting man has not changed, and will not in the foreseeable future.

There is nothing new to this—elite military forces are as old as history. The Bible tells of 300 soldiers who were 'The sword of the Lord, and of Gideon,' chosen out of 10,000 to lead an attack that defeated the army of Midian. Themistocles, leader of the Athenians, issued a decree that his navy '. . . enlist Marines, twenty to a ship

. . .;' these *Epibatas*, as they were called, helped turn back the Persian invasion. Rome, too, had special legions of *milites classiarii*, or 'soldiers of the fleet.' But the first true corps of Marines, and the ancestor of the United States Marines, was formed in 1664 when England's King Charles II decreed: *That twelve hundred land souldjers be forthwith raysed, to be in readinesse, to be distributed into his* [*Majesty's*] *Fleets prepared for Sea Service* [*which*] *twelve hundred men are to be putt into One Regiment. . . .* He gave this new group the ponderous name of 'The Duke of York and Albany's Maritime Regiment of Foot.' These were true salty soldiers, fully under the command of the Admiralty. They evolved over the next century into the British Marines; several Colonial battalions modeled on the British Marines were formed in America prior to the revolution against England.

The Marines were born to be maritime soldiers, and this definition of them is as true today as ever. The Corps consists of military specialists whose area of expertise is the beachhead where the sea touches the land. Here is where their combat training and their combat tradition are focused; the naval relationship goes bone deep. Not that this relationship hasn't been challenged—time and again during the past two centuries there have been attempts to sever the connection between the Corps and the Navy. Some of these actions originated, in fact, within the highest ranks of the Navy itself.

That the attempts failed is fortunate because, to paraphrase an old saying, 'If the Marine Corps didn't exist, it would have to be invented.' Every nation must possess the military capacity to support its international priorities, and for the United States, a world leader, this is preeminently the case. The assigned missions of the Corps provide important elements of this capacity; these missions are:

1 To keep itself ready to fight a land action anywhere in the world.
2 To maintain 'seaworthiness'—the proficient ability to coordinate with the Navy in the carrying out of amphibious operations, both during peace and war.
3 To set and maintain standards as a stable, professional combat force by which military comparisons may be made.

It is in this third area that an interesting challenge lies for the Marine Corps: to develop and perfect its proficiency in combined sea, land and air operations. Old interservice rivalries still make for difficulties in the smooth and successful carrying out of such actions, but the near future may see the Marine Corps, with its long experience in air-sea-land combat, serving as a catalyst for maximum operational cooperation among the three branches of Service.

Left: Marines of 3rd Battalion, First Marine Regiment, check a hut in Quang Tri province, Vietnam, during Operation Badger Tooth.

FROM THE REVOLUTION TO THE CIVIL WAR

'Drum, Fife and Colors'—1775-1783

In April of 1775 Governor Gage, England's man in Massachusetts, sent a strong force of British Redcoats marching toward Concord to destroy a colonist munition supply he'd learned was stored there. As the soldiers marched through the night, Paul Revere and others rode to spread the alarm, and when the British reached Lexington at dawn, grim-faced minute men were lined up to meet them. A shot rang out—fired by whom no one knows to this day—volleys were exchanged, and when the shooting ceased, eight patriots lay dead on the village green. The Redcoats pressed on to Concord where, in an incident made vivid by Ralph Waldo Emerson,

> . . . the embattled farmers stood,
> And fired the shot heard round the world.

Several weeks later, in an atmosphere of crisis, the Continental Congress convened in Philadelphia, a gathering of the most distinguished men in the colonies. Each Colony was a separate legal entity, independent of the others though answerable to the Crown, and each had its own ideas about what actions the Congress should take. Months of struggle then followed in an attempt to work out some basis for reconciliation between the Crown and the American people, and time after time these efforts were insultingly rebuffed by King George III. Gradually the conciliatory spirit of the Congress waned, to be replaced by a sterner attitude, and in November of the year this new spirit found expression in a landmark resolution in American military history.

Sitting in Tun Tavern, a popular Philadelphia inn of the day, a committee of the Congress drafted a resolution that the entire legislative body approved on 10 November 1775. It called for the creation of a new military force to be known as the Continental Marines. The owner of the Tun Tavern, Robert Mullan, a popular and energetic patriot, was named a Marine captain, and Samuel Nicholas, owner of another tavern, was designated commandant of the Continental Marines. Mullan began to actively recruit for the organization, and soon was able to report great success to his senior officer, Captain Nicholas; by early in 1776 the Continental Marines would be ready for their initial action.

Below : A more modern recruiting poster emphasizes Marine traditions.

The American Revolution saw service by three types of Marines: the ones belonging to each Colony's own navy (more about these units later); the Marines aboard privateer ships authorized by Congress to attack enemy vessels for personal profit; and, most importantly, the Continental or Regular Marines. Before detailing the exploits of the Continental Marines, it will be useful to briefly trace the military origins of this organization.

Forerunners of the Corps

Experience as 'sea soldiers' was nothing new to the American colonists; their previous experience was gained, ironically, in service for, rather than against, the Crown. The colonists were British by birth or ancestry, and they gave the English kings their loyalty until George III's increasingly harsh civil and economic actions against them finally turned loyalty into rebellion.

As early as 1740, four battalions made up of 3000 Colonial men were raised for service in England's war with Spain. Designated the 43rd Regiment of Foot, they came to be known as 'Gooch's Marines,' a reference to their popular leader, Colonel William Gooch. In 1741 Gooch led his regiment in an attack on Cartagena, Spain, where he was wounded. Several months later the Marines went ashore in Cuba and secured Guantanamo Bay for the British fleet as a base.

Another name associated with the regiment, that of Admiral Edward Vernon, the British commander, later was taken by a young Marine officer in the regiment for a home he built at Little Hunting Creek, Virginia; he called it 'Mount Vernon.' The officer was Lawrence Washington, and on his death the home passed to his younger brother, the first president.

With the end of warfare with Spain, the Marines found a role for themselves in the British Navy in skirmishes against the French. During ship-to-ship actions they served as marksmen, often firing down on the other vessel from perches in the rigging, and were the main force in boarding parties. They also were the ships' security detachments, keeping the hard-worked sailors in line; this duty engendered testy feelings between sailors and Marines, feelings that persist to a degree even to this day.

'The Original Eight'

Six months before the founding of the Continental Marines, in May 1775, the Continental Congress responded to news that American forces holding Fort Ticonderoga and Crown Point were 'in a feeble state' by requesting the governor of Connecticut to reinforce these garrisons in nearby upper New York with fresh troops from his Colony's forces. By direction of the Crown, many of the colonies had long maintained their own Army, naval and Marine forces modeled on British prototypes, in addition to providing men for service in British units.

A body of troops quickly left Hartford, and with them was 'money escorted with eight Marines [from the Connecticut Navy], well spirited and equipped.' The Marines and soldiers successfully made their way through hostile Indian and British forces to relieve the beleaguered garrisons. The 'Original Eight,' as they came to be known, were representative of Marines in service before the Revolution with the navies of eight colonies: Connecticut, Massachusetts,

Rhode Island, Pennsylvania, Maryland, Virginia, North Carolina and Georgia.

'Continental risque and pay'

On 15 June 1775, with the enthusiastic sponsorship of John Adams, the selection of George Washington as Commanding General of the military forces of all the colonies was very rapidly approved by the Congress.

Washington quickly discovered, on inventorying his available materials, that the total supply of gun powder for the Army was ninety kegs—which worked out to nine rounds per man and nothing for his artillery.

Pages 526-527: George Washington reviews his ragged troops at Valley Forge.
Left: Captain Porter's Marines on the attack during the Battle of Princeton in January 1777.
Below: Captain Nicholas and Lieutenant Parke look on as the first Marines are inspected in December 1775.

Above : Captain John Paul Jones of the *Bonhomme Richard*, one of the earliest supporters of the Marine Corps.

However, in October the Congress learned of two unescorted British ships sailing toward the colonies from England loaded with munitions. They ordered General Washington to obtain two armed vessels from Massachusetts and use them to capture the merchant ships, which was subsequently done. The vessels were placed on 'Continental risque and pay,' which meant that Congress would both pay the crews and be responsible for insuring the ships against loss or capture.

Congress further instructed Washington to give 'proper encouragement to the Marines and seamen' serving aboard the warships; this was penned just prior to the founding of the Continental Marines, and was the first time the Congress ever made written reference to 'Marines.'

By a masterful effort, General Washington was able to procure needed supplies and train men in time to put Colonial military forces into action early in 1776.

Operations of the Continental Marines

On 3 March 1776 the US frigate *Alfred* landed 268 Marines, under the command of Captain Samuel Nicholas, on New Providence Island in the Bahamas for their first military expedition. Within 13 days the Marine raiding party captured two forts, occupied Nassau town, took control of Government House and seized 88 guns, 16,535 shells and other supplies—an auspicious beginning for the new organization.

On the trip home the *Alfred* encountered the HMS *Glasgow*, a 20-gun British warship, off Block Island, and in a night action the ship's Marine unit experienced its first combat losses, Second Lieutenant John Fitzpatrick and six enlisted men. The *Glasgow* suffered four casualties, all caused by the muskets of Continental Marines.

Upon his return Nicholas was promoted to Major, and in December 1776 he and approximately 300 of his men joined Washington's Army in Pennsylvania just before the second battle of Trenton, in time to escape a trap set by Lord Cornwallis's forces. Soon after they fought alongside Army units in a successful strike at the enemy's flank and rear on 3 January 1777. This was the first instance recorded of Marines joining Army units in action; it would happen again many times in the Corps's history.

In the spring of that year Washington incorporated some of the Marines into artillery units of his reorganized Army, while the remainder went back to naval

Above : Marines raise the flag above one of the captured forts on New Providence in March 1776.

Below : The Marines come ashore at New Providence in the Corps' first amphibious operation.

duties. The Marine artillerymen participated in the defense of Fort Mifflin on the Delaware River. From 22 October until 15 November 1777, a force of twelve British ships, along with Hessian artillery batteries, pounded the fort into rubble, yet the stubborn defenders were able to fire back and prevent the enemy from relieving their units holding Philadelphia.

On 10 January 1778 a small force of Marines commanded by Captain James Willing set sail down the Mississippi aboard an ancient boat renamed by Willing the *Rattletrap*, headed for New Orleans. During the next year the detachment operated in the area of that city, primarily attacking British traders, until they returned north to join in actions against hostile Indians.

Some of the subsequent Marine land actions of the war were: participation in a joint Army-Navy attempt to seize a British fort established at Penobscot Bay, Maine (though the action was unsuccessful, the Marines were commended for their 'forcible charge on the enemy'); in May 1780, a gallant but futile attempt by 200 Marines and sailors to save Charleston, South Carolina, from a superior British force; an amphibious attack by Marines from the frigate *South Carolina* on the Isle of Jersey in the English Channel during the winter of 1780–1781, the last such attack of the war.

Above: The action between the *Bonhomme Richard* and the *Serapis* was one of the most closely contested of the War of Independence.

Aboard the Bonhomme Richard

Marines figured prominently in American naval actions of the war. They took part in the attacks on English ships in European waters of the American ship *Reprisal* until its loss. In April 1778 a Marine detachment took part in two raids on the soil of Great Britain conducted from the *Ranger*, commanded by John Paul Jones; this was among

Below: The British forces retreat during the action at Penobscot Bay.

the few such landings on British soil in over 700 years. Aboard another command of Jones's, the famous *Bonhomme Richard*, the Marine unit was not American but foreign, consisting of three Irish officers and 137 French Marines from Louis XVIs *Régiment Royaux d'Infanterie et d'Artillerie de Marine.* Louis's generosity had more to do with his ongoing war with England than with sympathy for the American cause. The French Marines were valiant fighters, however, and played a major part in accomplishing Jones's renowned victory over the British frigate HMS *Serapis* off Flamborough Head on 23 September 1779. Biographers of Captain Jones say he placed great reliance on Marines, both foreign and American, and expressed his admiration for their military discipline. He tried during the Revolution to persuade the Congress to build the Continental Marines into a larger body, but without success.

The Continental Marines' last significant action at sea took place in January 1783 when the Marine detachment aboard the American warship *Hague* boarded and seized the British ship *Baille* in the West Indies. The signing of the Treaty of Paris on 11 April 1783, brought about an end of the American Revolutionary War and, before long, of the Continental Marines as well. When the sale of the *Alliance*, last of the nation's warships, was authorized on 3 June 1785, the Continental Marines—which once had numbered 124 officers and about 3000 men—went out of existence along with the Navy.

After his release from service, Major Samuel Nicholas returned to Philadelphia and his tavern business. Though the Continental Marines preceded the Marine Corps as we know it today, that early organization's military prowess helped create the new nation, and for this reason Corps historians honor Nicholas with the designation of first Marine Commandant.

'An Act for Establishing a Marine Corps'—1798-1820

Among many concerns of the first United States Congress that met in 1789 were attacks on American merchant ships being made by Barbary pirates in the Mediterranean and by French privateers on the high seas; the privateers were unleashed by their government as a way of harassing sea commerce between America and France's enemies, the British. But so pressing were domestic matters facing the American legislators that not until 1794 did Congress get around to authorizing the reactivation of the Navy and the building of six frigates.

Another two years passed before the necessary funds were voted for constructing three ships, the *United States* the *Constellation* and the *Constitution*. All three vessels were launched the following year, 1797; by Congressional act each carried a Marine detachment consisting of five lieutenants, eight sergeants, eight corporals, three drummers, three fifers and 140 privates. Since there was then no Marine Corps as such, the Marines were considered part of the Navy crew.

The attacks on American shipping were on the mind of Alexander Hamilton when in 1798 he wrote to Secretary of War James McHenry:

> This is too much humiliation after all that has passed—Our merchants are very indignant—Our government very prostrate in the view of every man of energy.

McHenry subsequently recommended to House Naval Committee chairman Samuel Sewell of Massachusetts that an organization of Marines be formed, and before long the Committee sent to the House floor a bill calling for the creation of 'a battalion, to be called the Marine Corps.' The bill passed; the Senate changed the size of the proposed Corps to a regiment and, with House concurrence, *'An Act for Establishing and Organizing a Marine Corps'* went to President John Adams for his signature on 11 July 1798, the official 'birth date' of the Corps.

The table of organization of the fledgling

Top left: Capture of the *Sandwich* during the quasi-war with France, 11 May 1800.
Above left: Marines and seamen from Jones' *Ranger* raid the British port of Whitehaven, 22 April 1778.
Left: Replica of the Tun Tavern, birthplace of the Marines, built for the Sesquicentennial Fair in 1926.
Below: Marines and seamen aboard the *Bonhomme Richard* in action with the men of the *Serapis*.

Left : Lieutenant O'Bannon and his men raise the American flag above the citadel at Derna in Tripoli.

organization called for 33 officers and 848 'noncommissioned officers, musicians and privates.' Their uniforms were quite colorful; the shortcoats and trousers were blue edged in brilliant red, and their hats, with one turned-up side, displayed a yellow band and a cockade. Sergeants carried yellow epaulettes on their shoulders, officers wore long blue coats with red cuffs and golden epaulettes, and all the uniforms had stiff leather collars that earned the Marines their famous nickname, 'Leathernecks,' which remains to this day.

The Corps's mission was 'any . . . duty on shore as the President, at his discretion, shall direct.' The Corps was to be part of the Army or the Navy, 'according to the nature of the service in which they shall be employed,' and therefore regulated alternately by either the Articles of War or by Navy Regulations. This unwieldy proviso would create many difficulties for the Corps in the years ahead.

Scarcely a day after he signed the Act establishing the Corps, President Adams appointed William Ward Burrows of Philadelphia as its Major Commandant. Burrows, a well-reputed veteran of the Revolution, set to his recruiting job with zest and energy, and within six months had the Corps up to strength—this despite the fact that the pay for a private was only one dollar a week. Burrow's good work did not go unnoticed; he was promoted to lieutenant colonel and Congress authorized an increase in the Corps's strength of an additional eight officers and 196 men.

Two actions of Burrows worthy of particular note were his founding of the Marine Band and his decision to move Marine headquarters from his home city of Philadelphia to Washington, the new capital. On 31 March 1801, riding horseback with his friend, President Thomas Jefferson, he selected as the place for the Corps's Headquarters a location 'near the Navy Yard and within easy marching distance of the Capital,' the site at which it stands to this day. Burrows retired in 1804 for health reasons, replaced by Franklin Wharton; Burrows's commandancy would serve as a model for all those who followed him.

'To arms, especially by sea'

The leaders of the young nation, burdened with many governmental difficulties, had for years gritted their teeth and borne the attacks on American merchant ships of French privateers. The situation stung the pride of John Adams during his time as President; on 22 May 1798, he had rallied the Harvard graduating class with the patriotic cry, 'To arms, then, my young friends—to arms, especially by sea.' Six

Left : Marines are paid off at the end of the War of Independence. The permanent establishment of the Corps dates from 1798.

Above: Stephen Decatur, hero of actions against the Barbary pirates and during the War of 1812. *Right:* Decatur and his men during the action to burn the *Philadelphia* in Tripoli in 1804.

days later the President ordered an 'undeclared naval war' against France, and America's small navy went into action against one of the world's largest fleets.

Marine detachments served aboard every warship, and they participated in the many sea skirmishes that occurred. The Marines of the USS *Constitution* executed a daring attack on a French force lying in the ostensibly neutral port of Puerto Plata on the shore of Santo Domingo, then a Spanish colony. The French held a prize ship, the British vessel *Sandwich*, and in a maneuver reminiscent of the wooden horse ploy of the Trojans, 80 Marines and sailors entered the harbor hidden below-decks on the commandeered American sloop *Sally* and took the *Sandwich*. They then stormed and captured the Spanish fort, spiked its guns and sailed off with their prize. This was the first combat landing on foreign soil of the new Corps.

The USS *Constellation*, with 41 Marines aboard, engaged and severely damaged two French frigates, the *Insurgente* and *Vengeance*. The *Vengeance* limped into Dutch Curaçao seeking aid, but the neutral Dutch refused to get involved, whereupon a French unit landed, occupied part of the island and attacked the Dutch garrison in Willemstad, the capital. When the Dutch appealed to nearby American naval forces for help, the USS *Patapsco* and *Merrimack* responded, on 23 September 1800. Under covering cannon fire from the ships, Lieutenant James Middleton of the *Patapsco* and 70 Marines from both ships landed and engaged the French units laying siege to Willemstad. During that night the French broke off the action, boarded their badly-shattered ships and sailed away.

By the time peace was reached between the United States and France in February 1801, the young American war fleet had captured 85 French vessels, with the Marines contributing valiantly to this accomplishment. Within the year, however, a drive for peacetime economies and reduction of the national debt led President Jefferson to order the selling of naval vessels and the cessation of warship construction. The President also directed Secretary of the Navy Robert Smith to reduce Marine enlisted strength, an ill-advised move that brought Corps strength down to 26 officers and 453 men just at the time when the United States was entering the Tripolitan War in the Mediterranean.

Subduing the Barbary pirates

For many years the United States and European powers paid tribute to the Barbary pirates of the states of Morocco, Tunis, Algeria and Tripoli as the price for sailing their merchant ships on the Mediterranean. By 1801 the United States's payments equalled two million dollars, one-fifth of the nation's annual revenues. When the demand of Yusuf Caramanli, Pasha of Tripoli, for even larger payments from America was refused, he declared war in May 1801. Four vessels of the United States's now-tiny Navy—the USS *President*, *Philadelphia*, *Essex* and *Enterprise*—were formed into the Mediterranean Squadron and sent to protect American interests in that area. But the small force was hard-pressed to carry out its mission against the powerful Barbary pirate fleet.

On 31 October 1803 the frigate *Philadelphia* grounded on a reef off of Tripoli and was captured by pirate ships, floated free and towed into port as a prize. While negotiations went on regarding the payment of ransom for release of the crew Lieutenant Stephen Decatur, USN, and a force including Marines under the command of Sergeant Solomon Wren slipped into Tripoli Harbor, overcame the pirates aboard the *Philadelphia*, burned it to the waterline and escaped without a casualty. (The captured

Above: The battle between the American ship *Planter* and a French privateer during the quasi-war with France, 10 July 1799.

crew was subsequently released after the payment of a large ransom, another humiliation for the young nation.)

O'Bannon at Tripoli

The most extraordinary exploit of the war was that of Marine Lieutenant Presley N O'Bannon and William Eaton, American diplomatic agent and former army general. Hamet Bey, brother of Yusuf Caramanli and rightful ruler of Tripoli, was in exile in Egypt; Eaton persuaded Hamet to join in a land assault with the purpose of restoring him to his throne. To do this, Eaton and O'Bannon recruited a mercenary force in Alexandria and led them on a daring seven-week trek across 600 miles of the Libyan desert. Surviving mutiny, pilfery, religious clashes among the men and terrible thirst and hunger, the two Americans brought their motley force through the desert to the walls of Derna, Yusuf's capital, on 25 April 1805. They sent a messenger into the city with a note ordering the bey, or mayor, to surrender, to which he replied, 'Your head or mine.'

O'Bannon and Eaton informed him that they had no objection to his terms.

The Americans launched an attack supported by a bombardment of the city delivered from three warships in the harbor. O'Bannon's force, made up of Marines and mercenaries, was at the center of the attack on the walls, and quickly came under the heaviest fire. When the mercenaries began to panic, O'Bannon and Eaton led them in a charge against the enemy. Eaton fell wounded, along with three Marines and several mercenaries, but the surprise tactic worked—the startled enemy were caught off balance and began a retreat.

Pressing their advantage, O'Bannon's men soon drove the enemy from the walls. Hamet Bey then led his Arab troops in a successful attack on the bey's castle, and by 4:00 PM Lieutenant O'Bannon was able to raise the Stars and Stripes above the city, the first American flag to fly over a captured fortification in the Old World. This victory contributed to the signing of a favorable peace treaty with the Pasha of Tripoli on 4 June 1805.

In appreciation for O'Bannon's services, Hamet Bey presented him with his own sword, a handsome curved blade with ivory hilt topped by a golden eagle head. The Mameluk sword, so called after the Egyptian sect that forged it, subsequently served as the pattern for swords carried to this day by Marine officers.

War with Britain

To the great nations of Europe—England, France and Spain—the winning of independence by the United States in 1783 was of small importance, and they demonstrated this attitude by continuing to treat American merchant ships as though they belonged to a colony. Particularly flagrant in this regard was Great Britain, despite US trade with them; in the words of President James Madison to the Congress in June of 1812:

> They hover over and harass our entering and departing commerce. To the most insulting pretensions, they have added the most lawless proceedings in our very harbors, and have wantonly spilt American blood within the sanctuary of our territorial jurisdiction. . . .

The mood of the Congress was not with Madison, however; though they authorized an enlargement of the Marine Corps to 1869 officers and men, the Congress failed to vote an appropriation to make the increase possible. The Corps had not recovered from the Jefferson-imposed reductions in its size, and when war against Great Britain was declared by the Congress on 18 June 1812, the Corps consisted of 10 officers and 483 enlisted men, with less than half of them on sea duty. And though the popular slogan for the war was 'Free Trade and Sailors's Rights,' the American Navy consisted of a mere three first-line warships.

In actions on the Atlantic, this small force performed well. The USS *Constitution* destroyed HMS *Guerrière* on 19 August off Nova Scotia, the *United States* seized the *Macedonian* on 25 October and the *Constitution* sank the *Java* on 28 December off Brazil, earning for itself the now-famous accolade, 'Old Ironsides.' Marines figured in each of these engagements, delivering withering musket fire and playing a major role in boarding-party attacks.

Out of the War of 1812 came what is perhaps the most incredible saga in the history of the Marine Corps, that of a 23-year-old lieutenant named John Marshall

Below: British forces advance on Washington, as seen in a somewhat fanciful contemporary engraving.

Gamble. Gamble was in charge of a Marine detachment aboard the frigate *Essex*, commanded by Captain David Porter, when it sailed from the Delaware Capes on 28 October 1812; he would not see America again for almost three years. Off the Galapagos Islands the *Essex* encountered and captured three British whaling ships. Captain Porter placed cannon and a crew of 14 men aboard one of the ships, and used his authority to commission it as the USS *Greenwich*. He placed the vessel under the command of Lieutenant Gamble, making him the only Marine in history to captain a ship of the United States Navy.

In July of 1813 Gamble demonstrated impeccable seamanship when he closed with and captured a dreaded British raider, the *Seringapatam*. That October, Porter left Gamble on Nukuhiva in the Marquesas Islands in charge of a hastily-built fortification, three British prize ships, a number of prisoners, and supported by just 22 American officers and men. When several thousand hostile native Typees massed for an attack on his camp, Gamble promptly attacked them first with his handful of men and forced their withdrawal.

On 7 May 1814 British captives attacked the Americans, wounding Gamble in the process, but he managed to rally the Americans aboard one of the British prize ships, fight off a native attack that inflicted further casualties, then set sail without charts and with a crew of seven wounded men.

The Americans were taken captive by a British warship and, when news of peace came, set ashore in Rio de Janeiro, penniless and 5000 miles from home. Gamble finally managed to find a ship that would give passage to him and his six surviving men—three Marines and three sailors—and they arrived home in August 1815. For his heroism John Marshall Gamble soon was brevetted major.

The Battles for Washington and Baltimore

The British, along with their 'minor' war with the United States, had been engaged in a major struggle with the armies of Napoleon, and when they won a victory over the French in 1814 it released great numbers of Redcoats for action on the North American continent. The British strategy was to split the United States in two so that they might lay claim to New England during the protracted peace negotiations going on in Ghent, Belgium. They further decided that a strike against the capital, Washington, would devastate American morale; in overall charge of this operation they placed Rear-Admiral Sir George Cockburn, whose temperament can be judged by the fact that he later had his portrait painted with a flaming Washington as the background.

The British attack came on 19 August 1814, when 4000 men under Major General Robert Ross landed at Benedict, Maryland, joined up with two additional battalions and set out for Washington. American plans for the defense of the Capital were, to say the least, ill-conceived, dependent primarily on a rag-tag force of 6000 militia. The battle was joined at Bladensburg, a small town just outside Washington; at the first sound of fire from the British attackers the militia threw away their weapons and fled the field. However, the American defenders also included a battalion of 114 Marines led by Captain Samuel Miller, serving under Commodore Joshua Barney, whose force also included a few battle-experienced sailors. This group stood their ground, awaiting the British charge. As Barney later reported:

> I reserved our fire. In a few minutes the British advanced, when I ordered an 18-pounder to be fired, which completely cleared the road.

The effect of their fire was devastating, blowing away an entire British company. The Marines and sailors inflicted 249 casualties and delayed the attackers for two hours, but the British pressed forward and finally forced the defenders to fall back.

Before nightfall almost every public building in Washington had been burned, including both the White House and the Capital. The one bright note for Americans in the defeat was the performance of the small unit of sailors and Marines. A contemporary observer commented:

No troops could have stood better; and the fire of both artillery and musketry has been described as to the last degree severe. Commodore Barney himself, and Captain Miller of the Marines in particular, gained much additional reputation.

The Marines left Washington to join other Marine units in an attempt to defend Baltimore and its bastion, Fort McHenry. The British attacked by land and sea, and for days the air was filled with 'the rockets red glare, the bombs bursting in air'; the sight inspired an American prisoner aboard one of the British ships, Francis Scott Key, to pen what later became the nation's anthem.

Defending New Orleans

As the United States's principal city on the Gulf coast, New Orleans was an important military objective of the British. Vice-Admiral Sir Alexander Cochrane was assigned to capture the port, and given 9000 seasoned soldiers to serve in carrying out the task. Ironically, the attack force approached New Orleans on the same day, 14 December 1814, that the long-negotiated peace treaty was signed in far-off Ghent.

The defensive forces of General Andrew Jackson included 300 Marines under Major Daniel Carmick, as well as many pirates from the Creole band of Jean and Pierre Lafitte, all joined against their common enemy. Carmick was shot in an American counterattack against the British on December 28, and later died of his wounds. His men quickly moved into other units where, being true professionals, they served with distinction. The British struck again

Above: Marine uniforms of 1816. Drummers of military units of this period were often dressed in colors contrasting with those worn by the rank and file.
Below: The Battle of Lundy's Lane, 25 July 1814, an important engagement during the war with Britain.

and again, but without success, and by the time news finally came of the peace treaty, 2036 of their men were dead or wounded and over 500 of them prisoners. American casualties were fewer than 100. The Congress expressed its thanks 'for the valor and good conduct of Major Daniel Carmick, of the officers, noncommissioned officers, and Marines under his command.'

Unfortunately, the history of the Corps was marked by darker episodes during the war; foremost among these was the flight of Marine Commandant Franklin Wharton from Washington just prior to the British attack. Particularly incensed at Wharton's behavior was Marine Captain Archibald Henderson, who had commanded with distinction the Marine detachment aboard the *Constitution*. Henderson brought charges against the Commandant for neglect of duty and conduct unbecoming an officer and a gentleman. Though a trial held on

Above: A Marine officer (left) displays his finest uniform for a social occasion *c.* 1830.

22 September 1817 acquitted Wharton, the blot on his reputation marked him until his death the following year. His successor, Major Anthony Gale, lasted only two years, before he was court-martialed and eventually dismissed the service, cashiered for drunkenness and a number of other disreputable offences.

Fortune smiled on the Corps that same year, however, when Archibald Henderson was selected to be fifth Commandant of Marines. He took over a Corps rocked by the scandals created by its previous two Commandants, and pulled this way and that by demands from both the Army and Navy. Henderson would prove to be more than a match for these challenges.

'Gone to Fight The Indians'—1820-1859

Following the signing of the peace treaty of 1815, the Corps was at a peak of fighting efficiency, morale and public approval, but over the next five years the combined effects of peacetime economies and the abrupt loss of two Commandants under shabby circumstances threw the Corps into a state of confusion and disarray. That was how Major Archibald Henderson found it when he assumed the commandancy in 1820.

Commandant Archibald Henderson

At age 38 Henderson was, and has remained, the youngest man ever to become Commandant of the Marines. Enlisting in 1806, the slim redhead had served with distinction during the recent war, indicated by the fact that he was brevetted Major for his heroism. The Virginia-born officer was organized, direct and forceful in his manner, characteristics that come through in a phrase he once wrote: 'Take care to be right, and then they are powerless.' The problems he would face put Henderson's axiom to a stern test, and would make him work extremely hard and long for his Commandant's modest pay and perquisites of $2636.16 a year.

Right: Death of the British General Packenham during the Battle of New Orleans, 8 January 1815. *Below*: General Jackson inspires his defending forces to throw back the British attacks.

Above: The Marine barracks at Washington DC as seen in an illustration dating from *c.* 1830.

Small actions around the world

Henderson took command at a time when the political and economic interests of the United States were growing around the world, and with this expansion came much work for the Corps.

During 1821 and part of 1822, a force of 300 Marines serving with the Navy's West India Squadron took part in landings and assaults against pirates operating from strongholds on the north coast of Cuba, from which they attacked American commerce in the Caribbean in a manner reminiscent of the Barbary pirates. With cannon and muskets, the Marines put an end to this activity.

On 6 December 1831 President Andrew Jackson sent a message to Congress that presaged the military clash in 1982 between England and Argentina over Argentina's claim to the Falkland Islands. The message concerned the seizure of three American whaling ships for fishing near the Falklands and the holding of their crews on the islands

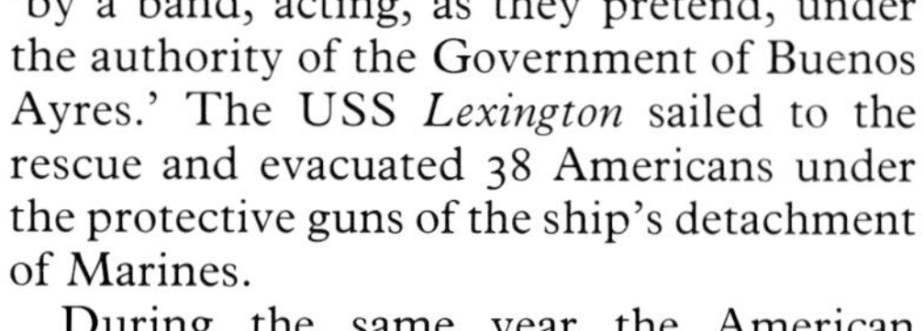

'by a band, acting, as they pretend, under the authority of the Government of Buenos Ayres.' The USS *Lexington* sailed to the rescue and evacuated 38 Americans under the protective guns of the ship's detachment of Marines.

During the same year the American merchant ship *Friendship* was attacked in the port of Kuala Batu in Sumatra by Malay pirates and several crewmen murdered. This was another of many attacks suffered by American ships in that area, and the administration in Washington decided that military action had to be taken. The warship *Potomac* commanded by Commodore John Downes was ordered to Sumatra.

The Malay pirates, 4000 in number, occupied four heavily-armed forts that overlooked the harbor of Kuala Batu. In the dim light of early morning on 7 February 1832, the *Potomac*, fitted out to look like a shabby merchant ship, dropped anchor off Kuala Batu and a landing force of Marines commanded by First Lieutenant Alvin Edson rowed ashore. Also with the detachment was Second Lieutenant George H Terrett, who would later conduct himself heroically at the San Cosme Gate of Mexico City. Edson was wounded in the assault on one of the four forts; Terrett assumed command and, after more than two hours of desperate fighting, the last fort fell to the Americans. Over 150 pirates were killed, along with their rajah leader, Po Mahomet.

For action and danger, the Marines didn't have to travel to such exotic, far-off places—some of their units found plenty of both right at home. Public safety organizations as we know them today, especially police and fire departments, were tiny in size in the early 19th century, and the Marines were regularly called on to help out.

In 1824 Marines from the Charlestown Navy Yard detachment helped put out a large fire in Boston. When arsonists set fire to the US Treasury in Washington, DC, Marines from 'Eighth and Eye'—Corps Headquarters located at Eighth and I Streets, SE—did double service as firefighters and as guards of the building's treasures. A great fire broke out in New York in December 1835, and Brooklyn Navy Yard sent Marines under Lieutenant Colonel John Marshal Gamble of War of 1812 fame, as well as seamen, to fight the blaze and guard against looters; the Marines were credited with blasting the firebreaks that saved Manhattan.

When inmates at Massachusetts State Prison rioted in 1824 and holed up in the mess hall with a guard as hostage, Marines from the Boston barracks came to help. Major R D Wainwright led 30 Marines into the mess hall to confront 283 armed and determined prisoners. Wainwright ordered his men to cock and level their muskets. 'You must leave this hall,' he told the inmates. 'I give you three minutes to decide.

Left: Uniforms of the 1840s. From right, a Marine lieutenant, a Marine staff officer and naval officers.

Above : A Colt revolving carbine used by the Marines during the war against the Creeks and Seminoles.
Below : Leatherneck. A leather stock of the type worn by Marines until 1875, which gave the Corps its nickname.

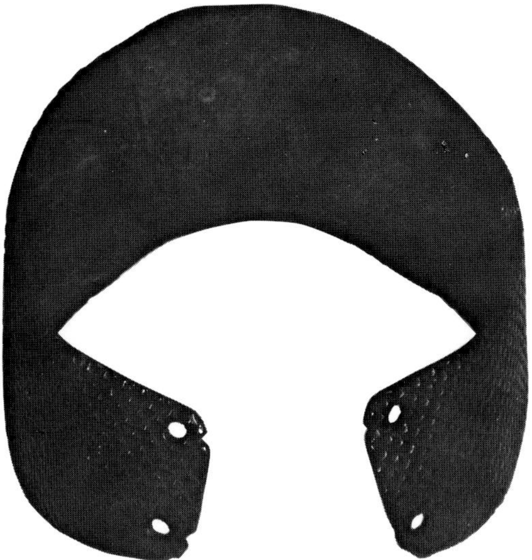

If at the end of that time a man remains, he will be shot dead. I speak no more.'

In two and a half minutes 'the hall was cleared as if by magic.'

A 'skirmish' of greater potential danger to the Marine Corps began on 8 December 1829, when President Andrew Jackson sent a message to the Congress recommending 'that the Marine Corps be merged into the artillery or infantry.' At the root of this executive assault were continuing difficulties with running the Corps under both Army and Navy regulations, financial irregularities resulting from that awkward arrangement, and the hostility of the Navy's Board of Commissioners, a group roughly equivalent to England's Admiralty.

Votes in both houses of Congress in 1830 resulted in shaky support for the Corps. But its attackers did not give up; the following year Secretary of the Navy John Branch recommended 'discontinuance of the Marine Corps . . . in its present fluctuating condition,' and its placement 'wholly under navy discipline and laws.' Commandant Henderson had no objection to such a proposal; as early as 1823 he had written: 'The Marine Corps is, and must continue to be, an appendage of the Navy, participating in its prosperity or sharing its adversity—in war braving with it the same dangers, and in peace asking nothing of it but sheer justice.'

On 30 June 1834 Henderson got his wish for justice—Congress passed 'an Act for the Better Organization of the Marine Corps,' which set the Corps's peacetime strength at 63 officers and 1224 enlisted men, made it a semi-autonomous part of the United States Navy with its own Headquarters and Commandant, and promoted Henderson to colonel. Though the Corps would come under many more political attacks, a watershed had been successfully passed.

War with the Seminoles and Creeks

Long the objects of unremitting pressures to force them off their ancestral lands, the Creek Indians of Georgia and Alabama and the Seminoles of Florida's Everglades joined in an uprising when attempts were begun to deport them to reservations west of the Mississippi River. On 23 May 1836, acting in his capacity as Commander in Chief of the Armed Forces, President Jackson detached all able-bodied Marines to service with the Army for the duration of the emergency.

Commandant Henderson was quick to respond; he reduced all Marine detachments at Navy installations to sergeants's guards, and in ten days had assembled a two-battalion regiment consisting of 38 officers and 424 enlisted men, more than half the Corps of that time. Before he strode out of Marine Headquarters gripping his gold-headed walking stick, legend has it Henderson tacked this note to his office door:

> Gone to fight the Indians. Will be back when the war is over.
>
> A. Henderson
> Col.Comdt.

By that summer's end the Creek uprising had been suppressed, and the Marines were moved south to Florida, arriving in September. When the Army commander, Major General T H Jesup, divided his forces into two brigades, Colonel Henderson was given command of one of them, a patchwork organization consisting of the Marine regiment, Creek Indian scouts, volunteers from Georgia, and infantry and artillery units from the Army. Henderson led his brigade in an action against the Seminoles northeast of Fort Brooke—now Tampa—on 27 January 1837, and won a victory, one of the few accomplished against a determined foe. For this, Henderson was brevetted brigadier general, making him the first general officer in the Corps's history.

The government forces tried with little success to pursue the Seminoles through the Everglades Swamp, and in 1842 the war dwindled to a conclusion—no treaty ever was signed—under conditions favorable to the Indians.

A Marine's Life

Life for the average American in the early part of the 19th century was stern and de-

Below : Seminole Indians watch from cover as a boatload of Marines passes by.

Above : American forces storm a Mexican fort at Churubusco in the final stages of the advance to Mexico City.

manding; for the enlisted Marine, it was even more so. The private's pay as late as 1843 still was only $6 a month, plus a $30 a year uniform allowance, with which he was expected to maintain himself in impeccable array. And discipline was severe. Drunks were made to drink several quarts of salt water, which had unpleasant and sobering effects; falling asleep on watch called for walking guard duty for several months while wearing an iron collar and dragging ankle chains-and-balls; disobeying the commands of a sentry earned twelve lashes from a cat-o'-nine-tails. Other minor violations could lose the offender his daily ration of a gill of grog, a concoction of rum and water which must have helped considerably to alleviate the harsh life.

With it all, men still signed up when the recruiter appeared, as recalled by one old Marine:

'the drummer and I would put on our red full dress tunics, with swallow tails, form a procession and down the street we'd go. The captain bought some bright colored ribbons for the drummer and me, which we tied in bows on our arms and to the buttons on the sides of our shakoes, and when the wind blew we certainly made a fine sight as we marched down Broadway to the Battery, then up the Bowery and back to the rendezvous on Chambers Street, ribbons flying and playing quick-steps all the way. Then the Captain would get up on a dry-goods box in front of the recruiting office and make a speech to the crowd, telling them what a fine place the Marine Corps was for a man and what a chance he'd have to visit foreign ports. That's the way we got recruits in those days.'

Below : General view of the fighting at Churubusco. The American success in this battle and at Chapultepec ensured the fall of the capital.

Against Mexico, ashore and afloat

Just as the push of Americans southward had precipitated hostilities with the Indians living in the area, so the expansion of the country's frontiers into the West and Southwest resulted in another war, this one with the Republic of Mexico.

The particular issues leading to it were America's desire for Mexico's territory of California and for the portion of Mexico called Texas, a name derived from the Indian word *techas*, which meant 'allies' and referred to the Caddo confederacy of tribes that lived in the area. Presidents John Adams and Andrew Jackson had pressed Mexico to sell Texas to the United States and had been refused with indignation; the continuing pressure from Washington for

such a purchase caused tension between the two governments. Curiously, however, Mexico encouraged the movement of Americans into the province in large numbers. When the Texans seceded in 1835 and took over the Alamo, a Mexican Army fortress in San Antonio, the Mexicans counterattacked and killed all the American defenders. A cry of 'Remember the Alamo!' was subsequently exploited by Presidents Tyler and Polk to move the nation toward war. When, on 28 February 1845, Congress voted to annex Texas into the United States, the stage was set for combat.

That October, President Polk sent Marine First Lieutenant Archibald H Gillespie to the West Coast with secret messages for Commodore John D Sloat, commander of the Navy's Pacific squadron; Thomas O Larkin, American consul at Monterey; and Captain John C Fremont, United States Army, engaged in a mapping expedition in California. The messages asked their aid in supporting and encouraging a secession movement in California similar to the one in Texas. Gillespie—described by a contemporary as 'an elegant, precise man with a stiff pointed beard and a temper of the same description'—memorized the President's message, disguised himself as a whisky salesman and set out.

His six month's journey took him by boat to Mexico, by stagecoach across that country to the Pacific, by warship to Honolulu—an unplanned sidetrip to deceive a watchful British admiral; England, too, coveted California—from Honolulu to Monterey, California, and finally into the Sierras by

Right: General Santa Anna commanded the Mexican forces defending the capital but misjudged the direction of the American attack. *Below:* The engagement at Cerro Gordo on 18 April 1847 during the advance from Vera Cruz to Mexico City.

Above: The last-man defense of the Alamo during the Texas War of Independence, a source of inspiration for events in the Mexican-American War.

Above: Dress (right) and working uniforms of a Marine private in 1847.

canoe and horseback to find Frémont. Gillespie's mission was a success, setting the stage for the birth of the California 'Bear Flag' republic on 14 June 1846.

On 11 May 1846 Polk asked Congress to declare war on Mexico, which it quickly did. The first military action of the war took place on May 18 when a Marine detachment fought a skirmish at Burrita, 15 miles up from the mouth of the Rio Grande River. Marines from the Navy's Gulf Coast Squadron next were involved in a series of landings at Mexican ports to establish and maintain a blockade in aid of the thrust toward Mexico City of the army of flamboyant General Zachary Taylor—'Old Rough and Ready.' When Commodore Matthew C Perry took command of the Squadron in March 1847, he initiated a series of amphibious landings, culminating in the attack on San Juan Bautista successfully carried off by 150 Marines and 60 seamen, a victory that closed the Mexicans's last remaining port of entry.

Angered over Taylor's self-promotional involvement with the press, suspecting that it represented presidential aspirations, Polk pinched off supplies to Taylor's forces and instead ordered an attack by Army Major General Winfield Scott—'Old Fuss and Feathers'—out of Vera Cruz toward Mexico City. On the way to this goal, the enlistment time of many of Scott's soldiers ran out and they left for home, bringing his march to a halt in the town of Puebla. Learning of this back in Washington, Marine Commandant Henderson—taking advantage of a 1000-man increase in Corps strength authorized by Congress on 3 March 1847—began a feverish recruiting drive, at the same time obtaining permission for Marines to join Scott to make up his losses. A battalion of Marines 357 strong joined Scott's forces at Puebla on 6 August 1847, and was attached to General John A Quitman's 4th Division, coming under the command of Marine Major Levi Twiggs, a decorated veteran of the Florida campaign.

The main defensive position before Mexico City was Chapultepec, a 200-foot-high promontory on top of which stood a stone castle surrounded by a wall that would have to be scaled. At eight in the morning on 13 September 1847 American troops in position below the walls began their attack up the rock face, including the Marines led by Major Twiggs, armed with his favorite double-barreled shotgun. Musket balls and cannon shot rained down on them; Twiggs was killed in an early volley—'the brave and lamented Twiggs,' General Quitman called him—but despite heavy casualties the assault carried to the base of the wall on top of the hill. Still under deadly fire, the Americans raised scaling ladders and swarmed up the walls, and before long the castle was theirs. Twenty-four Marines were casualties in the assault; among the wounded was Second Lieutenant C A Henderson, son of the Commandant.

Other 4th Division elements, including Marines, pressed on to Mexico City. When the Americans ran into strong enemy resistance, Marine Captain Terrett—who had distinguished himself in 1832 against Malay pirates at Kuala Batu—moved his Marine company forward on his own initiative to burst through a line of Mexican artillery and break up an attack by Mexican lancers; his company was accompanied by a small group of soldiers under Second Lieutenant Ulysses S Grant. The Americans pressed forward toward Mexico City; at dawn General Quitman was about to order an attack when a lone soldier emerged from the city under a white flag. The Mexican army, he said, had slipped away during the night; the city was theirs.

Exhausted and missing one shoe, Quitman led his ragged, bloodied force into Mexico City, where Marine Lieutenant Nicholson ran up the Stars and Stripes. 'The Capital is mine,' Quitman told Marine Captain Baker. 'My brave fellows have conquered it. . . !'

It is said that this victory inspired some unknown Marine to compose a brief lyric to a tune popular in that day, taken from the opera *Genevieve de Brabant* by Jacques Offenbach. The words went like this:

From the halls of Montezuma to the shores of
 Tripoli;
We fight our country's battles on land and on
 the sea.
First to fight for right and freedom and to keep
 our honor clean,
We are proud to claim the title of United States
 Marine.

And so the famous Marine Corps Hymn was born. In 1929 two additional stanzas were added to form the official version of the Hymn, and in 1942 a line of the first stanza was changed to read '. . . In the air, on land, and sea,' in recognition of the Corps's additional dimension of combat.

On 2 February 1848 the Treaty of Guadalupe Hidalgo brought the war to an end. The United States gained Texas, New Mexico—including what would later become Arizona—and California from San Diego north. The cost in American lives was 13,271 men killed in battle, or dead of wounds or disease—a significant number of these being Marines.

Fourteen troubled years

As has always happened following a war, the Corps's strength was cut back, in this instance to its authorized peacetime strength of 1224 enlisted men. But the workload of the Marines did not diminish during the 14-years period from the end of the War with Mexico to the Civil War, for it was a time of great expansion of America's commercial interests. Between 1846 and 1860, for example, the nation's foreign trade would grow by 300 percent, mostly transported by American ships, and Marines would be called on to protect those ships on the high seas and in ports around the world.

However, it became the Corps's duty to suppress rather than protect one part of this shipping, that of slavers sailing from the African coast. Congress had outlawed slave trade in 1808. In 1820 it declared such sea commerce by American-flag ships to be piracy. In 1842 the United States signed the Webster-Ashburton Treaty with England, specifying that the United States would station warships along the African coast to work against the slave trade. This the United States did with the Navy's African Squadron.

When the Squadron's commander, Commodore Matthew C Perry of Mexican War fame, landed in Liberia in 1843 to investigate slaver activities, he was attacked by Ben Crack-O, chief of the Berribees, a tribe involved in the slave traffic. A Marine sergeant sprang forward to Perry's defense and shot the chief, setting off a fight with the tribesmen that ended in a Marine victory. The last Marine landing in Africa against slavers took place in 1860 involving a detachment from the sloop *Marion*.

South America was another troubled area in the 1850s as the USA expanded its interests through the Southern Hemisphere. Marines from the *Congress* and the *Jamestown* landed at Buenos Aires in 1852 in response to reports of threats to American lives and property by rioting Argentines. Within days of that landing Marines from the *Albany* went to the aid of the citizens of San Juan del Sur, Nicaragua, to fight a fire that swept their city; two years later, in July 1854, Marines of the *Cyane* would land to bombard and burn the same city. Marines were in action repeatedly in Panama between 1856 and 1860 to protect the workers of an American company building a railroad across the isthmus to serve the booming California gold fields.

Above: Perry and his Marine escort during the negotiations with Liberian chiefs in 1843, shortly before violence erupted.

Battles of the Barrier Forts in China

China became inflamed during the mid-century with the bloody Taiping religious rebellion, a holocaust that would claim 20 million lives during the 15 years of its course. As this period began, attacks on foreign properties by both warring factions became more and more frequent, and Marines were called in repeatedly to provide protection. The situation came to a head in November 1856 when four so-called 'Barrier Forts' on the Pearl River near Canton—armed with 176 cannon up to ten inches in caliber, set behind granite-faced breastworks seven feet thick—opened fire on American ships.

The Navy steam frigate *San Jacinto* and the sloops-of-war *Portsmouth* and *Levant* sailed up the Pearl, and on 20 November a force of Marines commanded by Captain J D Simms—who had been brevetted for gallantry at Chapultepec—and seamen stormed ashore and splashed through rice fields toward the first of the forts. Supported by a bombardment from the ships, the force charged the walls and drove out the

Below: The US forces on the march from Puebla in early August 1847 in the final stages of the Mexican-American War.

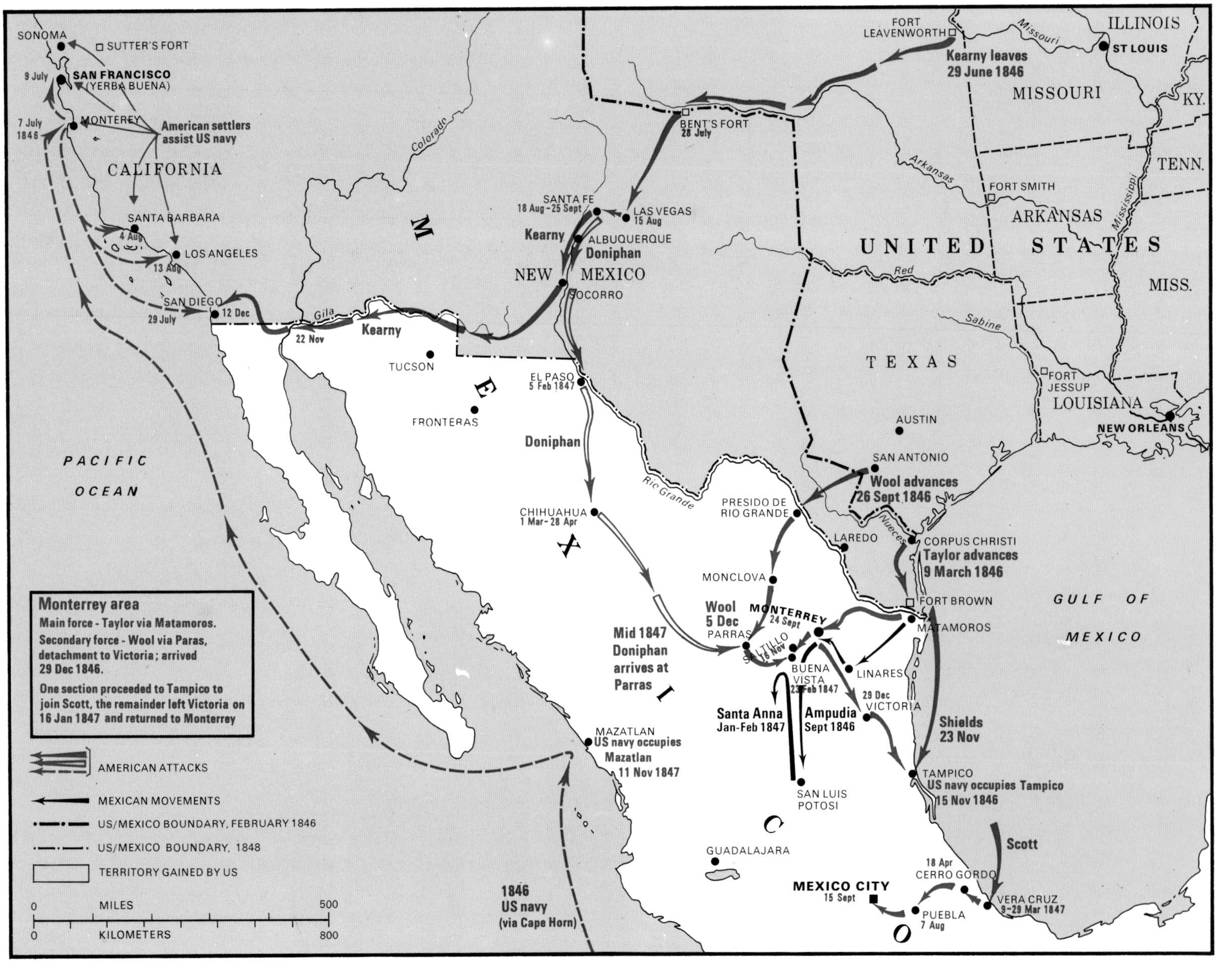

SONOMA
SUTTER'S FORT
9 July
SAN FRANCISCO (YERBA BUENA)
7 July 1846
MONTEREY
American settlers assist US navy
CALIFORNIA
SANTA BARBARA
4 Aug
13 Aug
LOS ANGELES
SAN DIEGO
29 July
12 Dec
Gila
22 Nov
Kearny
TUCSON
Colorado
FRONTERAS
PACIFIC OCEAN
FORT LEAVENWORTH
Missouri
Kearny leaves 29 June 1846
ST LOUIS
ILLINOIS
MISSOURI
KY.
TENN.
BENT'S FORT
28 July
Arkansas
FORT SMITH
ARKANSAS
Mississippi
SANTA FE
18 Aug – 25 Sept
LAS VEGAS
15 Aug
Kearny
ALBUQUERQUE
Doniphan
NEW MEXICO
SOCORRO
UNITED STATES
Red
MISS.
Sabine
TEXAS
FORT JESSUP
LOUISIANA
NEW ORLEANS
AUSTIN
EL PASO
5 Feb 1847
Doniphan
M E X I C O
SAN ANTONIO
Wool advances 26 Sept 1846
Rio Grande
PRESIDO DE RIO GRANDE
Nueces
CHIHUAHUA
1 Mar – 28 Apr
LAREDO
CORPUS CHRISTI
Taylor advances 9 March 1846
MONCLOVA
FORT BROWN
Wool 5 Dec
MONTERREY
24 Sept
MATAMOROS
PARRAS
SALTILLO
16 Nov
Mid 1847 Doniphan arrives at Parras
BUENA VISTA
23 Feb 1847
LINARES
29 Dec
VICTORIA
Santa Anna Jan–Feb 1847
Ampudia Sept 1846
Shields 23 Nov
GULF OF MEXICO
MAZATLAN
US navy occupies Mazatlan 11 Nov 1847
TAMPICO
US navy occupies Tampico 15 Nov 1846
SAN LUIS POTOSI
Scott
GUADALAJARA
18 Apr
CERRO GORDO
MEXICO CITY
15 Sept
VERA CRUZ
9–29 Mar 1847
PUEBLA
7 Aug
1846 US navy (via Cape Horn)
Monterrey area
Main force - Taylor via Matamoros.
Secondary force - Wool via Paras, detachment to Victoria; arrived 29 Dec 1846.
One section proceeded to Tampico to join Scott, the remainder left Victoria on 16 Jan 1847 and returned to Monterrey
AMERICAN ATTACKS
MEXICAN MOVEMENTS
US/MEXICO BOUNDARY, FEBRUARY 1846
US/MEXICO BOUNDARY, 1848
TERRITORY GAINED BY US
0 MILES 500
0 KILOMETERS 800

Left: Marines of Perry's squadron parade as the Commodore meets the Japanese Imperial Commissioner at Yokohama in March 1854.
Above: General Quitman leads his Marines and Army men into Mexico City.
Bottom: The entry into Mexico City.

fort's defenders, 'the Marines being in advance opened fire upon the fugitives with deadly effect.'

Over the following two days the Marines successively stormed and captured the remaining three forts, spiked some guns and threw others in the river, then blew up the fortifications with their own powder. Killed in the action: 500 enemy, 10 Americans.

In his report on the action, the captain of the *Portsmouth*, Commodore A H Foote, wrote this: 'It may be seen in this report how efficient our Marines are in service of this kind; and the inference is inevitable that an increase of that Corps, and of the number of officers and men attached to our ships, would tend to insure success in like expeditions.'

The 'Grand Old Man'

On 1 June 1857, the orderly process of elections in Washington, DC, was threatened by the arrival from Baltimore of a large gang of heavily-armed toughs, self-styled the 'Plug-Uglies,' who were determined to seize and control the polling places. When the city police were frightened off by the gang, Mayor Magruder sent out an emergency call for assistance from the Marines stationed at Corps Headquarters. Near Fifth and K Streets the two groups confronted one another, and the Plug-Uglies aimed a cannon at the line of Marines.

At that moment a white-whiskered man in civilian clothes and carrying a gold-headed cane stepped from the watching crowd and walked up to the line of toughs; it was Marine Commandant Brigadier General Archibald Henderson. The slim, erect 74-year-old man, standing in front of the cannon's muzzle, spoke calmly to the mob: 'Men, you had better think twice before you fire this piece at the Marines.'

A man thrust a pistol at Henderson two feet from his face; the Commandant seized the man and hauled him away to be placed under arrest. A volley of shots aimed at the Marines rang out, and 'they poured in an answering fire.' Within a few seconds the rioters fell back, then took to their heels and fled.

Two years later, on 6 January 1859, Archibald Henderson died while still in office. He had served as commandant for 39 years, under ten presidents, during the most tumultuous years of the nation's growth. Truly the 'Grand Old Man of the Corps,' as his contemporaries called him, Henderson set standards for rigorous training, professional discipline and courageous service that do honor to the Corps to this day.

Henderson also left a Corps that would shortly face an agonizing conflict of interest, one that would go beyond any previous test of the mettle of Marines—their own nation's Civil War.

FROM WAR TO BORROWED PEACE

'Rushing In Like Tigers'—1859–1865

As the decade of the 1850s drew to a close, the level of tension and confrontation in the United States between pro- and anti-slavery forces approached its climactic expression in the tragedy of the Civil War. The tension was manifest within the ranks of the Marine Corps as its members felt the pull of differing loyalties, depending mostly on the region of the country from which they came. Large numbers of Marines soon would resign to serve with the Confederacy, and this loss would leave the Corps poorly equipped to serve the Union effectively during the ensuing conflict.

Most of the resignations were by younger officers of company rank, with the result that the officer corps soon consisted heavily of elderly field-grade officers, some of whom were too feeble to serve in the field. The dash and spirit of another elderly Marine, Archibald Henderson, was nowhere to be seen in the senior ranks, and most particularly not in the person of Commandant Colonel John Harris, Henderson's successor.

As a result of these resignations, as well as of governmental pennypinching regarding the Marines, the Corps would consist in early 1861 of 1892 officers and enlisted men. And even with the subsequent increase authorized by Congress to a strength of 3167, the Corps never reached a size during the war that was adequate for carrying out the missions required of it. However, in one engagement on the eve of the Civil War the Marines did acquit themselves with honor.

Incident at Harpers Ferry

John Brown, a militant abolitionist from Kansas, was gripped by the idea of creating a refuge for runaway slaves in the rugged Southern hills, equipped with sufficient arms for the runaways to protect themselves against slave hunters. To procure the needed arms, Brown led a force of 18 armed men into the small town of Harpers Ferry, Virginia (now West Virginia) on the night of 16 October 1859, and seized the Federal arsenal located there, along with 40 hostages, one of whom was Colonel Lewis Washington, the first president's great-grandnephew.

Within the hour the new commandant of Marines, Colonel John Harris, had ordered into action from Corps headquarters First Lieutenant Israel Green and a force of 86 Marines. Green was told that Colonel Robert E Lee of the Army would be at the scene to assume overall command of the operation.

The Marine unit arrived at midnight of the same day; by the following dawn Colonel Lee had his plans made and a 24-man assault party briefed and ready to go. Lee asked the state militia unit that had arrived on the scene if they wished to conduct the attack on the heavily-fortified arsenal; they declined the offer vigorously. Colonel Lee then ordered Green and an Army cavalry lieutenant, J E B Stuart, to begin the operation.

Stuart walked to the arsenal door and read aloud an ultimatum of surrender, and when Brown would not comply, Stuart waved his cap as a signal to Lieutenant Green and his Marines. In Green's words, 'the men took hold bravely and made a tremendous assault upon the door' with heavy sledges and a battering ram, 'rushing in like tigers.' Green was first through the shattered doorway; a gun inside thundered, the round narrowly missed his head and struck the Marine behind him, Private Luke Quinn, mortally wounding him. Green saw Brown crouched and reloading a carbine; the lieutenant sprang forward and struck Brown down with a saber slash across the side of his neck. Within seconds the fight was won and John Brown's insurrection was over; he would subsequently hang for his attempt.

In a sense it might be said that the first serviceman to die in the Civil War was that unsung Marine, Private Quinn.

A time of low fortunes

This sort of cooperation between Southern and Northern members of American military units ended with the beginning of the Civil War; Colonel Lee and Lieutenant Stuart were distinguished examples of the many men who left Federal forces to join the Army of the Confederacy. Congress authorized Marine Corps expansion to 93 officers and 3074 enlisted men—President Lincoln raised this figure by 1000 more—but these increases could not make up for the losses in experienced personnel suffered by the Corps. As a result, the Marines did not play a major part in the ensuing conflict.

In the months immediately prior to the

Pages 550-551 : Men of the 1st Marines pose for the photographer near Olongapo during the Philippine Insurrection.
Above : A scene during the Battle of Bull Run, one of the least creditable in the Marines' history.
Left : Marines parading outside their barracks in Washington on the eve of the Civil War in 1861.
Right : Union forces on the march across the Potomac during the Civil War.

declaration of war on 15 April 1861, Marine units were employed to reinforce Federal garrisons located in Southern states. A unit of 100 Marines sent to Norfolk Navy Yards destroyed seven Union ships as well as arms and supplies to keep them from the Confederates.

Once war began, the first major action of the Marines was at the First Battle of Bull Run [Manassas] on 21 July 1861. The 353-man Marine unit, part of a 35,000-man Union force, was under Major John G Reynolds, with Major Jacob Zeilin of Mexican War renown in command of a company. The Marine unit that entered the battle consisted primarily of inexperienced

Right : The CSS *Virginia (Merrimack)* engages the Union blockading squadron in Hampton Roads on 8 March 1862, the day before the battle with the *Monitor*.

enlisted men and junior officers. After suffering 44 casualties in the course of three assaults on their position by the riflemen of the 33rd Virginia and the cavalry forces of J E B Stuart, now a Confederate colonel, the Marines broke and ran. This was reported by their commandant, Colonel Harris, to Secretary of the Navy Gideon Welles as 'the first instance in [Marine Corps] history where any portion of its members turned their backs to the enemy,'

Amphibious action along the Southern coast

The naval and amphibious uses to which Marines were put during the balance of the war were far more appropriate to the Corps's training and mission than was their disastrous action at Bull Run. A key strategy of the Union was to blockade Southern ports so as to prevent resupply of Confederate forces, and the Marines served well in the implementation of this strategy.

A month after Bull Run, Marines undertook the first of two operations aimed at gaining naval control of Hatteras Inlet, North Carolina; Confederate privateers were operating out of Puget Sound against Union shipping, and it was an entry point for British blockade runners carrying war materials to the South. On 28 August the Marine contingent from the USS *Minnesota*, along with Army regulars, scrambled from longboats to attack and, in a four-hour-long engagement, took Fort Clark on one side of the inlet. Soon afterward Fort Hatteras on the other side of the inlet fell to the Union attackers. This double loss shook Confederate morale, and the North gained a strategic foothold it would maintain for the rest of the war.

The concept of the Marines as an amphibious fighting force was held strongly

Below : The confused fighting at Bull Run which saw the Marines break and flee for one of very few times in their history.

by Naval Flag Officer Samuel F DuPont, commander of the South Atlantic Blockading Squadron, and together with Marine Major Reynolds he organized a 300-man battalion to that end. The group's first objective was to be Port Royal, South Carolina, but unfortunately, the Marines were given an unseaworthy boat as their transport, the sidewheeler *Governor*, and it foundered in a storm on the way to Port Royal, leaving the Marines unable to join the action.

In March 1862 Reynolds's battalion sailed to seize and occupy Fernandina, Georgia, only to discover when they arrived that Union troops already were there. Next they departed for St Augustine, Florida, to take it, but learned enroute that the Confederate garrison had abandoned the city. At this point DuPont decided there were no missions remaining that called for the special talents of the Marine amphibious battalion. The unit was broken up and the men assigned to various ships' detachments.

This wasn't the end of frustration for the Corps, however. In August 1863 Major Jacob Zeilin was sent with a battalion of 300 Marines to attack the nine fortifications guarding the port of Charleston, South Carolina. Zeilin tried to expand the unit to a regiment and train them in amphibious tactics, but found himself dissatisfied with the results. He was replaced by Major Reynolds, whose first action was to reduce the unit to battalion size and to then provide the men with further training.

On 8 September 1863 a Marine unit with sailors attached attacked Fort Sumter, the most celebrated of the Confederate-held strongholds at Charleston, in a night landing from small boats. The action went badly from the start, with many of the boats getting lost in the darkness; the 150 Marines and sailors who got ashore and were part of the unsuccessful assault took deadly accurate fire from the Confederate defenders, with the result that 44 Marines were killed, wounded or captured. The battalion was taken out of combat and sent to a rear area camp for rest and rehabilitation, but a sickness swept the unit and added to their misery. In early 1864 the battalion was broken up and its members reassigned.

The problems of the Corps at this time were many and pressing, not the least of them being the bitterness that existed between many members of the 'old guard' of staff officers and the younger line officers. These arguments visibly wore down John Harris, the Corps's Commandant, and his death on 12 May 1864, was not unexpected. Secretary of the Navy Welles seized on the event as an opportunity to 'retire the Marine officers who are past the legal age, and to bring in Zeilin as Commandant of the Corps. There seems no alternative.'

Top right: The bombardment and assault of Fort Fisher.
Right: The Marines storm ashore to take the Han River forts near Seoul in Korea in May 1871. Note the marshy terrain.

Above: Petersburg, Virginia, was an important supply base for Lee's Confederate Army of Northern Virginia.

This Welles did, with President Lincoln's approval; every Marine officer senior to Jacob Zeilin was retired, and on 10 June he was appointed as seventh Commandant of the Corps.

The Battle of Fort Fisher

By the end of 1864 Union attacks on Southern ports had neutralized all but that of Wilmington, North Carolina, which blockade runners continued to use as a point of resupply for the Confederacy. Entrance to the port was via Cape Fear River, and guarding that entrance was one of the South's more formidable fortifications, Fort Fisher, defended by 44 large-caliber cannon and more than a thousand troops.

Union action against the fort took place in two phases, the first of which resulted in embarrassment for all involved. It was commanded by an amateur soldier from Massachusetts, politician Major General Benjamin F Butler. On 24 December Butler ordered that a crewless ship filled with explosives be sailed to a point just offshore from the fort and blown up, with the hope of bringing down its walls. When the explosives went off, they did no damage whatsoever to Fort Fisher—the watching Confederates on the ramparts thought some unfortunate blockade runner had suffered an accident.

The following day, Christmas, under cover of heavy fire from Union Navy ships standing offshore, Butler's unit of 3000 men approached the huge fortification from the opposite side of the cape. They got within a few hundred yards of Fort Fisher's walls without drawing fire and apparently undetected—in fact, several daring Northerners actually scaled the walls, entered the fort and returned with trophies. Despite this, Butler showed little inclination to fight, instead ordering that the operation cease and his unit withdraw.

Union Commanding General Ulysses S Grant quickly relieved Butler of his command and replaced him with a professional soldier, Major General A H Terry, USA. Terry brought with him reinforcements of a number sufficient to swell the size of the attacking force to 8500 officers and men. Rear Admiral David D Porter, in overall command of the operation, decided that after a softening-up bombardment by his fleet, a force of 1600 seamen and 400 Marines would execute a diversionary attack from small boats against the front wall of the fort while Terry led his soldiers against the rear wall in the main assault.

The landing operation began at three o'clock in the afternoon of 15 January 1865. The idea of an attack on a fortification by seamen armed only with cutlasses and pistols was, in the words of one of Admiral Porter's own officers, 'sheer, murderous madness.' Once on the beach, the seamen were to wait until the Marines—a hastily-assembled group from the ships in Porter's command—took up positions from which they would deliver covering rifle fire. But neither the seamen nor their naval officers were experienced in land-based combat, and in the ensuing confusion the seamen launched their attack before the Marines were in place. The Confederate defenders in the fort let the attackers get within 40 yards of the walls, then cut them to ribbons with a hail of deadly gunfire. The Marines were ordered into the assault in support of the sailors, and they too were shot down in the attempt. When Porter finally gave the order to cease the attack and withdraw, 309 dead and wounded Marines and sailors were left on the beach. The diversion served its purpose, however—Terry's soldiers fought their way through the fort's defensive breastworks and over the walls to take it.

The bumbled assault on Fort Fisher loosened a storm of charges and countercharges from all the military services, with Admiral Porter at the center of the fire. Porter's defense tried to put the blame off onto the Marines: 'Had the covering party of Marines performed their duty, every one of the enemy would have been killed.' The final effect of the fiasco was to put back the cause of a separate, equal Corps of Marines, organized, trained and equipped to carry out its own unique form of military action, amphibious assaults. It would be many years before such a status would come into being.

Above: Major General Benjamin Frank Butler who led the first attack on Fort Fisher.

A few months later America's most soul-wrenching war ended, on 9 April 1865, when Lee presented his bejeweled sword to Grant in surrender at Appomattox Court House, and the United States, 'a house divided against itself,' began the long, painful process of coming back together.

As for the Corps, it had grown only slightly during the conflict, to a maximum strength of 4167 officers and men. The most telling indication of how lightly Marines had participated in the war could be seen in their casualty figures: 148 killed in combat, 312 dead as a result of other causes. The country's political and military higher authorities still had not decided on a basic mission for the Corps, and until that determination was made the Corps would continue to find its very reason-for-being under repeated assault.

'With a Blasted Muzzle-Fuzzle'—1871-1898

The Marine Corps came out of the Civil War with its reputation at a low point. Marines had not played a meaningful role in the war, most significantly not in their specialities of assaults and amphibious actions, as was obvious from the fact that only 148 Marines were killed in action during the war. Problems of low morale during the conflict had led to an inflated rate of desertions and to angry bickering between line and staff officers. But most shattering to the stability of the Corps had been the defections to the Confederacy of many Marine officers and men. These experiences combined to make the Corps vulnerable to its enemies, and on 18 June 1866 they struck: Marine Commandant Zeilin learned that the House of Representatives had just approved consideration of this resolution:

> Resolved, That the Committee on Naval Affairs be directed to consider the expediency of abolishing the Marine Corps, and transferring it to the Army, and making provision for supplying such military force as may at any time be needed in the Navy, by detail from the Army.

As his predecessors had before him, Commandant Zeilin instantly counter-attacked, soliciting and receiving from the highest-ranking officers in the Navy words of total support for the Corps. A friendly House Naval Affairs Committee reported out the hostile resolution adversely on 21 February 1867, saying that 'on the contrary, the Committee recommends that [the Marine Corps'] organization as a separate Corps be preserved and strengthened . . . [and] that its commanding officer shall hold the rank of a brigadier general.'

Postwar service on many seas

With its existence once again secured, the Corps was ready to take on whatever military assignments might come its way, and in the latter half of the 19th century there would be many. In addition to a number of major actions by the Marines, they made minor landings in Formosa, Japan and Uruguay in the 1860s; Mexico, Colombia and the Hawaiian Islands in the 1870s; Egypt, Korea, Haiti, Samoa and the Hawaiian Islands in the 1880s; Argentina, Chile, Navassa Island, Nicaragua, Korea, North China, the Isthmus of Panama and Nicaragua again in the 1890s. And, too, there were many challenging events for the Corps to deal with right at home in the United States.

Assaults in Korea

In many of the above-mentioned situations the mere presence of US Marines and warships in the region made fighting unnecessary, but this was not the case with Korea in the summer of 1871.

Korea was then known as 'The Hermit Kingdom,' and with good reason, for its people manifested a strong enmity toward any foreigners who dared to enter their territory, demonstrated by their attack upon and killing of the crew of the American vessel *General Sherman* after it was shipwrecked in the Han River. Washington quickly ordered America's Minister to China, Frederick Low, to go to Korea and negotiate a treaty of amity and accord with its people. In May of 1871 Low arrived off the west coast of Korea aboard the USS *Colorado*, flagship of the Asiatic Fleet, accompanied by four other warships, all under the command of Rear Admiral John Rodgers. They dropped anchor at the mouth of the Han River and Rodgers sent off a surveying party in a small boat to find an approach to the capital city of Seoul. As the party worked its way up the channel, it was fired on from one of five forts guarding the mouth of the river.

After demanding an apology from the

Below: Fort Sumter, scene of an unsuccessful Marine attack in September 1863.

Above: General Ulysses S Grant, commander of the Union forces in the Civil War.

Koreans and waiting ten days without receiving one, Low and Rodgers decided to exact retribution. A force of bluejackets and a Marine brigade of four officers and 105 enlisted men prepared to land and attack the Korean forts. The Marine commander, Captain McLane Tilton, was apprehensive about the suitability for the mission of the breech-loading muskets then carried by his men. Tilton was an advocate of the new breech-loading repeating rifle—in fact, he had earlier written Headquarters Marine Corps as follows:

One man with a breech loader is equal to 12 to 15 armed as we are and in the event of any landing, or even chasing Coreans armed with an excellent repeater, what ever could Americans do with a blasted *Muzzle Fuzzle*?

On 10 June the force landed on a mud flat south of the first fort, a small one, and the men promptly sank in the mud up to their knees; there might have been carnage had not the big guns of the warships provided covering fire until the Americans were able to extricate themselves and move forward. The naval cannonade had been too much for the defenders and they fled the fort, which the Marines and bluejackets then occupied and busied themselves with spiking its guns. The next day Tilton led his men to the second small fort and took it with as little effort as they had the first one.

Next came the major Korean fortification, 'The Citadel.' The Americans' approach path to the fort was over rugged terrain of steep hills and deep ravines, with a force of Korean riflemen firing at them from nearby ridges as they advanced. The final assault was straight up a 150-foot hillside with heavy fire raining down on the attackers, but despite these desperate conditions they finally made it to the top. During the ensuing hand-to-hand battle the Americans performed magnificently, which is obvious from the fact that six Marines received Medals of Honor for this action in which 243 Korean defenders were killed compared with just two Marine casualties. Frederick Low continued on to Seoul, and though no successful treaty came of his negotiations, hostile actions against Americans ceased.

Ashore in Alexandria

The next significant test of the Marines came in 1882. In the summer of that year the British Mediterranean Fleet bombarded Alexandria, Egypt, when an antiforeign movement in that city led to looting and murdering by *fellah* mobs. With part of Alexandria on fire and American nationals in danger, Marines from the European Squadron were dispatched to provide protection. Marine Captain H C Cochrane was chosen to head the landing force; Cochrane previously had won a small place in history when he accompanied President Lincoln on his trip to dedicate the Gettysburg cemetery. Henry Clay Cochrane was very much his own man, described by a fellow officer as

'. . . distinctly a gentleman and always extremely courteous in his social contacts, but "ornery" and meaner than hell on duty. . . . A man of no sympathy and no affection, but efficient to an unusual degree. A magnificent barracks and mess officer. Cordially hated by officers and men alike.'

On 14 July Cochrane led ashore a unit consisting of 73 Marines and 60 bluejackets, a tiny force compared with the city's great mobs. He marched them directly to the Grand Square of Mehemet Ali where the American Consulate was located and immediately set up a protective cordon around the building. This done, Cochrane sent units out in all directions with orders to work from street to street and gradually create a zone of order around the square. When reinforcements for the antiforeign rioters marched toward the city, Cochrane said he would 'stick by the British and take

Below: Contemporary sketch map of the American operations in Korea in 1871, showing the positions taken by the Marines.

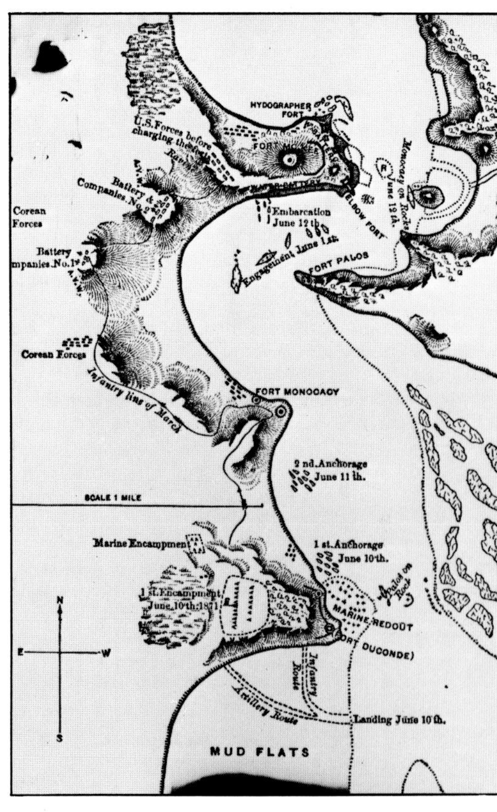

their chances.' Some 4000 British troops soon arrived to relieve the situation, and they and their political leaders were quick in expressing their appreciation for Cochrane's steadiness; the local British commander, Lord Charles Beresford, sent this message: 'To your smart, faithful force, great credit is due. . . . I have represented these facts to my government.'

Hot times in Panama

The year 1885 saw fighting explode on the Isthmus of Panama as its residents revolted against Colombia, which then ruled the area; the combat brought travel across the isthmus to a halt. Such traffic was of great importance to America's economic and military interests, and Washington quickly reacted to the stoppage. On 2 April 1885, Marine Commandant Zeilin received orders to organize and dispatch a battalion of Marines to Aspinwall (now Colón, a large city of Panama). Within 24 hours the force sailed out of New York Harbor, under the command of Brevet Lieutenant Colonel Charles Heywood, known as the 'boy colonel' because of his rapid rise through the officer ranks.

Above: Parade ground and, right, commandant's house at the Marine barracks during the Civil War. *Left:* Hats *c.* 1878. Clockwise from top left: field officer, full dress; company officer, fatigues; all officers, undress pattern; full dress, enlisted men; fatigue, enlisted men; undress, bandsmen; full dress, company officer.

Five days later a second battalion of Marines, along with a battalion of rifle-armed bluejackets under Commander Bowman H McCalla, departed from the United States for Panama; McCalla was designated by the Navy Department to be the commander of all American forces once they went ashore in Panama. The Marines were led by Captain J H Higbee; Captain Robert W Huntington, who would win fame at Guantanamo Bay, headed one company and a future Commandant, First Lieutenant George F Elliott, served with him.

The ship carrying the battalion headed by Colonel Heywood arrived off Panama while McCalla's force still was at sea. Heywood promptly ordered his unit ashore, and by sundown of the same day, 12 April, they had marched across the 47-mile wide isthmus, set up a camp outside Panama City, and Marine guards were aboard each train of the trans-Isthmus Panama Railroad. When Commander McCalla arrived three days later, a large degree of control already was established outside the city. Probably in recognition of this well-done piece of work, when another Marine battalion arrived from the United States, the three battalions were formed into a brigade and Colonel Heywood made its commander; this was the first organization of a Marine brigade.

By 20 April the military situation within Panama City had deteriorated badly, with the anti-government forces threatening to burn the city in a fight to the death. Hey-

Above: The Stars and Stripes flies above part of the Allied encampment at Alexandria during the expedition in 1882.

wood's Marines marched into the beleaguered city, destroyed all the street fortifications thrown up by the protestors and quickly gained military control of the city. The Marines maintained this control in the face of a numerically superior opposing force until 30 April, when Colombian regular army troops arrived in Panama City to take over the situation.

The sterling performance of the Marines affirmed the by-then widely held admiration of them; the captain of a British warship in the city's harbor, upon learning that a Marine unit was joining the action, had said, 'Tranquility is then assured.' But newspaper correspondent Richard Harding Davis provided the most memorable description of the episode: 'The Marines have landed and have the situation well in hand.'

Moonshine raids in Brooklyn

With the exception of such overseas expeditions, peacetime duty for the Corps was not very exciting, which is why the buoyant-spirited Marines appreciated the occasional stateside assignments that came their way, as unmilitary as some of these duties were. For example, after President Lincoln's assassination, Marines had been given the tension-filled job of providing detention security for the members of the murder plot as, one by one, they were captured and held for trial.

An even more unlikely assignment was that of performing as prohibition agents, which Marines did repeatedly between 1867 and 1871. Operators of illegal stills in the area of Brooklyn, New York, then known as 'Irishtown,' gave an inhospitable reception to federal revenue agents who attempted to shut down their bootlegging operations, and neither the city's police nor units of the Army's 8th Infantry had been able to provide the agents with sufficient protection. The local army commander, Major General Israel Vogdes, who had respectful memories of the Marines from his Civil War service, urged that the Leatherneck unit from the Brooklyn Navy Yard be assigned the task. This was done, and soon members of the Corps with bayonets fixed were marching through the area's streets, guarding revenue officers who searched out and smashed illegal stills. The Marines subsequently were thanked for the steadfastness of their service by everyone involved—everyone, that is, except the bootleggers.

Right and *above right:* The Marine guard from the USS *Boston* pictured in 1888 in full dress (right) and undress uniforms.
Below: Marine racing crew from the USS *Olympia*.

The railroad 'insurrection'

On the scorching summer afternoon of 21 July 1877, a trying episode began for the Marines. Orders came down from the highest level to Corps Headquarters in Washington for a battalion to hurry to Baltimore to restore order; striking railroad workers in nine states were tearing up rails, burning rolling stock and even attacking local authorities who attempted to control them. Army and Marine units under the overall command of Major General W S Hancock, USA, were ordered to aid police in what would prove to be one of the more tumultuous labor disputes in American history.

Under the command of Colonel Charles Heywood, of Panama fame, the Marine battalion proceeded to Baltimore's Camden Station by train, after some difficulty with finding an engineer courageous enough to operate the locomotive during the strike. It was night when the troop train arrived in Baltimore, a night lighted by the flames of blazing tank cars in the railroad yard; the Marines could see the running figures of the arsonists silhouetted against the flames. Throughout that chaotic night the Marines guarded Camden and Mount Clare Stations against violence; in the morning Heywood marched his small force, drums beating and colors flying, to Baltimore's prestigious Eutaw House for breakfast.

Heywood was awakened from sleep the following night by a Duty Officer holding a telegram; it contained urgent orders from the Secretary of the Navy for Heywood to move his battalion to Philadelphia, where striker violence had created a state of lawlessness similar to the situation in Baltimore. This time the trip was slowed by torn-up track, but at mid-day of 23 July the Marines were in action on Philadelphia's streets, and by nightfall a condition of orderliness had been imposed. The Marines were disconcerted when they were then ordered to stand inspection by General Hancock, since they had not been out of their uniforms for three days, but they need not have been concerned; Hancock, a seasoned combat soldier, conveyed his warm feelings regarding their performance in his General Order 46, which said:

> The major-general commanding desires to express his high appreciation of the excellent conduct and soldierly qualities of the Marines. . . .

During this same period, another battalion was assembled with Marines from Norfolk and Washington Marine Barracks as well as from ships' detachments, placed under the command of Brevet Lieutenant Colonel James Forney and given the mission of keeping open the railroad right-of-way between Washington and Martinsburg, West Virginia. Other Marine units were sent to Watervliet, New York, and Frankford, Pennsylvania, to guard the local arsenals against raids by striker gangs. In each of these instances, the Marine units carried out their assignments with quiet efficiency. In 1894 the Corps again sent men to restore peace in a railroad strike, this time involving the Central Pacific Railroad. Once again they demonstrated their efficiency and discipline.

Three innovative commandants

Fate smiled on the Marine Corps during the years between the Civil War and the Spanish-American War. The Marines had emerged from the earlier conflict torn both in organization and in morale, but they had the good fortune to get Jacob Zeilin as their leader following the dramatic forced retirement of every Marine officer senior to him. Zeilin brought the Corps back together both in body and spirit with his incisive leadership, as well as with such measures as the creation of a new standardized drill and tactics, and by the introduction of the annual inspection of every Marine station.

When Zeilin voluntarily retired himself on 1 November 1876, he had, with typical efficiency, seen to it that his successor was well prepared to take over as the eighth Commandant. Charles Grymes McCawley, who had served alongside Jacob Zeilin during the Civil War, had been ordered to Washington some time earlier so that he could learn first-hand what was involved in running the Corps. McCawley learned well, for among his administrative accomplishments were a number that would permanently improve the quality of the Marine Corps.

He vigorously led a four-year successful drive in the halls of Congress and with the Navy Department to have Marine Corps officers come from the ranks of Naval Academy graduates, with the result that all 50 officers who entered the Marine Corps between 1881 and 1897 were Academy graduates. McCawley supervised the creation of the first standard table of organization for the Corps; ordered the first factory mass production of uniforms to achieve standardization in sizes and appearance; brought about a thorough reorganization of the Headquarters Marine Corps cadre with the goals of improving soldierly skills and divesting junior commanders of independent authority; instituted a variety of promotion- and retirement-related measures for noncommissioned officers and enlisted men designed to make a career in the Corps a more attractive consideration.

Ironically, McCawley's most memorable contribution to the history of the Corps was not military but was, rather, a musical one involving the Marine band. Some time after he began his service as Commandant, McCawley was reported to have complained, 'The Band gives me more trouble than all the rest of the Corps put together.' When it became necessary in 1880 for him to dismiss Louis Schneider as the band's director following the report by an investigative board that Schneider was unfit for duty, McCawley appointed in his place, with wages of $23.50 a week, a musician by the name of John Philip Sousa. During his 12 years as leader of the Marine band, Sousa converted it into one of the world's finer musical groups.

McCawley, a teetotaler, did not win the hearts of some Marines, however, with his measures relating to intoxicating beverages; he forbade the sale of beer in Marine canteens, and he permitted the use of the Marine Band Hall for meetings by a group with the unlikely name of the Marines Temperance Union.

When McCawley stepped down on 30 January 1891, the 'boy colonel,' Charles Heywood, was selected to take his place and become the Corps's ninth Commandant. Heywood quickly instituted an important step toward the further professionalization of the Corps: he created the School of Application in Washington, forerunner of the Marine Basic School system. During his tour as Commandant the number of Marine bases increased from 12 to 21, one of them being a barracks at Port Royal, South Carolina, that would one day become the Corps' largest training area in the Eastern United States, Parris Island. Heywood instituted mandatory promotion examinations for officers and created a system of officers' schools. Finally, his stringent insistence on the fundamentals—physical fitness, marksmanship, field service and modern tactics—would serve the Corps well when America entered the Spanish-American War.

Below: Aboard the USS *Essex* in 1888, Marines and seamen drawn up for inspection.

Above: Marines at bayonet drill around 1890. Moored to the dock in the background is the receiving ship USS *New Hampshire*.

Navy-versus-Marines tension

By 1890 the Corps had never been more fit and ready, yet at that very moment plans were in the making by a group of junior Naval officers calculated to eliminate the Corps *per se* and convert it into an artillery adjunct of the Army. Behind this plot of the Naval officers was their frustration with the lack of meaningful duty for deck officers in the 'new Navy' of steam engines and other machinery. The spokesman for the Naval group was a brilliant young lieutenant, William F Fullam, USN, who in 1890 presented a paper to the United States Naval Institute in Annapolis in which he proposed the transfer of the Corps to the Army and the creation in its place of an amphibious infantry organization consisting of Naval officers and bluejackets. As in the past, this anti-Corps movement soon found sponsors in the Congress, and on 24 August 1894 a bill was introduced in the Senate that would have combined the Marine Corps with the Army's five regiments of artillery.

The bill died in the Military Affairs Committee, due largely to the testimony of the president of the Naval War College, Captain Henry C Taylor, USN, who made this telling point about the proposed Naval replacement organization for the Marine Corps:

> . . . I do not doubt that those seamen, and the officers [who] command them, would evolve . . . into a new Corps, identical to the present Marines.

The enemies of the Marine Corps in the Navy were not about to be dissuaded from their hostile purposes, however; between 1895 and 1897, three separate attempts were made to restrict or eliminate the role of the Corps within the United States Navy, with each of the attacks being defeated or turned aside. The Corps was secure—at least until the next assault.

Below: The wreck of the USS *Maine* in the harbor of Havana, Cuba. 28 Marines died in the explosion which is now believed to have been caused by spontaneous detonation of unstable ammunition.

Below: Commodore George Dewey, hero of the Battle of Manila Bay.

'Brave Hearts and Bright Weapons— 1898-1917

Brave Hearts

The angry interservice arguments with the Navy regarding the value of the Marine Corps were still taking place in 1898 when dramatic events brought the discussion to a temporary halt.

War with Spain: Manila, Guantanamo and Cuzco Valley

The evening of 15 February was pleasantly comfortable in Havana, Cuba. In the harbor the American battleship USS *Maine* lay at anchor; Charles D Sigsbee, the battleship's captain, sat at a table in his quarters composing a letter to his wife, and First Lieutenant A W Catlin, commander of the ship's Marine detachment, was busy with an inspection of extra sentry posts he had established on the captain's orders. The *Maine* had arrived in Havana several weeks previously, ostensibly for a routine courtesy call on the local Spanish authorities; however, anyone who followed current events knew that the visit was in fact the result of an emotional campaign against Spain being conducted in the newspapers of William Randolph Hearst. A revolution had been going on in Cuba for three years, and the headlines in Hearst newspapers regularly featured horrendous stories alleging atrocities committed by the Spanish against Cuban militants and civilians, with suggestions that Americans working on the island might be the next to be attacked. The United States had no meaningful stake in the Cuban events, but the emotional newspaper coverage finally had made the people at the State Department sufficiently uneasy that they arranged for the *Maine* to visit Havana to 'show the colors.'

Below right: Marine riflemen prepare to engage the enemy shortly after the landing at Guantanamo Bay.
Below: Marines entrenching on McCalla Hill near Guantanamo, Cuba in June 1898.

The provocation worked all too well; 20 minutes after Taps that evening the mighty warship was lifted by a gigantic explosion and its hull split open like a torn paper bag. The calm words of Marine Private William Anthony to Captain Sigsbee would make him a national hero: 'Sir, I beg to report that the Captain's ship is sinking.' Within a brief time the *Maine* went to the bottom by the bow, carrying 28 Marines and 238 bluejackets with it.

Given the hostile atmosphere of the time, the next events were predictable; on 21 April 1898, despite earnest attempts by President William McKinley to pacify the public, Congress passed a declaration of war against Spain, and three days later Spain declared war on the United States. By Congressional act the authorized strength of the Corps was increased to 4713 enlisted men and 119 officers, a new high, and Commandant Heywood's rank was raised to that of brigadier general.

While McKinley apparently was a reluctant participant in the war, his assistant secretary of the Navy, Theodore Roosevelt, was not. As early as 25 February Roosevelt had cabled orders to his protege, Commodore George Dewey, commander of the Asiatic Squadron of the US Navy fleet. The cable read as follows:

> Secret and confidential. Order the Squadron . . . to Hong Kong. Keep full of coal. In the event of declaration of war [with] Spain, your duty will be to see that the Spanish squadron does not leave the Asiatic coast and then offensive operations in Philippine Islands. . . . Roosevelt.

Dewey's temperament was perfectly suited to the assignment. Early in the morning of 1 May 1898, following a leisurely breakfast, he sent his seven ships into Manila Bay to attack the fleet of Admiral Montojo. After eight hours of furious fighting the Spanish admiral struck his colors, giving Dewey the most brilliantly-won naval victory until then in the age of steam-driven warships. Two days later Dewey sent ashore a contingent of Marines from the USS *Baltimore* under First Lieutenant Dion Williams to secure the Spaniards' Cavite Navy Yard on Manila Bay. The Marines accomplished the assignment with little difficulty, and soon were settled into their combat post. Williams remembered the situation thus:

> In the barracks storerooms were supplies of clothing and rations which reminded us of our own barracks at home, one feature which greatly interested our men being several barrels of red wine as this formed an important part of the Spanish ration. Cavite was evidently an old-time 'navy yard town' as shown by the number of liquor shops and other places of amusement for sailors, and some of our Marines said 'it was just like Vallejo,' the *Baltimore* having gone into commission at Mares Island.

Dewey's Marines had to wait in the Cavite Navy Yard for over two months

until Army troops arrived, much to Commodore Dewey's exasperation; in a later communication he complained, 'If there had been 5000 Marines under my command at Manila Bay, the city would have surrendered to me on May 1.'

Another American military officer to receive sealed orders even before hostilities erupted with the Spanish was Marine Corps Commandant Colonel Heywood. He was told to organize a battalion of crack Marines at the Brooklyn Navy Yard against the possibility of war, and hold them in readiness for action in Cuba. Heywood selected Lieutenant Colonel Robert W Huntington to head the new battalion. While Huntington, a full-bearded veteran of the Civil War, organized his 647 men into five infantry companies and one artillery battery, Heywood arrived in Brooklyn from Headquarters Marine Corps to personally see to it that:

> . . . [the battalion] was supplied with all the equipment and necessities for field service under conditions prevailing in Cuba, including mosquito netting, woolen and linen clothing, heavy and light weight underwear, three months' supply of provisions, wheelbarrows, pushcarts, pick-axes, shovels, barbed-wire cutters, wall and shelter tents, and a full supply of medical stores.

A merchant ship, the USS *Panther*, was fitted out as a transport for the Marine battalion, and it was ready for action when war came. The Marine battalion paraded through Brooklyn's streets to the blare of band music and the enthusiastic cries of spectators, boarded their transport and sailed for Key West. But the old rivalry between Navy and Marine Corps rose to haunt them; the *Panther*'s captain, Commander G C Reiter, saw the Marines as being under his command, and he put them ashore at night into a disease-ridden swamp at Key West. Making the most of a bad situation, Huntington set his battalion to practicing marksmanship and tactical maneuvering.

For a time the Marines feared they might spend the war in that hellish place, but when Commodore Schley's Flying Squadron needed a shore base to support a blockade of the Spanish fleet in Santiago Harbor, Navy Secretary Long asked Rear Admiral Sampson, the Atlantic Fleet commander, 'Can you not take possession of Guantanamo, occupy as a coaling station?' In response, Sampson ordered Huntington's Marines into action.

Guantanamo Bay lay about forty miles to the east of Santiago. On 7 June the USS

Right: Marines ready for inspection aboard the USS *Portsmouth* in 1885.

Above: The Battle of Manila Bay was a most one-sided engagement with almost the whole Spanish fleet destroyed at a cost of only eight Americans wounded.

Marblehead, a small cruiser accompanying the Marine's transport ship *Panther*, commenced shelling the Spanish defenses inshore, consisting of a gunboat, a few marine mines in the harbor and some 8000 Spanish troops. Three days later, with the additional covering fire of the newly-arrived battleship *Oregon*, the Marines waded ashore at Guantanamo into an eerie quiet. For unknown reasons, the Spanish defenders were nowhere to be seen; not a shot was fired against the Americans.

Then a difficulty arose; Reiter, the *Panther*'s captain, refused to send ashore the Marine's small-arms ammunitions, claiming he needed it as ballast for his ship. Huntington appealed to the senior Navy officer in the area, the *Marblehead*'s captain, who chanced to be Commander Bowman McCalla, a veteran of the Panama campaign. McCalla, who had fond memories of the Marines' performance in the Isthmus campaign, wired the *Panther*'s skipper in cold anger:

Sir, Break out immediately and land with the crew of the *Panther*, 50,000 rounds [small arms] ammunition. In future, do not require Colonel Huntington to break out or land his stores with members of his command. Use your own officers and men for this purpose, and supply the Commanding Officer of Marines promptly with anything he may desire.

The Marines ashore promptly named their bivouac area Camp McCalla. Within 24 hours of the landing, the Spanish defenders suddenly came alive, pouring deadly fire into the Marine encampment. To deprive the attackers of a vital supply, Huntington sent out two rifle companies together with friendly Cuban guerrillas to find and destroy the Spaniards' only water source at Cuzco, about six miles from the Marines' position. This well was located inside a heavily-defended blockhouse, and the Marine unit's commander, Captain George F Elliott, saw that he would need the support of fire from the heavy guns of a Navy ship, the USS *Dolphin*, then waiting offshore. When the fire came in, however, it began falling dangerously close to Elliott's own men. As the captain looked about for a signalman, Marine Sergeant John H Quick jumped to his feet with an improvised semaphore flag; with Spanish bullets and shells from the *Dolphin*'s cannons flying all about him, Quick calmly signalled the Navy vessel to redirect its fire onto the enemy, and the Marines soon moved in to take their objective. For his action Sergeant Quick received the Congressional Medal of

Below: The first ever photograph taken of US Marines on Guam in October 1899.

Honor. Stephen Crane, author of the classic war novel '*Red Badge of Courage*,' was at Cuzco as a correspondent and reported this about the heroic sergeant:

. . . I saw Quick betray only one sign of emotion. As he swung his clumsy flag to and fro, an end of it once caught on a cactus plant. He looked annoyed.

The success of Cuzco broke the back of enemy action at Guantanamo, and for the remainder of the Marines' stay in the area their patrols made little contact with Spanish forces. While Huntington's men dug in their defensive positions, Americans were active elsewhere in Cuba. The Army's Fifth Corps came ashore at Daiquiri and began a march toward Santiago, 20 miles to the east. Subsequently, a group of horsemen serving under the enthusiastic but amateur leadership of Colonel Theodore Roosevelt rode into fame and history with their wild charge up San Juan Hill. At dawn of 3 July the Spanish Navy, in a desperate bid for freedom, steamed out of Santiago Harbor with cannon blazing, but they were hopelessly and tragically outgunned and outclassed; the larger and heavier-gunned American ships cut the Spanish vessels to pieces and sent every one of them to the bottom. Within a month the war was over.

The superb performance of the Marines in the conflict was not lost on the American public. Where other services had experienced time-consuming delays in moving from peacetime slackness to combat readiness, the Marines had been capable of responding almost instantly and carried the war to the enemy, winning both time and territory. In combat fitness, too, the comparison was striking. The Marines were vastly better prepared for tropical warfare; whereas 50 percent of Army soldiers contracted yellow fever, malaria or enteric disease, only 2 percent of Marines suffered enteric disease and not one of them contracted yellow fever.

Recognition and reward for the Corps' fine performance came in a practical and meaningful form: on 3 March 1899 Congress passed a bill calling for a permanent Marine Corps consisting of 201 officers and 6062 men, which was a better than 100 percent increase in strength over just three years earlier.

Guam, Samoa, the Philippine Insurrection

While the country's attention was fixed on events in Cuba, other Marines were fighting battles on other islands. Guam was controlled by Spain at that time, which made it a target for the attentions of the United States Navy. A Marine contingent from the USS *Charleston* headed by First Lieutenant John Twiggs Myers—dubbed 'Handsome Jack' by his friends—landed and secured the island on 21 June 1898, after a preliminary bombardment by the American ship that the Spanish garrison at first took to be a courteous gun salute. Then, on 28 July the Marine detachment of the battleship USS *Massachusetts* went ashore at Ponce, Puerto Rico, and wrested control of the city from the Spanish garrison with virtually no effort.

Above: A group of officers from the 1st Marines in camp near the Portsmouth, New Hampshire, Navy Yard.

Samoa in the far-off South Pacific flared into violence in 1899 over an internal argument about the chieftancy of the island. Since Samoa then was a joint protectorate of Britain and the United States, the flare-up brought two British ships and an American cruiser to the scene. A landing party consisting of British and American Marines and sailors went ashore on 1 April to subdue the more violent of the contending factions, and the results were tragic. The joint force was ambushed near the village of Apia, and in the subsequent fire fight US Navy Lieutenant P V H Lansdale and Ensign John Monahagn were wounded. While the main Anglo-American force retreated, Marine Private H L Hulbert stayed with the wounded officers until both were dead, then he made his way to safety through heavy hostile fire. Marine First Lieutenant C M Perkins, who took over and led the withdrawal, said of Hulbert that 'His behavior throughout was worthy of all praise and honor.' The British and Americans responded to the defeat promptly with heavy reprisals against the factions involved, and within three weeks the Samoan uprising was terminated.

However, an uprising in another part of the Pacific was not nearly so easy to deal with. Commodore Dewey's desire for a sufficient number of Marines to finish the job in the Philippines soon turned out to be grimly appropriate; when the newly-liberated Filipinos saw that the Americans did not appear ready to give them their indepen-

Below: A sentry under the palms at Guantanamo Bay, Cuba. A picture taken shortly before World War II and symbolic of the continuing existence of the US base.

Above : A Marine firing line advances against insurgent positions in the fighting in the Philippines in 1901.
Left : Supposedly an action picture from the same campaign but more probably a scene specially composed for the camera.

dence, their cheers for the small Marine garrison at Cavite Navy Yard quickly turned into angry cries and then became rifle fire.

In March 1899 Dewey sent through an urgent request for a battalion of Marines to reinforce his hard-pressed detachment at Cavite. Within weeks a battalion consisting of 15 officers and 260 enlisted men sailed from the New York Naval Shipyard under the command of Colonel P C Pope, who had served Huntington at Guantanamo as his executive officer. A meaningful footnote to this expedition—one that presaged an end to the romantic era of warfare—was an item in the unit's orders that instructed officers, for the first time in Corps history, to leave their swords behind and take only their service pistols.

That September a second Marine battalion under Major G F Elliott departed hurriedly in response to messages from Dewey that the Philippine situation was worsening. Just three months later yet another battalion sailed for the Pacific, this one led by Major L W T Waller. By the end of 1900 a total of six Marine battalions would be in the Philippines, forming what subsequently would be designated the 1st Marine Brigade, consisting of two rifle regiments and two artillery companies with a total of 58 officers and 1547 enlisted men. Included in the unit were a number of officers who in later years would be Corps commandants.

The work of the Marines during the three years they spent in the Philippines consisted of long periods of boredom interspersed with episodes of the most harrowing and deadly sort of combat. Their first action took place on the main island of Luzon at Olongapo, on Subic Bay, on 23 September 1899, when a force of 70 Marines under Captain John T ('Handsome Jack') Myers landed under covering fire from Navy ships to seize and destroy formerly Spanish coast defense guns that had been captured by the insurgents and were in use against American vessels. Myers' group quickly overran the insurgents' positions and blew up the offending cannon.

The following month the regiment of Lieutenant Colonel G F Elliott was given the difficult assignment of attacking and driving from cover the insurgents of Novaleta, an inaccessible coastal area between Cavite and Manila; this was the same Elliott who only a year before had been a captain at Guantanamo Bay. His attack was to be so coordinated with a move by an Army column that it would deliver the fleeing enemy into the gunsights of the soldiers. On 8 October Elliott's 376 men approached Novaleta in two columns, struggling through a marshy tidal lagoon choked almost impenetrably by mangrove shrubs, and at that moment the waiting insurgents opened up with a hail of deadly fire from the Marine's front and left flank. Pressing forward through sometimes shoulder-deep water, the Marines managed to join up with the Army column, and by midday the combined forces had captured the fortified town. Reporting later to the Commander in Chief, Asiatic Station, Elliott wrote, 'A great deal of personal bravery among officers and men was shown'; but then he added with a combat veteran's wisdom, 'I respectfully request that the Admiral will admonish these young officers for bravado which might have caused a failure in carrying the fort provided these officers had been killed or wounded.'

'Stand, gentlemen, he served on Samar'

There were many instances of courage and resoluteness during the Philippine campaign, but none burned its way so deeply into Corps legend as did the expedition to Samar.

By 1901 peace had been brought to all of the scattered islands of the Philippine

group with the exception of Samar, far down in the southeast. There, legendary fighters known as Moros held the island and terrified the local farming people. On 28 September the Moros attacked an Army company's garrison as the soldiers sat at dinner and killed them almost to a man, many by means of unspeakable torture. A Marine battalion was ordered to hurry to Samar to stabilize the situation until the Army could reestablish its presence on the island. Commanding the battalion was Major Littleton Walter Tazewell Waller, a diminutive redhead who as a young lieutenant had served under Cochrane in the action at Alexandria, Egypt. 'A most excellent officer,' a colleague later said about him, 'who talked a lot about himself but who could always deliver the goods. The Marine Corps was his god. He never let you forget it.'

When Waller arrived off Samar the local US Army commander, Brigadier General 'Hell-Roaring Jake' Smith, to whose force Waller's battalion was attached, told him in no uncertain terms exactly what he wanted to see accomplished: 'I want no prisoners. I wish you to burn and kill; the more you burn and kill, the better it will please me.'

Waller set to his assignment with enthusiasm, and in less than three weeks his battalion had driven the Moros deep into the jungle and into their heavily-fortified stronghold in the cliffs of the Basey River, an area the Spanish Army had never dared penetrate. Approaching in three columns the Marines scaled a 200-foot cliff and, catching the Moros totally by surprise, captured their fortress. Two of the officers involved, Captains Porter and Bearss, earned Medals of Honor for extraordinary bravery.

This mission accomplished, Waller next was ordered by General Smith to determine the best route across Samar for a military telegraph line. Waller assembled a company-sized party and set out on 28 December 1901. Almost immediately the group began experiencing one disaster after another; boats swamped in jungle river, mutiny by bearers, illness and even madness suffered by the men. Finally Waller divided the expedition into two groups, with the weaker members to proceed at a slower pace. When all survivors finally emerged from the jungle on 15 January 1902, at Basey, site of the former Moros stronghold, Waller discovered that ten of his men had perished from fever or exhaustion. Still imperiled by the plotting of guides and bearers against the party, Waller conducted a drumhead court at Basey, sentenced 11 of the Filipinos to death, and had the sentences carried out on the spot. The events that followed caught Waller by surprise. In his words:

> Leaving Samar . . . we reached Cavite. . . . we expected a warm welcome home. . . . This welcome we received . . . cheer after cheer went up for us. . . . [then] I went to my Commander In Chief and was met with the charge of murder.

Incredibly, to Waller and his officers and men, it was true. A political decision had been made by a line of senior Army and civilian authorities reaching all the way back to Washington, and on 17 March Waller and one of his officers were tried by court-martial in Manila on 11 counts of murder. The Army's performance in the matter did it little credit; when the Marine officers were acquitted, the local commanding general, Adna R Chaffee, probably under pressure from Washington, disapproved the verdict. But then the Army Judge Advocate General's office threw out the entire case on the grounds that the Marines had never been detached for service with the Army by presidential order.

Though Waller's name was legally cleared, it is thought by Marine historians that the shadow of the case hung over his otherwise brilliant career, and quite possibly was the single reason why he never became Corps commandant. Within Waller's own brigade, however, a custom came into being that gave witness to the respect and affection in which he and the other members of the legendary expedition were held. Whenever one of them was present at brigade mess, this toast would be raised:

> 'Stand, gentlemen, he served on Samar.'

'The Fist of Righteous Amity': the Boxer Rebellion

The winds of social change that blew across the Pacific at the beginning of the twentieth century reached all the way to China. Disraeli had said, 'Let China sleep; when she awakes, the world will regret it.' The wild actions of *Yao* mobs seemed to affirm the wisdom of those words.

The *Yao* were groups scattered throughout China that shared a belief in magic and incantations; these spells, they believed, would shield them from harm in battle. The

Below: Marines hike into the jungle near Olongapo in 1900. Note the typical jungle terrain of the Bataan peninsula.

Above: A battalion of Marines on parade in the Forbidden City of Peking after the recapture of the city by the Allied expedition.

initial purpose of the groups was to oppose the dynasty of the Dowager Empress, but the ruling Manchus cleverly diverted the anger of the *Yao* onto the many foreigners in the country, and soon cities throughout China were literally aflame as angry mobs roamed the streets seeking to kill any Westerner they could find. The most militant of the *Yao* groups had a name that translated into English as the 'Fist of Righteous Amity'; this soon was shortened by Americans and British into the 'Boxers.'

As the spring of 1900 warmed into the heat of summer, so did the emotional temperature in China rise. On 27 May mobs of Boxers went on a destructive rampage, burning a number of railroad stations on the Belgian-built line between Peking and Paotingfu. The following day they put to the torch the Imperial Railway shops in Fengtai near Peking. At this point the legations of various Western nations became alarmed for their physical safety, and they wired their governments requesting military protection.

The American Minister, anticipating the violence, had asked for help even earlier, and on 24 May a force under Captain John T ('Handsome Jack') Myers of 48 Marines, one junior officer and an assistant surgeon had left the USS *Newark* at Taku and set off up the Heiho River in commandeered junks. Among those who greeted the Marines' arrival in Tientsin was a young engineer named Herbert Hoover who later recalled that, 'I do not remember a more satisfying musical performance than the bugles of the American Marines entering the settlement playing "There'll Be a Hot Time in the Old Town Tonight".' Overcoming the resistance of railroad officials, the US Marines and the military forces of Britain, Austria, Germany, France, Italy, Japan and Russia assembled a train and set off on 31 May for Peking. Arriving that night, the Marines marched to the American Legation building through huge mobs of angry but silent *Yao* members. 'The dense mass. . .,' reported Myers, 'seemed more ominous than a demonstration of hostility would have been.'

By 10 June the Boxers had torn up the track below Peking; the city was cut off. At this point the captain of the *Newark*, Captain Bowman H McCalla, the Marines' 'friend in need' in the Spanish-American War, declared 'I'll be damned if I sit here . . . and just wait.' McCalla and 112 bluejackets, joined by 2017 soldiers and Marines of the other nations, set off up the rail line toward Peking under the command of Vice Admiral Sir Edward Seymour, RN. But the Seymour party never reached its destination; unrelenting fire coming night and day from bands of Boxers so weakened the expedition that, though only 25 miles from their destination, they had to turn back and hole up at the Hsi-ku arsenal six miles north of Tientsin and await relief. Thirty-two of McCalla's 112-man force had been killed or wounded, and the captain himself was wounded three times.

This was on 22 June; two days later an international relief force that included 131 Marines and seven officers headed by Major Waller lifted the seige at the arsenal. Writing in his report afterwards, Waller said this:

> Our men . . . have gained the highest praise from all present, and have earned my love and confidence. They are like Falstaff's army in appearance, but with brave hearts and bright weapons. . . .

Back at Taku, warships of the Western Nations were arriving constantly with fresh troops. On 13 July these forces launched an attack to capture Tientsin which, after 24 hours of hard fighting, proved successful. By 3 August a new regiment of Marines was in Tientsin under the command of Major William P Biddle; a wounded 19-year old lieutenant named Smedley D Butler talked his way out of the hospital in time to join the regiment as it set off for Peking. The international force launched its final attack on 14 August; Smedley Butler scaled a wall and forced open the main gate of the British compound (in the process suffering a grazing wound that erased the map of South America from a Marine emblem tattooed above his heart). By nightfall the city was secured, the Americans having taken 17 killed or wounded. The fall of the Forbidden City took the last fight out of the Boxers, and by 10 October the 1st Marine Regiment was able to board ships for its base at Cavite in the Philippines.

From Panama to Addis Ababa

Upon General Charles Heywood's retirement as commandant in October 1903, George F Elliott came into the office. Elliott was a West Pointer, the last to become a Marine officer for almost one hundred years, and he had the astounding

Below: A section of the wall of the British Legation in Peking showing how it was reinforced by stone and timber. This was so effective that no shot penetrated the walls.

Above: A dramatic contemporary illustration showing street fighting in Peking between well-armed Marines and the Boxer forces.

record of having gone from company officer to commandant in just five years—after having been a lieutenant for 22 years! Hardly had Elliott assumed office when trouble for the Corps came his way. Negotiations between the United States and Colombia for the right to dig a canal across the Isthmus of Panama had broken down—Colombia then held Panama as a province—and on 3 November the Panamanian people, who very much wanted the canal, began wild rioting in Panama City, attacking in particular installations of the occupying Colombian authorities. Their actual objective was nothing less than full independence from Colombia.

President Theodore Roosevelt ordered the Marines into action. The gunboat USS *Nashville* raced to the scene and put ashore a small landing party with orders to 'prevent landing of any armed forces with hostile intent,' which meant the Colombians. When a group of 474 Colombian soldiers arrived and sought train passage to get to the scene of major rebel activity, the railway superintendent managed to delay them with bureaucratic red tape long enough for a battalion of Marines under Major Lejeune to arrive. When the Colombians saw the battle-hardened veterans march, bayonets fixed, down the gangplank of their transport, they quietly boarded a friendly merchant ship and sailed away.

President Roosevelt had the final word on the events: 'I took the Canal Zone and let Congress debate, and while the debate goes on, the Canal does also.'

Almost halfway around the world at about the same time, another Marine group under Captain G C Thorpe was escorting an American diplomatic mission on its way to Addis Ababa, capital of the ancient African nation of Ethiopia, for the purpose of negotiating a treaty with Emperor Menelik II. The march took the party across 300 miles of wild mountain country traveling by camel train. When the camel master took strong exception to the route selected by Thorpe and tried to lead them another way, the captain had him bound hand and foot and tied behind a camel. The officer

Below: Defending the American legation in Peking during the Boxer Rebellion, one of a series of photographs taken by Mrs Anna Woodward, a guest of the US Minister.

then informed the camel master he'd either lead them by the route he'd been told to or he'd travel the rest of the way dragged behind the camel. Faced with such clear logic, the *haban* quickly agreed to take them by Thorpe's route.

Outside Addis Ababa, Thorpe had his men put on special dress uniforms of blue blouses topped with scarlet collars, and a cap with a scarlet band, then they marched into the capital in dress parade style flanked by Abyssinian warriors wearing magnificent leopard skins. The Marines were put up in a royal palace, reviewed by the Emperor and each awarded the Menelik Medal; when the time for departure came, they set off on camels bearing with them a present for President Roosevelt of two live lions.

Trouble in Cuba

When the United States aided the Cubans in obtaining their independence from Spain and then established a protectorate relationship with the new country, the Washington administration didn't realize what a volatile 'foster child' it was taking on. But they soon found out.

In August 1906 the followers of Cuba's Liberal Party erupted into mob violence when a rigged election denied them office. President Tomas Estrada Palma, leader of the incumbent Moderate Party, beseeched President Roosevelt for aid, and Roosevelt agreed, though with reluctance. A battalion-strength group of Marines and sailors was hurried to Cuba and, on landing, set up their encampment directly in front of the Presidential palace. Shortly thereafter other Marine units arrived and took control of 24 towns across the island, protected ports and plantations, and rode as guards on every train in the country's rail system. Order was restored, but when the feuding political parties showed that they could not resolve their problems, Roosevelt ordered in a US Army of Cuban Pacification, set up a provisional government and named William Howard Taft, then Secretary of War, to be governor of the island.

There was a ridiculous footnote to the Cuban action: the *Ferrocarril Nacional de Cuba* sent the Navy Department a bill for tickets for every one of the Marines who had ridden 'shotgun' on their trains!

Under Presidential attack

Marines had suffered political attacks throughout their history, most of them by officers of the United States Navy, but as the Corps celebrated its 131st birthday on 10 November 1906, the first event in the most dangerous attack yet on their existence took place. Rear Admiral G A Converse, USN,

Above: President Teddy Roosevelt, despite his active foreign policy, fought to limit the Marine Corps.
Below: Marines on parade near the harbor at Vera Cruz during the intervention in 1914.

Above : Marines set to work to prepare their camp shortly after landing in Vera Cruz.

Above: Marines prepare their rations in the countryside outside Vera Cruz.

told the House Naval Affairs Committee that Marines should be taken off sea duty. Shortly thereafter the Corps' old enemy, William F Fullam, now a commander, endorsed Converse's views in a letter to the Secretary of the Navy. Over the next several years other persons in positions of power put forth similar ideas, all with the same goal: to obliterate the Corps as it had existed up to then.

In 1908 a stunning blow was struck: President Roosevelt ordered that Marine detachments be forthwith removed from all navy ships, and shortly thereafter he issued Executive Order 969 which, if carried out, would have had the effect of turning Marines into nothing more than night watchmen for naval stations, and eliminated their usefulness as amphibious infantry. The Marines promptly mounted a counterattack, an important element of which was the fact that one of the Corps' great heroes, Smedley Butler, was the son of the Chairman of the House Naval Affairs Committee, Congressman Thomas Butler. When the president's men and other enemies of the Marine Corps came before the Committee, they were stopped cold in their tracks: on 3 March 1909, a rider to the annual Naval Appropriations Bill bluntly told Roosevelt that he would receive no money for the Marines unless the men of that body continued to serve on warships as they always had in the past. Roosevelt roared with anger, but Congress's will prevailed.

The Marines had little chance to celebrate, for Roosevelt's successor in office, William Howard Taft, had no more love for the Corps than his predecessor had, and he made this clear in a private conversation with a Naval officer in which he alluded to 'the Government's . . . plans for the Corps.' Throughout his time in office he demonstrated that the 'plans' he had in mind involved the reduction of the Marine Corps into a meaningless non-entity.

Despite these harassments, Marine planning for continuing improvements in their organization went on. In 1901 General Heywood's Annual Report described a military exercise the Corps had conducted in small-unit beach landings and amphibious strategies and warfare. As a result of many such experimental exercises over the next 15 years under commandants Elliott, Biddle and Barnett, a vision gradually emerged of floating battalions aboard their own high-speed, heavily-armed transports, ready instantly to sail into combat with aviation support. Though these ideas, known as the Advance Base Force concept, were put into effect only loosely at that time, they would reappear and come fully into their own in warfare almost half a century later.

Double trouble in Hispaniola

The early years of the twentieth century, compared with the combat-ridden decades immediately preceding them, were relatively quiet ones for the Marine Corps.

In a flareup between political factions in Nicaragua, the United States took the side of the Catholic moderates, and in May 1910 a Marine force of 15 officers and 450 men under Major Smedley Butler landed from the gunboat USS *Paducah* to give witness to America's point of view. Another Marine force went into Veracruz, Mexico, in April 1914, this one commanded by a tough colonel, John Archer Lejeune. Washington had learned that a German ship soon was to deliver a cargo of arms to Victoriana Huerta, a general who had assassinated the elected president and seized power. The Marines landed and, after heavy house-to-house fighting over a three day period, secured the city. Huerta was persuaded to leave the country and a duly-elected government took over.

Trouble of a horrendously uglier nature followed in 1915 on the island of Hispaniola in the Caribbean, an island divided into the two countries of Haiti and Santo Domingo. Haiti, black and French-speaking, had a bloody political history; in the 29 years since 1886 it had run through 10 presidents, four of whom were killed in office and the others driven out in fear of their lives by rivals. In addition, the country's finances, never very good, had reached a state of total collapse. When, in March of 1915, a strongman named Vilbrun Guillaume Sam seized control in Port-au-Prince, the capital, another revolutionary named Dr Rosalvo Bobo began organizing an opposition force in the hills to the north. This instability caught the attention of Germany and France, and they began maneuvering for positions of power in the country; at this point the Washington administration became concerned about the growing possibility of a violation of the Monroe Doctrine if it did not take action.

In the dark morning hours of 27 July in Port-au-Prince, an attack began on the Presidential palace where President Sam lay sleeping; at the sound of gunfire the governor of the city personally began executing 167 political prisoners held in the local penitentiary; when his guns ran out of ammunition he continued the blood-bath with a machete. The mob finally broke in, seized the governor and killed him; they then discovered President Sam hiding in the French legation. The American *chargé d'affaires* described what happened next:

I could see that somebody or something was on the ground in the center of the crowd . . . a man disentangled himself from the crowd and rushed howling by me with a severed hand from which the blood was dripping, the thumb of which he had stuck in his mouth. Behind him came other men with the feet, the other hand, the head, and other parts of the body displayed on poles, each one followed by a mob of screaming men and women.

The following day a hastily-assembled regiment made up of sailors and ships-detachments Marines landed and won control of Port-au-Prince. They were followed in the ensuing months by the 2nd Marine Regiment under Colonel Eli K Cole and by the 1st Marine Regiment and Headquarters, 1st Marine Brigade, under Colonel Waller, hero of Samar. This American force, though somewhat patched together, represented a workable version of the Advance Base Force concept in action. Major Smedley Butler was one of Waller's officers, and serving under him was a fresh-cheeked

Right: Marines on an inland patrol after the fighting in Vera Cruz had died down.
Below, main picture: Men of the Marine Expeditionary Force land supplies on the beach at Carracao in the Philippine Islands in 1911.

Above: Marines come ashore at Port-au-Prince in the early stages of the long and controversial involvement in Haiti.

lieutenant named Alexander A Vandegrift.

The fighting that followed over the next three months was violent and dramatic as the Marines pursued and defeated the major troublemakers in Haiti, a criminal-*cum*-military group known as the *Cacos*; their name was taken from a local bird of prey. Butler's sterling performance earned him a second Medal of Honor to add to the one he had won at Veracruz. Once stability had been brought about and a government installed, elements of the 1st Marines stayed on in Haiti to see to it that things remained that way; in fact, it would not be until 21 August 1934 that the last Marine would depart the country.

As Haiti suffered its own violence, events on the eastern side of Hispaniola in Spanish-speaking Santo Domingo were coming to a head. The United States had exercised a financial receivership over the country since 1904 when Roosevelt had acted to block Santo Domingo's European creditors from closing in on it. But relationships between the two countries gradually had deteriorated, and in April 1916 civil war broke out in the capital, Ciudad Santo Domingo. Units of the Advanced Base Force were detached from duty in Haiti and sent to Santo Domingo to restore order. The two companies of Marines, along with 225 bluejackets, were commanded by Major Newt Hall, and his executive officer was Captain F M ('Dopey') Wise. The unit entered the city at dawn on 15 May and were greeted by an eerie silence; not a shot was fired and, when they searched the houses, not a weapon was to be found. Arias, the rebel leader, and his followers had slipped away during the night to their stronghold in Santiago, a city in the central mountains.

Sailing aboard the USS *Louisiana*, Wise

Right: Mounted Marines on patrol during the troubles in Santo Domingo.

circled the island to the north coast and on 26 May came ashore at Monte Cristo, seizing and holding the town against rebel attacks. When a combined force of Marines and sailors captured the nearby town of Puerta Plata on 1 June, this put the north coast of Santo Domingo into American hands and sent the last of the rebels into mountain hiding. For the moment at least, the situation was stabilized.

The Corps spent the next five years in Santo Domingo in operations against bandits, meanwhile working on public health and development projects. Beginning in 1919, the Marines' efforts incorporated six 'Jennies' of the 1st Air Squadron, whose pilots experimented with dive-bombing techniques when not occupied with bandits. A decision near the end of 1920 to end the occupation of Santo Domingo brought about a busy and successful roundup of bandits, followed by a period of amnesty. With the country in the process of settling down, the Marines began pulling out in 1922, but it would be September 1925 before the last company of US Marines left Santo Domingo.

But long before this, the United States and the rest of the Western world had slid into the abyss of World War I, by which time the Marine Corps had reached a high level of professionalism and military competency because of its varied experiences in the engagements of the past two decades. Ironically, while some recognition of these achievements was at least tacitly manifested by the US Navy, signs of future trouble for the Corps were revealed in comments and criticisms expressed by officers of the Army. But the Marines felt competent enough to take on and weather such assaults; combat, both on foreign fields and in the halls of Congress, had made the Corps tough, skilled, resilient, and ready for battle.

Right: Marine 3-inch field gun at full recoil during fighting near Santiago in 1916.

Below: Marines of the 8th Company form a skirmish line during fighting in the area between Monte Cristi and Santiago in June 1916.

THE GREAT WAR
AND ITS AFTERMATH

'Retreat, Hell! We Just Got Here!'—1917-1918

In November of 1916 Woodrow Wilson was reelected President on the campaign slogan, 'He kept us out of war.' By then war had been raging in Europe since the summer of 1914, when a Serbian student assassinated the Archduke of Austria-Hungary and his wife. This precipitated a Serbo-Austrian brawl that, because of various intricate military alliances as well as long-standing trade rivalries, quickly swept through Europe and other parts of the world.

The Germans began in the autumn of 1914 with a massive wheel through Belgium that was finally halted by the Allies. The conflict then settled down on the Western Front into a debilitating static trench warfare across a front some 600 miles long in Belgium and France. This was not an entirely new development in warfare; it had been a feature of several campaigns in the American Civil War, most notably the siege of Petersburg. But the military leaders of Europe had by no means addressed the demands of trench warfare; instead, their devotion to outmoded ideas—an obsession with the offensive, a reliance on the bayonet and on horse cavalry, among others—raised casualty lists to unprecedented numbers. It was to be some time before the generals learned that modern firepower—including the machine gun—had made trenches virtually invulnerable.

Previous page: Marines advance cautiously through a wood shattered by shellfire during the Meuse-Argonne campaign in France in 1918. *Below:* General Pershing is mobbed by enthusiastic French crowds.

Growth of the Corps

Wilson hoped to stay out of the war not only to avoid its ravages on the country but also to reserve for America a peacemaking role, which would be impossible if America became a belligerent. He wanted to keep America 'neutral in fact as well as in name.' But events in Europe as well as American public opinion made entry into the war steadily more likely. Thus, preparations had to be made.

The 1916 Naval Personnel Bill enlarged the US Marine Corps by almost 50 percent. It also recreated the rank of Brigadier General and made a number of promotions, most notably that of John A Lejeune, who was later to succeed Major General George Barnett as Commandant of the Corps. Further enlargements were soon instituted. Just before America's entry into the war, the Corps stood at 17,400 enlisted men and 693 officers, hardly enough to make a dent in a real conflict. Nonetheless, this Corps was larger, better trained and better led than any in the 142-year history of the Marines. They formed an ideal foundation for the rapid growth that was to come during wartime.

America enters the war

In 1915 a German submarine torpedoed the *Lusitania*, killing 128 Americans. After that, Germany, seeing the wisdom of not antagonizing America, made some pacifying agreements. Having weathered that crisis, Washington nonetheless instituted a program of preparedness. In addition to enlarging all the services in 1916, Congress allotted $7,000,000,000 for defense, the largest military budget in American history till then.

In 1917 Germany stepped up its submarine warfare, sinking a number of American merchantmen. Also that year it was learned that Germany had made overtures to Mexico to join the Central Powers if the United States entered the war, and had promised to pay them off for that service with American territory.

These actions of Germany, along with a rising tide of American public opinion in favor of the war and the declining fortunes of the Allies, brought about American entry into the conflict in April 1917. In his declaration, Wilson said to Congress, 'The

world must be made safe for democracy.' Significantly, the United States declared itself in support of the Allies but did not make a formal treaty with them. This perhaps reflected the determination of General John J Pershing, leader of the American Expeditionary Forces, that American troops would function essentially as an independent body, not merely as a reserve to be absorbed into British and French Forces.

The Marine enlistment slogan was the stirring, 'First to Fight!' It produced a wave of enlistments into the Corps, totalling some 46,000 by the end of the war. The training camps at Mare Island (California) and Parris Island (South Carolina) were swamped with recruits; accordingly, new centers were developed at Quantico, Virginia, and elsewhere.

For years Marines had been engaged primarily in chasing bandits around various jungles, but now the Corps had to face the exigencies of a new kind of war—and one that so far was imperfectly understood by the highest levels of command both in Europe and America. The Navy still saw the Marines only in light of their usual functions—ship's guards, security forces and advance base forces. No one but the Corps itself seemed to have great faith in its ability as an infantry force. It would take some hard fighting to prove that point.

As for training, the Marines between 1915 and 1917 had developed the institution of Boot Camp. Deciding that it did not want to tie up its officers running training camps, the position of non-commissioned Drill Instructor (DI) evolved, and these implacable men wielded an authority second only to that of the Almighty. The training program was designed to build the toughest fighters and best marksmen in the world, and to weed out anyone not up to the Marine standard. The camps became a legendary part of American military history, frequently criticized as brutal and sadistic, but nonetheless a vital element of the unique Marine *esprit de corps* as well as its fighting prowess.

TELL THAT TO THE MARINES!
AT 24 EAST 23rd STREET
HUNS KILL WOMEN AND CHILDREN!

Right: A Marine recruiting poster of the First World War.
Below: Applicants arriving at the recruit depot Paris Island SC in 1917. (The spelling was later changed to Parris Island).

Trouble with Pershing

It was decided by military authorities that the final training of all elements of the American Expeditionary Forces had best be in Europe, with the experienced trench fighters of Britain and France. In his dealings with the Marines, General Pershing quickly showed a discouraging attitude that was to persist throughout the war and after. To begin with, Pershing was not convinced that the Marines, despite their recruiting posters, would be 'First to Fight' among the American Forces in Europe. Commandant Barnett, trying to make good on that pledge, was repeatedly rebuffed by

Pershing and the War Department, who claimed that Marine weapons and tactics were incompatible with those of the Army. Having successfully put that notion to rest, Barnett secured an agreement from President Wilson that the Marines would go over in the first convoy. To make sure, Barnett rounded up the ships for their transportation himself. The Marines sailed on 14 June 1917, arriving in St Nazaire, France just under two weeks later.

This was the 5th Marine Regiment, which had been put together from men in service all around the globe. Later was to follow the 6th Marines, made up of new recruits added to a cadre of regulars, and a machine gun battalion. Eventually the 5th and 6th regiments were joined to form the 4th Marine Brigade, the largest tactical unit in Corps history.

Once in France, Marine leadership had to cope with further political barriers. The 5th Marines were scattered throughout France in support of the Army and used mainly for tasks behind the lines. As the irrepressible General Smedley Butler later wrote, Marines in this position were expected:

> . . . to sit in the rear and run this filthy mudhole [a camp near Brest]. Although 97 percent of my men were expert riflemen or sharpshooters, troops

Left : A privately-taken photograph of Marines resting near the front line during the Battle of Belleau Wood.
Below : Heavily-laden Marines pause in a French village while en route to join the fighting at at Belleau Wood.

that hardly knew which end of the gun to shoot were sent to the trenches. My crack regiment was broken up to do manual labor and guard duty.

Besides the recalcitrance of Pershing, there were also troubles with General Ferdinand Foch, French Commander-in-Chief of the Allied forces. Though the Allies desperately needed American manpower, they were not at all disposed to give Americans a position of strength in running the war or a unified command in fighting it. Not convinced of the fighting abilities of these fresh and over-enthusiastic new arrivals from a junior member of the coalition, Foch wanted to sprinkle the AEF among his own forces.

Pershing fought a tough and eventually successful battle to preserve the status of the Americans, insisting that they be an integrated component of the Allied command. Pershing's efforts were soon to be aided by the fighting performance of his men, most notably in the first major engagement of the Marines.

Belleau Wood: a turning point in Marine history

In March 1918 the Marines finally went into the Western Front, though they were considered to be only completing their training in the trenches. Thus a quiet sector was chosen at Toulon, just south of Verdun on the Meuse River. The first casualty of the fighting was the 5th Regiment Band's bass drum, punctured by a shell (the drummer, fortunately, was untouched). The Marines settled restlessly into the life of the trenches, becoming familiar with mud, gas alarms, rats and the regular rain of enemy shells, which accounted for 872 casualties before the Marines were pulled out, after 53 days for additional training. The French and British command soon began to realize that these newcomers were full of fight and fast learners—as compared to the warworn and often cynical French and British veterans.

In late May German commander Ludendorff unleashed a major offensive that created three large salients in the German line—one near Neuve-Chapelle in the north, one near Amiens in the middle of the front, the other along the Marne to the south. The latter salient threatened Paris itself; the French government prepared to flee. Now Foch had to use American troops. They were the only reserve he had. As the most battle-ready of the American units, the 4th Marine Brigade was ordered into the sector at Belleau Wood.

Above: German positions in Belleau Wood after their capture by the Marines.
Bottom: The Battle of Belleau Wood.

As the Marines tramped down the road to their goal on 5 June, they first met a stream of civilian refugees. One of the men remembered the sight:

Everything that a terrified peasantry would be likely to think of bringing from among their humble treasures was to be seen on that congested highway. Men, women, children, hurrying to the

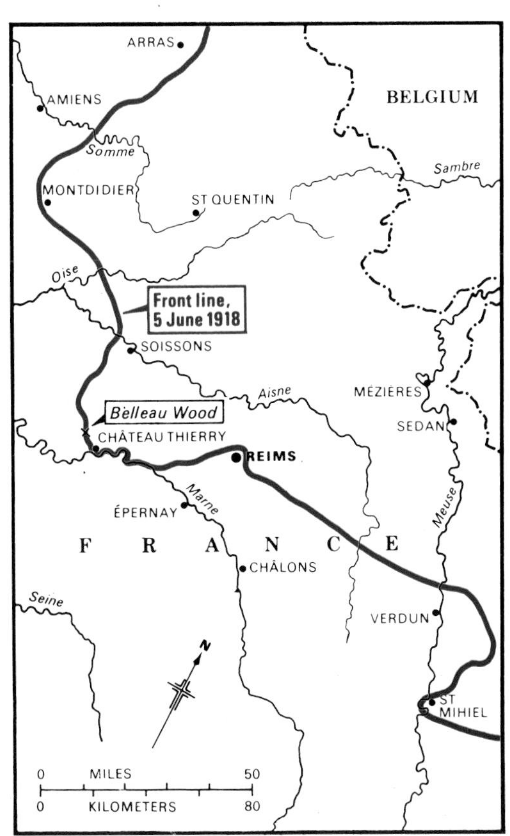

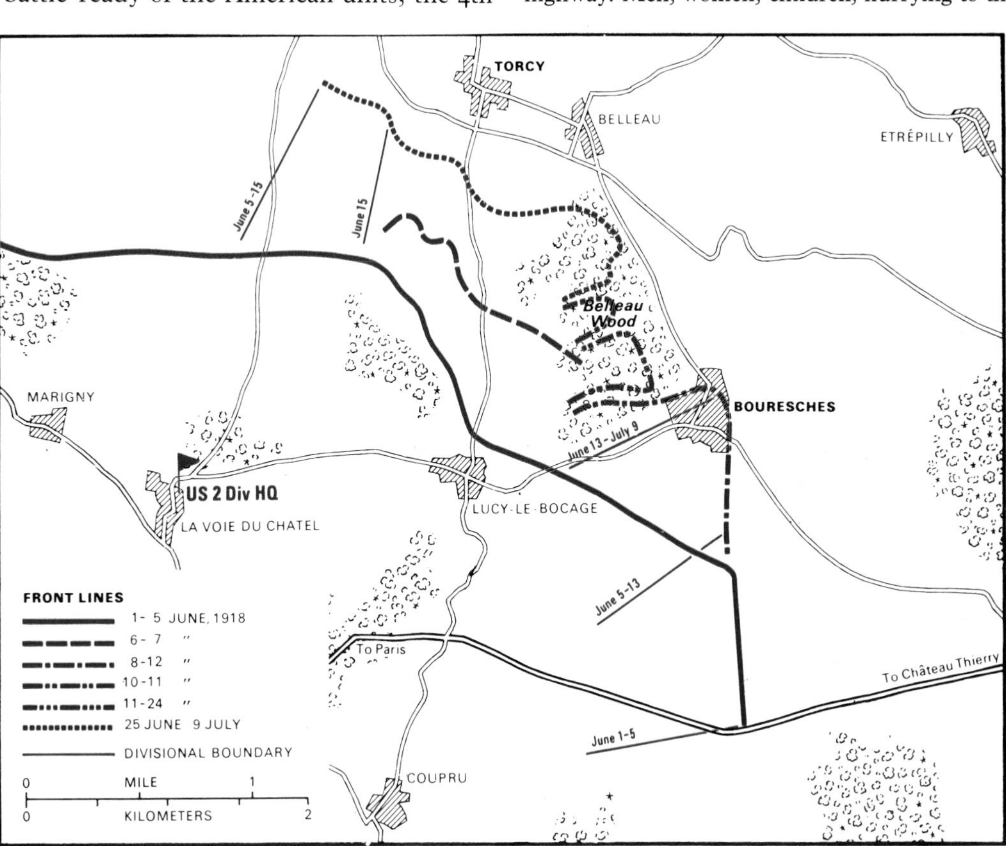

Above: Scenes of devastation in the woods near Chateau Thierry following a heavy German bombardment of Marine positions.

rear; tired and worn, with stark terror on their faces. Many were walking, an occasional woman wheeled a perambulator with the baby in it. Sick people were lying exhausted beside the road. Some were driving carts piled high with their worldly goods. . . . Little flocks of sheep, a led cow, crates of chicken on carts.

Soon they also encountered a bedraggled column of beaten French soldiers, retreating as fast as their exhaustion would allow. One Captain Lloyd W Williams, when advised by a French officer to join the retreat, replied with one of the great ripostes of the war: 'Retreat, hell! We just got here!'

Heading for the sound of gunfire, the Marines soon arrived on the outskirts of Belleau Wood, where the German advance had halted and erected a formidable defensive position in the square mile of woods and rocks, manned by 1200 of the veteran 461st Imperial German Infantry.

The Marines opened fire on advanced German units at 800 yards, to the amazement of the Germans, who considered fire at over 200 yards to be ineffective. The Corps' marksmanship had made its first impression on the enemy. As the 9444 men of the 4th Brigade advanced, firing steadily and accurately, the Germans began to wonder if the Americans were charging them with machine guns. They dug in to await developments.

In the morning of 6 June the 1st Battalion, 5th Marines, led the attack west of Belleau Wood. They moved out into a vicious machine-gun crossfire that drove them back and claimed 410 casualties. A second try gained a toehold in the edge of the woods and 1087 more casualties. In the day's fighting the losses were the worst the Marines would suffer until 1943, at Betio Island, Tarawa Atoll. The Marines had confidently expected to sweep through the woods in a few hours. Now they were about to learn the hard way that this war did not work that way. But Marine pluck was not diminished; Sergeant Dan Daly led a charge with the immortal exhortation, 'Come on, you sons of bitches! Do you want to live forever?'

Pulling in reinforcements to the edge of the wood, the Marines began a process of close, bloody fighting in brushy terrain against the well-armed and experienced foe. It was tough going indeed. And it took 20 days. Units from the 5th and 6th Marines pushed up through the woods from the south, slowly driving the Germans back until the third defense line had retreated and the enemy was all but gone from the woods. Then on 13 June the German infantry counterattacked, led by a storm of shell and gas. In spite of deadly accurate long-range American rifle fire, the Germans advanced steadily, until the village of Bouresches, within the wood, was about to be abandoned by the Marines. However, the 1st Battalion, 6th Marines, under Major John A Hughes, was not inclined to give up the town. They held on, taking 450 casualties, until the Germans gave up. On 15 June an Army regiment relieved the exhausted 5th Marines, who returned to action on the 22nd and once again took up the gruelling job of dislodging the enemy.

After a failed American assault on the evening of the 23rd, the following day saw an artillery barrage that softened up the German positions. Then the 3rd Battalion, 5th Marines, charged into the last German holdouts and emerged from the other side of the woods at last. The commander of the unit, Major Maurice Shearer, telegraphed AEF headquarters, 'Woods now US Marine Corps' entirely.'

Repercussions of the battle of Belleau Wood were significant both for the progress of the war and for the future of the Marine Corps. Above all, Paris was now out of danger. The action received its proper testimonials from the Allies—future President (then Assistant Secretary of the Navy) Franklin Delano Roosevelt cabled his enthusiasm to Washington in August, and the

Below: An artist's impression of the Marines storming into German machine gun nests during the fighting at Belleau Wood.

grateful French renamed the wood 'Bois de la Brigade de Marine.' But perhaps the most eloquent testimonial to the fighting prowess of the Americans at Belleau Wood came from German intelligence:

> The 2nd American Division must be considered a very good one, and may perhaps even be reckoned as storm troops. The different attacks on Belleau Wood were carried out with bravery and dash. The moral effect of our gunfire cannot seriously impede the advance of the American riflemen.

The battle of Belleau Wood was also to change the future thrust of the Marine Corps. Traditionally, the Corps had seen action largely in small campaigns against insurgents or guerrillas in various parts of the world. It was this tradition that had made the Army dubious about using them on the Western Front. Now the Marines had proven themselves against seasoned infantry using the latest arms and tactics. And they had shown a cutting edge possible only to an elite unit of high *esprit* and courage. Their effectiveness in this kind of warfare was not to go unnoticed in American military planning of the future.

Finally, there was one other gift to history from the action in Belleau Wood. As the Marines scraped out rifle pits in the lines, they took to calling them 'foxholes.'

Soissons, St Mihiel and Blanc Mont

After the German offensives in the spring of 1918, General Ludendorff had gained valuable territory, punching three huge salients into the Allied lines in the first major shift of positions since 1914. He had also lost 600,000 men in the process, and these were troops he sorely missed. In July Foch decided it was time to counterattack on those bothersome salients.

Along the Marne the Allied attack, called the Aisne-Marne offensive, was made with a mixture of French, British, Italian and

Above: A wounded Marine is given first aid in a front line trench.
Left: General Lejeune examines a battle plan at his command post.

American troops. The French used 300 tanks in the action. A British invention, tanks were to be one of the deciding factors in the war, especially in the coming Allied offensive at Amiens—the iron monsters could roll with impunity into enemy trenches, and thus, along with airplanes, were chiefly responsible for breaking the stalemate of trench warfare. (Failing to develop their own tanks was one of the biggest German mistakes of the war.) The Aisne-Marne offensive was the place where the American soldiers came of age, establishing themselves once and for all as reliable fighters and finally gaining Pershing's goal of maintaining the unity of his forces.

In mid-July the 5th Marines and US Army forces were on the march with a polyglot collection of forces in the French XX Corps. The troops staggered along in

Above: American troops pause by the roadside as a French cavalry unit passes by during the Meuse Argonne offensive.

heavy rains and mud, cannons sticking and slowing in the road, men falling into ditches and breaking limbs. One Marine remembered that march:

Cold, hungry, and wet, on we marched, hour after hour, each man bearing a pack weighing about 45 pounds, consisting of two blankets, a supply of underclothes, a pair of trousers, emergency rations of hardtack and 'monkey meat' (canned corn beef), besides a heavy belt with 100 rounds of ammunition, a canteen, wire cutters, gas mask, helmet, rifle and bayonet. Yes, and each man had around his neck, next to his body, two identification tags, one of which would mark his grave and the other his body.

On 18 July came the attack near Soissons, prepared by the customary artillery barrage. The Marines pressed out, sweeping over open ground against German entrenchments, but nonetheless gaining two miles by noon and another three by evening. Casualties were severe, the 2nd Battalion, 6th Marines, losing over 50 percent in 30 minutes. Next day they came afoul of a German counterattack, but still managed to make nearly two miles. A field message from Lieutenant C B Cates gives some idea of the severity of the action:

I am in an old abandoned French trench bordering on road leading out from your CP and 350 yards from an old mill. I have only two men left out of my company and 20 out of other companies. We need support but it is almost suicide to try to get it here as we are swept by machine gun fire and a constant artillery barrage is upon us. I have no one on my left and only a few on my right. I will hold.

Finally the regimental casualties passed 50 percent and the Americans dug in, the Marines overlooking the Soissons–Château Thierry road, a major German supply route. They had taken 1972 casualties in the fighting, but the salient had been pinched out as ordered. Just after the action, General John A Lejeune, future Commandant of the Corps, took command of the 2nd Division. It was to be the only time in history that a Marine was to command an Army division.

Another part of Foch's Allied offensive was in the Meuse–Argonne region. The St Mihiel operation was directed at a German salient to the southeast, along the Meuse, that had existed since 1914. General Pershing had had his eye on that salient for some time, seeing that it would be a good training ground for his forces and, if broken through, allow the Allies to penetrate deep into German territory. Foch scuttled the latter idea, but agreed that the Americans would lead the fighting, pinching in the sides of the salient while the French held the point. It was to be the first mainly-American show of the war.

The attack was led by two Army corps with the Marine 4th Brigade (under General Wendell C Neville) following up as divisional reserve. On 12 September the Army corps strode out to the attack. The Germans were, as it happened, already in the process of abandoning the salient; that fact, combined with a heavy fog and the freshness of the American troops, made for some confusion in the advance. Still the Army men pressed forward gallantly, gaining territory and capturing 3300 prisoners by nightfall. A number of these prisoners were rounded up by German-born Marine Major William Ulrich, who single-handedly chased them down, shouting vociferously in German, and returned to his lines leading 40 of them, explaining, 'They were willing to listen to reason.'

On the second day the Marines took over the task of reducing the fortifications that screened the Hindenburg Line, the German fallback position and a dreaded strongpoint. The strength of the German pillboxes was recalled by a participant:

These were strong fortifications built of concrete with walls about two feet thick ranging in size from about five feet to 20 feet square. They were about five feet underground with about two feet extending above the surface, were well camouflaged and the larger ones were designed for four or more compartments. We also came upon many large dugouts, some of them 50 feet underground, into which we entered with great caution.

Nonetheless, the Marines reduced the forts as ordered. Overhead during the battle flew an Allied air force commanded by American Colonel Billy Mitchell—planes were now joined with tanks to break the war out of the trenches. Meanwhile in the Bois de la Montagne, ostensibly unoccupied, the 2nd Battalion, 6th Marines, had to rout a substantial enemy force and then deal with four counterattacks, including artillery and gas. On 15 September the enemy gave up in the woods. The St Mihiel salient had been wiped out. But to their great surprise and

Below: Marines at rest alongside a light railway of the type often used during the First World War to bring ammunition and supplies close to the front; near Verdun 1918.

Above: Marines man 3-inch guns aboard the battleship *Pennsylvania* during World War I.
Right: Marine machine gunners on maneuvers in France in the winter of 1917–18.

relief, the Germans found that the Americans were not going to push in further. In the four days of fighting the Marines had been comparatively lightly engaged, but still lost 132 in killed and 574 wounded. Their next engagement would not let them off so lightly.

Now the Allies entered the next phase of the Meuse–Argonne offensive, the objective being to drive the Germans back across their railroad communications. The 2nd Division, under General Lejeune, joined Foch's Frenchmen in the operation. Since losing that area would be fatal to the German fallback position—the Hindenburg Line—they were prepared to mount maximum resistance. The result was to be the hardest fighting of the war for the Americans.

To the east of the Allied offensive the American attack was to fall on the Heights of the Meuse, a series of hills which had seen terrible fighting two years previously and from whence the German July offensive had begun. The hills were a forbidding natural

Above: Fully-armed Marines dismount from their trucks and march off during training maneuvers in France in 1917, before American forces were fully committed to the front line.

defensive line. The key feature of the hills was Blanc Mont Ridge, held by the enemy since 1914. By the end of September the French had fought their way to the village of Somme–Py, at the foot of Blanc Mont Ridge and right on the Hindenburg Line. The French command considered breaking up the American 2nd Division to replace the exhausted fighters in the line, but Lejeune proposed instead that the Yanks be given a crack at the ridge. The French agreed.

On the morning of 3 October the American attack kicked off after a short artillery barrage, the 6th Marines, followed by the 5th, aiming for the left side of the ridge. The right side was to be assaulted by the 3rd Infantry Brigade. Together they were to bypass a German strongpoint and pinch it off, a tricky maneuver that was much liked by commanders on both sides and little liked by soldiers.

After three hours of heavy fighting the Marines had broken through the Hindenburg Line and gained their objective. Meanwhile, a company of the 5th Regiment had fallen off to the left side of the ridge to help the French take a nest of German machine guns; this enemy position was taken by the Marines, then lost by the French, then retaken by the Marines. During the advance two Marines earned the Medal of Honor. Private John Kelley singlehandedly charged a machine-gun emplacement, killed two, and brought back eight prisoners, all done in the middle of an American artillery barrage. Corporal J H Pruitt accounted for two enemy machine guns and 40 prisoners before being killed.

Finally reaching the crest of Blanc Mont Ridge to the left, the 6th Marines found themselves weak on the left flank due to French slowness on the western slope. Following close behind, the 5th Marines fell into a flanking position at right angles to the 6th. Thus protected, the men waited for the next day. On 4 October the two regiments changed places, the 5th pressing forward some three miles while the 6th protected the flank, picking away at the German machine guns on the western slope.

In sight of the village of St Etienne, the 5th was struck hard by an enemy assault on the left flank. A thousand men of the 1st Battalion swung and charged into the onrushing enemy. A participant remembered those moments:

> All along the extended line the saffron shrapnel flowered, flinging death and mutilation down. Singing balls and jagged bits of steel spattered on the hard ground like sheets of hail; the line writhed and staggered, steadied and went on, closing toward the center as the shells bit into it. High explosive shells came with the shrapnel, and where they fell geysers of torn earth and black smoke roared up to mingle with the devilish yellow in the air. A foul murky cloud of dust and smoke formed and went with the thinning companies, a cloud lit with red flashes and full of howling death.

Nearly 900 Marines fell in that barrage, but the remainder charged into the Germans and drove them back to St Etienne.

The next days saw incessant and severe fighting, the 5th and 6th Regiments joining with French troops to drive the Germans from the village while the rest of the ridge fell to the 2nd Division. On 8 October Marines finally marched into St Etienne. After another determined German counterattack, the Marines were relieved from the front. They had helped break through the line the Germans had built to be impregnable, and done their part in breaking the back of the Central Powers. It had cost 2538 casualties; in one company only 23 remained of 230 that had begun the battle.

Thereafter the Marines received their third citation from the French Army, earning the right to carry the Croix de Guerre on their colors. And they earned this commendation from a Marshal of France: 'The taking of Blanc Mont Ridge is the greatest single achievement of the 1918 campaign.'

The development of Marine aviation

In July 1918 the first contingent of the 1st Marine Aviation Air Force arrived in Brest. The unit had grown from a modest stateside beginning in the summer of 1917. A year later they were in action over France and bombing German submarine bases in the English Channel.

One of the earliest missions was an odd 'bombing' raid on 1 October 1918. Flying borrowed French de Havillands, the bombers dropped a payload of French bread and canned goods onto a stranded French regiment. Despite heavy fire, this and four later runs supported the beleagured Allies.

By the end of the war the Marine Air Unit had 2500 men and 340 airplanes, had inflicted 330 enemy casualties and shot down 12 planes, and dropped 52,000 pounds of bombs on 57 raids. It was a vigorous Marine entry into the air age, which would flower in the next war.

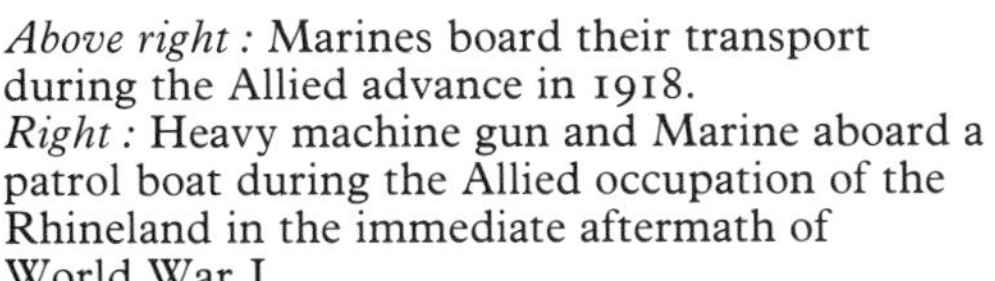

Above right: Marines board their transport during the Allied advance in 1918.
Right: Heavy machine gun and Marine aboard a patrol boat during the Allied occupation of the Rhineland in the immediate aftermath of World War I.

The final battle

As the Central Powers began to fall apart, Lejeune's 2nd Division, with some difficulty, joined the First Army in late October 1918, for final operations in the northern end of the Argonne Forest. The American forces in the area were given the task of punching through the Hindenburg Line and reducing two major fortifications—'Brünhilde' and 'Freya Stellung.'

On All Saints' Day the Marines of the 4th Brigade set out and pushed the demoralized Germans toward the Meuse, battalions leapfrogging one another to keep the attack moving steadily. German desertions increased, the retreating soldiers shouting at the incoming reserves that they were prolonging the war. Nonetheless, resistance remained stiff.

As was often the case, the Marines made faster progress than their Army compatriots; by mid-afternoon, units of the 4th Brigade were entrenching on high ground and waiting for the Army to catch up before resuming the advance. Some 1700 of the enemy had been captured. Then on 1 November the Marines outdid themselves, racing across the landscape at a rate that elicited this praise from an Army general:

> It was a brilliant advance of more than nine kilometers, destroying the last stronghold in the Hindenburg Line, capturing the Freya Stellung, one of the most remarkable achievements made by any troops in this war . . . These results must be

attributed to the great dash and speed of the troops, and to the irresistible force with which they struck and overcame the enemy.

After further rapid Allied advances, the Germans by 9 November had retreated over the Meuse and the 4th Brigade was ready to spearhead attacks across the river at Mouzon and Villemontry. On the night of the 10th, assault units crossed under heavy enemy fire on new Army footbridges. Next morning, as the Marines prepared to renew the advance, the artillery fire suddenly sank to a strange silence a little before 11 o'clock. That silence signaled the end of the war.

Action away from the Western Front

While the 4th Brigade was fighting in France, other segments of the Corps maintained their duties all around the world—in Haiti, Santo Domingo, and Cuba. Elsewhere, numbers of Marines served on Navy ships patroling the Atlantic. In the Azores, Marines guarded Navy antisubmarine bases; although no enemy submarine showed up in the area, this operation, involving artillery and planes, was a prototype of the kind of air-ground island operations which would be critical in World War II.

In June of 1918 Marines were sent to Vladivostok, helping to protect the United States Consulate in the wake of the Russian Revolution. Though most of the forces there gave way to Army Units in late August, a guard of Marines remained until 1922 at a Navy radio station in Vladivostok Bay.

A new Commandant

With the tour of command of George Barnett running out in early 1918, it was assumed as a matter of course that he would be reappointed. His men, everyone agreed, had done outstandingly well in their action. Navy Secretary Josephus Daniels indeed made the reappointment in February; but at the same time, to Barnett's surprise, Daniels prodded the Commandant to retire. Barnett refused and the Secretary backed down. But a few months later Barnett was astonished to hear himself denounced in the House of Representatives as a 'rocking-chair warrior.' (The Representative doing so happened to be the father of Marine General Smedley D Butler, no admirer of Barnett due partly to the fact that the Commandant himself had seen little combat action.)

Despite Barnett's stated outrage, the matter rested for two years, at which point Secretary Daniels summarily cashiered him and put General John A Lejeune in his place. The irregular nature of the affair was duly noted, but the respect and popularity commanded by Lejeune at length made it a moot question. General Lejeune became the 12th Commandant of the Corps on 30 June, 1920.

Right: A Marine Corps seaplane equipped for mapping work in the late 1920s.
Below: Marine infantry make a cautious advance on a German position in late 1918.
Bottom: Aerial mapping plane of the Cuban Aerial Survey takes off.

Above: Marines man a rudimentary air defense position in France in 1918.
Below: A Marine cameraman is caught at work filming captured German guns in 1919.

Peace: military lessons of World War I

The nature of war had changed. It had changed by the beginning of the war, when the tactics and imaginations of military leaders had not shown themselves up to the new demands of trench warfare, and it had changed again by the end of the war.

At the outset the spade and the bullet ruled the battlefield; traditional offensive tactics were all but impotent against that combination. This impasse had been broken at last by a new element of technology—the internal combustion engine, which made possible the tanks that drove through the trenches and the planes that assaulted them from the air. Added to these were wireless telegraphy, which speeded battlefield communications, and the new effectiveness of

Above: American forces march through the streets of Vladivostok during the Allied intervention in Russia after the Revolution. *Left:* Marines at ease in Santo Domingo in the World War I period.

submarines. Because of the new technology, war was to become a contest of machines as much as of men, of numbers of factories as much as numbers of soldiers. Battle in the future would move at a vastly increased tempo, and with considerably enhanced destructive power.

The leaders of the US Marine Corps pondered these changes, knowing that the new ways of war would still require an elite group of fighting men. The aviation branch had gotten its start; developing from that would be the techniques of close-air support which would be vital in the next conflict. Still to come were the important concepts and developments that would lead to modern Marine amphibious warfare. .

'Peace is Hell'—1918-1941

After the experience of the First World War, Commandant Lejeune began to take stock and to set in motion a good deal of thinking about the future function and tactics of the Corps. In this effort he was guided, as it turned out, by a mixture of planning, prophecy, and happenstance that would unite to transform the whole nature and mission of the Corps, turning it away from its traditional function as a colonial infantry and toward an integrated and vital role within the United States services. But before that could happen, there were still a few adventures in the 'colonies.'

Cuba, Haiti, and Santo Domingo

Early in 1917 unrest flared around the sugar-cane fields at Guacanayabo Bay, Cuba. Since sugar was considered necessary to the Allied war effort, the US Consul in Santiago called in the Marines to restore order. Thus came about the 'Sugar Intervention.'

In late February a fleet of US ships converged around the island and the Marines seized the north coast and Santiago in the east. The general idea was to protect the American-owned sugar mills while allowing the Cuban Army to round up dissidents. This strategy worked well enough, and things quickly cooled down around the countryside to the extent that a number of Marines were sent back stateside in May, to prepare for action in Europe.

But the relative tranquility proved short-lived. Encouraged, it was said, by German agents, rebels began a program of sabotage against the sugar plantations. In late 1917 two regiments of Marines were sent to the Oriente Province, again protecting the sugar plantations while the Cuban Army operated against the rebels. And once again things quickly calmed down. The Marines stayed on in Cuba as a visible but not particularly active force until 1919.

In Haiti things were not so easy. After a couple of years of relative peace, the Cacos took arms again in 1918. Their immediate grievance was the resurrection, by American authorities, of the practice of *corvée*, an old French dictate which required peasants to work unpaid on public roads. Not surprisingly, the peasants were enraged at this enforced peonage.

Into this unsettled situation stepped one Charlemagne Péralte, a dynamic leader who had been active with Cacos in central Haiti. He began recruiting peasants for organized revolt, and by 1918 had an army of some 5000 men and an active revolution in progress.

The American commandant of the Haitian Gendarmerie, realizing this was beyond their capabilities, called for the Marines in spring 1919. The 1st Brigade arrived and over the spring and summer engaged in some 131 engagements with Charlemagne's band of Cacos—without, however, making much of a dent in their operations.

The frustration of the campaign led Marine Sergeant Herman H Hanneken to decide on some rather under-the-table tactics to reach the elusive Caco chief. In August 1919 Hanneken set up his own bandit leader, a prominent local citizen who took to the field with a small band and began a series of phony 'battles' with Hanneken's men (the sergeant at one point sported a wound, also ersatz, from one of these mock battles). Slowly Hanneken's stooge, Conzé, earned the attention and the trust of Charlemagne.

Conzé then urged Charlemagne to join him in a raid on the town of Grande Rivière du Nord. This agreed to, Hanneken was duly informed; he made plans to defend the town and also to meet Charlemagne personally. On the day of the scheduled attack, Hanneken and Lieutenant William R Button, darkened with burnt cork and disguised as Cacos, led a group of similarly-disguised gendarmes into rebel territory. Guided by an informer, they made it through several near-exposures to Charlemagne's camp, which was manned by some 200 Cacos.

Charlemagne was pointed out by the informer, and Hanneken stepped up to him. As Charlemagne turned to address the stranger, he was greeted by two .45 slugs in the chest, which killed him instantly. The gendarme band immediately emptied their rifles into the crowd and settled down to repel several counterattacks during the night. Next day they made it back to Grande Rivière du Nord (which had successfully weathered the Caco attack) with the body of Charlemagne.

Though bandit activity continued for some time, its force had been broken. Hanneken and Button received the Congressional Medal of Honor. By mid-1920

Left: Marines on sentry duty in Santo Domingo, a deceptively peaceful view of an often violent intervention.

In midmorning two Marine planes happened to fly over the town on reconnaissance. Seeing the situation, they strafed the rebels, returned to base and came back loaded with bombs. They began dive-bombing Sandino's men, sending the rebels into a panic and accounting for considerable casualties. Though British and American pilots had previously experimented with dive-bombing, this was the world's first use of the technique in actual combat. Its effectiveness was dramatic, and it ended the rebel attack on Ocotal forthwith.

Thus began a new era of air-ground support that would be invaluable in World War II. This tactic would undergo considerable refinement from its first use in Nicaragua, but in Ocotal the principle had been firmly established. Other occasions soon followed. In January 1928, Marines besieged in Quilali were aided by 10 landings under fire onto an airstrip cut through the center of the town. The flights brought in supplies and took out wounded, and earned their pilot a Medal of Honor. As operations in Nicaragua went on—without managing to round up Sandino—it became regular practice to use planes in support of patrols and garrisons.

the last strongholds of Caco operations had been suppressed (some of it accomplished by a policy of amnesty). In 1924 the Marine force in Haiti was reduced to 500 men; these were finally withdrawn ten years later.

Nicaragua

The Marines had been in Nicaragua since 1913, helping that habitually troubled country to keep a lid on various internal problems. But in 1925 a Conservative faction took over the government by force. The Liberals took to arms, headed for the hills, and the ensuing conflict escalated steadily, finally threatening American business and property. The Marines appeared in 1926 their operations gradually took on the weight of an expedition.

Then there was a surprising and hopeful development. American political efforts, backed up by the presence of the Marines, led to talks between Conservative and Liberal leaders that in mid-1927 resulted in the Liberals laying down their arms and a general pacification agreement, with a promise of free elections. But this agreement, made under the shadow of American power, was not satisfactory to one of the Liberal leaders, Augusto Sandino. Refusing to accept the accord, Sandino slipped to the mountain jungles to carry on the guerrilla war.

A highly articulate man with a reported cruel streak, Sandino had a flair for publicity and the ability to cultivate connections all over the world (throughout his rebellion he had numbers of supporters in the United States). He also had considerable skill in building an army and maintaining them by appeals to ideology and patriotism. However, though he was able to elude capture for four years in spite of the best efforts of the Marines and Guardia Nacional, he was not able to lead his forces to a decisive victory.

In 1927 the Marines began setting up numbers of garrisons in the jungle, trying to contain Sandino in the highlands. All efforts to run him aground came to naught, however, frustrated by local sympathizers and the rebels' superior knowledge of the country. Nonetheless, instead of a successful campaign in its intended direction, the Marine experience in Nicaragua was to bear unexpected fruits: it became a major laboratory in the techniques of jungle warfare, which was to prove most valuable in the future.

This fact was not lost on Marine Captain Merrit A Edson, who divined that learning methodically to fight guerrillas in the bush might come in very handy (as he himself was later to prove in the Pacific). He developed new approaches, tactics and formations for ground fighting in rough territory. And most importantly, prodded by necessity, he stumbled on the beginnings of modern air-ground coordination.

It happened first in the village of Ocotal on 16 July 1927. In a surprise offensive against that fortified town, which was manned by 62 Marines and 48 of the new, poorly-trained Guardia Nacional, Sandino sent 600 men whooping to the attack just after midnight. When his initial assault was repulsed after two hours of hard fighting, Sandino turned to a tactic of attrition, trying to force the defenders to use up their ammunition.

Above: Red Cross ladies greet men of the 2nd Marines parading in New York in 1919 on their return from France.
Right: Marines in the hills of Haiti.

Right: Recruits being sworn in at the receiving station at Parris Island, a picture taken in 1919. The presiding officer is Captain Benjamin Fogg, USMC.

Despite frustrations regarding Sandino, the Marines did materially contribute to realizing the country's first free election in 1928, which placed the Liberals in power. The next year Sandino fled to Mexico for a year, where he successfully generated international support for his cause against his old Liberal compatriots (some, but by no means all, of this support came from Communist quarters—though Sandino himself was not a Communist). On his return the guerrilla war resumed; it ended only in 1934, when Sandino was lured into Managua and killed by the Guardia Nacional under Colonel Anastasio Somoza, later dictator of Nicaragua.

It had been a long and frustrating campaign for the Marines, and for the US as well. Though the tactics of jungle fighting and close-air support were to prove quite fruitful in the future, recognition of their real value also lay in the future. Meanwhile the government of the United States was beginning to rethink its paternal-interventionist policies in areas that would later be known as the Third World. The ramifications of traditional American policy were becoming increasingly complex and international, the effect on future American foreign relations increasingly unpredictable. The Marines left Nicaragua in 1933, after the third national election. It was to be the last of the 'banana wars.' But America was still to be haunted, in the 1980s, by the spirit of Augusto Sandino, when the anti-American ruling party of Nicaragua named themselves 'Sandianistas.'

Guns and letters

The early 1920s Stateside saw a nationwide crime wave that involved a series of robberies of US mail. The problem at length became serious enough that the Marines were assigned to try and do something about it. They proceeded to do so with customary directness. Secretary of the Navy Edwin Denby, a former Marine, sent a letter to Corps officers directing them to station their men, armed, alongside postmen, and included the exortation, '. . . if attacked, shoot and shoot to kill . . . When our men go in as guards over mail, that mail must be delivered or there must be a Marine dead at the post of duty.' Problems with mail robberies disappeared with notable promptness. A recurrence of robberies in 1926 was handled likewise, and with the same results.

Marines in China

In the middle 1920s China was in the grip of a civil war, with Cantonese and Northern Armies fighting it out all over the countryside. Under the leadership of Chiang Kai-shek, the Soviet-supported Cantonese threatened Shanghai early in 1927. To protect the International Settlement in the city, Marines were sent in February under the command of Smedley Butler. They spent two years troubleshooting effectively there and in other areas. By 1929 things had relaxed enough that much of the detachment was pulled out, leaving behind a force of 'China Marines' to protect American interests. They remained there until the outbreak of World War II.

Above: Marines search native huts on Santo Domingo for arms. The American involvement in Santo Domingo left a persistent legacy of bitterness and anti-American feeling on the island.
Main picture: Marines on Santo Domingo.

Inset, below: Marines on Santo Domingo find time to relax at a field day.

Above: Marines repack stores on board ship en route to Nicaragua in 1926.

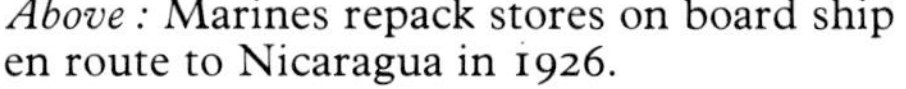

The 'Orange Plan'

Between the wars Commandant Lejeune directed a good deal of hard thinking about the implications of new wars, new kinds of terrain, new machines and the new tactics that would have to accompany them. As often happens, technology had advanced faster than the understanding of how to use it; and in the case of war, this can have most unpleasant results.

The process of rethinking was started by a strange, visionary, and ultimately tragic US Marine Corps staff officer named Earl Hancock ('Pete') Ellis. In 1913, well before the First World War, Ellis had given a series of highly classified lectures at the Naval War College. There he prophesied that America would someday fight a war with Japan, and that this conflict would involve the islands and atolls of the trans-Pacific (most of which, except for US-held Guam, became Japanese after the First World War). To deal with this eventuality, Ellis proposed a far-reaching development of amphibious warfare techniques. His predictions and concepts were so revolutionary that they were hardly noticed at the time.

Then the war intervened. After service in Europe, Ellis returned to his labors. His ideas, reinforced by the reality of Japanese gains after the war, found support among the leaders of the Corps, most notably in the person of Lejeune. The ensuing conceptual work came to be known under the heading of the 'Orange Plan.' These studies led in 1921 to a publication, mostly written by Ellis, called 'Advanced Base Operations in Micronesia,' which predicted with astonishing prescience the coming war in the Pacific and outlined the operations necessary to pursue it. In spite of much dubiousness in the other services, Lejeune approved the plan and proceeded to formulate the Marines' response to its challenge.

Meanwhile, Pete Ellis, obsessed with the Japanese threat to the point of neurosis, and drinking heavily, essayed an unofficial one-man reconnaissance of Japanese-held islands in the Pacific. During this journey he died, under mysterious circumstances, on the island of Koror. The Corps learned of his death through the Japanese authorities who meanwhile had cremated his body. The exact nature of his death was never cleared up, but the work he began went on.

Left: 1st Lieutenant Rogus and 1st Sergeant Belcher prepare their DH-4 aircraft for take off on a long-distance flight from Santo Domingo to Washington DC and San Francisco. The round trip took from 19 September to 9 November 1923. *Right:* F4B aircraft of VF10, part of the West Coast Expeditionary Force, around 1930.

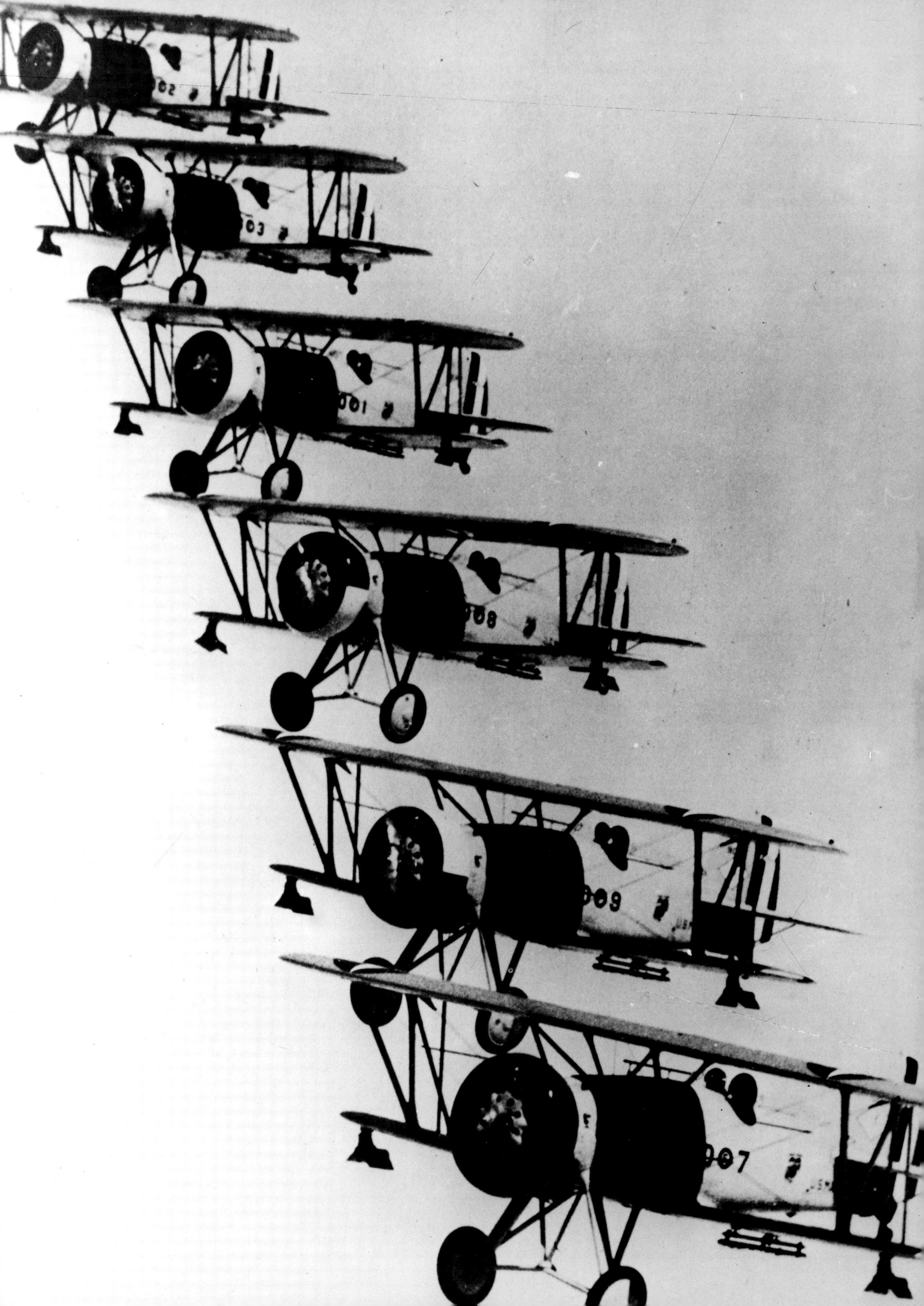

In light of Ellis's advocacy of amphibious warfare, Colonel Robert H Dunlap began an exhaustive study of the most elaborate amphibious operation of the First World War—the Allied debacle at Gallipoli. It was finally concluded, to the Marines' satisfaction if not that of the other services, that the operation had failed not because it was impossible (as current military doctrine had it) but because it was handled with utter ineptitude. History has amply confirmed this conclusion.

Now committed to developing its amphibious capabilities, the Corps held a series of exercises in Cuba and elsewhere during the years 1922 to 1925. These landing exercises served mainly to show that current tactics and landing craft—wooden navy launches—were spectacularly inadequate to the proposed tasks. Much work had to be done, then, in the planning and development of new technology.

After 1925 expeditionary duties were to divert the Corps from these studies for some years. But during that time there did appear a significant pamphlet called *Joint Action, Army and Navy*, which was another big step in the evolution of modern joint operations.

In March 1929 Lejeune stepped down as Commandant, leaving behind the most remarkable record of leadership since the days of Archibald Henderson. His tenure had seen the extraordinarily prescient development of amphibious capability, the strengthening of Marine officer education and procurement, a system of correspondence training, enhanced coordination with other services, and a resulting rise in the readiness and *esprit* of the Corps. Lejeune's immediate successor, General Wendell C Neville, died within a year of his appointment. From 1930 to 1936 the command was filled by two old colleagues, Ben H Fuller and then John H Russell, who continued the planning and modernization begun so ably by Lejeune.

Below: Marines huddle in the bottom of their landing craft during a training exercise in World War II.

Replaying the Civil War

While most of Lejeune's efforts had taken place within the confines of the Corps, a highly publicised series of exercises kept the Marines busy during the early 1920s. They recreated several Civil War battles—Gettysburg, Antietam, and New Market—on the actual battlefields. Besides entertaining politicians and reporters, these exercises were, or were claimed to be, useful workouts in ground operations. And they kept the Marines in the nation's mind as well.

Birth of the Fleet Marine Force

Under Ben Fuller and his Assistant—later Commandant—John Russell, the Marines again addressed the issue of amphibious warfare in the early 1930s. The developments that ensued were to constitute the most dramatic turning point in Corps history.

In 1932 was published the first American military text specifically dealing with doctrines of amphibious warfare—*Marine Corps Landing Operations*. In the same era there was a complete reevaluation of the functions of the Expeditionary Force concept, which at length concluded that the Marines needed more personnel, more stability of duty, more training and new concepts along the lines pioneered by Pete Ellis.

As a result of these conclusions, Russell stabilized the Expeditionary Force and staff as an integral part of the US Fleet, in the process changing its title to the Fleet Marine Force (FMF). Then he went ahead. The doctrines of amphibious warfare had been formed; now they had to be fleshed out with appropriate field tactics.

In 1934 came a small booklet entitled *Tentative Manual for Landing Operations*. It has been called by one historian a 'pioneer work of the most daring and imaginative sort,' and by another, the 'Pentateuch and Four Gospels' of modern amphibious warfare. In revised and perfected form, the manual's tenets were to be followed by all the services of the US and her allies in World War II. It dealt briefly but succinctly with every aspect of operations—command relations, ship-to-shore movement and communications, the relations of air and naval gunfire support, the basics of disembarking and of shore party organization.

The refining of this revolutionary document took place in the schoolroom, on the drawing board, and on the beach in a number of exercises. Once the tactics were stated on paper, however, there had to be created the technology to actualize it. In contrast to the situation before the First World War, theory had outstripped technology.

Above all there had to be some kind of new landing craft. After many false starts, this requirement finally came to rest with two people. One was ship designer Andrew Higgens, whose prototypes led to the World War II 'Landing Craft Vehicle and Personnel' (LCVP) and 'Landing Craft Mechanized' (LCM). Both featured a hinged bow that dropped to disgorge soldiers and equipment on the beach; they would become familiar from endless photos of the war. And there was Donald Roebling of Florida, whose amphibious 'Alligator,' developed for rescue work in the Everglades, became the familiar Amtrack, capable of sailing up to and then over the beaches on its finned tracks.

The clouds of war gather

These developments of the 1930s capped the history of what came to be known as the 'old Marine Corps.' They arrived none too soon, because the storm clouds were building in Europe and in the Pacific. Germany, demoralized by a dictated and vindictive peace agreement in the Treaty of Versailles, fell under the spell of Adolf Hitler. (When he first saw the treaty, Marshal Foch of France had exclaimed, 'This isn't peace! This is a truce for 20 years!' He was to be quite precisely correct.) And Japan was zeroing in on the Pacific as its dreams of conquest grew. There it was to be exactly as Pete Ellis had prophesied, and exactly as the Marines had marshaled all their powers, transforming the Corps in the process, to resist and finally to help defeat the Japanese.

Right: Marine Women Reserves pass a column of Leathernecks at Camp Lejeune in 1943, a token of the many changes that World War II was to bring to the Marine Corps.

330
330

WORLD WAR II
335
328

'Remember Pearl Harbor'—1941-1945

The decline of Rome in the 5th century. The discovery of the New World at the end of the 15th century. The Reformation in the 16th. The French Revolution of 1789–1799. World War I, the cataclysmic conflict of blood and futility that pitted the world-dominating European nations against one another between 1914 and 1918 only to weaken the system upon which they were built and lead to more conflict two decades later. All were events that shook and re-formed the entire world. Nothing was the same thereafter. Each event ushered in a new world where the powers of nations and the thinking of people were dramatically changed so that what had gone before seemed to be but fading memories of a simpler and less dangerous era in the history of mankind. Each demanded a fundamental readjustment of man's perception of him-self, his life, and his destiny upon this earth. And added to this list of time-shaping events in our age was the epic conflict of nations between 1939 and 1945 we call World War II.

World War II: The Event that Cut History in Two

By this war, the United States and the Soviet Union were catapulted into pre-eminence to stand astride the globe with weapons and powers of decision-making unthinkable in earlier times. Former great nations were weakened and lost their colonies. These colonies—taking advantage of the enfeebled political and economic conditions in the countries that had recently dominated them—now demanded their share of political freedom and material largess. War-induced technological changes not only in weaponry—crowned by the over-whelming destructive force of the atomic bomb—but also in transportation, computerization and miniaturization, to say nothing of new medicines and their life-saving and life-prolonging benefits, brought about problems undreamed of in former times. Problems of once all-but-unknown nations became problems of the world, and it was clear that they could draw into the jaws of limited or unlimited warfare even peace-loving peoples half a world away.

Taking part in, and in many ways the chief beneficiary of, all of these changes coming out of World War II was the United States. Having abandoned its essentially 'Fortress America' mentality early in the twentieth century to stand beside its European allies in World War I—only largely to retreat to its own shores in a fit of isolationism arising out of its disappointment with the outcome of that war—it found after the final defeat of the Axis powers in 1945 that such comfortable retreat was no longer possible. America was now a world power and the chief defender of the heritage of the Western World whether it welcomed this responsibility or not. Its friends and its interests encircled the globe. It could either stand up to those who would destroy its ideals and those of its friends or it could surrender itself to its ideological and political enemies. The stakes had been raised significantly by World War II; the dangers of miscalculation were even greater; the price of defeat was more and more unthinkable. Playing a major role in World War II from beginning to end by standing at the fore to defend the nation, and prepared to continue its service in the crisis-filled years that followed, was the United States Marine Corps.

Pearl Harbor

The Marines, like the other US military services, were in the process of preparing but hardly ready when war came in December 1941. As part of the mobilization program belatedly begun by the nation in the late 1930s, the Corps was anxious to move to a 50,000-man level at a minimum, but President Franklin D Roosevelt refused to make such a commitment until after the presidential election campaign of 1940. Accordingly, that level of manpower was reached only in mid-1941 (it would expand to almost 460,000 before the war was over). Nevertheless, vital steps were meanwhile being taken within the limitations imposed by political realities to prepare the Marines for action if events drew the United States into the conflicts already blazing in Europe, the Middle East and the Far East.

By late 1940 the Marine Aviation Wings (MAWs) were being expanded from their almost miniscule numbers of 452 officers and 3000 enlisted personnel. The call-up of reserve officers and enlisted men had added 5000 men to the Fleet Marine Force. On the Atlantic coast the 1st Marine Division was continuing its training exercises in amphibious operations, and a new training camp had been established in the pine barrens of North Carolina near the new port of Morehead City (it would later be named Camp Lejeune) to further the Corps' training missions and supplement Parris Island. And Cherry Point Marine Corps Air Station was under construction nearby. On the West Coast, Camp Elliot had recently been established at Kearney Mesa 12 miles outside San Diego for the training of recruits. (In 1942 the Corps purchased the 132,000-acre site some 48 miles outside San Diego that became Camp Pendleton. These two facilities were destined to become the Corps' primary West Coast training camps.) On the West Coast, too, amphibious warfare tactics were being developed. As in the East, these training exercises were conducted with the Army, but a lack of success in these dual-service operations led the Army to recommend that the Fleet Marine Force (FMF) look to the Pacific for possible areas of amphibious operations while the Army concentrated on possible European landings.

But despite its growing strength and newly-found concentration on amphibious landings for the FMF, US Marine personnel as of late 1941 were still spread far and wide across the globe at various duty stations. Of its 65,000 men, 18,000 were deployed overseas from Iceland to and beyond the Philippines, including China, Guam, Wake, Midway and various other locations. Another 4000 Marines were stationed on Navy ships or at naval stations, 20,000 were in training at land bases, and the remainder were at various other installations and duties. Although few if any of them suspected it would come so soon, the Marines' test of battle was about to descend upon

Previous page: Unloading ammunition from landing craft during the New Georgia campaign.
Left: Burned out fighter plane at Wheeler Field Hawaii in the aftermath of the Pearl Harbor attack.
Right: The destroyers *Cassin* and *Downes* and the battleship *Pennsylvania* at Pearl Harbor.

Above: Close up of the damage on the *Downes* in the drydock at Pearl Harbor. Remarkably she was repaired and returned to service in the later stages of the fighting in the Pacific.

them in the form of over 300 Imperial Japanese Navy bombers, torpedo planes, and fighters that lifted from the flight decks of their carriers in the clear morning air of 7 December 1941 while 200 miles north of Pearl Harbor on the island of Oahu in the Hawaiian Islands. Within hours the greatest surprise attack in history was carried out. America soon entered World War II, and the United States Marine Corps was forced to fight its way back from heartbreaking initial defeats to attain the greatest victories in its history.

At 7:55 AM that Sunday morning the Japanese planes struck. Before the air raids were over two hours later, the 4500 Marines stationed at Pearl Harbor had fought with unparalleled bravery with whatever weapons they could get their hands on, including machine guns salvaged from what was left of the 48 planes of Marine Air Group 21 (MAG-21), almost all having been destroyed on the ground in the first attacks by the diving Japanese Zeroes and Val dive bombers. In all, 112 Marines paid with their lives for their gallant if futile defensive efforts against the Japanese attackers. American casualties totaled more than 4000. And like their counterparts in the other services, the Marines stood bloody but unbowed in the aftermath of the Pearl Harbor attack and vowed that the Japanese —and their allies—would pay dearly for their treachery. For the Marines, the final payment for Pearl Harbor was never considered paid until the last Leatherneck put down his weapon in victory on Okinawa three-and-a-half years later and learned that the final assault on the Japanese home islands was no longer necessary. The price of vindication was high and bloodstained, but the Marines were prepared to pay that price in the months and years that followed until the stain of Pearl Harbor had been removed from the American flag.

Initial Defeats

Within hours of the attack on Pearl Harbor, Marines in China and on the American outposts of Guam, Wake and Midway were feeling the fury of Japanese attacks. The small garrison of less than 200 Marines scattered on the Chinese mainland was determined to fight back, but obeyed orders from their commanders to surrender to overwhelming power rather than sacrifice themselves to American honor as they desired to do. Guam was virtually defenseless. The Marines there, numbering only 153 officers and men, were reinforced by an Insular Guard of native Guamanians, but it numbered only 80 men. The heaviest weapons available to the Marines were a few .30-caliber machine guns. The small American naval detachment, consisting of a minesweeper, an old tanker, and two patrol boats, was sunk the first day by Japanese air attacks. Then, after two days of bombing, almost 6000 Japanese soldiers landed in three locations on Guam. After a futile defense near the capital of Agana, the naval governor of the island bowed to the inevitable and surrendered his forces to the Japanese invaders on 10 December. Four Marines and 15 Guamanians had died in the defense of the island.

Although the Marine garrisons at Midway, Johnston, and Palmyra islands in the Central Pacific were only lightly attacked by Japanese naval and air units in the first few days of the war, Wake Island, located about halfway between Hawaii and the Philippines and being prepared as a base for naval patrol planes, was subjected to direct invasion within days of Pearl Harbor. The Japanese had no intention of allowing Wake to remain in American hands. On the three small islands making up Wake Atoll there were only 449 Marines and a Marine fighter squadron, lately reinforced with a dozen new Grumman F4F Wildcats as a defense force. The only other persons on the islands were some 50 Army and Navy specialists and 1200 civilian construction personnel. The Japanese attacks on Wake began on 7 December with an initial attack on the small island defenses by 36 Japanese bombers. Seven of the new Wildcats, caught on the ground while refueling, were blasted into wreckage, and the aviation gasoline tank went up in flames. Twenty-three Marines were dead or dying after the attack. For the next two days the Japanese returned to bomb the garrison, only to be met by accurate anti-aircraft fire from the ground and gallant air attacks by the remaining Wildcat pilots. Although the Marine defenders were clearly acquitting themselves well against the enemy bombers, everyone on Wake Island waited for the amphibious attack that was sure to follow. It came on 10 December in the form of nine cruisers and destroyers escorting four transports. These were met by withering fire from Marine shore batteries and skillful air attacks by the four remaining Wildcats. The furious fighting that day ended with the Japanese invasion fleet limping away in disarray, having lost 700 troops and having had two ships sunk and eight damaged.

The Americans had won the first round at Wake, but the Japanese were determined that the tiny atoll would fall into their hands. Back they came, and from 12 December until 23 December the battle for Wake Island continued. Gradually the daily Japanese bombing—one raid at mid-day and another at dusk—began to take its toll, and soon the Marine aviators and their ground crews (decimated by injuries and unable to salvage any more spare parts) could no longer put even one airplane into the air to defend the island. Yet the Marines held on because a relief expedition consisting of the carrier *Saratoga*, three heavy cruisers, nine destroyers, a tanker and the USS *Tangier* loaded with Marine reinforcements and the supplies the defenders needed to hold out was on the way. Unfortunately, its progress was dilatory and it was fated to arrive too late. The powerful task force was only 425 miles from Wake when the Japanese began an amphibious landing in force covered by 12 cruisers and destroyers on 23 December. The order went out to the task force from Pearl Harbor to retire from the scene, and the convoy turned away. The Marines and civilians remaining on Wake resisted the 1500-man invasion force as best they could, but after 11 hours of embattled resistance the Navy officer commanding decided to surrender to the Japanese to save the lives of those who remained. Those Marines who survived the attacks on Wake Island joined their comrades from China and Guam in Japanese captivity, but not before they fought with everything possible to uphold the honor and territory of their country on the tiny mid-Pacific atoll.

Meanwhile the Marines and their Army and Navy comrades in the Philippines were writing their own tale of courage in the face of overwhelming odds in the first weeks of the war. Despite the fact that the islands' air force of Army B-17s was wiped out on the ground on 7 December and that the small US Asiatic Fleet was ordered south to join Allied fleets in the Netherlands East

Above: Marine antiaircraft crew aboard the carrier *Wasp* during a lull in operations near Guadalcanal on 7 August 1942.

Indies to try to hold off the Japanese naval offensives in that area soon thereafter, the American defenders were determined to fight as long as possible to delay the Japanese juggernaut while hoping that reinforcements would arrive. The Marines of the 4th Division, recently arrived from Shanghai, were put under the command of Army General Douglas MacArthur for the defense of the archipelago and were assigned the job of defending the beaches of Corregidor Island—'the Rock' at the entrance to Manila Bay—against Japanese attacks. As the Japanese landed in various spots on Luzon on 20 December 1941 and fought their way toward the capital of Manila, Bataan Peninsula and Corregidor nearby became the last bastions of the islands' defenses. American troops of all three services were thrown together to prevent or at least delay the all-but-inevitable fall of the archipelago. Much to the dismay of the Japanese attackers, the combined American forces with their Filipino allies held off the invading troops through December, then January, February and March 1942.

But despite the desperate heroism of the troops, Bataan fell in early April, rendering Corregidor completely vulnerable to fresh Japanese artillery, air, and naval gunnery attacks despite the determination of the defenders to resist to the last man. Almost incessant battering of the Corregidor defenses were preliminary to an amphibious assault upon the besieged fortress. Despite the best efforts of two battalions of the 4th Marine Regiment—aided by Army, Navy and Philippine troops to a total number of 3891 officers and men—the full-scale invasion of 4–5 May could not be held off. When the Japanese managed to land tanks, and Lieutenant General Jonathan Wainwright (who had succeeded General MacArthur when the Army commander was ordered to leave the Philippines to make his way to Australia to lead the Allied offensive back against the Japanese aggressors) was informed that half of the defenders of Corregidor were either dead or wounded, he made the heartrending decision to surrender the Philippine defense forces. Knowing that almost 700 of his Marines were either dead or wounded, the commander of the Marine forces on Corregidor, Colonel Samuel L Howard, ordered the colors of the 4th Marine Regiment burned and led his men into captivity on 5 May. All of the prisoners were then forced to undergo the infamous 'Bataan Death March' into captivity. It had taken the Japanese five months to overwhelm the defenders of the Philippines, and the Marines had displayed the valor that was their proud tradition. America—and its military forces—had taken a beating at Pearl Harbor, on Guam and Wake, and now in the Philippines in the early months of the war, but it was clear that the nation and her allies suffered no lack of courage and determination to turn the tables as time and circumstances permitted. The Japanese had indeed won the initial rounds, but the Pacific war was far from over.

Below: A Marine unit ready to move up to the front line during the unavailing defense of Bataan in March 1942. Few were to survive the fighting and the subsequent imprisonment by the Japanese.

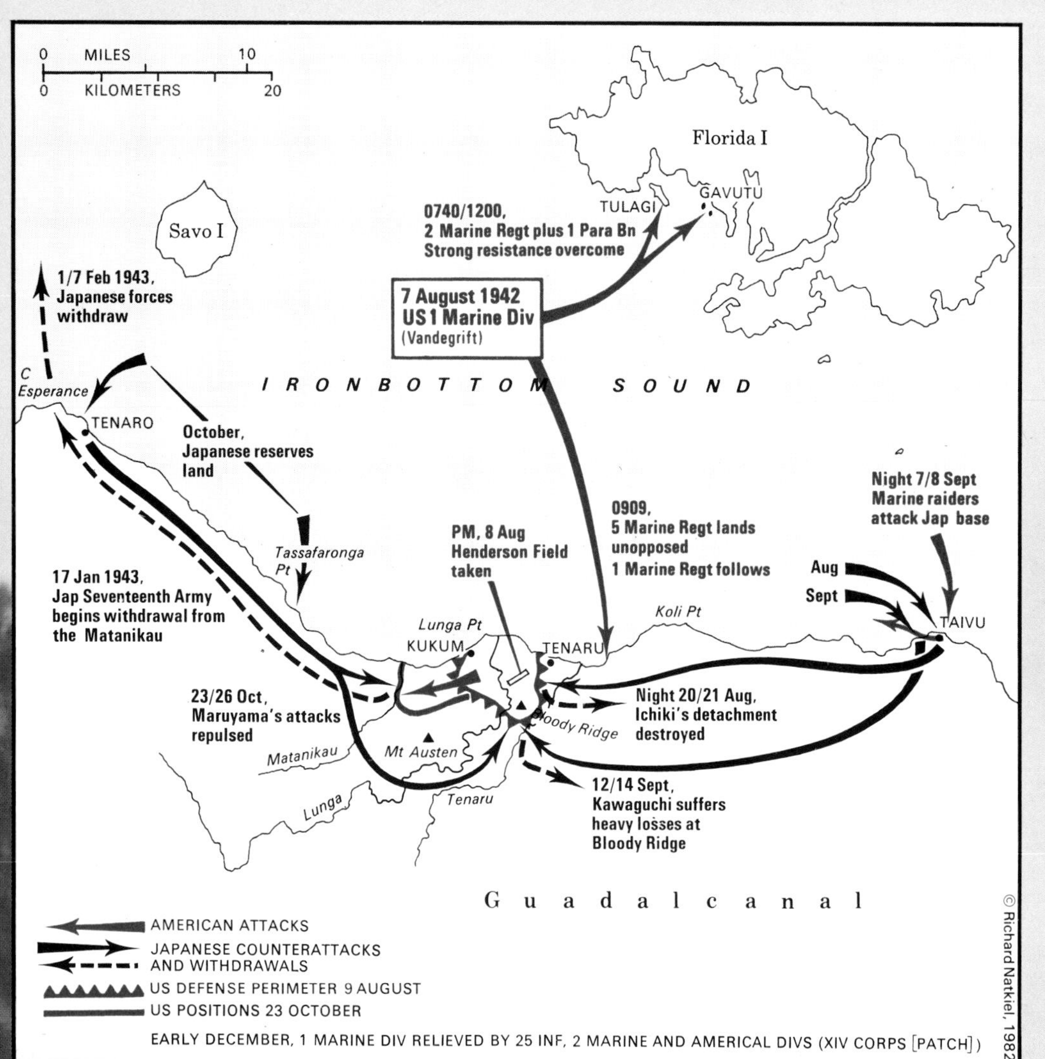

Start of the Long Road Back: Guadalcanal

During the first eight months of the war the Japanese had moved down through the Pacific islands on a path of conquest that seemed unstoppable. In spite of the monumental defeat the Japanese Imperial Navy had suffered at the hands of the US Navy off Midway early in June—aided by the gallant defenders of Midway Atoll which included Marine air units—the Japanese Army had not been stopped on its sweep south through the Pacific waters. The Americans had been driven from Guam, Wake and the Philippines. The British had suffered defeats in Burma, Malaya, Hong Kong and Singapore. The Dutch were driven out of the East Indies. And the Far East navies of all the Allied forces had been virtually destroyed in the process. Next in the path of Japanese conquest was New Guinea (the key to the conquest of Australia), the British islands of the Bismarck Archipelago, and then the 900-mile-long Solomon Island chain. If these could be taken, fortified, and turned into air and naval bases, the war in the South Pacific would be won for the Japanese. From these southerly locations supply lines from the United States mainland and Hawaii to Australia could be cut.

Determined to retain the initiative and consolidate their conquests, the Japanese landed and took New Britain Island and its important port of Rabaul in January 1942. Building it up as a naval and air base, they began the systematic bombing of Port Moresby on the coast of southeast New Guinea and landed troops on two locations on New Guinea itself. Australia was now in mortal peril. In March the Japanese began their invasion of the Solomons, meeting virtually no resistance from the hard-pressed British or Australians. In May they moved onto the island of Tulagi, off Florida Island in the southern Solomons, and made it their own. They now had possession of one of the best anchorages in the Solomons. Within a month they had crossed the bay to the south and had landed on the neighboring island of Guadalcanal, there to build an airfield on the north shore of the island just inland from Lunga Point. If this airfield was completed, Allied-held islands to the south would be in peril and the Japanese fleet anchored in Tulagi could move out at will to interdict the Allied fleets moving to Australia. If Australia, denied American men and supplies, fell to the Japanese, any American counter-offensives might have to come from Pearl Harbor thousands of miles away in the Central Pacific or even from the United States itself.

Out of these circumstances emerged one of the Marines' greatest battles of World War II. Denied support from its Australian and New Zealander allies who were busy fending off attacks on their own territories, the blunting of the Japanese moves in the Solomons by seizing Tulagi and Guadalcanal away from them would have to be an American affair. According to the plans drawn up by the American military commanders, the Navy would take in the invading American forces against Tulagi to the north and Guadalcanal to the south, the 1st Marine Division under Major General Alexander A Vandegrift would carry out the assault tactics, and the Army would come in to relieve the Marines as soon as a beachhead had been secured and reinforced. Vandegrift was forced to assemble his invading forces at Fiji from all over the Pacific and from bases at home. Many if not most were inadequately trained for the job they were to do (the Corps had been swollen to 143,000 men by June 1942 but few recruits were adequately trained for the tasks that lay ahead).

Unbelievable confusion reigned at Wellington, New Zealand, where the forces were assembled for the final push. Logistics broke down to the point that it was almost impossible to prepare for the amphibious operation. And because of too few supporting naval vessels, vital supplies of food, ammunition and fuel for the Guadalcanal and Tulagi landings were drastically cut back. If the landings in the southern Solomons were not too vigorously contested, if the Navy provided adequate protection against Japanese counterattacks, and if the Army and additional supplies followed soon after the initial attacks by the

Left : Map of the operations on Guadalcanal.
Right : General Vandegrift at work in his tent on Guadalcanal.
Below : A Marine Raider unit comes ashore on Guadalcanal in November 1942.

Leathernecks, Operation Watchtower stood some chance of success. Vandegrift had grave doubts, but given the consequences of further Japanese advances in the Solomons and their effects on the war in the Pacific, orders were tapped out and the Marines prepared to do their job. At last they were going on the offensive.

The Solomons assaults on 7 August 1942 came as a complete surprise to the Japanese. The defenders on Tulagi and on the nearby islands of Gavutu and Tanambogo had no forewarning before sighting the 76-ship invasion force but put up a furious defense from caves, natural redoubts and man-made dugouts until blasted out by grenades and dynamite. Before being quelled after three days of furious fighting, the defenders lost about 700 troops (almost 90 percent of their number), many by suicide charges. The Marines lost 144 dead or missing and almost 200 wounded. Valuable lessons were learned about the determination of Japanese forces to resist to the end from fortified emplacements and about the difficulty of assaulting heavily-defended islands. Across the bay, the landings on mountainous, jungled Guadalcanal to the south were virtually unopposed, and the Japanese airstrip (80 percent complete) was soon in American hands. It had been easy, almost too easy. The Japanese had lost not only their airfield but also precious supplies of trucks, repair facilities, gasoline and even food. But what the Marines did not realize—nor, almost fatally, did their naval counterparts—was that the Japanese, having lost Guadalcanal, had every intention of recovering it by all means possible. The battle for Guadalcanal was only beginning, not ending.

Bad news reached the Marines on Guadalcanal on 8 August. Because of his aircraft losses and the 'need to refuel' (although he had 17 days' fuel left), Vice-Admiral Frank Jack Fletcher was removing his carriers from the area (even before the landings he had promised only two days' support). This meant that Rear Admiral Richmond Kelly Turner, commander of the amphibious force, would have to remove his transports even though all the Marines had not debarked and more than half the vital supplies needed by the Marines on the beach were still in the ships' holds. Turner would leave the next day whether all the transports and supply ships were unloaded or not. But even an ordered hurry-up unloading operation was not destined to go smoothly because that night Japanese naval forces moved in through the Allied picket line undetected and the 40-minute Battle of Savo Island took place. Although the Japanese destroyed four Allied cruisers in the furious battle, their commander, believing the American carriers were still in the area and not wanting to be caught in daylight by their planes, pulled out of the fight and returned to Rabaul. The American transports were untouched, but weighed anchor the next morning nevertheless. The 10,000 Marines of the 1st Division were alone—for how long no one knew.

Above: A Vindicator dive bomber takes off from Midway to attack the Japanese fleet.

With Japanese bombers raiding every day at noon and with the Imperial Navy cruisers or destroyers showing up almost every night to shell the Lunga Point beachhead, the Marines wondered how long they could last, especially since their food supply could be counted only in terms of days and their heavy equipment and coastal defense guns had not been unloaded before the transports left for New Caledonia. Yet despite the constant enemy harassment, the Marines continued to hold out and complete the airstrip captured from the Japanese (which the Americans named Henderson Field after a Marine airman, Major Lofton R Henderson, killed at Midway). So successful were their efforts that on 20 August the first contingent of Marine aviators—in 12 SBD dive bombers—flew into Henderson Field. Other planes followed, and the 'Cactus Air Force' (the code-name for Guadalcanal was 'Cactus') was in business. It would have to be, for the 10,000 isolated Marines were about to taste the full fury of a Japanese counter-invasion.

On 18 August destroyers from Rabaul had landed 1000 Japanese soldiers 20 miles east of Lunga Point at a land projection called Taivu Point. Not waiting for reinforcements to arrive, the Japanese commander, Colonel Kiyono Ichiki, on the night of 21 August ordered an attack on the left flank of the American defense line fanning out from Lunga Point. The ensuing defense of the perimeter by the Marines came to be known as the Battle of the Tenaru River and was as bloody an assault as the Marines had ever tasted in their history. Wave after wave of Japanese troops swept on against the Marines' rifle, machine gun, antitank gun and artillery fire. Before the fight was over by early morning, 800 elite Japanese soldiers had died. Colonel Ichiki burned his regimental colors and committed suicide on Taivu Point. The reinforcements never arrived; their convoy subsequently was attacked and forced to abandon the landing in the Battle of the Eastern Solomons on 24 August.

The Japanese had been repulsed, the Cactus Air Force was proving its worth against enemy shipping, and supplies from naval transports began to move in once again. Still the issue was far from settled, and air raids on Henderson Field and the beachhead continued as daily occurrences while sickness began to decimate the Marines as they struggled to hold the island. Dysentery and malaria almost seemed a worse enemy than the Japanese. General Vandegrift wondered how long his men could hold out. One thing he knew: the Japanese would be back to attempt to retake the island and Henderson Field.

By mid-September 6000 more elite Japanese troops had been landed by destroyers near Taivu Point. Their commander, Major General Kiyotake Kawaguchi, decided that part of them would move west toward the American position at Lunga Point while another moved into the jungle to attack the Americans from the south. A third contingent would land west of Lunga Point near the village of Kokumbona and move on the Marines along the coast from that direction. Thus attacked from three sides, the Americans would be wiped out and Henderson Field would belong to the Japanese. Air units from Rabaul were scheduled to land on 13 September. (As in the previous attack on the American perimeter, the Japanese commander had been promised more men if needed, but he decided they were unnecessary.)

Everything went wrong with the three-prong attack. The Japanese moves were uncoordinated, troops got lost in the jungle and bogged down in the mud, and, most importantly, the Marines held off the main Japanese thrust from the south in the famous Battle of Bloody Ridge of 12–14 September 1942. The Japanese troops at one point got to within 1000 yards of the airfield, but furious Marine resistance pushed them back. The other two prongs of the attack—along the coast from the east and west—fared no better and never breached the Marine lines. What was left of the Japanese forces (about 1500 died in the attacks to only 143 Marine casualties) struggled off to the west through the mountains to areas held by their compatriots, fighting starvation and despair every step of the way.

Still the Japanese commanders refused to give up; they immediately began planning for a major invasion to take place the next month. Given their position on Rabaul and their supplies of manpower at this stage of the war, they might well have succeeded. But encouraged by developments on Guadalcanal, the American military commanders had beefed up Vandegrift's Marines with additional men (there were now 20,000 land and air Marines on Guadalcanal), supplies and airplanes. Furthermore, some Army troops had arrived to replace the Marines when conditions permitted, and a second airstrip had been added to Henderson Field. If the Battle of Guadalcanal, in the last analysis, was a battle of logistics as well as of courage and tenacity, the Americans were matching their enemy step by step. Still, control of the sea in the southern Solomons remained the crucial ingredient, and the Japanese Navy's sorties down 'the Slot' through the center of the Solomons every night—the Marines called these sorties the 'Tokyo Express'—hardly let up. Until the Japanese Navy had been driven off, the harassment of the Marines on Guadalcanal was ended, and the island was securely in American hands—or until the Americans had been driven out of the Solomons—the battle for Guadalcanal would continue. Too much was at stake for it to end without a clear victor.

Below: Lieutenant Mitchell Page receives the Medal of Honor from General Vandegrift for gallantry during the Guadalcanal fighting.

Frustrated at the failure of the two previous invasions of Guadalcanal to drive the Americans into the sea, Admiral Isoruko Yamamoto, commander of the Pacific Theater, from his headquarters at Truk far north in the eastern Carolines, assigned a full division to take the island from the Marines. He placed the troops under Lieutenant General Haruyoski Hyakutake. They landed at Kokumbona west of Lunga Point

Above: Admiral Yamamoto, Commander of the Japanese Combined Fleet and mastermind of Japanese strategy until his death in April 1943.

in October and began their move toward Lunga and Henderson Field on 16 October. But like the ill-fated west prong of the attack of a month before, the 8000-man force, poorly coordinated, slogged through the heavy jungle to attack the Marines on 26 October to no avail. Giving up on the attack after having 3500 of his men killed, Kyakutake moved his battered survivors to the western end of the island to hold out until the Imperial Navy took control of the waters around Guadalcanal. This too proved to be illusory, for in a series of naval battles around the island during the months of October and November (known as the Battle of the Santa Cruz Islands and the three Battles of Guadalcanal off Cape Esperance and Tassafaronga Point on the western part of the island) the American Navy—now under the aggressive Admiral William F Halsey—although severely battered (including the loss of the carriers *Hornet* and *Enterprise*), finally prevailed to turn the whole campaign around. So many ships had been sunk in the Sealark Channel between Guadalcanal and Tulagi by this time that the Americans called this expanse of water 'Ironbottom Sound.'

In one of the November battles 6000 Japanese troops were killed when their transports were attacked by American naval units and destroyed by planes from Henderson Field. During the months of the Guadalcanal campaign as they fought off air attacks and attacked enemy transports, the Cactus Air Force shot down 400 Japanese planes and sank ten transports while losing only 100 of their number. Thereafter Japanese supplies and reinforcements slowed to a trickle, Hyakutake and his men were isolated, and supplies and reinforcements began to flow into Vandegrift and his Marines in a steady stream. On 9 November 1942 Vandegrift and the 1st Marine Division were finally relieved—after four months of bloody fighting—by the 2nd Marine Divi-

Left: Putting out a small fire on a Marine Wildcat fighter following a Japanese air attack on Henderson Field, Guadalcanal. The 'Cactus Air Force' played a vital part in the battle.

sion and the Americal and 25th Divisions from the Army. (By the next year Vandegrift would be commandant of the Marine Corps.)

The Battle of Guadalcanal was over for the gallant but battered 1st Marine Division, although the Army spent the next few months mopping up Japanese forces in the vicinity of Lunga Point and extending their perimeters. They also moved towards Hyakutake's survivors on the western tip of the island. Early in February 1943 units of the Japanese Navy moved down 'the Slot' for the final time to evacuate the 13,000 sick and wounded survivors of the third major attack on the Marines on Guadalcanal. In all, a total of 36,000 Japanese had been assigned the task of removing the Marines from Guadalcanal. These 13,000 starving and demoralized soldiers hurriedly evacuated in the dead of night were all that were left on the 'island of death,' as they called it. Guadalcanal was securely in American hands; a foothold had been gained in the Solomons; and the sea lanes to Australia, and to her troops bravely holding off the Japanese on New Guinea, New Britain, and the nearby islands, had been secured.

The Pacific war had been turned around on land at Guadalcanal as it had been turned around on sea by the epic Battle of Midway earlier during those same crucial months of 1942. The US Marines, having faced their first major engagement of the war, having been left to their own devices against fanatical Japanese attacks, and having been forced to defend their lives and their nation's honor in the sour, steamy jungles of an island most had never heard of a few months before, had proved their effectiveness in the bloody cauldron of island warfare that was to be their lot in World War II. The cost had been 1152 Marines dead and 2799 wounded.

Above: Marines come ashore on Rendova Island, New Georgia at the start of the landings on 30 June 1943.
Below: Marine wounded being ferried offshore by landing craft.

Climbing the Solomons Ladder

As the American military planners contemplated their war efforts of 1943, three fundamental decisions were made. First, the campaign against the Japanese in the Pacific Theater would take the form of a giant two-pronged movement. One arm would advance upward from New Guinea and the Solomons toward the Philippines; the other would move across the Central Pacific in a series of island-hopping invasions of the Japanese-held islands. This right-hand prong would also be heading for the Philippines, but it would also place American forces within long-distance bombing range of the Japanese inner defenses and even the home islands. These giant pincers would move simultaneously toward their objectives.

Second, Army units would carry the fighting and make up the bulk of the landing forces in MacArthur's Southwest Pacific Theater, while the Marines would carry the landings in the Central Pacific with a Marine general in charge. To carry out these tasks, the Corps would be expanded to over 300,000 officers and men by mid-1943. It was within the context of this rapid build-up and the necessity of providing all fighting men possible to the Pacific war that the Marine Corps was forced to break its former all-segregated stance and allow blacks into

Above left : Marines on the beach at Bougainville ready to advance inland, November 1943.
Left : Dead Japanese on Bougainville. The 60,000 strong Japanese garrison reacted slowly to the Marine landings on 1 November 1943.
Below : Marines man the firing line, ready to repel one of the series of battalion-size attacks mounted on the beachhead on Bougainville in November 1943.

its ranks. This it did with great reluctance, initially assigning the blacks only to all-black units under white officers and non-commissioned officers and to defense and labor units. Women enlistees added to the Corps were detailed only to administrative and clerical jobs. As the war progressed, black Marines made combat landings and fought well. 15,000 blacks eventually wore Marine green before the war ended.

Third, facing a wartime strategy of island assaults, the Marine Corps requested and received new specialized landing craft invaluable for their assigned missions. By 1943 LSTs (Landing Ship, Tank), LSDs (Landing Ship, Dock), LCIs (Landing Craft, Infantry), LCTs (Landing Craft, Tank), and LVTs (Landing Vehicle, Tracked) were being added to the Marine arsenal of war. All except the LSDs could unload men and equipment directly on the beach of enemy-held territory. Thus the problems faced at Guadalcanal in getting onto a beach safely and then being rapidly reinforced were eliminated somewhat, although amphibious landings against enemy-held islands would continue to be a perilous undertaking—as the history of the Corps throughout the remainder of the war was to demonstrate dramatically.

The movement up the Solomons ladder began in February 1943 when an Army division and a Marine raider battalion seized the Russell Islands northwest of Guadalcanal. The islands proved to be undefended. Their seizure meant that fighter bases soon to be built there would be available for movements up through the central Solomons (plus three more airstrips had been added at Guadalcanal). But the principal targets were two islands in the New Georgia group in the central Solomons: New Georgia Island, which had a Japanese airfield at Munda on its southern shore, and nearby Rendova, from which artillery support could be supplied for the taking of Munda. The Marines were to aid two Army divisions in taking Munda on New Georgia by supplying two defense and two raider battalions to land with them. They were also assigned the task of helping the Army take Rendova. Although the campaign did not go well, particularly for the inexperienced Army units, and lasted from June until August 1943, the Marines were able to aid the Army appreciably by beating off Japanese counter-offensives around the airfield at Munda, by effecting artillery support from Rendova with their new 155-mm 'Long Toms,' and by playing a part in the air cover for the operation by supplying six of the 32 fighter and bomber squadrons flying out of Guadalcanal and the Russells assigned to the task.

The next step up the Solomons ladder was the island of Bougainville to the northwest. If Bougainville were taken, the great Japanese base at Rabaul would be within range of American fighters and dive bombers. Bougainville was as tempting an assault target as it was dangerous. The entire 125-mile length of the island was made up of swamps and jungle reaching up and across its mountainous interior. On Bougainville's southern tip at Buin the Japanese had built four airfields. Two more airfields were located at Buka and Bonis on the northern tip. And the island was defended by 40,000 seasoned troops. But the American military commanders fooled the Japanese completely as to their intentions by creating two diversionary landings, one taking place on the Treasury Islands nearby carried out by New Zealand troops and another on 27 October 1943 on the island of Choiseul to the southeast by the 2nd Marine Parachute Battalion (minus parachutes, as usual). And the Navy shelled both the northern and southern ends of the island just before the troops landed, convincing the Japanese commander that those would be the areas in which the Americans would land. Instead, they hit the beaches at Cape Torokina on Empress Augusta Bay halfway up the west coast of the island. The 3rd Marine Division and the Army's 37th Division met little initial resistance when landing on 1 November and had 14,000 troops ashore by nightfall, but they found that developing a perimeter in the impenetrable jungles hugging the shoreline was next to impossible. Fortunately, the Japanese commander, Lieutenant General Haruyoski Hyakutake (who had incurred the defeat of the third invasion of Guadalcanal), was not convinced that the Torokina landing was anything more than a diversion and thus held his troops back while the Americans fortified themselves around the landing site and began to prepare an airfield. There at Torokina they were forced to drive the Japanese off the surrounding hills from which they had a clear field of fire on the invasion forces. One such enclave, dubbed 'Helzapoppin Ridge,' was not taken until Christmas Day.

Finally convinced that the main American effort was indeed at Torokina—and that air assaults from Rabaul would not dislodge the soldiers and Marines from their positions—Hyakutake began to move his thousands of troops from the northern and

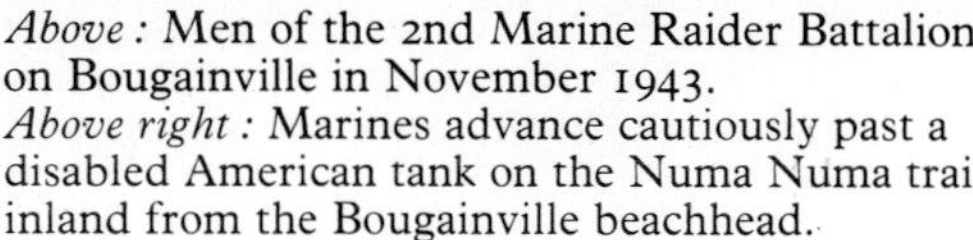

Above: Men of the 2nd Marine Raider Battalion on Bougainville in November 1943.
Above right: Marines advance cautiously past a disabled American tank on the Numa Numa trail inland from the Bougainville beachhead.

southern ends of the island. But it took weeks for the soldiers to make their way through the swampy morass that was the Bougainville jungle, and when they arrived, the Americans were ready with mined trails and well-dug emplacements. By the time the first Japanese attacks began on the Americans' perimeter in March, the 3rd Marine Division had been replaced by the Army's Americal Division, but the attacks were strenuously—if not fanatically— carried out. After 17 days of savage fighting, the Japanese had sustained 7000 casualties —to the Americans' 1000—and Bougainville had been secured. By the end of April 1944, aircraft from three airstrips carved out of the Torokina jungle had joined with naval carrier-based planes and Army Air Force units from MacArthur's forces to the west to begin pounding the crucial Japanese base at Rabaul on almost a daily basis.

In the meantime MacArthur had sent the 1st Marine Division, the tested and now rested veterans from Guadalcanal, to take another key base in his drive toward the Philippines. This was Cape Gloucester on the far western end of New Britain Island. Cape Gloucester controlled the Vitiaz and Dampier Straits between New Guinea and New Britain. With the straits in American hands, the sea path northwest was safe for passage. It was assaulted on 26 December 1943. Although well covered by Allied air power, which consistently beat off Japanese air attacks from Rabaul on the other end of the island, it took the Marines three weeks to subdue the 10,000 stubborn enemy troops in and around Cape Gloucester. But the job was done. (Thereafter, but not as a consequence of this operation, the 1st Marine Division was lifted from MacArthur's command and shifted to the Central Pacific campaign.)

Rabaul with its 135,000 troops had been designated as the next target, but having faced the jungle warfare of New Georgia, Bougainville and Cape Gloucester, and not wanting to repeat those agonizing experiences if possible—and with MacArthur's attention being returned to completing the domination of New Guinea to the southwest, while the Central Pacific drive was about to begin in earnest as the right arm of the two-prong strategy—the American military commanders made the decision to bypass Rabaul and let its troops, cut off from resupply, die on the vine. No longer usable as a naval anchorage—as countless air attacks had proved—and rapidly having its air forces destroyed by the American flyers of all three services, including Marines, Major General George Kenney's Fifth Air Force from New Guinea, and naval units from American carriers, Rabaul now represented no danger to the Allies as the left prong of the grand strategy moved to the northwest towards its destination in the Philippines.

The Gilbert Islands: The Horror of Tarawa

In order to move west across the Pacific from Hawaii toward the Philippines and possibly Formosa, and then to proceed northward toward the Japanese home islands, it was necessary for the American

forces to assault and capture the Central Pacific island chains known as the Marshalls and the Marianas. But first the Japanese would have to be removed from the Gilbert Islands to the southwest of Hawaii and almost due south of the Marshalls in order to clear the left flank of the movement. Like all the other Central Pacific islands, the Gilberts were far different from those found in the South Pacific with their mountainous ranges and lush jungle vegetation. The mid-Pacific islands were made up of atolls formed by volcanic eruptions below the sea. The islands making up the often diamond-shaped atolls were formed from the tops of the volcanic craters and were uniformly ringed with coral reefs but a few feet below the water, reefs that would tear to shreads anything that came in contact with their hard, crusty surface. The islands themselves were more or less flat, not mountainous, offering no protection to invading troops. And properly fortified with pillboxes and other deep emplacements made up of volcanic rock, coconut logs, and even reinforced concrete sides, they were almost impervious to artillery and bomb blasts—as the American attackers found in late 1943.

Two atolls in the Gilberts, Makin to the north and Tarawa 100 miles to the south, were the targets for the invasion fleet of 200 ships that made its way to the Gilberts to begin *Operation Galvanic* in November 1943. On board the transports were the 2nd Marine Division and part of the 27th Infantry Division. The men—totaling 35,000 in all—had their assignments: the Army would take Makin (with some of the Marines in reserve) and the Marines would take 18-mile-long Tarawa Atoll with Betio Island on the bottom of its triangular shape as the primary target. The amphibious force commander, Major General Holland M ('Howlin' Mad') Smith, decided he would stay with the Army for the taking of Makin Atoll as it was assumed this would be the easier target to pursue. An abortive Marine raid back in August 1942 carried out under Lieutenant Colonel Evans Carlson had revealed that Makin Atoll was lightly defended. Things should not have changed much in a little over a year.

But although there were few Japanese on the principal island of Butaritari on Makin, the operation took four days of hard fighting after the landings of 21 November. The 165th Regimental Combat Team of the 27th Division moved very cautiously across the island, too cautiously for 'Howlin' Mad' Smith who, believing in the Marine Corps practice of moving with all dispatch whatever the obstacles, personally intervened to get the operation moving at a faster pace despite whatever the Army thought of his methods. To Smith, having a 20-to-1 advantage over the Japanese defenders precluded any reason for slow movement. The delays on Makin, however, paled into insignificance when compared to the problems the Marines were running into at Betio to the south.

Bettio's less than 300 acres nowhere rose above ten feet in elevation but were fortified with coastal defense guns, 40 artillery pieces in bunkers, a long sea wall four feet in height on the lagoon or inner side (where most of the Marines were scheduled to land), and at least 100 machine guns in pillboxes. The Japanese pillboxes, bunkers, and supporting ammunition dumps were all interconnected with trenches for effective use by the 4300 troops on the island. And ringing Betio and the atoll was a submerged coral reef thoroughly mined with entanglements between the breaks in the sharp coral ridges. Most of the Marines were to approach Betio in shallow-draft LCVPs (Landing Craft, Vehicle and Personnel), or more commonly called 'Higgins Boats.' These, it was hoped, would clear the forbidding coral reefs. The first three waves of Marines were to be taken ashore in LVTs, or Amtracs, which could both 'swim' in the lagoon and then move on their caterpillar treads across the reefs and then onto the

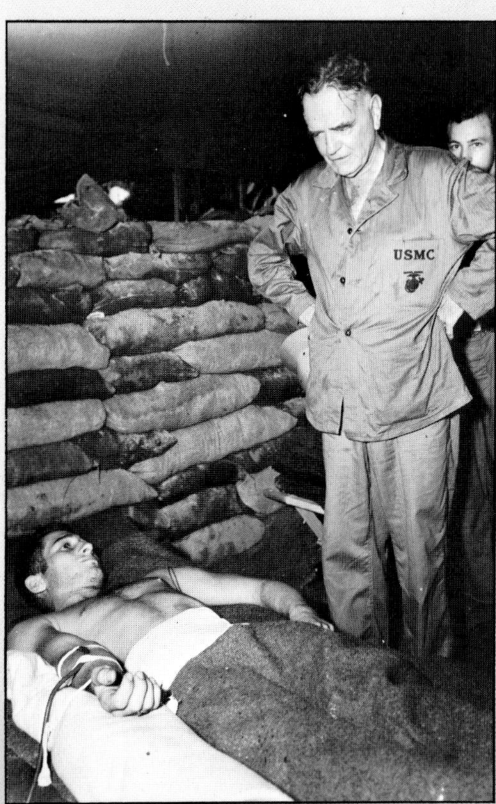

Above: Admiral Halsey talks with an injured Marine in a beachhead hospital on Bougainville. *Main picture, below:* Amtracs head for the shore, Tarawa, 20 November 1943.

Above: A wounded Marine is taken to a landing craft for evacuation to a hospital ship during the Tarawa operation.

beach, but only 125 of these were available. Most of the Marines and supplies would have to move into the beach in the Higgins boats. Four landing areas were designated on the northern shore of Betio: Green Beach on the outside of the atoll, and Red Beaches 1, 2, and 3 on the lagoon side. All would prove to be infernal stretches of real estate for the 76 hours following the landings on the morning of 20 November 1943.

As the amphibious landings proceeded, everything seemed to go wrong. The Navy lifted its gunfire too soon, allowing Japanese artillery to open up on the assembling landing craft. The planned half-hour air strikes were not only delayed but also lasted only seven minutes. And the leading boats of the invasion armada found themselves under murderous fire from shore as the naval bombardment and air strafing ended a full 18 minutes before the Marines hit the beach. Undaunted by the pre-invasion bombing, shelling and strafing—which had virtually no effect on them—the Japanese defenders rushed to their undamaged weapons and opened a withering fire upon the invaders. Not only were some of the LVTs destroyed in the water—over half never reached the beaches—but also the remainder either landed at the wrong beaches in the withering fire or found they could not traverse the four-foot sea wall. Their Marine occupants died in droves while trying to escape from them by jumping into the water and wading ashore. The Higgins boats following behind got hung up on the coral reefs, forcing their combat-laden occupants to endure fiery deaths from Japanese shore fire or from attempting to wade ashore in water often up to their armpits.

Those who made it to shore could only crouch down behind the sea wall unable to move because of murderous crossfire from the enemy guns. Some made it to the

Below: Men of the 2nd Marine Division being evacuated from Tarawa after the conclusion of the battle. The shattered trees attest to the violence of the fighting.

safety of a pier on Red Beach 3 where they hid under it and behind it trying to figure out their next move. The fears of the assault commander, Colonel David M Shoup, about the whole plan—including the coral reefs and the Higgins boats' ability to navigate over their jagged edges—now seemed to be coming to fruition. Control was rapidly vanishing on the beach—by now a confused expanse of dead and wounded men, wrecked equipment, and constant enemy fire—and communication with the areas on the beach and with the ships offshore broke down almost completely. The invasion was rapidly turning into a debacle of the first order. Standing in the command post he established at the end of the long pier, Shoup, although wounded, tried to make order out of the chaos as subsequent waves of Marines fell to the same grisly fate as their buddies had endured in the first waves.

The only way off the beach was for the Marines to fight their way forward inch by inch and yard by yard, taking whatever casualties as were necessary, until they could get close enough to the pillboxes to knock them out one by one. It was a grisly, bloody business, but the Marines did it. By noon General Smith, still back with the Army at Makin, had decided to send the 6th Marines to help out at Betio (the Army on Makin would have to get along without them). This allowed the reserves waiting off Tarawa to be committed to the fight ashore, but because of communications difficulties these reserves remained offshore during the first night because they had no orders as to where to land. When they began to come ashore the next morning they came under murderous fire as they slogged through the surf. Some 350 of the 800 men in the relief force were killed or wounded before touching the beach.

Above : Marines on the beach at Tarawa firing at Japanese positions around the island's airfield.

Fearful of complete annihilation of the relief Marines, Colonel Shoup ordered all the Marines on the beach to move forward against the Japanese emplacements despite the withering fire. Many Marine heroes died in those morning hours, but about noon of this second day the battle finally turned in favor of the Americans. The tide in the Tarawa lagoon shifted, allowing Higgins boats to clear the reefs with supplies. Two battalions on Red Beach 2 punched their way through to the south shore, and Green Beach on the outside of the lagoon was finally cleared. By evening the 6th Marines had arrived from Makin and were making their way across Green Beach.

By the morning of the third day on Tarawa the Marines had slugged their way out of Red Beach 3 and were approaching the bombproof blockhouse which served as the headquarters of Rear Admiral Meichi Shibasaki, the commander of the Japanese defense forces. This was soon reduced to ashes as Marine assault engineers dropped grenades down the air vents of the blockhouse, followed by gasoline poured down the vents to be detonated by TNT charges that followed in short order. By that evening hundreds of Japanese had fled to the eastern end of Betio, and as the night wore on they launched savage counterattacks against the Marine lines. More than 300

Below : On the beach at Tarawa. A heavily-laden squad of Marines moves off to attack Japanese positions around the airstrip.

died in savage hand-to-hand combat with the Marines.

By noon of the fourth day, 23 November 1943, it was all over. Betio was in American hands. The cost had been 1027 Marines dead or presumed dead and over 2200 wounded. On the other hand, only 17 Japanese were still alive on Betio, great numbers committing suicide by placing the muzzles of their rifles in their mouths and pulling the triggers with their toes rather than surrender. The remainder of Admiral Shibasaki's defenders and civilian construction workers on Tarawa—4700 in number—were dead. Makin and Tarawa Atolls were secure for the continuation of the trans-Pacific offensive.

Betio had been a hard lesson for the Marines and the American military commanders in the Pacific, and the military was flooded with condemnatory articles and letters when the pictures of the carnage and the casualty figures were released back home. But the military profited greatly by the bloody experience. More and better

Above: Crew of an LST opens the bow doors to allow the Marine LVTs to disembark for the assault landing on Roi, 1 February 1944.

LVTs would be produced for future operations and UDT (underwater demolition teams) would precede landings to clear obstacles for the landing craft from now on. The military also learned that massed artillery shelling and bombing would not destroy pillboxes and blockhouses. Tests conducted subsequent to the Tarawa experience proved that rockets and high-angle armor-piercing shells from naval guns alone would do the job. These and other lessons were not only learned but also applied as the Pacific war continued. In this sense, the Marine victims of Tarawa had indeed not died in vain.

Taking the Marshall Islands

The Tarawa and Makin campaigns caused no sidetracking of the drive to the west. On 1 February 1944, covered by a vast naval armada, American Forces stormed ashore in the Marshall Islands southwest of Hawaii and on the line to the Philippines. The newly-formed 4th Marine Division took the islands of Roi and Namur containing the main Japanese air base in the Marshalls at

Above: Seabees and Marines aboard an LVT wait for the order to land, 2 February 1944, Roi island.
Below, main picture: Marine reinforcements land on the Marshalls on the second day of the operation.

Above: Admiral Kelly Turner, naval commander of the Kwajalein landings and numerous other Marine operations of the Pacific War.

the northern tip of Kwajalein Atoll. At the same time the 7th Army Division attacked Kwajalein Island at the southern tip of the atoll. And simultaneously Majuro Atoll was taken without resistance by Army units, to be used as a base for the American Navy and its fast carrier task forces. By 4 February the central Marshalls had been taken with only slightly more than 300 lives lost. New, more heavily-armored LVTs (Amtracs) carried the troops to shore, better naval and air firepower made destruction of the enemy's fortifications more complete, and command ships stationed offshore with failsafe communications systems controlled the action without interruption. The Tarawa experience was not repeated.

Below: General Holland Smith, pointing, commander of the Marine landing force in the Kwajalein operation.

Because the Kwajalein landings had gone so smoothly, Admiral Nimitz decided to send the assaulting troops directly 300 miles farther to the northwest. Marshalls and specifically to Eniwetok Atoll, site of an important Japanese base and an excellent lagoon for a naval anchorage, but not before the Navy's fast carriers had punished the Japanese naval bastion at Truk in the eastern Carolines 770 miles away with two days and one night of punishing bombing raids. Forty-one ships and 200 Japanese planes were destroyed in the raids, and the fear of Japanese interference from Truk vanished. On Eniwetok, however, the soldiers of the 106th Infantry and 27th Division and the Marines of the 22nd Regiment who landed on 17 February found that the Japanese defenders had to be 'dug out' yard by yard despite the 'softening up' by artillery and bombing that had preceded their landings. Still, two of the principal islands fell to the Marines in four days, while the Army's campaign against Eniwetok Island itself ended early in March. The remainder of the Marshalls fell or were bypassed with little difficulty. The Americans suffered less than 600 killed. The sacrifices of Tarawa had indeed begun to pay immediate dividends for the Marines and soldiers who continued the Pacific war.

Fight for the Marianas

By June 1944 the American Military Forces were moving toward their next objective in the long road back across the Central Pacific; the Marianas Islands with their crucial island of Guam containing air bases and a superb harbor. Not only would the taking of the wooded and mountainous Marianas put them only 1500 miles east of the Philippines and only 1300 miles southeast of Japan itself, but also it would cut Japanese supply lines to the south (further isolating the great Japanese base at Truk in the eastern Carolines) and put their home islands within range of the Army Air Force's new long-range B-29 bombers. Reclaiming Guam would also represent a great moral victory as the island had fallen to the Japanese in the first days of the war. Retaking Guam from the occupying Japanese would be the first liberation of American territory in the Pacific.

Above: Marines of the 2nd Division dig in on the beach on Saipan on the first day of the landings.

Admiral Chester W Nimitz, commander of the Pacific Theater, decided that the islands of Saipan and Tinian to the north of Guam should be taken first. This would cut off Japanese air defense to Guam when that island was invaded three days later. Saipan was garrisoned by over 25,000 troops well dug in on the 15-by-5-mile island dominated by 1500-foot Mount Tapotchau at the center. Assigned to take it were three Marine divisions (the 2nd, 3rd and 4th), one Marine brigade, and the Army's 27th Division. The invasion plans called for the 2nd and 4th Marines to land on 15 June on the southwest coast, the 2nd turning left to assault Mount Tapotchau, the 4th racing across the island to Islito Airfield. The amphibious assault that bright and clear day did not go well as the Navy had not sufficiently softened up the landing area and the amtracs with the assault troops came under furious and deadly Japanese fire. More than 2000 casualties were suffered. Still, 20,000 Marines made it ashore and

Above : A wounded Marine is given treatment by a Navy corpsman on the beach at Namur, Kwajalein Atoll.
Left : Marines land on Aur Atoll in the Marshalls in April 1944. The atoll was in fact undefended by the Japanese.

that night held off the first of many suicide attacks launched by the Japanese. But if the initial landings were not reinforced, the soldiers and Marines would be in serious trouble on Saipan.

At this point the Navy came to the rescue by beating off a major Japanese attempt to disrupt the invasion of the Marianas. In what came to be known as the Battle of the Philippine Sea, Admiral Raymond Spruance and the Fifth Fleet intercepted the First Mobile Fleet under Vice Admiral Jisaburo Ozawa west of the Marianas and decimated it. Much of the glory rightly fell to the naval air crews who met the Japanese carrier plane onslaught west of Saipan on the first day in what soon came to be called 'the Great Marianas Turkey Shoot.' On the second day they pursued the Japanese fleet and inflicted even more damage. By the time it was over, the Americans had lost 130 planes and 76 of their crewmen, but the Japanese had lost almost 400 carrier planes, dozens of land-based airplanes from Guam, and three aircraft carriers. The Japanese carrier navy had been effectively destroyed in two days of furious combat. But this epic naval battle also meant that the Japanese defenders on Saipan would not be relieved. American efforts to dislodge them continued until all were wiped out. This proved to be a tremendous undertaking.

After eight days of fighting, the southern end of Saipan was in American hands, but the enemy forces on Mount Tapotchau and the northern end of the island remained to be subdued. As the 2nd Marines swung left to assault the mountain, the 4th Marines

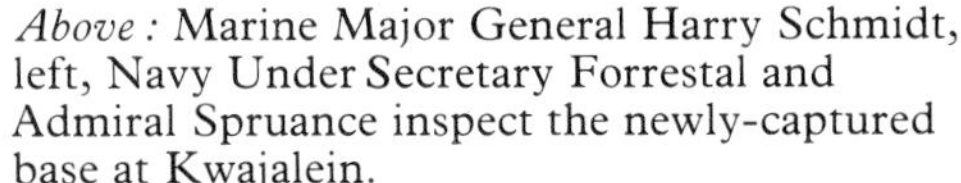

Above : Marine Major General Harry Schmidt, left, Navy Under Secretary Forrestal and Admiral Spruance inspect the newly-captured base at Kwajalein.

Above : Marines employ a captured Japanese mountain gun during the battle for Saipan.
Above right : A Navy corpsman gives aid to wounded Marines on 7 July 1944 during the last stages of the fighting on Saipan.
Right : A Marine flamethrowing tank attacks a Japanese pill box on Saipan. The vehicle is a modified version of the Stuart light tank.

swung out and then left to move up the far side of the island. The 27th Division was in the middle. When the Army units in the center could not keep up and threatened the two flanking movements, General 'Howlin' Mad' Smith demanded and received the dismissal of the Army's Major General Ralph Smith—with whom he had clashed on Makin for his dilatory approach to war—and the Army began to move.

By 6 July the sweep to the north was succeeding with Mount Tapotchau taken and the Japanese holding only the northern third of the island. Facing defeat, Admiral Chuichi Nagumo, commander of the carrier forces at Pearl Harbor, loser at the Battle of Midway, and now naval commander on Saipan, shot himself with a pistol. Lieutenant General Yoshitsugu Saito, commanding the Japanese Army forces, sliced himself in the stomach with a samurai sword; then an aide shot him in the back of the head. But before his ritualistic suicide, Saito had issued a message to his troops to follow him to glory against the enemy. They did so the next morning more than 2500 Japanese staged a massive banzai attack against the Americans. Their fanatical attack rolled forward against the 27th Division in particular. The Americans used every weapon available to stop them, including 105mm howitzers. When it was over, mounds of Japanese bodies lay in front of the American lines.

Still the carnage was not ended. Even though the Americans declared the island secure on 9 July, in the days that followed hundreds of Japanese civilians committed suicide at Marpi Point at the northernmost point of the island by throwing first their children, then themselves, off the 800-foot ledge into the sea. Hundreds of Japanese soldiers joined them despite repeated Japanese-language loudspeaker messages that captives would be treated well and would not be tortured and killed, as the military commanders had told them. Some of the soldiers jumped into the sea; others pulled the pins from grenades and held them against their bellies. Over 29,000 Japanese died on Saipan as war casualties or suicides before it was over. The Americans had also paid the price in blood with over 16,000 casualties, of whom over 3400 were killed in action. But the significance of the American victory on this island of blood was not lost on the Japanese government and its military; many were now sure the war was lost.

Tinian, just three-and-a-half miles to the south of Saipan, was the next objective because it contained three Japanese airfields. But while Tinian was fairly flat (unlike Saipan), it had a high rocky coastline well fortified with coastal batteries. The only break in the forbidding coastal wall was in front of Tinian Town on the southwest corner, but this area had been heavily fortified by the Japanese. To land there would mean very heavy casualties. Accordingly, the military commanders decided to land between the jagged coral cliffs on the northwest corner of the island through two gaps in their rugged face. These were undefended, but if the Japanese discovered that this was the landing site, the whole invasion might well fail as the tiny gaps in the coral cliffs could be easily plugged by the Japanese. Therefore, to allow the invasion a chance of success, on 24 July the invasion fleet containing the 2nd Marine Division appeared off Tinian Town, bombardment began, and the amtracs began moving toward shore. But instead of landing, they only milled about, convincing the Japanese that their shore batteries had discouraged any landing. Meanwhile, 15,000 Marines of the 4th Marine Division landed and made their way through the openings on the northwest corner and established a firm perimeter. When the Japanese reacted that evening, it was too late. With the 2nd Marines following them ashore, the Leathernecks of the 4th Marines were able to fend off their counterattacks, inflicting over 1400 deaths on the attacking Japanese. Within a week the Marines of these two divisions, aided by tanks, swept the island, and Tinian was in American hands.

Guam, 100 miles to the south, was meanwhile being assaulted by Marines and soldiers. On 21 July the 3rd Marine Division landed at Asan on the west coast of the island just below the capital of Agana to swing south and take Apra Harbor, while the 77th Army Division and the 1st Provisional Marine Brigade landed at Agat to the south to swing north to entrap the Japanese defenders on the Orote Peninsula where the main Japanese airfield was located. Progress away from the landing sites was agonizingly slow, but by 25 July Orote Peninsula had been cut off. That night, after apparently becoming thoroughly drunk to carry out their suicide mission of breaking out, the Japanese made a savage attack on the

Americans hemming them in. Carrying conventional weapons, bottles and even baseball bats, they assaulted the American lines. Artillery was ordered to fire directly into the charging lines of Japanese; they died in mounding clusters until the survivors fled back onto the peninsula. That same night a more carefully planned Japanese attack confronted the 3rd Marines to the north. Slipping through gaps in the American lines, the Japanese soldiers made a strenuous attempt to reach the beachhead. After desperate hand-to-hand fighting, the Marines repulsed the attack, but not until 3500 Japanese had paid with their lives. These were the last major actions on the valuable island.

Fighting went on for two more weeks, but the American hold on Guam was never seriously threatened. Many Japanese fled into the hills and hid out for months—and even years—thereafter, but by now Guam was securely in American hands, Saipan was being prepared as a major base for long-range bombers, and Truk to the southeast was cut off from support. The Americans could now look to the reconquest of the Philippines.

Above: Marines on the beach at Saipan. In the background a Buffalo amtrac modified to give fire support to the landing force.

Bloody Peleliu

Yet one obstacle remained. The Palau Islands, part of the western Carolines and 500 miles east of Mindanao in the southern Philippines, would stand astride the American left flank as it moved toward the Philippines. They would also threaten MacArthur's right flank as he moved northward toward the same goal. Some military planners, notably Admiral William F Halsey, argued that the islands should be bypassed as they represented no great danger to either movement. But Admiral Chester W Nimitz insisted that the Palaus be taken, and plans were made accordingly. Little did anyone know that the taking of Peleliu Island in the chain would rank in blood with Tarawa. Over 1200 Marines and 277 soldiers would die and another 6200 would be wounded before the island was taken after six weeks of fighting. Over 10,000 Japanese soldiers and civilians would also taste death in the carnage on Peleliu.

Peleliu is the major island in the Palau group. The whole is enclosed by a giant coral reef. Peleliu itself is an elongated island six miles by two. At its southern end was located the Japanese airfield. North of the airfield lay Umurbrogol Ridge, its mountainous spine making its way to the northern extremity of the island. The formidable ridge was honeycombed with coral caves. These old mining caves had been enlarged and perfected to aid and protect the defenders. Some of them had sliding steel doors behind which artillery pieces were hidden; after the guns fired their rounds, the doors could be slid closed so that they could neither be seen nor destroyed. All of the caves were well stocked with food and ammunition. The 10,000 Japanese troops on the island knew they could give the American invaders more than their money's worth. They were also under orders not to engage in pointless suicide attacks, but, rather, they were to try to contain the Americans on the beaches. If this was not possible, they were to pull back to defense lines from which mortar and artillery fire could enfilade the invaders. Furthermore,

Below: Fighting in Garapan village, Saipan, on 23 June 1944. The village was not completely captured until 2 July.

Above: During the fighting on Peleliu in September 1944, a Marine is picked off by a Japanese sniper.

troops about to be overrun were not to kill themselves, but were to remain hidden to strike the enemy from the rear after they passed. Lieutenant General Sadae Inoue, the overall commander in the Palaus, and Colonel Kunio Nakagawa, commanding on Peleliu, would not repeat the useless bloodletting of Saipan. They were determined to attain victory by stealth and effective military tactics.

The three-day preliminary air and naval bombardment of Peleliu was considered thorough and protracted. Little remained above ground near the landing area on the southwest coast of the island. The Navy was more than satisfied, yet the underground fortifications so carefully constructed by the Japanese had hardly been touched. The initial landings by the 1st Marine Division on the beaches west of the airfield on 15 September 1944 seemed easy, but as the Japanese emerged from their caves and began to pour mortar, artillery and machine gun fire on the waves of Marines, amtracs were hit and Leathernecks began to die by the score. Nor could the Navy support vessels help as their artillery could not penetrate the steel doors behind which the Japanese artillery was prepared to fire before emerging to rain its hellish fire on the Marines below on the beach. The Marines were able to hold the beach, but that was all.

Company K of the 1st Marine Regiment commanded by Colonel Lewis B 'Chesty' Puller was having a particularly difficult time at the north end of the beachhead because of furious fire coming from a Japanese emplacement on a rocky point of land that became famous that day, as afterwards, simply as 'the Point.' Dozens of men were dying and hundreds were taking wounds from five concrete pillboxes and a maze of trenches on that small stretch of land. Within two hours less than 30 men were still alive and unwounded from two entire platoons, but 'the Point' was being taken by the gutsy Marines. They gradually put the pillboxes out of action in the only way possible: crawling up to them through withering machine gun fire and throwing grenades through their firing slits. Still the left flank was in danger, so Puller threw up a defense line in case the Japanese counter attacked, for if this line was gapped the whole beachhead would be in danger.

The next crucial sector for the Marines, however, emerged at the airfield. At five o'clock in the afternoon hundreds of Japanese infantrymen emerged from beyond the airfield and began to move toward the Marine positions carefully and deliberately, taking cover where they could. This was no banzai attack but a well thought-out movement, for behind the infantry came tanks, over a dozen of them. Moving quickly through their infantry, they made straight for the lines of the 5th Marine Regiment. The charging Japanese tanks were stopped only by the appearance of a dozen more-heavily armed and armored Marine Sherman tanks that rumbled onto the airstrip to open fire on their Imperial counterparts. The Shermans and a Navy dive bomber stopped the Japanese charge, but it had been too close for comfort, and many Marines had died in desperate efforts to hold the center of the line. The airfield was still in American hands and the Japanese soldiers to the south of the airstrip had

Below: Marine landing craft drive ashore during the assault on Peleliu covered by the prelanding bombardment.

meanwhile been cut off by the 7th Marine Regiment. Yet the Japanese were far from finished on Peleliu.

Colonel Nakagawa decided at this point to withdraw his troops to the protecting caves and pillboxes on Umurbrogol Ridge. Since the 5th Marines had moved across the airfield toward the eastern side of the island and the 7th Marines were still cleaning out the Japanese from the southern tip of the island, it was up to Puller's 1st Marine Regiment to take on Nakagawa and his troops in their impregnable bastion, by now all but denuded of vegetation by gunfire and bombing but presenting a bloody challenge to his decimated forces as they faced artillery and mortar fire seemingly without end. On 17 September Puller's Marines began making their way up the coral ridges—'Horseshoe,' 'Death Valley,' and other deathtraps—that formed the mountainous stronghold. They were aided by naval gunfire, tanks, and bazookas. Cave after cave on the rocky mountainside was cleaned out the first day, only to be lost the next by a furious counterattack. Three days later, after more furious fighting on what the Corps came to call 'Bloody Nose Ridge,' Puller's 1st Marine Regiment had sustained 1700 casualties in the six days of fighting since the landings. Nor could the 7th Marine Regiment make any progress against the Japanese defenders when it relieved the battered 1st Marines on 20 September.

At this point units of the Army's 81st Division were moved onto the island. Then the 5th Marines swung back to the left of Umurbrogol and, covered by accurate naval gunfire, moved along the narrow west coast of the island. Utilizing their tanks and amtrac-mounted flamethrowers, they forced their way through and took the northern section of the island, then turned to assault Umurbrogol from the rear. Gradually the 321st Army Combat Team, the 5th Marines, and the 7th Marines moved in to surround, then work their way up, the formidable slopes of the forbidding ridge spining its way along Peleliu. Yard by yard the soldiers and Marines crawled their way up Umurbrogol, neutralizing pillboxes by flamethrowers, grenades and TNT as they went. By late October more Army troops had replaced the 5th and 7th Marines, but still the battle continued. Only after another full month of fighting was the cave-ridden citadel that was Umurbrogol finally taken by the Army. Only 700 of Colonel Nakagawa's 6500 men were still alive by that time. It had taken almost 1600 rounds of light and heavy ordnance to kill each of Nakagawa's 5800 men who died on Peleliu in 1944. The 1st Marines had sustained over 6000 casualties. Whatever glory the Marines—and their

Above: Explosions aboard the escort carrier *St Lo* after a kamikaze hit.
Below: The Battle of Leyte Gulf. The American escort carriers come under surface attack from Kurita's battleships.

Army compatriots—had gained on Peleliu they wanted to forget. Peleliu, along with Tarawa, stands even today as a gory lesson in the wretched warfare as it was fought in the Pacific coral islands on the way to eventual victory over the determined Japanese. After the savagery of Peleliu, it was imperative that the assaulting Marines be allowed to rest and refit before continuing the job they had been trained to do.

Marine Air in the Philippines

The reconquest of the Philippines was basically carried out by the Army. However, General MacArthur, the Southwest Pacific Theater commander, making his way up the northern shore of New Guinea in preparation for this return to his beloved Philippine Islands, requested and received the aid of the 1st Marine Aircraft Wing (1st MAW) for his landings in the archipelago. The 1st MAW, in turn, received from MacArthur's air commander, Lieutenant General George C Kenney, permission to assist the land forces by close air support and began training in the Solomons for this mission.

The 1st Marine Air Wing was not called into action initially as the American forces

Right: A Japanese fuel and oil store burns furiously as American troops move inland in the first hours of the landings on Leyte.

Right : Brewster Buffalo fighter aircraft in flight. The Buffalo served with Marine units in the early part of the war.

bypassed the landings on the island of Mindanao in the south and struck instead at Leyte in the center of the archipelago on 20 October 1944 as a preliminary to the main attack on Luzon to the north. However, the massive Japanese naval surface raid on the American invasion fleet known as the Battle of Leyte Gulf from 23–26 October and the *kamikaze* suicide raids on the fleet convinced MacArthur that more land-based air cover was absolutely necessary, and early in December the 1st MAW got the call to hurry to the Philippines from the Solomons.

The Marine dive bomber and fighter crews who reported to Leyte had their skills tested in the weeks that followed. They flew against Japanese reinforcements on the sea, flew night fighter cover for the Navy, and supported ground operations with verve. In ground support operations they demonstrated their skill at extremely low level bombing runs, a skill the Army Air Force was forced to emulate. When the Army moved on to attack the main Philippine island of Luzon in early January 1945 the Marine flyers were there, providing air cover for the Navy and striking Japanese bases both on Luzon and on Formosa to the north. In carrying out their close air support missions here, the Marines also taught their Army and Navy brethren a new technique in air support tactics. They utilized air liaison parties (ALPs) in radio-equipped jeeps with the ground units to direct air strikes with great precision, thereby assuring greater striking power with less chance of hitting friendly troops. The Army was quick to pick up the Marine innovation, and the use of ALPs became standard practice in the conquest of the remainder of the Philippines. The seven Marine squadrons on Luzon flew almost half of all sorties against the enemy between late January and April 1945 although they represented less than 15 percent of American aircraft available in the area.

Below : A Marine lieutenant briefs his platoon before the landings on Iwo Jima. The unit is from the 4th Marine Division.

Above : Men of the 5th Division in a forward position facing the Japanese defenses on Mount Suribachi.
Below right : The battle for Iwo Jima.

By March 1945, with Luzon gradually being cleared of Japanese, most of the Marine air units were shifted to the southern Philippines where they assisted the 8th Army and the Filipino guerrillas on Mindiano in clearing out the Japanese from that island. In this operation the Marines flew an excess of 10,000 sorties between March and July and again demonstrated their proficiency in close air support. Eventually all of the Philippines were brought back under American and Filipino control, and ALP-directed close air support had come to stay in the Pacific war. The Marines had made a valuable contribution to the liberation of the Philippines and to saving the lives of thousands of assault troops as the fighting wore on in the summer of 1945 with the Americans moving ever closer to the Japanese home islands.

Eight Square Miles of Hell: Iwo Jima

As the conquest of the Philippines was being carried out, military planners turned away from Formosa as the next possible target and decided, instead, to move north to Iwo Jima in the Bonin Islands and to Okinawa in the Ryukyus. From there the Japanese home islands would be within flying range of medium bombers, and Okinawa would be used as the staging area for the invasion of Japan. Furthermore, Iwo Jima was the site of two Japanese airfields with another being built which had to be taken, and the island would also be valuable as a base for fighter planes to escort the long-range B-29 'superfortresses' on their attacks on Japan from the Marianas. Iwo Jima was almost half way between the Marianas and Japan, being 650 miles from each. The invasion of Iwo Jima was set for 19 February 1945.

It would be hard to imagine a worse death-trap for an invading force than 'Iwo.' The small volcanic island of less than eight square miles was shaped like a porkchop with its tip to the south. At that tip Mount Suribachi rose 600 feet into the air, dominating the sandy beaches below. North of the southern coastal plain crowned by Suribachi rose the Motoyama Plateau, anchored at each end by cliffs dropping to the sea. Given the layout of the forbidding island, the landing would have to come at the south, Suribachi would have to be taken, and then the Marines of the assaulting V Amphibious Corps would have to work their way up Motoyama Plateau, blasting out the Japanese defenders as they went. And 21,000 Japanese troops, well dug in in over a thousand caves and well supplied with tanks, artillery and ammunition, were waiting. On Suribachi and the Motoyama Plateau the Japanese also had hundreds of concrete blockhouses. The Japanese commander, Lieutenant General Tadamichi Kuribayashi, had been fortifying his island for eight months and now ordered his troops to fight in place until death, killing as many Marines as they could. They succeeded. Before the fighting was over, more than 26,000 Marines had been killed or wounded —along with almost 3000 naval personnel—

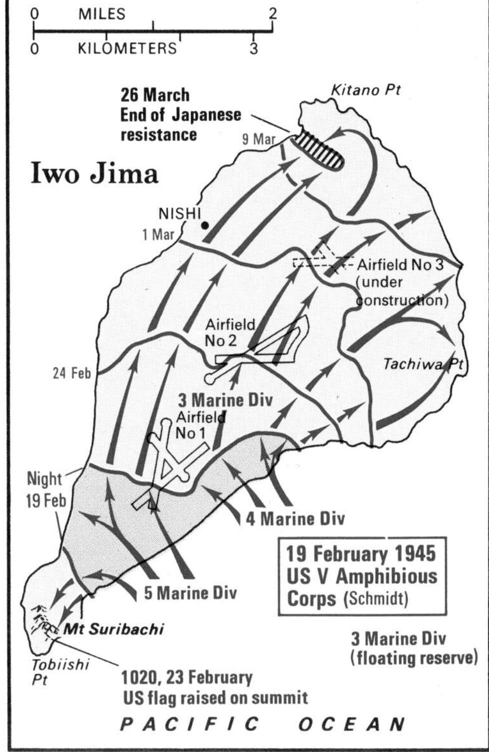

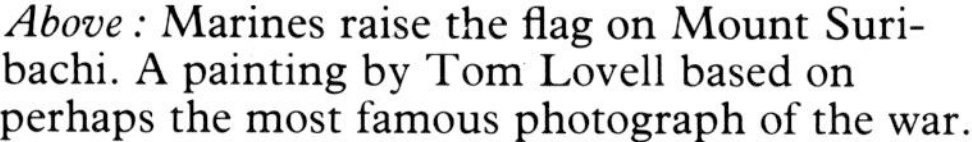

Above: Marines raise the flag on Mount Suribachi. A painting by Tom Lovell based on perhaps the most famous photograph of the war.

on the volcanic scrub wastes of the tiny island.

The Marines' 70,000-man assault force under General Holland M Smith, the V Amphibious Force, was made up of units of the veteran 3rd and 4th Marine Divisions and the newly-formed but veteran-packed 5th Marine Division. Learning their lessons from the cave warfare of Peleliu, the Marines had with them a large stock of bazookas, flamethrowers and flamethrower tanks, plus demolition teams. But first the landings had to take place on the southeastern shore of the island. The 4th and 5th Marine Divisions were assigned to make the landings with the 3rd Marines in reserve. Both would wheel to the north to assault Motoyama Plateau while the 28th Marine Regiment would take Mount Suribachi. This would mean that initially almost 50,000 Marines would be packed onto the small beachhead under the noses of Japanese gunners on Suribachi and the Plateau, but geography determined there was no other choice. The Marines would have to land and fight their way to their objectives as best they could since naval gunfire could do little against the blockhouse and cave defenses fashioned by the Japanese.

On the morning of 19 February the Marines in amtracs and landing boats moved toward the forbidding shore not knowing that preliminary bombing and shelling had knocked out only 17 of the more than 730 major defense installations on the island. The Japanese held their fire until the Marines began to crowd onto the beaches. Then all hell broke loose. Artillery and mortar fire began to decimate the Marine ranks almost at will. By nightfall over 2000 casualties had been sustained, and the beachhead was an incredible scene of crowding and confusion. There was no place to go on the beaches tangled with men, equipment, tanks and the mangled bodies

Above: General Holland Smith (nearer) and Admiral Kelly Turner during the Iwo Jima campaign.
Right: Marine wiremen at work on telephone lines leading up to the front.

of Marines blown into fragments by the withering Japanese fire. The surviving Marines dug in where they were, and the next morning began moving yard by yard into the interior, taking casualties in horrifying numbers as they ran and crawled forward against the enemy. Four days of slogging death were required before Mount Suribachi had been assaulted and the defenders wiped out. On 23 February patrols of the 28th Marine Regiment made it to the top of Mount Suribachi and raised a small American flag in

Below: Marines use explosives against Japanese positions near the foot of Mount Suribachi. Explosive charges were often the only way to attack the Japanese dugouts.

victory. Soon thereafter another patrol reached the summit of Suribachi; its Marines had with them a larger flag taken from an LST. This second flag-raising, dramatically captured for all time by an Associated Press photographer, became an overnight inspiration to the Corps and to the American nation and lives today as the most famous symbol of the Marines and their victories in the Pacific.

But at the moment the hard-pressed Marines on Iwo Jima had more important things to do than consider the symbolism of a flag-raising. The heights of the Motoyama Plateau had to be taken. On the Leathernecks went, moving up the face of the rise, sustaining appalling casualties with Marine blood flowing into the black volcanic dirt as they made their way forward. Of one 900-man battalion making the assault up the face of the plateau of death, only 150 were neither killed nor wounded in the hard fighting. For two more agonizing weeks the Marines clawed their way up the face of the plateau. Flamethrowers, grenades, TNT and air strikes were their constant companions as they blasted the Japanese defenders from their caves and blockhouses one by one. Marine artillery battalions pounded the Japanese positions around the clock. Before the main enemy lines had been penetrated and the high ground had been seized on 10 March, almost 13,000 Marines had been killed or wounded. Yet the fighting and dying continued as the Marines worked their way north to clear the tiny island of its stubborn defenders. Almost all of the island's 21,000 Japanese troops died in place as ordered. By the time the island was declared secure and the mangled remains of the 3rd, 4th and 5th Marine Divisions were pulled out on 16 March, 6000 Marines and Navy doctors and corpsmen had paid with their lives and another 20,000 had been wounded in taking the tiny chunk of volcanic Pacific real estate.

The ration between casualties taken to casualties inflicted on the enemy on Iwo had been the highest ratio ever recorded in the history of the Marine Corps. As Admiral Nimitz later remarked regarding the Marines on Iwo Jima, 'uncommon valor was a common virtue,' and 22 Marines received Congressional Medals of Honor for heroism—12 of the awards were presented posthumously—during the month-long campaign. This was more than a quarter of the total awarded to Marines during the course of World War II. The Marine Corps, in the face of determined resistance, had written one of the most glorious chapters in its proud history on tiny but crucial Iwo Jima in February and March 1945.

Okinawa: The Last Battle

Okinawa, the 60-mile-long major island in the Ryukyus chain and only 360 miles from Japan, was the next obvious target. While air units pounded the airfields and harbors of Japan, Formosa and the Ryukyus from the fast carrier task forces and land bases in the western Pacific in preparation for the invasion, a vast naval armada of more than 1200 vessels assembled for the landings. More than 183,000 men organized into the US Tenth Army (made up of the XXIV Army Corps and the III Marine Amphibious Corps) were gathered and prepared for the massive operation against the island and its 100,000 defenders. The Marine segment included the 1st, 2nd and 6th Marine Divisions. Several Marine air groups and squadrons were included in the covering Tactical Air Force. After the Okinawa beaches and airfields had been pounded for a full week, on 1 April 1945 the landing force of soldiers and Marines left their ships and headed for the Hagushi beaches on the southwest coast of the island north of the city of Naha. Almost 90,000 Marines were in a second landing force that made a feint at the southeastern beaches on the opposite side of the island and then landed at Hagushi.

Initially all went very well as Japanese resistance over the beach and island was light. Within four days the island had been split, and the 6th Marines moved northward while the Army moved south. On the basis of the light resistance encountered thus far, all dared to hope for an easy campaign, but the Japanese were prepared to defend Okinawa to the last man in a protracted war of attrition, particularly on the southern third of the island. Forcing the Tenth Army to bleed for Okinawa while their *kamikaze* attacks decimated the Fifth Fleet might well convince the Americans not to invade the home islands. At the least, the Japanese defenders would delay the invasion for a considerable length of time. They were prepared to concede the beachhead and to fight a delaying action in the north, but from that point on the Americans on Okinawa and with the fleet offshore would pay dearly for their efforts to dislodge them from their last bastion of resistance.

As the 6th Marine Division moved north it ran into the Japanese positions on the hilly Motobu Peninsula. Particularly difficult to assault was a hill complex known as Yae Take. The 4th and 29th Marine Regiments were finally able to take the hilly region by 20 April, but only at the cost of almost 1000 casualties. For the next week the Marines moved across the northern end of the island until all effective Japanese resistance had been ended.

The Japanese commander was determined that the southern third of Okinawa would be defended to the death. He had established an entire series of defensive positions across the island from west to east. The main defensive line began at Naha on the west, stretched across the heights of Shuri town and castle towards the center, and anchored itself around Yonabaru on the eastern shore. Fortified caves and emplacements on both the forward and reverse slopes of the ridges of the defensive line, complemented by limestone cliffs and ridges, constituted the Japanese defenses. During the first two weeks of April the American soldiers and Marines flung themselves against the Japanese line. Their three-division strength failed to crack it, and the Japanese even counterattacked on 12–14 April. So badly was the fighting going and so high were the casualty counts that the military commanders considered bypassing the Naha-Shuri-Yonabaru line by carrying out another amphibious assault. And in the meantime the Fifth Fleet was undergoing no less than ten large-scale *kamikaze* attacks of almost 1500 planes against their ships and men. These attacks, along with conventional air strikes, eventually sank 30 naval ships, damaged over 300 others, and killed or wounded almost 10,000 American naval personnel. On both land and sea the invasion of Okinawa was going very badly for the American forces. Something had to be done.

The amphibious end run was finally rejected by the military planners, and, instead, the 6th Marine Division from the north and the 1st Marine Division in reserve were thrown into the Naha-Shuri-Yonabaru line. Along with the Army units, they began the slow and bloody advance against the stubborn Japanese defenders in their emplacements. In fighting every bit as ferocious as that of Iwo Jima, the Americans threw massive artillery barrages, naval gunfire bombardments and tons of bombs against the Japanese positions (during the campaign American field artillery fired 1.7 million rounds against the enemy). Usually only flamethrowers and dynamite blasted the defenders from their caves and fortified positions as the Marines and soldiers climbed their way up the hills under machine gun fire and grenade poundings, hugging the ground as they went. The Marines of the 6th Division took tremendous casualties fighting for Sugar Loaf Hill, while the 1st Division did the same in taking Dakeshi Ridge and Wana Ridge. Only during the third week of May did the tide of battle begin to turn. One week later, having lost 50,000 men, the Japanese commander ordered a retreat from the remainder of the fortified positions along the Naha-Shuri-Yonabaru Line. By the end of the month Naha had fallen to the 6th Marine Division, and the 1st Marine Division had broken through near Shuri, although they had to beat off a fierce Japanese counterattack be-

Below: Major General Lemuel Shepherd, commanding the 6th Marine Division, studies a map shortly after the first landings on Okinawa.

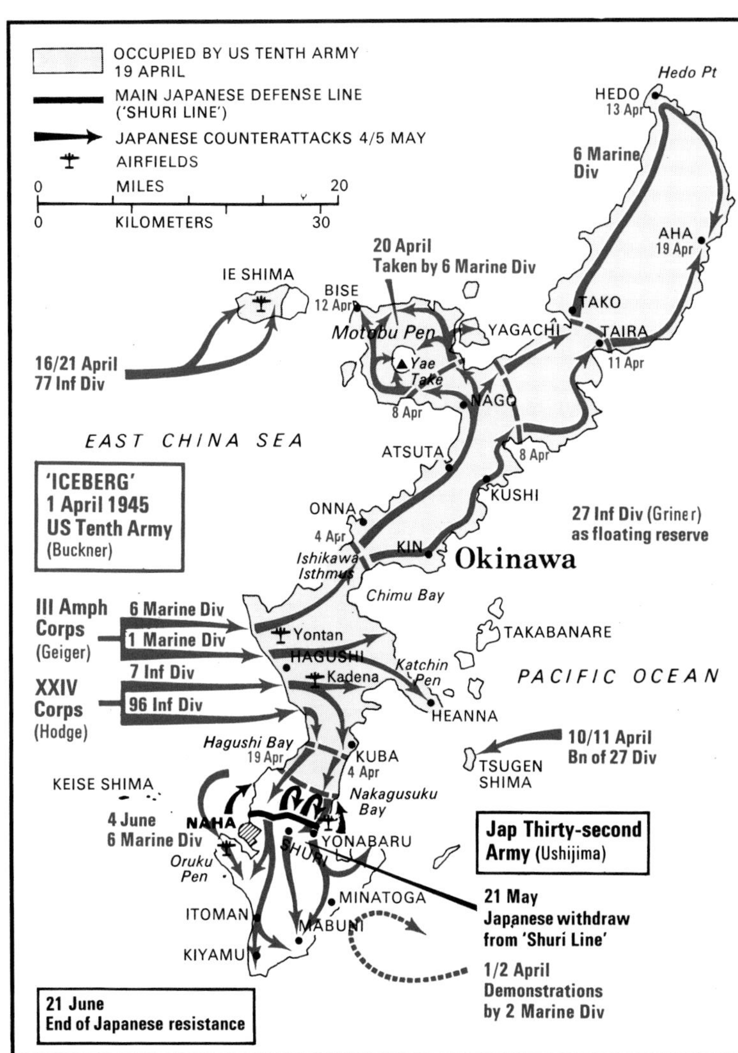

Above: A TEM Avenger bomber on a close support mission over Okinawa in June 1945. *Above right:* Map of the Okinawa campaign. *Right:* Marines close in on a Christian church near the Shuri castle on Okinawa which had been used by Japanese snipers.

fore planting the American flag on Shuri castle. The whole Naha-Shuri-Yonabaru line was in American hands by 31 May, but the Japanese, regrouping to the south, were far from finished as a fighting force even after two months of fighting.

The battles raged on in the south of Okinawa. The 6th Marine Division was given the task of clearing the Oroku Peninsula and its 2000 defenders. It took an amphibious assault and a solid week of bloody fighting before the peninsula fell. Meanwhile the 1st Marine Division was losing over 1000 men in taking Kunishi Ridge to the west. The southern shore of Okinawa was finally reached on 19 June, but mopping up of the remnants of the Japanese defenders continued for a few more days.

The battle for Okinawa was the last for the Marines in World War II. It had extended over 82 agonizing days. More than 100,000 Japanese defenders had died, inflicting over 19,000 casualties on the Marine Corps (including over 3000 dead). The entire US Tenth Army casualty list showed 65,000 killed and wounded, and the Navy had suffered 10,000 casualties. Okinawa,

the last campaign, was also by far the bloodiest campaign in the whole Pacific war. And if Japanese defensive efforts on Okinawa were any measure of that nation's willingness to defend itself against an American invasion of the home islands, the American military from the highest general or admiral down to the lowest private on the line knew what to expect when the next assault began, for it would be against Japan itself. Plans were being prepared. The Marines—along with their Army and Navy compatriots—could now look forward to the greatest task of the war, invading Japan and finally ending the long, bloody Pacific conflict with the complete subjugation of the enemy.

But this was not fated to be, for after the dropping of atomic bombs on Hiroshima and Nagasaki the Japanese finally surrendered in August 1945. Unspeakable relief spread over the six divisions of the Fleet Marine Force Pacific when news of the surrender arrived, for three divisions had already begun training for the invasion of Kyushu and the remaining three were scheduled to invade Honshu early in 1946. Now only occupation tasks remained. The Marines' greatest period of testing and valor had come to an end. *Semper Fidelis* had indeed been proved a worthy motto of the Corps, as it had so often before in its proud history.

The Tally

At the end of the war the Marine Corps had in uniform 458,000 officers, men, and women. During the course of World War II more than 669,000 wore the Marine green. These had represented some 5 percent of the total of over 16.3 million Americans who served in the armed forces during the war. From December 1941 until August 1945 some 19,733 Marines had given their lives for the cause of freedom. Another 67,207 had been wounded in action. Theirs had been a Pacific war. Approximately 98 percent of all Marine Corps officers served in the Pacific Theater during the course of the war; 89 percent of the enlisted ranks also served there.

Since the beginning of the conflict the Marines had made 15 landings utilizing six divisions across the broad expanse of the Pacific. The Army had made 26 landings with 18 divisions. Both had fought extremely well in the amphibious landing tactics new to warfare, but the Marines were widely recognized as the amphibious landing specialists. In developing in their mission during the Pacific campaigns, the Marines had developed and utilized new weapons and combat specialties to aid in their tasks. In fighting jungle wars in the South Pacific, atoll warfare in the Central Pacific, and cave warfare on Peleliu, Iwo Jima and Okinawa they had added greater firepower to aid their infantry in the form of bigger and better tanks, armored amphibians and massed artillery. Their air wings had over 2300 confirmed 'kills' to their credit and had created the whole field of modern, accurate close air support for ground troops. Above all, on V-J Day the Marines believed in themselves and their amphibious assault mission. And they believed in themselves as the elite of America's—if not the world's—fighting forces. Yet the postwar world, military planners and politicians were soon to challenge not only the Marine Corps' mission, but even its very existence as a fighting force.

Right: Men of the 15th Regiment (6th Marine Division) are brought up to the front line near Naha on 6 June 1945, Okinawa campaign. *Below:* A Marine photographer explains the workings of one of his cameras to an elderly Okinawan. Many Okinawan civilians believed that they would be mistreated by the Americans.

KOREA AND OTHER CONFLICTS

'Never Shone More Brightly'—1950-1955

During World War II, while the bulk of the Corps was distinguishing itself in the Pacific, Marines in other areas of the world were carrying out duties as couriers, intelligence operatives, support factions in the French and Belgian Resistance, and ships' detachments. Marine officers and advisers served with the British in Europe and the Middle East; other detachments raided the Japanese on the China coast and manned outposts in Cuba, the Virgin Islands, and Ireland. Finally, a group of 256 men and officers were designated combat correspondents, taking typewriters and cameras—along with their rifles—into combat in the Pacific.

Wrapping up

In the months following the end of World War II, Marines of the 4th, 2nd and 5th Marine Divisions debarked in Japan as part of the American occupation forces. Others went to China to repatriate Japanese troops and to try to keep the peace between the forces of the Nationalists and the Communists, warily eyeing one another and waiting for a chance to renew their civil war. Other Marine units were sent to garrison various Pacific islands. But despite these essentially constabulary duties, demobilization was proceeding apace as the American public demanded that the cry of 'bring the boys home' be answered immediately, even though the world situation called for caution in the face of forces released by the changed political situation, especially in Europe where dislocations among nations and peoples scarred the Continent and the power of the Soviet Union hung over Europe's horizon.

By January 1946 the 3rd, 4th and 5th Marine Divisions had been disbanded. By July of that year the Marine Corps had been cut from its wartime strength of 485,000 to only 156,000 officers and men, and more cuts were on the way. In another year the number would only total 92,000. Marine occupation troops were pulled out of Japan in 1946, and the units in China were being drastically cut back.

The Marine Corps survives

The greatest danger to the Corps came not from its cuts in personnel, which, after all, were expected and accepted in the aftermath of the war. The Corps could well live with its reduced numbers. The greatest threats came from the Corps' sister services. The Army wanted to take over all land-based military forces, thus wiping out the Marines' amphibious specialty. The Army leaders argued that amphibious warfare was now obsolete in the wake of the atomic bomb. Who would the Marines land against anyway, when threat of atomic destruction would force any aggressors back to the path of peace? And any land actions could well be handled by the Army. On the other hand, the Army Air Force, believing in the absolute supremacy of air power in the modern age, not only wanted to be an independent service but also was determined to take over all military air functions. This would wipe out the Navy's carrier-based air arm as well as the Marine Corps' carrier- and land-based units.

In order to protect itself and also to illustrate that fast assault tactics were not only practical but necessary, the Marine Corps began to develop the idea of using helicopters for swift envelopment tactics. They could come in from the sea by air rather than over the water. What would later be called 'vertical assault' tactics were thus born in the cauldron of necessity as the Marines faced the possibility of extinction from the Army and the Air Force and wondered at times whether or not it would be sacrificed to the Navy's determination to keep its air power even if something else—like its Marines—had to go.

Defense of the Marine Corps and its missions lay more in the political realm than in redefining and refining its missions in a highly complex world of unrest among the great superpowers and the restive lesser powers. Utilizing its best manpower available to make a case for itself; superb public relations abilities in the person of its Commandant, General Alexander A Vandegrift; and its political friends on Capitol Hill—and after two years of serious political infighting by the various services through their friends in Congress—the Marine Corps and the Navy won their battles. The National Defense Act of 1947 specifically stated that the Navy would retain its air wings and the Marine Corps would remain as a separate and distinct service as a branch of the Navy.

The Corps had won its right to exist with its prescribed missions recognized in law. Its greatest postwar challenge had been met. Its number continued to decline as a result of Congressional budget-cutting (by June

Previous page: Marine 105mm howitzer in action near Chinchon-ni, Korea, on 15 April 1951.
Right: Mao Tse-tung (second from left) and other Chinese Communist leaders in discussion with American officials during the US Government's unsuccessful attempts to mediate.
Below: General Marshall with Communist and Nationalist leaders at Yenan in April 1946.

1950 only 75,000 men and women wore the green and only 28,000 were with the Fleet Marine Force on station and combat ready), but the US Marine Corps was capable of expansion on land, at sea, and in the air.

Portents in North China

After the armistice, the civil war in China heated up, Communist forces beginning to gain the upper hand over the Nationalists. In 1945 Marines occupied four key cities in North China, including Peking. They were there not to fight the Communists but rather to maintain order and commerce, and to help in repatriating the Japanese. Nationalist forces began deploying in the area as General George C Marshall, President Truman's ambassador-at-large, tried unsuccessfully to bring the factions to the bargaining table.

Then in 1946 the Communists commenced a program of sabotage and harrassment which clearly endangered the widely-separated US Marine units. As was expected, it was not long before the Marines found bullets flying in their direction. It happened first on 29 July of that year, when a convoy heading for Peking was ambushed. A brisk firefight ensued in which the 40-man Marine escort suffered 16

Below: Men of the Chinese Communist 8th Route Army ready to welcome General Marshall shortly before his arrival in Yenan in April 1946.

casualties, including four killed, before getting away.

There followed a series of incidents in which Marines were attacked by Chinese Communists. The last major incident came near Tangku; an American supply depot was raided by 350 Communists, who were after ammunition. The small detachment drove them away, but not before five Marines had been killed and 16 wounded.

When the capital of Manchuria fell to the Communists in November 1948, the Nationalist cause was clearly in serious trouble. The Marines were withdrawn in May of 1949; but it was not to be long before they and the Communist Chinese were meeting again over the barrels of guns.

The price of unpreparedness

The United States had no combat forces in Korea when units of the North Korean Peoples Army (NKPA) struck across the 38th Parallel at 0400 hours on 25 June 1950, a rainy Sunday morning in Korea. It was the first Saturday afternoon of summer in Washington, where time is 14 hours earlier than in Korea and Japan. President Harry Truman had gone to his home in Independence, Missouri, for a brief vacation. After dismantling the greatest war machine in history, Americans felt smugly secure in the knowledge that any future war involving the US would be quickly terminated by the newly organized USAF's B-29s carrying atomic bombs.

The reality was that the condition of the US military, as described by General Matthew Ridgway, was one of 'shameful unpreparedness.' The United States had only 12 combat divisions, including two Marine Corps divisions, and only the US 1st Army Division in Europe was at full strength. Four US Army divisions were on duty in Japan as occupation forces, manned mainly by young recruits short on training, experience and physical condition.

US Marine Corps strength, which was at 485,113 at the end of World War II, had been whittled to 74,279 on the eve of hostilities in Korea. After World War II popular sentiment was against a large standing military establishment. And there was an eagerness, as after World War I, to trim the federal budget by skeletonizing the military. In his *A Brief History of the 10th Marines*, Major David N Bruckner notes that in the autumn of 1946 the unit had been reduced to 17 officers and 115 enlisted men. The total complement of a 4.5-inch Rocket Battery consisted of a captain, a sergeant major and a corporal. By the end of the year the manpower of the battery had been cut to one master sergeant.

The US had provided the Republic of Korea (ROK) army with several hundred members of a Korean Military Advisory Group (KMAG), scattered about South Korea for training a defensive force of about 70,000 men, including a Coast Guard. The ROK forces were equipped with about 90 105-mm howitzers plus some halftracks and scout cars. Many of the ROK officers had been given commissions for political reasons. Most could not speak English and few of the KMAG personnel could speak Korean. When communication between ROK and KMAG officers was possible, the Korean officers often refused to accept advice from the Americans for fear of 'losing face' with their own men. Except for a few ROK soldiers who had encountered North Korean infiltrators, the ROK army had never experienced hostile fire and was therefore unpredictable.

Top right: Troops of the 3rd ROK Division in the Diamond Mountains area during the advance to Wonsan in October 1950.
Below: United Nations' equipment is burned during the evacuation of Wonsan in December 1956.

The NKPA, in contrast to the ROK army, had a strength of 135,000, including eight full strength infantry divisions and two at half strength, five constabulary brigades, and an armored brigade with Soviet T-34 tanks. The NKPA also was supplied with 180 Soviet bombers, Yak fighters, and other aircraft and 122-mm guns with a range of 17 miles. The North Korean army was staffed by combat-tested cadres who had served with the USSR Red Army against the Japanese in Manchuria or with the Peoples Republic of China forces in the Chinese Civil War. Others had undergone three years of training under the direction of Soviet officers who served directly with NKPA troops at the division level.

North Korean Premier makes it official

More than seven hours elapsed between the start of the invasion of South Korea and receipt of official notice from the US Embassy in Seoul by the State Department in Washington. One reason for the delay was that the opening bombardment and border crossings by the NKPA were not unlike harassment and maneuvers that had been going on intermittently for months along the 38th Parallel. But any doubt was erased when North Korean Premier Kim Il Sung, a Soviet-trained general, announced in a radio broadcast at 0930 hours (1930 on 24 June in Washington) that his forces had begun an invasion.

As Soviet-built aircraft began strafing South Korea's capital city of Seoul, KMAG and the US Embassy activated a prepared emergency plan for evacuating American civilians. Orders began trickling through the chains of command within a few hours after official notice was received in Washington at 2126 hours. The US 7th Fleet began a blockade of the Korean coastline and USAF planes provided cover as approximately 600 US citizens and selected personnel from other countries were evacuated without incident aboard the SS *Reinholt*. President Truman authorized the contribution of whatever forces and equipment might be available for 'cover and support' of the ROK forces. Direct aid began 26 June 1950 when the US transferred 10 P-51 Mustang fighter planes to the South Koreans and convoys of military trucks started moving equipment and ammunition to USAF transport planes waiting at bases in Japan.

On 27 June 1950 North Korean tanks reached the outskirts of Seoul and the ROK government evacuated the capital. At the same time, KMAG personnel caught in Seoul hiked 16 miles through the mud to Kimpo Airport to catch the last flights to safety. By June 28 the Communist North Korean flag was flying over Seoul.

ROK troops delayed Communist advance

Two or three precious days were gained in delaying the advance of the North Korean Communist forces because of the canny intuition of one KMAG officer, Army Lieutenant Colonel Thomas McPhail, who convinced the commander of the ROK 6th Division to cancel all week-end passes beginning 23 June. Intelligence reports told of new NKPA units near the border with well-camouflaged tanks and artillery. When the attack came, only the ROK 6th Division was ready to respond. The division held its position until 28 June when faced with envelopment; as friendly flank units fled southward it withdrew. Some units of the ROK 1st Division also made a tough stand outside Seoul with one company fighting relentlessly until the last man was killed.

Above: A Marine sniper uses the telescopic sight on his M1 rifle to pick his targets carefully during street fighting in Seoul.

General Douglas MacArthur of the US Far East forces in Tokyo flew to Suwon, about 20 miles south of Seoul, on 29 June 1950 for a personal inspection of the area and briefings by KMAG officers. MacArthur radioed the Joint Chief of Staff that ROK forces were 'incapable of gaining the initiative' and recommended immediate commitment of US ground forces to prevent the complete loss of South Korea. President Truman at first authorized the use of one Regimental Combat Team (RCT) but later changed the authorization to the use of ground forces under MacArthur's command when it was learned that the nearest RCT was in Hawaii, more than 4000 miles away.

Thus was created a makeshift infantry battalion known as 'Task Force Smith,' named for its commanding officer, Lieutenant Colonel C B Smith. The Task Force was composed of 21st Regiment units of the 24th Infantry Division based in Japan and included a 105-mm howitzer battery, two rifle companies, two 4.2 mortar platoons, a 75-mm recoilless rifle unit, and six 2.36-inch bazooka teams. The Task Force was flown immediately to Pusan, the railhead for a train and truck ride to the front at Osan. From 1 July 1950 until other 24th Division units arrived by sea, Task Force Smith was the only US combat unit fighting the North Korean army.

Below: British Royal Marines land during a joint US/British raid behind enemy lines on Chinnapo on 14 June 1951. Such raiding missions were not uncommon after the first winter of the war.

Task Force Smith under Communist fire

The American unit, fresh from the soft life of occupation duty in Tokyo, made its first stand in a roadway between Seoul and Chonan on 5 July 1950 when a NKPA infantry division behind 30 T-34 tanks attacked. Despite their lack of training and experience, the makeshift army unit held off the entire North Korean division for seven hours, knocking out five of the T-34 tanks with howitzer shells. But they were greatly outnumbered, outgunned, outmaneuvered and finally out of ammunition.

As Task Force Smith withdrew to escape encirclement, units of the 24th Infantry Division's 34th Regiment were moving northward and provided rearguard action. But the NKPA troops continued their advance, catching the 34th Regiment in a bloody trap with fighting at such close quarters that the commanding officer, Colonel Robert R Martin was killed while dueling a T-34 tank with bazooka rockets from a distance of 15 yards. Survivors tried to withdraw to allied lines under cover of darkness, sometimes abandoning their boots which became stuck in the thick rice-paddy muck.

For more than two weeks during July 1950, the 24th Infantry Division units battled North Korean Communist forces almost continuously, going without sleep or food while fighting five separate delaying actions without reserves over a distance of 70 miles. Besides the enemy, the infantrymen had to fight mildew, rot and rust, flies, fleas and lice; often they went shoeless, hungry and bleeding in a country where any Korean in civilian clothing could be either a friend or a Communist infiltrator armed with hand grenades.

General Dean betrayed for five dollars

For several days after 20 July the fighting raged through the streets of Taejon where Communist snipers appeared suddenly on nearly every rooftop. The 24th Division commander, Major General William Dean, became separated from his men while assisting a wounded soldier. He was injured in a fall and blacked out. When General Dean recovered he found himself deep in Communist-held territory and tried to make his way back to American lines, dodging NKPA patrols and going without food for 20 days. Finally, he approached a Korean civilian to ask for food. The Korean turned General Dean into the Communists for the equivalent of $5.00 and the NKPA held him as a prisoner of war until September 1953. General Dean later said he 'kept his sanity' by counting the number of flies he killed during his imprisonment.

As the 24th Division units withdrew from Taejon, reinforcements from the 7th and 25th Infantry and 1st Cavalry Divisions began arriving in South Korea from Japan as General MacArthur rounded up most of the remaining army units on Japanese occupation duty for the fighting in Korea. The 5th RCT from Hawaii, authorized for the fighting in Korea on 30 June 1950, finally arrived on 1 August, along with the 2nd Infantry Division. Lieutenant General Walton Walker was named to replace General Dean as the entire ROK army and US ground forces in Korea were pushed back into the 'Pusan Perimeter,' a triangular-shaped corner of South Korea facing the Sea of Japan. From an apex at Taegu the friendly forces held a 75-mile defense line running to the east coast and another extending to the south coast of Korea. Although the US Navy and Air Force planes, accompanied by aircraft from other United Nations members, had cleared the skies over South Korea of Communist planes, the NKPA continued to advance toward Pusan by moving at night and hiding during daylight hours when they could be spotted by the planes.

First Marine units arrive

The NKPA advance finally was stopped by the arrival 2 August 1950 of the 1st Provisional Marine Brigade led by Brigadier General Edward A Craig. Army General Ridgway later credited Craig's crew with halting the enemy 'in its tracks.' The brigade included the 5th Marines and the Marine Aircraft Group 33, and although below strength like the army units—with two rifle companies per infantry battalion instead of three and four artillery batteries rather than six—it 'saved the day,' according to Ridgway, and 'provided real muscle.' TheMarine force was equipped with M-26 Pershing tanks with 90-mm guns, making them a fair match for the Soviet T-34s, which had hides generally too tough for the World War II bazooka shells issued the first army troops sent to Korea. Like the US 2nd Infantry Division, the Marine brigade had been dispatched by sea from the West Coast of the United States.

On 7 July 1950 the United Nations Security Council had authorized a UN military command with General MacArthur as Commander in Chief. Under a unified command, units from various countries were integrated into US Army company size and larger units. Each US Army company was authorized to utilize up to 100

Below : Scene during the epic retreat to Hungnam. Men of the 5th and 7th Marines are shown regrouping near Yudam-ni in a picture taken on 29 November 1950.

South Korean recruits. Larger non-US units, such as the 27th British Brigade, served as units of the US 8th Army. However, the US Marine Corps units were exempt from the order integrating South Korean recruits into company-size commands.

Marines join Task Force Kean

The 1st Marine Brigade went into action within five days after completing the sea voyage from Camp Pendleton, California. It was assigned with a ROK battalion and the 5th and 35th Army RCTs to a Task Force, named for 25th Infantry Division commander Major General William Kean, with a mission to block a drive by the veteran NKPA 6th Division to take Pusan from the southwest. On 7 August 1950 Task Force Kean launched a counteroffensive against the NKPA troops who held a mountain ridge near Chinju. In temperatures near 100 degrees Fahrenheit the Task Force battled the North Koreans for four days, at times firing 105-mm howitzers at point blank range at the Communist troops. The NKPA troops, sometimes dressed in civilian clothing, infiltrated the UN positions to locate the Marine command post and spot targets for the well-camouflaged North Korean guns. The NKPA units also used a favorite tactic of infiltrating to attack the Marine units from the rear. In addition to the killed and wounded, many casualties were caused by heat prostration.

After the initial engagement, the Marines captured Kosong on the southern coast of Korea, thereby securing the left flank of the US 8th Army position and forcing the North Koreans to retreat. General Walker then assigned the 1st Marine Brigade to duty along the southern portion of the Naktong River to fight alongside the battle-

Above: Men of the 1st Marine Division in Korea. In the background DUKWs and amtracs. *Above right:* A Korean and an American Military Policeman question a Korean refugee, to check for possible smuggled weapons. *Below:* Marine artillerymen of the 1st Marine Division in action in October 1952.

weary 24th Infantry Division. The safety of Pusan, which was rapidly growing into a large UN supply base, was virtually guaranteed by the Task Force victory.

More action to the north

While the UN forces had the advantage of shortened supply and communication lines within the Pusan Perimeter, the North Koreans were overextended. The NKPA had planned to forage and confiscate food from the South Korean areas they overran, but now found they had to resupply themselves from the north. When US B-26s destroyed their vehicles and supplies, the NKPA resorted to the use of ox carts and human porters to transport food and ammunition. Women were pressed into service as porters. Makeshift bridges were built from logs tied together and held beneath the water surface by large rocks; from the air they could not be detected because of the murky water covering the logs. The innocent looking oxcarts and A-frame backpacks of the Korean 'refugees' also concealed mortars and machine guns as well as rice for troops in the south.

In mid-August, as pressure built around the provincial capital of Taegu, near the apex of the Pusan Perimeter, the 1st Marine Brigade was shifted northward to the right flank of the US 24th Infantry Division, taking positions around Changnyong. This time the US Marines faced the

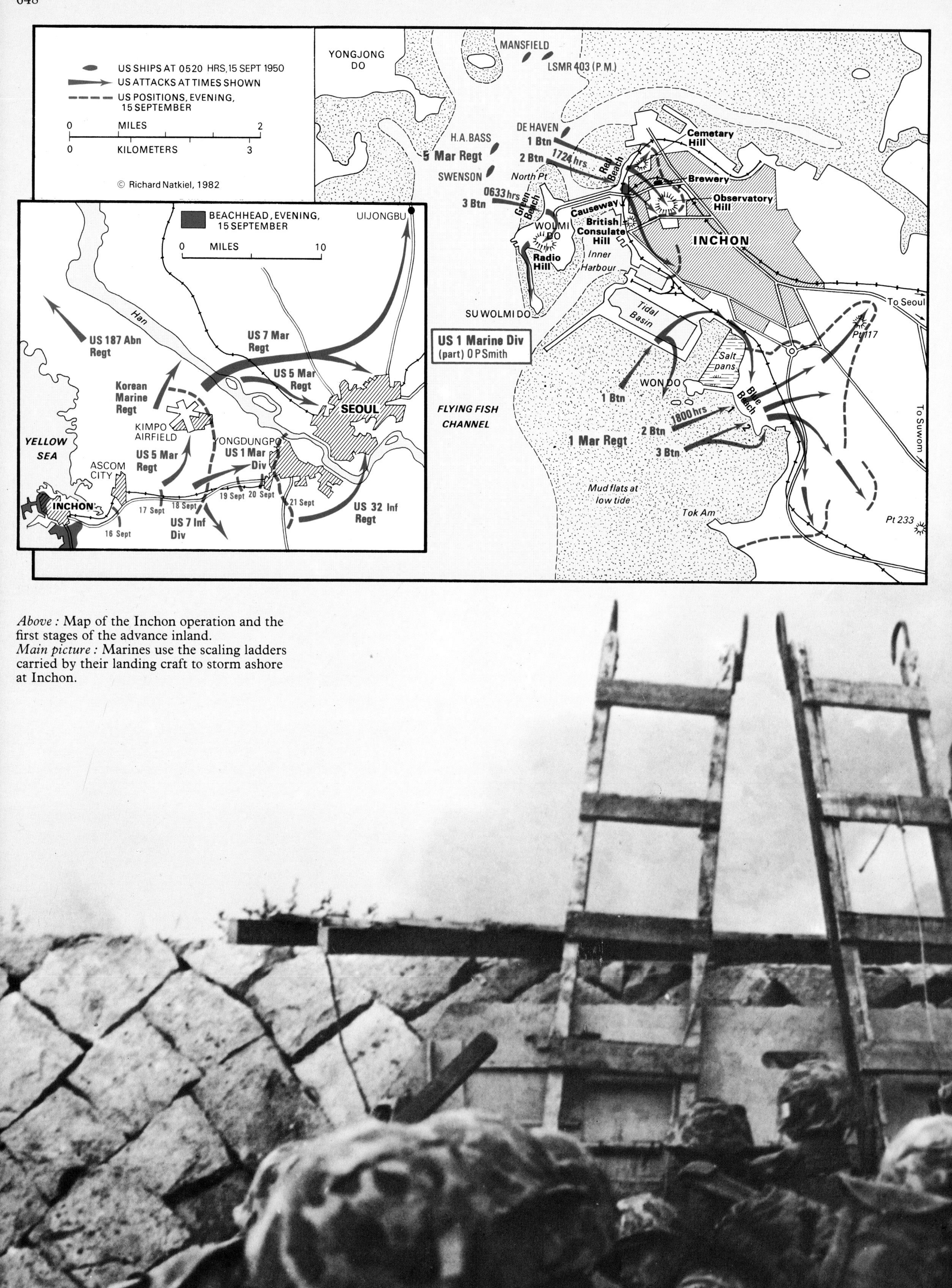

Above : Map of the Inchon operation and the first stages of the advance inland.
Main picture : Marines use the scaling ladders carried by their landing craft to storm ashore at Inchon.

NKPA 4th Division and after a number of determined counterattacks drove the North Koreans to the west bank of the Naktong River while ROK and US infantry troops prevented the fall of Taegu to three North Korean divisions. The 24th Division, which had fought alongside the Marines in two battles within two weeks was replaced by the US 2nd Infantry Division after the fight at Changnyong; the 24th had suffered 30 percent casualties in the first six weeks of the Korean War.

The last great battle along the Naktong River began 31 August 1950 as the Communist forces mounted their heaviest assault against the Pusan Perimeter. Fighting flared along most of the perimeter and breached the lines in many places, requiring the 24th Division to return to combat as the NKPA threatened to cut rail and highway lines. Fighting side-by-side with the 2nd Infantry, the men of the 1st Marine Brigade used rifles, grenades and bayonets to hold the Yongsan-Changnyong sector. They were helped by a rainstorm that flooded the Naktong River and disrupted North Korean efforts to ferry in reinforcements.

Marines lead Inchon Invasion

While UN army units fought along the Naktong River on the western edge of the Pusan Perimeter and the Taegu-Pohang line on the north, the 1st Marine Division was being formed in Japan by Major General Oliver P Smith. The 1st Provisional Marine Brigade was withdrawn from the Pusan Perimeter for the division, which also would include six battalions of Marines transferred from the Mediterranean, the United States and shipboard units. The 1st Marine Division would become a part of the newly activated X Corps which also would include the US 7th Infantry Division being fleshed out with 8000 South Korean soldiers.

X Corps would play the leading role in one of the most daring military ventures in history—the invasion of Inchon from the Yellow Sea. The Inchon landing was such a bold and seemingly impossible undertaking that many top officers in the Pentagon, experienced in World War II amphibious landings, doubted that it could be done. Because of Inchon's location on the Yellow Sea it was subjected to tides that varied by 30 feet during the day in a narrow circuitous channel through mile-wide mud flats. The harbor was guarded by shore batteries on the island of Wolmi-do, situated in the channel. And the date selected for the landing, 15 September, would fall during the typhoon season. There would only be two hours on 15 September when the tides would be high enough to effect an amphibious assault. And when General MacArthur presented the plan in early August, he only had six weeks to organize the men and equipment needed for the invasion.

Above: The landing force heads for the shore, Inchon, 15 September 1950.

Organization of X Corps

Creating a military corps with two freshly rebuilt wartime strength divisions on less than two months notice was something of a miracle in itself. On 19 July 1950 President Truman called up the Organized Marine Corps Reserve. Six days later, units from Camp Lejeune, North Carolina, began boarding trains for the West Coast of the US. On 30 July, the regimental Headquarters Battery, Service Battery, 4.5-inch Rocket Battery and the 1st and 2nd Battalions of the 10th Marine Regiment left for Camp Pendleton, followed by the regiment's 3rd Battalion. After arriving in California, the 10th Marines were redesignated the 11th Marines.

The US Army's 7th Infantry Division,

led by Major General David G Barr, had been on occupation duty in Japan since 1949. The original 7th Division had been cannibalized to provide troops for the 25th Infantry and 1st Cavalry Divisions after the loss of Taejon in late July. What was left of the 7th Division in Japan before South Korean soldiers were added was for a while the entire garrison remaining in Japan.

The situation back in the States was not much better until the call-up of reserves by the president. In July 1950 the entire General Military Reserve in the United States consisted of the 82nd Airborne Division and a poorly trained under-strength 3rd Infantry Division. The Joint Chiefs of Staff had rejected MacArthur's request for either one or both of those divisions, which would have left the nation without a combat division. And there was Genuine fear at the time that the Korean War itself was merely a Communist diversion to conceal a Soviet invasion elsewhere.

Far left: A Marine symbolically destroys a photograph of Stalin, found during the recapture of Seoul.
Left: General MacArthur and General Almond, commander of X Corps, on a visit to a 1st Marine Division command post, 20 September 1950. The Marine officer nearest the camera is Colonel L B Puller.
Below: Men of the 1st Marine Division move past a burning North Korean T34 tank as their own armor moves up the road in support, 17 September 1950.

Proving the impossible possible

It was because the Communists considered the capture of Inchon by an amphibious landing impossible that it succeeded. Once the plan was approved, Major General Edward Almond, a member of MacArthur's staff in Tokyo, was named commander of X Corps. A young navy lieutenant, Eugene Clark, was put ashore near Inchon two weeks before the planned invasion to gather information about gun emplacements, the sea wall and other details. Clark was so successful in his espionage effort that when the first UN landing craft approached the Inchon harbor, he was able to turn on the lighthouse lamp to help guide the ships.

As a diversion while planes and naval guns bombarded the Inchon area in advance of the landing, a fleet led by the battleship *Missouri* bombarded Communist installations on the east coast of Korea. Because the mission, given the code name 'Operation Chromite,' required 260 assorted vessels and high tide at Inchon could only be used for two hours to avoid stranding landing craft on the mud flats, men had to be put ashore in stages. The 3rd Battalion of the 5th Marine Regiment went ashore as the first wave at 0630 hours as bombarding naval guns ceased firing. Their objective was Wolmi Island, where shore batteries guarding the harbor were located.

The island was not as well fortified as had been anticipated and the Wolmi was secured within the first hour. When the afternoon tide came in, another wave of Marines attacked the sea wall which rose four feet above the prows of the landing craft. Some of the men scaled the wall with ladders, others rammed holes through the wall and still other units blasted openings with dynamite. By the end of the day the Marines had secured their Inchon beachhead.

The battle to retake Seoul

With each high tide for the next several days, units of the 1st Marine or 7th Infantry Division came ashore until the port area was in control of United Nations forces. Inchon fell with little resistance and the Marines advanced toward Kimpo Airport, Korea's largest airfield, located west of Seoul. The 7th Infantry advanced southeastward toward Suwon, Meanwhile, at Kimpo the Marines needed tanks to defeat NKPA troops who mounted an attack described in the official records as 'fanatical.' Once Kimpo was secured, however, US C-54 and C-119 transports began landing at intervals of a few minutes apart with ammunition, fuel and other supplies. If the scene was reminiscent of the 1948 Berlin Airlift it was because the same commander, Major General William H Tunner, had been sent to Tokyo to manage the Korean Airlift.

Marine and Navy aircraft had supported the Inchon landing and continued support

as X Corps Marines advanced toward Seoul. It was hoped the capital city, built around the base of a mountain, could be captured with the same light resistance encountered at Inchon and Kimpo. But the North Korean Communists had converted the tree-shrouded slopes of the mountain into a fortress. The NKPA intended to make the battle a street-by-street fight and had concentrated their best firepower in the area. Casualties among the X Corps troops became heavy before they even reached the city limits.

The North Korean defenders of Seoul included the NKPA 9th Division, which had been moved northward from the Pusan Perimeter to meet the UN forces on a new front. Marines fought yard by yard, and sometimes foot by foot, through sandbagged buildings and barbed-wired streets against small arms, machinegun and mortar fire. In the suburb of Yondungpo, advancing UN troops were subjected to heavy artillery fire. Although General MacArthur announced on 26 September 1950 that Seoul had been retaken, fighting was still going on and the capital could not be returned to the ROK government until 29 September.

The gap is narrowed

According to the original plan, the US 8th Army, composed of the ROK I and II Corps and the US I and IX Corps, was supposed to break out of the Pusan Perimeter with the start of the Inchon landing. Radio broadcasts and airdropped leaflets were used to urge the NKPA troops south of Seoul to surrender. The Communist radio, however, refrained from mentioning the UN success at Inchon so the psychological warfare effort had little success at first. On 20 September 1950 the US I Corps—composed of the US 1st Cavalry and 24th Infantry Divisions, the 27th British Commonwealth Brigade and ROK 1st Division—broke through the NKPA defenses along the Naktong River. The US IX Corps—consisting of the US 2nd and 25th Infantry Divisions and ROK units—forced the enemy back in the Masan-Chinju area. At about the same time, the ROK I and II Corps forced four NKPA divisions to withdraw 70 miles along the northern side of the Pusan Perimeter.

Caught between the 8th Army and X Corps, the NKPA troops abandoned weapons and tons of rice as they tried to escape to the north. Many simply changed to civilian clothing and mingled with the

general population. But the United Nations forces soon controlled all highway and rail routes to North Korea. As the gap between the 8th Army and X Corps narrowed, the 70th Tank Battalion of the US 1st Cavalry Division found forward elements of the US 7th Division south of Suwon and forged the link on 26 September. By the end of September the UN forces controlled an area of Korea four times that held before the Inchon landing.

The chase into North Korean turf

On 7 October 1950 the 8th Army relieved X Corps Marines in the Inchon area as the Marines were readied for a second amphibious assault elsewhere in Korea. On the previous day, the United Nations General Assembly had given approval to a request by General MacArthur for authority to pursue the NKPA in North Korea and destroy the remnants of the army. ROK President Syngman Rhee had already announced that his armies would continue to attack North Korean units, with or without United Nations permission, and the ROK 3rd Division began a push up the east coast of North Korea on 1 October. By mid-October the UN forces had captured 135,000 North Koreans—equal to the total NKPA army before the invasion—and had reached the North Korean capital of Pyongyang.

The 1st Marine Division had been scheduled to make an amphibious landing at the North Korean port of Wonsan, on the east coast, on 20 October 1950 after being withdrawn from the Inchon-Seoul area. Meanwhile, the ROK 3rd Division, which had jumped the gun by invading North Korea before the advance was authorized by the UN, had already taken Wonsan on 11 October 1950. When the 1st Marines arrived at Wonsan, the port was in UN hands but the Marines could not land until the Wonsan harbor had been cleared of some 2000 mines. The 1st Marine Division finally made an 'administrative' landing on 26 October 1950.

Above: M26 Pershing tanks and infantry of the 1st Marine Division pass by as a group of North Korean prisoners is led to the rear by South Korean troops, 26 September 1950.

The Drive to the Yalu River

Retrospective critiques suggest that later misfortunes could be traced to the master plan for invading North Korea by moving X Corps to the east side of the Korean

Above: Left to right, Admiral Radford, Commander in Chief Pacific Fleet, General MacArthur, Secretary of the Army Pace and Army Chief of Staff General Bradley during MacArthur's Wake Island conference with President Truman.

peninsula and the 8th Army to the Inchon-Seoul sector. The 8th Army had been assigned the responsibility for providing logistical support for X Corps as well as the 8th Army, but without giving the 8th Army tactical control over X Corps. The 8th Army experienced difficulty in obtaining supplies and transportation facilities. And the general north-south lines of mountain ridges in North Korea made communication between X Corps in the east and the 8th Army in the west virtually impossible. But the plan called for a second linkup of the 8th Army and X Corps south of the Yalu, with North Korean forces destroyed, before the onset of winter weather.

Actually, the 7th Regiment of the ROK 6th Division, attached to the 8th Army reached the Yalu River on 26 October 1950, the same day the 1st Marines finally were able to enter Wonsan. But the ROK troops encountered stubborn resistance from what appeared to be North Korean units making a last stand. Heavy fighting also developed at Unsan and Tokchon along the Chongchon River, south of the Yalu River, around 31 October 1950. Some of the captured enemy were found to be Chinese wearing North Korean uniforms but they were believed to be 'volunteers' from the Peoples Republic of China. During the first ten days of November, however, elements of 12 different Chinese Communist divisions had been identified in the area of the Changjin (Chosin) Reservoir. Then Chinese and NKPA units cut in behind X Corps' forward elements, including the 1st Marine Division.

Over the wild terrain yonder

The 1st Marine Division had been ordered to the Yalu over terrain as formidable as any likely to be encountered by a military unit. The only road leading to the objectives of Kanggye and Manpojin was a narrow winding path that in one sector rose 2500 feet above a canyon, a sheer granite cliff on the 'safe side' of the road. At another point, the road wound over a 4000-foot high pass where winter wind-chill factors usually were well below zero degrees Fahrenheit. The terrain was generally wild, rugged and trackless.

As General Smith proceeded northward along the mountain pathway, he had the foresight to have his men prepare an emergency airstrip at the southern end of the Changjin Reservoir. If necessary, it could be used to resupply the Marines and to evacuate casualties. Smith also stockpiled ammunition, fuel, and other supplies in case they were needed. His experience and intuition led him to believe his troops were extremely vulnerable to attack in the isolated granite gullies and gorges of northeastern Korea. His planning to insure a defensible route for withdrawal would pay dividends when and if the Chinese Communist armies struck, as they had been promising in radio propaganda broadcasts.

General MacArthur had expressed his confidence that the Chinese would not enter the Korean War and that the remnants of the NKPA could be eliminated 'in two weeks.' MacArthur even suggested that American troops could be 'home by Christmas,' a month away when the November offensive was scheduled to begin.

Right: Typically fierce Korean winter weather lashes Marines of the 1st Division as the retreat from Koto-ri begins in early December 1950.

The tide turns

Only one American unit ever reached the Yalu River. The 17th Regiment of the 7th Infantry Division captured the North Korean town of Hyesanjin during the last week of November 1950, about a month after ROK troops reached the Manchurian border town of Chosan. A ROK Capital Division unit attached to X Corps had progressed as far as Sodong along the northeast coast, the farthest point reached by any of the UN troops at that time.

The appearance of Chinese forces was at first something of an enigma. They would appear, then disappear, just as the first Soviet MiG-15s appeared briefly to oppose United Nations pilots near the Yalu, but just as suddenly jetted back to some airfield in Manchuria. X Corps, reinforced by the addition of the US 3rd Division, a group of British Royal Marines and two ROK Divisions, the 3rd and Capital, resumed its northward probe toward the Yalu, but this time with caution. As November temperatures dropped below freezing, a lull developed in the fighting and there was relatively little action for X Corps from about 10

November 1950 to 24 November. Radio Moscow had announced on 19 November 1950 that North Korean and Chinese forces had withdrawn to prepare a counteroffensive leading to a Communist victory—but the message was considered a bluff.

On 24 November 1950 General MacArthur announced the start of a major offensive to destroy the remnants of the NKPA. The 8th Army would advance northward through western and central Korea to the Manchurian border while X Corps would carry out an enveloping drive to the northwest. One day later Communist troops began a counteroffensive that broke the ranks of the ROK II Corps at Tokchon, exposing the right flank of the 8th Army. The 8th Army had engaged the 4th Field Army of the Peoples Republic of China. On 27 November X Corps was attacked along both sides of the Changjin Reservoir by the Chinese 3rd Field Army. The objective of the PRC armies was to pin the 8th Army against the west coast and X Corps against the east coast and open a route to the south for North Korean and Chinese division advancing through central Korea.

'An entirely new war'

General MacArthur summoned Generals Walker and Almond to Tokyo for a four-hour discussion of the situation. He explained that it was 'an entirely new war,' with Chinese armies that had entered the fighting without a declaration of war and without the official sanction of the Peoples Republic of China, which could not be held responsible for the actions of military 'volunteers.' Because of the conditions under which MacArthur had been allowed to pursue the NKPA into North Korea, United Nations planes could not conduct reconnaissance missions or attacks beyond the Yalu River frontier with China. Plans were made to withdraw the 8th Army by land and X Corps by sea through the port of Hungnam-Hamhung, below the Changjin Reservoir.

The US 2nd Division took the brunt of the fighting with the Chinese Communist forces for six days, providing a delaying action while the rest of General Walker's 8th Army withdrew below the North Korean capital of Pyongyang. The 2nd Division suffered so many casualties that it was declared combat ineffective and was withdrawn into South Korea. By the middle of December the 8th Army had withdrawn below the 38th Parallel and formed a defensive perimeter around Seoul.

The evacuation of X Corps

On the day following the crushing attack by the Chinese Communists on the ROK II Corps assigned to protect the right flank of the 8th Army, General Almond ordered the 1st Marine Division to attack northwest and cut the enemy lines of communication at Mupyong-ni. But before the Marines could execute the mission, the Chinese Communists began the second phase of their counteroffensive with the objective of destroying X Corps. From the snow-covered mountains around the Changjin Reservoir, six Chinese Communist Divisions attacked the Marines and neighboring battalions of the 7th Infantry Division. The 5th Marines under Lieutenant Colonel Raymond Murray and the 7th Marines commanded by Colonel Homer Litzenberg had started to relieve General Walker's troops when they were hit by hostile fire from assault batta-

Above: Marine infantry begin a counterattack near Hagaru-ri, 26 December 1950, after an air strike by Marine Corsair fighter-bombers.

lions of the Chinese 79th and 89th Divisions near the village of Yudam-ni. The two Chinese divisions then were given support by the Chinese 59th Division attacking from the south.

Fighting continued into the night with hand grenades and mortar fire in temperatures that dropped to 18 degrees below zero and froze BARs and carbines. The Marines fought on with M-1s and Browning machine guns, at one point setting fire to a building to provide enough light to see the waves of attacking Chinese. It was now that General Smith's advance planning helped prevent a withdrawal from turning into a disaster.

Battles of the Changjin Resezvoir

General Almond authorized General Smith to abandon his heavy equipment if such a move would speed his withdrawal. But General Smith announced he would not abandon any equipment he could use and he would withdraw only as rapidly as he was able to evacuate his wounded men.

It was a distance of nearly 60 miles from Yudam-ni at the north end of the Changjin Reservoir to the evacuation port of Hungnam, over the same treacherous mountain trails the Marines had traveled on their way toward the Manchurian border. Smith intended to fight all the way to Hungnam and to bring out all the equipment and personnel that could be moved. Only those killed in action would be left behind. He even conducted a burial service for the Marines killed in the first round of fighting at Yudam-ni.

The 5th and 7th Regiments joined forces in their withdrawal and acquired reinforcements along the way, including survivors of two battalions of the 7th Infantry Division who had fought the same Chinese Communist divisions near the Changjin Reservoir and a group of British Commandos.

Communist rifle and machinegun fire plagued the X Corps troops from every side and the enemy tried to trap the men numerous times with road blocks and

Above: 5th and 7th Regiment Marines near Yudam-ni at the start of the retreat to Hungnam. *Left:* MacArthur and, left, General Oliver Smith who led the 1st Marine Division.

blown bridges. Because the supply route had been cut in several places by Chinese Communists, the US Combat Cargo Command made daily airdrops of ammunition, food and medicines during the running battle along the western edge of the reservoir. Air Force and Marine transports and even Navy torpedo bombers were used to drop tons of supplies to the X Corps troops.

The greatest courage was required

In an official US Government report on the Korean War, the War Office said that for General Smith's Marines 'the greatest courage was required to effect the retreat to the coast,' where an evacuating fleet was gathering. As the Chinese battled to maintain their envelopment of the Marines, Task Force Dog commanded by Brigadier General Armistead Mead of the US 3rd Infantry Division fought inland from the coast to Chinhung-ni, on the road between Hungnam and the Changjin Reservoir, to clear a path for the 1st Marine Division.

General Smith's men were always under fire from Chinese Communists on the mountain slopes. Although the Marines tried to keep to high ground whenever possible, the men often had to move through open gorges and down steep mountain sides. For anyone who could walk, movement was by foot; only the dead and badly wounded were allowed to travel by vehicle. Meanwhile, Marine, Navy and Air Force fighters and bombers blasted away at Chinese troop concentrations which continued to shower death on the Marines 24 hours a day as they worked their way through the corkscrew corridor to safety.

In addition to the emergency airstrip built by the Marines at Koto-ri, the 1st Engineer Battalion worked through the night to build an additional emergency airstrip on the frozen ground at Hagaru, at the south end of the Changjin Reservoir. The airstrip was completed in 12 hours, including the occasional 'work breaks' required when the engineers had to put aside their construction equipment and take up rifles to fight Chinese Communist patrols that threatened to halt the project. The airstrips at Koto-ri and Hagaru served to evacuate more than 5000 casualties during the withdrawal, in addition to their use in supplementing air drops of supplies.

A bridge blown, a bridge built

After fighting their way through three Chinese Communist divisions between Yudam-ni and the 4000-foot Toktong Pass through the mountains west of the Changjin Reservoir, the 1st Marines encountered a fourth Chinese division, the PRC 58th, a part of General Chen Yi's 3rd Chinese Field Army, as they approached Hagaru on 6 December 1950. In five days of fighting the troops had moved about 12 miles closer to Hungnam and some of the more perilous miles were still ahead of the units. At one point the Marines had to fight on the frozen surface of the reservoir in order to rescue a 7th Infantry Division unit being decimated by Chinese Communist troops.

Near Koto-ri the Communists attempted to trap the Marines by blowing up a bridge that spanned a chasm. The bridge actually was a hydroelectric spillway apron but the only means of getting the division's mechanized equipment out of the North Korean mountains. Without the bridge the Marine transportation and wounded would have to be abandoned while the troops, carrying whatever light weapons they could pack, would have to cut back across the mountain ridges held by the Chinese Communists.

General Smith then ordered a military miracle. Although the task had never been performed before in the history of warfare, the Marine general requisitioned a 16-ton steel bridge to be air-dropped. The Combat Cargo Command responded by dispatching eight C-119 transports, each carrying a two-ton bridge section to Koto-ri. The flying boxcars dropped the spans, which were assembled by Marine engineers and moved into place across the narrow ravine. The bridge was built under heavy enemy fire as two Marine companies held the high ground commanding the crossing and prevented the Chinese troops from closing the trap. The span enabled the 1st Marines to continue their trek to Hungnam without leaving behind the heaviest of equipment.

Breakout at Chinhung-ni

After surviving attacks by the Chinese Communist 58th Division from the west and the Chinese 76th Division from the east on the road between Hagaru and Koto-ri, the 1st Marines had to face the Chinese 60th Division on the west and the Chinese 77th Division on the east to get beyond Koto-ri. The distance from Koto-ri to Chinhung-ni was ten miles and the 1st Marine Division with their entourage of 7th Division and British Commando remnants at one time were fighting along the entire length of the road, the advance elements striking the outskirts of Chinhung-ni while the rear guard was still battling Chinese Communists at Koto-ri. Each Marine unit had to fight its way back to join other Marine units to its rear.

Task Force Dog, meanwhile, had driven to Chinhung-ni and was able to meet up with a battalion of the 1st Marine Regiment working southward to open the last obstacle in the road to the plains below Chinhung-ni. It had taken 13 days of constant exposure to enemy fire in bitterly cold mountain terrain for the bearded survivors to reach the final leg of the road to Hungnam. The 3rd Infantry Division's 65th Regiment provided rear guard action for the Marines after they got beyond the range of Chinese Communist artillery near Chinhung-ni. Other 3rd Division units held defensive positions around the Hungnam Perimeter. Additional cover was provided by elements of the 7th Infantry Division that had not been involved in the Changjin Reservoir debacle.

Right : A Marine patrol ready to set out, Wonju sector, 22 February 1951.

Above : 5th Regiment Marines during the bitter retreat to Hungnam.
Below, main picture : Equipment and landing craft on the shore at Inchon, ready for the move of the 1st Marine Division to Wonsan in October 1950.

'In a superior manner'

General Smith and his half-frozen, exhausted Marines reached the Hungnam perimeter on 11 December 1950 as the nearly 200 vessels organized for evacuation of the beachhead got underway. General MacArthur flew to the beachhead on the same day and praised the men for their 'high morale and conspicuous self-confidence' throughout the heavy fighting. MacArthur added that 'Although highly outnumbered, you have come through in a superior manner.' The Marines not only brought out their wounded and all movable equipment but prisoners and captured enemy equipment.

But the fighting in North Korea was not ended for the X Corps troops. The scene at Hungnam was like a rerun of the British evacuation at Dunkirk in 1940. From Hungnam harbor General Almond established a perimeter extending in an arc with a 22-mile radius. The Chinese 3rd Field Army battered at the perimeter and was joined after the start of the evacuation by two North Korean divisions. Army, Navy and Marine Corps personnel, meanwhile, worked around the clock in subfreezing weather to load the Marines, 350,000 tons of cargo, 17,500 vehicles, ROK, US and British troops, 98,000 Korean refugees and even Soviet self-propelled 76-mm guns and other captured equipment onto the waiting vessels.

Final rounds of the year

The Hungnam evacuation required two weeks to complete. Each day the perimeter was allowed to shrink a bit as fully loaded ships departed. A 7th Fleet flotilla poured 34,000 rounds from 5-, 8- and 16-inch guns into the attacking Chinese and North Korean Communist troops. The guns were augmented by 5-inch rocket launchers. During the nights thousands of star shells and illuminating projectiles were fired to prevent a surprise night attack. The entire 1st Marine Air Wing, one fourth of the total USAF 5th Air Force and Navy and Marine planes from Rear Admiral E C Ewen's Fast Carrier Task Force 77 and Rear Admiral Richard Ruble's escort carrier group provided air cover.

As the perimeter became smaller each day, engineers destroyed anything in the port area that could have been used by the attacking Communist forces. Bridges, buildings, railroad equipment and rail lines were blown up. As Christmas Eve approached, only a small beachhead remained under a cloud of smoke and debris from demolition blasts. On 24 December 1950 rear guard elements of Major General Robert Soule's 3rd Infantry Division fired their final rounds of the year at the Communist enemy and while carrier-based planes and warships of the 7th Fleet pounded the approaching Chinese and NKPA troops, the 3rd Division men climbed into their landing craft and amphibious tractors and left the beachhead.

At 1436 hours on 24 December 1950, reported a message from the carrier *Philippine Sea*, all troops had been safely removed in the greatest sea evacuation in American history.

General Ridgway takes command

By 31 December 1950 all United Nations troops were back below the 38th Parallel and all of North Korea was once again in the hands of Communist military forces. The badly mauled 1st Marine Division had been evacuated to Pusan but would be back in action again within a month following the reorganization of X Corps and the 8th Army to form a single command. The reorganization was determined as a means of correcting the difficulties of operating X Corps and the 8th Army as separate but interdependent commands during the drive to the Yalu River. Meanwhile, General Walker, Commander of the United Nations ground forces, had been killed 23 December 1950 when his jeep collided with a ROK truck as he was traveling north of Seoul. Lieutenant General Matthew Ridgway, World War II commander of the 82nd Airborne Division, was named as Walker's replacement. General Ridgway arrived in Korea on 26 December to take command of the UN ground forces.

On 30 December 1950 General MacArthur advised the Joint Chiefs of Staff in Washington that the Communist forces could—if they wanted to make the effort—drive the United Nations troops out of Korea. It was estimated that the Chinese Communists had sent 21 divisions into Korea to aid 12 North Korean divisions and their total manpower was about 500,000. In addition, the Communists had massed a reserve force of about 1,000,000 troops along the Yalu, according to intelligence reports. The UN forces totaled 365,000, of which the largest single contingent was composed of ROK troops. The US 8th Army was the second largest UN force. And there were now token or larger contingents from Great Britain, Australia, Canada, New Zealand, India, South Africa, France, Greece, the Netherlands, the Philippines, Thailand, Turkey, Belgium and Sweden.

'Maximum punishment, maximum delay'

It was decided by the UN military commanders to establish a series of prepared defense perimeters extending as far back as the 1950 Pusan Perimeter. The strategy was to inflict as much damage on the attacking Communist forces as possible with a minimum of UN casualties, then withdraw in an orderly manner to the next prepared defense line to the rear. There was even a contingency plan to withdraw the UN troops to Japan if necessary. Some of the defense lines were prepared with trenches, barbed wire and sandbags. Fortunately, the deep defense lines were not needed because a later inspection revealed that Korean civilians had pilfered barbed wire and sandbags from the defenses for personal use. Nevertheless, the 'fight and roll' technique planned by Ridgway, based on a study of Chinese Communist tactics in the Chinese Civil War and again in the fighting north of the 38th Parallel, indicated it would achieve 'maximum punishment and maximum delay.'

The fight-and-roll tactic got its first test almost immediately as the Communist Armies began the New Year with a 1 January 1951 offensive in great force. Because the Chinese Communist troops moved as self-sufficient fighters, carrying enough food and ammunition to last several

Below: North Korean prisoners, captured by men of the 1st Marine Division.

Above: General Eisenhower, in his uniform as Supreme Allied Commander Europe, confers with President Truman in November 1951.

days and advancing by foot, they had to stop periodically to resupply themselves as their lines gradually became overextended. By inflicting maximum punishment, then falling back to a prepared defense line, Ridgway's troops were able to decimate the ranks of the Chinese Communist and NKPA forces.

The second drive to the north

Although the 1st Marine Division did not participate in the first week of the Communist January offensive, which forced the UN troops below the 37th Parallel, carrier-based US Marine aircraft covered the withdrawal of UN personnel through the Inchon area. By the end of the first week, contact with the enemy in the Suwon-Seoul area virtually disappeared, but pressure by the NKPA II Corps on the central and eastern defense lines increased considerably. On 10 January 1951 Communist troops had broken through the lines to the right of the US 2nd Division and infiltrated the ROK III Corps. To prevent further enemy penetration, General Smith's Marines were summoned to move northward from Masan to the Andong-Yongdok road where the Communist forces threatened to cut the supply routes of the ROK troops in the eastern sector.

With the mission to rescue the ROK III Corps executed and completed, the next major action involving the Marines in Korea was a contact with strong guerrilla forces south of the UN defense line on 23 January 1951 two days before Ridgway's Operation Thunderbolt was launched to take the United Nations forces back to the 38th Parallel. The Marines were busy with guerrilla groups in the south for nearly a month.

Large concentrations of guerrillas and remnants of the NKPA II Corps ranged between Andong and Usong, posing a serious constant threat to Ridgway's supply routes. The Communist forces would appear suddenly from the countryside, attack a truck convoy, then fade back into the countryside. All efforts to destroy the guerrilla groups had failed until units of the 1st Marine Division developed a technique of surrounding the guerrillas and preventing their escape. Once the hostile bands of guerrillas were encircled, the Marines would attack them with mortars and artillery. Observers estimated that such tactics reduced the strength of the Communist guerrillas in the south by 15 percent between January and February. The effectiveness of the Marine technique also was noticeable in a reduced level of activity. The guerrilla bands appeared less anxious to engage UN troops in large numbers, preferring to appear in brief skirmishes after which they would quickly disperse.

Operation Killer

On 21 February 1951 General Ridgway began a general assault on the Communist positions, an operation that required relieving the 1st Marine Division of its anti-guerrilla mission in the south. The new mission, dubbed Operation Killer, was frankly intended to produce a maximum number of enemy casualties with a minimum loss of UN troops. For this operation the Marines were committed near Wonju as part of IX Corps and during the first week of the advance General Smith, the commander of the 1st Marine Division, was named US IX Corps commander as a temporary replacement after army Major General Bryant Moore died of a heart attack following a helicopter crash into the Han River.

The Marines, meanwhile, had seized the high ground overlooking Hoengsong. Opposition was heavy but the enemy action was plainly an effort to delay the advance. As the UN troops moved northward through the Wonju area, the early Marine objective, they found the hills littered with dead Communist soldiers. It was estimated that 5000 Chinese troops were killed in the Wonju-Hoengsong offensive in seven days of fighting.

Below: Generals Ridgway (left) and MacArthur during a visit to the front in 1951.

Above: On the march in Korea. The harsh terrain and the poor roads in Korea meant that it was difficult for the United Nations' troops to make full use of their superior firepower. Greater emphasis was, therefore, placed on the training and determination of the individual foot soldier.

Above: 1st Marine Division in action near Hongchon.
Below: MacArthur at Wonju in February 1951.

Operation Ripper

Operation Killer had advanced the United Nations line to about halfway between the 37th and 38th Parallels by 1 March 1983 and was one of the more effective battle plans of the UN commanders. However, according to General Ridgway's retrospective of the event, he was advised by the Pentagon that there were objections in Washington to the use of the word 'killer' in the name of the operation because it had an adverse 'public relations' effect. Thus, beginning in early March 1951 the name was changed to 'Operation Ripper' but Ridgway's offensive continued.

By 15 March Operation Ripper had taken the UN forces back to the 38th Parallel and across the Han River in the west, and the capital city of Seoul changed hands a fourth time in less than nine months. Much of the city was rubble, including the US Embassy, there were no utilities and only 200,000 ragged civilians remained of the once bustling city's normal population of 1,500,000.

In the central zone Marines secured Hongchon and advanced toward Chunchon where fierce fighting erupted. NKPA troops had ensconced themselves in bunkers that were little affected by artillery and attacks by aircraft. Because Chunchon was a Communist supply and communications center it had to be destroyed. The 187th Airborne RCT was alerted to make a drop and assist the Marines but the project was cancelled when Marines went into the bunkers to dislodge the enemy with bayonets on 18 March 1951.

By the end of March, Operation Ripper was declared a qualified success. The geographical objectives had been achieved but the enemy had not been destroyed.

MacArthur is fired by President Truman

By early April 1951 some units of the US IX Corps had advanced beyond the 38th Parallel toward the so-called Iron Triangle bounded by Pyongyang, the North Korean capital, Chorwon and Kumhwa. The Communist forces, meanwhile, had massed 63 divisions with 500,000 men facing the United Nations troops. The Chinese Communists also were reported to have added at least a half-dozen new airbases in North Korea, including an airstrip built in Pyongyang by converting one of the main streets into a runway and tearing down the buildings on either side.

On 11 April 1951 General MacArthur was dismissed by President Truman from his four UN, Allied and US commands in the Far East. The five-star general was fired because of his public demands for a tougher stand against Communist China, contrary to policies of the United States and the

United Nations. Beginning in March, MacArthur had predicted a 'theoretical military stalemate' if his forces had to continue what he called a 'halfway war' against the Chinese Communists in Korea. MacArthur explained that under the conditions imposed by the US and the UN, his troops could not expel the Communists from Korea and the Communists could not run the UN forces from the peninsula. Every time the UN troops drove the Communist forces northward, their supply and communications improved because their lines between North Korea and China was shortened.

When it was suggested that the 38th Parallel be established as a truce line, MacArthur objected that there were 'no natural defense features anywhere near' the 38th Parallel, adding that to set up an impregnable defense 'on any line across the peninsula' would require so many men that, if he had that many, he could push the Communists back to the Manchurian frontier. As the US Senate approved sending four more divisions to General Eisenhower's NATO command in Europe, MacArthur recommended in a letter to House Minority Leader Joseph Martin the arming of Chiang Kai-shek's troops on Taiwan for an invasion of the Chinese mainland.

James Van Fleet replaces General Ridgway

When the Pentagon recommended arming South Koreans for guerrilla activity, MacArthur rejected the proposal, saying ROK guerrillas were ineffective and US interests would be better served if the weapons were used instead to arm the Japanese National Police Reserve. MacArthur further issued a public statement urging a direct attack on Communist China, a naval blockade of the Chinese coast and a face-to-face meeting in the field with the commander of the Chinese Communists to discuss peace. President Truman, in dismissing MacArthur, explained that MacArthur had violated rules governing the issuing of public statements that had not been cleared by the US Administration and for 'acts that could touch off World War III.' General Ridgway was sent to Tokyo to replace General MacArthur. Lieutenant General James A Van Fleet was dispatched to Korea to take command of the UN ground forces there; Van Fleet was commanding general of the US 90th Division in World War II and was credited with masterminding the Greek government's triumph over Communist forces between 1948 and 1950.

General Van Fleet arrived on the scene

Above: Marine recoilless rifle team attacking a strongpoint near Chinchon-ni, April 1951.

Below: Interdiction of communications was a vital part of the Allied war effort.

Above: Men of a 4.5-inch rocket battery attached to the 1st Marine Division wait to unload ammunition supplies, near Panjong-ni in August 1952.

14 April 1951 as the UN forces continued to edge northward while the enemy withdrew behind dense smokescreens created by burning off large areas of their front. The new commander continued the strategy of General Ridgway—'maximum punishment, maximum delay'—as the Communists broadcast radio messages promising a spring offensive either to drive the UN from the Korean peninsula or to destroy Van Fleet's troops in the field.

The enemy strikes back

The promised spring offensive began on the evening of 22 April 1951 with a four-hour artillery bombardment of the UN lines. It was a clear night with a full moon and by daybreak three Chinese Communist armies were moving across the entire peninsula. The Communist attacks followed the same pattern as in previous offensives, with 'human sea' assaults of massed infantry, blowing bugles and whistles, infiltrating to get behind the defense lines, and moving in so close that UN artillery and air support could not be used without endangering the UN's own frontline troops.

The Communists probed for a weak link, then struck at the ROK 6th Division which was between the US 24th Division on the left and the US 1st Marine Division on the right. As the ROK troops withdrew in confusion, the Communists attempted to move into the gap between the 1st Marine and 24th Infantry Divisions, which refused their exposed flanks and held their positions. The 27th Commonwealth Brigade rushed into the gap and stopped the Chinese advance south of the 38th Parallel. The 1st Marine Division retired southward and took up a new position near Chunchon.

When the Chinese cut the Seoul-Chunchon-Kansong highway near Kapyong on 26 April, Van Fleet ordered the entire IX Corps back to the Hongchon River, 20 miles south of the 38th Parallel. During the offensive, UN pilots flew 7420 missions in eight days and in one mission alone strafed 6000 Communist soldiers attempting to attack Seoul with an amphibious landing across the Han River. ROK marines on an embankment above the river finished off most of the Chinese troops that survived the air attacks.

Fighting on the No-Name-Line

Each of the defense lines originally established by General Ridgway had been given a code name identified with one of the states of the US—Wyoming, Utah, Kansas, Idaho. On 29 April 1951 General Van Fleet established a new line that was not given a state name and thereby became known as the No-Name-Line. It extended from north of Seoul in the generally northeastward direction across the 38th Parallel to Taepo-ri, on the east coast of North Korea. Van Fleet also shuffled the various units around to put more American troops on the west side of Korea, where the Chinese Communists had put the major weight of their offensive. The 1st Marine Division, however, was located near the center with the US 2nd Infantry and ROK 5th and 7th Divisions.

On 7 May 1951 the US Marines recaptured Chunchon after digging NKPA soldiers out of camouflaged bunkers along the highway to Wonju. Intelligence reports, meanwhile, indicated the Communists were planning a new drive. Fifty new airbases were being built and 1000 planes were sighted by reconnaissance cameras. The 1st Marine Aircraft Wing then stepped up its efforts in a coordinated attack with the 5th USAF. On 9 May 1951 a fleet of 312 F-80 Shooting Stars, F-84 Thunderjets, F-86 Sabrejets, F9F Panthers, F4U Corsairs and F51 Mustangs struck at airfields along the south bank of the Yaly River, destroying 15 Communist jet aircraft and more than 100 buildings. At about the same time, the No-Name-Line was turned into a No Man's Land with mine fields, artillery registered, bands of interlocking machine guns, 500 miles of barbed wire and 55-gallon drums of gasoline and napalm wired electronically for remote-control detonation. 'If the enemy comes,' said Van Fleet, 'I want to see so many artillery holes that a man can step from one to another.'

The second spring offensive

The enemy came on the night of 15 May 1951. Twenty-one Chinese divisions flanked by three North Korean divisions on the west and six on the east went for a sector in the center of the peninsula held by the US X Corps and ROK III Corps. The US 1st Marine Division held the left part of the line on terrain overlooking Chunchon plain. The US 2nd Infantry Division was to the right with the ROK 5th and 7th Divisions farther to the right. On 16 May, after holding their ground for a time, the ROK divisions fell back, broken and disorganized. The US 2nd Division, with French and Dutch battalions withstood enemy attacks until 18 May 1951. They, together with the US Marines, moved to fill the gap left by the two ROK divisions.

As the Chinese and North Koreans tried to encircle the 2nd Division, neighboring units rushed to help regain control. The 2nd Division held fast while the 38th Field Artillery Battalion fired 12,000 rounds of 105-mm shells at the Communist troops. Van Fleet's artillery use, which was five times the allowance of the previous ground forces commanders, led to later reports of an ammunition shortage and a Congressional inquiry. The 2nd Division suffered a total of 900 casualties but the Communist

Below: An HTL-4 training helicopter of the 1st Marine Air Wing in Korea in March 1951. Note the casualty evacuation litters fitted to the helicopter

Above: A Marine corpsman receives the Bronze Star for gallantry while serving with the 1st Marine Division.

attackers lost 35,000 dead, wounded or missing. By 20 May 1951 the US 1st Marine Division still held its position on the No-Name-Line and the US 2nd Division, with the 15th Infantry attached, began to retake its position on the line. The Communist spring offensive had been halted and the UN forces were preparing to take the offensive again.

'In hot pursuit of the enemy'

To help relieve enemy pressure on the US X Corps, General Van Fleet ordered several units—including the US 1st Marine Division—to send out patrols to a new phase line called the Topeka Line, just below the 38th Parallel. The following day, units of the UN forces began moving across the 38th Parallel toward the Hwachon Reservoir and the Iron Triangle. Van Fleet said the 38th Parallel 'has no significance in the present tactical situation' and his troops would 'go wherever the situation dictates in hot pursuit of the enemy.' Thus, the UN's own 1951 spring offensive rolled forward in May.

On 24 May 1951 General Almond ordered the 1st Marine Division to Yanggu and the 187th Airborne RCT to Inje to push the Communists farther away from the 38th Parallel and against the Hawachon Reservoir. Although rain, mud and the enemy slowed the offensive, the Marines made their final push toward their objective on 27 May. By June South Korea was virtually clear of Communist troops.

By June, General Van Fleet had lowered his sights a bit and it was explained that 'hot pursuit of the enemy' did not mean he intended another march to the Yalu River. In order to expend 'steel and fire, rather than human lives,' Van Fleet decided to find the most effective line across the Korean peninsula that offered optimum supply and communication lines and defensible terrain while making local advances in search of more favorable ground.

Operational Piledriver

On 1 June 1951 Van Fleet ordered reserve forces to begin building a virtually impregnable defense line at the position of the old Kansas phase line, running generally along the 38th Parallel for about the western half of Korea and swinging northward through Yanggu to a point above Kansong, approximately 30 miles above the parallel on the east coast of North Korea. All civilians were cleared out of the area, which was strung with barbed wire, laced with land mines and equipped with such amenities as covered shelters, road and trail blocks.

From this line, troops could work to the base of the Iron Triangle, which was a key supply and communications center for Communist troops, with terminals for rail and highway traffic coming from Manchuria. Operation Piledriver was the code name for the UN advances to Chorwon and Kumhwa, the base points of the triangle. Two tank-infantry task forces pushed all the way to Pyongyang on 13 June, but found it deserted and difficult to defend against Communist troops holding the high ground above the city. Chinese troops reoccupied Pyongyang four days later.

Probably the hardest fighting of Operation Piledriver involved the advance of the US Marines and the ROK 5th and 7th Divisions toward the 'punchbowl,' a volcano crater situated about 25 miles north of Inje and along the edge of the Kansas Line objective of Van Fleet. The route to the Punchbowl was blocked by a succession of well-entrenched NKPA II and V Corps troops who were adequately supplied with machine guns, mortars and artillery. After blasting the North Koreans out of one ridgeline of bunkers, the task had to be repeated at the next ridge. By 16 June 1958 the 1st Marine Division finally reached the Kansas Line. And for the rest of the month, the Marines fought a series of violent, bloody skirmishes about the Punchbowl, battles that were costly but did not result in a significant change in the positions of either side.

Call for a ceasefire

As the first anniversary of the Korean War approached, USSR Deputy Foreign Commissar and Soviet Delegate to the United Nations Jacob Malik proposed that the opposing sides in the war arrange for a

Below: Marines in training in a rear area try out a new pattern of winter clothing, Korea, December 1951.

ceasefire. The proposal was made on 23 June 1951, with indications that the ceasefire was actually requested on behalf of the Peoples' Republic of China. President Truman responded by authorizing General Ridgway to conduct negotiations with commanders of the Chinese and North Korean forces. A meeting was arranged at Kaesong, a town near Korea's west coast and between the front lines of the opposing armies, for 10 July 1951. Vice Admiral C Turner Joy, Far East Naval Commander for the US, was named delegate for the United Nations and Lieutenant General Nam Il, NKPA Chief of Staff, represented the Communist armies.

One of the conditions for the ceasefire negotiations agreed to by both sides was that hostilities would be continued until a truce was signed. However, neither side appeared willing to start any large-scale offensive while peace talks were underway. The front at that time extended from the Imjin River to Chorwon, parallel to the base of the Iron Triangle, swinging southeast along the southern edge of the Punchbowl, then north again to the Sea of Japan above Kansong. Van Fleet's troops improved their positions and consolidated the land they had just won. The US 1st Marine Division faced two strong NKPA Corps around the Punchbowl.

The Battle of Bloody Ridge

Much of the fighting in July 1951 centered about a 3980-foot peak west of the Punchbowl known as Hill 1179. It was defended by a regiment of NKPA troops and was being used to observe the UN lines during the ceasefire negotiations. ROK marines attacked Hill 1179 without success, after which Van Fleet ordered the US 2nd Division into the fight. The wooded slopes of Hill 1179 were so steep the American infantrymen had to climb hand over hand up the rocky cliffs while carrying full loads. Korean natives went with the troops, toting ammunition, armament and food on A-frame backpacks. After four days of struggle and supported by aircraft and artillery, the 2nd Division troops finally secured the crest of Hill 1179.

The next important round of fighting fell again to the US 1st Marine Division after the ROK 5th Division was driven off a mountain range, also west of the Punchbowl, called Bloody Ridge on the night of 27 August 1951. The 9th Regiment of the US 2nd Division was committed to retake the ridge in a seesaw battle that ran for five days, the infantrymen advancing only to be forced back. The Communist forces were well dug in and supported by artillery. The enemy did not yield its position until units of the 1st Marine Division joined in the battle, which became one of the bloodiest and most exhausting of the war. The fighting at times resembled scenes from a Hollywood movie, with Marines inching their way along rocky mountain slopes, carrying mortars as well as rifles and ammunition, to reach enemy foxholes. Much of the firing was at pointblank range after the Communist positions were reached.

Marines introduce helicopter troop lifts

Fighting for the many ridges along the UN line continued through September and into October 1951. After a seven-day mission by the 1st Marine Division to advance to the Soyang River above the Punchbowl, the Marines tried the first troop lift by helicopter in a combat zone. It was a military innovation that gave the troops a major tactical advantage in fighting that required hand over hand assaults over the knife-crested ridges of Korean terrain while carrying 60-mm mortars or 75-mm recoilless rifle rounds as well as their own rifles, ammunition and other supplies.

Below: Marine patrol returns to friendly lines, 1st Marine Division, 28 December 1951.

The helicopter was developed too late for effective use in World War II, but the Marines discovered the versatility of the rotary wing machines as early as August 1950 when they began to use helicopters for reconnaissance, rescue, casualty evacuation, liaison between units and laying communication wires.

The first Marine helicopters used in Korea were Sikorsky HO3S-1s, with room for three men. They were used during the Inchon invasion by unit commanders who could personally supervise fighting over a front of several hundred yards. Although there had been initial concern about the vulnerability of helicopters to enemy ground fire, losses turned out to be much less than expected. In fact, only two helicopter pilots were lost to enemy fire during the first six months of the Korean War.

During the fighting in the Bloody Ridge-Heartbreak Ridge-Punchbowl area above the 38th Parallel in late September 1951, the 1st Marine Division began transporting company-size units to the combat zones with the larger Sikorsky HRS-1 helicopters, each capable of carrying 1400 pounds of cargo or six fully-equipped combat troops. Using a squadron of the Sikorsky HRS-1s, the Marines could move a company 10 to 15 miles within a few hours over terrain that would have required a day or more by ground transportation. In October, the Marines began using helicopters to move whole battalions. After observing the success of the Marine experiments, the Army later began using helicopters for rapid troop transport to a battle zone.

Below: A Marine with Browning Automatic Rifle advances as his buddy prepares to give covering fire, Sintan-ni, December 1951.

Fighting and peace talks stalemated

The Communist delegation to the ceasefire negotiations broke off talks in August 1951 but called for a return to the peace table in mid-October after the UN firepower demonstrations in the Punchbowl area. Van Fleet had submitted plans for major offensive operations including an amphibious landing that would have taken the Marines to a point on the east coast of North Korea near Wonsan, the major port south of Hungnam. But General Ridgway in Tokyo vetoed the plans because of the optimistic outlook at that time for a truce and political discontent in the US about the price in American casualties for the amount of real estate gained. Van Fleet was instead ordered on 12 November 1951 to cease offensive operations and begin an active defense of the UN's main line of resistance.

As the year 1951 ended, fighting had tapered off into a routine of patrol clashes and skirmishes with the enemy over outpost positions along the 155-mile front. The US 45th Army Division arrived to replace the US 1st Cavalry Division and intelligence reports revealed that Chinese Communist troops had taken over the defense of the North Korean lines in the western and central sectors of the front. Communist attacks occurred sporadically at night. Conflict in the air also slowed as Communist pilots seemed reluctant to engage US Sabrejets. Navy planes from the carriers *Antietam* and *Valley Forge* bombed bridges and railyards. But the war generally ground into a stalemate that lasted into early 1952.

Marines reassigned to US I Corps

Because General Van Fleet believed the western sector had become more vulnerable during the spring of 1952, he shifted units along the front to concentrate greater US firepower in the area defended by the Chinese Communist troops. The changes required that the 1st Marine Division, which had been defending the Punchbowl area in the US X Corps zone, would be attached to the I Corps commanded by Lieutenant General John W O'Daniel. Small raids across the Imjin River were planned and the Marines were needed for the missions to utilize their amphibious experience and equipment. The ROK 1st Division, which was replaced by the US Marines, was moved to the right center sector and given greater responsibility for defending the battle line there.

As expected, the Chinese intensified their thrusts against the UN lines during May 1952. As measured in mortar and artillery rounds, the Chinese had increased their firepower from a total of 8000 rounds in July 1951 to 102,000 rounds in May 1952. They also moved their artillery closer to the UN lines and would mass eight to 10 guns on a single target. But the Marines encountered mainly patrol clashes and light probing attacks. The most ambitious Chinese attacks were directed against the US 45th Division, protecting O'Daniel's I Corps on the right wing. During June 1952 the 45th Division sustained 1004 casualties but cost the Chinese 5000 in a series of attacks and counterattacks.

Battles of the outposts

The 1st Marines saw action again after Major General Paul W Kendall became commander of the US I Corps in July 1952. Supported by mortar and artillery fire, two companies from the 7th Marine Regiment swept into Chinese Communist positions and inflicted 200 casualties on the surprised enemy before retiring. The battlefront had been relatively stable since the previous November but as summer followed spring, UN raids and Communist counterattacks increased. On 29 August 1952 the US 5th Air Force, accompanied by planes of the US Navy and Marine Corps, Australia and the United Kingdom, carried out the biggest air raid of the Korean War. Hundreds of planes flew over North Korea in a massive strike at the North Korean capital of Pyongyang, Communist supply installations, repair shops, troop concentrations, military headquarters and other targets. But Communist artillery bombardments also increased and in a single day in September 1952, 45,000 mortar and artillery rounds fell on UN defense positions. But even that record fell on 7 October 1952 when the US 8th Army received 93,000 mortar and artillery rounds from Chinese and North Korean guns.

In October 1952 Chinese troops that had concentrated their attacks during the late summer against US and ROK Army positions turned their attention to the sector of the front held by the US 1st Marine Division. In a series of harassing attacks, the Chinese Communists tried without success to overrun several of the Marine outposts.

The last offensive

At the end of 1952 General Van Fleet had 16 divisions manning the 8th Army's battle line. Included was the 1st Marine Division, which had acquired a ROK Marine regiment as an important adjunct. The UN also had four divisions available as reserve forces. During the stalemate that began in 1951, both sides had constructed such powerful defense lines that it would have been costly to either side to attempt to reduce the defenses of the opposing force. The Communists had suffered thousands of casualties attempting to breach the UN lines and Van Fleet advised that an occasional outpost could lose its usefulness if it became clear that the enemy was willing to capture it at any cost.

But through the spring and early summer of 1953, the Communist forces began signaling the start of a new offensive by attempting to seize outposts that overlooked the main defense line of the UN troops. By July 1953 the intensity of the enemy attacks had returned to the level of May 1951, before the start of ceasefire negotiations. The UN armies had a total strength of about 768,000, as opposed to nine Chinese and North Korean armies and corps on the enemy front line and an additional 11 armies and corps in reserve for a total of more than 1,000,000 men. About three-fourths of the frontline troops were Chinese.

General Van Fleet, meanwhile, retired after nearly two years as 8th Army commander and was replaced by Lieutenant General Maxwell Taylor.

The frequency and intensity of the Communist attacks began in March 1953, probing at sectors of the US I Corps line. On the evening of 26 March they assaulted several outposts of the 1st Marine Regiment. Two of three positions were overrun by enemy forces in regimental strength, and the Chinese advanced toward the main line of resistance until they were intercepted by a blocking force. The following morning, a Marine battalion counterattacked and recaptured one of the lost outposts. In fighting that continued through the day and into 28 March, the Marines drove the Chinese back and recaptured their other lost outpost.

However, the Chinese returned with a counterattack that drove the Americans back 400 yards. In the afternoon the US Marines once again drove back the Chinese and regained their outpost. Then the Marines dug in, reinforced their position and waited for the next Chinese attack. It came during the night of 28 March, spearheaded by a battalion of Chinese. More Marine reinforcements were poured into the battle while artillery fire was used to isolate the battlefield and prevent the Chinese from increasing the size of their force. By the next morning, the Chinese Communists withdrew after failing to make headway in their assault on the Marines.

An armistice is signed

The Communists continued their attacks into June and July 1953. On the night of 10 June 1953, the Chinese struck down both sides of the Pukhan River to drive the ROK II Corps back 4000 yards in six days of the heaviest fighting in more than two years. By mid-June, the Chinese had lost 6628 men and II Corps 7377 casualties in the fighting. General Taylor brought in the 187th Airborne Regimental Combat Team and the 34th Regimental Combat Team to reinforce the UN positions. In the following month, July 1953, the Communists experienced tremendous losses in an attempt to end the war with a victory. The estimated losses for the Chinese totaled 72,000, including 25,000 killed. The Chinese had sacrificed the equivalent of seven of their divisions in attacking the ROK II and US IX Corps.

Meanwhile, the negotiators at the peace table at Panmunjom finally reached an agreement on an armistice and a team began drawing up the boundaries of what was to become the DMZ, or Korean demilitarized zone. The armistice was signed by North Korean General Nam Il and US Lieutenant General William K Harrison, Jr, the senior United Nations delegate to the armistice negotiations, at 1000 hours on 27 July 1953.

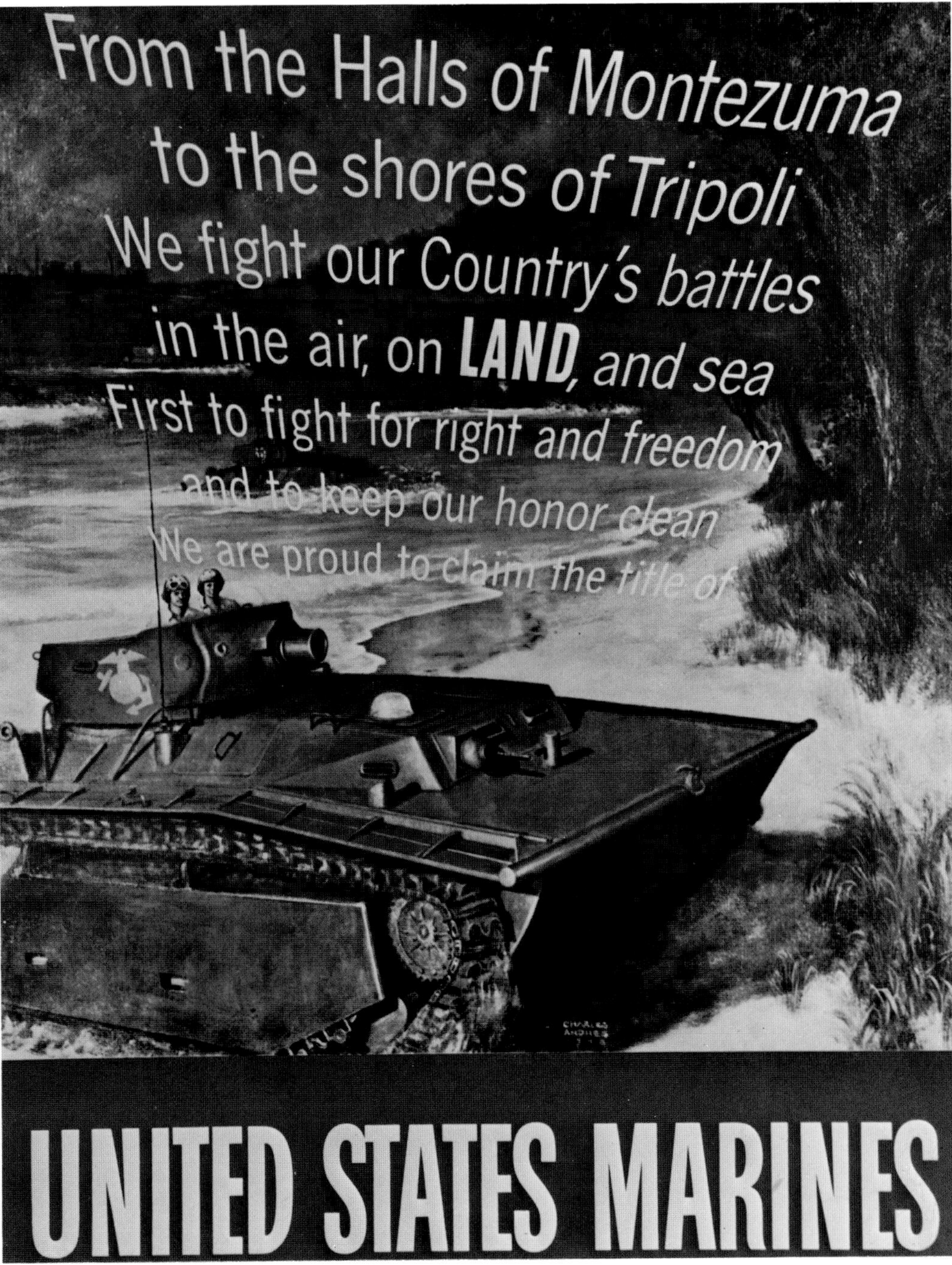

Above: A Marine recruiting poster of the Korean War period. Many of the recruits were veterans of World War II.

Above: Drill Instructor Sergeant Warren Plavets marches his platoon off after their graduation from basic training at Parris Island, a picture taken in May 1952.

The armistice took effect at 2200 hours on the same day, as a requirement of the agreement. The war had lasted three years, one month and two days. It had consumed the lives of hundreds of thousands of soldiers and civilians from two dozen nations around the world. Homes, fields and factories were destroyed, the nation's economy ruined and the populace threatened with famine and disease. General Dwight D Eisenhower, who had succeeded Harry Truman as President of the United States during the war, said: 'We have won an armistice on a single battleground—not peace in the world. We may not now relax our guard nor cease our quest.'

One of the greatest tributes paid to the members of the 1st Marine Division who served in the Korean War came later from a military chaplain who was with members of the Marine and Army troops who fought their way out of the Changjin Reservoir trap in North Korea in December 1950. The chaplain said he witnessed Army infantrymen who 'faked' injuries in order to be evacuated as casualties. But he also observed Marines who were wounded but who concealed their injuries so they would be allowed to continue fighting the Chinese Communist troops.

A different kind of peace

Another major war was over, but the next years of the Corps were not to be a replay of those after World War I and World War II, when its strength had been drastically cut. Even before the armistice was signed in 1953, the US Congress had passed in 1952 Public Law 416, which provided for three active Marine divisions and three air wings. Perhaps just as crucial for assuring the survival and integrity of the Corps, its Commandant was given a position on the Joint Chiefs of Staff, with co-equal status in decisions affecting the Marines. And in 1954 the Secretary of the Navy would further strength the Commandant's position by making him directly responsible to the Secretary, not to the Chief of Naval Operations. It was a recognition, if not a reward, of the fact that when the hostilities began in Korea, General MacArthur had called on the Marines, and they had done the job.

The Marines themselves had learned many lessons from the fighting in Korea, of which the versatility of the helicopter, already described, was only the most obvious. The Marines had also been confirmed in their high regard for amphibious landing forces and for the coordinated air support for Marine land operations. In the years that followed, the Corps would continue to develop its helicopter vertical-assault tactics, just as it had done with amphibious tactics in the 1930s (and with equal import for future operations). Training would also include both cold weather and jungle sessions. The Marines had developed a special thermal boot to protect feet from frostbite as a result of their early experiences in Korea; they had also learned the value of the 'flak jacket', or armored vest, developed by Marines to protect men in the front lines from abdominal and chest wounds. New weapons would also be adopted as a result of lessons learned in Korea: the M-14 would replace the old, familiar M-1, and the M-60 machine gun would replace the Browning automatic rifle.

Reflecting their firm respect and responsibilities, the Marines remained deployed around the world, with sizable units on Okinawa, Japan, and Hawaii, as well as at the home bases in the States. At Marine Headquarters in Washington, General Lemuel Shepherd Jr was replaced in 1956 as Commandant by General Randolph McCall Pate, who had been in office barely three months when, on 8 April 1956, an incident at the Parris Island training camp became one of the worst scandals in the Corps's history. An overzealous, if not downright irresponsible, Drill Instructor ordered an unauthorized night march, which led to six recruits drowning in Ribbon Creek. There was an immediate public outcry and protest over the Marines' traditional training methods—although most Marines were quick to defend them—and after Congressional hearings, numerous changes were made in these methods. Although individual cases of excessively rough, even brutal, training incidents would surface over the years, the Marines were at least credited with admitting to these failures. And the image of the Marines was enhanced, too, when in February 1962 Marine Lieutenant Colonel John H Glenn Jr became the first American to orbit the earth; Glenn went on to become a genuine

American hero, a Senator from his state of Ohio, and a candidate for nomination for the presidency, while many other Marines followed him into space.

But between the extremes, most Marines went about a more normal range of duties in the years following the Korean War. Some, for instance, found themselves performing essentially humanitarian tasks such as rescuing victims of natural disasters: in 1953, Greeks on the Ionian Islands, after an earthquake; in 1955, Mexicans, after a flood; in 1957, Ceylonese and Spanish, after floods; in 1960, Moroccans and foreigners, after an earthquake at the resort town of Agadir; in 1961, Turkish, after an earthquake; and British Hondurans, after a hurricane.

Marines also found themselves being assigned to another type of rescue mission in these years—helping individual Americans or friendly nationals when threatened by violence. Thus, in 1956, when war engulfed the Middle East briefly as a result of the Suez Crisis, Marines evacuated Americans from Alexandria, Egypt, and a UN truce team from Haifa, Israel, while two Marines held off a mob attacking the American consulate in Jerusalem. In 1958 a mob in Caracas, Venezuela, attacked the limousine carrying then-Vice President Richard Nixon, whose Latin American goodwill tour had run afoul of anti-*Yanqui* feelings (undoubtedly encouraged by leftist agitators); a battalion of Marines was put on standby on a cruiser off Caracas, but they did not have to go ashore. A somewhat similar incident occurred in Tokyo, Japan, in 1960, when Ambassador Douglas MacArthur II and the visiting White House Press Secretary James Hagerty were surrounded in their car by a mob; this time a US Marine helicopter actually rescued them.

Another type of rescue operation mounted by the Marines during these years came about when they were called in to display the full support or commitment of the USA when some friendly government seemed threatened by domestic or foreign violence. The most dramatic instance of this role for the Marines occurred in Lebanon in 1958. That summer, the pro-Western government headed by President Camille Chamoun felt threatened by a possible *coup d'etat* after a successful Communist coup in neighboring Iraq. On 14 July President Chamoun appealed to the USA and Britain for direct help; President Eisenhower consulted with his Joint Chiefs of Staff that day and then authorized a landing by Marines then in the Mediterranean. On the 15th the 2nd Battalion, 2nd Marines, part of the Sixth Fleet's landing force, went ashore some four miles south of Beirut; no shots were fired—indeed, the only obstacles were bathers at the beach. During the following two days, more Marines came ashore at other points around Beirut; although by no means welcomed by all Lebanese, the Marines ended up establishing an armed perimeter around Beirut by the end of July. The Marines did engage in some exchanges of fire with rebels (although the two Marine deaths came from accidental shootings by other Marines) but in general the American forces were praised for the restraint they showed. By the time the last Marines left at the end of September, a semblance of order had been restored to Lebanon, but events would conspire to bring the Marines back to Beirut many years later—and to a less peaceful rendezvous.

Marines in Central America and the Caribbean

One region of the world where the US Marines had a history of intervention was Central America and the Caribbean, where the United States had long taken it for granted that it would not stand by during certain manifestations of instability. Thus, in 1954, during a coup that overthrew the government of Colonel Jacobo Arbenz Guzman—a coup, not so incidentally, supported by the US government—a battalion of Marines was assigned to protect American nationals and American-owned property. That did not seem unreasonable, nor did it seem unreasonable in July 1958, when Fidel Castro was fighting his revolution against the Cuban government and the water supply of the US naval base at Guantanamo was threatened, that US Marines

Below: The intensification of the Cold War in the early 1950s led to renewed calls for Marine recruitment.

went into Cuban territory to protect that water supply.

A more controversial instance, however, came in April 1961, with the invasion of Cuba at the Bay of Pigs; although no Marines actively participated in the invasion, at least one high-ranking Marine officer played a significant part in the planning stage. Then, during the Cuban Missile Crisis of October 1962, when President Kennedy demanded that the USSR remove its missiles from Cuba and enforced a blockade, or quarantine, to effect this, the entire Marine Corps was placed on alert along with the entire US military throughout the world. More specifically, the 5th Marine Expeditionary Brigade, some 11,000 strong, actually sailed from Camp Pendleton, California, for the Caribbean, while the 2nd Marine Division was moved down to Key West, Florida, and various Caribbean stations.

Undoubtedly the most controversial intervention of the USA in Caribbean affairs in these years would come in 1965, when President Johnson ordered the US military into the Dominican Republic. The US Marines, of course, had occupied this nation between 1916–24, and ever since the assassination of Trujillo in May 1961, visits by US Navy ships and amphibious 'demonstrations' by US Marines had served to remind anyone who doubted it of the US commitment to maintaining order in this island state. Then, in late April 1965, a faction in the Dominican Army that was generally considered 'leftist' attempted a coup, and the US-backed president Donald J Reid Cabral asked for US aid. On 25 April a six-ship squadron of the US Navy's Caribbean Ready Group set out from Puerto Rico with some 1700 Marines aboard. The original, or at least announced, mission was simply to protect US nationals and aid in their evaucation should they become endangered. By 27 April there was such bloody fighting between the pro- and anti-government forces that the US ambassador asked that the Marines be assigned to assist in the evacuation. (There were already eight Marines comprising the security guard of the US Embassy, but they were powerless in the face of the violence in Santo Domingo.) Before that day was over, Marines, using helicopters and amphibious transports, managed to get some 1200 US nationals aboard US Navy ships.

But the fighting continued, and by 28 April it appeared that the leftist, anti-government forces were coming out on top. The military junta that now opposed these forces asked the US to provide military aid. At first, only platoons of Marines were brought to the US Embassy and to the evacuation site, where they could be regarded as still protecting US nationals. But soon they were engaged in firing back at the anti-government snipers. As reports of these developments were made to President Lyndon B Johnson, he and the Joint Chiefs of Staff decided to commit more Marines; by now it was clearly a decision to stop what was perceived as a pro-Communist coup.

Starting on the 29th, some 1500 Marines went ashore; the next day, elements of the US Airborne Infantry Division began to join them. As the American troops tried to make their way into the center of Santo Domingo, they engaged in some fairly intense fighting. In the days that followed, some 22,000 US Marines and Army personnel came ashore, and the anti-government forces were kept from taking over. A ceasefire was arranged through the agency of the Organization of American States (OAS); troops from five Latin-American nations began to arrive to take over from the US units, and by 6 June all the US Marines had left. But of the 6000 Marines who had gone ashore, nine were dead and 30 wounded.

Below: Apprehensive recruits arrive at Parris Island to begin training in 1951. As the picture shows the US armed forces were racially integrated by this time.

President Johnson and his advisers were criticized by many for committing US forces to fight on behalf of a particular government—especially since it had itself seized power by a coup. But Johnson and his supporters had the example of Cuba in mind, and were determined not to let another pro-Communist government become established on a Caribbean island. And although even some high-ranking Marines insisted that 'only a fraction of the force deployed was needed or justified,' no one denied that the Marines had once again done their duty like the professionals they were.

The Far East: dominoes or quagmire?
But of all the regions where the US Marines had so often found themselves assigned to defend America's interests, perhaps it was the Far East that would prove to be the most troublesome—and costly. After mainland China was taken over by the Communist Chinese, the USA decided to continue supporting the Nationalists on Taiwan, and this support sometimes meant calling in the Marines. Early in 1955, for instance, the Communist Chinese took over an offshore island of Ichiang; this move appeared to threaten Nationalist Chinese on the nearby Tachen Islands, so a battalion of Marines was assigned to help some 24,000 of them evacuate to Taiwan. In 1958, when the Communist Chinese began to bombard the offshore islands of Quemoy and Little Quemoy, a Marine Air Group was assigned to Taiwan to help bolster the Nationalist Chinese air defenses.

But it was in Southeast Asia that the United States found itself increasingly involved in commitments that had increasing implications. Behind all these commitments, in fact, was the determination not to let these lands fall under Communist domination. Thus, even in 1955, when some 300,000 North Vietnamese—mostly Catholics, but in any case opposed to the Communist government of Ho Chi Minh—chose to flee to the south, US Marines assisted in this mammoth refugee operation.

Above: Sporting their new Marine Corps haircuts recruits are issued with their uniforms, Parris Island 1955

Then a civil war broke out in Laos in 1959, and when it appeared that it might threaten the stability of neighboring Thailand, in 1961 the USA dispatched a Marine Expeditionary Brigade; eventually Marine helicopter units were also sent to Thailand, and before the Marines all left in August 1962, some 5000 had been assigned for duty there.

The justification, again, was that if one of these countries fell to the Communists, the others would begin to topple like a row of dominoes. Those opposed to American involvement, however, would employ another simile—that of a quagmire, into which America was sinking deeper and deeper. Whichever was the case, it was in another Southeast Asian land that the USA —and the Marines—were becoming increasingly involved. It was the troublespot to end all troublespots: Vietnam.

THE LONG STRUGGLE IN VIETNAM

'Our Tradition and Our Burden'—1955-1973

In early 1954 the Corps' total involvement in Vietnam was represented by the arrival there of one lone Marine advisor; by 1968 the number of Marines in Vietnam had grown to a peak strength of 85,755 men and women, more than a quarter of the total strength of the Corps. The circumstances that brought about the growth of Corps involvement in America's longest military action was a classic example of how deadly a brew the mixture of politics and warfare çan create.

In the beginning

In a sense, the Vietnam War was an 'adopted war' for the United States. What was then known as the Indochina War belonged to the French who, by the time the first American arrived, had been in combat with the North Vietnam-based Communist army of Ho Chi Minh for nearly a decade. During that period the French formed a union with the South Vietnamese that placed the conduct of the war against the Communists under the aegis of a group titled the Franco-Vietnamese High Committee, made up of military men of each nation. One of the plans generated by the committee called for the creation of a strong South Vietnamese Navy and Marine Corps, but political squabbling in Saigon, along with opposition by the country's large army, brought these plans to all but a halt, so that at the end of 1955 the South Vietnamese Marine Corps consisted of only 90 officers and 3730 men.

Previous page: Marine CH-53 helicopter in flight over Phnom Penh in April 1975.
Below: Viet Minh troops during the victory over the French at Dien Bien Phu in 1954, which signaled the end of French rule.

The American Marines in Vietnam at this time were served with an organization called MAAG—the US Military Assistance & Advisory Group, Indochina—which was set up by presidential order to support the efforts of the French and South Vietnamese military. At French insistance MAAG's role was strictly that of a supply depot; its advisory functions were limited to the demonstration of US equipment and not related to operations or combat training.

Major growth of the American presence did not come until after the signing of a peace agreement in 1954 ended the Indochina War and led to the subsequent gradual withdrawal of the French military. This reduction in French forces created great difficulty for the embryonic South Vietnamese military, since they had been receiving military supplies directly from the French, who in turn got the materials from the United States. With the French leaving, title to the military equipment reverted to the United States, and the American administration felt obliged to move in and see to its distribution.

Soon, however, the pressure of circumstances made it necessary for the United States to take on a major role previously filled by the French in regard to the South Vietnamese military forces, that of providing for their training, organization and administration. Toward the end of 1954 the United States told the Vietnamese government it was willing to provide equipment and training support for 90,000 Vietnamese troops. When Saigon strongly rejected this number, the US raised the figure in increments during the following year to 150,000.

Also, in 1955, Marines with the Seventh Fleet aided in the evacuation of 300,000 refugees from North Vietnam to the south. That same year, working in conjunction with the French, the United States provided personnel for two training missions with the acronym titles of ATOM and, its replacement later in 1955, TRIM. A plan for the organization of the South Vietnamese Navy and Marine Corps was developed by a committee of TRIM, with the naval portion of the plan coming from a French study group and the Marine proposals coming from US Marines assigned to TRIM. In December 1955, after a detailed presentation of the plans of Lieutenant General Lee Van Ty, Chief of Staff of the Vietnamese Armed Forces, Ty accepted the organizational plan. As part of the implementation of the plan, US Marine Corps drill instructors provided Basic School instruction for Vietnamese Marine Corps recruits; the best of the graduates from these classes became DIs themselves and soon took over much of the work of training recuirts.

Involvement by attrition: advisory campaign

The next decade of war in Vietnam at first saw American military forces play a 'bridesmaid' role to the combat, close to the center of action but never committed to aggressive combat by direct orders. However, this situation gradually changed in an evolutionary way as American military personnel—working with base-keeping forces, medical field units and helicopter elements in ever-closer support of Vietnamese combat

Right: A Sea Stallion helicopter carrying a water trailer to Hill 119, six miles from the Danang base, 1st Marine Division, during the Vietnam campaign in May 1970.

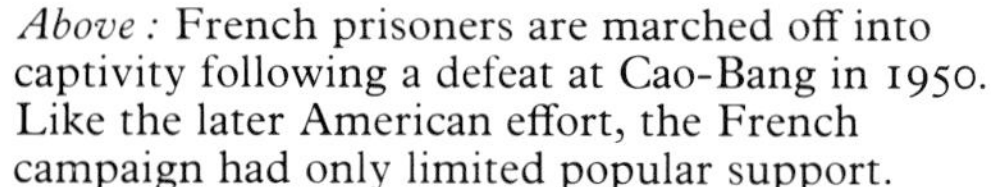

Above : French prisoners are marched off into captivity following a defeat at Cao-Bang in 1950. Like the later American effort, the French campaign had only limited popular support.

Above : Men of the 4th Marines during an amphibious landing at Danang.
Right : Marines move away from their transport helicopter during a search and destroy operation.

troops—began experiencing casualties from enemy action in steadily increasing numbers. Early in 1962 Marine Medium Helicopter Squadron 362 of the 1st Marine Aircraft Wing was ordered to Vietnam, in what was dubbed Operation Shu-Fly, to provide support for Vietnamese combat troops; Marine Corps commitment in the country at that time was approximately 600 personnel.

By far the largest number of American casualties were suffered in Viet Cong attacks on air bases from which planes of the US Air Force, beginning in February 1965, made strikes at North Vietnam; many of them operated out of the congested, ever-busy air base at Da Nang. Public indignation over these casualties grew steadily in the United States, and on 6 March 1965, it was announced in Washington that two battalions of Marines, about 3500 men, were being sent to South Vietnam to serve as security troops for the Da Nang air base, thereby freeing Vietnamese troops for combat duty. Secretary of State Dean Rusk, when questioned, said that the Marines would shoot back if fired upon; this was the first time an American administration had openly authorized ground forces in Vietnam to engage in fire fights with the enemy. It was a policy change of historic dimensions.

It was in the 'plan ahead' nature of the Marine Corps that it had well-formulated plans for exactly this mission—in fact, Da Nang was the objective area in the Corps Schools' well-practiced Amphibious Warfare Study No. XVI. The Bay of Da Nang above the air base was an excellent harbor—except during northeast monsoons—formed by the Hai Van Peninsula on the north and a sprawling promontory known as Mon Ky (or Monkey) Mountain to the south. The city of Da Nang, formerly the old French colonial city of Tourane, looked tattered and weary from years of warfare, yet its streets bustled with the noise and life of a population estimated at 200,000, more than half of them refugees and other displaced persons.

Involvement by attrition: defensive campaign

The seas were running rough before a northeast wind when the USS *Henrico*, *Union* and *Vancouver*, the ships carrying the 9th Marine Expeditionary Brigade, under Brigadier General Frederick J Karch, took up station 4000 yards off of Red Beach Two on the morning of 8 March 1965. The Marines had been warned that the refugees in Da Nang had been heavily infiltrated with Viet Cong, and that they therefore might receive fire from any quarter. But when the men in the first group ashore, Battalion Landing Team 3/9 came up the beach at 09:18, they were greeted instead by a crowd that included local dignitaries and slim Vietnamese girls who encircled the American's necks with strings of flowers. This friendly greeting was totally unexpected.

The arrival of BLT 3/9 by sea was coordinated with the arrival at Da Nang by air of BLT 1/3; this operation went off with such success that by the afternoon a halt was called to the airlift until the mountain of equipment on the ground could be cleared away; the inflights recommenced on 10 March and were completed by 12 March. Viet Cong interference with the operation was minimal, consisting only of some VC small-arms fire at incoming C-130 transport aircraft.

In addition to the 9th MEB's responsibility of sharing in the defense of Da Nang, it had the further mission of protecting the high ground directly to the west of the air base. When Company I, 3rd Battalion, 9th Marines, took over the hill, they nicknamed it '*the hungry i*' after their Company and a then-popular nightclub in San Francisco. After Company K dug in on Hill 268 to the north and engineers put in a road, a Hawk missile battery of the 1st Light Anti-Aircraft Missile Battalion under Lieutenant Colonel Bertram E Cook Jr took up firing positions. The defensive positions were text-book perfect; unfortunately for the Marines, the VC did not fight by text-book rules.

The problems of securing Da Nang were part of a larger problem, that of defending the military region known as I Corps Tactical Zone within which the air base was located. I Corps consisted of 10,000 square miles of variegated territory, about one-sixth of the total land area of South Vietnam. It was the farthest north of the four corps areas, with its upper boundary touching the border of North Vietnam, its eastern edge running along the China Sea, peaks of the Annamite mountains along the southern boundary, which continued upward at the Corps' western edge on a common border with Laos. The long, high stretch of the Annamites historically had separated the region designated as I Corps from the rest of Vietnam not only geographically but culturally as well; for example, one group of mountain people, the Montagnards, differed in a number of culturally significant

Force fighters and from Marine evacuation helicopters. With this aid, a total disaster for the ARVN forces was averted. However, it left a question in the minds of everyone involved: what would it take to bring American fighting men to the aid of their allies, the South Vietnamese?

Other events were at that moment bringing the question closer to being answered. Three months of defensive operations by the III MAF had resulted in almost 200 casualties, including 18 Marines dead; the feeling was growing among the officers and men in I Corps that if this was what constituted a static defensive role, they didn't like it. In fact, this opinion reached as high up the chain of command as the Commandant, Marine Corps, who on 28 April had told the press while on a visit to Da Nang that his Marines were not in Vietnam 'to sit on their ditty boxes,' they were there to 'kill Viet Cong.'

In Washington as well, a movement toward a more aggressive involvement

Above: Marines and an interpreter interview a Vietcong suspect. Distinguishing innocent civilians from Vietcong sympathizers was an endless problem in Vietnam.

ways from other Vietnamese. I Corps was a rural area; the basic social unit was the hamlet, of which there were literally hundreds. These, in turn, were combined in political units designated as villages, districts and provinces.

While command of military operations in I Corps was nominally under General Nguyen Chanh Thi, Vietnamese troops in fact controlled only the cities of Da Nang and Hoi An, and very little else other than outpost district headquarters which floated like warships in a sullen sea of Viet Cong. These outposts, fortified by surrounding breastworks of bamboo and mud, were scattered here and there throughout I Corps, most of them garrisoned with little more than a company-sized unit of Vietnamese troops who usually stayed within their protective mud walls.

By 12 April the Marine strength in the Da Nang area had reached about 5000. That day a reinforced company from 2nd Battalion, 3rd Marines, was lifted 42 miles north by helicopters to Phu Bai, seven miles from Hue, to secure an air base and communications facility; two days later other Marine units joined them in strength. Hué, South Vietnam's third largest city, once was the country's royal capital, and its people had never forgotten Hué's one-time splendor. Hué's students showed their proud, independent spirit by being a continuing source of political disquietude, as were the city's militant Buddhists.

On 7 May the designation of the Marine units in I Corps was changed from the 9th MEB into III MAF—Third Marine Amphibious Force. The organization was to have been called an 'Expeditionary' force, but it was decided all the way up at the level of the Joint Chiefs of Staff in Washington to change it to 'Amphibious' following the appearance of comments in Saigon newspapers that the term 'Expeditionary' evoked memories of the colonial days of the French Expeditionary Corps. General William C Westmoreland, Commander, United States Military Assistance Command, Vietnam (ComUSMACV), made it clear at this time that the mission of the Marines in Vietnam still was a defensive one, but he added that this included the task of undertaking, when authorized, limited offensive operations directly related to the security of their bases.

Also on 7 May, I Corps' string of coastal defensive positions was added to when the 3rd Marine Amphibious Brigade under Brigadier General Marion E Carl, the Corps' first air ace, came ashore on a barren beach at Chu Lai, 55 miles southeast of Da Nang, meeting no opposition. The specific purpose of this landing was to secure an area for the construction of a new air base that would relieve some of the growing congestion at busy Da Nang. Two days after the landing, Marine engineers and Seabees went to work on the site, and by the deadline date for flight operations, 1 June, the field went into operation with the arrival of four A-4 'Skyhawks' from Cubi Point in the Philippines.

Several weeks later the VC tested to find out what military difference all this activity might have made in the effectiveness of the ARVN—the Army of the Republic of Vietnam. On 30 May the 1st Battalion, 51st ARVN Regiment, was ambushed by the Viet Cong on Route 5 a short distance from their base at Ba Gia. Only three American advisors and 65 South Vietnamese escaped, of the 400 men in the unit. General Thi sent in his 39th Ranger Battalion and a Vietnamese Marine battalion against the enemy's estimated 5 battalions, with ensuing heavy losses for his units. Thi then asked Saigon for reinforcements, including an American Marine battalion; his request was refused, but he did get air support from US Air

could be detected between the lines of statements by Administration spokespeople. On 5 June Robert J McClosky of the State Department, speaking with the approval of the highest authorities, said about the role of American troops in Vietnam: 'In establishing and patrolling their defense perimeters, they come into contact with the Viet Cong and at times are fired upon. Our troops naturally return the fire. It should come as no surprise that our troops engage in combat in these and similar circumstances.'

There were then some 51,000 American servicepeople in Vietnam, about 16,500 of them Marines and 3500 Army Airborne troopers performing defensive missions and the rest doing jobs that could be lumped under the general description of 'advisory capacity.'

It was obvious that the White House was seeking a politically acceptable way out of a militarily unacceptable situation in Vietnam. President Johnson met with the soon-to-retire ambassador to South Vietnam, Maxwell D Taylor, and with his top political advisors prior to a meeting of the National Security Council. The consensus regarding prospects in Vietnam was one of concern; hopes were dimming that the ARVN could turn the tide on the Viet Cong, even in those areas where America was providing security troops, training and equipment, and the view was even gloomier regarding the central highlands area of Pleiku-Kontum, where there were as yet no US support troops. At the Washington meetings, the necessity of committing as many as half a million American troops began to be mentioned.

Against such a background, a statement released by the State Department on 8 June stirred up great excitement; it seemed to say that General Westmoreland had been given wider lattitude by the President to use US troops in offensive roles. The next day the White House released a statement that neither confirmed nor denied the previous day's information. It said: 'The President has issued no order of any kind in this regard to General Westmoreland recently or at any other time. . . . If help is requested by the appropriate Vietnamese commander, General Westmoreland also had authority within the assigned mission to employ . . . troops in support of Vietnamese forces faced with aggressive attack. . . .'

Faced with the cautious obliquity of political leaders, the country's press began its own speculation regarding America's military options in Vietnam. Two general viewpoints rose out of this, one the so-called 'Army' strategy and the other the 'Marine' strategy. The 'Army' strategy called for the aggressive employment of US troops on 'search and destroy' missions against the

Below: The Marines' assault landing craft hit the beach at Da Nang. Many of the Marines taking part had expected to have to make an opposed landing and were instead rather embarrassed by the friendly welcome they received.

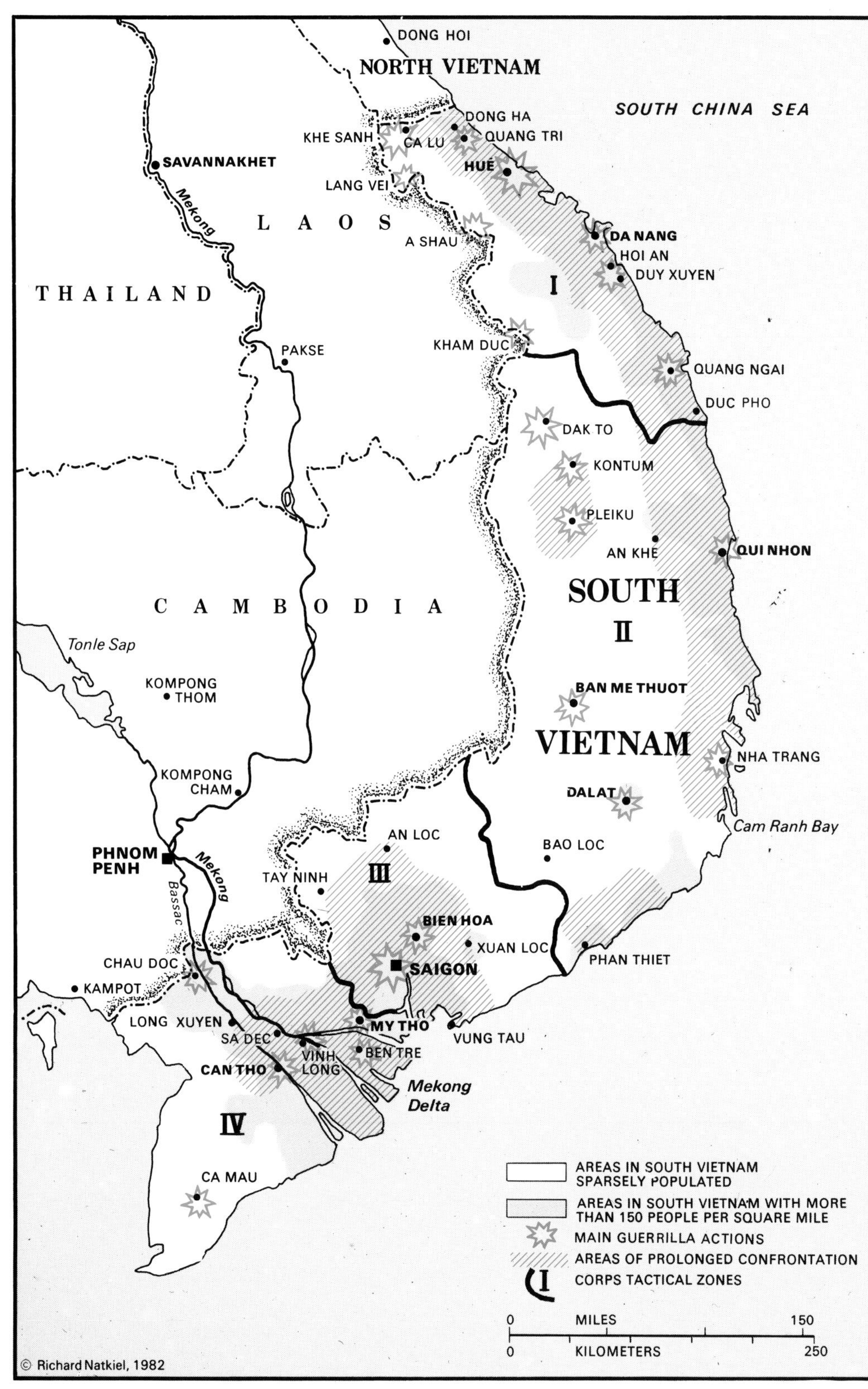

VC, while the 'Marine' strategy affirmed the status quo, giving priority to the establishment of secure coastal positions such as Da Nang from which forces could move out gradually in 'clear and hold' operations. As General Westmoreland had reminded his senior officers, the US government's official policy was then firmly on the side of the 'Marine' strategy.

This policy would gradually erode, in large measure due to the effects on the attitudes of politicians and the general public back in the United States of incidents such as that which occurred just before dawn of 1 July at Da Nang air base. A Viet Cong demolitions team slipped through the ARVN perimeter security south and east of the field and struck the parked aircraft with mortar and rocket fire and explosives, destroying or damaging three C-130s and three F-102s. A hastily-formed Provisional Base Defense Battalion was created out of support and service personnel to strengthen security until additional combat units arrived.

On 8 July Henry Cabot Lodge was sworn in by President Johnson as ambassador to Vietnam to replace the retiring Maxwell D Taylor, and immediately afterwards he and Defense Secretary Robert McNamara flew to Vietnam to inspect the American forces there and gain an up-dated sense of the situation. McNamara's comment on it while in Saigon was that 'In many respects it has deteriorated since 15 months ago, when I was last here.' On his return to Washington, McNamara joined President Johnson and his top advisors and long meetings stretching over several days, planning America's policy for its involvement in Vietnam. On 28 July the president announced that the country's military forces in Vietnam would be increased from 75,000 to 125,000 'almost immediately, that the draft quota would be increased from 17,000 to 35,000 a month, and enlistment programs would be stepped up. The next month, as a consequence of the President's July decisions, an increase of 30,000 Marines, up to 223,100, was authorized.

On 30 July General Westmoreland informed General Walt that he was to have operational control of all US ground elements in I Corps, and that ComUSMACV expected to see his forces undertake larger offensive operations that struck out farther from the protected bases. When Walt mentioned that his mission, as presently defined from Washington, called only for defensive operations, Westmoreland invited him to rewrite the instructions and make those changes he thought necessary to free up his forces for the kind of operations now being considered. This Walt did, and out of the new plan the concept of Tactical Areas of Responsibility was born. The TAORs presented some matters for thoughtful consideration: they made it necessary to work more carefully and closely with the office of General Thi, Vietnamese commander of I Corps, to avoid cross-purposes between his troops and the Americans; the TAORs growth was limited by the shortage of American troops; the Americans would be depending on ARVN troops to secure the territory within each TAOR as the Americans pushed its boundaries outward, and how well the ARVN could do this was an unknown factor.

As of that August the Corps had four regiments in Vietnam, as follows: 3rd Marines, with its 1st and 2nd Battalions at Da Nang and the 3rd Battalion, 4th Marines, attached and stationed at Phu Bai; 9th Marines, with its 2nd and part of the 1st Battalion guarding the area south of Da Nang; the rest of the 1st was on the air base itself; 4th Marines, at Chu Lai with its 1st and 2nd Battalions and 3rd Battalion, 3rd Marines, attached; 7th Marines, also at Chu Lai with its 1st Battalion; the 2nd Battalion was at Qui Nhon and the 3rd was at sea with the Fleet Special Landing Force. Additionally, four Marine Aircraft Groups were in Vietnam, MAG-11, 12, 16 and 36.

On line with the new point of view regarding offensive actions, III MAF Headquarters decided to enage the Viet Cong in a major battle, to take place in the area south of Chu Lai, where intelligence indicated that the 1st Viet Cong Regiment, some 2000 men, was gathering for an attack on the air strip. By chance two large fresh American units were in that area, and they became the basis for Operation Starlite, the first regimental-size American attack force since the Korean War. The attack began on 18 August with a three-pronged assault: a river landing from the north, a helilift on the west and an amphibious landing on the beaches to the southeast. In six days of battle the Marines caused 964 VC killed, broke up a probable attack on Chu Lai, and rendered a VC regiment unfit for combat.

Shortly afterwards Operation Pirhana was launched, beginning 7 September. The mission was a sweep of Batangan Peninsula south of Van Tuong, where reports said remnants of the 1st VC Regiment might be hiding out. This time the Marines coordinated their attack with Vietnamese military units, with a degree of operational success; in three days of fighting the Marines killed 183 Viet Cong and the South Vietnamese another 66.

While these victories took place, setbacks of a sort occurred as well. VC raiders struck on 5 August at an Esso tank farm near Da Nang at Lien Chu, setting afire and destroying two million gallons of fuel. The terminal lay outside the area of the Da Nang TAOR, and the Marines simply could not afford the manpower necessary to provide total security for the fuel depot; instead a rifle platoon was sent to guard the Nam O bridge on the road leading to Lien Chu. At the air base a number of changes were made in the disposition of the security forces which, on 21 August, made it finally possible to dissolve the Provisional Base Defense Battalion and send the clerks and maintenance personnel back to their regular duties.

The changes were not sufficient to keep out the VC however. On the night of 27 October a Viet Cong raiding party arrived at a village on China Beach between Monkey Mountain and Marble Mountain. From there they moved to a point near MAG-16's area of Da Nang air base, close by a Seabee camp, and opened up with mortar fire on the sleeping sailors. Under cover of this diversionary action, four demolition teams slipped onto the flight line and, with grenades and bangalore torpedoes, destroyed or damaged 47 helicopters; a nearby hospital was hit as well. Three Americans were killed and 91 wounded, while the VC suffered 41 dead. That same night 15 VC sappers attacked Chu Lai air base but did little damage, and most of the attackers were killed or captured; west and south of the Da Nang Marines struck and dispersed VC rifle units, one with artillery fire and the other in an ambush set by a Marine squad in which 15 Viet Cong died.

Operation Blue Marlin

The increasing activity was tied to the weather, for the VC were implementing what was called their 'monsoon strategy.' The monsoon season, which arrived a month late in I Corps that year, was an exceptionally heavy one, with rains averaging an inch each day. At III MAF headquarters this was seen as an opportunity to exploit the basic strength of the Corps, its ability to function efficiently in adverse circumstances and particularly those involving amphibious operations. Operation Blue Marlin went into effect on 10 November, the Corps' birthday, when BLT 2/7 and the 3rd Battalion, Vietnamese Marine Brigade, went ashore through storm-tossed surf onto the beach at Tam Ky, a village between Da Nang and Chu Lai. The force moved to Highway One, then turned and swept the area south to Chu Lai, concluding Phase One of Blue Marlin. In Phase Two, 17 November, the 3rd Battalion, 3rd Marines, joined with two Ranger battalions and two ARVN 'strike' forces on a 'search and destroy' movement through the VC-infested fishing villages below Song Gua Dai and 25 miles south of Da Nang. In three days of hit-and-run battles the allied force killed 25 VC and captured 15.

While Phase Two was in operation, the Viet Cong regiment that was badly mauled

Left: Map of South Vietnam showing the tactical zones of each American corps.
Below: A Marine sergeant investigates a Viet Cong tunnel in operations near An Hoa in May 1966.

in Operation Starlite attacked and captured Hiep Duc, a district capital 25 miles to the west of Tam Ky. Hiep Duc was in a mountain-surrounded valley that experienced even worse monsoon weather than the rest of I Corps, making it difficult to aid the town, and probably this was why the VC regiment had withdrawn to that area to regroup. The I Corps Vietnamese command sent two battalions of the 5th ARVN, with helilift support provided by MAG-16 and MAG-36. The Americans lifted in over 1000 ARVN troops and delivered heavy air-support fire on the target area, and after heavy fighting Hiep Duc was retaken, with the enemy slipping away into the mountains. It was subsequently decided by ARVN headquarters that they lacked sufficient manpower to hold the village, and it was abandoned to the VC.

The picture was becoming clearer as to the nature of the Viet Cong 'monsoon strategy;' it was to concentrate on attacking and destroying isolated government outposts with locally stronger VC forces, picking them off one by one, until such time that they might begin applying this strategy to larger communities such as district capitals. The objective was to wear down and exhaust the ARVN, both psychologically and militarily. Against the Americans the strategy was to avoid large-scale battles, but rather to pick away with constant attacks on smaller American units so as to create a climate of defensiveness and caution.

At Thatch Tru, on 22 November, the enemy performed what was for them a rare error in judgement, obviously based on poor military intelligence. They attacked the coastal village's outpost fort, apparently believing it to be garrisoned by poorly-trained and under-motivated Popular Force or Regional Force troops. But the fort was defended instead by part of an ARVN Ranger battalion, with two other Ranger

Below: An M-48 tank gives fire support to the 2nd Battalion 3rd Marines, 4 May 1966.

companies close by. The fight went through the night and into the next day, and by noon the VC had managed to make their way through the barbed wire, over the palisades and into the fort, where savage hand-to-hand fighting began.

Luckily for the defenders, three American warships, the USS *Bache*, *O'Brien* and *Fletcher*, were close by, and during the next 24 hours they delivered pounding fire on the VC forces still outside the fort. The 5-inch guns made the difference; the back of the attack was broken and the VC fled, leaving 175 dead on the ground. Next morning the 3rd Battalion, 7th Marines, flushed and struck units of the fleeing attackers. From prisoners it was learned that this was not a VC unit; these were North Vietnamese soldiers of the PAVN (Peoples' Army of Vietnam) belonging to the 95th Regiment, 325th Alpha Division.

The week after the Thach Tru attack Defense Secretary McNamara arrived back in Saigon, where he said in a press conference that the arrival of PAVN soldiers put a different completion on the war and on America's role in it. In a subsequent meeting of senior American officials it was accepted that there were then seven PAVN regiments in South Vietnam, the presence of an additional one more was considered 'probable' and that of another 'possible.' In ensuing discussions with the senior American military commanders in the area, the major part dealt with considerations of how much of an increase in US forces would be required to deal with the new circumstances.

One topic of discussion was the list of recommendations submitted to ComUSMACV by General Walt at General Westmoreland's request. It called for a strategy in I Corps balanced among the various military tasks facing the allies and the various military tools available to deal with these tasks. Walt proposed an increase in Marine infantry battalions from 12 up to at least 18; the number of fighter-attack squadrons should be increased to eight. He based these numbers on the tasks facing the allies rather than on considerations relating in combat terms to the enemy, the tasks being: first, to maintain secure base areas; second, to provide support for the offensive operations of the Vietnamese I Corps forces; third, to commit American units in offensive operations against the VC; fourth, to ready American forces for supportive roles in other regions of South Vietnam; fifth, to provide personnel and know-how for what came to be called 'pacification' operations.

There was at that time some difference of opinion between the Army and the Marines regarding the value of pacification efforts, with the Corps having more belief in its potential value; this resulted from the experience of Marines in earlier pacification efforts, some of it originating with small Marine units and even individual Marines, but most of it a well-planned product of III MAF headquarters. A particularly successful early example was My Lai, which developed into a model 'protected hamlet.' The techniques developed there were later applied in many villages: the village was liberated from VC occupation or domination, it was made secure, then programs designed to raise the village's quality of life in every way were carefully begun. While the process saw success in the thinly-populated area west of Da Nang, it had much less success in the heavily-populated region of rich ricelands south of the air base, strung along Highway One.

The Viet Cong were in this region in force for a number of reasons: the rich farmland took care of the VC's food needs, the adjacent coastline made resupply from North Vietnam by sea simpler, and the dense population of the area made it easier for the Viet Cong in their anonymous black pajamas to—as their leader, General Giap, was fond of saying—'swim like fish among the people.'

Operation Golden Fleece

To catch some of these 'fish' attempting to exact tribute from the farmers, III MAF ordered the 9th Marines to conduct Operation Golden Fleece between September and October when the rice crop was being gathered. The tactics of the operation involved saturation patrolling by small units, heavy use of night ambushes, and the stationing of Marine guards to protect the working harvesters. The harvest-protection function of 'Golden Fleece' was successful, and the name was used frequently afterwards for similar operations.

The 9th Marines continued their effort into October and succeeded in clearing half of Hoa Vang district of VC, a total of nine villages; then came the more difficult part of the operation, the pacification program. A trained government team of 350 people was ready for the job, but the South Vietnamese did not have the necessary security forces, to be stationed in each of the villages, that would make pacification possible. The Marines' job, as III MAF saw it, was limited to providing the outer perimeter of defense for the villages, some of the materials required to carry out the program and, of equal importance, the appropriate support structures within the American military and diplomatic organizations. To carry out the latter objective, III MAF made significant changes in its staff structure at headquarters; in addition, a Joint Coordinating Council was formed with both civilian and military members from the American and Vietnamese communities to provide contact and coordination among many agencies that dealt with related concerns. Both the concept and the organizational plan were brilliant; however, the abiding failure that worked to the detriment of all the other efforts was the inability of the South Vietnamese to provide Popular Forces of sufficient numbers and caliber to carry out the security job.

Involvement by attrition: counteroffensive campaign

Following the withdrawal of the Vietnamese from Hiep Duc in late November, the Viet Cong infiltrated eastward into the Phuoc Valley, threatening the government outposts at Viet An and Que Son. To relieve this pressure and perhaps entrap the VC, now thought to be the reestablished 1st Viet Cong Regiment with North Vietnamese reinforcements, Operation Harvest Moon was created. It called for a coordinated strike by ARVN and US Marine units that would catch the VC in a pincer action; it would develop into one of the war's turning points.

Units of the 5th ARVN and the 11th Vietnamese Ranger Battalion entered the contested zone the morning of 8 December and, after several uneventful hours of advancing, came under heavy fire. Within a half hour the South Vietnamese units were pinned down, and were relieved only when US helicopters brought in ARVN reinforcements. Next day the VC struck again, this time killing a battalion commander and sending the ARVN unit backwards in retreat.

At this point, Marine units were committed to the battle in force. Helicopters brought in the 2nd Battalion, 7th Marines; the 3rd Battalion, 3rd Marines; and the 2nd Battalion, 1st Marines to relieve ARVN units as well as to press the fight against the enemy. On 12 December the Marines began moving against the high ground at the southern rim of Phuoc Valley while ARVN forces attacked the northern rim. The Marines advanced steadily over the next five days, aided in their fire fights by precision bombing done by B-52s. The VC broke contact, and the Marine battalions moved out of the valley in a sweep of the country to the northeast of the original contact area; small Viet Cong units brought them under fire and were quickly cut down. At dusk of 19 December the Marines reached Highway One and Harvest Moon was completed. The Viet Cong dead totaled 407, and significant numbers of heavy and light weapons had been captured, as well as other supplies taken from a depot uncovered in a hill south of Que Son.

That year saw the first experiment by both sides in the war with a Christmas and Tet holiday truce; 'Tet' is a solemn Far East holiday celebrating the lunar new year. The Marines had no great enthusiasm for the entire idea, presuming that the VC would use the truce as an opportunity for some adventure against an American or South Vietnamese position; however, aside from three small attacks in the Da Nang and Chu Lai TAORs, the Christmas truce held, and the Tet truce was even better observed. However, immediately following the Tet

truce, Da Nang and Marble Mountain air bases were hit with mortar attacks; an ominous aspect of these attacks was the use by the VC of 120mm mortars, only the second time such large weapons had been used in I Corps.

As 1966 began there were 180,000 American military personnel in South Vietnam, 38,000 of them members of the Corps, but these numbers were about to change. As a follow-up on Secretary McNamara's latest visit, American troop strength was to be increased, and for the Marines, this meant the introduction of the 1st Marine Division to Vietnam, along with additional elements of units already in the country. The zones of action assigned to the 1st Division were the two southern provinces of I Corps, Quang Tin and Quanag Ngai.

Operation Double Eagle

Early in January of 1966 the most ambitious attempt yet at coordinated action against the enemy was activated; its name was Double Eagle. It would involve not only I Corps forces but also II Corps and the US Army's Field Force Victor, a special strike force. Their target: the 325A PAVN Division, believed to be encamped in an area adjoining both Quang Ngai province and Binh Dinh province.

The operation began when the 3rd Battalion, 1st Marines, landed near the site of the November battle with the PAVN, close to Thach Tru, in the largest amphibious operation of the war until that time, with three attack transports, an attack cargo ship, three LSTs, two LSDs, an LPH, a cruiser, a destroyer and two auxiliaries. Standing offshore were three other ships carrying the 2nd Battalion, 3rd Marines, as reserves; this unit was helilifted in on the second day of the operation to a site five miles west of the beaches. On D plus Four, the 2nd Battalion, 9th Marines, moved out of Quang Ngai airstrip into the mountains to the northwest of the beaches.

Marine attempts to make strong contact with the enemy were disappointing, and before long reports came in that the major part of the PAVN division had slipped south into Binh Dinh province. There, in Operation Masher (a name later toned down into White Wing), the enemy was engaged

Below: 3rd Regiment Marines during Operation Cormorant, a search and destroy mission conducted north of Da Nang in July 1966.

by the 1st Air Cavalry Division and II Corps troops in a big battle north of Bong Son and on into An Lao Valley. The total count of VC killed there and at later battles near Tam Ky came to 337.

Far from the battlefield, others were trying to shape the course of the war by diplomatic means. A conference was held in Honolulu early in February between President Johnson and the South Vietnamese leader, Premier Ky, out of which came a strong declaration for winning the war through a combination of military strength and expanded civic reforms for the country's peasants; a communique from the conference called the latter 'as important as the military battle itself.'

Efforts in the first so-called 'pacification' area had been disappointing, due as much to shortcomings on the part of the South Vietnamese as to aggressive efforts by the Viet Cong to see that it failed. However, things began to change for the better in February and early March when a concerned and intelligent Vietnamese, Lieutenant Colonel Lap, assumed overall command of security for the area and of the rural pacification program; Lap soon convinced the peasants that he truly cared about their welfare. A second and equally important factor in the turn-around was the invention by the 9th Marines of a new technique they called County Fair.

County Fair

On 24 and 25 February the first County Fair was held at Phong Bhac hamlet, just north of Song Cau Do river. Under cover of darkness the night before, units of the 9th Marines crept up on the hamlet and took up positions to seal it off totally; this was to make sure that any VC in the community could not escape and, of equal importance, no VC outside the cordon could enter later to provide reinforcements. At dawn, the hamlet dwellers were informed over loudspeakers that the hamlet was surrounded and about to be searched, and that the people should leave the hamlet and go to a designated assembly area nearby. There, in an atmosphere that was made as cheerful as possible under the circumstances, the people's identity cards were checked, then they met their district leader (perhaps for the first time) who explained what was going on. Next, the people experienced a 'County Fair' of speeches, events and such

strange foodstuffs as cokes and candy bars, sometimes along with movies, live entertainers and a Marine band. As this went on the hamlet was searched for VC. Some were found—hidden underground in tunnels, from which they had to be blasted out—but the searchers also discovered such evidence of their presence as propaganda leaflets, uniforms and arms.

Following this first County Fair, many more were conducted throughout the III MAF area, with heartening success.

In February and March, fighting in the area stepped up, with a number of vicious battles. Operation New York pitted the 810th Main Force Battalion of the VC against the 2nd Battalion, 1st Marines, who were called into the battle northeast of Phu Bai to support the hard-pressed 1st Battalion, 3rd ARVN Regiment. In a night helilift, the Marines landed in the objective area and moved in line across the Phu Thu Peninsula against well-prepared enemy positions. The battle lasted until 3 March; the final count was 122 Viet Cong killed.

Above : A watchful Marine radio operator on a jungle patrol. He is armed with an M14 rifle, soon to be replaced by the more modern M16. *Left :* The 9th Marine Expeditionary Brigade lands at Da Nang.

It was learned on 3 March that units of the 2nd ARVN had made contact with an enemy force northwest of Quang Ngai city, and that prisoners they had taken were members of the 36th PAVN Regiment, which the prisoners placed in the vicinity of Chau Nhai village. The Americans and South Vietnamese responded to this news the next morning with Operation Utah. Marine helicopters lifted the ARVN 1st Airborne Battalion to a point a short distance southeast of Chau Nhai, where they landed through blistering fire from the ground. The ARVN went into action; within hours they were joined in the battle by 2nd Battalion, 7th Marines on their right flank and the 3rd Battalion, 1st Marines to the north of the combat zone. That evening the trap was completed with the landing to the south of the 2nd Battalion, 4th Marines. The fight, a hard-fought one, lasted 24 hours, and at the end the Marines counted 359 PAVN dead in their sectors and the ARVN another 228 in theirs; almost a third of the enemy regiment had been destroyed.

An even more vicious fight happened on 9–11 March at a Special Forces camp near A Shau on the Laotian border. Three PAVN regiments attacked the camp, which was garrisoned by 17 Green Berets and about 400 Vietnamese irregulars, most of them local Montagnards. In the ensuing battle many of the irregulars refused to fight—in fact, some of them turned their weapons on the defenders, but were shot down. The defense, which lasted two days, was borne mostly by the Americans and a few loyal Vietnamese. Finally, Marine and Air Force helicopters managed to get to the camp through the terrible monsoon weather, land, and carry out a relatively successful evacuation; 12 Special Forces men and 178 irregular troops were airlifted to safety.

On 19 March the Marines of III MAF received a call for help from the Regional Force garrison at An Hoa, 30 kilometers northwest of Quang Ngai. This triggered Operation Texas. The 3rd Battalion, 7th Marines and the ARVN 5th Airborne Battalion were helilifted to within a kilometer north of the besieged outpost while the 2nd Battalion, 4th Marines came down at a point seven kilometers south of it. The enemy force, again the 1st Viet Cong Regiment, was caught between them and, following four days of fierce fighting, 405 VC dead were counted.

Another operation with a state name, Indiana, took place at almost the same spot on 28 March when the 5th ARVN Regiment came under heavy fire. This time the 1st Battalion, 7th Marines, flew in to help and, landing behind the enemy, they killed 69 of the VC in several hard hours of fighting.

While these traditional military missions were taking place, fighting of another sort went on among the South Vietnamese people themselves. A strong movement spearheaded by university students and Buddhists, in each case most particularly those in the city of Hué, called for the ouster of Premier Ky's government in Saigon. All through that spring a series of moves and countermoves by opposing groups kept the country in a turmoil as units loyal to Ky and other units aligned with the anti-government 'Struggle Force' came close to the point of bloody showdown. General Walt repeatedly stepped into the middle of these tense situations and, working skillfully as an arbitrator, prevented a bloodbath. A loser in this situation was the pacification effort as the VC infiltrated back into previously 'sanitized' hamlets.

In March Major General Wood B Kyle arrived in I Corps to assume command of the 3d Marine Division. A top-of-the-list priority for Kyle was to reduce the Viet Cong presence in the area south of Da Nang, and he soon made a number of changes in the disposition of several units in order to accomplish this. Operations Kings, Georgia and Liberty expanded the areas of responsibility of the 9th Marines and more closely connected its flanks with the 3rd and 1st Marines. Operation Jay was a sweep through an area 20 kilometers northwest of Hue by the 2nd Battalion, 4th Marines and the 2nd Battalions, 1st Marines, in a pincer movement that caught and killed 82 Viet Cong soldiers in a nine-day running battle.

Left: Men of the 2nd Marines during a search for Viet Cong suspects in the Mekong Delta area.

Above: Press photographers accompany a Marine patrol. Press and television coverage of the Vietnam War was more widespread than in any previous conflict.

Counteroffensive Phase II

On the 4th of July Operation Macon kicked off what turned out to be a grinding four-months' long series of battles against a particularly tough unit, the Doc Lap battalion, in the area north of An Hoa. Five Marine battalions were alternately involved, and the final kill count was 507 VC.

The next weeks saw a series of actions of a somewhat new and escalated nature. Reports said that a new North Vietnamese division, probably 324th Bravo, had entered the country into northern Quang Tri province. When 2nd Battalion, 1st Marines went into the area to investigate the reports, it precipitated the most savage large-scale fighting of the war to that date, involving 8000 Marines and 3000 South Vietnamese troops. Operation Hastings was the name given the action; other Marine units involved were the 2nd Battalion, 4th Marines; the 3rd Battalion, 4th Marines; the 3rd Battalion, 5th Marines; the 1st Battalion, 1st Marines and the 1st Battalion, 3rd Marines; five ARVN battalions also were involved, and B-52s repeatedly flew precision bombing support missions. The operation finished on 3 August with 824 of the enemy killed and large numbers of weapons captured.

The division had entered the country across the DMZ, or demilitarized zone, which was a 'first.' Speculation regarding the reason for the unusual line of march included it being an experiment to see if the PAVN could avoid the difficult and roundabout route through Laos, or an attempt to off-set the series of gains the allies had been making through the pacification program and the many Marine clean-sweep operations of recent months.

This action evolved into Operations Prairie I and Deckhouse IV. Prairie took place in the same area as Hastings and, in fact, involved the same PAVN unit, the 324B Division. Enemy losses by the end of August were an additional 110 killed. Deckhouse IV involved a landing at Dong Ha by the 1st Battalion, 26th Marines, on 15 September. Over ten days of battling

with units of the 324B Division, these Marines added 254 dead to the count. Prairie I would continue on and off into the following year.

The stepped-up pace of combat the Marines were experiencing required an associated increase in the Corps' strength, and a source for such growth had been set late in 1965 with an authorization for 55,000 additional Marines. The Corps' goal was 278,184 by mid-1967, somewhat more than half its all-time high of 485,113 reached during World War II. The Corps recruited 80,000 volunteers during 1966 and received about 19,000 draftees.

The basic success of America's efforts up to that time in South Vietnam was underscored on 11 September when national elections were held on schedule to elect members of the Constituent Assembly, who would draft a new constitution. The most extravagant guess as to the voter turnout had been 70 percent; in fact 80.8 percent of the electorate went to the polls despite deadly efforts by the Viet Cong to stop them.

Above left: Vietnamese civilians are escorted to a transport helicopter for evacuation from their village.
Below: Men of the 2nd Battalion, 7th Marines during an operation in the Da Nang area in June 1967.

And in Hué, center of student and Buddhist opposition to the central government, 84 percent of the voters cast ballots.

Concrete examples of the III MAF's contribution to this success, if tallied up in the Fall of 1966, would have revealed:

- a steady buildup during a year and a half period of the Marine presence to 60,000 soldiers;
- an expansion of the Corps' zone of responsibility from eight square miles and 1930 local people to 1800 square miles and nearly one million people;
- action in more than 150 operations of battalion or regimental size, resulting in 7300 enemy deaths;
- an additional 4000 enemy deaths resulting from 200,000 Marine patrols, ambushes and other small-unit actions;
- Marine losses in the period of 1700 killed and over 9000 wounded; better than 80 percent of the wounded returned to duty.

Out of the strife of 18 months one thing had become increasingly clear: fully as important as the military effort was the attempt to reach the hearts and minds of the people with the pacification effort, or Ngu Hanh Son as the Vietnamese called it. The government had committed 25,000 trained cadre to the effort, and this number was scheduled to more than double within a year. The number would be barely enough for the task, for there were 11,000 hamlets in South Vietnam, of which only 4500 were considered friendly to the government; the remaining 6500 either were uncommitted or under Viet Cong control.

Below: Clearing a helicopter landing zone. Although helicopters undoubtedly conferred greater mobility on Marine and Army combat troops, selecting suitable landing zones in Vietnam was often difficult.

1967: Heating up

As the year began, General Walt had 67,729 Marines under his command in III MAF. The force's 18 infantry battalions were committed in combat operations that ranged from one end of I Corps to the other, stretching 225 miles from the DMZ in the north down to Binh Dinh province and the border of II Corps in the south. Knowing this made it understandable why some people in Saigon referred to I Corps as 'Marineland.'

Operation Prairie I, which evolved out of Hastings, had continued in northern Quang Tri province since the previous July. This was a major operation; at its height six Marine battalions were engaged with large Viet Cong and North Vietnamese units. But the monsoon season had gradually squeezed the number of clashes down to only a few, and on 31 January Prairie I came to an end after 182 bloody days. Marine casualties were 225 killed 1159 wounded and 1 missing in action, while the enemy (PAVN and VC combined) lost 1397 killed and 29 captured.

Right: A Marine sits by his foxhole and camouflages his helmet in preparation for a patrol.

On 1 February Prairie II began in the same long-contested area, but it involved a less intense level of combat. The PAVN division had withdrawn back across the DMZ into North Vietnam, and reports indicated they were moving toward the longer route through Laos. Given this, Marine strength in the area was reduced, and the mission was changed from a search-and-destroy one into clear-and-secure. This meant that substantial support could be given once again to providing security for the rural pacification efforts of the 1st ARVN Division.

Operation Chinook had begun the previous 19 December with the 2nd and 3rd Battalions, 26th Marines, assigned to block infiltration routes used by the VC to come down through the mountains toward Hue. The Marines had no sooner disengaged when the Holiday truce went into effect, when they observed a thousand enemy troops moving down the approaches toward Hue. With their intent obvious, General Westmoreland gave permission for artillery and air strikes. These were carried out, but the heavy cloud cover and monsoon rains left the result in doubt. 3rd Battalion, 26th

Above: Marine on jungle patrol. Viet Cong booby traps were a continual hazard of all patrolling operations.

Marines, took over the mission but made only light contact with the enemy until 6 February when, in the last hours before the start of the Tet truce, 80 rounds of 81mm mortar fell on their headquarters, wounding five Marines.

The pulse beat of action and reaction by the Marines as well as the Viet Cong and the North Vietnamese accelerated through the winter and into the spring. The III MAF launched numerous operations against the enemy during that period, including Prairie II, III and IV, Tuscaloosa, Sierra, DeSoto, Independence, Stone, Beacon Hill, Newcastle, Union and Beaver Cage, most of which lasted only a few days or weeks while inflicting relatively high casualties on the enemy; down in the south of Vietnam in IV Corps, the 1st Battalion, 9th Marines, landed on 5 January in Operation Deckhouse V, the first use of US combat troops in the Mekong Delta. The results were modest, but in the subsequent Deckhouse VI landing and attack by 1st Battalion, 4th Marines, 204 enemy were left dead in nine days of battle.

The bloodiest fighting of the period began the morning of 24 April in what could be called the First Battle of Khe Sanh, located in the northwest corner of Quang Tri province. A platoon-sized patrol from 1st Battalion, 9th Marines, encountered an enemy force which did not return fire. When another American platoon moved up to join the first, the enemy attacked furiously, forcing the Marines to withdraw carrying their 13 dead with them. The following day, additional contacts indicated that an enemy force of at least battalion strength was entrenched on high ground before the Marines. Two additional Marine battalions were flown in and, over the next 18 days, the deeply dug-in enemy was hammered by artillery, repeated air strikes by the 1st Marine Aircraft Wing and repeated assaults by Marine infantry units. Both sides were badly hurt, with the Marines suffering 155 killed and 424 wounded, the enemy 940 dead and two prisoners.

Counteroffensive Phase III

On 1 June 1967 General Walt stepped down from his two year stint as commander of III MAF and was replaced by Lieutenant General Robert Cushman, holder of the Navy Cross. In his departing remarks, Walt commented on the changes he had seen take place in the individual Marine during his tenure with III MAF. Two years before the Marine infantryman had been armed with the M-14 rifle, actually a modified version of the old M-1 rechambered for the NATO 7.62mm cartridge, but by the time of the Khe Sanh battle the M-14 had been replaced with the M-16, a high-velocity weapon firing a 5.56mm round; after some initial difficulties, the weapon had proven itself to be a fine arm. The Marine combat uniform and footwear, too, had been modified for better service in Vietnam's terrain and climate.

The pace of action through spring into summer was a mixed one, with quiet periods in certain sectors suddenly torn apart by bursts of combat activity. Two Marine operations were directed, for the first time, against the DMZ in force. Operation Hickory, a massive Marine-Navy-Air Force operation, was begun on 19 May when five Marine battalions moved out from positions near Con Thien. In a well-coordinated assault, the enemy was pinned against the Ben Hai river by attacks from air, land and sea, losing a total of 815 dead. Operation Belt Tight followed Hickory, carrying the fight more deeply into the DMZ, and between 20 and 28 May it inflicted 71 deaths on the enemy.

Enemy activity in Quang Tin, Quang Tri, Thua Thien and Quang Nhai provinces was becoming more frequent and involving increasingly larger units. On 26 May the 5th Marines initiated Operation Union II with support from ARVN units. They engaged two PAVN regiments northwest of Tam Ky. After ten days of stiff action the enemy casualties, including those from the earlier Union I, were 1566 dead and 196 captured; Marine casualties for both operations were 220 killed, 714 wounded.

The Quang Tri actions involved three Marine operations, Crockett, Buffalo and Buffalo and Hickory II. Crockett was a response to continuous enemy probing of Marine positions in the Khe Sanh area; units of the 26th Marines took the enemy

Left: Keeping a close watch for approaching Viet Cong troops during Operation Deckhouse 5.

under fire repeatedly during the month of June until they finally broke off contact, with losses of 206 killed; Marine deaths totaled 52. Buffalo, which followed on 2 July, was a short but deadly battle. Five battalions of heavily-entrenched VC at a point northeast of Con Thien engaged what eventually became three battalions of Marines in a series of battles that included some of the most intense artillery fire by the enemy in the war to date, as well as the most intense air strikes by American planes. Between 2 and 10 July air support units dropped over 1066 tons or ordinance on enemy positions; the enemy lost 1301 dead in the operation, the Marines 159.

South of the DMZ, in Quang Tri province, Operation Kingfisher kicked off on 16 July with the objective of blocking enemy entrance into the province. Units of the 9th Marines repeatedly engaged enemy units in fire fights that served to scatter them. On 21 August and again on 7 September, major enemy units attempting ambushes were pounded by air and artillery support fire and fled, leaving a total of 554 dead.

Also on 7 September Secretary McNamara announced a decision to create a security wall below the DMZ running from Con Thien through Go Linh to the coast. Its purpose was to block the entrance into South Vietnam of PAVN forces and supplies for the Viet Cong. The barrier was to consist of barbed wire entanglements laced with land mines and electronic sensors to detect movement. Much of the US press was skeptical regarding the wall—they dubbed the project McNamara's Wall'—and their skepticisms was shared by the Marines in Vietnam.

'With these bastards,' explained one Marine officer, 'you'll have to build the zone all the way to India, and it would take the whole Marine Corps and half the Army to guard it.' And he added, 'Even then they'd probably burrow under it.' Despite

Below: A South Vietnamese patrol advances between rice paddies. Well defined paths were a favorite site for booby traps.

such comments, operations began to secure the area in which the wall would go.

Through the balance of the year the enemy pressed the fight at a number of points, all of them familiar targets for attack. For a four week period in September they directed a series of intense infantry and artillery attacks against the outpost at Con Thien, which the press had taken to calling a 'little Dien Bien Phu,' referring to the besieged French fortress of the Indochina War; during one six-day period Con Thien was shelled 24 times. Under intense pressure from B-52 bombings the enemy finally broke off in what General Westmoreland called a 'crushing defeat.' October saw Marine operations in the Hai Lang National Forest south of Quang Tri City, in Thua Thien province, and south of An Hoa near the area of the old Union operations. In each case the Viet Cong showed an undiminished zest for close and vicious fighting; they demonstrated this also with bloody raids against district headquarters and refugee settlements. As the year came to a close, reports suggested that some sort of major offensive was in the immediate offing.

Tet Offensive (1968)

As in previous years, a truce was arranged over the lunar New Year holiday of Tet. But then the North Vietnamese and VC broke the truce with the strongest all-out assault of the war.

It began with a major attack on Khe Sanh; the city had been relatively quiet since the hard fighting of the previous year, but intelligence indicated there now were four enemy regiments within 20 kilometers of the city. Westmoreland ordered reinforcements for the 26th Marine and ARVN troops at the strongpoint, for he considered it an important blocking position against enemy movements from the north.

On 20 January an enemy force of better than 20,000 hurled itself against Khe Sanh; on the second day they took the village itself and crowds of refugees moved for protection into the outpost fortification. The North Vietnamese moved toward the barricades, commencing a seige that would last 71 days. In their assaults the PAVN troops would suffer what were probably the heaviest casualties of the war from combined air and artillery strikes. The enemy in turn delivered intense shelling on the outpost, with the number of rounds numbering in the thousands, and though this continued through February and into March, the Marines held their ground. The defender's particular sense of appreciation went to the artillerymen and airmen who, with their deadly strikes, prevented the enemy from ever mounting a large-unit ground attack. On 6 April friendly ground forces were able to reach Khe Sanh; on 9 April no enemy fire fell on the outpost for the first time in 45 days. The siege was over.

In coordination with their attack against Khe Sanh, the enemy launched attacks against other American and ARVN strongpoints throughout South Vietnam, and against the civilian population as well, striking against undefended villages. In I Corps enemy forces consisting of both VC and PAVN units hit military and civilian targets, starting 30 and 31 January in the middle of the cease-fire. It was fortunate that American and ARVN units were in prime fighting readiness, as well as being alert to the enemy's move beforehand, for they were able to throw back their assaults in most instances. Quang Tri, Da Nang, Hoi An, Tam Ky and Quang Ngai—in these strongholds the Marines and ARVN met the enemy's best effort and threw them back. The only place where the North Vietnamese had success was in Hué. There they infiltrated soldiers dressed as civilians who, at midnight of 30 January, changed into uniforms and joined the attack on the defenders from within. The next day the city was taken, but soon three under-strength Marine battalions and 13 ARVN battalions counterattacked, and after weeks of bloody house-to-house fighting, they retook the city on 24 February. Enemy losses at Hué were over 5000.

Above: A platoon sergeant consults his map before calling in an artillery strike.
Right: Marine radiomen prepare to set out on a jungle patrol.
Previous page: An M60 machine gun team of the 5th Marines in a firefight in 1968.

The Tet offensive did not turn out as the Viet Cong and North Vietnamese had hoped. The overriding purpose had been to give the impression of their having overwhelming power and presence in South Vietnam; the enemy presumed that such an impression would weaken the allies' will to continue the fight, particularly the Americans, which might lead to an uprising against the government by the South Vietnamese people. None of this happened—in fact, the American and ARVN forces fought side by side with greater efficiency than ever before.

Immediately following cessation of the Tet attacks, III MAF prepared to strike back in force against the enemy. They were in a stronger position to do so; the 27th Marines were newly arrived in Vietnam, raising the Marine strength there to a record 163,000 as of 1 April. However, diplomatic events taking place in far-off places would effect these plans dramatically. Public enthusiasm for the war had required a number of years before it grew strong; now that enthusiasm had gradually eroded away. President Lyndon Johnson, a strong advocate of pursuing the war, responded to this new general will of the people on 31 March by announcing on national television that he would not seek another term in office. He also said that he had instructed the Defense Department to place specified limitations on the bombing of targets in North Vietnam; on 2 April the 20th Parallel was identified as the line north of which no further bombings by the US would take place. On that day also it was announced from Washington and Hanoi that the two countries would soon commence talks aimed at bringing the war to an end. Paris, France, was selected as the site for these discussions, and on 13 May W Averell Harriman for the United States and Xuan Thuy for North Vietnam held their first meeting.

The existence of the Paris peace talks, rather than diminishing the level of combat, obviously intensified it, as each side aimed at establishing its strength on the battlefield as leverage for establishing its strength in the negotiations. Westmoreland approved a three-pronged plan that included elimination of the enemy's capacity for repeated seiges of Khe Sanh, a major attack on enemy positions within the DMZ, and a raid into the A Shau valley. The relief of Khe Sanh, dubbed Operation Pegasus, was accomplished by means of a brilliant aerial operation that included tactical aircraft of the Air Force, Navy and Marines delivering over 35,000 tons of bombs and rockets on the enemy in a ten week period, and by Marine helicopters that flew in supplies and flew out the wounded. Operation Delaware Valley, a raid to oust the enemy from A Shau Valley, followed on 19 April and lasted a month, causing the enemy huge losses in war materials. A plan for an attack into the DMZ was pre-empted by a major enemy strike against Dong Ha, in the eastern side of the fighting zone below the DMZ, and then by what was referred to a 'mini-Tet,' begun on 5 May, a second major offensive by the enemy that year that included 119 rocket strikes against positions throughout South Vietnam. Though the attacks hurt many civilians, it was militarily of little merit.

Left: As well as the problems of personal hygiene illustrated above, the Vietnam climate required that great care be taken to maintain arms and ammunition. Here machine gun belts are checked over.

Above: The Vietnamese climate brought the Marines many problems with skin diseases and insects.

The success of Operation Pegasus contributed to an important decision on the part of General Creighton W Abrams, Westmoreland's replacement as ComUSMACV: the base at Khe Sanh would be abandoned, and in the future US ground forces would change from a defensive static-position strategy to one of using strong mobile forces to carry the war constantly to the enemy. The tactical mobility provided the US forces by this new strategy served to blunt the enemy's attacks; in just eight days of fighting, units of the 5th, 26th and 27th Marines in concert with ARVN forces scored 1072 dead. Despite such losses, the enemy continued to press toward their principal target, Da Nang, and on 18 August they began an attack on the air base in the 'Third Offensive' of 1968. By 28 August, when the 38th PAVN Regiment broke off and retreated, they had lost 1072 dead south of Da Nang.

Action during the fall months was widely scattered, and in many instances was fierce, but now the enemy's actions seemed more and more to be the expression of a political rather than a military strategy. Ironically, the coordinated actions of the US and ARVN units went off with previously unmatched success, and the performance of all South Vietnamese troops, including the semi-military Popular Forces and Regional Forces, were lauded by the US command. An outstanding example of this took place late in November in Operation Meade River. During a three-week period of hard fighting against the 36th PAVN Regiment, the 1st Marine Division and attached units, together with ARVN soldiers and Korean Marines, killed a total of 1210 enemy; a key element in the operation's success was

Above: A Marine from the 1st Regiment (3rd Marine Division) returns North Vietnamese fire during fighting in Hué, February 1968.

the carrying out of one of the largest helicopter assaults in Marine history.

But the war was winding down; its ultimate outcome was not to be determined on the battlefield but at the conference table. Early in October the USS *New Jersey* came on station of the DMZ and began pouring the devastating fire of its 16-inch guns into that area; on 31 October President Johnson announced that henceforth there would be no air, artillery or naval bombardment of North Vietnam. In the III MAF, the announcement was not well received, particularly by the men of the 3d Marine Division; located just south of the DMZ, they would bear the brunt of any advantage this decision gave the enemy.

Throughout this period the Marine efforts in the pacification program moved ahead at an accelerating pace; Marine units not immediately involved in combat operations built hospitals, schools and orphanages for the South Vietnamese, as well as homes for families and bridges to connect villages with the rest of the country. The well-proven technique of the County Fair, developed first in I Corps, was used throughout the country as a key part of the pacification effort. At year's end, as the peace talks went on in Paris, the Marines counted their dead—about 10,000 going back to the war's beginning—and made ready to press the war to the enemy.

As in years past, the Tet holiday of 1969 saw the truce violated by the enemy, but the effort was only a pale shadow of its former self. An attack was launched against Da Nang, a 'nut' the enemy had never been able to crack, and once again their effort foundered in the face of fierce Marine resistance that turned into counterstrikes against the retreating Viet Cong.

Marine units remained active throughout 1969, though at a reduced level to match the enemy's reversion from large-scale attacks to small-unit demolition attacks and anti-civilian terrorism. Operation Bold Mariner in January was the largest Marine Special Landing Force operation of the war, sweeping through the area south of Chu Lai in a successful sanitizing search for Viet Cong. Dewey Canyon I was a strike into Da Krong valley in Quang Tri's southwest corner; three battalions of the 9th Marines, over a month-long period of January and February, engaged heavily-entrenched North Vietnamese units and inflicted losses of 1617 dead on them. Other operations named Virginia Ridge, Oklahoma Hills, Utah Mesa, Daring Rebel, Pipestone Canyon, all bloodied the enemy with the same lopsided ratios of killed and wounded that had prevailed throughout the war. Defiant Stand, the last Special Landing Force strike of the war, was unique in being a combined landing of US and Korean Marines; coming ashore at Hoi An, the force killed 293 enemy and processed the documents of 2500 civilians.

1969 saw nearly 60,000 enemy killed by I Corps alone, yet at the end of the year their strength was greater than at the year's outset, almost totally as a result of fresh troops from North Vietnam. On the American side, the process of troop withdrawals had cut into its strength. The year had begun with 79,844 Marines in III MAF; it ended with 54,541.

Shortly after midnight on 6 January 1970, a hundred-member demolition team of the 409th PAVN Sapper Battalion, under cover of mortar fire, got through the wire around the headquarters of the 1st Battalion, 7th Marines, and though they took a loss of 38 killed, they inflicted casualties of 13 killed and 40 wounded on the defenders, which seems to have been an acceptable exchange for the enemy. It was an example of the enemy's will to press the fight even harder than ever despite the peace talks in Paris, probably as a means of hurrying the exit of Americans.

On 20 April a further reduction of 150,000 American troops in Vietnam was announced from Washington, with 41,800 of that number to come from the Marines. With Marine strength significantly reduced, ComUSMACV decided to reduce the Marine's TAOR—Tactical Area of Responsibility—in I Corps, with the ARVN taking over the relinquished area. General Lam, the ARVN commander, decided on a July offensive that he hoped would inflict major damage on the enemy's forces as a means of offsetting the negative effects of the reduced American force. In Operation Pickens Forest, the 7th Marines participated in this offensive, but little contact was made with enemy forces.

Heroic attempts were made to carry on US military operations in a professional manner, but the process of redeployment was accomplishing what years of enemy action had failed to do—hobble and curtail the ability of the Marine Corps to carry out its mission in Vietnam. Air support missions were becoming scarce. Combined action operations were drastically reduced. The burden of carrying out rural pacification programs was largely passed to the hard-pressed South Vietnamese.

But there was another side to the story, and that was the increasing indication that the enemy soldiers were suffering from exhaustion, hunger and sagging morale; a significant sign of this was the rising number of unburied enemy dead being found as well as unprotected caches of supplies, sure signs of a serious morale problem. Typhoon Kate, which struck in Quang Nam in October with the coming of the monsoon rains, added vastly to the enemy's misery.

Above: During the Tet Offensive a Marine fires on Viet Cong positions with an M79 grenade launcher.
Left: A scene from the fighting in Namo village during the Tet Offensive.

1971: The bleeding stops

During 1970 the level of combat for the Marine forces had declined steadily; this pattern continued in 1971. Contributing to this de-escalation was a conceptual change in the definition of Marine responsibility in Vietnam. For 'Tactical Areas of Responsibility' it substituted 'Tactical Areas of *Interest*.' This meant that local Marine commanders did not have primary responsibility for the area in which they operated—that now was passed to the local ARVN commander—and they could involve themselves in combat activities only as they chose to or were ordered to by ComUSMACV. From the point of view of the ordinary Marine rifleman, the difference this meant was that he went out on fewer patrols and ranged shorter distances away from his base.

Marine operations in the early part of the year were few and light. The 1st Marines Upshur Stream operation west of Da Nang in a search for enemy artillery positions turned up little. Marine support of Operation Lam Son 719, an ARVN strike into Laos against enemy bases and supply lines, was minimal on the ground, though Marine aircraft flew better than 500 sorties in support of it. Even a major North Vietnamese attack, the Easter Offensive,

Above : Marines lay down fire on a suspected North Vietnamese position. Because of the difficulty of detecting enemy positions the 'reconnaissance by fire' technique was often used, despite its drawbacks.
Left : Scene during Operation Lancaster II.
Right : Marines aboard an LCM during Deckhouse III. Amphibious operations were disappointingly ineffective in Vietnam.
Below : A typical fire support base with guns sited for all round defense.

saw no involvement by Marines in repulsing it; the enemy's message seemed to be, 'If we can do this while the Americans are here, imagine what we'll do when they are gone.' On 7 April the 1st Marines made one final foray, called Scott Orchard, sweeping the wild country west of An Hoa. There was little contact, and four enemy were killed.

The 14th of April was the day on which the III MAF, after six years of combat, left Vietnam; elsewhere throughout the country, other American units departed almost daily. However, a significant share of the duty of aiding the South Vietnamese military now passed to the guns of the ships of the Seventh Fleet, and to the Marine and Navy pilots operating from the carriers' decks. They seemed to be supporting a losing cause, for North Vietnamese units had for the first time captured a South Vietnamese province, Quang Tri, and were sweeping toward Hué. But by 28 June the South the South Vietnamese forces north of Hué were ready to strike back; an Airborne division and a Marine Division, their east

Above left : Tan Son Nhut Airbase burns in the background from North Vietnamese artillery strikes during the evacuation of Saigon, 29 April 1975.
Right : South Vietnamese refugees hurry off a CH-53 helicopter under the eyes of a watchful Marine aboard the USS *Hancock*.
Below : A Marine observation plane flies low over Hué in February 1968.

Above: Bewildered refugees on the deck of the USS *Hancock* during the evacuation of Saigon. They have been brought to the ship by the helicopters of Marine squadron HMH-463.

flank on the sea, moved north. The fighting was bitter; one month later the Airborne was relieved and the fight was left for the Marines to complete. They battered their way through massive enemy resistance to the walls of the Citadel, Quang Tri city's fortress where, on 16 September, they raised the red-striped yellow flag of South Vietnam above the shell-blasted west gate.

As the year ended a state of military equilibrium had been achieved; it would subsequently be destabilized not by military failures in the field but by decisions made at a far-off conference. Vietnam had been the longest and biggest war in Marine Corps history. At its peak size in 1968, III MAF had had one-quarter of the total Corps strength. Total Marine deaths due to enemy action totaled 12,936, and wounded in action came to 88,589; enemy deaths due to Marine actions came to 86,535.

Perhaps the most poignant footnote-comment on Vietnam was made by combat correspondent Keyes Beech on his departure after ten years of covering the war: 'I would like to offer a salute to that skinny little Viet Cong somewhere out there in the jungle shivering in the monsoon rains. . . . He is one hell of a fighting man.'

On 10 June 1968, General Westmoreland held his final news conference in Saigon as ComUSMACV. Most of his remarks and the queries from correspondents were routine and expected. Then some reporter raised his voice to ask Westmoreland one final question to end the news conference:

'General, can the war be won militarily?'

'Not in a classic sense, because—' Westmoreland paused, then continued in a deliberate, flat voice—'of our national policy of not expanding the war.'

Westmoreland placed his uniform cap on his head, and tugged the peak down at a slight angle. He looked around the room silently for an instant, then said one final word:

'Good-bye.'

The Marines left Vietnam with pride in how well the Corps had performed, but disappointment in how their efforts had been compromised politically. Before many years passed, they would know these feelings again.

The Mayaguez incident: 1975

With American aid gone from South Vietnam, the end was long, painful and inevitable. The ripple effect of the Communist victories in Vietnam spread to neighboring Cambodia where, in April 1975, the Khmer Rouge seized the capital of Phnom Penh. And in Saigon, at 0753 of the morning of 30 April, the last CH-46 helicopter lifted off from the roof of the burning American embassy building with the last 11 Marines.

At 1420 on 12 May, a Cambodian gunboat bearing the Khmer Rouge flag fired across the bow of the American container ship *Mayaguez*, on its way from Hong Kong to Thailand. The unarmed American ship hove to, and a boarding party of of Cambodian sailors ordered the crew to sail the ship to follow the gunboat. They finally dropped anchor off Koh Tang, a small jungle-covered island 34 miles off the Cambodian mainland, where the 39-member American crew was taken ashore. When they were later moved to the mainland on one of a small flotilla of gunboats, they narrowly escaped death at the hands of fellow Americans when the boats were strafed by Air Force jets and five were sunk.

Back in Washington, the National Security Council met the day after the seizing of the *Mayaguez* at President Gerald Ford's orders, and it was decided to retake the ship. Marines would make two assaults: one group would board and capture the

Above : Vietnamese troops during a river operation. Riverine rather than true amphibious operations were widely practiced but the Vietnamese proved uncertain allies in this as in other respects.
Right : Marines from the destroyer *Harold E Holt* board the *Mayaguez* only to find that the ship was deserted.
Below : Marines wearing gas masks and with M16 rifles at the ready during the capture of the *Mayaguez*. Another group of Marines landed on Koh Tang.

Mayaguez, the other group would land on Koh Tang and free the prisoners; it was not yet realized that they had been moved. 2nd Battalion, 9th Marines, reinforced, was airlifted from Okinawa to Utapao airfield in Thailand, over the protests of that neutral government. The attack carrier *Coral Sea*, the guided-missile destroyer *Henry B Wilson* and four destroyer escorts sailed at top speed into the Gulf of Siam.

The raiding party would go in aboard 16 helicopters. Lift-off was at 0415 on Wednesday, 15 May, only three days after seizure of the ship. Marines were helilifted to the destroyer-escort *Harold E Holt* which, at 0830, came alongside the captured ship. The Marines scrambled aboard, found the ship deserted, and took possession of it. Meanwhile, by remarkable good luck, just at that time the crew of the *Mayaguez* was being returned to Koh Tang aboard a captured Thai fishing boat by the Cambodians; the *Wilson* intercepted the boat, freed the captured Americans, took aboard the Cambodian guards and sent the Thai fishermen home to their village.

In the American attacks on Koh Tang and also on Kampong Som, as well as in the rescue operation itself, three helicopters were shot down and ten others damaged by the enemy; 11 Marines, two Navy men and two airmen died, 41 Marines, two Navy men and seven airmen were wounded.

PEACEKEEPING AND OTHER MODERN ROLES

Semper Fi . . . 1973-1984

On 10 November 1975 several hundred Marines stood silently in the cold and rain before the Marine Corps War Memorial—the great bronze statue of the Iwo Jima flag-raising on Mount Suribachi—at Arlington National Cemetery. The occasion: the 200th birthday of the United States Marine Corps. President Ford was there and spoke of the Corps as 'a living monument to devotion and self-sacrifice.' The new commandant of the Corps was there, General Louis H Wilson, as was the last surviving Marine portrayed in the statue itself, René A Gagnon. There were prayers for all the dead Marines, a rifle salute, and then Taps. That night there would be dancing and celebrations all around the world, wherever a few Marines or former Marines gathered. It was a momentous occasion, one little dreamed of when the Continental Congress back on 10 November 1775 called for a small unit of 'Continental Marines.'

Yet all thoughtful Marines, like all their fellow Americans, must have been somewhat troubled that day. For the United States was undergoing one of the most traumatic periods since those dark days of 1775. The nation had recently experienced two profound losses. One, the Vietnam War, which—whatever the role of the US military—had to be considered a national loss. The other, the resignation of President Nixon in a swirl of scandals and legal threats. And although the Marines were by no means singled out for any special blame, they undoubtedly shared in the malaise that now gripped the American people.

In particular, many Americans were raising disturbing questions about the performance of their military forces during the Vietnam War. Although far and away most individual Marines and units had performed to the highest standards, there were some few who had been involved in actions that were not. Some Marines had undoubtedly been unnecessarily destructive in their sweeps through Vietnamese villages: young men under stress had often been so. Meanwhile, in 1973, one former American officer who had been a prisoner of war in North Vietnam charged three Marine and five Army enlisted men with 'misconduct while in the prison camp': they had formed a 'Peace Committee.' And in a much publicized event, former Marine Private Robert Garwood returned in 1979 to face charges that he had collaborated with the enemy while in a prison camp and then chosen to stay in North Vietnam ever

If everybody could get in the Marines,

it wouldn't be the Marines.

WE'RE LOOKING FOR A FEW GOOD MEN.

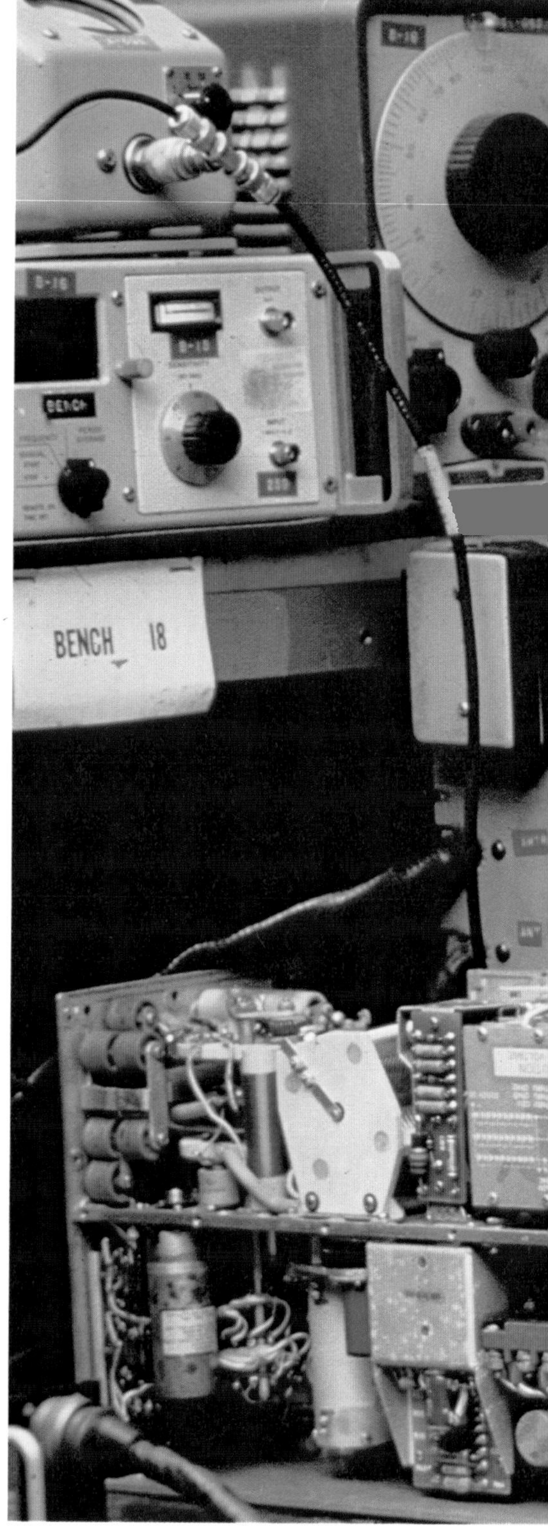

Above: Women are employed in many technical specialties in the modern Marine Corps.
Left: Contemporary recruiting poster.
Previous page: Marines of the 24th Amphibious unit come ashore to join the peacekeeping force in Beirut in November 1982.

since the other prisoners were allowed to return in 1973.

Throughout America, too, Marines—like all veterans of the Vietnam War—were being buffeted from all sides. There was a national debate raging over whether the deserters from the military should be given amnesty or pardon. Meanwhile, many former Vietnam veterans were complaining of ill-treatment from the very citizenry they had thought they were serving—treatment ranging from abusive remarks to just plain avoidance. Individual Marines were also beginning to show the first symptoms of what would become known as the 'Vietnam veterans syndrome,' a complex of psychological and emotional problems caused by the intensity of their experiences in Vietnam now recurring to prevent them from functioning in the civilian world.

The Corps itself was also finding itself experiencing various stresses and strains as it moved into the post-Vietnam world. The use of narcotics, which had undoubtedly been widespread in the military in Vietnam, was not to be tolerated in the peacetime Corps, and there were several well-publicized incidents of Marines being transferred from sensitive assignments. There were the usual cases of unnecessarily harsh Drill Instructors at Marine training camps, incidents that in some cases led to trials of the DIs involved.

There were also many more positive aspects to the Corps in these years. Women were rising in the ranks. In 1973 Colonel Mary E Bane became the first woman to command a unit, a company of some 2150 men and women. In 1977 the first women Marine officers began combat training with male Marines. And in 1978 Colonel Margaret E Brewer was promoted to Brigadier General, the first female general in the history of the Corps. Blacks, too, were rising in the Marines, and in 1979 Colonel Frank E Petersen Jr, became a brigadier general, the first black to achieve that rank in the Corps.

The fact was that the Corps could no longer, if it ever had been, be regarded as apart from American society as a whole. If it had an exceptionally high desertion rate in these years—and in 1976, the Marines reported a rate of 69.2 per 1000 enlistees, versus 31.7 per 1000 for the US Navy and 17.71 for the US Army—it was because young Americans had new attitudes about discipline and authority. And if the Marine Corps had a disproportionately high percentage of blacks—by 1982, 22 percent of the Corps, while they constituted only 12 percent of America's population as a whole—it was undoubtedly

Above: The amphibious assault ship USS *Inchon* and her six *Iwo Jima* class sisters can each carry 30 helicopters and over 2000 Marines.

because young black males were having a hard time finding other employment. Meanwhile, the Corps, like all branches of the US military, was having trouble attracting qualified volunteers now that the United States had eliminated the draft. Except in wartime, of course, the Marine Corps had prided itself on being an all-volunteer unit, but now the Marines found themselves recruiting within a society that was at least temporarily 'down on' the military. General Wilson, the Commandant, was so concerned that in 1978 he recommended the reinstatement of a draft—which would traditionally serve to steer some young men to enlist in the Marines. And in 1979, the new commandant of the Corps, General Robert H Barrow, proposed cutting back on the authorized strength of 190,000 to 179,000 Marines and putting more effort and budget into improving a trimmed-down and advanced Corps.

Again, though, the problems and issues that were current in the Corps during these years could not be divorced from those abroad in American society as a whole. Thus, the question of the numbers and qualifications of enlistees in the Marines was part of a national debate over just what role the traditional military would play in the future. Would not the weapons systems and wars of the future call for relatively few but highly trained personnel? Should so much money be budgeted for training, maintaining (and eventually retiring) conventional personnel when the new weapons, ships, planes and advanced technology required such large sums? In particular, were the Marines even required in the the wars of the future?

Now the Marines had often found their function, even existence, questioned, especially after a major war, and once again, in the 1970s, the Corps found its role being scrutinized. Some critics were claiming that if the Marines prime justification was as an amphibious landing force, the last true contested assault had been at Inchon, Korea, in 1950. (The several amphibious landings in Vietnam had been more for demonstration than for real.) In an age of nuclear weapons, missiles, versatile airplanes and advanced weapons of all kinds, would there be any need for Marines to storm ashore? Other critics were pointing out that both in Korea and in Vietnam, the Marines had essentially served as supplements—however valuable and courageous—to the regular army. Meanwhile, the Marines argued that their speciality——amphibious landings—required co-

Below: The assault transport *Spiegel Grove* (LSD.32) operates landing craft (as well as helicopters) to deploy heavy equipment during amphibious operations.

ordinated air support, while critics claimed it required a disproportionate amount of the Corps' budget to maintain its own air force. Perhaps the debate that raged around the Corps was best summed up in a much-publicized study made by one of the most prestigious 'think tanks,' the Brookings Institution, which in 1976 issued a report, *Where Does the Marine Corps Go From Here?*

The Marines stand by

Yet even as the debate was going on, the role of the Marines was made clear for all who would look. Even in a world of complex geopolitical and military decisions, there were the occasions when the old-fashioned US Marines seemed best suited to fulfilling America's goals. Thus, in the October 1973 war between Israel and Egypt and Syria, when the United States decided to supply planes and other military equipment to the beleagured Israelis, a force of 2000 Marines was sent from the USA to the Sixth Fleet in the Mediterranean—a clear signal to the Egyptians and Syrians, as well as to their patron, the USSR, that the USA 'meant business.' That was what the appearance of the US Marines had always meant.

In a somewhat different incident in 1974, the Marines also carried out their traditional role. The Greeks on Cyprus had overthrown their island's government in July, and the Turkish army had invaded the island to protect the Turkish minority there; a truce was soon arranged that left the island divided, and since the United States was perceived by the Greek Cypriots to have favored the Turks, a mob of Greeks attacked the US Embassy in the capital, Nicosia, on 19 August. Five Marines of the Security Guard Detachment defended the embassy with tear-gas grenades, although bullets fired by the Greek Cypriots killed the American ambassador and a woman secretary. No Marines were killed or wounded in this episode, nor were any in another attack on the embassy in Nicosia in January 1975, but there are times when the US Marines best serve America's interests by not getting killed—or killing.

This is particularly true for the Marines who serve in the Security Guard Battalion in some 125 embassies, consulate generals, and missions around the world (and occasionally with the American delegations to international conferences). This battalion was in fact created only in 1949, and its personnel serve under the arrangements made between the Corps and the US Department of State. Their basic assignment is to protect the official personnel, classified materials and government property at these posts, but on occasion the Marine guards find themselves bearing the brunt of foreigners' anger at the USA in general. Thus, in 1973, President Idi Amin, the violent and anti-American dictator of Uganda, demand that the Marines at the embassy leave—he claimed they were engaged in subversive activities. (The USA countered by closing the whole embassy.) And in 1974 the Communist Chinese government demanded that the six-man Marine unit at the new US liaison office in Peking be removed. And then, in 1978, Chinese Nationalists protesting the US recognition of Communist China attacked the US Embassy and military headquarters in Taipei, Taiwan, and it was the US Marine security guard that had to drive back the mob with tear gas.

The Iranian crisis

But perhaps the most dramatic episode in the Marines' history of service as security guards—and one that demonstrates so well the peculiarly delicate nature of this assignment—is the one that became known as the

Below: During the 1980 Bright Star exercises, Marines advance with support from their LVTP-7 amphibious personnel carriers.

Above: A modern recruiting poster but a traditional message.
Main picture: Marine M60 tank. The M60 entered service in the early 1960s but soldiers on today with more modern fire control systems among the many improved items of equipment.

Above: Physical fitness and discipline remain prime objectives of Marine Corps basic training. *Right:* Marines with an M110 8-inch self-propelled howitzer. Such weapons are normally not organic to Marine divisions but are controlled by higher echelons.

Iranian Hostage Crisis. In fact, for the US Marines, this crisis had both a prologue and an epilogue. The former came in February 1979, when in the turmoil that followed the overthrow of the Shah, forces supporting the Ayatollah Khomeini overthrew the government of Premier Shahpur Bakhtiar. President Jimmy Carter made plans to evacuate the 7800 Americans said to be in Iran, and a contingent of 69 Marines and six helicopters was stationed in an undisclosed location near Iran. But before any official evacuation began, leftist guerrillas stormed the US Embassy in Teheran; the compound was guarded by 19 US Marines of the Security Guard, and they fired tear gas grenades at the first attackers; outnumbered, they began to switch to shot guns loaded with birdshot, but they were soon overwhelmed by the sheer numbers of Iranians and were forced to surrender, along with some 100 embassy employees—including the US Ambassador, William Sullivan. Eventually representatives from Khomeini arrived, and after two hours the guerrillas were persuaded to release all the Americans. However, two Marines had been wounded in the attack—they claimed after

Above: The tank landing ship *Fairfax County* (nearest) and the *Inchon*, typical components of a force for Marine landing operations.

surrendering—and when one of them was taken to a Teheran hospital for treatment, he was then kidnapped by supporters of Khomeini. It was a week before US pressure on Khomeini brought about this Marine's release. At that time, it seemed a long while to hold an American hostage.

Following that incident, hundreds of Americans began to leave Iran, and the US government cut back its embassy staff to about 65, with a Marine Security Guard of 13. Some of the more experienced diplomatic personnel were warning the US government that continued support for the Shah would endanger any Americans at the Teheran Embassy, but on 22 October 1979, President Carter went ahead and allowed the Shah to enter the USA for medical treatment for cancer. From that day on, there were daily demonstrations in front of the entrance to the extensive compound where the US Embassy and its associated buildings were located.

So it was on Sunday morning, 4 November, when the embassy personnel saw and heard the usual mob shouting 'Death to America!' and similar slogans, there seemed nothing that different from other recent days. But for whatever reason—whether it was a totally planned and directed move or not—about 10:30 that morning the demonstrators began to force the gate and climb over the compound walls. The Marines on duty at the main gatehouse immediately realized that they would not be able to hold back this mob. As one member of the Marine Security Guard, Sergeant James M Lopez, would later say: 'To put it bluntly, all hell broke loose and we couldn't stop it.'

The Marines who could got inside the main chancery building and bolted its heavy front door. They then began to put on their flak jackets and helmets and to pass out rifles, shotguns, pistols and tear gas grenades. (Several of the 13-man Marine guard were elsewhere around the compound.)

Meanwhile, Bruce Laingen, chargé d'affaires at the US Embassy in Teheran (as there was no ambassador at that time), was at the Iranian Foreign Ministry. Informed by phone of the mob attacking the chancery, he gave orders that no Americans were to fire any weapons: this may have been one of the wisest decisions taken by anyone involved in the entire Iranian Hostage Crisis. And the US Marines there at the chancery deserve equal credit: trained to fight—to shoot—yes, to kill—to protect America's goals, Marines might have found it easy to start shooting. It would have made a heroic tale for the grandchildren—even if it had to be told by a widowed grandmother. For if any Marines had begun to shoot, the whole episode would almost certainly have ended in violence of a different kind, with many Americans equally certainly dead.

Instead, the Marines acted as the professionals they were, and as the civilian staff of the embassy began to retreat to higher floors and start to shred documents, the guards held off the Iranians who had broken in from the basement windows and were now forcing their way up the stairs of the chancery. Sergeant John D McKeel Jr and Corporal Westley Williams were the two Marines last in the stairway, and they were forced to don gas masks when tear gas began to spread. Sergeant McKeel did spray one young Iranian with chemical Mace (and would later be severely beaten for this) but neither Marine fired the shotguns they held. Gradually, all the Americans in the chancery were trapped and taken prisoner.

Other Americans, including some of the Marines, were at other stations in the compound, and one by one they were being captured by the Iranians now roaming free in the compound. One Marine was actually outside the compound on an errand, but when he heard that the mob had broken in, he rushed back into the grounds—only to be taken prisoner. At the consulate building, only one Marine, Sergeant James Lopez, was on duty, and he would later be singled out for praise by other Americans for his

Above: Marine training takes account of the possibility of biological or chemical attack. Practice routines with tear gas are common.

cool courage. Lopez not only took steps to make the consulate as secure as possible—at one point shoving an Iranian out of a second-floor window as he was about to climb in—but he calmly destroyed official consulate property while other Americans were slipping out a side door of the consulate. (Five of those eventually escaped from Iran with the help of Canadian Embassy officials.) Lopez was the last person to leave the consulate—he tried to disguise himself as an Iranian—but was caught as he was locking the door. One of the Americans who escaped would later say: 'By keeping the consulate secure, he made it possible for us to go. He was the one all of us looked to to tell us what to do. He may have been the most junior guy there, but he was certainly up to the occasion. He didn't get excited. He didn't lose his composure.' Marine Sergeant Lopez was 21 years old, and like the other Marines at the compound takeover that day, he may have performed his most courageous act by not firing his pistol.

By about 1:00 that afternoon, all 61 Americans in the compound were taken prisoner; two other Americans would be taken at the offices of the Iran-America Society elsewhere in Teheran, while three were held at the Foreign Ministry. Thus began the Hostage Crisis that would not end for most of them until 20 January 1981—444 days of captivity. (Thirteen of them would be released on 19–20 November 1979—five women secretaries and eight blacks, including five Marines: the Iranian revolutionaries were trying to show the world their support for 'oppressed' groups.) The US Marines held hostage did not suffer any more than the civilians—although, again, that would most certainly not have been the case had they killed even one Iranian. Indeed, in some respects, the individual Marines were less harassed by their Iranian captors than were certain civilians. It is not unreasonable to suggest that this was in tacit recognition that the US Marines were true professionals who carry out the orders of their government but do not make policy. If this was why the Marines were not bothered by the Iranians, it says something for the image—and performance—of the Corps.

But in the epilogue to the hostage crisis, other Marines were less fortunate. Almost immediately after it was clear that the Iranian government was not going to release the hostages, that very November 1979,

Left: Marine in full jungle camouflage aims his M16 rifle.
Right: Marine scout team. As the Vietnam experience proved, intensive patrol operations are vital in jungle terrain.

American military planners began to discuss possible ways of releasing them by force. The Carter administration insisted on using diplomatic and other channels to seek their release, but finally, convinced that all negotiations were at an end, at a secret meeting of his National Security Council on 11 April 1980, President Carter gave the go-ahead to a military rescue plan.

The plan had been rehearsed for some time, so it did not take that long to put it into effect. On 24 April, at 7:30 in the evening (Iranian time), eight Navy helicopters took off from the aircraft carrier *Nimitz* in the Arabian Sea off Iran. They were piloted and crewed by US Marines. About that same time, six US Air Force C-130 Hercules transports took off from an undisclosed base or aircraft carrier. The plan called for all these helicopters and planes to rendezvous at a desert site some 250 miles southeast of Teheran; at that point, troops aboard the transports would transfer to the helicopters, which would carry them to another point some 50 miles outside Teheran; from there they would be trucked into Teheran (the trucks arranged by CIA operatives), release the hostages, and then fly out on the helicopters. The plan called for a minimum of six helicopters to make it operational.

One of the helicopters was forced down only about 80 miles into Iranian airspace by rotorblade trouble. A second helicopter's navigation and flight instruments failed after flying through a dust storm, and the pilot returned to the *Nimitz*. And then, when the remaining six copters were at Desert One, the rendezvous site, a third one was revealed to have hydraulic failure. This meant that only five helicopters were available, so Colonel Charlie Beckwith, the US Army officer in command of the ground rescue team, recommended to the Defense Department in Washington that the mission be abandoned. At 3:15 in the morning of 25 April (Iranian time), President Carter ordered that the mission be canceled.

The helicopters now began to refuel from one of the C-130s, and as one was changing position, it collided with a C-130. As the two aircraft burst into flame, ammunition and shell casings from within the C-130 began to fall on the other helicopters. Colonel Beckwith gave orders for all the helicopters to be abandoned, and all surviving men were put aboard the C-130s, which then took off. But the intense fire had prevented them from carrying away the eight men who had been killed in the initial blast, and the charred bodies would be publicly displayed by Iranians at the embassy compound. (Later they were returned to America.)

Above: A Marine M60 tank comes ashore during joint maneuvers with Australian forces.
Left: Although scrambling nets are now used comparatively seldom in operational conditions they still feature in fitness training programs.

Debate over the mission—its very conception, its planning, its operation, the decisions made along the way—would continue for some time. But one point was undeniable: of the eight servicemen who died, three were US Marines—testifying once more to the prominent role played by the Marines whenever Americans were asked to make the extreme sacrifice.

The invasion of Grenada

In the months that followed the resolution of the Iranian Hostage Crisis, the US Marines, like all Americans, would have plenty of time to think about the cost to the US of its global commitments and of the uses and limits of its vast powers. The greatest test of this commitment—to the US Marines in particular—would come in Beirut, Lebanon, of course, but the nation was usually under some pressure in one part of the world or another. And where the US felt itself pressured, the US Marines were usually to be found. This holds especially, and traditionally, in the Caribbean and Central America, where at least since the Monroe Doctrine of 1823 the US has exerted a special concern. Since the intervention of the Marines in the Dominican Republic in 1965, there had been several incidents involving attacks on the US Embassy in El Salvador, and the Marine security guards had responded with their usual tear gas. But for the most part, the Marines were not involved in the training of the government's troops in El Salvador or of the anti-Sandinista forces in Guatemala. (Marines do train regularly in Panama, however, and they participated in the on-going training exercises known as Big Pine in Honduras in 1983–84.)

But Marines were called into action once again in the controversial intervention in Grenada in October 1983. The USA's problems with this tiny Caribbean island had been brewing for some time, ever since its Marxist Prime Minister Maurice Bishop had invited Cubans to help construct—with obvious Russian support—a 10,000-foot airfield; Bishop insisted it was simply to handle the large airplanes that would bring tourists, but the USA claimed it was designed to allow Russian airplanes to 'service' Caribbean nations. Then, in an unexpected development, the Prime Minister and about 100 other Grenadians were killed on 19 October by a group of even more radical leftists. They imposed a round-the-clock curfew on the island, yet seemed unable to provide any further leadership that might avoid anarchy. There were about 1000 Americans on Grenada, most of them students at St George's University School of Medicine, and there was genuine concern among some members of the US government that they could become hostages—just as had occurred in Iran during a similar time of turmoil.

So it was that President Ronald Reagan authorized the American military to go into Grenada. Meanwhile, six neighboring Caribbean nations had also asked the USA to intervene, as they feared the threat to their own people should a strong Marxist government take hold on Grenada. And there was no denying that the Reagan administration, aside from this appeal and the threat to the students, had its own determination not to let the USSR get any more of a foothold in the Caribbean.

The first ashore on 25 October 1983, were a small group of US Navy Seals, especially assigned to sneak ashore and rescue the Governor-General, Sir Paul Scoon, held under house arrest by the coup leaders. But at almost the same moment, on the opposite side of the island, some 400 Marines in troop helicopters from the amphibious assault ship *Guam* landed at Pearls Airport, the only really functional airstrip at that time. That was about 5:30 in the morning. About a half hour later, hundreds of Rangers, the Army's special force, parachuted onto the new 10,000-foot airstrip at Point Salines at the southeastern tip of Grenada. The Marines met little resistance and declared their airport secure within two hours. The Rangers, however, met unexpectedly heavy resistance, most of it apparently coming from the area where the Cuban workers lived. (The Pentagon had expected that some of the Cubans might fight but did not know that they were so well armed—including antiaircraft wea-

Below: The *Austin* class amphibious transport USS *Dubuque* can carry 900 Marines and their equipment, 6 transport helicopters and from 4 to 20 landing craft depending on type.

pons.) By 7:15, however, the Rangers had cleared the airstrip so that C-130s could land.

That afternoon, the *Guam*, which had moved around to the west coast, sent ashore 13 amphibious vehicles—with 250 Marines and five tanks—to take Fort Frederick and its Richmond Hill prison, on the high ground outside St George, the island's capital. As the Marines moved down from the north of the fort, Rangers moved from the south. Resistance from Grenadian revolutionaries was again unexpectedly heavy, and when night came that Tuesday, the US military could not really claim to be in control of Grenada. By Wednesday, however, most organized resistance was put down. Early that morning Marines stormed the mansion where the US Navy Seals were now besieged with the Governor-General. That evening, Marines were taking Fort Frederic at about the same time other Marines were relieving the campus of the medical school where hundreds of young Americans had been cut off by Grenadian revolutionaries.

On Thursday, 27 October, the Atlantic Fleet Commander was reporting that 'all major military objectives in the island were secured.' Pockets of resistance remained, however, for some days. By this time, there were some 50 Marines, 500 Rangers, and 5000 paratroopers from the 82nd Airborne Division on Grenada, plus about 400 members of the six-nation Caribbean force that served as a token of their support. The total American casualties for the operation were 18 dead and 67 wounded. A week later, all the US Marines and Rangers had left; and within another six weeks, only about 300 US Military Police and support troops were still on Grenada. As usual where American troops and casualties were involved, many Americans were left to raise many questions about this intervention. But when the large amounts of Russian-made arms and ammunition, not to mention 12 Soviet-built armored personnel carriers, were displayed; when the majority of the students expressed gratitude for being rescued; and when so many of the native Grenadians declared their joy of being freed from the repressive rule of their Marxist military revolutionaries—then most Americans conceded that it was one intervention that had succeeded.

The tragedy of Lebanon

America's involvement in Lebanon would not end so happily. It had begun in August 1982, when an agreement—negotiated by US envoy Philip Habib—called for the Israelis to pull their troops away from west Beirut, where they were besieging the Palestine Liberation Organization's (PLO) army, while an international peace-keeping force moved in to maintain order. On 19 August the Lebanese government formally requested that the USA, France and Italy send troops for such a force, and the USA assigned, quite naturally, 800 Marines. They were to be armed, but were to assume a 'carefully limited non-combat role,' and they were to stay no more than 30 days.

The first US Marines came ashore on 25 August—the French and Italian troops having come several days previously—and they relieved the French troops at the port.

Above: Men of the 6th Marines (2nd Marine Division) pause for orders in front of an M48 tank during the intervention in the Dominican Republic in 1965.
Right: A crate of Soviet AK-47 assault rifles found by the American forces on Grenada.
Below: Marine looks out for snipers near the town of Greenville, Grenada, 25 October 1983.

By 1 September all the Palestinians (and their Syrian supporters) were officially declared to be out of Beirut, and so on 10 September the 800 US Marines went back to their ships offshore. They had never fired a shot in action, and there were no casualties.

But then, on 14 September, the newly elected president of Lebanon, Bashir Gemayel, was assassinated by Moslem extremists opposed to Gemayel and his Christian-Phalangist party. To control the violence that everyone feared would ensue, the Israelis moved back into Beirut, but they made the mistake of allowing Christian-Phalangists into refugee camps housing Palestinians, and sometime between 16 and 18 September, Phalangist extremists massacred several hundred Palestinians in revenge. In the turmoil that followed, President Reagan agreed to send American troops back as part of an international peacekeeping force, and on 29 September, the first detachment of Marines once again came ashore at Beirut to join the French and Italian troops. The Americans were assigned to guard the Beirut International Airport, and they took up their posts around the airport.

As it happened, the first US Marine was killed within 24 hours by an 'accidental detonation' of some undetected explosive around the airport. This turned out to be significant in more ways than one, because the US Marine commander on the scene would later state that the Marines long considered such hidden explosives to be their greatest threat, along with the Israelis, who refused to leave Beirut so long as the Syrians also refused to leave. And in the weeks and then months that followed, several Marines were killed by various explosions, snipers, and shells fired into their midst. Americans began to raise questions about the role of the Marines there in Beirut; by 12 September 1983, there were 1200 Marines on shore and another 2000 in a backup force on ships off Beirut. The next day, President Reagan authorized the Marines to call in US naval artillery and air strikes if deemed

Below: LVTP-7s of the 32nd Marine Amphibious Brigade in Beirut on 15 November 1982. The 32nd Brigade was being relieved at that time by the 24th Marine Amphibious Unit.

Above: A 155mm howitzer of C Battery, 24th Marine Amphibious Unit, serving with the Beirut peacekeeping force in September 1983.

necessary, but the US Marine commander in Lebanon, Colonel Timothy J Geraghty, insisted that there was no change in the Marines' peace-keeping mission.' On 29 September the US Congress passed the War Powers Resolution allowing for US forces to remain in Lebanon only for another 18 months. For too many of the Marines, this would prove to be far too late a deadline.

At daybreak, 23 October, a large yellow Mercedes truck pulled into the parking lot at the south side of the compound where the Marines were headquartered on the edge of the Beirut airport. There was a roll of barbed wire bisecting the parking lot; behind this were two sentry posts, but at that time of morning only one sentry was on duty—and his rifle was not loaded; then there was a wrought-iron, six-foot high fence, with a knee-high cement base, with an iron grillwork gate through which vehicles had to enter; at the far end of a driveway was an 18-inch diameter pipe placed lengthwise as a barrier before the entrance to the headquarters building. All these devices seemed like reasonably adequate protection at the time.

No one noticed the Mercedes truck as it circled the parking lot two times, as most Marines were still asleep in the headquarters building. Suddenly the truck turned straight toward the building and crashed through the barbed wire, ran through the sentry posts, drove through the grillwork gate, and on over the pipe and went straight into the entryway. Later, the one Marine sentry who saw the driver would report that he appeared to be 'smiling.' If so, it was his last act, because his truck's cargo had the explosive force equal to 12,000 pounds of high explosives.

In the tremendous blast that followed, much of the headquarters building simply collapsed, floor by floor, onto itself, killing or trapping most of the 300 Marines inside. Those Marines who were outside began to dig frantically to save as many of their comrades as they could. Meanwhile, almost simultaneously, another truck had crashed

Left: Amphibious assault ships lie offshore as a Marine M48 tank lands.
Below left: The LVTP-7 is the Marines' standard amphibious assault vehicle.
Below: US Navy minesweeping RH-53 helicopter refuels from a Marine KC-130 tanker.

Above: Marines of the 24th MAU employ a MULE utility vehicle to transport communications equipment, Beirut, 15 November 1982.
Right: Fully-equipped Marines come ashore from their landing craft to join the Beirut peacekeeping force.

into the French troops' building and killed 58 of them. The American toll would eventually turn out to be 240 dead Marines. It was one of the worst single days in the entire history of the US Marine Corps. More Marines died in this one incident than had died in any single action in the entire Vietnam War, and on only one day in that bloody war had there been more US military fatalities.

What made it especially tragic to the Marines, at least, was that it seemed so unnecessary and so uncharacteristic. The Marines, who prided themselves on being so alert, so mobile, so combat-ready. To be caught, literally, in bed, with their defenses down. Inevitably there were charges, accusations, blame; inevitably, too, the Marine command—from the colonel in charge of the contingent in Beirut to the Commandant himself—came in for its share of criticism. There was a Congressional hearing, and later there was an official military review board. There seemed to be enough blame to go all around, but the simple conclusion was that there had not been adequate security measures, both in the literal sense of barriers and in the broader sense of alerting the Marines to all the potential threats from terrorists. Ironically, it turned out that it was less a lack of sufficient verbal warnings from intelligence sources but more a case of too many warnings: the Marines in Beirut had been receiving so many warnings of terrorist attacks that they were being disregarded. In the end, President Reagan tried to defuse the situation when in January 1984 he said he would assume final responsibility as Commander in Chief, and even if not all Americans felt this quite answered the charges, few were inclined to continue blaming the Marines who had already suffered more than their share of the sorrows that afflicted Lebanon.

Beirut Aftermath

The explosion at the Beirut headquarters marked one of the low points in the history of the Marines, and even in the weeks that followed, the killing of the Marines stationed in Beirut did not stop: in December 1983 one intensive artillery barrage by Syrian-backed Druze militiamen resulted in the deaths of eight US Marines. As Marine fatalities in Lebanon rose to 260, there was increasing doubt as to the viability of the US presence there. On 12 December a second truck loaded with explosives crashed into the US Embassy compound in Beirut. On 14 December President Reagan indicated that the Marines might be withdrawn because of a 'collapse of order,' meaning that no political solution could be found.

The following day US Marines came under attack from Druze positions in hills near Beirut, and the battleship *New Jersey* fired on Syrian positions in support of the Marines. US Warships and jet aircraft continued sporadic strikes against Muslim positions in and near Beirut until February 1984, when President Reagan finally ordered the 1400-man Marine contingent to withdraw. During a cease-fire, on 21 February the

Left: A Marine launches a Redeye antiaircraft missile. This type is now being phased out and replaced by the more modern Stinger.
Above: Marine C-130 Hercules employs a rocket pack to shorten its take-off run. Operating from restricted airfields is a Marine speciality.

Marines began boarding evacuation ships. The withdrawal was over by 26 February.

The experience of the Marines in Lebanon was not easily forgotten, and indeed was the subject of heated debates by candidates in the 1984 elections. When a third suicide bomber drove a van loaded with explosives into the US Embassy in Beirut in September 1984, the success of the attack was blamed by many on the February withdrawal of the US Marine guards.

Through all the debate about the mission of the Marines in Lebanon, these hardy warriors would remain on station and alert around the world. Perhaps their dedication is best expressed by an incident that followed the Beirut explosion. The Commandant of the Marines had gone to a US military hospital in West Germany to award purple hearts to some of the wounded survivors. As General Paul X Kelley was pinning the medal to the gown of Lance Corporal Jeffrey Nashton, the young Marine—who was unable to speak because of all the tubes in his face—indicated that he wanted a piece of paper to write on. He then scribbled something and handed it to General Kelley. What he wrote was 'Semper Fi,' the Marines' shorthand for their motto, *Semper Fidelis*. So long as Marines like this remained 'always faithful,' there was little doubt about the future of the Corps.

Below: Three Marine light attack squadrons were equipped with the AV-8A Harrier. The improved AV-8B has replaced it in service.

RETURN TO COMBAT

'On the Job for Country and Corps'

As the US Marines advanced into the last decade of the twentieth century they continued their proud tradition of service to the United States into a new period of history when responsibilities, objectives and methods of warfare were about to undergo dramatic changes. It was also a period of historic transition, when the final postscripts to earlier wars were being written: the last B-17 Flying Fortress used in combat in World War II was retired to a museum; the last surviving veteran of Teddy Roosevelt's 'Rough Riders,' Ralph Waldo Taylor, the last surviving American 'Ace' of World War I, Spad pilot A Raymond Brooks and General Lemuel C Shepherd, Jr, a Marine who fought in both World Wars I and II, died. Also, the last active-duty Marine who saw combat in World War II, Chief Warrant Officer Charles B Russell, who fought at Peleliu and Okinawa, retired at Camp Pendelton, California.

General Alfred M ('Al') Gray, the USMC's 28th Commandant, guided the Marines into the new era of high-technology combat in which warriors would go into battle wearing chemical protective clothing and carry nerve gas antidote along with their M-16 rifles. They would be supported by attack planes so technically sophisticated that computers would be the real pilots, while 'smart bombs' would find enemy bunkers hundreds of miles away and make pinpoint hits through their windows. Yet decisive battles would still be won by the grunts on the ground. Much of the new high-tech weaponry encountered by the Marines was developed for a third World War in Europe that never materialized.

Momentous Developments

Indeed, near the end of the 1980s and in the early 1990s, such tremendous political changes began to occur throughout the world that the role of all branches of the US military had to be thoroughly re-appraised. Specifically, the traditional role of the US Marines as 'troubleshooters' was being questioned. The Marine Corps had always been the 'branch of choice' when it came to America's taking the first steps in assuming a military role in foreign events. Now—overnight, historically speaking—both the nature of the events that might require US action and who the potential enemy might be had become unclear.

The first great rumblings of change began to erupt in Eastern Europe, followed by the startling decision by key Soviet leaders, especially the USSR President Mikhail Gorbachev, to end the Cold War and the costly game of military one-upmanship. Initially Gorbachev and President Reagan, at a May 1988 summit meeting in Moscow, agreed to reduce both NATO and Warsaw Pact forces in Europe by about 90,000 on each side. Almost simultaneously the USSR began to withdraw 100,000 troops from Afghanistan, ending a futile eight-year aggression.

Despite some opposition from conservative Red Army leaders, the USSR announced a program of *perestroika*, or restructuring economic, social, and political functions that had guided the Soviet government since the Bolshevik Revolution in 1917. One Soviet leader, Vaid Medvedev, even announced that Russia would no longer support its traditional objective of promoting the worldwide victory of socialism.

In the following months Soviet troops began loading their tanks and other military hardware onto trains that headed eastward beyond the Ural Mountains. After 45 years of facing each other across Germany's Fulda Gap, NATO and Warsaw Pact forces began to dismantle their gargantuan nuclear arsenals. The Cold War seemed suddenly to be fading away.

In September 1988 there began a 'swords into ploughshares' movement that would have been unthinkable at the beginning of the decade. Russian inspectors traveled to the Longhorn Army Ammunition Depot in Texas to watch the US destroy its Pershing Intermediate-Range Nuclear Missiles. Meanwhile, US inspectors supervised destruction of the USSR's Intermediate-Range Nuclear

Previous pages: Marines land on a Honduran beach in a 1985 amphibious exercise.
Above: Commandant Alfred M. Gray.
Below: Presidents Reagan and Gorbachev at the 1988 arms reductions summit.
Top right: Arms reduction begins: Elderly Soviet Mya-4s with bombsights removed.
Bottom right: The last Red Army units pull out of Afghanistan, 1989.

On 25 December 1991 the red banner flying over the Kremlin was lowered, and the red-blue-white flag of Russia took its place.

Missiles at Votkinsk, in eastern Russia. In early 1991 the US and Russia announced a mutual reduction in arsenals of long-range ballistic missiles, bombers, and other strategic armaments. But the significance even of such bilateral gestures would soon pale in comparison to events that were taking place inside the Soviet Union itself.

When Mikhail Gorbachev came to power in the USSR in 1985 he knew that the deeply-flawed Soviet economy was already beginning to disintegrate. His policy of *perestroika* had, in fact, been largely a last-minute effort to ward off the growing spectre of complete economic collapse. Whether *perestroika* could have succeeded even if it had been more consistently and courageously applied is moot, for in the event it did not. As economic chaos grew in the USSR, so did social and political turmoil. The overwhelming majority of the Soviet people lost faith first in Marxist-Leninist ideology and eventually in the central government itself. Throughout the autumn of 1991 all the major republics that composed the USSR, including Russia, the Ukraine, Byelorussia and Kazakhstan, rejected communism and declared their independence. The formal death of the once-mighty Soviet Union came on 25 December 1991, when Mikhail Gorbachev resigned as head of state, the red flag flying over the Kremlin was hauled down and the Commonwealth of Independent States, a loose confederation of now-sovereign ex-Soviet republics, was declared in being.

With the fall of the Soviet Union, the last vestiges of the nearly-50-year-old Cold War also expired. The United States would thenceforth confront a world that was radically altered. Unfortunately, as recent history had all too clearly demonstrated, it would not necessarily be a world either at peace or lacking in threats to US security.

Tension in Central America

Throughout the years when direct US–Soviet tensions were waning and the USSR was becoming ever more absorbed in its own internal problems, surrogate fighting continued between groups that favored communist governments and those that supported US-style democratic governments. And the US Marines continued to serve as frontline peacekeepers in that contest. On 19 June 1985 four off-duty US Marine embassy guards had been killed in San Salvador, the capital of El Salvador. A leftist guerilla group claimed responsibility for the attack in which a half-dozen men armed with automatic rifles leaped from the back of a pickup truck and fired at the Marines as they were seated at an outdoor cafe.

The shootings resulted in a pledge by President Reagan to increase military aid to El Salvador. Hostility between the US and leftist political factions in Latin America had built up gradually since the 1970s as a sideshow of the European Cold War. The USSR had supported the Sandanista regime of Nicaragua, and Nicaragua in turn helped Cuba's Fidel Castro support leftist guerilla activities in El Salvador and Honduras. On several occasions the conflict threatened to erupt into a war of the Americas.

In November 1984, in an episode reminiscent of the Cuban Missile Crisis of 1962, the US had warned Russia that it would intercept a reported shipment of MiG-21 combat jets en route to a Nicaraguan port. The threat moved Nicaragua to put its armed forces on full combat alert. President Reagan, in turn, declared Nicaragua a threat to US security, invoked his authority to declare a state of national emergency and ordered a trade embargo against Nicaragua. The dispute continued for the remainder of the decade, with the US actively supporting Nicaraguan 'contra' rebels who opposed the

Sandanista government. At one point, Nicaragua expelled the US Ambassador and part of his staff, and the US expelled the Nicaraguan Ambassador and a number of his assistants. But the crisis eventually faded away in early 1990 when the Sandanistas, bowing to both domestic and international pressure, agreed to hold a national election and were promptly voted out of power.

The Middle East and Libya

Tensions also remained high in the Middle East, where Shiite Muslim terrorists seized a TWA 727 and held 153 persons aboard, including 104 Americans, for 17 days in June 1985. The terrorists demanded the release of 766 (mostly Shiite) prisoners captured by Israel in fighting in Lebanon. During the siege the terrorists killed a US Navy diver, Robert Stephem and threw his body on to the runway in Beirut.

The US responded by massing Sixth Fleet warships off the coast of Lebanon. The US also threatened to blockade the country and close the Beirut airport. The situation was finally resolved when Israel agreed to release the Shiite prisoners in question, and the US agreed not to take military action.

In another terrorist episode that year, a

Right: An honor guard stands by the coffins of four Marines, among 11 people killed in a San Salvador cafe by terrorists in 1985.
Below: The scene of the 1985 massacre.

In 1986 Libyan Head of State Col Muammaar al-Qaddafi threatened to attack any US warships that entered the Gulf of Sidra.

group of Palestinians seized control of an Italian cruise ship, the *Achille Lauro*, as it crossed the Mediterranean Sea toward Port Said in Egypt. During the hijacking an American passenger was shot to death and his body thrown overboard. The hijackers agreed to surrender the ship only if they were offered safe conduct out of Egypt and were allowed to fly to Tunis. President Reagan however, ordered the US Navy to intercept the Egyptian 737 carrying the hijackers while it was traveling in international air space. The Navy F-14s forced the Egyptian plane to land at a NATO air base in Sicily, where the US also dispatched two military transports filled with commandos. As the US had neglected to get permission of the Italian government for this use of an Italian air base, a diplomatic furor followed, resulting in the resignation of Italian Prime Minister Bettino Craxi. The hijackers, meanwhile, were turned over to Italian authorities, who released the leader, Muhammed Abbas, on the grounds of PLO diplomatic immunity.

Anti-American hostility continued in the Middle East through the rest of the decade. In one airliner hijacking incident, three Americans were shot and thrown from a plane, and five Americans were killed in a terrorist attack at an airport in Rome. Intelligence sources indicated that Libya was involved in at least part of the terrorist activities. After a terrorist attack at a Vienna airport in which 40 civilians were killed or wounded, Libya praised the attack as 'heroic.' Meanwhile, President Reagan said Libyan actions constituted a threat to the national security of the US, and the Pentagon made contingency plans to attack targets in Libya if the terrorists could be identified and located in that North African nation.

On 24 January 1986 the US Navy announced plans to hold maneuvers off the coast of Libya. Libyan Head of State Colonel Muammar al-Qaddafi warned US warships against entering the Gulf of Sidra, claiming that Libyan territory included the Gulf and not just the waters within a 12-mile limit from shore. Qaddafi then drew a theoretical 'line of death' along the northern edge of the Gulf and dared the US fleet of 30 warships, including three aircraft carriers, to cross the line.

When the US ships called Libya's bluff and crossed the 'line of death,' Libya fired a half-dozen missiles from a shore battery near Syrte. None of the missiles hit a target, and US Navy planes responded by destroying a Libyan patrol boat with cluster bombs and an anti-ship missile. Navy planes then knocked out the radar system at Syrte and attacked three more Libyan patrol boats, sinking two of them. As the Navy ended maneuvers and withdrew from the Gulf of Sidra on 27 March 1986 Qaddafi promised to carry out a struggle against the US in all parts of the world.

A week later, on 2 April, four Americans were killed when a bomb exploded in a TWA passenger jet as it descended for a landing in Athens. A radical Arab group claimed responsibility, but no Libyan connection could be proven. Then a bomb exploded in a West Berlin discothèque on 5 April, and an American sergeant was killed and 60 other Americans were injured in the blast. Three different terrorist groups claimed responsibility for the bomb attack, but now intelligence reports indicated a direct involvement on the part of the Libyan government itself.

On 15 April 1986, at 2 am Libyan time, the US implemented one of its contingency

An Iraqi air-to-ground missile did severe damage to the Frigate USS *Stark* in May 1987 when it was on duty in the Persian Gulf.

A US *Spruance* class destroyer shells an Iranian offshore oil rig in October 1987.

plans. Air Force F-111 fighter-bombers based in Great Britain and carrier-based A-6 attack planes of the Sixth Fleet assaulted targets in Tripoli, including a barracks, a training site for terrorists and military airport facilities. The F-111s also attacked a military air base in Benghazi. (Because France refused permission for the US aircraft to overfly its territory, the F-111s based in England had had to fly over the Atlantic Ocean to Gibralter, then over the Mediterranean Sea, with aerial refueling along the way.) The attack involved a total of 32 US planes and lasted only 10 minutes. One F-111 and its two-man crew were lost. Libya retaliated by firing missiles at a US Coast Guard facility on the Italian island of Lampedusa; the missiles fell short of their target and splashed into the sea. However, two Britons and an American were found shot to death in Lebanon; a note found with the bodies claimed the men were executed as a protest against the raid on Libya. A more ominous reaction came from the new Gorbachev government in Moscow, which announced an offer to 'improve the defense capability' of Libya.

A US Marine officer, Lt Col William Higgins, became a victim of Middle East terrorism on 17 February 1988. Higgins disappeared while driving home alone after a meeting with an official of the Shiite Muslim Amal militia near the Lebanese port city of Tyre. An anonymous telephone caller on 18 February claimed Higgins was a CIA agent and would be put on trial. The US State Department denied that Higgins was associated with the CIA. At about the same time as the abduction of Higgins, United Nations representatives from Norway and Sweden were also kidnapped in Lebanon and a French agent was found shot to death. In July 1989 Muslim extremists announced the execution of Colonel Higgins.

The Iran-Iraq War

Warfare in the Persian Gulf originally began in September 1980 in a dispute between Iran and Iraq over control of Shatt al-Arab waterway that flows between the two countries. Each country began bombing attacks on the other's cities, and in 1984 the fighting spread to attacks on oil tankers in the Gulf. On 17 May 1987 an American frigate on station in the Gulf, the USS *Stark*, was struck by an Exocet missile fired by an Iraqi fighter, resulting in 37 US sailors killed. The frigate's electronic defenses were turned off because an Iraqi attack was not expected. Iraq claimed the attack was a mistake and apologized to the US government.

At about the same time, Iran attacked a Soviet ship in the Gulf. On 24 July 1987 a Kuwaiti tanker being escorted by the US Navy was damaged by a mine, and six days later a Navy helicopter with a crew of four was lost while escorting Kuwaiti tankers. Despite the efforts of the US to protect shipping in the Persian Gulf, sporadic attacks by Iran on ships using Iraqi ports, as well as Iraqi attacks on Iranian ships, continued. In one six-day period alone a total of 20 ships were attacked in this 'tanker war.' After an Iranian Silkworm missile struck a US-flagged Kuwaiti tanker on 16 October the US Navy warned Iran to abandon an offshore oil rig used as a gunboat base. Then four US destroyers trained their five-inch guns on the structure and demolished it.

On 6 March 1988 Iranian boats and batteries on an oil platform fired on US helicopters on patrol in the Gulf, and on 14 April 10 US sailors were injured when their frigate hit a mine in international waters. The next day two more mines were found in the same area. Because of evidence that the mines were Iranian, President Reagan authorized an attack on two Iranian offshore oil platforms. On 18 April three US warships began an attack on the Sassan platform, and US Marines moved in to finish its destruction. US forces also destroyed an oil platform near Sirri Island.

Iran retaliated with a series of attacks including an unsuccessful attempt to sink the USS *Wainright*. In another encounter, two ships repulsed an Iranian missile boat and sank it. Iran reported 15 of its sailors killed in the attacks; the US lost a helicopter gunship and its two-man crew. As Iran continued its attacks on commercial shipping, US A-6 attack planes sank one Iranian gunboat and damaged two others. Two Iranian frigates then attacked US Navy vessels, but both Iranian ships were struck, and one was presumed sunk.

Above: The cruiser *USS Vincennes* in error shot down an Iranian airliner in 1988.
Right: USAF C-5 Galaxies bring supplies to US troops in Panama in 1988. By the year's end 2100 Marines had been rushed to Panama.

US involvement in the fighting between Iran and Iraq in the Persian Gulf reached a climax on 3 July 1988, when a missile fired by the Navy's USS *Vincennes* accidentally brought down an Iranian airliner, killing all 290 passengers and crew members. The mishap occurred during a period when the *Vincennes* and the USS *Elmer Montgomery* had been fighting off a party of Iranian gunboats that had attacked a reconnaissance helicopter from the *Vincennes*.

The record showed the US warships had begun firing at the Iranian gunboats at 10:42 am and had sunk or damaged three of them. At 10:47, while tensions were still high, the airliner lifted off from a joint military-civilian airfield in Bandar Abbasm Iran, on a flight path across the Strait of Hormuz. At 10:49 the *Vincennes* began broadcasting warnings on three civilian and four military frequencies. When the airliner failed to acknowledge the warnings, it was declared hostile. Meanwhile, shipboard electronics equipment indicated erroneously that the airliner was an F-14 jet fighter, a type possessed by the Iranian air force. As the airliner approached to within nine miles of the *Vincennes* two surface-to-air heat-seeking missiles were fired at it, and at least one hit the airliner.

The US apologized for the unfortunate incident and offered to pay compensation to members of the families of the victims, who were from six countries besides Iran. As a possible side effect of the accident, Iran suddenly announced a dramatic reversal of policy and accepted a United Nations proposal to end the eight-year-old war with Iraq. On 5 August 1988, a month after the mishap, the UN announced a cease-fire and the start of discussions on a final settlement.

Anti-American terrorism did not end with the cease-fire. On 21 December 1988 a Pan Am 747 en route from London to New York exploded over Lockerbie, Scotland, killing 259 passengers aboard the plane and 11 persons on the ground. The explosion was traced to a plastic explosives bomb in an unaccompanied suitcase apparently put aboard the plane at a previous stop in Frankfurt. A pro-Iranian Islamic group claimed responsibility for the bombing, but intelligence officers later concluded that Libya had been, at the least, involved in the plot.

The Panamanian Connection

Meanwhile, fresh problems for the US were beginning to surface in Latin America, where Manuel Antonio Noriega, Panama's effective ruler and a key CIA link in the region, was publicly accused of being both a drug trafficker and double-agent, providing military intelligence to both Cuba's Castro and the CIA. Noriega was also accused of helping to launder money from narcotics sales through Panamanian banks and of supplying arms to leftist rebels in Colombia. Noriega denied the reports, but Federal grand juries in Miami and Tampa, Florida, returned indictments on 4 February 1988, charging Noriega with protecting and helping international drug traffickers and allowing drug profits to be laundered through state bank accounts.

The President of Panama, Eric Arturo Delvalle, now tried to fire Noriega. But Noriega refused to quit his government positions and instead persuaded the Panamanian National Assembly to remove Delvalle from office. Delvalle was ordered to leave Panama but instead went into hiding. A general strike began 29 February 1988. The US supported Delvalle but announced it would not intervene militarily. Nevertheless, this was the beginning of an eventual military showdown between the US and the Noriega-controlled Panamanian Defense Forces (PDF). Meanwhile, the US attempted to oust Noriega by economic and political pressures. On 2 March the US State Department advised US banks not to disburse funds to Noriega, and federal district courts the following day restrained US banks from transferring money to any accounts controlled by the Panamanian government.

These actions caused turmoil in Panama, which used the US dollar as its currency. The US tightened the screws further by putting in escrow a $7 million payment due the Panama Canal Commission, though the US did provide cash to pay Panama Canal workers. Street demonstrations and work slowdowns were now spreading throughout Panama, and Noriega's troops began to occupy docks, flour mills and other key economic facilities.

In April 1988 the US dispatched 1300 Marines to Panama to help provide security at American bases in the Panama Canal Zone. This action was followed by orders sending an additional contingent of 800 US Marines to Panama, ostensibly for 'jungle

training.' President Reagan next invoked the Emergency Economic Powers Act, thereby prohibiting any US business or individual from making any payments to the Noriega government. Noriega announced that the US was planing to invade Panama, a claim still denied by Washington. But after George Bush assumed the office of President of the US in 1989, one of his early moves was to send 2000 more combat troops to Panama to protect American civilians and economic interests in the Canal Zone.

In May 1989 Noriega tried to rig a Panamanian presidential election, but his efforts backfired as voters overwhelmingly chose anti-Noriega candidate Guillermo Endara. Noriega immediately declared the election results void, and the dictator's paramilitary squads attacked Endara and his winning vice-presidential candidate and beat them in the streets of Panama City. This episode was followed by an attempted coup, but the anti-Noriega plotters were arrested, and several senior military officials who were reported to be sympathetic to the plot were 'retired.'

On 3 October 1989 another coup was attempted by 240 officers and men of Noriega's own Panama Defense Forces. It was led by Major Moises Giroldi. US troops made an attempt to aid the coup by blocking two of three roads leading to Noriega's headquarters, and General Maxwell Thurman, commander of US Southern Command Headquarters at Quarry Heights in the Canal Zone, reportedly sought authorization to block the third road. But PDF troops on the third road managed to reach Noriega and rescue him before he could be captured by Giroldi's rebels. Giroldi and about 75 of his men were subsequently executed, and the US was much criticized for its failure to act quickly and decisively in the situation.

Left: Panamanian strongman Manuel Noriega defied, and then declared war on, the US.
Below: US Marines in Panama in 1988 train in jungle warfare, a skill they sense they will be called upon to use all too soon.

JCS Chairman Gen Colin Powell briefs the press on the progress of the US invasion of Panama in December 1989.

The political disorder in Panama worsened in December, when the National Assembly of Panama ignored the results of the legitimate presidential election and proclaimed Noriega 'Maximum Leader' and declared a 'state of war' between Panama and the US.

On the following day four off-duty US military officers became lost while driving through Panama City. They were stopped at a Panamanian Defence Forces checkpoint, and a PDF soldier tried to drag one of the Americans from the car. The driver gunned the engine in an attempt to elude the PDF troops, who opened fire. US Marine First Lieutenant Robert Paz, 25, of the US Southern Command Operations Directorate, was killed by the gunfire. The shooting was witnessed by a US Navy lieutenant and his wife, who were immediately seized and taken to PDF headquarters for questioning; the Navy officer was beaten and his wife brutalized. Meanwhile, Noriega ordered a 250-man guerilla unit to begin terrorist attacks on neighborhoods where 35,000 US citizens lived. President Bush reacted quickly to the new developments and called a meeting of key Pentagon and White House advisers, including General Colin Powell, head of the Joint Chiefs of Staff, and Army General Thomas W Kelly.

The generals and White House advisers dusted off a contingency plan developed during the Reagan administration for the

The coffin of a US soldier killed in Panama is delivered to Dover AFB in the US. Of 14 US fatalities in Panama, one was a Marine.

defense of the Panama Canal and US military bases in the Canal Zone. The plan, called 'Operation Blue Spoon,' outlined a blitzkrieg invasion of Panama in order to disable the Panama Defense Force quickly and to ensure the safety of Panama Canal facilities and US citizens working there. It called for deployment of five task forces that would capture the nation's capital and isolate it from reinforcements by troops stationed in outlying areas. On the recommendation of Defense Secretary Dick Cheney, the name of the mission was changed from 'Blue Spoon' to 'Operation Just Cause.'

Although the US had maintained a military presence in Panama since President Theodore Roosevelt sent the US Navy to 'protect' the tiny Republic in 1903, military officers posing as tourists flew to Panama to double-check the accuracy of current intelligence regarding the size and locations of PDF units and key military facilities.

'Operation Just Cause' called for the overnight movement of nearly 10,000 troops from six US military bases. The US had already positioned 12,700 well-equipped US Marines, Army, Air Force and Navy personnel at in Panama. On 19 December 1989 some 7000 troops began moving out from Fort Lewis, Washington; Ford Ord, California; Fort Bragg, North Carolina; Fort Benning and Fort Stewart, Georgia; and Fort Polk, Louisiana. They included units of the 82 Airborne Division, the Seventh Infantry and Ranger battalions. An additional 2500 service personnel followed the next day. Along with units already in Panama, the troops were divided up into Task Force Bayonet, Task Force Red, Task Force Atlantic, Task Force Pacific and Task Force Semper Fidelis,

Task Force Semper Fidelis was composed of 700 US Marines under the command of Col C E Richardson and was assisted by Army Engineers and military police. One of its objectives was to seize the Bridge of the Americas, the only direct route into Panama City across the Panama Canal. By controlling the bridge, the Marines could isolate the PDF headquarters, the Commandacia, in Panama City from the Panamanian Sixth and Seventh Infantry units based at Rio Hato on the opposite side of the Panama Canal.

Task Force Semper Fidelis also blocked road networks in an area that grew from 100 square kilometers to 600 square kilometers as the fighting progressed. They established a permanent presence in Vaca Monte, Vista Alegre, Nuevo Emperrador and Nuevo Arraijan. In Arraijan and Vera Cruz the Marines opened clinics and city government facilities, restored water service and distributed food and medical supplies. The good will of the Marines was reciprocated by the Panamanian civilians, who helped identify PDF members and helped to persuade more than 1000 PDF troops to surrender.

The fight for control of Arraijan was led by D Company, 2nd LAI Battalion, under the command of Captain Gerald Gaskins, and by the 1st FAST Platoon, commanded by 1st Lieutenant Wayne R Martin, and involved seizure of a PDF facility en route to the town. The PDF facility near the Arraijan tank farm required room-to-room firefighting. Outside Arraijan the Marines encountered a PDF roadblock in the form of a fuel tanker straddling the highway and protected by a platoon of armed PDF troops. Fire from LAVs (tank-like amphibious vehicles) helped break through the roadblock, after which the Marines had to fight their way through a second fortified PDF building. By 4:30 am, 20 December, the LAI-FAST task force had completed its mission.

Among Marine casualties were: Cpl Gareth C Isaak, 22, killed; and Sgt Gregory A Johnson, 24, PFC Aaron S Jenkins, 22, and 1st Lt Wayne R Martin, 26, wounded.

Marines also secured and protected Howard Air Force Base, a US-controlled facility used in the Operation as a base for ferrying troops by helicopter into Panama City. The helicopter trooplift was part of the Task Force Bayonet mission, which had, among its objectives, preventing reinforcements from Fort Amador, the nearest PDF military base, from entering the city.

A Marine gunner mans a machine-gun on a US Navy patrol boat guarding the Panama Canal in the aftermath of the Panama invasion.

Task Force Bayonet also had the objective of capturing the Commandacia headquarters facility inside Panama City. Equipped with Vietnam-era Sheridan light tanks and manned by Sixth Mechanized Infantry and 87th Infantry troops, Task Force Bayonet initiated its attack at 12:45 am on 20 December on the Commandacia. A second objective of Task Force Bayonet was capture of Paitilla Airport, where Noriega based his fleet of private aircraft, thereby blocking any airborne escape attempt by the Panamanian dictator. The mission required a midnight parachute jump into the ocean by US Navy SEALS equipped with lightweight motorboats. Once ashore, the SEALS encountered heavy resistance from PDF forces, and four of the SEALS were killed.

At 1:00 am US Army Ranger units of Task Force Red started low-altitude parachute jumps over the Rio Hato PDF base west of Panama City. After a brief engagement with the Sixth and Seventh Infantry Companies of the PDF, the Rangers captured Rio Hato and 250 PDF troops. In a second operation of Task Force Red, other US Army Rangers parachuted from an altitude of 500 feet on to the runways of Torrijos-Tocumen International Airport, east of Panama City. The low-altitude parachute jumps, intended to get the troops on the ground quickly, resulted in numerous injuries.

A winter storm far away in North Carolina nearly disrupted one phase of 'Operation Just Cause' in tropical Panama. A brigade of the 82nd Airborne Division was scheduled to arrive at the Torrijos-Tocumen Airport less than an hour after Army Rangers began their attack. But the storm delayed half the brigade of reinforcements three hours in starting from Fort Bragg. Meanwhile, PDF troops of Noriega's Battalion 2000, stationed at Fort Cimarron, began moving in a convoy toward the still-unsecured Pecora River Bridge, which lay between the airport and Panama City.

Control of the Pecora River Bridge was an objective of Task Force Pacific, which was relying upon the scheduled arrival of the 82nd Airborne troops from North Carolina. During the delay the Ranger battalion used AC-130 Specter gunships equipped with Gatling guns, 20 mm cannons and 105 mm side-door howitzers to discourage the Battalion 2000 convoy. The PDF convoy turned around and returned to Fort Cimarron after the first nine vehicles of the convoy were destroyed by Ranger gunfire.

Meanwhile, Task Force Atlantic, composed of units of the 82nd Airborne and the Seventh Light Infantry, seized vital objectives on the Atlantic Ocean side of the Canal, including the Madden Dam, which controls the flow of water through the locks, and the Sierre Tigre electric power generating station, which energizes the Canal facilities. US troops also captured Noriega's Radio Nacional Broadcasting Center and released a number of political prisoners, including two Americans, from Noriega jails.

'Operation Just Cause' established several military records. It was the largest US military airlift since the Vietnam War, and the 3000-man parachute attack was the largest combat jump since World War II. It was also the first military encounter in which American women played a combat role: the 988th Military Police Company, led by Captain Linda Bray, engaged PDF troops in a firefight for control of an attack dog compound. A total of 771 US Army women participated in the invasion. The operation also saw the first combat use of the F-117A Stealth aircraft; a total of six F-117As were deployed in the attack and two reportedly hit PDF barracks with 'pinpoint accuracy.' However, two other F-117s missed their targets because of pilot error.

'Operation Just Cause' made effective use of psychological warfare to produce surrenders of PDF forces without exposing US troops to gunfire. One technique employed the use of tape-recorded sound effects of Sherman tanks rumbling through the area and firing .50 cal machine guns. Another was the use of telephone calls to PDF garrisons advising the commanders to surrender immediately because American A-130 Spec-

An approving crowd looks on as two former PDF members are taken into custody by US Marines in Panama City in December 1989.

ter gunships were en route to destroy their positions (more than 1000 PDF troops lay down their arms after receiving such telephone calls). The US also collected 75,000 enemy weapons simply by offering cash for them, at about $150 per gun. One enterprising Panamanian delivered a PDF armored personnel carrier and collected $5000.

President Bush declared the basic mission 'pretty well wrapped up' by the second day, although sporadic fighting continued. On one occasion, Noriega loyalists lobbed mortar rounds at the Quarry Heights headquarters of General Thurman's Southern Command, but a greater threat was posed by Noriega's 'Dignity Battalions,' composed of some 8000 paramilitary troops who still roamed the city streets and countryside in civilian clothes, conducting hit-and-run terrorist attacks with automatic weapons.

At the end of the first week the US reported 23 soldiers killed and 322 wounded or injured, some casualties resulting from 'friendly fire.' The fighting had also resulted in four US civilian casualties. Panamanian

Below: Panamanians line up to surrender the weapons issued by the Noriega regime before the US invasion. The US cleared the guns from the streets by buying them @$1.50.
Right: Marines process PDF prisoners.

1964-1989
POR PANAMA: LA VIDA
25 ANIVERSARIO
DE LOS MARTIRES DE ENERO
NI UN PASO ATRAS

ATLAS

Previous pages: Some of the damage done in Panama City during the fighting.
Above: A Marine APC stands guard outside Noriega's sanctuary in the Vatican mission.
Right: US troops set up loudspeakers near Panama City's Vatican mission.

casualties tallied in March 1990 showed only 50 soldiers and 202 civilians killed, much lower figures than an earlier reported of 297 Panamanian soldiers and 400 civilians killed, (although the exact numbers of Panamanian casualties continued to be debated). In addition, about 5000 POWs were taken by the American troops. The US organized a new Panamanian police force, the Panama Public Forces (FPP) to replace Noriega's PDF.

PDF resistance collapsed when Noriega, after eluding capture by US forces for several days, sought sanctuary in the Vatican's diplomatic mission in Panama City on Christmas Eve. The capture of Noriega, who still faced criminal indictments in Florida, was one of the objectives of 'Operation Just Cause,' but despite the large US military presence in the country and a bounty of $1 million on his head, Noriega had managed to stay a jump ahead of the US commandos who searched airports and highways, back alleys and the known safe houses and hideaways of the Maximum Leader. Indeed, Noriega was able to slip through American lines on Christmas Eve because US forces watching embassies and other possible escape routes never expected that a uniformed PDF general carrying a Uzi machine pistol and accompanied by four bodyguards would seek assylum in a Vatican mission. Noriega had often been at odds with the Roman Catholic Church, had always protested when sanctuary was given to his political enemies and at one time had hired a 'witch' to put a hex on the papal nuncio, Monsignor Jose Sebastian Laboa.

Noriega's surrender began with a telephone call to the Vatican mission from a Dairy Queen ice cream store in Panama City. Monsignor Laboa responded by sending a car and driver to pick up Noriega and his bodyguards. Noriega surrendered his Uzi and was assigned a simple white room with opaque windows and only a crucifix for decoration. He was warned that if he and his supporters should attempt to take the papal nuncio or the mission hostage, the US Army had been authorized to storm the building. Units of the 82nd Airborne Division had, in fact, surrounded the nunciature. They shot out the streetlights, encircled the mission with loudspeakers, and began blasting the neighborhood with rock music and news bulletins reporting progress in restoring law and order in Panama.

There followed a week of diplomatic maneuvering between the US and the Vatican regarding the validity of Noriega's right to sanctuary as a political refugee. Monsignor Laboa, meanwhile, convinced Noriega that he would not face the death penalty if he surrendered to US authorities. Laboa described Noriega as a man who, 'without his pistol, could be handled by anyone.' Thus Noriega, who had arrived with a gun in his hand, left for Miami with a bible instead.

Other Troublespots

With the end of fighting in Panama, the US Southern Command returned to efforts to end the Latin American drug industry, using American troops to train soldiers in Bolivia, Colombia and Peru to destroy the production of cocaine and other narcotics in their own countries, so as not to 'Americanize' the drug war by direct US involvement. The effort was not popular among Latin Americans, who viewed narcotics as an 'American problem'—as long as Americans were willing to buy cocaine or other drugs for recreational use, the Latin American countries would produce them.

Elsewhere, a civil war that had begun in the West African nation of Liberia in 1989 with an invasion from the Ivory Coast had spread to the capital of Monrovia by May 1990, and this resulted in the dispatch of the 22nd Marine Expeditionary Unit (MEU) of the Mediterranean Amphibious Group to that trouble spot. The original rebel forces had split into tribal factions that fought each other as well as government troops, and tribal armies had slaughtered thousands of civilian members of other tribes. Liberian federal soldiers had also struck out wildly at unarmed civilians and at one point had killed 200 persons who had sought refuge in a Lutheran church in Monrovia. When one of the rebel leaders announced that all foreigners would be rounded up by his forces, President Bush ordered four ships of the Sixth Fleet, the USS *Saipan*, USS *Ponce*, USS *Sumter* and USS *Peterson*, plus 2300 US Marines under the command of Brigadier General Granville R Amos, to Liberia to protect the American population there. The force included a Ground Combat Element led by Lt Col Richard L Pugh (2nd Battalion, 4th Marines), an Aviation Combat Element headed by Lt Col Emerson N Gardner (HMM-261), a MEU Service Support Group (22nd MSSG) under Lt Col J W Head and a small Command Element.

About 2000 American citizens and 500 US Peace Corps workers lived in Liberia. A contingent of 237 of the Marines was helicoptered into Monrovia and evacuated 300 Americans who wanted to leave. The Marines suffered no casualties and, although well armed, completed the mission without firing a shot. About 225 Marines remained in Liberia after the evacuation to protect the US Embassy in Monrovia and the American citizens who chose to stay behind.

Iraq Becomes the Focus

At the same time, the political atmosphere in the Middle East was becoming increasingly belligerent: the White House described it as 'the most dangerous time in 20 years.' Iraq had appeared to be a US-friendly power during the Iran-Iraq War, despite Iraq's 'inadvertent' attack on the USS *Stark* in the Persian Gulf in 1987. Now it had suddenly replaced Libya as the major threat to peace in the Middle East. In 1990 US and British investigators found Iraq trying to purchase illegally the electronic triggers needed to detonate nuclear weapons. (Israeli warplanes in 1981 had destroyed a nuclear reactor near Baghdad said to be capable of producing atomic bombs.) Iraq also was discovered in 1990 to be assembling metal tubing to form the barrel of a 170-foot long 'Big Bertha' type of artillery weapon capable of firing conventional, nuclear or chemical weapon shells a distance of over 1000 miles, bringing Middle Eastern cities as Tel Aviv, Teheran and Cairo within its range. During the Iran-Iraq War, Iraq had developed one of the largest poison gas factories in the world and was reportedly developing biological weapons. It had acquired Soviet Scud missiles capable of hitting targets in Israel and had accumulated with its oil profits enough modern weapons to make Iraq's 1,000,000-man army one of the most powerful in the world. Indeed, Iraq's 5500 tanks, 3500 artillery pieces and 500 combat aircraft were rated as comparable in quality to those of NATO forces.

In July 1990, in a prelude to an invasion of neighboring Kuwait, Iraq accused the tiny sheikdom (it had a standing army of only 20,000), of being involved in an 'imperialist-zionist' plot to manipulate world oil prices and of stealing billions of dollars-worth of petroleum from Iraqi oilfields. On 2 August, Iraq claimed it was 'responding to a call' to aid Kuwaiti rebels and sent a force of 100,000 troops into Kuwait. Within six hours the invasion was complete.

By the following day Iraqi troops were also massed along the border of Saudi Arabia, raising the alarming possibility that Iraq might soon control 45 percent of the world's known oil reserves. While the United Nations condemned Iraq and

During Iraq's seizure of Kuwait in August 1990, Iraqi tanks line up along the shoreline to fire on Kuwaiti ships operating nearby in the Persian Gulf.

debated methods of resolving the crisis, President Bush ordered an aircraft battle group to the Persian Gulf and dispatched Defense Secretary Dick Cheney to Saudi Arabia to obtain permission for US military forces to be based on Saudi soil.

When Iraq invaded Kuwait, US Marine units were already actively engaged in several missions around the world. The 22nd Marine Expeditionary Unit (MEU) was protecting American interests in Liberia, the 13th MEU was afloat and en route to the Subic Bay area of the Philippines, while the Okinawa-based III Marine Expeditionary Force was on the ground in the Philippines for training and providing a deterrent against anti-American terrorist activity. Elsewhere, the 11th MEU was undergoing special operations training in California, and the 24th and 26th MEUs were in pre-deployment workup training in North Carolina. The 7th Marine Regiment was undergoing mountain warfare training in the Sierra Nevade Mountains, and the 1st Marine Expeditionary Brigade (MEB) was exercising in Hawaii. All these forces and more would soon be in the Middle East.

'Operation Desert Shield'

On 4 August, President Bush summoned key White House aides and the top generals in the Pentagon to a meeting at Camp David, Maryland. It was a day of decision. On 6 August the 26th MEU began loading for departure from Morehead City, North Carolina, and the 22nd MEU put ashore a rifle company to protect the US Embassy and then began evacuation from Liberia. The 1st MEB in Hawaii, the 4th MEB on the East Coast and the 7th MEB in California were alerted for possible deployment as the clock for 'Operation Desert Shield' began ticking. It was planned that the 1st and 7th MEBs would be airlifted to Saudi Arabia, taking only their individual arms and equipment: their heavy equipment and supplies would be brought to them by Maritime Prepositioning Squadron (MPS) ships based in Diego Garcia, in the Indian Ocean, and Guam, in the Western Pacific. (An MPS carries three brigade-size sets of equipment and 30 days-worth of supplies.) 'Desert Shield' was to be an acid test of the MPS concept of dispatching Marines and their combat equipment separately. Moving a single MEB of up to 17,000 men by air requires 250 C-141 sorties. To airlift a full Marine brigade *plus* their mechanized and armored equipment and ammunition would require nearly all the aircraft available to the whole US Department of Defense.

The first elements of the 7th MEB began moving out of California on 12 August and arrived at Al Jubayl, Saudi Arabia, on 14 August. The first MPS ships from Diego Garcia, loaded with tanks, howitzers, amphibious assault vehicles, light armored vehicles and other equipment, arrived on 15 August. By 20 August the 7th MEB, under the command of Major General John I Hopkins, had occupied its initial defensive position in northeastern Saudi Arabia and was ready for combat. Meanwhile, Major General Royal N Moore, Commanding General of the 3rd Marine Aircraft Wing, arrived on 16 August to determine bed-down sites for fixed-wing and helicopter squadrons, and the 4th MEB, under the command of Major General Harry W Jenkins, Jr, began sailing from North Carolina on 17 August. On 25 August the 1st MEB began an airlift from Hawaii, and MPS ships from Guam arrived the following day. And on 2 September, just one month after Iraq's invasion of Kuwait, the I Marine Expeditionary Force, under the command of Lieutenant General Walter Boomer, assumed operational control of all US

Below: Marines at Camp LeJeune, NC, train for combat in September 1990, the month following Iraq's invasion of Kuwait.
Top right: Marines at Camp LeJeune board a transport for the Middle East.
Bottom right: The military response to the Iraqi invasion of Kuwait was international. Shown here are British 7th Armoured Brigade Challenger tanks in Saudi Arabia.

Marine forces in the CentCom theater of operations. And still more Marine units were in the air or on the sea en route to join the largest operation in the history of the US Marine Corps.

By November 1990 a fifth of the total US force in this buildup phase, called 'Operation Desert Shield,' consisted of US Marines, and the 3rd Marine Aircraft Wing represented 25 percent of all US fixed-wing aircraft in the theater. At one point, Marine Commandant General Gray commented, 'There are four kinds of Marines: Those in Saudi Arabia, those going to Saudi Arabia, those who want to go to Saudi Arabia, and those who don't want to go to Saudi Arabia but are going anyway.' When 'Operation Desert Storm,' the combat phase, was launched on 16 January 1991 the US Marines had 24 infantry battalions, 40 air squadrons and more than 92,000 personnel committed in the Persian Gulf. The Marines were supported initially by 14,000 soldiers of the 7th Armoured Brigade of the British Army of the Rhine. The brigade, nicknamed the 'Desert Rats' after it defeated the Nazi Panzers in North Africa during World War II, arrived with Challenger tanks, roughly equivalent to the US M60A3, Warrior armored personnel carriers and Scimitar and Scorpion reconnaissance vehicles—very light tanks. The Desert Rats were later detached to rejoin the British 1st Armoured Division and were replaced by the US Army's 'Tiger Brigade,' some 4200 soldiers of the 2nd US Armored Division equipped with more than 100 M1A1 Abrams tanks and a large number of M2A2 Bradley infantry fighting vehicles. The main battle tank of the Marines was the M60A1, retrofitted with applique armor and mounting a 105 mm gun. It was rated as roughly equal to the lighter Soviet T-72, which carried a 125 mm smooth-bore gun.

Diversion in Somalia

As the January deadline for the removal of Iraqi troops from Kuwait approached, a detachment of Marines was diverted to Mogadishu, Somalia, where a rebellion had brought down the government and armed looters had entered the US Embassy compound. Orders went out to the Seventh Fleet in the Indian Ocean, and the USS *Trenton* launched two CH-53E helicopters loaded with 70 Marines. Because of the distance, 460 miles, nighttime aerial refueling was required twice by KC-130 tanker aircraft operating from Bahrain. The Marine detachment landed inside the embassy gate and began rounding up stranded Americans and other nationals, including the Soviet ambassador and 35 members of his staff. It may have been the first time in history that US Marines were sent to rescue officials of the USSR. When the USS *Guam* closed the distance to Mogadishu, it launched five CH-46 helicopters to evacuate 260 people, including 30 nationalities and senior diplomats from ten countries.

'Operation Desert Storm'

The air campaign of 'Desert Storm' was designed first to shape the Kuwaiti Theater of Operations (KTO) through the interdiction of Iraqi air activity in the KTO and the neutralization of Iraqi ground forces within it. As time for the start of the ground campaign approached, the air offensive shifted from pounding the Republican Guard strategic reserve in southern Iraq to attacking Iraqi armored divisions in central Kuwait and to striking Iraqi forward positions. A second objective of the air campaign was to mask the forward movement of allied ground forces to their attack positions. The theater commander, General H Norman Schwarzkopf, estimated the air campaign had reduced Iraqi frontline divisions by at least 50 percent.

Below: Clad in desert camouflage, US JCS Chairman Colin Powell (left) and CENTCOM head Gen H Norman Schwarzkopf receive a briefing at CENTCOM HQ in Saudi Arabia. *Right:* Marine 3rd Battalion M-60 tanks in Saudi Arabia during Operation Desert Shield.

Meanwhile, in the Persian Gulf, well-publicized amphibious rehearsals were held by the 4th and 5th MEBs and the 13th MEU. The 13th MEU had arrived from duty in the Philippines and was designated as Amphibious Ready Group 'A', or ARG Alpha. A second ready group, ARG Bravo, was activated in the Western Pacific. Landing rehearsals were held on the beaches of Oman using helicopters and AAV7A1 amphibious assault vehicles with land speeds of 45 mph and water speeds of up to eight mph when combat-loaded with a three-man crew and 25 Marines.

Although some 17,000 Marines afloat on G-Day were disappointed by being on the sea while their comrades were on the sand when ground fighting began, the importance of their amphibious ruse was apparent after Kuwait was captured: it was found that the

Right: An Iraqi battle map captured after the war shows the heavy defenses mounted against a possible Marine amphibious attack.

entire Kuwait City waterfront had been converted to a concrete fortress by the Iraqi army, and the potential invasion beaches had been liberally laced with land mines. The threat of a Marine invasion had tied down more than 50,000 Iraqi troops while General Schwarzkopf and his staff carefully maneuvered their forces westward and northward behind the Iraqi troops hunkered down in Kuwait. The Amphibious Ready Groups were prepared to hit the beaches if necessary, but they were not needed.

The Iraqi defense strategy was influenced by Soviet advisors and based on Russia's successful defence against the Nazi attack at Kursk in July 1943. It consisted of belts or echelons of huge sand berm barriers, oil-filled trenches and barbed wire, with open areas between systems of barricades. Any enemy armor that got trapped in a barricade or reached an open area before the next barricade would become an easy target for the defensive artillery and tanks. Saddam Hussein had used the technique effectively

Marines in a Hummer gaze at the smoke from a burning oil depot on the Kuwaiti border during the opening days of Desert Storm, the combat phase of the war with Iraq.

against Iran and apparently believed it would work against the allied forces. But for reasons unknown, Iraq did not extend its belts of barricades much beyond its western border with Kuwait, leaving its own right flank exposed.

During the allied air campaign the 1st Marine Division moved forward and slightly to the west. On its immediate right flank was the Joint Forces Command East, composed of Saudi, Kuwaiti, Oman and United Arab Emirate mechanized brigades. The 2nd Marine Division then passed to the rear and moved up, on the left flank of the 1st Marine Division. To the 2nd Marines' left was the Joint Forces Command North, composed of Egyptian and Syrian troops. Still farther west, the US Army VII Corps, which had been stationed in Germany, and the British 1st Armoured Division moved into position. On the VII Corps' left flank was the US XVIII Airborne Corps, and even farther to the west was the French 6th Light Armored Division.

Nearly a month before G-Day (24 February 1991), US Marines had battled Iraqi armor at a nearly-deserted coastal town of Al Khafji on the Saudi-Kuwait border. To test allied defenses, Iraq sent a mechanized column down the road, the tank turrets turned to the rear in a sign of surrender. Farther west, meanwhile, two other Iraqi columns approached. As the Iraqi tanks moved closer, the guns were swung around and began firing at the Marines. The Marines returned fire with TOW antitank missiles and called for artillery and air support. Marine AH-1 Cobra helicopter gunships and Navy A-6 Intruders, supported by Air Force A-10 Thunderbolts, attacked the tanks, destroying half of them. A group of Marines who became separated from their unit hid in a building and directed fire on an Iraqi unit still holding the town. The 1st Marine Division was prepared to retake the town, but General Schwarzkopf recommended that, as a matter of goodwill, Arab troops be allowed to drive the Iraqi soldiers from Khafji. The next day, Saudi and Qatari troops, with US fire support, restored allied control of Khafji.

The start of the ground campaign was announced at 1:00 am on 24 February by the firing of the 16-inch guns of USS *Wisconsin* and USS *Missouri* off the Kuwaiti coast, as if to signal a Marine amphibious assault. Three hours later, the 1st Marine Division began punching its way through two belts of Iraqi fortifications. And at 5:30 am the 2nd Marine Division, with the Tiger Brigade attached, crossed its own line of departure and had equal success in breaching the Iraqi defense system.

The action was the start of the offensive strategy that General Schwarzkopf called his 'Hail Mary' play, based on the football game ploy of sending one's teammates deep into the opposition flanks. By the end of the first day the 1st Marine Division had captured the Al Jaber airfield and the Al Burqan oilfield, had destroyed 21 Iraqi tanks and held 4000 POWs. The 2nd Marine Division engaged and defeated an Iraqi armored column coming out of Kuwait City and had taken 5000 prisoners. Meanwhile, in the XVIII Airborne Corps zone of action, the French 6th Light Armored Division, reinforced with a brigade of the US 101st Airborne Division, punched 60 miles into Iraq and destroyed the Iraqi 45th Division. Another brigade of the 101st, airlifted on 460 helicopters, leapfrogged 113 kilometers into Iraq and established a forward operating base which was given the designation 'Cobra.'

The 101st Airborne immediately spread out from 'Cobra' to cut the roads leading north from Kuwait along the Tigris and Euphrates river valleys. The US 24th Mechanized Division raced north to link up with the 101st, then swung eastward to engage the northernmost Republican Guard divisions of the Iraqi army. Next, the VII Corps started forward west of the Wadi al Batin border between Iraq and Kuwait.

As the US 1st Infantry Division, followed by the British 1st Armoured Division, the US 1st Cavalry, 1st and 3rd Armored Divisions and the 1st Armored Cavalry Regiment, swung northeastward to envelop the Iraqi Republican Guard, the 1st Marine Division destroyed 80 more tanks and took an additional 2000 POWs while clearing the Al Jaber airfield. The 2nd Marine Division attacked north through As Abdallya with similar success. Meanwhile, the 4th MEB, at sea, conducted an 'amphibious demonstration' in the vicinity of As Shuaybah with naval gunfire support from the USS *Mis-*

Below: Marines in the sharp battle for the Saudi town of Al Kafji, fought in January 1991. The Iraqi attackers were driven off with the loss of half their tanks.
Right: A Marine infantryman searches for hidden Iraqis in a liberated Kuwaiti town.

Prone on a Hummer, a First Division Marine directs artillery fire on Iraqi vehicles during the 100-hour liberation of Kuwait.

souri, and the 5th MEB began to fly in its ground combat element, Regimental Landing Team 5, to act as I MEF's reserve.

On 26 February, or G+2, the 1st Marine Division captured Kuwait International Airport, destroying 250 T-55/T-62 tanks and more than 70 T-72 tanks. The 2nd Marine Division took the city of Al Jahra, as well as Mutla Ridge, thereby cutting the major highways leading north and west from Kuwait City. The 4th MEB conducted another amphibious demonstration, this time against Bubiyan and Faylaka Islands controlling the seaward approaches to Kuwait City. The 5th Marine regiment moved up to Al Jaber to aid in POW control.

On the third day of ground fighting the 1st Marine Division completed capture of Kuwait International Airport and prepared for the passage of its lines by Joint Forces Command East to enter Kuwait City. Out in front, a platoon from the 2nd Force Reconnaissance Company reached the US Embassy and found the Stars and Stripes still flying there. The 2nd Marine Division, in the vicinity of Al Jahra, formed the bottom half of a box designed to trap the retreating Iraqi main force along a route dubbed the 'Highway of Death.' When the cease-fire was declared by President Bush at 5:00 am on 28 February almost the entire Iraqi army in the Kuwait theater of operations, estimated variously at between 300,000 and 500,000 strong, had been destroyed.

When the shooting stopped the I MEF had a strength of 92,990, making Desert Storm the biggest Marine Corps operation in history. It had included 24 Marine Infantry battalions and 40 Marine air squadrons. The Marines could claim 1040 enemy tanks, 608 armored personnel carriers, 432 artillery pieces and at least 20,000 POWs. The Marines afloat, meanwhile, had successfully held in place six divisions, or 50,000 Iraqis, on the Kuwait coast, waiting for an amphibious invasion that never came.

The ground fighting was not without losses: five Marines were killed and 48 wounded. Marine aircraft losses for the campaign were six fixed-wing aircraft and three helicopters. The total of US troop casualties in 'Desert Storm' was 148 killed, including 28 dead in a Scud missile attack, and 458 wounded. A military review of casualties noted that 20 of those killed were victims of 'friendly fire,' including seven Marines killed by an Air Force A-10 Thunderbolt in the fighting at Khafji.

The Lessons of 'Desert Storm'

'Desert Storm' provided a successful test of a new Marine Corps war-fighting doctrine that emphasizes maneuver-warfare rather than the attrition warfare of traditional Marine fighting tactics. Maneuver warfare relies on outsmarting the enemy and causing confusion and disorder in the enemy ranks. The maneuver-warfare doctrine was written into the 1988 revision of the official Marine Corps operations field manual by Colonel Mike Riley. It was based on his experiences as a rifle-company commander in Vietnam, where head-on fighting tactics resulted in greater than expected casualties. In Kuwait, the Marines attacked in narrow, multiple thrusts, maneuvering around and behind the Iraqi troops rather than attacking troops straight on.

The brief war was also a successful test of the new US 'AirLand' battle doctrine, emphasizing the close integration of air and land forces, particularly in the 38 days of continuous bombing that crippled the Iraqi military machine in advance of the ground offensive.

New Roles for the Marines

On 6 March, a week after the shooting stopped, the first US Army troops were aboard aircraft returning them home to the United States. But for some US Marines there was a new mission to be fulfilled before they could return home. A contingent of 4000 US Marines, 'Desert Storm' veterans, were assigned in May 1991 to 'Operation Sea Angel,' a 7500-member military mission to aid the survivors of a cyclone in Bangladesh. The storm had killed more than 138,000 persons living in Bay of Bengal coastal areas.

On 29 August 1991 the Marine Corps Reserve, whose members had fought in battles from Belleau Wood, Verdun and Meuse-Argonne in World War I to 'Operations Just

Marines occupied the airport in Kuwait City on 26 February 1991.

In May 1991 a cyclone devastated much of Bangladesh. Here, US Marines on an emergency relief mission land in Bangladesh from an LCAC air-cushion landing craft.

Cause' and 'Desert Storm', celebrated its 75th Anniversary of service 'on the job for Country and Corps.'

At about the same time, General Carl E Mundy, Jr, was nominated to be the 29th Commandant of the US Marines, to succeed retiring General Alfred M Gray, who had directed the swift, complex gathering of Marine Corps units from scattered outposts around the world to the Persian Gulf. Meanwhile, General H Norman Schwarzkopf, in an August 1991 ceremony at MacDill Air Force Base, Florida, handed over the reins of the US Central Command to Lieutenant General Joseph P Hoar, formerly Chief of Staff for Plans, Policies and Operations for the Marine Corps. Hoar, who had served in Vietnam and commanded the 31st Marine Amphibious Unit in Indian Ocean deployments, will supervise US military responsibilities in 18 Middle Eastern countries.

As the last National Guard medical units returned home from 'Operation Desert Storm' in October 1991 US Marines were again on the move to help fight for freedom and to protect American lives in Haiti after a military coup ousted the president of that Caribbean nation. More than 500 Marines were sent to the US Navy base in Guantanamo, Cuba, a short flight from Haiti. The mission was like a bit of *déja vu* for the US Marine Corps, whose troops landed in Haiti in 1915 to control an uprising after the assassination of a president.

Marines were never shy about audacious behavior in battle. The grunts of Task Force Ripper, First Battalion, Fifth Marine Regiment, kept that audacious spirit alive in 1991 as their high profile thinly armored vehicles breached the Saddam Line of fortifications at the start of 'Desert Storm.' The grunts were heard singing over the roar of the amtrac engines the Marine Corps Hymn. If the hymn is ever rewritten, it will surely include one or more lines about the deeds of the Marines in 'Operation Desert Storm.'

A New Role in the 1990s

In the aftermath of the destruction of the Marines' barracks in Beirut in 1983, there had inevitably been speculation that the US Marine Corps was in disfavor with the US military powers. There was even speculation that when the US military was assigned to go into Panama in 'Operation Just Cause,' the Marines were given a minor role because Washington was not convinced that the Marines could handle a really tough assignment. In 'Operation Desert Storm,' however, the Marines made a comeback, renewing their image as an elite and aggressive fighting service.

However, in the years following the Gulf War, the Marines – along with all branches of the US military – found themselves facing a new and different challenge. In a series of overlapping operations, the US service branches were called upon to function more as peacekeeping or humanitarian units. In these three operations – in Somalia, Haiti, and Bosnia – the Marines were asked to serve not as combat troops, not as strike force, but more like police intervening during a domestic dispute. The issues raised by this new role for the Marines were, in turn, part of a larger debate over the foreign policies of the United States in a changing world.

Somalia: A First for the Marines

The first of these new challenges came from Somalia, a country that few Americans had heard of until it collapsed into chaos. Somalia is located on the northeast corner, or Horn of Africa that juts into the Indian Ocean and Gulf of Aden. In the nineteenth century, Somalia was divided up by the British, French, Italians and Ethiopians, but in 1960 it gained its independence. In 1969 General Mohamed Siad Barre led a coup by the military; he soon declared it a 'socialist' state, but after Russia supported Ethiopia in its war against Somali guerrillas, Siad Barre turned to the United States for military and economic aid. Despite his autocratic rule, Somalia was rent by fighting, refugees and famine; in January 1991, Siad Barre was toppled from power and by April 1992 he was forced to flee to Kenya.

Meanwhile Somalia continued to be torn apart by two main warring factions and increasingly more people were forced to flee from their villages and farms, aggravating the famine conditions. By early 1992, the world began to become aware of the starving and dying Somalis as pictures were flashed across television screens. The international relief organizations were finding it increasingly more difficult to distribute food and medical supplies to the starving Somalis, who were gathering in a few areas that could not supply nearly enough food or water for such large populations. (Eventually some 350,000 Somalis are believed to have starved to death during these few years.) As the chorus of protest and outrage began to rise around the world, UN Secretary General Boutros Boutros-Ghali pressured the UN Security Council in July 1992 to approve Resolution 767, calling for UN intervention as needed.

At this point, the United States assumed the lead in organizing a multinational force, designated the United Task Force (UNITAF). President George Bush – perhaps influenced by his success in the Persian Gulf – made the decision to commit US military forces to what was to be a limited humanitarian operation, called 'Operation Restore Hope'. The first goal was simply to force the warlords to back off and allow the relief organizations to get the food and services to the masses of starving Somalis; the second goal was to get these refugees to return to their native villages; a third goal – to eliminate the warring factions and establish some form of stable government – was never clearly articulated.

Early on 3 December 1992, a US task force of four ships moved off the coast of Somali with 1,800 Marines aboard; they formed the lst Marine Expeditionary Force, part of the lst Marine Division. Just after midnight on 9 December, they began to land on the beaches on the edge of Mogadishu. Unfortunately, it was turned into something of a media circus because the international press and TV crews were already there to cover the Marines as they came ashore following their strict rules of landing. Inevitably this led to a certain amount of snickering – to see Marines earnestly acting as though they were threatened, while media people lounged about. But this was in fact an example of what made the Marines the elite branch they are: totally dedicated to discipline, always prepared for the worst.

The Marines moved quickly to secure the harbor and the airport – in fact the Marines did come under fire during these operations – and before the day was overr, giant Hercules C-130 transports and C-5A Galaxies were landing, carrying equipment, supplies, and US Army troops. Within the first few days, the Marines began to move into Somalia, taking another airbase at Bali Dogle, then moving into Baidoa, the largest city in the center of the region most stricken by famine. As these first Marines moved out in their traditional role of vanguard force, the US began to bring in another 5,000 Marines and 20,000 Army troops to mount the major operations. France, Australia, Belgium, India, Sweden and some 15 other nations eventually assigned units in Somalia.

Meanwhile, the Marines were assigned to various special operations. In one such, 'Operation Nutcracker' on 12 January 1993, the Marines made a surprise 'sweep' of the market in Mogadishu to seize as many arms as they could. The next day, the Marines took their only combat fatality, when Corporal Anthony Botello was killed by a sniper.

As the weeks and months passed, the Marines withdrew most of the original force and reassigned other units, but maintained their strength on ships of the US task force offshore. Finally, on 26 April 1993, almost all of the remaining 2,500 Marines in and around Mogadishu withdrew, handing over control of that city to the Pakistani troops operating under the aegis of the United Nations.

Marines patrolling in a M998 Hummer vehicle in the streets of Cap-Haitien during 'Operation Uphold Democracy' in September 1994.

Marines from the 24th Expeditionary Unit returning from exercises in Somalia.

But the Marines did not abandon Somalia. In June 1993, Somalis attacked Pakistani troops, killing 25 and wounding 59. The US dispatched the carrier *Wasp* with 2,200 Marines of the 24th Expeditionary Unit, which had been conducting a training exercise off Kuwait. These Marines went back into Somalia on 24 June to reinforce the UN forces; in the next two weeks another 600 Marines went ashore to perform special missions such as rebuilding roads and a school. In October 1993, 18 US soldiers were killed when they tried to arrest one of the warlords, and the Marines offshore went onto alert status. By December 1993, there were about 9,300 US troops still in Somalia, including some 1,200 US Marines.

Finally on 26 March 1994, the last of the 1,100 Marines of the 24th Marine Expeditionary Unit withdrew from Somalia. They left behind about 80 Marines to guard the civilian diplomats in the US Liaison Office in Somalia. (In September 1994 these diplomats and their Marine guards relocated to Nairobi, Kenya.) About 2,200 Marines remained on ships off the coast of Somalia in a Marine Amphibious Ready Group. In

November 1994, the United Nations voted to withdraw all military forces from Somalia. By that time, the total UN forces were down to some 15,000 and in the following weeks, most of these were withdrawn.

By the end of February 1995, the last UN troops left to be withdrawn from Somalia were some 2,400 Pakistani and Bangladeshi troops. The warring Somalis had become more aggressive and it was feared that some would attempt at least to seize arms and equipment and even to inflict casualties; it was decided to send in a force to serve as the rearguard for the withdrawing of troops. The units chosen were 500 men of the 13th Marine Expeditionary Unit along with 350 Italian Marines. They began to go ashore shortly after midnight on 28 February 1995; during 73 hours ashore, the Marines engaged in 24 minor fire-fights as the UN troops withdrew; by early morning of 3 March, all the UN troops as well as the US and Italian marines had left Somalia.

Although the main mission had been accomplished – namely, the elimination of starvation – the operation in Somalia had been frustrating for all involved, but especially for the US Marines. Here were troops trained specifically for combat as an aggressive, mobile, quick-strike force, yet in Somalia they had been forbidden to exchange fire except when directly attacked. It had taken great restraint; it had been a true test of the new posture of the US Marines.

A Marine Corps Ch-53E lands on the deck of the lead ship of an amphibious ready group in the Adriatic Sea off the coast of Bosnia.

Haiti: A Familiar Problem

Even before the last of the US Marines were out of Somalia, the US faced another crisis closer to home – the Caribbean island-nation of Haiti. Unlike Somalia, Haiti has a long history of dealings with the United States. In fact, the US Marines had effectively 'policed' Haiti from 1915 to 1934 (see pages 59-60, 77-78). After the Marines left, the island went through one dictator after another, the most notorious of which was 'Papa Doc' Duvalier, who ruled from 1957 until his death in 1971; his son Jean-Claude assumed power but was forced to go into exile in 1986. Another period of unrest followed, until in December 1990 a popular Roman-Catholic priest, Jean-Bertrand Aristide, won a free election for the presidency. However, he was overthrown in September 1991 in a military coup led by Lt Gen Raoul Cedras.

The Organization of American States immediately imposed an economic embargo on Haiti but this only intensified poverty and drove more people to flee the island. By the summer of 1994, conditions had become so bad on Haiti that the United States and several Latin American and Caribbean nations threatened to take military action unless Cedras allowed Aristide to return to office. Just before a scheduled air raid on Haiti on 18 September 1994, a three-man US negotiating team (former president Jimmy Carter, General Colin Powell, and Senator Sam Nunn) got Cedras to agree to go into exile. He left on 10 October and Aristide returned on 15 October.

Months before this, the US had dispatched to the Caribbean a 2,000-man Marine force on a small naval task force led by the USS *Mount Whitney*. They practiced their invasion skills and evacuation techniques on the beaches of Puerto Rico and the Bahamas in case they would be assigned to face hostile forces on Haiti. Instead, with Cedras's capitulation, on 19 September the first 2,000 US soldiers went quietly ashore at Port-au-Prince, Haiti's capital and main port. On the 20th and 21st, a force of 1,700 US Marines went ashore at Haiti's second city, Cap-Haitien.

The Marines' assignment was to disarm as many Haitians as possible and to ensure that no major resistance was mounted by anyone opposing Aristide, but they were told not to intervene if Haitians appeared to be attacking each other. This put considerable strain on the Marines, who found it hard to stand by during several incidents. The one major confrontation occurred on 24 September 1994, when a Marine unit felt that Haitian police were about to mount some kind of attack; in the ensuing firefight, 10 Haitian policemen were killed by the Marines.

The US Marines were intended to be simply the vanguard of a multinational force and there were some troops from other Caribbean and Latin American nations in Haiti. But the 23,000 US troops remained at the core of the military presence. By April 1996, most of the US soldiers and all the Marines were withdrawn from Haiti, but in the months that followed small Marine units were sent back into Haiti for what were officially called training exercises; more likely they were assigned to prevent the country from once more drifting into disorder and violence. It remained uncertain when the last of the US military would be withdrawn from Haiti, but there was determination not to let them become involved as they had been earlier in the century.

US Marines from 173rd Airborne Brigade, from the Southern European Task Force, on patrol in Southern Kosovo in April 2001.

Bosnia: The Marines to the Rescue

The third operation that involved the US Marines in some of the same issues as those raised by Somalia and Haiti came with the commitment of US troops to Bosnia. Bosnia-Herzegovina had been one of the six constituent republics of the Yugoslavia that emerged from World War II. In a referendum in March 1992, a majority of Bosnia's people voted to secede from Yugoslavia, but this was strongly opposed by the Serb minority in Bosnia-Herzegovina. Within a month, the Serbs launched what quickly grew into a bloody civil war against the Muslim majority; in July 1992, the Croats, another minority in Bosnia, decided to take advantage of this disorder and also turned against the Bosnian Muslims. Month after month, year after year, the fighting dragged on, leaving much of Bosnia destroyed and increasing numbers of people on all sides dead.

From the first months, the international diplomatic community had attempted to negotiate an end to hostilities, but all efforts failed. As early as June 1992, the first elements of a UN peacekeeping force had been inserted in Bosnia but they had a strictly defined mission of trying to protect shipments of food and medicine for the civilians. The United States chose not to assign any ground troops to this UN force, made up of European and Canadian troops, but did assign air support. By 1994, US Marine pilots were among those who flew reconnaisance missions from US aircraft carriers off the coast of Bosnia and from a US airbase at Aviano, Italy. By October 1994, NATO airplanes were bombing selected Serb targets such as weapons depots and artillery emplacements. Then, in November 1994, when it appeared that UN peacekeepers in Bosnia were being held hostage by Serbs, 2,000 Marines were dispatched as part of a US Navy amphibious group that took up station off the coast of Bosnia. Their assignment would have been to go ashore to rescue UN peacekeepers, but the Serbs released them and the Marines were not needed. They continued to conduct training exercises in Albania, which borders Yugoslavia, in case they would be asked to go into Bosnia. Near the end of May 1995, Serbs once more began to take UN peacekeepers hostage in retaliation for NATO air strikes. The US moved seven ships with some 2,000 Marines of the 24th Marine Expeditionary Unit off Bosnia but by 18 June the Serbs had released all the hostages.

Earlier in June, though, the Marines played a dramatic role in the Bosnian affair. On 2 June, US Air Force Captain Scott O'Grady, flying an F-16 on a patrol mission from Aviano, Italy, was shot down in Serb-occupied territory. His fate was unknown for several days, but on 8 June he was able to send a radio message establishing his whereabouts. A US Marine unit was selected to conduct the rescue operation, and as 40 US planes flew overhead, two CH-53 Sea Stallion helicopters with 40 Marines landed near the woods where O'Grady was hiding. O'Grady ran some 50 yards to get into one of the helicopters; at least one missle was fired at the departing helicopters, but the Marines had carried out their mission.

By the fall of 1995, increased international pressure was forcing the leaders of the warring factions finally to negotiate a truce. At this time, President Clinton stepped in and invited negotiators to the Wright-Patterson Air Force Base, outside Dayton, Ohio, where they were virtually locked up until on 21 November they reached an agreement. (It was formally signed in Paris on 14 December 1995.) Part of the Dayton Agreement called for assigning a NATO peacekeeping force of 60,000 (30,000 to be American troops) to Bosnia-Herzegovina and Croatia. In preparation for this major force, 22 US Marines (along with 78 other US military personnel) flew into Sarajevo on 10 December. These Americans were part of a NATO advance force assigned to perform security work at what was to become the NATO headquarters as of 19 December.

In the weeks that followed, some 20,000 US Army troops – most from Germany – were brought into Bosnia and Croatia. Consistent with their mission, the Marines did not join the NATO ground force in any numbers, but Amphibious Ready Group-4, with 2,000 US Marines of the 26th Marine Expeditionary Unit, had been stationed offshore since September 1995. They would go back to the States in February 1996 but would return again in November 1996 as part of the rotating 'special operations capable' force assigned to the Adriatic Sea off Bosnia. Between June and October 1996, the Marines' 1st Unmanned Aerial Vehicle Squadron (with 180 men and women) was stationed in Bosnia, the first Marine unit assigned there as part of the primary NATO operation.

In Harm's Way

As 1997 commenced, all but a handful of Marines had left Haiti, Kuwait/Saudi Arabia, and Bosnia, but some 4,400 combat-ready Marines remained 'forward deployed' on ships in the Mediterranean Sea and Persian Gulf. Other Marine units, assigned to the US Central Command that was responsible for US security interests from Africa to Central Asia, were also deployed on ships in the Atlantic Ocean, ready at a moment's notice to move into action. They did not have long to wait. In May 1997, a military coup overthrew President Ahmed Tejan Kabbah, the freely elected ruler of Sierra Leone. Intending to restore Kabbah to power, troops from neighboring Nigeria landed at the country's capital and major port, Freetown, and hundreds of foreigners found themselves trapped and at risk. Between 30 May and 3 June US Marine helicopters landed at a hotel in Freetown and ferried some 2,100 foreigners, including 360 Americans, to safety aboard the USS *Kearsarge* 12 miles offshore.

US Marines continued to find themselves on the front lines, at risk in unexpected places. On 7 August 1998, terrorists exploded bombs at two US embassies in Africa, one in Dar es Salaam, Tanzania, and the other at Nairobi, Kenya. In the former, 11 people were killed, all Tanzanians employed at the embassy. In the Nairobi bombing, among the 213 killed were 12 Americans, including a US Marine sergeant assigned there as a guard; another US Marine was wounded, as was a Marine's wife who worked in the embassy. High on the list of those suspected of involvement in these bombings was Osama bin Laden, the Saudi multimillionaire known even then to be providing support to militant Islamic terrorists.

In 1999, the US Marines were placed on full alert when NATO decided to intervene in Kosovo, where Serbians loyal to Slobodan Milosevic of Yugoslavia were committing genocide – under the abhorrent euphemism 'ethnic cleansing' – to rid the area of its majority population of ethnic Albanians. The NATO-sponsored bombing and air attacks on Serbian targets commenced on 24 March 1999, with USMC pilots among those participating. President Clinton also called up some Marine reserve personnel. In the end, Serbia agreed to terms before there was any need to introduce ground troops into combat in Kosovo, but in June some 2,000 US Marines went to the Former Yugoslavian Republic of Macedonia (FRYOM), part of a NATO contingent assigned there to take control of the eastern zone of Kosovo.

A different kind of incident that occurred back in February 1998 was to have long-term repercussions. A US Marine Corps EA-6B Prowler on a training mission was flying low in the Dolomite Mountains in northern Italy when it accidentally severed a cable carrying ski lift cable cars; one of the cars plummeted some 300 feet to the ground and all 20 people aboard were killed. In the military trials that followed, the pilot was acquitted of charges of involuntary manslaughter but was found guilty of removing and destroying a videotape made during the flight. His navigator was found guilty of the same charge, and both men were dismissed from the service. This tragedy raised serious issues as to whether there was adequate communication between the Marine and Air Force officials, proper training and briefing of flight crews, and provision of up-to-date maps. Similar questions had to be asked throughout the service branches, especially in an age when operations required instantaneous communication; the result was an agreement to provide hardware, training, and commitment to a unified inter-branch communications system.

Military aircraft are at risk – all service pilots accept it. But when there are a series of crashes involving the same model, it is no longer a matter of acceptable risk but one of equipment safety. Between 1991 and 2000, the V-22 Osprey, an innovative tilt-rotor aircraft designed to take off and land vertically like a helicopter but fly like an airplane, had been involved in 4 accidents in which 30 Marines died. The Marines had regarded this plane as critical to their aviation plans, because of its speed, cargo capacity, and ability to fly more than 2,100 miles without refueling, but after a crash in December 2000, all Ospreys were grounded. When its problems are identified and corrected, the Osprey will be restored to active service.

On 11 September 2001, two hijacked commercial airliners slammed into New York City's World Trade Center and another crashed into the Pentagon. No US Marines were among the casualties. President George W. Bush responded by announcing that the United States was committed to tracking down the terrorists responsible for the attacks, in particular the Taliban rulers of Afghanistan who harbored Osama bin Laden, the chief sponsor of the terrorists. The military phase of this commitment, OPERATION ENDURING FREEDOM, commenced on 7 October 2001, with aircraft and missiles targeting Taliban holdings in Afghanistan. Planes and missiles were launched from US Navy ships in the Arabian Sea off Pakistan, and by the end of October US Marine pilots had joined the action against the Taliban. Kandahar soon fell to the combined US forces and within a few weeks most Marines were able to withdraw from Afghanistan, their mission accomplished.

During the early weeks of this operation, with only a few US Army Special Operations troops on the ground in Afghanistan, US Marines were standing by, ready to join the first of any larger ground forces. It was not long before they were called to action. On 25 November, the first major U.S. ground units sent into Afghanistan were Marines from the 15th and 26th Expeditionary Units. Some exchanged fire with Taliban soldiers in the first 24 hours; within a few days, about 1,000 Marines had taken up position near the city of Kandahar and were preparing for the final assault on the Taliban forces there. As a self-contained force – with their own armored personnel carriers, Cobra attack helicopters, and Harrier jump jets – these Marines were expected to lay the groundwork that would allow both US Army and Air Force units to move in.

Commandant of the Marine Corps, Gen. James L. Jones salutes US Marines after their amphibious landing during Bright Star maneuvers in Egypt in October 2001.

Left: Charlie Co. 1/1 of the MEU (Marine Expeditionary Unit) board CH-53 helicopters on USS *Peleliu* for a raid into southern Afghanistan to seize a secret airstrip in November 2001.
Below: The 15th MEU load a HUMVEE equipped with a TOW missle launcher near their base in southern Afghanistan, November 2001.

Operation Iraqi Freedom

The conflict that was officially named "Operation Iraqi Freedom" was in many ways the outcome of three events already described: the Persian Gulf War of 1991, the disaster of 11 September 2001, and the Operation Enduring Freedom launched in October 2001 against the terrorists headed by Osama bin Laden. But to fully understand this relatively brief war and the controversy that it provoked both at home and abroad—although polls consistently showed that a heavy majority of Americans supported the war—it is necessary to locate its roots in those three events, for only then can it be clear why US Marines were dispatched to this Middle Eastern country in 2003.

To start with the Persian Gulf War of 1991, despite the success of the US-UN forces in driving the Iraqis under Saddam Hussein out of Kuwait, subsequent efforts to disarm Hussein met with continuing frustration in the years that followed. The United Nations Resolution 687 of April 1991 required Iraq to destroy or dismantle all biological, chemical, and nuclear weapons or nuclear-weapons-usable material. It also forbade the development of such weapons in the future. But the Iraqis continually failed to comply with this resolution despite UN economic sanctions in place and UN weapons inspectors being on the ground.

By 1998 the Iraqis were demanding an end to the economic sanctions imposed upon their country and forced the UN weapons inspectors to leave the country, allowing them to return only under the threat of US military intervention. Despite the fact that in 1999 a new UN weapons inspection organization was formed, the UN Monitoring, Verification and Inspection Commission (UNMOVIC), and Hans Blix of Sweden was named to head it the following year, Saddam Hussein's regime did not provide full cooperation. Evasion was the rule.

The terrorist attacks on New York City and the Pentagon on 11 September 2001, led not only to the war against the forces of the Taliban and al Qaeda in Afghanistan but to increased confrontations between the United States and Iraq, now labeled a supporter of radical Muslims. Unwilling to accept more possible terrorist attacks on the American people, in September 2002 President George W. Bush asked Congress for the authority to use force against Iraq. This authorization was forthcoming the following month with overwhelming majorities in both houses of Congress. Meanwhile, at the United Nations a new measure, Resolution 1441, was passed by the Security Council. It stated that Iraq was in "material breach" of the earlier UN resolutions and called for new inspections.

Above: During a house by house search on the outskirts of the southern Iraqi city of Nasiriyah a US Marine kicks open a door, March 2003. *Right:* A US Marines convoy passes through the southern Iraqi al-Ratka oilfield.

As all of this diplomatic interplay was taking place, plans were well underway by the American government to deploy an additional 62,000 troops to the Persian Gulf region to join the 60,000 already there. By late December 2002, increasing numbers of US Marine and Army units, US Navy ships and their crews, Air Force planes, weaponry, and crews were being deployed in and off-shore countries around the Persian Gulf. Eventually there would be some 250,000 military personnel standing by, 85,000 of them US Marines, another 30,000 British personnel. Most of the US Marines belonged to the 1st Marine Expeditionary Force, commanded by Lieut. General James T. Conway.

Standing firmly beside President Bush in his determination to challenge Iraq was Tony Blair, the prime minister of Great Britain. On 23 February the United States, Great Britain, and Spain proposed to the Security Council that a resolution be passed ordering Iraq to disarm. Blair backed this up on 7 March by proposing an amendment setting 17 March as the deadline for Iraq's compliance. France, however, made it clear that it would veto any resolution authorizing the use of force against Iraq, and Germany, China, and Russia stood with France on this issue.

Undeterred by this opposition, on 16 March President Bush met with Prime Minister Blair and Spanish Premier Jose Maria Aznar in the Azores. They announced they would give diplomacy one more day to work; then, they made it clear, they would go to war to disarm Iraq with or without UN approval. The next day Bush gave Saddam Hussein and his sons a final ultimatum: leave the country within 48 hours or face war. The president explained, "We are acting because the risks of inaction would be far greater." On 18 March the British House of Commons backed Blair on a 412-149 vote to use "all means necessary" to disarm Hussein.

The buildup of US military forces in the eastern Mediterranean and the Persian Gulf was by this time well in place. By the time the war began, the US had the support not only of military units from Great Britain and Australia but also at least indirect support by some 35 other nations the Bush administration claimed were in support of the use of armed force against Iraq. And by this time President Bush had widened the goals of the war, now asserting that the military action being taken was being carried out to help the Iraqi people achieve a "united, stable and free country."

What the United States chose to call Operation Iraqi Freedom began on 19 March 2003, with a surprise air assault on targets in Baghdad designed to eradicate Saddam Hussein and his closest group of leaders. Tomahawk Cruise missiles were fired from US Navy ships in the Persian Gulf and the Red Sea, and although it was not clear that they had killed any of their intended targets, this did announce to all doubters that this was to be a war to the finish. Less than 24 hours later, the first units of US Army and British Marines began to move from bases in Kuwait into southern Iraq. Marines of the First Marine Expeditionary Force were quick to follow—indeed, the first US soldier to die in the war was a Marine, shot while approaching an oil depot, for as part of the advance on Basra the Marines had moved to seize control of Iraq's southern oil fields.

The first days of the ground war were marked not only by the advance of coalition forces north from Kuwait into Iraqi territory, but with massive air support. US Marine planes—both fixed wing and rotary blade aircraft—were taking off from US Navy carriers in the Persian Gulf in a constant stream of sorties to provide air support for actions

Right: Shown through a night vision lens, US Marines spend their first night in southern Iraq, 21 March 2003.
Below: Iraqi soldiers surrender to US Marines in the desert in southern Iraq, 21 March 2003.

on the ground, to perform surveillance and reconnaissance missions, and to attack selected Iraqi targets. The 1st Marine Expeditionary Force, in fact, had more than 100 F-18 and AV-8B warplanes and 50 AH-1 Cobra helicopter gunships assigned to softening up Iraqi forces before the Marines themselves moved forward. Among the first casualties of the war were four Marines who went down with their Sea Knight helicopter carrying 12 British commandos back from a raid.

After the first few days of an unexpectedly quick advance, US forces including Marines seemed to come to a halt, in part due to blinding sandstorms, in part due to a need to allow supplies of all kinds to catch up with forward units, and in part due to unexpected opposition from irregular Iraqi forces—often posing as civilians. But within a few days, the troops were on their way again, with US Marines as always often taking the brunt of the Iraqi opposition. In the 300-mile race to Baghdad, in fact, the Marines made one of the longest continuous drives from a starting base in their history. And in one of the most daring operations, a small unit of Marines descended on a hospital where Army Private Jessica Lynch was being held as a wounded POW and managed to get her out alive. Marines were also the first to break through into the suburbs of Baghdad on 7 April. Two days later the world watched as a statue of Saddam Hussein in the center of Baghdad was toppled. By 21 April, when it was clear that Saddam Hussein's tyrannical rule was over and his country lay in ruins, US Marines were being pulled out of certain posts and replaced by US Army forces—Marines are not trained or equipped to oversee the rebuilding of the civil infrastructure.

The price in blood for the United States was 131 American troops losing their lives (113 in action with Iraqi forces), along with some 500 wounded. The Marines' toll of 62 dead reflects the leading role they take in combat. Much still had to be done to finish the war and put Iraq back together. The coalition forces now faced the tasks of ending the futile resistance of Saddam's remaining loyalists; finding and eliminating Iraq's weapons of mass destruction; capturing and eliminating terrorists both in the Middle East and worldwide, including those with tied to the al Qaeda terror network; and funneling in humanitarian aid to the Iraqi people and assisting them in establishing a representative government in their homeland.

The Marines in the New Millenium

Each of the operations conducted by the US Marines starting in the 1990s had a distinctive profile but they shared several characteristics that raised questions about the future role of the Corps – indeed, about all branches of the service. Among the most contentious was the ongoing debate about the use of highly trained military forces for humanitarian missions. Policy questions aside, also at issue was the cost of such spe-

Above: Members of the US 15 Marine Expeditionary Unit (MEU) fire a "javelin" rocket while engaged in battle at the port in Umm Qsar in southern Iraq, 23 March 2003.
Left: Marines move toward a path connecting with Highway One to Baghdad, 6 April 2003.

cial operations: At a time when overall defense spending was declining, they made severe demands on the Marine Corps' budget, forcing cutbacks in regular training exercises, maintenance and repair of equipment, and procurement of new weapons. Meanwhile, the Marines, like all the service branches, were forced to close down or combine several of their bases around the world.

In the wake of the September 11 disaster, the conventional wisdom was that warfare would never again be the same. Terrorism, biological/chemical warfare, electronic and other new weaponry: clearly these would make new demands on the military. But the time-tested methods and the tradition of valor that have always characterized the US Marines will never be obsolete.

Although no Marines lost their lives in the September 11 disaster, two Marine reservists did play a role in the events of that day, illustrating the ethic that makes the Corps all that it is. Working at his civilian job in Connecticut when he heard that the towers had collapsed, Marine Reserve Sergeant David Karnes immediately left his office, donned his uniform for identification purposes, and drove all the way to the site. There he met up with another volunteering Marine reservist identified only as Sergeant Thomas and together they began to search for survivors in the rubble. That afternoon, hearing voices from beneath the wreckage, they burrowed down as deep as they could to aid the survivors, who turned out to be two New York Port Authority policemen. Unable to free them on their own or to get the attention of anyone around to help, Sgt. Karnes used his cell phone to call his sister in Pittsburgh. She then called the NY Police Department, who alerted rescue workers at the site. Crawling into the pile of rubble at great personal risk, the two Marines remained with the trapped men for some 18 hours – a classic example of the courage and dedication that distinguish the US Marine Corps.

Perhaps it was best expressed by General Charles Krulak, who served as the 31st commandant of the Marine Corps (July 1996-June 1999) before being succeeded by Lt. General James L. Jones: 'The Marine Corps will be the nation's force of choice, a certain force for an uncertain world. No matter what the crisis or threat, the nation will have one thought: "Send in the Marines!"'

Right: A female member of the US Marines carries her weapon and combat pack. As the US combated Iraqi resistance on the way to Baghdad they flew in more troops on transport helicopters escorted by Cobra helicopters as seen in the background here. *Below:* A US soldier looks on as a statue of Saddam Hussein falls to the ground in Baghdad on 9 April 2003. Iraqis attacked the statue in Paradise Square and when US Marines noticed that they need some help in toppling it, they intervened.

EL
086

HISTORY OF THE US AIR FORCE

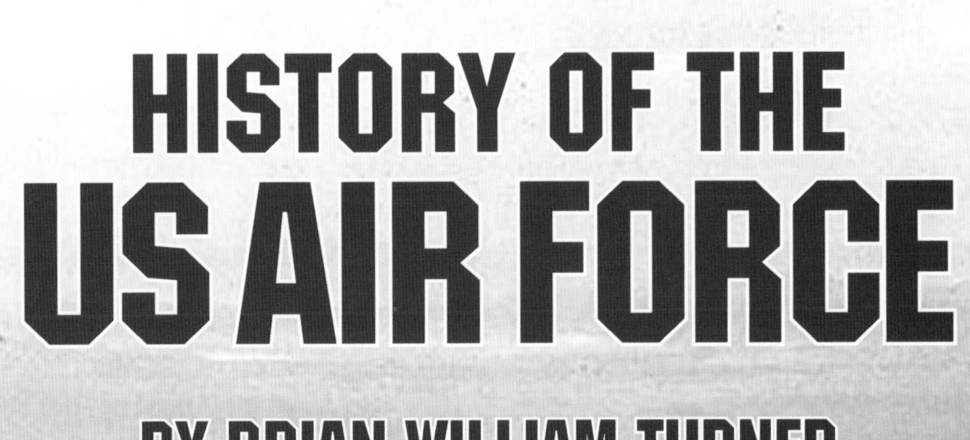

BY BRIAN WILLIAM TURNER
AND BROOKS ROBARDS

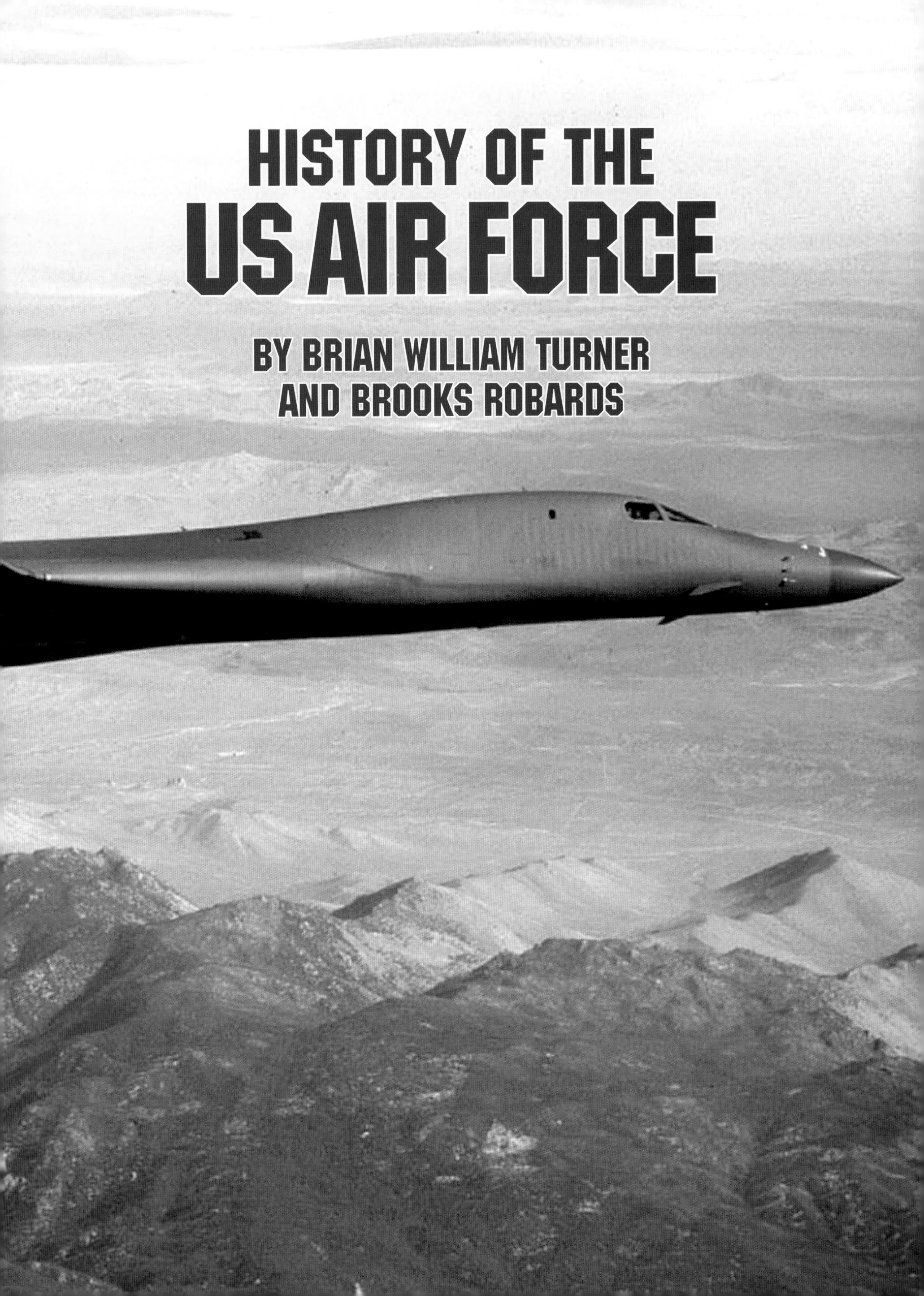

CONTENTS

INTRODUCTION

The United States Air Force is today respected—by friends and enemies alike—as one of the great military organizations in the world, a proud and powerful arm of the nation's military. Today, most Americans take this for granted—for them, the Air Force has always been there in the front line of the US defensive and offensive capabilities. Its planes are overhead and its personnel are everywhere. Yet few probably know of the true history of this grand institution.

In fact, a history of the United States military's air branch is, literally speaking, about two air forces: the air force that existed up until 1947—known, as this volume recounts, by a frequently changing series of names—and the United States Air Force that was formally established that year. But that said, it is basically the history of one continuous arm of the nation's military, and it is all the more fascinating for having passed through so many transformations in such a relatively short time.

That the USAF—to give it the acronym by which it is commonly known today—is the youngest service branch comes as no surprise, especially after December 2003 with its many public observances of the centennial of the Wright brothers' first flight. No one would expect an air force before then, and in fact it was 1907 before the Army created an Aeronautical Division. But as this history makes clear, the effort—the quest, really—to achieve free and controlled flight through the air began many centuries earlier, and the US Army actually had a balloon corps as early as 1861. The full story of the origins and evolution of the US military's air force is only one of the many special features of this book.

In addition to being the youngest, the USAF is arguably the most glamorous of the service branches. There is something special that accrues to members of the air force—any nation's air force—whether it be due to the risk assumed by pilots who take their planes aloft or the disdain for military formalities traditionally shown by air force personnel on the ground.

This 'specialness' is related to another aspect of the Air Force that at least pertained in its early decades, an aspect portrayed in early movies involving wartime aerial combat. In those first decades, airplanes as machines and flight as a skill were so new and so specialized that the relatively few men—and in the military they were all men—who mastered both saw themselves as forming a sort of fraternity, a brotherhood of knights of the

air. This emerged in the first war in which enemy pilots began to hunt each other down—World War I—when pilots sat in open cockpits and made eye contact with their opponents only yards away. There was a certain camaraderie among these pilots even as they tried to knock each other out of the sky. (For those who might find this hard to accept, they should be reminded that the most celebrated German fighter pilot of World War I, Manfred von Richthofen—whose role is discussed in this volume—shows up as the relatively congenial persona of the 'Red Baron' in the Peanuts comic strip.)

Of course this spirit has pretty much vanished in the world of modern air warfare. There is little chance for camaraderie when a plane is hurtling through the air at twice the speed of sound and firing missiles from miles away, or when planes flying at 35,000 feet can drop 'smart bombs' that devastate entire communities. The air force of the 21st Century is a dramatically different organization from that established in 1907. The sheer diversity and complexity of the technology behind the planes and weaponry available is beyond most people's comprehension. And the USAF's missions include far more than just standing by to fight wars—although, in fact, they continue to be called on for such duty even as this book goes to press. For example, the USAF is heavily involved in the nation's space program; it also is frequently called on to perform humanitarian missions for peoples in crisis around the world—even for some whose national leaders are regarded as potential threats.

Yes, the USAF has come a long way from the days when its sole mission was to prepare for and fight aerial 'dogfights' (a term that itself evokes a now vanished world). The complete story of how a small American air service emerged and then evolved into the mighty USAF is recounted in the narrative that follows, a narrative that also continually places this service branch's story into the context of broader currents of history. Finally, the story is supplemented and enhanced by hundreds of illustrations to make for a truly multidimensional history of the United States Air Force.

The combination of experience, technology, and raw firepower makes today's United States Air Force the best in the world. The F-15 Eagle (above left) enjoys air superiority with its speed and maneuverability, while the E-3 Sentry AWACS (above right) provides the eye in the sky for an advanced flying force that includes the radar-evading B-2 Spirit stealth bomber (left).

CHAPTER 1
THE BEGINNINGS OF FLIGHT AND MILITARY AIR FORCE

THE BEGINNINGS OF FLIGHT AND MILITARY AIR FORCE

'Given the proper power and inclined at the right angle, a barn door could be made to fly.'
-- *Wilbur Wright*

Previous page: **On 17 December 1903, at 10:35 am, Orville Wright took to the air for man's first powered flight. The Wright Flyer was in the air for 12 seconds and traveled a distance of 120 feet.**

Above: **An illustration of man's first free ascent from earth. The Montgolfier brothers' balloon took off from Versailles, France, on 21 November 1783.**

Below: **Leonardo da Vinci was dreaming of manned flight centuries before the Wright Brothers. Here, da Vinci drew his notion of what a helicopter might look like.**

The history of manned flight begins in 1783 with 'a cloud in an envelope,' a balloon over France. In 1903 the Wright brothers flew an engine-powered aircraft at Kitty Hawk, and six decades later, humans walked on the moon. The United States Air Force has formally existed only since 1947, but as a vital branch of the military, the air force is rooted in the history of the human endeavor to fly and to gain military advantage through air power.

The yearning to fly begins in universal dreams of escape and transformation. Such dreams come into our consciousness as questions, from which the theorems and equations of scientists and engineers ensue, followed by designs and models, then machines. However fast or high an aircraft flies, however sophisticated its instrumentation, a pilot knows that error or mechanical failure can bring a flight down—a risk complicated by the split-second demands of combat. Then as now, an airman places his faith in his aircraft, whether tested in a homemade wind tunnel in a bicycle shop in Dayton, Ohio, or virtually constructed by supercomputers in Houston, Texas.

But as dreams and reality go, flying is not an entirely modern human endeavor. In ancient times the power of flight was reserved for gods. Apollo, for one, lashed his chariot of the sun across the heavens. Legendary heroes of ancient cultures also flew, on a chair to which skyrockets were attached, or on a magic carpet, a winged steed, a giant bird. When mortals sought to emulate the gods by mechanical means, the results were mixed, as the ancient Greek myth of Icarus shows.

Daedalus and Icarus escaped from a tower on wings made of feathers and wax. Daedalus, who made the wings, warned his son Icarus not to fly too high. Icarus disobeyed, the sun melted the wax, and Icarus fell. For all its fatalism, the myth advances the dream of manned flight—namely, that a flyer's fate rests in his hands. However he may have grieved, Daedalus did manage to land safely.

Scientific Efforts at Flight

The science of flight began in classical times: Archytus of Tarentum, Italy, in 400 B.C. created a 'flying pigeon' (or 'stag' in some accounts) made of wood powered by steam—probably a model or toy. It stands to reason that Archytus was not an isolated instance, that other ancients explored aerodynamics and powered flight. Yet centuries passed before any texts appear that address the subject. In the thirteenth century, Roger Bacon, who was familiar with the Arabic manuscripts in which classical thought had been preserved, speculated on the possibility of aircraft, automobiles, and submarines in The Wonderful Power of Art and Nature. Bacon, who was imprisoned by his fellow Franciscans for teaching 'suspected novelties,' did not publish the book, and it only appeared in 1542.

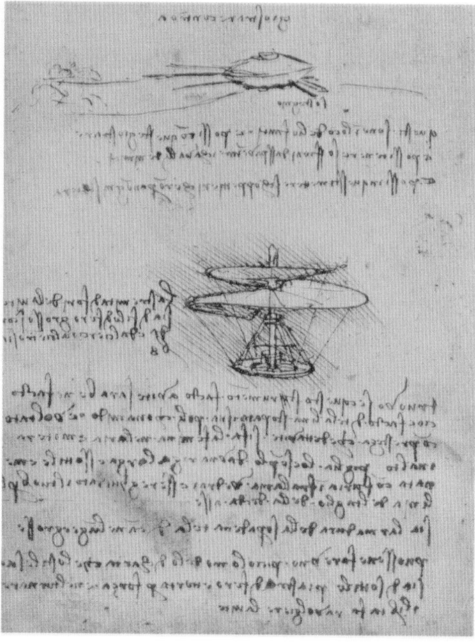

In 1486, Leonardo da Vinci sketched an 'ornithopter,' a machine that beats its wings like a bird. Leonardo also incorporated the "helical" or "Archimedes" screw in the design of a helicopter. Leonardo, like Bacon, kept these notions to himself. Millennia after the myth of Icarus, humankind was not ready to intrude upon the heavens. The principles of aerodynamics that had stirred ancient minds came to fruition only when the Enlightenment arrived and the scientific method tipped the scales in favor of flying.

Ballooning began in France on 19 September 1783, at Versailles, when Joseph and Jacques Montgolfier tested the effects of balloon ascent on a duck, a sheep, and a rooster. The Montgolfiers next launched a free ascent of a manned balloon on 21 November in Paris, with 400,000 people present (including Louis XVI and Marie Antoinette). During the flight, lasting 25 minutes, the brazier that heated the balloon caught fire, and the aeronauts, Marquis Francois d'Arlendes, a military officer, and Jean-Francois Pilatre de Rozier, a science teacher, spent their journey sponging down a smoldering balloon.

The Montgolfiers had rivals who advocated the use of hydrogen. On 1 December 1783, Jacques A. C. Charles flew in a balloon on a two-and-a-half hour journey of 27 miles; to further demonstrate the superiority of hydrogen, Charles descended to drop off his assistant, then re-ascended. On 7 January 1785, Dr. John Jeffries, an American, and French aeronaut Jean-Pierre Blanchard crossed the English Channel in a hydrogen balloon. Their craft very nearly went down in the channel, but they discarded everything they could, save for a package of mail that became the first international airmail delivery. (Not every "first" was a good thing. Pilatre de Rozier, the original aeronaut, became the first to die when his hydrogen and hot air balloon exploded in 1785.)

Despite an American's role in the channel crossing, the United States showed little interest. Not until 1793 did Blanchard launch a balloon on US soil, taking off in Philadelphia, as George Washington—along with Thomas Jefferson, James Madison, and James Monroe—watched. Blanchard landed 45 minutes later in New Jersey.

Aircraft in Early Warfare

The United States continued to lag behind the Europeans in aeronautical

Right: **A 1922 drawing showing the evolution of man's yearning to fly, from Icarus to the airplane. The French title reads, 'The most extraordinary conquest of humanity, wings.'**

la plus prodigieuse conquête
de l'Humanité
"les AILES"
Georges Villa
1922

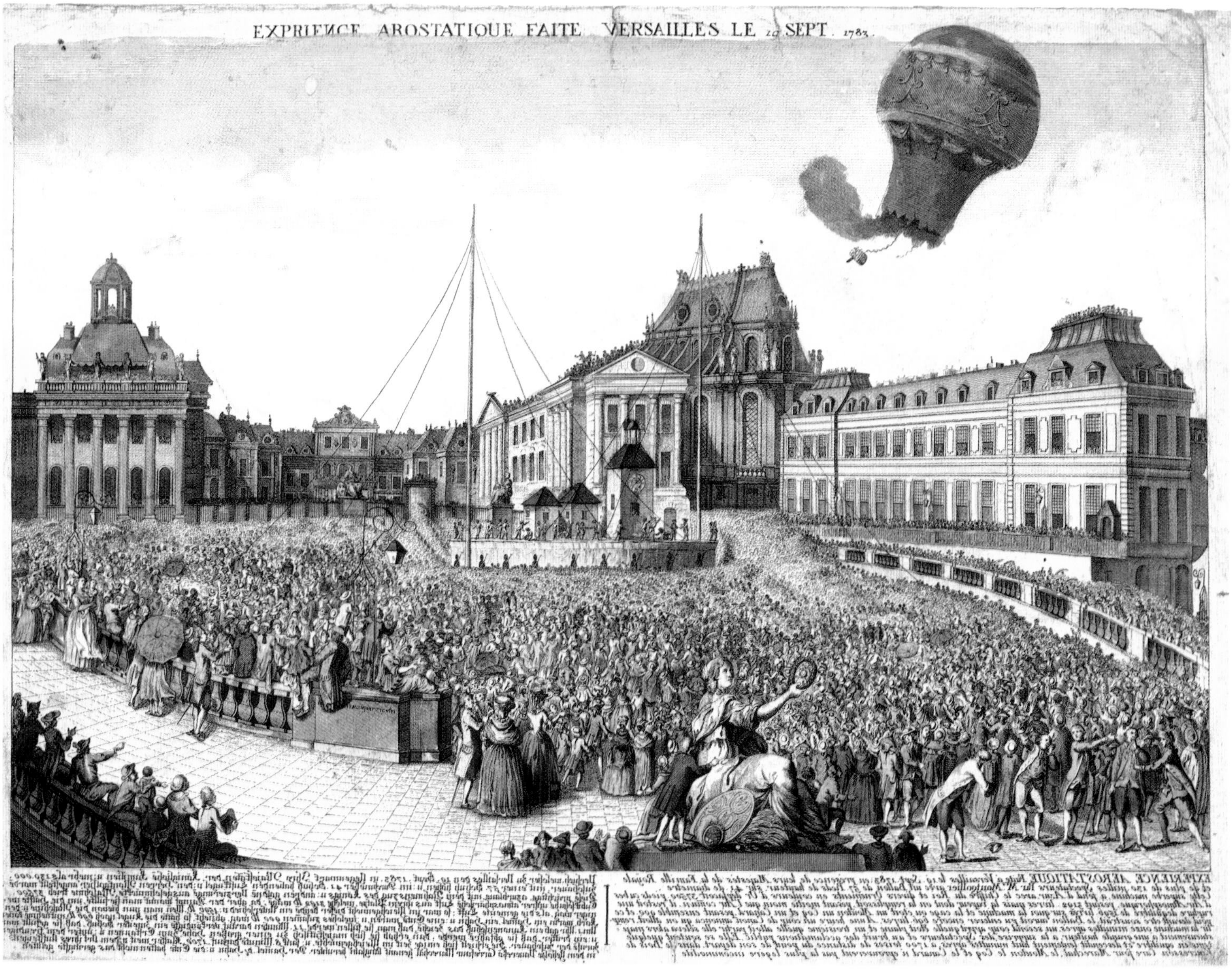

EXPRIENCE AROSTATIQUE FAITE VERSAILLES LE 19 SEPT. 1783.

developments. The French Aerostatic Corps became the world's first military air service and saw action against the Austrians at Mauberge in June 1794. The Corps saw action again in the French Revolutionary Army's victory over the Austrians, also in June, at the Battle of Fleurus in Belgium. (The Austrians protested that balloons were against the rules of war.) Napoleon used balloons during his Egyptian campaign, before disbanding the corps in 1799. Over the next decades there were glimpses of the uses to which an air service might be put. In 1849, for example, unmanned balloons launched from Habsburg ships bombarded Venice.

The American Civil War introduced many military innovations, such as machine guns, ironclad gunboats, trench warfare, and balloons capable of signaling intelligence. Shortly after the war started, Thaddeus Lowe, a balloonist-for-hire, embarked on a flight from Cincinnati, Ohio. Lowe made a forced landing in rebel territory in South Carolina. In spite of having observed Confederate troops, Lowe convinced his captors that he was not a spy. Upon his release, he went to Washington, D. C., and met with Abraham Lincoln in June of 1861. Lowe proposed that his balloons be placed in the service of the Union.

Not for the last time, the military application of aircraft was received with skepticism. General Winfield Scott, Commander of the Army, refused to meet Lowe until Lincoln directly interceded. By July, Winfield ordered the formation of a balloon corps, a civil organization under the Bureau of Topographical Engineers. Other organizational reshufflings followed. In 1862, the balloon corps was transferred to the Quartermaster Corps, and in 1863, it was transferred to the Corps of Engineers.

On 17 June 1861, Lowe inflated a balloon from the gas lines of Washington, D. C., and ascended 500 feet, from where he sent the first airborne telegraph to the War Department and White House. In September of that same year, a balloon was sent up on a tether above Arlington, Virginia, from which intelligence was telegraphed to the ground on Confederate deployments at Falls Church. For the first time, Union artillery was aimed and fired without a view of enemy positions. The War Department approved the construction of more balloons.

Lowe sought to solve the problem of transporting balloons, taken into battle, already inflated, by train or by horse and

Above left: **The Montgolfier brothers flew their hot air balloons before awed crowds in France. Their first passengers were a sheep, a duck, and a rooster.**

Left: **During the Napoleonic Wars, French General Morlot directed the Battle of Fleurus on 26 June 1794 from a balloon tethered overhead. Morlot received and sent orders through a cable leading to the ground.**

Above: **The Army Signal Corps used powered dirigibles in addition to their small fleet of early airplanes. Glenn Curtiss built the engine for the first powered dirigible in North America.**

Below: **Jean-Pierre Blanchard and John Jeffries were the first men to fly over the English Channel in their hydrogen balloon in 1785.**

wagon, and too often punctured or torn apart before reaching the front. In November of 1861, Lowe ascended from a barge in the Potomac—in effect, an early aircraft carrier. In that instance, as in others, the results were mixed. At Fair Oaks, Virginia, in 1862, the balloon corps observations proved crucial to Union victory. In the Peninsula Campaign, the balloon corps delivered vague reports on the strength and movements of Confederate forces, and General McClellan chose to withdraw rather than attack. By 1863 the corps was disbanded.

Above: **Samuel P. Langley's airplane was launched off of a specially constructed houseboat on the Potomac River. This earliest of floating aerial launch platforms led the US Navy to name its first aircraft carrier after Langley.**

Left: **In 1895, German inventor Otto Lilienthal was an early pioneer of manned flight with his experimental gliders. His writings and theories inspired and influenced the Wright Brothers.**

The Confederacy had its own aeronaut, Captain John Randolph Bryan. On 13 April 1862, Bryan launched a hot air balloon made of paper coated in varnish over Yorktown, Virginia. His next balloon, using hydrogen, was made of multi-colored silk, giving rise to the legend that southern ladies had donated their dresses. The military commanders of neither the Confederacy nor the Union were able to envision aircraft as an instrument of warfare. Without support from the military after 1863, balloonists resorted to barnstorming in carnivals.

Decades passed before balloons were reintegrated into US military thinking. In Europe there were sporadic deployments for military purposes. In 1871, the French used balloons to help break the Prussian siege of Paris. In the 1880s, balloons were used in colonial campaigns, by the British in Africa, by the French in Madagascar and Tonkin. In the 1890s, US Army Signal Corps commander General Adolphus Greely ordered the construction of balloons, one of which would see action on 1 July 1898 in Cuba during the Spanish-American War. Although the balloon provided observations that helped field commanders revise their tactics at

***Left:* Octave Chanute was an early flight pioneer in his biplane glider.**

***Below:* The US Army was slow to adopt the airplane as a military tool, partly due to the Wright Brothers' secrecy and sky-high asking price for their planes.**

Left: **A drawing of British inventor William Samuel Henson's proposed steam-powered airplane. The idea never got off the ground.**

Below left: **Glenn Curtiss won the Scientific American trophy for flight with his 'June Bug' in 1908. The plane incorporated the triangular wingtip aileron design of Alexander Graham Bell.**

Below: **Brigadier General James Allen is considered the father of the American air force. As chief of the Army Signal Corps, Allen authorized an aeronautical division to oversee 'all matters pertaining to military ballooning, air machines and all kindred subjects.'**

the Battle of San Juan Hill, it also drew fire upon the US troops stationed below. Ultimately, it was riddled with bullets and abandoned.

The Race to Heavier-than-Air Planes

Even as the debate over the usefulness of balloons continued, the race to invent a powered, heavier-than-air flying machine gathered force. Inventors, scientists, military men, and entrepreneurs who undertook the challenge came in two types: those who used gliders before installing an engine and those who built a machine with an engine in place.

Samuel Pierpont Langley belonged to the latter. Langley, the secretary of the Smithsonian Institution, designed an unmanned model powered by steam that flew and landed in 1896. In 1898 he received a grant of $50,000 from the War Department to work on a manned aircraft. Langley was encouraged by his friend, inventor Alexander Graham Bell, who formed the Aerial Experiment Association (AEA), a group that built several aircraft prototypes, including the 'Red Wing' and 'White Wing.' The AEA designed the first seaplane and introduced ailerons—movable flaps on wings to control flight.

In 1903, Langley made two attempts to catapult his aircraft from a platform on a houseboat in the Potomac. On 7 October the gas engine worked, but a strut caught on a part of the platform, causing the aircraft to nosedive into the river. On 8 December the aircraft cleared the platform, and for an instant achieved vertical lift. But the aircraft came apart at once from the stress placed upon it by the too-powerful engine.

On 17 December 1903, two bicycle mechanics from Dayton, Ohio, succeeded where Langley had failed. Wilbur and Orville Wright had been working on the problem of flight during the 1890s. Wilbur's research revealed that human flight with wings was occurring in Germany. Otto Lilienthal had flown gliders from hills outside Berlin more than 2000 times, and had widely publicized his accomplishments. The fact the Lilienthal was killed while gliding did not discourage the Wrights. Around the same time, Wilbur wrote to Octave Chanute, an early aeronautical theoretician and author of Progress in Flying Machines (1894). The two corresponded throughout the design process. With Chanute's encouragement, the Wrights constructed and tested a series of aircraft.

The Wrights were as patient (and as a secretive) as they were methodical. They started modestly, building and testing kites; by 1900, the kites had become full-scale gliders. They transported their prototypes to the dunes outside Kitty Hawk, where for the next four years they made flights, then returned to Dayton to improve their designs. They built a wind tunnel to test wing shapes in their bicycle shop, compiling tables of statistics on lift and drag in order to make an effective airfoil. The key challenge the Wrights faced was to maneuver an aircraft within multiple dimensions, and to achieve equilibrium while always in motion—then as now, a complicated task.

In 1903, aided by Charles E. Taylor, a hired mechanic, the Wrights produced a four-cylinder engine capable of nearly 12 horsepower. Propellers were placed behind the wings for thrust, the 'push' model with which the Wrights were closely identified. A critical innovation in their design was 'wing warping.' Warping, or twisting the wing's edge, served to improve lateral control and guard against roll. In the case of the Wright flyer, the pilot, who was lying down, swiveled between levers that pulled on cables, twisting the wings. In the front was a primitive elevator, referred to as a 'canard wing,' operated by a small lever to raise and lower the nose; in the rear was a double rudder. The Wrights did not catapult the aircraft, as Langley had, but used a rail for a smooth start. A pair of skids sufficed for landing gear.

The brothers tossed a coin to see who would go first, but when Wilbur attempted the first flight on 14 December, the plane stalled and came down at the

bottom of a hill, slightly damaged. After repairs were made, it was Orville's turn on 17 December. Orville succeeded in lifting off for 12 seconds and traveling 120 feet. (The only eyewitness account appeared months later in a beekeeping magazine, Gleanings in Bee-Culture.) For the next several hours the brothers took turns taking off, with Wilbur's fourth flight qualifying as the most impressive: 852 feet in 59 seconds. Upon landing, however, the skids broke. Seconds later, the world's first airplane was tossed about by a gust of wind and wrecked. It was disassembled and stored for years, until it was donated to the Smithsonian in the 1940s, where it has been on display ever since.

The US Military Adopts its First Airplanes

Initially, the US War Department showed limited interest in the Wrights' invention, because of the expensive failure of Langley's machine. Another factor was the control the Wrights exercised over their patent, Number 821,393, issued 22 May 1906. The Wrights repeatedly took rivals to court or responded to countersuits aimed at them, all to establish the primacy of their claim. The US government hesitated to offer the Wrights a contract until these legal matters were settled.

Europe, too, responded with skepticism. The British War Office required a demonstration and made no commitment to purchase the plane, even if it performed well. The Wrights were reluctant to place their invention on display, in part from a fear of piracy. Other nations balked at the price of a single plane: $200,000 (at least $4,000,000 in 2004 US dollars). The Wrights did not fly in public until May 1908, at which point, with an armaments race underway and growing animosity between European powers, the US government manifested more interest. President Theodore Roosevelt, eager to modernize all aspects of US military power, began the process of forming an air arm of the army and procuring a Wright airplane.

The Chief of the US Army Signal Corps, Brigadier General James Allen, signed a directive establishing the Aeronautical Division on 1 August 1907. On 27 December, the Board of Ordnance and Fortification set specifications for a military airplane's speed and weight. The Wrights' competitive bid was accepted, but accidents delayed delivery. In 1908, after a record-breaking test, Lieutenant Thomas E. Selfridge, the army's in-flight observer, was killed in a crash of a plane piloted by Orville. Thus Selfridge (who had tested the Baldwin dirigible, Signal Corps Dirigible No. 1) became the first casualty of a heavier-than-air accident.

Above: **Louis Blériot was the first man to cross the English Channel in a lighter-than-air craft. Blériot's historic flight from Les Barraques, France, to Dover, England, on 25 July 1909, lasted 37 minutes.**

Below: **Eugene Ely takes off from a platform aboard the USS *Pennsylvania* in San Francisco Bay just prior to making the first ever airplane landing aboard a ship on 18 January 1911.**

Orville Wright, who was badly injured, took weeks to recover.

Not until June and July 1909, did the official Army trials of the Wright aircraft take place. In one trial, Orville Wright and the Army observer Lieutenant Frank P. Lahm flew for one hour, 12 minutes and 40 seconds, a new endurance record. Later in the year, Orville and Lahm would achieve another aviation first, flying 10 miles from Fort Meyer to Alexandria, VA, the first cross-country flight. However, Lieutenant Lahm, the first Army airman to receive a Pilot Certificate, would not be regarded as the first Army pilot—that honor that would go to Lieutenant Benjamin D. Foulois.

Lieutenant Foulois was the observer for another Wright aircraft in 1909. Although he received his certificate later than Lahm, he taught himself to fly with instructions mailed from the Wright Brothers, qualifying him as the first Signal Corps pilot, and first navigator, instructor, and observer as well. (Foulois would command the first US air unit to take the field, with the 1916 Punitive Expedition in Mexico.) In the 1909 trial, flown by the now-recovered Orville Wright, the aircraft achieved an average speed of 42.5 mph. Foulois confirmed that the Wright 'push' flyer had met all specifications. In August the Army accepted 'Aeroplane No. 1,' and it was placed under the authority of the Aeronautical Division of the Signal Corps.

The Wright Company became a major supplier of commercial and military

& Ewing
.C.

aircraft during the period before World War I. Their competition came from a company formed by Glenn Curtiss, a motorcycle racer known as 'the fastest man alive.' Curtiss had worked with Bell and the Aerial Experiment Association and he designed his Model D with ailerons, the moveable flaps along a wing's edge, first conceived by Alexander Graham Bell, which replaced wing warping as a means of lateral control. The Curtiss D became the second purchase of the Signal Corps on 27 April 1911.

The U.S. Moves to Build an Air Force

US aviation lagged far behind Europe. France's Voison biplane, for example, took off on its own power and landed on wheels, whereas the Wright model was launched from a set of rails. In 1909, the Frenchman Louis Bleriot crossed the English Channel in a monoplane, using a 'fan type' air-cooled engine. From 1909 to 1910, Congress made little effort to close the aviation gap, repeatedly failing to allocate funds for the Aeronautical Division. The Wrights, like Curtiss, were forced to raise funds for their enterprises by staging air meets. The public appetite for spectacle was gratified, but the Wrights were shaken when several pilots were killed during their exhibitions. Not only was the loss of life regrettable, but the bad publicity did little to help their cause.

Even with limited funding, pilots experimented on military applications. In 1910 the first shot was fired from an airplane, in which a passenger took up a position on the wing and aimed his pistol while the pilot maneuvered around the target. The Army regarded such demonstrations as carnival stunts. The generals, who thought in terms of infantry and artillery, saw the airplane as a means of reconnaissance, as a faster, more flexible, less vulnerable balloon.

The Signal Corps established a flight school in College Park, Maryland, near Washington, D. C. It was at College Park that the young Henry 'Hap' Arnold, future CO of the Army Air Force in World War II, received his training, from the Wright Brothers no less. Arnold passed on what he had learned to new pilots and explored the tactical uses of aircraft, establishing records and taking early aviation prizes.

Many servicemen were intrigued by the promise of flight, but few aircraft were produced. A modified version of the Wright 'B' Flyer became Aeroplanes Number 3 and Number 4, purchased in 1911. The major modifications were the installation of an eight-cylinder engine, capable of a speed of 45 mph, and the addition of ailerons on the trailing edges of the wings in place of the Wrights' lever control system. Among other things, the Wright 'B' was used to conduct bombing trials at the College Park training grounds.

In 1912, the facilities at North Island, San Diego were designated the 'Signal Corps Aviation School,' the Army's first permanent training center for airmen. At the training centers, Wright B and Curtiss 'Jenny' planes were used on military maneuvers; to observe mortar and siege gunfire; to target enemy locations on land and at sea; to signal with small parachutes and pistol flares; to conduct aerial photography; and, most significantly, to experiment with two-way radio telegraphy.

One of the most important developments in aircraft design, apart from ailerons, was the debate over the placement of the engine and the propellers. Aircraft had two basic configurations: 'pusher' and 'tractor.' Pusher aircraft placed the propeller assembly behind the engine, where the thrust pushed the airplane forward. This was the design used by the Wrights. Tractor aircraft, by contrast, had the engine and propeller at the front of the aircraft where the thrust drew or pulled the airplane. The first tractor biplane procured by the military was a Burgess H. The Burgess H started out with a foot-operated throttle, manually operated rudder, no ailerons, and skids for landing gear; in these elements it closely resembled the Wright flyer. Wary of infringement on the patents held by the Wrights, who were notoriously litigious, Burgess introduced new lateral controls, eventually incorporating movable ailerons.

For fiscal year 1912, Congress appropriated $125,000 for military aviation. In 1913, the first bill to recommend a change in the status of military aviation was introduced into Congress. The bill did not pass, but that same year the 1st Aero Squadron was established, consisting of nine aircraft. 'Aeroplane No. 1,' a great stride forward in 1909, was already obsolete, and had been donated to the Smithsonian. The pace of technological change was speeding up, and the Signal Corps was hard pressed to keep up.

In 1912, Wilbur Wright died of typhoid fever. His death came on the eve of a world war that would force the evolution of his flying machine into an efficient military instrument. For now only war provided impetus for such a transformation, a pattern that held true not only for the Great War in Europe, but for the war to follow.

Opposite: **Orville Wright and Lieutenant Frank Lahm during one of their record-setting flights over Fort Myer, Virginia.**

D9516

CHAPTER 2
US AIRMEN IN WORLD WAR I: 1913-1918

US AIRMEN IN WORLD WAR I: 1913-1918

On 28 June 1914, in Sarajevo, as his chauffeur backed out from a dead-end street, the Archduke Franz Ferdinand was assassinated. Gavrillo Princip, who belonged to a Serbian nationalist group, must have been amazed to see the heir to the Austro-Hungarian Empire passing by. Austria-Hungary had long meddled in Balkan affairs, and in 1908 annexed Bosnia-Herzegovina. Princip drew his pistol and shot the Archduke dead. For reasons still debated by historians, Austria-Hungary declared war on Serbia on 28 August, and three days later declared war on Russia.

Within a week the Great War swallowed up a previous century's political arrangements. Germany, allied to Austria-Hungary, invaded Belgium, then drove south, hoping to knock France from the war. Britain cast its lot with France and Russia, forming the nucleus of what would become known as the Allied Powers. The Ottoman Empire aligned with Germany and Austria-Hungary to form the Central Powers. After the firing had ended in 1918, military deaths reached at least 9 million, with 21 million wounded, to which waves of influenza added millions of deaths, more than had been killed in battle.

From 1914 to early in 1917, President Woodrow Wilson would perform a diplomatic balancing act—keeping the United States both neutral and profitable. US industries supplied Britain and France with weaponry and materiel; the Atlantic sea lanes were clogged with US ships, upon which German U-boats preyed. So long as Wilson insisted on the right of the United States to neutral trade, the two nations remained on a collision course.

The Emerging Role of Aircraft

When war broke out in 1914, the newly renamed Air Section of the Army Signal Corps possessed fewer than a dozen military aircraft. Germany, on the other hand, had 180; England and France combined had 184. The major combatants soon recognized the value of aerial combat, and advances were made in design and performance, in gunnery and bombing, and in combat tactics and techniques. The novelty of 'flying machines' gave way to a new dimension of air strategy, and it soon became evident that fighters and bombers would be viable weapons in a nation's arsenal.

The European powers deployed airplanes as the 'eyes of the army.' Pilots on both sides went up each day to photograph the positions at the front. On 22 August 1914, as German troops poured into France, reconnaissance planes provided intelligence that enabled the British Expeditionary Force to organize a retreat, saving many lives. A week later, as the Germans pushed toward Paris, French aerial reconnaissance provided observa-

***Previous page:* The 148th Aero Squadron flew the Sopwith Camel F-1. The Camel was a fierce fighter, responsible for bringing down nearly 1,300 enemy aircraft in less than two years of service during WWI.**

***Above:* The Curtiss JN-3 'Jenny' was used for scouting the Mexican countryside in General John J. Pershing's Punitive Expedition in search of Francisco 'Pancho' Villa in 1916.**

***Below:* Glenn L. Martin in one of his early prototype fighter aircraft. Martin began building airplanes in his auto shop, eventually evolving his hobby into large-scale manufacture of aircraft, including the atomic B-29 'Enola Gay.'**

tions that sent French troops out to attack the exposed German flank. The resulting First Battle of the Marne halted the Germans 25 miles outside Paris.

After the Germans were driven back, the first trenches were dug. From then on the Germans used every means—long-distance shelling, unrestricted submarine warfare, strategic bombing by Zeppelins, gas warfare—to recover the ground they had lost. German Zeppelins conducted bombing runs upon England, 159 in all, resulting in 557 deaths and damages of $7,500,000. On 22 April 1915, Germany made the first truly successful use of poison gas, placing cylinders along the German lines in the Second Battle of Ypres, so that a greenish cloud of chlorine was released and drifted toward French and Canadian troops. On the seas, too, total war was waged. On 7 May 1915, a German U-Boat sank the British liner Lusitania, causing about 1200 civilian deaths, including as many as 120 Americans. Germany quickly promised that its U-Boats would not sink US ships without warning, but an undertow of economic and strategic interests drew the nations ever closer to war.

Lessons from an Expedition to Mexico

The inadequacy of US aerial operations became apparent in 1916. On 9 March, forces led by the Mexican revolutionary, Pancho Villa, crossed into Columbus, New Mexico, and killed 17 American miners. President Wilson directed Brigadier General John J. Pershing to organize the Mexican Punitive Expedition. It was the first time that a US tactical air unit took the field in support of troops. The 1st Aero Squadron had 11 officers, 84 enlisted men, and eight Curtiss JN3 'Jenny' airplanes, and was commanded by Captain Benjamin Foulois, the first Army pilot.

Foulois led his squadron into northern Mexico, from where the pilots (including Lieutenant Carl 'Tooey' Spaatz) patrolled the border, carried dispatches, and

Above: **The French-made Salmson 2A2 was built as a flying reconnaissance platform, as seen here, equipped with a camera for a photographic recon mission.**

Below: **The Burgess-Dunne 'Flying Wing' had a unique design for its day. It was the first plane used by the Canadian Army, mainly for training and reconnaissance, and could be fitted with pontoons for water landings.**

scouted for Villa's forces. Within a month, however, high winds, dust storms, and the inhospitable terrain brought about the destruction or abandonment of six planes; the two remaining planes were so damaged that they had to be condemned. The poor performance of the Jenny showed that it was unsuited for field operations.

Chastened by the Punitive Expedition, and spurred by events in Europe, the Army moved to expand and modernize the Aviation Section. In 1916, the Jenny was modified and re-designated the JN-4. The Signal Corps began ordering more JN-4s, primarily for flight training; some were equipped with machine guns and bomb racks for advanced training. Even so, with hostilities imminent, the Aviation Section was at least two years behind Germany in every aspect of military aviation, with 131 officers, slightly more than 1,000 enlisted men, and fewer than 300 airplanes, almost all of which were unsuitable for combat.

The Air War in Europe

High above the trenches in France, Allied pilots were at liberty to report on formations, munitions depots, and supply and reinforcement movements. Some units communicated to the ground by dropping messages in weighted bundles; others devised signal systems based on the movements of their planes. (Reconnaissance pilots, when required to defend themselves, were the first to fire at enemy planes and also the first to drop grenades.) By 1915, wireless telegraph equipment with which to send messages was added to standard aircraft design. The planes, weighed down by such equipment, became easy targets, so escort fighter planes were deployed for protection.

The trench-bound troops enjoyed no comparable freedom of movement. Every yard of territory cost blood, lungs, and lives. Beginning on 21 February 1916, the Battle of Verdun only came to an end in December with the advent of winter. The result, a draw; the cost, a million casualties. From 1 July to 18 November 1916, the Battle of the Somme produced another million casualties, again without a breakthrough. No military planner could have anticipated such astounding numbers. Given the slaughter overseas, and given the disproportionate means deployed to achieve dubious ends, President Wilson campaigned on, continued US neutrality, and won re-election.

The United States Enters the War

In spite of neutrality, US citizens joined the Allied forces; some enlisted in Canada so they could fight with Britain's Royal

Above: **Although the US Army chose not to buy the Blériot XI monoplane, Louis Blériot found great success building military aircraft during World War I as president of SPAD.**

Right: **Lt. Benjamin Foulois and Philip Parmalee make a reconnaissance run in a Wright Flyer. Foulois was the first US military officer assigned to fly an airplane, and would go on to serve as the Chief of the Army Air Service.**

Flying Corps, and others joined the French Foreign Legion. Members of the Legion transferred to the French Aviation Service, and in time American flyers in France requested permission to form their own squadron, the Escadrille Americaine. The Escadrille flew its first mission on 13 May 1916. Among its celebrated pilots were Raoul Lufbery, William Thaw, Norman Prince, and James Hall—Kiffin Rockwell scored the first victory by the Escadrille when he shot down a German reconnaissance plane. Eventually, Germany protested the use of 'Americaine,' since the United States was neutral: hence, Escadrille Lafayette.

On 1 February 1917, Germany reinstated unrestricted submarine warfare. For war to be avoided, the Germans had to back down from the policy, as they had done in 1915. Wilson's diplomatic efforts fell short; Germany refused to back down. On 6 April 1917, at Wilson's request, Congress passed a declaration of war on Germany. Congress also approved a budget of $640 million for air training and aircraft production, the largest single military appropriation to that point. Major General George O. Squier, Chief Signal Corps Officer, helped design the appropriations bill, and during his tenure, the Air Section expanded to 12,000 officers and 135,000 men.

In those first heady days, the US Air Section set absurdly optimistic goals, based on recommendations from a team headed by Major Foulois, the senior Army flying officer (with assistance from Major Hap Arnold, who was earning a reputation as a competent, even shrewd administrator). The team called for 345 air squadrons consisting of 22,625 airplanes, spare parts for another 17,600 airplanes, and 44,000 engines. The giddiness was contagious, even among the Allies. On 20 July, Winston Churchill, the British Minister for Munitions, promised to replace the attrition of men with a war of machines, 'a cloud of aeroplanes,' he said, with which to "darken the sky." In reality, only the roads of France were darkened, with trucks transporting troops to the Front, ambulances bearing the wounded to hospitals, and columns of refugees.

Production did not go as smoothly as the optimists hoped. The Wright Brothers may have been the first to fly, but US aircraft production had been hindered for years by their patent disputes. Dayton-Wright was formed by major automakers to bring assembly-line production techniques to aviation production, yet airplanes, made of thousands of parts, could not be produced like automobiles. The United States did produce the 12-cylinder Liberty engine that delivered 410 horsepower, surpassing all other engines. The United States also adapted the two-man British DeHavilland-4 design. The DH-4 was nicknamed 'The Flaming Coffin,' because the fuel tank was placed between its two cockpits, where it was vulnerable to enemy fire.

Above right: **Raoul Lufbery was the leading ace of the Lafayette Escadrille with 16 victories. The aerial combat maneuver, the Lufbery Circle, was named for the famous ace.**

Right: **Nobel prize-winning novelist William Faulkner joined the Canadian Royal Air Force during World War I. Although the war ended before he finished training, he allowed people to believe he had actually seen combat.**

The Air Service Established

In February 1918, the airplanes and equipment of the Escadrille Lafayette, together with its pilots, were absorbed by the United States and became the 103rd Aero Squadron. US military aviation in France acquired a new name: the Air Service of the American Expeditionary Force (AEF). Even as the 103rd joined the Air Service, it carried on its combat activity under French command, thereby qualifying as the first US unit to be engaged in aerial combat without interruption.

The Escadrille used the Spad VII, a French-designed fighter. The aircraft was rugged enough to dive at high speeds, a crucial maneuver for evading pursuit. During its existence, the Escadrille had downed 57 enemy aircraft, and had nine of its pilots killed. The American veterans from the French Aviation Service were assigned to newly-arrived US units where they could pass their knowledge about the Spad VII and other planes to pilots whose skills had not yet been tested in action.

The first US air unit sent to Europe arrived in France on 3 September 1917, the 1st Aero Squadron, and its commander, Benjamin Foulois, arrived in October. He had been promoted to temporary Brigadier General, and was placed in charge of maintenance, organization and operation of all Air Service equipment and people. The following month Foulois was named Chief of the Air Service of the AEF.

More squadrons arrived, but all had to be equipped and trained. Cadets now received advanced instruction from French pilots. US bomber pilots flew the French-designed and manufactured Breguet, used primarily for day bombardment. US fighter pilots also flew the Nieuport 28, another French plane. The Nieuport was highly maneuverable, but had a tendency to come apart during a steep dive, and even if the wings did not break off, the fabric covering them would peel away.

Flying in an open cockpit bi-plane could be a transformative experience for any young American. But a pilot had to resist complacency, for at any second an enemy flyer might drop through a break in the clouds, firing from above. (A pilot always took a box of matches with him, so that, if brought down, he could burn his plane rather than let it fall into the enemy's hands.) If the engine was stopped by bullets, the plane went into a dive, and the pilot fought to keep from spinning out of control, and to bring the aircraft level before the ground rushed up. If the plane

Over There!
Skilled Workers
PRO — PATRIA
LOUIS — FANCHER
On the ground behind the lines
In the Air Service
CHAUFFEURS WOOD WORKERS CARPENTERS
METAL WORKERS MACHINISTS TAILORS
AUTO MECHANICS PHOTOGRAPHERS MOTORCYCLISTS
AND MEN FROM 40 OTHER TRADES
Skilled Workers Registered in the Draft, or Under 40 Years of Age Can Still Join the
Aviation Section, Signal Corps, U. S. Army
FOR INSTRUCTIONS WRITE AIR PERSONNEL DIVISION, RECRUITING SECTION, SIGNAL CORPS, WASHINGTON, D.C.

leveled out, and if he had time to scout for a landing place, the chimney smoke from a nearby village had to suffice for some sense of the wind's direction. Rock-strewn fields and grazing livestock became visible; the wheels touched down—the next seconds determined a pilot's fate. The plane could disintegrate, leaving little more than the seat, with the pilot in it, and a trail of debris. US pilots, such as James Hall (upon whose account the above description is based), survived such landings, and if ambulatory, walked back to their lines, and took to the air again.

During the winter of 1917, some 2,500 U.S. pilots received advanced training, most in France; another 400 US pilots had been graduated from the Italian flying course at Foggia. Of these, 121 received training in bombardment, still regarded as an experimental tactic, and 65 remained in Italy, under the command of Captain Fiorello LaGuardia, still a Congressman from New York (and, later, Mayor of New York City). These 65 Americans, flying with Italian crews, engaged in the first combat bomber operations by the US Air Service.

All types of aircraft, including observation and fighter planes, were used for bombing. But the Italian Caproni bombers had the range and reliability to penetrate enemy defenses, defend from aerial attack, and deliver bombs behind the battle front. This biplane had three engines, and carried a load of 1,190 pounds for four hours.

Recruiting posters during World War I helped to romanticize pilots and airplanes. Columbia, who personifies the spirit of America, is depicted as leading a fleet of airplanes into battle (*above*). Americans are urged to join the Air Service in France during World War I (*left*). A US Army Signal Corps recruiting poster (*opposite*) entreats those 40 and under to go 'Over There!' to fight in Europe.

In France, untested US squadrons were sent north of Toul to acquire combat experience. Some American pilots had seen action with Allied air units. One of the officers directing combat activities was Colonel Billy Mitchell. Before the war, Mitchell had been an aeronautical observer with the British and French forces, and thus became the first American military man to fly behind enemy lines. Mitchell's superior was Major General William L. Kenly, who had arrived in France in July 1917 as CO of the 7th Field Artillery and worked with Britain's Royal Flying Corps. In April 1917, Kenly was chosen to head the Division of Military Aeronautics under the Signal Corps. Ground or artillery officers such as Kenly were often named to lead the aeronautic division, a sore point with airmen such as Mitchell. In turn, Mitchell tested the patience of his commanders (including Kenley's successor, Major General Charles Menoher).

Major organizational changes were brought about by the war. In 1918, the fighter squadrons were assigned to Pursuit Groups. The 27th, 147th, 95th, and 94th 'Hat in the Ring' squadrons were merged into the 1st Pursuit Group. Later, the 2nd Pursuit Group consisted of the 13th, 22nd, 49th, and 139th squadrons. The 3rd Pursuit consisted of the 93rd, 28th,

213th and 103rd ('Escadrille Lafayette') squadrons. In late October, a 4th Pursuit Group was formed, consisting of the 141st, 25th, 17th, 148th squadrons. Finally, a 5th Pursuit Group was formed, for training, consisting of the 138th, 41st, 638th squadrons. All these groups made up the 1st Pursuit Wing, commanded by Lieutenant Colonel Bert M. Atkinson.

Trench Warfare vs. Aerial Combat

The Germans sent 16 squadrons (Jagdstaffeln) to greet the new arrivals at Toul. The United States scored its first aerial victories on 14 April 1918 when Lieutenants Allan Winslow and Douglas Campbell were sent out to intercept a pair of German fighter planes. The pilots safely returned to the aerodrome, each with a victory. For all their training, it was in combat that pilots such as Winslow and Campbell learned the survival skills of aerial warfare, most of which they improvised.

Even at its most terrifying, aerial combat was preferable to the trenches. Infantrymen seemed to vanish by the thousands into an ocean of casualties. Rotting corpses, open latrines, lice, and rats made the trenches a vile place, and troops were rotated every week to spare their psyches from despair, their bodies from disease. In some battles, the trenches were literally cut off, the soldiers abandoned. Heavy bombardment left only pieces of trenches, without officers or tactical links, without stretcher bearers, without food. For the infantrymen who went 'over the top,' an advance was systematic, almost mechanistic, as they plodded shoulder-to-shoulder across 'No Man's Land,' and machine guns raked their lines, toppling soldiers by the score. With luck, a man might reach a shell hole where he cowered, not daring to raise his head.

Ironically, it was airmen, dependent on their flying machines, who seemed to retain their humanity. The contrast between infantrymen crouching in trenches and the aviators free to perform stunts—a barrel turn, a loop, two or three turns of a spinning dive—gave rise to one of the war's enduring myths: the 'Knights of the Air.' In illustrations and photographs and in movies, the airmen were portrayed as dashing gentlemen in their officers' hats with sharp visors, their double-breasted great coats, belts, breeches and boots; and when in flight, their flight jackets, eye goggles, and leather caps with earflaps captured the imagination of a hero-worshipping public.

Of all the 'Knights,' the most celebrated were the 'aces,' pilots who shot down five or more enemy aircraft or balloons. The top American ace, Lieutenant Eddie

Main picture: **Many World War I aces got their start in the Nieuport 17. The Nieuport was a quick and agile fighter plane that helped end Germany's air dominance.**

Inset: **A unique panoramic photo of the 'Flying Machines Aero Squadron' in Texas City, Texas, 1913. The First Aero Squadron was composed of eight pilots, twenty-one enlisted men, and one doctor.**

During World War I, the opposing armies were often bogged down in trench warfare, separated by no man's land. The airplane and the tank both helped to end that entrenched fighting style.

Opposite Left: **The French Caudron G. III was used as a trainer and reconnaissance plane by the US Air Service in 1917, but using wing-warping instead of ailerons, the Caudron was considered outdated.**

Opposite Below: **The SPAD XIII flown by ace pilot Lieutenant Jacques Michael Swaab of the 22nd Aero Squadron of the United States Air Service. Swaab had 10 victories during World War I.**

Above: **Due to its tricky handling characteristics, more men lost their lives learning to fly the Sopwith Camel F-1 than died in combat with enemy aircraft during World War I.**

Below left: **The artist Edward Penfield helped the war effort by drawing recruiting posters and stirring images for magazine covers, including this one from *Collier's* magazine in 1917.**

Below right: **A Clifford Berryman cartoon showing Uncle Sam, standing on shore, holding a paper reading 'Flying Orders U.S.' Before and during World War I the United States lagged behind European nations in the manufacture of warplanes.**

Rickenbacker, was an auto racing driver who had gone to France as a chauffeur to the Army command. Rickenbacker joined the 94th Aero Squadron and scored his first kill on 29 April 1918. He added five more during the month of May before an ear infection grounded him. In September he returned to combat, and notched an additional 20 victories to end the war with 26, the best record by a US flyer; in addition, he survived 134 dogfights, multiple crashes, and injuries. His fighting technique was to press in upon the foe, the throttles open, engine at capacity, firing from above and behind. On September 25, without any support, Rickenbacker attacked a group of Fokkers and Halberstadts, seven in all, and downed one of each type, for which he received his first Medal of Honor. In 1930, Rickenbacker's eight distinguished service crosses were upgraded to a Medal of Honor.

Other aces performed more specialized duties, such as Lieutenant Frank J. Luke, who in September 1918, shot down 14 observation balloons. A balloon

was dirigible-shaped, commonly called a 'sausage.' The target had to be hit on the first or second try; otherwise a ground crew would pull down the balloon by cables wound around a motor. A 'balloon buster' like Luke waited until he was directly overhead; then he shut the motor, pushed forward on the control-stick, and dove at an almost vertical angle, aiming rockets mounted on the wing-struts. Once hit, the balloon's hydrogen core exploded, and its skin shrank to a flaming ribbon of oily smoke. After being wounded during his final mission, Luke flew on into enemy territory, strafed troops, and after crashing, fired at his captors with a pistol until he was killed. Luke received a posthumous Medal of Honor, the only member of the Air Service to be so honored while the war was underway.

On 8 January 1918, in anticipation of the post-war era, President Wilson declared his 14 points as a path to world peace. But the Central Powers were not pacified. On 21 March, Germany launched the first of five offensives to win the war before American ground troops could be deployed. German troops drove into French territory held by the British, to drive them back to the English Channel, to leave France exposed. This was the blitzkrieg, which married the movements of infantry with the artillery, an approach favored by German commanders. But in the Spring Offensives of 1918, early German successes were offset by mounting losses, and the resulting fallback only reinforced the stalemate in place since 1914. The High Command on both sides seemed in thrall to some mythical breakthrough that might yet turn the tide.

As the US Air Service continued to expand, air power advocate Billy Mitchell deeply resented officers who did not see the wisdom of his strategic vision. Among

them was Brigadier General Benjamin Foulois, to whom Mitchell was, at least on paper, subordinate. Their relations deteriorated to the point that Foulois asked General Pershing to relieve Mitchell from duty. (Foulois would not be the last of Mitchell's superior officer to make such a request.) Pershing, who could not spare an officer of Mitchell's caliber, said that Foulois and Mitchell simply had to learn to get along.

On 29 May, mindful of the tensions among his air officers, General Pershing appointed Brigadier General Mason M. Patrick as Chief of the Air Service of the

Above: **A Depression Era mural shows a navy R-34 dirigible. A British R-34 was the first aircraft of any kind to make a round-trip crossing of the Atlantic Ocean in 1919.**

Right: **During World War I, Dutchman Anthony Fokker built airplanes for Germany at his factory in Schwerin. By the end of the war the Fokker D.VII was a legend in the air.**

AEF. Patrick, in his mid-50s, had a plain manner that calmed Mitchell and Foulois. (After the war, General Patrick became the service's oldest pilot at 59, a gesture that raised his stature in the eyes of the airmen.) In the end, Foulois recommended that Mitchell be put in command of the Air Service, First Army, and that he, Foulois, be made Mitchell's assistant. Thus reassured of his place in the hierarchy, Mitchell focused on the upcoming offensives. Foulois became chief of Air Service, Zone of Advance, in which he distinguished himself.

The Final Push to Armistice

Early in July the Germans built up their forces in Chateau-Thierry. US air units moved to reinforce the French on the Marne River. Two pursuit units, the 17th and 148th, saw combat with British forces near the English Channel. Although its pilots were members of the US Air Service, they flew British-designed Sopwith Camel fighters. The Sopwith Camel, with twin forward-firing machine guns, shot down more enemy aircraft than any other fighter in the field. It was a tricky plane to learn how to handle, however, and more of its flyers died in training than in combat. In experienced hands, and at its best altitude of 12,000 feet, the Sopwith Camel was difficult to pin down, let alone defeat.

One example of the plane's fighting potential came against the most fearsome bomber of the war, the German Gotha. The Gotha was more than twice the size of the Sopwith Camel fighter, with a capacity for half a ton of bombs. In 1917, Gothas raided the English coastal town of Folkestone and killed 95 people. Another Gotha fleet bombed London, a raid that met with little opposition. Within months, however, the unwieldy Gothas were limited to night raids because of losses inflicted by light, maneuverable Sopwith Camels. Before the war's end, the Gotha raids had been stopped.

However maneuverable a plane may have been, it had to withstand the German heavy guns. The shelling of air patrols from German batteries was persistent and methodical. Gunners routinely fired fifty shells during a two-hour patrol. One hundred and fifty shells an hour were not unusual, and a battery could even fire up to four hundred shells an hour. The experience of being shelled while flying in an open cockpit aircraft made from fabric and wood must have concentrated the mind of even the least excitable pilot. If air bursts came close, pilots forced themselves to feign indifference; if the shells fell well short, the pilots made their planes buck as if lifted up by the concussions, all to confound the spotters on the ground, who were seeking to narrow the target range.

FOKKER
FOKKER
SCHWERIN

For most of the war Germany enjoyed an advantage in artillery. In some battles, more than 100,000 shells were fired a day. Yet, at the close of each day's shelling, the lines of battle remained largely unchanged. Advocates of air power, such as Billy Mitchell and the British General Hugh M. Trenchard, made the argument for air power in terms of a cost-benefit analysis, in that air bombardments reaped benefits that exceeded firepower expended. Artillery and infantry officers disagreed, if for no other reason than to protect their interests, and the Army General Staff sided with the ground officers.

On 21 May 1918, President Wilson transferred the Air Service from the Signal Corps, under General Squier, to two agencies—the Bureau of Aircraft Production and the Division of Military Aeronautics, the latter under the command of Major General Kenly, just returned from France. (It wasn't until August, that a single person was placed in charge of both divisions: John D. Ryan, Second Assistant Secretary of War.) In July, US air units were recognized as a brigade and assigned to the Chateau-Thierry area. The commander was Billy Mitchell.

During the summer of 1918, the US

Top: **Eddie Rickenbacker was America's top ace in World War I with 26 victories. Rickenbacker went on to command the most successful American air wing of the war, the 94th Pursuit Squadron.**

Above: **Lt. Frank Luke was America's second-ranking ace of WWI with 18 victories, mostly over heavily defended German observation balloons. Luke preferred flying without a wingman and was killed behind enemy lines in 1918.**

Air Service entered an air engagement over the Marne. Combat intensified as American airmen faced Germany's best, including the 'Red Baron' Manfred von Richthofen. Richthofen and his men flew the Fokker D.VII, with its synchronized machine gun timed to fire between strokes of a propeller. (US planes had machine guns mounted above the propeller.) The first Jagdgeschwader (JG 1) flying group was dubbed the 'Richthofen Flying Circus' because the planes were painted bright red. On 21 April 1918, a bullet struck Richthofen's heart, killing him instantly. British forces recovered his body from his crashed plane, and he was buried with full military honors. Together with squadrons from Allied nations, the US pilots had halted the Germans and gained tactical confidence.

After victories at Cantigny, Chateau-Thierry and the Belleau Wood, the Allies had pushed the German forces back. The 1st US Army under General Pershing launched the St. Mihiel Offensive on September 12, deploying more than a half-million American soldiers and airmen. Until then, bombing campaigns conducted by Britain and France upon German civilian and industrial centers were largely in retaliation for 'savage and barbarous' German raids upon Paris and London. Such joint missions, precursors of the air doctrine of strategic bombardment used in WWII, were poorly executed, and little damage was done. Prior to the St. Mihiel Offensive, one US bombardment squadron had seen limited action, but starting on September 12 the Army compressed its entire air bombardment campaign into a period of four weeks.

Billy Mitchell (soon to become a Brigadier General) readied the greatest aerial force of the war: 26 US, 61 French, and 3 Italian squadrons, with 9 British squadrons for support, a total of 1,481 airplanes. When this armada took flight, Mitchell used a third of the planes to support front-line ground troops and the rest of the planes for bombing and strafing in rear areas. During the battle, Mitchell's airplanes downed 60 enemy planes and, most importantly, maintained air superiority. The Germans retreated, and St. Mihiel was regained for the first time since 1914.

US squadrons now prepared for an all-American operation, the Meuse-Argonne Offensive on 26 September. Mitchell's tactics were the same, and similarly effective, disrupting German troop formations at the rear to prevent a counteroffensive. For six weeks, Mitchell sent his planes into enemy territory, and losses mounted. One pilot, Lieutenant Carl Spaatz (pronounced "spots") of the 13th Squadron, was nearly killed when two Fokkers bore down upon him. Had a fellow airman not rescued Spaatz, he would never have gone on to command the US Strategic Air Forces in WWII, first in Europe, then the Pacific, and to become the first Commanding Officer of the post-war US Air Force.

As the Battle of Meuse-Argonne neared

the end, US airmen improvised techniques of observation and rescue. Contact patrols communicated with infantry units that had been cut off. In just such a mission, Lieutenants Harold Goettler and Erwin Bleckley conducted the first air re-supply drop for the legendary 'Lost Battalion.' During the first week in October, units of the 77th Division from New York were surrounded by German troops in a deep ravine in the Argonne forest. Of the more than 600 men who went into the ravine, some 200 eventually walked out. The battalion was never actually 'lost,' but its location could not be confirmed, and it wasn't clear where the relief parcels should be dropped. Goettler and Bleckley conducted their observations in a DeHavilland 4. Goettler flew in the forward cockpit with his observer Bleckley in the cockpit behind.

Their mission: to fly into the Argonne forest, locate the battalion, and re-supply the trapped soldiers. Under enemy fire, Goettler repeatedly reduced speed, and Bleckley leaned from his rear cockpit to drop parcels. When they returned to their aerodrome, more than 40 holes riddled their plane. Goettler and Bleckley volunteered to make one more trip before dark. Goettler flew lower than before, intentionally drawing enemy fire. (In fact, German gunners positioned on the ravine fired down into the plane.) Bleckley sketched enemy positions to eliminate the one spot devoid of incoming fire. Both men were mortally wounded, yet Goettler brought the plane around before he died so that it crashed in friendly territory. Before Lieutenant Bleckley died, he passed on a map of enemy firing positions. By process of elimination the battalion was found, and Bleckley and Goettler were awarded posthumous Medals of Honor. The Meuse-Argonne, in which they had given their lives, was the closing chapter of the war.

Now Assistant Executive Officer of the Air Service, Hap Arnold came to France in October to inspect all US air activities. At 31, Arnold was the youngest colonel in the service. The force that Arnold inspected had 45 squadrons, of which 38 had gone into combat. A total of 767 pilots, 504 observers and gunners, and 740 planes were assigned to the various armies. US aviators had logged more than 36,000 combat hours, made 13,000 pursuit flights, and 6,600 observation missions, taking more than 18,000 aerial reconnaissance photos of enemy positions. Bombardment sorties had dropped about 276,000 pounds of explosives. Seventy-two 'aces' had shot down at least five enemy planes and balloons. In all, the Air Service destroyed 781 enemy aircraft and 73 balloons. The United States lost 289 planes and 49 balloons in combat. In all, 237 flyers gave their lives in action, and 279 were wounded.

On 9 November, Kaiser Wilhelm abdicated. (On 10 November, Major Maxwell Kirby, with the 94th Squadron, shot down a Fokker, the final US kill.) On 11 November, when the Armistice took effect, even the most ardent advocate of air power had to admit that the Great War had been won by massed infantry, with artillery support. Americans had contributed manpower and fresh energy to the war effort, and for decades to come, the contributions of the US Air Service to victory, while modest, would fuel doctrinal disputes.

For one infantryman the war was revelatory. His sense of betrayal was complete, and his rage was reinforced by the Versailles Treaty. This man understood the humiliation felt by his countrymen. In the years to come Adolph Hitler fashioned a radical ideology that demonized all who had 'weakened' Germany. When selected Chancellor of Germany in 1933, he put his political program into action, and new levels of organized violence resulted, surpassing even the horrors of World War I.

Above left: **Manfred von Richthofen, the ace of aces, had 80 confirmed victories during WWI. Although most of his victories came in an Albatros D.III, the 'Red Baron' is remembered for his blood-red Fokker Dr.I tri-plane.**

Above: **As an ace with 22 victories, Hermann Goering took command of the Richthofen Squadron after the Red Baron was killed in action. Goering's status as a war hero helped propel him into the upper echelon of the Nazi party.**

Below: **LTC William 'Billy' Mitchell (second from left) was an early proponent of air power. Mitchell's views often clashed with those of superiors, eventually leading to his court martial in 1925.**

CHAPTER 3
BETWEEN THE WARS: 1918-1939

BETWEEN THE WARS: 1918-1939

With the end of the 'war to end all wars,' the US Air Service accepted peacetime duties such as flying forest-fire and border patrols, bombing ice jams, or dropping feed to snowbound livestock. The Air Service also provided air mail delivery, rather poorly, it must be said, and even as the Post Office revenues went down, so did airplanes.

In 1919, President Wilson suffered a stroke that forced him into seclusion, and in the vacuum of leadership that followed Congress rejected US entry into the League of Nations. Demobilization, isolationism, and bureaucratic infighting were the norm. Some in Congress even questioned how the Air Service had spent its $640 million wartime appropriation, since not a single US-made airplane had seen combat in the war.

Secretary of War Newton Baker formed a panel to report on the organization, technical development, and commercial development of the Air Service. The panel concluded that air activities should be formed into one service under a single government agency. But Congress was besieged by military funding requests lobbed into committee rooms with the frequency of mortar shells, and the political will to reorganize the Air Service did not exist. By 1919 the Air Service numbered 1,300 officers and 11,000 men, a mere 7 percent of the force active during the war.

Funding cuts also impeded the development of technology. Rather than invest in research, the Army organized a 'Round-

the-Rim Flight,' largely for publicity, but also to test the range of the Martin B-1 bomber. The flight started on 24 July 1919 in Washington, D.C., and went around the periphery of the then United States in 114 hours, 45 minutes. Another aerial event that year did not work out as well. Air Service pilots flew WWI surplus planes in the 'Transcontinental Reliability and Endurance Test.' About half of the 64 planes didn't finish, and 54 accidents resulted in seven deaths.

Mitchell Insists on the Superiority of Air Power

Such displays gave Billy Mitchell, now a colonel, ammunition to blast Army policy and practices. Mitchell, upon his promotion to Assistant Chief of the Air Services under Major General Charles Menoher, recommended the development of bombers to carry explosive ordnance anywhere in the world; the design of torpedoes and armor-piercing bombs to attack dreadnoughts; and the building of aircraft carriers. (Instructors at the Air Service Field Officers' School—later, Air Service Tactical School—promulgated similar doctrine based on independence for the Air Service.) Acting Secretary of the Navy Franklin D. Roosevelt invited Mitchell to share his ideas with the Navy. The admirals received Mitchell with interest, but his thesis that air power trumped the fleets of the Navy won few converts.

Air Service pilots continued to conduct field tests, to press the limits of speed, endurance, and distance. At McCook Field, Dayton, Ohio, on 28 April 1919, Lieutenant John A. Macready made the first jump with a free-fall parachute. For every first, however, there were failures. From 1920 to 1921, older airplanes were involved in 330 crashes and 69 US flyers died. Even Congress had to act, and on 4 June, the National Defense Act of 1920 was approved. The act allocated 1,516 officers and 16,000 men to the Air Service, and established it as a permanent branch, albeit still under Army command.

The national mood in 1920 was 'normalcy,' as defined by a Republican administration. Mitchell did little to endear himself to General Menoher, his superior, when he insisted that 'German militarism endangers the world.' After all, the Treaty at Versailles had dismantled the German military, and the London Ultimatum forbade Germany from manufacturing aircraft until 1922, and then only under restrictions.

Mitchell's warnings may have been hypothetical, but they were not unfounded. In Germany, on 29 July 1921, the National Socialists selected Adolph Hitler as their leader. Although the Nazis were a fringe movement, Hitler articulated with force two principal points of his program: to reject the Versailles Treaty and to restore the German military. Without openly supporting Hitler's call for rearmament, German military staff worked to refine air doctrine as the pace of technological development intensified. The German military were preparing to reemerge, rearmed.

Previous page: **The Keystone K-78D 'Patrician' was the largest passenger plane in 1929, seating twenty, including their baggage.**

Above: **A cartoon celebrating the first transatlantic flight by John Alcock and Arthur Brown, who flew their Vickers Vimy from Newfoundland to Ireland in 1919. A ship labeled '1492' urges the pilots to 'Sail on.'**

Left: **Billy Mitchell surveys bomb damage aboard the USS *Indiana*. Despite the considerable destruction, Mitchell failed to convince the military that a separate air force was necessary.**

In 1921, General Menoher requested that Mitchell be removed, and when General Pershing declined, Menoher resigned. Pershing placed General Mason Patrick in command of the Air Service. Patrick, who had served as Air Service Chief of the AEF in France, had shown that he could work with officers as temperamental as Mitchell. Patrick sought to divide military aviation into an air service (providing reconnaissance and artillery targeting in support of infantry) and an air force (engaged in pursuit and bombardment). The air force was not required to coordinate with the ground force, he reasoned, so independence was a logical step. Rather than press his case publicly, Patrick lobbied behind the scenes.

In February 1921, during an appearance in Congress, Mitchell offered to demonstrate that bombers alone could control both sea and air. At the war's end, the United States had seized several German ships, including the Ostfriesland with its watertight multi-layered bulkheads, displacing 27,000 tons. Under the Armistice, the Ostfriesland was to be scuttled soon, so the Navy agreed to tow the ship into the Atlantic where Mitchell could bomb it. The Navy insisted that the number and size of the bombs be limited, and that the test be conducted under a 'clinical setting' to ensure accurate documentation.

Mitchell formed the First Provisional Air Brigade (including Jimmy Doolittle), whose pilots were taught to bomb near a ship, not on it. The hammer effect, as it was called, depended upon a bomb's power being intensified by the compressed expansion of a ship's hull, causing its seams to split and rivets to pop. Restrictions placed by the Navy ruled out bombs as big as the ones Mitchell had designed, the largest to date at 2,000 pounds and up. Yet, on 21 July, Mitchell ordered his Martin B-2 bombers to drop the bombs anyway, and the Ostfriesland burst open as the "hammer effect" had posited. The Navy, outraged that Mitchell had flouted the rules, dismissed the test as unrealistic.

New Feats by Airplanes

During the early 1920s, trophy races were entertainment, and cash prizes motivated much derring-do. On 4 September 1922, Jimmy Doolittle completed the first transcontinental flight, covering 2,163 miles in 21 hours, 20 minutes with one stop. A month later, John A. Macready and O.G. Kelly set a world endurance record of 35 hours, 18 minutes, and 30 seconds. Macready also took an open-cockpit plane up to a lung-scalding 40,800 feet. Other achievements received scant attention. A helicopter, the H-1, made its first flight at McCook Field on 18 December 1922, rising six feet and remaining airborne for more than a minute. But the H-1 was unstable and difficult to control, and did not go into production.

In 1923, Air Service pilots developed a

Below: **In addition to high altitude testing, John Macready was the first to fly nonstop across the continental United States in 1923. This commemorative watercolor depicts Macready and Oakley Kelly's historic flight in their Fokker T-2.**

technique for mid-air refueling in aircraft interconnected by a length of hose. (The person in the rear seat of the receiving aircraft had to catch the hose by hand and connect it.) Using this technique, Lieutenants Macready and Kelly flew non-stop from New York to San Diego in 27 hours. A year later, in 1924, Lieutenant Russell L. Maughan completed a coast-to-coast, non-stop flight in 22 hours.

On 28 September 1924, after completing a mission that covered 26,345 miles in 175 days, two aptly-named Douglas World Cruisers completed the first flight around the world. Support systems were set up around the globe to accommodate the flyers, a demonstration that technology had turned even distant nations into neighbors. Ensuring that one's neighbors remained neighborly was another matter.

Above: **Four Douglas World Cruisers took off from Clover Field in Santa Monica, California, in 1924 for the first around-the-world flight. 175 days and more than 26,000 miles later, two of the planes completed the historic journey.**

Left: **In 1922 James Doolittle made the first transcontinental flight within a single day in a De Havilland DH-4. Doolittle only made one stop for refueling at Kelly Field near San Antonio, Texas.**

In 1924, primary and secondary role letters were assigned to military aircraft. The P-38, for example, was a pursuit plane, the thirty-eighth model in the sequence. Each stage would be assigned a suffix, P-38A or P-38B, to indicate modifications of the design. If 'experimental,' a plane was designated a prefix, XP-38, for example, the thirty-eighth version of a pursuit aircraft that never saw production. The most common designations included A (attack), B (bomber), C (cargo or transport), F (photographic), O (observation), and T (trainer). More numbers and letters identified not only the manufacturer, but the factory where the plane was produced.

Mitchell Presses His Case

In 1923, the Nazis staged a 'Beer Hall Putsch' an attempt to overthrow the Weimer Republic, and Hitler was arrested and imprisoned. In 1925, after Hitler was released, he published Mein Kampf, in which he spoke of restoring Germany to world power. Most of the world wanted peace, and so when the League of Nations admitted Germany on 8 September 1926, it was seen as a hopeful sign.

As Hitler was composing Mein Kampf in prison, Billy Mitchell was on an inspec-

tion tour of Hawaii and prepared a report critical of the facilities there. He plotted out air fields, anticipated enemy tactics, and even identified the culprit—Japan, a US ally! Mitchell specified the day of the week and the time of the day: '[Japan] could attack . . . by striking first at Hawaii, some fine Sunday morning.'

Mitchell's report earned him few friends in Washington. General Patrick, Chief of the Air Service, had promoted Hap Arnold to oversee aviation developments as the chief of information.

Above: **An aerial view of Charles Lindbergh's airplane, the *Spirit of St. Louis*, during his historic transatlantic flight. Lindbergh flew the nonstop journey solo from New York to Paris in 1927.**

Above right: **Members of Admiral Richard Byrd's South Pole Expedition flight crew receive medals for their accomplishment. Byrd's crew was the first to fly over the South Pole in 1929, although they were unable to land.**

Below: **Billy Mitchell's First Provisional Air Brigade bombed the Ostfriesland using the hammer effect of bombing in the water near a ship instead of directly on it. The Ostfriesland sank within minutes.**

Arnold brought his political experience in addition to flying and engineering skills, but his other task was to handle Mitchell, his friend. When Mitchell's term as Assistant Air Chief expired, he was not reappointed. He reverted to the rank of Colonel and was reassigned to Fort Sam Houston in Texas.

With every new air disaster, Mitchell expressed his outrage. In 1925, a Navy dirigible, Shenandoah, crashed in high winds, killing 14. The disaster, Mitchell declared, was a result of 'almost treasonable administration of the national defense by the Navy and War Departments.' President Coolidge himself preferred the charges of court-martial, 'conduct of a nature to bring discredit upon the military service.'

Mitchell's defense team ignored the charge of insubordination, which was inarguable; they focused on his critique, for if it could be validated, the charges against him might be negated. Starting on 28 September, officers such as Major Spaatz, Major Arnold, and Admiral William Sims did what they could within military rules to support Mitchell. Mayor of New York Fiorello La Guardia, a former airman, was less circumspect, and declared that his city would be defenseless before enemy attack. Eddie Rickenbacker, Ace of Aces, took the stand and excoriated military policy.

By the time Mitchell testified, the prosecution sought to pierce his celebrity

image. Mitchell's scenario for a Japanese attack upon Hawaii was ridiculed, his vision of air power lampooned, especially his predictions of a gliding bomb that could be directed to its target by remote control, or of bombers that could cruise oceans. Such 'fantasies' were suitable for pulp fiction, not air doctrine, the Army prosecutors declared.

The only issue before the court on 17 December was insubordination, and the six major generals found Mitchell guilty. Mitchell resigned from the Army, but continued to campaign for an independent Air Force until his death at the age of 59 in 1935.

New Developments in Airplanes and Flying

Shortly before the Mitchell trial, Coolidge had appointed Dwight Morrow to assess the feasibility of a separate air arm. Mitchell appeared before the panel, largely to read from his book, Winged Defense (1925), and to lend support to an air force with its own budget, headquarters, and staff. Benjamin Foulois, the US pilot with the longest flying record, agreed. Foulois described having to pay for airplane maintenance out of his own pocket. In the end, the Morrow Report did not recommend independence, but concluded that the Air Service was not to be regarded as an auxiliary to the Army.

General Patrick had been working to make the Air Service more closely resemble the Marine Corps in its autonomy, hence the name change to 'corps.' The Air Corps Act of 2 July 1926 set a goal of 1,800 planes and 16,650 personnel. The United States had ground to cover to catch up with other nations, who, because they were vulnerable, had made advances in air doctrine and technology. US air doctrine did not address fundamental issues such as bombing, strafing, or aerial combat until the mid-1920s.

In 1926, the Air Service Tactical School issued, 'Employment of Combined Air Force,' influenced by Italian General Giulio Douhet's Command of the Air (1921). The Tactical School officers argued that bombardment of an enemy's vital centers would depress morale and bring victory. Yet only 138 tons of bombs had been dropped in WWI, so the doctrine was an extrapolation from limited evidence. Even without Mitchell in the ranks, the Army now found itself engaged in a protracted air power debate.

Civilians, too, made their mark on aeronautics. On 16 March 1926, at Auburn, Massachusetts, physicist Robert H. Goddard fired the first rocket using liquid fuel. Goddard's rocket made little impression upon the military (until the Germans launched V-1 and V-2 ballistic missiles in WWII). Another mark was set on 21 May 1927, when Charles Lindbergh flew solo from New York to France in 33 hours, 30 minutes, nonstop. In the popular imagination, Lindbergh and his *Spirit of St. Louis* came to symbolize all that a 'Lone Eagle'

Above: **Nine Curtiss P-6E Hawks of the 17th Pursuit Squadron, 1st Pursuit Group, fly in formation in 1932. The P-6E was the last fighter biplane built in quantity for the Army Air Corps.**

Below: **Colonel Henry 'Hap' Arnold receiving the key to the city of Fairbanks, Alaska. Arnold led a fleet of ten Martin B-10 bombers from Washington, DC, to Fairbanks and back again in 1934.**

could achieve in an age of mass production and mass movements.

In 1927, General Patrick stepped down as Chief of the Army Air Corps, and his successor was Major General James Fechet. The Air Corps expanded its research and development facilities. McCook Field, Dayton, Ohio, was replaced by Wright Field, also in Dayton, as the Air Corps testing ground. Wright Field pilots flew airplane prototypes to test performance and reliability, such as the Curtiss Pursuit series, beginning with the P-1 Hawk. This pursuit series produced several dozen variations with more powerful engines, such as the Pratt & Whitney radial, capable of an average speed of 187 mph.

At Langley Memorial Aeronautical Laboratory in Virginia, researchers tested aircraft in the Propeller Research Tunnel. They found that non-retractable landing gear added 40 percent to aircraft drag. In addition to the need for retractable landing gear, researchers tested engine cowlings. Other subjects for research were variable-pitch propellers that adjusted pitch according to the needs of the airplane; gyroscopic equipment to control the attitude and direction of flight; and the 'Fowler flap' that slid back from the wing and rotated down, increasing the wing area as well as lift.

Through all these developments, Jimmy Doolittle was a bridge between the engineers and the flyers. After bombing the Ostfriesland, Doolittle earned a PhD in aeronautical engineering from the Massachusetts Institute of Technology. His dissertation held that a pilot required instrumentation to know the direction of the wind (as well as the direction in which he was flying). Doolittle worked on acceleration tests and the development of instruments that enabled pilots to take off and land at night. Research identified the problem, engineers responded with modifications, and pilots like Doolittle proved

Above: **Amelia Earhart and her navigator, Fred Noonan, board her Lockheed Model 10E Electra for their ill-fated around-the-world flight in 1937. With 7,000 miles left in the journey, the plane was thought to have ditched in the Pacific Ocean somewhere near the Howland Islands.**

Left: **Six Boeing B-17 bombers that made a goodwill trip to Buenos Aires, Argentina, in 1938. Their return to Langley Field, Virginia, was at that time the longest nonstop flight in Army Air Corps history.**

that technical advances worked. (Not every test was conducted with an airplane. One of the most audacious stunts took place on 15 June 1928, when an Air Corps blimp flew directly over a train, dipped down and passed off a mailbag to the postal clerk on board, thus completing the first airplane-to-train transfer.) On 24 September 1929, Doolittle made the first 'blind' flight, taking off, flying, and landing by instrument in a cockpit covered in fabric.

Military and civilian feats continued to validate new techniques. In 1929, the crew of The Question Mark, commanded by Major Spaatz, flew nonstop for 150 hours. In a triumph of logistics, 43 contacts were made, nine at night, so that a Douglas C-1 cargo plane could deliver 40 tons of fuel, food, and batteries to The Question Mark's crew. In July 1930, using mid-air refueling, a new record for endurance was set by a civilian crew, 647.5 hours without landing, a feat that required the pilots to eat and sleep for weeks in a pungent, droning cockpit. Such marathons yielded valuable data, and by 1934, the dangling-hose method would be replaced with calibrated fittings and hose connections that enabled aerial refueling to become routine.

The Buildup of the 1930s

The least welcome day of 1929 was Black Tuesday, 29 October. The stock market crash, and the depression that followed, roiled markets, devastated farmers, drove millions of workers into bread lines, and challenged officials at every level of government. In 1932, the Air Corps had

Top: **Adolf Hitler and Hermann Goering depart a Luftwaffe plane in Berlin, Germany. Goering had been a World War I ace fighter pilot before joining the Nazis.**

Above: **Benito Mussolini greets Adolf Hitler in 1934. Hitler flew to Venice to meet Mussolini just two months before he became the Fuhrer of Germany.**

1,709 planes and 14,705 personnel, well short of goals set in 1926.

In Germany, the National Socialists grew to become the second largest party. Although the Nazis lost seats in the 1932 elections, and never achieved a majority, Hitler was appointed Chancellor in 1933. On 27 February, the Reichstag was set afire, an act of 'subversion' that Hitler used to assume dictatorial powers. By 14 July the Nazis were the only political party. In October Germany withdrew from the League of Nations.

Sweeping change came to the United States. Democrat Franklin D. Roosevelt won the White House in 1932, and his party took control of Congress. Voters, preoccupied with the Depression, took little note of the rise of militant nationalists such as Hitler and Mussolini, who were caricatured in the press as buffoons. US military planners, however, could ill afford to dismiss such threats. Aircraft development was accelerated, evolving from modified biplane designs of the early 1930s to all-metal monoplanes.

The lower drag of a monoplane enabled it to fly faster than a biplane with the same engine. Yet, with few exceptions, metal wings weighed 25 to 36 percent more than wood wings, and all-metal airplanes were considerably more expensive. The P-30 was the first pursuit aircraft ordered by the Army Air Corps. It had retractable landing gear (manually operated by a crank in the cockpit), and an enclosed, heated cockpit. Even if the prototypes did not go into production, the pilots testing them made many valuable contributions. The XP-21 Hawk featured an air-cooled Pratt & Whitney 'Wasp' radial engine capable of 410 horsepower.

The Hawk XP-22, was the first US pursuit plane to exceed 200 mph. The Boeing XP-9 was a single wing pursuit aircraft rejected for its poor handling and visibility, but its framework had a 'stressed skin' construction, the standard in later years.

Building upon Doolittle's earlier experiments, Major A. F. Hegenberger made the first solo blind flight on 9 May 1932. In a Douglas BT-2 airplane equipped with standard instruments, Hegenberger made his airfield approach using a radio compass to line up on a pair of radio transmitters. In 1937, Captains Carl J. Crane and George V. Holloman made the first automatic landing using a ground radio system of transmitting beacons. Soon radio equipment would be installed in every plane and at every airfield.

Aviation pioneer Igor Sikorsky had experimented with helicopters since the turn of the century, and had succeeded in demonstrating rotary-wing lift before WWI. During the 1920s he designed flying boats and amphibians. In 1931, Sikorsky patented a design for a modern helicopter with a single large main rotor and small anti-torque tail rotor. The prototype was test-flown in 1938, and production began in 1939.

The Air Corps made significant advances in building bombers. One early bomber stood out, the Martin B-10 monoplane, with enclosed cockpits and gun turrets, internal bomb storage, retractable landing gear, and two-position variable-pitch propellers. The B-10 reached speeds of 200 mph. Colonel Hap Arnold commanded a group of B-10s on a flight to Alaska in 1934. By covering 23,000 square miles of uninhabited territory in three days, and by completing 8,300 mile round trip without losses, Arnold had proven that 'accidents of geography' no longer protected the United States from air invasion.

In March 1935, the War Department established the General Headquarters (GHQ) Air Force as a central striking force to defend US coasts and island possessions. Brigadier General Frank Andrews took command of GHQ Air Force. The GHQ reinforced the principle of an Air Force independent from ground action, but it also created the potential for internal rivalry. Air Corps Chief Benjamin Foulois remained in charge of production and supplies. On 31 December 1935, Foulois retired, and Major General Oscar Westover took his place. Westover took a dim view of the Army's critics, one of whom was Andrews.

To be effective, Andrews persisted, the

Above: **Adolf Hitler used the Nazi Party rallies at Nuremberg to showcase Germany's military and air power. Here a formation of Luftwaffe bombers flies over the 1937 rally.**

Below: **The Curtiss P-40 was the first single-seat fighter to be mass-produced in America. During World War II the P-40 was known by its pilots as a sturdy and trustworthy airplane.**

GHQ Air Force needed a weapon not yet available—the long-range bomber. The War Department, while skeptical, did allocate funds to develop a bomber that could carry a load of 2,000 pounds for at least 1,020 miles at 200 mph. Boeing proposed the all-metal, four-engine Model 299. It flew on 28 July 1935, earning the nickname 'Flying Fortress' because of the machine guns that bristled from its tail, its turrets, and its waists. Its bomb bays carried an average maximum load of 6,000 pounds, but could carry up to 17,600 pounds, if required. Its range was 1,850 miles, its ceiling 35,000 feet.

At altitudes above 30,000 feet, however, the air was thin and engine power lagged. Devices such as 'superchargers' took in air, compressed it, and fed it into the engine. Leaded gas enabled engines to use a supercharger more effectively and efficiently. After 1935, engines with superchargers provided full power at high altitudes. Airplanes were now free to go higher.

A New War Confronts the World

In Germany, the Luftwaffe served as a prop in Nazi pageantry, and air formations flew over the opening ceremonies of the 1936 Berlin Olympics. Hitler's swaggering affectation of military uniforms unnerved world leaders. At Nazi rallies Germans raised their arms to the Fuhrer, who had brought them prosperity (spending up to 23 percent of Germany's annual GNP on rearmament). The restorative aspects of the Nazi program, such as a focus on folk traditions, helped to revive national identity. Germany's sense of itself was also reinforced by unilateralist, preemptive military doctrine; regimentation of all societal activity, with the individual subsumed to the State; the suppression of dissent; and the construction of camps to imprison the disloyal (and non-Aryan). One Wehrmacht ('defense force') officer observed that the new order imposed upon Germany had created a 'machine from which no one could escape.'

The European peace since WWI came to an end in 1936. In Spain, a coalition of Communists, Socialists, and Basque and Catalonian separatists won control of the government. The Republicans, as the coalition was called, raised a prospect, unwelcome in many capitals, of a European state with an ideology similar to that of the Soviet Union. On 17 July General Francisco Franco seized a Spanish Army outpost in Morocco. A junta of generals, led by Franco, declared itself the legal government of Spain, henceforth the Nationalists. France helped supply the Republicans, as did the Soviet Union. The United States stayed neutral, but US citizens joined the International Brigade to fight for the Republican government, and three American pilots formed the Patrolla Americana, eventually fielding 20 pilots.

Mussolini sent Franco more than 700 airplanes and troops. Hitler sent 19,000 German 'volunteers' to Spain, including Luftwaffe flyers. The latter formed the Condor Legion, equipped with airplanes such as the Heinkel bomber and the Messerschmitt fighter, the finest aircraft of their time. When 20,000 Nationalist troops, including Franco, were trapped in Morocco, the Condor Legion evacuated the troops in 677 flights over two months, across the Strait of Gibraltar to Seville, with the loss of one airplane.

The Condor Legion was the first to use strategic bombing in an attempt to shock an enemy into surrender. In essence, the nation that emerged victorious from an air war was the one that endured (or escaped) strategic bombing of its cities, and visited devastation upon the cities of the other side. Of all the raids against Spanish cities, the one against Guernica drew the most attention. For three hours on 26 April 1937, the Condor Legion dropped 100,000 pounds of bombs, leaving 1,500 dead. The only military target, a bridge, had been left untouched. The attack raised grave ethical questions, but the most immediate effect was to cow the leaders of France and Great Britain, who in September 1938 chose to appease Hitler at Munich.

Above: **British Prime Minister Neville Chamberlain (center) flew to Munich in 1938 and left with a promise from Hitler not to make any further territorial demands. Hitler invaded Czechoslovakia six months later.**

Below: **In 1937, the Lockheed XC-35 was the first airplane to have a pressurized cabin, which allowed the plane to reach high altitudes in the sub-stratosphere without requiring pilots and passengers to use oxygen equipment or cold-weather clothes.**

Arnold Takes Command

On 21 October 1938, General Oscar Westover, Chief of the Army Air Corps, was killed in a plane crash. A week later, Major General Hap Arnold became the new Chief, and along with his position he inherited fewer than 2,000 airplanes and 21,000 men.

During Arnold's rise through the ranks, the Air Corps had achieved greater autonomy but not independence. Air doctrine was in flux, and the concept of strategic bombardment was gaining adherents, including Arnold. In order to implement such a doctrine, Arnold worked with aeronautic engineers and manufacturers to produce long range bombers such as the B-17 'Flying Fortress' and fast, maneuverable fighter planes such as the Curtiss P-40 for bomber escorts. The War Department and General Command saw air force in terms of quantity, and while they tolerated the concept of strategic bombardment, they did not endorse it. Arnold used his political acumen to advance strategic bombardment, which relied on fewer, bigger airplanes. Other more vocal advocates, such as Frank Andrews of GHQ Air Force or his subordinate George Kenney, were demoted, assigned to Billy Mitchell's old office at Fort Sam Houston in Texas, where they had to wait to be vindicated and reinstated during WWII.

Even as Andrews and Kenney suffered the consequences of their principled stand, behind the scenes the military planners in the United States and Britain continued to develop strategic bombing forces. Airplanes, it was hoped, could win a war with a relatively few bombing missions, saving the lives of soldiers. But the prospect of ruined cities and civilian casualties (today's 'collateral damage') intensified the American people's aversion to war. With an eye to public opinion, Hap Arnold adopted terminology that referred to 'precision daylight missions' against the enemy's 'vital' centers, if only to make the consequences sound less wantonly brutal.

Soon, however, the veterans of Germany's Condor Legion would be flying over Poland, Czechoslovakia, and France—an experienced air force fighting for Nazi goals. The United States would build its air force in every possible way, the better to forge an indispensable weapon with which to defeat Hitler's Germany.

Above: **The Lockheed P-38 Lightning first flew in 1939. It would become one of America's most versatile aircraft during World War II when nearly 10,000 were built.**

230681

CHAPTER 4
TAKE-OFF INTO WAR: 1939-1943

TAKE-OFF INTO WAR: 1939-1943

Hap Arnold took command of the US Army Air Corps at a critical time. Under Nazi rule Germany had undergone political and social revival, but the revival was predicated on expansionistic notions such as Lebensbraum, or 'living space,' a euphemistic reference to the annexation of territory. To his generals, Hitler argued that Germany required the resources and workforces of other nations in order to sustain the German economy.

In August 1939, Germany and the Soviet Union formed the Non-Aggression Pact, a moment of disillusionment for many, given that Hitler had portrayed himself as anti-Bolshevik. Britain rushed to form a Mutual Assistance Treaty with Poland, and word was sent to Hitler through a go-between that the British would not back down. Hitler's response revealed his faith in German industry and the Luftwaffe: 'I shall build airplanes, build airplanes, airplanes, airplanes!'

On 1 September 1939, Stuka dive bombers with wind-driven sirens howled through the air above Poland, bombing cities and attacking bridges and railroads. Airborne troops and Panzer units followed. The Luftwaffe lost 285 planes, a reminder that the price of air superiority had to be paid with every battle. Britain and France declared war, but it was a war that Germany, under Hitler, was ready to fight.

Isolationists in America had long opposed such a war, and mindful of their opposition, as well as the need to build military readiness, President Franklin D. Roosevelt declared neutrality. He also, more quietly, announced a 'limited national emergency,' permitting half a million Americans to be placed under arms. Moreover, the US Navy put its forces on an 'all but war' footing against German U-Boats, so that the Atlantic shipping lanes were kept open.

Previous page: **A shift change at a B-17 'Flying Fortress' plant. Even before the U.S. entered World War II, America was producing 500 of the heavy bombers per month.**

Above: **Top Nazi Commander Hermann Goering inspects Luftwaffe personnel on the French side of the English Channel, where Germany launched its blitzkrieg on Britain.**

Below: **Warsaw burns after the Luftwaffe bombarded the Polish city. This photograph was taken from the cockpit of a German fighter plane that participated in the attack.**

The United States Gears Up for War

The airplane prototypes of the 1930s had culminated in a unified modern design: fast, all-metal cantilever monoplanes with enclosed cockpits and retractable landing gear. Distributing such planes to Britain and France alarmed US Army Air Corps Chief Hap Arnold, who feared that US technological advances would be compromised if the Allies fell. Roosevelt bypassed Arnold by placing Secretary of Treasury Henry A. Morgenthau in charge of aircraft distribution. Unlike Billy Mitchell, Arnold knew when to withdraw from a confrontation with the Commander in Chief. He also knew how to maneuver through political thickets, and cultivated Republican allies in Congress and isolationists such as Charles Lindbergh.

The Germans regarded Lindbergh, the 'Lone Eagle,' as an ally in their campaign to influence American opinion. Lindbergh's pro-German sentiments were consistent with his double life during the 1930s: Only in 2003 would it be learned that he had fathered children by at least one German woman, even as he had a wife in the United States. During his frequent stays in Germany, Lindbergh toured munitions factories, met air commanders, and flew German planes. Now, with the United States supplying Britain and France, a policy Lindbergh opposed, he returned home for a secret meeting at West Point with Arnold and shared what he knew about the Luftwaffe, in which he urged Arnold not to meet the strength of the Luftwaffe, but to exceed it. Publicly, however, Lindbergh continued to speak out against US involvement in European affairs.

Arnold focused on heavy bombers for strategic campaigns, still a controversial idea for some. He started with the models in production, such as the B-17, and improved their effectiveness and safety. To avoid flak, the plane flew above 30,000 feet, so oxygen masks, pressure breathing equipment, and electric flight suits were developed. To reduce discomfort on long-range missions, designers simplified B-17 operations, redesigned the cockpit and turrets, and improved seating.

Roosevelt signed the National Defense Act of 1940, authorizing 6,000 airplanes, more than 3,000 officers, and 45,000 enlisted men. Research and development gave way to mass production, resulting in critical shortages in aluminum, machine tools, and skilled workers. In June 1940, only 400 warplanes were being produced a month. The goal, set by Roosevelt, was 50,000 planes a year. But mass production was at odds with the constant modifications required to achieve optimal performance in combat.

Industrial giant Henry Ford joined the effort to mass produce warplanes. For years Ford had lent his fortune and name to isolationist causes, but he rushed to increase war production, because doing nothing would cede the market to his competitors. He built the world's largest factory, 70 acres under one roof, to assemble one bomber an hour. The B-25 medium bomber—one half the size of heavy bombers such as the B-17—had to be assembled from 165,000 separate items, using 150,000 rivets. The haste with which airplanes were made became clear when the engines started up and loose rivets chattered on the wings.

General George Marshall, Army Chief of Staff, saw Air Corps autonomy as linked with overall decentralization of General Command. Marshall was determined to replace the horizontal bureaucratic structure with a vertical one. Marshall's plan to subordinate the GHQ Air Force to Hap Arnold was stymied when the War Department formed the Air Defense Command, a war planning agency. The GHQ Air Force, responsible for continental air defense, was placed under a General Headquarters with jurisdiction over four field armies. In other words, the combat arm of the Air Corps now answered to a field General.

Regional air districts, the Northeastern, Central, Southern, and Western Defense Commands, were designated the First, Second, Third, and Fourth Air Forces, respectively. An objective of 54 airplane groups for 1942 was set, and expanded to 84 groups. A training objective of 30,000 pilots per year required that the training center at Randolph Field start a class of 400 flyers every five weeks.

***Above:* The buildings of the British Parliament glow with the flames of German bombs in 1940. During the course of the war Londoners endured many months of bombings and V-1 rocket attacks.**

***Right:* The Douglas A-20 Havoc was admired for its speed and versatility as a light attack bomber and reconnaissance aircraft and was put into service by many of the Allied armies during World War II.**

On 20 June 1941, the US Army Air Corps became the US Army Air Force (USAAF). The GHQ Air Force shifted back to Hap Arnold's command, as Marshall had originally intended. Arnold, who was to sit on the Joint Chiefs of Staff (and later on the Allied Combined Chiefs of Staff), accompanied Roosevelt to the Atlantic Conference.

The War in Europe

On 10 May 1940, Winston Churchill was appointed British Prime Minister. Holland and Belgium had surrendered, and the roads to Paris were wide open. Between 27 May and 4 June, 850 ships of all sizes evacuated more than 300,000 English, French, and Belgian troops from the port city of Dunkirk. Using Spitfires, the Royal Air Force (RAF) provided air cover for the evacuation, and 177 Allied aircraft were lost, as were 240 German aircraft.

Italy declared war on Britain and France on 10 June. Ten days later, France surrendered, and was divided into occupied territory and a collaborationist Vichy government. Hap Arnold, like many in US command, doubted that the British could hold out, so he assumed that future air campaigns would have to originate from the US mainland. Arnold pushed

for a new generation of strategic bombers. The War Department resisted: Such a plane, with twice the range of a B-17, was a 'weapon of aggression' inconsistent with neutrality. The bomber Arnold envisioned was the B-29 'Superfortress,' a project over which he took personal command and which would come to fruition in the Pacific war, to sobering effect.

On 10 July, the 'Battle of Britain' began, a bombing campaign to soften the nation's defenses in preparation for a German invasion. The British had an extensive system of radios and radar and a central command office that coordinated radar reports. Yet German military intelligence asserted that the radar stations were unimportant and should not be targets. As a result, German fighters and bombers were brought down in large numbers. Still, the Royal Air Force, with far fewer planes, could not afford to engage in a war of attrition.

On 25 August, a Luftwaffe pilot mistakenly bombed central London. Churchill retaliated, sending 81 Hampden bombers to strike Berlin the next night. The damage to the German capital was minimal, yet Hitler ordered the Blitz (lightning strike), an unrelenting air assault upon London. The Luftwaffe had not been designed for daylight strategic bombing. (In fact, Germany's War Directive Number Two prohibited bombing cities in France and England except as reprisals.) Under the terms of the Versailles Treaty, Germany did not revitalize its aviation industry until the 1930s, and little had been done to develop the long-range heavy bombers favored by the United States and Britain. Moreover, German planners had seen the results of civilian bombing in the Spanish Civil War, and had opted for a force consisting of tactical fighters and medium bombers.

The Blitz was difficult for London—and Southampton, Bristol, Exeter, Portsmouth, Plymouth, and Coventry, which lost most of its city center, with hundreds dead. But all was not well for the Luftwaffe. Messerschmitts carried only enough fuel to remain over British airspace for 20 minutes, and Heinkel bombers flew without escort to Liverpool, Manchester, Cardiff, and Glasgow. Losses mounted, and the Blitz was shifted to a nighttime operation. But as civilians spent their nights in shelters, British air bases and aircraft factories were repaired. In this respect, the Blitz was a test of the doctrine of strategic bombardment, in particular the premise that bombing would paralyze the will of civilians. As it happened, civil-

Above: **A United States Army Air Force P-38 stationed in Iceland warms its engines for takeoff. Lt. Elza Shahan, flying a P-38 out of Iceland, became the first American to score a victory against a Luftwaffe plane when he downed an Fw 200 on 14 August 1942.**

Left: **A B-24 Liberator makes a low bombing pass over the Astra Romana refinery in Ploesti, Romania in 1943. Following a German occupation in October 1940, Romania joined the Axis powers a month later.**

Right: **This railway bridge over the river Seine between Rouen and Paris was bombed by Allied planes, forcing German troops to detour through Paris in order to reach the coast.**

ian morale strengthened, and their will to resist was fueled by indignation at having their homes and their places of work turned into targets.

The Blitz also evoked growing international sympathy for the British cause. The Royal Air Force announced the formation of the Eagle Squadron, an air unit for American volunteers who enlisted in Canada or in Britain. Three Eagle Squadrons were formed, and one flyer, Bill Dunn, became the first US 'ace' of WWII. At the same time, rearmament boosted US employment and helped to alleviate the effects of the Great Depression. Still, nearly three-quarters of Americans opposed US entry into the war.

Above: **Pilots of the 39th Squadron of the 31st Pursuit Group await takeoff in a new fleet of Bell P-39 Airacobras. The P-39 was essentially built around a 37mm cannon, which made for the unique position of the engine behind the pilot.**

Right: **Army Air Corps cadets take a group test, circa 1942. The tests were given to determine whether cadets were more suited to be pilots, navigators, or bombardiers in the variety of aircraft used during the war.**

The War Spreads

With Britain under assault, and with the United States on the sidelines, British imperial possessions in the Far East looked increasingly vulnerable. The Empire of Japan, having sent its military to seize the coastal cities of China, and having taken Korea and Manchuria, now saw an opportunity to claim its place as the dominant power in Asia. On 27 September 1940 Japan joined Germany and Italy in the Tripartite (Axis) Pact.

Churchill wanted to push back against the Axis. But his cash and gold reserves were exhausted, so he turned to Roosevelt, freshly re-elected, for new forms of support. Roosevelt responded with the Lend-Lease Act and a promise: for as long as the United States was not at war, planes from new plants were to go to Britain. Of 22,000 planes produced, 7,000 went to Britain and 10,000 to Army Air Force. Hap Arnold resisted sharing US aircraft production capability with Britain. The RAF, Arnold argued, wanted planes with more speed, less armament, lighter construction, not the sturdy planes his pilots preferred. If production were to be retooled to meet British needs, it would detract from the development of long-range heavy bombers such as the B-17, now being made at a rate of 500 per month.

Politically, Arnold was savvy enough to seek some measure of control over the Lend-Lease program. He proposed that US pilots ferry the aircraft across the North Atlantic, and in six months the Ferrying Command flew 1,350 planes to Britain. During the ferrying operation, women flyers joined the Women's Auxiliary Ferrying Squadron, with public support from Eleanor Roosevelt. Aviatrix Jacqueline Cochran prevailed upon Hap Arnold to form the Women's Flying Training Detachment to recruit and train women for ferrying duties. (Cochran also took women overseas to volunteer for the RAF's Air Transport Auxiliary.) In 1943, the organizations merged into the Women's Air Force Service Pilots (WASP), the members of which were civil service employees. With the end of the war in sight and a cutback in the USAAF, male pilots offered to perform ferrying duties; as a result, the

Top: **The light of dawn finds a fleet of Lockheed Hudson Bombers awaiting delivery to the Royal Air Force. The rugged Hudson was a specially modified Super Electra, nicknamed 'Boomerang' because it always returned home from missions.**

Right: **African-Americans flew fighters in the 332nd Fighter Group and were known as the Tuskegee Airmen. As bomber escorts, the Tuskegee Airmen lost 66 men to combat, but never lost a bomber to enemy aircraft.**

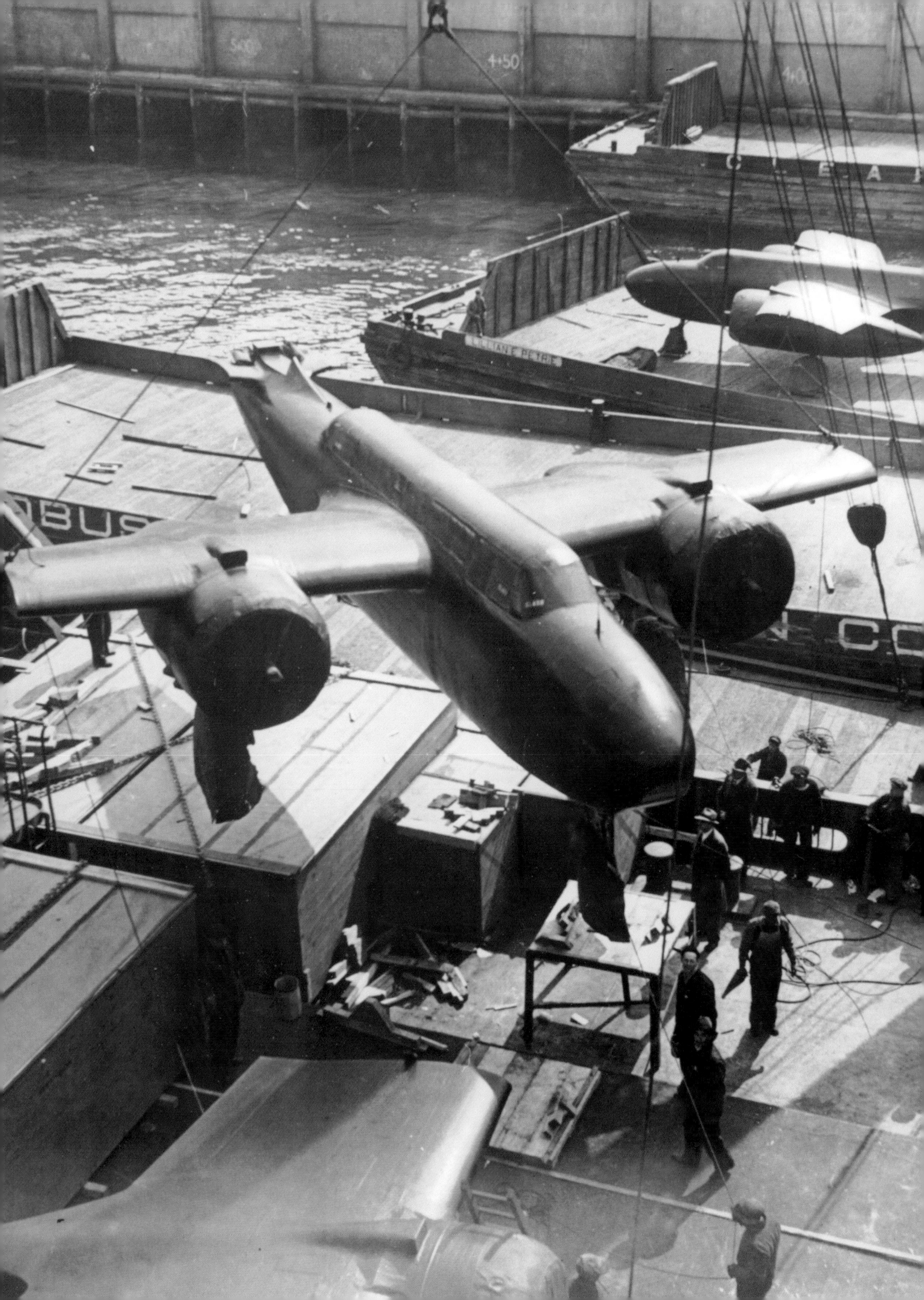

WASP were deactivated in 1944.

Women were not the only Americans to achieve a measure of social progress. The Selective Training and Service Act of 1940 prohibited discrimination because of 'race and color,' and the USAAF had to accept blacks for the first time. In 1941, thirteen cadets joined the first aviation class at the Tuskegee Institute in Alabama. Nine months later, five pilots completed training, including Captain Benjamin O. Davis, Jr., a West Point graduate. During the war, almost a thousand African-American pilots would be trained, collectively known as the Tuskegee Airmen.

The war in Europe took an unexpected turn. Hitler invaded the Soviet Union. On 22 June, Operation Barbarossa began, with Moscow as the primary objective. The Luftwaffe sent four of its five air fleets to the eastern front and destroyed 1000 Soviet aircraft on the first day. The German forces advanced with such rapidity that the Luftwaffe abandoned aircraft and spare parts. In time, logistical missteps would cause the Luftwaffe to lose more planes to malfunction than to combat. The only recourse for the Red Army was to fall back, burning everything as they went. By October, the Wehrmacht was outside Moscow.

Several factors interfered in Hitler's 'six week' strategy. Churchill, a staunch anti-Bolshevik, came to Stalin's aid. Roosevelt, too, extended Lend-Lease to the Soviets. Meanwhile, on the battlefield, weeks of rain turned roads to mud pits. Then came the subzero temperatures of the Russian winter—the worst in 20 years—and airplane engines became frozen blocks that would not start unless ground crews set fires to thaw them. Maintenance became impossible as mechanics' hands froze to metal surfaces. By 5 December, the attack on Moscow had to be abandoned.

The United States Enters the War

On Sunday, 7 December 1941, at 7:55 AM Hawaii time, the forces of Imperial Japan attacked US military installations at Pearl Harbor, Hawaii. The next day Roosevelt sought a declaration of war. Germany, assuming that Japan would be the primary target, declared war on the United States. Germany also assumed that it could finish its business in Russia before US forces reached the European theater.

On 22 December, Churchill and Roosevelt met in Washington, DC. Germany was to be defeated first, they agreed, even as Japan moved into New Guinea and threatened Australia. Roosevelt and Churchill also agreed that control of the Mediterranean affected key supply lines, aircraft routes, and oil fields. Churchill wanted the Allies to invade North Africa, something US commanders did not wish to do. Such a large-scale operation, they said, would be a nightmare of logistics and supply—and they were right.

On 9 March, the US Army Air Force achieved autonomy for the war's duration, plus six months. They were to operate replacement training centers and schools; organize tactical units; develop tactical and training doctrine, tables of organization, military characteristics of airplanes, weapons and equipment; develop ground air support, tactical training, and doctrine in conformity with policies prescribed by the War Department. Hap Arnold became the USAAF's first Commanding General.

The prototype for every warplane had been designed, tested, and cleared for production. Shell Oil executive, and reserve pilot, Jimmy Doolittle was reactivated and assigned to monitor the automobile industry's production of aircraft. Lieutenant Colonel Doolittle had long pressed for development of 100-octane fuel, and had convinced Shell to manufacture such fuel

Left: **Douglas A-20s being shipped to England as part of President Franklin Roosevelt's Lend-Lease program, which provided aircraft and arms to America's allies in the period before the US entered the war.**

Above: **A bomber crew reviews the details of their mission to destroy a rail center in central Italy. The mission was part of 'Operation Strangle,' which targeted German supply lines.**

Below: **Stalingrad, Russia shows the devastating effectiveness of Hitler's Luftwaffe. With buildings constructed mostly of wood, the city of 600,000 was reduced to wasteland of solitary walls and chimneys.**

and stockpile ingredients for more.

The US Eighth Air Force formed on 28 January when its headquarters was activated at Savannah Army Air Base in Georgia. At first known as the 'Fifth,' it became the 'Eighth' when units in US overseas possessions and protectorates were incorporated into the Fifth, Sixth, and Seventh Air Forces. Brigadier General Ira Eaker went to Britain to set up the Eighth headquarters, to be commanded by Major General Carl 'Tooey' Spaatz. (Spaatz and Eaker would play leading roles as commanders in the European and Mediterranean theaters.) With the help of the British Air Ministry and of RAF Bomber Command, a network of bases was organized for Eighth Air Force personnel, who sailed for Liverpool on 27 April. The first B-17s left on 23 June. By the end of August, P-38s and C-47 cargo planes had also arrived. Many of the aircrews were untutored in gunnery and navigation, and upon arriving, encountered conditions unfamiliar to them, such as haze and snow. Too many pilots had almost no experience in formation flying. But Hap Arnold was determined to demonstrate the effectiveness of his forces and to strike a blow for air force independence. Ready or not, the Eighth Air Force prepared for combat.

Royal Air Force doctrine, implemented by Air Marshal Sir Arthur Harris, had shifted to massive nighttime bombing, exemplified by the 1000 plane raid on May 30 against Cologne. By daylight the RAF deployed smaller bombers at low altitudes, flying to targets within a limited radius. Like Hap Arnold, Spaatz and Eaker were committed to long-range daylight bombing using the B-17 Flying Fortress. With engines that allowed for a bomb load of 8,000 pounds, B-17s were to deliver half of all bombs dropped in Europe. Before production stopped, more than 12,500 B-17s were built by Boeing, Douglas, and Lockheed-Vega. On 17 August, the first all-American bombing mission against French targets was conducted. Twelve B-17s of the 97th Bomb Group, Eighth Air Force, escorted by 108 Spitfires, hit the railroad yards at Rouen-Sotteville. The lead pilot was Paul W. Tibbets, Jr., who in 1945 would fly the B-29 that released the first atomic bomb.

Small formations of B-17s continued to attack France and Holland. During

Above: **The North American AT-6 'Texan' was used by American and other Allied forces to train their fighter pilots, but was also used in many other capacities, including bomber, strafer, and 'brass taxi.'**

Left: **An American soldier examines the wreckage of a Focke-Wulf Fw 200 Kondor, shot down somewhere over Iceland. The long-range bomber was used by Germany to attack Allied ships at sea.**

Above: **The Republic P-47 Thunderbolt was known for its speed and durability. Its original mission was as a high-altitude bomber escort, but the P-47 also saw duty as a fighter-bomber.**
Below: **Workers put the finishing touches on a North American B-25 Mitchell. In 1942 a fleet of B-25s, led by Jimmy Doolittle, took off for Tokyo from the deck of the USS *Hornet* to become the first US aircraft to attack the Japanese mainland.**

these first few probing missions two Fortresses were lost, on 6 September, when Luftwaffe fighters mounted a defense of German-occupied territory. To fend off the enemy attacks, Curtiss P-40s escorted the B-17s. The P-40 was a durable aircraft that could absorb punishment, but it was outclassed by the Messerschmitt Me-109s and Focke-Wulf 190s in speed and maneuverability. Too often, the limited range of the P-40s and RAF Spitfires forced B-17s to fly without escort, especially as the Allied target radius began to expand. More determined German resistance would cause the losses of B-17s to rise from 2 percent when escorted to almost 8 percent when unescorted.

The USAAF in North Africa

In mid-1942, elements of the US Eighth Air Force transferred to North Africa. The units that stayed in Britain shifted from strategic bombardment to striking U-Boat pens with bombs of up to 2,000 pounds, to little effect. Stalin had extracted a promise from Roosevelt that the Allies would open a second front, for until now the Red Army had fought a largely unassisted war against the German invaders. To placate Stalin, Roosevelt accepted Churchill's proposal to invade North Africa. For his part, Churchill wished to secure Egypt in order to protect British bases in the Mediterranean, such as Gibraltar, Malta, and Alexandria. Without these bases, or without the Suez Canal, Allied oil tankers from Iraq would be forced to circumnavigate South Africa.

The shift to the Mediterranean was opposed by Hap Arnold and Army Chief of Staff Marshall. North Africa, Marshall argued, would drain Allied resources and jeopardize the invasion of Europe. But along the northern edge of Africa, General Erwin Rommel's armored Afrika Korps staged fluid attacks and counterattacks, and regained control of hundreds of miles of desert from Egypt to Libya. Only the RAF Desert Air Force saved the British Eighth Army from being routed. By the spring, the British had retreated to El Alamein, west of Alexandria, Britain's easternmost Mediterranean base.

B-17 bombers from the US Tenth Air Force were diverted from India, and 'Liberator' B-24s were diverted from China. By October, the Middle East Air Force (MEAF) had 4000 airmen, including advance elements of the 376th Bomber Group and 79th Fighter Group. In western North Africa, Hap Arnold assigned Brigadier General Jimmy Doolittle to create the Twelfth Air Force. Three combat groups were transferred from the Eighth Air Force in Britain: the 57th Fighter group (P-40s), the 8th Bomber Group (B-24s), and the 12th Medium Bomber Group (B-25s). The USAAF and RAF coordinated attacks upon Axis supply lines, airfields, munitions and fuel dumps, convoys at sea, and harbor facilities. But it wasn't easy: heat sickened airmen, sand ruined engines, and the skin of the aircraft was too hot for ground crews to perform maintenance.

After six weeks, 200,000 men and 1,000 tanks had gathered under the command of General Bernard Montgomery. On 23 October, Allied fighters and bombers attacked Axis gun emplacements, tank groups, infantry positions, and supply lines, forcing the Afrika Korps to fall back. Prepared air fields were prized and too few. Troops on the advance were forced to use unprepared airfields, whereas the troops in retreat fell back to prepared ones, and the advantage in air power shifted accordingly. Allied aircraft struck at airfields to prevent Axis planes from contesting the ground battle. Once an airfield was abandoned, the Allies flew

in to occupy it. By hopping from field to field across the sands of North Africa, the Allies mimicked the island-hopping tactics used in the Pacific. Once the winter arrived, and the rains, unprepared airfields turned to muck.

On 8 November, the Allies launched Operation Torch, an amphibious landing by multiple task forces from Morocco to Tunisia. General Dwight Eisenhower had been given command of the Allied forces in this operation, but it was General George S. Patton who presented an 'American' face west of the Strait of Gibraltar, in the hope that the Vichy French forces would not resist. The airlift of British troops east of the Strait of Gibraltar did not go as well. Because the British lacked transports, US C-47s filled in. Faulty intelligence held that the Vichy forces in Algeria would give up without a fight. (French distaste for Britain had intensified when the Royal Navy surprised the Vichy fleet in Oran harbor, killing 2,400 sailors.) The C-47s arrived filled with equipment and troops, expecting no opposition. Instead, they were met by fighters and flak, and the airborne landings were scrapped or scattered into the desert. Vichy resistance ended on 12 November, having thoroughly disrupted the Allied landings.

Above: **The speed, maneuverability, and range of the North American P-51 Mustang made it possible to protect bombers making runs deep inside German territory.**

The landings in the northwest, together with Montgomery's advance from Egypt, created a pincer movement that drove the Axis army into Tunisia. Airlift provided ground commanders with the mobility to deploy troops and equipment as needed. Air carriers dropped troops one day, and returned with antiaircraft guns and gasoline the next. Equipment and support personnel were moved into the desert. Evacuation of the wounded was accomplished after supplies had been delivered to forward airfields.

In January 1943, at the Casablanca conference, Roosevelt declared there could be only one outcome, the 'unconditional surrender' of the Axis. A corresponding intransigence on the part of Hitler, as well as the reluctance of his generals to challenge him, meant a long fight. RAF Air Marshal Harris lobbied for the use of US B-17s on massive night raids against enemy power plants, aircraft factories, oil refineries, rubber factories, transportation hubs, and worker housing. General Eaker advocated daylight bombardment of very specific industries, such as ball bearing manufacturers. Churchill and Roosevelt reconciled the two approaches, declaring that Germany was to be subjected to 'round-the-clock' bombardment, as each air service went its own way.

In February, Rommel staged a final offensive, breaking through the Allied lines. Allied air operations were hampered as their forward bases were overrun. C-47s had to fly greater distances to transport fuel and munitions. In time, Rommel was pushed back, but his breakthrough had exposed defects in the combined air and ground operations, in particular US planning and practices, for which the USAAF assumed its share of blame.

Air Vice Marshal Arthur Coningham, a New Zealander, convinced General Eisenhower that close air support had to be organized on a basis of scarcity. Ground commanders could not expect air support on demand. Centralized control was fundamental, Coningham argued, for with limited resources, air units should be used only for the most crucial missions. Eisenhower agreed, but Coningham knew that convincing other Allied field generals, such as Patton, would be difficult, especially if, as a result, fewer Allied aircraft were to appear in support of ground troops.

The fury with which Tunisia was contested reflected its importance as the staging ground for an invasion of south-

ern Europe. Hitler had sent every man and machine he could spare from the eastern front, with as many as 500 planes airlifting reinforcements every night from Sicily and Sardinia. Allied fighters attacked the airlift on 5 April, reducing its strength by about 200 planes. Still, the Axis forces held on, with Stuka bombers and Messerschmitt fighters substituting for artillery. Speedy, well-armed German fighters, such as the FW-190, were rushed to North Africa, but too few arrived to prevent the Allies from achieving air superiority. When Tunisia fell in May, 250,000 Axis troops surrendered, mostly Germans. The USAAF losses were modest, 500 planes, 1,700 combat casualties.

On land, sea, and air, the North African campaign had strained Allied capabilities. The air forces had been sent on too many missions that served too many, often contradictory purposes. The USAAF and the RAF had found it difficult to coordinate command, since British and American officers were 'interleaved,' so that airmen of one nation were under the command of officers of another. Still, the combined forces, however inefficiently, had destroyed 60 percent of the fuel, food, and ammunition being shipped to North Africa; air supremacy had been won and a continent had been liberated.

Both the B-17 'Flying Fortress' and the B-24 'Liberator' had great range and bomb capacity, although the Flying Fortress (*top*) had better defenses than the B-24 (*below*), making unescorted bombing runs slightly less harrowing.

CHAPTER 5
TURBULENT TIMES: 1943–1944

Turbulent Times: 1943-1944

Early in 1943, Air Vice Marshal Coningham briefed Allied Command on the missteps, miscommunications, and tangled logistics that had prevented air power from achieving a speedy victory in North Africa. He asked that the commanders recognize the difference between air and ground forces, their coequality, and the need for each to cooperate and attack in unison. General Marshall approved a revision of doctrine, one that acknowledged flexibility of air power and centralized control under an air force commander. In mid-May, Hap Arnold (now a four-star general, a first for the USAAF) appointed Brigadier General Laurence S. Kuter as assistant air chief of staff for plans. Kuter, a veteran of North Africa, formed a committee of air and ground officers to produce Field Manual (FM) 100-20, Command and Employment of Air Power.

FM 100-20, issued by the War Department on 21 July, held that strategic bombardment, independent of surface forces, could win wars; that air superiority was necessary to enable all other air—and most surface—operations; that airpower should be centrally controlled by an airman. The primary function of the AAF, therefore, was to achieve superiority by degrading enemy air force. The basic tasks were to destroy hostile aircraft and existing bases; to operate against hostile land and sea forces; to wage offensive warfare against the sources of enemy military and economic strength; to operate as a part of task forces in military operations. In March, the AAF underwent its final wartime reorganization. Policymaking was combined with control of operations vested in six Chiefs of Air Staff: Personnel; Intelligence; Training; Materiel Maintenance and Distribution; Operations, Commitments, and Requirements; Plans.

The Sicily campaign was under overall command of General Dwight Eisenhower. Field commanders were General Montgomery with the British Eighth Army, and General Patton with the US Seventh Army. General Spaatz commanded the Northwest African Air Forces (NAAF), which included the Northwest African Strategic Air Force (NASAF), Jimmy Doolittle commanding, and Northwest African Tactical Air Force (NATAF) under Coningham. The first objective was to capture Pantelleria and Lampedusa, small islands between Sicily and Tunisia. Pantelleria, known as the 'Italian Gibraltar,' was defended by more than 10,000 Italian troops and fortified batteries. On 18 May, the aerial bombardment of Pantelleria began, supplemented by a naval blockade. Within weeks, the Italians surrendered, avoiding a full-scale invasion. On 11 June Allied bombers raided Lampedusa, a less well-defended target. Two days later, Lampedusa fell into Allied hands. Air power was the principal instrument of victory in each case.

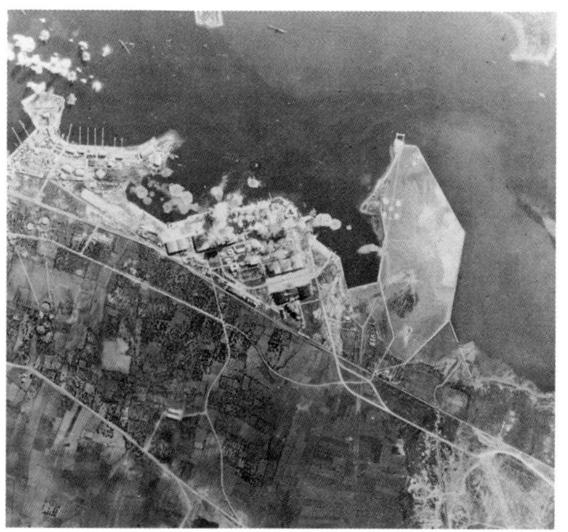

Previous page: **The Curtiss C-46 Commando was the Army's primary troop transport during World War II. Flying escort is a Curtiss P-40 fighter plane.**

Above: **The crew of the Snow White, a B-24D bomber, based in North Africa. The 343rd Bomber Squadron was know as the Snow White Squadron, with the planes named for characters from the fairy tale.**

Below left: **An aerial view of Allied bombs hitting an Axis naval base in Bizerte, Tunisia, in the spring of 1943. The North African campaign helped to erode Germany's fuel supplies.**

Below: **A Martin B-26 Marauder shows heavy anti-aircraft damage to her left wing after a bombing raid over Tunisia.**

The Battle for Sicily

On 9 July 1943, Operation Husky set forth from Tunisia, with 2600 vessels carrying 160,000 men. Allied aircraft from Pantelleria and Lampedusa patrolled from Gibraltar to Alexandria. Achieving and maintaining Allied air superiority was a critical factor, and therefore field generals did not receive the constant air cover that they wanted. With or without air cover, Patton's army was to land in the northwest and take Palermo, and Montgomery's army was to land in the east and take Syracuse. The Allied armies were to converge upon Messina, three miles by water off the coast of Italy.

The first troops to reach Sicily arrived in gliders. On 9 and 10 July, the C-47s of Troop Carrier Command towed as many as 140 Waco CG-4A gliders with 1,600 British airborne troops. The C-47 could absorb considerable punishment, which, when approaching a drop zone at 100 mph, and releasing gliders from as low as 500 to 1,500 feet, was a useful characteristic. High winds and flak forced the C-47s off course, so multiple passes were made in order to line up the release. At

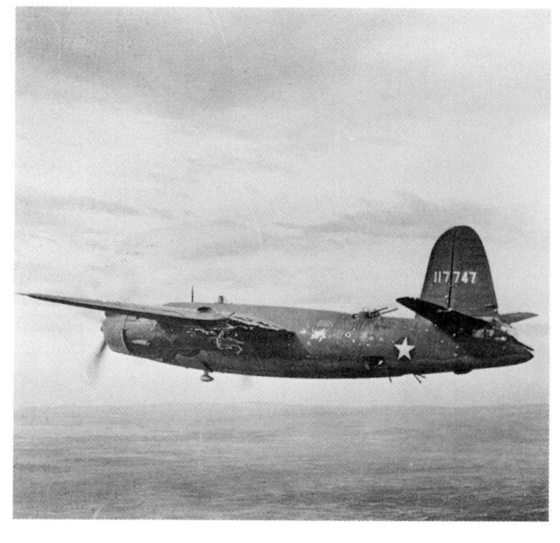

least 47 gliders came down at sea, and the British troops on board drowned. Only 12 gliders reached the objective, and the glider-men, 73 strong, took the bridge and held it until Montgomery's forces arrived. The paratroop drop of US troops in support of Patton's Seventh Army benefited from enemy confusion. An Allied bombing raid had hit the Italian headquarters, cutting off communication. Unsure where US troops were coming from, and without orders, the Italians withdrew, and Patton's forces moved up from the beachhead.

By 11 July, Montgomery and Patton had advanced 38 miles into Sicily. More paratroop drops were required, and with Allied battleships off-shore, Troop Carrier Command made an attempt to clear the way for the C-47s to fly over the fleet. Navy gunners, unaware of the formation's identity, opened fire, as did shore batteries. Twenty-three C-47s were lost, along with many of the troops on board. Two nights later, a British mission came under similar fire, and 11 C-47s were shot down and 50 damaged.

Infantry and artillery troops were no less embittered when Allied aircraft mistakenly attacked their positions. Such incidents, after the bloody fact, forced the US military to reform the ways in which its branches communicated and coordinated. Even though more than 60 percent of the paratroops had landed outside the drop zones, military airlift was now a weapon to be used in the Pacific and in the invasion of France.

***Above:* A B-17 Flying Fortress scores a direct hit on an Italian troop ship attempting evasive maneuvers in the Mediterranean sea. Bombs exploding in the water next to the hull of a ship often did more to sink the vessel than a direct hit.**

***Below:* The Curtiss P-40 was the Allied workhorse in the sky for much of WWII. Alternately called the 'Warhorse,' the 'Tomahawk,' and the 'Kittyhawk,' the P-40 underwent many model changes to improve performance and armament.**

On the ground in Sicily, the advance of Montgomery's Eighth Army had stalled. Patton's Seventh Army fought to Palermo and entered the city on 22 July. By now the Allies had air superiority and began operations over Italy, with the first raid on Rome conducted by B-17s and B-24s of Jimmy Doolittle's NASAF. On 26 July, with the loss of Sicily near, Mussolini was arrested. Pietro Badoglio was made head of state and offered to negotiate, an offer the Allies accepted in direct contradiction to the policy of 'unconditional surrender.'

On August 11, the Axis retreat began across the Strait of Messina, its rocky coast fortified by large guns. Hitler took command of the evacuation and deployed his troops to delay Montgomery and Patton's advance. Allied air forces did not attempt to interdict the retreat. Although 100,000 Axis troops were taken prisoner in Sicily, four German Divisions escaped, as did 70,000 Italians, for a total of 110,000 evacuees.

Sicily passed into Allied hands, at a cost of 16,000 casualties, with 27,000 casualties for the Axis. Patton, lauded in public for his wide flanking movements and amphibious end runs, had shown himself to be too eager to outrun his supplies. General Eisenhower, a more cautious commander, chose Gen. Mark Clark to command the US Fifth Army for the Italian invasion.

The War Proceeds on Several Fronts

The campaign in Sicily revealed deficits in Allied planning and operations, foremost of which was the lack of a coherent overall strategy. As always, the ground commanders had called for close air support and complained when it was not forthcoming. Eisenhower agonized over how to apply air power in support of land operations, when each commander demanded that USAAF resources be deployed according to parochial battlefield interests, especially when the battle was conducted on a continental scale, as would be the case for the invasion of Europe.

As the Allies conquered Sicily, Germany's war-making machine began to show strains, in particular its tenuous supply of oil. In 1939, Hitler had argued that Germany's need for resources justified going to war, but after four years of mechanized warfare, depleted fuel reserves threatened the Reich's survival. Small wonder, then, that the Russian Caucasus, with its abundance of oil, became an objective of the eastern front.

On 19 August 1942, the German Sixth Army attacked Stalingrad, and after weeks of street-fighting controlled 80 percent of the city. In mid-November, the Soviets routed the Italian, Hungarian, and Romanian forces protecting the German flank, and more than 300,000 of the German Sixth Army were trapped. Not until February 1943 did the 91,000 remaining Germans surrender, of whom only 6,000 survived captivity. The victory at Stalingrad had cost the Soviets 500,000 lives. In its merciless drive to expel the Germans from Russia, the Red Army waged a war of attrition on the ground and in the air, culminating with the Battle of Kursk, where the Luftwaffe forces there were almost completely destroyed.

At Germany's moment of vulnerability, the USAAF struck the oil refineries at Ploesti, Romania. On August 1, B-24s of the US Ninth Air Force set off from Libya to Ploesti. Clouds caused the formation to break up in route, and groups of bombers arrived at different times, coming in at treetop height, taking flak. Delayed action bombs dropped moments before exploded as B-24s arrived, a new form of friendly fire. The cost: 54 planes and 532 men. The raid earned five AAF pilots the Medal of Honor, the most given out for a single mission: Colonel Leon Johnson, Colonel John Kane, Lieutenant Col. Addison Baker, Major John Jerstad, and 2nd Lieutenant Lloyd Hughes.

Roosevelt and Churchill met in Quebec, Canada, in August. The two leaders were heartened by the downfall of Mussolini, but alarmed by the extent of Allied disorganization. The two men had begun to consider the shape of a postwar world. Churchill, in particular, had urged a Balkan invasion to discourage the Soviets from moving into the region, but Roosevelt declined. In turn, Roosevelt postponed a Burma offensive, a move that disappointed his commanders in the Pacific who were eager to bring the fight to the Japanese. Now that 600,000 Allied troops and 150,000 airmen were in the Mediterranean, the liberation of Italy took priority.

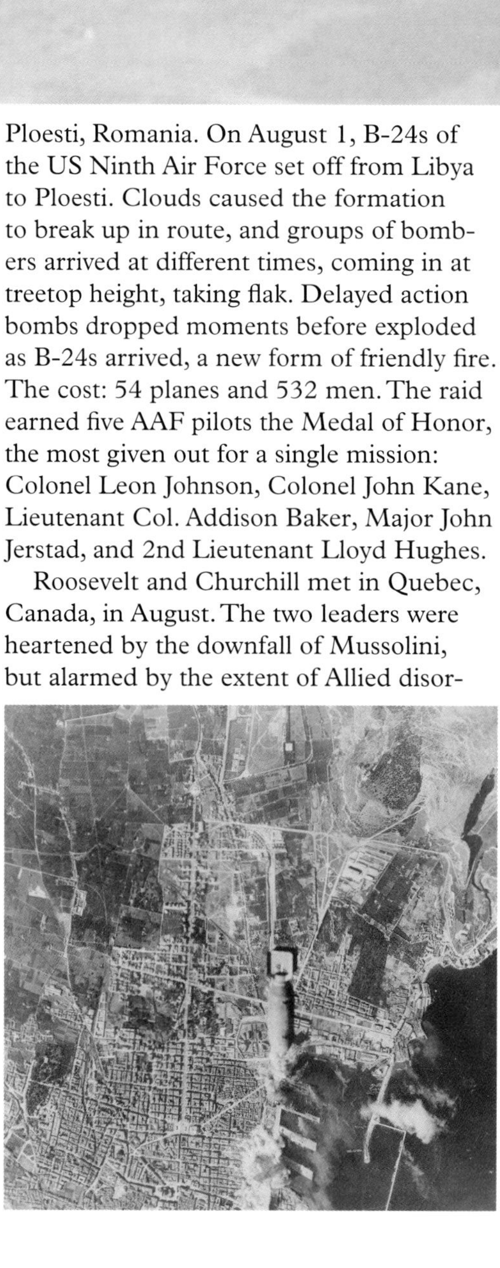

Above: **The Curtiss C-46 troop transport was originally built as a 36-seat civilian airliner. Modifications for military service included folding seats along the fuselage, larger cargo doors at the rear, and open space in the cabin for stretchers and cargo.**

Below: **A bomb dropped from the belly of a B-17 falls toward its target, the shipping and harbor installations at Palermo, Sicily. The bombing preceded the amphibious invasion by Allied forces on 10 July 1943.**

The Battle for Italy

During the weeks leading up to the Italy campaign, Allied bombers raided southern air bases until Italian and German air forces were in disarray. On 3 September, British troops led by Montgomery landed at Calabria on the toe of Italy. On 8 September, the US Fifth Army led by General Clark landed

at Salerno, south of Naples. Only with additional airborne interventions did Clark's Fifth Army secure the beachhead. More British troops landed at Taranto, near the top of Italy's heel. By the end of the month, German forces had been pushed out of the south, and the airfields there were used by Allied pilots to maintain air superiority over the beachheads.

The government of Italy had officially surrendered, but 16 German divisions remained in control of two-thirds of the

***Above:* Planes and crews with significant accomplishments, like the crew of the B-17 'Memphis Belle,' with 25 successful missions, were sent on tours of the United States to promote war bonds.**

***Left:* B-17s of the Army Eighth Air Force release their payloads over Meudon, France, in September 1943. The B-17G Flying Fortress had 13 machine guns for defense and could carry more than 17,500 pounds of bombs.**

The Douglas C-39 was used as a transport plane during WWII. The modified airliner participated in the evacuation of personnel from the Philippines to Australia in December 1941, just after the attack on Pearl Harbor.

***Opposite top:* During WWII the Women Airforce Service Pilots (WASP) ferried planes to destinations within the continental United States in order to free up male pilots for combat duty. Over 1,000 WASP flew over 60 million miles during the war.**

***Opposite middle:* The twin-engine Lockheed P-38 dominated the air in WWII with its speed and firepower. Major Richard I. Bong, America's ace of aces, had 40 victories over the Pacific flying the P-38.**

***Opposite bottom:* American ace Francis Gabreski had 28 victories in his P-47 Thunderbolt. Nicknamed 'Jug,' the P-47 was versatile and deadly in nearly all theaters of WWII.**

17

PISTOL
MAMA

2104309

country. Allied intelligence had indicated Hitler would not contest Rome, yet on 11 September, German troops occupied the city. The next day the Germans 'stole' Mussolini from his Italian captors. A Fascist government was installed with Mussolini as figurehead, but all orders came from Berlin. Throughout September, no matter where the Allies attacked and the Germans counterattacked, the battle for Italy devolved into a siege.

In October, the Allied Air Force bombed German supply lines, but the Germans ran night trains loaded with reinforcements and munitions, and engineers repaired bridges as quickly as Allied aircraft damaged them. As November began, 25 German divisions held well-fortified positions, against which 11 Allied divisions were arrayed. Repeated attempts over the next six months to outflank the Germans failed. The result was a winter stalemate.

The Bombing Campaign over Germany

The bombing raids by the US Eighth Air Force in Britain had been scaled back during the North African campaign. Once Tunisia and Sicily had fallen, and once German armies on the eastern front were in retreat, and with the stalemate in Italy, the Eighth Air Force, under General Eaker, again set its sights on Germany.

The USAAF and the RAF Bomber Command were joined in the Combined Bomber Offensive, in which two different strategies were used. The RAF preferred nighttime 'area bombing,' also called saturation or carpet-bombing, in which a very large number of bombs dropped in

Above: **Capt. Armour McDaniels examines battle damage on his P-51 Mustang. McDaniels, a member of the 332nd Pursuit Group, the Tuskegee Airmen, was shot down over Berlin in 1945 and taken prisoner but was later freed by Allied troops.**

Right: **A B-17 turns for home after completing a bombing raid on a Focke-Wulf factory in Marienburg, Germany. The attack demonstrates the relative degree of precision bombing crews were able to achieve on enemy targets.**

Inset: **A formation of B-25s have their bomb sights set on rail targets in northern Italy in order to cut off Axis supply lines.**

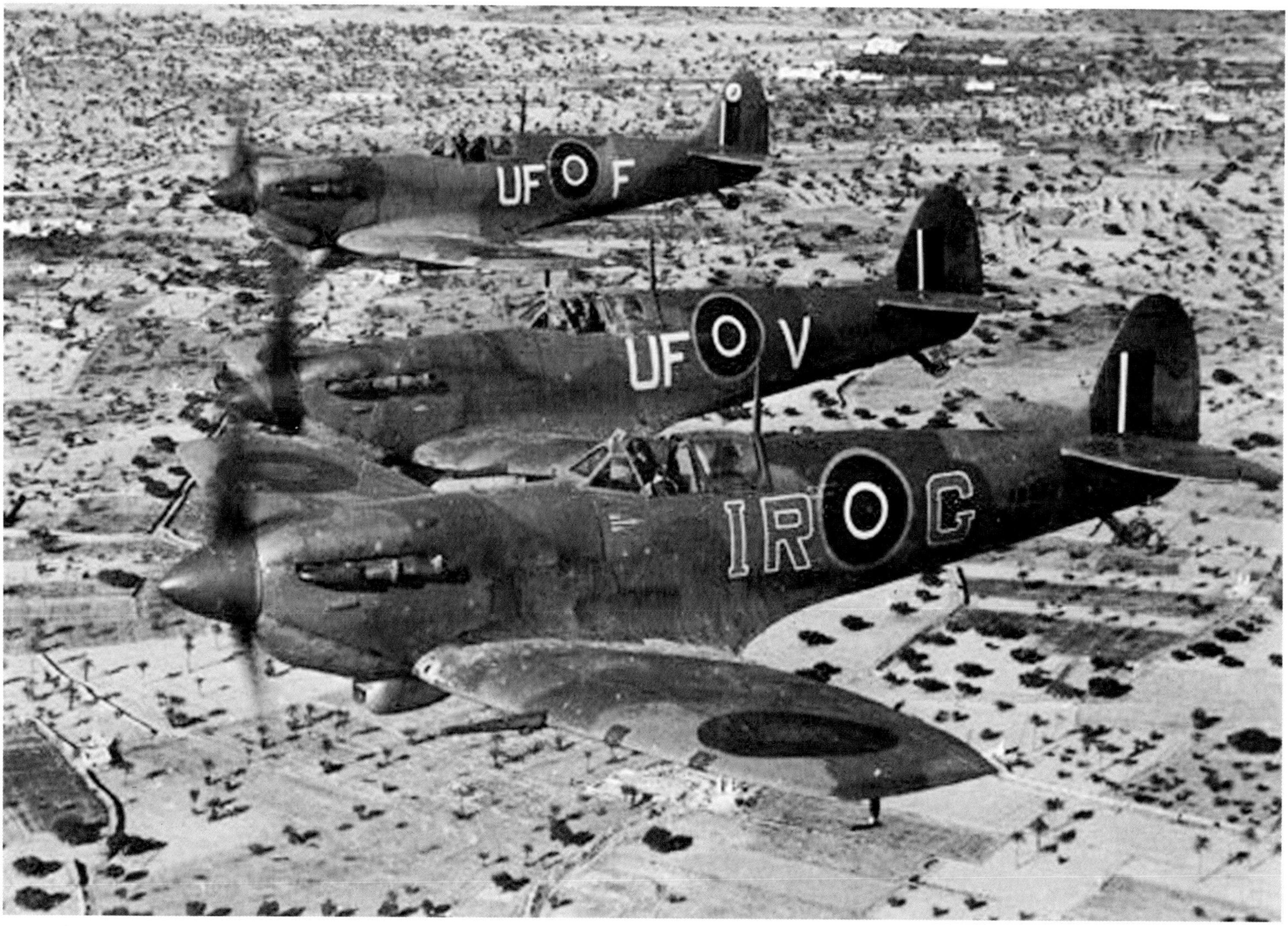

Above: **The British Royal Air Force and some American units flew the Supermarine MkII Spitfire. Here a formation of RAF Spitfires flies a mission over North Africa in 1943.**

Below: **An elated crew of the 'Memphis Belle' returns from their twenty-fifth bombing mission. The commander of the famous bomber, Colonel Robert Morgan, died in 2004 at the age of 84.**

a particular area ensured the destruction of a target. General Eaker held fast to US air doctrine, by which his bombardiers used the Norden bombsight to hit specific factories or transportation hubs, thereby minimizing damage to the surrounding areas. But loss rates on daylight missions were high, and British flyers referred to B-17s as 'bait' to draw German fighters into combat.

On 27 January, Eaker's B-17s hit Germany for the first time, striking Wilhelmshaven. On 4 February, in an attack on Emden, the B-17s were engaged by twin-engine Me-110s and Ju-88s, as well as single-engine Me-109s and Fw-190s. German pilots had observed that B-17s were lightly protected in the nose, so frontal attack became the tactic of choice. A German fighter flew straight for the nose of a B-17 at 500 mph, pouring machine gunfire and rockets dead ahead, and then veering at the last second. Under such attacks, B-17 losses on unescorted missions were mounting.

Early in 1943, the 4th Fighter Group, composed of the former American-volunteer Eagle Squadrons, received new P-47 fighters. The P-47s, while an improvement upon Spitfires, still could not escort bombers all the way to targets deep within Germany. On 13 June, 60 B-17s flew such a mission against Kiel on the Baltic Sea. As soon as the P-47s were forced to turn for home, the Luftwaffe attacked and shot down 22 Flying Fortresses.

On a typical daylight bombing raid, groups of B-17s climbed from British air bases to 25,000 feet, and massed in a fleet of 'box' formations. As the planes neared the shores of Holland (or Belgium or France) at 24,000 feet, German fighters appeared. The fighters swooped and fired on the bomber escorts, if any. B-17 gunners fired from the waists, the turrets, and the tail, as the pilot took care to stay in formation. Anti-aircraft bursts poured hot shrapnel through the wings and the fuselage. A B-17 could sustain tremendous damage and keep flying, but in an airplane filled with fuel, fires had to be put out immediately. A B-17 in its final throes was not a pretty sight, as it began to drift and then picked up speed as it dove down. When its structure exceeded its limits, parts broke away. Aircrews continuing on-

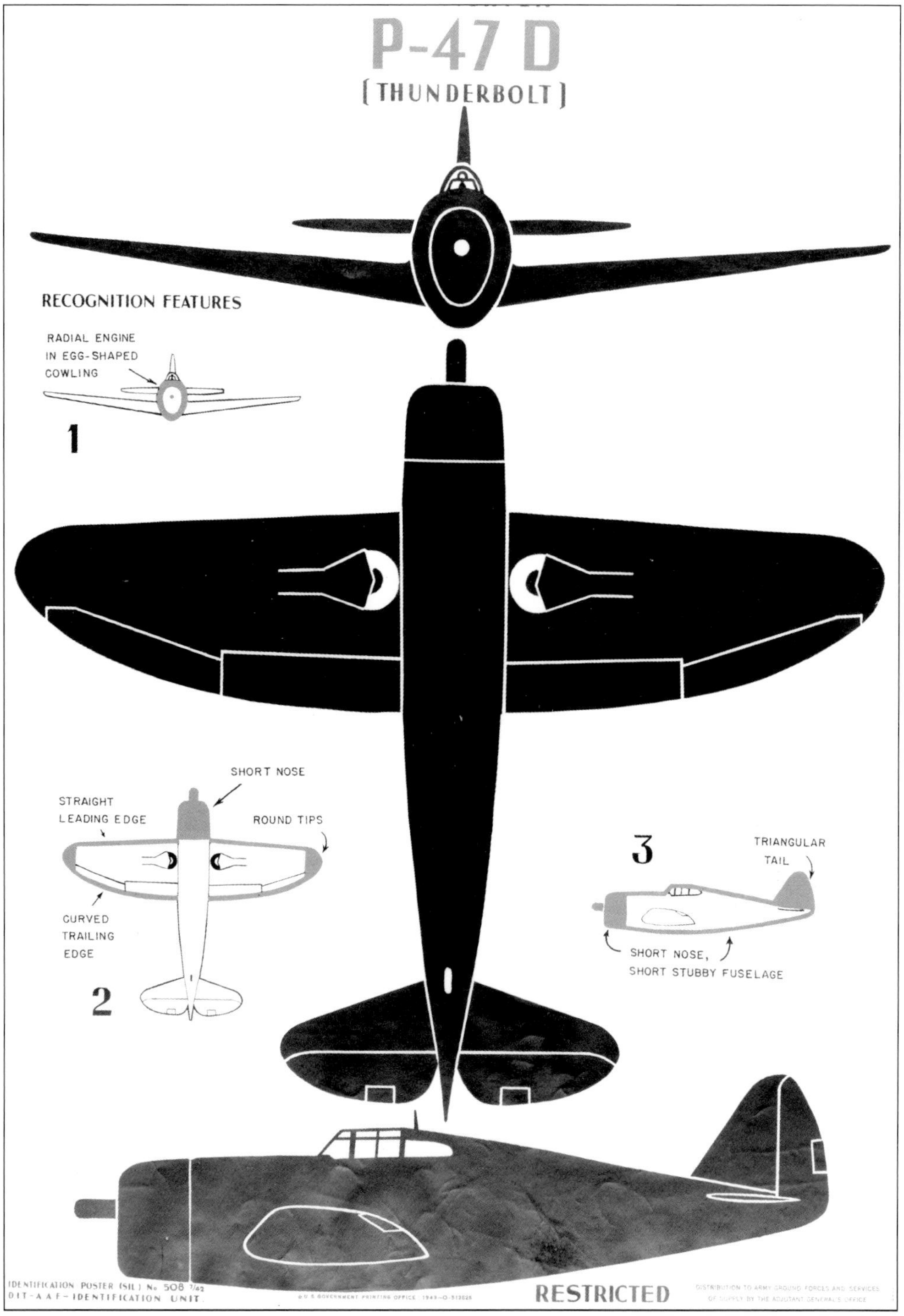

Above: **Posters like this one identifying a P-47 were distributed to aircraft spotters in cities in Europe and America. The posters helped spotters identify silhouettes and distinguishing markings of both Allied and enemy airplanes.**
Right: **A German tank works in Aschaffenburg shows the destruction of an American bombing raid. Such bombing raids crippled Germany's ability to replace arms destroyed in battle.**

Above: **A bombing run of marshalling yards at Hatvan, Hungary, by B-24 Liberators of the 15th Air Force on 20 September 1944. The strike was one of several on Hungarian cities in an attempt to weaken German supply lines.**

Below: **Glenn Miller (right) enlisted in the Army Air Force in October 1942 to lead the Allied Expeditionary Force Band. Miller was killed when his plane went down over the English Channel on 15 December 1944.**

ward could only hope that, amidst debris and flak, their comrades had bailed out. Upon returning to base, crew members were interrogated on what they had seen, as well as the bombing results, which were difficult to measure. AAF sorties continued to strike at the industrial heart of Germany, but aircrew morale suffered as the odds for survival over 25 to 30 missions seemed slim.

In June, a directive to improve Allied bombing strategy was issued: 'Pointblank' proposed six target systems, comprising 76 precision targets, to be destroyed by heavy bombers. The objective was to paralyze Germany's war effort and economy beyond any hope of recovery. Commanding General Eaker and his Eighth Air Force were charged with achieving air superiority over the Continent through strategic bombardment.

By summer, Air Marshal Harris had introduced incendiary nighttime bombing against the German cities of Lubeck and Rostock, attacks that were denounced by Germany as terrorangriff (terror raids). Churchill had written to Lord Beaverbrook calling for 'an absolutely devastating extermination attack by very heavy bombers.' Air Marshal Harris issued Bomber Command Operation Orders, No.173: the 'total destruction' of Hamburg, Germany's second largest city, using 10,000 tons of bombs 'to complete the obliteration.'

A case can be made that neither Churchill nor Harris anticipated the full destructive effects of the Feuersturm (firestorm) they were about to cause. Some analysts, with the benefit of hindsight, cited the weather conditions, a stagnant high-pressure system, a period of low humidity, and the lack of rain as primary causal factors. Yet, the code name Harris had selected, Operation Gomorrah, explicitly referred to a Biblical city destroyed by fire. Many officers and air crews of the USAAF disapproved of such firebombing, as did a good number of RAF airmen. The Combined Bomber Offensive was predicated on USAAF/RAF collaboration, and so US airmen flew daylight missions to complement the nighttime firebombing of Hamburg.

On the night of 24 July the first raid reached Hamburg, with almost 800 RAF aircraft and nearly 3,000 tons of bombs. The central and northwestern districts were hit by high-explosives, and 1,500 people were killed. On the day of 25 July, 68 B-17s of the US Eighth Air Force attacked shipyards, and on 26 July, 53 B-17s hit a power plant. The RAF had staged their raid at night with relative impunity, losing only 1.5 percent of their total force. The Eighth Air Force lost 19 Fortresses, an indication of the danger to which US flyers were exposed on their daylight raids.

On the night of 27 July, more than 700 RAF aircraft attacked the already burning city, this time with incendiaries. More fires broke out in the densely built-up working-class districts. As new fires merged with old, the air heated and rose; cool air rushed in to take its place, and fierce winds surged through the streets. The searing air suffocated many who had sought refuge in bomb shelters. Temperatures reached 1,800 degrees Fahrenheit, and anyone who fled from a shelter into the open was consumed by a vortex of flame. More RAF bombers returned on 29 July and 2 August. In all, seven air raids had been staged in nine days. An estimated 45,000 people were dead, roughly equal to the casualties suffered by the British in all the German bombing raids of the war.

For the next several months, in spite of continuing losses, the USAAF conducted daylight bombing raids upon Germany. The notion of 'precision' bombing offered an alternative to the annihilation of Hamburg, at least in theory. But when B-17s came under fighter pressure, or when a bombardier was confounded by poor visibility, daylight bombing raids

were imprecise. In time, as bombers flew tight formations through withering fire, aircrews no longer used bombsights individually. Instead, once the bombardier of the lead B-17 released his bombs, the other B-17s released theirs. In effect, 'precision' bombing gave way to 'pattern' bombing, and AAF aircrews continued to take high casualties.

On 17 August, the Eighth Air Force targeted the Messerschmitt works at Regensburg and ball bearing plants at Schweinfurt. The P-47 escorts fell away at the German border, leaving 376 B-17s on their own, 60 of which were shot down. The bombing did considerable destruction, yet ball bearing production at Schweinfurt did not stop. On September 6, similar factories around Stuttgart were bombed by 262 B-17s and B-24s. For this raid, P-47s were fitted with belly fuel tanks to increase their range, yet they still could not go all the way to the target, with the result that 45 bombers were lost. On 9 October, 352 AAF bombers flew to targets in Poland and East Prussia, including the Focke-Wulf Assembly Plant at Marienburg. The attack was made from between 11,000 and 13,500 feet, and the loss rate still reached 8 percent.

The climax of the Eighth Air Force bombing campaign came on 14 October, when the B-17s returned to hit Schweinfurt. The moment the P-47 escorts turned away, Luftwaffe fighters attacked the formation for hundreds of miles until the target had been reached. Once the B-17s dropped their bombs and turned for home, the German fighters, having refueled, struck again. Of the 251 B-17s on the mission, 60 were destroyed, 138 were damaged, and 600 airmen were lost, a day known as "Black Thursday."

New Planes, New Tactics

Eighth Air Force bombers were being lost at an unacceptable rate. The 'Pointblank' program was put on hold, as General Spaatz and Hap Arnold, among others, rethought the use of B-17s. They concluded that daylight missions were not to be staged until fighter escorts with greater range arrived. The effort to design more effective escorts had been underway for years. After much testing, the P-51 fighter was introduced. Originally intended for reconnaissance and ground support, the 'Mustang,' as the British termed the P-51, was soon outfitted with Rolls Royce 'Merlin' engines that reached 432 mph at 32,000 feet. The P-51 now had the range required to accompany raids all the way into Germany, and production of P-51s accelerated.

Until the P-51 Mustang reached the European theater, US bomber forces used the tight-formation combat flying techniques devised by Curtis LeMay, then a colonel. Before LeMay arrived, group commanders had used layered formations to defend against fighters. Pilots were allowed to maneuver ('jinking') to avoid flak, but the sharp, random 'jinking' caused bombs to fall off the mark. LeMay developed a box-type formation that he believed would solve the problem.

Above: **A bomber's view of a formation of P-51 Mustangs. Combat formations were designed so that each individual plane was always protected by another plane.**

Below: **A B-29 wings its way for home over the frozen landscape of Norway after a bombing run. Germany had invaded Denmark and Norway in 1940.**

Each group consisted of 21 planes. The top planes flew above and slightly to the right of the formation's middle layer of planes. The bottom planes flew below and slightly to the left of the formation's middle. Between those two layers of planes, the middle planes flew slightly ahead. In other words, no plane was directly above or below another. If German fighters made a run at the nose of a B-17, the gunners in all the planes in the 'box' created multiple fields of overlapping fire, a powerful deterrent.

Hap Arnold appointed the Eighth Air Force's General Eaker as deputy for Allied Air Operations in the Mediterranean, regarded by Eaker and others as a 'kick upstairs.' The Eighth was placed under

General Jimmy Doolittle. Doolittle was delighted by the prospect of becoming the first commander to bomb the capital cities of all three Axis powers, having already led raids upon Tokyo and Rome.

Meanwhile, the P-38 Lightning and P-51 Mustang fighter escorts began arriving. Long-range heavy bombers of the Ninth Air Force were absorbed by the Twelfth Air Force. The Ninth's medium and light bombers became the IX Bomber Command, its fighters and fighter-bombers (fighters with bomb racks and extra armor) became the IX Fighter Command. The IX Fighter Command shifted from long-distance escort missions to providing close air support, with aircraft specifically identified for ground attack.

Poor weather hampered bombing operations until 20 February when more than 1,000 heavies, escorted by hundreds of long-range fighters, struck at 12 airplane plants across Germany. For the next week the Eighth Air Force attacked by day from Britain, as did the Fifteenth Air Force from Italy, while the RAF attacked at night. By now, B-17s and B-24s had radar so that the bombs could be placed on target even when visibility was poor. During 'The Big Week,' the Combined Bomber Offensive deployed more than 3,000 bombers, of which 226 B-17s were lost, with US casualties of 2,600. The result was that three-quarters of Germany's airplane industry had been bombed. By the spring of 1944, the Luftwaffe had lost its ability to contest Allied air superiority. The Luftwaffe could still strike, but skilled fighter pilots were scarce and German fuel reserves were low. Fewer and fewer German fighters rose in defense of the Fatherland.

'The War Was Decided'

The Allies stepped up the bombing of Germany and German-occupied territory, striking from every side. The Soviets provided three airfields near Kiev, to facilitate strikes by USAAF heavy bombers against eastern Germany and the Balkans. On 22 January, Allied Air Forces flew 1,200 sorties from Mediterranean bases in support of the amphibious landings at Anzio, on the coast south of Rome. The assault on Anzio was intended to break the stalemate in Italy, but the landings turned into another siege, as US and British troops repulsed repeated counterattacks. The Germans held the high ground above the Allied beachhead, and were unable to retreat, in part because they were out of fuel. All the Germans could do was to ration food and ammunition, and hold on.

As the Allies faced down the Germans in central Italy, heavy and medium bombers, along with light bombers and fighters

were readied for raids upon Berlin. The German capital had key industrial targets, and the strength of the Luftwaffe would be sapped in rising to defend Berlin. Doolittle was disappointed to learn that he would not lead the Berlin mission; he knew too much, and were he to be captured, Operation Overlord, the invasion of Normandy, would be put at risk. The first major attack upon Berlin came on 6 March. Of more than 600 heavy bombers deployed, almost 70 were lost. On 8 March, nearly 400 Eighth Air Force heavy bombers returned to Berlin, escorted by P-51s. The Luftwaffe, as expected, rose to contest each raid and suffered losses that exceeded the rate at which their fighters, and their pilots, could be replaced.

AAF fighter escort to the target and back to base had become standard. By late spring, German flak claimed more AAF bombers than were claimed by Luftwaffe fighters. At Allied headquarters, air and ground commanders clashed over targeting priorities. British strategists proposed the large-scale bombardment of railroad centers in France. Air Marshal Harris did not care to pause in his nighttime bombing of German cities. Jimmy Doolittle feared that a shift away from the Eighth Air Force's execution of the Pointblank target program would give the Luftwaffe an opportunity to rebuild. General Spaatz opposed the bombing of railroad centers ('Operation Chattanooga Choo-Choo,' as US airmen called it) largely because he wanted to hit four synthetic oil plants and thirteen refineries that provided half of Hitler's oil. Eisenhower compromised: when weather was bad in France and good in Germany, Spaatz, Doolittle, and Harris would conduct strategic bombardment; when weather was good in France, the railroad centers were the objective. The new bombing strategy went into effect in May.

After the war, Albert Speer, Minister for Armaments (and the architect of Hitler's imperial Berlin), identified 12 May 1944 as the day the "war was decided. [T]he attack of nine hundred and thirty-five daylight bombers of the American Eighth Air Force upon several fuel plants in central and eastern Germany . . . meant the end of German armaments production."

Above: **Members of the Army Air Force stationed in England cheer on children in a game of tug-of-war at an Easter celebration. The children received candies that the soldiers had saved from their rations.**

Left: **In 1941 the US government asked American children to build scale models of airplanes for use in training military and civilian personnel to spot hostile aircraft. For some this hobby grew into a life-long passion for airplanes.**

5
22
13

CHAPTER 6
FLIGHTS TO VICTORY: 1944-1945

FLIGHTS TO VICTORY: 1944-1945

By June 1944, the Eighth Air Force had amassed 40 heavy bomber groups and 15 fighter groups with which to attack railroad yards and bridges across Belgium and northern France. In Italy, the US Fifth and Eighth Armies drove the Germans back to the southern edge of the Po River Valley. Staging from forward bases in Italy, the US Fifteenth Air Force raided factories, oil refineries, defensive fortifications, and air bases throughout German-occupied Europe. On 4 June, Allied troops entered Rome.

The Combined Bomber Offensive demonstrated day and night the relentlessness of strategic bombardment. The tactical uses of air force, helpful in preparing for amphibious landings in Sicily and Italy, were to prove indispensable during Operation Overlord and the Allied drive through France.

The Invasion of Europe

Supreme Allied Headquarters requested low-level photographic reconnaissance of specific beach defenses, 'dicing' missions to be conducted by pilots of the IX Tactical Air Command (TAC). Starting in May, aircraft with strip cameras flew as low as 15 feet across the Normandy beaches to bring back aerial mapping photos. The photographs would enable the precise application of bombing raids and also the deployment of amphibious force to secure any beachhead for the invasion of Europe, designated as Operation Overlord.

Below: **The bridge at Ludendorff escaped destruction by both Allied bombers and retreating German forces, allowing US troops their first foothold east of the Rhine.**

The IX and XIX Tactical Air Commands (TAC), with their P-47 Thunderbolts and P-51 Mustangs, were assigned to ground armies for the invasion. TAC commander Major General Elwood 'Pete' Quesada requisitioned radar and assigned air controllers in order to improve ground-air communications. Before the invasion, TAC pilots had sealed tunnels, brought down bridges, and blasted railways. By 6 June, with the bridges across the Seine River above Paris destroyed, the German Seventh Army in Normandy was separated from the Fifteenth Army in Pas de Calais.

On D-Day, 15,000 sorties were flown. Hundreds of C-47 transports carried paratroops and glider-men to secure the flanks and beach exits. Allied commanders, in an effort to avoid the friendly fire incidents of Sicily, arranged for safe passage above the Navy guns, and this time it worked. Clouds caused paratroops and gliders to miss their drop zones, but the airdrop (and thousands of fire-cracker-laden dummies) confused the German defenders. Shortly before Allied amphibious forces landed, more than 1,000 B-17s and B-24s struck German positions on the Normandy beaches with 3,000 tons of bombs. After the heavy bombers had passed through, medium bombers and fighter-bombers struck the beaches before attacking rear areas.

Beginning at 6:30 AM on 6 June, amphibious craft delivered 130,000 troops to five beaches in Normandy: in the east, Gold, Juno, and Sword; in the west, Utah and Omaha. At Omaha, TAC pilots had mistakenly flown past the German defenses and dropped bombs on dairy herds in the hedgerows beyond. As a result, US troops waded through the surf under killing fire. By mid-morning they were still at the water's edge, huddled behind wrecked vehicles. Infantrymen inched across the beach, being killed as they went, closing in on the bluffs where the machineguns were hidden. US destroyers came close to shore to shell the gun nests. After hours of losses the infantrymen secured the beach.

Previous page: **The Lockheed P-38 Lightning helped Allied forces to victory in World War II with its speed, agility, and range. In addition to long-range escort, the P-38 was also used in dive bombing, ground strafing, and photo reconnaissance.**

Above: **A Ninth Air Force reconnaissance photo taken one month before D-Day shows German 'dicing' of the beaches on the Cherbourg Peninsula to prevent a landing by Allied troops.**

In the end, the greatest assistance came from Hitler himself. The frequency of Allied bombing missions against Pas de Calais had convinced him that Normandy was a feint, so he held planes and troops in reserve. Only 300 German aircraft were in all of France, because Hitler believed he could rush reinforcements from Germany, if needed. But by 9 June, TAC fighter-bombers, flying from bases in France, interdicted German reinforcements, assaulted the fortifications around Cherbourg, and assisted operations south of Saint Lo. The Eighth Air Force performed tactical operations, its B-17s obliterating German positions around Caen, and a great deal of Caen itself. The only drawback to using the Flying Fortresses was that Allied tanks and infantry could not traverse the heavily cratered terrain.

Desperation in Germany

On 12 June, the Germans launched V-1 rockets (Vergeltungswaffen, 'weapons of vengeance') from ramps in the coastal areas of Belgium and Holland. The Combined Bomber Offensive had attempted to destroy the V-1 program in its infancy, by attacking research facilities in Germany where scientists (such as Werner Von Braun) were working on missile technology. After the first V-1 rockets landed, bombers were diverted to eliminate the launch sites, but the attacks would stop only when the Low Countries were retaken. Powered by a pulse-jet engine that ran on low-grade fuel oil, the unpiloted V-1 rocket made a tell-tale buzz; once the buzzing stopped it was time to take cover, for the engine had cut off and the warhead was on the way down. Up to 190 V-1s were launched each day, and by July 21, more than 4,000 'buzz bombs' had killed almost as many people.

Seemingly unaware of his own use of terror, and infuriated by the destruction being visited upon Germany, Hitler ordered that Allied Terrorflieger (terror fliers) be executed. Captured airmen were denied POW status and, if not executed, were sent to Buchenwald, in violation of international law. The Nazi regime was merely adding to its already long list of demonstrable war crimes, including the use of slave labor and the extermination of Jews. Those among the German elite who had countenanced such policies were coming to realize that, in the event of unconditional surrender, they, too, were to be held accountable for such crimes.

Above: A coastal battery at Pointe du Hoc burns after an attack by Douglas A-20 Havocs of the Ninth Air Force. Pointe du Hoc was one of the first objectives captured on D-Day.
Below: Oil refineries in Hamburg burn after a raid by the US Eighth Air Force. Both Hamburg and Dresden were nearly obliterated in intense firebombing campaigns by Allied forces.

For years, reports had appeared about attacks against Jews and Jewish-owned enterprises, the sealing off of the Jewish ghettoes, and eventually the transportation of Jews to the concentration camps. Ostensibly, European Jews were interned as ethnic nationals of divided loyalty, not unlike the Japanese Americans in the United States. But as early as 1942, British Foreign Secretary Anthony Eden had acknowledged the mass executions of Jews (and other 'undesirables'). More than once, Jewish leaders had asked the Allies to divert their bombers in order to disrupt the train transports. Roosevelt and Churchill asserted that nothing, not even genocide, should interfere with the war-winning strategy. Only total victory, they argued, would bring relief to the Jews of Europe.

Many Germans had come to blame Hitler for all that had befallen their nation. A plot to assassinate the Fuhrer was joined by high-level officers. On 20 July, Hitler attended a meeting, and a bomb in a briefcase was placed near where he sat. For whatever reason, when the bomb went off several of those present were killed, but not Hitler. Indeed, Hitler emerged in state of near-exhilaration, convinced of his invulnerability, and for the rest of war made increasingly irresponsible decisions.

The Relentless Air War

Hitler may have felt invulnerable, but the German people did not. On the eastern front, the Soviets advanced through the Baltic States. From the west, B-17s escorted by P-51s bombed German industry, using target lists provided by Hap Arnold's staff. From Italy, medium bombers and fighter-bombers attacked airfields northeast of Ploesti, then landed at Russian bases. In carrying out such missions, the USAAF lost 922 bombers and 674 fighters, but the losses were quickly replaced.

By the end of June, Allied forces in Normandy had advanced 20 miles inland, every foot of which the Germans contested. But Hitler and his generals were at a greater disadvantage than they knew. Their 'Enigma' encryption device had been compromised, so directives from Berlin were being read at Supreme Allied Headquarters. German troops were outflanked and overrun. TAC fighter-bombers disorganized any attempt the retreating Germans made to form a new defensive line. Some P-38s were fitted with five-inch rockets, armed with the

The North American B-25G Mitchell medium bomber had a crew of five: pilot, co-pilot, navigator, upper turret gunner, and radioman. All crewmembers pulled double duties as either gunners, or in the pilots' case, bombardier.

Inset: Significantly more advanced than earlier bombers, the Boeing B-29 Superfortress boasted a pressurized rear cabin that contained four bunks for its crew of 11 on long missions.

experimental jellied gasoline, napalm, first used on a fuel depot at Coutances, near Saint Lo on 17 July.

The strategic bombardment campaign continued, but when called upon, the Eighth Air Force helped level the maze-like hedgerows of Normandy which had confounded ground troops. The tactical use of strategic bombardment was applied again on 19 July in Operation Cobra to seize the crossroads at Saint Lo. For Cobra to succeed, the Allies had to dislodge a Panzer division that impeded the advance of the First Army, under General Omar Bradley. Bradley called for the area bombing of a three-mile long, 1.5-mile deep strip, even though such a narrow target area required that 1,500 heavies and 400 medium bombers line up in formation for miles, taking hours to pass through. Bradley set a buffer of 1,500 yards between the bombing target and the First Army. On 24 July, heavy and medium bombers saturated the target area, followed the next day by 600 P-47 fighter-bombers of IX TAC. In the process, the 30th infantry, located closest to the target area, took more than 600 casualties (including Lieutenant General Leslie J. McNair, who had been sent to take command of the European Theater). Operation Cobra was the first successful battlefield use of area bombing.

As the First Army broke through, TAC fighter-bombers and armored columns operated as teams, with airplanes bombing German defenses, and the pilots radioing the results back to the lead tank. If a lead tank were destroyed by artillery that the TAC fighters had missed, the radio man in the next tank called the pilots back. The complex dance of air and ground power was further enhanced by the scarcity of Luftwaffe planes in the air. Demoralized German armies withdrew to escape being surrounded by Allied tank columns, at which point the TAC fighters, in addition to bombing, began to strafe.

Strafing required that a pilot be neither faint of heart nor slow of reflex. In order to fire his guns to good effect, a TAC pilot had to come in as low as 50 feet, and close within yards of the target at top speed. German armored tanks, because of the fuel cans strapped to their sides, were a quick kill. But even so, small arms fire and flak took a toll upon low-flying TAC fighters assigned to strafe German positions. Strafing may have been the mission that fighter pilots least cared to carry out.

Through June and July, on behalf of Bradley's First Army, TAC P-47 Thunderbolts and P-51 Mustangs had provided tactical air cover. On 1 August, the fighter-bombers of XIX TAC, under General Otto 'Opie' Weyland, were assigned to the Patton's Third Army. Patton's distrust of air power was no secret. Yet when the Third Army broke out of Cotentin peninsula, they found only charred tanks and disabled artillery, courtesy of XIX TAC. With such results, Patton was better disposed toward the uses of air power. The Third Army split up, with half turning north to secure much-needed ports, and the rest flanking the First Army. In either direction, Patton's tanks moved freely with Thunderbolts flying overhead.

Allied Forces On the Move

On 15 August, the Allies staged an amphibious landing on the French Riviera, Operation Dragoon. Free French forces turned to take Marseilles. The US Seventh Army set out to prevent the reinforcement of German forces in Normandy and to provide a lifeline to Mediterranean ports. TAC pilots led the way, performing armed reconnaissance of forward positions. If a column of German troops and armor appeared, TAC pilots radioed to headquarters, and then, at great risk, attacked the column's lead elements, which, if destroyed, could halt its advance. Before long, a large group of TAC fighter-bombers arrived and bombed and strafed the column along its entire length.

Originally, Paris was to be bypassed, but when resistance fighters took to the

Above: **During the war the Army Air Force lost over 27,500 aircraft, including about 10,000 bombers, like this B-26 Marauder of the 9th Air Force, shot down over Germany by enemy anti-aircraft fire in 1945.**

Below: **Aerial photography shows the result of numerous USAAF and RAF bombing raids on Cologne, Germany.**

P-38 Lightnings of the 15th Army Air Force in formation over Yugoslavia.

Below left: **To cut off enemy supply lines and the ability for reinforcements to reach the front, Allied bombers destroyed many bridges. As a result, pontoon bridges had to be built by Allied forces in order to get their own equipment and supplies across the Rhine.**

Below right: **Fighter Control Centers of various Tactical Air Commands (TAC) coordinated their bombing runs with forces on the ground who requested the destruction of specific enemy targets.**

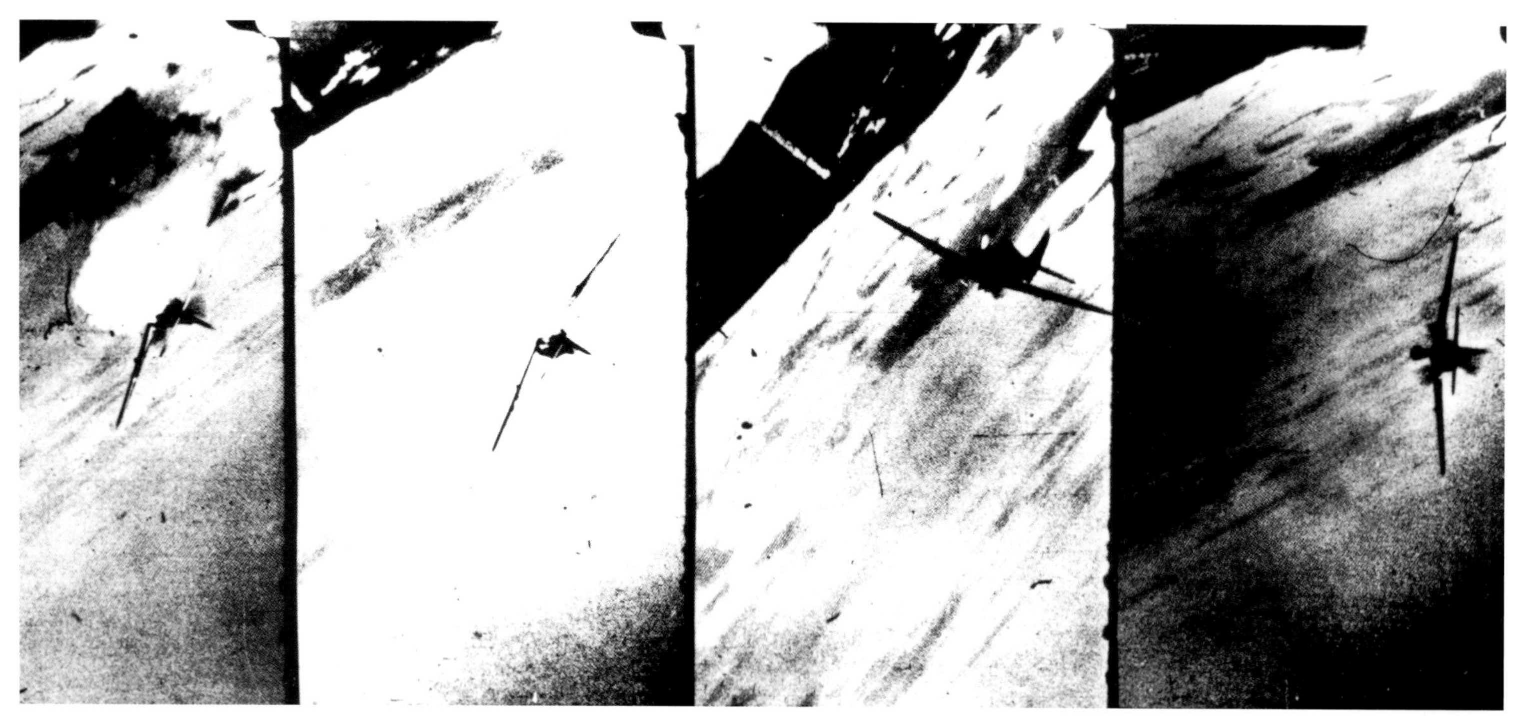

Left: **Still images taken from a camera in the nose of an Eighth Air Force fighter shows a German FW-190 losing an aerial dog fight. The sequence of the fight runs from right to left.**

Below left: **Belly gunner Sergeant William Watts fires his .50 caliber machine gun at enemy aircraft. Although not eligible for 'ace' status, bomber gunners shot down many thousands of enemy aircraft.**

streets, a column of US and Free French troops turned toward Paris, liberating the city on 25 August. Similarly, Eisenhower did not stop his forces at the Seine; he sent Montgomery north of the Ardennes and Bradley toward the Ruhr. Circling maneuvers and pincer movements were deployed along a broad front. Allied advances were rapid, and forces from southern France joined with Patton's Third Army in the rush toward Germany. Caught in a pincer movement, the Germans began to evacuate France. TAC pilots bombed in front of the advancing Allied troops, flew armed reconnaissance beyond the bomb line, and strafed targets on the way back. Allied columns advanced so rapidly that they outdistanced their supplies, and had to be re-supplied by airlift.

During the summer, the US Fifth Army had moved up through Italy. Allied bombers leveled the monastery at Monte Cassino, assuming that it served as an outlook, which it did not. Although USAAF commanders were willing to apply force with intensity on every front, in Italy care was taken to use 'precision' targeting to spare historic sites and cultural centers, such as Rome and Florence. By September, the Germans had retreated north of Florence. From forward bases, medium bombers disrupted supply centers and transportation routes. As a result, the German units being withdrawn required weeks to move out and left behind their equipment.

The Struggle Continues

German scientists had developed a faster, more powerful missile, the V-2, the first missile to break the sound barrier. On 8 September, V-2 rockets fell upon London and Antwerp. Allied bombers were sent to destroy the launch sites, but mobile launch platforms were improvised from within cities. Despite the deaths of 2,000 civilians, the V-2 was minimally effective. The development of the atomic bomb by Allied scientists raised a nightmarish possibility for Roosevelt and Churchill. If in the advanced research centers of Germany, scientists developed an atomic bomb and a rocket to deliver it, the war would come to a sudden conclusion—in Germany's favor.

To gain ground before bad weather slowed the Allied offensive, Eisenhower ordered Operation Market-Garden, an airborne assault into Holland. The plan called for US troops to break through to the Ruhr. If the Allies could outflank the West Wall, also known as the Seigfried Line, they could drive across the north plain and establish a bridgehead on the Rhine. On 17 September, Allied paratroops and glider-forces were airdropped at Eindhoven, Nijmegen, and Arnhem. For the plan to succeed, the paratroopers, supported by Allied fighter-bombers, had to keep open the roads and bridges for reinforcements. A shortage of transport planes delayed the airdrop, and poor weather suppressed tactical air support. The Germans counterattacked and forced a British withdrawal on 23 September. As weak as Germany was, Allied ground forces required air superiority in order to advance.

By 13 September, lead elements of Allied forces had reached the West Wall. Bad weather, difficult terrain, and the dense fortifications brought the Allied armies to a halt. As General Spaatz had foreseen, the use of heavy bombers for tactical purposes had given the Luftwaffe a chance to reorganize. Fighter production was dispersed from larger plants into hundreds of smaller plants. Germany turned out FW-190s and Me-109s, many of which operated from fields and roadways rather than airfields. Now Luftwaffe fighters began to intercept Allied heavy bomber formations in greater force.

In November, the US Third and Seventh Armies pushed to the West Wall. To prepare the way, a fleet of 1,000 heavy bombers struck Metz and its surrounding fortifications. The Third Army, led by Patton, bypassed Metz and moved along the Saar River. On 16 November, Allied tactical and strategic aircraft massed for Operation Queen, in which 5,000 planes

Above: **B-17s of the Army Eighth Air Force lumber towards their targets while fighter escorts leave zigzagging vapor trails through the sub-stratosphere.**

Below: **The USAAF used gliders like this one to drop troops, equipment, and supplies behind enemy lines in advance of invasions. The gliders were relatively inexpensive, expendable, and silent.**

were to strike German positions in front of the US First Army, as area bombing had been used in Operation Cobra at Saint Lo. The weather did not cooperate; the bombing raids were scattered, and their impact had been spread over too broad an area to be useful. As a result, Bradley's forces advanced only two miles. Not until a month later did the First and Ninth Armies reach the Roer River, east of Aachen, 22 miles inside Germany, but by then it was too late to take Berlin and end the war, as had been hoped, in 1944. Even at peak capacity, the Allied forces experienced setbacks when air power was misused or failed to accomplish its goals.

The Battle of the Bulge

The Allied armies settled in along the West Wall for Christmas, not expecting that a decisive battle was about to be joined. On 16 December, a major offensive in the Ardennes was launched, catching the Allies unprepared. Hitler's plan, strongly opposed by his generals, was to split the Allied armies and drive west to Antwerp. Had the gamble worked, and had the Germans secured more fuel to run their armored divisions, the Allies would have been in for a difficult time. The US First Army bore the brunt of the attack. Snow and fog limited the response of Allied airpower, and by 24 December, the Germans had penetrated 50 miles westward—creating what became known as 'the bulge.' The first days were vital, and although many Allied troops were overrun or surrendered, troops in Saint Vith and Bastogne resisted and slowed the German advance.

By Christmas Eve, the Germans had outrun their supply lines, and shortages of fuel and ammunition became critical. Improving weather brought Allied aircraft back into play, and in the tactical and strategic attacks that followed, the Luftwaffe used only its fighters, of which it had too few. The Allies used gliders and cargo planes to reinforce Bastogne, airdropping a medical team to treat the wounded. The Germans attempted to rush supplies and reinforcements by rail to the front, but Allied heavy bombers attacked the marshalling yards, hitting trains before they could leave. By the end of January 1945, the Battle of the Bulge had turned against Germany, as Hitler's generals had feared, though no one was so bold as to point out the foolhardiness of the Fuhrer's decision.

The First and Third Armies, along with their TAC forces, linked up after a month-long separation and prepared to drive into Germany. In the battle, more than 75,000 US troops were killed, wounded, missing or captured. The Germans lost 67,675 men, who had been held in reserve for the final defense of Berlin. The Bulge may have delayed Allied victory, but Berlin was soon to fall, if not to the Allies, then to the Red Army.

The Allies Advance

Ground forces steadily advanced to the Rhine during the first weeks of 1945. The broad front frustrated Patton and Montgomery, who wanted to beat each other (and the Red Army) to Berlin. Major air targets were becoming scarce, so the USAAF sent its fighters on sweeps into Germany to attack at low level. The Luftwaffe, lacking pilots and fuel, kept its aircraft grounded. TAC pilots were free to strafe targets of even limited value, such as the staff cars of German officers.

From time to time, USAAF missions were intercepted by an experimental aircraft—the jet. On 15 March, Me-262 jets took down 29 AAF bombers and fighters. The threat posed by these jet-propelled

fighters caused the Pointblank target list to include jet engine and aircraft plants. But the situation in Germany had deteriorated to the point that few jets were produced and fewer still deployed. Jets never posed a serious threat to Allied air superiority, now verging on supremacy.

At the Yalta Conference in February, Roosevelt, Churchill, and Stalin discussed post-war power arrangements. Serious political tensions surfaced, in particular between Stalin and Churchill (which did not prevent Churchill from trading away the Balkans in exchange for the preservation of the British sphere of influence in Greece). Roosevelt had been re-elected to a fourth term, though he had two months to live. Churchill, having been appointed a wartime leader, faced an election in peacetime, and without a war to fight his victory was not guaranteed.

The Big Three powers considered the facts. Soviet advantages on the ground—12 million soldiers in 300 divisions—were offset by Allied air power. As if to emphasize Allied air strength on the eve of the conference, 959 B-17 crews carried out the largest all-American raid to date against Berlin. It was probable that Berlin

Above: **Germany surrendered unconditionally to Allied command on 7 May 1945 in Reims, France. Adolph Hitler had committed suicide in a bunker in Berlin just one week earlier.**

would fall to the Soviets, and in dividing up Germany, and ceding much of Eastern Europe to Stalin, Roosevelt and Churchill recognized the reality of Soviet power.

Roosevelt and Churchill did not tell Stalin about the atomic bomb. Allied air power and industrial productivity, they felt, were sufficient to discourage the Red Army from advancing beyond Germany. Dresden further reinforced the point. Dresden was the only major German city to escape the Combined Bomber Offensive. The city contained an optical factory and a glass factory, both of which contributed to the production of bombsights. Other factories made components for radar, fuses for anti-aircraft shells, gas masks, aircraft engines and cockpit parts. Such facilities, while peripheral to the current German war effort, were verifiable military targets. The Soviets were poised to take the city, and Stalin had ordered a pause during Yalta, at which he had demanded that Allied air force come to the support of the Red Army.

Rather than interdict supply lines, or disrupt German defenses, the Allied air force launched a massive bombing raid against Dresden that lasted three days. On 13 February, RAF Bomber Command hit Dresden in two waves, dropping 1,478 tons of high explosive bombs to expose the timbers within buildings and 1,182 tons of incendiaries to burn the exposed timbers. A firestorm arose with the same intensity as the one that had consumed Hamburg. Official figures held that 35,000 people suffocated or were burned to death, but much higher estimates allowed for the fact the Dresden's population had been doubled by unregistered refugees. (The destruction of Dresden is described in Slaughterhouse Five, by Kurt Vonnegut, who as an American prisoner of war in that city lived through the firestorm.) The following two days, 600 US B-17 bombers struck the city's marshaling yards and attacked targets of opportunity, i.e. strafing.

Before Dresden, German civilians had proved resilient. Entire neighborhoods had vanished beneath Allied bombardment, but the emotional cores of the communities remained intact for as long as there was even the slightest hope of a favorable outcome. Hamburg, the first city to be firebombed, had not been subdued, and had to be hit by Allied raids again and again. But now that the Luftwaffe was incapable of mounting serious resistance, and now that German armies were in retreat on every front, the only outcome for the German people was disaster. Under such conditions, the doctrine of strategic bombardment received its validation, although the ultimate disposition of air power would be illustrated in Japan, at Hiroshima and Nagasaki.

The Final Stages

As spring drew near, the German military was disorganized and wholesale surrenders occurred. Allied air force was used for airlift and for tactical purposes, and the loss rate continued to fall. Allied armies arrived at the Rhine on 7 March. An airdrop of 2,800 US and British troops secured the bridgehead at Remagen, opening the way to Berlin. Patton broke through the West Wall, and before March had ended, the Third Army conquered 6,482 square miles, 3,072 towns and villages, and took a million prisoners.

Eisenhower chose not to advance toward Berlin. Projected casualties from a direct Allied assault ran as high as 100,000. On 11 April, Allied troops at Magdeburg had an opportunity to sprint 50 miles to Berlin, but Eisenhower declined. The next day, on 12 April, Franklin D. Roosevelt died, and Harry Truman became president. Roosevelt had said nothing to Truman about the atomic bomb project. Only after Truman took the oath of office did he learn of the decision that awaited him.

As April went on, Soviet troops took 317,000 German prisoners. Allied forces began to encounter the grisly reality of German concentration camps, and Army intelligence units gathered evidence for war crime tribunals. Army intelligence also set forth in a last-minute search of German scientists, such as Werner Von Braun, who brought his work on missile technology to the United States. On 21 April, the Soviets reached Berlin. The final USAAF bombing raid against an industrial target took place on 25 April against the Skoda works in Czechoslovakia. Also on 25 April, American and Soviet forces met at the Elbe River.

The end came for Mussolini on 28 April, when he was captured by Italian partisans, who executed Il Duce, and strung his body up by the feet. On 30 April, Hitler was in his bunker as the Red Army fought street to street through Berlin. The total number of Soviet dead from all causes in WW II was estimated at 20 million. The Soviet Air Force had flown 796,000 sorties and had lost more than 20,000 aircraft. Rather than face the Soviets, against whom he had railed all his political life, Hitler bit a cyanide pill and put a bullet into his head.

The USAAF air offensive against Germany and Italy was effective and costly. The AAF losses totaled 27,694 aircraft, of which 8,314 heavy bombers, 1,623 medium and light bombers, and 8,481 fighters were destroyed in combat. Total AAF battle casualties were more than 91,000 killed, wounded, and missing. On 7 May, the unconditional surrender of German forces was signed. 'The mission of this Allied force was fulfilled,' wrote Eisenhower, 'at 0241 local time, May 7, 1945.' On 8 May, V-E Day celebrations broke out in the major cities of Europe and the United States. Smaller, more somber observances took place elsewhere world, including in Germany. But there was another war to be won, and the United States Army Air Force began to shift operations to the Pacific theater.

Right: **New Yorkers celebrate V-E Day in Times Square on 8 May 1945. Victory in Europe also marked an end to the city's brownouts, bringing bright lights back to the Great White Way.**

UR ROSES
KINSEY
WHISKEY
LOEW'S STATE
RUPPERT
HOTEL STOR

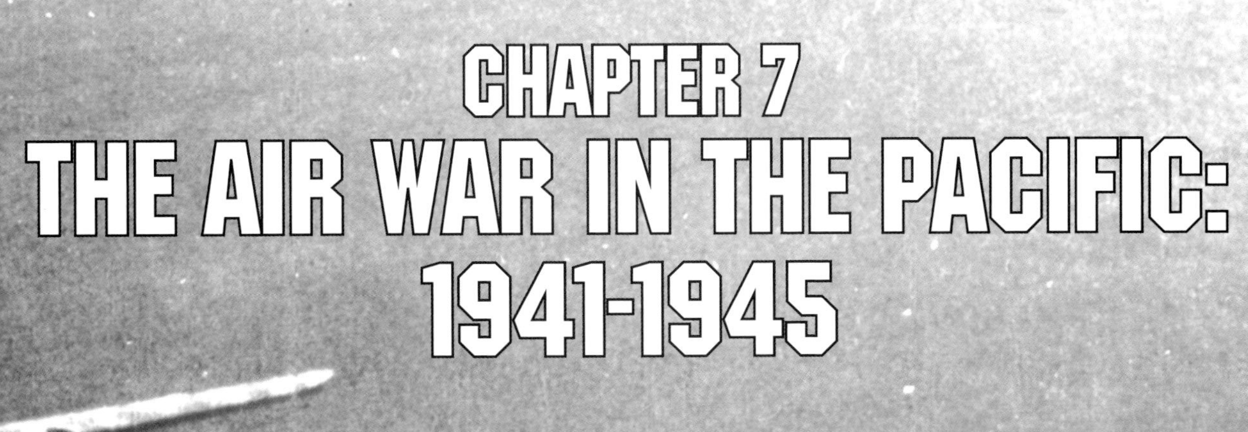

CHAPTER 7
THE AIR WAR IN THE PACIFIC: 1941-1945

THE AIR WAR IN THE PACIFIC: 1941-1945

In 1941, President Roosevelt froze Japanese assets, suspended diplomatic relations, and declared an oil embargo against the Axis Powers. The oil embargo was perceived as an act of aggression by Japan's political leaders, many of whom were generals and admirals, including Prime Minister Hideki Tojo. Once a decision was made to seize the oil-rich Dutch East Indies, Japan's military commanders devised a strategy to win air and sea superiority throughout the Pacific, beginning with the attack on Pearl Harbor.

Previous page: **A squadron of US Army Air Force B-24 Liberators crosses paths with a US Navy convoy in the South Pacific, pursuing different missions, but with the same goal—victory in the Pacific.**

Above: **An aerial view of the surprise attack on the American Pacific Fleet at Pearl Harbor on 7 December 1941, taken by a Japanese pilot participating in the raid.**

The Japanese Attack

On Sunday, 7 December 1941, at 6:45 AM, a Pearl Harbor radar station detected planes scouting ahead of the Japanese strike force. At 6:54, a Japanese midget submarine was sunk in the harbor mouth. At 7:55 the first wave of Japanese planes swept across Oahu, strafing and bombing aircraft at Hickam, Wheeler, and Bellows Fields. Dive bombers and torpedo planes, flying through flak, struck the ships of the Pacific Fleet.

A second wave of aircraft attacked the smaller airfields on Oahu, and also revisited the Pearl Harbor fleet, its battleships on fire and sinking. Pilots of the 47th Pursuit Squadron engaged the Japanese, but the Curtiss P-36 Hawks and Curtiss P-40 Warhawks lacked speed and maneuverability. Only 29 Japanese planes were brought down. A flight of B-17s arriving from the US mainland, low on fuel and without ammunition, took evasive action, one landing on a golf course.

In all, 188 USAAF planes were destroyed and 159 damaged. All eight Navy battleships were either sunk or damaged. Military casualties were 2,343 killed, 960 missing, and 1,272 wounded, with dead and wounded civilians as well. The Pacific Fleet's carriers were at sea and thus were spared. Pearl Harbor's oil storage tanks were also left intact. Had the Japanese struck the carriers, or had the oil tanks gone up in flames, the ability of the United States to recover would have taken longer.

The day after Pearl Harbor, the Japanese attacked the Philippines. The Far Eastern Air Force (FEAF) near Manila lost half of its B-17s and fighters. On 10 December, with Japanese forces landing on Luzon, General Douglas MacArthur withdrew his troops to Bataan peninsula, the rest taking refuge on the island of Corregidor guarding the approaches to Manila Bay. AAF ground crews, whose planes had been destroyed, were assigned to infantry units. Not until 9 April 1942 did the 12,000 Americans and 63,000 Filipinos surrender in Bataan, many of whom would die on the 'Bataan Death March.' Corregidor held out until 6 May.

In China, the American Volunteer Group (AVG) had already engaged Japan in sustained air combat. The 'Flying Tigers,' so-called because of the shark's teeth painted on their fighters, were recruited by ex-USAAF pilot Claire Chennault, who had gone to China at the outbreak of the Sino-Japanese War to train Chinese fighter pilots. Chennault trained the new American volunteers to fly in two-plane elements. Rather than engage the Japanese Zeros, they were to make a pass from above, fire a sustained burst, then get out. Three AVG squadrons patrolled opposite ends of the Burma Road: one in Rangoon; two others at Kumming, China, the headquarters of Generalissimo Chiang Kai-Chek.

The Japanese Advance

Over the next six months, Japan took Guam, Borneo, Burma, Malaysia, Thailand, Wake Island, and Hong Kong.

The Allies regrouped to hold the 'Malay Barrier,' a 2,000 mile stretch of land and sea from the fortress city of Singapore to Northern Australia. On 11 January, the Japanese invaded the Dutch East Indies, their air force bombing the airfields in Borneo and Java. The Allies transferred 142 P-40s to Java, only 39 of which arrived. Allied bombers conducted raids from the Malay Peninsula to the Celebes Islands, but without P-40 fighter escort, losses were high. On 8 February, Japanese forces landed at Singapore; a week later 130,000 British and Australian troops surrendered. The Malay barrier had been outflanked. As if to announce Australia's vulnerability, Japanese carrier-based aircraft attacked Darwin, Australia, on 19 February.

Given the geography of the Pacific, Japan (and the Allies) had little choice but to 'island hop.' Air and naval forces converged upon an island, at which point an assault began with long-range, land-based bombers, escorted by fighters. At the same time, battleships shelled the defenders from off-shore. An amphibious landing followed, and a ground campaign began. Even before the fighting ended, construction units began to build airstrips from which the next island could be attacked. To Hap Arnold, island-hopping was a surface campaign in support of his B-29s, to bring the 'Superfortresses' within range of Japan. Other commanders continued to deploy air, sea, and ground forces in complementary ways to recover the larger land masses of the Philippines or New Guinea, or to contest Japanese forces occupying much of Asia.

On 23 January 1942, the Japanese seized Rabaul on New Britain Island. Rabaul had a deep harbor and inland airfields, strategically located at the junction of the Bismarck Archipelago and Solomon Islands. From Rabaul, the Japanese could move south and east along the Solomons, and southwest to Papua, New Guinea. On New Guinea's northern shore, Japan took Lae and Salamaua. The southern coastal town of Port Moresby was Japan's next objective, from where Australia was to be attacked.

In late February, Japan won the Battle of the Java Sea, sinking the carrier USS Langley. On 11 March, General MacArthur was evacuated from the Philippines. The Japanese had possession of territory from eastern India across the Southwest Pacific islands to New Guinea, all of which, when added to Japan's other possessions, amounted to a quarter of the planet.

US strategists viewed the war against Japan primarily as a Navy war, to be fought with aircraft carriers, battleships, and Marines, supplemented by the Army infantry and its land-based Air Force. Admiral Chester Nimitz was given command of the central and southern Pacific. Remaining Allied forces were designated the Southwest Pacific Area (SWPA) and placed under General MacArthur. The AAF arm of SWPA had fewer than 200 flyable fighter aircraft and fewer than 30 heavy bombers, and one service depot in Australia. SWPA pilots, having returned from a mission, had to service their own planes.

The Air Force Strikes Back

In April, the carrier USS Hornet sailed toward Japan with 16 B-25s on board. The idea to stage USAAF bombers from a carrier was the brainchild of Navy Captain Francis Low, who had observed B-26 pilots in Norfolk, Virginia, performing full-throttle, short-distance take-offs on a 500-foot airstrip, the equivalent of a carrier deck. Hap Arnold approved the Navy-AAF mission, and Lieutenant Colonel Jimmy Doolittle was put in charge. B-25 medium bombers were to be used, stripped of armament, with a gas tank replacing the belly gun. The B-25s could not land on the Hornet because the tail section would have been torn off by the receiving hook, so the raiders had to land in China. On 18 April, the mission was launched, with Doolittle in the lead. Shortly after noon, the raiders bombed storage tanks, munitions factories, and military installations in Tokyo, and departed across the East China Sea. As the weather worsened and their fuel ran out, the raiders were forced to ditch at sea or crash-land. Of the 80 airmen, three died and eight were taken prisoner, three of whom were executed. Doolittle was promoted to brigadier general, but was ambivalent about receiving the Medal of Honor—as far as he was concerned, he had lost every aircraft under his command.

After Japan captured the Burma Road in 1942, the 'Flying Tigers' (AVG) joined the Fourteenth Air Force under Claire Chennault, now a brigadier general. Chennault proposed an airlift to supply Chiang's forces. Supplies had to be flown from India over the Himalayas, a five-hour, 700-mile flight subjected to monsoons and turbulence, called the 'Hump.' C-46 'Commando' transport planes were used to carry up to five tons of cargo, including smaller trucks and small light planes. With the Fourteenth Air Force defending the Chinese end of the Hump, tonnage delivered rose from 2,800 tons a month in February 1943 to 1,200 tons a day in November 1944. Some 900 flyers died during the operation, but sustained aerial transport enabled Chiang's forces to

Below: The battleship USS _Shaw_ explodes after a Japanese bomb hits the ship's forward magazines. Despite the destruction, the _Shaw_ was rebuilt with a new bow and served in the Pacific Fleet during World War II.

serve as a viable counterbalance to Japan in the China-Burma-India Theater (CBI).

A turning point came when the Navy broke Japan's secret code. In May of 1942, a Japanese carrier force sailed from Rabaul to prepare for an assault on Port Moresby at the southeastern tip of New Guinea. Having been forewarned, the US Navy moved its carriers to the Coral Sea, and the first major clash of carrier-based aircraft took place. In terms of aircraft and ships sunk, including the USS Lexington, Japan won a victory. Yet the Allies had caused the Japanese carriers to withdraw, and the Port Moresby invasion was cancelled.

The Navy code-breakers also learned of a plan devised by Admiral Isoruku Yamamoto, architect of the Pearl Harbor attack. In a diversionary tactic, Yamamoto sent light carriers to the Aleutian Islands. Meanwhile, the main Japanese carrier force sailed to Midway. Yamamoto believed that once Midway fell, the US fleet would be drawn out from Pearl Harbor and destroyed.

The Japanese arrived at Midway on 4 June. The Navy carriers Enterprise, Hornet, and Yorktown were waiting, a mid-ocean ambush, and sent out a first wave of torpedo aircraft. The Japanese sent up their air cover, leaving their ships unprotected. A second wave of US fighters and dive-bombers came in behind that engagement and sank three Japanese carriers, with a fourth sinking later. Midway cost Japan 250 planes. (The USS Yorktown, too, was lost.) Aircraft carriers, of which Japan had too few, were to be a deciding factor in the ocean war.

The Air War Rages

That summer, General George C. Kenney took command of the Fifth and Thirteenth Air Forces in the Southwest Pacific Area (SWPA). Kenney's first challenge was to retake the airfields at Buna and at Milne Bay on the southeastern tip of Papua, New Guinea. Japanese ground troops staging from Buna had advanced across the Owen Stanley Range to attack Port Moresby from the interior. Australian ground troops outside Port Moresby struggled to hack airfields from out of the bush. Japanese Zeros, flying from Buna, delayed the Australians by attacking them in the morning and again in the afternoon, and after dark. Japanese bombers undid what little progress had been made.

Above: **A formation of Brewster F2A fighters patrol the skies over Malaya. The 'Brewster Buffalo,' as the British called the plane, was slow and unstable and largely overmatched by the Japanese Zero. The Buffalo was relegated to duty in the Far East.**

Below: **General Douglas MacArthur pins a Distinguished Service Cross on Lieutenant Jack Dale of the USAAF. Dale received the medal for his heroism in fighting Japanese forces in the Philippines.**

Rather than reinforce Port Moresby directly, Kenney sent his B-17s to Milne Bay, to disrupt the Japanese reinforcements as they disembarked from a convoy. The Buna airstrip was also bombed to prevent Japanese fighter pilots from defending Milne Bay, as well as to prevent attacks upon the Australians at Port Moresby. Not until September were US troops airlifted by C-47s across the Coral Sea to fight alongside the Australians, and together they stopped the Japanese 30 miles from Port Moresby. The Japanese retreated back over the mountains to relieve Buna, now under siege. In this relatively minor land battle, in which the scales had been tipped by air power, the forces of Japan had reached the southernmost point in their Pacific-wide advance.

By mid-summer 1942, US strategists had identified Guadalcanal in the Solomon Islands as a pivot point in the island-hopping campaign. On Guadalcanal the Japanese rushed to complete an airfield from which to threaten the Allied supply lines. US Marines landed on Guadalcanal on 7 August and within a few days seized the partially-constructed airfield,; aviation engineers and construction battalions completed the job and renamed it Henderson Field. During the next months, the Japanese Navy and US Pacific Fleet engaged in repeated sea battles, with the Pacific Fleet retaining control of the sea lanes around Guadalcanal. USAAF fighters and B-17s assisted the Marines and Army infantry in the land battle, but the Japanese were re-supplied by sea, the

***Right*:** **The B-17 *Yankee Doodle, Jr.* displays the marks of her success in the South Pacific. *The Yankee Doodle, Jr.* sank a Japanese cruiser and transport ship, plus six Japanese flags representing Zero fighters downed by the planes' gunners.**

YANKEE DOODLE JR.
U.S. ARMY—MODEL B-17E
AIR CORPS SERIAL NO.
CREW WEIGHT 1200 LBS.

nightly 'Tokyo Express.' Even when air attacks disrupted the 'Tokyo Express,' Japanese troops continued to receive relief by submarines. Only in February 1943 did Japan finally evacuate Guadalcanal.

By January 1943, Japanese resistance on Papua had ceased, and Buna was in Allied hands. Yet the Japanese remained in northern New Guinea, at Lae. Early in March, at the Battle of the Bismarck Sea, Allied aircraft sank 12 of 16 Japanese ships in a troop convoy sent to reinforce the Huon Gulf. At most, 1,000 Japanese soldiers reached shore, while 4,000 died and 2,000 were captured. An aerial blockade of New Guinea was established. Air superiority over SWPA began to shift back to the Allies.

In the spring of 1943, SWPA was consolidated with the South Pacific (SOPAC) forces under command of Admiral Nimitz. MacArthur and Kenney were to advance by way of New Britain and the Admiralty Islands toward the Japanese supply center at Rabaul, which threatened MacArthur's flank. At the same time, SOPAC forces, under Nimitz, were to consolidate control over the Solomons, and stage a series of amphibious assaults upon the Gilberts, Marshalls, Admiralties, Carolines, and Marianas.

Under General Kenney, the Fifth and Thirteenth Air Forces, designated once more as the Far Eastern Air Force (FEAF), struck against Rabaul—indirectly. Kenney sent FEAF bombers on 1,400 sorties against New Britain's Cape Gloucester, after which 'Gloucesterizing' came to describe the total destruction of a target. Only after an air counterattack from Rabaul cost Japan more than 100 aircraft, did FEAF aircraft strike the Imperial Fleet at Rabaul harbor. The first planes arrived in darkness and dropped parachute flares. The rest of the attack force came in as low as 500 feet, releasing 'skip bombs' with short fuses that bounced across the water and exploded at the waterline of a ship. With Rabaul on the defensive, MacArthur staged landings along the New Guinea coast above Lae and took control of the Huon Gulf.

Above: **USAAF commander Gen. Henry 'Hap' Arnold (center) meets with other US and British commanders in New Delhi, India. From left are: Field Marshall Sir Archibald Wavell, Lt. Gen. Joseph Stilwell, Arnold, Lt. Gen. Brehon Somervell, and Field Marshal Sir John Dill.**
Below: **A Japanese aircraft carrier takes evasive maneuvers to avoid attack by US bombers in the Battle of Midway. The battle would prove decisive in the war in the Pacific.**

The US fleet off Guadalcanal had control of the sea and the sky. The Pacific island 'ladder' was ready for US forces to climb all the way to Japan. US Marines invaded Bougainville in November, with air cover provided by carrier-based aircraft and also the US Thirteenth Air Force under Major General Nathan Twining. Bomber runways and fighter airstrips were constructed on the beachhead at Bougainville, even as the ground battle continued. Also in November, Nimitz moved upon Tarawa and Makin in the Gilberts and the Marshalls. On 15 December, US troops landed on the Arawe Peninsula, and on 26 December, Marines landed on the much-bombed shores of Cape Gloucester, New Britain.

The Allies Move Toward Japan

Such rapid gains might have overextended the Allies, but US industry was producing one new aircraft carrier each month. By 1944, the US Pacific Fleet exceeded the rest of the world's navies combined. Aircraft were also produced, such as the versatile P-38 Lightning, the equal of Japan's Zeros. Thousands of US pilots were trained to fly the new planes, and by this measure, too, Japan was falling short. For all its initial successes, Japan lacked the resources and manpower to hold together its empire.

In January and February of 1944, Admiral Nimitz advanced into the central and western Marshalls. Army troops invaded Kwajalein Atoll, marking the first loss of territory that Japan had controlled before the war. From Kwajalein a naval task force sailed west and captured Eniwetok. In February, US warships shelled the Kurile Islands of Northern Japan, the first attack by ships on the Japanese homeland.

The Navy air campaign against the Marianas began on 23 February. For months the islands were bombed and strafed, culminating in June with the Battle of the Philippine Sea, known as the 'Marianas Turkey Shoot,' in which the Japanese lost three carriers and more than 400 carried-based aircraft. A Japanese counteroffensive in Burma, against Imphal and Kohima, was rebuffed. Allied transport aircraft rescued a large British force along the Indian border by flying in 10,000 reinforcements and 20,000 tons of supplies. The RAF and US Tenth Air Force won air superiority over Burma, and supplies to China once again flowed over the Burma Road. C-46 carrier transports continued to fly over the 'Hump,' with air cover from the Fourteenth Air Force, and Chiang's forces, assisted by B-24 bomber raids, advanced into Japanese-occupied China.

Once resistance had ended in the Admiralty Islands and the casualties had been counted, a disturbing pattern emerged, a pattern replicated throughout the Pacific: 3,820 Japanese defenders had been killed, and only 75 were taken prisoner. Some US soldiers, seeking retribution for Pearl Harbor, may not have taken many prisoners. But Japanese defenders preferred to die rather than surrender, and those who did not wish to die in combat committed suicide. The death rate remained exceptionally high for the amphibious assaults in the Marianas: Saipan on 15 June, Guam on 20 July, and Tinian on 23 July. Japanese troops had contested each island, killing 3,400 US troops. Yet 27,000 Japanese were killed and only 1,780 were taken prisoner. Such statistics cast a dark light upon the proposed Allied invasion of Japan. As MacArthur's army advanced, seizing or neutralizing Wewak, Hollandia, Biak, and Noemfoor, he scaled back the 'mopping up' operations against the Japanese defenders. If he judged that a stronghold had been isolated, he left the Japanese stranded and without supplies. The Marianas and Okinawa, however, could not be bypassed, since they were the staging areas for strategic bombardment of Japan and the invasion to follow.

Shifting Strategies in the Air War

Airmen such as Hap Arnold held out strategic bombardment as an alternative to the carnage of a ground invasion of Japan. On 15 June, B-29s based in India, staging through China, attacked the steel works at Yawata, the first such strike against the Japanese homeland. The B-29 Superfortress bomber incorporated all the technological advances of the previous decade. Its air-cooled Wright engines generated 2,200 horsepower, and it could carry bomb loads of up to 20,000 pounds at speeds of 360 to 380 miles per hour, and it had a range of more than 3,200 miles. When the Marianas Islands were recaptured, airfields were prepared to receive the B-29s. By late November, the strategic bombardment of Japan began.

***Above:* General Claire Chennault and Chinese leader Chiang Kai-Shek toast the formation of the 14th Air Force, which was formed after Pearl Harbor and absorbed Chennault's American Volunteer Group, the famed 'Fighting Tigers.'**

***Center:* A group of American pilots stationed in India check weather reports for their mission, flying supplies from India to China over the 'hump,' as the pilots fondly referred to the Himalayan mountain range.**

***Below:* A Boeing B-29 Superfortress drops its bomb load over Formosa (Taiwan), a geographically strategic island where the Japanese housed an airplane factory and airdrome.**

General Curtis LeMay was transferred from Europe to the XX Bomber Command in India, where he observed B-29 raids and concluded that the bombs were falling near the target only five percent of the time. LeMay attributed the low accuracy to erratic weather and poor visibility, and also to Japanese fighter attacks during daylight missions. LeMay was determined

A Curtis P-40 of the Flying Tigers readies for takeoff. The Flying Tigers are credited with 217 victories and 43 probables in just 31 engagements with Japanese aircraft.

to improve the performance of the Superfortresses.

In October 1944, MacArthur's Sixth Army landed on Leyte in the Philippines. Having been denied B-29s, General Kenney stripped his B-17s of armament to increase their range and carrying capacity. Kenney judged that Allied air superiority would keep casualties low on long-range missions to the Philippines. FEAF fighters shot down more than 300 Japanese planes over Leyte, losing only 16. The ground battle was bloodier still: 15,500 US dead compared to 70,000 Japanese dead. In late October, at the Battle of Leyte Gulf, the US Navy carried the day despite a frightening, new tactic: Kamikaze dive bombers. If such suicidal attacks were meant to discourage an invasion of Japan, then they worked—but with consequences impossible for the Japanese to foresee.

On 3 January 1945, MacArthur was made commander of US ground forces in the Pacific and Admiral Nimitz commander of naval forces there. MacArthur's Sixth Army landed in Lingayen Gulf on Luzon. Except for waves of suicide attacks by Kamikaze aircraft, little opposition in the air was encountered. Corregidor was recaptured in an amphibious operation, and paratroops used a two-hole golf course for a drop zone. Soon Kenney's pilots were free to roam against shipping in the South China Sea. By the end of February, the Philippines had fallen, with the most lopsided death-to-prisoner ratio yet: 21,000 Japanese dead, only 200 taken prisoner. But US commanders were also concerned with the number of American dead: 6,000.

In January 1945, Hap Arnold had another heart attack, less than a month after his promotion to five-star General of the Army. On 20 January, LeMay took over Arnold's project, the XXI Bomber Command based in the Marianas. LeMay's thinking coincided with Arnold's, though LeMay was more inclined to improvise, and began to experiment with incendiary bombing. Japanese urban centers, crowded with wood and paper buildings, were susceptible to incendiaries. Once incendiaries were introduced, the concept of precision became irrelevant—a target within the fire area would be destroyed as surely as if it had taken a direct hit. The first raid was on Kobe, when B-29s dropped 159 tons of incendiaries that burned more than a thousand buildings.

LeMay reversed three decades of airpower doctrine, shifting from daylight bombing at high altitudes to low-altitude night missions, from high-explosives to

Above left: **A dramatic photo taken aboard an American bomber flying a tree-top level bombing run over an enemy airfield on Boeroe Island. A camouflaged Japanese Mitsubishi Ki-21 'Sally' is about to be destroyed by a parafrag parachute bomb.**

Above: **A P-51 Mustang takes off from Iwo Jima, within striking distance of the Japanese islands. Iwo Jima fell into American hands after a bloody 36-day struggle between US Marines and Japanese soldiers.**

Below: **USAAF B-24 Liberators fly over a US naval convoy in the Southwest Pacific theater. The B-24s are on their way to Rabaul, an island made into a veritable fortress by the Japanese.**

incendiaries. On the night of 9 March, 334 B-29s with 2,000 tons of incendiary bombs took off from the Marianas against Tokyo, where the bombs were released at 5,000-9,000 feet. Aided by a strong wind, the fire in the city burned for four days. In the end, up to 84,000 people died and another 41,000 were injured. A 16-square-mile section of Tokyo burned, including more than 26,000 buildings.

The closest Japan was able to come to strategic bombardment of the US mainland was to launch paper or rubberized silk balloons carrying incendiary bombs, some of which reached as far east as Michigan. The US government asked the press to censor reports of these balloon-bombs. In 1945, a balloon bomb exploded and killed a group of six picnickers in Oregon, five of them children—the only known US civilian deaths as a result of enemy action from the air.

Closing In on Japan

On 19 February, Iwo Jima was invaded so that its airstrips would not be used to intercept B-29s flying every night to Japan. The Japanese defenders had dug into the volcanic mountains at one end of the island, and were subdued only at a cost of 6,800 US lives. From the airstrips at Iwo Jima, P-51 Mustangs began to escort B-29 bombing missions, and rarely met resistance from Japanese fighters. As the summer went on, flying bomber escort in a P-51 over Japan was the safest mission in the war.

In the spring of 1945, daylight bombing raids were resumed using conventional weapons against airfields and aircraft plants. In these raids, the B-29 loss rate was 1.9 percent. As the threat from enemy fighters decreased, armament was stripped from the planes to allow more weight for bombs. The USAAF also mined the Japanese harbors and straits to prevent Japan from mounting naval and air counterattacks against the US forces that were drawing ever nearer.

On 1 April, the US Tenth Army invaded Okinawa. The only counterattack by air came from Kamikaze pilots diving at US ships and ground forces, 1,900 suicide dive bombers in all, sinking 25 US ships. On land, the Japanese losses were staggering: 120,000 soldiers killed, 42,000 civilians killed. But 71,000 Japanese surrendered at Okinawa, the first indication that not every Japanese soldier was prepared to fight to the death. US casualties were 12,500 dead, 35,500 wounded. An extrapolation of casualties from an invasion of Japan would have troubled anyone,

Above: **On 9 August 1945 the B-29 'Bockscar' dropped its payload of a single atomic bomb over Nagasaki. The combined magnitude of devastation in Nagasaki and Hiroshima brought an end to World War II.**

and especially the US president. On 12 April, when Franklin D. Roosevelt died, Harry Truman succeeded him, and it was to Truman that the ultimate decision fell.

Once Germany surrendered, resources and manpower were transferred to the Pacific. General Carl Spaatz was given command of Pacific air forces. Bases on Okinawa became the staging ground for medium bombers and fighter-bombers to attack the home islands in vast sweeps, hitting targets of opportunity. The B-29s were released from providing air support for the island campaigns. Raids of as many as 1,000 bombers were staged against Japan's industrial cities. Without resistance, B-29s destroyed the industrial capability of Tokyo, Nagoya, Kobe, Osaka, Yokohama, and Kawasaki.

Although spared from the destruction of the atomic bomb, both Osaka (left) and Tokyo (right) suffered enormous destruction and losses from continual firebombing raids by American B-29s.

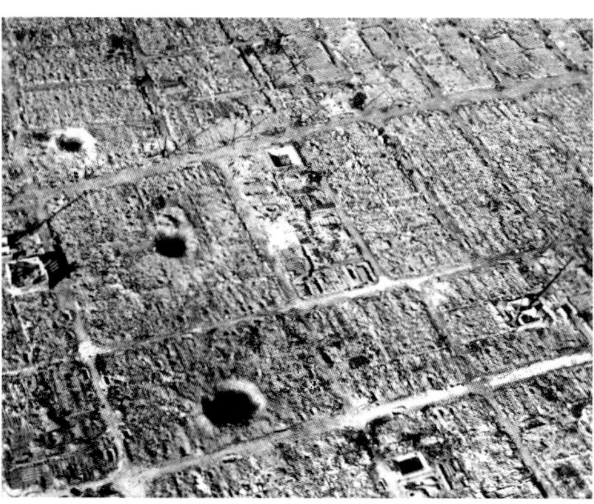

Atom Bombs and the End of the War

The first atomic bomb test took place on 16 July in New Mexico, and the results exceeded the hopes and fears of all who were present. Truman met with Churchill and Stalin at the Potsdam Conference and informed Stalin about the new weapon. The Potsdam Declaration was issued, calling for unconditional surrender. The Japanese military leaders found the terms insulting, and Prime Minister Suzuki announced that Japan would ignore the ultimatum.

Did the Japanese leaders intend for their intransigence to serve as a prelude to negotiation? If so, then they had to be impervious to the devastation, by conventional means, already visited upon their people, and the likelihood of more incendiary raids and firestorms to come. Whether their thinking would have been influenced by a 'peaceful demonstration' of the atomic bomb is difficult to say.

US commanders were divided over using the bomb, less for humanitarian reasons than for strategic ones. The Navy believed in the efficacy of a sea blockade. Hap Arnold opposed both the atomic bomb and a ground invasion. He believed that air supremacy and precision bombing would end the war. The Army, prepared to wage a ground war, faced an estimated 250,000 to 500,000 casualties, with the Japanese casualties estimated to be in the millions. These were the factors that played into Truman's decision, as well as the geopolitical reality of the Soviet Union, soon to declare war on Japan.

On 6 August, at 8:15 AM, the Enola Gay, commanded by Colonel Paul W. Tibbets, Jr., released the uranium-fueled 'Little Boy.' Hiroshima was consumed fifty seconds later. Approximately 78,000 people were killed instantly, and thousands more died over the next year from radiation. On 9 August, at 10:58 AM, 'Fat Man,' a plutonium-fueled bomb was released over Nagasaki with equally cataclysmic results. As many as 65,000 people died in Nagasaki, either instantaneously or from radiation. The Japanese signaled their willingness to accept the Potsdam Declaration, but when negotiations stalled, a final B-29 raid with conventional weapons was staged on 15 August. Before the last B-29 had returned, Emperor Hirohito announced Japan's unconditional surrender.

USAAF losses in the Pacific were 13,055 planes, of which 1,197 heavy bombers, 864 medium and light bombers, and 2,469 fighters were brought down in combat. AAF battle casualties were 24,230 killed in action, wounded, and missing, captured, or interned. The Navy and its carrier-based aircraft had achieved and maintained air superiority over the Pacific, but the future of air power had been written large in the skies above Hiroshima and Nagasaki. For the war's duration, plus six months, the US Army Air Force had been granted the autonomy it had always sought. Now, having played an indispensable role in history's most far-flung conflict, the airmen were united in their belief that they had earned independence.

Right: **Americans celebrate V-J Day in Times Square on August 15, 1945. World War II had proved the necessity for a strong, independent air force.**

PAPAYA DRINKS
FRESH FRUIT DRINKS
FRANKFURTERS

90135
0-90091
U.S. AIR FORCE

CHAPTER 8
THE COLD WAR HEATS UP: 1945-1964

THE COLD WAR HEATS UP: 1945-1964

In the years following World War II, America's Air Force truly came of age. During the war, cooperation had been a keynote for the nation's armed services as a result of the 9 March 1942, War Department revamp, which gave the Army Air Corps autonomy and equal command status. General Henry 'Hap' Arnold had built the Army Air Corps into an unbeatable fighting machine 2.4 million strong with 80,000 aircraft. In the years immediately following Pearl Harbor, the Air Force expanded fourfold, while still a component of the US Army. That devastating attack had made clear that the future of war would, in many ways, depend on dominance in the air. By March 1945, the Air Force reached its maximum World War II strength. In little more than two years, it would become a separate branch of the military.

The Air Force Established

Sentiment favoring a separate branch of the military for the Air Force had existed almost as long as American aviation itself. Indiana Congressman Charles Lieb introduced the first legislation that would have established a separate Air Force in 1916—only 14 years after Orville and Wilbur Wright's historic flight at Kitty Hawk.

Wartime did not, however, provide the proper climate for such a major bureaucratic step as formation of a separate air force. The 1942 War Department reorganization had come about by Executive Order. Once the war ended, the War Powers Act of 1941 called for reversion to the Air Force's pre-war position as a part of the Army six months after the end of hostilities.

Yet the Joint Chiefs of Staff recognized the need to re-align American military organization with the changes that became evident during wartime. In May of 1944, they created a committee of Navy and Army officers to determine the proper method of reorganization. After 10 months of study, the committee decided on one Department of Armed Forces with three equal components. The military leader who headed up the Armed Forces would also serve as the President's Chief of Staff. This plan met with determined resistance, particularly from the Navy, which felt it was in danger of being politically sidelined.

Two Congressional bills reorganizing the nation's military progressed to the hearing stage in 1945. With the bills stalled by political infighting, President Truman weighed in and made clear that

Previous page: **A squadron of Convair F-106 Delta Darts patrols the air space over Alaska's Mount McKinley. The F-106s were capable of Mach 2 and carried nuclear air-to-air missiles.**

Above: **In 1948 General Hoyt S. Vandenberg became the second Air Force Chief of Staff, the first head of the US Air Force during the Cold War, and oversaw the transition of the Air Force into the jet age.**

Below: **President Harry S. Truman signed the order creating the US Air Force in 1947, making Stuart Symington (on Truman's right) the first Secretary of the Air Force. The first Secretary of Defense, James Forrestal, is on Truman's left.**

he favored separate and equal status for the nation's air forces and a unified command system. When a new Congress convened in January 1947, the climate for compromise improved.

A new bill, featuring an organizational plan worked out by General Lauris Norstad and Vice Admiral Forrest P. Sherman, entered the approval process the next month, despite continued opposition from Navy and Marine advocates. What became the National Security Act of 1947 contained many changes from its original form. In sum, though, the new law established three separate military departments: Army, Navy (including the Marine Corps and a naval aviation unit), and Air Force. President Truman also issued Executive Order #9877 to clarify the individual responsibilities of the three military services. These were to be supervised by a civilian Secretary of Defense appointed by the president.

Transition of an air force from Army supervision had begun in July 1947 and

The insignia for the Strategic Air Command (SAC). The SAC was created with the mission of being able to deliver a long-range strike anywhere in the world, at any time.

Above: **This Douglas C-54 Skymaster, nicknamed the *Sacred Cow,* was the first airplane built especially for the President of the United States, Franklin Roosevelt. Appropriately, Harry S. Truman signed the Nation Security Act of 1947, creating the Air Force, aboard the *Sacred Cow.***

the new US Air Force came into existence officially on 18 September 1947, when W. Stuart Symington was sworn in as the first Secretary of the Air Force. On 26 September James V. Forrestal, the nation's first Secretary of Defense, approved Order #1, and both military and civilian staff officially became part of the US Air Force. That same day, General Carl Spaatz took office as the first US Air Force Chief of Staff.

When General Spaatz retired in April 1948, General Hoyt Vandenberg succeeded him as Chief of Staff. During his tenure, Vandenberg's responsibilities included the important public relations task of clarifying the new Air Force's role to Congress and to the general public. Aggression against the United States was to be met immediately through strategic air strikes on the enemy's bases. The Air Force was also given the responsibility of defending US bases against air attacks. In addition, the Air Force would offer tactical support to the Army and Navy.

In the years between the official end of World War II and the inauguration of the new US Air Force, the nation's military forces had been rapidly demobilized. Troops remained, for the most part, only in Germany and Japan, and even in those strategic locations their numbers were small. The Army Air Corps shrank from over two and a quarter million to barely 300,000 men. Air crew numbers dropped from over 400,000 to less than 25,000. By December 1946, only two Air Force combat units out of 52 could be called ready for deployment.

Because the US military returned so rapidly to peace-time numbers, air force strength in the immediate post-war years depended primarily on a few nuclear bombs and several hundred bombers well on their way to obsolescence. The United States Air Forces in Europe (USAFE) continued to exist but in severely truncated form. The Truman-appointed Air Policy Commission Report, released in January 1948, confirmed the central role air power needed to play in US defense and optimistically called for at least 12,000 aircraft including 700 bombers capable of carrying nuclear weapons. At the time, it seemed that the US budget could not support such an outlay.

The United States Confronts a New Challenge

The end of World War II saw the Soviet Union–America's ally against Germany and Japan–move to sever its ties to the free world. Russian air power had played a major role in the Allied victory, but in the post-war years the USSR shifted its military resources to the East European states that would become its satellites. The need grew urgent for the United States to meet this new challenge.

From the embers of the recently ended hot war emerged a new kind of conflict, soon to be dubbed the Cold War. While receiving an honorary degree at Westminster College in Fulton, Missouri, on 5 March 1946, Great Britain's Winston Churchill used his rhetorical eloquence to identify the threat that Russia posed:

> From Stettin in the Baltic to Trieste in the Adriatic, an iron curtain has descended across the Continent. Beyond that line lie all the capitals of the ancient states of Central and Eastern Europe. Warsaw, Berlin, Prague, Vienna, Budapest, Belgrade, Bucharest and Sofia; all these famous cities and the populations around them lie in what I must call the Soviet sphere, and all are subject, on one form or another, not only to Soviet influence but to a very high and in some cases increasing measure of control from Moscow.

In contrast to the United States, Russia did not dismantle its military machine but kept it at wartime levels. It was quick to extract whatever technological information it could from defeated German scientists, including data on poison

Left: **Although the concept of a 'flying wing' had been around since the 1920s, Northrop introduced the first jet-powered flying wing, the YB-49, in 1947. The bomber had a range of 4,000 miles with a 10,000-pound payload at 450 miles per hour.**

Below: **A photographer turns his camera on naval observers of an atomic test on Eniwetok Atoll in the Pacific. The age of the nuclear arms race had arrived.**

gas, swept wings, jet propulsion and, most ominously, atomic fission. It would detonate its first atomic bomb on 29 August 1949. In the meantime, the Soviets tightened their grip on Eastern Europe. They precipitated a coup in Hungary on 21 June 1947, and took over Czechoslovakia on 29 February 1948. In Romania, the Communists succeeded in pressuring King Michael to abdicate by the end of 1948. The march of communism through central Europe seemed relentless.

With the Cold War came new rules for conflict. The United States quickly responded to growing Soviet aggression with economic and military aid through the Truman Doctrine and the Marshall Plan. In Greece, a 1944 communist takeover attempt had failed, but by 1946, civil war was raging. Great Britain had given economic aid to both Greece and Turkey but told the United States early in 1947 that it no longer could do so. Congress overwhelmingly approved $400 million in aid for the two struggling nations, and the Truman Doctrine of 12 March 1947, was born. The US Air Force joined the Army and Navy to form a Joint US Military Advisory and Planning Group overseeing the aid programs to Greece and Turkey to stem the Communist tide. Soon Air Force personnel were on the ground and advising their Greek and Turkish counterparts.

But the key to containing the USSR in a reconfigured world arena remained the atomic bomb and US air power. Cold War rules required a constant level of high readiness. Well before he became the new Air Force Chief of Staff, General Spaatz had put into operation a plan to develop a combat force of 70 groups, with 22 specialized squadrons and the requisite supporting units. That size remained constant up to the Korean War. Spaatz opted to base these combat resources in the United States, and his plan, set up on 21 March 1946, provided the outline for future Air Force structure. Established were the Strategic Air Command, the Tactical Air Command, and the Air Defense Command. Three new commands were added in September 1947: Air Research and Development, Continental Air, and the Military Air Transport Service.

Probably best known to the general public is the Strategic Air Command (SAC). Strategic bombing played the decisive role in World War II by debilitating the German and Japanese economies before Allied ground troops prevailed. One of the architects of World War II air strategy, General Spaatz was committed to strategic air power. While still commanding general of the Army Air Force, he moved quickly to make SAC operational, and General George C. Kenney was appointed as its first commander. Kenney opened SAC's offices for business at Bolling Field in Washington, D.C., with the Fifteenth and Eighth air forces and 600 planes. The mission: readiness for long-range operations anywhere in the world at any time. Stationed at Roswell, New Mexico, the 509th Composite Group, which had delivered atomic bombs to Hiroshima and Nagasaki, provided the core of SAC's developing atomic strike force. Based on their capabilities at the time, Cold War intercontinental readiness meant one-way—in other words, suicide-missions.

From a technological standpoint, the Air Force had its eyes on the future and the necessity for ever-greater speed even before it officially came into existence. As early as 3 December 1945, the P-80 was introduced as its first jet fighter plane, and Colonel W. Council set a record on 26 January 1946, piloting a P-80 cross-country in a little over four hours. By 28 February 1947, an F-82B set another record flying non-stop from Hawaii to New York in 14 and a half hours. On 14 October 1947 Captain Charles E. Yeager broke the sound barrier in a Bell XS-1 rocket ship. Then the first B-50 Superfortress, a long-range bomber outfitted for in-flight refueling, was introduced on 20 February 1948. History was made on 2 March 1949, when the B-50 Lucky Lady II completed the first nonstop round-the-world flight, covering 23,452 miles in under four days.

Nor were personnel matters neglected. The Air Force attended to equity issues early in its development. Its plan for racial integration, released on 26 April 1948,

***Above:* The English Electric B-57 Canberra was contracted by the USAF to be built by the Glenn Martin Company. The B-57 served in the USAF for 25 years as a medium bomber and reconnaissance aircraft.**

***Below:* German children play with models in imitation of the American airplanes that brought supplies during the Berlin Airlift at Tempelhof Air Force Base. The game they play is called 'Luftbrucke,' or 'Air Bridge.'**

The Northrop F-89 Scorpion was a twin-engine, all-weather fighter-interceptor. First flying in 1948, the F-89 became the first airplane from which a Genie nuclear air-to-air missile was launched and detonated in 1957.

Above: A massive Douglas C-124 Globemaster II flies over San Francisco. The C-124, lovingly called 'Old Shakey,' first flew in 1949 and for a decade was the largest airlifter in the USAF fleet.

preceded President Truman's executive order on the matter by almost three months. Racial segregation ended in the Air Force on 29 June 1949, ahead of the other armed services. On 12 June 1948, Women in the Air Force came into existence, after Congress passed the Women's Armed Service Integration Act.

The Berlin Blockade

If any single event signaled new world conditions and the start of the Cold War, it was the 1948 Berlin blockade. That German city had been divided into four Allied-occupied quarters at the end of the war and was surrounded by Russian-occupied East Germany. In June 1948, the United States, Great Britain, and France were ready to advance the German reunification process by establishing a new currency. Soviet leaders balked, however, at the prospect of relinquishing any control over a nation that had invaded Russia twice. They engaged in a pattern of harassment and partial resistance, even causing the crash of a British transport plane and the death of its crew.

Less than 24 hours before the new German currency was supposed to begin circulating on 25 June, the Soviets introduced their own, separate currency for the East Berlin sector. At the same time, they instituted a full blockade, stopping all traffic by rail, canal, or road between East and West Berlin. They hoped to force the United States, France and Great Britain out of Berlin by starving its residents. The blockade seemed to leave the western sector with no way to re-supply itself with food and other provisions, in other words, a policy of starvation. Instead, in conjunction with its western allies, the United States came to West Berlin's rescue within a week.

US military governor General Lucius D. Clay called for an airlift to re-supply the two million-plus Berliners affected. General Curtis Le May, commander of the US. Air Force in Europe, supervised its initial setup using C-47s, and the airlift acquired nicknames like 'LeMay's Feed and Coal Company' and 'Operation Vittles.' By 30 July, Major General William H. Tunner--who had been responsible for World War II's celebrated "Over the Hump" supply mission to China and was commander of the new Military Air Transport Service (MATS)--took charge of what became the historic First Airlift Task Force. A candy drop for German children was dubbed 'Little Vittles.'

US Air Force C-54s began bringing in up to 7,000 tons of supplies per day to Tempelhof and other airfields along 20-mile corridors from Frankfurt and other West German locations. At the peak of the airlift, there were 319 C-54s in service. In what was a cooperative effort not just with Britain and France, the US Army Transportation Corps brought provisions to and from the cargo planes, the US Army Engineer Corps built new runways, and US Navy tanker ships supplied aviation fuel and additional planes. In April 1949, the 'Easter Parade' took place, with 1,398 planes delivering a record 12,940 tons. By 12 May 1949, Russian resistance caved in and they reopened the borders.

New Missions for the Air Force

What the Soviets had hoped would put an end to Allied plans for a reunified Germany failed on many fronts. Even though the blockade resulted in separate republics of East and West Germany, it alerted the Western world to the renewed prospects for war with a former ally. It also led to formation of the North Atlantic Treaty Organization (NATO) in April 1949. President Truman called NATO 'an expression of the desire of the people of the United States for peace and security, for the continuing opportunity to live and

Above: **The F-106 was developed from the F-102, the world's first supersonic all-weather interceptor. Both airplanes used the delta wing, allowing for decreased compressed airflow at supersonic speeds.**

Right: **Experimental aircraft on display at Edwards Air Force Base in 1954. Clockwise from bottom center: Douglas X-3, Bell X-1A, jet-powered Douglas D-558, Convair XF-92, Bell X-5, rocket-powered Douglas D-558, Northrop X-4.**

Above: **The Convair B-58, the US Air Force's first supersonic bomber, was built specifically for the new challenges of the Cold War, focusing on high technology and nuclear strategy.**

work in freedom.' It also put a stop to downsizing of Air Force resources abroad. US Air Force tactical units were deployed in Europe, primarily in Great Britain and France. The Air Force began transporting aircraft to nations receiving aid under the Truman and Marshall plans; it trained pilots and crews for countries receiving aid and supported Strategic Air Command training exercises in Europe and North Africa. Air command operations were also set up in the Far East, Alaska, the Northeast and the Caribbean. Development of the B-52 bomber went into high gear.

While it had little to do with the development of nuclear bombs, the Air Force had everything to do with testing them. Starting in July 1946, the Air Force cooperated with the Navy in Test Able of Operation Crossroads at Bikini Atoll in the Marshall Islands. A second one, called Test Baker, took place underwater on July 25. Other tests using Air Force aircraft and personnel continued in the Pacific and Nevada, initially above ground but later underground.

The news that the Soviets had exploded a nuclear device arrived on 23 September 1949, and President Truman stepped up production of American atomic bombs on 17 October, okaying the start of research on the even more lethal hydrogen bomb on 31 January 1950. The United States' first hydrogen bomb was detonated at Eniwetok Atoll in the Marshall Islands on 1 November 1952. While some felt the Russians remained a long way from acquiring functional nuclear weapons and the long-range aircraft capable of delivering them to US targets, other military experts saw the danger of one-way missions over the polar cap. As a result, Air Force power in Alaska, Canada, and Greenland was enhanced through the Alaskan and Northeast Air Commands. SAC increased its resources in the United Kingdom, North Africa and Spain.

New Responsibilities

While the Soviet nuclear build-up and the Berlin Blockade made it seem that America's only real post-war enemy would be the USSR, that was hardly the case. Confirming globalization of the communist threat, Communist leader Mao Zedong formed the People's Republic of China on 1 October 1949, ending a civil war the communists had waged since World War II against Chiang Kai-Chek and his Nationalist party. On the heels of Mao Zedong's rise to power came North Korea's attack on South Korea 25 June 1950. With onset of the Korean War, languishing US vigilance in the Far East ended, and the Air Force presence in Japan and Korea increased.

The death of Joseph Stalin in March 1953, followed by the ascension to power of Nikolai Khrushchev that fall, demonstrated how unstable world politics had become in the era of the Cold War. A series of popular revolts in Eastern bloc nations began with a demonstration in Berlin on 16-17 June that year against new workers quotas. Popular demonstrations followed in Hungary in 1956—and eventually in Czechoslovakia (1968) and in Poland (1970). They demonstrated that the Iron Curtain was not ideologically monolithic. Nevertheless, the United States maintained a neutral position politically.

In June 1953, General Nathan Twining took over as Air Force Chief of Staff and later became the first Joint Chiefs of Staff chairman from the Air Force. Although initially opposed to the use of atomic bombs, he came to favor nuclear weapons to aid the French in Indochina and established a role for tactical nuclear weapons in the Air Force. Harold Talbott had been appointed Secretary of the Air Force earlier that year and continued in that position until 1955. Both Twining and Talbott worked to help the Air Force acquire the funds it needed to support its expansion. Talbott also helped lay the

groundwork for the Air Force Academy, which Congress formally authorized on 1 April 1954, and which moved to its permanent site near Colorado Spring, Colorado, in 1955.

On 8 December 1953, President Eisenhower re-affirmed the American commitment to peace in a speech before the United Nations that alerted the American public to the growing threat of an international arms race and the very real possibility of a nuclear holocaust. The speech took a step, if small, toward nuclear disarmament by proposing a UN-based nuclear stockpile 'to serve the peaceful pursuits of mankind.' Direct outcomes of the Atoms for Peace initiative were formation of the International Atomic Energy Agency and US delivery by air transport of a nuclear reactor to a Geneva, Switzerland, conference on peaceful uses for atomic energy.

Eisenhower's peace initiative was balanced by Secretary of State John Foster Dulles's 1954 get-tough dealings with the Soviets. He warned that 'Local forces must be reinforced by the further deterrent of massive retaliation,' and 'massive retaliation' became the catch phrase for the times. That year Dulles also helped develop the Southeast Asia Treaty Organization (SEATO) in which the United States agreed to join Great Britain, France, Pakistan, Australia, New Zealand, the Philippines and Thailand to defend the participants against aggression. The Air Force added SEATO to its peacekeeping responsibilities.

Hostilities in Korea had ended in July 1953, but the first rumblings of a war that would soon preoccupy the US military came at the 1954 Geneva Conference on Indochina. The United States helped set the terms there for elections in the former French colonies of Laos, Cambodia, and—most importantly—Vietnam, which was officially divided along the 17th parallel into North and South Vietnam. Meanwhile, trouble brewed with Red China when it shelled two small islands, Quemoy and Matsu, that had been fortified by Nationalist China—now known as Taiwan but then called Formosa. The United States returned the 7th fleet to the Taiwan Straits to prevent further hostilities between the rival nations and in 1955 established Air Force bases on Formosa.

In the wake of the Korean War, the United States continued to extend the hand of friendship to other nations in anti-soviet alliances. The United States signed the Baghdad Pact, or Central

Left: **The Lockheed Martin U-2 Spy Plane made its first flight in August 1955. It has been involved in wars and several high-profile international conflicts, including the 1962 Cuban Missile Crisis.**

Above: **Soviet Premier Nikolai Khrushchev examines wreckage collected from the U-2 Spy Plane piloted by Francis Gary Powers in 1960. The U-2 Incident served to further fuel tensions of the Cold War.**

Air Force Captain Chuck Yeager (inset) became the first man to fly faster than the speed of sound in the Bell X-1 on 14 October 1947. Yeager piloted the Glamorous Glennis to a speed of Mach 1.06 at an altitude of 43,000 feet.

The jet age brought the hybrid Convair RB-36D, a reconnaissance version of the heavy bomber. The RB-36D had six push-prop engines, augmented by four General Electric J-47 jet engines, retrofitted on the wingtips. The North American B-45D (above) was the long-range version of the B-45, America's first four-engine jet bomber. Designed during World War II and first flying in 1947, the B-45 remained in USAF service until 1958, with a few seeing service in the Korean War.

Treaty Organization (CENTO), with Iraq and Turkey on 24 February 1955, and Great Britain, Iran and Pakistan joined later. A more coercive counterpart was the Warsaw Pact that Khrushchev strong-armed the Soviet satellite nations in Eastern Europe into signing on 14 May 1955. The Geneva Summit that year tried to thaw East-West relations, but the only important outcome was President Eisenhower's 'Open Skies' treaty proposal. It called for use of intelligence-gathering aircraft by East and West, but the Soviets rejected it.

Egypt seemed to tip toward Communism when Gamal Nasser took control of the Suez Canal on 26 July 1956, stunning the Western world. President Eisenhower put SAC on alert until the Egyptians backed down. More shockwaves followed when the Soviets launched Sputnik I on 4 October 1957. It was the first man-made satellite to orbit the earth and demonstrated that the USSR had an Intercontinental Ballistic Missile (ICBM) capable of launching it. The Air Force's own Atlas ICBM, designed by the Convair Division of General Dynamics Corporation and in the works since 1951, had failed twice in tests that year.

Scrambling to catch up with the Soviets, who had announced a successful ICBM test in August, the United States established the North American Air Defense Command (NORAD) on 12 September 1957, and extended it to include Canada through a cooperative agreement signed in May 1958. SAC took charge of ICBM operation on 1 January 1958, and the 672nd Strategic Missile Squadron became the first equipped with the Douglas Thor IRBM. The National Aeronautic and Space Act, signed into law on 28 July 1958, by President Eisenhower, brought NASA into existence, giving the nation a civilian space program.

The wisdom behind President Eisenhower's 'Open Skies' proposal demonstrated itself in a 1958 incident that occurred over Soviet Armenia. An American C-130, refitted for reconnaissance work, crossed the border from Turkey and was shot down by Soviet MiG's on 2 September. Seventeen crewmen were lost, and the Soviets never returned most of the bodies.

The year 1959 opened with dictator Fidel Castro's takeover of Cuba. The United States initially gave diplomatic recognition to Castro's government, but relations worsened. By October 1960, it instituted an embargo on Cuban goods that continues today. Establishment of a communist nation so close to home shocked Americans, and reaffirmed the importance of SAC's air defense role. US defenses were further enhanced when the Air Force successfully launched the first Titan I ICBM on 6 February 1959. Technological advances continued apace. The first Ballistic Missile Early Warning System (BMEWS) went into operation in 1959 to provide instant protection from missile incursions over the polar caps. The world's first nuclear weapons free zone also came into existence that year in December with signing of the Antarctic Treaty, which banned the use of Antarctica for military purposes like nuclear weapons testing.

By 1960, the United States signed a new mutual defense agreement with Japan. Japan assumed equal status with the United States for the first time since World War II in the Treaty of Mutual Cooperation and Security. It replaced the 1951 United States-Japan Defense Pact. But Cold War tensions remained high. President Eisenhower was meeting with Soviet Premier Nikolai Khrushchev at the Paris Summit of May 1960, when the news arrived that an American pilot, Francis Gary Powers, had been shot down over Russia. Powers was flying a U-2 reconnaissance plane on a joint mission by the CIA and the Air Force. After Khrushchev demanded an apology for the incident and Eisenhower refused to provide it, the Paris talks broke down. Powers was convicted of espionage and imprisoned in the Soviet Union almost two years before freed in exchange for a Soviet spy. Powers had gone through the Air Force's aviation cadet training program and flew F-84 Commandos as part of the 468th Strategic Fighter Squadron at Turner Air Force base in Georgia. But because the flight was CIA sponsored, Powers's heroism was not recognized until May 2000, when he received posthumously the Distinguished Flying Cross and two other medals.

The United States broke off diplomatic relations with Cuba in January 1961, after Castro 'nationalized' American holdings and moved closer to the Soviets. In April, a covert invasion of Cuba, planned by the CIA with a paramilitary force of Cuban exiles, proved disastrous. Almost 1,200 were taken prisoner, and four American pilots from the Alabama National Guard were killed. Although air strikes were considered a key element to the disastrous invasion at the Bay of Pigs, they were executed by Cuban exiles in conjunction with the US Navy. The Air Force was not directly involved, although SAC was put on alert.

In Europe, East Germany's isolation led to a flood of refugees through Berlin. To stop the exodus, the East German government sealed the border on 13 August 1961. The Berlin Wall began as a barbed wire barrier but quickly became solid, acquiring two concrete barriers with a death zone in between that contained tank traps, land mines, gun emplacements, and dog patrols.

The world veered toward possible nuclear holocaust in October 1962, after US surveillance discovered that the Soviets had installed ground-to-air missiles as part of a massive defense build-up in Cuba, 90 miles from the US Air Force Lieutenant General Gordon Blake, newly appointed as NSA director, established a 24-7 command post. On 22 October, President John F. Kennedy told the American public on television about the Cuban missiles and set up a naval blockade to keep further Soviet arms shipments out of Cuba. The world held its breath, waiting to see if the USSR would breech the blockade, but the Soviets backed down and war was averted.

Just as did the United States, the Soviets kept the pressure up through surveillance sorties, sometimes over Alaska. The Eleventh Air Force, based at Elmendorf in Alaska, had detected the first Soviet incursion of Alaskan airspace in 1958, and intercepted a Soviet TU-16 Badger on 5 December 1961. To prevent inadvertent 'Strangelove' attack orders, a telephone hotline was installed in 1962 to link Washington, D.C., and Moscow.

The Cold War state of mind turned tragic in November 1963, when President Kennedy was assassinated by Lee Harvey Oswald, a man who had spent time in the Soviet Union. Texan Lyndon Baines Johnson assumed the Presidency, and in 1964, the Cold War turned hot with the Gulf of Tonkin Resolution, the closest the United States came to declaring war on Vietnam. Appointed as Secretary of Defense under President Kennedy, Robert McNamara announced in 1964 a policy of 'assured destruction' for the enemy in light of a first strike on the United States. It meant that the development of nuclear weapons technology continued on a fast track.

Although the Cold War continued unabated in the years following 1964, two very 'hot' wars also required the total dedication of the US Air Force during these decades: the Korean War and the Vietnam War.

Above right: **The Soviet freighter *Anesov* leaves Cuba, escorted by the USS *Barry* and a Navy C-54. Aboard the *Anesov* are what appear to be missiles, being removed from Cuba after a tense fourteen-day standoff between the United States and the USSR.**

Right: **President John F. Kennedy mounts a platform to see over the Berlin Wall into communist territory. Kennedy flew to Germany aboard Air Force One in 1963 where he delivered his famous *Ich Bin Ein Berliner* speech.**

CHAPTER 9
THE AIR WAR IN KOREA: 1950-1953

THE AIR WAR IN KOREA: 1950-1953

When World War II ended after VJ Day on 15 August 1945, demobilization of the Army Air Corps happened rapidly. During the last four months of 1945, 1.2 million members of the Corps were discharged. Airplane manufacture stopped dead in its tracks, and by 1946 the nation did not have even one air corps group in operation. Ludicrously, Hollywood pilot Paul Mantz spent $50,000 to buy 500 surplus planes and earned it back by selling the fuel in their tanks. After helping the Koreans develop a domestic security organization, the United States withdrew from Korea except for a minimal military advisory group.

US foreign policy and military preoccupations remained focused on Europe, and American troops in Asia operated as little more than a garrison outpost. The outbreak of the Korean War would reveal how misguided this policy was. Fortunately, enough of the quarter-million pilots trained during World War II had remained in the Air Force Reserve and the National Guard. Many of these 'retread tigers' would return to serve in Korea, and they soon built a ten-to-one kill ratio against North Korean and Chinese pilots.

A War Breaks Out

Extending south from Soviet Siberia, the Korean Peninsula was divided along the 38th parallel by the United States and the USSR in the closing days of World War II. Although the 1945 Potsdam Agreement had called for reunification of Korea, the peninsula was divided simply at the outset to facilitate the surrender of Japanese soldiers to the Allied forces, but also with each nation's desire to prevent the other to seize complete control of Korea. Almost from the start, the USSR resisted reunification of North and South Korea and was unwilling to participate in national elections called for by the United Nations on 10 May 1948. By November 1948, all pretense of unification was discarded and instead there was recognized to be a Western-backed Republic of Korea (South Korea) and a Soviet-supported Democratic Republic of Korea (North Korea). Kim Il Sung, a former officer in the Russian Army, became premier of North Korea,

Previous page: **During the Korean War the P-51 was given new life. Re-designated as the F-51, Mustangs saw extensive duty in the war as low-level bombers, such as the *Sexy Sally,* seen here dropping a napalm bomb over a North Korean industrial target in 1951.**

Above: **A mechanic works on an engine of a B-29 Superfort based in Okinawa. During the Korean War, the USAF launched attacks on North Korea from bases in Okinawa and Japan.**

Below: **Mechanics test the .50 caliber machine guns on a Republic F-84 Thunderjet. Bright tracers, allowing pilots to see where their bullets were going, can be seen hitting a target and ricocheting.**

and the Soviets began a military build-up in their new Asian satellite.

Mao Zedong's rise to leadership of Communist China in 1949 offered one of the first signs that trouble was brewing in the Far East. The Potsdam conference had assured South Korea of US protection, but by 1947 the budget-conscious Joint Chiefs of Staff decided placement of troops in South Korea was not a high priority. They opted instead for Japan-based air force deterrence. US military presence in South Korea dwindled to a 500-member Korean Military Advisory Group, although the United States provided significant financial and materiel aid to a large South Korean army; likewise, although the USSR withdrew most of its troops from North Korea, they provided a great deal of aid to its military.

On 25 June 1950, North Korean troops invaded South Korea, and the conflict would continue until signing of the Korean Armistice on 17 July 1953. General Omar Bradley, then Chairman of the Joint Chiefs of Staff, called it 'the wrong war, in the wrong place at the wrong time with the wrong enemy.' The onset of the Korean War ended languishing US vigilance in the Far East, and Air Force presence in Japan and Korea increased.

Reinforced by 100 Soviet-made tanks, a North Korean force of 60,000 invaded South Korea. The UN Security Council went into emergency session and condemned the invasion. The Fifth Air Force, with aircraft in Okinawa and Japan, helped evacuate US citizens initially by providing air cover with F-82 jet fighters at the request of US Ambassador John J. Muccio. Within four days, North Korean forces arrived outside Seoul, the capital of South Korea. Fifth Air Force Commander Major General Earle E. Partridge ordered the 374th Troop Carrier Wing to complete the evacuation with C-54s. He also used fighter F-82 fighters for armed reconnaissance, a successful operation until the North Koreans began dispersing their

Above: **Little was known about the capabilities of the Soviet MiG-15 until a North Korean fighter pilot decided to defect to the West, landing at Kimpo Air Force Base in Seoul, South Korea, in 1953. The plane's number, 2057, was blocked out as classified.**

Right: **A formation of B-29s flies a mission over enemy territory in Korea. In July and August of 1950, over twenty-four million pounds of bombs were dropped from the Superfort.**

forces and operating at night.

At the start of the conflict, the US Far East Air Force (FEAF) consisted of the Fifth and Thirteenth Air Forces. Between them they had 535 working planes, including 32 F-82 Twin Mustangs and 365 F-80 Shooting Star fighter jets. The latter, developed in 1945, were already obsolete. Within a month, however, 145 National Guard F-51 aircraft left for Korea aboard the USS Boxer. A total of 764 National Guard F-51s went on active duty. By the end of the year, the Fourth Fighter Interceptor Wing's F-86A Sabrejets were also on their way. Setting a world speed record—670 mph—the Sabrejet became known as the 'fighter pilot's fighter.' The Sabrejet would produce the United States' first 39 jet aces, and seven of the top ten were World War II veterans.

The UN Security Council passed a resolution asking the North Koreans to withdraw to the 38th Parallel, but it was ignored. Fifteen countries, including Great Britain, Australia and Turkey, as well as the United States, responded to the UN call for troops. General Douglas MacArthur was appointed to head the UN Command, for what President Truman termed a 'police action.' General George Stratemeyer served as MacArthur's air commander. At this early stage, the war was seen as an effort to force North Korean troops back to the 38th parallel. It functioned as one of the United Nation's first tests as an international peacekeeping organization, and US air power played an important role. On 26 June, President Truman issued orders for US air and naval forces to aid the South Korean army but stipulated that neither group attack north of the 38th Parallel except for emergencies.

The next day, General MacArthur called for an FEAF strike on North Korean troops, and two Air Force groups, the 35th Fighter-Interceptor and the 49th Fighter-Bomber, left their Honshu bases, and flew to Itazuke and Ashiya on Japan's Kyushu Island. B-26 bombers from the Third Bombardment Group flew on to Korea but turned back because of poor weather. A squadron of F-82s sighted five North Korean YAK fighters en route to Seoul's Kimpo Airfield, where American passengers were being readied for evacuation, and shot down three of them. The Fifth Air Force's F-80s and F-82s eliminated a total of seven Soviet-made YAK fighters and IL-10s—all propeller driven—before they could reach Kimpo Airfield. The United States scored its first three air victories in Korea on 27 June, thanks to Lieutenant William Hudson of the 68th Fighter Squadron, as well as Lieutenant Charles Moran, and Major James Little.

Although the weather continued to be poor, on 28 June at Iazuke and Ashiya, F-80 jet fighter planes—unable to operate from unimproved South Korean air strips—and B-26s hit targets along roads north of the Han River outside Seoul. They were joined by four B-29s from the 19th Bombardment Group, based in Okinawa, which bombed Seoul's two main roads. After evacuation of American personnel, Kimpo Airfield was lost to the North Koreans, but on 29 June, Air Force B-29s bombed it.

When North Korean air power succeeded in strafing Air Force transports at Suwon Airfield while they were unloading ammunition, General MacArthur approved General Stratemeyer's request for retaliation against enemy air bases north of the 38th parallel. The 35th and another

Above: **By the end of the Korean War, the North American F-86 Sabrejets flown by the USAF enjoyed a 10 to 1 kill ratio over the Soviet MiG-15s flown by the North Korean Air Force.**

Right: **The North American P-82 was created by joining the fuselages of two P-51 Mustangs with a single wing. With a crew of two and a top speed of 475 miles per hour, the P-82 was one of the first planes to see action in the Korean War.**

squadron of B-26s from the Third Bombardment Group hit the North Korean airfield at Pyongyang.

The War Expands

By 30 June, President Truman approved air sorties against military targets in North Korea. Approval for US ground forces followed. FEAF planes were joined by Navy pilots from 11 US aircraft carriers to support ground troops. Their targets included railroads, refineries and factories, as well as airfields and enemy troops. After 12 July, the Fifth Air Force, along with B-29s, helped the 24th Division defend Taejon, a strategic communications site, until 20 July, when the North Koreans, who outnumbered US ground troops, overran it. From 1 to 10 August, the Fifth averaged 340 missions daily, giving the Eighth Army time to set up a defense for Pusan, a southeast port city on the Sea of Japan.

On 3 August, the Marine Fighting Squadron 214 entered the fray with Corsairs and VMF-323s. The Fifth destroyed most of the North Korean fleet of 70 YAKs and 62 IL-10s, primarily on the ground, by 10 August. Estimates put the figures at 110 planes destroyed with 22 remaining, and according to General Stratemeyer, the absence of effective enemy opposition in the air during the war's early stages was its 'paramount feature.'

An important aspect of the Air Force's role in Korea was to keep enemy troops and supplies from moving unimpeded into South Korea. To accomplish this aim, USAF Chief of Staff Hoyt Vandenberg in July ordered SAC B-29s from the 22nd and 92nd Groups to Asia. Major General Emmett O'Donnell, Jr., took command of the FEAF Bomber Command (Provisional) for supervision of medium bombers. General Stratemeyer ordered this new air power to be used against targets in North Korea. Additional support came in August with the SAC 98th and 307th Bombardment Groups. Although the FEAF command proposed the use of incendiaries and carpet bombing, the White House, fearing public reaction, vetoed incendiaries. General Stratemeyer opted to use high-explosive bombs instead in strategic bombing sorties and destroyed targets in Pyongyang and Chongjin, as well as Wonsan and Hungnam farther north.

North of Pusan near the Naktong River, North Korean troops began massing to attack Taegu, and on 16 August General O'Donnell directed a carpet-bombing raid by 98 B-29s to deflect the planned attack. Throughout most of August, the Fifth Air Force averaged almost 240 missions daily to support the thinly spread ground troops. By 31 August, when North Korean forces, six divisions strong, moved over the Naktong River to confront the US Second and 25th Infantry Divisions, the Fifth Air Force filled the breach, joined by B-29s and Navy planes.

The North Koreans ended their first major offensive 15 September 1950. While they had reached the southern end of South Korea and cornered South Korean troops with their UN compatriots in the region around Pusan, in fact the North Korean forces were in disarray. In a 9 September attack near Yongsan, many North Korean soldiers went into battle weaponless, with orders to retrieve guns from the dead.

Despite a typhoon raging nearby in Japan, UN troops initiated a counter-offensive 15 September, with US Marines making an amphibious landing at Inchon on the coast west of Seoul. General MacArthur masterminded the Inchon landing, and although opposed by a majority of the Joint Chiefs of Staff, it was dramatically successful. In preparation for the assault, General Stratemeyer arranged for additional air power in the form of C-119s from the Japan-based 314th Troop Carrier Group of the Eighth Air Force.

Above: **The Sikorsky H-5 Dragon Fly was used by the USAF during the Korean War for evacuating casualties and search and rescue missions of pilots who had been shot down behind enemy lines.**

Below: **A dramatic explosion, captured on film from a B-26 that just dropped its load on a marshalling yard in North Korea, shows the destructive power of napalm.**

He put Major General William H. Tunner in charge of the FEAF Combat Cargo Command (Provisional).

FEAF's role in the initiative was to provide air cover for the Eighth Army, perform cargo airlifts and complete an air sortie with the Eighth's 187th Airborne Regimental Combat Team. The Eighth and 18th Fighter-Bomber Groups shifted their F-51 Mustangs to Korea in time to escape the typhoon. The relocation enabled FEAF planes to fly 3,257 missions the week of the Inchon invasion. To keep the North Koreans from reinforcing their troops, B-29s flew missions from Seoul north to Pyongyang and Wonsan, bombing railroads and supply areas. Two RF-80s from the Eighth Tactical Reconnaissance Squadron provided crucial reconnaissance for the invasion by determining the height of an Inchon seawall the Marines would have to scramble over.

The first C-54 arrived at Kimpo Airfield in Seoul on 19 September, and FEAF's Combat Cargo Command began its airlift in earnest 20 September. Later in the month, air transports carried the 187th Airborne RCT to Kimpo. General MacArthur countermanded the plan to focus US air power on bombing North Korea in order to keep the B-29s nearer to the Eighth Army and bridges at the front. The region near Waegwan was bombed on 19 September, using 42 B-29s. By 22 September, the Fifth Air Force had cleared the way for the Eighth Army's attack and provided cover for South Korean soldiers moving up the east coast. The Eighth Army reached X Corps Marines outside Osan, south of Seoul, on 26 September, while South Korean soldiers continued up the eastern coast toward the 38th Parallel under protection of Fifth Air Force fighter planes. The fighters also strafed retreating North Korean soldiers. By 28 September, little was left to bomb, and North Korean forces had been ex-

***Above:* Direct hits are scored on a double bridge spanning the Kum River, 10 miles north of Taejon. In 1950, bridges were destroyed all along the Kum in an attempt to use the river as a natural barrier to halt the advancing North Korean army.**

***Below:* Unguided rockets are fired at enemy targets from Douglas B-26 Invaders of the Far East Air Force (FEAF) 452nd Light Bomb Wing.**

pelled from South Korea.

After the UN General Assembly called for taking all necessary steps 'to ensure conditions of peace throughout the whole of Korea,' on 7 October, the Eighth Army prepared to push past the 38th parallel toward North Korea's capital, Pyongyang, with support from FEAF. To provide the necessary air backup for such an incursion, General Partridge moved the Fifth Air Force into South Korea. Headquarters Fifth Air Force Korea set up shop 15 October in Seoul with the Joint Operations Center, and the Eighth, 18th and 35th Air Groups transferred their F-80 jet fighters from Japan to airfields at Pusan, Kimpo, and Pohang. The 502nd Tactical Control Group, from Pope Air Force Base in North Carolina, arrived to take over tactical control duties. Fighter jets from the Fifth Air Force scouted for the ground advance on Pyongyang 19 October.

In preparation for pushing northward after the capture of Pyongyang, five light bombers and 137 fighter jets strafed an area 30 miles north of the city. Then Combat Cargo Command, using 71 C-119s and 40 C-47s, dropped the 187th Airborne—2,860 soldiers—with their gear and supplies on roads near Sukchon and Sunchon. Using backup from the Fifth Air Force, South Korean forces won Wonsan on the east coast 10 October. A major engagement took place 23 October, when eight Superforts were attacked by MiGs, despite protection from 55 F-84s and another 34 Sabrejets. Three of the B-29s were lost, and the rest damaged. Demonstrating the level of heroism practiced by fighter-bomber pilots, Medal of Honor winners Major Louis Sebille and Captain Charles Loring dove their planes into their targets rather than turning back or bailing out.

The speed with which US and UN-forces entered North Korea led to a new interdiction plan, and FEAF destroyed all but six of 32 targeted highway and railway bridges north of Sinanju on the west coast. By 25 October, the 22nd and 92nd Bombardment Groups were able to return to the United States, and North Korean forces had been pushed back to the Yalu River, the dividing line between North Korea and Red China's Manchuria.

China Enters the War

An early warning of Red China's imminent entrance into the war came on 1 November, when six MiG-15s engaged F-51 Mustangs south of the Yalu River. Red China overtly entered the war on 3 November 1950, when 300,000 Chinese troops crossed the Yalu River. The Chinese brought with them 500 Soviet-made MiG-15 jet fighters, some Soviet piloted. The first all-jet dogfight in military history occurred on 8 November, when 51st Fighter-Interceptor Wing F-80s engaged MiG-15s. Although the obsolete F-80Cs were outclassed by the MiGs, Lieutenant Russell J. Brown from the 16th Fighter Interceptor Squadron took down the first MiG-15, which proved to be piloted by a Russian. The use of Russian pilots proved to be one of the dirty little secrets of the Korean engagement. The first kill occurred the following day by a Navy pilot. US Air Force and Navy planes supported the ground troops by strafing supply lines and kept North Korean and Chinese forces from massing.

By early November the FEAF had established aircraft warning radar near the front lines, begun air patrols over Sinuiju in western North Korea, and shifted three Mustang groups into North Korea. On 5 November, General MacArthur ordered a massive, two-week air campaign from the Yalu River south to the battle lines. FEAF planes hit cities, villages, communication equipment, factories and sections of the bridges between Red China and North Korea. By 8 November, Sinuiju was largely demolished in B-29 incendiary strikes, and the FEAF destroyed their

Above: **Supply warehouses and dock facilities such as these in Wonsan, North Korea, were prime bombing targets for the Far East Air Force.**

Right: **General Douglas MacArthur at the front lines in Suwon, Korea, in January 1951. President Harry S. Truman dismissed MacArthur as Allied Commander a few months later.**

A Lockheed F-80 Shooting Star drops a napalm bomb over an enemy target. From the road below, anti-aircraft fire can be seen streaking upward toward the fighter-bomber.

Left: **A MiG-15 pilot ejects after being hit by fire from a USAF F-86 Sabre. This victory was attributed to Lt. Edwin E. Aldrin, Jr., who would go on to later fame as an astronaut aboard Apollo 11, the first spacecraft to land on the Moon in 1969.**

other targets by 28 November. The bridge demolition proved tougher. MiG fighters fought back, and the B-29s were forbidden to fly into Manchurian China. With aid from carrier-based planes, however, four of the bridges were severed and the rest damaged.

The Eighth Army began a major foray on 18 November, but met Chinese resistance two days later, and UN soldiers were forced to retreat. FEAF planes fended off enemy air attacks, hit Chinese ground forces to enable safe retreat of ground troops and aided the retreat with air transport. Despite MiG superiority, the Fifth Air Force held its own. Arrival of the Fourth Fighter-Interceptor Wing's F-86 Sabre jets and the 27th Fighter-Escort Wing's F-84 Thunderjets changed the balance. F-86A Sabres downed four MiGs on 17 December. The skills of the US pilots surpassed those of the MiGs, and they shot down eight more MiGs in December.

Fifth Air Force fighter-bombers screened withdrawal of the US Second Infantry Division on 2 December. With Chinese troops gathering north of Seoul, US fighter-bombers cut down their advances, using rockets and napalm, and F-80s from the 49th Group strafed enemy soldiers crossing the Chongchun River. In the weeks that followed, UN air attacks destroyed some 40,000 Chinese soldiers.

Combat Cargo Command concurrently re-supplied the beleaguered X Corps Marines in the northeast. On 14 December, after the Marines reached Hamhung and Hungnam, Combat Cargo Command conducted a four-day evacuation from Yonpo Airfield. The Fifth Air Force moved south with ground troops. Mustangs went to southern Korea and those based out of Kimpo Airfield, to Japan.

With the prospects for a long-term conflict clear, FEAF reorganized as of 1 December. The Fifth Air Force's command post moved from Seoul to Teagu in the south and turned over air defense of Japan to the 314th Air Division. In January of 1951, the 315th Air Division (Combat Cargo) replaced FEAF's Combat Cargo Command (Provisional). It had become clear that military reunification of North Korea and South Korea stood a good chance of leading to a new world war. On 15 December, the UN General Assembly approved a US-sponsored declaration that every effort would be made to end the conflict and to resolve outstanding concerns peacefully. The UN Command's strategy became to push the Chinese and North Korea toward a truce by imposing the greatest possible losses, and President Truman warned China that the United States might employ atomic bombs.

By January 1951, the Chinese forced UN troops to retreat southward past Seoul. General MacArthur was eager to bring the war home to the Chinese by bombing their military factories, blockading the coast of China and sending Nationalist Chinese forces, led by Chiang Kai-Chek, from Formosa into mainland China. He argued, 'if we lose this war to communism in Asia, the fall of Europe is inevitable…there is no substitute for victory.' MacArthur's open defiance of President Truman's more cautious approach, in which US pilots were forbidden to cross the Yalu River, even in hot pursuit of enemy planes, would cost him his job.

For the first two months of 1951, the FEAF no longer could dominate northwest Korea from the air. The section of Korea between the Chongchon and Yalu Rivers became known as 'MiG Alley.' In a 23 January engagement close to the Yalu River, 33 F-84s nevertheless downed three out of 25 MiGs without any losses. The Chinese undertook a major air initiative in March 1951, after repairing damaged North Korean airfields.

On 11 April 1951, President Truman replaced General MacArthur with General Matthew Ridgeway. Brigadier General James E. Briggs, General O'Donnell's successor as commander of the FEAF Bomber Command, launched

Below: **An Indian paratrooper battalion boards a USAF C-124 Globemaster in Calcutta for deployment in the Korean demilitarized zone. The Indian Custodial Force was created in the Armistice of 1953.**

Above: **The Fairchild C-119 'Flying Boxcar' was used extensively in Korea, dropping supplies to soldiers on the ground, deployment of paratroopers, and transporting wounded soldiers and cargo.**

strikes against North Korean airfields that started on 13 April. Escorted by F-84s and F-86s, B-29s destroyed runways at nine enemy airfields, and more bombers hit Pyongyang airfields on 16 and 19 April. The air mission was completed with the destruction of 40 planes at Sinuiju by Fifth Air planes in conjunction with Army and Marine planes.

UN troops pushed into North Korea again, stopping at a line some 20 miles north of the 38th parallel. Attacks on enemy forces at the battlefront continued into the spring of 1951, impeding North Korean supply lines by up to 80 percent. At the North Korean-Chinese border, bombers destroyed most Yalu River bridges, but four planes were shot down by MiG fighter jets despite Thunderjet support. Major James 'Jabby' Jabara of the Fourth Fighter Wing downed 15 MiGs over MiG Alley, becoming the Air Force's first jet ace on 20 May. Captain Joseph McConnell, Jr., topped the ace score with 16 enemy planes downed. Combat Cargo Command C-46s and C-47s re-supplied the Eighth Army from air strips at Wonju, Andong, and Chungju, and, thanks to air support, the Eighth Army retook Suwon and Kimpo Airfields, as well as Inchon on the west coast. When the Second Division was surrounded in February, the Fifth Air Force re-supplied them, and they were able to hold firm.

In face of sustained enemy attack that spring, fighter-bombers patched a break in IX Corps lines that developed on 22 April. Over the next six weeks, the Fifth Air Force protected X Corps troops subjected to enemy attack in the central Korea region near Wonju, killing well over 16,000 enemy soldiers. Using radar, B-29s and B-26s stymied enemy troops, and in one case over 20 and 21 May, killed 4,000 members of an enemy regiment. The Eighth Army's demand for ammunition reached critical proportions, and supplies were delivered from Japan by the 315th Air Division in April, May, and June. In advance of a 23 June ceasefire, the Fifth Air Force buttressed a successful Eighth Army assault into the 'Iron Triangle.'

Truce Talks Commence

North Korean General Nam II told the UN 'Without the support of the indiscriminate bombing and bombardment of your air and naval forces, your ground forces would have long ago been driven out of the Korean peninsula.' While the cease-fire was in effect, FEAF was not allowed to undertake assault missions, and Chinese troops amassed large stockpiles of supplies. To prevent overwhelming enemy retaliation, the FEAF Bomber Command was called in, along with Naval Forces Far East (NFFE), on 18 August to destroy rail connections in large sections of central Korea, as well as at Pyongyang, Sonchun, Sinanju, and Sunchon. When the enemy shifted to nighttime truck convoys, the Third and 452nd Bombardment Wings flew sorties against them. The railroad interdiction was only partially successful, because of the enemy's speed at repairing bridges and key arteries at night. As a result, truce talks at Kaesong and Panmunjon went slowly.

In northwest Korea, the FEAF found itself outnumbered five to one, with the Chinese flying 525 MiG-15s against its 105 F-86 Sabrejets. Before the end of 1951, the MiGs destroyed 12 UN fighter-bombers. To bridge the gap, the Fifth Air Force provisioned the 51st Figher-Interceptor Wing with F-86s, which downed 31 MiG fighters at the beginning of 1952. Fifth Air Force Superfortresses bombed new jet airstrips near the Chongchon River in northwest Korea, losing four to MiG attacks. North Korean hydroelectric resources became an air target in June. One of the largest in the world, the Suiho on the Yahoo River was off limits because of its political sensitivity. Once President Eisenhower approved it, however, the facility was destroyed, starting 23 June.

FEAF announced a new plan on 10 July to apply continual pressure through selective destruction of cities and towns being used for military storage. Its goals were to sustain air superiority, destroy selected targets and minimize the enemy's

Below: **Captain James Jabara (center) demonstrates his flying technique to Captain Eddie Rickenbacker (left) and Air Force Chief of Staff General Hoyt Vandenberg. Rickenbacker became the first American ace in 1918, and Jabara became the first American jet ace in 1951.**

Above: **United Nations soldiers wounded in Korea are transported to Tokyo for treatment aboard a C-124. The Globemaster was able to carry as many as 135 patients at a time.**

ground troops. General Mark Clark, the new commander of US forces in the Far East, also emphasized the need to prevent civilian casualties whenever possible. When Lieutenant General Glenn O. Barcus assumed leadership of the Fifth Air Force on 30 May, he took aim at China's 22 air divisions in an effort to destroy as many enemy planes as possible. In the largest air attack of the war, 1,400 planes bombed Pyongyang. The improved F-86F made a more even match to the Chinese MiGs, and Sabre pilots downed 63 MiGs in September, losing only six of their own planes.

Talks had stalled for two years, when Dwight David Eisenhower was inaugurated as President in January 1953. Almost immediately, he warned Moscow, Pyongyang, and Beijing (then known as Peking or Peiping) that 'we intend to move decisively without inhibition in our use of weapons, and will no longer be responsible for confining hostilities to the Korean Peninsula.'

That same month, the Eighth and 18th Bomber Wings received F-86Fs and began interception campaigns against Chinese planes, downing a record 75 MiGs in June. A campaign of fighter-bomber attacks began in July, when the Fifth Air Force received the okay to fly against Pyongyang and other North Korean targets. Overlooked and rebuilt munitions factories were targeted by Short Range Navigation (SHORAN) equipped B-29s. On 20 July, B-26 bombers from the Third and 17th (452nd) Wings began a campaign to hit 78 towns used for supply, repair and troops. SHORAN-equipped B-20 also began elimination of 200 other locations suspected of harboring military supplies.

Although armistice talks resumed 26 April, there was no letup in air campaigns. Destruction of irrigation dams, first at Toksan by 59 F-84 Thunderjets and then at Chasan, Kusong, and Kuwongam, caused flash floods in May and severely hampered North Korea's agricultural production. FEAF Commander O. P. Weyland believed bombing of the dams was instrumental in leading to truce talks on 8 June 1953. Even after signing the initial truce, the Chinese organized a new onslaught. With Lieutenant General Samuel E. Anderson in place as head of the Fifth Air Force, the Fifth Air Force marshaled to support the Eighth Army with Navy Task Force 77 until 20 July, when the threat subsided.

The terms of the truce negotiated called for a ban on Chinese planes in North Korea, and General Weyland ordered bombing of North Korean airstrips to insure compliance. Flying an F-86, Captain Ralph S. Parr from the fourth Fighter-Interceptor Wing shot down the last enemy plane, an IL-12 transport. The Armistice Agreement ending the Korean War went into effect 27 July 1953, and established a military demarcation line running east-west from just sound of Kosong to just north of Kaesong.

Hostilities End

The war had lasted 37 months, with 95,000 South Korean and UN soldiers killed, including 54,246 Americans (33,629 of whom were killed in combat). Another 5,178 were declared missing or captured. Of the 1.5 million enemy casualties (killed, wounded, missing), 900,000 were Chinese. Civilian casualties were equally--probably 1 million in both North and South Korea.

One of the most tangible effects of the Korean War was to strengthen the NATO alliance. This virtually toothless organization had gained 50 divisions as well as air and naval forces by the end of the Korean War. The United States initiated an emergency program to build air bases in

Below: **In addition to its duties as a fighter-bomber, the subsonic Lockheed F-80C was used as a photographic reconnaissance platform during the Korean War.**

the Far East and elsewhere in the world. These included six Korean airfields, 13 enhanced air bases in Japan and airfields at Kadena and Naha on Okinawa, as well as gasoline storage facilities and housing for military and civilian support personnel.

Sometimes called the 'Forgotten War,' the battle for Korea employed 1,285,000 Air Force personnel. FEAF personnel grew from 33,600 to 112,000 by the end of the war. A total of 721,000 missions were flown, 1,180 airmen were killed and 1,466 planes lost. The helicopter turned into an effective military resource. North Korean Dictator Kim II Sung failed in his effort to unite the two Koreas under communist rule. Without Air Force tactical support, the Korean War might have gone another way. Despite their superior numbers so heavily enhanced by China, the North Koreans could not supply its troops effectively, and transports kept South Korean and UN—including the United States troops stocked. Strategic bombing remained a decisive tool, air power made the difference, and the US Air Force had proved its worth in its first war as a formal branch of the military.

Right: **The crew of a B-29 Superfort, shot down behind enemy lines and taken prisoner while on a mission to drop leaflets in North Korea, is shown here in Hong Kong following their release.**

Below: **Paratroopers of the 187th Airborne Regimental Combat Team suit up in parachutes and life preservers for a flight aboard a C-119 over the Sea of Japan.**

Airman Second Class Wilbur E. Baker, a gunner on a B-29 crew, celebrates the Armistice on 27 July 1953, by throwing practice .50-caliber ammunition in the air.

138
U.S. AIR FORCE

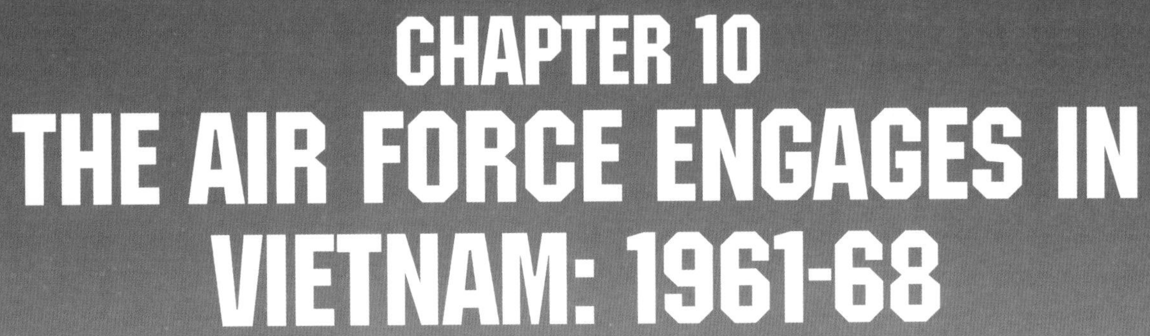

CHAPTER 10
THE AIR FORCE ENGAGES IN VIETNAM: 1961-68

The Air Force Engages in Vietnam: 1961-68

US involvement in Indochina—as Vietnam, Laos, and Cambodia were originally called in the West—dates back to the Truman administration. Nineteenth century European imperialism brought French domination to Indochina until World War II, when the Japanese invaded. After Japan was defeated, France tried to resume control of Indochina by establishing it as a federation, and the Truman administration supported its WW II ally, France.

During that war, Vietnam's legendary Communist leader Nguyen Ai Quoc, better known as Ho Chi Minh, and the Vietnam Independence League, popularly called the Viet Minh, had looked for and received help from the United States, even rescuing U.S. airmen who were shot down in Indochina. At the end of the war, Ho declared independence for Vietnam, but he was ignored by the United States and its Allied partners. By the end of 1946, nationalists from Annam, Tonkin, and Cochinchina (traditional names for regions of what would become Vietnam) plunged Indochina into civil war in an effort to free their lands from French rule. Concern for stopping the spread of Communism motivated Truman and, later, Eisenhower to finance France's struggle to hold onto its former Indochinese colonies.

The United States Becomes Involved in Vietnam

The onset of the Korean War in 1950 led Truman to boost the amount of aid the United States gave to France in Vietnam and to recognize France's token Vietnamese regent, Bao Dai. After Eisenhower became president, US aid to France for Vietnam increased steadily, until it constituted 80 percent of French costs there. As the French came closer to defeat at Dienbienphu in 1954, they requested US air and navy backup, but Congress opposed support of a colonialist regime. Despite that fact, the Air Force participated in undercover missions in Indochina, as well as Tibet, Iran, the USSR, and Cuba. Three US Air Force mechanics were captured at Dienbienphu but released by the Viet Minh after the battle.

After France had lost the military struggle at Dienbienphu in May 1954, the United States went to the peace talks in Geneva but did not sign the peace agreement, fearing the power of the USSR- and Red China-supported Viet Minh. The 1954 Geneva Accords temporarily separated Vietnam into North and South along the 17th parallel. North Vietnam was controlled by the Viet Minh, while South Vietnam remained in French hands, until elections could be held to unite the two in 1956. When the French pulled out of Vietnam in April 1956, US involvement in the Far East shifted there. In 1955, the United States sent a Military Assistance Advisory Group to help the South Vietnamese Army (ARVN).

Starting in the early 1950s, a Vietnamese Christian leader named Ngo Dinh Diem had been lobbying for American support and, with US financing, he replaced France's puppet Bao Dai in 1955. He quickly established an unpopular authoritarian regime that fought against the Viet Minh presence in South Vietnam. The result was a resurgence of the rebellion. By 1957, the insurgents organized themselves as the Vietcong. In effort to stop them, President Diem instituted a 'strategic hamlet' program, moving peasants into barbed-wire camps to isolate them from the Vietcong. It became clear that if elections were held, Ho Chi Minh and the Communists would win, so Diem cancelled them. Later, in 1963, Diem would be assassinated with tacit U.S. support and replaced with a series of military leaders.

After John F. Kennedy assumed office in 1961, French President Charles de Gaulle warned him the United States was moving into 'a bottomless quagmire.' Those words would come to haunt the United States. Nevertheless, Kennedy approved a mobile control and reporting post, set up at Tan Son Nhut Air Force Base outside Saigon. He would soon up the number of military advisors for Diem's forces to 1,000 and approve a limited combat role for American forces. General Curtis LeMay, Air Force Chief of Staff, established the Special Air Warfare Center (SAWC) at Eglin Air Force Base in Florida earlier that year. The goal was to organize US Air Force resources against guerrilla warfare tactics used by the Vietcong.

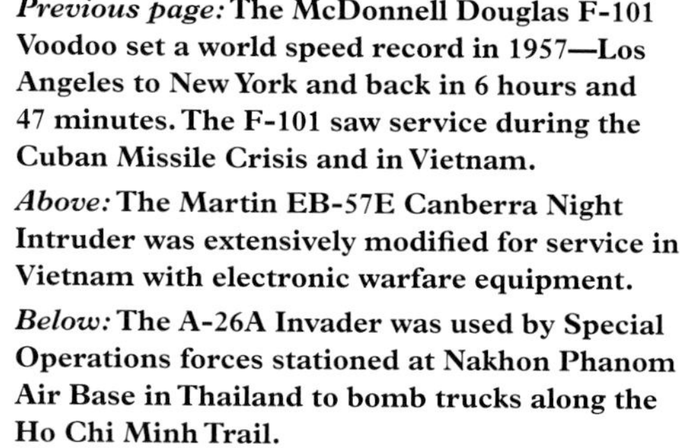
***Previous page:* The McDonnell Douglas F-101 Voodoo set a world speed record in 1957—Los Angeles to New York and back in 6 hours and 47 minutes. The F-101 saw service during the Cuban Missile Crisis and in Vietnam.**

***Above:* The Martin EB-57E Canberra Night Intruder was extensively modified for service in Vietnam with electronic warfare equipment.**

***Below:* The A-26A Invader was used by Special Operations forces stationed at Nakhon Phanom Air Base in Thailand to bomb trucks along the Ho Chi Minh Trail.**

Above: **President John F. Kennedy (right) holds a meeting in the Oval Office with Defense Secretary Robert McNamara (center) and Chairman of the Joint Chiefs General Maxwell Taylor to discuss the conflict in Southeast Asia.**

The US Air Force Enters Vietnam

On 5 October 1961, the 507th Tactical Control Group Detachment went into operation. It was the first Air Force commitment in Vietnam, and was followed by the 4400th Command Crew Training Squadron/First Air Commando Group. In November, the Second Advanced Air Echelon (later Division) began operations at Bien Hoa. The first US aircraft assigned to Vietnam included eight T-28 trainers, four SC-47 transports, and four B-26 light bombers, as well as C-119s and C-123s. Outfitted with red and yellow South Vietnamese Air Force markings, all were propeller driven and rapidly becoming obsolete, but they were considered adequate at the time because allegedly they were only going to be used to train South Vietnamese. The 4400th Combat Crew Training Squadron joined SAWC in April 1961. Designed for counterinsurgency missions throughout the Third World, it became known as 'Jungle Jim.' Its first mission, Sandy Beach One, had involved training Mali paratroopers in West Africa. In November 1961, it began its first Vietnam mission at Bien Hoa, Operation Farmgate, using the A-26 Invader, the oldest combat aircraft used in Vietnam.

The United States Strike Command (STRICOM) also came into existence that year to coordinate Air Force and Army resources. The earliest 155 Air Force personnel based in Saigon in 1961, used in addition to the T-28 trainers, Cessna spotter planes, and old A-1 Skyraiders, brought out of Navy surplus storage in Arizona. Their job was to advise—and train—the South Vietnamese Air Force. In one of the more bizarrely colorful sidelights of the war, Nguyen Cao Ky, who went on to serve as South Vietnam's premier from 1965 to 1967, headed a Skyraider squadron. His wife sometimes accompanied him dressed in lavender flight gear. While US Air Force pilots did most of the flying—even on combat missions—particularly in the early years, they had to be accompanied by South Vietnamese or Laotians because of their designation as advisors.

The Second Advanced Echelon (ADVON) of the Thirteenth Air Force came into existence on 15 November1961, with four detachments—three in South Vietnam and another in Thailand. The Second Air Division replaced it almost a year later.

By early 1962, two US Marine Corps helicopter companies began combat flights, as did an US Air Force Commando unit flying C-47s. The goal was to train the Vietnamese Armed Forces (VNAF) in guerrilla warfare. In the meantime, Operation Mule Train started up on 2 January1962, with Fairchild C-123 Providers. Military writer Walter J. Boyne points out that the Vietcong operated fundamentally as hit-and-run terrorists, and as a result, the VNAF needed more reconnaissance resources. The newly formed VNAF 716th Reconnaissance Squadron received Beech RC-45s, Douglas RC-47s, and North American RT-28s. These were backed up by McDonnell RF-101Cs flying in from Thailand.

Lieutenant Colonel Miles M. Doyle served as commandeer of Farmgate, which grew to include 275 airmen and over 40 planes in 1963. Operation Farmgate continued until 28 July 1963, when the C-47s were transferred to the US Air Commando Squadron (ACS) at Bien Hoa. By early 1964, all Farmgate's B-26s were out of commission, as were four of its T-28s. The reliance on obsolete aircraft was taking its toll. American planes based in Thailand and on aircraft carriers began flying surveillance over Vietnam, and a squadron of six Fairchild C-123 medium transports, modified to dispense up to 1,000 gallons of defoliant spray through

JV
315

Weapons of war: During the three years of Rolling Thunder, the U.S. dropped 634,000 tons of bombs, including 500 pound Snakeyes (left), and 750 pound bombs (right), both shown dropped by F-105s, and napalm bombs (below), shown here being dropped by an F-100 Super Sabre.

wing-mounted nozzles, started defoliation missions there as part of Operation Ranch Hand on 13 January1962.

Approved by President Kennedy, Operation Ranch Hand used Agent Orange (2,4, D and 2,4,5,T) for the first time in South Vietnam; its use would continue until 1971. Agent Orange was a code name derived from the orange bands on the defoliant's storage drums. This spray killed all foliage within five days. Its was a new strategy, designed to combat Vietcong guerrilla tactics in the Mekong Delta, and the aim was to clear out cover along roads and rivers, as well as some parts of wooded areas, and to eliminate Vietcong hiding places. With volunteer pilots at the controls, the planes had to fly approximately 150 feet above the trees at near-stall speeds. These planes—'Patches' was the name of the C-123 that took the most ground fire—became among the most targeted in the war. The first Air Force plane downed during the Vietnam War was one of Operation Ranch Hand's C-123s. The 2 February1962, crash killed Captains Fergus C. Groves and Robert D. Larson, as well as Staff Sergeant Milo B. Coghill.

Operation Ranch Hand became the most controversial aspect of the Air Force campaign in South Vietnam because of its potential for causing human chromosome damage. The pilots who flew these missions could not wear Air Force uniforms and were told that if they were captured, they would not be recognized as US Air Force personnel. Nineteen UC-123Ks were added to the operation as it expanded.

Left: An Air Force F-4 Phantom is armed for a bombing run over Southeast Asia in May 1970. The F-4 was one of the most versatile warplanes ever built, with many speed records to its credit.

Another agricultural contravention program employed an herbicide called Agent Blue to destroy crops and deprive the enemy of food. From 1962 to 1969, 688,000 acres of farmland were doused with Agent Blue by US Air Force planes, although evidence suggests that the destruction of rice crops harmed civilians more than the Vietcong. North Vietnam, China and the Soviet Union all complained about the use of herbicides, as did many Americans. American Ambassador to Vietnam Ellsworth D. Bunker formed a committee on the use of herbicides, Agents Orange, Blue, and White, which concluded they were not dangerous. By 22 December 1970, Defense Secretary Melvin Laird announced the United States would adhere to the same herbicide regulations that it did at home.

The US Air Force Ratchets Up

The US Air Force would send its first combat unit, the 509th Fighter Interceptor Squadron to South Vietnam in June 1962, but the first combat planes had arrived in Vietnam in 1961. That year, President Kennedy approved 'A Program of Action to Prevent Communist Domination of South Vietnam,' but the Vietnamese venture still seemed like a limited conflict to the US government and public, and the initial thrust was counterinsurgency. As Air Force historian Colonel C. V. Glines put it: 'An Air Force that had been preparing for possible nuclear warfare was required to reexamine its concepts and prepare a force capable of supporting ground forces operating in a jungle environment against an enemy determined to fight for a hundred years, if necessary.'

By the time of his November 1963 assassination, President Kennedy had increased the number of American advisors in South Vietnam to 16,500. After Lyndon Johnson assumed office, the US air war against Vietnam would begin in earnest. The Air Force acquired its first AC-47 gunships for use in Vietnam, and they were deployed in combat on 15 December1964. That year Secretary of Defense Robert McNamara ordered a study on the utility of bombing missions on North Vietnam. The Policy Planning Council argued against them on the grounds that 'the North was motivated by factors which were not affected by physical change and physical damage.' In May 1964 McNamara put a stop to combat

Above: **A C-130A Hercules gunship on the ground in Southeast Asia. The gunships were armed with two 7.62mm Gatling guns, two 20mm Vulcan cannons, and two 40mm cannons.**
Below: **A Fairchild AC-119G gunship on patrol over the Mekong River in 1968. The AC-119G was armed with four SUU-11 7.62mm 'mini-guns' and was capable of carrying up to 50,000 rounds of ammunition.**

flights using Air Force flyers. Instead, the VNAF was enlarged by two squadrons to six and were given Douglas A-1Hs. On 9 June, four SAC KC-135s, the Yankee Team Tanker Task Force, for the first time refueled F-100s on their way to targets in Laos. The F-100, which could carry four tons of bombs, saw service from the early 1960s until 1970.

The United States Undertakes a War in Vietnam

The 2 August 1964, incident that instigated what came closest to a declaration of war against Vietnam occurred in the Gulf of Tonkin. The United States had sent destroyers along the North Vietnamese coast to elicit the location of their radar stations. Three North Vietnamese torpedo boats attacked the US destroyer Maddox, and the US ship disabled two and destroyed one of them. After an alleged second attack two days later that has never been confirmed, Johnson presented Congress with the Tonkin Gulf Resolution, which called for 'all necessary steps, including the use of armed force, to assist any member or protocol state of the Southeast Asia Collective Defense Treaty requesting assistance in defense of its freedom.' (The Southeast Asia Treaty Organization-SEATO—had been formed in 1954, essentially a US initiative to halt Communist expansion in the region.) On 7 August, Congress passed the resolution. The Navy sent 64 fighter planes from the Seventh Fleet's USS Ticonderoga and Constellation to hit 30 boats, along with oil storage tanks at Vinh, on the coast of North Vietnam. Two US planes were downed and one pilot killed. Navy Lieutenant Everett Alvarez became the first Navy pilot captured by the North Vietnamese.

That fall, the Air Force relocated a squadron of B-57 bomber jets from Clark Air Force Base in the Philippines to Bien Hoa Air Base. An F-100 Super Sabre squadron went to Danang, and an F-105 Thunderbird squadron was relocated from Japan to Korat Royal Thai Air Force Base in Thailand. The F-105, built as a supersonic, long-range nuclear bomber, did most of the US bombing in Vietnam from 1965 until 1970. Air Force planes also flew reconnaissance over northern and southern Laos in Operation Barrel Roll, starting 24 December 1964. Almost immediately, Vietcong guerrillas, using rockets and mortar fire, destroyed six of the B-57s, damaged another 15 and hit four A-1s on the ground at Bien Hoa Air Base, leaving five Americans dead and 76 wounded. That incident persuaded the

United States it was not safe to position air resources in South Vietnam. In 1964, as Operation Waterpump, SAWC forces also trained Loatian and Thai pilots as part of the effort to stop the civil war in Laos. The bombings continued for three years, and one million tons of bombs were dropped. Yet Secretary of Defense McNamara predicted that year that the war would pretty much be over by the end of 1965.

Reflecting the transition from a predominantly advisory role to a combat one, US military forces rose eightfold from 23,310 in 1964, to 184,314 in 1965. The types of aircraft used shifted to jets—RB-57s, B-57s, RF-101s, Convair F102s, and F-105s. At the beginning of 1965, F-100 Super Sabres escorted South Vietnam Air Force planes on attack missions in North Vietnam. At this stage, crews operated under a 90-day rotation. Then Super Sabres and B-57s hit the Vietcong at An Khe in South Vietnam. On 13 February 1965, the question of a bombing campaign resurfaced, after a Vietcong attack on a US Army helicopter base at Camp Holloway, Pleiku, killed eight, wounded 126 and destroyed 10 planes.

President Johnson ordered immediate retaliation, and 132 Air Force jets, including F-100s and A-1s, bombed at Chap Le and other North Vietnamese targets until 2 March in Operation Flaming Dart, followed by Operation Flaming Dart II. Reconnaissance flights had given the United States photographic maps of strategic North Vietnamese targets. Despite the fact that Ho and the Viet Minh had been actively fighting in North Vietnam since the 1940s, they had not planned for air attacks. Key transportation sites, oil dumps, and munitions and materiel factories, as well as the country's electrical grid, were positioned in vulnerable locations.

Widening the War

Emboldened by his re-election in November 1964, President Johnson okayed Operation Rolling Thunder, the first regular bombing program against North Vietnam and selected Vietcong targets in South Vietnam, starting 2 March 1965.

Above: **Air Force F-4s sit at a distance from above-ground rubber fuel bladders at Phan Rang air base. The bladders were a favorite target of the Vietcong.**

Below: **A Douglas A1E Skyraider strafes enemy insurgents during Operation Buckskin in January 1966. The Skyraiders were used by the USAF for close air support and as escorts for rescue helicopters.**

At the time, the White House still saw the Vietnam conflict as a limited, short-term operation and was reluctant to destroy relations with the USSR and Red China, who supported North Vietnam. Captain Hayden J. Lockhart became the first Air Force pilot captured by the North Vietnamese on 2 March 1965. He would re-

main in captivity until 12 February 1973.

North Vietnamese pilots attacked Air Force planes for the first time April 3-5, 1965, and the first loss from Hanoi's SAMs came July 24, when an F-4C, flying out of Ubon, Thailand, was downed outside Hanoi. Captain Roscoe H. Fobair was killed, and Captain Richard P. Keirn, who had been a World War II flyer, was captured and imprisoned, as he had been in that previous war, this time for seven and a half years.

When General LeMay retired on 1 February 1965, General John P. McConnell took over as Chief of Staff. The Joint Chiefs of Staff had developed a list of 94 targets for a two- to three-week air campaign in North Vietnam, depending on weather. The US goals were to demoralize the enemy, avoid committing large numbers of ground troops, and cut off North Korean aid to the Vietcong. With the Second Air Division in charge, thirteen Air Force bases were planned, the largest of which was the Tactical Air Control Center (TACC) at Tan Son Nhut Air Base. Placement of these bases would enable pilots to be airborne in combat position within 30 minutes. The first base would be completed 16 November 1966, at Tuy Hoa. Other components consisted of Direct Air Support Centers, Forward Air Controllers (FACs), and Air Liaison Officers.

Although Johnson did up the ante in 1965, increasing the United States commitment in South Vietnam, he was not ready for as powerful a strike as was originally recommended. A modified bombing campaign began, with the White House calling the shots. According to military historian Herbert Molloy Mason, Jr., 'The air war was controlled from twelve thousand miles away by men interested in political repercussions and not with military realities.' Defense Secretary McNamara established rules of engagement that Air Force flyers found limiting. The pilots were not permitted to fly closer than 30 miles to the Chinese border, nor could pilots breach a 10-mile no-fly zone protecting Haiphong and Hanoi. Many bridges, strategic transit sites, power plants, oil tanks, and MiG bases were also off-limits. (MiG bases would become permissible targets in 1967.) So were

Above: **The size and speed of modern aircraft made it necessary to upgrade airport runways in Vietnam. A 9,000-foot runway was constructed of aluminum planking at the Tuy Hua Air Base in 1966, allowing this C-124 to have a smooth landing.**

Below: **The Fairchild UC-123 was used for Operation Ranch Hand, spraying herbicides, including Agent Orange, to defoliate the forest and deny the enemy cover.**

Right: **An RF-4C Phantom still smolders after a crash landing at Danang Air Base in 1969. Over 2,500 Air Force personnel lost their lives in Vietnam.**

Below: **An F-105G Thunderchief, affectionately nicknamed 'Thud,' patrols over the skies of North Vietnam. The F-105 was one of the very few fighter-bombers equipped with a bomb bay.**

numerous Surface-to-Air (SAM) missile sites. Pilots who disobeyed were threatened with court martial. Johnson relented partially in mid-1966, but, fearing public displeasure at hitting civilian targets, continued to veto attacks on Haiphong and Hanoi.

Ultimately the United States paid a high price for its bombing campaign in North Vietnam. With 300 bombers in use, the Air Force flew 26,000 bombing missions and lost 171 planes in 1965; by 1966, enemy antiaircraft fire downed 600 American combat planes. The weather also played a role, since Vietnam's monsoon season lasted six months of the year and led to operational losses. In response, the Vietcong focused on US air bases in South Vietnam, and General Westmoreland, Commander of the US Military Assistance Command (USMAC) asked for an increase in troops from the 23,000 then in country. On 8 March 1965, two battalions of Marines landed on China Beach at Danang, followed by members of the 173rd Airborne. These 3,500 soldiers became the first combat troops assigned officially to South Vietnam. The 173rd Airborne Brigade, the first Army combat force in Vietnam, arrived 3 May, after a US secret plan to go on the offensive, committing 40,000 troops. In a speech at Johns Hopkins University, President Johnson told the public the United States would not stop the bombing, 'We will not be defeated. We will not grow tired. We will not withdraw.' Public opinion polls taken at the time reported that 80 percent of the public supported both the bombings and the use of combat troops to Vietnam. On Christmas Day 1965, President Johnson temporarily stopped the bombing raids on North Vietnam, in hopes that he could bring the Viet Minh to the negotiating table, but when that did not produce the desired response, the US Air Force continued its bombing raids.

Beginning in 1965, the Air Force doubled the number of its aircraft in use. From a total of 9,500 in 1965, the number of Air Force personnel would grow to 59,000 in four years. Cargo transports flew highs of 6,000 pounds a minute, and the total cargo transport figure for the Korean War, 697,000 tons, was quickly surpassed. Korean-War-vintage Fairchild C-123s were used inside South Vietnam, as well as the Lockheed C-130 Hercules, which was larger and quicker and also served as a gunship. Lockheed C-141 Starlifter jets did transpacific duty, traveling inbound with supplies and personnel, returning with the wounded and dead. The first US plane downed by a Soviet-made SAM missile occurred 24 July1965.

As the war progressed, Thailand became more and more important to the Air Force, with bases at Ubon, Udorn, Korat, and U-Tapao. US Air Force numbers there leapt from 9,000 in 1965 to 26,000 in 1966. Thailand's capital, Bangkok, became the favored leave destination. That year Air Force special operations personnel numbers reached 10,000, with 19 squadrons and 500 aircraft by 1966. One of the Air Force's more memorable missions, Operation Bolo, took place on 2 January1967. To entice North Vietnamese MiGs, which preferred engaging bombers, into combat, World War II ace Colonel Robin Olds ordered his F-4 Phantom fighter jets into bomber formation. The deception worked. Before they were through, he and his Wolfpack, the Eighth Tactical Fighter Wing, shot down seven MiGs. In 1967, AC-119 gunships were introduced and in 1968, AC-130s. The US Air Force Special

Operations Force (USAFSOF) replaced SAWC in 1968.

The Air Force's Arsenal

The Air Force provided tactical support for the Army and Marines operating in the Mekong Delta area of South Vietnam. In aid of ground troops, pilots flew F-100 Super Sabre fighter bombers and A-1 Skyraiders, redesigned World War II AD-5s, which were also called Spads. The prop A-1E, nicknamed 'Sandy,' was especially effective close contact at low-altitude flying for long periods. Forward Air Controllers (FACs) played an especially important role by flying single-engine Cessna 0-1 Bird Dogs, 0-2s and OV-10s to locate targets for the larger planes. Flying at speeds as low as 100 mph, the FACs 'trolled' for the enemy. Radioing back information on Vietcong hideouts or troop placements, the FACs directed napalm bombing for gun emplacements, cluster bomb units for grassy areas or riverbanks and gunships for strafing. They used smoke rockets to place targets for the 'fast movers,' as the combat planes were called. The 1988 war movie Bat*21 provides a good illustration of the high risk jobs of the FACs. The movie stars Gene Hackman as a downed pilot, and Danny Glover as the spotter pilot who rescues him from 'Indian Territory,' as Vietcong enclaves were called. More than 200 FACs died during the war, and both FAC medals of honor were awarded posthumously.

Special bombs with three-foot nose extensions were used to ferret out Vietcong submerged in rice paddies. MiG fighters and Soviet-made ground-to-air missiles did not pose a problem in this section of South Vietnam, but automatic weapon fire did. SAC B-52 bombers, although designed for intercontinental use, played a new role in South Vietnam: carpet bombing. Once reconnaissance FACs uncovered concentrations of enemy troops, these Stratofortresses, nicknamed BUFFs (Big Ugly Fat Fellows), flew in from Anderson Air Force Base on Guam—for the first time on 18 June1965--more than 2,500 miles away, to drop over 50 750-lb bombs per plane from virtually undetectable altitudes of eight miles. The code name for the operation, which lasted for 10 months, was Arc Light. MACV Commander General Westmoreland stood behind use of the B-52s, even after two of them collided in midair early on. Their payload capacity increased in 1965 through the Big Belly program to 54,000 pounds in 500-pound bombs or 49,500 pounds in 750-pound bombs. Because the B-52s were dropping bombs into jungle, a mobile ground radar guidance system, called Combat Skyspot, was used. Guam-based B-52s were used to hit North Vietnam for the first time on 12 April1966, after a mortar attack on Tan Son Nhut Air Base.

The planes used most frequently north of the demilitarized zone (DMZ), single-seat Republic F-105Ds, acquired a variety of names: Thunderchiefs, Squash

The information war from high tech to low: The U-2 spy plane (above left) flew reconnaissance missions over Vietnam, as did the Mach 3-capable SR-71 Blackbird (above). Lower tech was the U-10 (left) dropping 'psywar' leaflets in 1967.

Bombers, Leads Sleds, and Thuds, the latter name reputedly mimicking the sound the F-105s made when they crashed. At 65 feet in length, the F-105s were the biggest single-seat planes the United States ever built. First built in 1955, they were modified in 1957 as the B model and were the first fighter planes with internal bomb bays. Based in Thailand, they were used on industrial targets, in part because of their ability to hit their targets and speed away at Mach 2.1. Almost 900 F-105s were produced during the war, but they were not without their problems. The F-105 was relatively high maintenance and prone to electronic snafus. By 1966, 130 F-105s were at Takhli and Korat bases in Thailand.

The first of the radar-suppressing 'Wild Weasels' was the F100F, with two seats. The Wild Weasel was a plane adapted with electronic detection and jamming equipment to use the enemy's anti-aircraft radar to locate and destroy the site. The F105F was used to scout for SAM locations in hunter-killer sorties. Once a missile was launched, the regular F-105 Thunderchief would take out the site. With a reputation for destroying MiGs, the McDonnell Douglas F-4 Phantom jet was also used against North Vietnam. The F-4 was introduced by the Navy in 1958, and a squadron joined the Air Force as the F-4C in 1964. With the capacity for aerial refueling, it quickly became the top MiG fighter for both the Air Force and the Navy, with 200 in use in Vietnam. The F-4E, a modification introduced in 1968, had the added advantage of an internal 20 mm M-61A1 multibarrel cannon and, by 1972, a telescopic device called the Target Identification System Electro Optical (TISEO).

In many ways, helicopters came to symbolize the Vietnam War. Used heavily by the Army and Marines to gain access to the enemy's jungle enclaves, they were a successful adjunct to combat at the platoon and company level. The Air Force also used them, starting in 1963 with the UH-1F. At first the CH-21 Flying Banana was utilized. It was followed in 1963 by the UH-1, a faster and more mobile machine. The nickname 'Huey' followed from the 'HU' designation used by the Army. The TH-1F saw service as a training and evacuation vehicle. In 1970, the HH-1H replaced the HH-43, or Huskie, for rescue work. Eventually the more heavily armed Huey Cobra was introduced.

In addition to conventional bombs, incendiaries were employed containing napalm, a mix of gasoline and chemicals like white phosphorus that create a gel, which attaches to the skin and can burn its victims down to the bone. The pineapple was yet another type of antipersonnel bomb often used. It consisted of small canisters containing hundreds of small metal pellets. As many as 250,000 pineapples might be used on a single bombing mission. Another innovation was utilizing plastic needles and pellets in antipersonnel bombs. The goal was to keep bomb fragments from being detected by X-ray scans, since undetectable injuries had a greater power to disrupt the enemy.

Some in the US military complained of inadequate ordnance supplies and other limits. Gatling gun ammunition was occasionally rationed, and the large, 750-lb bombs weren't available. The 250-lb Mk.81 and the 500-lb Mk.82 would be substituted, which meant that F4-Cs might be flying missions with loads at 10 percent capacity. The Air Force pilot training program was limited to 1,889 in 1966 and to 2,700 in 1967.

The Air Force also played an important role in the 'out-country' operations conducted outside Vietnam's borders. In Laos, the primary goal was to stop the movement of enemy supplies along the Ho Chi Minh Trail. A variety of techniques in addition to FACs were used, including electronic sensors, 'people sniffers,' defoliants and special-forces teams of trail watchers whose job was to call in fighters and gunships when they spotted enemy activity. Operation Steel Tiger began on 3 April1965, to stem the tide of enemy troops and supplies transported at night through Laos. Because Thailand refused to permit US bombers to fly out of its bases, the B-26K was renamed A-26A but not changed in any other way. At the end of the year, the Air Force was joined by the Army, Navy, VNAF and Royal Laotian Air Force in Operation Tiger Hound for an even more focused attack on supply routes near the Laotian-South Vietnamese border.

The Air Force claimed a big victory on 2 January1967, when F-4 Phantom jets downed seven MiGs near the enemy SAM sites at the Red River Delta. Early in 1967, the US forces began a strike in the strategic 'Iron Triangle,' the wedge of terrain, bounded roughly by the Saigon and Thi Tinh Rivers, south of Saigon. Beginning 8 January as Operation Cedar Falls, it was followed by the biggest American ground offensive of the war, called Operation Junction City, which hit Vietcong enclaves along the Cambodian border. Although an Army initiative, it relied on Air Force backup.

The year 1968 marked a major turning point in the war. The US bombing campaign in North Vietnam had destroyed the major railroad bridges and

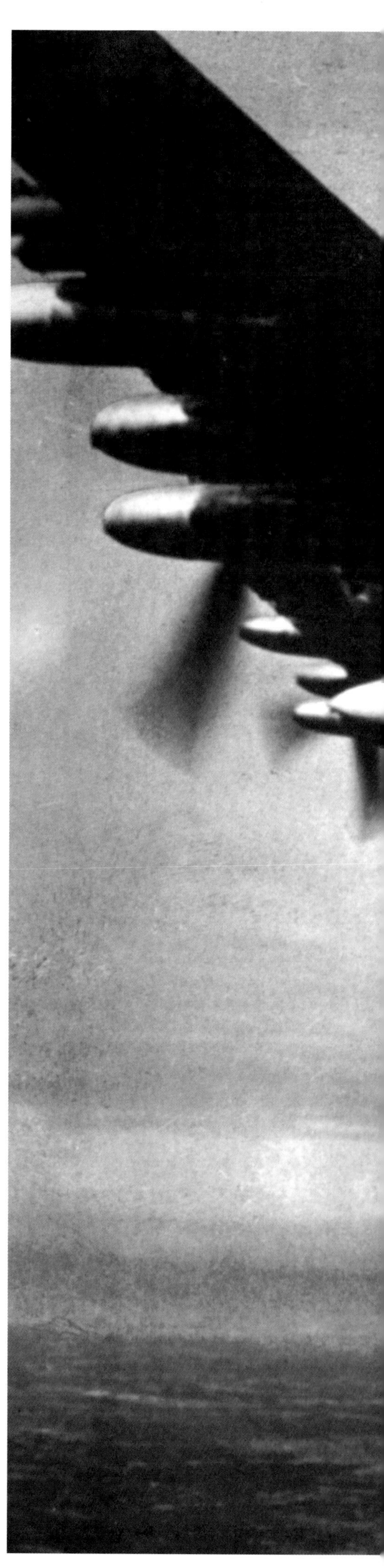

South Vietnamese pilots were trained to fly Douglas A1E Skyraiders, as seen here, flying a close air support sortie over the Mekong River.

473
NO SMOKING ON RAMP

fuel storage tanks, food was rationed, and a crew 300,000 strong including Chinese 'volunteers' was needed to repair bomb damage. Since the time of the French occupation, Tet had been a traditional occasion for a temporary cessation in hostilities to celebrate the traditional Vietnamese New Year, based on the lunar calendar. Instead on 30 January 1968, the North Vietnamese launched the Tet Offensive, a major attack on most of South Vietnam's cities, as well as the American bases at Dak To and Khe Sanh. Although the Vietcong suffered heavy losses, the Tet Offensive won them propaganda points.

Faced with a de facto war that was growing in unpopularity, President Johnson made an address to the nation on 31 March and announced he would start to de-escalate the war. Hoping to bring the North Vietnamese to the negotiating table, he said he was immediately limiting Operation Rolling Thunder to the southern portion of North Vietnam. The President declared that 80 percent of North Vietnam—with 90 percent of the population—would no longer be subject to bombing. Then, in what came as a total surprise to everyone except a few intimate advisers, Johnson announced that he was not going to run for president in November.

Johnson still hoped to stop the war by negotiations and sent a delegation to Paris in May 1968 to meet with North Vietnamese diplomats, but the talks quickly ran into snags. Ho, meanwhile, used the break in bombing to rebuild his supply lines along the Ho Chi Minh trail into South Vietnam, and on 1 July the bombing north of the DMZ resumed. On 31 October, just before Election Day in the United States and in what appeared to be a blatant attempt to help the cause of Democratic candidate, Hubert Humphrey, Johnson called a halt to all bombing of North Vietnam. However, it did not work: Richard M. Nixon was elected instead of Humphrey, and the bombing resumed on 8 November.

In January 1969 Nixon took office as president, and peace talks resumed the same month. The war in Vietnam would enter a new phase.

Above: **A US Air Force UH-1 Huey from the 211th Helicopter Squadron deploys soldiers for a combat assault mission in the Mekong Delta, 18 July 1970.**

Opposite bottom: **Sidewinder heat-seeking air-to-air missiles are readied for loading on F-4C fighter-bombers in Vietnam for combat with North Korean and Chinese MiG-17s.**

Left: **The North American F-100 Super Sabre made its combat debut flying air support missions over Vietnam.**

CHAPTER 11

THE VIETNAM WAR'S FINAL PHASE: 1968-1973

The Vietnam War's Final Phase: 1968-1973

As the Vietnam War entered a new phase in 1968, a number of events occurred. US Air Force numbers reached an all-time high of 904,000, although most personnel were stationed in the United States or at bases other than in Vietnam. The US troop level in Vietnam had reached 535,000, and when US-MAC Commander General Westmoreland asked for an additional 205,000, he was turned down. The war would soon be 'Vietnamized.'

By 1969, word began to leak out about a massacre of Vietnamese civilians at My Lai, adding fuel to growing protests over the war in the United States and Europe. With Vietnam costing $28 billion a year, a long economic boom had ended in the United States. Deficits and inflation set in. The US carrot-and-stick strategy—bombing attacks followed by cessation of air strikes--did not seem to produce the desired effect on Hanoi. The Paris peace talks stalled.

Operation Igloo White

Igloo White, an operation inspired by the work of Harvard Law School professor Roger Fisher, sounds more like science fiction than the actual warfare tactic used in Vietnam.

All of the US Armed Forces initially played a role in Igloo White, a 180-mile electronic barrier system to detect enemy movements. The Joint Chiefs of Staff opposed the high-tech operation on the grounds of its high cost and questionable efficacy, but Defense Secretary McNamara supported it and in 1966 formed the Defense Communications Planning Group (DCPG) to develop it. The Air Force took the program over in June 1968. A variety of electronic sensing devices, including Ground Seismic Intrusion Detectors (GSIDs), Air-delivered Seismic Detectors, acoustic and odor sensors were put in place. Once they sounded the alarm, air strikes were called into the area where movement had been detected. Aircraft received the signals from these devices and sent them on to Nakhon Phanom Royal Thai Air Force Base. After processing there, the information was passed along to what was called an airborne battlefield command and control center (ABCCC) flying over Laotian territory. ABCCCs then sent fighter planes to the places of detection. The program was said to cost nearly $3 billion. Planes used for Igloo White included 21 EC-121s used as ABCCCs, 18 F-4Ds, 18 A-1Es, 12 CH-3 helicopters and 34 O-2 Skymasters.

Previous page: **The B-52D was specially modified for high-density bombing in Vietnam with a modification call 'big belly,' which allowed the B-52D to carry a maximum load, inside and out, of 108 bombs.**

Above: **AIM-7 Sparrow AAM missiles ready for loading onto an Air Force F-4. The Sparrow was a guided missile that required the F-4's radar to illuminate its target.**

Below: **A grainy nose camera photo shows an AIM-9 Sidewinder heat-seeking missile scoring a direct hit on a MiG-17 over North Vietnam.**

USAF Cololnel (Ret.) Walter J. Boyne, in Beyond the Wild Blue, discusses the ways the North Vietnamese foiled the Igloo White sensors. 'They would cover some of the devices with the ubiquitous wicker baskets to mask their sensors; others they would trick by sending a truck back and forth to simulate a convoy.' Since the Ho Chi Minh Trail was not a single artery but a network of interconnected routes, all covered by a dense jungle canopy, there was no way to confirm Igloo White's detections visually.

The Battle of the Missiles

Air-to-air missile technology continued to evolve and play a role in the air war. The unguided missiles used during the post-WWII era lacked accuracy, but guided missiles proved more promising. The Navy produced the first effective guided missile, called the Sidewinder. Officially known as an air intercept missile (AIM-9), Sidewinders had an infrared head that zeroed in on the engine of the target plane. They had first been used in 1958 on Chinese MiGs engaging Taiwanese F-86s in the Taiwan Strait.

Another Navy-produced missile, the Sparrow (AIM-7), used radar to find its target. The launcher planes, however, had to track these 'beam riders' for them to reach their targets successfully. Both kinds of missiles were deployed in Vietnam, but their hit rates remained low. Their technical complexity and narrow target windows, as well as the enemy's effective evasion strategies, kept missile scores in the 10 percent range. Not until the 1980s did technological refinements produce the advanced medium-range air-to-air missile (AMRAAM) or AIM-120, a weapon that could reach its target without constant monitoring. Instead, Vietnam-era missile carriers like the F-4 Phantom acquired 20 mm gun pods for additional fire power.

Once the Vietcong began deploying SAMs on a regular basis, US planes operated at high risk. American flyers had three options. They could destroy the launchers on the ground, jam the missile's radar or conduct evasion maneuvers.

Above: The RF-101C reconnaissance aircraft was the only version of the Voodoo to see duty in Vietnam, flying intelligence gathering missions over South Vietnam and Laos.

Below: 15 B-52s were lost during Linebacker II in late 1972, a massive bombing assault on North Vietnam to bring 'peace with honor.' All 15 of the B-52s were brought down by surface-to-air missiles.

Otherwise, the commonly used SA-2, a two-stage, 35-foot missile, would knock them out of the sky. F-100s and F-105s began to be equipped with radar-warning systems, and their crews were specially trained. Over time and with experience, the Air Force learned to neutralize the enemy SAM threat. Some military analysts suggest that if the Air Force could have gotten permission to knock out Hanoi's SAMs when they were installed in 1965, the war would have ended then.

New Tactics, New Weapons

Because of White House sanctions against many targets in North Vietnam, the Air Force did not use conventional bombing strategy. Until 1972, Tactical Air Command (TAC) planes did most of the bombing 'Up North' (slang for North Vietnam). Usually sixteen F-105s, accompanied by F-4s, EB-66s, and Wild Weasels (the nickname for planes designed to counter hostile radar-controlled surface-to-air missiles) would carry some 75,000 pounds of bombs north to defined targets. Before the war was over, F-105 crews shot down 27 MiGs and shared another hit with an F-4D. SAC's long-range B-52s supported the ground war in South Vietnam with massive tactical strikes. The B-52s dropped as many as 560,000 pounds on indefinite, suppositional targets. They flew a total of 124,532 sorties. Military historian Barrett Tillman argues that many Air Force officers grew frustrated and concerned about this 'role-reversal' and the potential it provided for causing turf battles.

President Johnson's decision not to run for re-election in 1968 had put an end to bombing in North Vietnam during much of the last four years of the war. The kill ratio against enemy MiGs amounted to a disappointing 2-1 or less. In Korea, the ratio with F-86s had remained closer to 10-1. The cost differential on the Phantoms and Thuds used in Vietnam, compared to the Sabres and Thunderjets employed in Korea, was also considerable. At 2.5 to 1, the Navy record with its F-8 Crusader surpassed that of the Air Force in Vietnam.

Just as the Wild Weasels played an important role in neutralizing enemy SAMs, Air Force fighter pilots relied on the EC-121T to track MiG activity, along with the Navy's Red Crown, a radar warning ship stationed in the Gulf of Tonkin. In the early years of the war, the Air Force had supported the American campaign to prop up Laotian leader Souvanna Phouma with aging RB-26s, R-26s and T-28 trainers. By 1968, they switched to AC-130 Spectre gunships with TV, infrared surveillance, radar and 20 mm Gatlings. F-4 Phantoms and B-52s were also employed.

Daring Rescue Operations

Conventional Air Force Search and Rescue (SAR) operations played an important, if at first under-resourced role in Vietnam. Once a crewmember was on the ground, an A-1E Sandy flew to the area and began the hunt. A second Sandy accompanied two helicopters to the location, one for the pick-up and the other for back-up. Fighter jets performed rescue combat air patrol. When the downed flyer landed in enemy territory, the fighters and Sandys strafed the surrounding area for extra clout.

Captain J. R. Pardo and Lieutenant Stephen A. Wayne performed one of the most death-defying acts of air-born heroism during the entire war. Flying an F-4

Phantom out of the Eighth Wing over North Vietnam in March 1967, the two rescued Captain Earl Aman and Lieutenant Robert Houghton, whose own Phantom had been ready to crash in enemy territory. Because Aman and Houghton's jet was almost out of fuel, Pardo and Wayne had them shut off their engines and lower their tailhook. Pardo and Wayne, whose jet was also damaged, latched the other plane's tailhook onto their windscreen and kept the two jets in the air until they were both over safe ground in Laos. Then the four pilots bailed out and were rescued. Not until 22 years later were Pardo and Wayne awarded Silver Stars by the Air Force.

Marine Green Berets attempted one dramatic but sadly disappointing SAR rescue, Operation Kingpin, on 21 November 1970, at Son Tay prison camp near Hanoi. Air Force pilots in two HC-130 search-and-rescue tankers and an MC-130 Hercules Combat Talon supported the mission, as well as five A-1 Skyraiders. Despite the heroic effort, the North Vietnamese had moved the POWs days before.

Equally dramatic but far more successful, the SAR rescue of Captain Roger C. Locher took place in June 1972. Pilot Robert Lodge and Locher, his Weapons Systems Officer, both from the 555th Tactical Fighter Squadron, were shot down in their F4D 10 May, after dropping a MiG-21 near Yen Bai Airfield, an enemy stronghold. Three weeks later, Locher's radio signal was picked up. It took two days to locate the missing flyer, and because of the length of time that had passed since the plane was shot down, the SAR team grew concerned that it was a trap. Under heavy ground fire, an HH-53 helicopter, using the new electronic location finder (ELF) system, lowered a jungle penetrator, the rescue device used to lift men through jungle canopy, and secured Locher. He had stayed alive after walking 12 miles from his parachute drop and living on forage. The remains of Major Lodge were not returned by the North Vietnamese until 1977.

US Air Force and Navy Rivalry

One of the problems that became evident midway through the war was the impact of competition with Navy fliers. Tillman argues that it may have been exacerbated by Defense Secretary McNamara's preoccupation with statistics. Fighter jets might take off without a full bomb payload, leading to an increase in the number of planes sent out on a sortie. The numbers looked good, but an increase in overall flight hours exposed crews to unnecessary risk, according to one view. The Air Force did 'top' the Navy with two-thirds the total number of fixed-wing flights during the war.

In order to keep Air Force and Navy missions separate, Vietnam was divvied up geographically into seven regions, labeled 'route packages.' The low-number packages, beginning sequentially just above the 18th parallel, were not considered high priority. The 'hot' packages—Five, Six-A and Six-B—lay in the north. Six-

Above: **Pilots and crew of the 64th Fighter Interceptor Squadron scramble for their F-102 Delta Daggers at Danang Air Base. The F-102 was the world's first all-weather supersonic jet interceptor.**

Left: **Captain Richard S. Ritchie of the 555th Tactical Fighter Squadron was the only US Air Force ace of the Vietnam War with five victories over MiG-21s, each represented by a red star on the side of his F-4 Phantom.**

Right: **C-123s drop South Vietnamese paratroopers during Operation Phi Hoa II, a tactical air and ground strike against the Vietcong in March 1963.**

A included Hanoi and belonged to the Air Force, while Six-B, with Haiphong, was Navy property. These territorial divisions, similar to ones used in World War II and Korea, meant the US air war lacked the advantages of central control, in contrast to North Vietnam, which was highly centralized.

Operation Niagara, initiated in January 1968, offers an example of a key support operation complicated by Air Force coordination with Navy planes. Some 6,000 Marine and South Vietnamese forces found themselves facing off against 30,000 North Vietnamese regulars at Khe Sanh. The area had to be organized into the equivalent of route packages before the mission could begin. Then with help from Combat Skyspot, the code name for a ground-based radar system, B-52s hit their targets repeatedly in three-hour intervals. The limits on proximity to friendly troops dropped from 3,300 to 300 yards, a measure of bomber crew accuracy. A memorial at Andersen Air Force Base in Guam pays tribute to the Combat Skyspot and B-52 crews involved in this and other missions.

The Vietnamization of the War

Once Richard M. Nixon assumed the US presidency in January 1969, he called for 'Peace with Honor' in Vietnam, but that policy didn't prevent his authorization of bombing in Cambodia. Operation Menu sent out B-52s on 4,000 sorties there to wipe out Vietcong and North Vietnamese bases until 1973. More than 500,000 tons of bombs were dropped in Cambodia over the course of the campaign.

When the Communists started a major initiative in February 1969, Air Force bombs helped stem the enemy tide. At a Guam press conference in July 1969, Nixon announced what became known as the 'Nixon Doctrine'—namely, that although the United States would provide a broad 'shield' of defense, it expected Asian countries to defend themselves. In a November talk to the nation, he converted this doctrine into what became known as the 'Vietnamization' of the war, making clear that US troops would no longer sustain South Vietnam, when he said, 'we shall look to the nation directly threatened to assume the primary responsibility of providing the manpower for its defense.'

Nevertheless, an April 1970 foray sent 30,000 American ground troops into Cambodia, backed up by Air Force B-52 bombers. The consequences of the gradual US withdrawal quickly became clear. The next year in Operation Lam Son 719, hundreds of US aircraft were destroyed after South Vietnamese troops walked into an enemy trap in Laos.

By the beginning of 1972, the number of US ground troops in Vietnam had dropped to 133,000, and the American effort in Vietnam increasingly relied on US Air Force interdictions. In battle after battle, the South Vietnamese Army suffered major losses. In April 1972, North Vietnamese forces threatened to overrun the ancient city of Hue but were stopped with help from bombing attacks by US B-52s.

The enemy flew the MiG-17 Fresco, a descendant of the MiG-15 used during the Korean War. It was equipped with two 23 mm cannons and a 37 mm gun. Eventually the AA-2 Atoll missile, a close copy of the US Sidewinder, became standard MiG-17 armament. Another model, the MiG-19 Farmer, claimed to be the world's first supersonic fighter, dating from 1953, although the US Super Sabre had flown at a record-breaking 755-plus mph 29 October 1953. The MiG-19 carried 30 mm cannons as well as missiles. The MiG-21 Fishbed weighed only 13,500 pounds and could fly at more than Mach 2.

The efficacy of North Vietnam's central coordination helps explain why the US Air Force struggled along with such a low kill ratio. Other reasons include the paucity of radar-sensing planes like the EC 121T, rules of conduct that required actual sighting of the target before firing, inadequate armament, outdated training programs and the unwillingness of VNAF pilots to engage enemy aircraft.

As the North Vietnamese improved their response to US bombing raids, some Air Force officers did more than complain about the target constraints imposed by the White House. General John D. Lavelle, as commander of the Seventh Air Force in 1971, ordered fighter strikes against proscribed enemy air defensive sites. He was retired shortly after they ended and summoned to Washington for Congressional testimony. Deviating from the Rules of Engagement was not looked upon as acceptable.

On 23 March 1972, the United States cancelled peace talks in Paris for lack of progress. North Vietnamese troops were gathering above the demilitarized zone, and the South readied for an attack.

Above left: **The DeHavilland C-7 Caribou short take off and landing utility transport was ideally suited to the rugged conditions of Southeast Asia. The C-7 could carry 26 fully outfitted paratroopers or three tons of cargo.**

Opposite bottom: **A highway bridge northwest of Vinh is destroyed by bombs dropped from an F-105 Thunderchief.**

Below: **A North Vietnamese man gives directions to his countrymen from his perch atop the wreckage of at B-52, downed by enemy SAMs during Linebacker II.**

It came on 29 March, through Laos as well as the South Vietnam border. This last-ditch, all-out onslaught in the Spring of 1972, became known as the Easter Offensive, and the North Vietnamese used battle tanks, anti-aircraft guns and mobile SAMs. President Nixon's policy of Vietnamizing the war had led to a significant reduction of American troops, and the South Vietnamese were hard put to stop the offensive. US and Allied pilots helped keep the North Vietnamese from overrunning An Loc, 70 miles north of Saigon, when it was attacked on 2 April.

In a second enemy foray two weeks later, American forces faced more anti-aircraft weaponry, rockets and artillery fire. Fighter-bombers and AC-47 gunships, nicknamed 'Spookies,' flew with lightweight Cessna A-37 'Tweety Birds' to fend off the attacks on ground troops. B-52s contributed with carpet bombings. Lockheed C-130, or Hercules, transports kept the ground troops supplied during the siege, using the container delivery system (CDS) to drop cargo from low altitudes. Eventually air controllers utilized ground radar to direct the drops and allow the transports to fly above ground fire. Capable of carrying as many as 15 tons of cargo or 90 soldiers, the Hercules was a much-valued workhorse. By the end of the Easter Offensive, the Air Force had lost 39 aircraft.

***Above:* Colonel Robin Olds adjusts his parachute before a flight in Vietnam in 1967. Olds was a World War II ace with nine victories flying a P-38 and four more flying a P-51. Olds became the first American ace with victories in two non-consecutive wars, scoring four victories in Vietnam in a F-4 for a total of 17.**

The Air War Revived

When Nixon rescinded the United States' no-bombing policy and instituted Operation Freedom Train in 1972, it was the first US air retaliation in North Vietnam north of the 20th parallel since 1968. Navy aircraft moved in first, restricting their sorties to the section of North Vietnam between the 17th and 19th parallels. The targets were strategic communication locations, such as bridges, roads, railroad tracks and waterways, supply routes, industrial and electrical facilities, vehicles and air defense installations. The Navy planes flew missions from the carriers Kitty Hawk, Coral Sea, Constellation and Hancock. Both Air Force and Navy pilots fought bad weather by using instrumentation to direct their weapons. The goal was to stop North Vietnam's foray into the South.

The Air Force entered the fray as part of Operation Linebacker, with B-52s—used against the North for the first time—fighters and specialized planes equipped to contravene SAMs and employ other electronic countermeasures. On 16 April, they hit fuel storage tanks outside of Haiphong, and the smoke could be seen as far away as 110 miles. A second attack targeted Hanoi. When these activities didn't slow the North Vietnamese advance, Navy planes mined Haiphong Harbor. On 18 April, President Nixon approved bombing throughout North Vietnam.

By 1972, the laser-guided bombs (LGBs) introduced in Vietnam in 1968 with mixed results had been refined. The Paveway I enhanced regular 2,000-pound bombs fitted with laser guidance. They were used against bridges, and TV-guided bombs (precision-guided munitions or PGMs) carried by Phantom jets from the Eighth Tactical Fighter Wing brought down part of the 360-foot Thanh Hoa Bridge over the Song Ma River and the Paul Doumer Rail Bridge in Hanoi.

Since early April, the United States had concentrated on destroying the Thanh Hoa Bridge, nicknamed Dragon's Jaw. It took 871 Air Force and Navy sorties to complete the mission. The Eighth Tactical Fighter Wing completed the job on May 13, using F-4Ds with guided bombs. Eleven planes were been lost by the time the bridge was down. Five days later, the Air Force accomplished another important objective by hitting the Uong Bi electric power station outside Haiphong. These targets had been off-limits.

The Paul Doumer, or Long Bien Bridge, built by the French in 1902 and named after a French colonial governor-general, provided the only connection between Hanoi and North Vietnam's northeastern provinces at the time. Carrying both rail and automotive traffic, it was protected by 300 antiaircraft guns and 81 SAM installations. The US assault on the bridge had begun in 1967 with 20 F-105s and succeeded in destroying three of the 8,467-foot bridge's spans, but the North Vietnamese were able to repair it within two months. Then in 1972, as part of Operation Linebacker, F-4s used precision-guided Paveway I laser bombs to demolish the bridge.

Air Force losses during Operation Linebacker were even greater than with Rolling Thunder. In May 1972 during the Easter Offensive, pilots dropped six MiGs but lost 11 of their own planes. June brought an even worse record: two for seven; July produced an even six-six. As a result of the poor showing, the Seventh Air Force asked for Navy help. The Navy's Top Gun program had produced a 0-16 ratio. As a result of classes held at Udorn base, Thailand, under the leadership of Lieutenant Commander John B. Nichols, the 432nd Tactical Fighter Wing improved its hit ratio to 3-1, a top Air Force score for 1972.

Stopped on the battlefield, the North Vietnamese resumed peace talks in Paris, but when negotiations bogged down again in December 1972, President Nixon called for an all-out bombing attack on the North, dubbed Linebacker II. SAC headquarters in Omaha coordinated the bombing missions, calling in B-52s—120 during one three-day period—from many disparate locations—50 based at U-Tapao and another 150 at Andersen Air Force base in Guam. Other aircraft called in for the campaign included F-111s, F-4s, A-7s, EB-66s and KC-135s. The B-52s took unexpectedly heavy damage, with 15 downed and another two scrapped. A total of 26 American planes were lost in the 12-day campaign, and 20,000 tons of bombs were dropped. The enemy, however, ran out of SAMs before the raid ended, and their MiGs were put out of operation.

One unfortunate rumor claimed that the B-52 crews mutinied in response to the lack of imagination demonstrated by SAC's bombing strategies. In fact, only one crewmember would not fly. Tillman recounts how one bomber pilot blew a coach's whistle over the plane's radio and managed to stop SAM firings for a minute and a half. Linebacker II operated for the last two weeks of December 1972 and successfully brought the North Vietnamese back to the bargaining table. Peace talks resumed in Paris on 8 January 1973, and an accord was negotiated with a 27 January 1973 cease-fire.

The War Winds Down

Many felt that if Linebacker II had been initiated in 1965, the war might have ended seven years earlier. As it was, some military analysts believed that Linebacker II should have continued until the North Vietnamese were willing to accept total defeat.

US combat troops left South Vietnam in March 1973. Despite the Paris Peace Treaty, the North Vietnamese made steady encroachments into South Vietnam in 1974 and 1975, but the United States had ended its role in Vietnam. Two supervisory organizations formed as a result of the Paris Peace Accords—the Joint Military Commission with Saigon and Vietcong representatives and the International Commission for Control and Supervision consisting of Indonesia, Iran, Poland and Hungary—did little to stop the continued fighting. On 29 April1975, the remaining American civilians, along with 7,000 South Vietnamese refugees, were airlifted out of Saigon by US Marine, Navy and Air Force helicopters. The next day, the US Embassy in Saigon was looted. A long, bitter battle had ended, and it would continue to haunt both the American military and the American public.

While the Korean War produced 38 Aces—pilots who shot down five enemy aircraft—only three Air Force flyers received that honor. The rules for achieving Ace status in Vietnam allowed both the front- and back-seater to take credit. Captain Steve Ritchie became the first Air Force ace, shooting down five MiG-2s between May and August 1972. Weapons Systems Officer Charles DeBellevue helped destroy six MiGs, the most of any Vietnam flyer. Weapons Systems Officer Jeffrey Feinstein was the third Vietnam ace, and all three Aces flew in F-4s. World War II Ace Major Robin Olds also won four hits in Vietnam and was the only ace with wins in both World War II (12) and Vietnam.

Of the 660 American POWs at the war's end, most were flyers, and half of those were Air Force personnel. Major George 'Bud' Day won a Medal of Honor after escaping from captivity for two weeks before he was recaptured south of the DMZ and just two miles from freedom. Day was the only POW to escape even temporarily during the war. Captain Lance Sijan, another Medal of Honor winner, died in prison rather than yield to the enemy. Many were pressured to act as 'show' prisoners to demonstrate the allegedly good conditions. Some who refused were denied mail or given solitary confinement.

In the 11 years from 1962 to 1973, 2,257 Air Force planes were lost in the Vietnam War, 2118 personnel died and 300 were imprisoned or missing. Many thought Vietnam was a war run by White House administrators rather than generals. The final bombings of North Vietnam in Linebacker I and II demonstrated the Air Force's potential for defeating the North Vietnamese. Pilot and author Herbert Molloy Mason quotes Sir Robert Thompson, who masterminded Britain's 1950s counter-insurgency against the Communists in Malaysia on the Air Force's role at the end: 'You had them absolutely by the throat then.' Whether everyone would agree with that sentiment, all would say that the US Air Force had done its duty in Vietnam and served the nation with valor.

The rescuer and the rescued: The view up at a USAF HH-53 Super Jolly Green Giant helicopter (top) as it rescues a downed airman, and the view down at the airman (above) as he grabs the rescue winch.

HL
755

CHAPTER 12
THE COLD WAR COOLS DOWN: 1965-1990

THE COLD WAR COOLS DOWN: 1965-1990

Vietnam may have dominated American military minds during the 1960s and early 1970s, but that conflict was hardly the nation's only Cold War concern. The Soviet launch of Sputnik, the first satellite to orbit the earth, on 4 October 1957, had precipitated a race into space. With both the United States and the Soviet Union building a cache of nuclear weapons, and other forms of technological advances in aircraft and weaponry taking place, the US Air Force found itself playing a critical new role in the nation's defense.

A variety of short-term events other than Vietnam also preoccupied the Air Force during this time period. A military coup and civil war unsettled the Dominican Republic in 1965. With Cuba already a Communist enclave in the United States' 'backyard,' President Johnson ordered the Atlantic Command to send 23,000 Marines to Santo Domingo, along with 1,000 Air Force staff, to prevent a Communist takeover and re-establish order through Operation Powerpack. When President Charles de Gaulle withdrew France from the North Atlantic Treaty Organization (NATO) in 1966, the US Air Force took on the task of moving US planes and equipment from the French NATO base at Evreux to new NATO quarters at Mildenhall, England.

On 23 January 1968, a North Korean patrol boat boarded the Pueblo, a US Navy intelligence-gathering vessel, killed one crew member and took the other 82 captive, along with the boat. Within days, the Ninth Air Force responded to the incident, which shocked the world, by scrambling F-4Ds, F-100s, and RB 66 as well as F-4 Phantom II fighters as part of Operation Red Fox. No retaliation was authorized, however, and the Pueblo crewmembers were held captive for 11 months. The North Koreans returned them to the United States after the government admitted to conducting espionage. As late as 2004, the USS Pueblo, however, remains in Wonson Harbor.

Another spying incident with North Korea in April 1969 led to the destruction of a Navy EC-121 Reconnaissance plane. A North Korean MiG-17 jet fighter downed the American plane over the Sea of Japan, killing 31 people. President Nixon temporarily halted surveillance flights in the area after the incident.

The Air Force's 99th Reconnaissance Squadron contributed to American surveillance activities during the Cold War through its U-2 flights. In 1970, such surveillance operations helped uncover a Soviet base under construction at Cienfuegos, Cuba, disguised as a sugar terminal. After a warning from the United States, the Russians agreed to stop construction in return for a US guarantee to respect Cuba's sovereignty.

The Air Force and Space

Soviet successes in space exploration and their Cold-War ramifications led to rapid development of space research by the United States in these years. The Air Force's missile program shepherded the Atlas, capable of flying distances of 5,000 miles, through testing in December 1962. The Titan and Minutemen were not far behind. On 15 May 1963, Major L. Gordon Cooper, Jr., became the Air Force's first astronaut. Cooper orbited the earth 22 times as the last of the Project Mercury pilots, and he was the first American to circle the planet for more than 24 hours. In early 1964, two Air Force Captains, Albert R. Crews, and Richard E. Lawyer, spent two weeks in a simulated space vehicle as part of the testing that would lead to an Air Force-produced Manned Orbiting Laboratory (MOL).

The National Aeronautics and Space Administration (NASA) used Air Force rockets for launching space vehicles, including the Thor, Atlas, Agena, and Titan. In that era, space launchings took place at the Air Force's Eastern Test Range, with launch sites in Florida at Vandenberg Air Force Base, and at tracking stations from Newfoundland to Argentina. During the Gemini 4 space mission in June 1965, Air Force Majors James A. McDivitt and Edward H. White II set a record by orbiting 63 times, and White became the first US astronaut to walk outside a space capsule. Major L. Gordon Cooper helped break McDivitt's and White's endurance record by orbiting the earth 120 times during the Gemini 5 mission 21-29 August 1965. Then Air Force Lieutenant Colonel Frank Borman helped break 11 world records during 14 days orbiting in Gemini 7, 4-18 December 1965. The most remarkable and historic space event of the era, though, was the Apollo 11 flight to the moon on 20 July 1969. While Neil Armstrong was the first American to set foot on the moon, Air Force Colonel Edwin E. 'Buzz' Aldrin followed him to become the first member of the military to walk on the moon. One 'first' followed another, as the Air Force worked with NASA to develop the space program. On Apollo 15, launched 26 July 1971, the all-Air Force team of Colonel David R. Scott, Lieutenant Colonel James B. Irwin, and Major Alfred M. Worden explored the lunar surface, and then blasted off from the moon to the sound of Air Force anthem, 'Off We Go Into the Wild Blue Yonder,' catching the staff at Houston control center by surprise. Later that year, President Nixon dedicated the new Air Force Museum at Wright-Patterson Air Force Base in Dayton, Ohio. The Museum contains such space artifacts as the Apollo 15 Command Module and the McDonnell Gemini spacecraft, as well as conventional aircraft.

On 16 November 1973, when the final Skylab mission blasted off, Lieutenant

Previous page: **Two F-16Bs fly over Utah's Wasatch Mountains. The Lockheed Martin (General Dynamics) multirole fighter was first delivered to the 388th Tactical Fighter Wing at Hill Air Force Base, Utah, in January 1979.**

Above: **The McDonnell F-4 Phantom was one of the Air Force's most versatile airplanes. First flying in 1958, the F-4 has seen service in the air forces of 12 countries including the U.S., and was flown by the USAF flight demonstration team, the Thunderbirds, from 1969 to 1973.**

Right: **Two USAF F-4 Phantoms go 'bear hunting,' escorting a Soviet Tupelov Tu-95 Bear. The Tu-95 was Russia's Cold War intercontinental heavy bomber, with both nuclear free-fall bombing and nuclear missile capabilities.**

AIR FORCE
U.S. AIR FORCE

AF
78 119

Colonel William Pogue represented the Air Force on the crew. The Apollo-Soyez Test Project followed in July 1975, when Air Force General Thomas P. Stafford shook hands in space with Soviet cosmonauts.

An Air Force Titan III launched the Viking I mission to Mars on 20 August 1975. The Air Force reached another kind of milestone in September 1975, when Daniel 'Chappie' James, Jr., became the first African-American four-star general in American military history. The Air Force contributed the first African-American astronaut to the US space program, when Lieutenant Colonel Guion S. Bluford traveled into space on the Space Shuttle Challenger 30 August 1983.

The crash of the Space Shuttle Challenger on lift-off 28 January 1986, devastated everyone involved in the nation's space program. The spacecraft's commander was Francis R. 'Dick' Scobee, who had been an Air Force test pilot before entering the space program, and Mission Specialist Ellison S. Onizuka had also served in the Air Force before joining NASA as an astronaut. The Challenger disaster led to a stand-down in the US manned space program until launch of Space Shuttle Discovery on 29 September 1988. On 4 May 1989, Air Force Major Mark C. Lee, orbiting in the Space Shuttle Atlantis, sent the Magellan probe on its way to Venus.

New Planes, New Challenges

Air Force research and development continued alongside the space program. Not all the winged aircraft developed during the Vietnam War years saw service there. The XB-70 Valkyrie, termed 'one of the world's most exotic airplanes,' was first designed in the 1950s as a high-altitude bomber that could fly at speeds of Mach 3. Only two XB-70s were built, and they were used for aerodynamic research. The first flew 21 September 1964, while the second had its maiden flight 17 July 1965. The latter was destroyed in 1966 during a mid-air collision, while the first XB-70 ended up in the Air Force Museum at Wright-Patterson Base in Dayton, Ohio. The high-speed, rocket-propelled X-15 could fly higher than 50 miles. Such Air Force aircraft advances functioned as a deterrent to the Cold War's biggest bogeyman, nuclear war.

The F-111, which began life as the TFX under the reign of Robert McNamara as Defense Secretary in the 1960s, did see service in Vietnam, but it was an example of design compromises that satisfied no one. Conceived as a tactical fighter, it has been described as an attempt to cross a sports car with a truck. McNamara wanted it used by both the Air Force and the Navy with two versions and common parts to save money, but the Navy rejected the proposal. The Air Force was saddled with 270 F-111s. By the 1980s, it had acquired the F-15 Eagle as a tactical fighter, the A-10 for ground support, and the F-16 lightweight fighter, intended to cut the cost of the more expensive F-15. Aviation historian Joe Christy points out that at the same time new hi-tech aircraft are assets, the best planes are the ones that are ready to fly. Hi-tech too often means high maintenance. By 22 February 1978, the Air Force had moved on to development of its Navstar Global Positioning System and launched its first test satellite.

Above: **A Chinese Army honor guard greets Air Force One during President Richard M. Nixon's historic visit to the communist country in 1972.**

Opposite: **The F-15 Eagle fires an AIM-7 Sparrow missile, an air-to-air, radar-guided missile with all-weather and all-altitude capabilities.**

United States-USSR Relations

Meanwhile the arms race between the United States and the USSR sped up during the 1960s. In 1966, Defense Secretary Robert McNamara announced that the Soviet Union's Galosh anti-ballistic system was operative, and the United States continued to develop the Nike-X. By 1967, the United States announced deployment of its two-stage Sentinel ABM system with two interceptors. One, the long-range Spartan, carried a nuclear tip. The other was the short-range Sprint, and together they were designed to defend major cities.

Despite the accumulation of weaponry by both the United States and the Soviet Union, the Outer Space Treaty was signed in 1967 by the existing nuclear powers. Concern with the dangers of a nuclear holocaust went hand in hand with the Cold War. In 1968, the United States joined with the Soviet Union and Great Britain in signing a Nuclear Non-Proliferation Treaty to stop the spread of nuclear technology for military use. Ultimately, 186 nations signed the treaty, with only India, Pakistan, Israel and Cuba declining.

Once President Nixon took office in 1969, he shifted the ABM system to defense of ICBM installations and renamed it Safeguard. President Nixon and Soviet leader Leonid Brezhnev held Summit Talks that led a series of weapons-reduction accords designed to reduce the threat of nuclear war. Other Cold War activities between the United States and Soviet Union were not limited to saber rattling. In 1972, President Nixon arrived in Beijing, China, on Air Force One, to begin a series of historic talks aimed at improving relations. It was the start of an international thaw that would be encouraged by President Jimmy Carter later in the 1970s.

Conflicts Continue Around the World

Regional brush fires continued to ignite. The Middle East turned into the world's hot spot after Egypt and Syria attacked Israel on 6 October 1973. It became known as the Yom Kippur War because it was launched on a Jewish holy day. The United States, concerned that Israel might employ nuclear weapons, quickly became involved. The US Air Force initiated Operation Nickel Grass on 14 October, transporting to the Israelis 22,395 tons of supplies, including ammunition and tanks, until 14 November. The Operation flew out of Dover Air Force Base in Delaware, using the 436th Airlift Wing and flying C-5 Galaxies and C-141s.

President Nixon resigned on 9 Au-

gust 1974 as a result of the Watergate scandal, and his vice president, Gerald Ford, assumed office. Ford was left to preside over the evacuation of the last of US personnel from Saigon when it fell to the Communists on 30 April 1975. Then on 15 May 1975 he ordered Air Force helicopters to deliver 175 Marines to Kho Tang Island off Cambodia in a rescue operation, after hostile Cambodians boarded the SS Mayaguez, a US freighter, and captured its crew. Six months after President Ford visited China in December 1975, Mao Tse-tung died, temporarily destabilizing United States-Chinese relations.

Once President Jimmy Carter assumed office in 1977, the two nations moved a little closer towards détente. President Carter established diplomatic relations with mainland China, severing formal ties with Chiang Kai-Chek's Nationalist Chinese nation, Taiwan, and Prime Minister Deng Xiaoping visited the United States. President Carter and Secretary Brezhnev signed SALT II in Vienna on 18 June 1979, imposing ceilings on weapons systems. But when the Soviet Union invaded

Above: **Eight US service men, including five from the Air Force, died in the aborted attempt to rescue 53 American hostages from Iran on 26 April 1980 when a C-130 collided with a helicopter.**

Right: **A 'family portrait' of General Dynamics F-16s. From top, the AFTI/F-16 (Advanced Fighter Technology Integrator), the F-16/79, the F-16B, the F-16A, and the F-16XL.**

Below: **President Reagan and First Lady Nancy Reagan spend Memorial Day visiting casualty victims of the Lebanon and Grenada conflicts.**

The prototype B-1 bomber first flew in 1974. The USAF ordered four of the B-1s for flight tests before the program was canceled in 1977.

Below: **Air Force surveillance officers and US Customs personnel team up aboard a USAF E-3A AWACS Sentry in 1978 to detect smuggling aircraft.**

Afghanistan on 3 January 1980, President Carter asked Congress to delay ratification of the treaty. After President Reagan took office in 1981, the United States did, however, agree to comply with its terms so long as the Soviet Union did.

In response to the Soviet invasion of Afghanistan, the fall of the Shah of Iran, and the destabilization of the Persian Gulf at the end of the 1970s, US military leadership formed the Rapid Deployment Joint Task Force (RDJTF) to coordinate personnel from the Air Force and other military branches. When activated 1 March 1980, at MacDill Air Force Base in Florida, the RDJTF's goal was to form a military force that could be deployed as needed on a worldwide basis.

In his 1980 State of the Union Address, President Carter drew a line in the sand, warning, 'An attempt by any outside force to gain control of the Persian Gulf regions will be regarded as an assault on the vital interests of the United States. And such an assault will be repelled by any means necessary, including military force.' In 1980, President Carter also successfully pressured the US Olympic Committee into boycotting the Olympic Games that summer in Moscow because of the Soviet invasion of Afghanistan. After Iranian students seized hostages at the US Embassy in Iran, President Carter ordered a helicopter rescue mission in early 1980, when diplomatic efforts to free the hostages failed. Air Force General David C. Jones, as Chairman of the Joint Chiefs of Staff, began planning the rescue mission. Once the rescue got underway, three of the US helicopters failed, and the mission had to be scrapped. Eight men died, and five of them--Major Richard Bakke, Major Harold L. Lewis, Sergeant Joel C. Mayo, Captain Lyn D. McIntosh, and Captain Charles T. McMillan—came from the Air Force. They were killed when a helicopter from the aborted mission attempted takeoff in a desert sandstorm and slid into their C-130 Hercules transport. The attempted Hostage Rescue became the first US military conflict with Islamic militants.

New Strategies, New Weapons

By 1983, RDTJF had evolved into a regional unified command representing the United States in the Middle East and the

The Fighting Falcon spreads its wings: the assembly line at the mile-long General Dynamics aircraft factory in Fort Worth, Texas (top). The NATO European F-16 inaugural ceremony (second from top) at Hahn Air Force Base, Germany, 1982. F-16s fly in echelon formation (third from top), and an F-16 flashes its teeth with an impressive array of armaments (bottom).

An F-15E Strike Eagle breaks formation from his wingman. The F-15 maintains air superiority through a combination of speed, range, maneuverability, and adaptability.

Above: **The massive C-5 Galaxy is one of the largest aircraft in the world. Its cargo compartment measures 13.5 feet tall by 19 feet wide by 143 feet long, and can carry a load weighing 270,000 pounds.**

Opposite: **An Air Force A-7D Corsair II drops a load of Mark 82 high-drag bombs. The A-7D single-seat, tactical close air support fighter first flew in 1968 and was derived from the US Navy A-7.**

BOEING
U.S. AIR FORCE
084

U.S. AIR FORCE
CAUTION
CAUTION
CAUTION

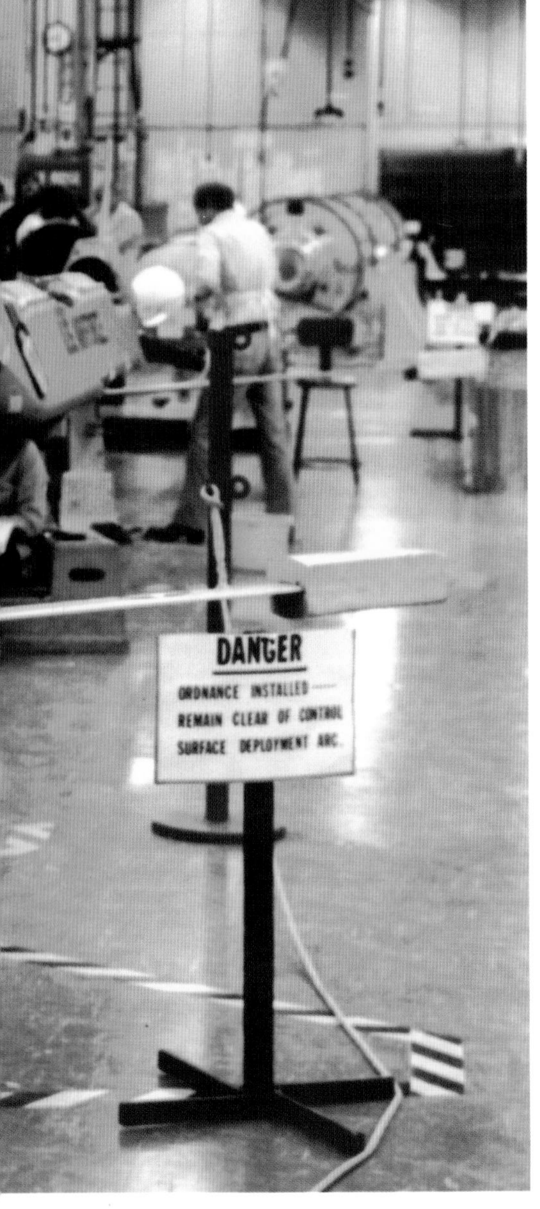

Left: **An Anti-Satellite Missile (ASAT) is loaded onto an F-15. The ASAT is launched at high altitudes from the F-15 while in a steep climb. The ASAT then uses its three rocket stages to propel a warhead into space where it impacts targeted satellites.**

Below left: **Inside a factory where air launched cruise missiles (ALCM) are assembled. The ALCM can be used to deliver either a nuclear warhead or a bunker buster with rocket-assisted penetration.**

African Horn. As a result, it was reformulated as the US Central Command, ready to intervene when the Middle East heated up again.

Responding in 1979 to Soviet development of 'killer satellites,' the United States initiated an anti-satellite missile program (ASAT). The Air Force began testing the F-15 Eagle-launched missile in 1982, with the first launch occurring in 1984. Although Congress resisted funding the ASAT, President Reagan continued to support it as an important form of deterrence.

In the early 1980s, the United States' arsenal included the Air Force's 1,053 ICBMs, consisting of 53 Titan IIs located in Arkansas, Arizona and Kansas; 450 solid-propellant Minuteman IIs: and 550 more Minuteman IIs with MIRV (multiple independently targetable re-entry vehicle) warheads. The Navy had its nuclear-powered submarine fleet with nuclear missiles, and SAC kept 290 of the more vulnerable manned B-52Gs and Hs, 70 FB-11s and 600 KC-135s for support. The B-52s carried Short Range Attack Missiles (SRAMs) with a range of about 100 miles in the early 1980s. They were replaced by the Air Launched Cruise Missile (ALCM), which began production in 1980. The advanced medium-range air-to-air missile (AMRAAM) or AIM-120 was also introduced in the 1980s. It improved on the Sidewinder, or AIM-9 and the Sparrow, or AIM-7, by using both heat-seeking and beam-riding technology. The AIM-120 was a 'launch-and-leave' missile that didn't need tracking from its launcher plane to reach the target successfully. Budget concerns delayed the Cruise missile, the MX and the B-1, which was scheduled to replace the B-52.

Plans for the MX dated back to 1966, when the Air Force decided it wanted to develop an advanced ICBM with a mobile basing system. The MX acquired its name in 1972 and was contracted for production in 1978. The first test came in 1982, and President Ronald Reagan, calling it the right missile at the right time, dubbed the MX 'Peacekeeper.' Congress, however, was initially unwilling to fund its development. Peacekeeper deployment finally began in 1986, using the so-called Rail Garrison system: under the operation of the USAF, 25 trains, each carrying two Peacekeepers, would move around the nation's rail system so as to foil any enemy's attempt to zero in on the missiles. (The Peacekeeper system was scheduled to be totally dismantled by 2005.) Production of the B-1A, proposed by President Nixon in 1970 as the first US supersonic bomber, was cancelled by President Carter in 1977. He said the continued utility of B-52 and cruise missiles made development of the B-1A variable-geometry bomber unnecessary. The Air Force would have used it to deliver nuclear bombs to the Soviet Union, but by the time the first prototype was built in 1974, anti-nuclear protesters were lying down in front of it to stop further production. Testing of the four existing prototypes continued, but the American climate had grown strongly anti nuclear.

After President Reagan came into office in 1981, though, the B-1 program was reactivated. In general, President Reagan took a more hawkish stance with the Soviets, and the 1970s thaw in the Cold War ended. When the Soviets invoked martial law in Poland on 13 December 1981, Reagan tried to enlist other nations to support an economic blockade of the Soviets. He coined the term 'Evil Empire' for the Soviet Union in his speeches and ratcheted up the arms race by stressing the 'deterrence of aggression through the promise of retaliation' approach. But in 1981 he also proposed meeting with Soviet leaders to work out a mutual reduction in nuclear weapons through a Strategic Arms Reduction Treaty (START). The START talks began on 29 June1982.

As these talks proceeded, President Reagan introduced a Strategic Defensive Initiative, nicknamed Star Wars, on 23 March 1983. The goal was to eliminate the threat of nuclear-armed ballistic missiles through research on advanced defensive technologies that would provide a shield against nuclear weapons. Scientist Edward Teller proposed an X-ray laser that could destroy nuclear-tipped missiles, while another system, called Brilliant Pebbles, used small orbiting missile interceptors. President Reagan's Star Wars program was controversial in the United States, where many thought it was impracticable and too costly.

Trying Incidents, Close Calls

While President Reagan worked on arms reduction, several international incidents made it clear that the Cold War was hardly over. On 1 September 1983, Soviet fighter jets shot down a Korean commercial airliner en route from New York to South Korea, killing its 283 pas-

sengers. Flight KAL 007 had flown off course and violated Soviet airspace over a sensitive military installation at Sakhalin Island. The Soviet Union insisted the Korean plane was spying and later claimed it had mistaken the plane for an American RC-135 reconnaissance plane.

Barely six weeks later, in Operation Urgent Fury, US Marines and Army troops, with Air Force and Navy support, landed on the tiny Caribbean nation of Grenada to quell a leftist uprising. The stated mission was evacuation of 1,100 American citizens, primarily medical students. The Air Force initially served strictly as transport for airborne troops and materiel, but at one point, when antiaircraft guns began to fire on US Army helicopters, Air Force AC-130 Spectre gunships were called in to destroy these guns.

The START talks were suspended in 1983 when the Soviets, fearing they could not compete with Star Wars, refused to accept strategic arms reduction unless the United States abandoned Star Wars. In January 1984, President Reagan called for renewed arms talks, including nuclear weapons and reduction of troops in Europe. It was considered to be a major policy shift. On 19 November 1985, summit talks—the first between the United States and Soviet Union since 1979—began in Geneva after Mikhail Gorbachev assumed Soviet leadership in March 1985.

Meanwhile, issues over nuclear force arose elsewhere. ANZUS, the post-World War II defense agreement among the United States, Australia and New Zealand ran aground in 1985, when New Zealand refused to allow American nuclear-armed or powered submarines enter its ports. As a result, the United States withdrew its defense commitment to New Zealand in 1986, although New Zealand remained in the ANZUS pact.

The Cold War Draws Down

Although no agreement on arms was reached in the 1985 Geneva talks, both President Reagan and Secretary Gorbachev did plan further talks leading to a 50-percent reduction in nuclear arms. Negotiations held in Reykjavik, Iceland, on 11 October 1986, ended without an accord again, because of the Soviet Union's resistance to Star Wars.

By 1987, the Soviet Union contained some 43,000 nuclear warheads, while the United States had 23,000. The Soviets seemed to soften their position by suggesting separate discussions of Intermediate Range Nuclear Missiles (INF), which the United States was committed to in Europe under the auspices of NATO. On 8 December 1987, Presidents Reagan and Gorbachev signed an INF Treaty. It went into effect 1 June 1988, with the United States destroying 846 intermediate and short-range missiles and the Soviet Union, 1,846. The last US Pershing missile was destroyed on 6 July 1989, at Longhorn Army Ammunition plant in Texas. On-site inspections ensured that all weapons were eliminated.

The remaining issues in the START talks were resolved after George Herbert Walker Bush took office in 1989. He and President Gorbachev signed the START Treaty on 31 July 1991. It limited each side to 1,600 strategic nuclear delivery systems (missiles, submarines and bombers) with a 6,000 cap on nuclear warheads, leading to a reduction of 20-30 percent.

Concurrent with the push to resolve arms reduction came American economic and political pressure on the Soviet Union. In a speech at the Brandenburg Gate of the Berlin Wall in West Germany on 12 June 1987, President Reagan called for Soviet leader Gorbachev, who had been preaching a policy of glasnost, or openness, to 'tear down this wall.' The challenge became one of the president's most quoted remarks and brought the first chink in the Wall, which was finally pulled down in November 1989. Its demolition marked the collapse of the Soviet Union's iron grip over Eastern Europe. No single event can be said to mark an absolute end of the Cold War, but the breaking down of the Berlin Wall on 11 November 1989 symbolized the collapse

Opposite top: **Cold War tensions eased when Mikhail Gorbachev became Soviet General Secretary. Here, he is given a tour of Governor's Island in New York harbor by President Ronald Reagan and Vice-President George Bush as Lady Liberty looks on.**

Opposite bottom: **The AC-130 Spectre gunship provides close air support, air interdiction, and armed reconnaissance. The heavily armed AC-130 saw duty protecting US Army helicopters during the Granada invasion in 1983.**

Above: **In 1987 Ronald Reagan traveled to Germany and spoke before the Brandenberg Gate, challenging Soviet leader Mikhail Gorbachev to tear down the Berlin Wall.**

Below: **F-15 Eagles fly patrol missions over the Middle East, soon to become a hot bed for US military action.**

of Soviet rule throughout Eastern Europe and signaled the end of the USSR as a threat in a 'hot' war.

The Air Force in Post-Cold War World

Without the Cold War to drive a weapons race, the United States began major cutbacks in troop deployments, predominantly in Europe. Two-thirds of the US bases there would be closed, and troops declined from 341,000 in 1989 to 109,000 by 1995. In 1990, the budget for Star Wars dropped from the $4.1 billion requested by President Reagan in 1988 to $3.8 billion approved by Congress. Congress also limited the Air Force's MX missile program to 50 weapons. The B-2 Stealth bomber, however, continued to move forward to the tune of $4.3 billion. The first plane was completed on 22 November 1988.

The US Air Force continued to be ready for combat. One such occasion came in 20-21 December 1989, when the United States invaded Panama to arrest its dictator Manuel Noriega on charges he was engaged in international drug traffic. The Air Force not only participated with airlift and airdrop activities, but AC-130 Spectre gunships were called on in two situations to support threatened US ground troops.

As the last decade of the 20th century began, the Western world took on a new shape. Eastern Europe freed itself from Soviet domination, and NATO began work on a treaty with Warsaw Pact nations. The Conventional Forces in Europe Treaty of 1990 (CFE) would, within a few years' time, reduce weaponry by more than 58,000 and complete 2,500 weapons inspections. The Air Force was changing, too. Forming its first new command since 1982, the Air Force established a Special Operations unit on 22 May 1990. Then on 13 July 1990, the Alaskan Air Command became the 11th Air Force as part of the Pacific Air Forces. On July 24, SAC's airborne alert status, designated Looking Glass and in operation continuously for 29 years, came to an end.

As Europe and the United States resolved its security issues, however, attention turned again to the Middle East. A crisis in the Persian Gulf was reaching the boiling point, and the United States began Operation Desert Shield, shifting US forces to the Middle East after Iraq's invasion of Kuwait on 1 August 1990.

An F-16 Fighting Falcon banks sharply while firing an AIM-9 Sidewinder, a supersonic, heat-seeking, air-to-air missile.

AMC
00532

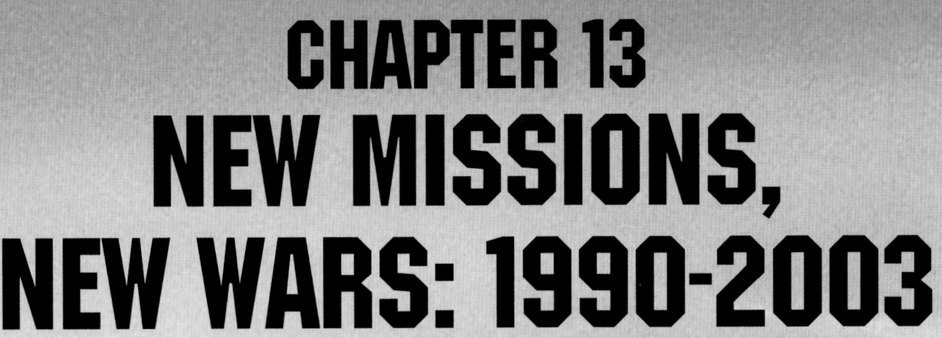

CHAPTER 13
NEW MISSIONS, NEW WARS: 1990-2003

NEW MISSIONS, NEW WARS: 1990-2003

The year 1990 began with US Air Force staff numbers at 535,000 and a total of 6,700 aircraft, some 3,500 of which were combat planes. A new Air Force analysis developed by Air Force Secretary Donald Rice and titled 'Global Reach, Global Power,' defined five components of military air power: speed, range, precision, flexibility, and lethalness. A revamped Air Force was ready to roll when called on for the largest US deployment since Vietnam when the Persian Gulf War ignited.

Lessons learned from Vietnam took the Air Force in the direction of integrated air-defense networks like the US Central Command (Centcom). At the end of the 20th century, a new form of warfare was coming into being through the development of electronic technology. Confounding enemy communications grew important, as well as 'signature reduction'—that is, reducing the ability of an enemy to identify the presence of attacking elements such as airplanes. Smart bombs introduced during the Vietnam conflict were refined, along with stealth weapons.

The Persian Gulf War

Seasoned by eight years of conflict with neighboring Iran, Iraq's army invaded Kuwait on 2 August 1990. The prelude to the invasion was Iraqi Dictator Saddam Hussein's call to the other Arab states to lower oil production and raise oil prices. When Kuwait in particular refused, Hussein, who had built up a large debt while fighting Iran and led the fourth largest army in the world, had massed 120,000 soldiers along the Kuwait border. In a week Iraq overwhelmed the tiny nation.

A shocked United States, with President George H. W. Bush at the helm, moved first to protect its interests in Saudi Arabia with Air Force and Navy aircraft and troops. The fear was that Saudi Arabia and its oil fields would be next. Lieutenant General Charles A. Horner oversaw the Air Force components, and a total of five fighter squadrons, an AWACS contingent and part of the 82nd Airborne Division arrived in Saudi Arabia in five days. F-15 Eagle fighter jets transferred from Langley Air Force Base in Virginia. Other Air Force combat aircraft employed included the F-15E Strike Eagle, A-10 Thunderbolt II, F-115 Stealth Fighter, B-52 Stratofortress, F-11, EF-111 Raven, F-4G Wild Weasel, and F-16 Fighting Falcon.

By the end of August, President Bush had called up military reserves, including the Air Force Reserve and the Air National Guard. The Air Force's Military Airlift Command (MAC) sent C-141s, C-5 Galaxies, C-130 Hercules, KC-135s, KC-10 Aerial Refuelers, and the Civil Reserve Air Fleet on 18,000 missions to Saudi Arabia with troops and supplies totaling 482,000 personnel and 513,000 tons of cargo.

Over 30 other nations quickly joined the United States to form a coalition against Iraq as part of Desert Shield. During the next six months, this coalition strengthened its position in Saudi Arabia, but Hussein would not back down; he kept his troops in Kuwait. Desert Shield turned into Desert Storm on 17 January 1991, when the United States and the Coalition went on the offensive. After Hussein fired seven SCUD missiles at Israel, the United States countered with the Patriot missile. The term 'surgical air strike' became common parlance.

The Air Force's first air-launched cruise missiles (ALCMs) arrived on seven B-52s from Barksdale Air Force Base in Louisiana, knocking out power stations and military communication sites. Army Apache helicopters went after Iraqi radar sites. Air Force MH-53J Pave Low helicopters led the way into Iraqi airspace for Army AH-64s and Air Force F-16s and A-10s, which fired Maverick missiles against the enemy's forward air defenses.

The Navy took responsibility for

Previous page: A C-17 Globemaster III of the 437th Airlift Wing out of Charleston Air Force Base flies over the South Carolina countryside. The transport's flexibility allows it to carry over a hundred paratroopers or a variety of cargo up to nearly 180,000 pounds.

Above: Various fighters used in Operation Desert Storm patrol the skies over Iraq.

Below: President George Bush meets with advisors in the Oval Office on 15 January 1991 during Operation Desert Shield.

Opposite top: Panama's General Manuel Noriega is escorted onto a US Air Force aircraft by DEA agents, transporting him to the U.S. for trial on drug charges in 1989.

Opposite bottom: Retreating Iraqi forces set hundreds of oil wells ablaze in Kuwait and southern Iraq.

neutralizing Iraqi command and control sites with Tomahawk missiles, while the Air Force sent its EF-111 Raven jets in to eliminate enemy radar and 19 Strike Eagles to destroy SCUD sites. Once Iraqi defenses were knocked out, F-117s flew directly to Baghdad, pinpointing targets like the Iraqi army and air force headquarters with precision-guided munitions (PGMs), or 'smart' bombs. PGM accuracy, tested in Vietnam, reached new levels of accuracy. Some, like the Walleye, were directed by TV cameras mounted on the missile tip; others, including the Paveways, used lasers to guide the weapon to its impact point (LGBs). Some 28 LGBs out of 49 launched struck their targets within 10 feet.

In the next stage of the air war, the Navy sent in BQM-74 drones to attract the remaining Iraqi radar stations. Air Force F-4G Phantoms and F-16C Fighting Falcons followed up with high-speed anti-radiation missiles (HARMs), virtually eliminating Iraqi radar by February 21. It did not take long to establish air dominance. On the first day of Operation Desert Storm, US planes downed eight Iraqi jets. Within a few days, a major contingent of the Iraqi air force fled to Iran. Many other enemy aircraft were hit on the ground, including Mirages, Sukhois, and MiGs.

Coalition air power ranged from Saudi Eagles and Kuwaiti Skyhawks to Royal Air Force Tornados and Jaguars, along with French and Arab Mirages. Components of the integrated air defense network that had evolved from the Vietnam conflict, like the E-3 Sentry Air Warning and Control System (AWACS) and the E-8 Joint Surveillance Target Attack Radar System (JSTARS) gave the United States the edge in surveillance and communication.

One of the challenges for pilots flying in Operation Desert Storm was navigating through the smoke from oil-well fires. Before fleeing from Kuwait, Iraqi forces ignited 700 oil fields on 23 February, creating lowered visibility and considerable air pollution. CENTCOM initially anticipated a total victory from the air, but Hussein opted to keep his troops in place even after six weeks of bombing. Iraqi forces took a heavy toll from Coali-

tion cluster bombs, which scattered their payloads. By 24 February, the Coalition Commander, Army General Norman Schwarzkopf, called for a ground offensive. The next day, an Iraqi SCUD missile hit the US barracks in Dhahran, Saudi Arabia, killing 28 soldiers. After three more days, the war was over; it was 28 February. On 1 March, the terms of the cease-fire were negotiated in Safwan, Iraq.

The A-10 Thunderbolt II, better known by its nickname 'Warthog,' came into its own during Operation Desert Storm. Designed for ground support and equipped with the giant 30-mm Gatling gun, it could pick off tanks with ease. In one case reported by military historian Barrett Tillman, Captain Eric 'Fish' Salmonson and First Lieutenant John 'Karl' Marks of the 23rd Tactical Fighter Wing polished off 23 armored vehicles and damaged another 10 tanks flying their A-10 on 25 February.

The statistics from this mini-war—direct US involvement lasted only 42 days—are impressive. The US Air Force flew 59 percent of the 110,000 sorties and lost 20 men in action and another six in accidents, out of 148 deaths and 467 wounded overall. Fifteen planes went down in combat, out of the total of 75 for the Coalition. In contrast, the Iraqis lost 39 aircraft in combat, 35 of which were downed by Air Force Eagles and two by A-10s. The number of friendly fire incidents remained low. While Desert Storm did not produce any aces, two of the Air Force's Eagle pilots took three kills each.

One of the problems remaining in the aftermath of Operation Desert Storm was the plight of the Kurdish peoples in Iraq, who had been persecuted by Hussein's government. In March after the ceasefire, Kurdish rebels took control of several northern Iraqi towns. The United States chose not to involve itself directly in the rebellion, and remaining Iraqi troops fought back with napalm and chemical weapons, quelling the revolt. But when one million Kurdish refugees fled to the mountains of northern Iraq and Turkey, President Bush authorized relief aid. On 7 April, 2,000 pounds of supplies were airdropped in Operation Provide Comfort, directed by Major General James L. Jamerson. On 11 April, Iraq signed the cease-fire terms. The United States continued to provide relief to the Kurds through Operation Provide Comfort, building a tent city outside Zakhu, Iraq. The United Nations took over on 7 June.

Once the cease-fire was in place, a no-fly zone, termed Operation Southern Watch, was put into effect, although General Schwarzkopf allowed the Iraqis to continue using their remaining helicopters. An unintended result was that the Iraqis employed the helicopters to attack Kurdish rebels, but enemy jets that entered the no-fly zone were shot down by US Air Force planes. Some analysts felt that Operation Desert Storm ended too soon and Hussein should have been ousted. Instead he stayed in power and was repeatedly able to put up obstacles for the UN inspectors who attempted to uncover weapons of mass destruction. The controversial decision to remove Hussein permanently from office would be made more than ten years later by a different Bush administration. Without debate, however, is the key role American air power played in the first Persian Gulf War. The 'Global reach/Global Power' document proved its mettle, as did the Air Force's new Total Force Policy, entailing use of both active and reserve forces.

Crisis in Somalia

Out-and out-war was not the only kind of military operation involving the US Air Force, which has always found itself involved in a variety of other military activities. Peacetime operations, humanitarian aid, crisis response, sanction enforcement and military intervention are some of the ways short of all-out war the United States employs its military resources. A number of civil crises in the early 1990s illustrate some of the forms of military deployment that include Air Force contingents.

The crisis in Somalia proved surprisingly messy. In 1992, the African nation, situated on the northeast coast of Africa next to Kenya and Ethiopia, found itself suffering from a famine so severe that half a million people had died. International relief efforts were hampered by civil unrest between Somali clans. Initially the

Above: **During Desert Storm, the B-52 Stratofortress delivered 40 percent of all the munitions dropped by coalition forces. The B-52 has been in service since 1955.**

Below: **Despite its enormous size, the C-17 Globemaster only requires a crew of three: a pilot, copilot, and loadmaster. 102 paratroopers can be deployed from the C-17.**

Air Force airlifted food and supplies as part of Operation Provide Relief. Then in August President Bush ordered troops to the region to protect relief workers as part of an international coalition called Operation Restore Hope.

The mission began on 9 December with US Marines creating a Civil Military Operations Center (CMOC) in conjunction with a UN Humanitarian Operations Center (HOC). USCENTCOM served as the unified command, directing Air Force as well as other military branch operations. US Air Forces in Europe (USAFE) provided air refueling, and Air Force AC-130 gunships gave cover to UN troops. Major General George N. Williams served as first air component commander for Somalia, as well as later in Kenya. Brigadier General Thomas R. Mikolajcik served as US Air Force component commander from December 1992 to March 1993.

After President Bill Clinton assumed office in January 1993, he concluded the Somali crisis had ameliorated and let the UN take over. US combat troops decreased to 1,200. One clan leader, Mohamed Farrah Aidid, continued to harass the remaining international forces, however, and after his forces killed 24 Pakistani soldiers, there was an outcry. When four American soldiers were also killed, Task Force Ranger was called into action, consisting of Delta Force commandos, Army Rangers and pilots from the 160th Special Operations Aviation Regiment. Their goal was to capture Aidid.

On 3 October, in the Somali capital, Mogadishu, 18 American soldiers were killed during the attempt to capture Aidid. Clan fighters shot down two American UH-60 Blackhawk helicopters, and the bodies of American soldiers were dragged through the streets. The 15-hour firefight was the longest for US forces since Vietnam. Pararescueman Technical Sergeant Tim 'Wilky' Wilkinson, who ministered to injured Army Rangers while dodging Somali gunfire, received the Air Force Cross for his heroism. His partner, Master Sergeant Scott Fales, and combat controller Staff Sergeant Jeffrey Bray both earned Silver Stars. (Ridley Scott's 2001 movie Black Hawk Down re-enacts the operation.) President Clinton withdrew all US forces after the incident. Aidid was never captured but later died of gunshot wounds.

***Above:* A C-130 Hercules from the 943rd Tactical Airlift Group, Air Force Reserves, responds to civilian firefighters calls for help in battling forest fires. The C-130 is capable of dumping 3,000 gallons of water or fire retardant in a single pass.**

Crisis in the Former Yugoslavia

The disintegration of the Soviet Union in 1989 led to a lack of stability in Eastern Europe that ultimately required US military involvement. In February 1992 after the Soviet Union had separated into 15 individual republics, the Air Force airlifted emergency aid in 70 sorties to former USSR capitals and Russian cities as part of Operation Provide Hope.

The six cobbled-together republics that made up Yugoslavia, which had only existed as one nation since World War I, also began to break apart. Slovenia, Croatia, Macedonia, and Bosnia-Herzegovina all declared their independence in 1991 and 1992. Montenegro and Serbia remained as the only republics constituting Yugoslavia, with Kosovo and Vojvodina functioning as provinces within Serbia. Ethnic and religious distinctions were deeply enmeshed in the political conflicts among these republics.

Above: **The Northrop Grumman B-2 Spirit stealth bomber was first delivered for service in 1993. The USAF has shown that two B-2s armed with precision weapons can do the job of 75 conventional aircraft.**

Left: **C-5 Galaxies wait in line for takeoff to deliver supplies to Mogadishu, Somalia, in 1993 during Operation Restore Hope.**

Below: **Two A-10 Thunderbolt IIs drop away after refueling. The 'Warthog' excels at close-air support with its array of armaments, including a 30mm cannon in the nose, capable of firing 70 rounds per second.**

Right: **The civil war in Rwanda forced refugees to flee into neighboring Zaire. Here a C-141 Starlifter from the 452nd Avionics Maintenance Wing of the Air Force Reserves distributes relief goods to Rwandan refugees.**

AMC
70026

When Bosnia-Herzegovina became independent in 1992, Serbia and Croatia both declared war on the new nation and undertook a pattern of 'ethnic cleansing,' or genocide. Initially the United States provided only humanitarian aid. In July 1992 with ethnic warfare underway in Bosnia, the Air Force cooperated in Operation Provide Promise to bring food and medical supplies to Sarajevo and other beleaguered parts of Bosnia.

Above: **The F-117A Nighthawk stealth fighter struck the initial blows of Operation Desert Storm on 17 January 1991, flying into Iraq undetected, taking out radar installations and the Iraqi Air Force headquarters in Baghdad.**

Below: **Captain Scott O'Grady returns to Andrews Air Force Base. O'Grady eluded capture for six days after his F-16C was shot down over Bosnia by a Serbian missile before he was eventually rescued by US Marines.**

US Air Force components of NATO's Allied Forces Southern Europe also participated in Operation Deny Flight, which enforced a ban on air traffic over Bosnia-Herzegovina, supported UN ground troops, and flew UN-approved air strikes. That phase of the war ended with signing of the December 1995 Dayton Peace Accords, which established a two-tier, multi-ethnic and democratic government in Bosnia-Herzegovina. A NATO-led Stabilization Force (SFOR), including US forces under Operation Joint Endeavor was put in place. During the 1995 Bosnian War, Bosnian Serbs shot down Air Force Captain Scott O'Grady's F-16 with an SA-6 mobile missile. O'Grady was later rescued by a US Marines air rescue unit. Despite the peace accords, the conflict continued to simmer, and the Air Force maintained a presence as part of Task Force Eagle in Operation Joint Guard.

Operation Joint Guard was followed in June 1998 by a smaller, NATO-led Stabilization Force in Bosnia-Herzegovina, called Operation Joint Forge. Unrest spread to Montenegro, which moved to separate itself from Serbia. In October 1998, the US Air Force stood poised for a strike against Serbia in cooperation with NATO. Slobodan Milosevic, who had been elected President of Serbia in 1989 and then President of Yugoslavia in 1997, refused to remove his troops from Kosovo province, where he was attempting to eliminate the ethnic Albanian majority.

Providing 60 percent of the strike force, the United States sent 260 aircraft, including two B-2 stealth bombers from Whiteman Air Force Base in Missouri, 12 F-117 stealth fighters from Holloman Air Force Base in New Mexico, and six B-52 bombers with air-launched cruise missile capability from Barksdale Air Force Base in Louisiana. The bombing of Serbia took place in 1999, and NATO peacekeepers were placed in Kosovo.

In February 1999, the United States and NATO offered a new peace plan, the Rambouillet Accord, to Milosevic, but he refused to sign on the grounds that it would subject all of Yugoslavia to NATO occupation. Federal elections in 2000 ousted Milosevic from office, and he was arrested in 2001, to be tried for crimes against humanity at the International Criminal Tribunal for the former Yugoslavia in The Hague. The Interim Administration Mission in Kosovo has governed Kosovo since June 1999. In 2003, Serbia and Montenegro became separate republics.

Diverse Missions

The Air Force has also participated in numerous, non-war-related humanitarian airlifts and those involving major natural disasters. Air Force humanitarian airlifts operated in Monrovia, Liberia, as Operation Sharp Edge in 1990-91; and in Zaire and Rwanda in 1994-1997, as part of the US Army Operations Support Hope. From November 1991 to May 1993, the Air Force was involved in Operation GITMO, providing humanitarian help to Haitians fleeing to Cuba. Operation Able Manner/Able Vigil aided in picking up Haitian and Cuban migrants in the Straits of Florida from January 1993 to October 1994. An Air Force Special Operations team led the evacuation of Americans in Liberia in 1996 and aided Zaire in 1996.

Natural disasters the Air Force has responded to include cyclones in Bangladesh; the eruption of Mount Pinatubo in the Philippines; and earthquakes in India and Armenia. The 910th Airlift Wing Crew flew aid to Algiers in May 2003 after a 6.1 earthquake and again in December to Bam, Iran, site of another earthquake. At home in the United States, the 709th Airlift Squadron stepped in after Hurricanes Hugo and Andrew in Florida and the Virgin Islands. There have been other airlifts after typhoons in Hawaii and Guam, flooding in the Midwest and forest fires in the Far West.

When four American commercial planes were hijacked on 11 September 2001, causing the most serious terrorist incident in US history, threat of war shifted to home ground. On the day of the al Qaeda attack, the Air Force's most immediate role was to protect the US President, who left Sarasota, Florida, on Air Force One and flew to Barksdale Air Force base in Louisiana. After speaking to the nation,

Above: **A US Air Force F-16 Fighting Falcon and a Royal Jordanian Air Force F-1 Mirage flying a joint patrol mission over Iraq enforcing the 'no-fly' zone.**

Below: **Pararescue members train for a pickup in the mountain ranges north of Nellis Air Force Base, Nevada. An HH-60G Pave Hawk swoops in for the rescue.**

Above: **An F-16 flies escort just off the wingtip of Air Force One returning President George W. Bush back to Washington, DC, following the terrorist attacks on 11 September 2001.**

Right: **A section of the Pentagon in Washington, DC, smolders after terrorists flew American Airlines Flight 77 into the Defense Department building on the morning of 11 September 2001.**

President George W. Bush, son of former President George H. W. Bush, then flew to Offutt Air Force base in Nebraska before landing later that day at Andrews Air Force Base in Maryland, with three fighter jets in escort, and returning to the White House.

As part of Operation Noble Eagle, 13,000 Air Force reserves were called up for home defense on 15 September, and the Air National Guard maintained two fighter jets over New York and four over Washington, D.C., 24 hours a day. Twenty-six air bases nationwide began to keep armed fighter jets ready to roll within 10 minutes.

In the post-9/11 quarterbacking, some argued that the North American Aerospace Defense Command (NORAD) had had the capacity to respond far more quickly than it did and send fighter jets like the lightning-fast F-15s at Otis Air Force Base in Massachusetts to intercept Flight 175 before it hit the South Tower of the World Trade Center. The same readiness argument has been made about interception of Flight 77, which hit the Pentagon. In both cases, the planes did not fly at maximum speed and theoretically could have overtaken the hijackers.

The War in Afghanistan

After Afghanistan refused to give up Osama bin Laden, the al Qaeda leader believed to be behind the 9/11 terrorist attacks, President Bush ordered retaliatory bombing, and the Air Force went into immediate action through US Central Command. The land and sea-based air attack, Operation Enduring Freedom, was launched on 7 October in partnership with Great Britain, which initiated Operation Veritas. The US operation employed some 15 Air Force jets, including F-16s, B-1, B-2 Stealth and B-52s, as well as 25 carriers and submarines launching 50 Tomahawk missiles. The air sorties focused on air defense and command posts, communications centers and power grids, as well as the Taliban's air force.

In an address to the nation that day, President Bush said the United States would also destroy terrorist training camps, capture al Qaeda leaders, and put an end to terrorist activity in Afghanistan. The Air Force used bases in Pakistan, and US troops were transported to an Uzbekistan air base near Khanabad. Humanitarian airlifts delivered food and medicine to the Afghani people.

Special Forces troops entered southern Afghanistan on 19 October, and by 20 October, US forces had destroyed the Taliban's air defenses. The US ground war officially began on 25 November at Kandahar. Working in conjunction with anti-Taliban forces, US troops took over one city after another: Mazar-e Sharif, Herat, Kabul, and Jalalabad. US CENTCOM Commander, General Tommy Franks, attended the inauguration of an interim government on 22 December. Operation Enduring Freedom continued, searching for chemical and biological weapons in March and eliminating remaining Taliban and al Qaeda enclaves in Operation Anaconda.

The US Transportation Command delivered all troops and most supplies. The Air Force, along with Navy and Marine pilots, fired 18,000 missiles and munitions, more than half of which were

UNITED STATES ARMY
POLICE
N407FC

An F-16CJ endures an Iraqi sandstorm during Operation Iraqi Freedom. Despite the conditions, aircrews still managed to launch planes for combat sorties in support of the operation.

Opposite: **A member of the Combined Weapons Effectiveness Assessment Team takes data regarding the pinpoint impact of a precision-guided 2,000 pound bomb on an Iraqi building. The team assessed the accuracy of precision weapons throughout Baghdad.**

precision-directed, and on average hit two targets per plane. During Desert Storm, it took 10 planes to eliminate one target. Another record came when US pilots flew a 15-hour combat fighter mission, the longest in US history, and a 26-hour surveillance mission, also the longest. NORAD conducted over 25,000 Operation Noble Eagle sorties and 17,600 combat air patrols. In memory of the many who lost their lives in the 9/11 disaster, a helmet that belonged to one of the firemen who died in the World Trade Towers attack traveled with many of the Air Force flyers from US CENTCOM in B-1s, B-52s, KC-10s, C-5s, and E-3s over Afghanistan and, later, in Operation Iraqi Freedom.

Improvements in smart bombs allowed the Air Force to pinpoint targets, and progress in communications technology meant pilots received target data more quickly and accurately. In contrast to missiles used in Kosovo, which were laser guided and therefore vulnerable to bad weather, those used in Afghanistan were guided by satellite and designed for all weather. Journalist Nancy Benac concluded that the 2001 Afghan airstrike 'demonstrated how U.S. air forces, whether land- or sea-based, have become the leading edge of American military power.

Particularly effective was the Joint Direct Attack Munition (JDAM), which adapted conventional bombs with payloads of 1,000 or 2,000 pounds into smart bombs guided by satellite-linked global positioning. In addition, the Predator unmanned drone was used not only for information relay, but to launch Hellfire anti-tank missiles. Ground forces also came into play significantly by relaying target information to aircraft. The US Army used the AH-64D Longbow Apache helicopter to fire Longbow Hellfire missiles.

By October 30, Air Force pilots, including active, Guard and Reserve members, flew over 85,000 sorties, three quarters of those flown in Operation Enduring Freedom. They dropped 9,650 tons of bombs. Airlift missions totaled 48,000 in that time period. In addition, there were 17,050 refuelings and another 3,025 reconnaissance flights using JSTARS, UAV, Rivet Joint, U-2, AWACS and Command Solo aircraft. Air Force fighters, tankers and early warning aircraft flew 28,600 sorties. The humanitarian aid statistics were also impressive: delivery of 2.5 million food rations, 1,700 tons of wheat, 328,200 blankets and 5,000 radios. The mission in Afghanistan continues.

Opposite top: **An F-16 of the 510th Fighter Squadron out of Aviano Air Base, Italy, flies a combat patrol mission over Serbia in 1999, armed with AIM-120 and AIM-9 air-to-air missiles.**

Opposite bottom: **The B-2 Spirit stealth bomber has seen duty in several conflicts, including NATO Operation Allied Force over the former Yugoslavia.**

Above: **General Norman Schwarzkopf allowed Iraqi forces to continue to use helicopters after the cease fire in 1991. The helicopters were then used by Saddam Hussein's forces to quash a Kurdish revolt in the north.**

Below: **The A-10 Thunderbolt II is known for its rugged reliability, its tank-busting weaponry, and its good looks, all captured in its nickname, 'Warthog.'**

The War in Iraq

Although Osama bin Laden had still not been apprehended, President Bush turned his attention to Iraq and the ousting of its President Saddam Hussein in 2002. Frustrated by the lack of cooperation with UN arms inspectors in their search for weapons of mass destruction, the Bush administration instituted a radical new policy that called for pre-emptive strikes. President Hussein claimed he had no weapons of mass destruction, but in an address before the United Nations, President Bush warned that if the United Nations did not act, the United States would. Congress authorized the use of force against Iraq, and the United States lobbied for UN support, but it was not forthcoming. UN weapons inspections resumed 27 November 2002, and the Air Force began bombing raids on Iraq in retaliation for no-fly zone violations.

The American proposal to invade Iraq grew increasingly controversial outside the United States, with Turkey voting down the US request to stage troops there for an invasion of Iraq, and the Arab League voting against war with Iraq in March 2003. Spain and Great Britain did support the ouster of Hussein, however, along with 47 other nations. Coalition support ranged from military forces to humanitarian aid. President Bush issued the order to attack Iraq on 19 March. On the first day, two F-117s dropped two Mk-84 bombs on a bunker where President Hussein was believed hiding, but the dictator was not found. The ground war began on 20

March 2003. The Air Force component of the US invasion was the Ninth Air and Space Expeditionary Task Force, led by Lieutenant General Michael Moseley.

The Iraqis were unable or unwilling to mount an air force defense but this did not mean that the USAF did not play an important role in the war. On 28 March, the longest air assault mission in history took place with troops from the 101st Airborne Division in 200 Black Hawk, Apache, Chinook and Kiowa helicopters, which landed at Najaf, Iraq. The Air Force 442nd Fighter Wing made history in April, when it became the first Air Force fighter unit to forward deploy into Iraq at Tallil Air Base near the Babylonian city Ur. In a speech on Thursday, 1 May, aboard the USS Abraham Lincoln, President Bush declared that major combat operations in Iraq were over.

By 30 October 2003, the Air Force had flown 30,000 sorties and dropped more than 21,300 bombs in Iraq. Another 5,700 airlift sorties were flown, with the Air Force transporting 40,000 tons or cargo and 55,000 passengers. Almost 70 percent of the bombs deployed were precision-guided. Space-based facilities provided for a high level of surveillance, reconnaissance, and global communication. The Air Force had moved one million troops during Operations Enduring Freedom and Iraqi Freedom and 2.75 million tons of cargo and equipment.

Saddam Hussein was finally captured on 13 December 2003, near Tikrit, Iraq. He had been hiding in an eight-foot hole on a farm. During a televised address announcing Hussein's capture, President Bush warned it did not mean the end of violence in Iraq. Hussein's supporters, foreign irregulars and others continued to resist the largely US occupation with high levels of violence in the form of car bombs, missiles, and suicide attacks. By 19 February 2004, the US death toll topped 500, over half incurred after President Bush announced the end of combat in Iraq. The United States aimed to turn control of the government over to the Iraq people by mid-year. Although the war continued to remain controversial, President Bush provided his best argument in the speech he delivered to the

Images of War: The 332nd AEG prepares an F-15E for battle in Afghanistan (top) during Operation Enduring Freedom. An F-15E of the 494th EFS (center) patrols the skies over Baghdad during Operation Iraqi Freedom. Airmen of the 447th AEG (left) lay down a temporary runway in a vicious Iraqi sandstorm. (Right) Left to right are Capt. Tally Parham, F-16 pilot with the 157th EFS, Capt. Mary Melfi and 1Lt. Julie Ayres, both weapons system officers aboard F-15Es with the 336th EFS.

SOUTH
CAROLINA
543
RESCUE

Various aircraft in the Air Force fleet: Both the B-2 Spirit stealth bomber and the B-52 Stratofortress (bottom) participated in the 'shock and awe' bombing campaign during Operation Iraqi Freedom. The F-15 (opposite bottom) flew thousands of sorties in both Iraq wars, watched over by the E-3 Sentry AWACS (opposite top). Downed pilots can await the HH-60G Pave Hawk (inset) for rescue.

nation 28 March 2003: 'We are sending a clear signal to the world that we will not submit to a future in which dictators and terrorists can arm and threaten the peace without consequence.'

Opposite top: **An F-117A stealth fighter flies over Lake Tahoe, Nevada. The F-117A relies on its ability to elude enemy radar rather than speed, with only high subsonic capability.**

Above: **Various printed materials show the struggle for hearts and minds. The poster at left depicts al Qaeda leader Osama bin Laden as a 'soldier of Islam.' On the right are cards dropped on Afghanistan by the US. The top card shows US aid helping Afghanis, while the lower card carries the caption, "This is what the Taliban has done?"**

Left: **An RQ-1 Predator unmanned aerial vehicle searches out enemy targets over Iraq and Afghanistan armed with Hellfire missiles.**

CHAPTER 14
THE WILD BLUE YONDER

The Wild Blue Yonder

To look back across the almost 60 years from the inception of the US Air Force as a separate branch of the military to its position at the beginning of the 21st century is to observe a remarkable pattern of growth and adaptation to prevailing conditions.

The Air Force as an Organization

The first building blocks of the newest military branch created a solid foundation. Since its establishment as a separate service in 1947, the Air Force has participated in several major restructurings of the US military. The Department of Defense Reorganization Act of 1958 removed the departments of Army, Navy, and Air Force from the chain of operational command. Instead, commanders reported to the Joint Chiefs of Staff (JCS), a panel comprising the highest-ranking members of each major branch of the armed forces. Then in 1986, another reorganization of the US military removed the operational command from the JCS. Responsibility for conducting military operations goes directly from the Secretary of Defense to the head of the United States regional commands and the chain of command bypasses the Joint Chiefs of Staff completely. Rather their primary responsibility is to ensure the readiness of their respective military services—to organize, train, equip, and support combat forces for the unified and specified commands.

The Joint Chiefs of Staff also act in an advisory military capacity for the President of the United States and the Secretary of Defense. In addition, the Chairman of the Joint Chiefs of Staff acts as the chief military advisor to the President. The presidentially-appointed civilian Secretary of the Air Force is advised by the chairman of the Joint Chiefs of Staff, who is appointed to a four-year term by the president with Senate approval. The Joint Chiefs of Staff also advise the president, the National Security Council, and the Secretary of Defense, as well as the Air Force secretary.

The Air Force's nine major commands operate on a functional basis in the United States and geographically overseas. They consist of Air Combat at Langley Air Force Base, Virginia; Air Education and Training at Randolph Air Force Base, Texas; Materiel at Wright-Patterson Air Force Base, Ohio; Reserve at Robins Air Force Base, Georgia; Space at Peterson Air Force Base, Colorado; Special Operations at Hurlbut Field, Florida; Air Mobility at Scott Air Force Base, Illinois; Pacific Air Forces at Hickam Air Force Base, Hawaii; and US Air Forces in Europe at Ramstein Air Base, Germany.

A dazzling array of 35 field-operation agencies are subsumed by these major commands. They include: Audit, Base Conversion, Center for Environmental Excellence, Civil Engineer Support, Communications, Cost Analysis, Flight Standards, Frequency Management, Historical Research, History Support, Inspection, Legal Services, Logistics Management, Manpower and Innovation, Medical Operations, Medical Support, National Security Emergency Preparedness, News,

***Previous page:* Dawn breaks on the future of US aviation. Three F/A-22 Raptors await deployment to join the ranks of the US Air Force in 2004.**

***Right:* The Air Force's aerial demonstration team, the Thunderbirds, have been flying the F-16 since 1983, the longest performance era of any aircraft used by the team.**

***Below:* An honor guard drills before Cadet Chapel at the United States Air Force Academy, Colorado.**

USAF
USAF
USAF
USAF
USAF
USAF

Special Investigations, Nuclear Weapons and Counterproliferation, Operations, Pentagon Communications, Personnel, Personnel Operations, Real Estate, Review Boards, Safety Center, Security Forces, Services, Studies and Analyses, Technical Applications, Weather, Intelligence, National Guard Readiness. In addition there are four direct-reporting units: the Doctrine Center, the Operational Test and Evaluation Center, and the Air Force Academy, and the 11th Wing (which oversees various USAF support operations including the USAF Band, the Honor Guard, and public relations). The development of this structure has enabled the Air Force to utilize its resources effectively over its 60-year history.

The Air Force Academy

Education has been part of the Air Force mission practically since its inception. President Eisenhower authorized the establishment of a US Air Force Academy on 1 April 1954. A site was selected that year near Colorado Springs, Colorado, and construction was completed in 1958, with 306 cadets entering in July 1955 and graduating in 1959. Since 1964, the total

Above: **Two generations of Air Force training aircraft: a vintage T-6 Texan and a new T-6A Texan II fly in formation over Randolph Air Force Base, Texas.**

Right: **The Tacit Rainbow loitering antiradar missile was an early experiment in unmanned aerial vehicles (UAVs). Although the project was cancelled in 1991, increasingly sophisticated UAVs like the Predator continue to be developed.**

annual enrollment has been about 4, 415. The first cadet class containing women entered the Academy on 28 June 1976. When the Academy graduated its first 97 female cadets on 28 May 1980, Lieutenant Kathleen Conly ranked eighth in her class. Hansford T. John, who graduated with the first class in 1959, became the first Academy graduate to make four-star general. The first women accepted for Air Force pilot training won their silver wings in 1977. After the combat-exclusion clause was terminated in 1993, women became eligible for duty on fighter, bomber and attack squadrons. By 1996, 1,218 cadets started their training.

One of the challenges of the new, sex-integrated military has been prevention of sexual harassment, assault, and even rape in what has traditionally been a male-dominated culture. In March 2003, the Air Force established that there had been 12 cases of sexual assault or rape at the Air Force Academy during its past 10 years. As other complainants came forward, the number of cases rose to 54. The controversy first arose when a Denver TV station reported that female cadets at the Air Force Academy had been disciplined or pressured to leave after filing sexual assault charges. It was part of a pattern of sexual misconduct that plagued all branches of the US military in the 1990s. Testifying before a Senate panel, Air Force Secretary James Roche said he was committed to changing the manner in which such charges were filed so that complainants would find it easier to come forward and that their complains would be listened to and no retaliation would take place. A report by National Organization of Women (NOW) staff indicated that women's rights leaders had praised the findings of a seven-member panel to investigate sex misconduct charges, after two panelists considered anti-feminist were removed. The reconstituted panel emphasized the importance of sexual assault education and stated that the top leadership was also an essential ingredient in ending sexual misconduct at the Air Force Academy.

Budget and Personnel Issues

One of the Air Force's crucial controlling factors is its budget, since without fiscal support from the White House and Congress, plans and dreams quickly dissolve. By 2002, the Air Force was operating with an $80.5 billion budget. With personnel costs taking 35 percent of it, modernization and operations and readiness followed at 30 percent each. Retention was a key personnel cost factor, and the budget aimed to increase Air Force pay levels by 5-10 percent, as well as to reduce pay gaps. The enlisted force at mid- and senior levels remained below staffing goals, as did skill levels, particularly among computer systems specialists, crypto-linguists, and air traffic controllers. In addition, pilot staffing stayed below required levels. The Air Force planned to use bonuses and improved promotion rates to boost retention, while advertising, enlistment bonuses, and recruitment resources were targeted for improving recruiting levels. Housing standards also received attention.

The primary budgetary concerns in the Operations and Readiness category were munitions replenishment, the cost of fleet growth and aging, and indicators of readiness. With the cost of mission capability rising, combat squadron readiness showed a drop from a high of 92 percent in 1996 to 69 percent in 2002. Modifications and upgrades of a number of aircraft and weapons systems were projected by the 2002 budget, including the C-5, C-135, F-16, T-38, F-15E, C-17, E-3, B-2 and MM-III. In the Modernization section of the budget, the primary goals were aerospace superiority, global mobility, precision weaponry, battlespace management, and transformation (this last named an issue to be discussed below). The bud-

Above: **In 2002, Boeing announced the existence of a previously highly classified aircraft, the Bird of Prey. The project, which ran from 1992 to 1999, pioneered low-observable technologies, now virtually an industry standard.**

Below: **Air Force One makes a low pass over Mount Rushmore. The VC-25A, a highly modified Boeing 747, is part of the Air Mobility Command's 89th Airlift Wing out of Andrews Air Force Base, Maryland.**

During operations Enduring Freedom and Iraqi Freedom, B-1B Lancers flew 497 combat sorties and dropped 4.56 million pounds of munitions.

Above: The U-2 Dragon Lady continues to be an invaluable asset to the Air Force with continual upgrades to engines, avionics, and sensors. The U-2 has been in service for nearly half a century.

Right: The Air Force Thunderbirds have been delighting audiences since 1953. Beginning with the F-84G, the team has flown nine different aircraft, including their present airplane, the F-16C.

get also anticipated the need to address degraded facilities.

In 2004, the Air Force had 370,000 men and women on active duty and 180,000 in the Air National Guard and Air Force Reserve. Dr. James G. Roche was serving as the 20th Secretary of the Air Force. A Navy retiree, Dr. Roche came to the Air Force from a career at Northup Grumman. Gen. John P. Jumper served as Air Force Chief of Staff and was responsible for the organization, training and equipping of Air Force personnel. General Jumper spent two tours of duty in Southeast Asia as a command fighter pilot.

Plans and Planes for the Future

In response to the demise of the Soviet Union and what appeared to be the end of the Cold War, the Air Force published in 1995 a visionary planning document called 'New World Vistas: Air and Space Power for the 21st Century.' This report suggested that the United States faced increasing pressure to act as a stabilizing force in the world as world alliances continued to shift. It called attention to the proliferation of dangerous humanitarian and peacekeeping operations as well as increasing numbers of anti-terrorist assignments. It suggested the fighting arena would move from earth into space and cyberspace. The blending of military and commercial applications would increase at high speed. 'The changes will be as profound as those experienced by the Army in moving from horse to tank or by the Navy in converting from sail to steam,' the authors of the document argued.

The newest blueprint for the Air Force's future came in the Transformation Flight Plan (TFP), initiated in May 2002 with annual updates. Transformation, according to Major General Daniel P. Leaf, is 'fundamental change in what we're able to do or how we do it.' According to Lieutenant Colonel James McCaw, the TFP 'can help all airmen, as well as our civilian members, understand where we are going and where the Air Force leadership believes emphasis must be placed in the future.'

The kind of rapid-fire change necessitating Air Force transformation is demonstrated by the F/A-22 Raptor, a new-generation stealth plane—that is, one designed and made from materials that allow a plane to go undetected by existent technologies. The high speed, advanced weaponry, and integrated avionics of this aircraft are revolutionizing air dominance. Use of unmanned aircraft—often referred to as 'drones'—while not inherently transformational, become so when used for warfare in new ways. The Expeditionary Air Force (EAF)—fast-acting, highly mobile, trimmed down units that can respond to crises anywhere in the world—is also not an entirely new concept, but the ways in which it is being used have been transformative.

The B-2 Spirit bomber provides another good example of how the Air Force is moving into the future. As a multiple-role stealth aircraft, it is able to carry a large payload of conventional and nuclear bombs yet maintain great aerodynamic efficiency. Composite materials, special coatings, and wing design enable it to avoid ready detection. On view for the first time in 1988, it had its first flight 17 July 1989 and the first one, Spirit of Missouri, rolled off the assembly line 17 December 1993. The B-2 demonstrated its mettle in Serbia during Operation Allied Force by eliminating 33 percent of all Serbian targets.

The role of unmanned aerial vehicles (UAVs) like the Predator also illustrates innovative directions for the Air Force. Advanced technology and miniaturization allow UAVs to hover in one place for up to 16 hours. The Global Hawk UAV offers 24-hour surveillance. Remote-piloted UAVs can carry weapons and launch them. Lieutenant General Ronald E. Keyes says of the UAV: 'It doesn't get tired and doesn't get hungry. It hangs there. It stares. It gives us an opportunity for predictive battle space awareness and time sensitive target engagement.' The Global Hawk was deployed in Germany for a three-week test operation on 15 October 2003.

Lockheed Martin's X-35C Joint Strike Fighter (JSF) is being developed for use with all branches of the US military as well as for the militaries of other countries. Individual models will vary by purpose and need.

Opposite left: The RQ-1 Predator unmanned aerial vehicle is a system, not just a single aircraft, consisting of four air vehicles (with sensors), a ground-control station, satellite link, and a crew of approximately 82 to keep the Predators flying 24 hours.

New Units, New Tasks

Special Operations expertise has also advanced light-years over the Air Force's 60-year history. As early as 1943, when the Air Force was still part of the Army, medics parachuted to aid fallen aircrew along the China-Burma border. Along the way to the 21st century, they became known as parajumpers, or PJs, incorporating scuba diving into their repertoire and jumping with as much as 170 pounds of equipment. As PJs turned into pararescuemen and their missions expanded, they rescued downed pilots in wartime, retrieved Gemini astronauts in the 1960s, and aided San Francisco earthquake victims in 1989. Today they have become some of the most highly trained emergency trauma specialists in the US military and can perform their duties in the remotest areas worldwide. Their specialized training includes combat diving, escape from planes sinking in water, and free-fall parachuting. In Special Tactics teams, they may work with combat controllers and combat weathermen to effect airfield capture and personnel recovery in hostile territory.

The Civil Air Patrol, founded 1 December 1941, now flies 80 percent of the search and rescue mission hours under direction of the Langley Air Force Base Air Force Rescue and Coordination Center, demonstrating the efficacy of a unified command system. Its duties have also been expanded to include air reconnaissance along US borders in cooperation with the US Customs Service, the Drug Enforcement Administration, and the US Forest Service.

At the 2004 Air Warfare Symposium, Air Force Secretary Roche provided a map for the Air Force's growth in the immediate future. It included upgrades of special operations, close air support, and battlefield management systems. The increased importance of special operations was demonstrated during Operation Enduring Freedom in Afghanistan, where bombers based halfway across the world performed in coordination with ground staff able to identify targets and direct attacks. To improve the effectiveness of special operations, Dr. Roche recommended replacement of the HH-60G Pave helicopter with a new medium-lift recovery aircraft. He also called for use of the CV-22 Osprey to replace the MH-35 Pave Low and replacement of the C-130

Above: **NASA's X-29 project from 1984 to 1992 tested an unusual forward swept wing and canard design, which showed improved maneuvering capabilities and less tendency to stall at high angles of attack.**

Left: **The MH-53J Pave Low III is the most technically advanced helicopter in the Air Force fleet. Designed for low-level penetration, the MH-53J can carry up to 35 Special Ops personnel undetected into denied areas.**

Development continues on a space-based particle beam weapon to shoot down enemy ICBMs. A technician inspects experimental particle beam equipment (below) at Los Alamos National Laboratory, and an artist's rendition (above) of what such a weapons system might look like.

NASA
008
U.S. AIR FORCE
HYPER-X

U.S AIR FORCE

A Titan IV B rocket lifts off from Cape Canaveral, Florida, carrying a classified payload for the National Reconnaissance Office, designed to enhance security and support troops on the battlefield.

Opposite top: For landing on the Red Planet, the Mars Rover Spirit used a radiation-resistant computer developed at the Air Force Research Laboratory at Kirtland Air Force Base, New Mexico.

Opposite center: NASA's Hyper-X project is experimenting with air-breathing engines that are capable of hypersonic speeds, defined as above Mach 5. The black Hyper-X vehicle rides on the tip of a modified Pegasus rocket under the wing of a B-52 mothership.

Opposite bottom: The RQ-4A Global Hawk is a high-altitude, long-endurance unmanned aerial vehicle, capable of ranging 13,500 nautical miles at an altitude of nearly 65,000 feet.

Hercules. Dr. Roche told his audience: 'We also envision a future that includes unmanned aerial vehicles and remotely piloted aircraft playing an expanded role in special operations.'

Close air support will have an increasingly important role in Air Force operations, according to Dr. Roche, to allow total integration with land forces. He identified 'battlefield airman' as a new way of thinking about Air Force personnel. 'We need to consolidate our battlefield airmen—combat controllers, pararescuemen, combat weather, special tactics, and tactical air controllers—under a common organizational and training structure, and strengthen the combat power they bring to the battlefield, whether it be in Air Combat Command or Air Force Special Operations Command.'

The Air Force Secretary also proposed development of more unmanned aerial vehicles and remote-piloted aircraft for use in land combat; upgrades for A-10 Thunderbolt IIs; development of a short take-off, vertical landing version of the F-35 Joint Strike Fighter. In addition, he envisioned a new role for wide-bodied planes in a new E-10 series.

At the symposium, the Air Force's Chief of Staff, Gen. John P. Jumper, stressed coordination of air and ground forces through a future force structure. The new organization would allow Air Force Air Operations Center weapons systems to monitor deployment of air expeditionary forces around the world 24-7. General Jumper also discussed joint warfight space, so that all military divisions with the capability for functioning in space, could launch micro-satellites and other rocket payloads quickly and efficiently. General Jumper foresaw shortening the response time of weapons from days or weeks to minutes or hours. Blended units could be another pattern for the future, with active duty personnel working side by side with Air National Guard in Joint Surveillance and Target Attack Radar System (JSTARS).

The Next Century

The 100th anniversary of Orville and Wilbur Wright's first flight at Kitty Hawk, North Carolina took place on 17 December 2003. To honor the occasion, a week of events, 'A Centennial of Flight,' was held at Kitty Hawk and included an air show by the US Air Force. Wright-Patterson Air Force Base in Ohio paid

***Right:* The CV-22 Osprey uses a pair of tilt-rotor engines that allow it to perform vertical take-offs and landings like a helicopter, and horizontal flight like traditional fixed-wing aircraft.**

DS

100 Years of Powered Flight: A replica of the Wright Flyer attempts to recreate the historic first flight during the 2003 Centennial Celebration at Kill Devil Hills, North Carolina. Meanwhile, high above, a heritage fly-by includes United States Air Force planes past and present.

An F/A-22 Raptor shows its vertical climb capability. The F/A-22 was designed to replace the aging fleet of F-15s (opposite top) as the America's frontline fighter. UAVs like the RQ-4A Global Hawk (opposite bottom) and the Predator will be increasingly relied upon on the battlefields of the future.

tribute to the centennial with Air Power 2003, an aerial demonstration on 10-11 May 2003. It included the Air Force's state-of-the-art F-15 Eagle, which flies at 1,875 miles per hour. Other planes featured were a T-6 Texan Warbird, used in World War II and the Korean War, flown by air performer Bill Lee. Also appearing was a P-38 Lightning. The Air Force Thunderbirds performed at air shows throughout the country in 2003 to celebrate the centennial.

This celebration demonstrated the remarkable speed with which the world has accustomed itself to sky travel. If we look equally as far into the future, we may find the US Air Force replaced by the US Aerospace Force. And the trend toward cooperative missions that has led to unified commands like Transportation, Strategic, and Space could evolve into one united US military. Just as humans dared to dream they might build flying machines, so their dreams will not be limited by today's technology. Only budgetary limitations will cloud the crystal ball of the Air Force's future. As a military force, the US Air Force dominates the world's skies today and will continue to do so in whatever future form it takes.

INDEX

Page numbers in italics refer to illustrations

ACKNOWLEDGMENTS

The publishers would like to thank John S. Bowman and Joel Carino for their contributions to this book.

History of the US Army
Many pictures throughout the text, and a majority of those relating to the 20th century, were supplied by the US Department of Defense, the US Army, the US Navy and the US Air Force. The publishers thank these agencies and the following whose picture appear in the pages noted:

AFP/Corbis: 260 middle and bottom, 262 bottom, 263
Anne S.K. Brown Military Collection, Brown University: 13 bottom, 26 bottom, 29 bottom right, 40 bottom, 45, 56 top right, 61 bottom, 65 bottom, 74 bottom, 77 top, 84-85, 94 top, 103 top, 121
Black Star: 209 bottom
Christopher Morris/Black Star/Timepix: 258 top
Dwight D. Eisenhower Library: 214
Library of Congress: 17 top, 25 top, 28, 36, 47, 57 top left, 66-67 bottom, 69 bottom, 70 bottom, 79 top, 87 top, 92 bottom, 98, 102-103, 114, 117, 120 top, 122 bottom, 124
Lincoln Library and Museum, Fort Wayne, Indiana: 71
Martin Marietta, Inc.: 227 top
National Archives: 19, 50 top, 72 top, 105 bottom, 102 bottom, 113 top, 118, 119, 126-7, 134 bottom, 145, 156-7, 185 bottom
National Gallery of Art, Washington, DC: 26 top
National Portrait Gallery, Smithsonian Institution: 60
New York Historical Society: 51 bottom
Peter Newark's Western Americana: 12 bottom, 18, 22, 23 bottom, 29 top, 30, 31 top, 34 bottom, 35, 39 bottom, 44 bottom, 46, 48, 52, 56, 58, 59, 62 bottom right, 63, 64 top, 69 top, 72 top, 76, 78, 81, 83 bottom, 85 top, 89, 92 top, 93, 95, 100, 101 bottom, 104 top, 105 top, 106, 107, 111
Remington Arms Company: 101 top, 118 top
Reuters NewMedia Inc./Corbis: 260 top, 261, 262 top
Reuters/Bettmann: 230-231, 234 top, 236, 244 both, 245, 246 both, 247 both, 248, 249 both, 250, 251, 252 all, 253 both, 254 both
Reuters/DOD/Timepix: 258 bottom, 259 top
Reuters/Timepix: 259 bottom
Roosevelt Library and Museum: 140 top
State Historical Society of Wisconsin: 21 top
UPI/Bettman: 240
US MilitaryAcademy Library: 96-7, 228 bottom
WWP: 205 bottom, 206, 207 top and bottom left, 214 top
Yale University Art Gallery: 40 top

HISTORY OF THE US NAVY
Many of the pictures throughout this text were supplied by the US Naval Public Affairs Department, the Naval Historical Center, and the Navy Department in the National Archives. Other photos were supplied by the following:

AFP/ Corbis: 514 top, 516
The Bettmann Archive: 501 bottom right, 518 top
Anne S.K. Brown Military Collection, Brown University: 268-9
Bundesarchiv: 346 top, 404-5, 405 top right, 408-9, 409 top right
Department of Defense: 508, 509 bottom
Library of Congress: 285 bottom, 306, 313bottom right, 329 top
General Dynamics Corporation: 447 top, 461, 462-3
Jim Hollander/Reuters/Timepix: 512 top
Imperial War Museum, UK: 381 bottom
MAI/Timepix: 512 bottom
Museum of the City of New York: 298-9 bottom left
National Army Museum, UK: 274
National Maritime Museum, UK: 272-3, 275, 283 top right, 284 bottom
New York Public Library: 270
Reuters/Bettmann: 485 top right and bottom, 488-9, 489 both, 490 top, 492 both, 493 bottom, 494, 495 top, 496 both, 497 bottom, 498 all, 499 both, 501 top and bottom left, 503 top, 504 bottom, 505 both, 506, 507 both
Reuters/Timepix: 511
Reuters NewMedia Inc./Corbis: 513 both, 514 bottom, 515 both
UPI/Bettmann: 284, 485 top left, 486 bottom, 487 both, 490 bottom, 491, 493 top, 495 bottom, 497 top, 452, 453 bottom, 454 top
US Air Force: 352 top left, 400 bottom
US Army: 425 top
US Coast Guard: 420 top
US Marine Corps: 303 top, 459 top, 509 top, 510

HISTORY OF THE US MARINES
Anne S. K. Brown Military Collection, Brown University: 538 top
AFP/Corbis: 780 both, 771 top, 772 bottom, 773 top
AP Worldwide: 712 bottom, 713 bottom
Jim Hollander/Reuters/Timepix: 769 both
Robert Hunt Library: 658 top, 659 top, 662-3
Imperial War Museum: 665 bottom
Library of Congress: 540-1, 544 top, 545 bottom, 553 top, 557
Aladin Abdel Naby/Reuters/Timepix: 768
National Archives: 522-3, 528, 529 top, 530 top and bottom, 531 top right and bottom, 532 bottom, 533 bottom, 534 bottom, 535 both, 536 both, 539 top, 541 inset, 542 both, 543 all three, 544 bottom, 546 both, 547 both, 548 top, 549 top, 550-1, 552 bottom, 553 bottom, 554 bottom, 555 both, 558 both, 559 both, 560 both, 561 both, 562, 563 top, 564 both, 567 both, 568 both, 570 bottom, 571 both, 576 both, 577 top, 578-9, 584 both, 585 both, 586 both, 587 bottom, 588, 589 both, 590, 591 top left, center, bottom, 592 both, 593, 595 bottom, 598 both, 602-3, 607 top, 628 top, 656 bottom, 681 both, 682, 683, 685, 690, 691, 692, 693, 694 inset, 696, 697, 698, 699 both, 700-701, 702, 703, 704, 705, 706 both, 798-9 all four, 713 top, 716, 717, 718 top, 719, 720 both, 722 both, 723, 724 both, 725, 729, 732 both, 736 , 737 top and bottom
Richard Natkiel (maps): 548 bottom, 631, 635, 648, 684
Naval Historical Photos: 545 top, 628 bottom
Peter Newark's Western Americana: 556
New York Historical Society: 537 bottom
New York Public Library: 554 bottom
Radu Sigheti/Timepix: 767
Reuters/Bettmann: 738-9, 741 both, 742, 743 both, 744 both, 745, 746, 747, 748, 749 both, 751, 753 both, 754-5, 756 both, 757, 759 bottom, 760, 761 both, 762 both, 763 both, 764
Reuters NewMedia Inc./Corbis: 771 bottom, 772 top, 773 bottom
UPI/Bettman: 740 both, 750. 758, 759 top, 267
US Army: 607 bottom, 629 top, 661 top, 664 bottom
US Air Force: 580, 604, 733 bottom, 738 bottom
US Marine Corps: 524-5, 529 bottom, 531 top left, 532 top left and right, 549 bottom, 552 top, 569, 570 top, 577 bottom, 581 both, 587 top, 591 top right, 594, 595 top, 599, 600, 601, 610, 611 top, 614-5 all three, 618 both, 619 both, 620-21 all three, 622-3 all five, 624-5 all four, 626-7 all four, 630, 631 top, 632-3 all four, 624-5 all four, 626, 627, 628-9, 646-7 all three, 648, 649, 650 top and bottom, 652-3, 655, 656 top, 657, 660, 664 top, 665 top, 666, 667, 668-9 all three, 670, 671, 672, 673, 674, 675, 676-7, 679, 686-7, 689, 694-5 main photo, 707 right, 710-11 all three, 712, 713-14, 728 top, 730-31, 733 top, 765, 766
US Signal Corps: 650 top right, 654 top, 661 bottom
Valley Forge Historical Society: 526-27

HISTORY OF THE US AIR FORCE
Alinari Archives/Corbis: 782 bottom
Bettmann/Corbis: 860-861 bottom, 863, 914 bottom, 938 top
Corbis: 942 bottom
Ellen Ozier/Reuters/Corbis: 988-989 bottom
Franklin D. Roosevelt Library: 805 top, 828
General Dynamics Corporation: 939, 975
Government of Vietnam: 929 bottom
Library of Congress: 780-781, 782 top, 783, 784-787, 788 top and center, 789-791, 794-804, 805 bottom, 807-813, 814 top, 815 top, 816-817, 818 top, 819, 822-827, 829, 830 bottom, 831 bottom, 832, 833 top, 834-839, 842 inset, 843, 844 top, 845, 847 bottom, 848-853, 856-857, 858 bottom, 859, 860 top, 861 top, 862, 864-875, 881 bottom, 887, 891 top, 897 bottom, 899 bottom, 909, 971 top
Lockheed Corporation: 818 bottom, 916 top
Los Alamos National Laboratory: 983

Markowitz Jeffrey/Corbis Sygma: 958 bottom
McDonnell Douglas Corporation: 906-907
NASA: 982 top, 984 top and center
United States Air Force: 778-779 all, 788 bottom, 814 bottom, 815 bottom, 830 top, 831 top, 840-841, 842 left, 844 bottom, 846, 847 top, 854-855, 858 top, 876-877, 878 top, 879-880, 881 top, 882-886, 888-889, 895 bottom, 896, 897 top) 902, 908, 910-912, 913 top, 914 top, 915, 917-923, 924 top, 925-928, 930, 932-936, 940-941, 942 top, 943-945, 946 bottom, 947 bottom, 948-951, 952 top, 953-957, 958 top, 959-970, 971 bottom, 972-974, 976 top, 977-981, 982 bottom, 984 bottom, 985-987, 988 top, 989 top, 990-991
United States Army: 913 bottom
United States Navy: 931
United States Department of Defense: 916 bottom, 976 bottom
United States National Archives & Records Administration:792-793, 806, 820-821, 833 top, 878 bottom, 891 bottom, 892-894, 895 top, 898, 899 top, 900-901, 903-905, 924 bottom, 938 bottom, 946 top, 947 top, 952 bottom
Wally McNamee/Corbis: 937